WESTMAR COLLEGE LIBRARY
W9-BVJ-956

CRITICISM

THE FOUNDATIONS OF MODERN LITERARY JUDGMENT

Revised Edition

EDITED BY

Mark Schorer

Josephine Miles

Gordon McKenzie

University of California

HARCOURT, BRACE & WORLD, INC.
NEW YORK AND BURLINGAME

~~801 S374~~
PN
81
.S23
1958

COPYRIGHT, 1948, © 1958, BY
HARCOURT, BRACE & WORLD, INC.

*All rights reserved. No part of this book
may be reproduced in any form, by mimeograph or any other means,
without permission in writing from the publisher.*

Printed in the United States of America

61014

Contents

INTRODUCTION

WE SHOULD like to call attention to the richness of literary criticism as it exists today, to its impressive learning, its great wit, its range of insights. Thus the primary purpose of this collection of critical essays is simply to make available to the general reader texts often referred to in literary discussion yet difficult to obtain. So many good volumes of the past decades are out of print and so many journals of intelligence endure but briefly, that their ideas, scattered in hundreds of scrapbooks and libraries, need a representative gathering place.

Literary criticism of the past half-century has been devoted with a singular fervor to the re-examination of principles and texts, and this collection attempts to represent the variety of principles criticism has examined and affirmed, and suggests the variety of literary works it has analyzed. There are certain strong and recurring interests: in close analysis as principle, in vividness and complexity as values, in seventeenth century poems and plays and nineteenth century novels as texts. There are at the same time other, and sometimes antagonistic, preoccupations with personal and institutional expressiveness or with social responsibility, which may involve the same or other works and standards. In these essays, both the multiplicity and the constancy of approach should be discernible.

We have hoped in other ways, too, to make the range of this collection as great as possible: in the genres (poetry, fiction, drama, and criticism itself) which the authors discuss; in tone and manner and method—formal and informal, austere and rhapsodic, academic and bohemian, rationalistic and impressionistic, subjective and objective; in the possible variety of positions within any of the three large categories under which we have ordered these selections; and in the relative purity and impurity of those positions.

These categories represent the second purpose of this collection: to arrange the materials in such a way as to suggest that, highly diverse as they are, the major preoccupations, the basic assumptions of literary criticism, are few and not necessarily far apart. The three categories present questions whose solutions are never in the nature of things quite right or finished, yet they seem to be the questions which critics perennially ask of literature, and by means of which they approach it and come to understand it.

Critics ask where art comes from, how it becomes what it is, and what it does; their questions are about the *Source*, the *Form*, the *End* of art. The first question, which concerns the artist's experience, emphasizes the matter that goes into art; the second, which analyzes the structural elements that compose the work as a whole, emphasizes the qualities of art in itself, the formal means; the third, which examines the response of the audience, emphasizes the function of art. Other emphases of course adhere to these; it is interesting to observe, for example, how frequently the first position regards art as "expression"; the second, as a mode of "imitation"; and the third, as "communication."

Yet these are varieties of emphasis only. The difference among the three categories is not radical, and it is probably a loss to insight whenever a critic takes so "pure" a position as to make his emphasis appear so. In the *Poetics*, Aristotle is no doubt most interested in the definition of the genre, tragedy, yet when he writes of pity and terror and the purgation which these induce in the beholder, he is concerned with its results. Even in the earliest examples, then, our categories are forms of emphasis, not mutually exclusive forms of understanding and judgment.

Since we are concerned with a broad representation of critical positions rather than with an exact representation of any individual's writing, readers should not be surprised to find a piece of criticism in a category to which they had not previously assigned its author. L. C. Knights, long a distinguished formalist, appears now, in the present, relatively recent essay, "Restoration Comedy," to be moving toward the category of *Source*. The work of T. S. Eliot, much of which derives from the author's intellectual program, might well appear in the category of *Source*, yet our particular selections from that work seem to place him rather in the category of *Form*. Of modern critics, I. A. Richards has been most clearly associated with the psychology of art, with literature as communication, and our selections from his work obviously belong in the category *End;* yet the work of his most notable predecessor, Coleridge, as well as of his most notable apostle, William Empson, is here included under *Form*. It is perhaps sufficient to point out that Mr. Richards would be a less considerable critic if his analysis of the psychology of art did not depend, in other works, on an exacting analysis of the formal means of art. Other critics who have been included in *Source*, notably Henry James and Allen Tate, might almost equally well—and, with other essays, would certainly—appear in *Form*. We hope, by calling attention to the interest these critics have in the source of literature, to point to the special virtues of their analysis of it.

Within the categories, the variety of critical emphasis should become apparent at a glance. In the first group, *Source*, we move from Plato to Longinus, both of whom think of the character of the artist, to Wordsworth, concerned with a due representation of nature, to Virginia Woolf, concerned with what is "really real" in the consciousness, to the political critics, Ralph Fox and George Orwell, determined that the artist make a proper analysis of society; or, again, we move from Professor Lovejoy's scholarly discussion of an intellectual source, which is perhaps not "criticism" at all, to Lionel Trilling's discussion of the general diffusion of an intellectual "influence" over modern literature, to Allen Tate's examination of the results of a philosophical deficiency in figurative language; and we conclude with Stephen Spender's discussion of the source of poetry in the very different terms of its composition. The second category, *Form*, represents perhaps less variety in position, but in degree of purity nearly as much becomes evident as we move from Aristotle, who, in the middle category, reaches out to both extremities, through John Crowe Ransom, who is deliberately and ascetically "pure," to Joseph Frank, who wishes to talk about "form" in literature in terms usually considered in the province of other arts. The third category, *End*, presents again a full panoply of possibility: for Sidney, art is an ennobling influence on character; for Pope and Hume, it is rather a matter of perfecting taste; for Johnson, Shelley, and Arnold, it provides three varieties of moral education; for Poe and Pater, nervous excitement; for Richards, nervous stability.

Under all this rich variety and individual emphasis in each category, there is, we yet hope to suggest, a real identity of interest between the three categories. *Source* is another way of saying *Experience*, the elements which go into art, without which it could not exist at all; yet without *Form*, its unique structural means, those elements would remain nothing but experience, neither beauty nor esthetic truth; and yet—in spite of the extremity of position which drives Mr. Auden to declare that art never re-enters history, or the purity of position which impels Mr. Ransom to suggest that esthetic value is of an entirely different order from all other value—the effectiveness of *Form* does enable art to enter the nervous system at least, and thus pertains to *Ends*. Only other kinds of criticism—religion or psychology—can tell us how far the nervous system reverberates.

Of the three categories, the second has been the great contemporary concern, and contemporary criticism has taught us that if we neglect art in its technical actualities, we are not talking about art at all, but about something else—life as the artist has lived it, or life as the critic would like it to be. Yet there are other modern voices, and these remind us that, autonomous as it may be, art is in itself one of the forms of human experience, and, being that, serves something else, and, in turn, rules something larger.

There are also the multiple, insistent voices of the past, wherefore—as a third purpose—it has seemed wise and useful to let some of them be heard here, behind the younger voices, to show that the new criticism has its roots in the past and that what it attacks are not so much different problems as the old problems in different forms. Obviously there has been no attempt here to provide even the essential texts in the history of literary criticism: except for Plato and Aristotle, Longinus and Jung, we have not gone beyond the limits of the English language, or, except for about a dozen others, beyond the limits of the present century. Yet these few will suffice to indicate the continuity of literary considerations. The style, vocabulary, and ideas of I. A. Richards or Harry Levin do not appear at first glance to have much in common with the ancients or the English critics of the eighteenth and nineteenth centuries, and, as a matter of fact, their differences give them their importance for us; but they have in common with older writers a concern with the same very large problems.

The formalism of Aristotle is to be recognized again in the different contexts of Hulme, Eliot, Tillyard, Blackmur, Brooks; his stress on tragic function, again in Bradley, Krutch, Yeats. The English Renaissance and the neoclassic concern with purposes and effects reappears in Shelley's social prophecy as in Pater's immediate sensation, in many discussions of the modern novel as in Richards' close analyses of poetic communication. The expressive soul of the artist is the responsible source not only for Poe and Yeats, but for Plato and Longinus, not only for the biographical speculations of Edmund Wilson, but for the milder autobiographical ones of Stephen Spender. Even though they take precisely opposite attitudes toward the particular problem which concerns them within their category, it is refreshing to note that Longinus implausibly provides the precedent in critical category for W. H. Auden.

We have meant, then, not to document history but to suggest it. To that end, chronology, even among modern critics, is useful in revealing changes of tastes and point of view, and we have therefore arranged our selections, within their categories, by date of publication or, occasionally, of composition.

It may, finally, be of some use to say that this book grew out of the needs of a college course in the theory and practice of criticism which the editors, among others, offer at the University of California at Berkeley, and that we have been in the habit of approaching criticism not directly, but by bringing it to bear on specially selected texts: a poet not ready-made to student taste (Herrick, Collins, or Landor); a drama, usually *The Duchess of Malfi;* a novel, usually *Wuthering Heights.* We have examined these texts intensively (and others around them less intensively) in an effort to understand the critic's problem and apply his principles; and we have tested him and his principles by these samples of the art which he claims as his special province.

In making this selection, we are therefore indebted to our students in English 100, who have proved its usefulness; and to our colleagues, especially Professors George R. Potter and James R. Caldwell. After using this book for ten years, we have felt most need of change in the first section, *Source,* in the foundations of modern anthropological and mythological interest. For this section, most suggestions have been sent to us, and we thank the senders.

February, 1958 M. S., J. M., G. McK.
BERKELEY, CALIFORNIA

Note: Footnotes which are introduced by reference symbols or which appear in brackets are the editors'; all others are reproduced from the original text.

1. SOURCE

PLATO: The Poet in the Republic*

OF THE many excellences which I perceive in the order of our State, there is none which upon reflection pleases me better than the rule about poetry.

To what do you refer?

To the rejection of imitative poetry, which certainly ought not to be received; as I see far more clearly now that the parts of the soul have been distinguished.

What do you mean?

Speaking in confidence, for I should not like to have my words repeated to the tragedians and the rest of the imitative tribe—but I do not mind saying to you, that all poetical imitations are ruinous to the understanding of the hearers, and that the knowledge of their true nature is the only antidote to them.

Explain the purport of your remark.

Well, I will tell you, although I have always from my earliest youth had an awe and love of Homer, which even now makes the words falter on my lips, for he is the great captain and teacher of the whole of that charming tragic company; but a man is not to be reverenced more than the truth, and therefore I will speak out.

Very good, he said.

Listen to me then, or rather, answer me.

Put your question.

Can you tell me what imitation is? for I really do not know.

A likely thing, then, that I should know.

* Plato's *Republic* was composed in about 373 B.C. The present selection is a portion of Book X, and appears here in the translation of Benjamin Jowett, reprinted from *The Dialogues of Plato*, third edition, 1892, by permission of the Oxford University Press. Plato's other famous comment on poets and poetry is in the *Ion*, which was composed about 390 B.C. The passage is appended to our selection from *The Republic;* it is taken from the same edition of Jowett's translation, and reprinted by permission of the Oxford University Press.

Why not? for the duller eye may often see a thing sooner than the keener.

Very true, he said; but in your presence, even if I had any faint notion, I could not muster courage to utter it. Will you enquire yourself?

Well then, shall we begin the enquiry in our usual manner: Whenever a number of individuals have a common name, we assume them to have also a corresponding idea or form. Do you understand me?

I do.

Let us take any common instance; there are beds and tables in the world—plenty of them, are there not?

Yes.

But there are only two ideas or forms of them—one the idea of a bed, the other of a table.

True.

And the maker of either of them makes a bed or he makes a table for our use, in accordance with the idea—that is our way of speaking in this and similar instances—but no artificer makes the ideas themselves: how could he?

Impossible.

And there is another artist,—I should like to know what you would say of him.

Who is he?

One who is the maker of all the works of all other workmen.

What an extraordinary man!

Wait a little, and there will be more reason for your saying so. For this is he who is able to make not only vessels of every kind, but plants and animals, himself and all other things—the earth and heaven, and the things which are in heaven or under the earth; he makes the gods also.

He must be a wizard and no mistake.

Oh! you are incredulous, are you? Do you mean that there is no such maker or creator, or that in one sense there might be a maker of all these things but in another not? Do you see that there is a way in which you could make them all yourself?

What way?

An easy way enough; or rather, there are many ways in which the feat might be quickly and easily accomplished, none quicker than that of turning a mirror round and round—you would soon enough make the sun and the heavens, and the earth and yourself, and other animals and plants, and all the other things of which we were just now speaking, in the mirror.

Yes, he said; but they would be appearances only.

Very good, I said, you are coming to the point now. And the painter too is, as I conceive, just such another—a creator of appearances, is he not?

Of course.

But then I suppose you will say that what he creates is untrue. And yet there is a sense in which the painter also creates a bed?

Yes, he said, but not a real bed.

And what of the maker of the bed? Were you not saying that he too makes, not the idea which, according to our view, is the essence of the bed, but only a particular bed?

Yes, I did.

Then if he does not make that which exists he cannot make true existence, but only some semblance of existence; and if any one were to say that the work of the maker of the bed, or of any other workman, has real existence, he could hardly be supposed to be speaking the truth.

At any rate, he replied, philosophers would say that he was not speaking the truth.

No wonder, then, that his work too is an indistinct expression of truth.

No wonder.

Suppose now that by the light of the examples just offered we enquire who this imitator is?

If you please.

Well then, here are three beds: one existing in nature, which is made by God, as I think that we may say—for no one else can be the maker?

No.

There is another which is the work of the carpenter?

Yes.

And the work of the painter is a third?

Yes.

Beds, then, are of three kinds, and there are three artists who superintend them: God, the maker of the bed, and the painter?

Yes, there are three of them.

God, whether from choice or from necessity, made one bed in nature and one only; two or more such ideal beds neither ever have been nor ever will be made by God.

Why is that?

Because even if He had made but two, a third would still appear behind them which both of them would have for their idea, and that would be the ideal bed and not the two others.

Very true, he said.

God knew this, and He desired to be the real maker of a real bed, not a particular maker of a particular bed, and therefore He created a bed which is essentially and by nature one only.

So we believe.

Shall we, then, speak of Him as the natural author or maker of the bed?

Yes, he replied; inasmuch as by the natural process of creation He is the author of this and of all other things.

And what shall we say of the carpenter—is not he also the maker of the bed?

Yes.

But would you call the painter a creator and maker?

Certainly not.

Yet if he is not the maker, what is he in relation to the bed?

I think, he said, that we may fairly designate him as the imitator of that which the others make.

Good, I said; then you call him who is third in the descent from nature an imitator?

Certainly, he said.

And the tragic poet is an imitator, and therefore, like all other imitators, he is thrice removed from the king and from the truth?

That appears to be so.

Then about the imitator we are agreed. And what about the painter?—I would like to know whether he may be thought to imitate that which originally exists in nature, or only the creations of artists?

The latter.

As they are or as they appear? You have still to determine this.

What do you mean?

I mean, that you may look at a bed from different points of view, obliquely or directly or from any other point of view, and the bed will appear different, but there is no difference in reality. And the same of all things.

Yes, he said, the difference is only apparent.

Now let me ask you another question: Which is the art of painting designed to be—an imitation of things as they are, or as they appear—of appearance or of reality?

Of appearance.

Then the imitator, I said, is a long way off the truth, and can do all things because he lightly touches on a small part of them, and that part an image. For example: A painter will paint a cobbler, carpenter, or any other artist, though he knows nothing of their arts; and, if he is a good artist, he may deceive children or simple persons, when he shows them his picture of a carpenter from a distance, and they will fancy that they are looking at a real carpenter.

Certainly.

And whenever any one informs us that he has found a man who knows all the arts, and all things else that anybody knows, and every single thing with a higher degree of accuracy than any other man—whoever tells us this, I think that we can only imagine him to be a simple creature who is likely to have been deceived by some wizard or actor whom he met, and whom he thought all-knowing, because he himself was unable to analyze the nature of knowledge and ignorance and imitation.

Most true.

And so, when we hear persons saying that the tragedians, and Homer, who is at their head, know all the arts and all things human, virtue as well as vice, and divine things too, for that the good poet cannot compose well unless he knows his subject, and that he who has not this knowledge can never be a poet, we ought to consider whether here also there may not be a similar illusion. Perhaps they may have come across imitators and been deceived by them; they may not have remembered when they saw their works that these were but imitations thrice removed from the truth, and could easily be made without any knowledge of the truth, because they are appearances only and not realities? Or, after all, they may be in the right, and poets do really know the things about which they seem to the many to speak so well?

The question, he said, should by all means be considered.

Now do you suppose that if a person were able to make the original as well as the image, he would seriously devote himself to the image-making branch? Would he allow imitation to be the ruling principle of his life, as if he had nothing higher in him?

I should say not.

The real artist, who knew what he was imitating, would be interested in realities and not in imitations; and would desire to leave as memorials of himself works many and fair; and, instead of being the author of encomiums, he would prefer to be the theme of them.

Yes, he said, that would be to him a source of much greater honour and profit.

Then, I said, we must put a question to Homer; not about medicine, or any of the arts to which his poems only incidentally refer: we are not going to ask him, or any other poet, whether he has cured patients like Asclepius, or left behind him a school of medicine such as the Asclepiads were, or whether he only talks about medicine and other arts at second hand; but we have a right to know respecting military tactics, politics, education, which are the chiefest and noblest subjects of his poems, and we may fairly ask him about them. "Friend Homer," then we say to him, "if you are only in the second remove from truth in what you say of virtue, and not in the third—not an image maker or imitator—and if you are able to discern what pursuits make men better or worse in private or public life, tell us what State was ever better governed by your help? The good order of Lacedaemon is due to Lycurgus, and many other cities great and small have been similarly benefited by others; but who says that you have been a good legislator to them and have done them any good? Italy and Sicily boast of Charondas, and there is Solon who is renowned among us; but what city has anything to say about you?" Is there any city which he might name?

I think not, said Glaucon; not even the Homerids themselves pretend that he was a legislator.

Well, but is there any war on record which

was carried on successfully by him, or aided by his counsels, when he was alive?

There is not.

Or is there any invention of his, applicable to the arts or to human life, such as Thales the Milesian or Anacharsis the Scythian, and other ingenious men have conceived, which is attributed to him?

There is absolutely nothing of the kind.

But, if Homer never did any public service, was he privately a guide or teacher of any? Had he in his lifetime friends who loved to associate with him, and who handed down to posterity an Homeric way of life, such as was established by Pythagoras who was so greatly beloved for his wisdom, and whose followers are to this day quite celebrated for the order which was named after him?

Nothing of the kind is recorded of him. For surely, Socrates, Creophylus, the companion of Homer, that child of flesh, whose name always makes us laugh, might be more justly ridiculed for his stupidity, if, as is said, Homer was greatly neglected by him and others in his own day when he was alive?

Yes, I replied, that is the tradition. But can you imagine, Glaucon, that if Homer had really been able to educate and improve mankind—if he had possessed knowledge and not been a mere imitator—can you imagine, I say, that he would not have had many followers, and been honoured and loved by them? Protagoras of Abdera, and Prodicus of Ceos, and a host of others, have only to whisper to their contemporaries: "You will never be able to manage either your own house or your own State until you appoint us to be your ministers of education"—and this ingenious device of theirs has such an effect in making men love them that their companions all but carry them about on their shoulders. And is it conceivable that the contemporaries of Homer, or again of Hesiod, would have allowed either of them to go about as rhapsodists, if they had really been able to make mankind virtuous? Would they not have been as unwilling to part with them as with gold, and have compelled them to stay at home with them? Or, if the master would not stay, then the disciples would have followed him about everywhere, until they had got education enough?

Yes, Socrates, that, I think, is quite true.

Then must we not infer that all these poetical individuals, beginning with Homer, are only imitators; they copy images of virtue and the like, but the truth they never reach? The poet is like a painter who, as we have already observed, will make a likeness of a cobbler though he understands nothing of cobbling; and his picture is good enough for those who know no more than he does, and judge only by colours and figures.

Quite so.

In like manner the poet with his words and phrases [1] may be said to lay on the colours of the several arts, himself understanding their nature only enough to imitate them; and other people, who are as ignorant as he is, and judge only from his words, imagine that if he speaks of cobbling, or of military tactics, or of anything else, in metre and harmony and rhythm, he speaks very well—such is the sweet influence which melody and rhythm by nature have. And I think that you must have observed again and again what a poor appearance the tales of poets make when stripped of the colours which music puts upon them, and recited in simple prose.

Yes, he said.

They are like faces which were never really beautiful, but only blooming; and now the bloom of youth has passed away from them?

Exactly.

Here is another point: The imitator or maker of the image knows nothing of true existence; he knows appearances only. Am I not right?

Yes.

Then let us have a clear understanding, and not be satisfied with half an explanation.

Proceed.

Of the painter we say that he will paint reins, and he will paint a bit?

Yes.

And the worker in leather and brass will make them?

Certainly.

But does the painter know the right form of the bit and reins? Nay, hardly even the workers in brass and leather who make them; only the horseman who knows how to use them—he knows their right form.

Most true.

[1] Or, "with his nouns and verbs."

And may we not say the same of all things?

What?

That there are three arts which are concerned with all things: one which uses, another which makes, a third which imitates them?

Yes.

And the excellence or beauty or truth of every structure, animate or inanimate, and of every action of man, is relative to the use for which nature or the artist has intended them.

True.

Then the user of them must have the greatest experience of them, and he must indicate to the maker the good or bad qualities which develop themselves in use; for example, the flute-player will tell the flute-maker which of his flutes is satisfactory to the performer; he will tell him how he ought to make them, and the other will attend to his instructions?

Of course.

The one knows and therefore speaks with authority about the goodness and badness of flutes, while the other, confiding in him, will do what he is told by him?

True.

The instrument is the same, but about the excellence or badness of it the maker will only attain to a correct belief; and this he will gain from him who knows, by talking to him and being compelled to hear what he has to say, whereas the user will have knowledge?

True.

But will the imitator have either? Will he know from use whether or no his drawing is correct or beautiful? Or will he have right opinion from being compelled to associate with another who knows and gives him instructions about what he should draw?

Neither.

Then he will no more have true opinion than he will have knowledge about the goodness or badness of his imitations?

I suppose not.

The imitative artist will be in a brilliant state of intelligence about his own creations?

Nay, very much the reverse.

And still he will go on imitating without knowing what makes a thing good or bad, and may be expected therefore to imitate only that which appears to be good to the ignorant multitude?

Just so.

Thus far then we are pretty well agreed that the imitator has no knowledge worth mentioning of what he imitates. Imitation is only a kind of play or sport, and the tragic poets, whether they write in Iambic or in Heroic verse, are imitators in the highest degree?

Very true.

And now tell me, I conjure you, has not imitation been shown by us to be concerned with that which is thrice removed from the truth?

Certainly.

And what is the faculty in man to which imitation is addressed?

What do you mean?

I will explain: The body which is large when seen near, appears small when seen at a distance?

True.

And the same object appears straight when looked at out of the water, and crooked when in the water; and the concave becomes convex, owing to the illusion about colours to which the sight is liable. Thus every sort of confusion is revealed within us; and this is that weakness of the human mind on which the art of conjuring and of deceiving by light and shadow and other ingenious devices imposes, having an effect upon us like magic.

True.

And the arts of measuring and numbering and weighing come to the rescue of the human understanding—there is the beauty of them—and the apparent greater or less, or more or heavier, no longer have the mastery over us, but give way before calculation and measure and weight?

Most true.

And this, surely, must be the work of the calculating and rational principle in the soul?

To be sure.

And when this principle measures and certifies that some things are equal, or that some are greater or less than others, there occurs an apparent contradiction?

True.

But were we not saying that such a contradiction is impossible—the same faculty cannot have contrary opinions at the same time about the same thing?

Very true.

Then that part of the soul which has an opinion contrary to measure is not the same with that which has an opinion in accordance with measure?

True.

And the better part of the soul is likely to be that which trusts to measure and calculation?

Certainly.

And that which is opposed to them is one of the inferior principles of the soul?

No doubt.

This was the conclusion at which I was seeking to arrive when I said that painting or drawing, and imitation in general, when doing their own proper work, are far removed from truth, and the companions and friends and associates of a principle within us which is equally removed from reason, and that they have no true or healthy aim.

Exactly.

The imitative art is an inferior who marries an inferior, and has inferior offspring.

Very true.

And is this confined to the sight only, or does it extend to the hearing also, relating in fact to what we term poetry?

Probably the same would be true of poetry.

Do not rely, I said, on a probability derived from the analogy of painting; but let us examine further and see whether the faculty with which poetical imitation is concerned is good or bad.

By all means.

We may state the question thus:—Imitation imitates the actions of men, whether voluntary or involuntary, on which, as they imagine, a good or bad result has ensued, and they rejoice or sorrow accordingly. Is there anything more?

No, there is nothing else.

But in all this variety of circumstances is the man at unity with himself—or rather, as in the instance of sight there was confusion and opposition in his opinions about the same things, so here also is there not strife and inconsistency in his life? Though I need hardly raise the question again, for I remember that all this has been already admitted; and the soul has been acknowledged by us to be full of these and ten thousand similar oppositions occurring at the same moment?

And we were right, he said.

Yes, I said, thus far we were right; but there was an omission which must now be supplied.

What was the omission?

Were we not saying that a good man, who has the misfortune to lose his son or anything else which is most dear to him, will bear the loss with more equanimity than another?

Yes.

But will he have no sorrow, or shall we say that although he cannot help sorrowing, he will moderate his sorrow?

The latter, he said, is the truer statement.

Tell me: will he be more likely to struggle and hold out against his sorrow when he is seen by his equals, or when he is alone?

It will make a great difference whether he is seen or not.

When he is by himself he will not mind saying or doing many things which he would be ashamed of any one hearing or seeing him do?

True.

There is a principle of law and reason in him which bids him resist, as well as a feeling of his misfortune which is forcing him to indulge his sorrow?

True.

But when a man is drawn in two opposite directions, to and from the same object, this, as we affirm, necessarily implies two distinct principles in him?

Certainly.

One of them is ready to follow the guidance of the law?

How do you mean?

The law would say that to be patient under suffering is best, and that we should not give way to impatience, as there is no knowing whether such things are good or evil; and nothing is gained by impatience; also, because no human thing is of serious importance, and grief stands in the way of that which at the moment is most required.

What is most required? he asked.

That we should take counsel about what has happened, and when the dice have been thrown order our affairs in the way which reason deems best; not, like children who have had a fall, keeping hold of the part struck and wasting time in setting up a howl, but always accustoming the soul forthwith to apply a remedy, raising up that which is sickly and fallen, banishing the cry of sorrow by the healing art.

Yes, he said, that is the true way of meeting the attacks of fortune.

Yes, I said; and the higher principle is ready to follow this suggestion of reason?

Clearly.

And the other principle, which inclines us to recollection of our troubles and to lamentation, and can never have enough of them, we may call irrational, useless, and cowardly?

Indeed, we may.

And does not the latter—I mean the rebellious principle—furnish a great variety of materials for imitation? Whereas the wise and calm temperament, being always nearly equable, is not easy to imitate or to appreciate when imitated, especially at a public festival when a promiscuous crowd is assembled in a theatre. For the feeling represented is one to which they are strangers.

Certainly.

Then the imitative poet who aims at being popular is not by nature made, nor is his art intended, to please or to affect the rational principle in the soul; but he will prefer the passionate and fitful temper, which is easily imitated?

Clearly.

And now we may fairly take him and place him by the side of the painter, for he is like him in two ways: first, inasmuch as his creations have an inferior degree of truth—in this, I say, he is like him; and he is also like him in being concerned with an inferior part of the soul; and therefore we shall be right in refusing to admit him into a well-ordered State, because he awakens and nourishes and strengthens the feelings and impairs the reason. As in a city when the evil are permitted to have authority and the good are put out of the way, so in the soul of man, as we maintain, the imitative poet implants an evil constitution, for he indulges the irrational nature which has no discernment of greater and less, but thinks the same thing at one time great and at another small—he is a manufacturer of images and is very far removed from the truth.

Exactly.

But we have not yet brought forward the heaviest count in our accusation:—the power which poetry has of harming even the good (and there are very few who are not harmed), is surely an awful thing?

Yes, certainly, if the effect is what you say.

Hear and judge: The best of us, as I conceive, when we listen to a passage of Homer, or one of the tragedians, in which he represents some pitiful hero who is drawling out his sorrows in a long oration, of weeping, and smiting his breast—the best of us, you know, delight in giving way to sympathy, and are in raptures at the excellence of the poet who stirs our feelings most.

Yes, of course I know.

But when any sorrow of our own happens to us, then you may observe that we pride ourselves on the opposite quality—we would fain be quiet and patient; this is the manly part, and the other which delighted us in the recitation is now deemed to be the part of a woman.

Very true, he said.

Now can we be right in praising and admiring another who is doing that which any one of us would abominate and be ashamed of in his own person?

No, he said, that is certainly not reasonable.

Nay, I said, quite reasonable from one point of view.

What point of view?

If you consider, I said, that when in misfortune we feel a natural hunger and desire to relieve our sorrow by weeping and lamentation, and that this feeling which is kept under control in our own calamities is satisfied and delighted by the poets;—the better nature in each of us, not having been sufficiently trained by reason or habit, allows the sympathetic element to break loose because the sorrow is another's; and the spectator fancies that there can be no disgrace to himself in praising and pitying any one who comes telling him what a good man he is, and making a fuss about his troubles; he thinks that the pleasure is a gain, and why should he be supercilious and lose this and the poem too? Few persons ever reflect, as I should imagine, that from the evil of other men something of evil is communicated to themselves. And so the feeling of sorrow which has gathered strength at the sight of the misfortunes of others is with difficulty repressed in our own.

How very true!

And does not the same hold also of the ridiculous? There are jests which you would be ashamed to make yourself, and yet on the comic stage, or indeed in private, when you hear them, you are greatly amused by them, and are not at all disgusted at their unseemliness;—the case of pity is repeated;—there is a principle in human nature which is disposed to raise a laugh, and this which you once restrained by reason, because you were afraid of being thought a buffoon, is now let out again; and having stimulated the risible faculty at the theatre, you are betrayed unconsciously to yourself into playing the comic poet at home.

Quite true, he said.

And the same may be said of lust and anger and all the other affections, of desire and pain and pleasure, which are held to be inseparable from every action—in all of them poetry feeds and waters the passions instead of drying them up; she lets them rule, although they ought to be controlled, if mankind are ever to increase in happiness and virtue.

I cannot deny it.

Therefore, Glaucon, I said, whenever you meet with any of the eulogists of Homer declaring that he has been the educator of Hellas, and that he is profitable for education and for the ordering of human things, and that you should take him up again and again and get to know him and regulate your whole life according to him, we may love and honour those who say these things—they are excellent people, as far as their lights extend; and we are ready to acknowledge that Homer is the greatest of poets and first of tragedy writers; but we must remain firm in our conviction that hymns to the gods and praises of famous men are the only poetry which ought to be admitted into our State. For if you go beyond this and allow the honeyed muse to enter, either in epic or lyric verse, not law and the reason of mankind, which by common consent have ever been deemed best, but pleasure and pain will be the rulers in our State.

That is most true, he said.

And now since we have reverted to the subject of poetry, let this our defence serve to show the reasonableness of our former judgment in sending away out of our State an art having the tendencies which we have described; for reason constrained us. But that she may not impute to us any harshness or want of politeness, let us tell her that there is an ancient quarrel between philosophy and poetry; of which there are many proofs, such as the saying of "the yelping hound howling at her lord," or of one "mighty in the vain talk of fools," and "the mob of sages circumventing Zeus," and the "subtle thinkers who are beggars after all"; and there are innumerable other signs of ancient enmity between them. Notwithstanding this, let us assure our sweet friend and the sister arts of imitation that if she will only prove her title to exist in a well-ordered State we shall be delighted to receive her—we are very conscious of her charms; but we may not on that account betray the truth. I dare say, Glaucon, that you are as much charmed by her as I am, especially when she appears in Homer?

Yes, indeed, I am greatly charmed.

Shall I propose, then, that she be allowed to return from exile, but upon this condition only—that she make a defence of herself in lyrical or some other metre?

Certainly.

And we may further grant to those of her defenders who are lovers of poetry and yet not poets the permission to speak in prose on her behalf: let them show not only that she is pleasant but also useful to States and to human life, and we will listen in a kindly spirit; for if this can be proved we shall surely be the gainers—I mean, if there is a use in poetry as well as a delight?

Certainly, he said, we shall be the gainers.

If her defence fails, then, my dear friend, like other persons who are enamoured of something, but put a restraint upon themselves when they think their desires are opposed to their interests, so too must we after the manner of lovers give her up, though not without a struggle. We too are inspired by that love of poetry which the education of noble States has implanted in us, and therefore we would have her appear at her best and truest; but so long as she is unable to make good her defence, this argument of ours shall be a charm to us, which we will repeat to ourselves while we listen to her strains; that we may not fall away into the childish love of her which captivates the many. At all events we are well aware that poetry being such as we have described is not to be regarded seriously as attaining to the truth; and he who listens to her, fearing for the safety of the city which is within him, should be on his guard against her seductions and make our words his law.

Yes, he said, I quite agree with you.

Yes, I said, my dear Glaucon, for great is the issue at stake, greater than appears, whether a man is to be good or bad. And what will any one be profited if under the influence of honour or money or power, aye, or under the excitement of poetry, he neglect justice and virtue?

Yes, he said; I have been convinced by the argument, as I believe that any one else would have been.

FROM THE *Ion*

SOCRATES: I perceive, Ion; and I will proceed to explain to you what I imagine to be the reason of this. The gift which you possess of speaking excellently about Homer is not an art, but, as I was just saying, an inspiration; there is a divinity moving you, like that contained in the stone which Euripides calls a magnet, but which is commonly known as the stone of Heraclea. This stone not only attracts iron rings, but also imparts to them a similar power of attracting other rings; and sometimes you may see a number of pieces of iron and rings suspended from one another so as to form quite a long chain: and all of them derive their power of suspension from the original stone. In like manner the Muse first of all inspires men herself; and from these inspired persons a chain of other persons is suspended, who take the inspiration. For all good poets, epic as well as lyric, compose their beautiful poems not by art, but because they are inspired and possessed. And as the Corybantian revellers when they dance are not in their right mind, so the lyric poets are not in their right mind when they are composing their beautiful strains: but when falling under the power of music and metre they are inspired and possessed; like Bacchic maidens who draw milk and honey from the rivers when they are under the influence of Dionysus but not when they are in their right mind. And the soul of the lyric poet does the same, as they themselves say; for they tell us that they bring songs from honeyed fountains, culling them out of the gardens and dells of the Muses; they, like the bees, winging their way from flower to flower. And this is true. For the poet is a light and winged and holy thing, and there is no invention in him until he has been inspired and is out of his senses, and the mind is no longer in him: when he has not attained to this state, he is powerless and is unable to utter his oracles. Many are the noble words in which poets speak concerning the actions of men; but like yourself when speaking about Homer, they do not speak of them by any rules of art: they are simply inspired to utter that to which the Muse impels them, and that only; and when inspired, one of them will make dithyrambs, another hymns of praise, another choral strains, another epic or iambic verses—and he who is good at one is not good at any other kind of verse: for not by art does the poet sing, but by power divine. Had he learned by rules of art, he would have known how to speak not of one theme only, but of all; and therefore God takes away the minds of poets, and uses them as his ministers, as he also uses diviners and holy prophets, in order that we who hear them may know them to be speaking not of themselves who utter these priceless words in a state of unconsciousness, but that God himself is the speaker, and that through them he is conversing with us. And Tynnichus the Chalcidian affords a striking instance of what I am saying: he wrote nothing that any one would care to remember but the famous paean which is in every one's mouth, one of the finest poems ever written, simply an invention of the Muses, as he himself says. For in this way the God would seem to indicate to us and not allow us to doubt that these beautiful poems are not human, or the work of man, but divine and the work of God; and that the poets are only the interpreters of the Gods by whom they are severally possessed. Was not this the lesson which the God intended to teach when by the mouth of the worst of poets he sang the best of songs? Am I not right, Ion?

LONGINUS: On the Sublime *

I

You will remember, my dear Postumius Terentianus,[1] that when we examined together the treatise of Caecilius, On the Sublime, we found that it fell below the dignity of the whole subject, while it failed signally to grasp the essential points, and conveyed to its readers but little of that practical help which it should be a writer's principal aim to give. In every systematic treatise two things are required. The first is a statement of the subject; the other, which although second in order ranks higher in importance, is an indication of the methods by which we may attain our end. Now Caecilius seeks to show the nature of the sublime by countless instances as though our ignorance demanded it, but the consideration of the means whereby we may succeed in raising our own capacities to a certain pitch of elevation he has, strangely enough, omitted as unnecessary. 2. However, it may be that the man ought not so much to be blamed for his shortcomings as praised for his happy thought and his enthusiasm. But since you have urged me, in my turn, to write a brief essay on the sublime for your special gratification, let us consider whether the views I have formed contain anything which will be of use to public men. You will yourself, my friend, in accordance with your nature and with what is fitting, join me in appraising each detail with the utmost regard for truth; for he answered well who, when asked in what qualities we resemble the Gods, declared that we do so in benevolence and truth.

* "Longinus" is the name commonly assigned to the unidentified author of "On the Sublime" because of its long but mistaken association with Cassius Longinus (third century A.D.). The real author was almost certainly of the first century and probably flourished in its last quarter. The present translation, by W. Rhys Roberts, was first published by the Cambridge University Press, with whose permission it is here reprinted.

[1] Probably this name (together with another which has disappeared) underlies the reading of P.

3. As I am writing to you, my good friend, who are well versed in literary studies, I feel almost absolved from the necessity of premising at any length that sublimity is a certain distinction and excellence in expression, and that it is from no other source than this that the greatest poets and writers have derived their eminence and gained an immortality of renown. 4. The effect of elevated language upon an audience is not persuasion but transport. At every time and in every way imposing speech, with the spell it throws over us, prevails over that which aims at persuasion and gratification. Our persuasions we can usually control, but the influences of the sublime bring power and irresistible might to bear, and reign supreme over every hearer. Similarly, we see skill in invention, and due order and arrangement of matter, emerging as the hard-won result not of one thing nor of two, but of the whole texture of the composition, whereas sublimity flashing forth at the right moment scatters everything before it like a thunderbolt, and at once displays the power of the orator in all its plenitude. But enough; for these reflexions, and others like them, you can, I know well, my dear Terentianus, yourself suggest from your own experience.

II

First of all, we must raise the question whether there is such a thing as an art of the sublime or lofty. Some hold that those are entirely in error who would bring such matters under the precepts of art. A lofty tone, says one, is innate, and does not come by teaching; nature is the only art that can compass it. Works of nature are, they think, made worse and altogether feebler when wizened by the rules of art. 2. But I maintain that this will be found to be otherwise if it be observed that, while nature as a rule is free and independent in matters of passion and elevation, yet is she wont not to act at random and utterly without system. Further, nature is the original and vital underlying principle in all cases, but system can define limits and fitting seasons, and can also contribute the safest rules for use and practice. Moreover, the expression of the sublime is more exposed to danger when it goes its own way without the guidance of knowledge—when it is suffered to be unstable and unballasted—when it is left at the mercy of mere momentum and ignorant audacity. It is true that it often needs the spur, but it is also true that it often needs the curb. 3. Demosthenes expresses the view, with regard to human life in general, that good fortune is the greatest of blessings, while good counsel, which occupies the second place, is hardly inferior in importance, since its absence contributes inevitably to the ruin of the former. This we may apply to diction, nature occupying the position of good fortune, art that of good counsel. Most important of all, we must remember that the very fact that there are some elements of expression which are in the hands of nature alone, can be learnt from no other source than art. If, I say, the critic of those who desire to learn were to turn these matters over in his mind, he would no longer, it seems to me, regard the discussion of the subject as superfluous or useless. . . .

III

Quell they the oven's far-flung splendour-glow!
Ha, let me but one hearth-abider mark—
One flame-wreath torrent-like I'll whirl on high;
I'll burn the roof, to cinders shrivel it!—
Nay, now my chant is not of noble strain.[2]

Such things are not tragic but pseudo-tragic—"flame-wreaths," and "belching to the sky," and Boreas represented as a "flute-player," and all the rest of it. They are turbid in expression and confused in imagery rather than the product of intensity, and each one of them, if examined in the light of day, sinks little by little from the terrible into the contemptible. But since even in tragedy, which is in its very nature stately and prone to bombast, tasteless tumidity is unpardonable, still less, I presume, will it harmonise with the narration of fact. 2. And this is the ground on which the phrases of Gorgias of Leontini are ridiculed when he describes Xerxes as the "Zeus of the Persians" and vultures as "living tombs." So is it with some of the expressions of Callisthenes which are not sublime but high-flown, and still more with those of Cleitarchus, for the man is frivolous and blows, as Sophocles has it,

On pigmy hautboys: mouthpiece have they none.[3]

Other examples will be found in Amphicrates and Hegesias and Matris, for often when these writers seem to themselves to be inspired they are in no true frenzy but are simply trifling. 3. Altogether, tumidity seems particularly hard to avoid. The explanation is that all who aim at elevation are so anxious to escape the reproach of being weak and dry that they are carried, as by some strange law of nature, into the opposite extreme. They put their trust in the maxim that "failure in a great attempt is at least a noble error." 4. But evil are the swellings, both in the body and in diction, which are inflated and unreal, and threaten us with the reverse of our aim; for nothing, say they, is drier than a man who has the dropsy. While tumidity desires to transcend the limits of the sublime, the defect which is termed puerility is the direct antithesis of elevation, for it is utterly low and mean and in real truth the most ignoble vice of style. What, then, is this puerility? Clearly, a pedant's thoughts, which begin in learned trifling and end in frigidity. Men slip into this kind of error because, while they aim at the uncommon and elaborate and most of all at the attractive, they drift unawares into the tawdry and affected. 5. A third, and closely allied, kind of defect in matters of passion is that which Theodorus used to call *parenthyrsus*. By this is meant unseasonable and empty passion, where no passion is required, or immoderate, where moderation is needed. For men are often carried away, as if by intoxication, into displays of emotion which are not caused by the nature of the subject, but are purely personal and wearisome. In consequence they seem to hearers who are in no wise affected to act in an ungainly way. And no wonder; for they are beside themselves, while their hearers are not. But the question of the passions we reserve for separate treatment.

[2] Aeschylus, tr. by A. S. Way.

[3] Tr. by A. S. Way.

IV

Of the second fault of which we have spoken—frigidity—Timaeus supplies many examples. Timaeus was a writer of considerable general ability, who occasionally showed that he was not incapable of elevation of style. He was learned and ingenious, but very prone to criticise the faults of others while blind to his own. Through his passion for continually starting novel notions, he often fell into the merest childishness. 2. I will set down one or two examples only of his manner, since the greater number have been already appropriated by Caecilius. In the course of a eulogy on Alexander the Great, he describes him as "the man who gained possession of the whole of Asia in fewer years than it took Isocrates to write his Panegyric urging war against the Persians." Strange indeed is the comparison of the man of Macedon with the rhetorician. How plain it is, Timaeus, that the Lacedaemonians, thus judged, were far inferior to Isocrates in prowess, for they spent thirty years in the conquest of Messene, whereas he composed his Panegyric in ten. 3. Consider again the way in which he speaks of the Athenians who were captured in Sicily. "They were punished because they had acted impiously towards Hermes and mutilated his images, and the infliction of punishment was chiefly due to Hermocrates the son of Hermon, who was descended, in the paternal line, from the outraged god." I am surprised, beloved Terentianus, that he does not write with regard to the despot Dionysius that "Dion and Heracleides deprived him of his sovereignty because he had acted impiously towards Zeus and Heracles." 4. But why speak of Timaeus when even those heroes of literature, Xenophon and Plato, though trained in the school of Socrates, nevertheless sometimes forget themselves for the sake of such paltry pleasantries? Xenophon writes in the Polity of the Lacedaemonians: "You would find it harder to hear their voice than that of busts of marble, harder to deflect their gaze than that of statues of bronze; you would deem them more modest than the very maidens in their eyes." [4]

It was worthy of an Amphicrates and not of a Xenophon to call the pupils of our eyes "modest maidens." Good heavens, how strange it is that the pupils of the whole company should be believed to be modest notwithstanding the common saying that the shamelessness of individuals is indicated by nothing so much as the eyes! "Thou sot, that hast the eyes of a dog," as Homer has it.[5] 5. Timaeus, however, has not left even this piece of frigidity to Xenophon, but clutches it as though it were hid treasure. At all events, after saying of Agathocles that he abducted his cousin, who had been given in marriage to another man, from the midst of the nuptial rites, he asks, "Who could have done this had he not had wantons, in place of maidens, in his eyes?" 6. Yes, and Plato (usually so divine) when he means simply *tablets* says, "They shall write and preserve *cypress memorials* in the temples." [6]

And again, "As touching walls, Megillus, I should hold with Sparta that they be suffered to lie asleep in the earth and not summoned to arise." [7] The expression of Herodotus to the effect that beautiful women are "eye-smarts" is not much better.[8] This, however, may be condoned in some degree since those who use this particular phrase in his narrative are barbarians and in their cups, but not even in the mouths of such characters is it well that an author should suffer, in the judgment of posterity, from an unseemly exhibition of triviality.

V

All these ugly and parasitical growths arise in literature from a single cause, that pursuit of novelty in the expression of ideas which may be regarded as the fashionable craze of the day. Our defects usually spring, for the most part, from the same sources as our good points. Hence, while beauties of expression and touches of sublimity, and charming elegances withal, are favourable to effective composition, yet these very things are the elements and foundation, not only of success, but also of the contrary. Something of the kind is true also of variations and hyperboles and the use of the plural number, and we shall show subsequently the dangers to which these seem severally to be exposed. It is necessary now to seek and to suggest means by

[4] III, 5.

[5] *Iliad*, I, 225.
[6] *Laws*, V, 741c.
[7] *Ibid.*, VI, 778d.
[8] V, 18.

which we may avoid the defects which attend the steps of the sublime.

VI

The best means would be, my friend, to gain, first of all, clear knowledge and appreciation of the true sublime. The enterprise is, however, an arduous one. For the judgment of style is the last and crowning fruit of long experience. None the less, if I must speak in the way of precept, it is not impossible perhaps to acquire discrimination in these matters by attention to some such hints as those which follow.

VII

You must know, my dear friend, that it is with the sublime as in the common life of man. In life nothing can be considered great which it is held great to despise. For instance, riches, honours, distinctions, sovereignties, and all other things which possess in abundance the external trappings of the stage, will not seem, to a man of sense, to be supreme blessings, since the very contempt of them is reckoned good in no small degree, and in any case those who could have them, but are high-souled enough to disdain them, are more admired than those who have them. So also in the case of sublimity in poems and prose writings, we must consider whether some supposed examples have not simply the appearance of elevation with many idle accretions, so that when analysed they are found to be mere vanity—objects which a noble nature will rather despise than admire. 2. For, as if instinctively, our soul is uplifted by the true sublime; it takes a proud flight, and is filled with joy and vaunting, as though it had itself produced what it has heard. 3. When, therefore, a thing is heard repeatedly by a man of intelligence, who is well versed in literature, and its effect is not to dispose the soul to high thoughts, and it does not leave in the mind more food for reflexion than the words seem to convey, but falls, if examined carefully through and through, into disesteem, it cannot rank as true sublimity because it does not survive a first hearing. For that is really great which bears a repeated examination, and which it is difficult or rather impossible to withstand, and the memory of which is strong and hard to efface. 4. In general, consider those examples of sublimity to be fine and genuine which please all and always. For when men of different pursuits, lives, ambitions, ages, languages, hold identical views on one and the same subject, then that verdict which results, so to speak, from a concert of discordant elements makes our faith in the object of admiration strong and unassailable.

VIII

There are, it may be said, five principal sources of elevated language. Beneath these five varieties there lies, as though it were a common foundation, the gift of discourse, which is indispensable. First and most important is the power of forming great conceptions, as we have elsewhere explained in our remarks on Xenophon. Secondly, there is vehement and inspired passion. These two components of the sublime are for the most part innate. Those which remain are partly the product of art. The due formation of figures deals with two sorts of figures, first those of thought and secondly those of expression. Next there is noble diction, which in turn comprises choice of words, and use of metaphors, and elaboration of language. The fifth cause of elevation—one which is the fitting conclusion of all that have preceded it—is dignified and elevated composition. Come now, let us consider what is involved in each of these varieties, with this one remark by way of preface, that Caecilius has omitted some of the five divisions, for example, that of passion. 2. Surely he is quite mistaken if he does so on the ground that these two, sublimity and passion, are a unity, and if it seems to him that they are by nature one and inseparable. For some passions are found which are far removed from sublimity and are of a low order, such as pity, grief and fear; and on the other hand there are many examples of the sublime which are independent of passion, such as the daring words of Homer with regard to the Aloadae, to take one out of numberless instances,

Yea, Ossa in fury they strove to upheave on Olympus on high,
With forest-clad Pelion above, that thence they might step to the sky.[9]

[9] *Odyssey*, XI, 315-16.

And so of the words which follow with still greater force:

Ay, and the deed had they done.[10]

3. Among the orators, too, eulogies and ceremonial and occasional addresses contain on every side examples of dignity and elevation, but are for the most part void of passion. This is the reason why passionate speakers are the worst eulogists, and why, on the other hand, those who are apt in encomium are the least passionate. 4. If, on the other hand, Caecilius thought that passion never contributes at all to sublimity, and if it was for this reason that he did not deem it worthy of mention, he is altogether deluded. I would affirm with confidence that there is no tone so lofty as that of genuine passion, in its right place, when it bursts out in a wild gust of mad enthusiasm and as it were fills the speaker's words with frenzy.

IX

Now the first of the conditions mentioned, namely elevation of mind, holds the foremost rank among them all. We must, therefore, in this case also, although we have to do rather with an endowment than with an acquirement, nurture our souls (as far as that is possible) to thoughts sublime, and make them always pregnant, so to say, with noble inspiration. 2. In what way, you may ask, is this to be done? Elsewhere I have written as follows: "Sublimity is the echo of a great soul." Hence also a bare idea, by itself and without a spoken word, sometimes excites admiration just because of the greatness of soul implied. Thus the silence of Ajax in the Underworld is great and more sublime than words.[11] 3. First, then, it is absolutely necessary to indicate the source of this elevation, namely, that the truly eloquent must be free from low and ignoble thoughts. For it is not possible that men with mean and servile ideas and aims prevailing throughout their lives should produce anything that is admirable and worthy of immortality. Great accents we expect to fall from the lips of those whose thoughts are deep and grave. 4. Thus it is that stately speech comes naturally to the proudest spirits. [You will remember the answer of] Alexander to Parmenio when he said "For my part I had been well content." [12] . . .

. . . the distance from earth to heaven; and this might well be considered the measure of Homer no less than of Strife. 5. How unlike to this the expression which is used of Sorrow by Hesiod, if indeed the Shield is to be attributed to Hesiod:

Rheum from her nostrils was trickling.[13]

The image he has suggested is not terrible but rather loathsome. Contrast the way in which Homer magnifies the higher powers:

And far as a man with his eyes through the sea-line haze may discern,
On a cliff as he sitteth and gazeth away o'er the wine-dark deep,
So far at a bound do the loud-neighing steeds of the Deathless leap.[14]

He makes the vastness of the world the measure of their leap. The sublimity is so overpowering as naturally to prompt the exclamation that if the divine steeds were to leap thus twice in succession they would pass beyond the confines of the world. 6. How transcendent also are the images in the Battle of the Gods:

Far round wide heaven and Olympus echoed his clarion of thunder;
And Hades, king of the realm of shadows, quaked thereunder.
And he sprang from his throne, and he cried aloud in the dread of his heart
Lest o'er him earth-shaker Poseidon should cleave the ground apart,
And revealed to Immortals and mortals should stand those awful abodes,
Those mansions ghastly and grim, abhorred of the very Gods.[15]

You see, my friend, how the earth is torn from its foundations, Tartarus itself is laid bare, the whole world is upturned and parted asunder, and all things together—heaven and hell, things mortal and things immortal—share in the conflict and the perils of that battle!

7. But although these things are awe-inspiring, yet from another point of view, if they be not

[10] *Ibid.*, XI, 317.
[11] *Ibid.*, XI, 543.

[12] Quotation from Arrian.
[13] *Shield of Heracles*, 267.
[14] *Iliad*, V, 770.
[15] *Ibid.*, XXI, 388; XX, 61-65.

taken allegorically, they are altogether impious, and violate our sense of what is fitting. Homer seems to me, in his legends of wounds suffered by the gods, and of their feuds, reprisals, tears, bonds, and all their manifold passions, to have made, as far as lay within his power, gods of the men concerned in the Siege of Troy, and men of the gods. But whereas we mortals have death as the destined haven of our ills if our lot is miserable, he portrays the gods as immortal not only in nature but also in misfortune. 8. Much superior to the passages respecting the Battle of the Gods are those which represent the divine nature as it really is—pure and great and undefiled; for example, what is said of Poseidon in a passage fully treated by many before ourselves:

Her far-stretching ridges, her forest-trees, quaked in dismay,
And her peaks, and the Trojans' town, and the ships of Achaia's array,
Beneath his immortal feet, as onward Poseidon strode.
Then over the surges he drave: leapt sporting before the God
Sea-beasts that uprose all around from the depths, for their king they knew,
And for rapture the sea was disparted, and onward the car-steeds flew.[16]

9. Similarly, the legislator of the Jews,[17] no ordinary man, having formed and expressed a worthy conception of the might of the Godhead, writes at the very beginning of his Laws, "God said"—what? "Let there be light, and there was light; let there be land, and there was land." 10. Perhaps I shall not seem tedious, my friend, if I bring forward one passage more from Homer—this time with regard to the concerns of *men*—in order to show that he is wont himself to enter into the sublime actions of his heroes. In his poem the battle of the Greeks is suddenly veiled by mist and baffling night. Then Ajax, at his wits' end, cries:

Zeus, Father, yet save thou Achaia's sons from beneath the gloom,
And make clear day, and vouchsafe unto us with our eyes to see!
So it be but in light, destroy us! [18]

[16] *Ibid.*, XIII, 18; XX, 60; XIII, 19, 27-29.
[17] Moses.
[18] *Iliad*, XVII, 645-47.

That is the true attitude of an Ajax. He does not pray for life, for such a petition would have ill beseemed a hero. But since in the hopeless darkness he can turn his valour to no noble end, he chafes at his slackness in the fray and craves the boon of immediate light, resolved to find a death worthy of his bravery, even though Zeus should fight in the ranks against him. 11. In truth, Homer in these cases shares the full inspiration of the combat, and it is neither more nor less than true of the poet himself that

Mad rageth he as Ares the shaker of spears, or as mad flames leap
Wild-wasting from hill unto hill in the folds of a forest deep,
And the foam-froth fringeth his lips.[19]

He shows, however, in the Odyssey (and this further observation deserves attention on many grounds) that, when a great genius is declining, the special token of old age is the love of marvellous tales. 12. It is clear from many indications that the Odyssey was his second subject. A special proof is the fact that he introduces in that poem remnants of the adventures before Ilium as episodes, so to say, of the Trojan War. And indeed, he there renders a tribute of mourning and lamentation to his heroes as though he were carrying out a long-cherished purpose. In fact, the Odyssey is simply an epilogue to the Iliad:

There lieth Ajax the warrior wight, Achilles is there,
There is Patroclus, whose words had weight as a God he were;
There lieth mine own dear son.[20]

13. It is for the same reason, I suppose, that he has made the whole structure of the Iliad, which was written at the height of his inspiration, full of action and conflict, while the Odyssey for the most part consists of narrative, as is characteristic of old age. Accordingly, in the Odyssey Homer may be likened to a sinking sun, whose grandeur remains without its intensity. He does not in the Odyssey maintain so high a pitch as in those poems of Ilium. His sublimities are not evenly sustained and free from the liability to sink; there is not the same profusion of accumulated passions, nor the supple and oratorical style, packed with images drawn from real life. You

[19] *Ibid.*, XV, 605-07.
[20] *Odyssey*, III, 109-11.

seem to see henceforth the ebb and flow of greatness, and a fancy roving in the fabulous and incredible, as though the ocean were withdrawing into itself and were being laid bare within its own confines. 14. In saying this I have not forgotten the tempests in the Odyssey and the story of the Cyclops and the like. If I speak of old age, it is nevertheless the old age of Homer. The fabulous element, however, prevails throughout this poem over the real. The object of this digression has been, as I said, to show how easily great natures in their decline are sometimes diverted into absurdity, as in the incident of the wine-skin and of the men who were fed like swine by Circe (*whining porkers*, as Zoilus called them), and of Zeus like a nestling nurtured by the doves, and of the hero who was without food for ten days upon the wreck, and of the incredible tale of the slaying of the suitors.[21] For what else can we term these things than veritable dreams of Zeus? 15. These observations with regard to the Odyssey should be made for another reason—in order that you may know that the genius of great poets and prose-writers, as their passion declines, finds its final expression in the delineation of character. For such are the details which Homer gives, with an eye to characterisation, of life in the home of Odysseus; they form as it were a comedy of manners.

X

Let us next consider whether we can point to anything further that contributes to sublimity of style. Now, there inhere in all things by nature certain constituents which are part and parcel of their substance. It must needs be, therefore, that we shall find one source of the sublime in the systematic selection of the most important elements, and the power of forming, by their mutual combination, what may be called one body. The former process attracts the hearer by the choice of the ideas, the latter by the aggregation of those chosen. For instance, Sappho everywhere chooses the emotions that attend delirious passion from its accompaniments in actual life. Wherein does she demonstrate her supreme excellence? In the skill with which she selects and binds together the most striking and vehement circumstances of passion:

[21] *Ibid.*, IX, 182; X, 17, 237; XII, 62, 447; XXII, 79.

2. Peer of Gods he seemeth to me, the blissful
Man who sits and gazes at thee before him,
Close beside thee sits, and in silence hears thee
Silverly speaking,

Laughing love's low laughter. Oh this, this only
Stirs the troubled heart in my breast to tremble!
For should I but see thee a little moment,
Straight is my voice hushed;

Yea, my tongue is broken, and through and through me
'Neath the flesh impalpable fire runs tingling;
Nothing see mine eyes, and a noise of roaring
Waves in my ear sounds;

Sweat runs down in rivers, a tremor seizes
All my limbs, and paler than grass in autumn,
Caught by pains of menacing death, I falter,
Lost in the love-trance.

3. Are you not amazed how at one instant she summons, as though they were all alien from herself and dispersed, soul, body, ears, tongue, eyes, colour? Uniting contradictions, she is, at one and the same time, hot and cold, in her senses and out of her mind, for she is either terrified or at the point of death. The effect desired is that not one passion only should be seen in her, but a concourse of the passions. All such things occur in the case of lovers, but it is, as I said, the selection of the most striking of them and their combination into a single whole that has produced the singular excellence of the passage. In the same way Homer, when describing tempests, picks out the most appalling circumstances. 4. The author of the Arimaspeia thinks to inspire awe in the following way:

A marvel exceeding great is this withal to my soul—
Men dwell on the water afar from the land, where deep seas roll.
Wretches are they, for they reap but a harvest of travail and pain,
Their eyes on the stars ever dwell, while their hearts abide in the main.
Often, I ween, to the Gods are their hands upraised on high,
And with hearts in misery heavenward-lifted in prayer do they cry.[22]

It is clear, I imagine, to everybody that there is more elegance than terror in these words. 5. But what says Homer? Let one instance be quoted from among many:

[22] Aristeas.

And he burst on them like as a wave swift-rushing beneath black clouds,
Heaved huge by the winds, bursts down on a ship, and the wild foam shrouds
From the stem to the stern her hull, and the storm-blast's terrible breath
Roars in the sail, and the heart of the shipmen shuddereth
In fear, for that scantly upborne are they now from the clutches of death.[23]

6. Aratus has attempted to convert this same expression to his own use:

And a slender plank averteth their death.

Only, he has made it trivial and neat instead of terrible. Furthermore, he has put bounds to the danger by saying *A plank keeps off death.* After all, it *does* keep it off. Homcr, however, does not for one moment set a limit to the terror of the scene, but draws a vivid picture of men continually in peril of their lives, and often within an ace of perishing with each successive wave. Moreover, he has in the words ὑπὲκ θανάτοιο,[24] forced into union, by a kind of unnatural compulsion, prepositions not usually compounded. He has thus tortured his line into the similitude of the impending calamity, and by the constriction of the verse has excellently figured the disaster, and almost stamped upon the expression the very form and pressure of the danger, ὑπὲκ θανάτοιο φέρονται.[25] 7. This is true also of Archilochus in his account of the shipwreck, and of Demosthenes in the passage which begins "It was evening," where he describes the bringing of the news.[26] The salient points they selected, one might say, according to merit and massed them together, inserting in the midst nothing frivolous, mean, or trivial. For these faults mar the effect of the whole, just as though they introduced chinks or fissures into stately and co-ordered edifices, whose walls are compacted by their reciprocal adjustment.

XI

An allied excellence to those already set forth is that which is termed *amplification*. This figure is employed when the narrative or the course of a forensic argument admits, from section to section, of many starting-points and many pauses, and elevated expressions follow, one after the other, in an unbroken succession and in an ascending order. 2. And this may be effected by way of the rhetorical treatment of commonplaces, or by way of intensification (whether events or arguments are to be strongly presented), or by the orderly arrangement of facts or of passions; indeed, there are innumerable kinds of amplification. Only, the orator must in every case remember that none of these methods by itself, apart from sublimity, forms a complete whole, unless indeed where pity is to be excited or an opponent to be disparaged. In all other cases of amplification, if you take away the sublime, you will remove as it were the soul from the body. For the vigour of the amplification at once loses its intensity and its substance when not resting on a firm basis of the sublime. 3. Clearness, however, demands that we should define concisely how our present precepts differ from the point under consideration a moment ago, namely the marking-out of the most striking conceptions and the unification of them; and wherein, generally, the sublime differs from amplification.

23 *Iliad,* XV, 624-28.
24 ["up out of death"]
25 ["they were borne up out of death"]
26 Demosthenes, *On the Crown,* 169.

XII

Now the definition given by the writers on rhetoric does not satisfy me. Amplification is, say they, discourse which invests the subject with grandeur. This definition, however, would surely apply in equal measure to sublimity and passion and figurative language, since they too invest the discourse with a certain degree of grandeur. The point of distinction between them seems to me to be that sublimity consists in elevation, while amplification embraces a multitude of details. Consequently, sublimity is often comprised in a single thought, while amplification is universally associated with a certain magnitude and abundance. 2. Amplification (to sum the matter up in a general way) is an aggregation of all the constituent parts and topics of a subject, lending strength to the argument by dwelling upon it, and differing herein from proof that, while the latter demonstrates the matter under investigation. . . †

† A section and a half on Plato is here omitted.

XIV

Accordingly it is well that we ourselves also, when elaborating anything which requires lofty expression and elevated conception, should shape some idea in our minds as to how perchance Homer would have said this very thing, or how it would have been raised to the sublime by Plato or Demosthenes or by the historian Thucydides. For those personages, presenting themselves to us and inflaming our ardour and as it were illumining our path, will carry our minds in a mysterious way to the high standards of sublimity which are imaged within us. 2. Still more effectual will it be to suggest this question to our thoughts, "What sort of hearing would Homer, had he been present, or Demosthenes have given to this or that when said by me, or how would they have been affected by the other?" For the ordeal is indeed a severe one, if we presuppose such a tribunal and theatre for our own utterances, and imagine that we are undergoing a scrutiny of our writings before these great heroes, acting as judges and witnesses. 3. A greater incentive still will be supplied if you add the question, "In what spirit will each succeeding age listen to me who have written thus?" But if one shrinks from the very thought of uttering aught that may transcend the term of his own life and time, the conceptions of his mind must necessarily be incomplete, blind, and as it were untimely born, since they are by no means brought to the perfection needed to ensure a futurity of fame.

XV

Images, moreover, contribute greatly, my young friend, to dignity, elevation, and power as a pleader. In this sense some call them mental representations. In a general way the name of *image* or *imagination* is applied to every idea of the mind, in whatever form it presents itself, which gives birth to speech. But at the present day the word is predominantly used in cases where, carried away by enthusiasm and passion, you think you see what you describe, and you place it before the eyes of your hearers. 2. Further, you will be aware of the fact that an image has one purpose with the orators and another with the poets, and that the design of the poetical image is enthralment, of the rhetorical—vivid description. Both, however, seek to stir the passions and the emotions.

Mother!—'beseech thee, hark not thou on me
Yon maidens gory-eyed and snaky-haired!
Lo there!—lo there!—they are nigh—they leap on me! [27]

And:

Ah! she will slay me! whither can I fly? [28]

In these scenes the poet himself saw Furies, and the image in his mind he almost compelled his audience also to behold. 3. Now, Euripides is most assiduous in giving the utmost tragic effect to these two emotions—fits of love and madness. Herein he succeeds more, perhaps, than in any other respect, although he is daring enough to invade all the other regions of the imagination. Notwithstanding that he is by nature anything but elevated, he forces his own genius, in many passages, to tragic heights, and everywhere in the matter of sublimity it is true of him (to adopt Homer's words) that

The tail of him scourgeth his ribs and his flanks to left and to right,
And he lasheth himself into frenzy, and spurreth him on to the fight.[29]

4. When the Sun hands the reins to Phaethon, he says,

"Thou, driving, trespass not on Libya's sky,
Whose heat, by dews untempered, else shall split
Thy car asunder."

And after that,

"Speed onward toward the Pleiads seven thy course."
Thus far the boy heard; then he snatched the reins;
He lashed the flanks of that wing-wafted team;
Loosed rein; and they through folds of cloudland soared.
Hard after on a fiery star his sire
Rode, counselling his son—"Ho! thither drive!
Hither thy car turn—hither!"

Would you not say that the soul of the writer enters the chariot at the same moment as Phaethon and shares in his dangers and in the rapid flight of his steeds? For it could never have con-

[27] Euripides, *Orestes,* 255.
[28] Euripides, *Iphigenia in Tauris,* 291.
[29] *Iliad,* XX, 170.

ceived such a picture had it not been borne in no less swift career on that journey through the heavens. The same is true of the words which Euripides attributes to his Cassandra:

O chariot-loving Trojans.

5. Aeschylus, too, ventures on images of a most heroic stamp. An example will be found in his Seven Against Thebes, where he says,

For seven heroes, squadron-captains fierce,
Over a black-rimmed shield have slain a bull,
And, dipping in the bull's blood each his hand,
By Ares and Enyo, and by Panic
Lover of blood, have sworn.[30]

In mutual fealty they devoted themselves by that joint oath to a relentless doom. Sometimes, however, he introduces ideas that are rough-hewn and uncouth and harsh; and Euripides, when stirred by the spirit of emulation, comes perilously near the same fault, even in spite of his own natural bent. 6. Thus in Aeschylus the palace of Lycurgus at the coming of Dionysus is strangely represented as *possessed:*

A frenzy thrills the hall; the roofs are bacchant
With ecstasy:

an idea which Euripides has echoed, in other words, it is true, and with some abatement of its crudity, where he says:

The whole mount shared their bacchic ecstasy.[31]

7. Magnificent are the images which Sophocles has conceived of the death of Oedipus, who makes ready his burial amid the portents of the sky.[32] Magnificent, too, is the passage where the Greeks are on the point of sailing away and Achilles appears above his tomb to those who are putting out to sea—a scene which I doubt whether anyone has depicted more vividly than Simonides. But it is impossible to cite all the examples that present themselves. 8. It is no doubt true that those which are found in the poets contain, as I said, a tendency to exaggeration in the way of the fabulous and that they transcend in every way the credible, but in oratorical imagery the best feature is always its reality and truth. Whenever the form of a speech is poetical and fabulous and breaks into every kind of impossibility, such digressions have a strange and alien air. For example, the clever orators forsooth of our day, like the tragedians, see Furies, and—fine fellows that they are—cannot even understand that Orestes when he cries,

Unhand me!—of mine Haunting Fiends thou art—
Dost grip my waist to hurl me into hell! [33]

has these fancies because he is mad. 9. What, then, can oratorical imagery effect? Well, it is able in many ways to infuse vehemence and passion into spoken words, while more particularly when it is combined with the argumentative passages it not only persuades the hearer but actually makes him its slave. Here is an example. "Why, if at this very moment," says Demosthenes, "a loud cry were to be heard in front of the courts, and we were told that the prison-house lies open and the prisoners are in full flight, no one, whether he be old or young, is so heedless as not to lend aid to the utmost of his power; aye, and if anyone came forward and said that yonder stands the man who let them go, the offender would be promptly put to death without a hearing." [34] 10. In the same way, too, Hyperides on being accused, after he had proposed the liberation of the slaves subsequently to the great defeat, said, "This proposal was framed, not by the orator, but by the battle of Chaeroneia." The speaker has here at one and the same time followed a train of reasoning and indulged a flight of imagination. He has, therefore, passed the bounds of mere persuasion by the boldness of his conception. 11. By a sort of natural law in all such matters we always attend to whatever possesses superior force; whence it is that we are drawn away from demonstration pure and simple to any startling image within whose dazzling brilliancy the argument lies concealed. And it is not unreasonable that we should be affected in this way, for when two things are brought together, the more powerful always attracts to itself the virtue of the weaker. 12. It will be enough to have said thus much with regard to examples of the sublime in thought, when produced by greatness of soul, imitation, or imagery.

[30] Aeschylus, *Seven Against Thebes,* 42.
[31] *Bacchae,* 726.
[32] 1586.

[33] Euripides, *Orestes,* 264.
[34] *Against Timocrates,* 208.

XVI

Here, however, in due order comes the place assigned to Figures; for they, if handled in the proper manner, will contribute, as I have said, in no mean degree to sublimity. But since to treat thoroughly of them all at the present moment would be a great, or rather an endless task, we will now, with the object of proving our proposition, run over a few only of those which produce elevation of diction. 2. Demosthenes is bringing forward a reasoned vindication of his public policy. What was the natural way of treating the subject? It was this. "You were not wrong, you who engaged in the struggle for the freedom of Greece. You have domestic warrant for it. For the warriors of Marathon did no wrong, nor they of Salamis, nor they of Plataea."[35] When, however, as though suddenly inspired by heaven and as it were frenzied by the God of Prophecy, he utters his famous oath by the champions of Greece ("assuredly ye did no wrong; I swear it by those who at Marathon stood in the forefront of the danger"), in the public view by this one Figure of Adjuration, which I here term *Apostrophe*, he deifies his ancestors. He brings home the thought that we ought to swear by those who have thus nobly died as we swear by Gods, and he fills the mind of the judges with the high spirit of those who there bore the brunt of the danger, and he has transformed the natural course of the argument into transcendent sublimity and passion and that secure belief which rests upon strange and prodigious oaths. He instils into the minds of his hearers the conviction—which acts as a medicine and an antidote—that they should, uplifted by these eulogies, feel no less proud of the fight against Philip than of the triumph at Marathon and Salamis. By all these means he carries his hearers clean away with him through the employment of a single figure. 3. It is said, indeed, that the germ of the oath is found in Eupolis:

> For, by the fight I won at Marathon,
> No one shall vex my soul and rue it not.

But it is not sublime to swear by a person in any chance way; the sublimity depends upon the place and the manner and the circumstances and the motive. Now in the passage of Eupolis there is nothing but the mere oath, addressed to the Athenians when still prosperous and in no need of comfort. Furthermore, the poet in his oath has not made divinities of the men in order so to create in his hearers a worthy conception of their valour, but he has wandered away from those who stood in the forefront of the danger to an inanimate thing—the fight. In Demosthenes the oath is framed for vanquished men, with the intention that Chaeroneia should no longer appear a failure to the Athenians. He gives them at one and the same time, as I remarked, a demonstration that they have done no wrong, an example, the sure evidence of oaths, a eulogy, an exhortation. 4. And since the orator was likely to be confronted with the objection, "You are speaking of the *defeat* which has attended your administration, and yet you swear by *victories*," in what follows he consequently measures even individual words, and chooses them unerringly, showing that even in the revels of the imagination sobriety is required. "Those," he says, "who stood in the forefront of the danger at Marathon, and those who fought by sea at Salamis and Artemisium, and those who stood in the ranks at Plataea." Nowhere does he use the word "conquered," but at every turn he has evaded any indication of the result, since it was fortunate and the opposite of what happened at Chaeroneia. So he at once rushes forward and carries his hearer off his feet. "All of whom," says he, "were accorded a public burial by the state, Aeschines, and not *the successful only*." ‡

XXXIX

The fifth of those elements contributing to the sublime which we mentioned, my excellent friend, at the beginning, still remains to be dealt with, namely the arrangement of the words in a certain order. In regard to this, having already in two treatises sufficiently stated such results as our inquiry could compass, we will add, for the purpose of our present undertaking, only what is absolutely essential, namely the fact that harmonious arrangement is not only a natural source of persuasion and pleasure among men but also a wonderful instrument of lofty utterance and of passion. 2. For does not the flute instil certain emotions into its hearers and as it were make

[35] *On the Crown*, 208.

‡ Sections on technical detail are omitted here.

them beside themselves and full of frenzy, and supplying a rhythmical movement constrain the listener to move rhythmically in accordance therewith and to conform himself to the melody, although he may be utterly ignorant of music? Yes, and the tones of the harp, although in themselves they signify nothing at all, often cast a wonderful spell, as you know, over an audience by means of the variations of sounds, by their pulsation against one another, and by their mingling in concert. 3. And yet these are mere semblances and spurious copies of persuasion, not (as I have said) genuine activities of human nature. Are we not, then, to hold that composition (being a harmony of that language which is implanted by nature in man and which appeals not to the hearing only but to the soul itself), since it calls forth manifold shapes of words, thoughts, deeds, beauty, melody, all of them born at our birth and growing with our growth, and since by means of the blending and variation of its own tones it seeks to introduce into the minds of those who are present the emotion which affects the speaker and since it always brings the audience to share in it and by the building of phrase upon phrase raises a sublime and harmonious structure: are we not, I say, to hold that harmony by these selfsame means allures us and invariably disposes us to stateliness and dignity and elevation and every emotion which it contains within itself, gaining absolute mastery over our minds? But it is folly to dispute concerning matters which are generally admitted, since experience is proof sufficient. 4. An example of a conception which is usually thought sublime and is really admirable is that which Demosthenes associates with the decree: "This decree caused the danger which then beset the city to pass by just-as a cloud." [36] But it owes its happy sound no less to the harmony than to the thought itself. For the thought is expressed throughout in dactylic rhythms, and these are most noble and productive of sublimity; and therefore it is that they constitute the heroic, the finest metre that we know. For if you derange the words of the sentence and transpose them in whatever way you will, as for example "This decree just-as a cloud caused the danger of the time to pass by"; nay, if you cut off a single syllable only and say "caused to pass by as a cloud," you will perceive to what an extent harmony is in unison with sublimity. For the very words "just-as a cloud" begin with a long rhythm, which consists of four metrical beats; but if one syllable is cut off and we read "as a cloud," we immediately maim the sublimity by the abbreviation. Conversely, if you elongate the word and write "caused to pass by just-as-if a cloud," it means the same thing, but no longer falls with the same effect upon the ear, inasmuch as the abrupt grandeur of the passage loses its energy and tension through the lengthening of the concluding syllables.

[36] *Ibid.*, 188.

XL

Among the chief causes of the sublime in speech, as in the structure of the human body, is the collocation of members, a single one of which if severed from another possesses in itself nothing remarkable, but all united together make a full and perfect organism. So the constituents of grandeur, when separated from one another, carry with them sublimity in distraction this way and that, but when formed into a body by association and when further encircled in a chain of harmony they become sonorous by their very rotundity; and in periods sublimity is, as it were, a contribution made by a multitude. 2. We have, however, sufficiently shown that many writers and poets who possess no natural sublimity and are perhaps even wanting in elevation have nevertheless, although employing for the most part common and popular words with no striking associations of their own, by merely joining and fitting these together, secured dignity and distinction and the appearance of freedom from meanness. Instances will be furnished by Philistus among many others, by Aristophanes in certain passages, by Euripides in most. 3. In the last-mentioned author, Heracles, after the scene in which he slays his children, uses the words:

Full-fraught am I with woes—no space for more.[37]

The expression is a most ordinary one, but it has gained elevation through the aptness of the structure of the line. If you shape the sentence in a different way, you will see this plainly, the fact being that Euripides is a poet in virtue of his power of composition rather than of his inven-

[37] *Mad Heracles*, 1245.

tion. 4. In the passage which describes Dirce torn away by the bull:

> Whitherso'er he turned
> Swift wheeling round, he haled and hurled withal
> Dame, rock, oak, intershifted ceaselessly,

the conception itself is a fine one, but it has been rendered more forcible by the fact that the harmony is not hurried or carried as it were on rollers, but the words act as buttresses for one another and find support in the pauses, and issue finally in a well-grounded sublimity.

XLI

There is nothing in the sphere of the sublime, that is so lowering as broken and agitated movement of language, such as is characteristic of pyrrhics and trochees and dichorees, which fall altogether to the level of dance music. For all over-rhythmical writing is at once felt to be affected and finical and wholly lacking in passion owing to the monotony of its superficial polish. 2. And the worst of it all is that, just as petty lays draw their hearer away from the point and compel his attention to themselves, so also over-rhythmical style does not communicate the feeling of the words but simply the feeling of the rhythm. Sometimes, indeed, the listeners, knowing beforehand the due terminations, stamp their feet in time with the speaker, and as in a dance give the right step in anticipation. 3. In like manner those words are destitute of sublimity which lie too close together, and are cut up into short and tiny syllables, and are held together as if with wooden bolts by sheer inequality and ruggedness.

XLII

Further, excessive concision of expression tends to lower the sublime, since grandeur is marred when the thought is brought into too narrow a compass. Let this be understood not of proper compression, but of what is absolutely petty and cut into segments. For concision curtails the sense, but brevity goes straight to the mark. It is plain that, *vice versa,* prolixities are frigid, for so is everything that resorts to unseasonable length.

XLIII

Triviality of expression is also apt to disfigure sublimity. In Herodotus, for example, the tempest is described with marvellous effect in all its details, but the passage surely contains some words below the dignity of the subject. The following may serve as an instance—"when the sea seethed." [38] The word "seethed" detracts greatly from the sublimity because it is an ill-sounding one. Further, "the wind," he says, "grew fagged," and those who clung to the spars met "an unpleasant end." [39] The expression "grew fagged" is lacking in dignity, being vulgar; and the word "unpleasant" is inappropriate to so great a disaster. 2. Similarly, when Theopompus had dressed out in marvellous fashion the descent of the Persian king upon Egypt, he spoilt the whole by some petty words. "For which of the cities (he says) or which of the tribes in Asia did not send envoys to the Great King? Which of the products of the earth or of the achievements of art was not, in all its beauty or preciousness, brought as an offering to his presence? Consider the multitude of costly coverlets and mantles, in purple or white or embroidery; the multitude of pavilions of gold furnished with all things useful; the multitude, too, of tapestries and costly couches. Further, gold and silver plate richly wrought, and goblets and mixing-bowls, some of which you might have seen set with precious stones, and others finished with care and at great price. In addition to all this, countless myriads of Greek and barbaric weapons, and beasts of burden beyond all reckoning and victims fattened for slaughter, and many bushels of condiments, and many bags and sacks and sheets of papyrus and all other useful things, and an equal number of pieces of salted flesh from all manner of victims, so that the piles of them were so great that those who were approaching from a distance took them to be hills and eminences confronting them." 3. He runs off from the more elevated to the more lowly, whereas he should, on the contrary, have risen higher and higher. With his wonderful description of the whole outfit he mixes bags and condiments and sacks, and conveys the impression of a confectioner's shop! For just as if, in the case

[38] VII, 188.
[39] VII, 191; VIII, 13.

of those very adornments, between the golden vessels and the jewelled mixing-bowls and the silver plate and the pavilions of pure gold and the goblets, a man were to bring and set in the midst paltry bags and sacks, the proceeding would have been offensive to the eye, so do such words when introduced out of season constitute deformities and as it were blots on the diction. 4. He might have described the scene in broad outline just as he says that hills blocked their way, and with regard to the preparations generally have spoken of "waggons and camels and the multitude of beasts of burden carrying everything that ministers to the luxury and enjoyment of the table," or have used some such expression as "piles of all manner of grain and things which conduce preeminently to good cookery and comfort of body," or if he must necessarily put it in so uncompromising a way, he might have said that "all the dainties of cooks and caterers were there." 5. In lofty passages we ought not to descend to sordid and contemptible language unless constrained by some overpowering necessity, but it is fitting that we should use words worthy of the subject and imitate nature the artificer of man, for she has not placed in full view our grosser parts or the means of purging our frame, but has hidden them away as far as was possible, and as Xenophon says has put their channels in the remotest background, so as not to sully the beauty of the entire creature. 6. But enough; there is no need to enumerate, one by one, the things which produce triviality. For since we have previously indicated those qualities which render style noble and lofty, it is evident that their opposites will for the most part make it low and base.

XLIV

It remains however (as I will not hesitate to add, in recognition of your love of knowledge) to clear up, my dear Terentianus, a question which a certain philosopher has recently mooted. "I wonder," he says, "as no doubt do many others, how it happens that in our time there are men who have the gift of persuasion to the utmost extent, and are well fitted for public life, and are keen and ready, and particularly rich in all the charms of language, yet there no longer arise really lofty and transcendent natures unless quite exceptionally. So great and world-wide a dearth of high utterance attends our age." 2. "Can it be," he continued, "that we are to accept the trite explanation that democracy is the kind nursing-mother of genius, and that literary power may be said to share its rise and fall with democracy and democracy alone? For freedom, it is said, has power to feed the imaginations of the lofty-minded and to inspire hope, and where it prevails there spreads abroad the eagerness of mutual rivalry and the emulous pursuit of the foremost place. 3. Moreover, owing to the prizes which are open to all under popular government, the mental excellences of the orator are continually exercised and sharpened, and as it were rubbed bright, and shine forth (as it is natural they should) with all the freedom which inspires the doings of the state. To-day," he went on, "we seem in our boyhood to learn the lessons of a righteous servitude, being all but enswathed in its customs and observances, when our thoughts are yet young and tender, and never tasting the fairest and most productive source of eloquence (by which," he added, "I mean freedom), so that we emerge in no other guise than that of sublime flatterers." 4. This is the reason, he maintained, why no slave ever becomes an orator, although all other faculties may belong to menials. In the slave there immediately burst out signs of fettered liberty of speech, of the dungeon as it were, of a man habituated to buffetings. 5. "For the day of slavery," as Homer has it, "takes away half our manhood." [40] "Just as," he proceeded, "the cages (if what I hear is true) in which are kept the Pygmies, commonly called *nani*, not only hinder the growth of the creatures confined within them, but actually attenuate them through the bonds which beset their bodies, so one has aptly termed all servitude (though it be most righteous) the cage of the soul and a public prison-house." 6. I answered him thus: "It is easy, my good sir, and characteristic of human nature, to find fault with the age in which one lives. But consider whether it may not be true that it is not the world's peace that ruins great natures, but far rather this war illimitable which holds our desires in its grasp, aye, and further still those passions which occupy as with troops our present age and utterly harry and

[40] *Odyssey*, XVII, 322.

plunder it. For the love of money (a disease from which we all now suffer sorely) and the love of pleasure make us their thralls, or rather, as one may say, drown us body and soul in the depths, the love of riches being a malady which makes men petty, and the love of pleasure one which makes them most ignoble. 7. On reflexion I cannot discover how it is possible for us, if we value boundless wealth so highly, or (to speak more truly) deify it, to avoid allowing the entrance into our souls of the evils which are inseparable from it. For vast and unchecked wealth is accompanied, in close conjunction and step for step as they say, by extravagance, and as soon as the former opens the gates of cities and houses, the latter immediately enters and abides. And when time has passed the pair build nests in the lives of men, as the wise say, and quickly give themselves to the rearing of offspring, and breed ostentation, and vanity, and luxury, no spurious progeny of theirs, but only too legitimate. If these children of wealth are permitted to come to maturity, straightway they beget in the soul inexorable masters—insolence, and lawlessness, and shamelessness. 8. This must necessarily happen, and men will no longer lift up their eyes or have any further regard for fame, but the ruin of such lives will gradually reach its complete consummation and sublimities of soul fade and wither away and become contemptible, when men are lost in admiration of their own mortal parts and omit to exalt that which is immortal. 9. For a man who has once accepted a bribe for a judicial decision cannot be an unbiassed and upright judge of what is just and honourable (since to the man who is venal his own interests must seem honourable and just), and the same is true where the entire life of each of us is ordered by bribes, and huntings after the death of others, and the laying of ambushes for legacies, while gain from any and every source we purchase—each one of us—at the price of life itself, being the slaves of pleasure. In an age which is ravaged by plagues so sore, is it possible for us to imagine that there is still left an unbiassed and incorruptible judge of works that are great and likely to reach posterity, or is it not rather the case that all are influenced in their decisions by the passion for gain? 10. Nay, it is perhaps better for men like ourselves to be ruled than to be free, since our appetites, if let loose without restraint upon our neighbours like beasts from a cage, would set the world on fire with deeds of evil. 11. Summing up, I maintained that among the banes of the natures which our age produces must be reckoned that half-heartedness in which the life of all of us with few exceptions is passed, for we do not labour or exert ourselves except for the sake of praise and pleasure, never for those solid benefits which are a worthy object of our own efforts and the respect of others. 12. But " 'tis best to leave these riddles unresolved,"[41] and to proceed to what next presents itself, namely the subject of the Passions, about which I previously undertook to write in a separate treatise. These form, as it seems to me, a material part of discourse generally and of the Sublime itself. . . .

[41] Euripides, *Electra,* 379.

THOMAS HOBBES:

Answer to Sir William Davenant's Preface to *Gondibert* *

SIR,

If to commend your Poem I should onely say, in general Termes, that in the choice of your Argument, the disposition of the parts, the maintenance of the Characters of your Persons, the dignity and vigor of your expression, you have performed all the parts of various experience, ready memory, clear judgement, swift and well govern'd fancy, though it were enough for the truth, it were too little for the weight and credit of my testimony. For I lie open to two Exceptions, one of an incompetent, the other of a corrupted Witness. Incompetent, because I am not a Poet; and corrupted with the Honor done me by your Preface. The former obliges me to say something, by the way, of the Nature and differences of Poesy.

As Philosophers have divided the Universe, their subject, into three Regions, *Celestiall, Aëriall,* and *Terrestriall,* so the Poets (whose worke it is, by imitating humane life in delightful and measur'd lines, to avert men from vice and incline them to vertuous and honorable actions) have lodg'd themselves in the three Regions of mankinde, *Court, City,* and *Country,* correspondent in some proportion to those three Regions of the World. For there is in Princes and men of conspicuous power, anciently called *Heroes,* a lustre and influence upon the rest of men resembling that of the Heavens; and an insincereness, inconstancy, and troublesome humor of those that dwell in populous Cities, like the mobility, blustring, and impurity of the Aire; and a plainness, and though dull, yet a nutritive faculty in rurall people, that endures a comparison with the Earth they labour.

From hence have proceeded three sorts of Poesy, *Heroique, Scommatique,* and *Pastorall.* Every one of these is distinguished again in the manner of *Representation,* which sometimes is *Narrative,* wherein the Poet himself relateth, and sometimes *Dramatique,* as when the persons are every one adorned and brought upon the Theater to speak and act their own parts. There is therefore neither more nor less then six sorts of Poesy. For the Heroique Poem narrative, such as is yours, is called an *Epique Poem.* The Heroique Poem Dramatique is *Tragedy.* The Scommatique Narrative is *Satyre,* Dramatique is *Comedy.* The Pastorall narrative is called simply *Pastorall,* anciently *Bucolique;* the same Dramatique, *Pastorall Comedy.* The Figure therefore of an Epique Poem and of a Tragedy ought to be the same, for they differ no more but in that they are pronounced by one or many Persons. Which I insert to justifie the figure of yours, consisting of five books divided into Songs, or Cantoes, as five Acts divided into Scenes has ever been the approved figure of a Tragedy.

They that take for Poesy whatsoever is writ in Verse will think this Division imperfect, and call in Sonets, Epigrams, Eclogues, and the like peeces, which are but Essayes and parts of an entire Poem, and reckon *Empedocles* and *Lucretius* (natural Philosophers) for Poets, and the moral precepts of *Phocylides, Theognis,* and the Quatraines of *Pyrbrach* and the History of *Lucan,* and others of that kind amongst Poems, bestowing on such Writers for honor the name of Poets rather then of Historians or Philosophers. But the subject of a Poem is the manners of men, not natural causes; manners presented, not dictated; and manners feigned, as the name of Poesy imports, not found in men. They that give entrance to Fictions writ in Prose err not so much, but they err: For Prose requireth delightfulness, not onely of fiction, but of stile, in which, if Prose contend with Verse, it is with disadvantage and, as it were, on foot against the strength and wings of *Pegasus.*

* First published in 1650.

For Verse amongst the *Greeks* was appropriated anciently to the service of their Gods, and was the Holy stile, the stile of the Oracles, the stile of the Laws, and the stile of men that publiquely recommended to their Gods the vowes and thanks of the people, which was done in their holy songs called Hymnes, and the Composers of them were called Prophets and Priests before the name of Poet was known. When afterwards the majestie of that stile was observed, the Poets chose it as best becoming their high invention. And for the Antiquity of Verse, it is greater then the antiquity of Letters. For it is certain *Cadmus* was the first that from *Phoenicia,* a country that neighboureth *Judea,* brought the use of Letters into *Greece.* But the service of the Gods and the Laws, which by measured Sounds were easily committed to the memory, had been long time in use before the arrivall of *Cadmus* there.

There is, besides the grace of stile, another cause why the ancient Poets chose to write in measured language, which is this. Their Poems were made at first with intention to have them sung, as well Epique as Dramatique—which custom hath been long time laid aside, but began to be revived, in part, of late years in *Italy*—and could not be made commensurable to the Voyce or Instruments in Prose, the ways and motions whereof are so uncertain and undistinguished, like the way and motion of a Ship in the Sea, as not onely to discompose the best Composers, but also to disappoint some times the most attentive Reader and put him to hunt counter for the sense. It was therefore necessary for Poets in those times to write in Verse.

The verse which the *Greeks* and *Latines,* considering the nature of their own Languages, found by experience most grave, and for an Epique Poem most decent, was their *Hexameter,* a Verse limited not onely in the length of the line, but also in the quantity of the syllables. In stead of which we use the line of ten Syllables, recompencing the neglect of their quantity with the diligence of Rime. And this measure is so proper for an Heroique Poem as without some losse of gravity and dignity it was never changed. A longer is not far from ill Prose, and a shorter is a kinde of whisking, you know, like the unlacing rather then the singing of a Muse. In an Epigram or a Sonnet a man may vary his measures, and seek glory from a needlesse difficulty, as he that contrived Verses into the formes of an Organ, a Hatchet, an Egg, an Altar, and a paire of Wings; but in so great and noble a worke as is an Epique Poem, for a man to obstruct his own way with unprofitable difficulties is great imprudence. So likewise to chuse a needlesse and difficult correspondence of Rime is but a difficult toy, and forces a man sometimes for the stoping of a chink to say somewhat he did never think; I cannot therefore but very much approve your *Stanza,* wherein the syllables in every Verse are ten, and the Rime Alternate.

For the choyce of your subject, you have sufficiently justified your self in your Preface. But because I have observed in *Virgil,* that the Honor done to *Æneas* and his companions has so bright a reflection upon *Augustus Cæsar* and other great *Romans* of that time as a man may suspect him not constantly possessed with the noble spirit of those his *Heroes,* and beleeve you are not acquainted with any great man of the Race of *Gondibert,* I add to your justification the purity of your purpose, in having no other motive of your labour but to adorn vertue and procure her Lovers, then which there cannot be a worthier designe, and more becoming noble Poesy.

In that you make so small account of the example of almost all the approved Poets, ancient and modern, who thought fit in the beginning, and sometimes also in the progress of their Poems, to invoke a Muse or some other Deity that should dictate to them or assist them in their writings, they that take not the laws of Art from any reason of their own but from the fashion of precedent times will perhaps accuse your singularity. For my part, I neither subscribe to their accusation, nor yet condemn that Heathen custom otherwise then as accessary to their false Religion. For their Poets were their Divines, had the name of Prophets; Exercised amongst the People a kinde of spiritual Authority, would be thought to speak by a divine spirit, have their works which they writ in Verse (the divine stile) pass for the word of God and not of man, and to be hearkened to with reverence. Do not our Divines (excepting the stile) do the same, and by us that are of the same Religion cannot justly be reprehended for it? Besides, in the use of the spiritual calling of Divines, there is danger sometimes to be feared from want of skill, such as is reported of unskilful Conjurers, that mistaking the rites and ceremonious points of their art, call up such spirits as they cannot at their pleasure allay again, by whom storms are raised that overthrow buildings and are the cause of miserable wracks at sea. Unskilful Divines do often times the like: For when they call unseasonably for *Zeal* there appears a Spirit of *Cruelty;* and by the like error, instead of *Truth* they raise *Discord;* instead of *Wisdom, Fraud;* instead of *Reformation, Tumult;* and *Controversie* instead of *Religion.* Whereas in the Heathen Poets, at least in those whose works have lasted to the time we are in, there are none of those indiscretions to be found that tended to subversion or disturbance of the Commonwealths wherein they lived. But why a Christian should think it an ornament to his Poem, either to profane the true God or invoke a false one, I can imagine no cause but a reasonless imitation of Custom, of a foolish custome, by which a man, enabled to speak wisely from the principles of nature and his own meditation, loves rather to be thought to speak by inspiration, like a Bagpipe.

Time and Education begets experience; Experience begets memory; Memory begets Judgement and Fancy: Judgment begets the strength and structure, and Fancy begets the ornaments of a Poem. The Ancients therefore fabled not absurdly in making memory the Mother of the Muses. For memory is the World (though not really, yet so as in a looking glass) in which the Judgment, the severer Sister, busieth her self in a grave and rigid examination of all the parts of Nature, and in registring by Letters their order, causes, uses, differences, and resemblances; Whereby the Fancy, when any work of Art is to be performed, findes her materials at hand and prepared for use, and needs no more then a swift motion over them, that what she wants, and is there to be had, may not lie too long unespied. So that when she seemeth to fly from one *Indies* to the other, and from Heaven to Earth, and to penetrate into the hardest matter and obscurest places, into the future and into her self, and all this in a point of time, the voyage is not very great, her self being all she seeks; and her wonderful celerity consisteth not so much in motion as in copious Imagery discreetly ordered & perfectly registered in the memory, which most men under the name of Philosophy have a glimpse of, and is pretended to by many that, grosly mistaking her, embrace contention in her place. But so far forth as the Fancy of man has traced the ways of true Philosophy, so far it hath produced very marvellous effects to the benefit of mankinde. All that is beautiful or defensible in building, or marvellous in Engines and Instruments of motion, whatsoever commodity men receive from the observations of the Heavens, from the description of the Earth, from the account of Time, from walking on the Seas, and whatsoever distinguisheth the civility of *Europe* from the Barbarity of the *American* savages, is the workmanship of Fancy but guided by the Precepts of true Philosophy. But where these precepts fail, as they have hitherto failed in the doctrine of Moral vertue, there the Architect, *Fancy,* must take the Philosophers part upon her self. He therefore that undertakes an Heroick Poem, which is to exhibite a venerable & amiable Image of Heroick vertue, must not only be the Poet, to place & connect, but also the Philosopher, to furnish and square his matter, that is, to make both Body and Soul, colour and shadow of this Poem out of his own Store: Which how well you have performed I am now considering.

Observing how few the Persons be you introduce in the beginning, and how in the course of the actions of these (the number increasing) after several confluences they run all at last into the two principal streams of your Poem, *Gondibert* and *Oswald,* methinks the Fable is not much unlike the Theater. For so, from several and far distant Sources, do the lesser Brooks of *Lombardy,* flowing into one another, fall all at last into the two main Rivers, the *Po* and the *Adice.* It hath the same resemblance also with a mans veins, which, proceeding from different parts, after the like concourse insert themselves at last into the two principal veins of the Body. But when I considered that also the actions of men, which singly are inconsiderable, after many conjunctures grow at last either into one great protecting power or into two destroying factions, I could not but approve the structure of your Poem, which ought to be no other then such as an imitation of humane life requireth.

In the Streams themselves I finde nothing but setled Valor, cleane Honor, calm Counsel, learned diversion, and pure Love, save onely a torrent or two of Ambition, which, though a fault, has somewhat Heroick in it, and therefore must have a place in an Heroick Poem. To shew the reader in what place he shall finde every excellent picture of vertue you have drawn is too long. And to shew him one is to prejudice the rest; yet I cannot forbear to point him to the Description of Love in the person of *Birtha,* in the seventh *Canto* of the second Book. There has nothing been said of that Subject neither by the Ancient nor Modern Poets comparable to it. Poets are Painters: I would fain see another Painter draw so true, perfect, and natural a Love to the Life, and make use of nothing but pure Lines, without the help of any the least uncomely shadow, as you have done. But let it be read as a piece by it self, for in the almost equal height of the whole the eminence of parts is Lost.

There are some that are not pleased with fiction, unless it be bold, not onely to exceed the *work,* but also the *possibility* of nature: they would have impenetrable Armors, Inchanted Castles, invulnerable bodies, Iron Men, flying Horses, and a thousand other such things, which are easily feigned by them that dare. Against such I defend you (without assenting to those that condemn either *Homer* or *Virgil*) by dissenting onely from those that think the Beauty of a Poem consisteth in the exorbitancy of the fiction. For as truth is the bound of Historical, so the Resemblance of truth is the utmost limit of Poetical Liberty. In old time amongst the Heathen such strange fictions and Metamorphoses were not so remote from the Articles of their Faith as they are now from ours, and therefore were not so unpleasant. Beyond the actual works of nature a Poet may now go; but beyond the conceived possibility of nature, never. I can allow a Geographer to make in the Sea a Fish or a Ship which by the scale of his Mapp would be two or three hundred mile long, and think it done for ornament, because it is done without the precincts of his undertaking; but when he paints an Elephant so, I presently apprehend it as ignorance, and a plain confession of *Terra incognita.*

As the description of Great Men and Great Actions is the constant designe of a Poet, so the descriptions of worthy circumstances are necessary accessions to a Poem, and being well performed are the Jewels and most precious ornaments of Poesy. Such in *Virgil* are the Funeral games of Anchises, The duel of Æneas and Turnus, etc.; and such in yours are The Hunting, The Bataile, The City Mourning, The Funeral, The House of Astragon, The Library, and the Temple, equal to his, or those of *Homer* whom he imitated.

There remains now no more to be considered but the Expression, in which consisteth the countenance and colour of a beautiful Muse, and is given her by the Poet out of his own provision, or is borrowed from others. That which he hath of his own is nothing but experience and knowledge of Nature, and specially humane nature, and is the true and natural Colour. But that which is taken out of Books (the ordinary boxes of Counterfeit Complexion) shews well or ill, as it hath more or less resemblance with the natural, and are not to be used without examination unadvisedly. For in him that professes the imitation of Nature, as all Poets do, what greater fault can there be then to bewray an ignorance of nature in his Poem—especially having a liberty allowed him, if he meet with any thing he cannot master, to leave it out?

That which giveth a Poem the true and natural Colour consisteth in two things, which are, *To know well,* that is, to have images of nature in the memory distinct and clear, and *To know much.* A signe of the first is perspicuity, property, and decency, which delight all sorts of men, either by instructing the ignorant or soothing the learned in their knowledge. A signe of the latter is novelty of expression, and pleaseth by exitation of the minde; for novelty causeth admiration, and admiration curiosity, which is a delightful appetite of knowledge.

There be so many words in use at this day in the English Tongue, that though of magnifique sound, yet (like the windy blisters of a troubled water) have no sense at all, and so many others that lose their meaning by being ill coupled, that it is a hard matter to avoid them; for having been obtruded upon youth in the Schools by such as make it, I think, their business there (as 'tis exprest by the best Poet)

With terms to charm the weak and pose the wise,

they grow up with them, and, gaining reputation with the ignorant, are not easily shaken off.

To this palpable darkness I may also add the ambitious obscurity of expressing more then is perfectly conceived, or perfect conception in fewer words then it requires. Which Expressions, though they have had the honor to be called strong lines, are indeed no better then Riddles, and, not onely to the Reader but also after a little time to the Writer himself, dark and troublesome.

To the property of Expression I referr that clearness of memory by which a Poet, when he hath once introduced any person whatsoever speaking in his Poem, maintaineth in him to the end the same character he gave him in the beginning. The variation whereof is a change of pace that argues the Poet tired.

Of the Indecencies of an Heroick Poem the most remarkable are those that shew disproportion either between the persons and their actions, or between the manners of the Poet and the Poem. Of the first kinde is the uncomliness of representing in great persons the inhumane vice of Cruelty or the sordid vice of Lust and Drunkenness. To such parts as those the Ancient approved Poets thought it fit to suborn, not the persons of men, but of monsters and beastly Giants, such as *Polyphemus, Cacus,* and the *Centaures.* For it is supposed a Muse, when she is invoked to sing a song of that nature, should maidenly advise the Poet to set such persons to sing their own vices upon the Stage, for it is not so unseemly in a *Tragedy.* Of the same kinde it is to represent scurrility or any action or language that moveth much laughter. The delight of an *Epique* Poem consisteth not in mirth, but in admiration. Mirth and Laughter is proper to *Comedy* and *Satyre.* Great persons that have their mindes employed on great designes have not leasure enought to laugh, and are pleased with the contemplation of their own power and vertues, so as they need not the infirmities and vices of other men to recommend themselves to their own favour by comparison, as all men do when they laugh. Of the second kinde, where the disporportion is between the Poet and the Persons of his Poem, one is in the Dialect of the Inferior sort of People, which is alwayes different from the language of the Court. Another is to derive the Illustration of any thing from such Metaphors or Comparisons as cannot come into mens thoughts but by mean conversation and experience of humble or evil Arts, which the Person of an *Epique* Poem cannot be thought acquainted with.

From *Knowing much,* proceedeth the admirable variety and novelty of Metaphors and Similitudes, which are not possible to be lighted on in the compass of a narrow knowledge. And the want whereof compelleth a Writer to expressions that are either defac'd by time or sullied with vulgar or long use. For the Phrases of Poesy, as the airs of musick, with often hearing become insipide, the Reader having no more sense of their force then our Flesh is sensible of the bones that sustain it. As the sense we have of bodies consisteth in change and variety of impression, so also does the sense of language in the variety and changeable use of words. I mean not in the affectation of words newly brought home from travail, but in new and with all significant translation to our purposes of those that be already received, and in far fetch't but withal apt, instructive, and comly similitudes.

Having thus, I hope, avoided the first Exception against the incompetency of my Judgement, I am but little moved with the second, which is of being bribed by the honor you have done me by attributing in your Preface somewhat to my Judgment. For I have used your Judgment no less in many things of mine, which coming to light will thereby appear the better. And so you have your bribe again.

Having thus made way for the admission of my Testimony, I give it briefly thus: I never yet saw Poem that had so much shape of Art, health of Morality, and vigour and beauty of Expression as this of yours. And but for the clamour of the multitude, that hide their Envy of the present under a Reverence of Antiquity, I should say further that it would last as long as either the *Æniad* or *Iliad,* but for one Disadvantage; and the Disadvantage is this: The languages of the *Greeks* and *Romans,* by their Colonies and Conquests, have put off flesh and blood, and are becom immutable, which none of the modern tongues are like to be. I honor Antiquity, but that which is commonly called *old time* is young time. The glory of Antiquity is due, not to the Dead, but to the Aged.

And now, whilst I think on't, give me leave with a short discord to sweeten the Harmony of the approaching close. I have nothing to object against your Poem, but dissent onely from something in your Preface sounding to the prejudice of Age. 'Tis commonly said that old Age is a return to childhood: Which methinks you insist on so long, as if you desired it should be believed. That's the note I mean to shake a little. That saying, meant onely of the weakness of body, was wrested to the weakness of minde by froward children, weary of the controulment of their parents, masters, and other admonitors. Secondly, the dotage and childishness they ascribe to Age is never the effect of Time, but sometimes of the excesses of youth and not a returning to, but a continual stay with, childhood. For they that, wanting the curiosity of furnishing their memories with the rarities of nature in their youth, and pass their time in making provision onely for their ease and sensual delight, are children still at what years soever, as they that coming into a populous City, never going out of their Inn, are strangers still, how longsoever they have bin there. Thirdly, there is no reason for any man to think himself wiser to day then yesterday, which does not equally convince he shall be wiser to morrow then to day.

Fourthly, you will be forced to change your opinion hereafter when you are old; and in the mean time you discredit all I have said before in your commendation, because I am old already. But no more of this.

I beleeve, Sir, you have seen a curious kinde of perspective, where he that looks through a short hollow pipe upon a picture containing divers figures sees none of those that are there painted, but some one person made up of their parts, conveyed to the eie by the artificial cutting of a glass. I finde in my imagination an effect not unlike it from your Poem. The vertues you distribute there amongst so many noble Persons represent in the reading the image but of one mans vertue to my fancy, which is your own, and that so deeply imprinted as to stay for ever there, and govern all the rest of my thoughts and affections in the way of honouring and serving you to the utmost of my power, that am,

Sir,

Your most humble and obedient Servant,

THOMAS HOBBES.

WILLIAM WORDSWORTH:

Observations Prefixed to "Lyrical Ballads"*

THE FIRST volume of these Poems has already been submitted to general perusal. It was published, as an experiment, which, I hoped, might be of some use to ascertain, how far, by fitting to metrical arrangement a selection of the real language of men in a state of vivid sensation, that sort of pleasure and that quantity of pleasure may be imparted, which a Poet may rationally endeavour to impart.

I had formed no very inaccurate estimate of the probable effect of those Poems: I flattered myself that they who should be pleased with them would read them with more than common pleasure: and, on the other hand, I was well aware, that by those who should dislike them, they would be read with more than common dislike. The result has differed from my expectation in this only, that a greater number have been pleased than I ventured to hope I should please.

Several of my Friends are anxious for the success of these Poems, from a belief, that, if the views with which they were composed were indeed realized, a class of Poetry would be produced, well adapted to interest mankind permanently, and not unimportant in the quality, and in the multiplicity of its moral relations: and on this account they have advised me to prefix a systematic defence of the theory upon which the Poems were written. But I was unwilling to undertake the task, knowing that on this occasion the Reader would look coldly upon my arguments, since I might be suspected of having been principally influenced by the selfish and foolish hope of *reasoning* him into an approbation of these particular Poems: and I was still more unwilling to undertake the task, because, adequately to display the opinions, and fully to enforce the arguments, would require a space wholly disproportionate to a preface. For, to treat the subject with the clearness and coherence of which it is susceptible, it would be necessary to give a full account of the present state of the

* The "Observations" first appeared in the 1800 edition of *Lyrical Ballads;* the "Appendix," in the edition of 1802.

public taste in this country, and to determine how far this taste is healthy or depraved; which, again, could not be determined, without pointing out in what manner language and the human mind act and re-act on each other, and without retracing the revolutions, not of literature alone, but likewise of society itself. I have therefore altogether declined to enter regularly upon this defence; yet I am sensible, that there would be something like impropriety in abruptly obtruding upon the Public, without a few words of introduction, Poems so materially different from those upon which general approbation is at present bestowed.

It is supposed, that by the act of writing in verse an Author makes a formal engagement that he will gratify certain known habits of association; that he not only thus apprises the Reader that certain classes of ideas and expressions will be found in his book, but that others will be carefully excluded. This exponent or symbol held forth by metrical language must in different eras of literature have excited very different expectations: for example, in the age of Catullus, Terence, and Lucretius, and that of Statius or Claudian; and in our own country, in the age of Shakespeare and Beaumont and Fletcher, and that of Donne and Cowley, or Dryden, or Pope. I will not take upon me to determine the exact import of the promise which, by the act of writing in verse, an Author in the present day makes to his reader: but it will undoubtedly appear to many persons that I have not fulfilled the terms of an engagement thus voluntarily contracted. They who have been accustomed to the gaudiness and inane phraseology of many modern writers, if they persist in reading this book to its conclusion, will, no doubt, frequently have to struggle with feelings of strangeness and awkwardness: they will look round for poetry, and will be induced to inquire by what species of courtesy these attempts can be permitted to assume that title. I hope therefore the reader will not censure me for attempting to state what I have proposed to myself to perform; and also (as far as the limits of a preface will permit) to explain some of the chief reasons which have determined me in the choice of my purpose: that at least he may be spared any unpleasant feeling of disappointment, and that I myself may be protected from one of the most dishonourable accusations which can be brought against an Author; namely, that of an indolence which prevents him from endeavouring to ascertain what is his duty, or, when his duty is ascertained, prevents him from performing it.

The principal object, then, proposed in these Poems was to choose incidents and situations from common life, and to relate or describe them, throughout, as far as was possible in a selection of language really used by men, and, at the same time, to throw over them a certain colouring of imagination, whereby ordinary things should be presented to the mind in an unusual aspect; and, further, and above all, to make these incidents and situations interesting by tracing in them, truly though not ostentatiously, the primary laws of our nature: chiefly, as far as regards the manner in which we associate ideas in a state of excitement. Humble and rustic life was generally chosen, because, in that condition, the essential passions of the heart find a better soil in which they can attain their maturity, are less under restraint, and speak a plainer and more emphatic language; because in that condition of life our elementary feelings coexist in a state of greater simplicity, and, consequently, may be more accurately contemplated, and more forcibly communicated; because the manners of rural life germinate from those elementary feelings, and, from the necessary character of rural occupations, are more easily comprehended, and are more durable; and, lastly, because in that condition the passions of men are incorporated with the beautiful and permanent forms of nature. The language, too, of these men has been adopted (purified indeed from what appear to be its real defects, from all lasting and rational causes of dislike or disgust) because such men hourly communicate with the best objects from which the best part of language is originally derived; and because, from their rank in society and the sameness and narrow circle of their intercourse, being less under the influence of social vanity, they convey their feelings and notions in simple and unelaborated expressions. Accordingly, such a language, arising out of repeated experience and regular feelings, is a more permanent, and a far more philosophical language, than that which is frequently substituted for it by Poets, who think that they are conferring honour upon themselves and their art, in proportion as they separate themselves from the sympathies of men, and indulge in arbitrary and capricious habits of expression, in order to furnish food for fickle tastes, and fickle appetites, of their own creation.[1]

I cannot, however, be insensible to the present outcry against the triviality and meanness, both of thought and language, which some of my contemporaries have occasionally introduced into their metrical compositions; and I acknowledge that this defect, where it exists, is more dishonourable to the Writer's own character than false refinement or arbitrary innovation, though I should contend at the same time, that it is far less pernicious in the sum of its consequences. From such verses the Poems in these volumes will be found distinguished at least by one mark of difference, that each of them has a worthy *purpose.* Not that I always began to write with a distinct purpose formally conceived; but habits of meditation have, I trust, so prompted and regulated my feelings, that my descriptions of such objects as strongly excite those feelings, will be found to carry along with them a *purpose.* If this opinion be erroneous, I can have little right to the name of a Poet. For all good poetry is the spontaneous overflow of powerful feelings: and though this be true, Poems to which any value can be attached were never produced on any variety of subjects but by a man who, being possessed of more than usual organic sensibility, had also thought long and deeply. For our continued influxes of feeling are modified and directed by our thoughts, which are indeed the representatives of all our past feelings; and, as by contemplating the relation of these general representatives to each other, we discover what is really important to men, so, by the repetition and continuance of this act, our feelings will be connected with important subjects, till at length, if we be originally possessed of much sensibility, such habits of mind will be produced, that, by obeying blindly and mechanically the impulses of those habits, we shall describe objects, and utter sentiments, of such a nature, and in such connexion with each other, that the understanding of the Reader must necessarily be in some degree enlightened, and his affections strengthened and purified.

It has been said that each of these poems has a purpose. Another circumstance must be mentioned which distinguishes these Poems from the popular Poetry of the day; it is this, that the feeling therein developed gives importance to the action and situation, and not the action and situation to the feeling.

A sense of false modesty shall not prevent me from asserting, that the Reader's attention is pointed to this mark of distinction, far less for the sake of these particular Poems than from the general importance of the subject. The subject is indeed important! For the human mind is capable of being excited without the application of gross and violent stimulants; and he must have a very faint perception of its beauty and dignity who does not know this, and who does not further know, that one being is elevated above another, in proportion as he possesses this capability. It has therefore appeared to me, that to endeavour to produce or enlarge this capability is one of the best services in which, at any period, a Writer can be engaged; but this service, excellent at all times, is especially so at the present day. For a multitude of causes, unknown to former times, are now acting with a combined force to blunt the discriminating powers of the mind, and, unfitting it for all voluntary exertion, to reduce it to a state of almost savage torpor. The most effective of these causes are the great national events which are daily taking place, and the increasing accumulation of men in cities, where the uniformity of their occupations produces a craving for extraordinary incident, which the rapid communication of intelligence hourly gratifies. To this tendency of life and manners the literature and theatrical exhibitions of the country have conformed themselves. The invaluable works of our elder writers, I had almost said the works of Shakespeare and Milton, are driven into neglect by frantic novels, sickly and stupid German Tragedies, and deluges of idle and extravagant stories in verse. —When I think upon this degrading thirst after outrageous stimulation, I am almost ashamed to have spoken of the feeble endeavour made in these volumes to counteract it; and, reflecting

[1] It is worth while here to observe, that the affecting parts of Chaucer are almost always expressed in language pure and universally intelligible even to this day.

upon the magnitude of the general evil, I should be oppressed with no dishonourable melancholy, had I not a deep impression of certain inherent and indestructible qualities of the human mind, and likewise of certain powers in the great and permanent objects that act upon it, which are equally inherent and indestructible; and were there not added to this impression a belief, that the time is approaching when the evil will be systematically opposed, by men of greater powers, and with far more distinguished success.

Having dwelt thus long on the subjects and aim of these Poems, I shall request the Reader's permission to apprise him of a few circumstances relating to their *style,* in order, among other reasons, that he may not censure me for not having performed what I never attempted. The Reader will find that personifications of abstract ideas rarely occur in these volumes; and are utterly rejected, as an ordinary device to elevate the style, and raise it above prose. My purpose was to imitate, and, as far as possible, to adopt the very language of men; and assuredly such personifications do not make any natural or regular part of that language. They are, indeed, a figure of speech occasionally prompted by passion, and I have made use of them as such; but have endeavoured utterly to reject them as a mechanical device of style, or as a family language which Writers in metre seem to lay claim to by prescription. I have wished to keep the Reader in the company of flesh and blood, persuaded that by so doing I shall interest him. Others who pursue a different track will interest him likewise; I do not interfere with their claim, but wish to prefer a claim of my own. There will also be found in these volumes little of what is usually called poetic diction; as much pains has been taken to avoid it as is ordinarily taken to produce it; this has been done for the reason already alleged, to bring my language near to the language of men; and further, because the pleasure which I have proposed to myself to impart, is of a kind very different from that which is supposed by many persons to be the proper object of poetry. Without being culpably particular, I do not know how to give my Reader a more exact notion of the style in which it was my wish and intention to write, than by informing him that I have at all times endeavoured to look steadily at my subject; consequently, there is I hope in these Poems little falsehood of description, and my ideas are expressed in language fitted to their respective importance. Something must have been gained by this practice, as it is friendly to one property of all good poetry, namely, good sense: but it has necessarily cut me off from a large portion of phrases and figures of speech which from father to son have long been regarded as the common inheritance of Poets. I have also thought it expedient to restrict myself still further, having abstained from the use of many expressions, in themselves proper and beautiful, but which have been foolishly repeated by bad Poets, till such feelings of disgust are connected with them as it is scarcely possible by any art of association to overpower.

If in a poem there should be found a series of lines, or even a single line, in which the language, though naturally arranged, and according to the strict laws of metre, does not differ from that of prose, there is a numerous class of critics, who, when they stumble upon these prosaisms, as they call them, imagine that they have made a notable discovery, and exult over the Poet as over a man ignorant of his own profession. Now these men would establish a canon of criticism which the Reader will conclude he must utterly reject, if he wishes to be pleased with these volumes. And it would be a most easy task to prove to him, that not only the language of a large portion of every good poem, even of the most elevated character, must necessarily, except with reference to the metre, in no respect differ from that of good prose, but likewise that some of the most interesting parts of the best poems will be found to be strictly the language of prose when prose is well written. The truth of this assertion might be demonstrated by innumerable passages from almost all the poetical writings, even of Milton himself. To illustrate the subject in a general manner, I will here adduce a short composition of Gray, who was at the head of those who, by their reasonings, have attempted to widen the space of separation betwixt Prose and Metrical composition, and was more than any other man curiously elaborate in the structure of his own poetic diction.

In vain to me the smiling mornings shine,
And reddening Phœbus lifts his golden fire:
The birds in vain their amorous descant join,
Or cheerful fields resume their green attire.
These ears, alas! for other notes repine;
A different object do these eyes require;
My lonely anguish melts no heart but mine;
And in my breast the imperfect joys expire;
Yet morning smiles the busy race to cheer,
And new-born pleasure brings to happier men;
The fields to all their wonted tribute bear;
To warm their little loves the birds complain,
I fruitless mourn to him that cannot hear,
And weep the more because I weep in vain.

It will easily be perceived, that the only part of this Sonnet which is of any value is the lines printed in Italics; it is equally obvious, that, except in the rhyme, and in the use of the single word "fruitless" for fruitlessly, which is so far a defect, the language of these lines does in no respect differ from that of prose.

By the foregoing quotation it has been shown that language of Prose may yet be well adapted to Poetry; and it was previously asserted, that a large portion of the language of every good poem can in no respect differ from that of good Prose. We will go further. It may be safely affirmed, that there neither is, nor can be, any *essential* difference between the language of prose and metrical composition. We are fond of tracing the resemblance between Poetry and Painting, and, accordingly, we call them Sisters: but where shall we find bonds of connexion sufficiently strict to typify the affinity betwixt metrical and prose composition? They both speak by and to the same organs; the bodies in which both of them are clothed may be said to be of the same substance, their affections are kindred, and almost identical, not necessarily differing even in degree; Poetry [2] sheds no tears "such as Angels weep," but natural and human tears; she can boast of no celestial ichor that distinguishes her vital juices from those of prose; the same human blood circulates through the veins of them both.

If it be affirmed that rhyme and metrical arrangement of themselves constitute a distinction which overturns what has just been said on the strict affinity of metrical language with that of prose, and paves the way for other artificial distinctions which the mind voluntarily admits, I answer that the language of such Poetry as is here recommended is, as far as possible, a selection of the language really spoken by men; that this selection, wherever it is made with true taste and feeling, will of itself form a distinction far greater than would at first be imagined, and will entirely separate the composition from the vulgarity and meanness of ordinary life; and, if metre be superadded thereto, I believe that a dissimilitude will be produced altogether sufficient for the gratification of a rational mind. What other distinction would we have? Whence is it to come? And where is it to exist? Not, surely, where the Poet speaks through the mouths of his characters: it cannot be necessary here, either for elevation of style, or any of its supposed ornaments: for, if the Poet's subject be judiciously chosen, it will naturally, and upon fit occasion, lead him to passions the language of which, if selected truly and judiciously, must necessarily be dignified and variegated, and alive with metaphors and figures. I forbear to speak of an incongruity which would shock the intelligent Reader, should the Poet interweave any foreign splendour of his own with that which the passion naturally suggests: it is sufficient to say that such addition is unnecessary. And, surely, it is more probable that those passages, which with propriety abound with metaphors and figures, will have their due effect, if, upon other occasions where the passions are of a milder character, the style also be subdued and temperate.

But, as the pleasure which I hope to give by the Poems now presented to the Reader must depend entirely on just notions upon this subject, and, as it is in itself of high importance to our taste and moral feelings, I cannot content myself with these detached remarks. And if, in what I am about to say, it shall appear to some that my labour is unnecessary, and that I am like a man fighting a battle without enemies, such persons may be reminded, that, whatever be the

[2] I here use the word "Poetry" (though against my own judgement) as opposed to the word Prose, and synonymous with metrical composition. But much confusion has been introduced into criticism by this contradistinction of Poetry and Prose, instead of the more philosophical one of Poetry and Matter of Fact, or Science. The only strict antithesis to Prose is Metre; nor is this, in truth, a *strict* antithesis, because lines and passages of metre so naturally occur in writing prose, that it would be scarcely possible to avoid them, even were it desirable.

language outwardly holden by men, a practical faith in the opinions which I am wishing to establish is almost unknown. If my conclusions are admitted, and carried as far as they must be carried if admitted at all, our judgements concerning the works of the greatest Poets both ancient and modern will be far different from what they are at present, both when we praise, and when we censure: and our moral feelings influencing and influenced by these judgements will, I believe, be corrected and purified.

Taking up the subject, then, upon general grounds, let me ask, what is meant by the word Poet? What is a Poet? To whom does he address himself? And what language is to be expected from him?—He is a man speaking to men: a man, it is true, endowed with more lively sensibility, more enthusiasm and tenderness, who has a greater knowledge of human nature, and a more comprehensive soul, than are supposed to be common among mankind; a man pleased with his own passions and volitions, and who rejoices more than other men in the spirit of life that is in him; delighting to contemplate similar volitions and passions as manifested in the goings-on of the Universe, and habitually impelled to create them where he does not find them. To these qualities he has added a disposition to be affected more than other men by absent things as if they were present; an ability of conjuring up in himself passions, which are indeed far from being the same as those produced by real events, yet (especially in those parts of the general sympathy which are pleasing and delightful) do more nearly resemble the passions produced by real events, than anything which, from the motions of their own minds merely, other men are accustomed to feel in themselves:—whence, and from practice, he has acquired a greater readiness and power in expressing what he thinks and feels, and especially those thoughts and feelings which, by his own choice, or from the structure of his own mind, arise in him without immediate external excitement.

But whatever portion of this faculty we may suppose even the greatest Poet to possess, there cannot be a doubt that the language which it will suggest to him, must often, in liveliness and truth, fall short of that which is uttered by men in real life, under the actual pressure of those passions, certain shadows of which the Poet thus produces, or feels to be produced, in himself.

However exalted a notion we would wish to cherish of the character of a Poet, it is obvious, that while he describes and imitates passions, his employment is in some degree mechanical, compared with the freedom and power of real and substantial action and suffering. So that it will be the wish of the Poet to bring his feelings near to those of the persons whose feelings he describes, nay, for short spaces of time, perhaps, to let himself slip into an entire delusion, and even confound and identify his own feelings with theirs; modifying only the language which is thus suggested to him by a consideration that he describes for a particular purpose, that of giving pleasure. Here, then, he will apply the principle of selection which has been already insisted upon. He will depend upon this for removing what would otherwise be painful or disgusting in the passion; he will feel that there is no necessity to trick out or to elevate nature: and, the more industriously he applies this principle, the deeper will be his faith that no words, which *his* fancy or imagination can suggest, will be to be compared with those which are the emanations of reality and truth.

But it may be said by those who do not object to the general spirit of these remarks, that, as it is impossible for the Poet to produce upon all occasions language as exquisitely fitted for the passion as that which the real passion itself suggests, it is proper that he should consider himself as in the situation of a translator, who does not scruple to substitute excellencies of another kind for those which are unattainable by him; and endeavours occasionally to surpass his original, in order to make some amends for the general inferiority to which he feels that he must submit. But this would be to encourage idleness and unmanly despair. Further, it is the language of men who speak of what they do not understand; who talk of Poetry as of a matter of amusement and idle pleasure; who will converse with us as gravely about a *taste* for Poetry, as they express it, as if it were a thing as indifferent as a taste for rope-dancing, or Frontiniac or Sherry. Aristotle, I have been told, has said, that Poetry is the most philosophic of all writing: it is so: its object is truth, not individual and local, but general, and operative; not standing upon external testimony, but carried alive into the heart by passion; truth which is its own testimony, which gives competence and confidence to the tribunal to which it appeals, and receives them from the same tribunal. Poetry is the image of man and nature. The obstacles which stand in the way of the fidelity of the Biographer and Historian, and of their consequent utility, are incalculably greater than those which are to be encountered by the Poet who comprehends the dignity of his art. The Poet writes under one restriction only, namely, the necessity of giving immediate pleasure to a human Being possessed of that information which may be expected from him, not as a lawyer, a physician, a mariner, an astronomer, or a natural philosopher, but as a Man. Except this one restriction, there is no object standing between the Poet and the image of things; between this, and the Biographer and Historian, there are a thousand.

Nor let this necessity of producing immediate pleasure be considered as a degradation of the Poet's art. It is far otherwise. It is an acknowledgement of the beauty of the universe, an acknowledgement the more sincere, because not formal, but indirect; it is a task light and easy to him who looks at the world in the spirit of love: further, it is a homage paid to the native and naked dignity of man, to the grand elementary principle of pleasure, by which he knows, and feels, and lives, and moves. We have no sympathy but what is propagated by pleasure: I would not be misunderstood; but wherever we sympathize with pain, it will be found that the sympathy is produced and carried on by subtle combinations with pleasure. We have no knowledge, that is, no general principles drawn from the contemplation of particular facts, but what has been built up by pleasure, and exists in us by pleasure alone. The Man of science, the Chemist and Mathematician, whatever difficulties and disgusts they may have had to struggle with, know and feel this. However painful may be the objects with which the Anatomist's knowledge is connected, he feels that his knowledge is pleasure; and where he has no pleasure he has no knowledge. What then does the Poet? He considers man and the objects that surround him as acting and reacting upon each other, so as to produce an infinite complexity of pain and pleasure; he considers man in his own nature and in his ordinary life as contemplating this with a certain quantity of immediate knowledge, with certain convictions, intuitions, and deductions, which from habit acquire the quality of intuitions; he considers him as looking upon this complex scene of ideas and sensations, and finding everywhere objects that immediately excite in him sympathies which, from the necessities of his nature, are accompanied by an overbalance of enjoyment.

To this knowledge which all men carry about with them, and to these sympathies in which, without any other discipline than that of our daily life, we are fitted to take delight, the Poet principally directs his attention. He considers man and nature as essentially adapted to each other, and the mind of man as naturally the mirror of the fairest and most interesting properties of nature. And thus the Poet, prompted by his feeling of pleasure, which accompanies him through the whole course of his studies, converses with general nature, with affections akin to those, which, through labour and length of time, the Man of science has raised up in himself, by conversing with those particular parts of nature which are the objects of his studies. The knowledge both of the Poet and the Man of science is pleasure; but the knowledge of the one cleaves to us as a necessary part of our existence, our natural and unalienable inheritance; the other is a personal and individual acquisition, slow to come to us, and by no habitual and direct sympathy connecting us with our fellow-beings. The Man of science seeks truth as a remote and unknown benefactor; he cherishes and loves it in his solitude: the Poet singing a song in which all human beings join with him, rejoices in the presence of truth as our visible friend and hourly companion. Poetry is the breath and finer spirit of all knowledge; it is the impassioned expression which is in the countenance of all Science. Emphatically may it be said of the Poet, as Shakespeare hath said of man, "that he looks before and after." He is the rock of defence for human nature; an upholder and preserver, carrying everywhere with him relationship and love. In spite of difference of soil and climate, of language and manners, of laws and customs: in spite of things silently gone out of mind, and things violently destroyed; the Poet binds together by passion and knowledge the vast empire of human society, as it is spread over the whole earth, and over all time. The objects of the Poet's thoughts are everywhere; though the eyes and senses of man are, it is true, his favourite guides, yet he will follow wheresoever he can find an atmosphere of sensation in which to move his wings. Poetry is the first and last of all knowledge—it is as immortal as the heart of man. If the labours of Men of science should ever create any material revolution, direct or indirect, in our condition, and in the impressions which we habitually receive, the Poet will sleep then no more than at present; he will be ready to follow the steps of the Man of science, not only in those general indirect effects, but he will be at his side, carrying sensation into the midst of the objects of the science itself. The remotest discoveries of the Chemist, the Botanist, or Mineralogist, will be as proper objects of the Poet's art as any upon which it can be employed, if the time should ever come when these things shall be familiar to us, and the relations under which they are contemplated by the followers of these respective sciences shall be manifestly and palpably material to us as enjoying and suffering beings. If the time should ever come when what is now called science, thus familiarized to men, shall be ready to put on, as it were, a form of flesh and blood, the Poet will lend his divine spirit to aid the transfiguration, and will welcome the Being thus produced, as a dear and genuine inmate of the household of man.—It is not, then, to be supposed that any one, who holds that sublime notion of Poetry which I have attempted to convey, will break in upon the sanctity and truth of his pictures by transitory and accidental ornaments, and endeavour to excite admiration of himself by arts, the necessity of which must manifestly depend upon the assumed meanness of his subject.

What has been thus far said applies to Poetry in general; but especially to those parts of composition where the Poet speaks through the mouths of his characters; and upon this point it appears to authorize the conclusion that there are few persons of good sense, who would not allow that the dramatic parts of composition are defective, in proportion as they deviate from the real language of nature, and are coloured by a diction of the Poet's own, either peculiar to him as an individual Poet or belonging simply to Poets in general; to a body of men who, from the circumstance of their compositions being in metre, it is expected will employ a particular language.

It is not, then, in the dramatic parts of composition that we look for this distinction of language; but still it may be proper and necessary where the Poet speaks to us in his own person and character. To this I answer by referring the Reader to the description before given of a Poet. Among the qualities there enumerated as principally conducing to form a Poet, is implied nothing differing in kind from other men, but only in degree. The sum of what was said is, that the Poet is chiefly distinguished from other men by a greater promptness to think and feel without immediate external excitement, and a greater power in expressing such thoughts and feelings as are produced in him in that manner. But these passions and thoughts and feelings are the general passions and thoughts and feelings of men. And with what are they connected? Undoubtedly with our moral sentiments and animal sensations, and with the causes which excite these; with the operations of the elements, and the appearances of the visible universe; with storm and sunshine, with the revolutions of the seasons, with cold and heat, with loss of friends and kindred, with injuries and resentments, gratitude and hope, with fear and sorrow. These, and the like, are the sensations and objects which the Poet describes, as they are the sensations of other men, and the objects which interest them. The Poet thinks and feels in the spirit of human passions. How, then, can his language differ in any material degree from that of all other men who feel vividly and see clearly? It might be *proved* that it is impossible. But supposing that this were not the case, the Poet might then be allowed to use a peculiar language when expressing his feelings for his own gratification, or that of men like himself. But Poets do not write for Poets alone, but for men. Unless therefore we are advocates for that admiration which subsists upon ignorance, and that pleasure which arises from hearing what we do not understand, the Poet must descend from this supposed height; and, in order to excite rational sympathy, he must express himself as other men express themselves. To this it may be added, that while he is only selecting from the real language of men, or, which amounts to the same thing, composing accurately in the spirit of such selection, he is treading upon safe ground, and we know what we are to expect from him. Our feelings are the same with respect to metre; for, as it may be proper to remind the Reader, the distinction of metre is regular and uniform, and not, like that which is produced by what is usually called POETIC DICTION, arbitrary, and subject to infinite caprices upon which no calculation whatever can be made. In the one case, the Reader is utterly at the mercy of the Poet, respecting what imagery or diction he may choose to connect with the passion; whereas, in the other, the metre obeys certain laws, to which the Poet and Reader both willingly submit because they are certain, and because no interference is made by them with the passion, but such as the concurring testimony of ages has shown to heighten and improve the pleasure which co-exists with it.

It will now be proper to answer an obvious question, namely, Why, professing these opinions, have I written in verse? To this, in addition to such answer as is included in what has been already said, I reply, in the first place, Because, however I may have restricted myself, there is still left open to me what confessedly constitutes the most valuable object of all writing, whether in prose or verse; the great and universal passions of men, the most general and interesting of their occupations, and the entire world of nature before me—to supply endless combinations of forms and imagery. Now, supposing for a moment that whatever is interesting in these objects may be as vividly described in prose, why should I be condemned for attempting to superadd to such description the charm which, by the consent of all nations, is acknowledged to exist in metrical language? To this, by such as are yet unconvinced, it may be answered that a very small part of the pleasure given by Poetry depends upon the metre, and that it is injudicious to write in metre, unless it be accompanied with the other artificial distinctions of style with which metre is usually accompanied, and that, by such deviation, more will be lost from the shock which will thereby be given to the Reader's associations than will be counterbalanced by any pleasure which he can derive from the general power of numbers. In answer to those who still contend for the necessity of accompanying metre with certain appropriate colours of style in order to the accomplishment of its appropriate end, and who also, in my opinion, greatly underrate the power of metre in itself, it might, perhaps, as far as relates to these Volumes, have been almost sufficient to observe, that poems are extant, written upon more humble subjects, and in a still more naked and simple style, which have continued to give pleasure from generation to generation. Now, if nakedness and simplicity be a defect, the fact here mentioned affords a strong presumption that poems somewhat less naked and simple are capable of affording pleasure at the present day; and, what I wish *chiefly* to attempt, at present, was to justify myself for having written under the impression of this belief.

But various causes might be pointed out why, when the style is manly and the subject of some importance, words metrically arranged will long continue to impart such a pleasure to mankind as he who proves the extent of that pleasure will be desirous to impart. The end of Poetry is to produce excitement in co-existence with an overbalance of pleasure; but, by the supposition, excitement is an unusual and irregular state of the mind; ideas and feelings do not, in that state, succeed each other in accustomed order. If the words, however, by which this excitement is produced be in themselves powerful, or the images and feelings have an undue proportion of pain connected with them, there is some danger that the excitement may be carried beyond its proper bounds. Now the co-presence of something regular, something to which the mind has been accustomed in various moods and in a less excited state, cannot but have great efficacy in tempering and restraining the passion by an inter-texture of ordinary feeling, and of feeling not strictly and necessarily connected with the passion. This is unquestionably true; and hence, though the opinion will at first appear paradoxical, from the tendency of metre to divest language, in a certain degree, of its reality, and thus to throw a sort of half-consciousness of unsubstantial existence over the whole composition, there can be little doubt but that more pathetic situations and sentiments, that is, those which have a greater proportion of pain connected with them, may be endured in metrical composition, especially in rhyme, than in prose. The metre of the old ballads is very artless; yet they contain many passages which would illustrate this opinion; and, I hope, if the following Poems be attentively perused, similar instances will be found in them. This opinion may be further illustrated by appealing to the Reader's own experience of the reluctance with which he comes to the re-perusal of the distressful parts of *Clarissa Harlowe,* or *The Gamester;* while Shakespeare's writings, in the most pathetic scenes, never act upon us, as pathetic, beyond the bounds of pleasure—an effect which, in a much greater degree than might at first be imagined, is to be ascribed to small, but continual and regular impulses of pleasurable surprise from the metrical arrangement.—On the other hand (what it must be allowed will much more frequently happen) if the Poet's words should be incommensurate with the passion, and inadequate to raise the Reader to a height of desirable excitement, then (unless the Poet's choice of his metre has been grossly injudicious), in the feelings of pleasure which the Reader has been accustomed to connect with metre in general, and in the feeling, whether cheerful or melancholy, which he has been accustomed to connect with that particular movement of metre, there will be found something which will greatly contribute to impart passion to the words, and to effect the complex end which the Poet proposes to himself.

If I had undertaken a SYSTEMATIC defence of the theory here maintained, it would have been my duty to develop the various causes upon which the pleasure received from metrical language depends. Among the chief of these causes is to be reckoned a principle which must be well known to those who have made any of the Arts the object of accurate reflection; namely, the pleasure which the mind derives from the perception of similitude in dissimilitude. This principle is the great spring of the activity of our minds, and their chief feeder. From this principle the direction of the sexual appetite, and all the passions connected with it, take their origin: it is the life of our ordinary conversation; and upon the accuracy with which similitude in dissimilitude, and dissimilitude in similitude are perceived, depend our taste and our moral feelings. It would not be a useless employment to apply this principle to the consideration of metre, and to show that metre is hence enabled to afford much pleasure, and to point out in what manner that pleasure is produced. But my limits will not permit me to enter upon this subject, and I must content myself with a general summary.

I have said that poetry is the spontaneous overflow of powerful feelings: it takes its origin from emotion recollected in tranquillity: the emotion is contemplated till, by a species of reaction, the tranquillity gradually disappears, and an emotion, kindred to that which was before the subject of contemplation, is gradually produced, and does itself actually exist in the mind. In this mood successful composition generally begins, and in a mood similar to this it is carried on; but the emotion, of whatever kind, and in whatever degree, from various causes, is qualified by various pleasures, so that in describing any passions whatsoever, which are voluntarily described, the mind will, upon the whole, be in a state of enjoyment. If Nature be thus cautious to preserve in a state of enjoyment a being so employed, the Poet ought to profit by the lesson held forth to him, and ought especially to take care, that, whatever passions he communicates to his Reader, those passions, if his Reader's mind be sound and vigorous, should always be accompanied with an overbalance of pleasure. Now the music of harmonious metrical language, the sense of difficulty overcome, and the blind association of pleasure which has been previously received from works of rhyme or metre of the same or similar construction, an indistinct perception perpetually renewed of language closely resembling that of real life, and yet, in the circumstance of metre, differing from it so widely—all these imperceptibly make up a complex feeling of delight, which is of the most important use in tempering the painful feeling always found intermingled with powerful descriptions of the deeper passions. This effect is always produced in pathetic and impassioned poetry; while, in lighter compositions, the ease and gracefulness with which the Poet manages his numbers are themselves confessedly a principal source of the gratification of the Reader. All that it is *necessary* to say, however, upon this subject, may be effected by affirming, what few persons will deny, that, of two descriptions, either of passions, manners, or characters, each of them equally well executed, the one in prose and the other in verse, the verse will be read a hundred times where the prose is read once.

Having thus explained a few of my reasons for writing in verse, and why I have chosen subjects from common life, and endeavoured to bring my language near to the real language of men, if I have been too minute in pleading my own cause, I have at the same time been treating a subject of general interest; and for this reason a few words shall be added with reference solely to these particular poems, and to some defects which will probably be found in them. I am sensible that my associations must have sometimes been particular instead of general, and that, consequently, giving to things a false importance, I may have sometimes written upon unworthy subjects; but I am less apprehensive on this account, than that my language may frequently have suffered from those arbitrary connexions of feelings and ideas with particular words and phrases, from which no man can altogether protect himself. Hence I have no doubt, that, in some instances, feelings, even of the ludicrous, may be given to my Readers by expressions which appeared to me tender and pathetic. Such faulty expressions, were I convinced they were faulty at present, and that they must necessarily continue to be so, I would willingly take all reasonable pains to correct. But it is dangerous to make these alterations on the simple authority of a few individuals, or even of certain classes of men; for where the understanding of an Author is not convinced, or his feelings altered, this cannot be done without great injury to himself: for his own feelings are his stay and support; and, if he set them aside in one instance, he may be induced to repeat this act till his mind shall lose all confidence in itself, and become utterly debilitated. To this it may be added, that the critic ought never to forget that he is himself exposed to the same errors as the Poet, and, perhaps, in a much greater degree: for there can be no presumption in saying of most readers, that it is not probable they will be so well acquainted with the various stages of meaning through which words have passed, or with the fickleness or stability of the relations of particular ideas to each other; and, above all, since they are so much less interested in the subject, they may decide lightly and carelessly.

Long as the Reader has been detained, I hope he will permit me to caution him against a mode of false criticism which has been applied to Poetry, in which the language closely resembles that of life and nature. Such verses have been triumphed over in parodies, of which Dr. Johnson's stanza is a fair specimen:—

> I put my hat upon my head
> And walked into the Strand,
> And there I met another man
> Whose hat was in his hand.

Immediately under these lines let us place one of the most justly admired stanzas of the "Babes in the Wood."

> These pretty Babes with hand in hand
> Went wandering up and down;
> But never more they saw the Man
> Approaching from the Town.

In both these stanzas the words, and the order of the words, in no respect differ from the most unimpassioned conversation. There are words in both, for example, "the Strand," and "the Town," connected with none but the most familiar ideas; yet the one stanza we admit as admirable, and the other as a fair example of the superlatively contemptible. Whence arises this difference? Not from the metre, not from the language, not from the order of the words; but the *matter* expressed in Dr. Johnson's stanza is contemptible. The proper method of treating trivial and simple verses, to which Dr. Johnson's stanza would be a fair parallelism, is not to say, this is a bad kind of poetry, or, this is not poetry; but, this wants sense; it is neither interesting in itself nor can *lead* to anything interesting; the images neither originate in that sane state of feeling which arises out of thought, nor can excite thought or feeling in the Reader. This is the only sensible manner of dealing with such verses. Why trouble yourself about the species till you have previously decided upon the genus? Why take pains to prove that an ape is not a Newton, when it is self-evident that he is not a man?

One request I must make of my reader, which is, that in judging these Poems he would decide by his own feelings genuinely, and not by reflection upon what will probably be the judgement of others. How common is it to hear a person say, I myself do not object to this style of composition, or this or that expression, but, to such and such classes of people it will appear mean or ludicrous! This mode of criticism, so destructive of all sound unadulterated judgement, is almost universal: let the Reader then abide, independently, by his own feelings, and, if he finds himself affected, let him not suffer such conjectures to interfere with his pleasure.

If an Author, by any single composition, has impressed us with respect for his talents, it is useful to consider this as affording a presumption, that on other occasions where we have been displeased, he, nevertheless, may not have written ill or absurdly; and further, to give him so much credit for this one composition as may induce us to review what has displeased us, with more care than we should otherwise have bestowed upon it. This is not only an act of justice, but, in our decisions upon poetry especially, may conduce, in a high degree, to the improvement of our own taste; for an *accurate* taste in poetry, and in all the other arts, as Sir Joshua Reynolds has observed, is an *acquired* talent, which can only be produced by thought and a long continued intercourse with the best models of composition. This is mentioned, not with so ridiculous a purpose as to prevent the most inexperienced Reader from judging for himself (I have already said that I wish him to judge for himself), but merely to temper the rashness of decision, and to suggest, that, if Poetry be a subject on which much time has not been bestowed, the judgement may be erroneous; and that, in many cases, it necessarily will be so.

Nothing would, I know, have so effectually contributed to further the end which I have in view, as to have shown of what kind the pleasure is, and how that pleasure is produced, which is confessedly produced by metrical composition essentially different from that which I have here endeavoured to recommend: for the Reader will say that he has been pleased by such composition; and what more can be done for him? The power of any art is limited; and he will suspect, that, if it be proposed to furnish him with new friends, that can be only upon condition of his abandoning his old friends. Besides, as I have said, the Reader is himself conscious of the pleasure which he has received from such composition, composition to which he has peculiarly attached the endearing name of Poetry; and all men feel an habitual gratitude, and something of an honourable bigotry, for the objects which have long continued to please them: we not only wish to be pleased, but to be pleased in that particular way in which we have been accustomed to be pleased. There is in these feelings enough to resist a host of arguments; and I should be the less able to combat them successfully, as I am willing to allow, that, in order entirely to enjoy the Poetry which I am recommending, it would be necessary to give up much of what is ordinarily enjoyed. But, would my limits have permitted me to point out how this pleasure is produced, many obstacles might have been removed, and the Reader assisted in perceiving that the powers of language are not so limited as he may suppose; and that it is possible for poetry to give other enjoyments, of a purer, more lasting, and more exquisite nature. This part of the subject has not been altogether neglected, but it has not been so much my present aim to prove, that the interest excited by some other kinds of poetry is less vivid, and less worthy of the nobler powers of the mind, as to offer reasons for presuming, that if my purpose were fulfilled, a species of poetry would be produced, which is genuine poetry; in its nature well adapted to interest mankind permanently, and likewise important in the multiplicity and quality of its moral relations.

From what has been said, and from a perusal of the Poems, the Reader will be able clearly to perceive the object which I had in view: he will determine how far it has been attained; and, what is a much more important question, whether it be worth attaining: and upon the decision of these two questions will rest my claim to the approbation of the Public.

APPENDIX TO "LYRICAL BALLADS"

Perhaps, as I have no right to expect that attentive perusal, without which, confined, as I have been, to the narrow limits of a preface, my meaning cannot be thoroughly understood, I am anxious to give an exact notion of the sense in which the phrase poetic diction has been used; and for this purpose, a few words shall here be added, concerning the origin and characteristics of the phraseology, which I have condemned under that name.

The earliest poets of all nations generally wrote from passion excited by real events; they wrote naturally, and as men: feeling powerfully as they did, their language was daring, and figurative. In succeeding times, Poets, and Men ambitious of the fame of Poets, perceiving the influence of such language, and desirous of producing the same effect without being animated by the same passion, set themselves to a mechanical adoption of these figures of speech, and made use of them, sometimes with propriety, but much more frequently applied them to feelings and thoughts with which they had no natural connexion whatsoever. A language was thus insensibly produced, differing materially from the real language of men in *any situation.* The Reader or Hearer of this distorted language found himself in a perturbed and unusual state of mind: when affected by the genuine language of passion he had been in a perturbed and unusual state of mind also: in both cases he was willing that his common judgement and understanding should be laid asleep, and he had no instinctive and infallible perception of the true to make him reject the false; the one served as a passport for the other. The emotion was in both cases delightful, and no wonder if he confounded the one with the other, and believed them both to be produced by the same, or similar causes. Besides, the Poet spake to him in the character of a man to be looked up to, a man of genius and authority. Thus, and from a variety of other causes, this distorted language was received with admiration; and Poets, it is probable, who had before contented themselves for the most part with misapplying only expressions which at first had been dictated by real passion, carried the abuse still further, and introduced phrases composed apparently in the spirit of the original figurative language of passion, yet altogether of their own invention, and characterized by various degrees of wanton deviation from good sense and nature.

It is indeed true, that the language of the earliest Poets was felt to differ materially from ordinary language, because it was the language of extraordinary occasions; but it was really spoken by men, language which the Poet himself had uttered when he had been affected by the events which he described, or which he had heard uttered by those around him. To this language it is probable that metre of some sort or other was early superadded. This separated the genuine language of Poetry still further from common life, so that whoever read or heard the poems of these earliest Poets felt himself moved in a way in which he had not been accustomed to be moved in real life, and by causes manifestly different from those which acted upon him in real life. This was the great temptation to all the corruptions which have followed: under the protection of this feeling succeeding Poets constructed a phraseology which had one thing, it is true, in common with the genuine language of poetry, namely, that it was not heard in ordinary conversation; that it was unusual. But the first Poets, as I have said, spake a language which, though unusual, was still the language of men. This circumstance, however, was disregarded by their successors; they found that they could please by easier means: they became proud of modes of expression which they themselves had invented, and which were uttered only by themselves. In process of time metre became a symbol or promise of this unusual language, and whoever took upon him to write in metre, according as he possessed more or less of true poetic genius, introduced less or more of this adulterated phraseology into his compositions, and the true and the false were inseparately interwoven until, the taste of men becoming gradually perverted, this language was received as a natural language: and at length, by the influence of books upon men, did to a certain degree really become so. Abuses of this kind were imported from one nation to another, and with the progress of refinement this diction became daily more and more corrupt, thrusting out of sight the plain humanities of nature by a motley masquerade of tricks, quaintnesses, hieroglyphics, and enigmas.

It would not be uninteresting to point out the causes of the pleasure given by this extravagant and absurd diction. It depends upon a great variety of causes, but upon none, perhaps, more than its influence in impressing a notion of the peculiarity and exaltation of the Poet's character, and in flattering the Reader's self-love by bringing him nearer to a sympathy with that character; an effect which is accomplished by unsettling ordinary habits of thinking, and thus assisting the Reader to approach to that perturbed and dizzy state of mind in which if he does not find himself, he imagines that he is *balked* of a peculiar enjoyment which poetry can and ought to bestow.

The sonnet quoted from Gray, in the Preface, except the lines printed in italics, consists of little else but this diction, though not of the worst kind; and indeed, if one may be permitted to say so, it is far too common in the best writers both ancient and modern. Perhaps in no way, by positive example could more easily be given a notion of what I mean by the phrase *poetic diction* than by referring to a comparison between the metrical paraphrase which we have of passages in the Old and New Testament, and those passages as they exist in our common Translation. See Pope's *Messiah* throughout; Prior's "Did sweeter sounds adorn my flowing tongue," &c. &c. "Though I speak with the tongues of men and of angels," &c. &c., 1st Corinthians, ch. xiii. By way of immediate example take the following of Dr. Johnson:

Turn on the prudent Ant thy heedless eyes,
Observe her labours, Sluggard, and be wise;
No stern command, no monitory voice,
Prescribes her duties, or directs her choice;
Yet, timely provident, she hastes away
To snatch the blessings of a plenteous day;
When fruitful Summer loads the teeming plain,
She crops the harvest, and she stores the grain.
How long shall sloth usurp thy useless hours,
Unnerve thy vigour, and enchain thy powers?
While artful shades thy downy couch enclose,
And soft solicitation courts repose,
Amidst the drowsy charms of dull delight,
Year chases year with unremitted flight,
Till Want now following, fraudulent and slow,
Shall spring to seize thee, like an ambush'd foe.

From this hubbub of words pass to the original. "Go to the Ant, thou Sluggard, consider her ways, and be wise: which having no guide, overseer, or ruler, provideth her meat in the summer, and gathereth her food in the harvest. How long wilt thou sleep, O Sluggard? when wilt thou arise out of thy sleep? Yet a little sleep, a little slumber, a little folding of the hands to sleep. So shall thy poverty come as one that travelleth, and thy want as an armed man." Proverbs, ch. vi.

One more quotation, and I have done. It is from Cowper's Verses supposed to be written by Alexander Selkirk:

Religion! what treasure untold
Resides in that heavenly word!
More precious than silver and gold,
Or all that this earth can afford.
But the sound of the church-going bell
These valleys and rocks never heard,
Ne'er sighed at the sound of a knell,
Or smiled when a sabbath appeared.
Ye winds, that have made me your sport
Convey to this desolate shore
Some cordial endearing report
Of a land I must visit no more.
My Friends, do they now and then send
A wish or a thought after me?
O tell me I yet have a friend,
Though a friend I am never to see.

This passage is quoted as an instance of three different styles of composition. The first four lines are poorly expressed; some Critics would call the language prosaic; the fact is, it would be bad prose, so bad, that it is scarcely worse in metre. The epithet "church-going" applied to a bell, and that by so chaste a writer as Cowper, is an instance of the strange abuses which Poets have introduced into their language, till they and their Readers take them as matters of course, if they do not single them out expressly as objects of admiration. The two lines "Ne'er sighed at the sound," &c., are, in my opinion, an instance of the language of passion wrested from its proper use, and, from the mere circumstance of the composition being in metre, applied upon an occasion that does not justify such violent expressions; and I should condemn the passage, though perhaps few Readers will agree with me, as vicious poetic diction. The last stanza is throughout admirably expressed: it would be equally good whether in prose or verse, except that the Reader has an exquisite pleasure in seeing such natural language so naturally connected with metre. The beauty of this stanza tempts me to conclude with a principle which ought never to be lost sight of, and which has been my chief guide in all I have said,—namely, that in works of *imagination and sentiment,* for of these only have I been treating, in proportion as ideas and feelings are valuable, whether the composition be in prose or in verse, they require and exact one and the same language. Metre is but adventitious to composition, and the phraseology for which that passport is necessary, even where it may be graceful at all, will be little valued by the judicious.

HENRY JAMES: The Art of Fiction*

I SHOULD not have fixed so comprehensive a title to these few remarks, necessarily wanting in any completeness upon a subject the full consideration of which would carry us far, did I not seem to discover a pretext for my temerity in the interesting pamphlet lately published under this name by Mr. Walter Besant. Mr. Besant's lecture at the Royal Institution—the original form of his pamphlet—appears to indicate that many persons are interested in the art of fiction, and are not indifferent to such remarks as those who practice it may attempt to make about it. I am therefore anxious not to lose the benefit of this favorable association, and to edge in a few words under cover of the attention which Mr. Besant is sure to have excited. There is something very encouraging in his having put into form certain of his ideas on the mystery of story-telling.

It is a proof of life and curiosity—curiosity on the part of the brotherhood of novelists as well as on the part of their readers. Only a short time ago it might have been supposed that the English novel was not what the French call *discutable.* It had no air of having a theory, a conviction, a consciousness of itself behind it—of being the expression of an artistic faith, the result of choice and comparison. I do not say it was necessarily the worse for that: it would take much more courage than I possess to intimate that the form of the novel as Dickens and Thackeray (for instance) saw it had any taint of incompleteness. It was, however, *naïf* (if I may help myself out with another French word); and evidently if it be destined to suffer in any way for having lost its *naïveté* it has now an idea of making sure of the corresponding advantages. During the period I have alluded to there was a comfortable good-humored feeling abroad that a novel is a novel, as a pudding is a pudding, and that our only business with it could be to swallow it. But within a year or two, for some reason or other, there have been signs of returning animation—the era of discussion would appear to have been to a certain extent opened. Art lives upon discussion, upon experiment, upon curiosity, upon variety of attempt, upon the exchange of views and the comparison of standpoints; and there is a presumption that those times when no one has anything particular to say about it, and has no reason to give for practice or preference, though they may be times of honor, are not times of development—are times, possibly, even a little of dullness. The successful application of any art is a delightful spectacle, but the theory too is interesting; and though there is a great deal of the latter without the former I suspect there has never been a genuine success that has not had a latent core of conviction. Discussion, suggestion, formulation, these things are fertilizing when they are frank and sincere.

* "The Art of Fiction" was first published in *Longman's Magazine* in 1884, and republished in 1888 in James's *Partial Portraits.* James (1843-1916) was the author of *French Poets and Novelists* (1878), *Hawthorne* (1879), *Views and Reviews* (1908), *Notes on Novelists* (1914), *Within the Rim and Other Essays* (1918), and *Notes and Reviews* (1921), but his most famous criticism is in his prefaces to his own novels, collected by R. P. Blackmur under the title, *The Art of the Novel* (1934).

Mr. Besant has set an excellent example in saying what he thinks, for his part, about the way in which fiction should be written, as well as about the way in which it should be published; for his view of the "art," carried on into an appendix, covers that too. Other laborers in the same field will doubtless take up the argument, they will give it the light of their experience, and the effect will surely be to make our interest in the novel a little more what it had for some time threatened to fail to be—a serious, active, inquiring interest, under protection of which this delightful study may, in moments of confidence, venture to say a little more what it thinks of itself.

It must take itself seriously for the public to take it so. The old superstition about fiction being "wicked" has doubtless died out in England; but the spirit of it lingers in a certain oblique regard directed toward any story which does not more or less admit that it is only a joke. Even the most jocular novel feels in some degree the weight of the proscription that was formerly directed against literary levity: the jocularity does not always succeed in passing for orthodoxy. It is still expected, though perhaps people are ashamed to say it, that a production which is after all only a "make-believe" (for what else is a "story"?) shall be in some degree apologetic—shall renounce the pretension of attempting really to represent life. This, of course, any sensible, wide-awake story declines to do, for it quickly perceives that the tolerance granted to it on such a condition is only an attempt to stifle it disguised in the form of generosity. The old evangelical hostility to the novel, which was as explicit as it was narrow, and which regarded it as little less favorable to our immortal part than a stage-play, was in reality far less insulting. The only reason for the existence of a novel is that it does attempt to represent life. When it relinquishes this attempt, the same attempt that we see on the canvas of the painter, it will have arrived at a very strange pass. It is not expected of the picture that it will make itself humble in order to be forgiven; and the analogy between the art of the painter and the art of the novelist is, so far as I am able to see, complete. Their inspiration is the same, their process (allowing for the different quality of the vehicle) is the same, their success is the same. They may learn from each other, they may explain and sustain each other. Their cause is the same, and the honor of one is the honor of another. The Mahometans think a picture an unholy thing, but it is a long time since any Christian did, and it is therefore the more odd that in the Christian mind the traces (dissimulated though they may be) of a suspicion of the sister art should linger to this day. The only effectual way to lay it to rest is to emphasize the analogy to which I just alluded—to insist on the fact that as the picture is reality, so the novel is history. That is the only general description (which does it justice) that we may give of the novel. But history also is allowed to represent life; it is not, any more than painting, expected to apologize. The subject-matter of fiction is stored up likewise in documents and records, and if it will not give itself away, as they say in California, it must speak with assurance, with the tone of the historian. Certain accomplished novelists have a habit of giving themselves away which must often bring tears to the eyes of people who take their fiction seriously. I was lately struck, in reading over many pages of Anthony Trollope, with his want of discretion in this particular. In a digression, a parenthesis or an aside, he concedes to the reader that he and this trusting friend are only "making believe." He admits that the events he narrates have not really happened, and that he can give his narrative any turn the reader may like best. Such a betrayal of a sacred office seems to me, I confess, a terrible crime; it is what I mean by the attitude of apology, and it shocks me every whit as much in Trollope as it would have shocked me in Gibbon or Macaulay. It implies that the novelist is less occupied in looking for the truth (the truth, of course I mean, that he assumes, the premises that we must grant him, whatever they may be) than the historian, and in doing so it deprives him at a stroke of all his standing-room. To represent and illustrate the past, the actions of men, is the task of either writer, and the only difference that I can see is, in proportion as he succeeds, to the honor of the novelist, consisting as it does in his having more difficulty in collecting his evidence, which is so far from being purely literary. It seems to me to give him a great character, the fact that he has at once so much in common with the philosopher and the painter; this double analogy is a magnificent heritage.

It is of all this evidently that Mr. Besant is full when he insists upon the fact that fiction is one of the *fine* arts, deserving in its turn of all the honors and emoluments that have hitherto been reserved for the successful profession of music, poetry, painting, architecture. It is impossible to insist too much on so important a truth, and the place that Mr. Besant demands for the work of the novelist may be represented, a trifle less abstractly, by saying that he demands not only that it shall be reputed artistic, but that it shall be reputed very artistic indeed. It is excellent that he should have struck this note, for his doing so indicates that there was need of it, that his proposition may be to many people a novelty. One rubs one's eyes at the thought; but the rest of Mr. Besant's essay confirms the revelation. I suspect in truth that it would be possible to confirm it still further, and that one would not be far wrong in saying that in addition to the people to whom it has never occurred that a novel ought to be artistic, there are a great many others who, if this principle were urged upon them, would be filled with an indefinable mistrust. They would find it difficult to explain their repugnance, but it would operate strongly to put them on their guard. "Art," in our Protestant communities, where so many things have got so strangely twisted about, is supposed in certain circles to have some vague injurious effect upon those who make it an important consideration, who let it weigh in the balance. It is assumed to be opposed in some mysterious manner to morality, to amusement, to instruction. When it is embodied in the work of the painter (the sculptor is another affair!) you know what it is: it stands there before you, in the honesty of pink and green and a gilt frame; you can see the worst of it at a glance, and you can be on your guard. But when it is introduced into literature it becomes more insidious—there is danger of its hurting you before you know it. Literature should be either instructive or amusing, and there is in many minds an impression that these artistic preoccupations, the search for form, contribute to neither end, interfere indeed with both. They are too frivolous to be edifying, and too serious to be diverting; and they are moreover priggish and paradoxical and superfluous. That, I think, represents the manner in which the latent thought of many people who read novels as an exercise in skipping would explain itself if it were to become articulate. They would argue, of course, that a novel ought to be "good," but they would interpret this term in a fashion of their own, which indeed would vary considerably from one critic to another. One would say that being good means representing virtuous and aspiring characters placed in prominent positions; another would say that it depends on a "happy ending," on a distribution at the last of prizes, pensions, husbands, wives, babies, millions, appended paragraphs, and cheerful remarks. Another still would say that it means being full of incident and movement, so that we shall wish to jump ahead, to see who was the mysterious stranger, and if the stolen will was ever found, and shall not be distracted from this pleasure by any tiresome analysis or "description." But they would all agree that the "artistic" idea would spoil some of their fun. One would hold it accountable for all the description, another would see it revealed in the absence of sympathy. Its hostility to a happy ending would be evident, and it might even in some cases render any ending at all impossible. The "ending" of a novel is, for many persons, like that of a good dinner, a course of dessert and ices, and the artist in fiction is regarded as a sort of meddlesome doctor who forbids agreeable aftertastes. It is therefore true that this conception of Mr. Besant's of the novel as a superior form encounters not only a negative but a positive indifference. It matters little that as a work of art it should really be as little or as much of its essence to supply happy endings, sympathetic characters, and an objective tone, as if it were a work of mechanics: the association of ideas, however incongruous, might easily be too much for it if an eloquent voice were not sometimes raised to call attention to the fact that it is at once as free and as serious a branch of literature as any other.

Certainly this might sometimes be doubted in presence of the enormous number of works of fiction that appeal to the credulity of our generation, for it might easily seem that there could be no great character in a commodity so quickly and easily produced. It must be admitted that good novels are much compromised by bad ones, and that the field at large suffers discredit from overcrowding. I think, however, that this injury is only superficial, and that the superabundance of written fiction proves nothing against the principle itself. It has been vulgarized, like all other kinds of literature, like everything else today, and it has proved more than some kinds accessible to vulgarization. But there is as much difference as there ever was between a good novel and a bad one: the bad is swept with all the daubed canvases and spoiled marble into some unvisited limbo, or infinite rubbish-yard beneath the back-windows of the world, and the good subsists and emits its light and stimulates our desire for perfection. As I shall take the liberty of making but a single criticism of Mr. Besant, whose tone is so full of love of his art, I may as well have done with it at once. He seems to me to mistake, in attempting to say so definitely beforehand, what sort of an affair the good novel will be. To indicate the danger of such an error as that has been the purpose of these few pages; to suggest that certain traditions on the subject, applied *a priori*, have already had much to answer for, and that the good health of an art which undertakes so immediately to reproduce life must demand that it be perfectly free. It lives upon exercise, and the very meaning of exercise is freedom. The only obligation to which in advance we may hold a novel, without incurring the accusation of being arbitrary, is that it be interesting. That general responsibility rests upon it, but it is the only one I can think of. The ways in which it is at liberty to accomplish this result (of interesting us) strike me as innumerable, and such as can only suffer from being marked out or fenced in by prescription. They are as various as the temperament of man, and they are successful in proportion as they reveal a particular mind, different from others. A novel is in its broadest definition a personal, a direct impression of life: that, to begin with, constitutes its value, which is greater or less according to the intensity of the impression. But there will be no intensity at all, and therefore no value, unless there is freedom to feel and say. The tracing of a line to be followed, of a tone to be taken, of a form to be filled out, is a limitation of that freedom and a suppression of the very thing that we are most curious about. The form, it seems to me, is to be appreciated after the fact: then the author's choice has been made, his standard has been indicated; then we can follow lines and directions and compare tones and resemblances. Then in a word we can enjoy one of the most charming of pleasures, we can estimate quality, we can apply the test of execution. The execution belongs to the author alone; it is what is most personal to him, and we measure him by that. The advantage, the luxury, as well as the torment and responsibility of the novelist, is that there is no limit to what he may attempt as an executant—no limit to his possible experiments, efforts, discoveries, successes. Here it is especially that he works, step by step, like his brother of the brush, of whom we may always say that he has painted his picture in a manner best known to himself. His manner is his secret, not necessarily a jealous one. He cannot disclose it as a general thing if he would; he would be at a loss to teach it to others. I say this with a due recollection of having insisted on the community of method of the artist who paints a picture and the artist who writes a novel. The painter *is* able to teach the rudiments of his practice, and it is possible, from the study of good work (granted the aptitude), both to learn how to paint and to learn how to write. Yet it remains true, without injury to the *rapprochement*, that the literary artist would be obliged to say to his pupil much more than the other, "Ah, well, you must do it as you can!" It is a question of degree, a matter of delicacy. If there are exact sciences, there are also exact arts, and the grammar of painting is so much more definite that it makes the difference.

I ought to add, however, that if Mr. Besant says at the beginning of his essay that the "laws of fiction may be laid down and taught with as much precision and exactness as the laws of harmony, perspective, and proportion" he mitigates what might appear to be an extravagance by applying his remark to "general" laws, and by expressing most of these rules in a manner with which it would certainly be unaccommodating to disagree. That the novelist must write from his experience, that his "characters must be real and such as might be met with in actual life"; that "a young lady brought up in a quiet country village should avoid descriptions of garrison life," and "a writer whose friends and personal experiences belong to the lower middle-class should carefully avoid introducing his characters into society"; that one should enter one's notes in a common-place book; that one's figures should be clear in outline; that making them clear by some trick of speech or of carriage is a bad method, and "describing them at length" is a worse one; that English Fiction should have a "conscious moral purpose"; that "it is almost impossible to estimate too highly the value of careful workmanship—that is, of style"; that "the most important point of all is the story," that "the story is everything": these are principles with most of which it is surely impossible not to sympathize. That remark about the lower middle-class writer and his knowing his place is perhaps rather chilling; but for the rest I should find it difficult to dissent from any one of these recommendations. At the same time, I should find it difficult positively to assent to them, with the exception, perhaps, of the injunction as to entering one's notes in a common-place book. They scarcely seem to me to have the quality that Mr. Besant attributes to the rules of the novelist—the "precision and exactness" of "the laws of harmony, perspective, and proportion." They are suggestive, they are even inspiring, but they are not exact, though they are doubtless as much so as the case admits of: which is a proof of that liberty of interpretation for which I just contended. For the value of these different injunctions—so beautiful and so vague—is wholly in the meaning one attaches to them. The characters, the situation, which strike one as real will be those that touch and interest one most, but the measure of reality is very difficult to fix. The reality of Don Quixote or of Mr. Micawber is a very delicate shade; it is a reality so colored by the author's vision that, vivid as it may be, one would hesitate to propose it as a model: one would expose one's self to some very embarrassing questions on the part of a pupil. It goes without saying that you will not write a good novel unless you possess the sense of reality; but it will be difficult to give you a recipe for calling that sense into being. Humanity is immense, and reality has a myriad forms; the most one can affirm is that some of the flowers of fiction have the odor of it, and others have not; as for telling you in advance how your nosegay should be composed, that is another affair. It is equally excellent and inconclusive to say that one must write from experience; to our suppositious aspirant such a declaration might savor of mockery. What kind of experience is intended, and where does it begin and end? Experience is never limited, and it is never complete; it is an immense sensibility, a kind of huge spider-web of the finest silken threads suspended in the chamber of consciousness, and catching every air-borne particle in its tissue. It is the very atmosphere of the mind; and when the mind is imaginative—much more when it happens to be that of a man of genius—it takes to itself the faintest hints of life, it converts the very pulses of the air into revelations. The young lady living in a village has only to be a damsel upon whom nothing is lost to make it quite unfair (as it seems to me) to declare to her that she shall have nothing to say about the military. Greater miracles have been seen than that, imagination assisting, she should speak the truth about some of these gentlemen. I remember an English novelist, a woman of genius, telling me that she was much commended for the impression she had managed to give in one of her tales of the nature and way of life of the French Protestant youth. She had been asked where she learned so much about this recondite being, she had been congratulated on her peculiar opportunities. These opportunities consisted in her having once, in Paris, as she ascended a staircase, passed an open door where, in the household of a *pasteur*, some of the young Protestants were seated at table round a finished meal. The glimpse made a picture; it lasted only a moment, but that moment was experience. She had got her direct personal impression, and she turned out her type. She knew what youth was, and what Protestantism; she also had the advantage of having seen what it was to be French, so that she converted these ideas into a concrete image and produced a reality. Above all, however, she was blessed with the faculty which when you give it an inch takes an ell, and which for the artist is a much greater source of strength than any accident of residence or of place in the social scale. The power to guess the unseen from the seen, to trace the implication of things, to judge the whole piece by the pattern, the condition of feeling life in general so completely that you are well on your way to knowing any particular corner of it—this cluster of gifts may almost be said to constitute experience, and they occur in country and in town, and in the most differing stages of education. If experience consists of impressions, it may be said that impressions *are* experience, just as (have we not seen it?) they are the very air we breathe. Therefore, if I should certainly say to a novice, "Write from experience and from experience only," I should feel that this was rather a tantalizing monition if I were not careful immediately to add, "Try to be one of the people on whom nothing is lost!"

I am far from intending by this to minimize the importance of exactness—of truth of detail. One can speak best from one's own taste, and I may therefore venture to say that the air of reality (solidity of specification) seems to me to be the supreme virtue of a novel—the merit on which all its other merits (including that conscious moral purpose of which Mr. Besant speaks) helplessly and submissively depend. If it be not there they are all as nothing, and if these be there, they owe their effect to the success with which the author has produced the illusion of life. The cultivation of this success, the study of this exquisite process, form, to my taste, the beginning and the end of the art of the novelist. They are his inspiration, his despair, his reward, his torment, his delight. It is here in very truth that he competes with life; it is here that he competes with his brother the painter in *his* attempts to render the look of things, the look that conveys their meaning, to catch the color, the relief, the expression, the surface, the substance of the human spectacle. It is in regard to this that Mr. Besant is well inspired when he bids him take notes. He cannot possibly take too many, he cannot possibly take enough. All life solicits him, and to "render" the simplest surface, to produce the most momentary illusion, is a very complicated busi- [illegible] His case would be easier, and the rule [illegible]ore exact, if Mr. Besant had been [illegible]what notes to take. But this, [illegible] in any manual; it is the business of his life. He has to take a great many in order to select a few, he has to work them up as he can, and even the guides and philosophers who might have most to say to him must leave him alone when it comes to the application of precepts, as we leave the painter in communion with his palette. That his characters "must be clear in outline" as Mr. Besant says—he feels that down to his boots; but how he shall make them so is a secret between his good angel and himself. It would be absurdly simple if he could be taught that a great deal of "description" would make them so, or that on the contrary the absence of description and the cultivation of dialogue, or the absence of dialogue and the multiplication of "incident," would rescue him from his difficulties. Nothing, for instance, is more possible than that he be of a turn of mind for which this odd, literal opposition of description and dialogue, incident and description, has little meaning and light. People often talk of these things as if they had a kind of internecine distinctness, instead of melting into each other at every breath, and being intimately associated parts of one general effort of expression. I cannot imagine composition existing in a series of blocks, nor conceive, in any novel worth discussing at all, of a passage of description that is not in its intention narrative, a passage of dialogue that is not in its intention descriptive, a touch of truth of any sort that does not partake of the nature of incident, or an incident that derives its interest from any other source than the general and only source of the success of a work of art—that of being illustrative. A novel is a living thing, all one and continuous, like any other organism, and in proportion as it lives will it be found, I think, that in each of the parts there is something of each of the other parts. The critic who over the close texture of a finished work shall pretend to trace a geography of items will mark some frontiers as artificial, I fear, as any that have been known to history. There is an old-fashioned distinction between the novel of character and the novel of incident which must have cost many a smile to the intending fabulist who was keen about his work. It appears to me as little to the point as the equally celebrated distinction between the novel and the romance—to answer as little to any reality. There are bad novels and good novels, as there are bad pictures and good pictures; but that is the only distinction in which I see any meaning, and I can as little imagine speaking of a novel of character as I can imagine speaking of a picture of character. When one says picture one says of character, when one says novel one says of incident, and the terms may be transposed at will. What is character but the determination of incident? What is incident but the illustration of character? What is either a picture or a novel that is *not* of character? What else do we seek in it and find in it? It is an incident for a woman to stand up with her hand resting on a table and look at you in a certain way; or if it be not an incident I think it will be hard to say what it is. At the same time it is an expression of character. If you say you don't see it (character in *that—allons donc!*), this is exactly what the artist who has reasons of his own for thinking he *does* see it undertakes to show you. When a young man makes up his mind that he has not faith enough after all to enter the Church as he intended, that is an incident, though you may not hurry to the end of the chapter to see whether perhaps he doesn't change once more. I do not say that these are extraordinary or startling incidents. I do not pretend to estimate the degree of interest proceeding from them, for this will depend upon the skill of the painter. It sounds almost puerile to say that some incidents are intrinsically much more important than others, and I need not take this precaution after having professed my sympathy for the major ones in remarking that the only classification of the novel that I can understand is into that which has life and that which has it not.

The novel and the romance, the novel of incident and that of character—these clumsy separations appear to me to have been made by critics and readers for their own convenience, and to help them out of some of their occasional predicaments, but to have little reality or interest for the producer, from whose point of view it is of course that we are attempting to consider the art of fiction. The case is the same with another shadowy category which Mr. Besant apparently is disposed to set up—that of the "modern English novel"; unless indeed it be that in this matter he has fallen into an accidental confusion of standpoints. It is not quite clear whether he intends the remarks in which he alludes to it to be didactic or historical. It is as difficult to suppose a person intending to write a modern English as to suppose him writing an ancient English novel: that is a label which begs the question. One writes the novel, one paints the picture, of one's language and of one's time, and calling it modern English will not, alas! make the difficult task any easier. No more, unfortunately, will calling this or that work of one's fellow-artist a romance—unless it be, of course, simply for the pleasantness of the thing, as for instance when Hawthorne gave this heading to his story of *Blithedale*. The French, who have brought the theory of fiction to remarkable completeness, have but one name for the novel, and have not attempted smaller things in it, that I can see, for that. I can think of no obligation to which the "romancer" would not be held equally with the novelist; the standard of execution is equally high for each. Of course it is of execution that we are talking—that being the only point of a novel that is open to contention. This is perhaps too often lost sight of, only to produce interminable confusions and cross-purposes. We must grant the artist his subject, his idea, his *donnée:* our criticism is applied only to what he makes of it. Naturally I do not mean that we are bound to like it or find it interesting: in case we do not our course is perfectly simple—to let it alone. We may believe that of a certain idea even the most sincere novelist can make nothing at all, and the event may perfectly justify our belief; but the failure will have been a failure to execute, and it is in the execution that the fatal weakness is recorded. If we pretend to respect the artist at all, we must allow him his freedom of choice, in the face, in particular cases, of innumerable presumptions that the choice will not fructify. Art derives a considerable part of its beneficial exercise from flying in the face of presumptions, and some of the most interesting experiments of which it is capable are hidden in the bosom of common things. Gustave Flaubert has written a story about the devotion of a servant-girl to a parrot, and the production, highly finished as it is, cannot on the whole be called a success. We are perfectly free to find it flat, but I think it might have been interesting; and I, for my part, am extremely glad he should have written it; it is a contribution to our knowledge of what can be done—or what cannot. Ivan Turgénieff has written a tale about a deaf and dumb serf and a lap-dog, and the thing is touching, loving, a little masterpiece. He struck the note of life where Gustave Flaubert missed it—he flew in the face of a presumption and achieved a victory.

Nothing, of course, will ever take the place of the good old fashion of "liking" a work of art or not liking it: the most improved criticism will not abolish that primitive, that ultimate test. I mention this to guard myself from the accusation of intimating that the idea, the subject, of a novel or a picture, does not matter. It matters, to my sense, in the highest degree, and if I might put up a prayer it would be that artists should select none but the richest. Some, as I have already hastened to admit, are much more remunerative than others, and it would be a world happily arranged in which persons intending to treat them should be exempt from confusions and mistakes. This fortunate condition will arrive only, I fear, on the same day that critics become purged from error. Meanwhile, I repeat, we do not judge the artist with fairness unless we say to him, "Oh, I grant you your starting-point, because if I did not I should seem to prescribe to you, and heaven forbid I should take that responsibility. If I pretend to tell you what you must not take, you will call upon me to tell you then what you must take; in which case I shall be prettily caught. Moreover, it isn't till I have accepted your data that I can begin to measure you. I have the standard, the pitch; I have no right to tamper with your flute and then criticize your music. Of course I may not care for your idea at all; I may think it silly, or stale, or unclean; in which case I wash my hands of you altogether. I may content myself with believing that you will not have succeeded in being interesting, but I shall, of course, not attempt to demonstrate it, and you will be as indifferent to me as I am to you. I needn't remind you that there are all sorts of tastes: who can know it better? Some people, for excellent reasons, don't like to read about carpenters; others, for reasons even better, don't like to read about courtesans. Many object to Americans. Others (I believe they are mainly editors and publishers) won't look at Italians. Some readers don't like quiet subjects; others don't like bustling ones. Some enjoy a complete illusion, others the consciousness of large concessions. They choose their novels accordingly, and if they don't care about your idea they won't, *a fortiori,* care about your treatment."

So that it comes back very quickly, as I have said, to the liking: in spite of M. Zola, who reasons less powerfully than he represents, and who will not reconcile himself to this absoluteness of taste, thinking that there are certain things that people ought to like, and that they can be made to like. I am quite at a loss to imagine anything (at any rate in this matter of fiction) that people *ought* to like or to dislike. Selection will be sure to take care of itself, for it has a constant motive behind it. That motive is simply experience. As people feel life, so they will feel the art that is most closely related to it. This closeness of relation is what we should never forget in talking of the effort of the novel. Many people speak of it as a factitious, artificial form, a product of ingenuity, the business of which it is to alter and arrange the things that surround us, to translate them into conventional, traditional moulds. This, however, is a view of the matter which carries us but a very short way, condemns the art to an eternal repetition of a few familiar *clichés,* cuts short its development, and leads us straight up to a dead wall. Catching the very note and trick, the strange irregular rhythm of life, that is the attempt whose strenuous force keeps Fiction upon her feet. In proportion as in what she offers us we see life *without* rearrangement do we feel that we are touching the truth; in proportion as we see it *with* rearrangement do we feel that we are being put off with a substitute, a compromise and convention. It is not uncommon to hear an extraordinary assurance of remark in regard to this matter of rearranging, which is often spoken of as if it were the last word of art. Mr. Besant seems to me in danger of falling into the great error with his rather unguarded talk about "selection." Art is essentially selection, but it is a selection whose main care is to be typical, to be inclusive. For many people art means rose-colored window-panes, and selection means picking a bouquet for Mrs. Grundy. They will tell you glibly that artistic

considerations have nothing to do with the disagreeable, with the ugly; they will rattle off shallow commonplaces about the province of art and the limits of art till you are moved to some wonder in return as to the province and the limits of ignorance. It appears to me that no one can ever have made a seriously artistic attempt without becoming conscious of an immense increase—a kind of revelation—of freedom. One perceives in that case—by the light of a heavenly ray—that the province of art is all life, all feeling, all observation, all vision. As Mr. Besant so justly intimates, it is all experience. That is a sufficient answer to those who maintain that it must not touch the sad things of life, who stick into its divine unconscious bosom little prohibitory inscriptions on the end of sticks, such as we see in public gardens—"It is forbidden to walk on the grass; it is forbidden to touch the flowers; it is not allowed to introduce dogs or to remain after dark; it is requested to keep to the right." The young aspirant in the line of fiction whom we continue to imagine will do nothing without taste, for in that case his freedom would be of little use to him; but the first advantage of his taste will be to reveal to him the absurdity of the little sticks and tickets. If he have taste, I must add, of course he will have ingenuity, and my disrespectful reference to that quality just now was not meant to imply that it is useless in fiction. But it is only a secondary aid; the first is a capacity for receiving straight impressions.

Mr. Besant has some remarks on the question of "the story" which I shall not attempt to criticize, though they seem to me to contain a singular ambiguity, because I do not think I understand them. I cannot see what is meant by talking as if there were a part of a novel which is the story and part of it which for mystical reasons is not—unless indeed the distinction be made in a sense in which it is difficult to suppose that any one should attempt to convey anything. "The story," if it represents anything, represents the subject, the idea, the *donnée* of the novel; and there is surely no "school"—Mr. Besant speaks of a school—which urges that a novel should be all treatment and no subject. There must assuredly be something to treat; every school is intimately conscious of that. This sense of the story being the idea, the starting-point, of the novel, is the only one that I see in which it can be spoken of as something different from its organic whole; and since in proportion as the work is successful the idea permeates and penetrates it, informs and animates it, so that every word and every punctuation-point contribute directly to the expression, in that proportion do we lose our sense of the story being a blade which may be drawn more or less out of its sheath. The story and the novel, the idea and the form, are the needle and thread, and I never heard of a guild of tailors who recommended the use of the thread without the needle, or the needle without the thread. Mr. Besant is not the only critic who may be observed to have spoken as if there were certain things in life which constitute stories, and certain others which do not. I find the same odd implication in an entertaining article in the *Pall Mall Gazette,* devoted, as it happens, to Mr. Besant's lecture. "The story is the thing!" says this graceful writer, as if with a tone of opposition to some other idea. I should think it was, as every painter who, as the time for "sending in" his picture looms in the distance, finds himself still in quest of a subject—as every belated artist not fixed about his theme will heartily agree. There are some subjects which speak to us and others which do not, but he would be a clever man who should undertake to give a rule—an *index expurgatorius*—by which the story and the no-story should be known apart. It is impossible (to me at least) to imagine any such rule which shall not be altogether arbitrary. The writer in the *Pall Mall* opposes the delightful (as I suppose) novel of *Margot la Balafrée* to certain tales in which "Bostonian nymphs" appear to have "rejected English dukes for psychological reasons." I am not acquainted with the romance just designated, and can scarcely forgive the *Pall Mall* critic for not mentioning the name of the author, but the title appears to refer to a lady who may have received a scar in some heroic adventure. I am inconsolable at not being acquainted with this episode, but am utterly at a loss to see why it is a story when the rejection (or acceptance) of a duke is not, and why a reason, psychological or other, is not a subject when a cicatrix is. They are all particles of the multitudinous life with which the novel deals, and surely no dogma which pretends to make it lawful to touch the one and unlawful to touch the other will stand for a moment on its feet. It is the special picture that must stand or fall, according as it seems to possess truth or to lack it. Mr. Besant does not, to my sense, light up the subject by intimating that a story must, under penalty of not being a story, consist of "adventures." Why of adventures more than of green spectacles? He mentions a category of impossible things, and among them he places "fiction without adventure." Why without adventure, more than without matrimony, or celibacy, or parturition, or cholera, or hydropathy, or Jansenism? This seems to me to bring the novel back to the hapless little *rôle* of being an artificial, ingenious thing—bring it down from its large, free character of an immense and exquisite correspondence with life. And what *is* adventure when it comes to that, and by what sign is the listening pupil to recognize it? It is an adventure—an immense one—for me to write this little article; and for a Bostonian nymph to reject an English duke is an adventure only less stirring, I should say, than for an English duke to be rejected by a Bostonian nymph. I see dramas within dramas in that, and innumerable points of view. A psychological reason is, to my imagination, an object adorably pictorial; to catch the tint of its complexion—I feel as if that idea might inspire one to Titianesque efforts. There are few things more exciting to me, in short, than a psychological reason, and yet, I protest, the novel seems to me the most magnificent form of art. I have just been reading, at the same time, the delightful story of *Treasure Island*, by Mr. Robert Louis Stevenson, and, in a manner less consecutive, the last tale from M. Edmond de Goncourt, which is entitled *Chérie*. One of these works treats of murders, mysteries, islands of dreadful renown, hairbreadth escapes, miraculous coincidences, and buried doubloons. The other treats of a little French girl who lived in a fine house in Paris, and died of wounded sensibility because no one would marry her. I call *Treasure Island* delightful, because it appears to me to have succeeded wonderfully in what it attempts; and I venture to bestow no epithet upon *Chérie*, which strikes me as having failed deplorably in what it attempts—that is, in tracing the development of the moral consciousness of a child. But one of these productions strikes me as exactly as much of a novel as the other, and as having a "story" quite as much. The moral consciousness of a child is as much a part of life as the islands of the Spanish Main, and the one sort of geography seems to me to have those "surprises" of which Mr. Besant speaks quite as much as the other. For myself (since it comes back in the last resort, as I say, to the preference of the individual), the picture of the child's experience has the advantage that I can at succesive steps (an immense luxury, near to the "sensual pleasure" of which Mr. Besant's critic in the *Pall Mall* speaks) say Yes or No, as it may be, to what the artist puts before me. I have been a child in fact, but I have been on a quest for a buried treasure only in supposition, and it is a simple accident that with M. de Goncourt I should have for the most part to say No. With George Eliot, when she painted that country with a far other intelligence, I always said Yes.

The most interesting part of Mr. Besant's lecture is unfortunately the briefest passage—his very cursory allusion to the "conscious moral purpose" of the novel. Here again it is not very clear whether he be recording a fact or laying down a principle; it is a great pity that in the latter case he should not have developed his idea. This branch of the subject is of immense importance, and Mr. Besant's few words point to considerations of the widest reach, not to be lightly disposed of. He will have treated the art of fiction but superficially who is not prepared to go every inch of the way that these considerations will carry him. It is for this reason that at the beginning of these remarks I was careful to notify the reader that my reflections on so large a theme have no pretension to be exhaustive. Like Mr. Besant, I have left the question of the morality of the novel till the last, and at the last I find I have used up my space. It is a question surrounded with difficulties, as witness the very first that meets us, in the form of a definite question, on the threshold. Vagueness, in such a discussion, is fatal, and what is the meaning of your morality and your conscious moral purpose? Will you not define your terms and explain how (a novel being a picture) a picture can be either moral or immoral? You wish to paint a moral picture or carve a moral statue: will you not tell us how you would set about it? We are discussing the Art of Fiction; questions of art are questions (in the widest sense) of execution; questions of morality are quite another affair, and will you not let us see how it is that you find it so easy to mix them up? These things are so clear to Mr. Besant that he has deduced from them a law which he sees embodied in English Fiction, and which is "a truly admirable thing and a great cause for congratulation." It is a great cause for congratulation indeed when such thorny problems become as smooth as silk. I may add that in so far as Mr. Besant perceives that in point of fact English Fiction has addressed itself preponderantly to these delicate questions he will appear to many people to have made a vain discovery. They will have been positively struck, on the contrary, with the moral timidity of the usual English novelist; with his (or with her) aversion to face the difficulties with which on every side the treatment of reality bristles. He is apt to be extremely shy (whereas the picture that Mr. Besant draws is a picture of boldness), and the sign of his work, for the most part, is a cautious silence on certain subjects. In the English novel (by which of course I mean the American as well), more than in any other, there is a traditional difference between that which people know and that which they agree to admit that they know, that which they see and that which they speak of, that which they feel to be a part of life and that which they allow to enter into literature. There is the great difference, in short, between what they talk of in conversation and what they talk of in print. The essence of moral energy is to survey the whole field, and I should directly reverse Mr. Besant's remark and say not that the English novel has a purpose, but that it has a diffidence. To what degree a purpose in a work of art is a source of corruption I shall not attempt to inquire; the one that seems to me least dangerous is the purpose of making a perfect work. As for our novel, I may say lastly on this score that as we find it in England today it strikes me as addressed in a large degree to "young people," and that this in itself constitutes a presumption that it will be rather shy. There are certain things which it is generally agreed not to discuss, not even to mention, before young people. That is very well, but the absence of discussion is not a symptom of the moral passion. The purpose of the English novel—"a truly admirable thing, and a great cause for congratulation"—strikes me therefore as rather negative.

There is one point at which the moral sense and the artistic sense lie very near together; that is in the light of the very obvious truth that the deepest quality of a work of art will always be the quality of the mind of the producer. In proportion as that intelligence is fine will the novel, the picture, the statue partake of the substance of beauty and truth. To be constituted of such elements is, to my vision, to have purpose enough. No good novel will ever proceed from a superficial mind; that seems to me an axiom which, for the artist in fiction, will cover all needful moral ground: if the youthful aspirant take it to heart it will illuminate for him many of the mysteries of "purpose." There are many other useful things that might be said to him, but I have come to the end of my article, and can only touch them as I pass. The critic in the *Pall Mall Gazette,* whom I have already quoted, draws attention to the danger, in speaking of the art of fiction, of generalizing. The danger that he has in mind is rather, I imagine, that of particularizing, for there are some comprehensive remarks which, in addition to those embodied in Mr. Besant's suggestive lecture, might without fear of misleading him be addressed to the ingenuous student. I should remind him first of the magnificence of the form that is open to him, which offers to sight so few restrictions and such innumerable opportunities. The other arts, in comparison, appear confined and hampered; the various conditions under which they are exercised are so rigid and definite. But the only condition that I can think of attaching to the composition of the novel is, as I have already said, that it be sincere. This freedom is a splendid privilege, and the first lesson of the young novelist is to learn to be worthy of it. "Enjoy it as it deserves," I should say to him; "take possession of it, explore it to its utmost extent, publish it, rejoice in it. All life belongs to you, and do not listen either to those who would shut you up into corners of it and tell you that it is only here and there that art inhabits, or to those who would persuade you that this heavenly messenger wings her way outside of life altogether, breathing a superfine air, and turning away her head from the truth of things. There is no impression of life, no manner of seeing it and feeling it, to which the plan of the novelist may not offer a place; you have only to remember that talents so dissimilar as those of Alexandre Dumas and Jane Austen, Charles Dickens and Gustave Flaubert have worked in this field with equal glory. Do not think too much about optimism and pessimism; try and catch the color of life itself. In France today we see a prodigious effort (that of Emile Zola, to whose solid and serious work no explorer of the capacity of the novel can allude without respect), we see an extraordinary effort, vitiated by a spirit of pessimism on a narrow basis. M. Zola is magnificent, but he strikes an English reader as ignorant; he has an air of working in the dark; if he had as much light as energy, his results would be of the highest value. As for the aberrations of a shallow optimism, the ground (of English fiction especially) is strewn with their brittle particles as with broken glass. If you must indulge in conclusions, let them have the taste of a wide knowledge. Remember that your first duty is to be as complete as possible—to make as perfect a work. Be generous and delicate and pursue the prize."

ANDREW CECIL BRADLEY: Hegel's Theory of Tragedy*

SINCE Aristotle dealt with tragedy, and, as usual drew the main features of his subject with those sure and simple strokes which no later hand has rivalled, the only philosopher who has treated it in a manner both original and searching is Hegel.[1] I propose here to give a sketch of Hegel's theory, and to add some remarks upon it. But I cannot possibly do justice in a sketch to a theory which fills many pages of the *Aesthetik;* which I must tear from its connections with the author's general view of poetry, and with the rest of his philosophy;[2] and which I must try to exhibit as far as possible in the language of ordinary literature. To estimate this theory, therefore, from my sketch would be neither safe nor just—all the more because, in the interest of immediate clearness, I have not scrupled to insert without warning various remarks and illustrations for which Hegel is not responsible.

On certain characteristics of tragedy the briefest reminder will suffice. A large part of the nature of this form of drama is common to the drama in all its forms; and of this nothing need be said. It will be agreed, further, that in all tragedy there is some sort of collision or conflict—conflict of feelings, modes of thought, desires, wills, purposes; conflict of persons with one another, or with circumstances, or with themselves; one, several, or all of these kinds

* "Hegel's Theory of Tragedy" was first delivered as a lecture in 1901 and later revised for publication in *Oxford Lectures on Poetry* (1909) by A. C. Bradley, from which it is here reprinted by permission of The Macmillan Company of New York, publishers. A. C. Bradley (1851-1934) was also the author of *A Commentary on Tennyson's "In Memoriam"* (1901), *Shakespearean Tragedy* (1904), and *A Miscellany* (1929).

[1] See, primarily, *Aesthetik,* iii. 479-581, and especially 525-581. There is much in *Aesthetik,* i. 219-306, and a good deal in ii. 1-243, that bears on the subject. See also the section on Greek religion in *Religionsphilosophie,* ii. 96-156, especially 131-6, 152-6; and the references to the death of Socrates in *Geschichte der Philosophie,* ii. 81 ff., especially 102-5. The works so far cited all consist of posthumous redactions of lecture-notes. Among works published by Hegel himself, the early essay on "Naturrecht" (*Werke,* i. 386 ff.), and *Phaenomenologie d. Geistes,* 320-348, 527-542, deal with or bear on *Greek* tragedy. See also *Rechtsphilosophie,* 196, note. There is a note on *Wallenstein* in *Werke,* xvii. 411-4. These references are to the second edition of the works cited, where there are two editions.

[2] His theory of tragedy is connected with his view of the function of negation in the universe. No statement therefore which ignores his metaphysics and his philosophy of religion can be more than a fragmentary account of that theory.

of conflict, as the case may be. Again, it may be taken for granted that a tragedy is a story of unhappiness or suffering, and excites such feelings as pity and fear. To this, if we followed the present usage of the term, we should add that the story of unhappiness must have an unhappy end; by which we mean in effect that the conflict must close with the death of one or more of the principal characters. But this usage of the word "tragedy" is comparatively recent; it leaves us without a name for many plays, in many languages, which deal with unhappiness without ending unhappily; and Hegel takes the word in its older and wiser sense.

Passing on from these admitted characteristics of tragedy, we may best approach Hegel's peculiar view by observing that he lays particular stress on one of them. That a tragedy is a story of suffering is probably to many people the most obvious fact about it. Hegel says very little of this; partly, perhaps, because it is obvious, but more because the essential point to him is not the suffering but its cause, namely, the action or conflict. Mere suffering, he would say, is not tragic, but only the suffering that comes of a special kind of action. Pity for mere misfortune, like fear of it, is not tragic pity or fear. These are due to the spectacle of the conflict and its attendant suffering, which do not appeal simply to our sensibilities or our instinct of self-preservation, but also to our deeper mind or spirit (*Geist*, a word which, with its adjective, I shall translate "spirit," "spiritual," because our words "mind" and "mental" suggest something merely intellectual).

The reason why the tragic conflict thus appeals to the spirit is that it is itself a conflict of the spirit. It is a conflict, that is to say, between powers that rule the world of man's will and action—his "ethical substance." The family and the state, the bond of parent and child, of brother and sister, of husband and wife, of citizen and ruler, or citizen and citizen, with the obligations and feelings appropriate to these bonds; and again the powers of personal love and honour, or of devotion to a great cause or an ideal interest like religion or science or some kind of social welfare—such are the forces exhibited in tragic action; not indeed alone, not without others less affirmative and perhaps even evil, but still in preponderating mass. And as they form the substance of man, are common to all civilised men, and are acknowledged as powers rightfully claiming human allegiance, their exhibition in tragedy has that interest, at once deep and universal, which is essential to a great work of art.

In many a work of art, in many a statue, picture, tale, or song, such powers are shown in solitary peace or harmonious co-operation. Tragedy shows them in collision. Their nature is divine, and in religion they appear as gods; but, as seen in the world of tragic action, they have left the repose of Olympus, have entered into human wills, and now meet as foes. And this spectacle, if sublime, is also terrible. The essentially tragic fact is the self-division and intestinal warfare of the ethical substance, not so much the war of good with evil as the war of good with good. Two of these isolated powers face each other, making incompatible demands. The family claims what the state refuses, love requires what honour forbids. The competing forces are both in themselves rightful, and so far the claim of each is equally justified; but the right of each is pushed into a wrong, because it ignores the right of the other, and demands that absolute sway which belongs to neither alone, but to the whole of which each is but a part.

And one reason why this happens lies in the nature of the characters through whom these claims are made. It is the nature of the tragic hero, at once his greatness and his doom, that he knows no shrinking or half-heartedness, but identifies himself wholly with the power that moves him, and will admit the justification of no other power. However varied and rich his inner life and character may be, in the conflict it is all concentrated in one point. Antigone *is* determination to do her duty to her dead brother; Romeo is not a son or a citizen as well as a lover, he is lover pure and simple, and his love is the whole of him.

The end of the tragic conflict is the denial of both the exclusive claims. It is not the work of chance or blank fate; it is the act of the ethical substance itself, asserting its absoluteness against the excessive pretensions of its particular powers. In that sense, as proceeding from an absolute right which cancels claims based on right but pushed into wrong, it may be called the act of "eternal justice." Sometimes it can end the conflict peacefully, and the tragedy closes with a solution. Appearing as a divine being, the spiritual unity reconciles by some adjustment the claims of the contending powers (*Eumenides*); or at its bidding one of them softens its demand (*Philoctetes*); or again, as in the more beautiful solution of the *Oedipus Coloneus,* the hero by his own self-condemnation and inward purification reconciles himself with the supreme justice, and is accepted by it. But sometimes the quarrel is pressed to extremes; the denial of the one-sided claims involves the death of one or more of the persons concerned; and we have a catastrophe. The ultimate power thus appears as a destructive force. Yet even here, as Hegel insists, the end is not without an aspect of reconciliation. For that which is denied is not the rightful powers with which the combatants have identified themselves. On the contrary, those powers, and with them the only thing for which the combatants cared, are affirmed. What is denied is the exclusive and therefore wrongful assertion of their right.

Such in outline is Hegel's main view. It may be illustrated more fully by two examples, favourites of his, taken from Aeschylus and Sophocles. Clytemnestra has murdered Agamemnon, her husband and king. Orestes, their son, is impelled by filial piety to avenge his father, and is ordered by Apollo to do so. But to kill a mother is to sin against filial piety. The spiritual substance is divided against itself. The sacred bond of father and son demands what the equally sacred bond of son and mother forbids. When, therefore, Orestes has done the deed, the Furies of his murdered mother claim him for their prey. He appeals to Apollo, who resists their claim. A solution is arrived at without a catastrophe. The cause is referred to Athene, who institutes at Athens a court of sworn judges. The votes of this court being equally divided, Athene gives her casting-vote for Orestes; while the Furies are at last appeased by a promise of everlasting honour at Athens.

In the *Antigone,* on the other hand, to Hegel the "perfect exemplar of tragedy," the solution is negative. The brother of Antigone has brought against his native city an army of foreigners bent on destroying it. He has been killed in the battle, and Creon, the ruler of the city, has issued an edict forbidding anyone on pain of death to bury the corpse. In so doing he not only dishonours the dead man, but violates the rights of the gods of the dead. Antigone without hesitation disobeys the edict, and Creon, despite the remonstrance of his son, who is affianced to her, persists in exacting the penalty. Warned by the prophet Teiresias, he gives way, but too late. Antigone, immured in a rocky chamber to starve, has anticipated her death. Her lover follows her example, and his mother refuses to survive him. Thus Antigone has lost her life through her absolute assertion of the family against the state; Creon has violated the sanctity of the family, and in return sees his own home laid in ruins. But in this catastrophe neither the right of the family nor that of the state is denied; what is denied is the absoluteness of the claim of each.

The danger of illustrations like these is that they divert attention from the principle illustrated to questions about the interpretation of particular works. So it will be here. I cannot stay to discuss these questions, which do not affect Hegel's principle; but it will be well, before going further, to remove a misunderstanding of it which is generally to be found in criticisms of his treatment of the *Eumenides* and the *Antigone.* The main objection may be put thus: "Hegel talks of equally justified powers or claims. But Aeschylus never meant that Orestes and the Furies were equally justified; for Orestes was acquitted. Nor did Sophocles mean that Antigone and Creon were equally right. And how can it have been equally the duty of Orestes to kill his mother and not to kill her?" But, in the first place, it is most important to observe that Hegel is not discussing at all what we should generally call the moral quality of the acts and persons concerned, or, in the ordinary sense, what it was their duty to do. And, in the second place, when he speaks of "equally justified" powers, what he means, and, indeed, sometimes says, is that these powers are *in themselves* justified. The family and the state, the bond of father and son, the bond of mother and son, the bond of citizenship, these are each and all, one as much as another, powers rightfully claiming human allegiance. It is tragic that observance of one should involve the violation of another. These are Hegel's propositions, and surely they are true. Their truth is quite unaffected by the fact (assuming it is one) that in the circumstances the act combining this observance of one and violation of another was morally right, or by the fact (if so it is) that one such act (say Antigone's) was morally right, and another (say Creon's) was morally wrong. It is sufficient for Hegel's principle that the violation should take place, and that we should feel its weight. We do feel it. We may approve the act of Antigone or Orestes, but in approving it we still feel that it is no light matter to disobey the law or to murder a mother, that (as we might say) there is much justice in the pleas of the Furies and of Creon, and that the *tragic* effect depends upon these facts. If, again, it is objected that the underlying conflict in the *Antigone* is not between the family and the state, but between divine and human law, that objection, if sound, might touch Hegel's interpretation,[3] but it would not affect his principle, except for those who recognise no obligation in human law; and it will scarcely be contended that Sophocles is to be numbered among them. On the other hand, it is, I think, a matter for regret that Hegel employed such words as "right," "justified," and "justice." They do not mislead readers familiar with his writings, but to others they suggest associations with criminal law, or our everyday moral judgments, or perhaps the theory of "poetic justice"; and these are all out of place in a discussion on tragedy.

Having determined in outline the idea or principle of tragedy, Hegel proceeds to give an account of some differences between ancient and modern works. In the limited time at our disposal we shall do best to confine ourselves to a selection from his remarks on the latter. For in speaking of ancient tragedy Hegel, who finds something modern in Euripides, makes accordingly but little use of him for purposes of contrast, while his main point of view as to Aeschylus and Sophocles has already appeared in the illustrations we have given of the general principle. I will only add, by way of preface, that the pages about to be summarised leave on one, rightly or wrongly, the impression that to his mind the principle is more adequately realised in the best classical tragedies than in modern works. But the question whether this really was his deliberate opinion would detain us too long from weightier matters.[4]

Hegel considers first the cases where modern tragedy resembles ancient in dealing with conflicts arising from the pursuit of ends which may be called substantial or objective and not merely personal. And he points out that modern tragedy here shows a much greater variety. Subjects are taken, for example, from the quarrels of dynasties, of rivals for the throne, of kings and nobles, of state and church. Calderon shows the conflict of love and honour regarded as powers imposing obligations. Schiller in his early works makes his characters defend the rights of nature against convention, or of freedom of thought against prescription—rights in their essence universal. Wallenstein aims at the unity and peace of Germany; Karl Moor attacks the whole arrangement of society; Faust seeks to attain in thought and action union with the Absolute. In such cases the end is more than personal; it represents a power claiming the allegiance of the individual; but, on the other hand, it does not always or generally represent a great *ethical* institution or bond like the family or the state. We have passed into a wider world.

But secondly, he observes, in regard to modern tragedy, that in a larger number of instances such public or universal interests either do not appear at all, or, if they appear, are scarcely more than a background for the real subject. The real subject, the impelling end or passion, and the ensuing conflict, is personal,—these particular characters with their struggle and their fate. The importance given to subjectivity—this is the distinctive mark of modern sentiment, and so of modern art; and such tragedies bear its impress. A part at least of Hegel's meaning may be illustrated thus. We are interested in the personality of Orestes or Antigone, but chiefly as it shows itself in one aspect, as identifying itself with a certain ethical relation; and our interest in the personality is inseparable and indistinguishable from our interest in the power it represents. This is not so with Hamlet, whose position so closely resembles that of Orestes. What engrosses our attention is the whole per-

[3] I say "might," because Hegel himself in the *Phaenomenologie* uses those very terms "divine" and "human law" in reference to the *Antigone.*

[4] See Note at end of lecture.

sonality of Hamlet in his conflict, not with an opposing spiritual power, but with circumstances and, still more, with difficulties in his own nature. No one could think of describing Othello as the representative of an ethical family relation. His passion, however much nobility he may show in it, is personal. So is Romeo's love. It is not pursued, like Posa's freedom of thought, as something universal, a right of man. Its right, if it could occur to us to use the term at all, is Romeo's right.

On this main characteristic of modern tragedy others depend. For instance, that variety of subject to which reference has just been made depends on it. For when so much weight is attached to personality, almost any fatal collision in which a sufficiently striking character is involved may yield material for tragedy. Naturally, again, characterisation has become fuller and more subtle, except in dramas which are more or less an imitation of the antique. The characters in Greek tragedy are far from being types or personified abstractions, as those of classical French tragedy tend to be: they are genuine individuals. But still they are comparatively simple and easy to understand, and have not the intricacy of the characters in Shakespeare. These, for the most part, represent simply themselves; and the loss of that interest which attached to the Greek characters from their identification with an ethical power, is compensated by an extraordinary subtlety in their portrayal, and also by their possession of some peculiar charm or some commanding superiority. Finally, the interest in personality explains the freedom with which characters more or less definitely evil are introduced in modern tragedy. Mephistopheles is as essentially modern as Faust. The passion of Richard or Macbeth is not only personal, like that of Othello; it is egoistic and anarchic, and leads to crimes done with a full knowledge of their wickedness; but to the modern mind the greatness of the personality justifies its appearance in the position of hero. Such beings as Iago and Goneril, almost portents of evil, are not indeed made the heroes of tragedies; but, according to Hegel, they would not have been admitted in Greek tragedy at all. If Clytemnestra had been cited in objection as a parallel to Lady Macbeth, he would have replied that Lady Macbeth had not the faintest ground of complaint against Duncan, while in reading the *Agamemnon* we are frequently reminded that Clytemnestra's husband was the sacrificer of their child. He might have added that Clytemnestra is herself an example of the necessity, where one of the principal characters inspires hatred or horror, of increasing the subtlety of the drawing or adding grandeur to the evil will.

It remains to compare ancient and modern tragedy in regard to the issue of the conflict. We have seen that Hegel attributes this issue in the former to the ethical substance or eternal justice, and so accounts for such reconciliation as we feel to be present even where the end is a catastrophe. Now, in the catastrophe of modern tragedy, he says, a certain justice is sometimes felt to be present; but even then it differs from the antique justice. It is in some cases more "abstract": the end pursued by the hero, though it is not egoistic, is still presented rather as his particular end than as something rightful though partial; and hence the catastrophe appears as the reaction, not of an undivided ethical totality, but merely of the universal turning against a too assertive particular.[5] In cases, again, where the hero (Richard or Macbeth) openly attacks an ethical power and plunges into evil, we feel that he meets with justice, and only gets what he deserves; but then this justice is colder and more "criminalistic" than that of ancient tragedy. Thus even when the modern work seems to resemble the ancient in its issue, the sense of reconciliation is imperfect. And partly for this reason, partly from the concentration of our interest on individuality as such, we desire to see in the individual himself some sort of reconciliation with his fate. What shape this will take depends, of course, on the story and the character of the hero. It may appear in a religious form, as his feeling that he is exchanging his earthly being for an indestructible happiness; or again, in his recognition of the justice of his fall; or at least he may show us that, in face of the forces that crush him to death, he maintains untouched the freedom and strength of his own will.

But there remain, says Hegel, many modern tragedies where we have to attribute the catas-

[5] This interpretation of Hegel's "abstract" is more or less conjectural and doubtful.

trophe not to any kind of justice, but to unhappy circumstances and outward accidents. And then we can only feel that the individual whose merely personal ends are thwarted by mere particular circumstances and chances, pays the penalty that awaits existence in a scene of contingency and finitude. Such a feeling cannot rise above sadness, and, if the hero is a noble soul, it may become the impression of a dreadful external necessity. This impression can be avoided only when circumstance and accident are so depicted that they are felt to coincide with something in the hero himself, so that he is not simply destroyed by an outward force. So it is with Hamlet. "This bank and shoal of time" is too narrow for his soul, and the death that seems to fall on him by chance is also within him. And so in *Romeo and Juliet* we feel that the rose of a love so beautiful is too tender to bloom in the stormswept valley of its birth. But such a feeling of reconciliation is still one of pain, an unhappy blessedness.[6] And if the situation displayed in a drama is of such a kind that we feel the issue to depend *simply* on the turn the dramatist may choose to give to the course of events, we are fully justified in our preference for a happy ending.

In this last remark (or rather in the pages misrepresented by it) Hegel, of course, is not criticising Shakespeare. He is objecting to the destiny-dramas of his own time, and to the fashionable indulgence in sentimental melancholy. Strongly as he asserted the essential function of negation throughout the universe, the affirmative power of the spirit, even in its profoundest divisions, was for him the deepest truth and the most inspiring theme. And one may see this even in his references to Shakespeare. He appreciated Shakespeare's representation of extreme forms of evil, but, even if he was fully satisfied of its justification, his personal preference lay in another direction, and while I do not doubt that he thought *Hamlet* a greater work than *Iphigenie,* I suspect he loved Goethe's play the best.

Most of those who have thought about this subject will agree that the ideas I have tried to sketch are interesting and valuable; but they suggest scores of questions. Alike in the account of tragedy in general, and in that of the differences between ancient and modern tragedy, everyone will find statements to doubt and omissions to regret; and scarcely one of Hegel's interpretations of particular plays will escape objection. It is impossible for me to touch on more than a few points; and to the main ideas I owe so much that I am more inclined to dwell on their truth than to criticise what seem to be defects. But perhaps after all an attempt to supplement and amend may be the best way of throwing some part of Hegel's meaning more into relief. And I will begin with the attempt to supplement.

He seems to be right in laying emphasis on the action and conflict in tragedy rather than on the suffering and misfortune. No mere suffering or misfortune, no suffering that does not spring in great part from human agency, and in some degree from the agency of the sufferer, is tragic, however pitiful or dreadful it may be. But, sufficient connection with these agencies being present, misfortune, the fall from prosperity to adversity, with the suffering attending it, at once becomes tragic; and in many tragedies it forms a large ingredient, as does the pity for it in the tragic feeling. Hegel, I think, certainly takes too little notice of it; and by this omission he also withdraws attention from something the importance of which he would have admitted at once; I mean the way in which suffering is borne. Physical pain, to take an extreme instance, is one thing: Philoctetes, bearing it, is another. And the noble endurance of pain that rends the heart is the source of much that is best worth having in tragedy.

Again, there is one particular kind of misfortune *not* obviously due to human agency, which undoubtedly may affect us in a tragic way. I mean that kind which suggests the idea of fate. Tragedies which represent man as the mere plaything of chance or a blank fate or a malicious fate, are never really deep: it is satisfactory to see that Maeterlinck, a man of true genius, has now risen above these ideas. But, where those factors of tragedy are present which Hegel emphasises, the impression of something fateful in what we call accident, the impression that the hero not only invites misfortune by his

[6] Hegel's meaning does not fully appear in the sentences here condensed. The "blessedness" comes from the sense of the greatness or beauty in the characters.

exceptional stature and exceptional daring, but is also, if I may so put it, strangely and terribly unlucky, is in many plays a genuine ingredient in tragic effect. It is so, for example, in the *Oedipus Tyrannus.* It is so even in dramas like Shakespeare's, which exemplify the saying that character is destiny. Hegel's own reference to the prominence of accident in the plot of *Hamlet* proves it. Othello would not have become Iago's victim if his own character had been different; but still, as we say, it is an extraordinary fatality which makes him the companion of the one man in the world who is at once able enough, brave enough, and vile enough to ensnare him. In the *Antigone* itself, and in the very catastrophe of it, accident plays its part; we can hardly say that it depends solely on the characters of Creon and Antigone that the one yields just too late to save the life of the other. Now, it may be said with truth that Hegel's whole account of the ultimate power in tragedy is a rationalisation of the idea of fate, but his remarks on this particular aspect of fate are neither sufficient nor satisfactory.

His insistence on the need for some element of reconciliation in a tragic catastrophe, and his remarks on the various forms it assumes, have the greatest value; but one result of the omissions just noticed is that he sometimes exaggerates it, and at other times rates it too low. When he is speaking of the kind of tragedy he most approves, his language almost suggests that our feeling at the close of the conflict is, or should be, one of complete reconciliation. This it surely neither is nor can be. Not to mention the suffering and death we have witnessed, the very existence of the conflict, even if a supreme ethical power is felt to be asserted in its close, remains a painful fact, and, in large measure, a fact not understood. For, though we may be said to see, in one sense, how the opposition of spiritual powers arises, something in us, and that the best, still cries out against it. And even the perception or belief that it must needs be that offences come would not abolish our feeling that the necessity is terrible, or our pain in the woe of the guilty and the innocent. Nay, one may conjecture, the feeling and the pain would not vanish if we fully understood that the conflict and catastrophe were by a rational necessity involved in the divine and eternally accomplished purpose of the world. But this exaggeration in Hegel's language, if partly due to his enthusiasm for the affirmative, may be mainly, like some other defects, an accident of lecturing. In the *Philosophy of Religion,* I may add, he plainly states that in the solution even of tragedies like the *Antigone* something remains unresolved (ii. 135).

On the other hand, his treatment of the aspect of reconciliation in modern tragedy is in several respects insufficient. I will mention only one. He does not notice that in the conclusion of not a few tragedies pain is mingled not merely with acquiescence, but with something like exultation. Is there not such a feeling at the close of *Hamlet, Othello,* and *King Lear;* and that although the end in the last two cases touches the limit of legitimate pathos? This exultation appears to be connected with our sense that the hero has never shown himself so great or noble as in the death which seals his failure. A rush of passionate admiration, and a glory in the greatness of the soul, mingle with our grief; and the coming of death, so far from destroying these feelings, appears to leave them untouched, or even to be entirely in harmony with them. If in such dramas we may be said to feel that the ultimate power is no mere fate, but a spiritual power, then we also feel that the hero was never so near to this power as in the moment when it required his life.

The last omission I would notice in Hegel's theory is that he underrates the action in tragedy of what may be called by a rough distinction moral evil rather than defect. Certainly the part played by evil differs greatly in different cases, but it is never absent, not even from tragedies of Hegel's favourite type. If it does not appear in the main conflict, it appears in its occasion. You may say that, while Iago and Macbeth have evil purposes, neither the act of Orestes nor the vengeance of the Furies, neither Antigone's breach of the edict nor even Creon's insistence on her punishment, springs from evil in them; but the situation with which Orestes or Antigone has to deal, and so in a sense the whole tragedy, arises from evil, the murder of Agamemnon, and the attempt of Polyneices to bring ruin on his native city. In fact, if we confine the title "tragedy" to plays ending with a catastrophe, it will be found difficult to name great tragedies, ancient or modern, in which evil has not directly or indirectly a prominent part. And its presence has an important bearing on the effect produced by the catastrophe. On the one hand, it deepens the sense of painful awe. The question why affirmative spiritual forces should collide is hard enough; but the question why, together with them, there should be generated violent evil and extreme depravity is harder and more painful still. But, on the other hand, the element of reconciliation in the catastrophe is strengthened by recognition of the part played by evil in bringing it about; because our sense that the ultimate power cannot endure the presence of such evil is implicitly the sense that this power is at least more closely allied with good. If it rejects the exaggerated claims of its own isolated powers, that which provokes from it a much more vehement reaction must be still more alien to its nature. This feeling is forcibly evoked by Shakespeare's tragedies, and in many Greek dramas it is directly appealed to by repeated reminders that what is at work in the disasters is the unsleeping Ate which follows an ancestral sin. If Aristotle did not in some lost part of the *Poetics* discuss ideas like this, he failed to give a complete rationale of Greek tragedy.

I come lastly to the matter I have most at heart. What I take to be the central idea in Hegel's theory seems to me to touch the essence of tragedy. And I will not assert that his own statement of it fails to cover the whole field of instances. For he does not teach, as he is often said to do, that tragedy portrays only the conflict of such ethical powers as the family and the state. He adds to these, as we have seen, others, such as love and honour, together with various universal ends; and it may even be maintained that he has provided in his general statement for those numerous cases where, according to himself, no substantial or universal ends collide, but the interest is centered on "personalities." Nevertheless, when these cases come to be considered more fully—and, in Hegel's view they are the most characteristically modern cases—we are not satisfied. They naturally tend to appear as declensions from the more ideal ancient form; for how can a personality which represents only itself claim the interest of one which represents something universal? And further, they are sometimes described in a manner which strikes the reader, let us say, of Shakespeare, as both insufficient and misleading. Without raising, then, unprofitable questions about the comparative merits of ancient and modern tragedy, I should like to propose a restatement of Hegel's general principle which would make it more obviously apply to both.

If we omit all reference to ethical or substantial powers and interests, what have we left? We have the more general idea—to use again a formula not Hegel's own—that tragedy portrays a self-division and self-waste of spirit, or a division of spirit involving conflict and waste. It is implied in this that on *both* sides in the conflict there is a spiritual value. The same idea may be expressed (again, I think, not in Hegel's own words) by saying that the tragic conflict is one not merely of good with evil, but also, and more essentially, of good with good. Only, in saying this, we must be careful to observe that "good" here means anything that has spiritual value, not moral goodness alone,[7] and that "evil" has a similarly wide sense.

Now this idea of a division of spirit involving conflict and waste covers the tragedies of ethical and other universal powers, and it covers much besides. According to it the collision of such powers would be one kind of tragic collision, but only one. *Why* are we tragically moved by the conflict of family and state? Because we set a high value on family and state. Why then should not the conflict of anything else that has sufficient value affect us tragically? It does. The value must be sufficient—a moderate value will not serve; and other characteristics must be present which need not be considered here. But, granted these conditions, *any* spiritual conflict involving spiritual waste is tragic. And it is just one greatness of modern art that it has shown the tragic fact in situations of so many and such diverse kinds. These situations have not the peculiar effectiveness of the conflicts preferred by Hegel, but they may have an equal effectiveness peculiar to themselves.

Let me attempt to test these ideas by choosing a most unfavourable instance—unfavourable because the play seems at first to represent

[7] Hegel himself expressly guards against this misconception.

a conflict simply of good and evil, and so, according both to Hegel's statement and the proposed restatement, to be no tragedy at all: I mean *Macbeth.* What is the conflict here? It will be agreed that it does not lie between two ethical powers or universal ends, and that, as Hegel says, the main interest is in personalities. Let us take it first, then, to lie between Macbeth and the persons opposing him, and let us ask whether there is not spiritual value or good on both sides—not an equal amount of good (that is not necessary), but enough good on each to give the impression of spiritual waste. Is there not such good in Macbeth? It is not a question merely of moral goodness, but of good. It is not a question of the use made of good, but of its presence. And such bravery and skill in war as win the enthusiasm of everyone about him; such an imagination as few but poets possess; a conscience so vivid that his deed is to him beforehand a thing of terror, and, once done, condemns him to that torture of the mind on which he lies in restless ecstasy; a determination so tremendous and a courage so appalling that, for all this torment, he never dreams of turning back, but, even when he has found that life is a tale full of sound and fury, signifying nothing, will tell it out to the end though earth and heaven and hell are leagued against him; are not these things, in themselves, good, and gloriously good? Do they not make you, for all your horror, admire Macbeth, sympathise with his agony, pity him, and see in him the waste of forces on which you place a spiritual value? It is simply on this account that he is for you, not the abstraction called a criminal who merely "gets what he deserves" (art, like religion, knows no such thing), but a tragic hero, and that his war with other forces of indubitable spiritual worth is a tragic war.[8]

It is required by the restatement of Hegel's principle to show that in the external conflict of persons there is good on both sides. It is not required that this should be true, secondly, of both sides in the conflict within the hero's soul; for the hero is only a part of the tragedy. Nevertheless in almost all cases, if not in all, it is true. It is obviously so where, as in the hero and also the heroine of the *Cid,* the contending powers in this internal struggle are love and honour. Even when love is of a quality less pure and has a destructive force, as in Shakespeare's Antony, it is clearly true. And it remains true even where, as in Hamlet and Macbeth, the contest seems to lie, and for most purposes might conveniently be said to lie, between forces simply good and simply the reverse. This is not really so, and the tragic effect depends upon the fact. It depends on our feeling that the elements in the man's nature are so inextricably blended that the good in him, that which we admire, instead of simply opposing the evil, reinforces it. Macbeth's imagination deters him from murder, but it also makes the vision of a crown irresistibly bright. If he had been less determined, nay, if his conscience had been less maddening in its insistence that he had thrown the precious jewel of his soul irretrievably away, he might have paused after his first deed, might even have repented. Yet his imagination, his determination, and his conscience were things good. Hamlet's desire to do his duty is a good thing, but what opposes this desire is by no means simply evil. It is something to which a substantial contribution is made by the qualities we most admire in him. Thus the nature of tragedy, as seen in the external conflict, repeats itself on each side of this conflict, and everywhere there is a spiritual value in both the contending forces.

In showing that *Macbeth,* a tragedy as far removed as possible from the *Antigone* as understood by Hegel, is still of one nature with it, and equally answers to the account of tragedy proposed, it has been necessary to ignore the great difference between the two plays. But when once the common essence of all tragedies has been determined, their differences become the interesting subject. They could be distinguished according to the character of the collisions on which they are built, or of the main forces which move the principal agents. And it may

[8] The same point may be put thus, in view of that dangerous word "personality." Our interest in Macbeth may be called interest in a personality; but it is not an interest in some bare form of self-consciousness, nor yet in a person in the legal sense, but in a personality full of matter. This matter is not an ethical or universal end, but it must in a sense be universal—human nature in a particular form—or it would not excite the horror, sympathy, and admiration it does excite. Nor, again, could it excite these feelings if it were not composed largely of qualities on which we set a high value.

well be that, other things being equal (as they never are), the tragedy in which the hero is, as we say, a good man, is more tragic than that in which he is, as we say, a bad one. The more spiritual value, the more tragedy in conflict and waste. The death of Hamlet or Othello is, so far, more tragic than that of Macbeth, that of Macbeth than that of Richard. Below Richard stands Iago, a figure still tragic, but unfit for the hero's part; below him persons like Regan or, in the very depth, Oswald, characters no longer (at least in the dramatic sense) tragic at all. Moral evil, that is to say, so greatly diminishes the spiritual value we ascribe to the personality that a very large amount of good of some kind is required to bring this personality up to the tragic level, the destruction of evil as such being in no degree tragic. And again, it may well be that, other things being equal, the more nearly the contending forces approach each other in goodness, the more tragic is the conflict; that the collision is, so far, more tragic in the *Antigone* than in *Macbeth*, and Hamlet's internal conflict than his struggle with outward enemies and obstacles. But it is dangerous to describe tragedy in terms that even appear to exclude *Macbeth*, or to describe *Macbeth*, even casually or by implication, in terms which imply that it portrays a conflict of mere evil with mere good.

The restatement of Hegel's main principle as to the conflict would involve a similar restatement as to the catastrophe (for we need not consider here those "tragedies" which end with a solution). As before, we must avoid any reference to ethical or universal ends, or to the work of "justice" in the catastrophe. We might then simply say that, as the tragic action portrays a self-division or intestinal conflict of spirit, so the catastrophe displays the violent annulling of this division or conflict. But this statement, which might be pretty generally accepted, would represent only half of Hegel's idea, and perhaps nothing of what is most characteristic and valuable in it. For the catastrophe (if I may put his idea in my own way) has two aspects, a negative and an affirmative, and we have ignored the latter. On the one hand it is the act of a power immeasurably superior to that of the conflicting agents, a power which is irresistible and unescapable, and which overbears and negates whatever is incompatible with it. So far, it may be called, in relation to the conflicting agents,[9] necessity or fate; and unless a catastrophe affects us in ways corresponding with this aspect it is not truly tragic. But then if this were all and this necessity were merely infinite, characterless, external force, the catastrophe would not only terrify (as it should), it would also horrify, depress, or at best provoke indignation or rebellion; and these are not tragic feelings. The catastrophe, then, must have a second and affirmative aspect, which is the source of our feelings of reconciliation, whatever form they may assume. And this will be taken into account if we describe the catastrophe as the violent self-restitution of the divided spiritual unity. The necessity which acts and negates in it, that is to say, is yet of one substance with both the agents. *It* is divided against itself in them; they are *its* conflicting forces; and in restoring its unity through negation it affirms them, so far as they are compatible with that unity. The qualification is essential, since the hero, for all his affinity with that power, is, as the living man we see before us, not so compatible. He must die, and his union with "eternal justice" (which is more than "justice") must itself be "eternal" or ideal. But the qualification does not abolish what it qualifies. This is no occasion to ask how in particular, and in what various ways in various works, we feel the effect of this affirmative aspect in the catastrophe. But it corresponds at least with that strange double impression which is produced by the hero's death. He dies, and our hearts die with him; and yet his death matters nothing to us, or we even exult. He is dead; and he has no more to do with death than the power which killed him and with which he is one.

I leave it to students of Hegel to ask whether he would have accepted the criticisms and modifications I have suggested. Naturally I think he would, as I believe they rest on truth, and am sure he had a habit of arriving at truth. But in

[9] In relation to *both* sides in the conflict (though it may not need to negate life in both). For the ultimate agent in the catastrophe is emphatically not the finite power of one side. It is beyond both, and, at any rate in relation to them, boundless.

any case their importance is trifling, compared with that of the theory which they attempt to strengthen and to which they owe their existence.

NOTE

Why did Hegel, in his lectures on Aesthetics, so treat of tragedy as to suggest the idea that the kind of tragedy which he personally preferred (let us for the sake of brevity call it "ancient") is also the most adequate embodiment of the idea of tragedy? This question can be answered, I think, only conjecturally, but some remarks on it may have an interest for readers of Hegel (they are too brief to be of use to others).

One answer might be this. Hegel did not really hold that idea. But he was lecturing, not writing a book. He thought the principle of tragedy was more clearly and readily visible in ancient works than in modern; and so, for purposes of exposition, he emphasised the ancient form. And this fact, with his personal enthusiasm for certain Greek plays, leads the reader of the *Aesthetik* to misconstrue him.

Again, we must remember the facts of Hegel's life. He seems first to have reflected on tragedy at a time when his enthusiasm for the Greeks and their "substantial" ethics was combined, not only with a contemptuous dislike for much modern "subjectivity" (this he never ceased to feel), but with a certain hostility to morality. His first view of tragedy was thus, in effect, a theory of Aeschylean and Sophoclean tragedy; and it appears in the early essay on *Naturrecht* and more fully in the *Phaenomenologie*. Perhaps, then, when he came to deal with the subject more generally, he insensibly regarded ancient form as the typical form, and tended to treat the modern rather as a modification of this type than as an alternative embodiment of the general idea of tragedy. The note in the *Rechtsphilosophie* (p. 196) perhaps favours this idea.

But, whether it is correct or no, I believe that the impression produced by the *Aesthetik* is a true one, and that Hegel did deliberately consider the ancient form the more satisfactory. It would not follow, of course, from that opinion that he thought the advantage was all on one side, or considered this or that ancient poet greater than this or that modern, or wished that modern poets had tried to write tragedies of the Greek type. Tragedy would, in his view, be in somewhat the same position as Sculpture. Renaissance sculpture, he might say, has qualities in which it is superior to Greek, and Michael Angelo may have been as great an artist as Pheidias; but all the same for certain reasons Greek sculpture is, and probably will remain, sculpture *par excellence.* So, though not to the same extent, with tragedy.

And such a view would cohere with his general view of Art. For he taught that, in a sense, Classical Art is Art *par excellence,* and that in Greece beauty held a position such as it never held before and will not hold again. To explain in a brief note how this position bears upon his treatment of modern tragedy would be impossible: but if the student of Hegel will remember in what sense and on what grounds he held it; that he describes Beauty as the "*sinnliches* Scheinen der Idee";[10] that for him the new idea that distinguished Christianity and Romantic Art from Greek religion and Classical Art is that "*unendliche* Subjektivität"[11] which implies a negative, though not merely negative, relation to sense; and that in Romantic Art this idea is not only exhibited in the religious sphere, but appears in the position given to personal honour, love, and loyalty, and indirectly in what Hegel calls "die formelle Selbstständigkeit der individuellen Besonderheiten," and in the fuller admission of common and un-beautiful reality into the realm of Beauty,—he will see how all this is connected with those characteristics of modern tragedy which Hegel regards as necessary and yet as, in part, drawbacks. This connection, which Hegel has no occasion to work out, will be apparent even from consideration of the introductory chapter on "die romantische Kunstform," *Aesthetik,* ii. 120-135.

There is one marked difference, I may add, between ancient and modern tragedy, which should be considered with reference to this subject, and which Hegel, I think, does not explicitly point out. Speaking roughly, we may say that the former includes, while the latter tends to ignore, the accepted religious ideas of the time. The ultimate reason of this difference,

10 ["Material appearance of the Idea."]
11 ["Infinite subjectivity."]

on Hegel's view, would be that the Olympian gods are themselves the "*sinnliches* Scheinen der Idee," and so are in the same element as Art, while this is, on the whole, not so with modern religious ideas. One result would be that Greek tragedy represents the total Greek mind more fully than modern tragedy can the total modern mind.

VIRGINIA WOOLF: Mr. Bennett and Mrs. Brown*

It seems to me possible, perhaps desirable, that I may be the only person in this room who has committed the folly of writing, trying to write, or failing to write, a novel. And when I ask myself, as your invitation to speak to you about modern fiction made me ask myself, what demon whispered in my ear and urged me to my doom, a little figure rose before me—the figure of a man, or of a woman, who said, "My name is Brown. Catch me if you can."

Most novelists have the same experience. Some Brown, Smith, or Jones comes before them and says in the most seductive and charming way in the world, "Come and catch me if you can." And so, led on by this will-o'-the-wisp, they flounder through volume after volume, spending the best years of their lives in the pursuit, and receiving for the most part very little cash in exchange. Few catch the phantom; most have to be content with a scrap of her dress or a wisp of her hair.

My belief that men and women write novels because they are lured on to create some character which has thus imposed itself upon them has the sanction of Mr. Arnold Bennett. In an article from which I will quote he says: "The foundation of good fiction is character-creating and nothing else. . . . Style counts; plot counts; originality of outlook counts. But none of these counts anything like so much as the convincingness of the characters. If the characters are real the novel will have a chance; if they are not, oblivion will be its portion. . . ." And he goes on to draw the conclusion that we have no young novelists of first-rate importance at the present moment, because they are unable to create characters that are real, true, and convincing.

These are the questions that I want with greater boldness than discretion to discuss tonight. I want to make out what we mean when we talk about "character" in fiction; to say something about the question of reality which Mr. Bennett raises; and to suggest some reasons why the younger novelists fail to create characters, if, as Mr. Bennett asserts, it is true that fail they do. This will lead me, I am well aware, to make some very sweeping and some very vague assertions. For the question is an extremely difficult one. Think how little we know about character—think how little we know about art. But, to make a clearance before I begin, I will suggest that we range Edwardians and Georgians into two camps; Mr. Wells, Mr. Bennett, and Mr. Galsworthy I will call the Edwardians; Mr. Forster, Mr. Lawrence, Mr. Strachey, Mr. Joyce, and Mr. Eliot I will call the Georgians. And if I speak in the first person, with intolerable egotism, I will ask you to excuse me. I do not want to attribute to the world at large the opinions of one solitary, ill-informed, and misguided individual.

My first assertion is one that I think you will grant—that every one in this room is a judge of character. Indeed it would be impossible to live for a year without disaster unless one practised character-reading and had some skill in

* "Mr. Bennett and Mrs. Brown" first appeared in 1924 and is reprinted here by permission of The Hogarth Press, London. Virginia Woolf (1882-1941) was the author of *The Common Reader* (1925), *The Second Common Reader* (1932), *A Room of One's Own* (1929), *Three Guineas* (1938), *The Death of the Moth and Other Essays* (1942), *The Moment and Other Essays* (1948).

the art. Our marriages, our friendships depend on it; our business largely depends on it; every day questions arise which can only be solved by its help. And now I will hazard a second assertion, which is more disputable perhaps, to the effect that on or about December 1910 human character changed.

I am not saying that one went out, as one might into a garden, and there saw that a rose had flowered, or that a hen had laid an egg. The change was not sudden and definite like that. But a change there was, nevertheless; and, since one must be arbitrary, let us date it about the year 1910. The first signs of it are recorded in the books of Samuel Butler, in *The Way of All Flesh* in particular; the plays of Bernard Shaw continue to record it. In life one can see the change, if I may use a homely illustration, in the character of one's cook. The Victorian cook lived like a leviathan in the lower depths, formidable, silent, obscure, inscrutable; the Georgian cook is a creature of sunshine and fresh air; in and out of the drawing-room, now to borrow *The Daily Herald*, now to ask advice about a hat. Do you ask for more solemn instances of the power of the human race to change? Read the *Agamemnon*, and see whether, in process of time, your sympathies are not almost entirely with Clytemnestra. Or consider the married life of the Carlyles, and bewail the waste, the futility, for him and for her, of the horrible domestic tradition which made it seemly for a woman of genius to spend her time chasing beetles, scouring saucepans, instead of writing books. All human relations have shifted —those between masters and servants, husbands and wives, parents and children. And when human relations change there is at the same time a change in religion, conduct, politics, and literature. Let us agree to place one of these changes about the year 1910.

I have said that people have to acquire a good deal of skill in character-reading if they are to live a single year of life without disaster. But it is the art of the young. In middle age and in old age the art is practised mostly for its uses, and friendships and other adventures and experiments in the art of reading character are seldom made. But novelists differ from the rest of the world because they do not cease to be interested in character when they have learnt enough about it for practical purposes. They go a step further; they feel that there is something permanently interesting in character in itself. When all the practical business of life has been discharged, there is something about people which continues to seem to them of overwhelming importance, in spite of the fact that it has no bearing whatever upon their happiness, comfort, or income. The study of character becomes to them an absorbing pursuit; to impart character an obsession. And this I find it very difficult to explain: what novelists mean when they talk about character, what the impulse is that urges them so powerfully every now and then to embody their view in writing.

So, if you will allow me, instead of analysing and abstracting, I will tell you a simple story which, however pointless, has the merit of being true, of a journey from Richmond to Waterloo, in the hope that I may show you what I mean by character in itself; that you may realise the different aspects it can wear; and the hideous perils that beset you directly you try to describe it in words.

One night some weeks ago, then, I was late for the train and jumped into the first carriage I came to. As I sat down I had the strange and uncomfortable feeling that I was interrupting a conversation between two people who were already sitting there. Not that they were young or happy. Far from it. They were both elderly, the woman over sixty, the man well over forty. They were sitting opposite each other, and the man, who had been leaning over and talking emphatically to judge by his attitude and the flush on his face, sat back and became silent. I had disturbed him, and he was annoyed. The elderly lady, however, whom I will call Mrs. Brown, seemed rather relieved. She was one of those clean, threadbare old ladies whose extreme tidiness—everything buttoned, fastened, tied together, mended and brushed up—suggests more extreme poverty than rags and dirt. There was something pinched about her—a look of suffering, of apprehension, and, in addition, she was extremely small. Her feet, in their clean little boots, scarcely touched the floor. I felt that she had nobody to support her; that she had to make up her mind for herself; that, having been deserted, or left a widow, years ago, she had led an anxious, harried life, bringing up an only son, perhaps, who, as likely as not, was by this time beginning to go to the bad. All this shot through my mind as I sat down, being uncomfortable, like most people, at travelling with fellow passengers unless I have somehow or other accounted for them. Then I looked at the man. He was no relation of Mrs. Brown's I felt sure; he was of a bigger, burlier, less refined type. He was a man of business I imagined, very likely a respectable corn-chandler from the North, dressed in good blue serge with a pocket-knife and a silk handkerchief, and a stout leather bag. Obviously, however, he had an unpleasant business to settle with Mrs. Brown; a secret, perhaps sinister business, which they did not intend to discuss in my presence.

"Yes, the Crofts have had very bad luck with their servants," Mr. Smith (as I will call him) said in a considering way, going back to some earlier topic, with a view to keeping up appearances.

"Ah, poor people," said Mrs. Brown, a trifle condescendingly. "My grandmother had a maid who came when she was fifteen and stayed till she was eighty" (this was said with a kind of hurt and aggressive pride to impress us both perhaps).

"One doesn't often come across that sort of thing nowadays," said Mr. Smith in conciliatory tones.

Then they were silent.

"It's odd they don't start a golf club there—I should have thought one of the young fellows would," said Mr. Smith, for the silence obviously made him uneasy.

Mrs. Brown hardly took the trouble to answer.

"What changes they're making in this part of the world," said Mr. Smith, looking out of the window, and looking furtively at me as he did so.

It was plain, from Mrs. Brown's silence, from the uneasy affability with which Mr. Smith spoke, that he had some power over her which he was exerting disagreeably. It might have been her son's downfall, or some painful episode in her past life, or her daughter's. Perhaps she was going to London to sign some document to make over some property. Obviously against her will she was in Mr. Smith's hands. I was beginning to feel a great deal of pity for her, when she said, suddenly and inconsequently,

"Can you tell me if an oak-tree dies when the leaves have been eaten for two years in succession by caterpillars?"

She spoke quite brightly, and rather precisely, in a cultivated inquisitive voice.

Mr. Smith was startled, but relieved to have a safe topic of conversation given him. He told her a great deal very quickly about plagues of insects. He told her that he had a brother who kept a fruit farm in Kent. He told her what fruit farmers do every year in Kent, and so on, and so on. While he talked a very odd thing happened. Mrs. Brown took out her little white handkerchief and began to dab her eyes. She was crying. But she went on listening quite composedly to what he was saying, and he went on talking, a little louder, a little angrily, as if he had seen her cry often before; as if it were a painful habit. At last it got on his nerves. He stopped abruptly, looked out of the window, then leant towards her as he had been doing when I got in, and said in a bullying menacing way, as if he would not stand any more nonsense,

"So about that matter we were discussing. It'll be all right? George will be there on Tuesday?"

"We shan't be late," said Mrs. Brown, gathering herself together with superb dignity.

Mr. Smith said nothing. He got up, buttoned his coat, reached his bag down, and jumped out of the train before it had stopped at Clapham Junction. He had got what he wanted, but he was ashamed of himself; he was glad to get out of the old lady's sight.

Mrs. Brown and I were left alone together. She sat in her corner opposite, very clean, very small, rather queer, and suffering intensely. The impression she made was overwhelming. It came pouring out like a draught, like a smell of burning. What was it composed of—that overwhelming and peculiar impression? Myriads of irrelevant and incongruous ideas crowd into one's head on such occasions; one sees the person, one sees Mrs. Brown, in the centre of all sorts of different scenes. I thought of her in a seaside house, among queer ornaments: sea-urchins, models of ships in glass cases. Her husband's medals were on the mantelpiece. She popped in and out of the room, perching on the edges of chairs, picking meals out of saucers, indulging in long, silent stares. The caterpillars and the oak-trees seemed to imply all that. And then, into this fantastic and secluded life, in broke Mr. Smith. I saw him blowing in, so to speak, on a windy day. He banged, he slammed. His dripping umbrella made a pool in the hall. They sat closeted together.

And then Mrs. Brown faced the dreadful revelation. She took her heroic decision. Early, before dawn, she packed her bag and carried it herself to the station. She would not let Smith touch it. She was wounded in her pride, unmoored from her anchorage; she came of gentlefolks who kept servants—but details could wait. The important thing was to realise her character, to steep oneself in her atmosphere. I had no time to explain why I felt it somewhat tragic, heroic, yet with a dash of the flighty, and fantastic, before the train stopped, and I watched her disappear, carrying her bag, into the vast blazing station. She looked very small, very tenacious; at once very frail and very heroic. And I have never seen her again, and I shall never know what became of her.

The story ends without any point to it. But I have not told you this anecdote to illustrate either my own ingenuity or the pleasure of travelling from Richmond to Waterloo. What I want you to see in it is this. Here is a character imposing itself upon another person. Here is Mrs. Brown making someone begin almost automatically to write a novel about her. I believe that all novels begin with an old lady in the corner opposite. I believe that all novels, that is to say, deal with character, and that it is to express character—not to preach doctrines, sing songs, or celebrate the glories of the British Empire, that the form of the novel, so clumsy, verbose, and undramatic, so rich, elastic, and alive, has been evolved. To express character, I have said; but you will at once reflect that the very widest interpretation can be put upon those words. For example, old Mrs. Brown's character will strike you very differently according to the age and country in which you happen to be born. It would be easy enough to write three different versions of that incident in the train, an English, a French, and a Russian. The English writer would make the old lady into a "character"; he would bring out her oddities and mannerisms; her buttons and wrinkles; her ribbons and warts. Her personality would dominate the book. A French writer would rub out all that; he would sacrifice the individual Mrs. Brown to give a more general view of human nature; to make a more abstract, proportioned, and harmonious whole. The Russian would pierce through the flesh; would reveal the soul—the soul alone wandering out into the Waterloo Road, asking of life some tremendous question which would sound on and on in our ears after the book was finished. And then besides age and country there is the writer's temperament to be considered. You see one thing in character, and I another. You say it means this, and I that. And when it comes to writing each makes a further selection on principles of his own. Thus Mrs. Brown can be treated in an infinite variety of ways, according to the age, country, and temperament of the writer.

But now I must recall what Mr. Arnold Bennett says. He says that it is only if the characters are real that the novel has any chance of surviving. Otherwise, die it must. But, I ask myself, what is reality? And who are the judges of reality? A character may be real to Mr. Bennett and quite unreal to me. For instance, in this article he says that Dr. Watson in *Sherlock Holmes* is real to him: to me Dr. Watson is a sack stuffed with straw, a dummy, a figure of fun. And so it is with character after character—in book after book. There is nothing that people differ about more than the reality of characters, especially in contemporary books. But if you take a larger view I think that Mr. Bennett is perfectly right. If, that is, you think of the novels which seem to you great novels—*War and Peace, Vanity Fair, Tristram Shandy, Madame Bovary, Pride and Prejudice, The Mayor of Casterbridge, Villette*—if you think of these books, you do at once think of some character who has seemed to you so real (I do not by that mean so lifelike) that it has the power to make you think not merely of it itself, but of all sorts of things through its eyes—of religion, of love, of war, of peace, of family life, of balls in county towns, of sunsets, moonrises, the immortality of the soul. There is hardly any subject of human experience that is left out of *War and Peace* it seems to me. And in all these novels all these great novelists have brought us to see whatever they wish us to see through some character. Otherwise, they would not be novelists; but poets, historians, or pamphleteers.

But now let us examine what Mr. Bennett went on to say—he said that there was no great novelist among the Georgian writers because they cannot create characters who are real, true, and convincing. And there I cannot agree. There are reasons, excuses, possibilities which I think put a different colour upon the case. It seems so to me at least, but I am well aware that this is a matter about which I am likely to be prejudiced, sanguine, and near-sighted. I will put my view before you in the hope that you will make it impartial, judicial, and broad-minded. Why, then, is it so hard for novelists at present to create characters which seem real, not only to Mr. Bennett, but to the world at large? Why, when October comes round, do the publishers always fail to supply us with a masterpiece?

Surely one reason is that the men and women who began writing novels in 1910 or thereabouts had this great difficulty to face—that there was no English novelist living from whom they could learn their business. Mr. Conrad is a Pole; which sets him apart, and makes him, however admirable, not very helpful. Mr. Hardy has written no novel since 1895. The most prominent and successful novelists in the year 1910 were, I suppose, Mr. Wells, Mr. Bennett, and Mr. Galsworthy. Now it seems to me that to go to these men and ask them to teach you how to write a novel—how to create characters that are real—is precisely like going to a bootmaker and asking him to teach you how to make a watch. Do not let me give you the impression that I do not admire and enjoy their books. They seem to me of great value, and indeed of great necessity. There are seasons when it is more important to have boots than to have watches. To drop metaphor, I think that after the creative activity of the Victorian age it was quite necessary not only for literature but for life, that someone should write the books that Mr. Wells, Mr. Bennett, and Mr. Galsworthy have written. Yet what odd books they are! Sometimes I wonder if we are right to call them books at all. For they leave one with so strange a feeling of incompleteness and dissatisfaction. In order to complete them it seems necessary to do something—to join a society, or more desperately, to write a cheque. That done, the restlessness is laid, the book finished: it can be put upon the shelf, and need never be read again. But with the work of other novelists it is different. *Tristram Shandy* or *Pride and Prejudice* is complete in itself; it is self-contained; it leaves one with no desire to do anything, except indeed to read the book again, and to understand it better. The difference perhaps is that both Sterne and Jane Austen were interested in things in themselves; in character in itself; in the book in itself. Therefore everything was inside the book, nothing outside. But the Edwardians were never interested in character in itself; or in the book in itself. They were interested in something outside. Their books, then, were incomplete as books, and required that the reader should finish them, actively and practically, for himself.

Perhaps we can make this clearer if we take the liberty of imagining a little party in the railway carriage—Mr. Wells, Mr. Galsworthy, Mr. Bennett are travelling to Waterloo with Mrs. Brown. Mrs. Brown, I have said, was poorly dressed and very small. She had an anxious, harassed look. I doubt whether she was what you call an educated woman. Seizing upon all these symptoms of the unsatisfactory condition of our primary schools with a rapidity to which I can do no justice, Mr. Wells would instantly project upon the windowpane a vision of a better, breezier, jollier, happier, more adventurous and gallant world, where these musty railway carriages and fusty old women do not exist; where miraculous barges bring tropical fruit to Camberwell by eight o'clock in the morning; where there are public nurseries, fountains, and libraries, dining-rooms, drawing-rooms, and marriages; where every citizen is generous and candid, manly and magnificent, and rather like Mr. Wells himself. But nobody is in the least like Mrs. Brown. There are no Mrs. Browns in Utopia. Indeed I do not think that Mr. Wells, in his passion to make her what she ought to be, would waste a thought upon her as she is. And what would Mr. Galsworthy see? Can we doubt that the walls of Doulton's factory would take his fancy? There are women in that factory who make twenty-five dozen earthenware pots every day. There are mothers in the Mile End Road who depend upon the farthings which those women earn. But there are employers in Surrey who are even now smoking rich cigars while the nightingale sings. Burning with indignation, stuffed with information, arraigning civilisation, Mr. Galsworthy would only see in Mrs. Brown a pot broken on the wheel and thrown into the corner.

Mr. Bennett, alone of the Edwardians, would keep his eyes in the carriage. He, indeed, would observe every detail with immense care. He would notice the advertisements; the pictures of Swanage and Portsmouth; the way in which the cushion bulged between the buttons; how Mrs. Brown wore a brooch which had cost three-and-ten-three at Whitworth's bazaar; and had mended both gloves—indeed the thumb of the left-hand glove had been replaced. And he would observe, at length, how this was the non-stop train from Windsor which calls at Richmond for the convenience of middleclass residents, who can afford to go to the theatre but have not reached the social rank which can afford motor-cars, though it is true, there are occasions (he would tell us what), when they hire them from a company (he would tell us which). And so he would gradually sidle sedately towards Mrs. Brown and would remark how she had been left a little copyhold, not freehold, property at Datchet, which, however, was mortgaged to Mr. Bungay the solicitor—but why should I presume to invent Mr. Bennett? Does not Mr. Bennett write novels himself? I will open the first book that chance puts in my way—*Hilda Lessways*. Let us see how he makes us feel that Hilda is real, true, and convincing, as a novelist should. She shut the door in a soft, controlled way, which showed the constraint of her relations with her mother. She was fond of reading *Maud;* she was endowed with the power to feel intensely. So far, so good; in his leisurely, sure-footed way Mr. Bennett is trying in these first pages, where every touch is important, to show us the kind of girl she was.

But then he begins to describe, not Hilda Lessways, but the view from her bedroom window, the excuse being that Mr. Skellorn, the man who collects rents, is coming along that way. Mr. Bennett proceeds:

"The bailiwick of Turnhill lay behind her; and all the murky district of the Five Towns, of which Turnhill is the northern outpost, lay to the south. At the foot of Chatterley Wood the canal wound in large curves on its way towards the undefiled plains of Cheshire and the sea. On the canal-side, exactly opposite to Hilda's window, was a flour-mill, that sometimes made nearly as much smoke as the kilns and the chimneys closing the prospect on either hand. From the flour-mill a bricked path, which separated a considerable row of new cottages from their appurtenant gardens, led straight into Lessways Street, in front of Mrs. Lessways' house. By this path Mr. Skellorn should have arrived, for he inhabited the farthest of the cottages."

One line of insight would have done more than all those lines of description; but let them pass as the necessary drudgery of the novelist. And now—where is Hilda? Alas. Hilda is still looking out of the window. Passionate and dissatisfied as she was, she was a girl with an eye for houses. She often compared this old Mr. Skellorn with the villas she saw from her bedroom window. Therefore the villas must be described. Mr. Bennett proceeds:

"The row was called Freehold Villas: a consciously proud name in a district where much of the land was copyhold and could only change owners subject to the payment of 'fines,' and to the feudal consent of a 'court' presided over by the agent of a lord of the manor. Most of the dwellings were owned by their occupiers, who, each an absolute monarch of the soil, niggled in his sooty garden of an evening amid the flutter of drying shirts and towels. Freehold Villas symbolised the final triumph of Victorian economics, the apotheosis of the prudent and industrious artisan. It corresponded with a Building Society Secretary's dream of paradise. And indeed it was a very real achievement. Nevertheless, Hilda's irrational contempt would not admit this."

Heaven be praised, we cry! At last we are coming to Hilda herself. But not so fast. Hilda may have been this, that, and the other; but Hilda not only looked at houses, and thought of houses; Hilda lived in a house. And what sort of a house did Hilda live in? Mr. Bennett proceeds:

"It was one of the two middle houses of a detached terrace of four houses built by her grandfather Lessways, the teapot manufacturer; it was the chief of the four, obviously the habitation of the proprietor of the terrace. One of the corner houses comprised a grocer's shop, and this house had been robbed of its just proportion of garden so that the seigneurial garden-plot might be triflingly larger than the other. The terrace was not a terrace of cottages, but of houses rated at from twenty-six to thirty-six pounds a year: beyond the means of artisans and petty insurance agents and rent-collectors. And further, it was well built, generously built; and its architecture, though debased, showed some faint traces of Georgian amenity. It was admittedly the best row of houses in the newly settled quarter of the town. In coming to it out of Freehold Villas Mr. Skellorn obviously came to something superior, wider, more liberal. Suddenly Hilda heard her mother's voice. . . ."

But we cannot hear her mother's voice, or Hilda's voice; we can only hear Mr. Bennett's voice telling us facts about rents and freeholds and copyholds and fines. What can Mr. Bennett be about? I have formed my own opinion of what Mr. Bennett is about—he is trying to make us imagine for him; he is trying to hypnotise us into the belief that, because he has made a house, there must be a person living there. With all his powers of observation, which are marvellous, with all his sympathy and humanity, which are great, Mr. Bennett has never once looked at Mrs. Brown in her corner. There she sits in the corner of the carriage—that carriage which is travelling, not from Richmond to Waterloo, but from one age of English literature to the next, for Mrs. Brown is eternal, Mrs. Brown is human nature, Mrs. Brown changes only on the surface, it is the novelists who get in and out—there she sits and not one of the Edwardian writers has so much as looked at her. They have looked very powerfully, searchingly, and sympathetically out of the window; at factories, at Utopias, even at the decoration and upholstery of the carriage; but never at her, never at life, never at human nature. And so they have developed a technique of novel writing which suits their purpose; they have made tools and established conventions which do their business. But those tools are not our tools, and that business is not our business. For us those conventions are ruin, those tools are death.

You may well complain of the vagueness of my language. What is a convention, a tool, you may ask, and what do you mean by saying that Mr. Bennett's and Mr. Wells's and Mr. Galsworthy's conventions are the wrong conventions for the Georgians? The question is difficult: I will attempt a short cut. A convention in writing is not much different from a convention in manners. Both in life and in literature it is necessary to have some means of bridging the gulf between the hostess and her unknown guest on the one hand, the writer and his unknown reader on the other. The hostess bethinks her of the weather, for generations of hostesses have established the fact that this is a subject of universal interest in which we all believe. She begins by saying that we are having a wretched May, and, having thus got into touch with her unknown guest, proceeds to matters of greater interest. So it is in literature. The writer must get into touch with his reader by putting before him something which he recognises, which therefore stimulates his imagination, and makes him willing to cooperate in the far more difficult business of intimacy. And it is of the highest importance that this common meeting-place should be reached easily, almost instinctively, in the dark, with one's eyes shut. Here is Mr. Bennett making use of this common ground in the passage which I have quoted. The problem before him was to make us believe in the reality of Hilda Lessways. So he began, being an Edwardian, by describing accurately and minutely the sort of house Hilda lived in, and the sort of house she saw from the window. House property was the common ground from which the Edwardians found it easy to proceed to intimacy. Indirect as it seems to us, the convention worked admirably, and thousands of Hilda Lessways were launched upon the world by this means. For that age and generation, the convention was a good one.

But now, if you will allow me to pull my own anecdote to pieces, you will see how keenly I felt the lack of a convention, and how serious a matter it is when the tools of one generation are useless for the next. The incident had made a great impression on me. But how was I to transmit it to you? All I could do was to report as accurately as I could what was said, to describe in detail what was worn, to say, despairingly, that all sorts of scenes rushed into my mind, to proceed to tumble them out pell-mell, and to describe this vivid, this overmastering impression by likening it to a draught or a smell of burning. To tell you the truth, I was also strongly tempted to manufacture a three-volume novel about the old lady's son, and his adventures crossing the Atlantic, and her daughter, and how she kept a milliner's shop in Westminster, the past life of Smith himself, and his house at Sheffield, though such stories seem to me the most dreary, irrelevant, and humbugging affairs in the world.

But if I had done that I should have escaped the appalling effort of saying what I meant. And to have got at what I meant I should have had to go back and back and back; to experiment with one thing and another; to try this sentence and that, referring each word to my vision, matching it as exactly as possible, and knowing that somehow I had to find a common ground between us, a convention which would not seem to you too odd, unreal, and far-fetched to believe in. I admit that I shirked that arduous undertaking. I let my Mrs. Brown slip through my fingers. I have told you nothing whatever about her. But that is partly the great Edwardians' fault. I asked them—they are my elders and betters—How shall I begin to describe this woman's character? And they said, "Begin by saying that her father kept a shop in Harrogate. Ascertain the rent. Ascertain the wages of shop assistants in the year 1878. Discover what her mother died of. Describe cancer. Describe calico. Describe—" But I cried, "Stop! Stop!" And I regret to say that I threw that ugly, that clumsy, that incongruous tool out of the window, for I knew that if I began describing the cancer and the calico, my Mrs. Brown, that vision to which I cling though I know no way of imparting it to you, would have been dulled and tarnished and vanished for ever.

That is what I mean by saying that the Edwardian tools are the wrong ones for us to use. They have laid an enormous stress upon the fabric of things. They have given us a house in the hope that we may be able to deduce the human beings who live there. To give them their due, they have made that house much better worth living in. But if you hold that novels are in the first place about people, and only in the second about the houses they live in, that is the wrong way to set about it. Therefore, you see, the Georgian writer had to begin by throwing away the method that was in use at the moment. He was left alone there facing Mrs. Brown without any method of conveying her to the reader. But that is inaccurate. A writer is never alone. There is always the public with him—if not on the same seat, at least in the compartment next door. Now the public is a strange travelling companion. In England it is a very suggestible and docile creature, which, once you get it to attend, will believe implicitly what it is told for a certain number of years. If you say to the public with sufficient conviction, "All women have tails, and all men humps," it will actually learn to see women with tails and men with humps, and will think it very revolutionary and probably improper if you say, "Nonsense. Monkeys have tails and camels humps. But men and women have brains, and they have hearts; they think and they feel,"—that will seem to it a bad joke, and an improper one into the bargain.

But to return. Here is the British public sitting by the writer's side and saying in its vast and unanimous way, "Old women have houses. They have fathers. They have incomes. They have servants. They have hot water bottles. That is how we know that they are old women. Mr. Wells and Mr. Bennett and Mr. Galsworthy have always taught us that this is the way to recognise them. But now with your Mrs. Brown—how are we to believe in her? We do not even know whether her villa was called Albert or Balmoral; what she paid for her gloves; or whether her mother died of cancer or of consumption. How can she be alive? No; she is a mere figment of your imagination."

And old women of course ought to be made of freehold villas and copyhold estates, not of imagination.

The Georgian novelist, therefore, was in an awkard predicament. There was Mrs. Brown protesting that she was different, quite different, from what people made out, and luring the novelist to her rescue by the most fascinating if fleeting glimpse of her charms; there were the Edwardians handing out tools appropriate to house building and house breaking; and there was the British public asseverating that they must see the hot water bottle first. Meanwhile the train was rushing to that station where we must all get out.

Such, I think, was the predicament in which the young Georgians found themselves about the year 1910. Many of them—I am thinking of Mr. Forster and Mr. Lawrence in particular—spoilt their early work because, instead of throwing away those tools, they tried to use them. They tried to compromise. They tried to combine their own direct sense of the oddity and significance of some character with Mr. Galsworthy's knowledge of the Factory Acts, and Mr. Bennett's knowledge of the Five Towns. They tried it, but they had too keen, too overpowering a sense of Mrs. Brown and her peculiarities to go on trying it much longer. Something had to be done. At whatever cost of life, limb, and damage to valuable property Mrs. Brown must be rescued, expressed, and set in her high relations to the world before the train stopped and she disappeared for ever. And so the smashing and the crashing began. Thus it is that we hear all round us, in poems and novels and biographies, even in newspaper articles and essays, the sound of breaking and falling, crashing and destruction. It is the prevailing sound of the Georgian age—rather a melancholy one if you think what melodious days there have been in the past, if you think of Shakespeare and Milton and Keats or even of Jane Austen and Thackeray and Dickens; if you think of the language, and the heights to which it can soar when free, and see the same eagle captive, bald, and croaking.

In view of these facts—with these sounds in my ears and these fancies in my brain—I am not going to deny that Mr. Bennett has some reason when he complains that our Georgian writers are unable to make us believe that our characters are real. I am forced to agree that they do not pour out three immortal masterpieces with Victorian regularity every autumn. But instead of being gloomy, I am sanguine. For this state of things is, I think, inevitable whenever from hoar old age or callow youth the convention ceases to be a means of communication between writer and reader, and becomes instead an obstacle and an impediment. At the present moment we are suffering, not from decay, but from having no code of manners which writers and readers accept as a prelude to the more exciting intercourse of friendship. The literary convention of the time is so artificial—you have to talk about the weather and nothing but the weather throughout the entire visit—that, naturally, the feeble are tempted to outrage, and the strong are led to destroy the very foundations and rules of literary society. Signs of this are everywhere apparent. Grammar is violated; syntax disintegrated; as a boy staying with an aunt for the weekend rolls in the geranium bed out of sheer desperation as the solemnities of the sabbath wear on. The more adult writers do not, of course, indulge in such wanton exhibitions of spleen. Their sincerity is desperate, and their courage tremendous; it is only that they do not know which to use, a fork or their fingers. Thus, if you read Mr. Joyce and Mr. Eliot you will be struck by the indecency of the one, and the obscurity of the other. Mr. Joyce's indecency in *Ulysses* seems to me the conscious and calculated indecency of a desperate man who feels that in order to breathe he must break the windows. At moments, when the window is broken, he is magnificent. But what a waste of energy! And, after all, how dull indecency is, when it is not the overflowing of a superabundant energy or savagery, but the determined and public spirited act of a man who needs fresh air! Again, with the obscurity of Mr. Eliot. I think that Mr. Eliot has written some of the loveliest single lines in modern poetry. But how intolerant he is of the old usages and politenesses of society —respect for the weak, consideration for the dull! As I sun myself upon the intense and ravishing beauty of one of his lines, and reflect that I must make a dizzy and dangerous leap to the next, and so on from line to line, like an acrobat flying precariously from bar to bar, I cry out, I confess, for the old decorums, and envy the indolence of my ancestors who, instead of spinning madly through mid-air, dreamt quietly in the shade with a book. Again, in Mr. Strachey's books, *Eminent Victorians* and *Queen Victoria,* the effort and strain of writing against the grain and current of the times is visible too. It is much less visible, of course, for not only is he dealing with facts, which are stubborn things, but he has fabricated, chiefly from eighteenth-century material, a very discreet code of manners of his own, which allows him to sit at table with the highest in the land and to say a great many things under cover of that exquisite apparel which, had they gone naked, would have been chased by the men-servants from the room. Still, if you compare *Eminent Victorians* with some of Lord Macaulay's essays, though you will feel that Lord Macaulay is always wrong, and Mr. Strachey always right, you will also feel a body, a sweep, a richness in Lord Macaulay's essays which show that his age was behind him; all his strength went straight into his work; none was used for purposes of concealment or of conversion. But Mr. Strachey has had to open our eyes before he made us see; he has had to search out and saw together a very artful manner of speech; and the effort, beautifully though it is concealed, has robbed his work of some of the force that should have gone into it, and limited his scope.

For these reasons, then, we must reconcile ourselves to a season of failures and fragments. We must reflect that where so much strength is spent on finding a way of telling the truth the truth itself is bound to reach us in rather an exhausted and chaotic condition. Ulysses, Queen Victoria, Mr. Prufrock—to give Mrs. Brown some of the names she has made famous lately—is a little pale and dishevelled by the time her rescuers reach her. And it is the sound of their axes that we hear—a vigorous and stimulating sound in my ears—unless of course you wish to sleep, when, in the bounty of his concern, Providence has provided a host of writers anxious and able to satisfy your needs.

Thus I have tried, at tedious length, I fear, to answer some of the questions which I began by asking. I have given an account of some of the difficulties which in my view beset the Georgian writer in all his forms. I have sought to excuse him. May I end by venturing to remind you of the duties and responsibilities that are yours as partners in this business of writing books, as companions in the railway carriage, as fellow travellers with Mrs. Brown? For she is just as visible to you who remain silent as to us who tell stories about her. In the course of your daily life this past week you have had far stranger and more interesting experiences than the one I have tried to describe. You have overheard scraps of talk that filled you with amazement. You have gone to bed at night bewildered by the complexity of your feelings. In one day thousands of ideas have coursed through your brains; thousands of emotions have met, collided, and disappeared in astonishing disorder. Nevertheless, you allow the writers to palm off upon you a version of all this, an image of Mrs. Brown, which has no likeness to that surprising apparition whatsoever. In your modesty you seem to consider that writers are of different blood and bone from yourselves; that they know more of Mrs. Brown than you do. Never was there a more fatal mistake. It is this division between reader and writer, this humility on your part, these professional airs and graces on ours, that corrupt and emasculate the books which should be the healthy offspring of a close and equal alliance between us. Hence spring those sleek, smooth novels, those portentous and ridiculous biographies, that milk and watery criticism, those poems melodiously celebrating the innocence of roses and sheep which pass so plausibly for literature at the present time.

Your part is to insist that writers shall come down off their plinths and pedestals, and describe beautifully if possible, truthfully at any rate, our Mrs. Brown. You should insist that she is an old lady of unlimited capacity and infinite variety; capable of appearing in any place; wearing any dress; saying anything and doing heaven knows what. But the things she says and the things she does and her eyes and her nose and her speech and her silence have an overwhelming fascination, for she is, of course, the spirit we live by, life itself.

But do not expect just at present a complete and satisfactory presentment of her. Tolerate the spasmodic, the obscure, the fragmentary, the failure. Your help is invoked in a good cause. For I will make one final and surpassingly rash prediction—we are trembling on the verge of one of the great ages of English literature. But it can only be reached if we are determined never, never to desert Mrs. Brown.

JOSEPH WOOD KRUTCH: The Tragic Fallacy*

THROUGH the legacy of their art the great ages have transmitted to us a dim image of their glorious vitality. When we turn the pages of a Sophoclean or a Shakespearean tragedy we participate faintly in the experience which created it and we sometimes presumptuously say that we "understand" the spirit of these works. But the truth is that we see them, even at best and in the moments when our souls expand most nearly to their dimensions, through a glass darkly.

It is so much easier to appreciate than to create that an age too feeble to reach the heights achieved by the members of a preceding one can still see those heights towering above its impotence, and so it is that, when we perceive a Sophocles or a Shakespeare soaring in an air which we can never hope to breathe, we say that we can "appreciate" them. But what we mean is that we are just able to wonder, and we can never hope to participate in the glorious vision of human life out of which they were created—not even to the extent of those humbler persons for whom they were written; for while to us the triumphant voices come from far away and tell of a heroic world which no longer exists, to them that spoke of immediate realities and revealed the inner meaning of events amidst which they still lived.

When the life has entirely gone out of a work of art come down to us from the past, when we read it without any emotional comprehension whatsoever and can no longer even imagine why the people for whom it was intended found it absorbing and satisfying, then, of course, it has ceased to be a work of art at all and has dwindled into one of those deceptive "documents" from which we get a false sense of comprehending through the intellect things which cannot be comprehended at all except by means of a kinship of feeling. And though all works from a past age have begun in this way to fade there are some, like the great Greek or Elizabethan tragedies, which are still halfway between the work of art and the document. They no longer can have for us the immediacy which they had for those to whom they originally belonged, but they have not yet eluded us entirely. We no longer live in the world which they represent, but we can half imagine it and we can measure the distance which we have moved away. We write no tragedies today, but we can still talk about the tragic spirit of which we would, perhaps, have no conception were it not for the works in question.

An age which could really "appreciate" Shakespeare or Sophocles would have something comparable to put beside them—something like them, not necessarily in form, or spirit, but at least in magnitude—some vision of life which would be, however different, equally ample and passionate. But when we move to put a modern masterpiece beside them, when we seek to compare them with, let us say, a *Ghosts* or a *Weavers,* we shrink as from the impulse to commit some folly and we feel as though we were about to superimpose Bowling Green upon the Great Prairies in order to ascertain which is the larger. The question, we see, is not primarily one of art but of the two worlds which two minds inhabited. No increased powers of expression, no greater gift for words, could have

* "The Tragic Fallacy" first appeared in a slightly different version from this in *The Atlantic Monthly,* November 1928. It then appeared as Chapter Five of *The Modern Temper: A Study and a Confession.* It is reprinted here from *The Modern Temper* by Joseph Wood Krutch, Copyright 1929, by Harcourt, Brace and Company, Inc. Mr. Krutch(*b.* 1893) is also the author of *Comedy and Conscience after the Restoration* (1924), *Edgar Allan Poe: A Study in Genius* (1926), *Five Masters: A Study in the Mutations of the Novel* (1930), *Experience and Art: Some Aspects of the Esthetics of Literature* (1932), *Was Europe a Success?* (1934), *The American Drama since 1918* (1939), and *Samuel Johnson* (1944).

transformed Ibsen into Shakespeare. The materials out of which the latter created his works—his conception of human passions, his vision of the amplitude of human life—simply did not and could not exist for Ibsen, as they did not and could not exist for his contemporaries. God and Man and Nature had all somehow dwindled in the course of the intervening centuries, not because the realistic creed of modern art led us to seek out mean people, but because this meanness of human life was somehow thrust upon us by the operation of that same process which led to the development of realistic theories of art by which our vision could be justified.

Hence, though we still apply, sometimes, the adjective "tragic" to one or another of those modern works of literature which describe human misery and which end more sadly even than they begin, the term is a misnomer since it is obvious that the works in question have nothing in common with the classical examples of the genre and produce in the reader a sense of depression which is the exact opposite of that elation generated when the spirit of a Shakespeare rises joyously superior to the outward calamities which he recounts and celebrates the greatness of the human spirit whose travail he describes. Tragedies, in that only sense of the word which has any distinctive meaning, are no longer written in either the dramatic or any other form and the fact is not to be accounted for in any merely literary terms. It is not the result of any fashion in literature or of any deliberation to write about human nature or character under different aspects, any more than it is of either any greater sensitiveness of feeling which would make us shrink from the contemplation of the suffering of Medea or Othello or of any greater optimism which would make us more likely to see life in more cheerful terms. It is, on the contrary, the result of one of those enfeeblements of the human spirit not unlike that described in the previous chapter of this essay, and a further illustration of that gradual weakening of man's confidence in his ability to impose upon the phenomenon of life an interpretation acceptable to his desires which is the subject of the whole of the present discussion.

To explain that fact and to make clear how the creation of classical tragedy did consist in the successful effort to impose such a satisfactory interpretation will require, perhaps, the special section which follows, although the truth of the fact that it does impose such an interpretation must be evident to any one who has ever risen from the reading of *Oedipus* or *Lear* with that feeling of exultation which comes when we have been able, by rare good fortune, to enter into its spirit as completely as it is possible for us of a remoter and emotionally enfeebled age to enter it. Meanwhile one anticipatory remark may be ventured. If the plays and the novels of today deal with littler people and less mighty emotions it is not because we have become interested in commonplace souls and their unglamorous adventures but because we have come, willy-nilly, to see the soul of man as commonplace and its emotions as mean.

2

Tragedy, said Aristotle, is the "imitation of noble actions," and though it is some twenty-five hundred years since the dictum was uttered there is only one respect in which we are inclined to modify it. To us "imitation" seems a rather naive word to apply to that process by which observation is turned into art, and we seek one which would define or at least imply the nature of that interposition of the personality of the artist between the object and the beholder which constitutes his function and by means of which he transmits a modified version, rather than a mere imitation, of the thing which he has contemplated.

In the search for this word the estheticians of romanticism invented the term "expression" to describe the artistic purpose to which apparent imitation was subservient. Psychologists, on the other hand, feeling that the artistic process was primarily one by which reality is modified in such a way as to render it more acceptable to the desires of the artist, employed various terms in the effort to describe that distortion which the wish may produce in vision. And though many of the newer critics reject both romanticism and psychology, even they insist upon the fundamental fact that in art we are concerned, not with mere imitation, but with the imposition of some form upon the material which it would not have if it were merely copied as a camera copies.

Tragedy is not, then, as Aristotle said, the *imitation* of noble actions, for, indeed, no one knows what a *noble* action is or whether or not such a thing as nobility exists in nature apart from the mind of man. Certainly the action of Achilles in dragging the dead body of Hector around the walls of Troy and under the eyes of Andromache, who had begged to be allowed to give it decent burial, is not to us a noble action, though it was such to Homer, who made it the subject of a noble passage in a noble poem. Certainly, too, the same action might conceivably be made the subject of a tragedy and the subject of a farce, depending upon the way in which it was treated; so that to say that tragedy is the *imitation* of a *noble* action is to be guilty of assuming, first, that art and photography are the same, and, second, that there may be something inherently noble in an act as distinguished from the motives which prompted it or from the point of view from which it is regarded.

And yet, nevertheless, the idea of nobility is inseparable from the idea of tragedy, which cannot exist without it. If tragedy is not the imitation or even the modified representation of noble actions it is certainly a representation of actions *considered* as noble, and herein lies its essential nature, since no man can conceive it unless he is capable of believing in the greatness and importance of man. Its action is usually, if not always, calamitous, because it is only in calamity that the human spirit has the opportunity to reveal itself triumphant over the outward universe which fails to conquer it; but this calamity in tragedy is only a means to an end and the essential thing which distinguishes real tragedy from those distressing modern works sometimes called by its name is the fact that it is in the former alone that the artist has found himself capable of considering and of making us consider that his people and his actions have that amplitude and importance which make them noble. Tragedy arises then when, as in Periclean Greece or Elizabethan England, a people fully aware of the calamities of life is nevertheless serenely confident of the greatness of man, whose mighty passions and supreme fortitude are revealed when one of these calamities overtakes him.

To those who mistakenly think of it as something gloomy or depressing, who are incapable of recognizing the elation which its celebration of human greatness inspires, and who, therefore, confuse it with things merely miserable or pathetic, it must be a paradox that the happiest, most vigorous, and most confident ages which the world has ever known—the Periclean and the Elizabethan—should be exactly those which created and which most relished the mightiest tragedies; but the paradox is, of course, resolved by the fact that tragedy is essentially an expression, not of despair, but of the triumph over despair and of confidence in the value of human life. If Shakespeare himself ever had that "dark period" which his critics and biographers have imagined for him, it was at least no darkness like that bleak and arid despair which sometimes settles over modern spirits. In the midst of it he created both the elemental grandeur of Othello and the pensive majesty of Hamlet and, holding them up to his contemporaries, he said in the words of his own Miranda, "O brave new world that hath *such* creatures in it."

All works of art which deserve their name have a happy end. This is indeed the thing which constitutes them art and through which they perform their function. Whatever the character of the events, fortunate or unfortunate, which they recount, they so mold or arrange or interpret them that we accept gladly the conclusion which they reach and would not have it otherwise. They may conduct us into the realm of pure fancy where wish and fact are identical and the world is remade exactly after the fashion of the heart's desire or they may yield some greater or less allegiance to fact; but they must always reconcile us in one way or another to the representation which they make and the distinctions between the genres are simply the distinctions between the means by which this reconciliation is effected.

Comedy laughs the minor mishaps of its characters away; drama solves all the difficulties which it allows to arise; and melodrama, separating good from evil by simple lines, distributes its rewards and punishments in accordance with the principles of a naive justice which satisfies the simple souls of its audience, which are neither philosophical enough to question its primitive ethics nor critical enough to object to the way in which its neat events violate the laws of probability. Tragedy, the greatest and the most difficult of the arts, can adopt none of these methods; and yet it must reach its own happy end in its own way. Though its conclusion must be, by its premise, outwardly calamitous, though it must speak to those who know that the good man is cut off and that the fairest things are the first to perish, yet it must leave them, as *Othello* does, content that this is so. We must be and we are glad that Juliet dies and glad that Lear is turned out into the storm.

Milton set out, he said, to justify the ways of God to man, and his phrase, if it be interpreted broadly enough, may be taken as describing the function of all art, which must, in some way or other, make the life which it seems to represent satisfactory to those who see its reflection in the magic mirror, and it must gratify or at least reconcile the desires of the beholder, not necessarily, as the naiver exponents of Freudian psychology maintain, by gratifying individual and often eccentric wishes, but at least by satisfying the universally human desire to find in the world some justice, some meaning, or, at the very least, some recognizable order. Hence it is that every real tragedy, however tremendous it may be, is an affirmation of faith in life, a declaration that even if God is not in his Heaven, then at least Man is in his world.

We accept gladly the outward defeats which it describes for the sake of the inward victories which it reveals. Juliet died, but not before she had shown how great and resplendent a thing love could be; Othello plunged the dagger into his own breast, but not before he had revealed that greatness of soul which makes his death seem unimportant. Had he died in the instant when he struck the blow, had he perished still believing that the world was as completely black as he saw it before the innocence of Desdemona was revealed to him, then, for him at least, the world would have been merely damnable, but Shakespeare kept him alive long enough to allow him to learn his error and hence to die, not in despair, but in the full acceptance of the tragic reconciliation to life. Perhaps it would be pleasanter if men could believe what the child is taught—that the good are happy and that things turn out as they should—but it is far more important to be able to believe, as Shakespeare did, that however much things in the outward world may go awry, man has, nevertheless, splendors of his own and that, in a word, Love and Honor and Glory are not words but realities.

Thus for the great ages tragedy is not an expression of despair but the means by which they saved themselves from it. It is a profession of faith, and a sort of religion; a way of looking at life by virtue of which it is robbed of its pain. The sturdy soul of the tragic author seizes upon suffering and uses it only as a means by which joy may be wrung out of existence, but it is not to be forgotten that he is enabled to do so only because of his belief in the greatness of human nature and because, though he has lost the child's faith in life, he has not lost his far more important faith in human nature. A tragic writer does not have to believe in God, but he must believe in man.

And if, then, the Tragic Spirit is in reality the product of a religious faith in which, sometimes at least, faith in the greatness of God is replaced by faith in the greatness of man, it serves, of course, to perform the function of religion, to make life tolerable for those who participate in its beneficent illusion. It purges the souls of those who might otherwise despair and it makes endurable the realization that the events of the outward world do not correspond with the desires of the heart, and thus, in its own particular way, it does what all religions do, for it gives a rationality, a meaning, and a justification to the universe. But if it has the strength it has also the weakness of all faiths, since it may—nay, it must—be ultimately lost as reality, encroaching further and further into the realm of imagination, leaves less and less room in which that imagination can build its refuge.

3

It is, indeed, only at a certain stage in the development of the realistic intelligence of a people that the tragic faith can exist. A naiver people may have, as the ancient men of the north had, a body of legends which are essentially tragic, or it may have only (and need only) its happy and childlike mythology which arrives inevitably at its happy end, and where the only ones who suffer "deserve" to do so and in which, therefore, life is represented as directly and easily acceptable. A too sophisticated society on the other hand—one which, like ours, has outgrown not merely the simple optimism of the child but also that vigorous, one might almost say adolescent, faith in the nobility of man which marks a Sophocles or a Shakespeare, has neither fairy tales to assure it that all is always right in the end nor tragedies to make it believe that it rises superior in soul to the outward calamities which befall it.

Distrusting its thought, despising its passions, realizing its impotent unimportance in the universe, it can tell itself no stories except those which make it still more acutely aware of its trivial miseries. When its heroes (sad misnomer for the pitiful creatures who people contemporary fiction) are struck down it is not, like Oedipus, by the gods that they are struck but only, like Oswald Alving, by syphilis, for they know that the gods, even if they existed, would not trouble with them, and they cannot attribute to themselves in art an importance in which they do not believe. Their so-called tragedies do not and cannot end with one of those splendid calamities which in Shakespeare seem to reverberate through the universe, because they cannot believe that the universe trembles when their love is, like Romeo's, cut off or when the place where they (small as they are) have gathered up their trivial treasure is, like Othello's sanctuary, defiled. Instead, mean misery piles on mean misery, petty misfortune follows petty misfortune, and despair becomes intolerable because it is no longer even significant or important.

Ibsen once made one of his characters say that he did not read much because he found reading "irrelevant," and the adjective was brilliantly chosen because it held implications even beyond those of which Ibsen was consciously aware. What is it that made the classics irrelevant to him and to us? Is it not just exactly those to him impossible premises which make tragedy what it is, those assumptions that the soul of man is great, that the universe (together with whatever gods may be) concerns itself with him and that he is, in a word, noble? Ibsen turned to village politics for exactly the same reason that his contemporaries and his successors have, each in his own way, sought out some aspect of the common man and his common life—because, that is to say, here was at least something small enough for him to be able to believe.

Bearing this fact in mind, let us compare a modern "tragedy" with one of the great works of a happy age, not in order to judge of their relative technical merits but in order to determine to what extent the former deserves its name by achieving a tragic solution capable of purging the soul or of reconciling the emotions to the life which it pictures. And in order to make the comparison as fruitful as possible let us choose *Hamlet* on the one hand and on the other a play like *Ghosts,* which was not only written by perhaps the most powerful as well as the most typical of modern writers but which is, in addition, the one of his works which seems most nearly to escape that triviality which cannot be entirely escaped by any one who feels, as all contemporary minds do, that man is relatively trivial.

In *Hamlet* a prince ("in understanding, how like a god!") has thrust upon him from the unseen world a duty to redress a wrong which concerns not merely him, his mother, and his uncle, but the moral order of the universe. Erasing all trivial fond records from his mind, abandoning at once both his studies and his romance because it has been his good fortune to be called upon to take part in an action of cosmic importance, he plunges (at first) not into action but into thought, weighing the claims which are made upon him and contemplating the grandiose complexities of the universe. And when the time comes at last for him to die he dies, not as a failure, but as a success. Not only has the universe regained the balance which had been upset by what *seemed* the monstrous crime of the guilty pair ("there is nothing either good nor ill but thinking makes it so"), but in the process by which that readjustment is made a mighty mind has been given the opportunity, first to contemplate the magnificent scheme of which it is a part, and then to demonstrate the greatness of its spirit by playing a rôle in the grand style which it called for. We do not need to despair in *such* a world if it has *such* creatures in it.

Turn now to *Ghosts*—look upon this picture and upon that. A young man has inherited syphilis from his father. Struck by a to him mysterious malady he returns to his northern village, learns the hopeless truth about himself, and persuades his mother to poison him. The incidents prove, perhaps, that pastors should not endeavor to keep a husband and wife together unless they know what they are doing. But what a world is this in which a great writer can deduce nothing more than that from his greatest work and how are we to be purged or reconciled when we see it acted? Not only is the failure utter, but it is trivial and meaningless as well.

Yet the journey from Elsinore to Skien is precisely the journey which the human spirit has made, exchanging in the process princes for invalids and gods for disease. We say, as Ibsen would say, that the problems of Oswald Alving are more "relevant" to our life than the problems of Hamlet, that the play in which he appears is more "real" than the other more glamorous one, but it is exactly because we find it so that we are condemned. We can believe in Oswald but we cannot believe in Hamlet, and a light has gone out in the universe. Shakespeare justifies the ways of God to man, but in Ibsen there is no such happy end and with him tragedy, so called, has become merely an expression of our despair at finding that such justification is no longer possible.

Modern critics have sometimes been puzzled to account for the fact that the concern of ancient tragedy is almost exclusively with kings and courts. They have been tempted to accuse even Aristotle of a certain naiveté in assuming (as he seems to assume) that the "nobility" of which he speaks as necessary to a tragedy implies a nobility of rank as well as of soul, and they have sometimes regretted that Shakespeare did not devote himself more than he did to the serious consideration of those common woes of the common man which subsequent writers have exploited with increasing pertinacity. Yet the tendency to lay the scene of a tragedy at the court of a king is not the result of any arbitrary convention but of the fact that the tragic writers believed easily in greatness just as we believe easily in meanness. To Shakespeare, robes and crowns and jewels are the garments most appropriate to man because they are the fitting outward manifestation of his inward majesty, but to us they seem absurd because the man who bears them has, in our estimation, so pitifully shrunk. We do not write about kings because we do not believe that any man is worthy to be one and we do not write about courts because hovels seem to us to be dwellings more appropriate to the creatures who inhabit them. Any modern attempt to dress characters in robes ends only by making us aware of a comic incongruity and any modern attempt to furnish them with a language resplendent like Shakespeare's ends only in bombast.

True tragedy capable of performing its function and of purging the soul by reconciling man to his woes can exist only by virtue of a certain pathetic fallacy far more inclusive than that to which the name is commonly given. The romantics, feeble descendants of the tragic writers to whom they are linked by their effort to see life and nature in grandiose terms, loved to imagine that the sea or the sky had a way of according itself with their moods, of storming when they stormed and smiling when they smiled. But the tragic spirit sustains itself by an assumption much more far-reaching and no more justified. Man as it sees him lives in a world which he may not dominate but which is always aware of him. Occupying the exact center of a universe which would have no meaning except for him and being so little below the angels that, if he believes in God, he has no hesitation in imagining Him formed as he is formed and crowned with a crown like that which he or one of his fellows wears, he assumes that each of his acts reverberates through the universe. His passions are important to him because he believes them important throughout all time and all space; the very fact that he can sin (no modern can) means that this universe is watching his acts; and though he may perish, a God leans out from infinity to strike him down. And it is exactly because an Ibsen cannot think of man in any such terms as these that his persons have so shrunk and that his "tragedy" has lost that power which real tragedy always has of making that infinitely ambitious creature called man content to accept his misery if only he can be made to feel great enough and important enough. An Oswald is not a Hamlet chiefly because he has lost that tie with the natural and supernatural world which the latter had. No ghost will leave the other world to warn or encourage him, there is no virtue and no vice which he can possibly have which can be really important, and when he dies neither his death nor the manner of it will be, outside the circle of two or three people as unnecessary as himself, any more important than that of a rat behind the arras.

Perhaps we may dub the illusion upon which the tragic spirit is nourished the Tragic, as opposed to the Pathetic, Fallacy, but fallacy though it is, upon its existence depends not merely the writing of tragedy but the existence of that religious feeling of which tragedy is an expression and by means of which a people aware of the dissonances of life manages nevertheless to hear them as harmony. Without it neither man nor his passions can seem great enough or important enough to justify the sufferings which they entail, and literature, expressing the mood of a people, begins to despair where once it had exulted. Like the belief in love and like most of the other mighty illusions by means of which human life has been given a value, the Tragic Fallacy depends ultimately upon the assumption which man so readily makes that something outside his own being, some "spirit not himself"—be it God, Nature, or that still vaguer thing called a Moral Order—joins him in the emphasis which he places upon this or that and confirms him in his feeling that his passions and his opinions are important. When his instinctive faith in that correspondence between the outer and the inner world fades, his grasp upon the faith that sustained him fades also, and Love or Tragedy or what not ceases to be the reality which it was because he is never strong enough in his own insignificant self to stand alone in a universe which snubs him with its indifference.

In both the modern and the ancient worlds tragedy was dead long before writers were aware of the fact. Seneca wrote his frigid melodramas under the impression that he was following in the footsteps of Sophocles, and Dryden probably thought that his *All for Love* was an improvement upon Shakespeare, but in time we awoke to the fact that no amount of rhetorical bombast could conceal the fact that grandeur was not to be counterfeited when the belief in its possibility was dead, and turning from the hero to the common man, we inaugurated the era of realism. For us no choice remains except that between mere rhetoric and the frank consideration of our fellow men, who may be the highest of the anthropoids but who are certainly too far below the angels to imagine either that these angels can concern themselves with them or that they can catch any glimpse of even the soles of angelic feet. We can no longer tell tales of the fall of noble men because we do not believe that noble men exist. The best that we can achieve is pathos and the most that we can do is to feel sorry for ourselves. Man has put off his royal robes and it is only in sceptered pomp that tragedy can come sweeping by.

4

Nietzsche was the last of the great philosophers to attempt a tragic justification of life. His central and famous dogma—"Life is good *because* it is painful"—sums up in a few words the desperate and almost meaningless paradox to which he was driven in his effort to reduce to rational terms the far more imaginative conception which is everywhere present but everywhere unanalyzed in a Sophocles or a Shakespeare and by means of which they rise triumphant over the manifold miseries of life. But the very fact that Nietzsche could not even attempt to state in any except intellectual terms an attitude which is primarily unintellectual and to which, indeed, intellectual analysis is inevitably fatal, is proof of the distance which he had been carried (by the rationalizing tendencies of the human mind) from the possibility of the tragic solution which he sought; and the confused, half-insane violence of his work will reveal, by the contrast which it affords with the serenity of the tragic writers whom he admired, how great was his failure.

Fundamentally this failure was, moreover, conditioned by exactly the same thing which has conditioned the failure of all modern attempts to achieve what he attempted—by the fact, that is to say, that tragedy must have a hero if it is not to be merely an accusation against, instead of a justification of, the world in which it occurs. Tragedy is, as Aristotle said, an imitation of noble actions, and Nietzsche, for all his enthusiasm for the Greek tragic writers, was palsied by the universally modern incapacity to conceive man as noble. Out of this dilemma, out of his need to find a hero who could give to life as he saw it the only possible justification, was born the idea of the Superman, but the Superman is, after all, only a hypothetical being, destined to become what man actually was in the eyes of the great tragic writers—a creature (as Hamlet said) "how infinite in capacities, in understanding how like a god." Thus Nietzsche lived half in the past through his literary enthusiasms and half in the future through his grandiose dreams, but for all his professed determination to justify existence he was no more able than the rest of us to find the present acceptable. Life, he said in effect, is not a Tragedy now but perhaps it will be when the Ape-man has been transformed into a hero (the *Übermensch*), and trying to find that sufficient, he went mad.

He failed, as all moderns must fail when they attempt, like him, to embrace the tragic spirit as a religious faith, because the resurgence of that faith is not an intellectual but a vital phenomenon, something not achieved by taking thought but born, on the contrary, out of an instinctive confidence in life which is nearer to the animal's unquestioning allegiance to the scheme of nature than it is to that critical intelligence characteristic of a fully developed humanism. And like other faiths it is not to be recaptured merely by reaching an intellectual conviction that it would be desirable to do so.

Modern psychology has discovered (or at least strongly emphasized) the fact that under certain conditions desire produces belief, and having discovered also that the more primitive a given mentality the more completely are its opinions determined by its wishes, modern psychology has concluded that the best mind is that which most resists the tendency to believe a thing simply because it would be pleasant or advantageous to do so. But justified as this conclusion may be from the intellectual point of view, it fails to take into account the fact that in a universe as badly adapted as this one to human as distinguished from animal needs this ability to will a belief may bestow an enormous vital advantage as it did, for instance, in the case at present under discussion where it made possible for Shakespeare the compensations of a tragic faith completely inaccessible to Nietzsche. Pure intelligence, incapable of being influenced by desire and therefore also incapable of choosing one opinion rather than another simply because the one chosen is the more fruitful or beneficent, is doubtless a relatively perfect instrument for the pursuit of truth, but the question (likely, it would seem, to be answered in the negative) is simply whether or not the spirit of man can endure the literal and inhuman truth.

Certain ages and simple people have conceived of the action which passes upon the stage of the universe as of something in the nature of a Divine Comedy, as something, that is to say, which will reach its end with the words "and they lived happily ever after." Others, less naive and therefore more aware of those maladjustments whose reality, at least so far as outward events are concerned, they could not escape, have imposed upon it another artistic form and called it a Divine Tragedy, accepting its catastrophe as we accept the catastrophe of an *Othello,* because of its grandeur. But a Tragedy, Divine or otherwise, must, it may again be repeated, have a hero, and from the universe as we see it both the Glory of God and the Glory of Man have departed. Our cosmos may be farcical or it may be pathetic but it has not the dignity of tragedy and we cannot accept it as such.

Yet our need for the consolations of tragedy has not passed with the passing of our ability to conceive it. Indeed, the dissonances which it was tragedy's function to resolve grow more insistent instead of diminishing. Our passions, our disappointments, and our sufferings remain important to us though important to nothing else and they thrust themselves upon us with an urgency which makes it impossible for us to dismiss them as the mere trivialities which, so our intellects tell us, they are. And yet, in the absence of tragic faith or the possibility of achieving it, we have no way in which we may succeed in giving them the dignity which would not only render them tolerable but transform them as they were transformed by the great ages into joys. The death of tragedy is, like the death of love, one of those emotional fatalities as the result of which the human as distinguished from the natural world grows more and more a desert.

Poetry, said Santayana in his famous phrase, is "religion which is no longer believed," but it depends, nevertheless, upon its power to revive in us a sort of temporary or provisional credence and the nearer it can come to producing an illusion of belief the greater is its power as poetry. Once the Tragic Spirit was a living faith and out of it tragedies were written. Today these great expressions of a great faith have declined, not merely into poetry, but into a kind of poetry whose premises are so far from any we can really accept that we can only partially and dimly grasp its meaning.

We read but we do not write tragedies. The tragic solution of the problem of existence, the reconciliation to life by means of the tragic spirit is, that is to say, now only a fiction surviving in art. When that art itself has become, as it probably will, completely meaningless, when we have ceased not only to write but to *read* tragic works, then it will be lost and in all real senses forgotten, since the devolution from Religion to Art to Document will be complete.

CONSTANCE ROURKE: The American*

THE CIVIL WAR has been considered a prime destructive agent in the life of the nation, warping or even destroying a native culture. But the literature of the '50's had never been truly complete. Uncalculating digressions might have followed even though there had been no catastrophe. In spite of the disruption of the War a determined experiment continued through the '60's, '70's, and '80's. The international scene became a great American scene, even in a sense *the* great American scene.

Few ideas had disturbed the American mind more acutely than those which had to do with the European relationship. In the '60's the early commentaries of European travelers still rankled: Tuckerman gathered them into a compendious volume, with rejoinders. But the old fable had undergone a change. In its last notable version, *Our American Cousin*, the nationalistic hero had exhibited his character and enjoyed his adventures in England, and possessed an English heritage. He was in fact one of those "dispossessed princes and wandering heirs" of whom Henry James was to write. In spite of the burlesque the gesture of disseverance had grown less positive in Mark Twain's long skits. The American went abroad, often to stay; sentiment overspread his return to "our old home," and that preoccupation with art which had been satirized in *Innocents Abroad* became one of his larger preoccupations.

This was mixed with a consideration which had long since been borne in upon the American mind by British criticisms. Culture was an obvious proof of leisure, of long establishment, of half a hundred desirable assurances that had been lacking in American life; it even seemed to resolve the vexing problem of manners. Culture was sought abroad as a tangible emblem. The resultant "pillage of the past" was to mount to monstrous proportions, and to include the play of many unworthy instincts—ostentation, boredom, a morbid inversion of personal desires; often, no doubt, it represented a natural response to the fine accumulations of time. Yet surely on the wide scale it was something more

* "The American" first appeared in 1931 in *American Humor: A Study of the National Character*, by Constance Rourke, copyright 1931, by Harcourt, Brace and Company, Inc. Constance Rourke (1885-1941) was the author of *Trumpets of Jubilee* (1927), *Troupers of the Gold Coast* (1928), *Davy Crockett* (1934), *Audubon* (1936), *Charles Sheeler* (1938), and *The Roots of American Culture* (1942).

than these. Fumbling and fantastic, the restless habit seemed an effort to find an established tradition, with the solidity, assurance, and justification which traditions may bring. The American wish for establishment had often seemed a fundamental wish, with all the upheaval.

Many Americans continued to make the extravagant denials of *Innocents Abroad,* but the exodus was unbroken, and found an interpreter in Henry James. His talk of "dispossessed princes and wandering heirs" was not without a personal connotation. As a young man, considering Europe, he had wondered how he was to come into his "own." "The nostalgic poison had been distilled for him," he declared, speaking of himself. James became indeed, as Van Wyck Brooks has said, "an immortal symbol." Strangely enough in this connection, he was something more: an American artist who worked within native sequence.

Henry James has been pictured as a troubled evasionist without a country; and the charge has been turned to a militant charge against American civilization. Yet this theory can hardly account for the long engagement of a major talent. Such talent usually has only one great subject; the choice of that subject will be instinctive, resting upon innumerable elements of heritage and of intimate experience. The consciousness of the European relationship had been binding in America. Given favoring observation, some considerable artist was bound to use the international scene and to find its richest content.

But even a major talent will need the impetus which may come from other imaginative approaches. As formal literary expression of the time is scanned nothing arises to account for the scope and intention of James. He had none of those slightly inferior forerunners in his own medium by which the great writer is often heralded. He wrote as from a fresh impulse; yet the way for his achievement had been opened by a popular vanguard with whose efforts he had some contact. As a small boy he frequented Barnum's, where the Yankee farces were often performed, where the whole American legend was racily sketched, with the backwoodsman and the minstrel as occasional figures, and with melodrama well to the fore. *Our American Cousin* achieved its first great success when James was a lad of fifteen; the play created an immense volume of talk, and was continued for many years. During James's boyhood the streets of New York were alive with the color of the California adventure, with its outlining of the composite American character.

Somewhere James has spoken of the novelist's aptitude for judging the whole piece by a small bit of pattern. Such hints as those abroad in New York during the '50's could go far with a sensitive young mind like his; and others existed to complement them, in the London magazines read before the fire in the New York house, in the visits of Thackeray there, in the glimpses of the great foreign world afforded by the constant voyaging of the family to Europe. James never lost the sense of romance with which his youthful apprehensions of Europe were tinged. He was to write of the European scene with warmth and luster and enchantment; even his dull passages have their inner glow. But he began on humble, even primitive ground in his consideration of the American character as this appeared within the European scene; and he kept throughout his life convictions which he must have drawn from the fund of a common native experience.

2

James was bent upon a purpose that had absorbed many American fabulists, that of drawing the large, the generic, American character. Deliberately, it seems, he abandoned the portrayal of local figures, though for this he had a singular genius: in regions familiar to him he caught the local speech, the manner, the inevitable effect of background. Barring the characters in *The Europeans* and *The Bostonians* and a scattering few elsewhere, his Americans are nomadic and rootless; even when they are seen on American soil they belong to no special locality; they are the composite type; the broad lineaments are unmistakable. He wrote of an American "confidence that broke down . . . a freedom that pulled up nowhere . . . an idyllic ease that was somehow too ordered for a primitive social consciousness and too innocent for a developed." In drawing Roderick Hudson, with his "instinctive quickness of observation and his free appropriation of whatever might serve his purpose," James seemed to have in mind something more than a character: his young sculptor becomes a national type. "His appetite for novelty was insatiable, and for everything characteristically foreign, as it presented itself, he had an extravagant greeting; but in half an hour the novelty had faded, he had guessed the secret, he had plucked out the heart of the mystery, and was clamoring for a keener sensation. . . . The boy was living too fast . . . and giving alarming pledges of ennui in his later years. . . ."

James was candid, as the early fabulists had been candid. He wrote of Americans who treated Europe "collectively, as a vast painted and gilded holiday toy, serving its purpose on the spot, but to be relinquished, sacrificed, broken and cast away, at the dawn of any other convenience." Using the familiar symbolism of the comic name, he pictured the conquering Mrs. Headway, who by a gross energy and with impenetrable surfaces achieved an external European triumph.

He pictured Mr. Leavenworth, "a tall, expansive, bland gentleman, with a carefully brushed whisker and a spacious, fair, well-favored face, which seemed somehow to have more room in it than was occupied by a smile of superior benevolence, so that (with his smooth white forehead) it bore a resemblance to a large parlor with a very florid carpet but no pictures on the walls." Mr. Leavenworth was in fact the pretentious consummation of a dominating American idea. "You may be sure that I have employed a native architect for the large residential structure that I am erecting on the banks of the Ohio," he said to Roderick Hudson. "In a tasteful home, surrounded by the memorials of my wanderings, I hope to recover my moral tone. I ordered in Paris the complete appurtenances of a dining-room. Do you think you could do something for my library? It is to be filled with well-selected authors, and I think a pure white image in this style"—he pointed to one of Roderick's statues—"standing out against the morocco and gilt, would have a noble effect. The subject I have already fixed upon. I desire an allegorical representation of Culture. Do you think now," Mr. Leavenworth inquired, "you could rise to the conception?"

These questing Americans—James showed some of them full of an eager pathos, others as indifferent and lost, moving about the world for lack of another occupation. He made an inclusion that went far beyond the efforts of any American before his time, except that of Hawthorne in *The Scarlet Letter*. He drew American women at full length. With the exception of Christopher Newman and Roderick Hudson and a few others the most significant of James's characters are women: it is they who engage in disastrous encounters abroad, they who embody diverse and contradictory American elements. Isabel Archer, Milly Theale, Mary Garland—their number could be extended: their close and delicate portraiture seemed James's greatest preoccupation. Some of his lesser feminine figures reveal hardy American habits; it is they who most often indulge in the monologue. "I don't apologize, Lord Lambeth," said Mrs. Westgate; "some Americans are always apologizing; you must have noticed that. We've the reputation of always boasting and 'blowing' and waving the American flag; but I must say that what strikes me is that we're perpetually making excuses and trying to smooth things over. The American flag has quite gone out of fashion; it's very carefully folded up, like a tablecloth the worse for wear. Why should we apologize? The English never apologize—do they? No, I must say *I* never apologize. You must take us as we come—with all our imperfections on our heads. Of course we haven't your country life and your old ruins and your great estates and all that. . . ." On she went at immense length, this pretty lady, then and later, "with a mild merciless monotony, a paucity of intonation, an impartial flatness that suggested a flowery mead scrupulously 'done over' by a steam roller that had reduced its texture to that of a drawing-room carpet."

The true heroines of James usually possess a bias of temperament which had appeared more than once in the fable of the contrast and casually elsewhere: Poe had stressed it. "Morella's erudition was profound." "I have spoken of the learning of Ligeia: it was immense—such as I have never known in women." The shadow is not deep in James's novels, but it exists. Mrs. Westgate's sister was little Bessie Alden, a great reader, who united native inquisitiveness with a sturdy integrity. There was Mary Garland, a prim and pretty bluestocking. The young women in *The Europeans*—the true Americans—appear against a background of high thinking; and those in *The Bostonians* form a galaxy absorbed in esoteric knowledge. When these women are not directly absorbed in books they are likely to fulfill the general intention by a definite leaning toward the arts: Isabel Archer walked blindly to her fate because of her belief in the fine accumulations of time. Occasionally James pictured the child of nature—fully feminine at last—as in Daisy Miller or Pandora Day, thus following another tradition; but in the main the women with whom he was most deeply engaged took the aloof, the conscious, the slightly studious part.

Portrait after portrait becomes clear in the great range of his novels and short stories. An entire gallery of characters is created to which Americans may well turn for knowledge and social experience and enlargement, or even for a sense of renewal. They are more than types: they are a whole society of typical individuals: they appear with narrow aggressions and an insular nobility, a careless honesty, a large and delicate purpose. Their ambitions are often blind, or have grown hard and unerring. This society of migratory Americans was a provincial society, transcending provincialism only by fine character. Race, history, even a sense of the future, is upon these people; they still remain singularly inclusive. They offer indeed a legible critique of the American character for those who care to read it; and in the end they reveal more than one unmistakable bias which had appeared in earlier years.

The wilderness and the farm had gone: only their faint traces were discernible in these narratives. James noted in Mr. Westgate a face of toil, a voice of leisure; he remarked a peculiar blankness on the faces of older women who may have belonged to a pioneer society. But for the most part the level has changed; these are people of leisure; they are distinctly urban. The range was wide, the innovation profound; the accomplishment of James, who began to write soon after the Civil War, seems little short of miraculous when set against the spare and simple portraiture of earlier years. Yet his illumination of the American character may have grown bright and deep because he accumulated energy from that portraiture, because he possessed the momentum which a tradition may give. He was grounded in the Yankee fable; his basic apprehension of the American character was that which had been drawn there. He was acutely sensitive to foreign criticism, as a long line of popular writers had been before him.

"It was not in the least of American barbarism that she was afraid," he wrote of Lady Barberina. "Her dread was all of American civilization." The satirical recognition included the familiar foreign charge. In *Pandora's Box* the German envoy was on his way "to explore a society abounding in comic aspects"—an American society comic to the European. Repeatedly James set the wickedness or subtlety or deceit of Europeans against American innocence. The contrast is clear in the small encounters of *Four Meetings;* it lies at the basis of *An International Episode;* it is dramatically posed, with all the implications of a wounding British scorn, in *The Modern Warning.* Even such fine characters as Kate Croy and Merton Densher reveal an ancestral blackness, against which is drawn the touching and exquisite nobility of Milly Theale, an American.

In later years James denied that the innocent Americans in *The Wings of the Dove* and *The Golden Bowl* were exhibited as Americans; yet the contrast remains. James never presented its opposite terms with imaginative force; and the pattern was repeated too often to be anything but the outgrowth of a profound conviction. He was captivated by the vision of American innocence. In *The Europeans* the American characters appear as the very perfection of a delicate and straitened purity—those indigenous Americans who were being contrasted with vagrant others born and bred in Europe. They were "charming," these true characters, as Felix said, "in a style of their own. How shall I describe it? It's primitive; it's patriarchal; it's the *ton* of the golden age." In one of his later prefaces James wrote with an almost hysterical emphasis of "the comparative *state of innocence* of my country folk."

Truly enough, this preoccupation may have been strengthened by influences outside the old view. The endowment of innocence for heroes and heroines alike had been present in the English novels of his period in a fanciful extreme, and it was not unnatural for the son of the elder Henry James to be concerned with moral and ethereal qualities. Truly enough too, his portrayals often reach far beyond simple effects of contrast and comprise a revelation of moral beauty transcending national considerations altogether; and the pattern was often broken by gross contradictions and incongruities. Yet innocence as drawn by Henry James remains rooted in an established idea. In *The American* he wrote the complete fable, with an altered ending.

3

Even the title was a fulfillment. Who ever heard of a significant English novel called *The Englishman* or an excellent French novel called *Le Français?* The simple and aggressive stress belonged to an imagination perennially engaged by the problem of the national type. The name Newman had significance, faintly partaking of that comic symbolism by which a hero in one of the Yankee fables was called Jedidiah Homebred.

At the opening of the story, as Newman strolled through the Salon Carré examining masterpieces, James declared that no one with an eye for types could have failed to perceive that he was an American. "Indeed such an observer might have made an ironic point of the almost ideal completeness with which he filled out the mold of race. . . . He had the flat jaw and firm, dry neck which are frequent in the American type. . . . Long, lean, and muscular, he suggested an intensity of unconscious resistance. . . . His usual attitude and carriage had a liberal looseness; but when, under a special intensity of inspiration, he straightened himself, he looked like a grenadier on parade." Newman was of the familiar build; he had the familiar consciousness of costume; in an ensuing scene he appeared in a blue satin cravat of too light a shade and with a shirt front obtrusively wide. But according to James it was the eye, of a clear cold gray, that told the final story: "an eye in which the unacquainted and the expert were singularly blended"—the innocent and the shrewd. "I can't make you out," said Mrs. Tristram, "whether you are very simple or very deep."

Newman's local origin was never given; though he stemmed from the Yankee, he was not of New England, certainly not of Boston. The Pacific Coast had been the scene of his financial successes; and these were fixed as occurring before 1868, that is, during the period of the gold rush. He might have been in San Francisco or Virginia City with Mark Twain; he had habits of the time and place. "He had sat with western humorists in circles around cast-iron stoves and had seen tall stories grow taller without toppling over, and his imagination had learnt the trick of building straight and high." Young Madame de Bellegarde said that if she had not known who Newman was she could have taken him for a duke—an American duke, the Duke of California. "The way you cover ground!" said Valentin de Bellegarde. However, being as you are a giant, you move naturally in seven league boots. . . . You're a man of the world to a livelier tune than ours."

Fabulous stories were told about Newman. At the great ball given by the Bellegardes he was presented to the Duchess, whose nodding tiara and triple chins and vast expanse of bosom troubled him, and who looked at him "with eyes that twinkled like a pair of polished pinheads in a cushion." "With her little circle of admirers this remarkable woman reminded him of a Fat Lady at a fair." "I've heard all sorts of extraordinary things about you," she said, fixing her small unwinking gaze upon him. "*Voyons,* are they true? . . . Oh, you've had your *légende.* You've had a career of the most chequered, the most *bizarre.* What's that about your having founded a city some ten years ago in the great West, a city which contains today half a million inhabitants? Isn't it half a million, messieurs? You're exclusive proprietor of the wonderful place and are consequently fabulously rich, and you'd be richer still if you didn't grant lands and houses free of rent to all newcomers who'll pledge themselves never to smoke cigars. At this game, in three years, we're told, you're going to become President of all the Americas."

"He liked doing things that involved his paying for people," said James; "the vulgar truth is he enjoyed 'treating' them. . . . Just as it was a gratification to him to be nobly dressed, just so it was a private satisfaction (for he kept the full flavor of it quite delicately to himself) to see people occupied and amused at his pecuniary expense and by his profuse interposition. To set a large body of them in motion and transport them to a distance, to have special conveyances, to charter railway-carriages and steamboats, harmonized with his relish for bold processes and made hospitality the potent thing it should ideally be."

Newman preserved a negligent air in such enterprises just as he casually gave an order for copies of half a dozen masterpieces to Mademoiselle Noémie in order to provide money for her *dot.* But he clearly saw the direction of Mademoiselle Noémie's purpose when she announced to him that her paintings were daubs in the hope that her candor might bring her a more considerable profit. He passed over her declaration with his customary blankness, dropping into some hidden cavern of his mind the revelation that his taste had been at fault. "You've got something it worries me to have missed," said Valentin. "It's not money, it's not even brains, though evidently yours have been excellent for your purpose. It's not your superfluous stature, though I should have rather liked to be a couple of inches taller. It's a sort of air you have of being imperturbably, being irremovably and indestructibly (that's the thing) at home in the world. When I was a boy my father assured me it was by just such an air that people recognized a Bellegarde. He called my attention to it. He didn't advise me to cultivate it; he said that as we grew up it always came of itself. . . . But you who, as I understand it, have made and sold articles of vulgar household use—you strike me —in a fashion of your own, as a man who stands about at his ease and looks straight over ever so many high walls. I seem to see you move everywhere like a big stockholder on his favorite railroad. You make me feel awfully my want of shares. And yet the world used to be supposed to be ours. What is it I miss?"

Newman's reply was resounding, and might have been taken out of many an American oration of the past. "It's the proud consciousness of honest toil, of having produced something yourself that somebody has been willing to pay for—since that's the definite measure. Since you speak of my washtubs—which were lovely—isn't it just they and their loveliness that make up my good conscience?"

"Oh, no; I've seen men who had gone beyond washtubs, who had made mountains of soap—strong-smelling yellow soap, in great bars; and they've left me perfectly cold."

"Then it's just the regular treat of being an American citizen," said Newman. "That sets a man right up."

The tone, as one knows Newman, was jocose, with an admixture of serious conviction. It was the comic belligerent tone that had spread through the assertive nationalism of the Yankee fables; and James seemed to enjoy the mixed quality. He glossed over nothing, writing with gusto of Newman's early preoccupation with money, which had also been dominant in Yankee swapping and bargaining. He admitted that his hero considered "what he had been placed in the world for was . . . simply to gouge a fortune, the bigger the better, out of its hard material. This idea completely filled his horizon and contented his imagination. Upon the uses of money, upon what one might do with a life into which one had succeeded in injecting the golden stream, he had up to the eve of his fortieth year very scantly reflected."

"I cared for money-making, but I have never cared so very terribly about money," Newman told Madame de Cintré with expansive confidence, launching into self-revelation. As he sat in her drawing-room he stretched his legs; his questions had a simple ease. "Don't you find it rather lifeless here," he inquired, "so far from the street?" "Your house is tremendously old then?" he asked a little later. When Valentin had found the date, 1627, over the mantelpiece, Newman announced roundly, "Your house is of a very fine style of architecture." "Are you interested in questions of architecture?" asked Valentin. "Well, I took the trouble this summer to examine—as well as I can calculate—some four hundred and seventy churches. Do you call that interested?" "Perhaps you're interested in religion," answered his host. Newman considered for a moment. "Not actively." He spoke as though it were a railroad or a mine; and he seemed quickly to feel the apparent lack of nicety. To correct this he turned to Madame de Cintré and asked whether she was a Roman Catholic.

Satire invaded the portrait—a deep satire—but James loved Newman. Toward the end of his life he spoke of his young "infatuation" with his subject, and though by this he particularly meant an artistic absorption, his personal devotion was likewise plain. He revealed his hero as a man whom Madame de Cintré could love—that creature "tall, slim, imposing, gentle, half *grande dame* and half an angel; a mixture of 'type' and simplicity, of the eagle and the dove." It was Newman's goodness which drew her; but this alone would not have sufficed for the daughter of an old race if goodness had not been joined with an essential dignity.

But while Madame de Cintré and Valentin perceived the genuine stature of Newman others of his family remembered their prejudices. When Madame de Bellegarde first received Newman, knowing his wish to marry her daughter, she sat small and immovable. "You're an American," she said presently. "I've seen several Americans." "There are several in Paris," said Newman gaily. "Oh, really? It was in England I saw these, or somewhere else; not in Paris. I think it must have been in the Pyrenees many years ago. I'm told your ladies are very pretty. One of these ladies was very pretty—with such a wonderful complexion. She presented me with a note of introduction from some one—I forget whom—and she sent with it a note of her own. I kept her letter a long time afterwards, it was so strangely expressed. I used to know some of the phrases by heart. But I've forgotten them now—it's so many years ago. Since then I've seen no more Americans. I think my daughter-in-law has; she's a great gadabout; she sees every one."

Even the gentle Madame de Cintrĕ furthered the critical note, perhaps from a mild notion that Newman would be amused. "I've been telling Madame de la Rochefidèle that you're an American," she said as he came up to her in her salon. "It interests her greatly. Her favorite uncle went over with the French troops to help you in your battles in the last century, and she has always, in consequence, wanted greatly to see one of your people. But she has never succeeded until tonight. You're the first—to her knowledge—that she has ever looked upon." Madame de la Rochefidèle lifted an antique eye-glass, looked at Newman from head to foot, and at last said something to which he listened with deference but could not understand, for Madame de la Rochefidèle had an aged and cadaverous face with a falling of the lower jaw that impede her utterance. Madame de Cintré offered an interpretation. "Madame de la Rochefidèle says she's convinced that she must have seen Americans without knowing it." Newman considered that she might have seen many things without knowing it; and the French visitor, again speaking in an inarticulate guttural, said that she wished she *had* known it. This interchange was followed by the polite approach of a very elderly gentleman who declared that almost the first person he had looked upon after coming into the world was an American, no less than the celebrated Doctor Franklin. But he too, in the circumstances, could hardly have known it.

The animus of James, who has so often been pictured as a happy expatriate, mounted as such episodes recurred. At the great reception given by the Bellegardes for Newman after the announcement of his engagement to Madame de Cintré, he was introduced to their friends by her elder brother. "If the Marquis was going about as a bear-leader," wrote James stormily, "the general impression was that the bear was a very fair imitation of humanity." James even made a comment on worldly society which might have derived from one of the early wise, wandering Yankees; its like had been heard in *Fashion.* "Every one gave Newman extreme attention: every one lighted up for him regardless, as he would have said, of expense: every one looked at him with that fraudulent intensity of good society which puts out its bountiful hand but keeps the fingers closed over the coin." Nearly fifty years later James could betray an enduring bitterness. "Great and gilded was the whole trap set, in fine, for his wary freshness and into which it would blunder upon its fate."

When the catastrophe came, when the Bellegardes broke their word and Claire was commanded to withdraw from her engagement, Newman was rejected and publicly humiliated because he was American: they found themselves unable to tolerate that circumstance in relation to their family. He was rejected on the score of manners—the old and vexing score. He should have known that to ask the old Marquise to parade through her own rooms on his arm the evening of the ball would be almost an affront. When the journey was accomplished and she said, "This is enough, sir," he might have seen the gulf widening before his eyes. His commercial connections were held against him; and James pointed the irony of the objection. The Bellegardes were shown as sordidly commercial; in shrewdness they far outdistanced Newman. He was beaten indeed because he was incapable of suspecting the treachery accumulating against him. At the end Newman was unable to maintain his purpose of revenge against the Bellegardes; he destroyed the scrap of evidence which would have proved their earlier inhuman crime. His act is not overstressed; a deep-lying harshness gave stringency to Newman's generous impulses. But the contrast is firmly kept.

With all the preordained emphasis these characters are rounded and complete. The integrity of Valentin was placed against the unscrupulous coldness of his older brother. Claire, with her lovely purity, lights the black picture created by the Marquise. If the balance seems to be tipped down by the inclusion of Mademoiselle Nioche and her deplorable father, there is always Mrs. Bread. As a great artist James had moved immeasurably beyond the simple limits of the original fable. A genuine tragedy was created whose elements were tangled deep in inalienable differences. At the last Newman was unable to understand either the character or the decision of the woman he so deeply loved. Circling across the sea and the American continent, he returned again to Paris by an irresistible compulsion, and at twilight one evening, a gray time, walked to the convent of the Carmelite order in the Rue d'Enfer and gazed at the high blank wall which surrounded it. Within, his beloved was forever enclosed, engaged in rites which he could never understand, withdrawn for reasons which he could not fathom. He could never pass beyond that wall, in body or in spirit. The image was final, and became a dramatic metaphor: in the spelling of the old fable the outcome had changed from triumph to defeat. Defeat had become at last an essential part of the national portraiture.

4

Almost invariably the opening moods and even the later sequences of James's novels were those of comedy. He instinctively chose the open sunny level; the light handling of his early *Confidence*, uncomplicated by the international situation, shows what he could do in maintaining this when his materials permitted. He ran indeed through a wide gamut of humor, from that of the happy and easy view and a delicate satire to a broad caricature and irony. Social comedy appeared in Henry James. For the first time an American writer drew a society and infused his drawing with an acute sense of human disparities. Yet the aggregation of his novels does not spell comedy, but a kind of *tragédie Américaine*, which was in large part a tragedy of manners. "I have the instincts—have them deeply—if I haven't the forms of a high old civilization," Newman told Claire de Cintré; but the instincts, if he possessed them, were not enough. *Daisy Miller*, bringing down a storm of angry reproof upon James's head, was a classic instance which he multiplied with variations of subtlety and range.

Defeat for the American adventurer was new, at least in wide transcription. Triumph had hitherto been the appointed destiny in American portraiture, except for vagabonds and common adventurers. Yet with all the tragic implications the ultimate ending of these latter-day fables was not that of tragedy. In the midst of his final encounters with the forces of the opposition Newman gathered his energies; his spirits rose. When he confronted the Marquis de Bellegarde he "had a singular sensation; he felt his sense of wrong almost brim into gaiety." He could laugh during the momentous interview with Mrs. Bread; at one moment in their plotting his face "lighted with the candor of childhood." The mood was unreasoning, beyond reason: it was a typical mood, that of resilience under opposition or criticism. Finally, after all the conflict, after his searching and baffled effort to understand inscrutable forces, this mood was resolved into something subtler and more enduring than resilience. When Newman stood before the wall that forever enclosed Claire de Cintré "the barren stillness of the place represented somehow his own release from ineffectual desire." Touching the nadir of despair and disillusionment, he was "disburdened"—free at last from those dark personalities by whom he had been cruelly wronged. He reached a moment of profound recognition, not perhaps of the inner character of the forces that worked against him—these he could never understand—but of his own final plight. He achieved that laden balance of mind and feeling from which an enduring philosophical comedy may spring. As one sees Newman beyond the end of the book he has become a far graver character, but for him something of humor might play quietly once more.

Again and again James pictured this low-keyed humor of defeat. For Isabel Archer more than one way of escape lay open; fronting these possibilities, she made the choice which meant renunciation; and the outcome is not tragic, for all the wrench which it produces at the end, since James has revealed that free poise and nobility of her character which made renunciation inevitable and acceptance of her lot tolerable. Even *The Wings of the Dove* cannot be called tragedy. Milly Theale learned the worst there was to know of those to whom she was attached, their betrayal, their base purpose; yet with knowledge she still could keep a magnanimous love. James repeated this stress again in the recognition which finally lay between Kate Croy and Merton Densher. Each had plumbed a deep and even dangerous knowledge of the other; yet an indissoluble acceptance remained between them; and their final alliance had a touch of the secure upward swing which belongs to comedy.

In comedy reconcilement with life comes at the point when to the tragic sense only an inalienable difference or dissension with life appears. Recognition is essential for the play of a profound comedy; barriers must be down; perhaps defeat must lie at its base. Yet the outcome in these novels was in a sense the traditional outcome, for triumph was comprised in it; but the sphere had altered from outer circumstances to the realm of the mind and spirit; and triumph was no longer blind and heedless, but achieved by difficult and even desperate effort.

In this outcome James transcended the nationalistic altogether—that obsession which had had so long a history. Yet in the aggregate of his novels he repeated a significant portion of the old fable. He showed that the American was in truth what the belligerent Yankee had always declared him to be, a wholly alien, disparate, even a new character. In the end the primary concern of James was with that character; and he kept a familiar touch of the fabulous in his narratives. "I had been plotting arch-romance without knowing it," he said of *The American;* and by romance he meant what Hawthorne had meant, life with a touch of the marvelous, an infusion which can be apprehended only imperfectly by the sense of fact. Romance appeared in the generality and scale which James gave to his characters and to his situations. Such titles as *The Wings of the Dove* and *The Golden Bowl* suggest a poetized conception completing the romantic character of the themes; and his handling is kept free from complicated circumstance. Poetry indeed overspread much of James's writing. Like that of the popular fabulists, it was packed with metaphor. "The morning was like a clap of hands." "She carried her three and thirty years as a light-wristed Hebe might have carried a brimming wine-cup." His figures could also be ironical; the romantic feeling is constantly enclosed by a close drawing. Recognition is fundamental in all of James's portraiture; yet a basic poetry of outline and expression remains clear, most of all in his later novels. Few writers have had so deep a sense of the poetry of character; and his poetical penetration was the rarer achievement because his approaches were not those of the primary emotions.

In commentary James once spoke of one of the women whom he had drawn as "unaware of life." Elsewhere he wondered "what it might distinguishably be in their own flourishing Order that could *keep* them, the passionless pilgrims, so unaware?" "Passionless" surely was not meant to include his major characters; yet even they could not be called passionate in the sense that the characters in *Wuthering Heights* are passionate; it is significant of his obsessions that elsewhere James could give the attribute "passionate" to a pilgrim in quest of the past. For the most part emotion in these Americans in his wide gallery is frustrated, buried, or lost. Instead, renunciation, tenderness, pity, are likely to be dominant among them. The finest of these feelings do not belong to the primary emotions; they are restrained or delicate or withdrawn. These characters indeed are of an established native mold; this diminution had prevailed elsewhere. In a fashion James himself revealed the same qualities; a profound tenderness suffuses the greatest of his writing, but not the compulsion of a deep and natural, simple emotion. He gains power by integrity, by a close intensity of view, often by intensity of the mind. His portrayals gain every possible concentration from the high art by which they are revealed. "Dramatize! dramatize!" he said again and again; and the dramatic quality belonged to his writings at every point, in the ready immediacy of the talk, in the swift juxtapositions, in swift and daring ellipses, particularly in his later novels. At one point he considered that the drama was his true form. "I feel at last as if I had found my *real* form, which I am capable of carrying far, and for which the pale little art of fiction, as I have practiced it, has been, for me, but a limited and restricted substitute." James failed in writing drama; nothing of true dramatic expression had appeared in American literature, and he was not to transcend its tendency. He necessarily failed, lacking a depth of simple emotion; the approach to the drama had been made before without completion, perhaps for the same reason. James returned to the novel, and kept the dramatic organization.

The highly conscious artist was uppermost in Henry James; and he joined in the traditional bias toward the inward view. Strangely enough, though he had no New England ancestry and was likely to be positive in his declarations to the contrary, he came closer than any of the earlier American writers to that introspective analysis which had belonged to the Puritan, closer even than Hawthorne. His scrutiny of motives, while delicate, was intense. He never used that direct revelation of elements in the stream of consciousness which had been ventured by Whitman and Hawthorne before him; yet his later novels are full of the unsaid and understated; they are full of complex moods and states of inner feeling revealed by the slightest and most ephemeral of notations. Whether or not James was subject to some untraceable Puritan influence, whether he touched popular sources, whether perhaps he gained greatly from the initial experiments of Hawthorne and Poe, his novels vastly amplified this new subject of the mind lying submerged beneath the scope of circumstance, which had long engaged the American imagination.

5

Nearly always the mark of that era in which an artist is young will in some way lie upon his work, however far he may advance into the future. Henry James bore the mark of that deeply experimental era which came to a culmination in the late '40's and early '50's. Like Poe, Hawthorne, Melville, Whitman, he performed that difficult and elliptical feat by which a writer both invades a province and occupies it. Like them he was in a sense a primary writer.

No American before him had made a full imaginative approach to living characters and the contemporary scene; the view hitherto had been mainly the retrospective view. He greatly extended the areas of native comedy; he all but created a new subject for the novel in his stress upon the inward view; he discovered the international scene, as Van Wyck Brooks has said, "for literature." There is irony in the fact that so wide and subtle an accomplishment should have been produced within a tradition that still bore the print of the pioneer. There is a further irony in the circumstance that the American character should first have been fully realized within the European scene. This remoteness has been considered a flight and a loss; and truly enough to have perceived that character with equal amplitude against the native background would have meant an immense gain in imaginative understanding. Yet James's choice fulfilled the consciousness of a fundamental relationship; only the denial had been abortive.

The great experimental writer is like to betray signs of incompletion, to cover more than one era, to show hesitation as well as an unmistakable security. James showed some of these signs. They are apparent in the great division between his later and his earlier writing, and in the incalculable abysms of his later style. In a strange fashion after the middle of his career he showed a partial reversal of his sense of language, which took on an extreme gentility even while it attempted that colloquialism which had been part of the American tradition. He strove for elegances like a minor writer of the '30's who sought to prove that Americans too could enter the stately domain of English literature. He used quotation marks to set off such phrases as "detective story," and the attempted grace of his movements through the great morass of his words was often elephantine. In his final revisions of the earlier novels he often emasculated a vigorous speech. The result was a form of writing which was neither English nor American in character. Yet few experimental writers have maintained so fine an artistry or encompassed with that artistry so great a scope. His failures are minor failures within a great original accomplishment.

Howells was the only other measurable American writer of this time to employ the novelistic form; the concerns of Howells were largely regional; he was engaged by small portions of the American scene and of the American character; he never fused these into an unmistakable and moving whole. The real situation in *Silas Lapham* lay between the Yankee and the Bostonian, between Lapham and the Coreys, between Penelope and young Corey. Here were elements of social comedy or tragedy, which Howells pictured in one scene which remains a high scene in American humor, full of comedy indeed, full of pathos and hurt—the scene of the Coreys' dinner-party. But Howells evaded the full scope of the indicated differences, packing Lapham off to Vermont and Penelope and young Corey to South America. He made the same evasion in *The Lady of the Aroostook,* never showing Lydia in any prolonged contact with the superior Americans with whom her destinies were linked, never exploring the social situation beyond its superficial aspects, and again at the end sending his two major characters to far parts, where the manners and speech of the country girl need trouble nobody, and where Howells at any rate was not troubled by ensuing complications.

In spite of lapses in local observation, Howells had a striking aptitude for seizing essential elements in the native tradition: he knew the Yankee, the backwoodsman, the itinerant revivalist. His narratives are full of prime comic sketches, full of a racy contemporary and local speech. They reveal too that acute and expressive awareness with which the American constantly viewed himself, his fellow countrymen, his nation. His young men are always theorizing about America, and often have superior attitudes. "What a very American thing!" exclaims one of them when he heard Lydia saying, "I want to know." "It's incredible," he continued. "Who in the world can she be?" The American quarrel with America, the product of a long self-consciousness, was beginning.

Howells had it in his power to draw social comedy of breadth and the first order, for disparities of background were included within his view; he was grounded within the comic tradition. He might have been the great artist to picture the American against the native scene, complementing the portrayals of James abroad. He had all the gifts except a passionate concern with his subject. Whether from lassitude or from a fundamental lack of imagination he never truly explored his materials; not one of his novels can be put beside *The Portrait of a Lady* or *The American.* He veered from one theme to another, from one locale to another. His novels were in the end not novels at all but an invaluable collection of minor notations on the American character.

Henry James stands alone in his time, not wholly to be accounted for, not in any immediate sense productive as an influence. He began writing in the '60's; his work was hardly a force among other writers for nearly half a century. In later years other American writers have followed him in using the international scene; yet his other great achievement, that of portraying the inner mind, cannot be said to have given any notable impetus to the American novel. It is abroad that the implications of his work have been pushed to their furthest boundaries. Proust and Joyce, Dorothy Richardson and Virginia Woolf, may or may not have been influenced by James; but they have carried the whole stress of an American intention far beyond anything achieved by American writers, in their portrayal of the inner consciousness.

The fate of Henry James has been that of other primary writers within the American tradition. Each of these had stormed some battlement without a following sequence of writers. The prolific energies that create an entire literature were lacking in this long period, though a widely flung pattern had been created which had freshness and even magnificence.

HERBERT READ: Surrealism and the Romantic Principle*

JUNE, 1936. After a winter long drawn out into bitterness and petulance, a month of torrid heat, of sudden efflorescence, of clarifying storms. In this same month the International Surrealist Exhibition broke over London, electrifying the dry intellectual atmosphere, stirring our sluggish minds to wonder, enchantment and derision. The press, unable to appreciate the significance of a movement of such unfamiliar features, prepared an armoury of mockery, sneers and insults. The duller desiccated weeklies, no less impelled to anticipate the event, commissioned their polyglot gossips, their blasé globe-trotters, their old-boy-scouts, to adopt their usual pose of I know all, don't be taken in, there's nothing new under the sun—a pose which merely reflected the general lack of intellectual curiosity in this country. But in the event they were all deceived; their taunts fell on deaf ears, and though for a time there was no lack of the laughing jackass—an animal extinct in most parts of the world and even in this country generally emerging only from beyond the pale of the ineffectual Cheviots—in the outcome people, and mostly young people, came in their hundreds and their thousands not to sneer, but to learn, to find enlightenment, to live. When the foam and froth of society and the press had subsided, we were left with a serious public of scientists, artists, philosophers and socialists. Ten years have now passed by, bringing with them death, destruction, and the diaspora of another world war; but that serious public still remains.

From the moment of its birth Surrealism was an international phenomenon—the spontaneous generation of an international and fraternal *organism* in total contrast to the artificial manufacture of a collective *organisation* such as the League of Nations. It would therefore be contrary to the nature of the movement to present, as some have suggested, a specifically English version of Surrealism. We who in England have supported this movement have had no other desire than to pool our resources in the general effort. Nevertheless, there is an English contribution to be made to this effort, and its strength and validity can only be shown by tracing its sources in the native tradition of our art and literature. The evidences on which we base the claims of Surrealism are scattered through the centuries, the partial and incoherent revelations of permanent human characteristics; and nowhere are these evidences so plentiful as in England. My main purpose in this essay will be to present this English evidence, to unite it with the general theory of Surrealism, and to reaffirm on this wider basis the truths which other writers, above all André Breton, have already declared.

In an Introduction which I contributed to the catalogue of the exhibition I asserted, in the cryptic and exiguous manner demanded by the occasion, that "superrealism in general is the romantic principle in art." It will be noted

* "Surrealism and the Romantic Principle" first appeared as the Introduction to *Surrealism* (1936) by André Breton and others, and is reprinted here in a specially revised version by permission of Mr. Read and Faber and Faber, Ltd. Mr. Read (b. 1893) is the author of *Reason and Romanticism* (1926), *English Prose Style* (1928), *Phases of English Poetry* (1928), *The Sense of Glory* (1929), *Julien Benda and the New Humanism* (1930), *Wordsworth* (1930), *Form in Modern Poetry* (1932), *Collected Essays in Literary Criticism* (1938), and *Poetry and Anarchism* (1939).

that I used a variation of the word "surrealism." When it first became essential to find an English equivalent for the original French word, I made an attempt to establish "superrealism." Pedantically, euphonically and logically I think I was right; "superrealism" is not only simple to say, but self-explanatory to the meanest intelligence ("super" is slang, "sur" is a purely grammatical affix). But I was defeated by that obscure instinct which determines word-formation in the life of a language, and for which I have the greatest respect. The very clarity of the term "superrealism" was against it; the public wanted a strange and not too intelligible word for a strange and not too intelligible thing; and I bow to that decree. But I do not propose to abandon the word "superrealism" altogether; I propose rather to make a distinction between superrealism in general and Surrealism in particular, employing the first word for the tentative and historical manifestations of what has now become a conscious and deliberate artistic principle. And those tentative and historical manifestations of superrealism I shall identify with some of the essential characteristics of romanticism—but of romanticism understood in a certain strict and not too comprehensive sense.

No critic of experience will return to a discussion of the terms "romanticism" and "classicism" with anything but extreme reluctance; no subject has provoked so much weary logomachy since the Scholastics argued themselves out on the question of nominalism. I only take up the discussion again (eating my own words in the process) because I think that Surrealism has settled it. So long as romanticism and classicism were considered as alternative attitudes, rival camps, professions of *faith*, an interminable struggle was in prospect, with the critics as profiteers. But what in effect Surrealism claims to do is to resolve the conflict—not, as I formerly hoped, by establishing a synthesis which I was prepared to call "reason" or "humanism" —but by liquidating classicism, by showing its complete irrelevance, its anaesthetic effect, its contradiction of the creative impulse. Classicism, let it be stated without further preface, represents for us now, and has always represented, the forces of oppression. Classicism is the intellectual counterpart of political tyranny. It was so in the ancient world and in the medieval empires; it was renewed to express the dictatorships of the Renaissance and has ever since been the official creed of capitalism. Wherever the blood of martyrs stains the ground, there you will find a doric column or perhaps a statue of Minerva.

Academic critics have not been unaware of this alignment, but have united, of course, to give living colours to the corpse they have embalmed. I have often praised Sir Herbert Grierson's clean handling of this problem; like Brunetière, whose main line of demarcation he follows, he is not altogether unsympathetic towards romanticism, but there is a question of values involved which must be challenged. A classical literature, he writes, "is the product of a nation and a generation which has consciously achieved a definite advance, moral, political, intellectual; and is filled with the belief that its view of life is more natural, human, universal and wise than that from which it has escaped. It has effected a synthesis which enables it to look round on life with a sense of its wholeness, its unity in variety; and the work of the artist is to give expression to that consciousness; hence the solidity of his work and hence too its definiteness, and in the hands of great artists its beauty. . . . The work of the classical artist is to give individual expression, the beauty of form, to a body of common sentiments and thoughts which he shares with his audience, thoughts and views which have for his generation the validity of universal truths.

"Classical and romantic—these are the systole and diastole of the human heart in history. They represent on the one hand our need of order, of synthesis, of a comprehensive yet definite, therefore *exclusive* as well as inclusive, ordering of thought and feeling and action; and on the other hand the inevitable finiteness of every human synthesis, the discovery that, in Carlyle's metaphor, our clothes no longer fit us, that the classical has become the conventional, that our spiritual aspirations are being starved, or that our secular impulses are 'cribb'd, cabin'd, and confined.' "[1]

The particular danger of this argument is due to its false dialecticism. A certain type of society is regarded as a "synthesis," a natural order or

[1] *The Background of English Literature.* London, 1925. Pp. 266, 287-8.

balance of forces, a state of equilibrium; and any deviation from that standard is regarded as abnormal, degenerate or revolutionary. Actually such types of society merely represent the dominance of one particular class—the economic dominance and therefore the cultural dominance of that class. For the stability of such a society a certain uniformity of ideas and modes of expression is a fundamental necessity; and the less novelty these ideas and modes of expression show the better. This explains the constant return to the norms of classical art; for these norms (in architecture we call them the "orders") are the typical patterns of order, proportion, symmetry, equilibrium, harmony and of all static and inorganic qualities. They are intellectual concepts which control or repress the vital instincts on which growth and therefore change depend, and in no sense represent a freely determined preference, but merely an imposed ideal.

The fallacy we are discussing is logical in its origin. It is a sophism by means of which two terms are conceived as dialectical opposites whereas actually they represent types of action and reaction. This is a very important distinction, and its neglect is the cause of much confusion. In dialectics the thesis and the antithesis are both objective facts, and the necessity for a resolution or synthesis is due to the real existence of a contradiction. But "classic" and "romantic" do not represent such a contradiction. They correspond rather to the husk and the seed, the shell and the kernel. There is a principle of life, of creation, of liberation, and that is the romantic spirit; there is a principle of order, of control and of repression, and that is the classical spirit. Naturally there is some purpose in the latter principle—the instincts are curbed in the interest of some particular ideal or set of values; but on analysis it always resolves into the defence of some particular structure of society, the perpetuation of the rule of some particular class. To identify romanticism with revolt as Grierson does is true enough as an historical generalisation; but it merely distorts the values involved if such revolt is conceived in purely literary or academic terms. It would be much nearer the truth to identify romanticism with the artist and classicism with society; classicism being the political concept of art to which the artist is expected to conform.

It may be as well to forestall at once the criticism that on this showing the artist is merely the individualist in conflict with society. To a certain extent, as I have shown elsewhere,[2] this is true; the mental personality of the artist is originally determined by a failure in social adaptation. But his whole effort is directed towards a reconciliation with society, and what he offers to society is not a bagful of his own tricks, his idiosyncrasies, but rather some knowledge of the secrets to which he has had access, the secrets of the self which are buried in every man alike, but which only the sensibility of the artist can reveal to us in all their actuality. This "self" is not the personal possession we imagine it to be; it is largely made up of elements from the unconscious, and the more we learn about the unconscious, the more collective it appears to be—in fact, "a body of common sentiments and thoughts . . . universal truths" such as Grierson assumes to be the exclusive concern of the classical artist. But whereas the universal truths of classicism may be merely the temporal prejudices of an epoch, the universal truths of romanticism are coeval with the evolving consciousness of mankind.

It is in this sense, then, that Surrealism is a reaffirmation of the romantic principle; and though poets and painters in all ages have clung to a belief in the inspirational and even the obsessional nature of their gifts, repudiating in deeds if not in words the rigid bonds of classical theory, it is only now, with the aid of modern dialectics and modern psychology, in the name of Marx and Freud, that they have found themselves in a position to put their beliefs and practices on a scientific basis, thereby initiating a continuous and deliberate creative activity whose only laws are the laws of its own dynamics.

Before passing on to a more precise examination of the romantic principle as actually manifested in English art and literature, there is one further interpretation of the classic-romantic antithesis which is worth referring to, especially as it finds its justification in modern psychology —I mean the theory that the two terms correspond to the general distinction between "extravert" and "introvert" types of personality. The comparison is valid enough if it has refer-

[2] *Art and Society*, Chap. VI.

ence to the personalities involved; what is questionable is the very existence of such a type as an extravert *artist.* To the degree in which he becomes extravert the artist, we would say, ceases to be, in any essential sense of the word, an artist. Now admittedly there is much in the process of producing a work of art which involves, or may involve, an objective attitude towards the materials the artist is using; only the purely automatic text or drawing is purely subjective, and though the Surrealist insists on the significance of such automatic expression, he is far from asserting that all art must of necessity be produced under such conditions. What he does assert, however, is the absolute impossibility of producing a work of art by the conscious exercise of talents. The notion that a work of art can be created by observing a set of rules is only to be compared with the notion that a human being can be produced in a test-tube.

"Verbal and graphic automatism," Breton has said, "only represents a *limit* towards which the poet or artist should tend." The opposed limit is represented by all those "arts of poetry," those academic discourses on painting, in which various ages have sought to codify for all time the laws of art. Between these limits we find the whole range of aesthetic expression, but it is towards the limit of automatism, and away from the limit of rational control, that we find the most enduring vitality, the words which live when poet is dead, when ever his name is forgotten—

A rose-red city half as old as time

—a single line surviving from the complete works of a poet and surviving precisely by virtue of its irrationality.

It is very difficult to determine the factors which lead to the survival of any particular work of art. There is a considerable element of chance, even under modern conditions of publishing and propaganda. We know that contemporary judgment is very uncertain, very arbitrary; every age has its Ossians and there may still be Donnes to be redeemed from a neglected past. We ascribe this fickleness of public estimation to changes in sensibility, but sensibility itself does not change, only the control of it. The sensibility which appreciated the poems of Donne at the time of their first appearance was lively and direct; it needed the colossal irrelevance of a Johnsonian intellect and the general diffusion of a rational spirit to throw them into obscurity. The sensibility which we have now recovered and by virtue of which we once more appreciate the poetry of Donne is the identical sensibility for which his poems were written; and it is no gust of fashion which has re-established his fame, but a revival of poetic sensibility itself—the same revival which has once more placed Shakespeare at the utmost pinnacle of fame, which has given Blake his due eminence and has secured immediate recognition for Hopkins and Eliot. No doubt we are age-bound like the rest and our standards are relative to our circumstances; but it is difficult to imagine, in any form of society congenial to our elementary demands of economic security and intellectual liberty, any return to the standards which tended to exalt a Dryden or a Pope above Shakespeare, and which misled so genuine a poet as Milton into the barren wastes of his later works.

Some recognition of the truth which I am affirming—the identity of art and romanticism—has been given by the philosophers of art; not by all philosophers, but particularly by those who have shown the greatest appreciation of art, or who have been like Plato, great artists themselves. Plato's description of the poet in *Ion* is well known; I have quoted it before, but I think it should be read again in the present context. Socrates is the speaker:

"For all good poets, epic as well as lyric, compose their beautiful poems not by art, but because they are inspired and possessed. And as the Corybantian revellers when they dance are not in their right mind, so the lyric poets are not in their right mind when they are composing their beautiful strains; but when falling under the power of music and metre they are inspired and possessed; like Bacchic maidens who draw milk and honey from the rivers when they are under the influence of Dionysus but not when they are in their right mind. And the soul of the lyric poet does the same, as they themselves say; for they tell us that they bring songs from honeyed fountains, culling them out of the gardens and dells of the Muses; they, like the bees, winging their way from flower to flower. And this is true. For the poet is a light and winged and holy thing, and there is no invention in him until he has been inspired and is out of his senses, and the mind is no longer in him: when he has not attained to this state, he is powerless and is unable to utter his oracles." [3]

It is pointless to observe that because of their irrational character Plato excluded poets from his ideal republic. Within the logic of his rational philosophy, this was inevitable; just as later it was inevitable that Hegel, for quite similar reasons, should come to the conclusion that "the fair days of Greek art, as also the golden time of the later middle ages, are over." Both philosophers held the view that a reflective, idealistic and ratiocinative culture was not merely desirable, but actually represented a higher stage in human evolution. They were both right in considering that the sensuous phenomena of art—the completely irrational basis of the imaginative faculty—are inconsistent with such a reflective culture. But what we now assert with the strongest conviction is our disbelief in either the inevitability or desirability of such a culture. The whole evidence of history, as well as of modern psychology, causes us to reject without hesitation such a fool's paradise of idealism. For good or for evil the instinctive and impulsive components of our being are irreducible and irreplaceable, and we ignore them or repress them at our peril. Not merely the neuroses of individuals result from such repression, but there is more and more reason to believe that the mass hysteria manifested, for example, in such a nation as Germany, is the collective aspect of general repressions. The only absolutely pacifist races (if any such still exist) are those which live in a golden age of hedonism such as, apparently, the Minoan civilisation enjoyed for many centuries. Unfortunately we do not know enough about the Minoan civilisation to relate its freedom from war to, for example, its freedom from morality; but we are beginning to know sufficient about our own civilisation to be sure that war has no simple explanation in economic forces, but is most probably not unrelated to the frustration of certain primitive impulses during childhood, a frustration which is prolonged and reinforced by adult codes of morality. War is, in theory as in fact, the correlative of religion. Above all, the Christian religion in its Calvinistic rigour has induced the bloodiest epoch in the world's history. Piety and asceticism are inevitably accompanied by masochism and sadism, and the more Christianity has been deprived of a ritualistic and occult indulgence of the senses, rationalising itself in the form of moral precepts and social conventions, the deeper the world has plunged into compensatory orgies of hatred and bloodshed.[4]

Those who have not experienced war at first hand may perhaps entertain illusions about its comparative evil; they may entertain the idea, that is to say, that even its modern intensity of horror is sanctioned by some nobler effects of heroism, of national awakening, of personal regeneration. Such a belief is a pestilential idiocy. There is in modern war neither grace nor dignity. It is mad and inconsequential in its inception; beyond the scope of human control in its conduct—a dreary shattering of human flesh in conditions of physical and mental disgust, a long agony which can only be ended in exhaustion. In spite of this truth, which must be evident to millions of people, we today contemplate a political situation (it would be more exact to say a psychological situation) whose inevitable outcome seems to be another world war even more stupid, more purposeless and more horrible than the last. Everywhere in all countries we meet apparently friendly and peaceful human beings; we exchange visits, books, ideas—not to insist too much on manufactures; we slowly build up an international understanding in which there is no thought of anything but mutual help and general well-being—an indivisible peace. Yet in a few days the face of the world may change. Bugles blow, klaxons screech, an immense machine begins to move and we find ourselves segregated, regimented, drafted into armies and navies and workshops. Bull-necked demagogues inject a poisonous propaganda into our minds and then the storm of steel breaks above us; our bodies become so much manure for an acid soil, and our ideas, our aspirations, the whole structure

[3] Jowett's translation.

[4] It is impossible to ignore the evidence on this question presented by Dr. Edward Glover in *War, Sadism and Pacifism* (London, 1933). Cf. also C. G. Jung, *Aufsätze zur Zeitgeschichte* (Zürich, 1946).

61014

of our civilisation, becomes a history which the future may not even record.

The astonishing fact is that men can contemplate such a fate and remain passive. Nothing in the world is so disturbing as human docility. Man is indeed a wild animal tamed; broken in and made to trot obediently in a ring, to respond to every crack of the whip. In Europe, Asia and America, millions of people live below a decent subsistence level; millions, indeed, now exist on the verge of starvation. At the other end of the scale a few thousand people expend three-quarters of the total income of the country. It is true that these few thousand protect themselves with armed forces, but these armed forces are the same flesh and blood as the starving millions. Against the passive resistance of the millions they might fire a few solitary shots, but the blood of their innocent brothers and sisters would spread like a fire of desolation through their ranks, and their guns would be turned against the tyrants of a system which exacted such vicarious suffering.

But the human animal remains docile. He accepts the tips and the kicks, the doles and the charity of these indifferent and cynical masters. Only the fact that history shows that the goad may be driven too deep, that out of extreme suffering will come general revolt—only this melancholy thought saves us from complete despair.

Underlying this condition of humanity are motives no less irrational than those which promote war-mindedness; the capitalist and the socialist no less than the militarist and the pacifist are moved by obscure instincts. Admittedly it is not a very obscure instinct that makes a man desire to triumph over his fellows, to enjoy a position of comparative wealth and ease, to command the admiration of the loveliest women—such desires are elementary and we are only ashamed of them in the degree of our sensibility and altruism. But the individuals who possess this altruism, this sensibility, are certainly not the priests and preceptors whose position and authority is assured by the social system of which they are an integral part. Nothing is simpler to demonstrate than the dependency, in every age, of the official codes of morality on the class interests of those who possess the economic power. The only individuals who protest against injustices—or who make their protest vocal—are in effect the poets and artists of each age, who to the extent that they rely on their imaginative capacities and powers, despise and reject the acquisitive materialism of men of action.[5]

I am not leaving it open for anyone to suggest that in this respect—in its adoption of a revolutionary political attitude, its protest against injustice and inhumanity—Surrealism merely represents a sentimental movement of the heart. Surrealism is anti-rational, but it is equally anti-emotional. If you wish to reduce Surrealism to its foundations you will find the only basic elements on which any useful structure can be built—the basic elements of natural science and psychology. We build on that materialistic basis. But we build. We create. And we have our method of building, our craft of logic, our dialectic.

The philosophical justification of Surrealism is to be found, if anywhere in the past, in Hegel. But it is a Hegel deprived for the most part of those elements which he would have considered of the greatest importance. Just as Marx, for his purposes, turned Hegel upside down, "sloughed off" the mystical form of Hegel's dialectic, so the Surrealist, for his purposes, subjects the philosopher to the same indignity. If I am asked why, in this matter, we should return to Hegel rather than start our philosophy of art afresh, there are various answers to give—answers similar to those which have to be given in the field of political philosophy. One is that Hegel represents a convenient *crux* in philosophy: all previous philosophies seem to meet in him, to be sorted and smelted and reduced to the purest and least contradictory elements of human thought. Hegel is the great scavenger of philosophical systems; he cleans them up and leaves a tidy piece of ground on which we can build. More than that, he provides a scaffolding within which we can build—the scaffold of his dialectic.

This dreaded word *dialectic*—a word which the English-speaking public finds difficult to digest and which even our so-called socialists, with a few exceptions, would willingly forget

[5] It is obvious that the few revolutionary priests who may be included (St. Francis of Assisi, Wycliffe, Huss) were in our sense of the word no less poets than priests.

—this word is actually the name of a very simple and very necessary process of thought. If we consider the natural world, we soon become aware that its most striking characteristic is not permanency, solidity or stability, but continuous change or development. Physicists now affirm that not merely the organic world, not merely this earth we live on, but the whole universe is undergoing a process of continuous change. Dialectics is nothing more than a logical explanation of how such a change takes place. It does not suffice to say that "it grows," or "it decays," "it runs down," "it expands"; these phrases are vague abstractions. The change must take place in a definite way. Between one phase and another of that development there must intervene an active principle, and Hegel suggested that this principle was actually one of opposition and interaction. That is to say, to produce any new situation (i.e., any departure from an existing condition of equilibrium) there must previously exist two elements so opposed to each other and yet so related to each other that a solution or resolution is demanded; such a solution being in effect a new phase of development (temporary state of equilibrium) which preserves some of the elements of the interacting phases, eliminates others, but is qualitatively different from the previously existing state of opposition.

Such is the dialectical logic, elaborated by Hegel for idealistic purposes and brilliantly adapted by Marx for materialistic purposes. As an instrument of thought it enabled Marx to explain the evolution of human society from primitive communism to feudalism and through the various stages of capitalism; it enabled him, moreover, to predict the self-extinction of capitalism and the coming of the socialist state. But that is by the way. What I wish to stress now is that Surrealism is an application of the same logical method to the realm of art. By the dialectical method we can explain the development of art in the past and justify a revolutionary art at the present time.

In dialectical terms we claim that there is a continual state of opposition and interaction between the world of objective fact—the sensational and social world of active and economic existence—and the world of subjective fantasy. This opposition creates a state of disquietude, a lack of spiritual equilibrium, which it is the business of the artist to resolve. He resolves the contradiction by creating a synthesis, a work of art which combines elements from both these worlds, eliminates others, but which for the moment gives us a qualitatively new experience—an experience on which we can dwell with equanimity. Superficial critics may pretend to be unable to distinguish such a qualitatively new state from an ordinary compromise, and it is to be feared that in practice most dialectical solutions are of this kind. But a true synthesis is never a reversion; it is always a progression.

That is the central core of the surrealist claim, and any attempt to discredit or criticise Surrealism must present an adequate philosophical alternative; just as any criticism of dialectical materialism as embodied in the socialism of Marx must present an adequate philosophical alternative. At present any alternatives worthy of our consideration are lacking.

To return for a moment to Hegel. He dealt with the subject of art at such length (in his *Aesthetik*) that one would expect to find there some approach to the dialectical interpretation of art which the Surrealist now advances. Actually we no more find that than, in his other works, we find an anticipation of Marx. Everything, in his philosophy, is sacrificed to the necessity of making "ideas," or states of self-consciousness, the supreme forces in creative development. As Marx observed in his Preface to the first edition of *Kapital,*

"My dialectic method is not only different from the Hegelian, but its direct opposite. To Hegel, the life-process of the human brain, i.e., the process of thinking, which, under the name of 'the Idea,' he even transforms into an independent subject, is the demiurgos of the real world, and the real world is only the external, phenomenal form of 'the Idea.' With me, on the contrary, the ideal is nothing else than the material world reflected by the human mind, and translated into forms of thought."

With the Surrealists, we might also say, the ideal is nothing else than the material world reflected by the human mind, and translated into images. But "reflection" and "translation" are not, for us today, such simple mechanical processes as perhaps Marx implies. For us the process is infinitely complicated: a passage through a series of distorting mirrors and underground labyrinths.

When Hegel generalises his logic in relation to art, the result is not far from our present point of view. In one place he says:

"This universal need for artistic expression (Bedürfniss zur Kunst) is based on the rational impulse in man's nature to exalt both the world of his inner experience and that of nature into the conscious embrace of mind, as an object in which he rediscovers himself. He satisfies the demand of this spiritual freedom by making explicit to his *inner* life all that exists, no less than by giving correspondingly a realised *external* embodiment to the self made thus explicit. And by this reduplication of what is his own he places before the vision and within the cognition of himself and others what is within him. This is the free rationality of man, in which art as also all action and knowledge originates." (*Aesthetik*, III, Id.)

But Hegel was not able to continue to treat art as an integral activity. In the name of the Idea he must differentiate between three types of beauty—the symbolic, the classical and the romantic. If in high hope that at least within his romantic category we shall find some anticipation of our theory we turn to that part of his work which deals with romantic art, we find that the terms do not apply to qualities of art in general, but denote specific arts; symbolic art being identified with architecture, classical art with sculpture, and romantic art with painting, music and poetry. In short, Hegel is only concerned to denote the degree of sensuousness in art—which is the negation of the degree in which the Idea, in all its immateriality, is adequately realised. And the Idea is, of course, precisely that mystical emanation of German idealism which the Surrealists, no less than the Marxians, repudiate and reject.

It is my ambition some day to submit Hegel's *Aesthetik* to a detailed examination—to do for the realm of art on the basis of Hegel's dialectic something analogous to what Marx on the same basis did for the realm of economics. With such a philosophy of art one could then proceed to a complete revaluation of aesthetic values. I am convinced that the general body of existing aesthetic judgments are *conventional*. For the most part they consist of dogmas handed down by tradition or inculcated by education. They rarely have any real basis in personal experience. We pay lip-service, perhaps to Homer and Sophocles, perhaps to Virgil and Lucretius, Ariosto and Dante, Racine and Boileau, Shakespeare and Milton, and many other names in poetry and the other arts; but very few of these names represent for us *active influences*. I am not suggesting that the whole façade of our culture is false; but it has an architectonic completeness which is historical rather than actual. We look up at this façade and see a magnificent array of saints, all ordered in their appropriate niches; we recognise Homer, Dante, Shakespeare and several others; but for the most part we are ignorant of the identity of the figures and have to consult the guide-book. Our culture is altogether on the guide-book model; Shakespeare has four stars, Milton three, Donne and Blake one. We do not stop to ask on what system, and by whom, the stars were awarded. If we did, we should discover some dusty college of pedants, their noses buried in a profit and loss account of bibliographical data, critical overdrafts and vested interests. If we dared to travel without a guide, to trust our eyes and ears and our contemporary sensibility, the result would be catastrophic. Schoolmasters and professors would wander about helplessly like myopic men deprived of their glasses; textbooks would be irrelevant and teaching an impudent imposition.

Surrealism demands nothing less than such a revaluation of all aesthetic values. It has no respect for any academic tradition, least of all for the classical-capitalist tradition of the last four hundred years. It believes that as a general rule even men of genius during this period—and it has no difficulty in conceding genius where it is due—have been hampered and repressed by the conventions of their education and by their social environment. For poets like Dryden and Pope, for painters like Michelangelo and Poussin, and for many lesser artists, we can only have an angry and in no sense patronising pity. The spectacle of the immense genius of Michelangelo, for example, caught in the toils of the rational ideas of the Grand Manner, is a titanic tragedy. On the other hand the exaltation of conforming mediocrities in every age into a position of authority is a melancholy farce. It is true that only a small proportion of them survive the inevitable ridicule of posterity, but there still remain on every self-styled Parnassus stuffed corpses that should be thrown on the dunghill.

That such a revaluation would be in effect merely a rehabilitation of romanticism is true enough, if the definition of romanticism I have already given is borne in mind. I would suggest, merely as examples of the tasks awaiting us, and merely in the restricted field of English literature, the following:

(1) *A fuller acknowledgment of the supreme poetic quality of our ballads and anonymous literature.* I do not refer to the actual work of recovering and editing the material; to that ghoulish activity it is time to cry halt. The ballads have become the happy hunting ground of academic competence; they must be rescued from such dead hands and be fully recognised as the most fundamental and authentic type of all poetry. Ballads are partly collective (if not in origin, at least in development) and to some degree automatic, and illustrate the intrinsic nature of surrealist poetry. I include in this category, not merely the familiar Border Ballads, but the popular ballads of more recent times (even Woolworth's Song Sheets) and the vast store of primitive poetry mostly still hidden in anthropological works.

(2) *Driving home the inescapable significance of Shakespeare.* To claim Shakespeare as an ally will be treated as an act of impudence by academic critics, but to justify our claim it is only necessary to point to the history of Shakespearean criticism. The rehabilitation of Shakespeare's genius, after the class and classical denigration of the seventeenth and eighteenth centuries, has been the work of specifically romantic critics, beginning with Coleridge and ending, for the moment, with Middleton Murry. Other critics have tinkered with his text—usually to little purpose—or have elaborated the historical background. But the poetic status of Shakespeare—his relative position among the poets of England and of the world—that depends on the romantic theory of poetry. It is impossible—the very attempt is absurd—to establish the genius of Shakespeare on any classical basis. He breaks all the academic rules.

A critic who would not be described as romantic—Professor Dover Wilson—recently published a long book on a vexed question: the problem of Hamlet.[6] Most critics have been puzzled by the incoherency of this, the most famous of Shakespeare's plays—an incoherency which affects not only the action of the play, but also the character of the hero. Various solutions have been proposed, and Professor Wilson reviews them all and finds them wanting. He has great fun demolishing the clumsy or ingenious attempts which have been made to explain the inexplicable; and ends where they might all have begun—by accepting the inexplicable at its face-value, its value as inexplicableness, as irrationality. The heart of the mystery proves to be the mystery itself:

"In fine, we were never intended to reach the heart of the mystery. That it has a heart is an illusion; the mystery itself is an illusion; Hamlet is an illusion. The secret that lies behind it all is not Hamlet's, but Shakespeare's; the technical devices he employed to create this supreme illusion of a great and mysterious character, who is at once mad and the sanest of geniuses, at once a procrastinator and a vigorous man of action, at once a miserable failure and the most adorable of heroes. The character of Hamlet, like the appearance of his successive impersonators on the stage, is a matter of 'make-up.' "

Not since Wharton defended the irrational imagery of Milton has such light streamed into the dark cloisters of the academic mind! It is really a very significant event in the history of scholarship. Professor Wilson is not a stray wolf in academic robes—such do occasionally find their way into the fold. He is the authentic type, the adept of a modern apparatus of the most efficient kind. He moves his apparatus into position; sets it in motion to do its carding and sorting and tidy ordering and then discovers that it will not work. Abandoning his apparatus he approaches the work of genius with his naked eyes, and is dazzled. Rest, rest, perturbed spirit.[7]

[6] *What Happens in Hamlet.* By J. Dover Wilson. Cambridge, 1935.

[7] This critic's acknowledgment of the irrationality of Shakespeare's genius is not confined to this one instance. For example, what can he mean in saying that in *King Lear* Shakespeare "has fashioned a mirror of art in which, more successfully than any man before or since, he has caught the whole of life and focussed

(3) *The exact relations between metaphysics and poetry.* This is a subject to which I have devoted a good deal of attention in the past, but I am by no means satisfied that I have exhausted its interest.

e il pensamento in sogno transmutai—[8]

Dante's line is the perfect description of a process which has yet to be given a full psychological explanation. We think we know how one kind of poetry originates—in inspiration, directly from the sensational awareness of the objective world, or no less directly from the promptings of the unconscious. But we have to admit—it is the only justification of the poetic elements in classical verse—that poetry may be generated by discursive reasoning or metaphysical speculation. In an early essay I described metaphysical poetry as "felt thought," and I still think that no thought can become poetic unless it is apprehended in its mental configuration—we lack the equivalent of the more exact German word *Gestalt.* But what is still necessary is some explanation of why thoughts or ideas should evoke, not merely a metaphorical imagery, but a sensuous identification with visual images: thought transmuted into dream. Obviously it is some extension of the "association of ideas" upon which psychoanalysis relies; the poet passes from the idea to the image unconsciously, and for reasons which might be revealed in analysis. But from our present point of view it is only necessary to affirm and prove that even in its most intellectual forms poetry acquires its poetic quality by a process which brings it into line with the irrational sources of lyrical and romantic poetry.

This fact has not been generally acknowledged by critics in the past, but one who enjoys great respect in quarters where the Surrealists expect none had some inkling of the truth. "Although poets often have unusual powers of reflective thought," wrote A. C. Bradley, "the specific genius of a poet does not lie there, but in the imagination. Therefore his deepest and most original interpretation is likely to come by way of the imagination. And the specific way of imagination is not to clothe in imagery consciously held ideas; *it is to produce half-consciously a matter* from which, when produced, the reader may, if he chooses, extract ideas."

Some further tasks of revaluation must be referred to more generally and quite briefly.

(4) *Lifting the moral ban.* Though something has been accomplished during the last twenty or thirty years, it is still true to say that poets like Shelley, Byron and Swinburne are judged by standards which must be repudiated. If we can agree that a poet's work is to be judged by purely aesthetic standards, as in general we judge a painter's work, then we can proceed to the task unimpeded by the irrelevant standards of morality. But if we prove incapable of such detachment—and I admit it is almost inhuman to expect it—if, like Mr. Eliot, we believe that "literary criticism should be completed by criticism from a definite ethical and theological standpoint," then a revaluation becomes all the more necessary. For the ethical and theological standpoint from which we should then judge Shelley would be much nearer to Shelley's ethics and theology than to the ethics and theology of the Church. And the moral shudder that the very name of Byron sends through our bourgeois homes would be intensified by our acclamation. Byron is not, in any obvious degree, a superrealist poet; but he is a superrealist personality. He is the only English poet who might conceivably occupy, in our hierarchy, the position held in France by the Marquis de Sade. The function of such figures is to be so positive in their immorality, that morality becomes negative by comparison. They show, by the more-than-human energy of their evil, that evil too, as Milton was compelled to admit, has its divinity. In short, they reveal the conventionality of all systems of morality. They prove that the most deeply rooted taboos, such as incest, can be thwarted by the individual will; and the courage they manifest in such defiance is so absolute that a figure like Byron becomes the unconfessed hero of humanity. How else explain the enduring fascination of Byron's personality? By all the rules which condemn such lives as worthless and without honour, he should long ago have sunk into an oblivion from which his poetry would not have rescued him. But it is safe to say that no statue in the temple of fame

it to one intense and burning point of terror and beauty"? (*The Essential Shakespeare.* Cambridge, 1932. Page 127.) It is not in such terms that the academic critic is wont to award his marks.

[8] ["And I changed the thought into a dream."]

is so securely lodged as Byron's; irrational in his life, he is now the object of irrational devotion.

The case of Swinburne is no less interesting. Though the public is still kept in ignorance of the true nature of Swinburne's character—or wilfully or unwittingly keeps itself in such ignorance—it is no longer to be disguised that the best of Swinburne's poetry is precisely that part of it which most openly celebrates what most people regard as unnatural aspects of human passion—poems like "Anactoria," "Faustine" and "Dolores." Swinburne during his life was bullied into conformity and bad verse, and his fate is one more unforgivable crime committed in the name of the bourgeois God. It was a crime against beauty, against honesty, against life itself. For let it be clearly understood that, in taking up such an attitude towards the case of Swinburne or Byron, our policy is not to encourage vice as such; unnatural behavior is not in itself interesting or admirable, and is only made anything but dull and distressing by the active aggression of moralists. But Swinburne himself expressed the truth of the matter in a self-defence he was compelled to publish in 1866:[9]

"The question at issue is wider than any between a single writer and his critics, or it might well be allowed to drop. It is this: whether or not the first and last requisite of art is to give no offence; whether or not all that cannot be lisped in the nursery or fingered in the schoolroom is therefore to be cast out of the library; whether or not the domestic circle is to be for all men and writers the outer limit and extreme horizon of their world of work. For to this we have come; and all students of art must face the matter as it stands. Who has not heard it asked, in a final and triumphant tone, whether this book or that can be read aloud by her mother to a young girl? whether such and such a picture can properly be exposed to the eyes of young persons? If you reply that this is nothing to the point, you fall at once into the ranks of the immoral. Never till now, and nowhere but in England, could so monstrous an absurdity rear for one moment its deformed and eyeless head. In no past century were artists ever bidden to work on these terms; nor are they now, except among us. The disease, of course, afflicts the meanest members of the body with most virulence. Nowhere is cant at once so foul-mouthed and so tight-laced as in the penny, twopenny, threepenny or sixpenny press. Nothing is so favourable to the undergrowth of real indecency as this overshadowing foliage of fictions, this artificial network of proprieties. *L'Arioste rit au soleil, L'Aretin ricane à l'ombre.*[10] The whiter the sepulchre without, the ranker the rottenness within. Every touch of plaster is a sign of advancing decay."

Swinburne speaks the language of his age, but the case would be no different if we were to translate it into the more technical terms of modern psychology. The dilemma which faces all moralists is that the repression of instincts is apt to breed a worse disease than their free expression; incidentally it entails a feebler art.

(5) That last sentence may, however, need a certain qualification in this sense: that what is repressed may nevertheless find a disguised outlet. Without subscribing to the view that art is in every respect a sublimation of repressed instincts (for sublimation usually involves a conformity to collective ideals which completely submerges the individuality of the artist), one must nevertheless recognise—it is indeed one of our main theses—that art is closely linked with these same instincts. Actually it is a question of consciousness. If we are conscious of our instincts and repress them, then we act under duress and produce nothing but intellectual reactions. We try to be good and only succeed in being dull. But if we are not conscious of our instincts, and at the same time allow them to be expressed in a disguised form, then the result may well be interesting. I will return to the psychological aspect of the question presently; for the moment I only want to suggest that certain kinds of literature which are tolerated because they are described as mad or nonsensical—the Prophetic Books of Blake, the nonsense verse and tales of Lear and Lewis Carroll—are actually charged with this unconscious significance. Nothing would be so angrily resented as a revelation of the psychoanalytical significance of *Alice in Wonderland*—the work of a strongly repressed individual; but such

[9] *Notes on Poems and Reviews*. London, 1866.

[10] ["Ariosto laughs at the sun; Aretino sneers at the shadow."]

significance is obvious and the resistance which its exposure would evoke is only a confirmation of its reality. In our opinion such significance only adds to the value of such literature, and in revealing it we have no other desire than to affirm its importance; that is to say, among the tasks of revaluation we include a reconsideration of all such literature. From our point of view, Lear is a better poet than Tennyson; Lewis Carroll has affinities with Shakespeare.

Many other tasks of revaluation will suggest themselves to the reader who has seized our point of view. I am sure, for example, that the whole field of English fiction must be reviewed, though I do not feel competent to make any proposals myself. It is possible that "Monk" Lewis, Maturin and Mrs. Radcliffe should, relatively to Scott, Dickens and Hardy, occupy a much higher rank. For myself I find them all equally difficult to read. I prefer the *Arabian Nights,* or Franz Kafka. It seems to me that fiction, that is to say the prose narrative, awaits a complete transformation. In so far as it is to justify itself as art, it must be transformed into poesy. For fundamentally there is no distinction between prose art and verse art; there is only the one verbal art which is poesy.

As for English Painting, there too we must insist on a complete revision of values. The pen is more irresponsible than the brush; we print things which we dare not depict. That is a crude aspect of the general truth that poetry is an art of wider scope and deeper significance than painting, and this will remain the truth even when the art of painting is completely emancipated from the prejudice of naturalism. But during the many centuries in which painting has been hampered by this prejudice, it is obvious that its close adherence to a standard of objective verisimilitude would give only a minor and exceptional scope to any superrealist elements. I would, of course, claim that the art of the Middle Ages, except in so far as occupied with the mass-production of ecclesiastical symbols, was wholly of a superrealist character; for before the age of reason art was supernatural. Between the superreal and the supernatural there is only a difference of age, of evolution. The supernatural is associated with the mysticism of a religious view of life. But both agree in rejecting the "real" or the "natural" as the only aspect of existence. Supernaturalism, it is true, implies a dualism of spirit and matter; whereas superrealism implies a monism or identity of spirit and matter. Nevertheless, there is sufficient resemblance in the two attitudes to give more than a surface resemblance to their arts. Medieval religion required the plastic realisation of irrational concepts. An angel or a devil could not be copied from a living model; the artist was compelled to use his imagination. Medieval sculpture, and above all medieval manuscripts, offer a wealth of material which it would be only too easy to call surrealist. I do not draw on this material, because I respect the difference of intention. Nevertheless, as an example of what I mean, we find that a subject like "Christ in Limbo" is often treated in a manner recalled by Picasso's recent etching "Minotauromachia."

Between the end of the Middle Ages and the beginning of the Romantic Movement, the plastic arts in England were almost completely dead: a significant fact. Interest begins again with Gainsborough and Blake. Blake I will leave aside for the moment; I shall have something to say about him here in another connection, and I have written about him elsewhere. The early paintings of Gainsborough have a naive spontaneity which brings them close to the Douanier Rousseau; as he increased in technical efficiency, he scarcely added to his aesthetic appeal. At least, his dullest works were done to rival the academic standards of Reynolds or to flatter the bourgeois desire for "finish." The same is true of Constable, and the history of Turner is actually the history of the emancipation of a great artist from the fetters of naturalism. Turner is certainly a subject for revaluation; from the first the victim of Ruskin's enthusiasm, and in our own day the blind spot of influential critics like Roger Fry, this painter actually transformed the topographical canvas which he had inherited into a veritable torch of sensational fury. A little dogged in spirit, he lacked the final courage to take leave of his senses—the vacation which every hard-working artist owes to himself. But he remains a very significant figure—far more significant than any of the French Impressionists, the compeer of Delacroix and Cézanne. There are other painters to be rescued from the dustbin of the nineteenth century: Samuel Palmer and John Martin; but the most serious task is a reconsideration of the Pre-Raphaelites. I doubt if any Englishman—at least, any Englishman still so near to them—can approach these artists with the freshness and freedom that Salvador Dali, for example, brings to their revaluation. But certain truths may be admitted. First, the Pre-Raphaelites were integral artists; like the Surrealists, they had a philosophy of life which embraced painting, poetry, philosophy and politics. They were also convinced of the imbecility of most of their contemporaries, and reacted in the strongest possible way to the academic naturalism of the time. They were not afraid to experiment with their sensations; they acknowledged the primacy of the imagination. But they were incapable of a really comprehensive reaction—a revolution. They had no dialectic, no scientific method, no real energy. In a word, they were sentimentalists. They should have developed romanticism from the stage where Coleridge left it; instead, they developed nostalgia. They read the *Ancient Mariner* and Keats and Blake, and merely indulged in the easy path of repetition. They might have read instead the *Biographia Literaria* and even Hegel, and produced a more vital movement of thought. One has only to contrast Morris with Marx, contemporaries almost, to measure the failure of the Pre-Raphaelites and their followers.

Their followers degenerated into soulful weavers, mock-medieval craftsmen, bookbinders and harpists. English plastic arts had to wait for the inspiration of Picasso to show any real revival. In the last twenty years we have produced potentially great artists—Wyndham Lewis is the typical example—but they have suffered from a disastrous form of individualism. The English sin has always been eccentricity; by which I do not mean a lack of conformity, but simply a lack of social coherence. Surrealism does not, like Communism, call upon artists to surrender their individuality; but it does insist that artists have common problems to solve and common dangers to avoid, and that a certain coherence, even a certain mutuality, is one of the conditions of the efficacity of art.

The fact that the Surrealists inherited from the Dadaists a certain scorn for the "formalism" and "purism" of the later stages of impressionism has led to some misunderstanding of their attitude towards the technique of art. Surrealism is opposed to any intellectualisation of art—to any preference, that is to say, for rational as opposed to imaginative elements. Nothing, in their opinion, could be more futile and unnecessary than an art exclusively concerned with the rendering of some aspect of natural fact—effects of light, of space, of mass or solidity. This seems to them to be a purely mechanical or muscular preoccupation, and the result entirely without artistic interest. Was it not Monet who painted the same haystack in thirty-two different degrees of light? Well, there is always a haystack to be seen somewhere at whatever time and in whatever light you like. It does not seem worth recording at immense pains the passive mutations of such a banal object. It would be just as interesting to record the artist's reaction to thirty-two different degrees of toothache. Even the preoccupation of a Cézanne, though it invested nature with a structure that in actual appearance it lacks, and to that extent contributed a mental and even an imaginative element; and though this preoccupation led to the discovery of perfect relations between intellectual order and sensuous colour; yet even such an art is deceptive if it does not extend our sensibility on more than a sensational level. Cézanne himself seemed to realise this, and was not satisfied with his apples. The series of "Baigneuses" which he painted at the end of his career marks the wider imaginative range of his genius. Seurat is a special case, too complex and too unresolved to dogmatise about—we must not forget that he died at the age of thirty-two; but obviously, in paintings like "Le Cirque" and "La Parade," he was creating a new world, a world of imagination or fantasy which owed no more than its primary elements to the world of objective vision. Since their day, painters not so great as Cézanne or Seurat have seized on one part of their achievement, and that the least interesting part, and have elaborated it into an exclusive method. They have made painting an ocular exercise; a decorative variation on the data of physical vision. Against such an art it was necessary to protest; and the best protest, which should have been final in its effect, was the invention of the collage by Picasso or Braque

—the work of art made of any old pieces of string or newspaper but which, nevertheless, in spite of its complete lack of the fiddling kind of finesse that threatened to become the sole aim of painting, was undeniably a work of art. Max Ernst, taking rubbings from the surfaces of wood and other natural materials, went a step further and reproduced *mechanically* the actual effect of sensibility so much prized as a personal quality by bourgeois amateurs. In this manner the physique of art was seen in its proper proportions; not as a thing which could be dispensed with or despised, but as an instrument subordinate to the sovereign power of the imagination.

The Surrealist, therefore, by no means denies or ridicules aesthetic values as such. To him, no less than to any other sensitive creature, there is good art and bad art, good painting and bad painting, *good Surrealism and bad Surrealism.* He has a scale of values and these values are aesthetic. But aesthetic values are not necessarily objective values—in painting they are not necessarily what the Germans call *malerisch* or painterly values: they do not belong so much to the paint as to the person. Like the pitch of a voice, the "hand" in handwriting or even the gait in walking, they are the expression of a personality —a mentality. Dali's neat, tight Vermeerish *facture* has its aesthetic as well as Picasso's bold, plangent viscous brushwork. There is no one style of using paint, no one criterion of perfection: the artist is using a medium to express certain sensations or ideas and he is not to be judged by the manner in which he uses the medium but by the success with which he conveys the sensations or ideas (I do not suggest that in practice there is any possibility of making the distinction). This is even true of so-called "abstract" art, where the ideas are contained within the formal relations: are, that is to say, the direct expression of formal relations. The alternative which must otherwise be admitted is an art tending towards one uniform standard of perfection: a form of idealism contradicted by history no less than by common sense.

This explanation made, it will perhaps be seen how certain "found objects" which are not the work of human artists, but the products of natural (or unnatural) forces, come to be cherished by Surrealists. If I am walking along the beach and my eye catches a sea-worn and sun-bleached knot of wood whose shape and colour strongly appeal to me, the act of identification (which may in any case have a psychological explanation) makes that object as expressive of my personality as if I had actually carved the wood into that shape. Selection is also creation. Nothing is so expressive of a man as the fetishes he gathers round him—his pipe, his pens, his pocket-knife—even the pattern of his suit. Art in its widest sense is an extension of the personality: a host of artificial limbs.

To the plastic objects which we find by the aid of our eyes correspond, on another plane of consciousness, the images found in dreams. The direct use of dream imagery has not been frequent in the past, for the good psychological reason that the conscious mind is a jealous guardian of the secrecy of this world. But now we turn to the dream with the same confidence that formerly men placed in the objective world of sensation, and we weave its reality into the synthesis of our art. It is possible that in the integral dream—the dream as entire myth rather than as a series of fragmentary symbols—the work of synthesis is already done. In most dreams we find elements that are merely the casual residues of the day's anxieties; but we find also the day-world transformed, and occasionally this new reality presents itself to us as a poetic unity. But to make this distinction clear I will relate the history of an experiment.

Hitherto poets and critics have shown singularly little curiosity about the actual mechanism of poetic inspiration. There are, of course, many disjointed statements which throw light on the subject, such as Wordsworth's quasi-psychological description of emotion recollected in tranquillity, and Keats and Rilke have observed themselves to some profit. Not long before his death A. E. Housman disconcerted his academic cronies by confessing that inspiration was most often induced in him by a pint of beer; that in any case it had physical symptoms. My own suggestion is that poetic inspiration has an exact parallel in dream-formation. In what respect the two processes differ can only be shown by the analysis of a particular case of inspiration, which is what I propose to undertake. But first I must make sure that the reader has a clear picture of the process of dream-formation as described by Freud.

In his latest "Revision of the Theory of Dreams" (*New Introductory Lectures*, 1933. Chapter 1) Freud gives the following schematic summary of the process:

"The introduction: the wish to sleep, the voluntary withdrawal from the outside world. Two things follow from this: firstly, the possibility for older and more primitive modes of activity to manifest themselves, i.e., regression; and secondly, the decrease of the repression-resistance which weighs on the unconscious. As a result of this latter feature an opportunity for dream-formation presents itself, which is seized upon by the factors which are the occasion of the dream; that is to say, the internal and external stimuli which are in activity. The dream which thus eventuates is already a compromise formation; it has a double function: it is on the one hand in conformity with the ego ('ego-syntonic'), since it subserves the wish to sleep by draining off the stimuli which would otherwise disturb it, while on the other hand it allows to a repressed impulse the satisfaction which is possible in these circumstances in the form of an hallucinatory wish-fulfilment. The whole process of dream-formation, which is permitted by the sleeping ego, is, however, under the control of the censorship, a control which is exercised by what is left of the forces of repression."

What is allowed to emerge as a dream—that is to say, what is remembered as a dream—Freud calls the dream-text or the *manifest* dream; but what the analyst suspects to lie beyond the dream, its motive force, these are the *latent* dream-thoughts. "Their dominating element is the repressed impulse, which has obtained some kind of expression, toned down and disguised though it may be, by associating itself with stimuli which happen to be there and by tacking itself on to the residue of the day before." The rest of Freud's description should be followed with close attention, because its bearing on the process of poetic inspiration is direct and immensely significant:

"Just like any other impulse this one presses forward towards satisfaction in action, but the path to motor discharge is closed to it on account of the physiological characteristics of the state of sleep, and so it is forced to travel in the retrograde direction to perception, and content itself with an hallucinatory satisfaction. The latent dream-thoughts are therefore turned into a collection of sensory images and visual scenes. As they are travelling in this direction something happens to them which seems to us new and bewildering. All the verbal apparatus by means of which the more subtle thought-relations are expressed, the conjunctions and prepositions, the variations of declension and conjugation, are lacking, because the means of portraying them are absent: just as in primitive grammarless speech, only the raw material of thought can be expressed, and *the abstract is merged again in the concrete from which it sprang*. What is left over may very well seem to lack coherence. It is as much the result of the archaic regression in the mental apparatus as of the demands of the censorship that so much use is made of the representation of certain objects and processes by means of symbols which have become strange to conscious thought. But of more far-reaching import are the other alterations to which the elements comprising the dream-thoughts are subjected. Such of them as have any point of contact are *condensed* into new unities. When the thoughts are translated into pictures those forms are indubitably preferred which allow of this kind of telescoping, or condensation; it is as though a force were at work which subjected the material to a process of pressure or squeezing together. As a result of condensation one element in a manifest dream may correspond to a number of elements of the dream-thoughts; but conversely one of the elements from among the dream-thoughts may be represented by a number of pictures in the dream."

This spate of quotation is already too long, but there are two further refinements in the process of dream-formation which are still relevant. The first is *displacement* or transference of accent. The individual ideas which make up the dream-thoughts are not all of equal value; "they have various degrees of affective tone attached to them, and, corresponding to these, they are judged as more or less important, and more or less worthy of attention. In the dream-work these ideas are separated from their affects; the affects are treated separately. They may be transferred to something else, they may remain where they were, they may undergo transformation, or they may disappear from the dream entirely. *The importance of the ideas which have been shorn of their affect reappears in the dream in the form of the sensuous vividness of the dream-pictures;* but we notice that this accent, which should lie on important elements, has been transferred to unimportant ones, so that what seems to be pushed to the forefront in the dream, as the most important element in it, only plays a subsidiary role in the dream-thoughts, and conversely, what is important among the dream-thoughts obtains only incidental and rather indistinct representation in the dream."

The other refinement in the process is, from our point of view, perhaps the most important of all. "After these operations on the dream-thoughts the dream is almost ready. There is still, however, a more or less non-constant factor, the so-called secondary elaboration, that makes its appearance after the dream has come into consciousness as an object of perception. When the dream has come into consciousness, we treat it in exactly the same way that we treat any content of perception; we try to fill in the gaps, we add connecting links, and often enough we let ourselves in for serious misunderstandings. But this, as it were, rationalising activity, which at its best provides the dream with a smooth façade, such as cannot correspond to its real content, may be altogether absent in some cases, or only operate in a very feeble way, in which case the dream displays to view all its gaps and inconsistencies. . . ."

To trace the parallel between dream-formation and poem-formation it is necessary to analyse a particular poem, and of necessity such a poem must be one of my own (or otherwise I should have to conduct a long and searching analysis of another poet). The poem I shall take is actually based on a dream. On December 31, 1935, I was present at a family gathering in Yorkshire, and at midnight we celebrated the passing of the Old Year and the birth of the New Year by drinking a rum-punch (I am, it will be seen, about to confirm Housman's diagnosis). I retired to bed and dreamt a vivid dream. It was still vivid to me when next day I travelled by train back to London, and since, like several poets of my acquaintance, I have always found the rhythm of a train journey conducive to poetic composition, I began to transfer to paper the haunting images of my dream. The following poem was the result—I will explain the significance of the italics presently:

The narrow labyrinth has light
which casts our shadows on the wall
as in extremity of flight
I follow one whose face I have not seen.

The walls are white
and turn at intervals to make a screen
on which our racing shadows rise and fall
like waves against the bleached cliff.

Anxious to make my mentor turn
I lift my hands and make a pass
which casts upon the facing wall
a silhouette hovering like a baffled bird.

But on he leads unmoved
and fatally I follow till at last
we leave the labyrinth and I find myself
alone, upon a plinth.

The houses in the square below
stand newly built, brick-rough, bright
bathed in some *Castilian* light.
In the unpaved area a few children play.

This must be a foreign land, I say,
and gaze about with eager eyes.
Then suddenly know that it is *Heaven*
to which *Death* has led me in disguise.

What I described in this poem was, of course, the *manifest* content of my dream; the *latent* content could only be elicited by analysis, and is of no immediate interest. But our poetic analysis of the poem should begin by asking to what extent I succeeded in conveying the manifest content. Is the poem efficient merely as the narrative of an experience? As far as the events of the poem are concerned, I think it is only towards the end that I myself am conscious of any failure. I fancy that in the dream the identity of the unknown figure was revealed to me, and that immediately I awoke—in the process of awaking—this identity slipped from me and I was left with a sense of being baffled. The notion of suddenly finding myself in a Heaven was present in the dream, but identifying the figure with Death was a subsequent rationalisation; it did not, if I can trust my memory, occur to me until I began to write the poem.

Let us now examine the images in the poem. In the dream the labyrinth was real; an intricate maze always turning at right angles and full of an evenly diffused white light; the figure, clad rather like a harlequin in close-fitting tights, never turned. I made the pass by lifting my hands above my head and making a shadow on the wall in the manner of the shadow-game played by children; the image of the baffled bird —the fluttering shadow like a bird beating against a window-pane—*occurred to me in my dream.* In this it differs from the wave-image I have used to describe the shadows of our bodies on the walls of the labyrinth, which is a conscious image produced in the process of writing the poem; I would on that account call it a metaphor rather than an image. In a similar way the word "Castilian," used to describe the peculiar light which was diffused over the square, is an epithet derived from my conscious experience; the nearest equivalent in my memory being certain effects of sunlight in Spain. I have not conveyed exactly enough the vivid impression I have of the effect of this dream-light on the houses; I have distinct sensuous image of the porous quality of the brick into which the light seemed to soak, as if absorbed. The children in the square (it was a new square, not yet paved or laid out in any way, rough and uneven) seemed to be self-centred, detached, in a different perspective to the rest of the scene; an effect which Salvador Dali often conveys in his paintings.

It will be observed that there are several rhymes, but no regular rhyme system; these rhymes were not sought by me, but came unconsciously in the act of writing the poem. If I had sought for rhymes I should inevitably have been compelled to distort my narrative and my imagery, and to that extent to be false to my inspiration. And such, indeed, has always been my practice in writing poetry. I neither seek rhymes nor avoid them, for either attitude would involve a too conscious control of my expression—would defeat the desirable automatism. But this does not prevent me from recognising that when there is no total inspiration— when a poet is writing line by line—the search for rhymes may lead to the discovery of surprising images. That is merely a different method of composition; a mosaic as opposed to a reflection. If a poet wishes to remain faithful to a myth—a myth presented to him integrally—he cannot afford to go off in pursuit of surface ornaments.

Perhaps the most important distinction which this analysis reveals is that between images and metaphors—a distinction which has already been made by Pierre Reverdy and which I have referred to before (Breton also quotes it in the First Surrealist Manifesto):

"L'image est une création pure de l'esprit.

"Elle ne peut naître d'une comparaison mais du rapprochement de deux réalités plus ou moins éloignées.

"Plus les rapports des deux réalités rapprochées seront lointains et justes, plus l'image sera forte— plus elle aura de puissance émotive et de réalité poétique. . . ." [11]

In my poem the metaphor of the waves against the bleached cliff, though to my mind accurate enough as description, has not the same force as the image of the baffled bird; and actually, of course, the whole content of the poem —labyrinth, square, light, children—is a series of images, but of images whose counterpart is not manifest, and which therefore we call symbols.

The metaphor may have its associational significance within the psychological unity of the poem; if it is purely intellectual in origin it is apt to stick out of the poem like an irrelevant ornament.

This type of poem, then, we might describe, to adopt Freud's terminology, as the manifest content of a dream whose latent thoughts have been turned into sensory images or visual scenes; the abstract, that is to say, is merged again in the concrete form from which it sprang.[12] Cer-

[11] ["The Image is a pure creation of the mind.

"It cannot grow out of a comparison but only out of a union of two more or less distant realities.

"The more distant and true the connection between the two realities which are being united, the stronger will be the image and the more emotional power and poetic truth will it have."]

[12] Compare Vico's theory of poetry, especially the following passage: "[So for us] the whole art of Poetry reduces itself to this, that anyone who wishes to excel as a poet must unlearn all his native language, and return to the pristine beggary of words; by this necessity he will express the feelings of his mind by means of the most obvious and easily perceived aspects of things; he will, by the aid of the senses and the imagination, paint the most striking and lovely images

tain of the dream-thoughts have been condensed into images or symbols, whose latent significance resists any analysis, but which nevertheless, *and perhaps precisely on that account,* have extreme poetic force. Then, to disguise any gaps or incoherency, the conscious mind of the poet has worked over the poem, and given it that smooth façade which is generally demanded by the literary conventions of an age, and which in any case makes for ease of communication.

It is not every poem that has the integral character of a dream, but every authentic image is conceived in the unconscious; that is to say, the two realities of which Reverdy speaks, though more or less distantly separated, cohere as an image and gain their emotive power from the presence in the unconscious of a hidden connecting link. There is no need, in any poetic analysis, to reveal that repressed connection; the poetic reality lies in the evident power of the image, and is no stronger—indeed, may be much weaker—if its latent meaning is made manifest. The whole irrationality of art, and the surrealist defence of irrationality, is explained by the Freudian theory of regression. An unconscious impulse creates the poem no less than the dream; it provides, that is to say, the mental energy required for its formation. That impulse seeks in the poem, no less and no otherwise than in the dream, its desired satisfaction. The latent ideas or thoughts are turned into visual images, are dramatised and illustrated, are finally liberated in the hallucinatory reality of the poem.

That the actual choice of words—the poet's language as distinct from his imagery—is formed by a similar process of unconscious association, would seem to be a fair deduction from the evidence of psychoanalysis. In the degree that they are poetic such words are automatic associations of an aural rather than a visual nature. It may be that some poets search the dictionary of their conscious memory for the apt epithet, and in that way display an inventive wit; but such a faculty—the faculty of a Pope or a Dryden—is not the essentially poetic gift. Poetry, to adapt a saying of Picasso's, is found, not sought. It emerges, perhaps not easily but at any rate directly, from the well of the unconscious. It may be elaborated or distorted by the exercise of conscious skill, but there is no evidence at all to show that as a result the poem ever gains in its specifically poetic power.

We are so uncertain of the limits of mental activity—its actual range and effectiveness—that even as materialists we must not exclude the possibility of hitherto unsuspected modes of operation. For example, psychoanalysis has already been compelled to admit the scientific possibility of thought-transference or telepathy. On the analogy of such "occult" phenomena, it is possible that the mind of the poet or painter, during the course of its ordinary activity, picks up and transmits "messages" in a wholly unconscious manner. I think it is possible that such "messages" are always in the form of "images"—that is to say, the ideas they deal with are not verbalised. In this way, for example, the "residues" of the day's activity, in their least unimportant and unobserved details, are taken up and "used" in the course of the dream activity. A pattern in a wall, a patch of lichen, or any abstract pattern which I have for a moment stared at, may in this way sink into my mind and determine the form of my unconscious images, which when called up in the activity of painting, emerge in this apparently inexplicable and illogical shape. That process is comparatively easy to understand; but in the contrary direction it is also possible that ideas, with which we may have been obsessed during the activity of thought, may, when conscious thought is for the time being superseded by instinctive modes of expression, so guide such expression that it corresponds to the latent thought. Salvador Dali relates how a splash of paint on his palette had assumed *unknown to his conscious mind* the shape of a distorted skull which he had consciously and vainly been trying to discover. It is another aspect of automatism; and all that it is necessary to admit is the super-reality, the something-more-than-conscious naturalism, which encompasses all our actions. At this moment I have an intimation that I shall

of things, manners and feelings; and just as anyone who wishes to be a philosopher must first purge himself of the prejudices of children and common people, so anyone who would write a poem must feel and think entirely according to the childlike and common views of the world. In this way he will become really imaginative, and will compose at once sublimely and in accordance with the popular understanding." *De Constantia Philologiae.* (Trans. by H. S. Davies.)

find in Blake a verse or a sentence bearing on this question. I take the book from the shelf; it opens at page 562 and I read:

"... Condens'd his Emanations into hard opake substances,
And his infant thoughts & desires into cold dark cliffs of death.
His hammer of gold he seiz'd, and his anvil of adamant;
He seiz'd the bars of condens'd thoughts to forge them
Into the sword of war, into the bow and arrow,
Into the thundering cannon and into the murdering gun.
I saw the limbs form'd for exercise contemn'd, & the beauty of
Eternity look'd upon as deformity, & loveliness as a dry tree.
I saw disease forming a Body of Death around the Lamb
Of God to destroy Jerusalem & to devour the body of Albion,
By war and stratagem to win the labour of the husbandman.
Awkwardness arm'd in steel, folly in a helmet of gold,
Weakness with horns & talons, ignorance with a rav'ning beak,
Every Emanative joy forbidden as a Crime
And the Emanations buried alive in the earth with pomp of religion,
Inspiration deny'd, Genius forbidden by laws of punishment,
I saw terrified. I took the sighs & tears & bitter groans,
I lifted them into my Furnaces to form the spiritual sword
That lays open the hidden heart. I drew forth the pang
Of sorrow red hot: I work'd on my resolute anvil:
I heated it in the flames of Hand & Hyle & Coban
Nine times. . . ."

Jerusalem, i, 9.

Thus Blake labours in hope that Enthusiasm and Life may not cease. In the whole of his writings I feel the presence of an instinctive dialecticism which is of the greatest interest. I know that some of my fellow Surrealists have many reserves to make about Blake; they are suspicious of his obscurity, which wears the too obvious mask of mysticism. I am equally suspicious; but I must confess that the more I have studied Blake the more these mists have dispersed. It would be absurd to call Blake a materialist (it would be absurd to call the Surrealist anything but a *dialectical* materialist); nevertheless, in works like *The Marriage of Heaven and Hell* and *Jerusalem* there is a realisation of the fundamental contradictions of reality, and a movement towards a synthesis which is anything but idealistic.

From much the same point of view the metaphysical element in Shelley should be re-examined. In Shelley's case there is no doubt of the point of departure—a materialistic determinism of the most antitheist type. But it is generally assumed that Shelley abandoned his early antitheism and ended in the clouds of neo-platonic idealism. But actually he too arrived at a dialectical synthesis of the real and the unreal, actuality and hallucination, as the following quotation from his *Speculations on Metaphysics* will make clear:

"Thoughts, or ideas, or notions, call them what you will, differ from each other, not in kind, but in force. It has commonly been supposed that those distinct thoughts which affect a number of persons, at regular intervals, during the passage of a multitude of other thoughts, which are called *real* or *external objects*, are totally different from those which affect only a few persons, and which recur at irregular intervals, and are usually more obscure and indistinct, such as hallucinations, dreams, and the ideas of madness. No essential distinction between any one of these ideas, or any class of them, is founded on a correct observation of the nature of things, but merely on a consideration of what thoughts are most invariably subservient to the security and happiness of life; and if nothing more were expressed by the distinction, the philosopher might safely accommodate his language to that of the vulgar. But they pretend to assert an essential difference, which has no foundation in truth, and which suggests a narrow and false conception of universal nature, the parent of the most fatal errors in speculation. A specific difference between every thought of the mind, is, indeed, a necessary consequence of that law by which it perceives diversity and number; but a generic and essential difference is wholly arbitrary."

In an essay of this kind I am mainly concerned with presenting the positive aspects of

Surrealism; all that necessary part of a critical activity which consists in removing misunderstandings and replying to criticism made on the basis of such misunderstandings may be left to more fugitive forms of publication. But one form of attack may be mentioned here because it is of a serious nature and because it will serve to introduce an aspect of Surrealism which yet remains to be dealt with. During the London Exhibition Mr. J. B. Priestley was commissioned to write an article for the evening paper famous for its betting news. Now, that Mr. Priestley should be made to feel, as he confesses, "not too comfortable," in fact, "profoundly disturbed" by our activities is exactly as we would have it. But when he goes on to ascribe to the Surrealists in general all kinds of moral perversion, he is merely indulging in the abortive vituperation of his kind:

> As if a man should spit against the wind;
> The filth returns in's face.

The Surrealists, he said, "stand for violence and neurotic unreason. They are truly decadent. You catch a glimpse behind them of the deepening twilight of barbarism that may soon blot out the sky, until at last humanity finds itself in another long night." In that fuliginous perspective, and knowing what a man of Mr. Priestley's prejudices means by decadence, the Surrealists might willingly stand. But that is not the end of Mr. Priestley's insinuations. "There are about far too many effeminate or epicene young men, lisping and undulating. Too many young women without manners, balance, dignity—greedy and slobbering sensation-seekers. Too many people who are steadily lapsing into shaved and powdered barbarism. . . . Frequently they have strong sexual impulses that they soon contrive to misuse or pervert."

Mr. Priestley no doubt feels none too comfortable on his bed of roses, and sympathy for the under-dog flows in a copious if somewhat muddled stream from his generous heart. But Mr. Priestley is not personally acquainted with the Surrealists, in this country or any other; and as a novelist he ought to have enough penetration to realise that the least repressed of people are generally the most moral; or, as Huysmans put it, "au fond . . . il n'y a de réellement obscènes que les gens chastes."[13] As a matter of fact, the Surrealists are no less aware than Mr. Priestley of undesirable elements in their midst; but they are not themselves to be identified with such elements. It is true that they cannot protest against the perversions of a moral code for which they have no respect. But they despise the kind of people who indulge in perversion just as much as they despise people who indulge in hypocrisy. They despise any kind of weakness, any lack of personal integrity. Their principle of liberty allows to each the free exercise of his natural propensities so long as this does not infringe the equal rights of others. On the subject of homosexuality, for example (a subject which the evening papers do not mention, though it is one of the most acute questions of the day), the Surrealists are not in the least prejudiced; they recognise that inversion is an abnormal condition due to a certain psychological or physiological predisposition for which the individual is in no way responsible. But they protest when such individuals form a sodality or freemasonry for the purpose of imposing their special ethos upon the social and intellectual life of the day. It leads in particular to an intolerance for women which is certainly no part of the surrealist creed.

In short, the Surrealists admit the disciplinary truth that, if you have to attack a diseased body for the purpose of healing it, your own body should be in a healthy state. The kind of insult which Mr. Priestley hurls at the Surrealists is the kind of insult that used to be insinuated about the Bolsheviks until the purity and disinterestedness of their lives could no longer be disguised.

The Surrealist is opposed to current morality because he considers that it is rotten. He can have no respect for a code of ethics that tolerates extremes of poverty and riches; that wastes or deliberately destroys the products of the earth amidst a starving or undernourished people; that preaches a gospel of universal peace and wages aggressive war with all the appendages of horror and destruction which its evil genius can invent; that so distorts the sexual impulse that thousands of unsatisfied men and women

[13] ["Ultimately, the only really obscene people are the chaste."]

go mad, millions waste their lives in unhappiness or poison their minds with hypocrisy. For such a morality (and these are merely its most general features) the Surrealist has nothing but hatred and scorn.

His own code of morality is based on liberty and love. He sees no reason why the frailties of the human race should be erected into a doctrine of original sin, but he realises that most men are born imperfect and are made less perfect still by their circumstances. Such evils and imperfections cannot wholly be eradicated in any conceivable span of human development. But it is our belief that the whole system of organized control and repression which is the social aspect of present-day morality is psychologically misconceived and positively harmful. We believe, that is to say, in the fullest possible liberation of the impulses and are convinced that what law and oppression have failed to achieve will in due time be brought about by love and fraternity.

The Surrealist is not a sentimental humanitarian; the superrealism of his art has its counterpart in the realism of his science. He is a psychologist of the strictest type, and if he uses words like "love" and "fraternity," it is because his analysis of the sexual and affective and of the economic life of man has given him the right to use such words cleanly, without the least surplus of sentimentality.

To close this essay without a personal note of explanation would be discreet, perhaps, but unnecessarily indefinite. I am often accused of contradictions, and do not doubt that these exist in my critical writings. But I must confess that I am not particularly uneasy about them. They are related to the contradictions of my personality, and, if I am then told that it is very wrong or weak of me to possess such a personality, the objection is meaningless to me. For I am conscious that, such as it is, my personality is integral, and I do not choose to present a falsely regular façade. I have a strong dislike for people with symmetrical faces; if not criminals (an attested fact), they are at any rate stupid or depraved. I do not necessarily glory in contradictions, but if they come as a natural consequence of a natural disposition I leave them to be reconciled in that synthetic judgment which is the Last Judgment.

In that judgment it will be seen that my main affiliations have always been romantic, in the sense in which I have interpreted romanticism in this essay. I have always had an instinctive preference for those poets and painters who have exceeded the limits of convention, which are the limits of moral experience; and in the history of criticism my interest quickens from the moment that romanticism begins to acquire a rational and scientific basis in psychology and philosophy: the line of development from Vico to Freud. That in the present desperate circumstances, when at any moment every poet and artist may be called upon to find his position *in the line,* that at such a time I should in spite of all my past pontifical detachment declare for Surrealism—that, I assert, should be regarded as merely an affirmation of all that is most real and active in my work.

In so far as such an attitude involves a political alignment and is thereby a clerk's *trahison,* such treason is committed in full awareness of the consequences. In normal circumstances the *detachment* of the artist from a party and therefore a partial point of view is a condition of his *attachment* to an integral view of life. But the conditions of the present time are not normal.[14] It is the presumption of modern dictatorships to challenge in a most direct manner the artist's creative freedom. Whether done in the cause of "socialist realism" or "racial purity" or nationalism, the menace is the same —not merely repression and economic servitude such as the artist has suffered in all ages, but the actual extermination of the artist as such. Not since the Iconoclastic Controversy has the artist been forced into the position usually occupied by religious martyrs and political enemies. To the degree that the artist is directly attacked as an artist, he must actively defend himself; and to defend himself he must ally himself with whatever political forces seem to him to promise the requisite intellectual liberty. That choice

14 It is significant that Julien Benda, who was responsible for the phrase "la trahison des clercs," has himself long since abandoned his attitude of intellectual detachment.

may be a difficult one, for even Communism, the creed of liberty and fraternity, has made the exigences of a transitional epoch the excuse for an unnecessary and stupid form of aesthetic intolerance.

The contradictions of the personality are resolved in the work of art: that is one of the first principles of romanticism. One might even go so far as to say that the personality without contradictions is incapable of creating a work of art. It is incapable of entering into dialectical activity—of moving from the state of equilibrium which is the state of mental passivity. Art is more than description or "reportage"; it is an act of renewal. It renews vision, it renews language; but most essentially it renews life itself by enlarging the sensibility, by making men more conscious of the terror and the beauty, the *wonder* of the possible forms of being.

The renascence of wonder—I remember this as the title of an essay by Watts-Dunton, the friend of Swinburne. I should not be afraid to adopt such a grandiloquent phrase to describe the general aim of Surrealism as I conceive it. Just as curiosity is the faculty which drives man to seek out the hidden structure of the external universe, thereby enabling him to build up that body of knowledge which we call Science, so wonder is the faculty which dares man to create what has not before existed, which dares man to use his powers in new ways and for new effects. We have lost this sense of the word "wonderful"—it is one of the most outworn clichés in the language. But actually "wonder" is a better and more inclusive word than "beauty," and what is full of wonder has the most compelling force over the imagination of men. "We cease to wonder at what we understand," said Dr. Johnson, a man indifferent to the cost of complacency. It would have been much more to the point to have observed that understanding ceases when we cease to wonder, that, as Pascal, a less complacent man, observed "there are reasons of the heart of which Reason knows nothing."

C. G. JUNG: Psychology and Literature*

THERE is a fundamental difference of approach between the psychologist's examination of a literary work, and that of the literary critic. What is of decisive importance and value for the latter may be quite irrelevant for the former. Literary products of highly dubious merit are often of the greatest interest to the psychologist. For instance, the so-called "psychological novel" is by no means as rewarding for the psychologist as the literary-minded suppose. Considered as a whole, such a novel explains itself. It has done its own work of psychological interpretation, and the psychologist can at most criticize or enlarge upon this. The important question as to how a particular author came to write a particular novel is of course left unanswered, but I wish to reserve this general problem for the second part of my essay.

The novels which are most fruitful for the psychologist are those in which the author has not already given a psychological interpretation of his characters, and which therefore leave room for analysis and explanation, or even invite it by their mode of presentation. Good examples of

* Reprinted from *Modern Man in Search of a Soul* by C. G. Jung by permission of Harcourt, Brace and Company, Inc. Carl Gustav Jung, born in 1875, the founder of an important school of psychotherapy that he designated by the term "analytical psychology" (as distinguished from Freud's term "psychoanalysis"), has written little that is explicitly concerned with literature but has exerted a profound influence on the modern interpretation of literature. "Psychology and Literature" is a selection from the chapter of that name in *Modern Man in Search of a Soul.*

this kind of writing are the novels of Benoît, and English fiction in the manner of Rider Haggard, including the vein exploited by Conan Doyle which yields that most cherished article of mass-production, the detective story. Melville's *Moby Dick,* which I consider the greatest American novel, also comes within this class of writings. An exciting narrative that is apparently quite devoid of psychological exposition is just what interests the psychologist most of all. Such a tale is built upon a groundwork of implicit psychological assumptions, and, in the measure that the author is unconscious of them, they reveal themselves, pure and unalloyed, to the critical discernment. In the psychological novel, on the other hand, the author himself attempts to reshape his material so as to raise it from the level of crude contingency to that of psychological exposition and illumination—a procedure which all too often clouds the psychological significance of the work or hides it from view. It is precisely to novels of this sort that the layman goes for "psychology"; while it is novels of the other kind that challenge the psychologist, for he alone can give them deeper meaning.

I have been speaking in terms of the novel, but I am dealing with a psychological fact which is not restricted to this particular form of literary art. We meet with it in the works of the poets as well, and are confronted with it when we compare the first and second parts of the Faust drama. The love-tragedy of Gretchen explains itself; there is nothing that the psychologist can add to it that the poet has not already said in better words. The second part, on the other hand, calls for explanation. The prodigious richness of the imaginative material has so overtaxed the poet's formative powers that nothing is self-explanatory and every verse adds to the reader's need of an interpretation. The two parts of *Faust* illustrate by way of extremes this psychological distinction between works of literature.

In order to emphasize the distinction, I will call the one mode of artistic creation *psychological,* and the other *visionary.* The psychological mode deals with materials drawn from the realm of human consciousness—for instance, with the lessons of life, with emotional shocks, the experience of passion and the crises of human destiny in general—all of which go to make up the conscious life of man, and his feeling life in particular. This material is psychically assimilated by the poet, raised from the commonplace to the level of poetic experience, and given an expression which forces the reader to greater clarity and depth of human insight by bringing fully into his consciousness what he ordinarily evades and overlooks or senses only with a feeling of dull discomfort. The poet's work is an interpretation and illumination of the contents of consciousness, of the ineluctable experiences of human life with its eternally recurrent sorrow and joy. He leaves nothing over for the psychologist, unless, indeed, we expect the latter to expound the reasons for which Faust falls in love with Gretchen, or which drive Gretchen to murder her child! Such themes go to make up the lot of humankind; they repeat themselves millions of times and are responsible for the monotony of the police-court and of the penal code. No obscurity whatever surrounds them, for they fully explain themselves.

Countless literary works belong to this class: the many novels dealing with love, the environment, the family, crime and society, as well as didactic poetry, the larger number of lyrics, and the drama, both tragic and comic. Whatever its particular form may be, the psychological work of art always takes its materials from the vast realm of conscious human experience—from the vivid foreground of life, we might say. I have called this mode of artistic creation psychological because in its activity it nowhere transcends the bounds of psychological intelligibility. Everything that it embraces—the experience as well as its artistic expression—belongs to the realm of the understandable. Even the basic experiences themselves, though non-rational, have nothing strange about them; on the contrary, they are that which has been known from the beginning of time—passion and its fated outcome, man's subjection to the turns of destiny, eternal nature with its beauty and its horror.

The profound difference between the first and second parts of Faust marks the difference between the psychological and the visionary modes of artistic creation. The latter reverses all the conditions of the former. The experience that furnishes the material for artistic expression is no longer familiar. It is a strange something that derives its existence from the hinterland of man's mind—that suggests the abyss of time separating us from pre-human ages, or evokes a super-human world of contrasting light and darkness. It is a primordial experience which surpasses man's understanding, and to which he is therefore in danger of succumbing. The value and the force of the experience are given by its enormity. It arises from timeless depths; it is foreign and cold, many-sided, demonic and grotesque. A grimly ridiculous example of the external chaos —a *crimen laesae majestatis humanae,*[1] to use Nietzsche's words—it bursts asunder our human standards of value and of aesthetic form. The disturbing vision of monstrous and meaningless happenings that in every way exceed the grasp of human feeling and comprehension makes quite other demands upon the powers of the artist than do the experiences of the foreground of life. These never rend the curtain that veils the cosmos; they never transcend the bounds of the humanly possible, and for this reason are readily shaped to the demands of art, no matter how great a shock to the individual they may be. But the primordial experiences rend from top to bottom the curtain upon which is painted the picture of an ordered world, and allow a glimpse into the unfathomed abyss of what has not yet become. Is it a vision of other worlds, or of the obscuration of the spirit, or of the unborn generations of the future? We cannot say that it is any or none of these.

> Shaping—re-shaping—
> The eternal spirit's eternal pastime.[2]

We find such vision in *The Shepherd of Hermas,* in Dante, in the second part of *Faust,* in Nietzsche's Dionysian exuberance, in Wagner's *Nibelungenring,* in Spitteler's *Olympischer Frühling,* in the poetry of William Blake, in the *Ipnerotomachia* of the monk Francisco Colonna, and in Jacob Boehme's philosophic and poetic stammerings. In a more restricted and specific way, the primordial experience furnishes material for Rider Haggard in the fiction-cycle that turns upon *She,* and it does the same for Benoît, chiefly in *L'Atlantide,* for Kubin in *Die Andere Seite,* for Meyrink in *Das Grüne Gesicht*—a book whose importance we should not undervalue—for Goetz in *Das Reich ohne Raum,* and for Barlach in *Der Tote Tag.* This list might be greatly extended. . . .

The psychologist who follows Freud will of course be inclined to take the writings in question as a problem in pathology. On the assumption that an intimate, personal experience underlies what I call the "primordial vision"—an experience, that is to say, which cannot be accepted by the conscious outlook—he will try to account for the curious images of the vision by calling them cover-figures and by supposing that they represent an attempted concealment of the basic experience. This, according to his view, might be an experience in love which is morally or aesthetically incompatible with the personality as a whole or at least with certain fictions of his conscious mind. In order that the poet, through his ego, might repress this experience and make it unrecognizable (unconscious), the whole arsenal of a pathological fantasy was brought into action. Moreover, this attempt to replace reality by fiction, being unsatisfactory, must be repeated in a long series of creative embodiments. This would explain the proliferation of imaginative forms, all monstrous, demonic, grotesque and perverse. On the one hand they are substitutes for the unacceptable experience, and on the other they help to conceal it. . . .

Creativeness, like the freedom of the will, contains a secret. The psychologist can describe both these manifestations as processes, but he can find no solution of the philosophical problems they offer. Creative man is a riddle that we may try to answer in various ways, but always in vain, a truth that has not prevented modern psychology from turning now and again to the question of the artist and his art. Freud thought that he had found a key in his procedure of deriving the work of art from the personal experiences of the artist.[3] It is true that certain possibilities lay in this direction, for it was conceivable that a work of art, no less than a neurosis, might be traced back to those knots in psychic life that we call the complexes. It was Freud's great discovery that neuroses have a causal origin in the psychic realm—that they take their rise from emotional states and from real or imagined childhood experiences. Certain of his followers, like Rank and

[1] ["Crime of offending human dignity."]

[2] *Gestaltung, Umgestaltung,*
Des ew'gen Sinnes ew'ge Unterhaltung. (Goethe.)

[3] See Freud's essay on Jensen's *Gradiva* and on Leonardo da Vinci.

Stekel, have taken up related lines of enquiry and have achieved important results. It is undeniable that the poet's psychic disposition permeates his work root and branch. Nor is there anything new in the statement that personal factors largely influence the poet's choice and use of his materials. Credit, however, must certainly be given to the Freudian school for showing how far-reaching this influence is and in what curious ways it comes to expression.

Freud takes the neurosis as a substitute for a direct means of gratification. He therefore regards it as something inappropriate—a mistake, a dodge, an excuse, a voluntary blindness. To him it is essentially a shortcoming that should never have been. Since a neurosis, to all appearances, is nothing but a disturbance that is all the more irritating because it is without sense or meaning, few people will venture to say a good word for it. And a work of art is brought into questionable proximity with the neurosis when it is taken as something which can be analysed in terms of the poet's repressions. In a sense it finds itself in good company, for religion and philosophy are regarded in the same light by Freudian psychology. No objection can be raised if it is admitted that this approach amounts to nothing more than the elucidation of those personal determinants without which a work of art is unthinkable. But should the claim be made that such an analysis accounts for the work of art itself, then a categorical denial is called for. The personal idiosyncrasies that creep into a work of art are not essential; in fact, the more we have to cope with these peculiarities, the less is it a question of art. What is essential in a work of art is that it should rise far above the realm of personal life and speak from the spirit and heart of the poet as man to the spirit and heart of mankind. The personal aspect is a limitation—and even a sin—in the realm of art. When a form of "art" is primarily personal it deserves to be treated as if it were a neurosis. There may be some validity in the idea held by the Freudian school that artists without exception are narcissistic—by which is meant that they are undeveloped persons with infantile and auto-erotic traits. The statement is only valid, however, for the artist as a person, and has nothing to do with the man as an artist. In his capacity of artist he is neither auto-erotic, nor hetero-erotic, nor erotic in any sense. He is objective and impersonal—even inhuman—for as an artist he is his work, and not a human being.

Every creative person is a duality or a synthesis of contradictory aptitudes. On the one side he is a human being with a personal life, while on the other side he is an impersonal, creative process. Since as a human being he may be sound or morbid, we must look at his psychic make-up to find the determinants of his personality. But we can only understand him in his capacity of artist by looking at his creative achievement. We should make a sad mistake if we tried to explain the mode of life of an English gentleman, a Prussian officer, or a cardinal in terms of personal factors. The gentleman, the officer and the cleric function as such in an impersonal role, and their psychic make-up is qualified by a peculiar objectivity. We must grant that the artist does not function in an official capacity—the very opposite is nearer the truth. He nevertheless resembles the types I have named in one respect, for the specifically artistic disposition involves an overweight of collective psychic life as against the personal. Art is a kind of innate drive that seizes a human being and makes him its instrument. The artist is not a person endowed with free will who seeks his own ends, but one who allows art to realize its purposes through him. As a human being he may have moods and a will and personal aims, but as an artist he is "man" in a higher sense—he is "collective man"—one who carries and shapes the unconscious, psychic life of mankind. To perform this difficult office it is sometimes necessary for him to sacrifice happiness and everything that makes life worth living for the ordinary human being.

All this being so, it is not strange that the artist is an especially interesting case for the psychologist who uses an analytical method. The artist's life cannot be otherwise than full of conflicts, for two forces are at war within him—on the one hand the common human longing for happiness, satisfaction and security in life, and on the other a ruthless passion for creation which may go so far as to override every personal desire. The lives of artists are as a rule so highly unsatisfactory—not to say tragic—because of their inferiority on the human and personal side, and not because of a sinister dispensation. There are hardly any exceptions to the rule that a person must pay dearly for the divine gift of the creative fire. It is as though each of us were endowed at birth with a certain capital of energy. The strongest force in our make-up will seize and all but monopolize this energy, leaving so little over that nothing of value can come of it. In this way the creative force can drain the human impulses to such a degree that the personal ego must develop all sorts of bad qualities—ruthlessness, selfishness and vanity (so-called "auto-erotism") —and even every kind of vice, in order to maintain the spark of life and to keep itself from being wholly bereft. The auto-erotism of artists resembles that of illegitimate or neglected children who from their tenderest years must protect themselves from the destructive influence of people who have no love to give them—who develop bad qualities for that very purpose and later maintain an invincible egocentrism by remaining all their lives infantile and helpless or by actively offending against the moral code or the law. How can we doubt that it is his art that explains the artist, and not the insufficiencies and conflicts of his personal life? These are nothing but the regrettable results of the fact that he is an artist—that is to say, a man who from his very birth has been called to a greater task than the ordinary mortal. A special ability means a heavy expenditure of energy in a particular direction, with a consequent drain from some other side of life.

It makes no difference whether the poet knows that his work is begotten, grows and matures with him, or whether he supposes that by taking thought he produces it out of the void. His opinion of the matter does not change the fact that his own work outgrows him as a child its mother. The creative process has feminine quality, and the creative work arises from unconscious depths —we might say, from the realm of the mothers. Whenever the creative force predominates, human life is ruled and moulded by the unconscious as against the active will, and the conscious ego is swept along on a subterranean current, being nothing more than a helpless observer of events. The work in process becomes the poet's fate and determines his psychic development. It is not Goethe who creates *Faust,* but *Faust* which creates Goethe. And what is *Faust* but a symbol? By this I do not mean an allegory that points to something all too familiar, but an expression that stands for something not clearly known and yet profoundly alive. Here it is something that lives in the soul of every German, and that Goethe has helped to bring to birth. Could we conceive of anyone but a German writing *Faust* or *Also sprach Zarathustra?* Both play upon something that reverberates in the German soul—a "primordial image," as Jacob Burckhardt once called it—the figure of a physician or teacher of mankind. The archetypal image of the wise man, the saviour or redeemer, lies buried and dormant in man's unconscious since the dawn of culture; it is awakened whenever the times are out of joint and a human society is committed to a serious error. When people go astray they feel the need of a guide or teacher or even of the physician. These primordial images are numerous, but do not appear in the dreams of individuals or in works of art until they are called into being by the waywardness of the general outlook. When conscious life is characterized by one-sidedness and by a false attitude, then they are activated—one might say, "instinctively"—and come to light in the dreams of individuals and the visions of artists and seers, thus restoring the psychic equilibrium of the epoch.

In this way the work of the poet comes to meet the spiritual need of the society in which he lives, and for this reason his work means more to him than his personal fate, whether he is aware of this or not. Being essentially the instrument for his work, he is subordinate to it, and we have no reason for expecting him to interpret it for us. He has done the best that in him lies in giving it form, and he must leave the interpretation to others and to the future. A great work of art is like a dream; for all its apparent obviousness it does not explain itself and is never unequivocal. A dream never says: "You ought," or: "This is the truth." It presents an image in much the same way as nature allows a plant to grow, and we must draw our own conclusions. If a person has a nightmare, it means either that he is too much given to fear, or else that he is too exempt from it; and if he dreams of the old wise man it may mean that he is too pedagogical, as also that he stands in need of a teacher. In a subtle way both meanings come to the same thing, as we perceive when we are able to let the work of art act upon us as it acted upon the artist. To grasp its meaning, we must allow it to shape us as it once shaped him. Then we understand the nature of his experience. We see that he has drawn upon the healing and redeeming forces of the collective psyche that underlies consciousness with its isolation and its painful errors; that he has penetrated to that matrix of life in which all men are embedded, which imparts a common rhythm to all human existence, and allows the individual to communicate his feeling and his striving to mankind as a whole.

The secret of artistic creation and of the effectiveness of art is to be found in a return to the state of *participation mystique*—to that level of experience at which it is man who lives, and not the individual, and at which the weal or woe of the single human being does not count, but only human existence. This is why every great work of art is objective and impersonal, but none the less profoundly moves us each and all. And this is also why the personal life of the poet cannot be held essential to his art—but at most a help or a hindrance to his creative task. He may go the way of a Philistine, a good citizen, a neurotic, a fool or a criminal. His personal career may be inevitable and interesting, but it does not explain the poet.

FRANCIS FERGUSSON:

Oedipus Rex: The Tragic Rhythm of Action*

. . . quel secondo regno dove l'umano spirito si purga.†—*Purgatorio,* CANTO I

I SUPPOSE there can be little doubt that *Oedipus Rex* is a crucial instance of drama, if not *the* play which best exemplifies this art in its essential nature and its completeness. It owes its position partly to the fact that Aristotle founded his definitions upon it. But since the time of Aristotle it has been imitated, rewritten, and discussed by many different generations, not only of dramatists, but also of moralists, psychologists, historians, and other students of human nature and destiny.

Though the play is thus generally recognized as an archetype, there has been little agreement about its meaning or its form. It seems to beget, in every period, a different interpretation and a different dramaturgy. From the seventeenth century until the end of the eighteenth, a Neoclassic and rationalistic interpretation of *Oedipus,* of Greek tragedy, and of Aristotle, was generally accepted; and upon this interpretation was based the dramaturgy of Corneille and Racine. Nietzsche, under the inspiration of Wagner's *Tristan und Isolde,* developed a totally different view of it, and thence a different theory of drama. These two views of Greek tragedy, Racine's and Nietzsche's, still provide indispensable perspectives upon *Oedipus.* They show a great deal about modern principles of dramatic composition; and they show, when compared, how central and how essential Sophocles' drama is. . . .

In our day a conception of *Oedipus* seems to be developing which is neither that of Racine nor that of Nietzsche. This view is based upon the studies which the Cambridge School, Fraser, Cornford, Harrison, Murray, made of the ritual origins of Greek tragedy. It also owes a great deal to the current interest in myth as a way of ordering human experience. *Oedipus,* we now see, is both myth and ritual. It assumes and employs these two ancient ways of understanding and representing human experience, which are prior to the arts and sciences and philosophies of modern times. To understand it (it now appears)

* "*Oedipus Rex:* The Tragic Rhythm of Action" is the first chapter of Francis Fergusson's *The Idea of a Theater,* published by Princeton University Press in 1949 and reprinted here with the permission of that press. Mr. Fergusson, born in 1904, is the author of many essays and critical reviews and of another book, *Dante's Drama of the Mind* (1953).

† ". . . that second realm where the human spirit is purged."

we must endeavor to recapture the habit of significant make-believe, of the direct perception of action, which underlies Sophocles' theater.

If *Oedipus* is to be understood in this way, then we shall have to revise our ideas of Sophocles' dramaturgy. The notion of Aristotle's theory of drama, and hence of Greek dramaturgy, which still prevails (in spite of such studies as Butcher's of the *Poetics*) is largely colored by Neoclassic taste and rationalistic habits of mind. If we are to take it that Sophocles was imitating action before theory, instead of after it, like Racine, then both the elements and the form of his composition appear in a new light.

In the present essay the attempt is made to draw the deductions, for Sophocles' theater and dramaturgy, which the present view of *Oedipus* implies. We shall find that the various traditional views of this play are not so much wrong as partial.

OEDIPUS, MYTH AND PLAY

When Sophocles came to write his play he had the myth of Oedipus to start with. Laius and Jocasta, King and Queen of Thebes, are told by the oracle that their son will grow up to kill his father and marry his mother. The infant, his feet pierced, is left on Mount Kitharon to die. But a shepherd finds him and takes care of him; at last gives him to another shepherd, who takes him to Corinth, and there the King and Queen bring him up as their own son. But Oedipus—"Club-foot"—is plagued in his turn by the oracle; he hears that he is fated to kill his father and marry his mother; and to escape that fate he leaves Corinth never to return. On his journey he meets an old man with his servants; gets into a dispute with him, and kills him and all his followers. He comes to Thebes at the time when the Sphinx is preying upon that City; solves the riddle which the Sphinx propounds, and saves the City. He marries the widowed Queen, Jocasta; has several children by her; rules prosperously for many years. But, when Thebes is suffering under a plague and a drought, the oracle reports that the gods are angry because Laius' slayer is unpunished. Oedipus, as King, undertakes to find him; discovers that he is himself the culprit and that Jocasta is his own mother. He blinds himself and goes into exile. From this time forth he becomes a sort of sacred relic, like the bones of a saint; perilous, but "good medicine" for the community that possesses him. He dies, at last, at Athens, in a grove sacred to the Eumenides, female spirits of fertility and night.

It is obvious, even from this sketch, that the myth, which covers several generations, has as much narrative material as *Gone with the Wind*. We do not know what versions of the story Sophocles used. It is the way of myths that they generate whole progenies of elaborations and varying versions. They are so suggestive, seem to say so much, yet so mysteriously, that the mind cannot rest content with any single form, but must add, or interpret, or simplify—reduce to terms which the reason can accept. Mr. William Troy suggests that "what is possibly most in order at the moment is a thoroughgoing refurbishment of the medieval fourfold method of interpretation, which was first developed, it will be recalled, for just such a purpose—to make at least partially available to the reason that complex of human problems which are embedded, deep and imponderable, in the Myth." [1] It appears that Sophocles, in his play, succeeded in preserving the suggestive mystery of the Oedipus myth, while presenting it in a wonderfully unified dramatic form; and this drama has all the dimensions which the fourfold method was intended to explore.

Everyone knows that when Sophocles planned the plot of the play itself, he started almost at the end of the story, when the plague descends upon the City of Thebes which Oedipus and Jocasta had been ruling with great success for a number of years. The action of the play takes less than a day, and consists of Oedipus' quest for Laius' slayer—his consulting the Oracle of Apollo, his examination of the Prophet, Tiresias, and of a series of witnesses, ending with the old Shepherd who gave him to the King and Queen of Corinth. The play ends when Oedipus is unmistakably revealed as himself the culprit.

At this literal level, the play is intelligible as a murder mystery. Oedipus takes the role of District Attorney; and when he at last convicts himself, we have a twist, a *coup de théâtre,* of unparalleled excitement. But no one who sees or reads the play can rest content with its literal coherence. Questions as to its meaning arise at

[1] "Myth, Method and the Future," by William Troy. *Chimera*, spring, 1946.

once: Is Oedipus really guilty, or simply a victim of the gods, of his famous complex, of fate, of original sin? How much did he know, all along? How much did Jocasta know? The first, and most deeply instinctive effort of the mind, when confronted with this play, is to endeavor to reduce its meanings to some set of rational categories.

The critics of the Age of Reason tried to understand it as a fable of the enlightened moral will, in accordance with the philosophy of that time. Voltaire's version of the play, following Corneille, and his comments upon it, may be taken as typical. He sees it as essentially a struggle between a strong and righteous Oedipus, and the malicious and very human gods, aided and abetted by the corrupt priest Tiresias; he makes it an antireligious tract, with an unmistakable moral to satisfy the needs of the discursive intellect. In order to make Oedipus "sympathetic" to his audience, he elides, as much as possible, the incest motif; and he adds an irrelevant love story. He was aware that his version and interpretation were not those of Sophocles but, with the complacent provinciality of his period, he attributes the difference to the darkness of the age in which *Sophocles* lived.

Other attempts to rationalize *Oedipus Rex* are subtler than Voltaire's, and take us further toward an understanding of the play. Freud's reduction of the play to the concepts of his psychology reveals a great deal, opens up perspectives which we are still exploring. If one reads *Oedipus* in the light of Fustel de Coulanges' *The Ancient City,* one may see it as the expression of the ancient patriarchal religion of the Greeks. And other interpretations of the play, theological, philosophical, historical, are available, none of them wrong, but all partial, all reductions of Sophocles' masterpiece to an alien set of categories. For the peculiar virtue of Sophocles' presentation of the myth is that it preserves the ultimate mystery by focusing upon the tragic human at a level beneath, or prior to, any rationalization whatever. The plot is so arranged that we see the action, as it were, illumined from many sides at once.

By starting the play at the end of the story, and showing on-stage only the last crucial episode in Oedipus' life, the past and present action of the protagonist are revealed together; and, in each other's light, are at last felt as one. Oedipus' quest for the slayer of Laius becomes a quest for the hidden reality of his own past; and as that slowly comes into focus, like repressed material under psychoanalysis—with sensory and emotional immediacy, yet in the light of acceptance and understanding—his immediate quest also reaches its end: he comes to see himself (the Savior of the City) and the guilty one, the plague of Thebes, at once and at one.

This presentation of the myth of Oedipus constitutes, in one sense, an "interpretation" of it. What Sophocles saw as the essence of Oedipus' nature and destiny, is not what Seneca or Dryden or Cocteau saw; and one may grant that even Sophocles did not exhaust the possibilities in the materials of the myth. But Sophocles' version of the myth does not constitute a "reduction" in the same sense as the rest.

I have said that the action which Sophocles shows is a quest, the quest for Laius' slayer; and that as Oedipus' past is unrolled before us his whole life is seen as a kind of quest for his true nature and destiny. But since the object of this quest is not clear until the end, the seeking action takes many forms, as its object appears in different lights. The object, indeed, the final perception, the "truth," looks so different at the end from what it did at the beginning that Oedipus' action itself may seem not a quest, but its opposite, a flight. Thus it would be hard to say, simply, that Oedipus either succeeds or fails. He succeeds; but his success is his undoing. He fails to find what, in one way, he sought; yet from another point of view his search is brilliantly successful. The same ambiguities surround his effort to discover who and what he is. He seems to find that he is nothing; yet thereby finds himself. And what of his relation to the gods? His quest may be regarded as a heroic attempt to escape their decrees, or as an attempt, based upon some deep natural faith, to discover what their wishes are, and what true obedience would be. In one sense Oedipus suffers forces he can neither control nor understand, the puppet of fate; yet at the same time he wills and intelligently intends his every move.

The meaning, or spiritual content of the play, is not to be sought by trying to resolve such ambiguities as these. The spiritual content of the play is the tragic action which Sophocles directly presents; and this action is in its essence *zweideutig:* triumph and destruction, darkness and enlightenment, mourning and rejoicing, at any moment we care to consider it. But this action has also a shape: a beginning, middle, and end, in time. It starts with the reasoned purpose of finding Laius' slayer. But this aim meets unforeseen difficulties, evidences which do not fit, and therefore shake the purpose as it was first understood; and so the characters suffer the piteous and terrible sense of the mystery of the human situation. From this suffering or passion, with its shifting visions, a new perception of the situation emerges; and on that basis the purpose of the action is redefined, and a new movement starts. This movement, or *tragic rhythm of action,* constitutes the shape of the play as a whole; it is also the shape of each episode, each discussion between principals with the chorus following. Mr. Kenneth Burke has studied the tragic rhythm in his *Philosophy of Literary Form,* and also in *A Grammar of Motives,* where he gives the three moments traditional designations which are very suggestive: *Poiema, Pathema, Mathema.* They may also be called, for convenience, Purpose, Passion (or Suffering) and Perception. It is this tragic rhythm of action which is the substance or spiritual content of the play, and the clue to its extraordinarily comprehensive form.

In order to illustrate these points in more detail, it is convenient to examine the scene between Oedipus and Tiresias with the chorus following it. This episode, being early in the play (the first big agon), presents, as it were, a preview of the whole action and constitutes a clear and complete example of action in the tragic rhythm.

HERO AND SCAPEGOAT: THE AGON BETWEEN OEDIPUS AND TIRESIAS

The scene between Oedipus and Tiresias comes after the opening sections of the play. We have seen the citizens of Thebes beseeching their King to find some way to lift the plague which is on the City. We have had Oedipus' entrance (majestic, but for his tell-tale limp) to reassure them, and we have heard the report which Creon brings from the Delphic Oracle: that the cause of the plague is the unpunished murder of Laius, the former king. Oedipus offers rewards to anyone who will reveal the culprit, and he threatens with dire punishment anyone who conceals or protects him. In the meantime, he decides, with the enthusiastic assent of the chorus, to summon Tiresias as the first witness.

Tiresias is that suffering seer whom Sophocles uses in *Antigone* also to reveal a truth which other mortal find it hard and uncomfortable to see. He is physically blind, but Oedipus and chorus alike assume that if anyone can see who the culprit is, it is Tiresias, with his uncanny inner vision of the future. As Tiresias enters, led by a boy, the chorus greets him in these words: [2]

CHORUS. But the man to convict him is here. Look: they are bringing the one human being in whom the truth is native, the godlike seer.

Oedipus is, at this point in the play, at the opposite pole of experience from Tiresias: he is hero, monarch, helmsman of the state; the solver of the Sphinx's riddle, the triumphant being. He explains his purpose in the following proud clear terms:

OED. O Tiresias, you know all things: what may be told, and the unspeakable: things of earth and things of heaven. You understand the City (though you do not see it) in its present mortal illness—from which to save us and protect us, we find, Lord, none but you. For you must know, in case you haven't heard it from the messengers, that Apollo, when we asked him, told us there was one way only with this plague: to discover Laius' slayers, and put them to death or send them into exile. Therefore you must not jealously withhold your omens, whether of birds or other visionary way, but save yourself and the City—save me, save all of us—from the defilement of the dead. In your hand we are. There is no handsomer work for a man, than to bring, with what he has, what help he can.

This speech is the prologue of the scene, and the basis of the agon or struggle which follows. This struggle in effect analyzes Oedipus' purpose; places it in a wider context, reveals it as faulty and dubious. At the end of the scene Oedipus loses his original purpose altogether, and suffers a wave of rage and fear, which will have to be rationalized in its turn before he can "pull himself together" and act again with a clear purpose.

[2] I am responsible for the English of this scene. The reader is referred to *Oedipus Rex,* translated by Dudley Fitts and Robert Fitzgerald (New York: Harcourt, Brace and Co., 1949), a very handsome version of the whole play.

In the first part of the struggle, Oedipus takes the initiative, while Tiresias, on the defensive, tries to avoid replying:

TIR. Oh, oh. How terrible to know, when nothing can come of knowing! Indeed, I had lost the vision of these things, or I should never have come.

OED. What things? . . . In what discouragement have you come to us here!

TIR. Let me go home. I shall endure this most easily, and so will you, if you do as I say.

OED. But what you ask is not right. To refuse your word is disloyalty to the City that has fed you.

TIR. But I see that your demands are exorbitant, and lest I too suffer such a—

OED. For the sake of the gods, if you know, don't turn away! Speak to us, we are your suppliants here.

TIR. None of you understands. But I—I never will tell my misery. Or yours.

OED. What are you saying? You know, but tell us nothing? You intend treachery to us, and death to the City?

TIR. I intend to grieve neither myself nor you. Why then do you try to know? You will never learn from me.

OED. Ah, evil old man! You would anger a stone! You will say *nothing?* Stand futile, speechless before us?

TIR. You curse my temper, but you don't see the one that dwells in you; no, you must blame me.

OED. And who would *not* lose his temper, if he heard you utter your scorn of the City?

TIR. It will come. Silent though I be.

OED. Since it will come, it is your duty to inform me.

TIR. I shall say no more. Now, if you like, rage to your bitter heart's content.

OED. Very well: in my "rage" I shall hold back nothing which I now begin to see. I think you planned that deed, even performed it, though not with your own hands. If you could see, I should say that the work was yours alone.

In the last speech quoted, Oedipus changes his tack, specifying his purpose differently; he accuses Tiresias, and that makes Tiresias attack. In the next part of the fight the opponents trade blow for blow:

TIR. You would? I charge you, abide by the decree you uttered: from this day forth, speak neither to these present, nor to me, unclean as you are, polluter of the earth!

OED. You have the impudence to speak out words like these! And now how do you expect to escape?

TIR. I have escaped. The truth strengthens and sustains me.

OED. Who taught you the truth? Not your prophet's art.

TIR. You did; you force me against my will to speak.

OED. Speak what? Speak again, that I may understand better.

TIR. *Didn't* you understand? Or are you goading me?

OED. I can't say I really grasp it: speak again.

TIR. I say you are the murderer of the man whose murderer you seek.

OED. You won't be glad to have uttered that curse twice.

TIR. Must I say more, so you may rage the more?

OED. As much as you like—all is senseless.

TIR. I say you do not know your own wretchedness, nor see in what shame you live with those you love.

OED. Do you think you can say that forever with impunity?

TIR. If the truth has power.

OED. It has, with all but you: helpless is truth with you: for you are blind, in eye, in ear, in mind.

TIR. You are the impotent one: you utter slanders which every man here will apply to you.

OED. You have your being only in the night; you couldn't hurt me or any man who sees the sun.

TIR. No. Your doom is not to fall by me. Apollo suffices for that, he will bring it about.

OED. Are these inventions yours, or Creon's?

TIR. Your wretchedness is not Creon's, it is yours.

OED. O wealth, and power, and skill—which skill, in emulous life, brings low—what envy eyes you! if for this kingly power which the City gave into my hands, unsought—if for *this* the faithful Creon, my friend from the first, has stalked me in secret, yearning to supplant me! if he has bribed this juggling wizard, this deceitful beggar, who discerns his profit only, blind in his own art!

Tell me now, tell me where you have proved a true diviner? Why, when the song-singing sphinx was near, did you not speak deliverance to the people? Her riddles were not for any comer to solve, but for the mantic art, and you were apparently instructed neither by birds nor by any sign from the gods. Yet when I came, I, Oedipus, all innocent, I stopped her song. No birds taught me, by my own wit I found the answer. And it is I whom you wish to banish, thinking that you will then stand close to Creon's throne.

You and your ally will weep, I think, for this attempt; and in fact, if you didn't seem to be an old man, you would already have learned, in pain, of your presumption.

In this part the beliefs, the visions, and hence the purposes of the antagonists are directly contrasted. Because both identify themselves so completely with their visions and purposes, the fight descends from the level of dialectic to a level below the rational altogether: it becomes cruelly *ad hominem*. We are made to see the absurd incommensurability of the very beings of Oedipus and Tiresias; they shrink from one another as from the uncanny. At the end of the round, it is Oedipus who has received the deeper wound; and his great speech, "O wealth and power," is a far more lyric utterance than the ordered exposition with which he began.

The end of this part of the fight is marked by the intervention of the chorus, which endeavors to recall the antagonists to the most general version of purpose which they supposedly share: the discovery of the truth and the service of the gods:

CHORUS. To us it appears that this man's words were uttered in anger, and yours too, Oedipus. No need for that: consider how best to discharge the mandate of the god.

The last part of the struggle shows Tiresias presenting his whole vision, and Oedipus, on the defensive, shaken to the depths:

TIR. Although you rule, we have equally the right to reply; in that I too have power. Indeed, I live to serve, not you, but Apollo; and I shall not be enrolled under Creon, either. Therefore I say, since you have insulted even my blindness, that though you have eyesight, you do not see what misery you are in, nor where you are living, nor with whom. Do you know whence you came? No, nor that you are the enemy of your own family, the living and the dead. The double prayer of mother and father shall from this land hound you in horror—who now see clearly, but then in darkness.

Where then will your cry be bounded? What part of Kitharon not echo it quickly back, when you shall come to understand that marriage, to which you sailed on so fair a wind, homelessly home? And many other evils which you do not see will bring you to yourself at last, your children's equal.

Scorn Creon, therefore, and my words: you will be struck down more terribly than any mortal.

OED. Can I really hear such things from him? Are you not gone? To death? To punishment? Not fled from this house?

TIR. I should never have come if you hadn't called me.

OED. I didn't know how mad you would sound, or it would have been a long time before I asked you here to my house.

TIR. This is what I am; foolish, as it seems to you; but wise, to the parents who gave you birth.

OED. To whom? Wait: *who* gave me birth?

TIR. This day shall give you birth, and death.

OED. In what dark riddles you always speak.

TIR. Aren't you the best diviner of riddles?

OED. Very well: mock that gift, which, you will find, is mine.

TIR. That very gift was your undoing.

OED. But if I saved the City, what does it matter?

TIR. So be it. I am going. Come, boy, lead me.

OED. Take him away. Your presence impedes and trips me; once you are gone, you can do no harm.

TIR. I shall go when I have done my errand without fear of your frowns, for they can't hurt me. I tell you, then, that the man whom you have long been seeking, with threats and proclamations, Laius' slayer, is here. He is thought to be an alien, but will appear a native Theban, and this circumstance will not please him. Blind, who once could see; destitute, who once was rich, leaning on a staff, he will make his way through a strange land. He will be revealed as brother and father of his own children; of the woman who bore him, both son and husband; sharer of his father's bed; his father's killer.

Go in and ponder this. If you find it wrong, say then I do not understand the prophetic vision.

Oedipus rushes off-stage, his clear purpose gone, his being shaken with fear and anger. Tiresias departs, led by his boy. The chorus is left to move and chant, suffering the mixed and ambivalent feelings, the suggestive but mysterious images, which the passion in which the agon eventuated produces in them:

CHORUS.

Strophe I. Who is it that the god's voice from the Rock of Delphi says
Accomplished the unspeakable with murderous hands?
Time now that windswift
Stronger than horses
His feet take flight.
In panoply of fire and lightning
Now springs upon him the son of Zeus
Whom the dread follow,
The Fates unappeasable.

Antistrophe I. New word, like light, from snowy Parnassus:

Over all the earth trail the unseen one.
For in rough wood,
In cave or rocks,
Like bull bereft—stampeded, futile
He goes, seeking with futile foot to
Flee the ultimate
Doom, which ever
Lives and flies over him.

Strophe II. In awe now, and soul's disorder, I neither accept
The augur's wisdom, nor deny: I know not what to say.
I hover in hope, see neither present nor future.
Between the House of Laius
And Oedipus, I do not hear, have never heard, of any feud:
I cannot confirm the public charge against him, to help
Avenge the dark murder.

Antistrophe II. Zeus and Apollo are wise, and all that is mortal
They know: but whether that human seer knows more than I
There is no way of telling surely, though in wisdom
A man may excel.
Ah, never could I, till I see that word confirmed, consent to blame him!
Before all eyes the winged songstress, once, assailed him;
Wise showed he in that test, and to the City, tender; in my heart
I will call him evil never.

The chorus is considered in more detail below. At this point I merely wish to point out that Oedipus and Tiresias show, in their agon, the "purpose" part of the tragic rhythm; that this turns to "passion," and that the chorus presents the passion and also the new perception which follows. This new perception is that of Oedipus as the possible culprit. But his outlines are vague; perhaps the vision itself is illusory, a bad dream. The chorus has not yet reached the end of its quest; that will come only when Oedipus, in the flesh before them, is unmistakably seen as the guilty one. We have reached merely a provisional resting-place, the end of the first figure in which the tragic rhythm is presented. But this figure is a reduced version of the shape of the play as a whole, and the fleeting and unwelcome image of Oedipus as guilty corresponds to the final perception or epiphany, the full-stop, with which the play ends.

OEDIPUS: RITUAL AND PLAY

The Cambridge School of Classical Anthropologists has shown in great detail that the form of Greek tragedy follows the form of a very ancient ritual, that of the *Enniautos-Daimon,* or seasonal god.[3] This was one of the most influential discoveries of the last few generations, and it gives us new insights into *Oedipus* which I think are not yet completely explored. The clue to Sophocles' dramatizing of the myth of Oedipus is to be found in this ancient ritual, which had a similar form and meaning—that is, it also moved in the "tragic rhythm."

Experts in classical anthropology, like experts in other fields, dispute innumerable questions of fact and of interpretation which the layman can only pass over in respectful silence. One of the thornier questions seems to be whether myth or ritual came first. Is the ancient ceremony merely an enactment of the Ur-Myth of the year-god—Attis, or Adonis, or Osiris, or the "Fisher-King"—in any case that Hero-King-Father-High-Priest who fights with his rival, is slain and dismembered, then rises anew with the spring season? Or did the innumerable myths of this kind arise to "explain" a ritual which was perhaps mimed or danced or sung to celebrate the annual change of season?

For the purpose of understanding the form and meaning of *Oedipus,* it is not necessary to worry about the answer to this question of historic fact. The figure of Oedipus himself fulfills all the requirements of the scapegoat, the dismembered king or god-figure. The situation in which Thebes is presented at the beginning of the play—in peril of its life; its crops, its herds, its women mysteriously infertile, signs of a mortal disease of the City, and the disfavor of the gods—is like the withering which winter brings, and calls, in the same way, for struggle, dismemberment, death, and renewal. And this tragic sequence is the substance of the play. It is enough to know that myth and ritual are close together in their genesis, two direct imitations of the perennial experience of the race.

But when one considers *Oedipus* as a ritual one understands it in ways which one cannot by

[3] See especially Jane Ellen Harrison's *Ancient Art and Ritual,* and her *Themis* which contains an "Excursus on the Ritual Forms Preserved in Greek Tragedy" by Professor Gilbert Murray.

thinking of it merely as a dramatization of a story, even that story. Harrison has shown that the Festival of Dionysos, based ultimately upon the yearly vegetation ceremonies, included *rites de passage*, like that celebrating the assumption of adulthood—celebrations of the mystery of individual growth and development. At the same time, it was a prayer for the welfare of the whole City; and this welfare was understood not only as material prosperity, but also as the natural order of the family, the ancestors, the present members, and the generations still to come, and, by the same token, obedience to the gods who were jealous, each in his own province, of this natural and divinely sanctioned order and proportion.

We must suppose that Sophocles' audience (the whole population of the City) came early, prepared to spend the day in the bleachers. At their feet was the semicircular dancing-ground for the chorus, and the thrones for the priests, and the altar. Behind that was the raised platform for the principal actors, backed by the all-purpose, emblematic façade, which would presently be taken to represent Oedipus' palace in Thebes. The actors were not professionals in our sense, but citizens selected for a religious office, and Sophocles himself had trained them and the chorus.

This crowd must have had as much appetite for thrills and diversion as the crowds who assemble in our day for football games and musical comedies, and Sophocles certainly holds the attention with an exciting show. At the same time his audience must have been alert for the fine points of poetry and dramaturgy, for *Oedipus* is being offered in competition with other plays on the same bill. But the element which distinguishes this theater, giving it its unique directness and depth, is the *ritual expectancy* which Sophocles assumed in his audience. The nearest thing we have to this ritual sense of theater is, I suppose, to be found at an Easter performance of the *Matthias Passion.* We also can observe something similar in the dances and ritual mummery of the Pueblo Indians. Sophocles' audience must have been prepared, like the Indians standing around their plaza, to consider the playing, the make-believe it was about to see—the choral invocations, with dancing and chanting; the reasoned discourses and the terrible combats of the protagonists; the mourning, the rejoicing, and the contemplation of the final stage-picture or epiphany—as imitating and celebrating the mystery of human nature and destiny. And this mystery was at once that of individual growth and development, and that of the precarious life of the human City.

I have indicated how Sophocles presents the life of the mythic Oedipus in the tragic rhythm, the mysterious quest of life. Oedipus is shown seeking his own true being; but at the same time and by the same token, the welfare of the City. When one considers the ritual form of the whole play, it becomes evident that it presents the tragic but perennial, even normal, quest of the whole City for its well-being. In this larger action, Oedipus is only the protagonist, the first and most important champion. This tragic quest is realized by all the characters in their various ways; but in the development of the action as a whole it is the chorus alone that plays a part as important as that of Oedipus; its counterpart, in fact. The chorus holds the balance between Oedipus and his antagonists, marks the progress of their struggles, and restates the main theme, and its new variation, after each dialogue or agon. The ancient ritual was probably performed by a chorus alone without individual developments and variations, and the chorus, in *Oedipus,* is still the element that throws most light on the ritual form of the play as a whole.

The chorus consists of twelve or fifteen "Elders of Thebes." This group is not intended to represent literally all of the citizens either of Thebes or of Athens. The play opens with a large delegation of Theban citizens before Oedipus' palace, and the chorus proper does not enter until after the prologue. Nor does the chorus speak directly for the Athenian audience; we are asked throughout to make-believe that the theater is the agora at Thebes; and at the same time Sophocles' audience is witnessing a ritual. It would, I think, be more accurate to say that the chorus represents the point of view and the faith of Thebes as a whole, and, by analogy, of the Athenian audience. Their errand before Oedipus' palace is like that of Sophocles' audience in the theater: they are watching a sacred combat, in the issue of which they have an all-important and official stake. Thus they represent the audience and the citizens in a particular way—not as a mob formed in response to some momentary feeling, but rather as an organ of a highly self-conscious community: something closer to the "conscience of the race" than to the overheated affectivity of a mob.

According to Aristotle, a Sophoclean chorus is a character that takes an important role in the action of the play, instead of merely making incidental music between the scenes, as in the plays of Euripides. The chorus may be described as a group personality, like an old Parliament. It has its own traditions, habits of thought and feeling, and mode of being. It exists, in a sense, as a living entity, but not with the sharp actuality of an individual. It perceives; but its perception is at once wider and vaguer than that of a single man. It shares, in its way, the seeking action of the play as a whole; but it cannot act in all the modes; it depends upon the chief agonists to invent and try out the detail of policy, just as a rather helpless but critical Parliament depends upon the Prime Minister to act but, in its less specific form of life, survives his destruction.

When the chorus enters after the prologue, with its questions, its invocation of the various gods, and its focus upon the hidden and jeopardized welfare of the City—Athens or Thebes—the list of essential *dramatis personae,* as well as the elements needed to celebrate the ritual, is complete, and the main action can begin. It is the function of the chorus to mark the stages of this action, and to perform the suffering and perceiving part of the tragic rhythm. The protagonist and his antagonists develop the "purpose" with which the tragic sequence begins; the chorus, with its less than individual being, broods over the agons, marks their stages with a word (like that of the chorus leader in the middle of the Tiresias scene), and (expressing its emotions and visions in song and dance) suffers the results, and the new perception at the end of the fight.

The choral odes are lyrics but they are not to be understood as poetry, the art of words, only, for they are intended also to be danced and sung. And though each chorus has its own shape, like that of a discrete lyric—its beginning, middle, and end—it represents also one passion or pathos in the changing action of the whole. This passion, like the other moments in the tragic rhythm, is felt at so general or, rather, so deep a level that it seems to contain both the mob ferocity that Nietzsche felt in it and, at the other extreme, the patience of prayer. It is informed by faith in the unseen order of nature and the gods, and moves through a sequence of modes of suffering. This may be illustrated from the chorus I have quoted at the end of the Tiresias scene.

It begins (close to the savage emotion of the end of the fight) with images suggesting that cruel "Bacchic frenzy" which is supposed to be the common root of tragedy and of the "old" comedy: "In panoply of fire and lightning/The son of Zeus now springs upon him." In the first antistrophe these images come together more clearly as we relish the chase; and the fleeing culprit, as we imagine him, begins to resemble Oedipus, who is lame, and always associated with the rough wilderness of Kitharon. But in the second strophe, as though appalled by its ambivalent feelings and the imagined possibilities, the chorus sinks back into a more dark and patient posture of suffering, "in awe," "hovering in hope." In the second antistrophe this is developed into something like the orthodox Christian attitude of prayer, based on faith, and assuming the possibility of a hitherto unimaginable truth and answer: "Zeus and Apollo are wise," etc. The whole chorus then ends with a new vision of Oedipus, of the culprit, and of the direction in which the welfare of the City is to be sought. This vision is still colored by the chorus's human love of Oedipus as Hero, for the chorus has still its own purgation to complete, cannot as yet accept completely either the suffering in store for it, or Oedipus as scapegoat. But it marks the end of the first complete "purpose-passion-perception" unit, and lays the basis for the new purpose which will begin the next unit.

It is also to be noted that the chorus changes the scene which we, as audience, are to imagine. During the agon between Oedipus and Tiresias, our attention is fixed upon their clash, and the scene is literal, close, and immediate: before Oedipus' palace. When the fighters depart and the choral music starts, the focus suddenly widens, as though we had been removed to a distance. We become aware of the interested City around the bright arena; and beyond that, still more dimly, of Nature, sacred to the hidden gods. Mr. Burke has expounded the fertile notion that human action may be understood in terms of the scene in which it occurs, and vice versa: the scene is defined by the mode of action. The chorus's action is not limited by the sharp, rationalized purposes of the protagonist; its mode of action, more patient, less sharply realized, is cognate with a wider, if less accurate, awareness of the scene of human life. But the chorus's action, as I have remarked, is not that of passion itself (Nietzsche's cosmic void of night) but suffering informed by the faith of the tribe in a human and a divinely sanctioned natural order: "If such deeds as these are honored," the chorus asks after Jocasta's impiety, "why should I dance and sing?" (lines 894, 895). Thus it is one of the most important functions of the chorus to reveal, in its widest and most mysterious extent, the theater of human life which the play, and indeed the whole Festival of Dionysos, assumed. Even when the chorus does not speak, but only watches, it maintains this theme and this perspective—ready to take the whole stage when the fighters depart.

If one thinks of the movement of the play, it appears that the tragic rhythm analyzes human action temporally into successive modes, as a crystal analyzes a white beam of light spatially into the colored bands of the spectrum. The chorus, always present, represents one of these modes, and at the recurrent moments when reasoned purpose is gone, it takes the stage with its faith-informed passion, moving through an ordered succession of modes of suffering, to a new perception of the immediate situation.

SOPHOCLES AND EURIPIDES, THE RATIONALIST

Oedipus Rex is a changing image of human life and action which could have been formed only in the mirror of the tragic theater of the Festival of Dionysos. The perspectives of the myth, of the rituals, and of the traditional *hodos*, the way of life of the City—"habits of thought and feeling" which constitute the traditional wisdom of the race—were all required to make this play possible. That is why we have to try to regain these perspectives if we are to understand the written play which has come down to us: the analysis of the play leads to an analysis of the theater in which it was formed.

But though the theater was there, everyone could not use it to the full: Sophocles was required. This becomes clear if one considers the very different use which Euripides, Sophocles' contemporary, makes of the tragic theater and its ritual forms.

Professor Gilbert Murray has explained in detail how the tragic form is derived from the ritual form; and he has demonstrated the ritual forms which are preserved in each of the extant Greek tragedies. In general, the ritual had its agon, or sacred combat, between the old King, or god or hero, and the new, corresponding to the agons in the tragedies, and the clear "purpose" moment of the tragic rhythm. It had its *Sparagmos,* in which the royal victim was literally or symbolically torn asunder, followed by the lamentation and/or rejoicing of the chorus: elements which correspond to the moments of "passion." The ritual had its messenger, its recognition scene, and its epiphany; various plot devices for representing the moment of "perception" which follows the "pathos." Professor Murray, in a word, studies the art of tragedy in the light of ritual forms, and thus, throws a really new light upon Aristotle's *Poetics.* The parts of the ritual would appear to correspond to parts of the plot, like recognitions and scenes of suffering, which Aristotle mentions, but, in the text which has come down to us, fails to expound completely. In this view, both the ritual and the more highly elaborated and individualized art of tragedy would be "imitating" action in the tragic rhythm; the parts of the ritual, and the parts of the plot, would both be devices for showing forth the three moments of this rhythm.

Professor Murray, however, does not make precisely these deductions. Unlike Aristotle, he takes the plays of Euripides, rather than Sophocles' *Oedipus,* as the patterns of the tragic form. That is because his attitude to the ritual forms is like Euripides' own: he responds to their purely theatrical effectiveness, but has no interest or belief in the prerational image of human nature and destiny which the ritual conveyed; which Sophocles felt as still alive and significant for his generation, and presented once more in *Oedipus.* Professor Murray shows that Euripides restored the literal ritual much more accurately than Sophocles—his epiphanies, for example, are usually the bodily showing-forth of a very human god, who cynically expounds his cruel part in the proceedings; while the "epiphany" in *Oedipus,* the final tableau of the blind old man with his incestuous brood, merely conveys the moral truth which underlay the action, and implies the anagoge: human dependence upon a mysterious and divine order of nature. Perhaps these distinctions may be summarized as follows: Professor Murray is interested in the ritual forms in abstraction from all content; Sophocles saw also the spiritual content of the old forms: understood them at a level deeper than the literal, as imitations of an action still "true" to life in his sophisticated age.

Though Euripides and Sophocles wrote at the same time and for the same theater, one cannot understand either the form or the meaning of Euripides' plays on the basis of Sophocles' dramaturgy. The beautiful lyrics sung by Euripides' choruses are, as I have said, incidental music rather than organic parts of the action; they are not based upon the feeling that all have a stake in the common way of life and therefore in the issue of the present action. Euripides' individualistic heroes find no light in their suffering, and bring no renewal to the moral life of the community: they are at war with the very clear, human, and malicious gods, and what they suffer, they suffer unjustly and to no good end. Where Sophocles' celebrated irony seems to envisage the *condition humaine* itself—the plight of the psyche in a world which is ultimately mysterious to it—Euripides' ironies are all aimed at the incredible "gods" and at the superstitions of those who believe in them. In short, if these two writers both used the tragic theater, they did so in very different ways.

Verral's *Euripides the Rationalist* shows very clearly what the basis of Euripides' dramaturgy is. His use of myth and ritual is like that which Cocteau or, still more exactly, Sartre makes of them—for parody or satirical exposition, but without any belief in their meaning. If Euripides presents the plight of Electra in realistic detail, it is because he wants us to feel the suffering of the individual without benefit of any objective moral or cosmic order—with an almost sensational immediacy: he does not see the myth, as a whole, as significant as such. If he brings Apollo, in the flesh, before us, it is not because he "believes" in Apollo, but because he disbelieves in him, and wishes to reveal this figment of the Greek imagination as, literally, incredible. He depends as much as Sophocles upon the common heritage of ritual and myth: but he "reduces" its form and images to the uses of parody and metaphorical illustration, in the manner of Ovid and of the French Neoclassic tradition. And the human action he reveals is the extremely modern one of the psyche caught in the categories its reason invents, responding with unmitigated sharpness to the feeling of the moment, but cut off from the deepest level of experience, where the mysterious world is yet felt as real and prior to our inventions, demands, and criticisms.

Though Sophocles was not using the myths and ritual forms of the tragic theater for parody and to satirize their tradition, it does not appear that he had any more naïve belief in their literal validity than Euripides did. He would not, for his purpose, have had to ask himself whether the myth of Oedipus conveyed any historic facts. He would not have had to believe that the performance of *Oedipus,* or even the Festival of Dionysos itself, would assure the Athenians a good crop of children and olives. On the contrary he must have felt that the tragic rhythm of action which he discerned in the myth, which he felt as underlying the forms of the ritual, and which he realized in so many ways in his play, was a deeper version of human life than any particular manifestation of it, or any conceptual understanding of it, whether scientific and rationalistic, or theological; yet potentially including them all. If one takes Mr. Troy's suggestion, one might say, using the Medieval notion of fourfold symbolism, that Sophocles might well have taken myth and ritual as literally "fictions," yet still have accepted their deeper meanings—trope, allegory, and anagoge—as valid.

OEDIPUS: THE IMITATION OF AN ACTION

The general notion we used to compare the forms and spiritual content of tragedy and of ancient ritual was the "imitation of action." Ritual imitates action in one way, tragedy in another; and Sophocles' use of ritual forms indicates that he sensed the tragic rhythm common to both.

But the language, plot, characters of the play may also be understood in more detail and in relation to each other as imitations, in their various media, of the one action. I have already quoted Coleridge on the unity of action: "not properly a rule," he calls it, "but in itself the great end, not only of the drama, but of the epic, lyric, even to the candle-flame cone of an epigram—not only of poetry, but of poesy in general, as the proper generic term inclusive of all the fine arts, as its species."[4] Probably the influence of Coleridge partly accounts for the revival of this notion of action which underlies the recent studies of poetry which I have mentioned. Mr. Burke's phrase, "language as symbolic action," expresses the idea, and so does his dictum: "The poet spontaneously knows that 'beauty *is* as beauty *does*' (that the 'state' must be embodied in an 'actualization')." (*Four Tropes.*)

This idea of action, and of the play as the imitation of an action, is ultimately derived from the *Poetics*. . . . I wish to show how the complex form of *Oedipus*—its plot, characters, and discourse—may be understood as the imitation of a certain action.

The action of the play is the quest for Laius' slayer. That is the over-all aim which informs it—"to find the culprit in order to purify human life," as it may be put. Sophocles must have seen this seeking action as the real life of the Oedipus myth, discerning it through the personages and events as one discerns "life in a plant through the green leaves." Moreover, he must have seen this particular action as a type, or crucial instance, of human life in general; and hence he was able to present it in the form of the ancient ritual which also presents and celebrates the perennial mystery of human life and action. Thus by "action" I do not mean the events of the story but the focus or aim of psychic life from which the events, in that situation, result.

If Sophocles was imitating action in this sense, one may schematically imagine his work of composition in three stages, three mimetic acts: 1. He makes the plot: i.e., arranges the events of the story in such a way as to reveal the seeking action from which they come. 2. He develops the characters of the story as individualized forms of "quest." 3. He expresses or realizes their actions by means of the words they utter in the various situations of the plot. This scheme, of course, has nothing to do with the temporal order which the poet may really have followed in elaborating his composition, nor to the order we follow in becoming acquainted with it; we start with the words, the "green leaves." The scheme refers to the "hierarchy of actualizations" which we may eventually learn to see in the completed work.

1. The first act of imitation consists in making the plot or arrangement of incidents. Aristotle says that the tragic poet is primarily a maker of plots, for the plot is the "soul of a tragedy," its formal cause. The arrangement which Sophocles made of the events of the story—starting near the end, and rehearsing the past in relation to what is happening now—already to some degree actualizes the tragic quest he wishes to show, even before we sense the characters as individuals or hear them speak and sing.

(The reader must be warned that this conception of the plot is rather unfamiliar to us. Usually we do not distinguish between the plot as the form of the play and the plot as producing a certain effect upon the audience—excitement, "interest," suspense, and the like. Aristotle also uses "plot" in this second sense. The mimicry of art has a further purpose, or final—as distinguished from its formal—cause, i.e., to reach the audience. Thinking of the Athenian theater, he describes the plot as intended to show the "universal," or to rouse and purge the emotions of pity and terror. . . . I am using the word *plot* in the first sense: as the form, the first actualization, of the tragic action.)

2. The characters, or agents, are the second actualization of the action. According to Aristotle, "the agents are imitated mainly with a view to the action"—i.e., the soul of the tragedy is there already in the order of events, the tragic rhythm of the life of Oedipus and Thebes; but this action may be more sharply realized and more elaborately shown forth by developing individual variations upon it. It was with this principle in mind that Ibsen wrote to his publisher, after two years of work on *The Wild Duck*, that the play was nearly complete, and he could now proceed to "the more energetic individuation of the characters."

If one considers the Oedipus-Tiresias scene which I have quoted, one can see how the characters serve to realize the action of the whole. They reveal, at any moment, a "spectrum of action" like that which the tragic rhythm spread before us in temporal succession, at the same time offering concrete instances of almost photographic sharpness. Thus Tiresias "suffers" in the

[4] The essay on *Othello*.

darkness of his blindness while Oedipus pursues his reasoned "purpose"; and then Tiresias effectuates his "purpose" of serving his mantic vision of the truth, while Oedipus "suffers" a blinding passion of fear and anger. The agents also serve to move the action ahead, develop it in time, through their conflicts. The chorus meanwhile, in some respects between, in others deeper, than the antagonists, represents the interests of that resolution, that final chord of feeling, in which the end of the action, seen ironically and sympathetically as one, will be realized.

3. The third actualization is in the words of the play. The seeking action which is the substance of the play is imitated first in the plot, second in the characters, and third in the words, concepts, and forms of discourse wherein the characters "actualize" their psychic life in its shifting forms, in response to the everchanging situations of the play. If one thinks of plotting, characterization, and poetry as successive "acts of imitation" by the author, one may also say that they constitute, in the completed work, a hierarchy of forms; and that the words of the play are its "highest individuation." They are the "green leaves" which we actually perceive; the product and the sign of the one "life of the plant" which, by an imaginative effort, one may divine behind them all.

At this point one encounters again Mr. Burke's theory of "language as symbolic action," and the many contemporary studies of the arts of poetry which have been made from this point of view. It would be appropriate to offer a detailed study of Sophocles' language, using the modern tools of analysis, to substantiate my main point. But this would require the kind of knowledge of Greek which a Jebb spent his life to acquire; and I must be content to try to show, in very general terms, that the varied forms of the poetry of *Oedipus* can only be understood on a histrionic basis: i.e., as coming out of a direct sense of the tragic rhythm of *action*.

In the Oedipus-Tiresias scene, there is a "spectrum of the forms of discourse" corresponding to the "spectrum of action" which I have described. It extends from Oedipus' opening speech —a reasoned exposition not, of course, without feeling but based essentially upon clear ideas and a logical order—to the choral chant, based upon sensuous imagery and the "logic of feeling." Thus it employs, in the beginning, the principle of composition which Mr. Burke calls "syllogistic progression," and, at the other end of the spectrum, Mr. Burke's "progression by association and contrast." When the Neoclassic and rationalistic critics of the seventeenth century read *Oedipus*, they saw only the order of reason; they did not know what to make of the chorus. Hence Racine's drama of "Action as Rational": a drama of static situations, of clear concepts and merely illustrative images. Nietzsche, on the other hand, saw only the passion of the chorus; for his insight was based on *Tristan*, which is composed essentially in sensuous images, and moves by association and contrast according to the logic of feeling: the drama which takes "action as passion." Neither point of view enables one to see how the scene, as a whole, hangs together.

If the speeches of the characters and the songs of the chorus are only the foliage of the plant, this is as much as to say that the life and meaning of the whole is never literally and completely present in any one formulation. It takes *all* of the elements—the shifting situation, the changing and developing characters, and their reasoned or lyric utterances, to indicate, in the round, the action Sophocles wishes to convey. Because this action takes the form of reason as well as passion, and of contemplation by way of symbols; because it is essentially moving (in the tragic rhythm); and because it is shared in different ways by all the characters, the play has neither literal unity nor the rational unity of the truly abstract idea, or "univocal concept." Its parts and its moments are one only "by analogy"; and just as the Saints warn us that we must believe in order to understand, so we must "make believe," by a sympathetic and imitative act of the histrionic sensibility, in order to get what Sophocles intended by his play.

It is the histrionic basis of Sophocles' art which makes it mysterious to us, with our demands for conceptual clarity, or for the luxury of yielding to a stream of feeling and subjective imagery. But it is this also which makes it so crucial an instance of the art of the theater in its completeness, as though the author understood "song, spectacle, thought, and diction" in their primitive and subtle roots. And it is the histrionic basis of drama which "undercuts theology and science."

RALPH FOX: Marxism and Literature*

Marxism is a materialist philosophy. It believes in the primacy of matter and that the world exists outside of us and independently of us. But Marxism also sees all matter as changing, as having a history, and accepts nothing as fixed and immutable. In the seventeenth century few English writers would have quarrelled with a materialist view of life, though their view of materialism would not have been the same as that of Marx and Engels. To Shakespeare, drawing his philosophical views from Rabelais and Montaigne, there would have appeared nothing outrageous in the Marxian view of life. For the greater part of the eighteenth century a materialist view of life would have been accepted without question by many of the greatest British writers.

It is not so today. It has not been so for more than a century. Today the literary journalist protests that materialism and imagination cannot go to bed together. The result, they suggest, would not be creation, but simply an unholy row. It is a curiously perverted view, for it would appear to be the most natural thing in the world for the imaginative writer, and particularly the novelist, to adopt a materialist view of life.

"Being determines consciousness" is the Marxist definition of the ultimate relation between matter and spirit. Whether or not this is the actual view of the artist it must, in fact, be the basis of his creative work. For all imaginative creation is a reflection of the real world in which the creator lives. It is the result of his contact with that world and his love or hate for what he finds in that world.

* "Marxism and Literature" is the first chapter of *The Novel and the People* (1937) and is reprinted here by permission of International Publishers Company, Inc. The fugitive writings of Ralph Fox (1900-1937) were posthumously collected by John Lehman in *Ralph Fox: A Writer in Arms* (1937).

It is the lights and colours, the forms and shapes, the breath of the winds, the scents of life, the physical beauty or the physical ugliness of animal life, including the lives of human beings, the acts, the thoughts, the dreams of actual men and women, including the creator himself, that form the stuff of art.

Milton demanded three things of poetry, that it be "simple, sensuous and passionate." Art that is not sensuous, that is not concerned with perception of the real world, with sensible objects, is not art at all, not even the shadow of art. The essence of the creative process is the struggle between the creator and external reality, the urgent demand to master and re-create that reality. "But does not Marxism claim that works of art are merely a reflection of economic needs and economic processes?" it will be objected.

No, this is not the view of Marxism, though it is the view of a number of materialists of the nineteenth century of the positivist school whose views have nothing in common with Marxian, dialectical materialism. Marx has clearly stated his ideas on the relationship between the spiritual processes of life, of which artistic creation is one, and the material basis of life, in the famous Preface to his "Critique of Political Economy." Here is the passage:

> The mode of production of the material means of existence conditions the whole process of social, political and intellectual life. It is not the consciousness of men that determines their existence, but, on the contrary, their social existence determines their consciousness. At a certain stage of their development the material forces of production in society come in conflict with the existing relations of production, or—what is but a legal expression for the same thing—with the property relations within which they had been at work before. From forms of development of the forces of production these relations turn into their fetters. Then opens an epoch of social revolution. With the

change of the economic foundation the entire immense superstructure is more or less rapidly transformed. In considering such revolutions the distinction should always be between the material revolution in the economic conditions of production which can be determined with the precision of natural science, and the juridical, political, religious, aesthetic, or philosophic—in short, ideological forms—in which men become conscious of this conflict and fight it out.

Marx, then, certainly believed that the material mode of life in the end determined the intellectual. But he never for a moment considered the connection between the two was a direct one, easily observed and mechanically developing. He would have laughed to scorn the idea that because capitalism replaces feudalism, therefore a "capitalist" art immediately replaces "feudal" art, and that all great artists must in consequence directly reflect the needs of the new capitalist class. Nor, as will appear later, did he consider that because the capitalist mode of production was a more progressive one than the feudal, capitalist art must therefore always stand on a higher level than feudal art, while feudal art in turn must stand above the art of the slave States of Greece and Rome, or the ancient Eastern monarchies. Such crude and vulgar views are foreign to the whole spirit of Marxism.

Changes in the material basis of society, Marx rightly urged, can be determined by the economic historian with the precision of natural science (which, of course, is not the same thing as saying that these changes are scientifically determined). But no such scientific measurement of the resulting changes in the social and spiritual superstructure of life is possible. The changes take place, men become conscious of them, they "fight out" the conflict between old and new in their minds, but they do so unevenly, burdened by all kinds of past heritage, often unclearly, and always in such a way that it is not easy to trace the changes in men's minds.

It is true, for example, that the Code Napoleon is the legal expression of the social and economic changes wrought by the French Revolution. Yet the knowledge of this does not in itself explain the Code Napoleon. One must understand also the past history of France and the relation of classes in that country before the Revolution, one must understand the course of the Revolution itself and the changes in class relationships which the Revolution brought about, and finally, one must understand Napoleon's military dictatorship. Then only does the Code become comprehensible as the legal expression of the new bourgeois society and the French industrial revolution which began during the Napoleonic period. And law is perhaps the most responsive part of the ideal superstructure, it changes most easily in accordance with changes in the mode of production. But art is much farther from the basis, responds far less easily to the changes in it.

Engels in a letter to J. Bloch written in 1890, was quite emphatic about this point. "According to the materialist conception of history," he wrote,

the determining element in history is *ultimately* the production and reproduction in real life. More than this neither Marx nor I have ever asserted. If therefore somebody twists this into a statement that the economic element is the *only* determining one, he transforms it into a meaningless, abstract and absurd phrase. The economic situation is the basis, but the various elements of the superstructure—political forms of the class struggle and its consequences, constitutions established by the victorious class after a successful battle, etc.—forms of law—and then even the reflexes of all these actual struggles in the brains of the combatants: political, legal, philosophical theories, religious ideas and their further development into systems of dogma—also exercise their influence upon the course of the historical struggles and in many cases preponderate in determining their *form*. There is an interaction of all these elements, in which, amid all the endless *host* of accidents (i.e., of things and events whose inner connection is so remote or so impossible to prove that we regard it as absent and can neglect it), the economic movement finally asserts itself as necessary. Otherwise the application of the theory to any period of history one chose would be easier than the solution of a simple equation of the first degree.

Marxism, therefore, while reserving the final and decisive factor in any change for economic causes, does not deny that "ideal" factors can also influence the course of history and may even preponderate in determining the *form* which changes will take (but only the form). It is only a caricature of Marxism to suggest that it underestimates the importance of such a spiritual factor in human consciousness as artistic creation, or to make the absurd claim that Marx considered works of art to be the direct reflexion of material and economic causes. He did not. He understood perfectly well that religion, or philosophy, or tradition can play a great part in the creation of a work of art, even that any one of these or other "ideal" factors may preponderate in determining the *form* of the work in question. Among all the elements which go to make a work of art it is, however, only the economic movement which asserts itself as *finally* necessary, for what Marx and Engels considered to be true of historical changes they also considered true of aesthetic creation.

It is often objected against Marxism that it denies the individual, who is merely the prey of abstract economic forces which drive him to his doom with the inevitability of a Greek fate. We will leave aside the question of whether or not the conception that man is driven by external fate to an inevitable end makes the creation of a work of art impossible. Perhaps Calvinism has never produced great art, but the idea of doom and fate has done so—in the Greek tragedies, in the works of Hardy, to mention only two instances. It is nevertheless possible that the objection, if it really represented the Marxian view, would be a valid one. At least this objection is prompted by the humanist tradition of the great art of the western world, and is therefore worthy of respect, even though it is based on a grave misunderstanding.

For Marxism does not deny the individual. It does not see only masses in the grip of inexorable economic forces. True, some Marxist literary works, particularly some "proletarian" novels, have given innocent critics cause to believe that this is the case, but here perhaps the weakness has been in the novelists who have failed to rise to the greatness of their theme of man changing himself through the process of changing nature and creating new economic forces. Marxism places man in the centre of its philosophy, for while it claims that material forces may change man, it declares most emphatically that it is man who changes the material forces and that in the course of so doing he changes himself.

Man and his development is the centre of the Marxist philosophy. How does man change? What are his relations with the external world? These are the questions to which the founders of Marxism have sought and found answers. I do not wish here to outline Marxist philosophy, for that is done more capably elsewhere, but let us examine for a moment this question of man as an active historical agent, man at work and struggling with life, for this is the man who is at once artistic creator and the object of art. This is the way in which Engels explained the part of the individual in history:

> History makes itself in such a way that the final result always arises from conflicts between many individual wills, of which each again has been made what it is by a host of particular conditions of life. Thus there are innumerable intersecting forces, an infinite series of parallelograms of forces which give rise to one resultant—the historical event. This again may itself be viewed as the product of a power which, taken as a whole, works *unconsciously* and without volition. For what each individual wills is obstructed by everyone else, and what emerges is something that no one willed. Thus past history proceeds in the manner of a natural process and is also essentially subject to the same laws of movement. But from the fact that individual wills—of which each desires what he is impelled to by his physical constitution and external, in the last resort economic, circumstances (either his own personal circumstances or those of society in general)—do not attain what they want, but are merged into a collective mean, a common resultant, it must not be concluded that their value = 0. On the contrary, each contributes to the resultant and is to this degree involved in it.

Here is not only a formula for the historian, but also for the novelist. For the one concern of the novelist is, or should be, this question of the individual will in its conflict with other wills on the battleground of life. It is the fate of man that his desires are never fulfilled, but it is also his glory, for in the effort to obtain their fulfilment he changes, be it ever so little, in ever so limited a degree, life itself. Not X = 0 is the Marxist formula for the fate of man, but "on the contrary, each contributes to the resultant and is to this degree involved in it."

The conflict of wills, of desires and passions, is not, however, a conflict of abstract human beings, for Engels is careful to emphasise that man's desires and actions are conditioned by his physical constitution and, finally, by economic circumstances, either his personal circumstances or those of society in general. In his social history it is, in the last resort again, the class to which he belongs, the psychology of that class, with its contradictions and conflicts, which plays the determining part. So that each man has, as it were, a dual history, since he is at the same time a type, a man with a social history, and an individual, a man with a personal history. The two, of course, even though they may be in glaring conflict, are also one, a unity, in so far as the latter is eventually conditioned by the former, though this does not and should not imply that in art the social type must dominate the individual personality. Falstaff, Don Quixote, Tom Jones, Julien Sorel, Monsieur de Charlus, are all types, but they are types in whom the social characteristics constantly reveal the individual, and in whom the personal hopes, hungers, loves, jealousies and ambitions in turn light up the social background.

The novelist cannot write his story of the individual fate unless he also has this steady vision of the whole. He must understand how his final result arises from the individual conflicts of his characters, he must in turn understand what are the manifold conditions of lives which have made each of those individuals what she or he is. "What emerges is something that no one willed," how exactly that sums up each great work of art, and how well it expresses the pattern of life itself, since behind the event that no one willed a pattern does exist. Marxism gives to the creative artist the key to reality when it shows him how to discern that pattern and the place which each individual occupies in it. At the same time it consciously gives to man his full value, and in this sense is the most humanist of all world outlooks.

ARTHUR O. LOVEJOY:

Milton and the Paradox of the Fortunate Fall*

To many readers of *Paradise Lost* in all periods the most surprising lines in the poem must have been those in the Twelfth Book in which Adam expresses a serious doubt whether his primal sin—the intrinsic enormity and ruinous consequences of which had elsewhere been so copiously dilated upon—was not, after all, rather a ground for self-congratulation. The Archangel Michael, it will be remembered, has been giving Adam a prophetic relation of the history of mankind after the Fall. This, though for the greater part a most unhappy story, concludes with a prediction of the Second Coming and the Final Judgment, when Christ shall reward

His faithful and receive them into bliss,
Whether in Heav'n or Earth, for then the Earth
Shall all be Paradise, far happier place
Than this of Eden, and far happier days.
So spake the Archangel Michael; and then paused,
As at the world's great period, and our Sire
Replete with joy and wonder thus replied:
"O Goodness infinite, Goodness immense,
That all this good of evil shall produce,
And evil turn to good—more wonderful
Than that which by creation first brought forth
Light out of darkness! Full of doubt I stand,
Whether I should repent me now of sin
By me done or occasioned, or rejoice
Much more that much more good thereof shall spring—

* "Milton and the Paradox of the Fortunate Fall" first appeared in *A Journal of English Literary History*, September 1937, and is reprinted here by permission of the editors, of the Manager of The Johns Hopkins Press, and of Mr. Lovejoy. Mr. Lovejoy (*b.* 1873) is the author of *The Revolt Against Dualism* (1930) and of *The Great Chain of Being* (1936), and is one of the editors of *A Documentary History of Primitivism and Related Ideas* (1935-).

To God more glory, more good will to men
From God—and over wrath grace shall abound. . . ."

The last six lines are Milton's expression of what may be called the Paradox of the Fortunate Fall. It is a paradox which has at least the look of a formal antinomy. From the doctrinal premises accepted by Milton and implicit in the poem, the two conclusions between which Adam is represented as hesitating were equally inevitable; yet they were mutually repugnant. The Fall could never be sufficiently condemned and lamented; and likewise, when all its consequences were considered, it could never be sufficiently rejoiced over. Adam's eating of the forbidden fruit, many theologians had observed, contained in itself all other sins; [1] as the violation by a rational creature of a command imposed by infinite wisdom, and as the frustration of the divine purpose in the creation of the earth, its sinfulness was infinite; and by it the entire race became corrupted and estranged from God. Yet if it had never occurred, the Incarnation and Redemption could never have occurred. These sublime mysteries would have had no occasion and no meaning; and therefore the plenitude of the divine goodness and power could neither have been exercised nor have become known to men. No devout believer could hold that it would have been better if the moving drama of man's salvation had never taken place; and consequently, no such believer could consistently hold that the first act of that drama, the event from which all the rest of it sprang, was really to be regretted. Moreover, the final state of the redeemed, the consummation of human history, would far surpass in felicity and in moral excellence the pristine happiness and innocence of the first pair in Eden—that state in which, but for the Fall, man would presumably have remained.[2] Thus Adam's sin—and also, indeed, the sins of his posterity which it "occasioned"—were the *conditio sine qua non* [3] both of a greater manifestation of the glory of God and of immeasurably greater benefits for man than could conceivably have been otherwise obtained.

Necessary—upon the premises of orthodox Christian theology—though this conclusion was, its inevitability has certainly not been always, nor, it may be suspected, usually, apparent to those who accepted those premises; it was a disturbing thought upon which many even of those who were aware of it (as all the subtler theologians must have been) were naturally reluctant to dwell; and the number of theological writers and religious poets who have given it entirely explicit and pointed expression has apparently not been great. Nevertheless it had its own emotional appeal to many religious minds —partly, no doubt, because its very paradoxicality, its transcendence of the simple logic of common thought, gave it a kind of mystical sublimity; between logical contradiction (or seeming contradiction) and certain forms of religious feeling there is a close relation, of which the historic manifestations have never been sufficiently studied. And for writers whose purpose, like Milton's, was a religious interpretation of the entire history of man, the paradox served, even better than the simple belief in a future millennium or celestial bliss, to give to that history as a whole the character, not of tragedy, but of a divine comedy.[4] Not only should the drama have (for the elect—and about the unredeemed the elect were not wont to be greatly concerned) a happy ending, but the happy ending had been implicit in the beginning and been made possible by it. The Paradox of the Fortunate Fall has consequently found

[1] So Milton himself in *De doctrina chr.* 1, ch. 11 in *Milton's Prose Wks.*, Bohn ed., 4, p. 258: "What sin can be named, which was not included in this one act? It comprehended at once distrust in the divine veracity, and a proportionate credulity in the assurances of Satan; unbelief; ingratitude; disobedience; gluttony; in the man excessive uxoriousness, in the woman a want of proper regard for her husband, in both an insensibility to the welfare of their offspring, and that offspring the whole human race; parricide; theft, invasion of the rights of others, sacrilege, deceit, presumption in aspiring to divine attributes, fraud in the means employed to attain the object, pride and arrogance."

[2] On this last point, however, there were, in the early Fathers and later theologians, differing opinions; the view that the primeval state was not that in which man was intended to remain, but merely a phase of immaturity to be transcended, had ancient and respectable supporters. Into the history of this view I shall not enter here.

[3] ["Indispensable condition."]

[4] The application of the phrase here is borrowed from Professor C. A. Moore, *PMLA* 12 (1921). 11.

recurrent expression in the history of Christian religious thought; the idea was no invention, or discovery, of Milton's. In the present paper, I shall note a few earlier phrasings of the same idea, which it is of interest to compare with Milton's. They may or may not be "sources" of *P. L.* 12. 469-478; they are in any case illustrations of a long tradition lying behind that passage.

1

To Milton-specialists the occurrence of a similar passage in Du Bartas is, of course, well known; but to facilitate comparison it seems worth while to cite the lines here. In the section of the *Seconde Semaine* entitled "The Imposture," after the Creator has pronounced sentence upon Adam, the poet interrupts his narrative to introduce a disquisition of his own, designed to answer the usual complaints against the justice of God in his dealings with Adam and his descendants:

Here I conceive, that flesh and bloud will brangle,
And murmuring Reason with th'Almighty wrangle.[5]

The ensuing essay in theodicy is apparently addressed primarily to mankind in general, though the poet sometimes rather confusedly seems, when he uses the second person singular, to be thinking of those whose errors he is refuting, sometimes of Adam, sometimes of departed saints in general, sometimes of all the elect. The lines which concern us are the following:

For, thou complainest of God's grace, whose Still
Extracts from dross of thine audacious ill,
Three unexpected goods; praise for his Name;
Bliss for thy self; for Satan endless shame:
Sith, but for sin, *Justice* and *Mercy* were
But idle names: and but that thou didst erre,
CHRIST had not come to conquer and to quell,
Upon the Cross, Sin, Satan, Death, and Hell;
Making thee blessèd more since thine offence,
Then in thy primer happy innocence . . .
In Earth thou liv'dst then; now in heav'n thou beest:
Then, thou didst hear God's word; it now thou seest:
Then pleasant fruits; now, CHRIST is thy repast:
Then might'st thou fall; but now thou standest fast.[6]

Since, as we shall see, the thought was not original with Du Bartas, the passage in *P. L.* 12 is not one of those which can confidently be cited among the evidences of Milton's utilization of *La Semaine.* There is, however, a similarity in one detail which perhaps lends a slight probability to the supposition of a conscious or unconscious reminiscence by Milton of the corresponding passage in the French poet: the fact that both specify three "greater goods" which sprang from the evil inherent in the Fall.[7] Of these, two are identical in both passages—greater "glory" to God, greater benefits conferred by God upon man. The third is different; for the defeat and humiliation of Satan Milton substitutes, as the last happy consequence, the manifestation of the predominance of God's grace over his wrath—religiously a more mov-

[5] *The Complete Works of Joshua Sylvester,* ed. Grosart (1880), 1. 111. Sylvester's tr., 1611 ed., p. 249.

[6] Grosart 1. 111-2; in 1611 ed., p. 249. The original in Du Bartas, whom Sylvester here follows closely, is as follows:

. . . sa grace
Dont l'alambic extrait de ta rebelle audace
Trois biens non esperez: sçavoir, gloire pour soy,
Vergongne pour Sathan, felicité pour toy.
Veu que sans le peché sa Clemence et Justice
Ne seroient que vains noms; et que sans ta malice
Christ ne fust descendu, qui d'un mortel effort
A vaincu les Enfers, les Pechez, et la Mort,
Et te rend plus heureux mesme apres ton offence,
Qu'en Eden tu n'estois pendant ton innocence . . .
Tu viuois icy-bas, or tu vis sur le Pole.
Dieu parloit avec toy: or tu vois sa Parole.
Tu vivois de doux fruicts: Christ ore est ton repas.
Tu pouvois trebucher: mais or tu ne peux pas.

(*La Seconde Semaine,* Rouen, 1592, p. 53.) It is to be remembered that not only were the poem of Du Bartas, and Sylvester's English version of it, famous and familiar in the 17th century, but also Simon Goulart's prose *Commentaires et Annotations sur la Sepmaine . . .* (1582, 1584) and Thomas Lodge's translation of Goulart: *A learned Summarie of the famous Poeme of William of Saluste, Lord of Bartas, wherein are discovered all the excellent Secrets in Metaphysicall, Physicall, Morall and Historicall Knowledge . . .*, 2 vols., 1637. The 1584 ed. of Goulart in the Harvard University Library does not contain the commentary on *The Second Week,* but the passage corresponding to Du Bartas's lines may be found in Lodge, *ed. cit.,* 2. 69-70: "The Poet expresseth this in the Verse 509, saying, That without sinne the Mercy and Justice of God had not so much been manifested," *etc.* The comparison of this pasage of Du Bartas with *P. L.* 12. 468 ff. is not made by G. C. Taylor in *Milton's Use of Du Bartas,* 1934.

[7] This detail is not found in other expressions of the paradox known to me.

ing and edifying conception, though less apposite to the plot of Milton's epic of the war between God and the rebel angels.[8] There are two other differences worth nothing: (a) Milton gains greater dramatic effect by putting the paradox into the mouth of Adam himself—a ground for this being laid in the device of the preceding recital of the future history of man by the Archangel.[9] (b) In Milton, however, the paradox is not so sharply expressed. Du Bartas puts quite categorically the point that but for the Fall there *could* have been no Incarnation and Redemption and that, "but for sin, Justice and Mercy were but idle names"; Milton's Adam is made to express merely a doubt whether he should repent his sin or "rejoice much more" over its consequences. Yet the logic of the paradox remains clear enough in Milton's lines; Adam could have had no reason for his doubt except upon the assumption that the sin was truly prerequisite to the "much more good" that was to follow—was, in Milton's own significant term, to "spring" from it; and an intelligent reader could hardly have failed to conclude that the doubt was to be resolved in favor of the second alternative.

Du Bartas, however, was not the only poetic precursor of Milton in the use of the paradox. It was peculiarly adapted both to the theme and the style of Giles Fletcher in his most ambitious poem, *The Triumph of Christ.* It naturally occurred to a devout but reflective mind when it dwelt rapturously upon that theme; the more intense the feeling of the sublimity of the redemptive act and the magnitude of the good both inherent in it and resultant from it, the more apparent the impossibility of regarding as merely evil the sin which had evoked it. And to a writer whose poetic method consisted chiefly in the multiplication of conceits and rhetorical antitheses, even when dealing with the gravest articles of his faith, such a paradox naturally had a special attraction. Consequently in *Christ's Triumph over Death* (1610) Fletcher, descanting upon the Passion of Christ in a series of what may be called antithetic parallels between the Fall and the Redemption—the two trees (i.e., the forbidden tree and the cross), the two gardens (Eden and Gethsemane), etc.—introduces the paradox—and converts it into a play upon words:

Such joy we gained by our parentalls,
That good, or bad, whither I cannot wiss,
To call it a mishap, or happy miss
  That fell from Eden and to heav'n did rise.[10]

Fletcher, however, while raising the question clearly, is, like Milton's Adam, ostensibly noncommittal about the answer to it; yet it is so put that the reader could hardly remain in doubt about the answers. A fall from Eden which made the greater joys of heaven possible was plainly no "mishap." [11]

The last act of Andreini's *L'Adamo* (1613) has a good deal in common with the last book of *Paradise Lost,* including a long speech by Michael in which, after reproachfully reminding Eve of her guilt—

Tu cagionera a l'huomo
E di doglia et di pianto—[12]

he proceeds to a prophecy of the final triumph of grace and of the future bliss to be enjoyed

[8] This eventual consequence of the Incarnation and Resurrection had, however, been dwelt upon by Milton in *P. L.* 3. 250-8. If in writing the passage in Bk. 12, Milton was recasting that of Du Bartas, the change of the third "good" may be attributable to a desire to avoid repetition.

[9] Du Bartas employs the same device of a prophetic recital of subsequent history (*Seconde Semaine,* 1611 ed., p. 293); but here the prophet is Adam himself, who tells the story of things to come to Seth, and his prediction abruptly ends with the Deluge. If we were sure that Milton was, in Books 11-12, consciously recasting Du Bartas, the comparison between his and the earlier poet's use of the same group of themes would significantly illuminate the working of Milton's mind in the construction of his poem.

[10] *Op. cit.,* stanza 12; in *Giles and Phineas Fletcher: Poetical Works,* ed. F. S. Boas (1908), 1. 61.

[11] The second stanza following might be construed as a more affirmative expression of the paradox:

Sweet Eden was the arbour of delight,
Yet in his honey flowres our poyson blew,
Sad Gethseman the bowre of baleful night
Whear Christ a health of poyson for us drew;
Yet all our honey in that poyson grewe.

If the "poyson" in the last two lines is that referred to in the second—i.e., the forbidden fruit, or the consequences of eating it—the final line is a figurative way of asserting once more the dependence of the Redemption upon the Fall. But it is possible that the "poyson" in the penultimate line signifies the Agony in the Garden and that the last line is merely a repetition of this. The former interpretation seems the more likely.

[12] ["You will cause man suffering and sorrow."] *Op. cit.,* tercentenary ed. E. Allodoli (1913). Act 5, Sc. 9, p. 140, ll. 4122-3; cf. "cagionera" with Milton's "occasioned" in 12. 475, apparently his only use of the word as a verb.

by the first pair and their progeny, both on earth, which will then be like Paradise, and in heaven.[13] In their response to this archangelic discourse, Andreini's Adam and Eve, like Milton's Adam, expand with gratitude and wonder over the benignant power which can so "unite" good with evil:

Con la morte, la vita,
Con la guerra la pace,
Col perder la Vittoria,
Con l'error la salute
E con l'Inferno il Cielo
Insieme unir, non è poter umano,
Ma de l'eterno mano
Omnipotenza summa. Ondè, Signore,
Ch' Eva trafitta è sana,
E perdendo trionfa, et vinta hà gloria.[14]

There is in these lines, especially in "perdendo trionfa," an evident adumbration of the paradox, but they hardly give it unequivocal expression.[15]

2

Some of Milton's precursors, then, in the century preceding *Paradise Lost,* had dwelt upon the idea that the Fall had not only been over-ruled for good by the divine beneficence, but had been the indispensable means to the attainment of far greater good for man and—if it may be so put—for God than would have been possible without it. Milton's eighteenth century annotators and editors soon began to point out—though with a characteristic and exasperating neglect to give definite references—that the idea had already been expressed in the patristic period. The earliest suggestion of such a source seems to have been given in J. Richardson's *Explanatory Notes and Remarks on Milton* (1734), in which line 473 is annotated: *"O felix culpa, quae talem ac tantum meruit habere Redemptorem!*[16] 'tis an exclamation of St. Gregory."[17] Newton and other annotators in the same century were, prudently, still more vague in citation: "He seems to remember the rant of one of the Fathers, *O felix culpa," etc.*[18] So far as I have observed, no modern editor has given any more precise reference for this yet more striking phrasing of the Paradox of the Fall. An extensive, though not exhaustive, search of the writings of St. Gregory[19] fails to disclose it. But it is to be found in a probably earlier, more noteworthy, and, at least to non-Protestants, more widely familiar source—a passage in the Roman Liturgy.[20] In the service for Easter Even (Holy Saturday) there is a hymn, sung by the deacon

[13] *Ibid.,* p. 143, ll. 4235 ff.: "per la gioia D'esser rapito l'uomo A l'artiglio infernale il tutto gode, E pel diletto sembra Il Cielo in terra, e'n Paradiso il Mondo": cf. *P. L.* 12.462-5. The supreme good, however, Andreini, unlike Milton, expressly says, will be the beatific vision: "di Dio . . . il sacrosanto viso, . . . il sommo bel del Paradiso."

[14] *Ibid.,* p. 141, ll. 4157 ff. ["To unite life with death, war with peace, victory with defeat, sin with salvation, and Heaven with Hell, is not within man's power, but the highest omnipotence of the eternal hand. Thus, O Lord, Eve, mortally wounded and yet safe, has triumphed through perdition, and, conquered, has glory."]

[15] The later scenes of the fifth act of Salandra's *Adamo Caduto* (1647), especially in a dialogue between two personified divine attributes, Omnipotence and Mercy, dwell upon the happy ending which was to follow the disaster of the Fall; the Incarnation and Atonement are foretold, and, as in Milton, there are devout ejaculations over *la gran Bontade* which is to be made manifest through this outcome; and it is remarked that other attributes of deity—Infinity and Charity—would thereby obtain wider scope for their exercise:

L'Infinitade
In compartirsi sin fra Creature.
Applaudarà la Caritade, mentre
Verrà più dilatato il suo bel Regno.

But the essence of the paradox—the dependence of the possibility of all this upon the Fall—is not emphasized. In the equally cheerful outlook upon the future with which Vondel's *Lucifer* (1654) concludes, there is no hint of the paradox. That poems about the Fall should be given a happy ending by the introduction, through one device or another, of a prevision of the coming of Christ and the future bliss of the redeemed, may be said to have been a convention of this *genre;* and, as Professor C. A. Moore has pointed out in *PMLA* 12 (1921). 463 ff. the accepted dogma itself made it virtually incumbent upon the author of such a poem to foreshadow the "far happier place, far happier days," which the elect should know. To end upon a tragic note was to depart from both literary and theological orthodoxy. But a recognition of the Paradox of the Fortunate Fall was not a necessary or invariable part of a happy ending.

[16] ["O happy fault which has deserved to have so great a redeemer."]

[17] *Op. cit.,* p. 521.

[18] Fourth ed. (1757) of Thomas Newton's ed. of *P. L.,* 2, 429 (note). The parallel is not indicated in the earliest commentary, Patrick Hume's *Annotations on Paradise Lost* (1695).

[19] Richardson's "St. Gregory" presumably refers to Gregory the Great (d. 604), since the citation is in Latin.

[20] For my knowledge of this fact, and for other valued assistance in this section, I am indebted to Professor G. La Piana of Harvard University.

in the rite of blessing the paschal candle, which bears the title of *Praeconium* but is better known, from the word with which it opens, as the *Exultet* (*exultet iam angelica turba caelorum*); [21] in it, a Catholic writer has remarked, "the language of the liturgy rises into heights to which it is hard to find a parallel in Christian literature." [22] In this rapturous exultation over the mystery of the Redemption the sentence already cited is preceded by another expressing the same paradox yet more pointedly: *"O certe necessarium Adae peccatum, quod Christi morte deletum est! O felix culpa, quae talem ac tantum meruit habere redemptorem!"* [23] Adam's sin was not only a "happy fault" but "certainly necessary"—necessary to the very possibility of the redemptive act, which, it may be supposed, was by the author of the hymn conceived as itself a necessary, and the central, event in the divine plan of terrestrial history.

The date of composition of the *Exultet* and that of its incorporation in the service of Easter Even can be determined only approximately.[24] It was originally no part of the Roman Liturgy, but appears first in the Gallican, which, as some liturgiologists hold, was probably in existence by the beginning of the fifth century; [25] but the earliest manuscript of this liturgy which includes the hymn in question is of the seventh century.[26] Certain conjectures concerning its authorship have been made, but none is supported by any substantial evidence; [27] in the words of the most careful modern study of the subject, "in the present state of the sources, one must give up the attempt to determine the authorship and even the place of origin of this famous hymn." [28] All that can be said, then, on the question of date, is that the passage which some of Milton's editors have regarded as the probable source of *P. L.* 12. 473 ff. was in liturgical use as early as the seventh and possibly as early as the fourth century, in the churches employing the Gallican sacramentary. It is, however, certain that the popularity of the hymn was so great that it presently drove out, even in the Roman Liturgy—apparently after some hesitancies on the part of the popes—all rival formulas in the rite of blessing the Easter candle. It evidently "owed its triumph," as a Catholic historian of the liturgy has said, "to the fact that it was far superior to all these rivals both in expression and content." [29] In certain medieval missals there are some interesting variations in the wording of the two sentences relevant to the theme of this paper; [30] and it is of interest to note that these sentences were by some ecclesiastical authorities considered dangerous, and were omitted from the hymn—rather generally in German and not infrequently in French and Italian sacramentaries.[31] But with the establishment of liturgical uniformity since the late sixteenth century, both sentences found

[21] ["Let the angelical crowd of the Heavens exult forthwith."]

[22] C. B. Walker, in *Catholic Encycl.*, art. *"Exultet."*

[23] ["O surely the sin of Adam, which was washed away by the death of Christ, was necessary. O happy fault which has deserved to have so great a redeemer!"]

[24] For the text of the hymn (in its oldest known form) see Duchesne, *Christian Worship*, 5th ed. (1923), p. 254; Migne, *Patr. Lat.*, 72, col. 269 f. For its history cf. Duchesne, *loc. cit.*: A. Franz, *Die kirchliche Benediktionen im Mittelalter* (1909) 1. 519-553; V. Thalhofer and L. Eisenhofer, *Handbuch der katholischen Liturgik* (1912) 1. 643 ff.; A. Gastoué, *Les vigiles nocturnes* (1908), p. 18; C. B. Walker, *loc. cit.*; J. Braun, *Liturgisches Handlexikon* (1922), art. "Praeconium paschale." An English version of the entire hymn may be found in I. Schuster, *The Sacramentary* (1925), 2. 293-5.

[25] Duchesne, *op. cit.*, p. 86, thinks the hymn may be as early as the middle of the fourth century.

[26] Cf. the liturgiological authorities cited.

[27] Some ancient manuscripts credit it to St. Augustine "when he was deacon," a highly improbable ascription (cf. Thalhofer and Eisenhofer, 1. 644; Franz, 1. 534). It is probably due to the fact that Augustine, as he himself records (*De civ. Dei*, 15. 22), once wrote a short *laus cerei* in verse; but this was not the *Exultet.* It appears to have been originally the custom for the deacon to compose his own *praeconium* for the rite of blessing the Easter candle (Braun, *loc. cit.*), a practice of which the *locus* in Augustine gives probable evidence. One of Migne's editors (H. Menard in *Pat. Lat.*, 78, col. 335) suggests that the hymn may perhaps have been written by St. Ambrose, which is perhaps possible, but incapable of proof. Gastoué's suggestion of St. Ennodius of Pavia (d. 521) as the author appears to be due to a confusion of the *Exultet* with two quite different formulas of benediction composed by that Father (v. *Corp. script. lat. eccles.* 6. 415-419).

[28] Franz, *op. cit.*, 1. 534.

[29] Thalhofer and Eisenhofer, *op. cit.*, p. 644.

[30] E.g., in the Missal of Westminster Abbey (ed. Lagg, 1893, 2, 581) the words *et nostrum* follow *Adae peccatum.*

[31] See Franz, 1. 540 f., for examples, of which I cite only one: Hugo, Abbot of Cluny (d. 1109), commanded that these sentences should be "deleted and no longer read, *cum aliquando non bene haberetur 'O felix culpa,' et quod peccatum Adae necessarium esset.*"

an accepted and permanent place in the Missal of the Roman Church.

3

That the Protestant religious poets of the sixteenth and seventeenth centuries who gave expression to the Paradox of the Fortunate Fall had heard or read the part of the Catholic liturgy containing the *Exultet* is, of course, possible; but there is no need to suppose them to have done so. It is rather more likely that they—or at all events the earliest of them, Du Bartas—became acquainted with the idea through the reading of one of the Fathers, whose writings still had among Protestant theologians much authority. St. Ambrose, for example, (4th c.) had flatly asserted that Adam's sin "has brought more benefit to us than harm" (*amplius nobis profuit culpa quam nocuit*),[32] and had even permitted himself the more generalized and hazardous apophthegm that "sin is more fruitful than innocence" (*fructuosior culpa quam innocentia*).[33] God "knew that Adam would fall, *in order that* he might be redeemed by Christ (*ut redimeretur a Christo*). *Felix ruina, quae reparatur in melius.*" [34] The identity of the thought and the approximation of the phrasing here to those of the two sentences quoted from the *Exultet* are evident; and it is probable that these Ambrosian passages are the primary source of the expressions of the paradox, alike in that hymn and in Du Bartas, Fletcher and Milton. To the last two the idea may or may not have been transmitted through Du Bartas; [35] or to any of them it is possible that the medium of transmission may have been some later patristic repetition or amplification of the theme. In the century after Ambrose his enunciation of it was echoed, with some weakening, by one of the greatest of the Popes, Leo I, in his *First Sermon on the Lord's Ascension:*

> Today we [in contrast with the first of our race] are not only confirmed in the possession of Paradise, but have even penetrated to the higher things of Christ; we have gained more by the ineffable grace of Christ than we had lost by the envy of the Devil.[36]

And in the next century Gregory the Great (d. 604) expressed the paradox with all possible explicitness.[37]

> What greater fault than that by which we all die? And what greater goodness than that by which we are freed from death? And certainly, unless Adam had sinned, it would not have behooved our Redeemer to take on our flesh. Almighty God saw beforehand that from that evil because of which men were to die, He would bring about a good which would overcome that evil. How wonderfully the good surpasses the evil, what faithful believer can fail to see? Great, indeed, are the evils we deservedly suffer in consequence of the first sin; but who of the elect would not willingly endure still worse evils, rather than not have so great a Redeemer? [38]

4

In the foregoing examples, the writers who enunciated the paradox, it is evident, usually had chiefly in mind the relation of causal dependence between specific historical events, the

[32] *De institutione virginis,* ch. 17. 104 (*MPL,* 16. 331).

[33] *De Jacob,* 6. 21 (*MPL,* 14. 607).

[34] *In Ps. XXXIX,* 20 (*MPL,* 14. 1065). ["Happy is the downfall which is restored for the better."]

[35] That Du Bartas "used Ambrose's *Hexaemeron*" is said by U. T. Holmes and his associates to be a certainty (*The Works of Du Bartas* (1935), 1. 128); it is improbable that Du Bartas's reading in Ambrose was confined to this writing. Cf. Thibaut de Maisières, *Les poèmes inspirés du début de la Genèse* (1931), p. 26. Milton, however, was acquainted with Ambrose at first hand; cf. *Tetrachordon* in *Prose Works,* Bohn ed. (1848), 3. 418.

[36] *MPL,* 54. 396: ampliora adepti per ineffabilem Christi gratiam quam per diaboli amiseramus invidiam.

[37] Richardson, therefore, was perhaps not wholly wrong in indicating Gregory as a source of the passage in *P. L.,* though in error in attributing the *O felix culpa* to that saint.

[38] *In Primum Regum Expositiones,* 4. 7; *MPL,* 79. 222: "Quae maior culpa, quam illa, qua omnes morimur? Et quae maior bonitas, quam illa, per quam a morte liberamur? Et quidem nisi Adam peccaret, Redemptorem nostrum carnem suscipere nostram non oporteret. . . . Ex illo malo, quo morituri erant, bonum quod malum illum vinceret, omnipotens Deus sese facturum providerat. Cuius profecto boni magnitudo, quis fidelis non videat quam mirabiliter excellat. Magna quippe sunt mala, quae per primae culpae meritum patimur, sed quis electus nollet peiora mala perpeti, quam tantum Redemptorem non habere?" The echo of the last clause in the *Exultet* suggests that the author of the hymn may have been remembering *both* this passage of Gregory and those of Ambrose; in which case a seventh century date for the hymn, or at least for the part of it which here concerns us, would be indicated. But it is, of course, possible, that Gregory was echoing the *Exultet.*

Fall and the Redemption; and the argument was that the latter, or consequent, being preponderatingly a good, the former, as its necessary (though not sufficient) cause, must have been preponderatingly a good. Yet the Fall none the less remained, upon orthodox principles, a moral evil. These considerations, taken together, tended to suggest two larger, and awkward, questions. Was it true in general that the existence of moral evils is, from another and more comprehensive point of view, a good? And if, from such a point of view, the Fall was preponderatingly a good, was it not necessary to assume that its occurrence must after all have been in accordance with God's will? These questions, implicit in the notion of the *felix culpa,* were fairly explicitly raised and considered by Augustine; and his answers to both were, at least sometimes, in the affirmative; in other words, he not only accepted the paradox but gave it a more generalized form. Thus in his *Enchiridion ad Laurentium* he writes:

Although those things that are evil, in so far as they are evil, are not good; nevertheless, it is good that there should be not only goods but evils as well. For unless this—namely, that there be also evils—were not a good, men would under no circumstances fall away from the omnipotent Good; [39]

i.e., neither Adam nor any man would ever have sinned. And again:

The works of God are so wisely and exquisitely contrived that, when an angelic and human creature sins, that is, does, not what God wished it to do, but what itself wishes, yet by that very will of the creature whereby it does what the Creator did not will, it fulfills what he willed—God, as supremely good, putting even evils to good use, for the damnation of those whom he has justly predestined to punishment and for the salvation of those whom he has benignantly predestined to grace.[40]

The greatest of the Latin Fathers was here manifestly skating on rather thin ice. It was always difficult for an acute-minded theologian with a strong sense of the divine sovereignty to admit that Adam's sin had really frustrated the will of God, and had compelled the deity to perform, unwillingly, acts which he would not otherwise have performed; it was therefore not easy, when dealing with these matters, always to avoid the thought that the Fall itself, with its consequences—so happy for the elect—was but a part of the eternal and ineluctable divine purpose for mankind. These passages of Augustine's thus reveal more clearly some of the moral difficulties and metaphysical pitfalls which lay behind the conception of the *felix culpa*—difficulties and pitfalls which Augustine himself cannot be said to have wholly escaped.[41]

The familiarity of the idea in the fourteenth century is shown by its occurrence both in *The Vision of Piers the Plowman, ca.* 1378, and in Wyclif's *Sermons.* In the former it is put into the mouth of Repentance, after the Seven Deadly Sins have made their confessions: God created man "most like to himself, and afterwards suffered him to sin,"

And al for the best, as I bileve · what euer the
boke telleth,
O *felix culpa! o necessarium peccatum ade! etc.*

[39] *Op. cit.,* ch. 96 (*MPL* 40. 276): Quamvis ergo ea quae mala, in quantum mala sunt, non sint bona; tamen ut non solum bona, sed etiam sint et mala, bonum est. Nam nisi esset hoc bonum, ut essent et malla, nullo modo sinerentur ab omnipotente bono.

[40] *Ibid.* ch. 100 (*MPL* 40. 279): Opera domini [sunt] . . . tam sapienter exquisita, ut cum angelica et humana creatura peccasset, id est, non quod ille, sed quod voluit ipsa fecisset, etiam per eamdem creaturae voluntatem, qua factum est quod Creator noluit, impleret ipse quod voluit; bene utens et malis, tamquam summe bonus, ad eorum damnationem quos iuste praedestinavit ad poenam, et ad eorum salutem quos benigne praedestinavit ad gratiam.

[41] Donne in one of his sermons bases upon the authority of Augustine as well as of Scripture a similar remark that matters have been so ordered that sin in general—not specifically the sin of Adam—is made conducive to moral good: "If I cannot find a foundation for my comfort in this subtilty of the Schoole, that sin is nothing, . . . yet I can raise a second step for my consolation in this, that be sin what it will be in the nature thereof, yet my sin shall conduce and cooperate to my good. So *Ioseph* saies to his Brethren, *You thought evill against me, but God meant it unto good*: which is not onely good to *Ioseph,* who was not partaker in the evill, but good even to them who meant nothing but evill." What Donne has in mind here at least in part, however, is the more special idea that, after many little sins, a good round sin may be a means of grace, by bringing the sinner to a realization of his own state. "Though it be strangely said, yet I say it, That God's anger is good; so saies S. Augustine, *Audeo dicere,* Though it be boldly said yet must I say it, *Utile est cadere in aliquid manifestum peccatum,* Many sinners would not have been saved if they had not committed some greater sin at last, then before; for, the punishment of that sin, hath brought them to a remorse of all their other sins formerly neglected" (LXXX *Sermons* (1640), p. 171).

For thourgh that synne thi sone · sent was to this erthe,
And bicam man of a mayde · mankind to save.[42]

Wyclif in a Christmas sermon preached, perhaps, to his rustic flock at Lutterworth in the early 1380s, did not shrink from the paradox, but on the contrary joined with it a still more sweeping optimism, of very dubious orthodoxy: all things, including sin, are for the best in the best of possible worlds, since all happens in accordance with God's will:

And so, as many men seien, alle thingis comen for the beste; for alle comen for Goddis ordenance, and so thei comen for God himsilf; and so alle thingis that comen fallen for the beste thing that mai be. Moreover to another witt men seien, that this world is betterid bi everything that fallith therinne, where that it be good or yvel . . . and herfore seith Gregori, that it was a blesful synne that Adam synnede and his kynde, for bi this the world is beterid; but the ground of this goodnesse stondith in grace of Jesus Crist.[43]

An interesting late-medieval lyrical poem gives to the paradox a turn not found in any of the other examples here cited; it is presented in its relation to the cult of the Virgin. Since there would have been no Incarnation without the Fall, all that phase of Catholic piety and religious emotion which centers about the figure of the Virgin Mother manifestly owed its possibility to Adam's eating the forbidden fruit. There is also in the poem, if I am not mistaken, a touch of sly humor; the anonymous author hints that poor Adam, to whom not only mankind in general but the Queen of Heaven herself are so deeply indebted, has been rather badly treated. This further inference from the idea of the *felix culpa* would, one may suspect, hardly have been approved by St. Ambrose and St. Gregory. Adam, the poet recalls, lay bound for four thousand winters:

And all was for an appil,
An appil that he tok . . .
Ne hadde the appil takė ben,
The appil taken ben,
Ne haddė never our lady
A bene hevene quene.
Blessed be the time
That appil takė was.
Therefore we moun singen
"Deo gracias."[44]

A sixteenth century illustration of the vogue of the concept of the *felix culpa* is to be found in the widely used Latin *Commentary on Genesis* of the Jesuit Benito Pereira (Pererius). The commentator is dilating, *à propos* of Genesis 1, 31, upon the manner in which God transmutes evils—even moral evils (*mala culpae*)—into good.

A signal proof and example of this is exhibited to us in the sin of Adam. How grave this sin was, how far and wide it spread poison and destruction, how severely it was punished, is acknowledged by all men. Yet this so great sin, such is the goodness and power of God, has been wonderfully converted into the greatest good and the most glorious of God's works, namely, the incarnation, passion and death of the Son of God. So that Gregory not unadvisedly or rashly somewhere exclaims, *O felix culpa, quae talem ac tantum meruit habere Redemptorem*."[45]

Upon the crucial point of the paradox, however—that God could not have performed this *praeclarissimum opus* if Adam had remained innocent—Pereira does not dwell.

5

For a final example, which will bring us back to Milton's century, I will cite one of the

[42] B. Ms., *Passus V*, 489 ff., in Skeat, *The Vision of William Concerning Piers the Plowman* (1886).

[43] *Select English Works of John Wyclif*, ed. Thomas Arnold (1869), Sermon XC, 1. 320-321. There is no corresponding passage in the Latin sermon from the same text and for the same festival: *Ioannis Wyclif Sermones*, ed. Loserth (1888) 2. 1 ff. Wyclif also apparently confused in his memory the *Exultet* and the passage of Gregory above cited, or else believed Gregory to have composed the hymn.

[44] Professor Douglas Bush has kindly brought this poem to my notice. It is printed in Chambers and Sidgwick's *Early English Lyrics* (1907), p. 102, and is believed to have been written in the early fifteenth century.

[45] *Benedicti Pererii Valentini Commentariorum et disputationum in Genesim tomus primus* (Leyden, 1594), p. 168. Pereira, like Wyclif, it will be observed, either attributes the *Exultet* to St. Gregory or has confused the phrase from the hymn with the dictum of Gregory above cited. The passage is a highly probable source of Richardson's similar error previously noted; and it is a conceivable source of the *locus* in Milton. On the importance of this and similar Renaissance commentaries on Genesis for the background of *P. L.*, see the article of Arnold Williams in *Studies in Philology*, April, 1937, pp. 191-208. But it is to be borne in mind that Pereira's work and the others mentioned by Williams were later than Du Bartas's poem.

most famous and widely read of Catholic devotional works, the *Traité de l'amour de Dieu* of St. Francis de Sales (1616).[46]

> The mercy of God [he writes] has been more salutary for the redemption of the race of men than the wretchedness of Adam has been poisonous for its destruction. And so far is it from being true that the sin of Adam has overcome the benevolence (*debonnaireté*) of God, that on the contrary it has served to excite and provoke it: so that, by a gentle and most loving antiperistasis[47] and opposition, that benevolence has been re-invigorated by the presence of its adversary: and, so to say, gathering together its forces in order to win the victory, it has caused grace "to abound more exceedingly where sin abounded."[48] Therefore the Church, in a holy excess of admiration, exclaims on the Eve of Easter: "O sin of Adam, truly necessary" *etc.* [quotes the two sentences from the *Exultet*]. Of a truth, we can say with that man of ancient times: "We should be lost (*perdus*) if we had not been lost;"[49] that is to say, our loss has been our gain, since human nature has received more gifts of grace (*plus de graces*) from its redemption by its Savior than it would ever have received from the innocence of Adam, if he had persevered in it. . . . The redemption of our Lord, touching our miseries, renders them more useful and amiable than the original innocence would ever have been. The Angels, the Savior tells us, "have more joy over one sinner that repenteth than over ninety-and-nine just persons that need no repentance"; and in the same way, the state of redemption is one hundred times greater in value than the state of innocence.[50]

[46] The passage is therefore of later date than those cited from Du Bartas and Giles Fletcher.

[47] A technical term of the physics of the period, signifying a process by which a quality or force in a substance is increased or intensified by the action of an opposing quality or force. Milton expresses the same idea in the hymn of the celestial choirs, 7. 613 ff.

> Who seeks
> To lessen thee, against his purpose serves
> To manifest the more thy might: his evil
> Thou usest, and from thence creat'st more good.

The "more good" here, however, is the creation of "this new-made world" and of man, to "repair that detriment" resulting from the defection of the rebel angels —not the Redemption and its consequences.

[48] *Romans* 5.20. The Pauline text gave a seeming biblical sanction to the paradox, though it does not in fact express the essential point of it.

[49] The reference is to a saying of Themistocles in Plutarch's *Life of Themistocles*, 39.

[50] *Op. cit.*, Bk. 2, ch. 5.

Here the strangest aspect of the paradox is even more pointedly brought out than by Du Bartas or Milton: not only did the Fall make possible more good for man, but God himself *needed* a fallen race to evoke fully the divine attributes and powers.

6

It is unlikely that the pre-Miltonic expressions of the Paradox of the Fortunate Fall which I have noted are the only ones to be found in Christian literature from the fourth to the seventeenth centuries, but they pretty certainly include the most important; all but one of them could have been known to Milton at first hand; and they are sufficient to place in its proper historical perspective the passage of the Twelfth Book of *Paradise Lost* cited at the beginning. In that perspective, the passage ceases to be surprising, or indicative of any originality or of any great boldness in Milton's thought. A paradox which had been embraced by Ambrose, Leo the Great, Gregory the Great, Francis de Sales, and Du Bartas, had for at least ten centuries had a place in many missals, and had finally been officially adopted by the Roman Church, was, obviously, sufficiently orthodox; and it had been put more sharply and boldly by at least two of the Doctors of the Church, by the composer of the *Exultet,* by the French mystic, and by the author of *La Semaine,* than by Milton. Though the hint of antinomianism latent in it had made many writers to whom it was probably familiar avoid expressing it, it had nevertheless a recognized and natural place in the treatment of the topic in Christian theology—that of the culmination of the redemptive process in human history—which was also for Milton the culminating theme in his poem. Yet it undeniably placed the story of the Fall, which was the subject of the poem announced at the outset, in a somewhat ambiguous light; when it was borne in mind, man's first disobedience could not seem the deplorable thing which for the purposes of the poet—and of the theologian—it was important to make it appear. The only solution was to keep the two themes separate. In the part of the narrative dealing primarily with the Fall, the thought that it was after all a *felix culpa* must not be permitted explicitly to intrude; that was to be reserved for the conclusion, where it could heighten the happy final consummation by making the earlier and unhappy episodes in the story appear as instrumental to that consummation, and, indeed, as its necessary conditions.

EDMUND WILSON: The Ambiguity of Henry James*

A DISCUSSION of Henry James's ambiguity may appropriately begin with "The Turn of the Screw." This story, which seems to have proved more fascinating to the general reading public than anything else of James's except "Daisy Miller," apparently conceals another horror behind the ostensible one. I do not know who first propounded the theory; but Miss Edna Kenton, whose insight into James is profound, has been one of its principal exponents, and the late Charles Demuth did a set of illustrations for the story based on this interpretation.

According to this theory, the young governess who tells the story is a neurotic case of sex repression, and the ghosts are not real ghosts at all but merely the hallucinations of the governess.

Let us go through the story from the beginning. It opens with an introduction. The man who is presenting the governess's manuscript tells us first who she is. She is the youngest daughter of a poor country parson, but "the most agreeable woman I've ever known in her position," who would have been "worthy of any whatever." She had come up to London and answered an advertisement and found a man who wanted a governess for his orphaned nephew and niece. "This prospective patron proved a gentleman, a bachelor in the prime of life, such a figure as had never risen, save in a dream or an old novel, before a fluttered, anxious girl out of a Hampshire vicarage." It is made clear that the young woman has become thoroughly infatuated with her employer. He is charming to her and lets her have the job on condition that she will never bother him about the children; and she goes down to the house in the country where they have been left with a housekeeper and some other servants.

The boy, she finds, has been sent home from school for reasons into which she does not inquire but which she colors, on no evidence at all, with a significance somehow sinister. She learns that the former governess left, and that she has since died, under circumstances which are not explained but which are made in the same way to seem ominous. She is alone with the illiterate housekeeper, a good and simple soul, and the children, who seem innocent and charming. As she wanders about the estate, she thinks often how delightful it would be to come suddenly round the corner and find that the master had arrived: there he would stand, smiling, approving and handsome.

She is never to meet her employer again, but what she does meet are the apparitions. One day when his face has been vividly in her mind, she comes out in sight of the house and sees the figure of a man on the tower, a figure which is not the master's. Not long afterwards, the figure appears again, toward the end of a rainy Sunday. She sees him at closer range and more clearly: he is wearing smart clothes but is not a gentleman. The housekeeper, meeting the governess immediately afterwards, behaves as if the governess herself were a ghost: "I wondered

* "The Ambiguity of Henry James" first appeared in a different and shorter version in the Henry James number of *Hound & Horn* (April-June 1934). The complete version appeared in 1938 and is here reprinted from *The Triple Thinkers: Ten Essays on Literature,* by Edmund Wilson, copyright, 1938, by Harcourt, Brace and Company, Inc. Mr. Wilson (*b.* 1895) is also the author of *Axel's Castle: A Study in the Imaginative Literature of 1870-1930* (1931), *The Boys in the Back Room* (1941), and *The Wound and the Bow: Seven Studies in Literature* (1941).

why she should be scared." The governess tells her about the apparition and learns that it answers the description of one of the master's valets who had stayed down there and used to wear his clothes. The valet had been a bad character, who used "to play with the boy . . . to spoil him"; he had been found dead, having slipped on the ice coming out of a public house: it is impossible to say that he wasn't murdered. The governess believes that he has come back to haunt the children.

Not long afterwards, she and the little girl are out on the shore of a lake, the little girl playing, the governess sewing. The latter becomes aware of a third person on the opposite side of the lake. But she looks first at the little girl, who is turning her back in that direction and who, she notes, has "picked up a small flat piece of wood, which happened to have in it a little hole that had evidently suggested to her the idea of sticking in another fragment that might figure as a mast and make the thing a boat. This second morsel, as I watched her, she was very markedly and intently attempting to tighten in its place." This somehow "sustains" the governess so that she is able to raise her eyes: she sees a woman "in black, pale and dreadful." She concludes that it is the former governess. The housekeeper tells her that her predecessor, though a lady, had had an affair with the valet. The boy had used to go off with the valet and then lie about it afterwards. The governess concludes that the boy must have known about the valet and the woman—the boy and girl have been corrupted by them.

Observe that there is never any real reason for supposing that anybody but the governess sees the ghosts. She believes that the children see them, but there is never any proof that they do. The housekeeper insists that she does not see them; it is apparently the governess who frightens her. The children, too, become hysterical; but this is evidently the governess's doing, too. Observe, also, from the Freudian point of view, the significance of the governess's interest in the little girl's pieces of wood and of the fact that the male apparition first appears on a tower and the female apparition on a lake. There seems here to be only a single circumstance which does not fit into the hypothesis that the ghosts are hallucinations of the governess: the fact that the governess's description of the first ghost at a time when she has never heard of the valet, but it has been suggested to her in a conversation with the housekeeper that there has been some other male somewhere about who "liked everyone young and pretty," and the idea of this other person has been ambiguously confused with the master and with the master's possible interest in her, the present governess. And has she not, in her subconscious imagination, taking her cue from this, identified herself with her predecessor and conjured up an image who wears the master's clothes but who (the Freudian "censor" coming into play) looks debased, "like an actor," she says (would he not have to stoop to love her!)? The apparition had "straight, good features" and his appearance is described in detail. When we look back, we find that the master's appearance has never been described at all: we have merely been told that he was "handsome." It is impossible for us to know how much the ghost resembles the master—certainly the governess would never tell us.

The apparitions now begin to appear at night, and the governess becomes convinced that the children get up to meet them, though they are able to give plausible explanations of their behavior. The housekeeper tells the governess that she ought to report these phenomena to the master, if she is so seriously worried about them. The governess, who has promised not to bother him, is afraid he would think her insane; and she imagines "his derision, his amusement, his contempt for the breakdown of my resignation at being left alone and for the fine machinery I had set in motion to attract his attention to my slighted charms." The housekeeper threatens to send for the master herself; the governess threatens to leave if she does. After this, for a considerable period, the visions no longer appear.

The children become uneasy: they begin to wonder when their uncle is coming down; they want to write to him—but the governess suppresses their letters. The boy finally asks her frankly when she is going to send him to school, intimates that if he had not been so fond of her he would have written to his uncle long ago about her failure to do so, threatens to write him at once.

This upsets her: she thinks for a moment of leaving, but decides that this would be deserting them. She is apparently now in love with the boy. The ghost of the other governess immediately appears again, looking "dishonored and tragic," full of "unutterable woe." The new governess feels now—the morbid half of her split personality is getting the upper hand of the other—that it is she who is intruding upon the spirit instead of the spirit who is intruding upon her: "You terrible miserable woman!" she cries. The apparition disappears. She tells the housekeeper, who looks at her oddly, that the soul of the former governess is damned and wants the little girl to share her damnation. She finally agrees to write to the master, but no sooner has she sat down to the paper than she gets up and goes to the boy's bedroom, where she finds him lying awake. When he demands to go back to school, she embraces him and begs him to tell her why he was sent away; appealing to him with what seems to her desperate tenderness but what must seem queer and disquieting to the child, she insists that all she wants is to save him. There is the sudden gust of wind—it is a windy night outside—the casement rattles, the boy shrieks. She has been kneeling beside the bed: when she gets up, she finds the candle extinguished. "It was I who blew it, dear!" says the boy. For her, it has been the evil spirit disputing her domination. It does not occur to her that the boy may really have blown the candle out in order not to have to tell her with the light on about his disgrace at school. (Here, however, occurs the only detail which is not readily susceptible of double explanation: the governess has *felt* a "gust of frozen air" and yet sees that the window is "tight." Are we to suppose she merely fancied that she felt it?)

The next day, the little girl disappears. They find her beside the lake. The young woman now for the first time speaks openly to one of the children about ghosts. "Where, my pet, is Miss Jessel?" she demands—and immediately answers herself. "She's there, she's there!" she cries, pointing across the lake. The housekeeper looks with a "dazed blink" and asks where she sees anything; the little girl turns upon the governess "an expression of hard, still gravity, an expression absolutely new and unprecedented and that appeared to read and accuse and judge me." The governess feels her "situation horribly crumble." The little girl breaks down, becomes feverish, begs to be taken away from the governess; the housekeeper sides with the child and hints that the governess had better go. But the young woman forces her, instead, to take the little girl away; and she tries to make it impossible, before their departure, for the children to see each other.

She is now left alone with the boy. A strange and dreadful scene ensues. "We continued silent while the maid was with us—as silent, it whimsically occurred to me, as some young couple who, on their wedding-journey, at the inn, feel shy in the presence of the waiter." When the maid has gone, and she presses him to tell her why he was expelled from school, the boy seems suddenly afraid of her. He finally confesses that he "said things"—to "a few," to "those he liked." It all sounds very harmless: there comes to her out of her "very pity the appalling alarm of his being perhaps innocent. It was for the instant confounding and bottomless, for if he *were* innocent, what then on earth was *I?*" The valet appears at the window—it is "the white face of damnation." (But is the governess condemning the spirits to damnation or is she succumbing to damnation herself?) She is aware that the boy does not see it. "No more, no more, no more!" she shrieks to the apparition. "Is she *here?*" demands the boy in panic. (He has, in spite of the governess's efforts, succeeded in seeing his sister and has heard from her of the incident at the lake.) No, she says, it is not the woman; "But it's at the window—straight before us. It's *there!*" . . . "It's *he?*" then. Whom does he mean by "he"? " 'Peter Quint—you devil!' His face gave again, round the room, its convulsed supplication. 'Where?' " "What does he matter now, my own?" she cries. "What will he *ever* matter? *I* have you, but he has lost you forever!" Then she shows him that the figure has vanished: "There, *there!*" she says, pointing toward the window. He looks and gives a cry; she feels that he is dead in her arms. From her point of view, the disappearance of the spirit has proved too terrible a shock for him and "his little heart, dispossessed, has stopped"; but if we study the dialogue from the other point of view, we see that he must have taken her "There, *there!*" as an answer to his own "Where?" Instead of persuading him that there is nothing to be frightened of, she has, on the contrary, finally convinced him either that he has actually seen or that he is on the point of seeing something. He gives "the cry of a creature hurled over an abyss." She has literally frightened him to death.

When one has once been given this clue to "The Turn of the Screw," one wonders how one could ever have missed it. There is a very good reason, however, in the fact that nowhere does James unequivocally give the thing away: almost everything from beginning to end can be read equally in either of two senses. In the preface to the collected edition, however, as Miss Kenton has pointed out, James does seem to want to put himself on record. He asserts here that "The Turn of the Screw" is "a fairy-tale pure and simple"—but adds that the apparitions are of the order of those involved in witchcraft cases rather than of those in cases of psychic research. And he goes on to tell of his reply to one of his readers, who had complained that he had not characterized the governess sufficiently. At this criticism, he says, "One's artistic, one's ironic heart shook for the instant almost to breaking"; and he answered: "It was '*déjà très-joli*' . . . please believe, the general proposition of our young woman's keeping crystalline her record of so many intense anomalies and obscurities—*by which I don't of course mean her explanation of them, a different matter*. . . . She has 'authority,' which is a good deal to have given her" . . . The italics above are mine: these words seem impossible to explain except on the hypothesis of hallucination. And note, too, in the collected edition that James has not included "The Turn of the Screw" in the volume with his other ghost stories but in a volume of stories of another kind, between "The Aspern Papers" and "The Liar"—this last the story of a pathological liar, whose wife protects his lies against the world, acting with very much the same sort of deceptive "authority" as the governess in "The Turn of the Screw."

When we look back in the light of these hints, we become convinced that the whole story has been primarily intended as a characterization of the governess: her visions and the way she behaves about them, as soon as we look at them from the obverse side, present a solid and unmistakable picture of the poor country parson's daughter, with her English middle-class class-consciousness, her inability to admit to herself her sexual impulses and the relentless English "authority" which enables her to put over on inferiors even purposes which are totally deluded and not at all to the other people's best interests. Add to this the peculiar psychology of governesses, who, by reason of their isolated position between the family and the servants, are likely to become ingrown and morbid. The writer knows of an actual case of a governess who used to frighten the servants by opening doors and smashing mirrors and who tortured the parents by mythical stories of kidnappers. The poltergeist, once a figure of demonology, is now a recognized neurotic type.

When we examine "The Turn of the Screw" in this light, we understand for the first time its significance in connection with Henry James's other fiction—(the story, on any other hypothesis, would be, so far as I remember, the only thing James ever wrote which did not have some more or less serious point). We see now that it is simply a variation on one of James's familiar themes: the frustrated Anglo-Saxon spinster; and we remember that he has presented other cases of women who deceive themselves and others about the sources and character of their emotions. The most obvious example is that remarkable and too little read novel, "The Bostonians." The subject of "The Bostonians" is the struggle for the attractive daughter of a poor evangelist between a young man from the South who wants to marry her and a well-to-do Boston lady with a Lesbian passion for her. The strong-minded and strong-willed spinster is herself apparently quite in the dark as to the real reason for her interest in the girl: she is convinced that her desire to dominate her, to make her live with her, to teach her to make speeches on women's rights, to prevent the eligible young Southerner from marrying her, is all ardor for the Feminist cause. But James does not leave the reader in doubt—and he presents Olive Chancellor in a setting of other self-deluded New England idealists.

There is a theme of the same kind in the

short story called "The Marriages," which amused Robert Louis Stevenson so hugely. But here the treatment is comic. A young English girl, described by one of the characters as of the unmarriageable type, much attached to an attractive father and obsessed by the memory of a dead mother, breaks up her father's projected second marriage. She goes to his fiancée and tells her that her father is an impossible character who had made her late mother miserable. When her brother calls her a raving maniac, she remains serene in the conviction that, by ruining the happiness of her father, she has been loyal to her duty to her mother.

James's world is full of these women. They are not always emotionally perverted. Sometimes they are emotionally apathetic—like the amusing Francie Dosson of "The Reverberator," who, though men are always falling madly in love with her, seems never really to understand what courtship and marriage mean and is apparently quite content to go on all her life eating *marrons glacés* with her father and sister in their suite in a Paris hotel. Sometimes they are emotionally starved—like the pathetic Milly Theale of "The Wings of the Dove," who wastes away in Venice and whose doctor recommends a lover.

2

James's men are not precisely neurotic; but they are the masculine counterparts of his women. They have a way of missing out on emotional experience, either through timidity or caution or through heroic renunciation.

The extreme and fantastic example is the hero of "The Beast in the Jungle," who is finally crushed by the realization that his fate is to be the man in the whole world to whom nothing at all is to happen. Some of these characters are presented ironically: Mr. Wentworth of "The Europeans," so smug and secure in his neat little house, deciding not to marry the baroness who has proved such an upsetting element in the community, is a perfect comic portrait of a certain kind of careful Bostonian. Others are made sympathetic: the starved and weary Lambert Strether of "The Ambassadors," who comes to Paris too late in life.

Sometimes, however, the effect is ambiguous. Though the element of irony in Henry James is often underestimated by his readers, there are stories which leave us in doubt as to whether or not the author knew how his heroes would strike his readers. Is the fishy Bernard Longueville of the early novel "Confidence" really intended for a sensitive and interesting young man or is he a prig in the manner of Jane Austen? And some of James's later heroes are just as unsympathetic. The very late short story "Flickerbridge," in which a young American painter decides not to marry a young newspaper woman (the men are always deciding *not* to marry the women in Henry James) because he is afraid she will spoil by publicizing it a delightful old English house, the property of her own family, in which he has greatly enjoyed living without her, affects us in the same unpleasant way.

But "Flickerbridge" seems merely a miscue: evidently James intends it to be taken seriously. How is "The Sacred Fount" to be taken? This short novel, surely one of the curiosities of literature, which inspired the earliest parody—by Owen Seaman—I ever remember to have seen of James and which apparently marked his passing over some borderline into a region where he was to become for the public unassimilably exasperating and ridiculous, was written not long after "The Turn of the Screw" and is a sort of companionpiece to it. There is the same setting of an English country house, the same passages of a sad and strange beauty, the same furtive and disturbing goings-on in an atmosphere of clarity and brightness, the same dubious central figure, the same almost inscrutable ambiguity. As in the case of "The Turn of the Screw," the fundamental question presents itself and never seems to get definitely answered: What is the reader to think of the protagonist?—who is here a man instead of a woman.

It would be tedious to analyze "The Sacred Fount" as I have done with "The Turn of the Screw"—and it would be a somewhat more difficult undertaking. "The Sacred Fount" is mystifying, even maddening. But I believe that if anyone really got to the bottom of it, he would throw a good deal of light on Henry James. Rebecca West has given a burlesque account of this novel as the story of how "a week-end visitor spends more intellectual force than Kant can have used on 'The Critique of Pure Reason' in an unsuccessful attempt to discover whether there exists between certain of his fellow-guests a relationship not more interesting among these vacuous people than it is among sparrows." A gentleman, who tells the story, goes to a week-end party in the country; there he observes that certain of his friends appear to have taken a new lease on life whereas others seem to have been depleted. He evolves a theory about them: the theory is that the married couples have been forming new combinations and that the younger individuals have been feeding the older individuals from the sacred fount of their youth at the price of getting used up themselves.

This theory seems obviously academic: older people feed younger people with their vitality quite as often as younger people feed older ones—and does James really mean us to accept it? Are not the speculations of the narrator intended to characterize the narrator as the apparitions characterize the governess? As this detached and rather eerie individual proceeds to spy on and cross-examine his friends in order to find out whether the facts fit his theory, we decide, as we do in "The Turn of the Screw," that there are two separate things to be kept straight: a false hypothesis which the narrator is putting forward and a reality which we are supposed to guess from what he tells us about what actually happens. We remember the narrator of "The Aspern Papers," another inquisitive and annoying fellow, who is finally foiled and put to rout by the old lady whose private papers he is trying to get hold of. In the case of "The Aspern Papers," there is no uncertainty about James's attitude toward the narrator: James lets us know that the papers were none of the journalist's business and that the rebuff served him right. And the amateur detective of "The Sacred Fount" is foiled and rebuffed in precisely the same manner by one of his recalcitrant victims. "My poor dear, you *are* crazy, and I bid you good-night!" she says to him at the end of the story. "Such a last word," the narrator remarks, "the word that put me altogether nowhere—was too inacceptable not to prescribe afresh that prompt test of escape to other air for which I had earlier in the evening seen so much reason. I *should* certainly never again, on the spot, quite hang together, even though it wasn't really that I hadn't three times her method. What I too fatally lacked was her tone." But why *did* he lack her tone?—why *would* he never again hang together? What are we supposed to conclude about his whole exploit?

Mr. Wilson Follett, the only writer on James who has given "The Sacred Fount" special attention (in "Henry James's Portrait of Henry James," *New York Times Book Review,* August 23, 1936), believes that the book is a parable—even a conscious parody—of James's own role as an artist. The narrator may or may not have been right as to the actual facts of the case. The point is that, in elaborating his theory, he has constructed a work of art, and that it is a mistake to make the validity of works of art depend on a correspondence with actuality. Art has only its own kind of validity, and a collision with actuality would destroy it and put an end to the activities of the artist.

Certainly James has put himself into "The Sacred Fount," and certainly he has intended some sort of fable about the imaginative mind and the material with which it works. But it seems to me that Mr. Follett's theory assumes on James's part a conception of artistic truth which would hardly be worthy of him. After all, the novelist must know what people are actually up to, however much he may rearrange actuality; and it is not clear in "The Sacred Fount" whether the narrator really knew what he was talking about. If "The Sacred Fount" is a parody, what is the point of the parody? Why should James have represented the artist as defeated by the breaking-in of life?

The truth is, I believe, that Henry James was not clear about the book in his own mind. Already, with "The Turn of the Screw," he has carried his ambiguous procedure to a point where it seems almost as if he did not want the reader to get through to the hidden meaning. See his curious replies in his letters to correspondents who write him about the story: to what seem to have been leading questions, he seems to have given evasive answers, dismissing the tale as a mere "pot-boiler," a mere *"jeu d'esprit.*" Olive Chancellor in "The Bostonians," though tragic perhaps, is horrid, and she is vanquished by Basil Ransom. But he was willing to leave his readers in doubt as to whether the governess was horrid or nice. And now in "The Sacred Fount," we do not know whether the week-end guest, though he was unquestionably obnoxious to the other guests, is intended to be taken as one of the élite, a fastidious highly civilized sensibility, or merely as a little bit cracked and a bore. The man who wanted to get the Aspern papers was fanatically inquisitive and a nuisance; but many of James's inquisitive observers who never take part in the action are presented as most superior people. James confessed to being this sort of person himself. Ambiguity was certainly growing on James. It was to pass all bounds in those scenes in his later novels (of which the talks in "The Turn of the Screw" between the housekeeper and the governess are only comparatively mild examples) in which the characters are able to carry on long conversations with each consistently mistaking the other's meaning and neither ever yielding to the impulse to say any of the obvious things which would clear the situation up.

What if the hidden theme of "The Sacred Fount" is simply sex again? What if the real sacred fount, from which the people observed by the narrator have been drawing their new vitality, is love instead of youth? They have something which he has not had, know something which he does not know; and, lacking the clue of love, he can only pedantically misunderstand them. And they, since they have the forces of life on their side, are able to frighten him away.

This theory may be dubious, also; but there is certainly involved in "The Sacred Fount" the conception of a man shut out from love and doomed to barren speculation on human relations, who will be shocked by direct contact with reality.

Hitherto, it has usually been quite plain what James wanted us to think of his characters; but now there appears in his work a morbid element which is not always handled objectively but has invaded the story-teller himself. He seems to be dramatizing the frustrations of his own life without quite being willing to confess it, without always fully admitting it to himself.

But before we pursue this line of inquiry, let us look at him in a different connection.

3

Who *are* these characters of Henry James's about whom we come to be less and less certain as to precisely what he means us to think?

The type is the cultivated American bourgeois, like Henry James himself, who lives on an income derived from some form (usually left extremely vague) of American business activity but who has taken no part in the achievements which made the income possible. These men turn their backs on business; they attempt to enrich their experience through the society and art of Europe. But they bring to it the bourgeois qualities of timidity, prudence, primness, the habits of mind of a narrow morality which, even when they wish to be open-minded, cause them to be easily shocked. They wince alike at the brutalities of the aristocracy and at the vulgarities of the working-class; they shrink most of all from the "commonness" of the less cultivated bourgeoisie, who, having acquired their incomes more recently, are not so far advanced in self-improvement. The women have the corresponding qualities: they are innocent, conventional and rather cold—sometimes they suffer from Freudian complexes or a kind of arrested development, sometimes they are neglected or cruelly cheated by the men to whom they have given their hearts. And even when James's heroes and heroines are English, they assimilate themselves to these types.

It is illuminating in this connection to compare James's attitude to Flaubert's. The hero of "L'Education Sentimentale" is a perfect Henry James character: he is sensitive, cautious, afraid of life, he lives on a little income and considers himself superior to the common run. But Flaubert's attitude toward Frédéric Moreau is devastatingly ironic. Frédéric has his aspects of pathos, his occasional flashes of spirit: but Flaubert is quite emphatic in his final judgment of Frédéric. He considers Frédéric a worm.

Now James has his own kind of irony, but it is not Flaubert's kind. Frédéric Moreau is really the hero of most of James's novels, and you can see very plainly how James's estimate of him usually differs from Flaubert's if you compare certain kinds of scenes which tend to recur in Henry James with scenes in "L'Education Sentimentale" from which James has evidently imitated them: those situations of a sensitive young man immersed in some kind of gathering or having a succession of meetings with various characters without being able in his innocence precisely to figure out what they are up to. The reader is able to guess that they are more worldly and unscrupulous persons than the hero and that they are talking over his head, acting behind his back. You have this pattern, as I say, both in Flaubert and in James; but the difference is that, whereas in James the young man is made wondering and wistful and is likely to turn out a pitiful victim, in Flaubert he is made to look like a fool and is as ready to double-cross these other people who seem to him so inferior to himself as they are to double-cross him.

In this difference between Flaubert's attitude toward Frédéric and James's attitude toward, say, Hyacinth Robinson of "The Princess Casamassima" is to be discovered, I believe, the real reason for James's peculiar resentment of Flaubert. Flaubert interested James deeply: they had in common that they were both trying to give dignity to the novel of modern life by bringing it to intense esthetic form. And James returned to Flaubert again and again, wrote three essays on him at different periods. But though he obviously cannot help admiring Flaubert, he usually manages in the long run to belittle him—and he is especially invidious on the subject of "L'Education Sentimentale." His great complaint is that Flaubert's characters are so ignoble that they do not deserve to have so much art expended on them and that there must have been something basically wrong with Flaubert ever to have supposed that they did. James never seems to understand that Flaubert intends all his characters to be "middling" and that the greatness of his work arises from the fact that it constitutes a criticism of something bigger than they are. James praises the portrait of Mme. Arnoux: thank God at least, he exclaims, that here Flaubert was able to muster the good taste to deal delicately with a pure and fine-grained woman! He seems completely unaware that Mme. Arnoux is treated as ironically as any of the other characters—that the virtuous bourgeois wife with her inhibitions and superstitions is pathetic only as a part of the bigger thing of which Flaubert is showing the failure. Henry James mistakes Mme. Arnoux for a refined portrait of an American lady and he is worried because Frédéric isn't a quietly vibrating young American. Yet at the same time he must have his uneasy suspicion that young Americans of that kind are being made fun of. I believe that James's antagonism to Flaubert may be primarily due to the fact that Flaubert's criticism of the pusillanimity of the bourgeois has really touched James himself. James's later heroes are always regretting having lived and loved too meagerly; and James distills from these sensitive non-participants all the sad self-effacing nobility, all the fine and thin beauty, he can get out of them. Whereas Flaubert extracts something quite different and bitter: when Frédéric recalls in middle age his first clumsy and frightened visit to a brothel as the best that life has had to offer him, it is a damnation of a whole society.

But there was another kind of modern society which Flaubert did not know and which Henry James did know. Henry James was that new anomalous thing, an American. He is an American who has spent much of his childhood and youth in Europe, and he is imbued to a considerable extent with the European point of view. The monuments of feudal and ancient Europe, the duchesses and princesses and princes who seem to carry on the feudal tradition, are still capable of making modern life look to him dull, undistinguished and tame. But the past for him does not completely dwarf the present, as the vigil of Saint Anthony and the impacts of pagan armies dwarf Flaubert's Frédéric Moreau. The American in Henry James insistently asserts himself against Europe. After all, Frédéric Moreau and Madame Arnoux are the best people of Albany and Boston!—but they are not characters in Flaubert there. There their scruples and their renunciations possess a real value—for Frédéric Moreau at home possesses a real integrity; and when they visit Europe, they judge the whole thing in a new way. Henry James speaks somewhere of his indignation at an Englishwoman's saying to him in connection with something: "That is true of the aristocracy, but in one's own class it is quite different." As an American, it had never occurred to him that he could be described as a middle-class person. When Edith Wharton accused him in his later years of no longer appreciating Flaubert and demanded of him why Emma Bovary was not as good a subject for a novel as Anna Karenina, he replied: "Ah, but one paints the fierce passions of a luxurious aristocracy; the other deals with the petty miseries of a little bourgeoise in a provincial town!" But if Emma Bovary is small potatoes, what about Daisy Miller? Why, Daisy Miller is an American girl! Emma Bovary has her debts and adulteries, but she is otherwise a conventional person, she remains in her place in the social scheme, even when she dreams of rising out of it: when she goes to visit the château, the sugar seems to her whiter and finer than elsewhere. Whereas Daisy Miller represents something which has walked quite out of the frame of Europe. When it comes back to Europe again, it disregards the social system. Europe is too much for Daisy Miller: she catches cold in the Coliseum, where according to European conventions she oughtn't to have been at that hour. But the great popularity of her story was certainly due to her creator's having somehow conveyed the impression that her spirit went marching on.

In Henry James's mind, there disputed all his life the European and the American points of view; and their debate, I believe, is closely connected with his inability sometimes to be clear as to what he thinks of a certain sort of person. It is quite mistaken to talk as if James had uprooted himself from America in order to live in England. He had traveled so much from his earliest years that he had never had any real roots anywhere. His father had himself been a wandering intellectual, oscillating back and forth between the United States and Europe. And even in America, the Jameses oscillated back and forth between Boston and New York. They were not New Englanders but New Yorkers, and they had none of the tight local ties of New Englanders—they always came to Boston from a larger outside world and their attitude toward it was critical and objective.

To James's critical attitude toward Boston was probably partly due the failure in America of "The Bostonians"; and to this failure is possibly due his discouragement with his original ambition of becoming the American Balzac. At any rate, it marks the moment of his taking up his residence in England and of his turning from the Americans to the English.

He was in London, and he found he liked living in London better than living in Boston or New York. His parents in the States had just died, and his sister came over to join him.

4

And this brings us to what seems to have been the principal crisis in Henry James's life and work. We know so little about his personal life that it is impossible to give any account of it save as it reflects itself in his writings.

Up to the period of his playwriting his fiction has been pretty plain sailing. He has aimed to be a social historian, and, in a rather limited field, he has succeeded. His three long novels of the later eighties—"The Bostonians," "The Princess Casamassima," and "The Tragic Muse" —are, indeed, as social history, his most ambitious undertakings and, up to a point, his most brilliant. The first hundred pages of "The Bostonians," with the arrival of the Mississippian in Boston and the crowded picture of the meeting of reformers is, in its way, one of the most masterly things that Henry James ever did. "The Princess Casamassima," with its prison and its revolutionary exiles in London, deals with issues and social contrasts of a kind that James had never before attempted. The familiar criticism of Henry James—the criticism made by H. G. Wells—does not, in fact, hold true of these books. Here his people do have larger interests and functions aside from their personal relations: they have professions, missions, practical aims; and they also engage in more drastic action than in his novels of any other period. Basil Ransom pursues Verena Tarrant and rescues her from the terrible Olive Chancellor; Hyacinth Robinson pledges himself to carry out a political assassination, then kills himself instead; Miriam Rooth makes her career as a great actress. Here there is a genuine will to do rather than a mere disposition to observe. Up to a point these three books are quite triumphant.

But there *is* a point—usually about half way through—at which every one of these novels begins strangely to run into the sands; the excitement seems to lapse at the same time that the color fades from the picture; and the ends are never up to the beginnings. This is most obvious, and even startling, in "The Tragic Muse," the first volume of which, when we read it, makes us think that it must be James's best novel, so solid and alive does it seem. There are in it a number of things which he has never given us before: a wonderful portrait of a retired parliamentarian with an implied criticism of British Liberal politics, a real scene—what one might have thought he could never do—between a man and a woman (Nick Dormer and Julia Dallow) instead of the polite conversations to which he has accustomed us; and Miriam Rooth, the Muse herself, comes nearer to carrying Henry James out of the enclosure of puritan scruples and prim prejudices on to the larger stage of human creative effort than any other character he has drawn. Here at least we seem to find ourselves with real people, who have the same appetites and ambitions as other people—in comparison, the characters of his earlier works are real only in a certain convention. Then suddenly the story stops short: after the arrival of Miriam in London, "The Tragic Muse" is an almost total blank. Of the two young men who have been preoccupied with Miriam, one renounces her because she will not leave the stage and the other apparently doesn't fall in love with her. Miriam, to be sure, makes a great success as an actress, but we are never taken into her life, we know nothing at first hand about her emotions. And with nothing but these negative decisions in sight, the author himself seems to lose interest.

The first half of "The Tragic Muse" is the high point of the first part of James's career, after which something snaps. He announces that he will write no more long novels, but only fiction of shorter length. He may have been aware that a long novel demands a mounting-up to a point of intensity and revelation of a kind which he was unable to give it, whereas a short story need not go so deep. At any rate, he set himself to write plays, and for five years he produced little else.

Why did he do this? He complained at this time that he had difficulty in selling his fiction, and he confessed that his plays were written in the hope of a popular success, that they were intended merely to entertain and were not to be taken too seriously. Yet this is surely an inadequate explanation of the phenomenon of a novelist of the first order giving up the art in which he has perfected himself to write plays which do not even aim to be serious.

That there was something incomplete and unexplained about James's emotional life seems to appear unmistakably from his novels. I believe it may be said that up to this point there are no consummated love affairs in his fiction—that is, none among the principal actors and during the action of the story; and this fact must certainly have contributed to his increasing loss of hold on his readers. It is not merely that he gave in "The Bostonians" an unpleasant picture of Boston, and in "The Tragic Muse" an equally unpleasant picture of the English; it is not merely that "The Princess Casamassima" treated a social-revolutionary subject from a point of view which gave neither side best. It was not merely that he was thus at this period rather lost between America and England. It was also that you cannot long hold an audience with stories about men wooing women in which the parties either never get together or are never seen as really functioning as lovers. And you will particularly discourage your readers with a story about two men and a girl in which neither man ever gets her and in which she marries a third person, totally uninteresting. There is, as I have said, in "The Tragic Muse," a much more convincing man-and-woman relationship. Julia Dallow is really female and she really behaves like a woman with Nick Dormer; but here her political ambitions get between Nick and her, so that this, too, never comes to anything: here the man, again, must renounce. (In James's later novels, these healthily female women are always invested with a value frankly sinister and usually animated by evil designs: Kate Croy and Charlotte Stant.) Years later, Henry James explained in his preface to "The Tragic Muse" that he had been prevented from allowing Miriam Rooth to have a genuine love affair with anybody by the prudery of the American magazines; and certainly the skittishness of a reading public which was scandalized by "Jude the Obscure" is not to be underestimated. But, after all, Hardy and Meredith did write about Jude and Lord Ormont and his Aminta and let the public howl; and it would certainly have enhanced rather than diminished Henry James's reputation—as to which his ambitions seem by no means to have been modest—if he had done the same thing himself. Problems of passion in conflict with convention and law were coming to be subjects of burning interest; but James could not deal with that kind of passion and was much too honest to try to fake it.

One feels about the episode of his playwriting that it was an effort to put himself over, an effort to make himself felt, as he had never succeeded in doing before. His brother William James wrote home in the summer of 1889, at the beginning of Henry's playwriting period, that Henry, beneath the "rich sea-weeds and rigid barnacles and things" of "strange heavy alien manners and customs" with which he had covered himself like a "marine crustacean," remained the "same dear old, good, innocent and at bottom very powerless-feeling Harry." He had injured his back in an accident in his boyhood, and it was still necessary for him to lie down for regular rests. And now it is as if he were putting his back into playwriting as he had never been able to put it into a passion. His heroine Miriam Rooth in the novel has turned away from the Philistine English world, which rejects her, and taken into the theater the will of the artist, which will enable her to conquer that world; and her creator is now to imitate her.

But his plays were not produced or did not go. At the first night of "Guy Domville," he ran foul of a hissing and booing British audience (the play contained another of his confounded renunciations); and these five years put him under a severe strain. When he recovers from his disappointment, he is seen to have passed through a kind of crisis.

Now he enters upon a new phase, of which the most obvious feature is a subsidence back into himself. And now sex *does* appear in his work—and even becomes something like an obsession—in a queer and left-handed way. We have "The Turn of the Screw" and "The Sacred Fount"—and "What Maisie Knew" and "In the Cage." There are plenty of love affairs now and plenty of irregular relations, but there are always barriers between them and us; they are the chief object of interest but they are seen from a distance.

For the Jamesian central observer, through whose intelligence the story is usually relayed to us, has undergone a strange diminution. This observer is no longer a complete and interesting person more or less actively involved in the events, but a small child, a telegraph operator who lives vicariously through the senders of telegrams, a week-end guest who seems not to exist in any other capacity except that of a week-end guest and who lives vicariously through his fellow visitors. The people who surround this observer tend to take on the diabolic value of the specters of "The Turn of the Screw," and this diabolic value is almost invariably connected with their concealed and only guessed-at sexual relations. The innocent Nanda Brookenham of "The Awkward Age," a work of the same period and group, has a whole host of creepy creatures around her. James is ceasing to sustain the objectivity which has kept the outlines of his stories pretty definite up through his middle novels: he has relapsed into a dreamy inner world, where values are often uncertain and where it is not even possible for him any longer to judge the effect of his stories on his audience—that audience which, as a matter of fact, has almost ceased to exist. One is dismayed in reading his comments on "The Awkward Age," which he seems to have considered highly successful, to realize that he is unaware of the elements in the book which, in spite of the technical virtuosity displayed in it, make it unpleasant and irritating. The central figure of "The Sacred Fount" may perhaps have been presented ironically; but James could never have known how we should feel about the gibbering disemboweled crew who hover about one another with sordid shadowy designs in "The Awkward Age."

This is accompanied by a kind of expansion of the gas of the psychological atmosphere—an atmosphere which has now a special odor. With "What Maisie Knew," as F. M. Ford says, the style first becomes a little gamey; and then, dropping off its old formality and what sometimes amounted to a mechanical hardness, it becomes progressively, in the conventional sense, more poetic.

With all this, his experience of playwriting has done him no good in his fiction. He had set himself to emulate the most stultifying models of the mechanically well-made play. He turned certain of these pieces into novels—"Covering End" and "The Other House"—and dreadful novels they made; and in "The Awkward Age" and other works of this period, an artificial dramatic technique persists. It is one of the elements that make some of them so exasperating. They combine a lifeless trickery of logic with the ambiguous subjectivity of a nightmare.

In this period certainly originates that tendency on James's part to exploit the mysteries of technique for the purpose of diverting attention from his shortcomings which has imposed on some of his critics and which must of course have imposed on himself. One can see from his comments of various periods how a method like that of Tolstoy in "War and Peace" became more and more distasteful to him. Tolstoy, he insisted, was all over the shop, entering the minds of far too many of his characters and failing to exercise the principle of selection. He speaks in the preface to "The Tragic Muse" of his own difficulty in handling a complex subject—though here it is a question of going into the minds of only two of the characters. But, obviously, the question of whether the novelist enters into a variety of points of view has nothing to do with his technical proficiency or even with his effect of concentration. One trouble with "The Tragic Muse" is that James does not show us the inside of Miriam Rooth; and if he fails to do so, it is because, here as elsewhere, he does not know, as Tolstoy did, what the insides of such people are like. So, in "The Wings of the Dove," the "messengering," as the drama courses say, of Kate Croy's final scene with Merton Densher is evidently due to James's increasing incapacity for dealing directly with scenes of emotion rather than to the esoteric motives he alleges. And so his curious constant complaint that he is unable to do certain things because there is no longer space within the prescribed limits of the story is certainly only another hollow excuse: he never seems to be aware of the amount of space he is wasting through the roundabout locutions or quite gratuitous verbiage with which he habitually pads out his sentences—and which is itself a form of staving off his main problems. His censure of Tolstoy for his failure to select is a defensive reflex action on Henry James's part for his own failure to fill in his picture.

5

What happens after this, however, is interesting. In "The Ambassadors," "The Wings of the Dove" and "The Golden Bowl," the psychological atmosphere thickens, fills up the stories with the Jamesian gas instead of with detail and background. The characters (though usually apprehended as convincing personal entities) are seen dimly through a phantasmagoria of dream-like metaphors and similes, which seem sometimes, as Rebecca West has said, more vivid and solid than the settings.

But a positive element reappears. The novels of "The Awkward Age" period were written not merely from James's international limbo between the United States and Europe but under the oppression of defeat and self-doubt. But in these queer and neurotic stories—(some of them, of course—"The Turn of the Screw" and "What Maisie Knew"—among James's masterpieces)—moral values begin to assert themselves again. They sprout first in the infantile form of Maisie and Nanda Brookenham, whose innocence is the test of the other characters. Then in the longer novels that follow, in figures of a more mature innocence, they completely take the field; and these figures are now invariably Americans. We are back to the pattern of his earlier novels, where the typical conflict was between glamorous people who were also worldly and likely to be wicked, and people of superior scruples who were likely to be more or less homely, and where the former usually represented Europe and the latter the United States. In these novels, it was sometimes the Americans—as in "The Portrait of a Lady"—who were left with the moral advantage; sometimes—as in "The Europeans"—the Europeans. But in these late novels it is always the Americans who have the better of it from the moral point of view—scoring heavily off a fascinating Italian prince, an equally fascinating French lady and a formidable group of middle-class English people. Yes: there *was* a beauty and there was also a power in the goodness of these naive and open people, which had not existed for Flaubert and his group. It *is* something different and new which does not fit into the formulas of Europe. What if Lambert Strether *had* missed in Woollett, Mass., many things that he would have enjoyed in Paris: he had brought to Paris something it did not have. And the burden of the book on "William Wetmore Story and His Friends," which was also written during this time—rather different from that of his early book on Hawthorne—is that American artists might much better stay at home.

And now—in 1904—Henry James revisits America, writes "The American Scene," returns to it in a novel, "The Ivory Tower," left unfinished at his death.

In his other unfinished novel, the fantasia called "The Sense of the Past," he makes a young contemporary American go back into eighteenth-century England. Here the Jamesian ambiguity serves an admirable artistic purpose. Is it the English of the past who are the ghosts or is it the American himself who is a dream?—will the moment come when *they* will vanish or will he himself cease to exist? And, as before, there is a question of James's own asking at the bottom of the ambiguity: Which is real—America or Europe? It was, however, in the novel, the American who was to remain real. (It is curious to compare "The Sense of the Past" with "A Connecticut Yankee in King Arthur's Court," with which it really has a good deal in common.)

Yes: in spite of the popular assumption founded on his expatriation, it is America which gets the better of it in Henry James. His warmest tributes to American genius come out of these later years. Though he could not, in "Notes of a Son and Brother," resist the impulse to remove references to Lincoln as "old Abe" from William James's early letters of the wartime, it contains pages on Lincoln's death of a touching appreciation and pride. "It was vain to say," he writes of Andrew Johnson, of whom he says that the American people felt him unworthy to represent them, "that we had deliberately invoked the 'common' in authority and must drink the wine we had drawn. No countenance, no salience of aspect nor composed symbol, could superficially have referred itself less than Lincoln's mold-smashing mask to any mere matter-of-course type of propriety; but his admirable unrelated head had itself revealed a type—as if by the very fact that what made in it for roughness of kind looked out only less than what made in it for splendid final stamp; in other words for commanding Style." And of the day when the news reached Boston: "I was fairly to go in shame of its being my birthday. These would have been the hours of the streets if none others had been—when the huge general gasp filled them like a great earth-shudder and people's eyes met people's eyes without the vulgarity of speech. Even this was, all so strangely, part of the lift and the swell, as tragedy has but to be of a pure enough strain and a high enough connection to sow with its dark hand the seed of greater life. The collective sense of what had occurred was of a sadness too noble not somehow to inspire, and it was truly in the air that, whatever we had as a nation produced or failed to produce, we could at least gather round this perfection of classic woe." In "The American Scene," he writes of Concord: "We may smile a little as we 'drag in' Weimar, but I confess myself, for my part, much more satisfied than not by our happy equivalent, 'in American money,' for Goethe and Schiller. The money is a potful in the second case as in the first, and if Goethe, in the one, represents the gold and Schiller the silver, I find (and quite putting aside any bi-metallic prejudice) the same good relation in the other between Emerson and Thoreau. I open Emerson for the same benefit for which I open Goethe, the sense of moving in large intellectual space, and that of the gush, here and there, out of the rock, of the crystalline cupful, in wisdom and poetry, in *Wahrheit* and *Dichtung;* and whatever I open Thoreau for (I needn't take space here for the good reasons) I open him oftener than I open Schiller." Edith Wharton says that he used to read Walt Whitman aloud "in a mood of subdued ecstasy" and with tremendous effect on his hearers.

Henry James's career had been affected by the shift in the national point of view which occurred after the Civil War. It is being shown by Mr. Van Wyck Brooks in his cultural history of New England how the Bostonian of the first part of the century was inspired—as, in our time, the Russians have been—to present the world with a new humanity, set free from the caste-barriers and poverties of Europe, which should return to the mother-country only to plunder her for elements of culture which might contribute to the movement at home; and how, with the triumph of the industrial system, the persons who were occupied with art and thought became gradually ashamed of the United States and tended to take refuge in Europe. Henry James belonged to this second phase, but he had a good deal of the idealism of the first one. It appears in the name of the hero of "The American": Newman, and in his phrase about Lincoln's "mold-smashing mask"; and, after a period of partial abeyance, when he had been writing largely about Europeans, it cropped up again, as I have shown, and took the field.

But Henry James is a reporter, not a prophet. With less political philosophy even than Flaubert, he can only chronicle the world as it passes, and in his picture the elements are mixed. In the Americans of Henry James's later novels—the Milly Theales, the Lambert Strethers, the Maggie Ververs—he shows us all that was magnanimous, reviving and human in the Americans at the beginning of the new century along with all that was frustrated, sterile, excessively refined, depressing—all that they had in common with the Frédéric Moreaus and with the daughters of poor English parsons. There they are with their ideals and their blights. Milly Theale, for example—quite real at the core of the cloudy integument with which James has swathed her about—is one of the best portraits of a rich New Yorker in fiction. It is the great period of the heyday of Sargent; but compare these figures of Henry James's with Sargent's and see with what profounder insight as well as with what superior delicacy James has caught the rich Americans of this race.

6

And between the first and the second blooming something tragic has happened to these Americans. What has become of Cristopher Newman? He is Lambert Strether now: he has been worn down by the factories of Woollett. And these Americans of the later novels, who still bring Europe the American sincerity—what has happened to them to make them so wan? Well, for one thing, they have become very rich, and being rich is a terrible burden: in the process of getting rich, they have starved themselves spiritually at home; and now that they are trying to get something for their money, they find that they have put themselves at the mercy of all the schemers and adventurers of Europe. It seems to me foolish to reproach Henry James for having neglected the industrial background. Like sex, we never get very close to it, but its effects are a part of his picture. James's tone is more often old-maidish than his sense of reality is feeble; and the whole development of American society during his absence is implied in these later books.

Now when he returns—late in the day though it is for him—he reacts strongly and reports vividly what he finds.

The returning New Yorker of "The Jolly Corner" encounters the apparition of himself as he would have been if he had stayed in America: "Rigid and conscious, spectral yet human, a man of his own substance and stature waited there to measure himself with his power to dismay." At first the apparition covers its face with its hands; then it advances upon the returned native "as for aggression, and he knew himself give ground. Then harder pressed still, sick with the force of his shock, and falling back as under the hot breath and the sensed passion of a life larger than his own, a rage of personality before which his own collapsed, he felt the whole vision turn to darkness," and he fainted.

But at contact with the harsh new America, the old Balzac in James revives. I do not know why more has not been made by James's critics—especially by the critics of the Left, who are so certain that there is nothing in him—of his unfinished novel, "The Ivory Tower." The work of his all but final period has been "poetic" rather than "realistic"; but now he passes into still a further phase, in which the poetic treatment is applied to what is for James a new kind of realism. The fiction of his latest period is preoccupied in a curious way with the ugly, the poor and the old, even with—what is unprecedented for James—the grotesque. It is perhaps the reflection of his own old age, his own lack of worldly success, the strange creature that he himself has become. This new vein begins, I think, with "The Papers," with its fantastically amusing picture of the sordid lives of journalists in London. "Fordham Castle," in which he said he had attempted to do some justice to the parents of the Daisy Millers, whose children had left them behind, is an excursion into the America of Sinclair Lewis. "The Bench of Desolation"—one of the most beautifully written and wonderfully developed pieces in the whole range of Henry James's work, and, I believe, the last piece of fiction he published—is a sort of poem of loneliness and poverty among the nondescript small shopkeepers and former governesses of an English seaside resort.

And now the revelation of Newport, as it presented itself in the nineteen hundreds—so different from the Newport which he had described years ago in "An International Episode"—stimulates him to something quite new: a kind of nightmare of the American new rich. Here his gusto for the varied forms of life, his interest in social phenomena for their own sake, seems suddenly to wake up from its reveries. The actual appearances of things become suddenly vivid again. In the novels which preceded "The Ivory Tower," the carefully selected and charming old-world settings had been steadily fading out; but now, to our amazement, there starts into relief the America of the millionaires, at its crudest, corruptest and phoniest: the immense summer mansions full of equipment which no one ever seems to have selected or used, the old men of the Rockefeller-Frick generation, landed, with no tastes and no interests, amidst an unlimited magnificence which dwarfs them, the silly or clumsy young people of the second generation with their off-color relationships, their enormous meaningless parties, their touching longings and resolute strivings for an elegance and cultivation they cannot manage. The apparition in "The Jolly Corner" came upon the Europeanized American "quite as one of those expanding fantastic images projected by the magic lantern of childhood"; and in the same way, for the reader of James, with the opening of "The Ivory Tower," there emerges the picture of old Abner Gaw sitting and rocking his foot and looking out on the sparkling Atlantic while he waits for his partner to die.

"The Ivory Tower" is immensely comic, deeply human and brilliantly observed—and it is poetic in the highest sense, like all these later novels: in the sense that its characters and images, individualized though they are, shine out with the incandescence which shows them as symbols of phases through which the human soul has passed.

The moral of the book—which seems quite plain from the scenario left by James—is also of particular interest. The ivory tower itself, a fine piece of Chinese carving, figures the spiritual isolation, the cultivation of sensations and the literary activity which are to be made possible for the young American, returned from Europe, who has inherited his uncle's fortune; but it contains, also, the fatal letter in which the vindictive Mr. Gaw has revealed all the swindles and perfidies by which the fortune has been created. So that the young man (he has always had a *little* money) is to come finally to be glad enough to give up the ivory tower with the fortune.

James dropped "The Ivory Tower" when the War broke out in 1914, because it seemed to him too remote from the present. The War seems to have presented itself to him as simply a struggle between, on the one hand, French and English civilization and, on the other, German barbarism. He had believed in, and had been writing rather vaguely about, the possible salutary effect on human affairs of a sort of international élite such as he tended to depict in his novels; and now he spoke of the past as "the age of the mistake," the time when people had thought that things would be all right. He now became violently nationalistic, or at least violently pro-Ally, and took out citizen's papers in England, because America had not yet gone into the War. It never seems to have occurred to him that in "The Ivory Tower" he had been much closer to contemporary realities than in becoming an English citizen, that the partnership of Betterman and Gaw was a European phenomenon, too—any more than it ever occurred to him that the class antagonisms of "The Princess Casamassima"—his response to the depression of the eighties—must inevitably appear again. But as Hyacinth Robinson died of the class struggle, so Henry James died of the War.

Before he died, the English gave him the

Order of Merit. But I do not think that anybody has yet done justice to the genius that, overriding personal deficiencies of a peculiarly disabling kind, finding its bearings in a social situation almost as bewildering as the astronomical one with which the mathematics of relativity deals, surviving the ridicule and indifference of the two peoples whose critic he had made himself, was able to re-create itself to the end and actually to break fresh ground at seventy.

For Henry James *is* a great artist, in spite of everything. His deficiencies are obvious enough. He was certainly rather short on invention; and he tended to hold life at arm's-length. Yet when a novelist with a real inventive gift—say Compton Mackenzie—can invent till the cows come home without his inventions' making any lasting impression on us, the things that James *does* invent have so perfect an appropriateness and beauty, even floating though they sometimes are in rather a gray sea of abstract exposition, that they remain in our minds as luminous symbols; and the objects and beings at the end of James's arm, or rather, at the end of his antennae, are grasped with an astonishing firmness, gauged with a marvelous intelligence. His work is incomplete as his experience was; but it is in no respect second-rate, and he can be judged only in the company of the greatest. My argument has not given me an occasion to call attention to the classical equanimity, the classical combination of realism with harmony—I have tried to describe them in writing about Pushkin—which have been so rare in American and in English literature alike and of which James is one of the only examples.*

* The reader may be interested in James's own statement of the inception of "The Turn of the Screw." It is reprinted here by permission of the publishers from *The Notebooks of Henry James*, edited by F. O. Matthiessen and Kenneth B. Murdock. Copyright 1947 by Oxford University Press.

Saturday, January 12th, 1895. Note here the ghost-story told me at Addington (evening of Thursday 10th), by the Archbishop of Canterbury; the mere vague, undetailed faint sketch of it—being all he had been told (very badly and imperfectly), by a lady who had no art of relation, and no clearness: the story of the young children (indefinite number and age) left to the care of servants in an old country-house, through the death, presumably, of parents. The servants, wicked and depraved, corrupt and deprave the children; the children are bad, full of evil, to a sinister degree. The servants *die* (the story vague about the way of it) and their apparitions, figures, return to haunt the house *and* children, to whom they seem to beckon, whom they invite and solicit, from across dangerous places, the deep ditch of a sunk fence, etc.—so that the children may destroy themselves, lose themselves, by responding, by getting into their power. So long as the children are kept from them, they are not lost; but they try and try and try, these evil presences, to get hold of them. It is a question of the children 'coming over to where they are.' It is all obscure and imperfect, the picture, the story, but there is a suggestion of strangely gruesome effect in it. The story to be told—tolerably obviously—by an outside spectator, observer.

Lamb House, August 9th, 1900. . . . The ideal [of *The Sense of the Past*] is something as simple as "The Turn of the Screw," only different and less grossly and merely apparitional."

GEORGE ORWELL: Politics and the English Language*

MOST people who bother with the matter at all would admit that the English language is in a bad way, but it is generally assumed that we cannot by conscious action do anything about it. Our civilization is decadent and our language—so the argument runs—must inevitably share in the general collapse. It follows that any struggle against the abuse of language is a sentimental archaism, like preferring candles to electric light or hansom cabs to aeroplanes. Underneath this lies the half-conscious belief

* From *Shooting an Elephant, and Other Essays* by George Orwell, copyright, 1945, 1946, 1949, 1950, by Sonia Brownell Orwell. Reprinted by permission of Harcourt, Brace and Company, Inc. "George Orwell" was the pseudonym of Eric Blair (1903-1950), the author of many literary essays, most of them collected in *Dickens, Dali and Others* (1946), *Such, Such Were the Joys* (1953), *England Your England* (1953), and *Shooting an Elephant, and Other Essays.*

that language is a natural growth and not an instrument which we shape for our own purposes.

Now, it is clear that the decline of a language must ultimately have political and economic causes: it is not due simply to the bad influence of this or that individual writer. But an effect can become a cause, reinforcing the original cause and producing the same effect in an intensified form, and so on indefinitely. A man may take to drink because he feels himself to be a failure, and then fail all the more completely because he drinks. It is rather the same thing that is happening to the English language. It becomes ugly and inaccurate because our thoughts are foolish, but the slovenliness of our language makes it easier for us to have foolish thoughts. The point is that the process is reversible. Modern English, especially written English, is full of bad habits which spread by imitation and which can be avoided if one is willing to take the necessary trouble. If one gets rid of these habits one can think more clearly, and to think clearly is a necessary first step towards political regeneration: so that the fight against bad English is not frivolous and is not the exclusive concern of professional writers. I will come back to this presently, and I hope that by that time the meaning of what I have said here will have become clearer. Meanwhile, here are five specimens of the English language as it is now habitually written.

These five passages have not been picked out because they are especially bad—I could have quoted far worse if I had chosen—but because they illustrate various of the mental vices from which we now suffer. They are a little below the average, but are fairly representative samples. I number them so that I can refer back to them when necessary:

(1) I am not, indeed, sure whether it is not true to say that the Milton who once seemed not unlike a seventeenth-century Shelley had not become, out of an experience ever more bitter in each year, more alien [*sic*] to the founder of that Jesuit sect which nothing could induce him to tolerate.

Professor Harold Laski
(Essay in *Freedom of Expression*).

(2) Above all, we cannot play ducks and drakes with a native battery of idioms which prescribes such egregious collocations of vocables as the Basic *put up with* for *tolerate* or *put at a loss* for *bewilder*.

Professor Lancelot Hogben (*Interglossa*).

(3) On the one side we have the free personality: by definition it is not neurotic, for it has neither conflict nor dream. Its desires, such as they are, are transparent, for they are just what institutional approval keeps in the forefront of consciousness; another institutional pattern would alter their number and intensity; there is little in them that is natural, irreducible, or culturally dangerous. But *on the other side*, the social bond itself is nothing but the mutual reflection of these self-secure integrities. Recall the definition of love. Is not this the very picture of a small academic? Where is there a place in this hall of mirrors for either personality or fraternity?

Essay on psychology in *Politics* (New York).

(4) All the "best people" from the gentlemen's clubs, and all the frantic fascist captains, united in common hatred of Socialism and bestial horror of the rising tide of the mass revolutionary movement, have turned to acts of provocation, to foul incendiarism, to medieval legends of poisoned wells, to legalize their own destruction of proletarian organizations, and rouse the agitated petty-bourgeoisie to chauvinistic fervor on behalf of the fight against the revolutionary way out of the crisis.

Communist pamphlet.

(5) If a new spirit *is* to be infused into this old country, there is one thorny and contentious reform which must be tackled, and that is the humanization and galvanization of the B.B.C. Timidity here will bespeak canker and atrophy of the soul. The heart of Britain may be sound and of strong beat, for instance, but the British lion's roar at present is like that of Bottom in Shakespeare's *Midsummer Night's Dream*—as gentle as any sucking dove. A virile new Britain cannot continue indefinitely to be traduced in the eyes, or rather ears, of the world by the effete languors of Langham Place, brazenly masquerading as "standard English." When the Voice of Britain is heard at nine o'clock, better far and infinitely less ludicrous to hear aitches honestly dropped than the present priggish, inflated, inhibited, school-ma'amish arch braying of blameless bashful mewing maidens!

Letter in *Tribune*.

Each of these passages has faults of its own, but, quite apart from avoidable ugliness, two qualities are common to all of them. The first is staleness of imagery; the other is lack of precision. The writer either has a meaning and cannot express it, or he inadvertently says something else, or he is almost indifferent as to whether his words mean anything or not. This mixture of vagueness and sheer incompetence is the most marked characteristic of modern English prose, and especially of any kind of political writing. As soon as certain topics are raised, the concrete melts into the abstract and no one seems able to think of turns of speech that are not hackneyed: prose consists less and less of *words* chosen for the sake of their meaning, and more and more of *phrases* tacked together like the sections of a prefabricated hen-house. I list below, with notes and examples, various of the tricks by means of which the work of prose-construction is habitually dodged:

Dying metaphors. A newly invented metaphor assists thought by evoking a visual image, while on the other hand a metaphor which is technically "dead" (e.g. *iron resolution*) has in effect reverted to being an ordinary word and can generally be used without loss of vividness. But in between these two classes there is a huge dump of worn-out metaphors which have lost all evocative power and are merely used because they save people the trouble of inventing phrases for themselves. Examples are: *Ring the changes on, take up the cudgels for, toe the line, ride roughshod over, stand shoulder to shoulder with, play into the hands of, no axe to grind, grist to the mill, fishing in troubled waters, on the order of the day, Achilles' heel, swan song, hotbed.* Many of these are used without knowledge of their meaning (what is a "rift," for instance?), and incompatible metaphors are frequently mixed, a sure sign that the writer is not interested in what he is saying. Some metaphors now current have been twisted out of their original meaning without those who use them even being aware of the fact. For example, *toe the line* is sometimes written *tow the line.* Another example is *the hammer and the anvil,* now always used with the implication that the anvil gets the worst of it. In real life it is always the anvil that breaks the hammer, never the other way about: a writer who stopped to think what he was saying would be aware of this, and would avoid perverting the original phrase.

Operators or *verbal false limbs.* These save the trouble of picking out appropriate verbs and nouns; and at the same time pad each sentence with extra syllables which give it an appearance of symmetry. Characteristic phrases are *render inoperative, militate against, make contact with, be subjected to, give rise to, give grounds for, have the effect of, play a leading part (role) in, make itself felt, take effect, exhibit a tendency to, serve the purpose of, etc., etc.* The keynote is the elimination of simple verbs. Instead of being a single word, such as *break, stop, spoil, mend, kill,* a verb becomes a *phrase,* made up of a noun or adjective tacked on to some general-purpose verb such as *prove, serve, form, play, render.* In addition, the passive voice is wherever possible used in preference to the active, and noun constructions are used instead of gerunds (*by examination of* instead of *by examining*). The range of verbs is further cut down by means of the *-ize* and *de-* formations, and the banal statements are given an appearance of profundity by means of the *not un-* formation. Simple conjunctions and prepositions are replaced by such phrases as *with respect to, having regard to, the fact that, by dint of, in view of, in the interests of, on the hypothesis that;* and the ends of sentences are saved by anticlimax by such resounding common-places as *greatly to be desired, cannot be left out of account, a development to be expected in the near future, deserving of serious consideration, brought to a satisfactory conclusion,* and so on and so forth.

Pretentious diction. Words like *phenomenon, element, individual* (as noun), *objective, categorical, effective, virtual, basic, primary, promote, constitute, exhibit, exploit, utilize, eliminate, liquidate,* are used to dress up simple statement and give an air of scientific impartiality to biased judgments. Adjectives like *epoch-making, epic, historic, unforgettable, triumphant, age-old, inevitable, inexorable, veritable,* are used to dignify the sordid processes of international politics, while writing that aims at glorifying war usually takes on an archaic color, its characteristic words being: *realm, throne, chariot, mailed fist, trident, sword, shield, buckler, banner, jackboot, clarion.* Foreign words and expressions such as *cul de sac, ancien régime, deus ex machina, mutatis mutandis, status quo, gleichschaltung, weltanschauung,* are used to give an air of culture and elegance. Except for the useful abbreviations *i.e., e.g.,* and *etc.*, there is no real need for any of the hundreds of foreign phrases now current in English. Bad writers, and especially scientific, political and sociological writers, are nearly always haunted by the notion that Latin or Greek words are grander than Saxon ones, and unnecessary words like *expedite, ameliorate, predict, extraneous, deracinated, clandestine, subaqueous* and hundreds of others constantly gain ground from their Anglo-Saxon opposite numbers. The jargon peculiar to Marxist writing (*hyena, hangman, cannibal, petty bourgeois, these gentry, lacquey, flunkey, mad dog, White Guard*, etc.) consists largely of words and phrases translated from Russian, German or French; but the normal way of coining a new word is to use a Latin or Greek root with the appropriate affix and, where necessary, the size formation. It is often easier to make up words of this kind (*deregionalize, impermissible, extramarital, nonfragmentary* and so forth) than to think up the English words that will cover one's meaning. The result, in general, is an increase in slovenliness and vagueness.

Meaningless words. In certain kinds of writing, particularly in art criticism and literary criticism, it is normal to come across long passages which are almost completely lacking in meaning. Words like *romantic, plastic, values, human, dead, sentimental, natural, vitality*, as used in art criticism, are strictly meaningless, in the sense that they not only do not point to any discoverable object, but are hardly ever expected to do so by the reader. When one critic writes, "The outstanding feature of Mr. X's work is its living quality," while another writes, "The immediately striking thing about Mr. X's work is its peculiar deadness," the reader accepts this as a simple difference of opinion. If words like *black* and *white* were involved, instead of the jargon words *dead* and *living*, he would see at once that language was being used in an improper way. Many political words are similarly abused. The word *Fascism* has now no meaning except in so far as it signifies "something not desirable." The words *democracy, socialism, freedom, patriotic, realistic, justice*, have each of them several different meanings which cannot be reconciled with one another. In the case of a word like *democracy*, not only is there no agreed definition, but the attempt to make one is resisted from all sides. It is almost universally felt that when we call a country democratic we are praising it: consequently the defenders of every kind of régime claim that it is a democracy, and fear that they might have to stop using the word if it were tied down to any one meaning. Words of this kind are often used in a consciously dishonest way. That is, the person who uses them has his own private definition, but allows his hearer to think he means something quite different. Statements like *Marshal Pétain was a true patriot, The Soviet Press is the freest in the world, The Catholic Church is opposed to persecution*, are almost always made with intent to deceive. Other words used in variable meanings, in most cases more or less dishonestly, are: *class, totalitarian, science, progressive, reactionary, bourgeois, equality*.

Now that I have made this catalogue of swindles and perversions, let me give another example of the kind of writing that they lead to. This time it must of its nature be an imaginary one. I am going to translate a passage of good English into modern English of the worst sort. Here is a well-known verse from *Ecclesiastes:*

"I returned and saw under the sun, that the race is not to the swift, nor the battle to the strong, neither yet bread to the wise, nor yet riches to men of understanding, nor yet favour to men of skill; but time and chance happeneth to them all."

Here it is in modern English:

"Objective consideration of contemporary phenomena compels the conclusion that success or failure in competitive activities exhibits no tendency to be commensurate with innate capacity, but that a considerable element of the unpredictable must invariably be taken into account."

This is a parody, but not a very gross one. Exhibit (3), above, for instance, contains several patches of the same kind of English. It will be seen that I have not made a full translation. The beginning and ending of the sentence follow the original meaning fairly closely, but in the middle the concrete illustrations—race, battle, bread—dissolve into the vague phrase "success or failure in competitive activities." This had to be so, because no modern writer of the kind I am discussing—no one capable of using phrases like "objective consideration of contemporary phenomena"—would ever tabulate his thoughts in that precise and detailed way. The whole tendency of modern prose is away from concreteness.

Now analyse these two sentences a little more closely. The first contains forty-nine words but only sixty syllables, and all its words are those of everyday life. The second contains thirty-eight words of ninety syllables: eighteen of its words are from Latin roots, and one from Greek. The first sentence contains six vivid images, and only one phrase ("time and chance") that could be called vague. The second contains not a single fresh, arresting phrase, and in spite of its ninety syllables it gives only a shortened version of the meaning contained in the first. Yet without a doubt it is the second kind of sentence that is gaining ground in modern English. I do not want to exaggerate. This kind of writing is not yet universal, and outcrops of simplicity will occur here and there in the worst-written page. Still, if you or I were told to write a few lines on the uncertainty of human fortunes, we should probably come much nearer to my imaginary sentence than to the one from *Ecclesiastes.*

As I have tried to show, modern writing at its worst does not consist in picking out words for the sake of their meaning and inventing images in order to make the meaning clearer. It consists in gumming together long strips of words which have already been set in order by someone else, and making the results presentable by sheer humbug. The attraction of this way of writing is that it is easy. It is easier—even quicker, once you have the habit—to say *In my opinion it is not an unjustifiable assumption that* than to say *I think.* . . . A speaker who uses that kind of phraseology has gone some distance towards turning himself into a machine. The appropriate noises are coming out of his larynx, but his brain is not involved as it would be if he were choosing his words for himself. If the speech he is making is one that he is accustomed to make over and over again, he may be almost unconscious of what he is saying, as one is when one utters the responses in church. And this reduced state of consciousness, if not indispensable, is at any rate favorable to political conformity.

In our time, political speech and writing are largely the defence of the indefensible. Things like the continuance of British rule in India, the Russian purges and deportations, the dropping of the atom bombs on Japan, can indeed be defended, but only by arguments which are too brutal for most people to face, and which do not square with the professed aims of political parties. Thus political language has to consist largely of euphemism, question-begging and sheer cloudy vagueness. Defenceless villages are bombarded from the air, the inhabitants driven out into the countryside, the cattle machine-gunned, the huts set on fire with incendiary bullets: this is called *pacification.* Millions of peasants are robbed of their farms and sent trudging along the roads with no more than they can carry: this is called *transfer of population* or *rectification of frontiers.* People are imprisoned for years without trial, or shot in the back of the neck or sent to die of scurvy in Arctic lumber camps: this is called *elimination of unreliable elements.* Such phraseology is needed if one wants to name things without calling up mental pictures of them. Consider for instance some comfortable English professor defending Russian totalitarianism. He cannot say outright, "I believe in killing off your opponents when you can get good results by doing so." Probably, therefore, he will say something like this:

"While freely conceding that the Soviet régime exhibits certain features which the humanitarian may be inclined to deplore, we must, I think, agree that a certain curtailment of the right to political opposition is an unavoidable concomitant of transitional periods, and that the rigors which the Russian people have been called upon to undergo have been amply justified in the sphere of concrete achievement."

The inflated style is itself a kind of euphemism. A mass of Latin words falls upon the facts like soft snow, blurring the outlines and covering up all the details. The great enemy of clear language is insincerity. When there is a gap between one's real and one's declared aims, one turns as it were instinctively to long words and exhausted idioms, like a cuttlefish squirting out ink. In our age there is no such thing as "keeping out of politics." All issues are political issues, and politics itself is a mass of lies, evasions, folly, hatred and schizophrenia. When the general atmosphere is bad, language must suffer. I should expect to find—this is a guess which I have not sufficient knowledge to verify—that the German, Russian and Italian languages have all deteriorated in the last ten or fifteen years, as a result of dictatorship.

But if thought corrupts language, language can

also corrupt thought. A bad usage can spread by tradition and imitation, even among people who should and do know better. The debased language that I have been discussing is in some ways very convenient. Phrases like *a not unjustifiable assumption, leaves much to be desired, would serve no good purpose, a consideration which we should do well to bear in mind,* are a continuous temptation, a packet of aspirins always at one's elbow. Look back through this essay, and for certain you will find that I have again and again committed the very faults I am protesting against. By this morning's post I have received a pamphlet dealing with conditions in Germany. The author tells me that he "felt impelled" to write it. I open it at random, and here is almost the first sentence that I see: "[The Allies] have an opportunity not only of achieving a radical transformation of Germany's social and political structure in such a way as to avoid a nationalistic reaction in Germany itself, but at the same time of laying the foundations of a cooperative and unified Europe." You see, he "feels impelled" to write—feels, presumably, that he has something new to say—and yet his words, like cavalry horses answering the bugle, group themselves automatically into the familiar dreary pattern. This invasion of one's mind by ready-made phrases (*lay the foundations, achieve a radical transformation*) can only be prevented if one is constantly on guard against them, and every such phrase anaesthetize's a portion of one's brain.

I said earlier that the decadence of our language is probably curable. Those who deny this would argue, if they produced an argument at all, that language merely reflects existing social conditions, and that we cannot influence its development by any direct tinkering with words and constructions. So far as the general tone or spirit of a language goes, this may be true, but it is not true in detail. Silly words and expressions have often disappeared, not through any evolutionary process but owing to the conscious action of a minority. Two recent examples were *explore every avenue* and *leave no stone unturned,* which were killed by the jeers of a few journalists. There is a long list of flyblown metaphors which could similarly be got rid of if enough people would interest themselves in the job; and it should also be possible to laugh the *not un-* formation out of existence,[1] to reduce the amount of Latin and Greek in the average sentence, to drive out foreign phrases and strayed scientific words, and, in general, to make pretentiousness unfashionable. But all these are minor points. The defence of the English language implies more than this, and perhaps it is best to start by saying what it does *not* imply.

To begin with it has nothing to do with archaism, with the salvaging of obsolete words and turns of speech, or with the setting up of a "standard English" which must never be departed from. On the contrary, it is especially concerned with the scrapping of every word or idiom which has outworn its usefulness. It has nothing to do with correct grammar and syntax, which are of no importance so long as one makes one's meaning clear, or with the avoidance of Americanisms, or with having what is called a "good prose style." On the other hand it is not concerned with fake simplicity and the attempt to make written English colloquial. Nor does it even imply in every case preferring the Saxon word to the Latin one, though it does imply using the fewest and shortest words that will cover one's meaning. What is above all needed is to let the meaning choose the word, and not the other way about. In prose, the worst thing one can do with words is to surrender to them. When you think of a concrete object, you think wordlessly, and then, if you want to describe the thing you have been visualizing you probably hunt about till you find the exact words that seem to fit it. When you think of something abstract you are more inclined to use words from the start, and unless you make a conscious effort to prevent it, the existing dialect will come rushing in and do the job for you, at the expense of blurring or even changing your meaning. Probably it is better to put off using words as long as possible and get one's meaning as clear as one can through pictures or sensations. Afterwards one can choose—not simply *accept*—the phrases that will best cover the meaning, and then switch round and decide what impression one's words are likely to make on another person. This last effort of the mind cuts out all stale or mixed images, all prefabricated phrases, needless

[1] One can cure oneself of the *not un-* formation by memorizing this sentence: *A not unblack dog was chasing a not unsmall rabbit across a not ungreen field.*

repetitions, and humbug and vagueness generally. But one can often be in doubt about the effect of a word or a phrase, and one needs rules that one can rely on when instinct fails. I think the following rules will cover most cases:

(i) Never use a metaphor, simile or other figure of speech which you are used to seeing in print.

(ii) Never use a long word where a short one will do.

(iii) If it is possible to cut a word out, always cut it out.

(iv) Never use the passive where you can use the active.

(v) Never use a foreign phrase, a scientific word or a jargon word if you can think of an everyday English equivalent.

(vi) Break any of these rules sooner than say anything outright barbarous.

These rules sound elementary, and so they are, but they demand a deep change of attitude in anyone who has grown used to writing in the style now fashionable. One could keep all of them and still write bad English, but one could not write the kind of stuff that I quoted in those five specimens at the beginning of this article.

I have not here been considering the literary use of language, but merely language as an instrument for expressing and not for concealing or preventing thought. Stuart Chase and others have come near to claiming that all abstract words are meaningless, and have used this as a pretext for advocating a kind of political quietism. Since you don't know what Fascism is, how can you struggle against Fascism? One need not swallow such absurdities as this, but one ought to recognize that the present political chaos is connected with the decay of language, and that one can probably bring about some improvement by starting at the verbal end. If you simplify your English, you are freed from the worst follies of orthodoxy. You cannot speak any of the necessary dialects, and when you make a stupid remark its stupidity will be obvious, even to yourself. Political language—and with variations this is true of all political parties, from Conservatives to Anarchists—is designed to make lies sound truthful and murder respectable, and to give an appearance of solidity to pure wind. One cannot change this all in a moment, but one can at least change one's own habits, and from time to time one can even, if one jeers loudly enough, send some worn-out and useless phrase—some *jackboot, Achilles' heel, hotbed, melting pot, acid test, veritable inferno* or other lump of verbal refuse—into the dustbin where it belongs.

W. H. AUDEN:

The Public *v.* the Late Mr. William Butler Yeats*

THE PUBLIC PROSECUTOR:

Gentlemen of the jury. Let us be quite clear in our minds as to the nature of this case. We are here to judge, not a man, but his work. Upon the character of the deceased, therefore, his affectations of dress and manner, his inordinate personal vanity, traits which caused a fellow countryman and former friend to refer to him as the greatest literary fop in history, I do not intend to dwell. I must only remind you that there is usually a close connection between the personal character of a poet and his work, and that the deceased was no exception.

Again I must draw your attention to the exact nature of the charge. That the deceased had talent is not for a moment in dispute; so much is freely admitted by the prosecution. What the defense are asking you to believe,

* "The Public *v.* the Late Mr. William Butler Yeats" first appeared in *Partisan Review*, Spring 1939, and was later included in *The Partisan Reader* (1946). It is reprinted here by permission of the editors of *Partisan Review*, copyright, 1939, and the author. Mr. Auden (*b.* 1907) has written many essays and reviews which remain uncollected.

however, is that he was a great poet, the greatest of this century writing in English. That is their case, and it is that which the prosecution feels bound most emphatically to deny.

A great poet. To deserve such an epithet, a poet is commonly required to convince us of these things: firstly a gift of a very high order for memorable language, secondly a profound understanding of the age in which he lived, and thirdly a working knowledge of and sympathetic attitude toward the most progressive thought of his time.

Did the deceased possess these? I am afraid, gentlemen, that the answer is, no.

On the first point I shall be brief. My learned friend, the counsel for the defense, will, I have no doubt, do his best to convince you that I am wrong. And he has a case, gentlemen. O yes, a very fine case. I shall only ask you to apply to the work of the deceased a very simple test. How many of his lines can you remember?

Further, it is not unreasonable to suppose that a poet who has a gift for language will recognize that gift in others. I have here a copy of an Anthology edited by the deceased entitled *The Oxford Book of Modern Verse.* I challenge anyone in this court to deny that it is the most deplorable volume ever issued under the imprint of that highly respected firm which has done so much for the cause of poetry in this country, The Clarendon Press.

But in any case you and I are educated modern men. Our fathers imagined that poetry existed in some private garden of its own, totally unrelated to the workaday world, and to be judged by pure aesthetic standards alone. We know that now to be an illusion. Let me pass, then, to my second point. Did the deceased understand his age?

What did he admire? What did he condemn? Well, he extolled the virtues of the peasant. Excellent. But should that peasant learn to read and write, should he save enough money to buy a shop, attempt by honest trading to raise himself above the level of the beasts, and O, what a sorry change is there. Now he is the enemy, the hateful huxter whose blood, according to the unseemly boast of the deceased, never flowed through *his* loins. Had the poet chosen to live in a mud cabin in Galway among swine and superstition, we might think him mistaken, but we should admire his integrity. But did he do this? O dear no. For there was another world which seemed to him not only equally admirable, but a deal more agreeable to live in, the world of noble houses, of large drawing rooms inhabited by the rich and the decorative, most of them of the female sex. We do not have to think very hard or very long, before we shall see a connection between these facts. The deceased had the feudal mentality. He was prepared to admire the poor just as long as they remained poor and deferential, accepting without protest the burden of maintaining a little Athenian band of literary landowners, who without their toil could not have existed for five minutes.

For the great struggle of our time to create a juster social order, he felt nothing but the hatred which is born of fear. It is true that he played a certain part in the movement for Irish Independence, but I hardly think my learned friend will draw your attention to that. Of all the modes of self-evasion open to the well-to-do, nationalism is the easiest and most dishonest. It allows to the unjust all the luxury of righteous indignation against injustice. Still, it has often inspired men and women to acts of heroism and self-sacrifice. For the sake of a free Ireland the poet Pearse and the countess Markovitz gave their all. But if the deceased did give himself to this movement, he did so with singular moderation. After the rebellion of Easter Sunday, 1916, he wrote a poem on the subject which has been called a masterpiece. It is. To succeed at such a time in writing a poem which could offend neither the Irish Republicans nor the British Army was indeed a masterly achievement.

And so we come to our third and last point. The most superficial glance at the last fifty years is enough to tell us that the social struggle toward a greater equality has been accompanied by a growing intellectual acceptance of the scientific method and the steady conquest of irrational superstition. What was the attitude of the deceased toward this? Gentlemen, words fail me. What are we to say of a man whose earliest writings attempted to revive a belief in fairies and whose favorite themes were legends of barbaric heroes with unpronounceable names, work which has been aptly and wittily described as Chaff about Bran!

But you may say, he was young: youth is always romantic; its silliness is part of its charm. Perhaps it is. Let us forgive the youth, then, and consider the mature man, from whom we have a right to expect wisdom and common sense. Gentlemen, it is hard to be charitable when we find that the deceased, far from outgrowing his folly, has plunged even deeper. In 1900 he believed in fairies; that was bad enough; but in 1930 we are confronted with the pitiful, the deplorable spectacle of a grown man occupied with the mumbo-jumbo of magic and the nonsense of India. Whether he seriously believed such stuff to be true, or merely thought it pretty, or imagined it would impress the public, is immaterial. The plain fact remains that he made it the center of his work. Gentlemen, I need say no more. In the last poem he wrote, the deceased rejected social justice and reason, and prayed for war. Am I mistaken in imagining that somewhat similar sentiments are expressed by a certain foreign political movement which every lover of literature and liberty acknowledges to be the enemy of mankind?

THE COUNSEL FOR THE DEFENSE:

Gentlemen of the Jury. I am sure you have listened with as much enjoyment as I to the eloquence of the prosecution. I say enjoyment because the spectacle of anything well done, whether it be a feat of engineering, a poem, or even an outburst of impassioned oratory, must always give pleasure.

We have been treated to an analysis of the character of the deceased which for all I know, may be as true as it is destructive. Whether it proves anything about the value of his poetry is another matter. If I may be allowed to quote my learned friend, "We are here to judge, not a man but his work." We have been told that the deceased was conceited, that he was a snob, that he was a physical coward, that his taste in contemporary poetry was uncertain, that he could not understand physics and chemistry. If this is not an invitation to judge the man I do not know what is. Does it not bear an extraordinary resemblance to the belief of an earlier age that a great artist must be chaste? Take away the frills, and the argument of the prosecution is reduced to this: "A great poet must give the right answers to the problems which perplex his generation. The deceased gave the wrong answers. Therefore the deceased was not a great poet." Poetry in such a view is the filling up of a social quiz; to pass with honors the poet must score not less than 75 per cent. With all due respect to my learned friend, this is nonsense. We are tempted so to judge contemporary poets because we really do have problems which we really do want solved, so that we are inclined to expect everyone, politicians, scientists, poets, clergymen, to give us the answer, and to blame them indiscriminately when they do not. But who reads the poetry of the past in this way? In an age of rising nationalism, Dante looked back with envy to the Roman Empire. Was this socially progressive? Will only a Catholic admit that Dryden's "The Hind and the Panther" is a good poem? Do we condemn Blake because he rejected Newton's theory of light, or rank Wordsworth lower than Baker, because the latter had a deeper appreciation of the steam engine?

Can such a view explain why

Mock Emmet, Mock Parnell
All the renown that fell

is good; and bad, such a line as

Somehow I think that you are rather like a tree

In pointing out that this is absurd, I am not trying to suggest that art exists independently of society. The relation between the two is just as intimate and important as the prosecution asserts.

Every individual is from time to time excited emotionally and intellectually by his social and material environment. In certain individuals this excitement produces verbal structures which we call poems; if such a verbal structure creates an excitement in the reader, we call it a good poem. Poetic talent, in fact, is the power to make personal excitement socially available. Poets, i.e. persons with poetic talent, stop writing good poetry when they stop reacting to the world they live in. The nature of that reaction, whether it be positive or negative, morally admirable or morally disgraceful, matters very little, what is essential is that the reaction should genuinely exist. The later Wordsworth is not inferior to the earlier because the poet had altered his political opinions, but because he had ceased to feel and think so strongly, a change which happens, alas, to most of us as we grow older. Now, when we turn to the deceased, we are confronted by the amazing spectacle of a man of great poetic talent, whose capacity for excitement not only remained with him to the end, but actually increased. In two hundred years when our children have made a different and, I hope, better social order, and when our science has developed out of all recognition, who but a historian will care a button whether the deceased was right about the Irish Question or wrong about the transmigration of souls? But because the excitement out of which his poems arose was genuine, they will still, unless I am very much mistaken, be capable of exciting others, different though their circumstances and beliefs may be from his.

However, since we are not living two hundred years hence, let us play the schoolteacher a moment, and examine the poetry of the deceased with reference to the history of our time.

The most obvious social fact of the last forty years is the failure of liberal capitalist democracy, based on the premises that every individual is born free and equal, each an absolute entity independent of all others. And that a formal political equality, the right to vote, the right to a fair trial, the right of free speech, is enough to guarantee his freedom of action in his relations with his fellow men. The results are only too familiar to us all. By denying the social nature of personality, and by ignoring the social power of money, it has created the most impersonal, the most mechanical, and the most unequal civilization the world has ever seen, a civilization in which the only emotion common to all classes is a feeling of individual isolation from everyone else, a civilization torn apart by the opposing emotions born of economic injustice, the just envy of the poor and the selfish terror of the rich.

If these latter emotions meant little to the deceased, it was partly because Ireland compared with the rest of western Europe was economically backward, and the class struggle was less conscious there. My learned friend has sneered at Irish nationalism, but he knows as well as I that nationalism is a necessary stage towards socialism. He has sneered at the deceased for not taking arms, as if shooting were the only honorable and useful form of social action. Has the Abbey Theater done nothing for Ireland?

But to return to the poems. From first to last they express a sustained protest against the social atomization caused by industrialism, and both in their ideas and their language a constant struggle to overcome it. The fairies and heroes of the early work were an attempt to find through folk tradition a binding force for society; and the doctrine of Anima Mundi found in the later poems is the same thing, in a more developed form, which has left purely local peculiarities behind, in favor of something that the deceased hoped was universal; in other words, he was working for a world religion. A purely religious solution may be unworkable, but the search for it is, at least, the result of a true perception of a social evil. Again, the virtues that the deceased praised in the peasantry and aristocracy, and the vices he blamed in the commercial classes were real virtues and vices. To create a united and just society where the former are fostered and the latter cured is the task of the politician, not the poet.

For art is a product of history, not a cause. Unlike some other products, technical inventions for example, it does not re-enter history as an effective agent, so that the question whether art should or should not be propaganda is unreal. The case for the prosecution rests on the fallacious belief that art ever makes anything happen, whereas the honest truth, gentlemen, is that, if not a poem had been written, not a picture painted, not a bar of music composed, the history of man would be materially unchanged.

But there is one field in which the poet is a man of action, the field of language, and it is precisely in this that the greatness of the deceased is most obviously shown. However false or undemocratic his ideas, his diction shows a continuous evolution toward what one might call the true democratic style. The social virtues of a real democracy are brotherhood and intelligence, and the parallel linguistic virtues are strength and clarity, virtues which appear even more clearly through successive volumes by the deceased.

The diction of *The Winding Stair* is the diction of a just man, and it is for this reason that just men will always recognize the author as a master.

LIONEL TRILLING: Freud and Literature*

THE FREUDIAN psychology is the only systematic account of the human mind which, in point of subtlety and complexity, of interest and tragic power, deserves to stand beside the chaotic mass of psychological insights which literature has accumulated through the centuries. To pass from the reading of a great literary work to a treatise of academic psychology is to pass from one order of perception to another, but the human nature of the Freudian psychology is exactly the stuff upon which the poet has always exercised his art. It is therefore not surprising that the psychoanalytical theory has had a great effect upon literature. Yet the relationship is reciprocal and the effect of Freud upon literature has been no greater than the effect of literature upon Freud. When, on the occasion of the celebration of his seventieth birthday, Freud was greeted as the "discoverer of the unconscious," he corrected the speaker and disclaimed the title. "The poets and philosophers before me discovered the unconscious; what I discovered was the scientific method by which the unconscious can be studied."

A lack of specific evidence prevents us from considering the particular literary "influences" upon the founder of psychoanalysis; and besides, when we think of the men who so clearly anticipated many of Freud's own ideas—Schopenhauer and Nietzsche, for example—and then learn that he did not read their works until after he had formulated his own theories, we must see that particular influences cannot be in question here but that what we must deal with is nothing less than a whole *Zeitgeist*, a direction of thought. For psychoanalysis is one of the culminations of the Romanticist literature of the nineteenth century. If there is perhaps a contradiction in the idea of a science standing upon the shoulders of a literature which avows itself inimical to science in so many ways, the contradiction will be resolved if we remember that this literature was, despite its avowals, itself scientific, for it was passionately devoted to a research into the self.

In showing the connection between Freud and this Romanticist tradition, it is difficult to know where to begin, but there might be a certain aptness in starting even back of the tradition, as far back as 1762 with that dialogue of Diderot's called "Rameau's Nephew." At any rate, certain men at the heart of nineteenth century thought were agreed in finding a peculiar importance in this brilliant little work: Goethe translated it, Marx admired it, Hegel—as Marx reminded Engels in the letter which announced that he was sending the book as a gift—praised and expounded it at length, Shaw was impressed by it and Freud himself, as we know from a quotation in his *Introductory Lectures,* read it with the pleasure of agreement.

The dialogue takes place between Diderot himself and a nephew of the famous composer. The protagonist, the younger Rameau, is a despised, outcast, shameless fellow; Hegel calls him the "disintegrated consciousness" and credits him with great wit, for it is he who breaks down all the normal social values and makes

* "Freud and Literature" first appeared in *The Kenyon Review,* Spring 1941, and, somewhat revised for the present collection, is reprinted here by permission of the editor and Mr. Trilling. Mr. Trilling (*b.* 1905) is the author of *Matthew Arnold* (1939) and *E. M. Forster* (1943).

new combinations with the pieces. As for Diderot, the deuteragonist, he is what Hegel calls the "honest consciousness" and Hegel considers him reasonable, decent and dull. It is quite clear that the author does not despise his Rameau and does not mean us to; Rameau is lustful and greedy, arrogant yet self-abasing, perceptive yet "wrong," like a child—still, Diderot seems actually to be giving the fellow a kind of superiority over himself, as though Rameau represents the elements which, dangerous but wholly necessary, lie beneath the reasonable decorum of social life. It would perhaps be pressing too far to find in Rameau Freud's *id* and in Diderot Freud's *ego;* yet the connection does suggest itself; and at least we have here the perception which is to be the common characteristic of both Freud and Romanticism, the perception of the hidden element of human nature and of the opposition between the hidden and the visible.

From the self-exposure of Rameau to Rousseau's account of his own childhood is no great step; society might ignore or reject the idea of the "immorality" which lies concealed in the beginning of the career of the "good" man, just as it might turn away from Blake struggling to expound a psychology which would include the forces beneath the propriety of social man in general, but the idea of the hidden thing went forward to become one of the dominant notions of the age. The hidden element takes many forms and it is not always "dark" and "bad"; for Blake, Wordsworth and Coleridge what was hidden and unconscious was wisdom and power, working even in despite of the conscious intellect, and for Matthew Arnold the mind was fed by streams buried deeper than we can know.

The mind has become far less simple; the devotion to the various forms of autobiography —itself an important fact in the tradition—provides abundant examples of the change that has taken place. Poets, making poetry by what seems to them almost a freshly discovered faculty, find that this new power may be conspired against by other agencies of the mind and even deprived of its freedom; the names of Wordsworth, Coleridge and Arnold at once occur to us again and Freud quotes Schiller on the danger to the poet which lies in the merely analytical reason. And it is not only the poets who are threatened; educated and sensitive people throughout Europe become aware of the depredations the reason might make upon the affective life, as in the classic instance of John Stuart Mill.

We must also take into account the preoccupation—it began in the eighteenth century, even in the seventeenth—with children, women, peasants and savages, because their mental life, it is felt, is less overlaid than that of the educated adult male by the proprieties of social habit. With this preoccupation goes a concern with education and personal development, so consonant with the historical and evolutionary bias of the time. And we must certainly note the revolution in morals which took place at the instance (we might almost say) of the *Bildungsroman,* for in the novels fathered by *Wilhelm Meister* we get the almost complete identification of author and hero and of reader with both, and this identification suggests a leniency of moral judgment. The autobiographical novel has a further influence upon the moral sensibility by its exploitation of all the modulations of motive and by its hinting that we may not judge a man by any single moment in his life without taking into account the determining past and the expiating and fulfilling future.

It is difficult to know how to go on, for the further we look the more literary affinities to Freud we find, and even if we limit ourselves to bibliography we can at best be incomplete. Yet we must mention the sexual revolution that was being demanded—by Shelley, for example, by the Schlegel of *Lucinde,* by George Sand, and later and more critically by Ibsen; the belief in the sexual origin of art, baldly stated by Tieck, more subtly by Schopenhauer; the investigation of sexual maladjustment by Stendhal, the quality of whose observations on erotic feeling are in the direct line of Freud. Again and again we see the effective, utilitarian ego being relegated to an inferior position and the plea being made on behalf of the anarchic and self-indulgent id. We find the energetic exploitation of the idea of the mind as a divisible thing, one part of which can contemplate and mock the other. It is no far remove from this to Dostoievsky's brilliant instances of ambivalent feeling. Novalis brings in the preoccupation with the death-wish, and this is linked on the one hand with sleep and, on the other hand, with the perception of the perverse, self-destroying impulses, which in turn leads us to that fascination by the horrible which we find in Shelley. Poe and Baudelaire. And always there is the profound interest in the dream—"Our dreams," said Gerard de Nerval, "are a second life"—and in the nature of metaphor, which reaches its climax in Rimbaud and the later Symbolists, of metaphor becoming less and less communicative as it approaches the relative autonomy of the dream life.

But perhaps we must stop to ask whether, since these are the components of the *Zeitgeist* from which Freud himself developed, it can be said that Freud did indeed produce a wide literary effect? What is it that Freud added that the tendency of literature itself would not have developed without him? If we were looking for a writer who showed the Freudian influence, Proust would perhaps come to mind as readily as anyone else; the very title of his novel—in French more than in English—suggests an enterprise of psychoanalysis and scarcely less so does his method—the investigation of sleep, of sexual deviation, of the ways of association, the almost obsessive interest in metaphor: at these and at many other points the "influence" might be shown. Yet I believe it is true that Proust did not read Freud. Or again, exegesis of *The Waste Land* reads remarkably like the interpretation of a dream, yet we know that Eliot's methods were prepared for him not by Freud but by other poets.

Nevertheless, it is of course true that Freud's influence on literature has been very great. Much of it is so pervasive that its extent is scarcely to be determined; in one form or another, frequently in perversions or absurd simplifications, it has been infused into our life and become a component of our culture of which it is now hard to be specifically aware. In biography its effect was sensational but not fortunate. The Freudian biographers were for the most part Guildensterns who seemed to know the pipes but could not pluck out the heart of the mystery. In criticism the situation has been sad, for reasons which I shall try to suggest later in this essay.

The names of the creative writers who have been more or less Freudian in tone or assumption would, of course, be legion. Only a relatively small number, however, have made serious use of the Freudian ideas. Freud himself seems to have thought this was as it should be: he is said to have expected very little of the works that were sent to him by writers with inscriptions of gratitude for all they had learned from him. The Surrealists have, with a certain inconsistency, depended upon Freud for the scientific sanction of their program. Kafka, with an apparent awareness of what he was doing, has explored the Freudian conceptions of guilt and punishment, of the dream and of the fear of the father. Thomas Mann, whose tendency, as he himself says, was always in the direction of Freud's interests, has been most susceptible to the Freudian anthropology, finding a special charm in the theories of myths and magical practices. James Joyce, with his interest in the numerous states of receding consciousness, with his use of words as things and of words which point to more than one thing, with his pervading sense of the interrelation and interpenetration of all things, and, not least important, his treatment of familial themes, has perhaps most thoroughly and consciously exploited Freud's ideas.

2

Yet although it will be clear enough how much of Freud's thought has significant affinity with the Romanticist tradition, we must see with no less distinctness how much of his system is militantly rationalistic. Thomas Mann is at fault when, in his first essay on Freud, he makes it seem that the "Apollonian," the rationalistic, side of psychoanalysis is, while certainly important and wholly admirable, somehow secondary and even accidental. He gives us a Freud who is committed to the "night side" of life. Not at all: the rationalistic element of Freud is foremost; before everything else he is positivistic. If the interpreter of dreams came to medical science through Goethe, as he tells us he did, he entered not by way of the Walpurgisnacht but by the essay which played so important a part in the lives of so many scientists of the nineteenth century, the famous disquisition on Nature.

This correction is needed not only for accuracy but also for any understanding of Freud's attitude to art. And for that understanding we must see how intense is the passion with which

Freud believes that positivistic rationalism, in its golden-age, pre-Revolutionary purity, is the very form and pattern of intellectual virtue. The aim of psychoanalysis, he says, is the control of the night-side of life. It is "to strengthen the ego, to make it more independent of the super-ego, to widen its field of vision and so to extend the organization of the id. Where id was,"—that is, where all the irrational, non-logical, pleasure-seeking dark forces were—"there shall ego be," —that is, intelligence and control. "It is," he concludes, with a reminiscence of Faust, "reclamation work, like the draining of the Zuyder Zee." This passage is quoted by Mann when, in taking up the subject of Freud a second time, he does indeed speak of Freud's positivistic program; but even here the bias induced by Mann's artistic interest in the "night side" prevents him from giving this aspect of Freud its proper emphasis. Freud would never have accepted the role which Mann seems to give him as the legitimizer of the myth and the dark irrational ways of the mind. If Freud discovered the darkness for science he never endorsed it. On the contrary, his rationalism supports all the ideas of Enlightenment that deny validity to myth or religion; he holds to a simple materialism, to a simple determinism, to a rather limited sort of epistemology. No great scientist of our day has thundered so articulately and so fiercely against all those who would sophisticate with metaphysics the scientific principles that were good enough for the nineteenth century. Conceptualism or pragmatism are anathema to him, and this, when we consider the nature of his own brilliant scientific methods, has surely an element of paradox in it.

From his rationalistic positivism comes much of Freud's strength and all of his weakness. The strength is the fine, clear tenacity of his positive aims, the goal of therapy, the desire to bring to men a decent measure of earthly happiness. But upon the rationalism must also be placed the blame for his rather naive scientific principles which consist largely of claiming for his theories a perfect correspondence with an external reality, a position which, for those who admire Freud, and especially for those who take seriously his views on art, is troublesome in the extreme.

Now Freud has, I believe, much to tell us about art, but whatever is suggestive in him is not to be found in those of his works in which he deals expressly with art itself. Freud is neither insensitive to art—on the contrary—nor does he ever intend to speak of it with contempt. Indeed, he speaks of it with a real tenderness and counts it one of the true charms of the good life. Of artists, especially of writers, he speaks with admiration and even a kind of awe, though perhaps what he most appreciates in literature are specific emotional insights and observations; he often speaks of literary men, because they have understood the part played in life by the hidden motives, as the precursors and coadjutors of his own science.

And yet eventually Freud speaks of art with what we must indeed call contempt. Art, he tells us, is a "substitute gratification" and as such is "an illusion in contrast to reality." Unlike most illusions, however, art is "almost always harmless and beneficent" for the reason that "it does not seek to be anything but an illusion. Save in the case of a few people who are, one might say, obsessed by Art, it never dares make any attack on the realm of reality." One of its chief functions is to serve as a "narcotic." It shares the characteristics of the dream, whose element of distortion Freud calls a "sort of inner dishonesty." As for the artist he is virtually in the same category with the neurotic. "By such separation of imagination and intellectual capacity," Freud says of the hero of a novel, "he is destined to be a poet or a neurotic, and he belongs to that race of beings whose realm is not of this world."

Now there is nothing in the logic of psychoanalytical thought which requires Freud to have these opinions. But there is a great deal in the practice of the psychoanalytical therapy which makes it understandable that Freud, unprotected by an adequate philosophy, should be tempted to take the line he does. The analytical therapy deals with illusion. The patient comes to the physician to be cured, let us say, of a fear of walking in the street. The fear is real enough, there is no illusion on that score, and it produces all the physical symptoms of a more rational fear, the sweating palms, pounding heart and shortened breath. But the patient knows that there is no cause for the fear—or, rather, that there is, as he says, no "real cause": there are no machine-guns, man-traps or tigers in the street. The physician knows, however, that there is indeed a "real" cause for the fear, though it has nothing at all to do with what is or is not in the street; the cause is within the patient and the process of the therapy will be to discover, by gradual steps, what this real cause is and so free the patient from its effects.

Now the patient, in coming to the physician, and the physician in accepting the patient, make a tacit compact about reality; for their purpose they agree to the limited reality by which we get our living, win our loves, catch our trains and our colds. The therapy will undertake to train the patient in proper ways of coping with this reality. The patient, of course, has been dealing with this reality all along, but in the wrong way. For Freud there are two ways of dealing with external reality. One is practical, effective, positive; this is the way of the conscious self, of the ego which must be made independent of the super-ego and extend its organization over the id, and it is the right way. The antithetical way may be called, for our purpose now, the "fictional" way. Instead of doing something about, or to, external reality, the individual who uses this way does something to, or about, his affective states. The most common and "normal" example of this is day-dreaming in which we give ourselves a certain pleasure by imagining our difficulties solved or our desires gratified. Then too, as Freud discovered, sleeping dreams are, in much more complicated ways and even though quite unpleasant, at the service of this same "fictional" activity. And in ways yet more complicated and yet more unpleasant, the actual neurosis—from which our patient suffers—deals with an external reality which the mind considers still more unpleasant than the painful neurosis itself.

For Freud as psychoanalytic practitioner there are, we may say, the polar extremes of reality and illusion. Reality is an honorific word and it means what is *there;* illusion is a pejorative word and it means a response to what is *not there.* The didactic nature of a course of psychoanalysis no doubt requires a certain firm crudeness in making the distinction; it is, after all, aimed not at theoretical refinement but at practical effectiveness. The polar extremes are practical reality and neurotic illusion, the latter judged by the former. This, no doubt, is as it should be; the patient is not being trained in metaphysics and epistemology.

We may say, however, that Freud has two views of the mind. One view assumes that the mind, for good as well as bad, helps create its reality by selection and evaluation. In this view, which is the typically Freudian one, reality is malleable and subject to creation; it is not static but is, rather, a series of situations which are dealt with in their own terms. But beside this view of the mind stands the view which arises from Freud's therapeutic-practical assumptions; in this view, the mind deals with a reality which is quite fixed and static, a reality that is wholly "given" and not (to use a phrase of Dewey's) "taken." In his epistemological utterances, Freud insists on this second view, although it is not easy to see why he should do so. For the reality to which he wishes to reconcile the neurotic patient is, after all, a "taken" and not a "given" reality. It is the reality of social life and of value, conceived and maintained by the human mind and will. Love, morality, honor, esteem—these are the components of a created reality. If we are to call art an illusion then we must call most of the activities and satisfactions of the ego illusions; Freud, of course, has no desire to call them that.

What then is the difference between, on the one hand, the dream and the neurosis, and, on the other hand, art? That they have certain common elements is of course clear; that unconscious processes are at work in both would be denied by no poet or critic; they share too, though in different degrees, the element of fantasy. But there is a vital difference between them which Charles Lamb saw so clearly in his defense of the sanity of true genius: "The . . . poet dreams being awake. He is not possessed by his subject but has dominion over it."

That is the whole difference: for the poet is in command of his fantasy, while it is exactly the mark of the neurotic that he is possessed by his fantasy. And there is a further difference which Lamb states; speaking of the poet's relation to reality (he calls it Nature), he says, "He is beautifully loyal to that sovereign directress, even when he appears most to betray her": the illusions of art are made to serve the purpose of a closer and truer relation with reality.

Jacques Barzun, in an acute and sympathetic discussion of Freud, puts the matter well: "A good analogy between art and *dreaming* has led him to a false one between art and *sleeping*. But the difference between a work of art and a dream is precisely this, that the work of art *leads us back to the outer reality by taking account of it.*" Freud's assumption of the almost exclusively hedonistic nature and purpose of art bar him from the perception of this.

Of the distinction that must be made between the artist and the neurotic Freud is, of course, aware; he tells us that the artist is not like the neurotic in that he knows how to find a way back from the world of imagination and "once more get a firm foothold in reality." This, however, seems to mean no more than that reality is to be dealt with when the artist suspends the practice of his art; and at least once when Freud speaks of art dealing with reality, he actually means the rewards that a successful artist can win. He does not deny to art its function and its usefulness: it has a therapeutic effect in releasing mental tension; it serves the cultural purpose of acting as a "substitute gratification" to reconcile men to the sacrifices they have made for culture's sake; it promotes the social sharing of highly valued emotional experiences and it recalls men to their cultural ideals. This is not everything that some of us would find that art does, yet even this is a good deal for a "narcotic" to do.

3

I started by saying that Freud's ideas could tell us something about art but so far I have done little more than try to show that Freud's very conception of art is inadequate. Perhaps, then, the suggestiveness lies in the application of the analytic method to specific works of art, or to the artist himself? I do not think so; and it is only fair to say that Freud himself was aware both of the limits and the limitations of psychoanalysis in art, even though he does not always, in practice, submit to the former or admit the latter.

Freud has, for example, no desire to encroach upon the artistic autonomy; he does not wish us to read his monograph on Leonardo and then say of the Madonna of the Rocks that it is a fine example of homosexual, autoerotic painting. If he asserts that in investigation the "psychiatrist cannot yield to the author," he immediately insists that the "author cannot yield to the psychiatrist," and he warns the latter not to "coarsen everything" by using for all human manifestations the "substantially useless and awkward terms" of clinical procedure. He admits, even while asserting that the sense of beauty probably derives from sexual feeling, that psychoanalysis "has less to say about beauty than about most other things." He confesses to a theoretical indifference to the form of art and restricts himself to its content. Tone, feeling, style and the modification that part makes upon part he does not consider. "The layman," he says, "may expect perhaps too much from analysis . . . for it must be admitted that it throws no light upon the two problems which probably interest him the most. It can do nothing toward elucidating the nature of the artistic gift, nor can it explain the means by which the artist works—artistic technique."

What then does the analytical method claim to do? Two things: explain the "inner meanings" of the work of art and explain the temperament of the artist as man.

A famous example of the method is the attempt to solve the "problem" of *Hamlet* as suggested by Freud and as carried out by Dr. Ernest Jones, his early and distinguished follower. Dr. Jones's monograph is a work of painstaking scholarship and of really masterly ingenuity. The research undertakes not only the clearing up of the mystery of Hamlet's character but also the discovery of "the clue to much of the deeper workings of Shakespeare's mind." Part of the mystery in question is, of course, why Hamlet, after he had so definitely resolved to do so, did not avenge upon his hated uncle his father's death. But there is another mystery to the play—what Freud calls "the mystery of its effect," its magical appeal that draws so much interest toward it. Recalling the many failures to solve the riddle of the play's charm, he wonders if we are to be driven to the conclusion "that its magical appeal rests solely upon the impressive thoughts in it and the splendor of its language." Freud believes that we can find a source of power beyond this.

We remember that Freud has told us that the

meaning of a dream is its intention, and we may assume that the meaning of a drama is its intention too. The Jones research undertakes to discover what it was that Shakespeare intended to say about Hamlet. It finds that the intention was wrapped by the author in a dream-like obscurity because it touched so deeply both his personal life and the moral life of the world; what Shakespeare intended to say is that Hamlet cannot act because he is incapacitated by the guilt he feels at his unconscious attachment to his mother. There is, I think, nothing to be quarrelled with in the statement that there is an Oedipus situation in Hamlet; and if psychoanalysis has indeed added a new point of interest to the play, that is to its credit.[1] And just so there is no reason to quarrel with Freud's conclusion when he undertakes to give us the meaning of *King Lear* by a tortuous tracing of the mythological implications of the theme of the three caskets, of the relation of the caskets to the Norns, the Fates and the Graces, of the connection of these triadic females with Lear's daughters, of the transmogrification of the death-goddess into the love-goddess and the identification of Cordelia with both, all to the conclusion that the meaning of *King Lear* is to be found in the tragic refusal of an old man to "renounce love, choose death and make friends with the necessity of dying." There is something both beautiful and suggestive in this, but it is not *the* meaning of *King Lear* any more than the Oedipus motive is *the* meaning of *Hamlet.*

It is not here a question of the validity of the evidence, though that is of course important. We must, rather, object to the conclusions of Freud and Dr. Jones on the ground that its proponents do not have an adequate conception of what an artistic meaning is. There is no single meaning to any work of art; this is true not merely because it is better that it should be true —that is, because it makes art a richer thing—but because historical and personal experience show it to be true. Changes in historical context and in personal mood change the meaning of a work and indicate to us that artistic understanding is not a question of fact but of value. Even if the author's intention were—as it cannot be—precisely determinable, the meaning of a work cannot lie in the author's intention alone. It must also lie in its effect. We can say of a volcanic eruption on an inhabited island that it "means terrible suffering" but if the island is uninhabited or easily evacuated it means something else. In short, the audience partly determines the meaning of the work. But although Freud sees something of this when he says that in addition to the author's intention we must take into account the mystery of *Hamlet's* effect, he nevertheless goes on to speak as if historically *Hamlet's* effect had been single and brought about solely by the "magical" power of the Oedipus motive to which, unconsciously, we so violently respond. Yet there was, we know, a period when *Hamlet* was relatively in eclipse, and it has always been scandalously true of the French, a people not without filial feeling, that they have been somewhat indifferent to the "magical appeal" of *Hamlet.*

I do not think that anything I have said about the inadequacies of the Freudian method of interpretation limits the number of ways we can deal with a work of art. Bacon remarked that experiment may twist nature on the rack to wring out its secrets, and criticism may use any instruments upon a work of art to find its meanings. The elements of art are not limited by art. They reach into life and whatever extraneous knowledge of them we gain—for example, by research into the historical context of the work —may quicken our feelings for the work itself and even enter legitimately into those feelings. Then too, anything we may learn about the artist himself may be enriching and legitimate. But one research into the mind of the artist is simply not practicable, however legitimate it may theoretically be. That is the investigation of his unconscious intention as it exists apart from the work itself. Criticism understands that the artist's statement of his conscious intention, though it is sometimes useful, cannot finally

[1] However, A. C. Bradley in his discussion of Hamlet (*Shakespearean Tragedy*) states clearly the intense sexual disgust which Hamlet feels and which, for Bradley, helps account for his uncertain purpose; and Bradley was anticipated in this view by Löning. It is well known, and Dover Wilson has lately emphasized the point, that to an Elizabethan audience Hamlet's mother was not merely, as to a modern audience she seems, tasteless in hurrying to marry Claudius but actually adulterous in marrying him at all because he was, as her brother-in-law, within the forbidden degrees.

determine meaning. How much less can we know from his unconscious intention considered as something apart from the whole work. Very little that goes beyond interesting speculation; certainly very little that can be called conclusive or scientific. For, as Freud himself points out, we are not in a position to question the artist; we must apply the technique of dream analysis to his symbols, but as Freud says, with some heat, those people do not understand his theory who think that a dream may be interpreted without the dreamer's free-association with the multitudinous details of his dream.

We have so far ignored the aspect of the method which finds the solution to the "mystery" of such a play as *Hamlet* in the temperament of Shakespeare himself and then illuminates the mystery of Shakespeare's temperament by means of the solved mystery of the play. Here it will be amusing to remember that by 1935 Freud had become converted to the theory that it was not Shakespeare of Stratford but the Earl of Oxford who wrote the plays, thus invalidating the important bit of evidence that Shakespeare's father died shortly before the composition of Hamlet. This is destructive enough to Dr. Jones's argument but the evidence from which Dr. Jones draws conclusions about literature fails on grounds more relevant to literature itself. For when Dr. Jones, by means of his analysis of *Hamlet,* takes us into "the deeper workings of Shakespeare's mind," he does so with a perfect confidence that he knows what *Hamlet* is and what its relation to Shakespeare is. It is, he tells us, Shakespeare's "chief masterpiece," so far superior to all his other works that it may be placed on "an entirely separate level." And then, having established his ground on an entirely inacceptable literary judgment, Dr. Jones goes on to tell us that *Hamlet* "probably expresses the core of Shakespeare's philosophy and outlook as no other work of his does." That is, all the contradictory or complicating or modifying testimony of the other plays is dismissed on the basis of Dr. Jones's acceptance of the peculiar position which, he believes, *Hamlet* occupies in the Shakespeare canon. And it is upon this entirely inadmissable judgment that Dr. Jones bases his argument: "it may be expected *therefore,* that anything which will give us the key to the inner meaning of the play will *necessarily* give us the clue to much of the deeper workings of Shakespeare's mind."

I should be sorry if it appeared that I am trying to say that psychoanalysis can have nothing to do with literature. I am sure that the opposite is so. For example, the whole notion of rich ambiguity in literature, of the interplay between the apparent meaning and the latent—not "hidden"—meaning, has been reinforced by the Freudian concepts, perhaps even received its first impetus from them. Of late years, the more perceptive psychoanalysts have surrendered the early pretensions of their teachers to deal "scientifically" with literature and that is all to the good, and when a study as modest and precise as Dr. Alexander's essay on *Henry IV* comes along, an essay which pretends not to "solve" but only to illuminate the subject, we have something worth having. Dr. Alexander undertakes nothing more than to say that in the development of Prince Hal we see the classic struggle of the ego to come to normal adjustment, beginning with the rebellion against the father, going on to the conquest of the superego (Hotspur, with his rigid notions of honor and glory), then to the conquest of the id (Falstaff, with his anarchic self-indulgence), then to the identification with the father (the crown scene) and the assumption of mature responsibility. An analysis of this sort is not momentous and not exclusive of other meanings; perhaps it does no more than point up and formulate what we all have already seen. It has the tact to *accept* the play and does not, like Dr. Jones's study of *Hamlet,* search for a "hidden motive" and a "deeper working" and thus imply that there is a reality to which the play stands in the relation that a dream stands to the wish that generates it and from which it is separable; it is this reality, this "deeper working" which, according to Dr. Jones, produced the play. But *Hamlet* is not merely the product of Shakespeare's thought, it is the very instrument of his thought; and if meaning is intention, Shakespeare did not intend the Oedipus motive or anything less than *Hamlet;* if meaning is effect, then it is *Hamlet* which affects us, not the Oedipus motive: *Coriolanus* also deals, and very terribly, with the Oedipus motive but the effect of the one drama is very different from the effect of the other.

4

If, then, we can accept neither Freud's conception of the place of art in life nor his application of the analytical method, what is it that he contributes to our understanding of art or to its practice? In my opinion, what he contributes quite outweighs his errors; it is of the greatest importance and it lies in no specific statement that he makes about art but is, rather, implicit in his whole conception of the mind.

For, of all mental systems, the Freudian psychology is the one which makes poetry indigenous to the very constitution of the mind. Indeed, the mind, as Freud sees it, is in the greater part of its tendency, exactly a poetry-making organ. This puts the case too strongly no doubt, for it seems to make the working of the unconscious mind equivalent to poetry itself, forgetting that between the unconscious mind and the finished poem there supervene the social intention and the formal control of the conscious mind. Yet the statement has at least the virtue of counterbalancing the belief, so commonly expressed or implied, that the very opposite is true and that poetry is a kind of beneficent aberration of the mind's right course.

Freud has not merely naturalized poetry; he has discovered its status as a pioneer settler and he sees it as a method of thought. Often enough he tries to show how, as a method of thought, it is unreliable and ineffective for conquering reality; yet he himself is forced to use it in the very shaping of his own science, as when he speaks of the topography of the mind and tells us with a kind of defiant apology that the metaphors of space-relationship which he is using are really most inexact since the mind is not a thing of space at all, but that there is no other way of conceiving the difficult idea except by metaphor. In the eighteenth century Vico spoke of the metaphorical, imagistic language of the early stages of culture; it was left to Freud to discover how, in a scientific age, we still feel and think in figurative formations and to create, what psychoanalysis is, a science of tropes, of metaphor and its variants, synecdoche and metonomy.

Freud showed too how the mind, in one of its parts, could work without logic, yet not without that directing purpose, that control of intent from which, perhaps it might be said, logic springs. For the unconscious mind works without the syntactical conjunctions which are logic's essence. It recognizes no *because*, no *therefore*, no *but;* such ideas as similarity, agreement and community, for example, are expressed in dreams imagistically by compressing the elements into a unity. The unconscious mind in its struggle with the conscious always turns from the general to the concrete and finds the tangible trifle more congenial than the large abstraction. Freud discovered in the very organization of the mind those mechanisms by which art makes its effects, such devices as the condensations of meanings and the displacement of accent.

All this is perhaps obvious enough and, though I should like to develop it in proportion both to its importance and to the space I have given to disagreement with Freud, I will not press it further. For there are two other elements in Freud's thought which, in conclusion, I should like to introduce as of great weight in their bearing on art.

Of these, one is a specific idea which, in the middle of his career (1920), Freud put forward in his essay, *Beyond the Pleasure Principle.* The essay itself is a speculative attempt to solve a perplexing problem in clinical analysis, but its relevance to literature is inescapable, as Freud sees well enough even though his perception of its critical importance is not sufficiently strong to make him revise his earlier views of the nature and function of art. The idea is one which stands beside Aristotle's notion of the catharsis, in part to supplement, in part to modify it.

Freud has come upon certain facts which are not to be reconciled with his earlier theory of the dream. According to this theory, all dreams, even the unpleasant ones, could be understood upon analysis to have the intention of fulfilling the dreamer's wishes. They were in the service of what Freud calls the Pleasure-principle, which is opposed to the Reality-principle. It is, of course, this explanation of the dream which had so largely conditioned Freud's theory of art. But now there is thrust upon him the necessity for reconsidering the theory of the dream, for it was found that in cases of war-neurosis—what we call shell-shock—the patient, with the utmost anguish, recurred in his dreams to the very situation, distressing as it was, which had precipitated his neurosis. It seemed impossible to interpret these dreams by any assumption of a hedonistic intent. Nor did there seem to be the usual amount of distortion in them: the patient recurred in the terrible initiatory situation with great literalness. And the same pattern of psychic behavior could be observed in the play of children; there were some games which, far from fulfilling wishes, seemed to concentrate upon the representation of those aspects of the child's life which were most unpleasant and threatening to his happiness.

To explain such mental activities Freud evolved a theory for which he refuses to claim much but to which, it is obvious, he attaches the greatest importance. He first makes the assumption that there is indeed in the psychic life a repetition-compulsion which goes beyond the Pleasure-principle. Such a compulsion cannot be meaningless, it must have an intent. And that intent, Freud comes to believe, is exactly and literally the developing of fear. "These dreams," he says, "are attempts at restoring control of the stimuli by developing apprehension, the pretermission of which caused the traumatic neurosis." The dream, that is, is the effort to reconstruct the bad situation in order that the failure to meet it may be recouped; in these dreams there is no obscured intent to evade but only an attempt to meet the situation, to make a new effort of control. And in the play of children it seems to be that "the child repeats even the unpleasant experiences because through his own activity he gains a far more thorough mastery of the strong impression than was possible by mere passive experience."

Freud, at this point, can scarcely help being put in mind of tragic drama; nevertheless, he does not wish to believe that this effort to come to mental grips with a situation is involved in the attraction of tragedy. He is, we might say, under the influence of the Aristotelean tragic theory which emphasizes a qualified hedonism through suffering. But the pleasure involved in tragedy is perhaps an ambiguous one; and sometimes we must feel that the famous sense of cathartic resolution is perhaps the result of glossing over terror with beautiful language rather than an evacuation of it. And sometimes the terror even bursts through the language to stand stark and isolated from the play, as does Oedipus' sightless and bleeding face. At any rate, the Aristotlean theory does not deny another function for tragedy (and for comedy too) which is suggested by Freud's theory of the traumatic neurosis—what might be called the mithradatic function, by which tragedy is used as the homeopathic administration of pain to inure ourselves to the greater pain which life will force upon us. There is in the cathartic theory of tragedy, as it is usually understood, a conception of tragedy's function which is too negative and which inadequately suggests the sense of active mastery which tragedy can give.

In this essay, in which he sets forth the conception of the mind embracing its own pain for some vital purpose, Freud also expresses a provisional assent to the idea (earlier stated, as he reminds us, by Schopenhauer) that there is perhaps a human drive which makes of death the final and desired goal. The two ideas form the crown of Freud's broader speculation on the life of man. Their quality of grim poetry is characteristic of Freud's system and the ideas it generates for him.

And as much as anything else that Freud gives to literature, this quality of his thought is, I feel, important. Although the artist is never finally determined in his work by the intellectual systems about him, he cannot avoid their influence; and it can be said of various competing systems that some hold more promise for the artist than others. When, for example, we think of the simple humanitarian optimism which, for a decade, has been so pervasive, we must see that not only has it been politically and philosophically inadequate but also that it implies by the smallness of its view of the varieties of human possibility, a kind of check on the creative faculties. There is, in Freud's view of life, no such limitation implied. To be sure, certain elements of his system seem hostile to the usual notions of man's dignity. Like every great critic of human nature—and Freud is that—he finds in human pride the ultimate cause of human wretchedness and he takes pleasure in knowing that his ideas stand with those of Copernicus and Darwin in making pride more difficult to maintain. Yet the Freudian man is, I venture to think, a creature of far more dignity and far more interest than the man which any other modern system has been able to conceive. Despite popular belief to the contrary, man, as Freud conceives him, is not to be understood by any simple formula (such as sex) but is rather an inextricable tangle of culture and biology. And not being simple, he is not simply good; he has, as Freud says somewhere, a kind of hell within him from which rise everlastingly the impulses which threaten his civilization. He has the faculty of imagining for himself more in the way of pleasure and satisfaction than he can possibly achieve. Everything that he gains he pays for in more than equal coin; compromise and the compounding with defeat constitute his best way of getting through the world. His best qualities are the result of a struggle whose outcome is tragic. Yet he is a creature of love; it is Freud's sharpest criticism of the Adlerian psychology that to aggression it gives everything and to love nothing at all.

What one senses always in Freud is how little cynicism there is in his thought, his desire for man is only that he should be human and to this end his science is devoted. No view of life to which the artist responds can insure the quality of his work—how true this is can be proved from the innumerable novels made up of Freudian tags—but the poetic qualities of Freud's own principles, which are so clearly in the line of the classic tragic realism, suggest that this is a view which does not narrow and simplify the human world for the artist but, on the contrary, opens and complicates it.

ALLEN TATE: Hardy's Philosophic Metaphors*

AFTER Thomas Hardy had become a great literary figure on the British model—that is to say, a personage to whom one makes pilgrimages—criticism of his works languished: once the battle over the obscenity of Jude and the pessimism of his "philosophy" had been won, nobody had very much to say, except that one admired him. So far as I know, only two critical works on Hardy exist: Lionel Johnson's fine study of the novels, *The Art of Thomas Hardy*, which, first published in 1894, appeared before Hardy was known as a poet; and Lascelles Abercrombie's *Thomas Hardy*, a book of considerable value for the criticism of the novels but of not much use for the poetry. One must add to these works the excellent essay, "The Poetry of Thomas Hardy," by J. E. Barton, which appears as an appendix to the John Lane edition of Johnson's book (1923). The centennial biography, *Hardy of Wessex*, by C. J. Weber, no doubt adds to our store of facts about Hardy; yet Mr. Weber's critical ineptitude contributes little to our understanding of either the poetry or the novels.

For two reasons I have wished to make this comment upon the critics of Hardy's poetry: they have given us very little to start with, and their assertion of Hardy's greatness as a poet is worse than nothing to start with. I do not intend in this commentary to deny the "greatness" of Hardy's poetry, nor to deny meaning to the pious enthusiasm of two generations of devoted readers, among whom intermittently I count myself. But I do think at the same time that the enthusiasm is partly sentimental; it implies an equivocal judgment of both the poetry and the man. It is sentimental because it does not distinguish man from poet or tell us upon what terms we may talk about them together. We have here in the case of Hardy—though for no

* "Hardy's Philosophic Metaphors" first appeared in *The Southern Review*, Summer 1941, and was included in the book of essays, *Reason in Madness*, Copyright, 1941, by Allen Tate. It is reprinted here by courtesy of G. P. Putnam's Sons. Mr. Tate (*b.* 1899) is also the author of *Reactionary Essays on Poetry and Ideas* (1936).

doubt quite different reasons—the figure of the poet-sage not unlike that of Mr. Robert Frost, whose admirers will not permit the critics to dissociate the poetry from the wise man who wrote it. When without the admirers' permission a critic like Mr. R. P. Blackmur assumes that his task is to discuss Mr. Frost's language, he suffers the fanatical obloquy of a popular spellbinder, Mr. Bernard DeVoto, who promptly calls Mr. Blackmur a fool.

Now very much the same sort of thing went on towards the end of Thomas Hardy's life, and one must suspect very strongly, from all the evidence, that he liked it, and that he liked it because, like most critically naive minds, he could accept the personal tribute as tribute to the power of his message, which was the message of a "philosopher." Hardy was a great poet, but I arrive at that conclusion after disposing of a strong prejudice against the personal qualities that have led his admirers to believe him a great man. I see him as a somewhat complacent and tiresome old gentleman, mellow and wise; a man who in his youth had set about conquering a career; who married a woman his inferior but above him socially, and could never forget the social difference—a fact that forbids us to forget it; who permitted his literary reputation to lead him into the tow of society hostesses who could have seen in him only his fame and from whom, as he frequently confessed, he got nothing. Yet he continued until late in life to appear as the literary lion. Why did he do it? It is useless to pretend that Thomas Hardy's social sense was distinguished (a distinction that has nothing to do with "class") or that he was not lacking in a certain knowledge of the world that would have been valuable even to the historian of a yeoman society: in so far as historical and biographical criticism will illuminate Hardy's poetry, it is i nportant to keep his defects steadily in mind, for he never overcame them. Shakespeare's origins were humbler than Hardy's, yet they are irrelevant in the criticism of Shakespeare, because the confusion of feeling that one finds in Hardy cannot be found in Shakespeare. Hardy's background and education, like other backgrounds and other educations for poetry, will give us a clew to the defects of the work, but not to its merits, and it is with the merits that criticism must be specifically occupied. Literature can be written from any background, and Hardy wrote literature.

Mr. Weber quotes from Hardy's famous description of Clym Yeobright the following passage, and applies it to Hardy's own young manhood:

> Mentally he was in a provincial future, that is, he was in many points abreast with the central town thinkers of his date. Much of this development he may have owed to his studious life in Paris, where he had become acquainted with ethical systems popular at the time. In consequence of this relatively advanced position, Yeobright might have been called unfortunate. The rural world was not ripe for him.

From this and other passages in the novels, in which Hardy presents himself in the disguise of certain characters, we get a portrait of the young Hardy against the background from which he sprang. Like Yeobright he was a young man "educated" out of the folk culture of his region: he had read Darwin, Huxley, Hume, Gibbon—the Victorian agnostics and their naturalistic forerunners of the eighteenth century. He began to see the world through "ethical systems popular at the time"; more than that, he began to see the people of Dorset in terms of the metaphysical bias of these systems; so that when he came back to Dorset from his studies in London he must have felt that his "advanced position" had cut him off from his people.

Yet there can be no doubt that, if this situation actually confronted Hardy at the outset of his literary career, it offered him tremendous advantages. He had been possessed from birth of an immense, almost instinctive knowledge of the life of a people rooted in ancient folk-traditions and fixed, also, in the objective patterns of nature and of the occupations close to nature. This knowledge of a provincial scene, where "life had bared its bones" to him, must have toughened his skepticism against the cruder aspects of Victorian thought, liberalism, optimism, and the doctrine of progress, and he could concentrate with a sort of classical purity upon the permanent human experiences.

Yet he did have a philosophical view of the significance of the human situation. As William R. Rutland indicates in his *Thomas Hardy* (the best general book on the subject), Hardy maintained with great consistency, from the beginning of his literary career, a philosophical attitude. The attitude did not change. Mr. Rutland makes an astute analysis of it:

> It is an interesting paradox that Hardy should have placed so high a value upon intellectual reason, while his own mental life was almost entirely governed by emotion . . . he criticized J. H. Newman for failing to provide logical support for his beliefs. The outlook upon life of his mature manhood was almost wholly due to emotional reactions against suffering and injustice; but he sought for intellectual explanations of the universe in the writing of the philosophers. He went on reading philosophy till he was old, but he never advanced beyond what had been in the forefront of thought during his early manhood. When, in 1915, he read that no modern philosopher subscribes to Herbert Spencer's doctrine of "the Unknowable" (which had greatly influenced him) he declared himself "utterly bewildered."

How much this philosophical reading did towards making the young Hardy, like Clym Yeobright, an outsider in his own region, nobody could calculate accurately; but that it did affect him in this manner I believe no one will deny. His "advanced position" is only another way of saying that he had very early come to be both inside and outside his background, which was to be the material of his art: an ambivalent point of view that, in its infinite variations from any formula that we may state for it, is at the center of the ironic consciousness. While Hardy had a direct "emotional reaction" to his Wessex people, who were the human substance of the only world he really knew, he nevertheless tried to philosophize about them in the terms of Victorian materialism.

This, I think, was his intellectual situation, and Mr. Rutland has given us a clew to its meaning that ought to receive at some future time a more detailed analysis than I can give it here. In setting forth the experiences of people deeply involved with the cycle of the earth and "conditioned" in their emotional relations by close familiarity with the processes of nature, he had constantly before him a kind of "naturalism" that only an astute philosophical mind could have kept, in that period, distinct from a naturalism of a wholly different order: the philosophic naturalism of Huxley and Spencer which, according to Mr. Rutland, Hardy tended to look upon as "explanations" of the world, not as theories. When he was shocked in 1915 by the decline of Spencer's reputation, he doubtless felt that a final conclusion had been upset; his outlook was not philosophical but brooding and ruminative; and I believe that here, again, we get the image of Clym Yeobright, the young man ill-prepared to digest the learning of the great world, the provincial amateur who sees farther than his neighbors but who, if he had seen still farther, might not have accepted, *in an act of faith,* the Darwinian naturalism of his time. As late as 1922 he wrote in the "Apology" to *Late Lyrics and Earlier* that "when belief in witches of Endor is displacing the Darwinian theory and 'the truth that shall make you free,' men's minds appear, as above noted, to be moving backwards rather than on." The witches of Endor were doubtless presiding over the irrational passions of the War; but at any rate the going backwards instead of forwards indicates, I believe, a somewhat greater belief in one of the leading Victorian ideas, Progress, than is usually attributed to Hardy.

Perhaps Hardy's intense awareness of the folk-realism of his people modified the liberal optimism of his time, and checked his assent to the enthusiasm of his age at a particular stage, which he described as "evolutionary meliorism." Nevertheless, the reader of Hardy's novels gets a total impression in which this doctrine of "meliorism" is occasionally stated but in which it plays little part in terms of the characters and their plots. It has often been said that Hardy's two leading ideas, Necessity and Chance, Fate and "Crass Casualty," continue the Greek tradition; but it seems more likely that his Necessity is only Victorian Mechanism, and that Chance represents the occasional intercession into the mechanical routine of the universe, of Spencer's Unknowable.

It is a curious feature of Hardy's treatment of the Dorchester peasantry that not one of them is permitted to have a religious experience: their religious emotions are thoroughly "psychologized" and naturalistic. It would seem then that Hardy, like Clym, had reached an "advanced position" which forbade him to take seriously the religious life of his people. Their peculiar compound of pagan superstition and

Christianity which issued in a simple miraculism (as opposed to Hardy's mechanism of fate interrupted by blind chance) he tended from the first to look at from the outside, where it seemed quaint and picturesque. This, of course, is not quite the whole story of Hardy's profound insight into human character, or of his mastery of dramatic form which he achieved in spite of technical limitations and of a high-falutin' prose style of which the best that can be said is that it has an occasional descriptive grandeur and a frequent bathos. (He once said that while poetry requires technique, prose writes itself—perhaps a British as well as a personal blindness.) I have offered this brief simplification of Hardy's intellectual "position" not as an explanation of his work, but merely as a pointer towards a certain kind of meaning that I have seen in his poetry.

2

One of Hardy's most powerful poems is "Nature's Questioning." It is written in a four-line stanza that seems characteristically to be derived from a hymn meter in the first two lines, but instead of completing the 4-3-4-3 stanza that the first two lines have led us to expect, he boldly finishes it off, 3-6, thus:

When I look forth at dawning, pool,
Field, flock, and lonely tree,
All seem to gaze at me
Like chastened children sitting silent in school;

Their faces dulled, constrained, and worn,
As though the master's ways
Through the long teaching days
Had cowed them till their early zest was overborne.

The Alexandrines in these stanzas are prosodically among the most successful in English: the sense overlaps the caesura, imparting to the structure a firmness that keeps the line from breaking down into two trimeters—the usual result of the attempt to write English hexameter. The poem proceeds, after two stanzas setting forth cosmic questions from nature:

Or come we of an Automaton
Unconscious of our pains? . . .
Or are we live remains
Of Godhead dying downwards, brain and eye now gone?

The two last lines are often cited as Hardy's most brilliant, and I think there can be no doubt of their magnificence. The phrase *now gone* could not be better: one is reminded of Henry James's tact concerning the presentation of supernatural beings in fiction, that "weak specifications" limit their credibility. *Now gone* is just specific enough, its colloquial tone bringing the idea of God within the range of familiarity without the risks of a too concrete image: brain and eye are no images, but rather objects denoted. The rhythm of the line seems to me to be masterly. The prevailing falling rhythm is suddenly shifted from "brain" to the end of the line, to a counter, mounting rhythm; moreover, the trimeter line latent in the hexameter becomes explicit—"Of Godhead dying downwards"—and the shock of *downwards* has the prolonged effect of the feminine ending; when the hexameter is resumed, *brain* strikes with tremendous force, with a secondary stress on *eye;* and *now gone* reads to my ear almost as spondee. In this last feature it seems to me that the final proof of the technical mastery appears (conscious in Hardy, or not). The rhythmic conflict in the line is never quite resolved. There has been a regular alternation of stressed and unstressed syllables, so that when we reach *now* we are under a strong compulsion to pass it over lightly; yet we cannot do it; the quantity of the syllable, reinforced by its rhetoric, stops us. Could we pass it lightly, *now gone* as an iambus would restore the prevailing pattern of mounting rhythm; as a spondee it suspends the conflict, the particular effect of meaning and rhythm being a kind of kinesthetic sensation that we soon discover that we have been attributing to the agony of the dying Godhead.

I do not apologize for laboring this point. Great passages of poetry are rare; because they are exceptionally rare in Hardy we must exert ourselves to the utmost to understand their value. There is nothing else in "Nature's Questioning" to reward our close attention—if we are looking for poetry; but there is a great deal that will illuminate our understanding of Hardy's poetry. The two last stanzas:

Or is it that some high Plan betides,
As yet not understood,
Of Evil stormed by Good,

We the Forlorn Hope over which Achievement strides?

Thus things around. No answerer I . . .
Meanwhile the winds, and rains,
And Earth's old glooms and pains
Are still the same, and Life and Death are neighbors nigh.

Now this poem as a whole fairly represents a use of metaphor practiced by certain Victorian poets. The inanimate "things around" that have asked the questions appear in the first stanza as pool, field, flock, and a tree whose sole quality is its loneliness; these objects quickly become school children, before they have been sufficiently particularized to be themselves. The transformation of the natural objects into persons is initiated with some degree of tact in terms of simile—"Like chastened children"—that we can accept because not too much is claimed for it at that stage. But in the second stanza what appeared to be simile becomes completed metaphor. We have here, in the terms of Mr. I. A. Richards, an instance of metaphor in which the "vehicle" replaced the "tenor"; the natural objects (tenor) are so weakly perceived that the children (vehicle), who appear as the conveyance of their significance, cancel out the natural objects altogether; so that, as the poem proceeds to the fourth stanza, we get a group of inanimate objects as school children asking this question:

Has some vast Imbecility,
Mighty to build and blend,
But impotent to tend,
Framed us in jest, and left us now to hazardy?

Now Hardy is saying that the children are Nature, or would like to say, since he is a nineteenth-century monist, that they are also mechanically determined, as Nature is; both human and nonhuman nature suffer the neglect of the absentee God of Deism, who is:

Mighty to build and blend,
But impotent to tend . . .

This God is the schoolmaster of line two, stanza two; here again the metaphorical vehicle replaces the tenor; and in view of the deistic character of this God, the figure of the "master," who is the personal, anthropomorphic representation of the Unknowable, contradicts his logical significance: to render this God dramatically, Hardy has made him the God of theism, a personal, if not the Christian, God, but if he is the Automaton of stanza five, he is not equipped to teach a class; he cannot even be present if he is "impotent to tend."

Throughout this poem (and I should risk the guess, in most of the "philosophical" poems of Hardy) the margin of intelligible meaning achieved by the union of the tenor and the vehicle is very narrow. Even in the magnificent image of the "Godhead dying downwards" we get a certain degree of contradiction between tenor and vehicle: in order to say that God has left the universe to chance after setting it in motion, Hardy can merely present us with the theistic God as blind and imbecile.

So generally of Hardy it may perhaps be said that his "philosophy" tends to be a little beyond the range of his feeling: his abstractions are thus somewhat irresponsible, since he rarely shows us the experience that ought to justify them, that would give them substance, visibility, meaning. The visible embodiment of the meaning of "Nature's Questioning" ought doubtless to be "pool, field, flock, and lonely tree," which are not experienced objects of nature, but only universals of so thinly perceived quality that Hardy apparently had no trouble at all in absorbing them into the analogy of the school children; and likewise the schoolmaster is so thinly particularized that the next analogical development, master into God, is easy and unconvincing.

It is likely that other critics will from time to time examine other types of Hardy's verse; it will probably be many years before a comprehensive study of all his poetry can appear. I have a strong impression that the ballads, songs, and occasional lyrics, as well as the versified tales and the ironic incidents of the *Satires of Circumstance*, exhibit the greatest freedom of sensibility of which Hardy, the poet, was capable: in the vast number of these slighter pieces Hardy is at his least philosophical; he is closer to the immediate subject, he is free to observe directly and to record the direct impression. But when he begins to think, when he begins to say what the impression, the observation, the incident means, he can only bring in his ill-digested philosophy—a *mélange* of Schopenhauer, Darwin, and Spencer, against a cosmological background of eighteenth-century Deism that he could not project imaginatively into his immediate experience.

Is this not the common situation of the Victorian poets and, with some differences, our predicament today? Our chief difference seems to consist in a greater awareness of the problem—not in its solution. Hardy's philosophical limitations permitted him to accept as "truth" Spencer's *Synthetic Philosophy,* with the result that he held to the mechanistic theories of his time with greater single-mindedness than Spencer or Browning ever achieved. This single-mindedness probably kept him immune to the eclectic miscellany of easy solutions and speculations that his more sensitive contemporaries succumbed to. There can be no doubt that the poetic language of Hardy, particularly in poems like "God's Funeral" and "The Convergence of the Twain," achieves a weight and solidity that only Arnold of the Victorians—and then only in his best moments—could rival: perhaps his lack of a university training in literature permitted him to seize the language afresh, so that even his heavily Latinized vocabulary is capable of effects that a better educated poet in his age would have missed. It is as dangerous as it is meaningless to wish that a great poet might have either made up or suppressed his deficiencies. Had he been "better educated" he might have been like Browning or Swinburne—both men his inferiors; had he been worse educated, it is not inconceivable that he should have been even more like James Thomson (B.V.) than he was; but fortunately he was Thomas Hardy.

STEPHEN SPENDER: The Making of a Poem*

Apology

IT WOULD be inexcusable to discuss my own way of writing poetry unless I were able to relate this to a wider view of the problems which poets attempt to solve when they sit down at a desk or table to write, or walk around composing their poems in their heads. There is a danger of my appearing to put across my own experiences as the general rule, when every poet's way of going about his work and his experience of being a poet are different, and when my own poetry may not be good enough to lend my example any authority.

Yet the writing of poetry is an activity which makes certain demands of attention on the poet and which requires that he should have certain qualifications of ear, vision, imagination, memory and so on. He should be able to think in images, he should have as great a mastery of language as a painter has over his palette, even if the range of his language be very limited. All this means that, in ordinary society, a poet has to adapt himself, more or less consciously, to the demands of his vocation, and hence the peculiarities of poets and the condition of inspiration which many people have said is near to madness. One poet's example is only his adaptation of his personality to the demands of poetry, but if it is clearly stated it may help us to understand other poets, and even something of poetry.

Today we lack very much a whole view of poetry, and have instead many one-sided views of certain aspects of poetry which have been advertised as the only aims which poets should attempt. Movements such as free verse, imagism, surrealism, expressionism, personalism and so

* "The Making of a Poem" appeared in *Partisan Review,* Summer 1946, and is reprinted here by courtesy of the editors and Mr. Harold Matson. Mr. Spender (*b.* 1909) is the author of *The Destructive Element: A Study of Modern Writers and Beliefs* (1935), *Forward from Liberalism* (1937), and *European Witness* (1946), and editor of *A Choice of English Romantic Poetry* (1947).

on, tend to make people think that poetry is simply a matter of not writing in metre or rhyme, or of free association, or of thinking in images, or of a kind of drawing room madness (surrealism) which corresponds to drawing room communism. Here is a string of ideas: Night, dark, stars, immensity, blue, voluptuous, clinging, columns, clouds, moon, sickle, harvest, vast camp fire, hell. Is this poetry? A lot of strings of words almost as simple as this are set down on the backs of envelopes and posted off to editors or to poets by the vast army of amateurs who think that to be illogical is to be poetic, with that fond question. Thus I hope that this discussion of how poets work will imply a wider and completer view of poets.

Concentration

The problem of creative writing is essentially one of concentration, and the supposed eccentricities of poets are usually due to mechanical habits or rituals developed in order to concentrate. Concentration, of course, for the purposes of writing poetry, is different from the kind of concentration required for working out a sum. It is a focussing of the attention in a special way, so that the poet is aware of all the implications and possible developments of his idea, just as one might say that a plant was not concentrating on developing mechanically in one direction, but in many directions, towards the warmth and light with its leaves, and towards the water with its roots, all at the same time.

Schiller liked to have a smell of rotten apples, concealed beneath the lid of his desk, under his nose when he was composing poetry. Walter de la Mare has told me that he must smoke when writing. Auden drinks endless cups of tea. Coffee is my own addiction, besides smoking a great deal, which I hardly ever do except when I am writing. I notice also that as I attain a greater concentration, this tends to make me forget the taste of the cigarette in my mouth, and then I have a desire to smoke two or even three cigarettes at a time, in order that the sensation from the outside may penetrate through the wall of concentration which I have built round myself.

For goodness' sake, though, do not think that rotten apples or cigarettes or tea have anything to do with the quality of the work of a Schiller, a de la Mare, or an Auden. They are a part of a concentration which has already been attained rather than the causes of concentration. De la Mare once said to me that he thought the desire to smoke when writing poetry arose from a need, not of a stimulus, but to canalize a distracting leak of his attention away from his writing towards the distraction which is always present in one's environment. Concentration may be disturbed by someone whistling in the street or the ticking of a clock. There is always a slight tendency of the body to sabotage the attention of the mind by providing some distraction. If this need for distraction can be directed into one channel—such as the odor of rotten apples or the taste of tobacco or tea—then other distractions outside oneself are put out of competition.

Another possible explanation is that the concentrated effort of writing poetry is a spiritual activity which makes one completely forget, for the time being, that one has a body. It is a disturbance of the balance of body and mind and for this reason one needs a kind of anchor of sensation with the physical world. Hence the craving for a scent or taste or even, sometimes, for sexual activity. Poets speak of the necessity of writing poetry rather than of a liking for doing it. It is spiritual compulsion, a straining of the mind to attain heights surrounded by abysses and it cannot be entirely happy, for in the most important sense, the only reward worth having is absolutely denied: for, however confident a poet may be, he is never quite sure that all his energy is not misdirected nor that what he is writing is great poetry. At the moment when art attains its highest attainment it reaches beyond its medium of words or paints or music, and the artist finds himself realizing that these instruments are inadequate to the spirit of what he is trying to say.

Different poets concentrate in different ways. In my own mind I make a sharp distinction between two types of concentration: one is immediate and complete, the other is plodding and only completed by stages. Some poets write immediately works which, when they are written, scarcely need revision. Others write their poems by stages, feeling their way from rough draft to rough draft, until finally, after many revisions, they have produced a result which may seem to have very little connection with their early sketches.

These two opposite processes are vividly illustrated in two examples drawn from music: Mozart and Beethoven. Mozart thought out symphonies, quartets, even scenes from operas, entirely in his head—often on a journey or perhaps while dealing with pressing problems—and then he transcribed them, in their completeness, onto paper. Beethoven wrote fragments of themes in notebooks which he kept beside him, working on and developing them over years. Often his first ideas were of a clumsiness which makes scholars marvel how he could, at the end, have developed from them such miraculous results.

Thus genius works in different ways to achieve its ends. But although the Mozartian type of genius is the more brilliant and dazzling, genius, unlike virtuosity, is judged by greatness of results, not by brilliance of performance. The result must be the fullest development in a created aesthetic form of an original moment of insight, and it does not matter whether genius devotes a lifetime to producing a small result if that result be immortal. The difference between two types of genius is that one type (the Mozartian) is able to plunge the greatest depths of his own experience by the tremendous effort of a moment, the other (the Beethovenian) must dig deeper and deeper into his consciousness, layer by layer. What counts in either case is the vision which sees and pursues and attains the end; the logic of the artistic purpose.

A poet may be divinely gifted with a lucid and intense and purposive intellect; he may be clumsy and slow; that does not matter, what matters is integrity of purpose and the ability to maintain the purpose without losing oneself. Myself, I am scarcely capable of immediate concentration in poetry. My mind is not clear, my will is weak, I suffer from an excess of ideas and a weak sense of form. For every poem that I begin to write, I think of at least ten which I do not write down at all. For every poem which I do write down, there are seven or eight which I never complete.

The method which I adopt therefore is to write down as many ideas as possible, in however rough a form, in notebooks (I have at least twenty of these, on a shelf beside my desk, going back over fifteen years). I then make use of some of the sketches and discard others.

The best way of explaining how I develop the rough ideas which I use, is to take an example. Here is a Notebook begun in 1944. About a hundred pages of it are covered with writing, and from this have emerged about six poems. Each idea, when it first occurs, is given a number. Sometimes the ideas do not get beyond one line. For example No. 3 (never developed) is the one line:—

A language of flesh and roses.

I shall return to this line in a few pages, when I speak of inspiration. For the moment, I turn to No. 13, because here is an idea which has been developed to its conclusion. The first sketch begins thus:—

a) *There are some days when the sea lies like a harp*
Stretched flat beneath the cliffs. The waves
Like wires burn with the sun's copper glow
[all the murmuring blue
every silent]

Between whose spaces every image
Of sky [field and] *hedge and field and boat*
Dwells like the huge face of the afternoon.
[Lies]

When the heat grows tired, the afternoon
Out of the land may breathe a sigh
[Across these wires like a hand. They vibrate
With]
Which moves across those wires like a soft hand
[Then the vibration]
Between whose spaces the vibration holds
Every bird-cry, dog's bark, man-shout
And creak of rollock from the land and sky
With all the music of the afternoon.

Obviously these lines are attempts to sketch out an idea which exists clearly enough on some level of the mind where it yet eludes the attempt to state it. At this stage, a poem is like a face which one seems to be able to visualize clearly in the eye of memory, but when one examines it mentally or tries to think it out, feature by feature, it seems to fade.

The idea of this poem is a vision of the sea. The faith of the poet is that if this vision is clearly stated it will be significant. The vision is of the sea stretched under a cliff. On top of the cliff there are fields, hedges, houses. Horses draw carts along lanes, dogs bark far inland, bells ring in the distance. The shore seems laden with hedges, roses, horses and men, all high above the sea, on a very fine summer day when the ocean seems to reflect and absorb the shore. Then the small strung-out glittering waves of the sea lying under the shore are like the strings of a harp which catch the sunlight. Between these strings lies the reflection of the shore. Butterflies are wafted out over the waves, which they mistake for the fields of the chalky landscape, searching them for flowers. On a day such as this, the land, reflected in the sea, appears to enter into the sea, as though it lies under it, like Atlantis. The wires of the harp are like a seen music fusing seascape and landscape.

Looking at this vision in another way, it obviously has symbolic value. The sea represents death and eternity, the land represents the brief life of the summer and of one human generation which passes into the sea of eternity. But let me here say at once that although the poet may be conscious of this aspect of his vision, it is exactly what he wants to avoid stating, or even being too concerned with. His job is to recreate his vision, and let it speak its moral for itself. The poet must distinguish clearly in his own mind between that which most definitely must be said and that which must not be said. The unsaid inner meaning is revealed in the music and the tonality of the poem, and the poet is conscious of it in his knowledge that a certain tone of voice, a certain rhythm, are necessary.

In the next twenty versions of the poem I felt my way towards the clarification of the seen picture, the music and the inner feeling. In the first version quoted above, there is the phrase in the second and third lines

The waves
Like wires burn with the sun's copper glow.

This phrase fuses the image of the sea with the idea of music, and it is therefore a key-phrase, because the theme of the poem is the fusion of the land with the sea. Here, then, are several versions of these one and a quarter lines, in the order in which they were written:—

b) *The waves are wires*
Burning as with the secret song of fires

c) *The day burns in the trembling wires*
With a vast music golden in the eyes

d) *The day glows on its trembling wires*
Singing a golden music in the eyes

e) *The day glows on its burning wires*
Like waves of music golden to the eyes.

f) *Afternoon burns upon its wires*
Lines of music dazzling the eyes

g) *Afternoon gilds its tingling wires*
To a visual silent music of the eyes

In the final version, these two lines appear as in the following stanza:—

h) *There are some days the happy ocean lies*
Like an unfingered harp, below the land.
Afternoon gilds all the silent wires
Into a burning music of the eyes.

On mirroring paths between those fine-strung fires
The shore, laden with roses, horses, spires,
Wanders in water, imaged above ribbed sand.

Inspiration

The hard work evinced in these examples, which are only a fraction of the work put into the whole poem, may cause the reader to wonder whether there is no such thing as inspiration, or whether it is merely Stephen Spender who is uninspired. The answer is that everything in poetry is work except inspiration, whether this work is achieved at one swift stroke, as Mozart wrote his music, or whether it is a slow process of evolution from stage to stage. Here again, I have to qualify the word 'work,' as I qualified the word 'concentration': the work on a line of poetry may take the form of putting a version aside for a few days, weeks or years, and then taking it up again, when it may be found that the line has, in the interval of time, almost rewritten itself.

Inspiration is the beginning of a poem and it is also its final goal. It is the first idea which drops into the poet's mind and it is the final idea which he at last achieves in words. In between this start and this winning post there is the hard race, the sweat and toil.

Paul Valéry speaks of the "*une ligne donnée*" of a poem. One line is given to the poet by

God or by nature, the rest he has to discover for himself.

My own experience of inspiration is certainly that of a line or a phrase or a word or sometimes something still vague, a dim cloud of an idea which I feel must be condensed into a shower of words. The peculiarity of the key word or line is that it does not merely attract, as, say, the word "braggadocio" attracts. It occurs in what seems to be an active, male, germinal form as though it were the centre of a statement requiring a beginning and an end, and as though it had an impulse in a certain direction. Here are examples:—

A language of flesh and roses

This phrase (not very satisfactory in itself) brings to my mind a whole series of experiences and the idea of a poem which I shall perhaps write some years hence. I was standing in the corridor of a train passing through the Black Country. I saw a landscape of pits and pitheads, artificial mountains, jagged yellow wounds in the earth, everything transformed as though by the toil of an enormous animal or giant tearing up the earth in search of prey or treasure. Oddly enough, a stranger next to me in the corridor echoed my inmost thought. He said: "Everything there is man-made." At this moment the line flashed into my head

A language of flesh and roses.

The sequence of my thought was as follows: the industrial landscape which seems by now a routine and act of God which enslaves both employers and workers who serve and profit by it, is actually the expression of man's will. Men willed it to be so, and pitheads, slag-heaps and the ghastly disregard of anything but the pursuit of wealth, are a symbol of modern man's mind. In other words, the world which we create—the world of slums and telegrams and newspapers—is a kind of language of our inner wishes and thoughts. Although this is so, it is obviously a language which has got outside our control. It is a confused language, an irresponsible senile gibberish. This thought greatly distressed me, and I started thinking that if the phenomena created by humanity are really like words in a language, what kind of language do we really aspire to? All this sequence of thought flashed into my mind with the answer which came before the question: *A language of flesh and roses.*

I hope this example will give the reader some idea of what I mean by inspiration. Now the line, which I shall not repeat again, is a way of thinking imaginatively. If the line embodies some of the ideas which I have related above, these ideas must be further made clear in other lines. That is the terrifying challenge of poetry. Can I think out the logic of images? How easy it is to explain here the poem that I would have liked to write! How difficult it would be to write it. For writing it would imply living my way through the imaged experience of all these ideas, which here are mere abstractions, and such an effort of imaginative experience requires a lifetime of patience and watching.

Here is an example of a cloudy form of thought germinated by the word *cross,* which is the key word of the poem which exists formlessly in my mind. Recently my wife had a son. On the first day that I visited her after the boy's birth, I went by bus to the hospital. Passing through the streets on the top of the bus, they all seemed very clean, and the thought occurred to me that everything was prepared for our child. Past generations have toiled so that any child born today inherits, with his generation, cities, streets, organization, the most elaborate machinery for living. Everything has been provided for him by people dead long before he was born. Then, naturally enough, sadder thoughts colored this picture for me, and I reflected how he also inherited vast maladjustments, vast human wrongs. Then I thought of the child as like a pin-point of present existence, the moment incarnate, in whom the whole of the past, and all possible futures *cross.* This word *cross* somehow suggested the whole situation to me of a child born into the world and also of the form of a poem about his situation. When the word *cross* appeared in the poem, the idea of the past should give place to the idea of the future and it should be apparent that the *cross* in which present and future meet is the secret of an individual human existence. And here again, the unspoken secret which lies beyond the poem, the moral significance of other meanings of the word "cross" begins to glow with its virtue that should never be said and yet should shine through every image in the poem.

This account of inspiration is probably weak beside the accounts that other poets might give. I am writing of my own experience, and my own inspiration seems to me like the faintest flash of insight into the nature of reality beside that of other poets whom I can think of. However, it is possible that I describe here a kind of experience which, however slight it may be, is far truer to the real poetic experience than Aldous Huxley's account of how a young poet writes poetry in his novel *Time Must Have a Stop.* It is hard to imagine anything more self-conscious and unpoetic than Mr. Huxley's account.

Memory

If the art of concentrating in a particular way is the discipline necessary for poetry to reveal itself, memory exercised in a particular way is the natural gift of poetic genius. The poet, above all else, is a person who never forgets certain sense-impressions which he has experienced and which he can re-live again and again as though with all their original freshness.

All poets have this highly developed sensitive apparatus of memory, and they are usually aware of experiences which happened to them at the earliest age and which retain their pristine significance throughout life. The meeting of Dante and Beatrice when the poet was only nine years of age is the experience which became a symbol in Dante's mind around which the *Divine Comedy* crystallized. The experience of nature which forms the subject of Wordsworth's poetry was an extension of a childhood vision of "natural presences" which surrounded the boy Wordsworth. And his decision in later life to live in the Lake District was a decision to return to the scene of these childhood memories which were the most important experiences in his poetry. There is evidence for the importance of this kind of memory in all the creative arts, and the argument certainly applies to prose which is creative. Sir Osbert Sitwell has told me that his book *Before the Bombardment,* which contains an extremely civilized and satiric account of the social life of Scarborough before and during the last war, was based on his observations of life in that resort before he had reached the age of twelve.

It therefore is not surprising that although I have no memory for telephone numbers, addresses, faces and where I have put this morning's correspondence, I have a perfect memory for the sensation of certain experiences which are crystallized for me around certain associations. I could demonstrate this from my own life by the overwhelming nature of associations which, suddenly aroused, have carried me back so completely into the past, particularly into my childhood, that I have lost all sense of the present time and place. But the best proofs of this power of memory are found in the odd lines of poems written in notebooks fifteen years ago. A few fragments of unfinished poems enable me to enter immediately into the experiences from which they were derived, the circumstances in which they were written, and the unwritten feelings in the poem that were projected but never put into words.

. . . Knowledge of a full sun
That runs up his big sky, above
The hill, then in those trees and throws
His smiling on the turf.

That is an incomplete idea of fifteen years ago, and I remember exactly a balcony of a house facing a road, and, on the other side of the road, pine trees, beyond which lay the sea. Every morning the sun sprang up, first of all above the horizon of the sea, then it climbed to the tops of the trees and shone on my window. And this memory connects with the sun that shines through my window in London now in spring and early summer. So that the memory is not exactly a memory. It is more like one prong upon which a whole calendar of similar experiences happening throughout years, collect. A memory once clearly stated ceases to be a memory, it becomes perpetually present, because every time we experience something which recalls it, the clear and lucid original experience imposes its formal beauty on the new experiences. It is thus no longer a memory but an experience lived through again and again.

Turning over these old notebooks, my eye catches some lines, in a projected long poem, which immediately re-shape themselves into the following short portrait of a woman's face:—

Her eyes are gleaming fish
Caught in her nervous face, as if in a net.
Her hair is wild and fair, haloing her cheeks
Like a fantastic flare of Southern sun.
There is madness in her cherishing her children.
Sometimes, perhaps a single time in years,
Her wandering fingers stoop to arrange some flowers—
Then in her hands her whole life stops and weeps.

It is perhaps true to say that memory is the faculty of poetry, because the imagination itself is an exercise of memory. There is nothing we imagine which we do not already know. And our ability to imagine is our ability to remember what we have already once experienced and to apply it to some different situation. Thus the greatest poets are those with memories so great that they extend beyond their strongest experiences to their minutest observations of people and things far outside their own self-centredness (the weakness of memory is its self-centredness: hence the narcissistic nature of most poetry).

Here I can detect my own greatest weakness. My memory is defective and self-centred. I lack the confidence in using it to create situations outside myself, although I believe that, in theory, there are very few situations in life which a poet should not be able to imagine, because it is a fact that most poets have experienced almost every situation in life. I do not mean by this that a poet who writes about a Polar Expedition has actually been to the North Pole. I mean, though, that he has been cold, hungry, etc., so that it is possible for him by remembering imaginatively his own felt experiences to know what it is like to explore the North Pole. That is where I fail. I cannot write about going to the North Pole.

Faith

It is evident that a faith in their vocation, mystical in intensity, sustains poets. There are many illustrations from the lives of poets to show this, and Shakespeare's sonnets are full of expressions of his faith in the immortality of his lines.

From my experience I can clarify the nature of this faith. When I was nine, we went to the Lake District, and there my parents read me some of the poems of Wordsworth. My sense of the sacredness of the task of poetry began then, and I have always felt that a poet's was a sacred vocation, like a saint's. Since I was nine, I have wanted to be various things, for example, Prime Minister (when I was twelve). Like some other poets I am attracted by the life of power and the life of action, but I am still more repelled by them. Power involves forcing oneself upon the attention of historians by doing things and occupying offices which are, in themselves, important, so that what is truly powerful is not the soul of a so-called powerful and prominent man but the position which he fills and the things which he does. Similarly, the life of "action" which seems so very positive is, in fact, a selective, even a negative kind of life. A man of action does one thing or several things because he does not do something else. Usually men who do very spectacular things fail completely to do the ordinary things which fill the lives of most normal people, and which would be far more heroic and spectacular perhaps, if they did not happen to be done by many people. Thus in practice the life of action has always seemed to me an act of cutting oneself off from life.

Although it is true that poets are vain and ambitious, their vanity and ambition are of the purest kind attainable in this world, for the saint renounces ambition. They are ambitious to be accepted for what they ultimately are as revealed by their inmost experiences, their finest perceptions, their deepest feelings, their uttermost sense of truth, in their poetry. They cannot cheat about these things, because the quality of their own being is revealed not in the noble sentiments which their poetry expresses, but in sensibility, control of language, rhythm and music, things which cannot be attained by a vote of confidence from an electorate, or by the office of Poet Laureate. Of course, work is tremendously important, but, in poetry, even the greatest labor can only serve to reveal the intrinsic qualities of soul of the poet as he really is.

Since there can be no cheating, the poet, like the saint, stands in all his works before the bar of a perpetual day of judgment. His vanity of course is pleased by success, though even success may contribute to his understanding that popularity does not confer on him the favorable judgment of all the ages which he seeks. For what does it mean to be praised by one's own age, which is soaked in crimes and stupidity, except perhaps that future ages, wise where we are foolish, will see him as a typical expression of this age's crimes and stupidity? Nor is lack of success a guarantee of great poetry, though there are some who pretend that it is. Nor can the critics, at any rate beyond a certain limited point of technical judgment, be trusted.

The poet's faith is therefore, firstly, a mystique of vocation, secondly, a faith in his own truth, combined with his own devotion to a task. There can really be no greater faith than the confidence that one is doing one's utmost to fulfil one's high vocation, and it is this that has inspired all the greatest poets. At the same time this faith is coupled with a deep humility because one knows that, ultimately, judgment does not rest with oneself. All one can do is to achieve nakedness, to be what one is with all one's faculties and perceptions, strengthened by all the skill which one can acquire, and then to stand before the judgment of time.

In my Notebooks, I find the following Prose Poem, which expresses these thoughts:

Bring me peace bring me power bring me assurance. Let me reach the bright day, the high chair, the plain desk, where my hand at last controls the words, where anxiety no longer undermines me. If I don't reach these I'm thrown to the wolves, I'm a restless animal wandering from place to place, from experience to experience.

Give me the humility and the judgment to live alone with the deep and rich satisfaction of my own creating: not to be thrown into doubt by a word of spite or disapproval.

In the last analysis don't mind whether your work is good or bad so long as it has the completeness, the enormity of the whole world which you love.

Song

Inspiration and song are the irreducible final qualities of a poet which make his vocation different from all others. Inspiration is an experience in which a line or an idea is given to one, and perhaps also a state of mind in which one writes one's best poetry. Song is far more difficult to define. It is the music which a poem as yet unthought of will assume, the empty womb of poetry for ever in the poet's consciousness, waiting for the fertilizing seed.

Sometimes, when I lie in a state of half-waking half-sleeping, I am conscious of a stream of words which seem to pass through my mind, without their having a meaning, but they have a sound, a sound of passion, or a sound recalling poetry that I know. Again sometimes when I am writing, the music of the words I am trying to shape takes me far beyond the words, I am aware of a rhythm, a dance, a fury, which is as yet empty of words.

In these observations, I have said little about headaches, midnight oil, pints of beer or of claret, love affairs, and so on, which are supposed to be stations on the journeys of poets through life. There is no doubt that writing poetry, when a poem appears to succeed, results in an intense physical excitement, a sense of release and ecstasy. On the other hand, I dread writing poetry, for, I suppose, the following reasons: a poem is a terrible journey, a painful effort of concentrating the imagination; words are an extremely difficult medium to use, and sometimes when one has spent days trying to say a thing clearly one finds that one has only said it dully; above all, the writing of a poem brings one face to face with one's own personality with all its familiar and clumsy limitations. In every other phase of existence, one can exercise the orthodoxy of a conventional routine: one can be polite to one's friends, one can get through the day at the office, one can pose, one can draw attention to one's position in society, one is—in a word—dealing with men. In poetry, one is wrestling with a god.

Usually, when I have completed a poem, I think "this is my best poem," and I wish to publish it at once. This is partly because I only write when I have something new to say, which seems more worth while than what I have said before, partly because optimism about my present and future makes me despise my past. A few days after I have finished a poem, I relegate it to the past of all my other wasted efforts, all the books I do not wish to open.

Perhaps the greatest pleasure I have got from poems that I have written is when I have heard some lines quoted which I have not at once recognized. And I have thought "how good and how interesting," before I have realized that they are my own.

In common with other creative writers I pretend that I am not, and I am, exceedingly affected by unsympathetic criticism, whilst praise usually makes me suspect that the reviewer does not know what he is talking about. Why are writers so sensitive to criticism? Partly, because it is their business to be sensitive, and they are sensitive about this as about other things. Partly, because every serious creative writer is really in his heart concerned with reputation and not with success (the most successful writer I have known, Sir Hugh Walpole, was far and away the most unhappy about his reputation, because the "highbrows" did not like him). Again, I suspect that every writer is secretly writing for *someone*, probably for a parent or teacher who did not believe in him in childhood. The critic who refuses to "understand" immediately becomes identified with this person, and the understanding of many admirers only adds to the writer's secret bitterness if this one refusal persists.

Gradually one realizes that there is always this someone who will not like one's work. Then, perhaps, literature becomes a humble exercise of faith in being all that one can be in one's art, of being more than oneself, expecting little, but with a faith in the mystery of poetry which gradually expands into a faith in the mysterious service of truth.

Yet what failures there are! And how much mud sticks to one; mud not thrown by other people but acquired in the course of earning one's living, answering or not answering the letters which one receives, supporting or not supporting public causes. All one can hope is that this mud is composed of little grains of sand which will produce pearls.

2. FORM

ARISTOTLE: Poetics*

I PROPOSE to treat of Poetry in itself and of its various kinds, noting the essential quality of each; to inquire into the structure of the plot as requisite to a good poem; into the number and nature of the parts of which a poem is composed; and similarly into whatever else falls within the same inquiry. Following, then, the order of nature, let us begin with the principles which come first.

2. Epic poetry and Tragedy, Comedy also and Dithyrambic poetry, and the music of the flute and of the lyre in most of their forms, are all in their general conception modes of imitation. 3. They differ, however, from one another in three respects,—the medium, the objects, the manner or mode of imitation, being in each case distinct.

4. For as there are persons who, by conscious art or mere habit, imitate and represent various objects through the medium of colour and form, or again by the voice; so in the arts above mentioned, taken as a whole, the imitation is produced by rhythm, language, or "harmony," either singly or combined.

Thus in the music of the flute and of the lyre, "harmony" and rhythm alone are employed; also in other arts, such as that of the shepherd's pipe, which are essentially similar to these. 5. In dancing, rhythm alone is used without "harmony"; for even dancing imitates character, emotion, and action, by rhythmical movement. 6. There is another art which imitates by means of language alone, and that either in prose or verse—which verse, again, may either combine different metres or consist of but one kind —but this has hitherto been without a name. 7. For there is no common term we could apply to the mimes of Sophron and Xenarchus and the Socratic dialogues on the one hand; and, on the other, to poetic imitations in iambic, elegiac, or any similar metre. People do, indeed, add the word "maker" or "poet" to the name of the metre, and speak of elegiac poets, or epic (that is, hexameter) poets, as if it were not the imitation that makes the poet, but the verse that entitles them all indiscriminately to the name. 8. Even when a treatise on medicine or natural science is brought out in verse, the name of poet is by custom given to the author; and yet Homer and Empedocles have nothing in common but the metre, so that it would be right to call the one poet, the other physicist rather than poet. 9. On the same principle, even if a writer in his poetic imitation were to combine all metres, as Chaeremon did in his Centaur, which is a medley composed of metres of all kinds, we should bring him too under the general term poet. So much then for these distinctions.

10. There are, again, some arts which employ all the means above mentioned,—namely, rhythm, tune and metre. Such are Dithyrambic and Nomic poetry, and also Tragedy and Comedy; but between them the difference is, that in the first two cases these means are all employed in combination, in the latter, now one means is employed, now another.

Such, then, are the differences of the arts with respect to the medium of imitation.

2

Since the objects of imitation are men in action, and these men must be either of a higher or a lower type (for moral character mainly answers to these divisions, goodness and badness

* The *Poetics* was composed between 335 and 322 B.C., the year of Aristotle's death. The present translation is the corrected version of the 4th edition (1911) by S. H. Butcher, and is reprinted here by permission of The Macmillan Company, publishers, from S. H. Butcher's *Aristotle's Theory of Poetry and Fine Art* (1932).

being the distinguishing marks of moral differences), it follows that we must represent men either as better than in real life, or as worse, or as they are. It is the same in painting. Polygnotus depicted men as nobler than they are, Pauson as less noble, Dionysius drew them true to life.

2. Now it is evident that each of the modes of imitation above mentioned will exhibit these differences, and become a distinct kind in imitating objects that are thus distinct. 3. Such diversities may be found even in dancing, flute-playing, and lyre-playing. So again in language, whether prose or verse unaccompanied by music. Homer, for example, makes men better than they are; Cleophon as they are; Hegemon the Thasian, the inventor of parodies, and Nicochares, the author of the Deiliad, worse than they are. 4. The same thing holds good of Dithyrambs and Nomes; here too one may portray different types, as Timotheus and Philoxenus differed in representing their Cyclopes. The same distinction marks off Tragedy from Comedy; for Comedy aims at representing men as worse, Tragedy as better than in actual life.

3

There is still a third difference—the manner in which each of these objects may be imitated. For the medium being the same, and the objects the same, the poet may imitate by narration—in which case he can either take another personality as Homer does, or speak in his own person, unchanged—or he may present all his characters as living and moving before us.

2. These, then, as we said at the beginning, are the three differences which distinguish artistic imitation—the medium, the objects and the manner. So that from one point of view, Sophocles is an imitator of the same kind as Homer—for both imitate higher types of character; from another point of view, of the same kind as Aristophanes—for both imitate persons acting and doing. 3. Hence, some say, the name of "drama" is given to such poems, as representing action. For the same reason the Dorians claim the invention both of Tragedy and Comedy. The claim to Comedy is put forward by the Megarians,—not only by those of Greece proper, who allege that it originated under their democracy, but also by the Megarians of Sicily, for the poet Epicharmus, who is much earlier than Chionides and Magnes, belonged to that country. Tragedy too is claimed by certain Dorians of the Peloponnese. In each case they appeal to the evidence of language. The outlying villages, they say, are by them called κῶμαι, by the Athenians δῆμοι: and they assume that Comedians were so named not from κωμάζειν, "to revel," but because they wandered from village to village (κατὰ κώμας), being excluded contemptuously from the city. They add also that the Dorian word for "doing" is δρᾶν, and the Athenian, πράττειν.

4. This may suffice as to the number and nature of the various modes of imitation.

4

Poetry in general seems to have sprung from two causes, each of them lying deep in our nature. 2. First, the instinct of imitation is implanted in man from childhood, one difference between him and other animals being that he is the most imitative of living creatures, and through imitation he learns his earliest lessons; and no less universal is the pleasure felt in things imitated. 3. We have evidence of this in the facts of experience. Objects which in themselves we view with pain, we delight to contemplate when reproduced with minute fidelity: such as the forms of the most ignoble animals and of dead bodies. 4. The cause of this again is, that to learn gives the liveliest pleasure, not only to philosophers but to men in general; whose capacity, however, of learning is more limited. 5. Thus the reason why men enjoy seeing a likeness is, that in contemplating it they find themselves learning or inferring, and saying perhaps, "Ah, that is he." For if you happen not to have seen the original, the pleasure will be due not to the imitation as such, but to the execution, the colouring, or some such other cause.

6. Imitation, then, is one instinct of our nature. Next, there is the instinct for "harmony" and rhythm, metres being manifestly sections of rhythm. Persons, therefore, starting with this natural gift developed by degrees their special aptitudes, till their rude improvisations gave birth to Poetry.

7. Poetry now diverged in two directions, according to the individual character of the writers. The graver spirits imitated noble actions, and the actions of good men. The more trivial sort imitated the actions of meaner persons, at first composing satires, as the former did hymns to the gods and the praises of famous men. 8. A poem of the satirical kind cannot indeed be put down to any author earlier than Homer; though many such writers probably there were. But from Homer onward, instances can be cited,—his own Margites, for example, and other similar compositions. The appropriate metre was also here introduced; hence the measure is still called the iambic or lampooning measure, being that in which people lampooned one another. 9. Thus the older poets were distinguished as writers of heroic or of lampooning verse.

As, in the serious style, Homer is pre-eminent among poets, for he alone combined dramatic form with excellence of imitation, so he too first laid down the main lines of Comedy, by dramatising the ludicrous instead of writing personal satire. His Margites bears the same relation to Comedy that the Iliad and Odyssey do to Tragedy. 10. But when Tragedy and Comedy came to light, the two classes of poets still followed their natural bent: the lampooners became writers of Comedy, and the Epic poets were succeeded by Tragedians, since the drama was a larger and higher form of art.

11. Whether Tragedy has as yet perfected its proper types or not; and whether it is to be judged in itself, or in relation also to the audience,—this raises another question. 12. Be that as it may, Tragedy—as also Comedy—was at first mere improvisation. The one originated with the authors of the Dithyramb, the other with those of the phallic songs, which are still in use in many of our cities. Tragedy advanced by slow degrees; each new element that showed itself was in turn developed. Having passed through many changes, it found its natural form, and there it stopped.

13. Aeschylus first introduced a second actor; he diminished the importance of the Chorus, and assigned the leading part to the dialogue. Sophocles raised the number of actors to three, and added scene-painting. 14. Moreover, it was not till late that the short plot was discarded for one of greater compass, and the grotesque diction of the earlier satyric form for the stately manner of Tragedy. The iambic measure then replaced the trochaic tetrameter, which was originally employed when the poetry was of the satyric order, and had greater affinities with dancing. Once dialogue had come in, Nature herself discovered the appropriate measure. For the iambic is, of all measures, the most colloquial: we see it in the fact that conversational speech runs into iambic form more frequently than into any other kind of verse; rarely into hexameters, and only when we drop the colloquial intonation. 15. The additions to the number of "episodes" or acts, and the other accessories of which tradition tells, must be taken as already described; for to discuss them in detail would, doubtless, be a large undertaking.

5

Comedy is, as we have said, an imitation of characters of a lower type—not, however, in the full sense of the word bad, the Ludicrous being merely a subdivision of the ugly. It consists in some defect or ugliness which is not painful or destructive. To take an obvious example, the comic mask is ugly and distorted, but does not imply pain.

2. The successive changes through which Tragedy passed, and the authors of these changes, are well known, whereas Comedy has had no history, because it was not at first treated seriously. It was late before the Archon granted a comic chorus to a poet; the performers were till then voluntary. Comedy had already taken definite shape when comic poets, distinctively so called, are heard of. 3. Who introduced masks, or prologues, or increased the number of actors,—these and other similar details remain unknown. As for the plot, it came originally from Sicily; but of Athenian writers Crates was the first who, abandoning the "iambic" or lampooning form, generalised his themes and plots.

4. Epic poetry agrees with Tragedy in so far as it is an imitation in verse of characters of a higher type. They differ, in that Epic poetry admits but one kind of metre, and is narrative in form. They differ, again, in their length: for Tragedy endeavours, as far as possible, to confine itself to a single revolution of the sun, or

but slightly to exceed this limit; whereas the Epic action has no limits of time. This, then, is a second point of difference; though at first the same freedom was admitted in Tragedy as in Epic poetry.

5. Of their constituent parts some are common to both, some peculiar to Tragedy. Whoever, therefore, knows what is good or bad Tragedy, knows also about Epic poetry. All the elements of an Epic poem are found in Tragedy, but the elements of a Tragedy are not all found in the Epic poem.

6

Of the poetry which imitates in hexameter verse, and of Comedy, we will speak hereafter. Let us now discuss Tragedy, resuming its formal definition, as resulting from what has been already said.

2. Tragedy, then, is an imitation of an action that is serious, complete, and of a certain magnitude; in language embellished with each kind of artistic ornament, the several kinds being found in separate parts of the play; in the form of action, not of narrative; through pity and fear effecting the proper purgation of these emotions. 3. By "language embellished," I mean language into which rhythm, "harmony," and song enter. By "the several kinds in separate parts," I mean, that some parts are rendered through the medium of verse alone, others again with the aid of song.

4. Now as tragic imitation implies persons acting, it necessarily follows, in the first place, that Spectacular equipment will be a part of Tragedy. Next, Song and Diction, for these are the medium of imitation. By "Diction" I mean the mere metrical arrangement of the words: as for "Song," it is a term whose sense every one understands.

5. Again, Tragedy is the imitation of an action; and an action implies personal agents, who necessarily possess certain distinctive qualities both of character and thought; for it is by these that we qualify actions themselves, and these—thought and character—are the two natural causes from which actions spring, and on actions again all success or failure depends. 6. Hence, the Plot is the imitation of the action:—for by plot I here mean the arrangement of the incidents. By Character I mean that in virtue of which we ascribe certain qualities to the agents. Thought is required wherever a statement is proved, or, it may be, a general truth enunciated. 7. Every Tragedy, therefore, must have six parts, which parts determine its quality—namely, Plot, Character, Diction, Thought, Spectacle, Song. Two of the parts constitute the medium of imitation, one the manner, and three the objects of imitation. And these complete the list. 8. These elements have been employed, we may say, by the poets to a man; in fact, every play contains Spectacular elements as well as Character, Plot, Diction, Song, and Thought.

9. But most important of all is the structure of the incidents. For Tragedy is an imitation, not of men, but of an action and of life, and life consists in action, and its end is a mode of action, not a quality. 10. Now character determines men's qualities, but it is by their actions that they are happy or the reverse. Dramatic action, therefore, is not with a view to the representation of character: character comes in as subsidiary to the actions. Hence the incidents and the plot are the end of a tragedy; and the end is the chief thing of all. 11. Again, without action there cannot be a tragedy; there may be without character. The tragedies of most of our modern poets fail in the rendering of character; and of poets in general this is often true. It is the same in painting; and here lies the difference between Zeuxis and Polygnotus. Polygnotus delineates character well: the style of Zeuxis is devoid of ethical quality. 12. Again, if you string together a set of speeches expressive of character, and well finished in point of diction and thought, you will not produce the essential tragic effect nearly so well as with a play which, however deficient in these respects, yet has a plot and artistically constructed incidents. 13. Besides which, the most powerful elements of emotional interest in Tragedy—Peripeteia or Reversal of the situation, and Recognition scenes—are parts of the plot. 14. A further proof is, that novices in the art attain to finish of diction and precision of portraiture before they can construct the plot. It is the same with almost all the early poets.

The Plot, then, is the first principle, and, as it were, the soul of a tragedy: Character holds the second place. 15. A similar fact is seen in painting. The most beautiful colours, laid on confusedly, will not give as much pleasure as the chalk outline of a portrait. Thus Tragedy is the imitation of an action, and of the agents mainly with a view to the action.

16. Third in order is Thought,—that is, the faculty of saying what is possible and pertinent in given circumstances. In the case of oratory, this is the function of the political art and of the art of rhetoric: and so indeed the older poets make their characters speak the language of civic life; the poets of our time, the language of the rhetoricians.

17. Character is that which reveals moral purpose, showing what kind of things a man chooses or avoids. Speeches, therefore, which do not make this manifest, or in which the speaker does not choose or avoid anything whatever, are not expressive of character. Thought, on the other hand, is found where something is proved to be or not to be, or a general maxim is enunciated.

18. Fourth among the elements enumerated comes Diction; by which I mean, as has been already said, the expression of the meaning in words; and its essence is the same both in verse and prose.

19. Of the remaining elements Song holds the chief place among the embellishments.

The Spectacle has, indeed, an emotional attraction of its own, but, of all the parts, it is the least artistic, and connected least with the art of poetry. For the power of Tragedy, we may be sure, is felt even apart from representation and actors. Besides, the production of spectacular effects depends more on the art of the stage machinist than on that of the poet.

7

These principles being established, let us now discuss the proper structure of the Plot, since this is the first and most important thing in Tragedy.

2. Now, according to our definition, Tragedy is an imitation of an action that is complete, and whole, and of a certain magnitude; for there may be a whole that is wanting in magnitude. 3. A whole is that which has a beginning, a middle, and an end. A beginning is that which does not itself follow anything by causal necessity, but after which something naturally is or comes to be. An end, on the contrary, is that which itself naturally follows some other thing, either by necessity, or as a rule, but has nothing following it. A middle is that which follows something as some other thing follows it. A well constructed plot, therefore, must neither begin nor end at haphazard, but conform to these principles.

4. Again, a beautiful object, whether it be a picture of a living organism or any whole composed of parts, must not only have an orderly arrangement of parts, but must also be of a certain magnitude; for beauty depends on magnitude and order. Hence an exceedingly small picture cannot be beautiful; for the view of it is confused, the object being seen in an almost imperceptible moment of time. Nor, again, can one of vast size be beautiful; for as the eye cannot take it all in at once, the unity and sense of the whole is lost for the spectator; as for instance if there were one a thousand miles long. 5. As, therefore, in the case of animate bodies and organisms a certain magnitude is necessary, and a magnitude which may be easily embraced in one view; so in the plot, a certain length is necessary, and a length which can be easily embraced by the memory. 6. The limit of length in relation to dramatic competition and sensuous presentment, is no part of artistic theory. For had it been the rule for a hundred tragedies to compete together, the performance would have been regulated by the water-clock,—as indeed we are told was formerly done. 7. But the limit as fixed by the nature of the drama itself is this: —the greater the length, the more beautiful will the piece be by reason of its size, provided that the whole be perspicuous. And to define the matter roughly, we may say that the proper magnitude is comprised within such limits, that the sequence of events, according to the law of probability or necessity, will admit of a change from bad fortune to good, or from good fortune to bad.

8

Unity of plot does not, as some persons think, consist in the unity of the hero. For infinitely various are the incidents in one man's life, which cannot be reduced to unity; and so, too, there are many actions of one man out of which we cannot make one action. 2. Hence the error, as it appears, of all poets who have composed a Heracleid, a Theseid, or other poems of the kind. They imagine that as Heracles was one man, the story of Heracles must also be a unity. 3. But Homer, as in all else he is of surpassing merit, here too—whether from art or natural genius—seems to have happily discerned the truth. In composing the Odyssey he did not include all the adventures of Odysseus—such as his wound on Parnassus, or his feigned madness at the mustering of the host—incidents between which there was no necessary or probable connexion: but he made the Odyssey, and likewise the Iliad, to centre round an action that in our sense of the word is one. 4. As therefore, in the other imitative arts, the imitation is one when the object imitated is one, so the plot, being an imitation of an action, must imitate one action and that a whole, the structural union of the parts being such that, if any one of them is displaced or removed, the whole will be disjointed and disturbed. For a thing whose presence or absence makes no visible difference, is not an organic part of the whole.

9

It is, moreover, evident from what has been said, that it is not the function of the poet to relate what has happened, but what may happen,—what is possible according to the law of probability or necessity. 2. The poet and the historian differ not by writing in verse or in prose. The work of Herodotus might be put into verse, and it would still be a species of history, with metre no less than without it. The true difference is that one relates what has happened, the other what may happen. 3. Poetry, therefore, is a more philosophical and a higher thing than history: for poetry tends to express the universal, history the particular. 4. By the universal I mean how a person of a certain type will on occasion speak or act, according to the law of probability or necessity; and it is this universality at which poetry aims in the names she attaches to the personages. The particular is —for example—what Alcibiades did or suffered. 5. In Comedy this is already apparent: for here the poet first constructs the plot on the lines of probability, and then inserts characteristic names;—unlike the lampooners who write about particular individuals. 6. But tragedians still keep to real names, the reason being that what is possible is credible: what has not happened we do not at once feel sure to be possible: but what has happened is manifestly possible: otherwise it would not have happened. 7. Still there are some tragedies in which there are only one or two well known names, the rest being fictitious. In others, none are well known,—as in Agathon's Antheus, where incidents and names alike are fictitious, and yet they give none the less pleasure. 8. We must not, therefore, at all costs keep to the received legends, which are the usual subjects of Tragedy. Indeed, it would be absurd to attempt it; for even subjects that are known are known only to a few, and yet give pleasure to all. 9. It clearly follows that the poet or "maker" should be the maker of plots rather than of verses; since he is a poet because he imitates, and what he imitates are actions. And even if he chances to take an historical subject, he is none the less a poet; for there is no reason why some events that have actually happened should not conform to the law of the probable and possible, and in virtue of that quality in them he is their poet or maker.

10. Of all plots and actions the epeisodic are the worst. I call a plot "epeisodic" in which the episodes or acts succeed one another without probable or necessary sequence. Bad poets compose such pieces by their own fault, good poets, to please the players; for, as they write show pieces for competition, they stretch the plot beyond its capacity, and are often forced to break the natural continuity.

11. But again, Tragedy is an imitation not only of a complete action, but of events inspiring fear or pity. Such an effect is best produced when the events come on us by surprise; and the effect is heightened when, at the same time, they follow as cause and effect. 12. The tragic wonder will then be greater than if they happened of themselves or by accident; for even coincidences are most striking when they have an air of design. We may instance the statue of Mitys at Argos, which fell upon his murderer while he was a spectator at a festival, and killed him. Such events seem not to be due to mere

chance. Plots, therefore, constructed on these principles are necessarily the best.

10

Plots are either Simple or Complex, for the actions in real life, of which the plots are an imitation, obviously show a similar distinction. 2. An action which is one and continuous in the sense above defined, I call Simple, when the change of fortune takes place without Reversal of the Situation and without Recognition.

A Complex action is one in which the change is accompanied by such Reversal, or by Recognition, or by both. 3. These last should arise from the internal structure of the plot, so that what follows should be the necessary or probable result of the preceding action. It makes all the difference whether any given event is a case of *propter hoc* or *post hoc*.[1]

11

Reversal of the Situation is a change by which the action veers round to its opposite, subject always to our rule of probability or necessity. Thus in the Oedipus, the messenger comes to cheer Oedipus and free him from his alarms about his mother, but by revealing who he is, he produces the opposite effect. Again in the Lynceus, Lynceus is being led away to his death, and Danaus goes with him, meaning to slay him; but the outcome of the action is, that Danaus is killed and Lynceus saved.

2. Recognition, as the name indicates, is a change from ignorance to knowledge, producing love or hate between the persons destined by the poet for good or bad fortune. The best form of recognition is coincident with a Reversal of the Situation, as in the Oedipus. 3. There are indeed other forms. Even inanimate things of the most trivial kind may sometimes be objects of recognition. Again, we may recognise or discover whether a person has done a thing or not. But the recognition which is most intimately connected with the plot and action is, as we have said, the recognition of persons. 4. This recognition, combined with Reversal, will produce either pity or fear; and actions producing these effects are those which, by our definition, Tragedy represents. Moreover, it is upon such situations that the issues of good or bad fortune will depend. 5. Recognition, then, being between persons, it may happen that one person only is recognised by the other—when the latter is already known—or it may be necessary that the recognition should be on both sides. Thus Iphigenia is revealed to Orestes by the sending of the letter; but another act of recognition is required to make Orestes known to Iphigenia.

6. Two parts, then, of the Plot—Reversal of the Situation and Recognition—turn upon surprises. A third part is the Scene of Suffering. The Scene of Suffering is a destructive or painful action, such as death on the stage, bodily agony, wounds, and the like.

12

[The parts of Tragedy which must be treated as elements of the whole, have been already mentioned. We now come to the quantitative parts—the separate parts into which Tragedy is divided—namely, Prologue, Episode, Exode, Choric song; this last being divided into Parode and Stasimon. These are common to all plays: peculiar to some are the songs of actors from the stage and the Commoi.

2. The Prologue is that entire part of a tragedy which precedes the Parode of the Chorus. The Episode is that entire part of a tragedy which is between complete choric songs. The Exode is that entire part of a tragedy which has no choric song after it. Of the Choric part the Parode is the first undivided utterance of the Chorus: the Stasimon is a Choric ode without anapaests or trochaic tetrameters: the Commos is a joint lamentation of Chorus and actors. 3. The parts of Tragedy which must be treated as elements of the whole have been already mentioned. The quantitative parts—the separate parts into which it is divided—are here enumerated.]

13

As the sequel to what has already been said, we must proceed to consider what the poet should aim at, and what he should avoid, in constructing his plots; and by what means the specific effect of Tragedy will be produced.

[1] ["because of this" or "after this."]

2. A perfect tragedy should, as we have seen, be arranged not on the simple but on the complex plan. It should, moreover, imitate actions which excite pity and fear, this being the distinctive mark of tragic imitation. It follows plainly, in the first place, that the change of fortune presented must not be the spectacle of a virtuous man brought from prosperity to adversity: for this moves neither pity nor fear; it merely shocks us. Nor, again, that of a bad man passing from adversity to prosperity: for nothing can be more alien to the spirit of Tragedy; it possesses no single tragic quality; it neither satisfies the moral sense, nor calls forth pity or fear. Nor, again, should the downfall of the utter villain be exhibited. A plot of this kind would, doubtless, satisfy the moral sense, but it would inspire neither pity nor fear; for pity is aroused by unmerited misfortune, fear by the misfortune of a man like ourselves. Such an event, therefore, will be neither pitiful nor terrible. 3. There remains, then, the character between these two extremes,—that of a man who is not eminently good and just, yet whose misfortune is brought about not by vice or depravity, but by some error or frailty. He must be one who is highly renowned and prosperous, —a personage like Oedipus, Thyestes, or other illustrious men of such families.

4. A well constructed plot should, therefore, be single in its issue, rather than double as some maintain. The change of fortune should be not from bad to good, but, reversely, from good to bad. It should come about as the result not of vice, but of some great error or frailty, in a character either such as we have described, or better rather than worse. 5. The practice of the stage bears out our view. At first the poets recounted any legend that came in their way. Now, the best tragedies are founded on the story of a few houses,—on the fortunes of Alcmaeon, Oedipus, Orestes, Meleager, Thyestes, Telephus, and those others who have done or suffered something terrible. A tragedy, then, to be perfect according to the rules of art should be of this construction. 6. Hence they are in error who censure Euripides just because he follows this principle in his plays, many of which end unhappily. It is, as we have said, the right ending. The best proof is that on the stage and in dramatic competition, such plays, if well worked out, are the most tragic in effect; and Euripides, faulty though he may be in the general management of his subject, yet is felt to be the most tragic of the poets.

7. In the second rank comes the kind of tragedy which some place first. Like the Odyssey, it has a double thread of plot, and also an opposite catastrophe for the good and for the bad. It is accounted the best because of the weakness of the spectators; for the poet is guided in what he writes by the wishes of his audience. 8. The pleasure, however, thence derived is not the true tragic pleasure. It is proper rather to Comedy, where those who, in the piece, are the deadliest enemies—like Orestes and Aegisthus—quit the stage as friends at the close, and no one slays or is slain.

14

Fear and pity may be aroused by spectacular means; but they may also result from the inner structure of the piece, which is the better way, and indicates a superior poet. For the plot ought to be so constructed that, even without the aid of the eye, he who hears the tale told will thrill with horror and melt to pity at what takes place. This is the impression we should receive from hearing the story of the Oedipus. 2. But to produce this effect by the mere spectacle is a less artistic method, and dependent on extraneous aids. Those who employ spectacular means to create a sense not of the terrible but only of the monstrous, are strangers to the purpose of Tragedy; for we must not demand of Tragedy any and every kind of pleasure, but only that which is proper to it. 3. And since the pleasure which the poet should afford is that which comes from pity and fear through imitation, it is evident that this quality must be impressed upon the incidents.

Let us then determine what are the circumstances which strike us as terrible or pitiful.

4. Actions capable of this effect must happen between persons who are either friends or enemies or indifferent to one another. If an enemy kills an enemy, there is nothing to excite pity either in the act or the intention,—except so far as the suffering in itself is pitiful. So again with indifferent persons. But when the

tragic incident occurs between those who are near or dear to one another—if, for example, a brother kills, or intends to kill, a brother, a son his father, a mother her son, a son his mother, or any other deed of the kind is done—these are the situations to be looked for by the poet. 5. He may not indeed destroy the framework of the received legends—the fact, for instance, that Clytemnestra was slain by Orestes and Eriphyle by Alcmaeon—but he ought to show invention of his own, and skilfully handle the traditional material. Let us explain more clearly what is meant by skilful handling.

6. The action may be done consciously and with knowledge of the persons, in the manner of the older poets. It is thus too that Euripides makes Medea slay her children. Or, again, the deed of horror may be done, but done in ignorance, and the tie of kinship or friendship be discovered afterwards. The Oedipus of Sophocles is an example. Here, indeed, the incident is outside the drama proper; but cases occur where it falls within the action of the play: one may cite the Alcmaeon of Astydamas, or Telegonus in the Wounded Odysseus. 7. Again, there is a third case,—<to be about to act with knowledge of the persons and then not to act. The fourth case is> when some one is about to do an irreparable deed through ignorance, and makes the discovery before it is done. These are the only possible ways. For the deed must either be done or not done,—and that wittingly or unwittingly. But of all these ways, to be about to act knowing the persons, and then not to act, is the worst. It is shocking without being tragic, for no disaster follows. It is, therefore, never, or very rarely, found in poetry. One instance, however, is in the Antigone, where Haemon threatens to kill Creon. 8. The next and better way is that the deed should be perpetrated. Still better, that it should be perpetrated in ignorance, and the discovery made afterwards. There is then nothing to shock us, while the discovery produces a startling effect. 9. The last case is the best, as when in the Cresphontes Merope is about to slay her son, but, recognising who he is, spares his life. So in the Iphigenia, the sister recognises the brother just in time. Again in the Helle, the son recognises the mother when on the point of giving her up. This, then, is why a few families only, as has been already observed, furnish the subjects of tragedy. It was not art, but happy chance, that led poets to look for such situations and so impress the tragic quality upon their plots. They are compelled, therefore, to have recourse to those houses whose history contains moving incidents like these.

Enough has now been said concerning the structure of the incidents, and the proper constitution of the plot.

15

In respect of Character there are four things to be aimed at. First, and most important, it must be good. Now any speech or action that manifests moral purpose of any kind will be expressive of character: the character will be good if the purpose is good. This rule is relative to each class. Even a woman may be good, and also a slave; though the woman may be said to be an inferior being, and the slave quite worthless. 2. The second thing to aim at is propriety. There is a type of manly valour; but valour in a woman, or unscrupulous cleverness, is inappropriate. 3. Thirdly, character must be true to life: for this is a distinct thing from goodness and propriety, as here described. 4. The fourth point is consistency: for though the subject of the imitation, who suggested the type, be inconsistent, still he must be consistently inconsistent. 5. As an example of motiveless degradation of character, we have Menelaus in the Orestes: of character indecorous and inappropriate, the lament of Odysseus in the Scylla, and the speech of Melanippe: of inconsistency, the Iphigenia at Aulis,—for Iphigenia the suppliant in no way resembles her later self.

6. As in the structure of the plot, so too in the portraiture of character, the poet should always aim either at the necessary or the probable. Thus a person of a given character should speak or act in a given way, by the rule either of necessity or of probability; just as this event should follow that by necessary or probable sequence. 7. It is therefore evident that the unravelling of the plot, no less than the complication, must arise out of the plot itself, it must not be brought about by the *Deus ex Machina*—as in the Medea, or in the Return of the Greeks

in the Iliad. The *Deus ex Machina* should be employed only for events external to the drama,—for antecedent or subsequent events, which lie beyond the range of human knowledge, and which require to be reported or foretold; for to the gods we ascribe the power of seeing all things. Within the action there must be nothing irrational. If the irrational cannot be excluded, it should be outside the scope of the tragedy. Such is the irrational element in the Oedipus of Sophocles.

8. Again, since Tragedy is an imitation of persons who are above the common level, the example of good portrait-painters should be followed. They, while reproducing the distinctive form of the original, make a likeness which is true to life and yet more beautiful. So too the poet, in representing men who are irascible or indolent, or have other defects of character, should preserve the type and yet ennoble it. In this way Achilles is portrayed by Agathon and Homer.

9. These then are rules the poet should observe. Nor should he neglect those appeals to the senses, which, though not among the essentials, are the concomitants of poetry; for here too there is much room for error. But of this enough has been said in our published treatises.

16

What Recognition is has been already explained. We will now enumerate its kinds.

First, the least artistic form, which, from poverty of wit, is most commonly employed—recognition by signs. 2. Of these some are congenital,—such as "the spear which the earth-born race bear on their bodies," or the stars introduced by Carcinus in his Thyestes. Others are acquired after birth; and of these some are bodily marks, as scars; some external tokens, as necklaces, or the little ark in the Tyro by which the discovery is effected. 3. Even these admit of more or less skilful treatment. Thus in the recognition of Odysseus by his scar, the discovery is made in one way by the nurse, in another by the swineherds. The use of tokens for the express purpose of proof—and, indeed, any formal proof with or without tokens—is a less artistic mode of recognition. A better kind is that which comes about by a turn of incident, as in the Bath Scene in the Odyssey.

4. Next come the recognitions invented at will by the poet, and on that account wanting in art. For example, Orestes in the Iphigenia reveals the fact that he is Orestes. She, indeed, makes herself known by the letter; but he, by speaking himself, and saying what the poet, not what the plot requires. This, therefore, is nearly allied to the fault above mentioned:—for Orestes might as well have brought tokens with him. Another similar instance is the "voice of the shuttle" in the Tereus of Sophocles.

5. The third kind depends on memory when the sight of some object awakens a feeling: as in the Cyprians of Dicaeogenes, where the hero breaks into tears on seeing the picture; or again in the "Lay of Alcinous," where Odysseus, hearing the minstrel play the lyre, recalls the past and weeps; and hence the recognition.

6. The fourth kind is by process of reasoning. Thus in the Choëphori:—"Some one resembling me has come: no one resembles me but Orestes: therefore Orestes has come." Such too is the discovery made by Iphigenia in the play of Polyidus the Sophist. It was a natural reflexion for Orestes to make, "So I too must die at the altar like my sister." So, again, in the Tydeus of Theodectes, the father says, "I came to find my son, and I lose my own life." So too in the Phineidae: the women, on seeing the place, inferred their fate:—"Here we are doomed to die, for here we were cast forth." 7. Again, there is a composite kind of recognition involving false inference on the part of one of the characters, as in the Odysseus Disguised as a Messenger. A said <that no one else was able to bend the bow; . . . hence B (the disguised Odysseus) imagined that A would> recognise the bow which, in fact, he had not seen; and to bring about a recognition by this means—the expectation that A would recognise the bow—is false inference.

8. But, of all recognitions, the best is that which arises from the incidents themselves, where the startling discovery is made by natural means. Such is that in the Oedipus of Sophocles, and in the Iphigenia; for it was natural that Iphigenia should wish to dispatch a letter. These recognitions alone dispense with the artificial

aid of tokens or amulets. Next come the recognitions by process of reasoning.

17

In constructing the plot and working it out with the proper diction, the poet should place the scene, as far as possible, before his eyes. In this way, seeing everything with the utmost vividness, as if he were a spectator of the action, he will discover what is in keeping with it, and be most unlikely to overlook inconsistencies. The need of such a rule is shown by the fault found in Carcinus. Amphiaraus was on his way from the temple. This fact escaped the observation of one who did not see the situation. On the stage, however, the piece failed, the audience being offended at the oversight.

2. Again, the poet should work out his play, to the best of his power, with appropriate gestures; for those who feel emotion are most convincing through natural sympathy with the characters they represent; and one who is agitated storms, one who is angry rages, with the most life-like reality. Hence poetry implies either a happy gift of nature or a strain of madness. In the one case a man can take the mould of any character; in the other, he is lifted out of his proper self.

3. As for the story, whether the poet takes it ready made or constructs it for himself, he should first sketch its general outline, and then fill in the episodes and amplify in detail. The general plan may be illustrated by the Iphigenia. A young girl is sacrificed; she disappears mysteriously from the eyes of those who sacrificed her; she is transported to another country, where the custom is to offer up all strangers to the goddess. To this ministry she is appointed. Some time later her own brother chances to arrive. The fact that the oracle for some reason ordered him to go there, is outside the general plan of the play. The purpose, again, of his coming is outside the action proper. However, he comes, he is seized, and, when on the point of being sacrificed, reveals who he is. The mode of recognition may be either that of Euripides or of Polyidus, in whose play he exclaims very naturally:—"So it was not my sister only, but I too, who was doomed to be sacrificed"; and by that remark he is saved.

4. After this, the names being once given, it remains to fill in the episodes. We must see that they are relevant to the action. In the case of Orestes, for example, there is the madness which led to his capture, and his deliverance by means of the purificatory rite. 5. In the drama, the episodes are short, but it is these that give extension to Epic poetry. Thus the story of the Odyssey can be stated briefly. A certain man is absent from home for many years; he is jealously watched by Poseidon, and left desolate. Meanwhile his home is in a wretched plight—suitors are wasting his substance and plotting against his son. At length, tempest-tost, he himself arrives; he makes certain persons acquainted with him; he attacks the suitors with his own hand, and is himself preserved while he destroys them. This is the essence of the plot; the rest is episode.

18

Every tragedy falls into two parts,—Complication and Unravelling or *Dénouement.* Incidents extraneous to the action are frequently combined with a portion of the action proper, to form the Complication; the rest is the Unravelling. By the Complication I mean all that extends from the beginning of the action to the part which marks the turning-point to good or bad fortune. The Unravelling is that which extends from the beginning of the change to the end. Thus, in the Lynceus of Theodectes, the Complication consists of the incidents presupposed in the drama, the seizure of the child, and then again * * <The Unravelling> extends from the accusation of murder to the end.

2. There are four kinds of Tragedy, the Complex, depending entirely on Reversal of the Situation and Recognition; the Pathetic (where the motive is passion),—such as the tragedies on Ajax and Ixion; the Ethical (where the motives are ethical),—such as the Phthiotides and the Peleus. The fourth kind is the Simple. <We here exclude the purely spectacular element>, exemplified by the Phorcides, the Prometheus, and scenes laid in Hades. 3. The poet should endeavour, if possible, to combine all poetic elements; or failing that, the greatest number and those the most important; the more so, in face of the cavilling criticism of the day. For whereas there have hitherto been good poets,

each in his own branch, the critics now expect one man to surpass all others in their several lines of excellence.

In speaking of a tragedy as the same or different, the best test to take is the plot. Identity exists where the Complication and Unravelling are the same. Many poets tie the knot well, but unravel it ill. Both arts, however, should always be mastered.

4. Again, the poet should remember what has been often said, and not make an Epic structure into a Tragedy—by an Epic structure I mean one with a multiplicity of plots—as if, for instance, you were to make a tragedy out of the entire story of the Iliad. In the Epic poem, owing to its length, each part assumes its proper magnitude. In the drama the result is far from answering to the poet's expectation. 5. The proof is that the poets who have dramatised the whole story of the Fall of Troy, instead of selecting portions, like Euripides; or who have taken the whole tale of Niobe, and not a part of her story, like Aeschylus, either fail utterly or meet with poor success on the stage. Even Agathon has been known to fail from this one defect. In his Reversals of the Situation, however, he shows a marvellous skill in the effort to hit the popular taste,—to produce a tragic effect that satisfies the moral sense. 6. This effect is produced when the clever rogue, like Sisyphus, is outwitted, or the brave villain defeated. Such an event is probable in Agathon's sense of the word: "it is probable," he says, "that many things should happen contrary to probability."

7. The Chorus too should be regarded as one of the actors; it should be an integral part of the whole, and share in the action, in the manner not of Euripides but of Sophocles. As for the later poets, their choral songs pertain as little to the subject of the piece as to that of any other tragedy. They are, therefore, sung as mere interludes,—a practice first begun by Agathon. Yet what difference is there between introducing such choral interludes, and transferring a speech, or even a whole act, from one play to another?

19

It remains to speak of Diction and Thought, the other parts of Tragedy having been already discussed. Concerning Thought, we may assume what is said in the Rhetoric, to which inquiry the subject more strictly belongs. 2. Under Thought is included every effect which has to be produced by speech, the subdivisions being,—proof and refutation; the excitation of the feelings, such as pity, fear, anger, and the like; the suggestion of importance or its opposite. 3. Now, it is evident that the dramatic incidents must be treated from the same points of view as the dramatic speeches, when the object is to evoke the sense of pity, fear, importance, or probability. The only difference is, that the incidents should speak for themselves without verbal exposition; while the effects aimed at in speech should be produced by the speaker, and as a result of the speech. For what were the business of a speaker, if the Thought were revealed quite apart from what he says?

4. Next, as regards Diction. One branch of the inquiry treats of the Modes of Utterance. But this province of knowledge belongs to the art of Delivery and to the masters of that science. It includes, for instance,—what is a command, a prayer, a statement, a threat, a question, an answer, and so forth. 5. To know or not to know these things involves no serious censure upon the poet's art. For who can admit the fault imputed to Homer by Protagoras,—that in the words, "Sing, goddess, of the wrath," he gives a command under the idea that he utters a prayer? For to tell some one to do a thing or not to do it is, he says, a command. We may, therefore, pass this over as an inquiry that belongs to another art, not to poetry.

20

[Language in general includes the following parts:—Letter, Syllable, Connecting word, Noun, Verb, Inflexion or Case, Sentence or Phrase.

2. A Letter is an indivisible sound, yet not every such sound, but only one which can form part of a group of sounds. For even brutes utter indivisible sounds, none of which I call a letter. 3. The sound I mean may be either a vowel, a semi-vowel, or a mute. A vowel is that which without impact of tongue or lip has an audible sound. A semi-vowel, that which with such impact has an audible sound, as S and R. A mute, that which with such impact has by itself no sound, but joined to a vowel sound becomes

audible, as G and D. 4. These are distinguished according to the form assumed by the mouth and the place where they are produced; according as they are aspirated or smooth, long or short; as they are acute, grave, or of an intermediate tone; which inquiry belongs in detail to the writers on metre.

5. A Syllable is a non-significant sound, composed of a mute and a vowel: for GR without A is a syllable, as also with A,—GRA. But the investigation of these differences belongs also to metrical science.

6. A Connecting word is a non-significant sound, which neither causes nor hinders the union of many sounds into one significant sound; it may be placed at either end or in the middle of a sentence. Or, a non-significant sound, which out of several sounds, each of them significant, is capable of forming one significant sound,—as ἀμφί, περί, and the like. 7. Or, a non-significant sound, which marks the beginning, end, or division of a sentence; such, however, that it cannot correctly stand by itself at the beginning of a sentence,—as μέν, ἤτοι, δέ.

8. A Noun is a composite significant sound, not marking time, of which no part is in itself significant: for in double or compound words we do not employ the separate parts as if each were in itself significant. Thus in Theodorus, "god-given," the δῶρον or "gift" is not in itself significant.

9. A Verb is a composite significant sound, marking time, in which, as in the noun, no part is in itself significant. For "man," or "white" does not express the idea of "when"; but "he walks," or "he has walked" does connote time, present or past.

10. Inflexion belongs both to the noun and verb, and expresses either the relation "of," "to," or the like; or that of number, whether one or many, as "man" or "men"; or the modes or tones in actual delivery, e.g. a question or a command. "Did he go?" and "go" are verbal inflexions of this kind.

11. A Sentence or Phrase is a composite significant sound, some at least of whose parts are in themselves significant; for not every such group of words consists of verbs and nouns—"the definition of man," for example—but it may dispense even with the verb. Still it will always have some significant part, as "in walking," or "Cleon son of Cleon." A sentence or phrase may form a unity in two ways,—either as signifying one thing, or as consisting of several parts linked together. Thus the Iliad is one by the linking together of parts, the definition of man by the unity of the thing signified.]

21

Words are of two kinds, simple and double. By simple I mean those composed of non-significant elements, such as γῆ. By double or compound, those composed either of a significant and non-significant element (though within the whole word no element is significant), or of elements that are both significant. A word may likewise be triple, quadruple, or multiple in form, like so many Massilian expressions, e.g. "Hermo-caico-xanthus <who prayed to Father Zeus.>"

2. Every word is either current, or strange, or metaphorical, or ornamental, or newly-coined, or lengthened, or contracted, or altered.

3. By a current or proper word I mean one which is in general use among a people; by a strange word, one which is in use in another country. Plainly, therefore, the same word may be at once strange and current, but not in relation to the same people. The word σίγυνον, "lance," is to the Cyprians a current term but to us a strange one.

4. Metaphor is the application of an alien name by transference either from genus to species, or from species to genus, or from species to species, or by analogy, that is, proportion. 5. Thus from genus to species, as: "There lies my ship"; for lying at anchor is a species of lying. From species to genus, as: "Verily ten thousand noble deeds hath Odysseus wrought"; for ten thousand is a species of large number, and is here used for a large number generally. From species to species, as: "With blade of bronze drew away the life," and "Cleft the water with the vessel of unyielding bronze." Here ἀρύσαι, "to draw away," is used for ταμεῖν, "to cleave," and ταμεῖν again for ἀρύσαι,—each being a species of taking away. 6. Analogy or proportion is when the second term is to the first as the fourth to the third. We may then use the fourth for the second, or the second for the fourth. Sometimes too we qualify the meta-

phor by adding the term to which the proper word is relative. Thus the cup is to Dionysus as the shield to Ares. The cup may, therefore, be called "the shield of Dionysus," and the shield, "the cup of Ares." Or, again, as old age is to life, so is evening to day. Evening may therefore be called "the old age of the day," and old age, "the evening of life," or, in the phrases of Empedocles, "life's setting sun." 7. For some of the terms of the proportion there is at times no word in existence; still the metaphor may be used. For instance, to scatter seed is called sowing: but the action of the sun in scattering his rays is nameless. Still this process bears to the sun the same relation as sowing to the seed. Hence the expression of the poet "sowing the god-created light." 8. There is another way in which this kind of metaphor may be employed. We may apply an alien term, and then deny of that term one of its proper attributes; as if we were to call the shield, not "the cup of Ares," but "the wineless cup."

<An ornamental word . . .>

9. A newly-coined word is one which has never been even in local use, but is adopted by the poet himself. Some such words there appear to be: as ἐρνύγες, "sprouters," for κέρατα, "horns," and ἀρητήρ, "supplicator," for ἱερεύς, "priest."

10. A word is lengthened when its own vowel is exchanged for a longer one, or when a syllable is inserted. A word is contracted when some part of it is removed. Instances of lengthening are,—πόληος for πόλεως, and Πηληιάδεω for Πηλείδου: of contraction,—κρῖ, δῶ and ὄψ as in μία γίνεται ἀμφοτέρων ὄψ.

11. An altered word is one in which part of the ordinary form is left unchanged, and part is re-cast; as in δεξιτερὸν κατὰ μαζόν, δεξιτερόν is for δεξιόν.

12. [Nouns in themselves are either masculine, feminine, or neuter. Masculine are such as end in ν, ρ, ς, or in some letter compounded with ς,—these being two, ψ and ξ. Feminine, such as end in vowels that are always long, namely η and ω, and—of vowels that admit of lengthening—those in α. Thus the number of letters in which nouns masculine and feminine end is the same; for ψ and ξ are equivalent to endings in ς. No noun ends in a mute or vowel short by nature. Three only end in ι,—μέλι, κόμμι, πέπερι: five end in υ. Neuter nouns end in these two latter vowels; also in ν and ς.]

22

The perfection of style is to be clear without being mean. The clearest style is that which uses only current or proper words; at the same time it is mean:—witness the poetry of Cleophon and of Sthenelus. That diction, on the other hand, is lofty and raised above the commonplace which employs unusual words. By unusual, I mean strange (or rare) words, metaphorical, lengthened,—anything, in short, that differs from the normal idiom. 2. Yet a style wholly composed of such words is either a riddle or a jargon; a riddle, if it consists of metaphors; a jargon, if it consists of strange (or rare) words. For the essence of a riddle is to express true facts under impossible combinations. Now this cannot be done by any arrangement of ordinary words, but by the use of metaphor it can. Such is the riddle:—"A man I saw who on another man had glued the bronze by aid of fire," and others of the same kind. A diction that is made up of strange (or rare) terms is a jargon. 3. A certain infusion, therefore, of these elements is necessary to style; for the strange (or rare) word, the metaphorical, the ornamental, and the other kinds above mentioned, will raise it above the commonplace and mean, while the use of proper words will make it perspicuous. 4. But nothing contributes more to produce a clearness of diction that is remote from commonness than the lengthening, contraction, and alteration of words. For by deviating in exceptional cases from the normal idiom, the language will gain distinction; while, at the same time, the partial conformity with usage will give perspicuity. 5. The critics, therefore, are in error who censure these licenses of speech, and hold the author up to ridicule. Thus Eucleides, the elder, declared that it would be an easy matter to be a poet if you might lengthen syllables at will. He caricatured the practice in the very form of his diction, as in the verse:

Ἐπιχάρην εἶδον Μαραθῶνάδε βαδίζοντα,

or,

οὐκ ἄν γ' ἐράμενος τὸν ἐκείνου ἐλλέβορον.

6. To employ such license at all obtrusively is, no doubt, grotesque; but in any mode of poetic diction there must be moderation. Even metaphors, strange (or rare) words, or any similar forms of speech, would produce the like effect if used without propriety, and with the express purpose of being ludicrous. 7. How great a difference is made by the appropriate use of lengthening, may be seen in Epic poetry by the insertion of ordinary forms in the verse. So, again, if we take a strange (or rare) word, a metaphor, or any similar mode of expression, and replace it by the current or proper term, the truth of our observation will be manifest. For example Aeschylus and Euripides each composed the same iambic line. But the alteration of a single word by Euripides, who employed the rare term instead of the ordinary one, makes one verse appear beautiful and the other trivial. Aeschylus in his Philoctetes says:

φαγέδαινα <δ'> ἥ μου σάρκας ἐσθίει ποδός.[2]

Euripides substitutes θοινᾶται "feasts on" for ἐσθίει "feeds on." Again, in the line,

νῦν δέ μ' ἐὼν ὀλίγος τε καὶ οὐτιδανὸς καὶ ἀεικής,[3]

the difference will be felt if we substitute the common words,

νῦν δέ μ' ἐὼν μικρός τε καὶ ἀσθενικὸς καὶ ἀειδής.[4]

Or, if for the line,

δίφρον ἀεικέλιον καταθεὶς ὀλίγην τε τράπεζαν,[5]

we read,

δίφρον μοχθηρὸν καταθεὶς μικράν τε τράπεζαν.[6]

Or, for ἠιόνες βοόωσιν, ἠιόνες κράζουσιν.[7]

8. Again, Ariphrades ridiculed the tragedians for using phrases which no one would employ in ordinary speech: for example, δωμάτων ἄπο instead of ἀπὸ δωμάτων, σέθεν, ἐγὼ δέ νιν, Ἀχιλλέως πέρι instead of περὶ Ἀχιλλέως, and the like. It is precisely because such phrases are not part of the current idiom that they give distinction to the style. This, however, he failed to see.

9. It is a great matter to observe propriety in these several modes of expression as also in compound words, strange (or rare) words, and so forth. But the greatest thing by far is to have a command of metaphor. This alone cannot be imparted by another; it is the mark of genius, for to make good metaphors implies an eye for resemblances.

10. Of the various kinds of words, the compound are best adapted to dithyrambs, rare words to heroic poetry, metaphors to iambic. In heroic poetry, indeed, all these varieties are serviceable. But in iambic verse, which reproduces, as far as may be, familiar speech, the most appropriate words are those which are found even in prose. These are,—the current or proper, the metaphorical, the ornamental.

Concerning Tragedy and imitation by means of action this may suffice.

23

As to that poetic imitation which is narrative in form and employs a single metre, the plot manifestly ought, as in a tragedy, to be constructed on dramatic principles. It should have for its subject a single action, whole and complete, with a beginning, a middle, and an end. It will thus resemble a living organism in all its unity, and produce the pleasure proper to it. It will differ in structure from historical compositions, which of necessity present not a single action, but a single period, and all that happened within that period to one person or to many, little connected together as the events may be. 2. For as the sea-fight at Salamis and the battle with the Carthaginians in Sicily took place at the same time, but did not tend to any one result, so in the sequence of events, one thing sometimes follows another, and yet no single result is thereby produced. Such is the practice, we may say, of most poets. 3. Here again, then, as has been already observed, the transcendent excellence of Homer is manifest. He never attempts to make the whole war of Troy the subject of his poem, though that war had a beginning and an end. It would have been too vast a theme, and not easily embraced in a single view. If, again, he had kept it within

[2] ["The cancer feeds on my foot."]

[3] [Homer's "and now being paltry, powerless, of no account."]

[4] ["And now being small, puny, vile."]

[5] [Homer's "having placed an ignoble seat and a paltry table."]

[6] ["Having placed a poor seat and a small table."]

[7] ["The shores bellow," "the shores cry out."]

moderate limits, it must have been overcomplicated by the variety of the incidents. As it is, he detaches a single portion, and admits as episodes many events from the general story of the war—such as the Catalogue of the ships and others—thus diversifying the poem. All other poets take a single hero, a single period, or an action single indeed, but with a multiplicity of parts. Thus did the author of the Cypria and of the Little Iliad. 4. For this reason the Iliad and the Odyssey each furnish the subject of one tragedy, or, at most, of two; while the Cypria supplies materials for many, and the Little Iliad for eight—the Award of the Arms, the Philoctetes, the Neoptolemus, the Eurypylus, the Mendicant Odysseus, the Laconian Women, the Fall of Ilium, the Departure of the Fleet.

24

Again, Epic poetry must have as many kinds as Tragedy: it must be simple, or complex, or "ethical," or "pathetic." The parts also, with the exception of song and spectacle, are the same; for it requires Reversals of the Situation, Recognitions, and Scenes of Suffering. 2. Moreover, the thoughts and the diction must be artistic. In all these respects Homer is our earliest and sufficient model. Indeed each of his poems has a twofold character. The Iliad is at once simple and "pathetic," and the Odyssey complex (for Recognition scenes run through it), and at the same time "ethical." Moreover, in diction and thought they are supreme.

3. Epic poetry differs from Tragedy in the scale on which it is constructed, and in its metre. As regards scale or length, we have already laid down an adequate limit:—the beginning and the end must be capable of being brought within a single view. This condition will be satisfied by poems on a smaller scale than the old epics, and answering in length to the group of tragedies presented at a single sitting.

4. Epic poetry has, however, a great—a special—capacity for enlarging its dimensions, and we can see the reason. In Tragedy we cannot imitate several lines of actions carried on at one and the same time; we must confine ourselves to the action on the stage and the part taken by the players. But in Epic poetry, owing to the narrative form, many events simultaneously transacted can be presented; and these, if relevant to the subject, add mass and dignity to the poem. The Epic has here an advantage, and one that conduces to grandeur of effect, to diverting the mind of the hearer, and relieving the story with varying episodes. For sameness of incident soon produces satiety, and makes tragedies fail on the stage.

5. As for the metre, the heroic measure has proved its fitness by the test of experience. If a narrative poem in any other metre or in many metres were now composed, it would be found incongruous. For of all measures the heroic is the stateliest and the most massive; and hence it most readily admits rare words and metaphors, which is another point in which the narrative form of imitation stands alone. On the other hand, the iambic and the trochaic tetrameter are stirring measures, the latter being akin to dancing, the former expressive of action. 6. Still more absurd would it be to mix together different metres, as was done by Chaeremon. Hence no one has ever composed a poem on a great scale in any other than heroic verse. Nature herself, as we have said, teaches the choice of the proper measure.

7. Homer, admirable in all respects, has the special merit of being the only poet who rightly appreciates the part he should take himself. The poet should speak as little as possible in his own person, for it is not this that makes him an imitator. Other poets appear themselves upon the scene throughout, and imitate but little and rarely. Homer, after a few prefatory words, at once brings in a man, or woman, or other personage; none of them wanting in characteristic qualities, but each with a character of his own.

8. The element of the wonderful is required in Tragedy. The irrational, on which the wonderful depends for its chief effects, has wider scope in Epic poetry, because there the person acting is not seen. Thus, the pursuit of Hector would be ludicrous if placed upon the stage—the Greeks standing still and not joining in the pursuit, and Achilles waving them back. But in the Epic poem the absurdity passes unnoticed. Now the wonderful is pleasing: as may be inferred from the fact that every one tells a story with some addition of his own, knowing that his hearers like it. 9. It is Homer who has

chiefly taught other poets the art of telling lies skilfully. The secret of it lies in a fallacy. For, assuming that if one thing is or becomes, a second is or becomes, men imagine that, if the second is, the first likewise is or becomes. But this is a false inference. Hence, where the first thing is untrue, it is quite unnecessary, provided the second be true, to add that the first is or has become. For the mind, knowing the second to be true, falsely infers the truth of the first. There is an example of this in the Bath Scene of the Odyssey.

10. Accordingly, the poet should prefer probable impossibilities to improbable possibilities. The tragic plot must not be composed of irrational parts. Everything irrational should, if possible, be excluded; or, at all events, it should lie outside the action of the play (as, in the Oedipus, the hero's ignorance as to the manner of Laius' death); not within the drama,—as in the Electra, the messenger's account of the Pythian games; or, as in the Mysians, the man who comes from Tegea to Mysia and is still speechless. The plea that otherwise the plot would have been ruined, is ridiculous; such a plot should not in the first instance be constructed. But once the irrational has been introduced and an air of likelihood imparted to it, we must accept it in spite of the absurdity. Take even the irrational incidents in the Odyssey, where Odysseus is left upon the shore of Ithaca. How intolerable even these might have been would be apparent if an inferior poet were to treat the subject. As it is, the absurdity is veiled by the poetic charm with which the poet invests it.

11. The diction should be elaborated in the pauses of the action, where there is no expression of character or thought. For, conversely, character and thought are merely obscured by a diction that is over brilliant.

25

With respect to critical difficulties and their solutions, the number and nature of the sources from which they may be drawn may be thus exhibited.

The poet being an imitator, like a painter or any other artist, must of necessity imitate one of three objects,—things as they were or are, things as they are said or thought to be, or things as they ought to be. 2. The vehicle of expression is language,—either current terms or, it may be, rare words or metaphors. There are also many modifications of language, which we concede to the poets. 3. Add to this, that the standard of correctness is not the same in poetry and politics, any more than in poetry and any other art. Within the art of poetry itself there are two kinds of faults,—those which touch its essence, and those which are accidental. 4. If a poet has chosen to imitate something, <but has imitated it incorrectly> through want of capacity, the error is inherent in the poetry. But if the failure is due to a wrong choice—if he has represented a horse as throwing out both his off legs at once, or introduced technical inaccuracies in medicine, for example, or in any other art—the error is not essential to the poetry. These are the points of view from which we should consider and answer the objections raised by the critics.

5. First as to matters which concern the poet's own art. If he describes the impossible, he is guilty of an error; but the error may be justified, if the end of the art be thereby attained (the end being that already mentioned),—if, that is, the effect of this or any other part of the poem is thus rendered more striking. A case in point is the pursuit of Hector. If, however, the end might have been as well, or better, attained without violating the special rules of the poetic art, the error is not justified: for every kind of error should, if possible, be avoided.

Again, does the error touch the essentials of the poetic art, or some accident of it? For example,—not to know that a hind has no horns is a less serious matter than to paint it inartistically.

6. Further, if it be objected that the description is not true to fact, the poet may perhaps reply,—"But the objects are as they ought to be": just as Sophocles said that he drew men as they ought to be; Euripides, as they are. 7. In this way the objection may be met. If, however, the representation be of neither kind, the poet may answer,—"This is how men say the thing is." This applies to tales about the gods. It may well be that these stories are not higher than fact nor yet true to fact: they are, very possibly, what Xenophanes says of them. But any-

how, "this is what is said." Again, a description may be no better than the fact: "still, it was the fact"; as in the passage about the arms: "Upright upon their butt-ends stood the spears." This was the custom then, as it now is among the Illyrians.

8. Again, in examining whether what has been said or done by some one is poetically right or not, we must not look merely to the particular act or saying, and ask whether it is poetically good or bad. We must also consider by whom it is said or done, to whom, when, by what means, or for what end; whether, for instance, it be to secure a greater good, or avert a greater evil.

9. Other difficulties may be resolved by due regard to the usage of language. We may note a rare word, as in οὐρῆας μὲν πρῶτον, where the poet perhaps employs οὐρῆας not in the sense of mules, but of sentinels. So, again, of Dolon: "ill-favoured indeed he was to look upon." It is not meant that his body was ill-shaped, but that his face was ugly; for the Cretans use the word εὐειδές, "well-favoured," to denote a fair face. Again, ζωρότερον δὲ κέραιε, "mix the drink livelier," does not mean "mix it stronger" as for hard drinkers, but "mix it quicker."

10. Sometimes an expression is metaphorical, as "Now all gods and men were sleeping through the night,"—while at the same time the poet says: "Often indeed as he turned his gaze to the Trojan plain, he marvelled at the sound of flutes and pipes." "All" is here used metaphorically for "many," all being a species of many. So in the verse,—"alone she hath no part . . . ," οἴη, "alone," is metaphorical; for the best known may be called the only one.

11. Again, the solution may depend upon accent or breathing. Thus Hippias of Thasos solved the difficulties in the line,—δίδομεν (διδόμεν) δέ οἱ, and τὸ μὲν οὗ (οὐ) καταπύθεται ὄμβρῳ.

12. Or again, the question may be solved by punctuation, as in Empedocles,—"Of a sudden things became mortal that before had learnt to be immortal, and things unmixed before mixed."

13. Or again, by ambiguity of meaning,—as in παρῴχηκεν δὲ πλέω νύξ, where the word πλέω is ambiguous.

14. Or by the usage of language. Thus any mixed drink is called οἶνος, "wine." Hence Ganymede is said "to pour the wine to Zeus," though the gods do not drink wine. So too workers in iron are called χαλκέας, or workers in bronze. This, however, may also be taken as a metaphor.

15. Again, when a word seems to involve some inconsistency of meaning, we should consider how many senses it may bear in the particular passage. 16. For example: "there was stayed the spear of bronze"—we should ask in how many ways we may take "being checked there." The true mode of interpretation is the precise opposite of what Glaucon mentions. Critics, he says, jump at certain groundless conclusions; they pass adverse judgment and then proceed to reason on it; and, assuming that the poet has said whatever they happen to think, find fault if a thing is inconsistent with their own fancy. The question about Icarius has been treated in this fashion. The critics imagine he was a Lacedaemonian. They think it strange, therefore, that Telemachus should not have met him when he went to Lacedaemon. But the Cephallenian story may perhaps be the true one. They allege that Odysseus took a wife from among themselves, and that her father was Icadius not Icarius. It is merely a mistake, then, that gives plausibility to the objection.

17. In general, the impossible must be justified by reference to artistic requirements, or to the higher reality, or to received opinion. With respect to the requirements of art, a probable impossibility is to be preferred to a thing improbable and yet possible. Again, it may be impossible that there should be men such as Zeuxis painted. "Yes," we say, "but the impossible is the higher thing; for the ideal type must surpass the reality." To justify the irrational, we appeal to what is commonly said to be. In addition to which, we urge that the irrational sometimes does not violate reason; just as "it is probable that a thing may happen contrary to probability."

18. Things that sound contradictory should be examined by the same rules as in dialectical refutation—whether the same thing is meant, in the same relation, and in the same sense. We should therefore solve the question by reference

to what the poet says himself, or to what is tacitly assumed by a person of intelligence.

19. The element of the irrational, and, similarly, depravity of character, are justly censured when there is no inner necessity for introducing them. Such is the irrational element in the introduction of Aegeus of Euripides, and the badness of Menelaus in the Orestes.

20. Thus, there are five sources from which critical objections are drawn. Things are censured either as impossible, or irrational, or morally hurtful, or contradictory, or contrary to artistic correctness. The answers should be sought under the twelve heads above mentioned.

26

The question may be raised whether the Epic or Tragic mode of imitation is the higher. If the more refined art is the higher, and the more refined in every case is that which appeals to the better sort of audience, the art which imitates anything and everything is manifestly most unrefined. The audience is supposed to be too dull to comprehend unless something of their own is thrown in by the performers, who therefore indulge in restless movements. Bad flute-players twist and twirl, if they have to represent "the quoit-throw," or hustle the coryphaeus when they perform the "Scylla." 2. Tragedy, it is said, has this same defect. We may compare the opinion that the older actors entertained of their successors. Mynniscus used to call Callippides "ape" on account of the extravagance of his action, and the same view was held of Pindarus. Tragic art, then, as a whole, stands to Epic in the same relation as the younger to the elder actors. So we are told that Epic poetry is addressed to a cultivated audience, who do not need gesture; Tragedy, to an inferior public. 3. Being then unrefined, it is evidently the lower of the two.

Now, in the first place, this censure attaches not to the poetic but to the histrionic art; for gesticulation may be equally overdone in epic recitation, as by Sosistratus, or in lyrical competition, as by Mnasitheus the Opuntian. Next, all action is not to be condemned—any more than all dancing—but only that of bad performers. Such was the fault found in Callippides, as also in others of our own day, who are censured for representing degraded women. Again, Tragedy like Epic poetry produces its effect even without action; it reveals its power by mere reading. If, then, in all other respects it is superior, this fault, we say, is not inherent in it.

4. And superior it is, because it has all the epic elements—it may even use the epic metre—with the music and spectacular effects as important accessories; and these produce the most vivid of pleasures. Further, it has vividness of impression in reading as well as in representation. 5. Moreover, the art attains its end within narrower limits; for the concentrated effect is more pleasurable than one which is spread over a long time and so diluted. What, for example, would be the effect of the Oedipus of Sophocles, if it were cast into a form as long as the Iliad? 6. Once more, the Epic imitation has less unity; as is shown by this, that any Epic poem will furnish subjects for several tragedies. Thus if the story adopted by the poet has a strict unity, it must either be concisely told and appear truncated; or, if it conform to the Epic canon of length, it must seem weak and watery. <Such length implies some loss of unity,> if, I mean, the poem is constructed out of several actions, like the Iliad and the Odyssey, which have many such parts, each with a certain magnitude of its own. Yet these poems are as perfect as possible in structure; each is, in the highest degree attainable, an imitation of a single action.

7. If, then, Tragedy is superior to Epic poetry in all these respects, and, moreover, fulfils its specific function better as an art—for each art ought to produce, not any chance pleasure, but the pleasure proper to it, as already stated—it plainly follows that Tragedy is the higher art, as attaining its end more perfectly.

8. Thus much may suffice concerning Tragic and Epic poetry in general; their several kinds and parts, with the number of each and their differences; the causes that make a poem good or bad; the objections of the critics and the answers to these objections.

JOHN DRYDEN: An Essay of Dramatic Poesy*

It was that memorable day, in the first summer of the late war, when our navy engaged the Dutch; a day wherein the two most mighty and best appointed fleets which any age had ever seen, disputed the command of the greater half of the globe, the commerce of nations, and the riches of the universe. While these vast floating bodies, on either side, moved against each other in parallel lines, and our countrymen, under the happy conduct of his Royal Highness, went breaking, by little and little, into the line of the enemies; the noise of the cannon from both navies reached our ears about the City, so that all men being alarmed with it, and in a dreadful suspense of the event which they knew was then deciding, every one went following the sound as his fancy led him; and leaving the town almost empty, some took towards the park, some cross the river, others down it; all seeking the noise in the depth of silence.

Among the rest, it was the fortune of Eugenius, Crites, Lisideius, and Neander, to be in company together; three of them persons whom their wit and quality have made known to all the town; and whom I have chose to hide under these borrowed names, that they may not suffer by so ill a relation as I am going to make of their discourse.

Taking then a barge, which a servant of Lisideius had provided for them, they made haste to shoot the bridge, and left behind them that great fall of waters which hindered them from hearing what they desired: after which, having disengaged themselves from many vessels which rode at anchor in the Thames, and almost blocked up the passage towards Greenwich, they ordered the watermen to let fall their oars more gently; and then, every one favouring his own curiosity with a strict silence, it was not long ere they perceived the air to break about them like the noise of distant thunder, or of swallows in a chimney: those little undulations of sound, though almost vanishing before they reached them, yet still seeming to retain somewhat of their first horror, which they had betwixt the fleets. After they had attentively listened till such time as the sound by little and little went from them, Eugenius, lifting up his head, and taking notice of it, was the first who congratulated to the rest that happy omen of our Nation's victory: adding, that we had but this to desire in confirmation of it, that we might hear no more of that noise, which was now leaving the English coast. When the rest had concurred in the same opinion, Crites, a person of a sharp judgment, and somewhat too delicate a taste in wit, which the world have mistaken in him for ill-nature, said, smiling to us, that if the concernment of this battle had not been so exceeding great, he could scarce have wished the victory at the price he knew he must pay for it, in being subject to the reading and hearing of so many ill verses as he was sure would be made upon it. Adding, that no argument could scape some of those eternal rhymers, who watch a battle with more diligence than the ravens and birds of prey; and the worst of them surest to be first in upon the quarry: while the better able either out of modesty writ not at all, or set that due value upon their poems, as to let them be often called for and long expected! "There are some of those impertinent people you speak of," answered Lisideius, "who to my knowledge are already so provided, either way, that they can produce not only a Panegyric upon the victory, but, if need be, a Funeral Elegy on the Duke; and, after they have crowned his valour with many laurels, they will at last deplore the odds under which he fell, conclud-

* Dryden's "Essay of Dramatic Poesy" was published in 1668. It is reprinted here in the edition of W. P. Ker, from *The Essays of John Dryden*, by permission of the publishers, The Clarendon Press, Oxford.

ing that his courage deserved a better destiny." All the company smiled at the conceipt of Lisideius; but Crites, more eager than before, began to make particular exceptions against some writers, and said, the public magistrate ought to send betimes to forbid them; and that it concerned the peace and quiet of all honest people, that ill poets should be as well silenced as seditious preachers. "In my opinion," replied Eugenius, "you pursue your point too far; for as to my own particular, I am so great a lover of poesy, that I could wish them all rewarded, who attempt but to do well; at least, I would not have them worse used than Sylla the Dictator did one of their brethren heretofore:—*Quem in concione vidimus* (says Tully), *cum ei libellum malus poeta de populo subjecisset, quod epigramma in eum fecisset tantummodo alternis versibus longiusculis, statim ex iis rebus quas tunc vendebat jubere ei praemium tribui, sub ea conditione ne quid postea scriberet.*" [1] "I could wish with all my heart," replied Crites, "that many whom we know were as bountifully thanked upon the same condition,—that they would never trouble us again. For amongst others, I have a mortal apprehension of two poets, whom this victory, with the help of both her wings, will never be able to escape." "'Tis easy to guess whom you intend," said Lisideius; "and without naming them, I ask you, if one of them does not perpetually pay us with clenches upon words, and a certain clownish kind of railery? if now and then he does not offer at a catachresis or Clevelandism, wresting and torturing a word into another meaning: in fine, if he be not one of those whom the French would call *un mauvais buffon;* one that is so much a well-willer to the satire, that he spares no man; and though he cannot strike a blow to hurt any, yet ought to be punished for the malice of the action, as our witches are justly hanged, because they think themselves so; and suffer deservedly for believing they did mischief, because they meant it." "You have described him," said Crites, "so exactly, that I am afraid to come after you with my other extremity of poetry. He is one of those who, having had some advantage of education and converse, knows better than the other what a poet should be, but puts it into practice more unluckily than any man; his style and matter are every where alike: he is the most calm, peaceable writer you ever read: he never disquiets your passions with the least concernment, but still leaves you in as even a temper as he found you; he is a very Leveller in poetry: he creeps along with ten little words in every line, and helps out his numbers with *For to,* and *Unto,* and all the pretty expletives he can find, till he drags them to the end of another line; while the sense is left tired half way behind it: he doubly starves all his verses, first for want of thought, and then of expression; his poetry neither has wit in it, nor seems to have it; like him in Martial:

Pauper videri Cinna *vult, et est pauper.*[2]

"He affects plainness, to cover his want of imagination: when he writes the serious way, the highest flight of his fancy is some miserable antithesis, or seeming contradiction; and in the comic he is still reaching at some thin conceit, the ghost of a jest, and that too flies before him, never to be caught; these swallows which we see before us on the Thames are the just resemblance of his wit: you may observe how near the water they stoop, how many proffers they make to dip, and yet how seldom they touch it; and when they do, it is but the surface: they skim over it but to catch a gnat, and then mount into the air and leave it."

"Well, gentlemen," said Eugenius, "you may speak your pleasure of these authors; but though I and some few more about the town may give you a peaceable hearing, yet assure yourselves, there are multitudes who would think you malicious and then injured: especially him whom you first described; he is the very Withers of the city: they have bought more editions of his works than would serve to lay under all their pies at the Lord Mayor's Christmas. When his famous poem first came out in the year 1660, I have seen them reading it in the midst of 'Change time; nay so vehement they were at it, that they lost their bargain by the candles' ends; but what will you say if he has been received

[1] ["We saw him once in a popular gathering when from the crowd a bad poet offered him an epigram in elegiac verse which he had just composed attacking him; immediately he ordered the poet to be given a reward out of the articles he was then selling on the condition that he not write anything afterwards."]

[2] ["Cinna wants to appear a pauper, and, in fact, he is a pauper."]

amongst the great ones? I can assure you he is, this day, the envy of one who is lord in the art of quibbling; and who does not take it well, that any man should intrude so far into his province." "All I would wish," replied Crites, "is, that they who love his writings, may still admire him, and his fellow poet: *Qui Bavium non odit, etc.*,[3] is curse sufficient." "And farther," added Lisideius, "I believe there is no man who writes well, but would think himself very hardly dealt with, if their admirers should praise anything of his: *Nam quos contemnimus, eorum quoque laudes contemnimus.*"[4] "There are so few who write well in this age," says Crites, "that methinks any praises should be welcome; they neither rise to the dignity of the last age, nor to any of the Ancients: and we may cry out of the writers of this time, with more reason than Petronius of his, *Pace vestrâ liceat dixisse, primi omnium eloquentiam perdidistis:*[5] you have debauched the true old poetry so far, that Nature, which is the soul of it, is not in any of your writings."

"If your quarrel," said Eugenius, "to those who now write, be grounded only on your reverence to antiquity, there is no man more ready to adore those great Greeks and Romans than I am: but on the other side, I cannot think so contemptibly of the age I live in, or so dishonourably of my own country, as not to judge we equal the Ancients in most kinds of poesy, and in some surpass them; neither know I any reason why I may not be as zealous for the reputation of our age as we find the Ancients themselves in reference to those who lived before them. For you hear your Horace saying,

Indignor quidquam reprehendi, non quia crassé
Compositum, illepidève putetur, sed quia nuper.[6]

And after:

Si meliora dies, ut vina, poemata reddit,
Scire velim, pretim chartis quotus arroget annus?[7]

[3] ["Who does not hate Bavius."]

[4] ["For those whom we despise, their praises we despise too."]

[5] ["With your permission, may we say that you were the first of all to lose eloquence."]

[6] ["I grow indignant when anything is censored not because it is considered to have been written crudely and tastelessly but because it has been written recently."]

[7] ["If time improves poems, like wines, I should like to know how many years it takes to bestow value upon writings."]

"But I see I am engaging in a wide dispute, where the arguments are not like to reach close on either side; for Poesy is of so large an extent, and so many both of the Ancients and Moderns have done well in all kinds of it, that in citing one against the other, we shall take up more time this evening than each man's occasions will allow him: therefore I would ask Crites to what part of Poesy he would confine his arguments, and whether he would defend the general cause of the Ancients against the Moderns, or oppose any age of the Moderns against this of ours?"

Crites, a little while considering upon this demand, told Eugenius he approved his propositions, and if he pleased, he would limit their dispute to Dramatic Poesy; in which he thought it not difficult to prove, either that the Ancients were superior to the Moderns, or the last age of this of ours.

Eugenius was somewhat surprised, when he heard Crites make choice of that subject. "For ought I see," said he, "I have undertaken a harder province than I imagined; for though I never judged the plays of the Greek or Roman poets comparable to ours, yet, on the other side, those we now see acted come short of many which were written in the last age: but my comfort is, if we are overcome, it will be only by our own countrymen: and if we yield to them in this one part of poesy, we more surpass them in all the other: for in the epic or lyric way, it will be hard for them to show us one such amongst them, as we have many now living, or who lately were so: they can produce nothing so courtly writ, or which expresses so much the conversation of a gentleman, as Sir John Suckling; nothing so even, sweet, and flowing as Mr. Waller; nothing so majestic, so correct, as Sir John Denham; nothing so elevated, so copious, and full of spirit as Mr. Cowley; as for the Italian, French, and Spanish plays, I can make it evident, that those who now write surpass them; and that the Drama is wholly ours."

All of them were thus far of Eugenius his opinion, that the sweetness of English verse was never understood or practised by our fathers; even Crites himself did not much oppose it; and every one was willing to acknowledge how much our poesy is improved by the happiness of some writers yet living; who first taught us to mould our thoughts into easy and significant words; to retrench the superfluities of expression, and to make our rhyme so properly a part of the verse, that it should never mislead the sense, but itself be led and governed by it.

Eugenius was going to continue this discourse, when Lisideius told him that it was necessary, before they proceeded further, to take a standing measure of their controversy; for how was it possible to be decided who writ the best plays, before we know what a play should be? But, this once agreed on by both parties, each might have recourse to it, either to prove his own advantages, or to discover the failings of his adversary.

He had no sooner said this, but all desired the favour of him to give the definition of a play; and they were the more importunate, because neither Aristotle, nor Horace, nor any other, who had writ of that subject, had ever done it.

Lisideius, after some modest denials, at last confessed he had a rude notion of it; indeed, rather a description than a definition; but which served to guide him in his private thoughts, when he was to make a judgment of what others writ: that he conceived a play ought to be, *A just and lively image of human nature, representing its passions and humours, and the changes of fortune to which it is subject, for the delight and instruction of mankind.*

This definition, though Crites raised a logical objection against it—that it was only *a genere et fine,*[8] and so not altogether perfect, was yet well received by the rest; and after they had given order to the watermen to turn their barge, and row softly, that they might take the cool of the evening in their return, Crites, being desired by the company to begin, spoke on behalf of the Ancients, in this manner:

"If confidence presage a victory, Eugenius, in his own opinion, has already triumphed over the Ancients: nothing seems more easy to him, than to overcome those whom it is our greatest praise to have imitated well; for we do not only build upon their foundations, but by their models. Dramatic Poesy had time enough, reckoning from Thespis (who first invented it) to Aristophanes, to be born, to grow up, and to flourish in maturity. It has been observed of arts and sciences, that in one and the same century they have arrived to great perfection; and no wonder, since every age has a kind of universal genius, which inclines those that live in it to some particular studies: the work then, being pushed on by many hands, must of necessity go forward.

"Is it not evident, in these last hundred years, (when the study of philosophy has been the business of all the Virtuosi in Christendom), that almost a new nature has been revealed to us? That more errors of the school have been detected, more useful experiments in philosophy have been made, more noble secrets in optics, medicine, anatomy, astronomy, discovered, than in all those credulous and doting ages from Aristotle to us?—so true it is, that nothing spreads more fast than science, when rightly and generally cultivated.

"Add to this, the more than common emulation that was in those times of writing well; which though it be found in all ages and all persons that pretend to the same reputation, yet Poesy, being then in more esteem than now it is, had greater honours decreed to the professors of it, and consequently the rivalship was more high between them; they had judges ordained to decide their merit, and prizes to reward it; and historians have been diligent to record of Eschylus, Euripides, Sophocles, Lycophron, and the rest of them, both who they were that vanquished in these wars of the theatre, and how often they were crowned: while the Asian kings and Grecian commonwealths scarce afforded them a nobler subject than the unmanly luxuries of a debauched court, or giddy intrigues of a factious city:—*Alit æmulatio ingenia* (says Paterculus), *et nunc invidia, nunc admiratio incitatio nem accendit:* Emulation is the spur of wit; and sometimes envy, sometimes admiration, quickens our endeavours.

"But now, since the rewards of honour are taken away, that virtuous emulation is turned into direct malice; yet so slothful, that it contents itself to condemn and cry down others, without attempting to do better: it is a reputation too unprofitable, to take the necessary pains for it; yet, wishing they had it, is incitement enough to hinder others from it. And this, in short, Eugenius, is the reason why you have now so few good poets, and so many severe

[8] ["By general classification and purpose."]

judges. Certainly, to imitate the Ancients well, much labour and long study is required; which pains, I have already shown, our poets would want encouragement to take, if yet they had ability to go through with it. Those Ancients have been faithful imitators and wise observers of that Nature which is so torn and ill represented in our plays; they have handed down to us a perfect resemblance of her; which we, like all copiers, neglecting to look on, have rendered monstrous, and disfigured. But, that you may know how much you are indebted to those your masters, and be ashamed to have so ill requited them, I must remember you, that all the rules by which we practise the Drama at this day, (either such as relate to the justness and symmetry of the plot, or the episodical ornaments, such as descriptions, narrations, and other beauties, which are not esential to the play,) were delivered to us from the observations which Aristotle made, of those poets, which either lived before him, or were his contemporaries: we have added nothing of our own, except we have the confidence to say our wit is better; of which, none boast in this our age, but such as understand not theirs. Of that book which Aristotle has left us, περὶ τῆς Ποιηικῆς, Horace his *Art of Poetry* is an excellent comment, and, I believe, restores to us that Second Book of his concerning *Comedy*, which is wanting in him.

"Out of these two have been extracted the famous Rules, which the French call *Des Trois Unitez*, or, The Three Unities, which ought to be observed in every regular play; namely, of Time, Place, and Action.

"The Unity of Time they comprehend in twenty-four hours, the compass of a natural day, or as near as it can be contrived; and the reason of it is obvious to every one,—that the time of the feigned action, or fable of the play, should be proportioned as near as can be to the duration of that time in which it is represented: since, therefore, all plays are acted on the theatre in the space of time much within the compass of twenty-four hours, that play is to be thought the nearest imitation of nature, whose plot or action is confined within that time; and, by the same rule which concludes this general proportion of time, it follows, that all the parts of it are to be equally subdivided; as namely, that one act take not up the supposed time of half a day, which is out of proportion to the rest; since the other four are then to be straitened within the compass of the remaining half: for it is unnatural that one act, which being spoke or written is not longer than the rest, should be supposed longer by the audience; it is therefore the poet's duty, to take care that no act should be imagined to exceed the time in which it is represented on the stage; and that the intervals and inequalities of time be supposed to fall out between the acts.

"This rule of time, how well it has been observed by the Ancients, most of their plays will witness; you see them in their tragedies, (wherein to follow this rule is certainly most difficult), from the very beginning of their plays, falling close into that part of the story which they intend for the action or principal object of it, leaving the former part to be delivered by narration: so that they set the audience, as it were, at the post where the race is to be concluded; and, saving them the tedious expectation of seeing the poet set out and ride the beginning of the course, you behold him not till he is in sight of the goal, and just upon you.

"For the second Unity, which is that of Place, the Ancients meant by it, that the scene ought to be continued through the play, in the same place where it was laid in the beginning: for the stage on which it is represented being but one and the same place, it is unnatural to conceive it many, and those far distant from one another. I will not deny but, by the variation of painted scenes, the fancy, which in these cases will contribute to its own deceit, may sometimes imagine it several places, with some appearance of probability; yet it still carries the greater likelihood of truth, if those places be supposed so near each other as in the same town or city; which may all be comprehended under the larger denomination of one place; for a greater distance will bear no proportion to the shortness of time which is allotted in the acting, to pass from one of them to another; for the observation of this, next to the Ancients, the French are to be most commended. They tie themselves so strictly to the Unity of Place that you never see in any of their plays a scene changed in the middle of an act: if the act begins in a garden, a street, or chamber, 'tis ended in the same place; and that you may know it to be the same, the stage is so supplied with persons, that it is never empty all the time: he that enters second, has business with him who was on before; and before the second quits the stage, a third appears who has business with him. This Corneille calls *la liaison des scenes,* the continuity or joining of the scenes; and 'tis a good mark of a well-contrived play, when all the persons are known to each other, and every one of them has some affairs with all the rest.

"As for the third Unity, which is that of Action, the Ancients meant no other by it than what the logicians do by their *finis,* the end or scope of any action; that which is the first in intention, and last in execution: now the poet is to aim at one great and complete action, to the carrying on of which all things in his play, even the very obstacles, are to be subservient; and the reason of this is as evident as any of the former. For two actions, equally laboured and driven on by the writer, would destroy the unity of the poem; it would be no longer one play, but two: not but that there may be many actions in a play, as Ben Jonson has observed in his *Discoveries;* but they must be all subservient to the great one, which our language happily expresses in the name of *under-plots:* such as in Terence's *Eunuch* is the difference and reconcilement of Thais and Phædria, which is not the chief business of the play, but promotes the marriage of Chærea and Chremes's sister, principally intended by the poet. There ought to be but one action, says Corneille, that is, one complete action, which leaves the mind of the audience in a full repose; but this cannot be brought to pass but by many other imperfect actions, which conduce to it, and hold the audience in a delightful suspence of what will be.

"If by these rules (to omit many other drawn from the precepts and practice of the Ancients) we should judge our modern plays, 'tis probable that few of them would endure the trial: that which should be the business of a day, takes up in some of them an age; instead of one action, they are the epitomes of a man's life; and for one spot of ground, which the stage should represent, we are sometimes in more countries than the map can show us.

"But if we allow the Ancients to have contrived well, we must acknowledge them to have writ better. Questionless we are deprived of a great stock of wit in the loss of Menander among the Greek poets, and of Cæcilius, Aranius, and Varius, among the Romans; we may guess at Menander's excellency by the plays of Terence, who translated some of his; and yet wanted so much of him, that he was called by C. Cæsar the half-Menander; and may judge of Varius, by the testimonies of Horace, Martial, and Velleius Paterculus. 'Tis probable that these, could they be recovered, would decide the controversy; but so long as Aristophanes in the old Comedy, and Plautus are extant, while the tragedies of Euripides, Sophocles, and Seneca, are to be had, I can never see one of those plays which are now written but it increases my admiration of the Ancients. And yet I must acknowledge further, that to admire them as we ought, we should understand them better than we do. Doubtless many things appear flat to us, whose wit depended on some custom or story, which never came to our knowledge; or perhaps on some criticism in their language, which being so long dead, and only remaining in their books, 'tis not possible they should make us understand perfectly. To read Macrobius, explaining the propriety and elegancy of many words in Virgil, which I had before passed over without consideration, as common things, is enough to assure me that I ought to think the same of Terence; and that in the purity of his style (which Tully so much valued that he ever carried his works about him) there is yet left in him great room for admiration, if I knew but where to place it. In the meantime I must desire you to take notice that the greatest man of the last age (Ben Jonson) was willing to give place to them in all things: he was not only a professed imitator of Horace, but a learned plagiary of all the others; you track him everywhere in their snow: if Horace, Lucan, Petronius Arbiter, Seneca, and Juvenal, had their own from him, there are few serious thoughts which are new in him: you will pardon me, therefore, if I presume he loved their fashion, when he wore their clothes. But since I have otherwise a great veneration for him, and you, Eugenius, prefer him above all other poets, I will use no farther argument to you than his example: I will produce Father Ben to you, dressed in all the ornaments and colours of the Ancients; you will need no other guide to our party, if you follow him; and whether you consider the bad plays of our age, or regard the good ones of the last, both the best and worst of the modern poets will equally instruct you to esteem the Ancients."

Crites had no sooner left speaking, but Eugenius, who had waited with some impatience for it, thus began:

"I have observed in your speech, that the former part of it is convincing as to what the Moderns have profited by the rules of the Ancients; but in the latter you are careful to conceal how much they have excelled them; we own all the helps we have from them, and want neither veneration nor gratitude, while we acknowledge that, to overcome them, we must make use of the advantages we have received from them: but to these assistances we have joined our own industry; for, had we sat down with a dull imitation of them, we might then have lost somewhat of the old perfection, but never acquired any that was new. We draw not therefore after their lines, but those of Nature; and having the life before us, besides the experience of all they knew, it is no wonder if we hit some airs and features which they have missed. I deny not what you urge of arts and sciences, that they have flourished in some ages more than others; but your instance in philosophy makes for me: for if natural causes be more known now than in the time of Aristotle, because more studied, it follows that poesy and other arts may, with the same pains, arrive still nearer to perfection; and, that granted, it will rest for you to prove that they wrought more perfect images of human life than we; which seeing in your discourse you have avoided to make good, it shall now be my task to show you some part of their defects, and some few excellencies of the Moderns. And I think there is none among us can imagine I do it enviously, or with purpose to detract from them; for what interest of fame or profit can the living lose by the reputation of the dead? On the other side, it is a great truth which Velleius Paterculus affirms: *Audita visis libentius laudamus; et præsentia invidia præterita admiratione prosequimur; et his nos obrui, illis instrui credimus:* [9] that praise or censure is certainly the most sincere, which unbribed posterity shall give us.

"Be pleased then in the first place to take notice, that the Greek poesy, which Crites has affirmed to have arrived to perfection in the reign of the Old Comedy, was so far from it, that the distinction of it into acts was not known to them; or if it were, it is yet so darkly delivered to us that we cannot make it out.

"All we know of it is, from the singing of their Chorus; and that too is so uncertain, that in some of their plays we have reason to conjecture they sung more than five times. Aristotle indeed divides the integral parts of a play into four. First, the *Protasis,* or entrance, which gives light only to the characters of the persons, and proceeds very little into any part of the action. Secondly, the *Epitasis,* or working up of the plot; where the play grows warmer, the design or action of it is drawing on, and you see something promising that it will come to pass. Thirdly, the *Catastasis,* or counter-turn, which destroys that expectation, imbroils the action in new difficulties, and leaves you far distant from that hope in which it found you; as you may have observed in a violent stream resisted by a narrow passage,—it runs round to an eddy, and carries back the waters with more swiftness than it brought them on. Lastly, the *Catastrophe,* which the Grecians called λύσις, the French *le dénouement,* and we the discovery, or unravelling of the plot: there you see all things settling again upon their first foundations; and, the obstacles which hindered the design or action of the play once removed, it ends with that resemblance of truth and nature, that the audience are satisfied with the conduct of it. Thus this great man delivered to us the image of a play; and I must confess it is so lively, that from thence much light has been derived to the forming it more perfectly into acts and scenes: but what poet first limited to five the number of the acts, I know not; only we see it so firmly established in the time of Horace, that he gives it for a rule in comedy,—*Neu brevior quinto, neu sit productior actu.*[10] So that you see the Grecians cannot be said to have consummated this art; writing rather by entrances than by acts, and having rather a general indigested

9 ["We praise more willingly what we have heard than what we have seen; and we pursue the present with envy and the past with admiration; we feel oppressed by the former and uplifted by the latter."]

10 ["Let it be neither shorter than five acts, nor longer."]

notion of a play, than knowing how and where to bestow the particular graces of it.

"But since the Spaniards at this day allow but three acts, which they call *Jornadas,* to a play, and the Italians in many of theirs follow them, when I condemn the Ancients, I declare it is not altogether because they have not five acts to every play, but because they have not confined themselves to one certain number: it is building an house without a model; and when they succeeded in such undertakings, they ought to have sacrificed to Fortune, not to the Muses.

"Next, for the plot, which Aristotle called τὸ μῦθος, and often τῶν πραγμάτων σύνθεσις,[11] and from him the Romans *Fabula;* it has already been judiciously observed by a late writer, that in their tragedies it was only some tale derived from Thebes or Troy, or at least something that happened in those two ages; which was worn so threadbare by the pens of all the epic poets, and even by tradition, itself of the talkative Greeklings (as Ben Jonson calls them), that before it came upon the stage it was already known to all the audience: and the people, so soon as ever they heard the name of Œdipus, knew as well as the poet, that he had killed his father by a mistake, and committed incest with his mother, before the play; that they were now to hear of a great plague, an oracle, and the ghost of Laius: so that they sat with a yawning kind of expectation, till he was to come with his eyes pulled out, and speak a hundred or two verses in a tragic tone, in complaint of his misfortunes. But one Œdipus, Hercules, or Medea, had been tolerable: poor people, they escaped not so good cheap; they had still the *chapon bouille*[12] set before them, till their appetites were cloyed with the same dish, and, the novelty being gone, the pleasure vanished; so that one main end of Dramatic Poesy in its definition, which was to cause delight, was of consequence destroyed.

"In their comedies, the Romans generally borrowed their plots from the Greek poets; and theirs was commonly a little girl stolen or wandered from her parents, brought back unknown to the same city, there [falling into the hands of] some young fellow, who, by the help of his servant, cheats his father; and when her time comes, to cry,—*Juno Lucina, fer opem,*[13]—one or other sees a little box or cabinet which was carried away with her, and so discovers her to her friends, if some god do not prevent it, by coming down in a machine, and take the thanks of it to himself.

"By the plot you may guess much of the characters of the persons. An old father, who would willingly, before he dies, see his son well married; his debauched son, kind in his nature to his wench, but miserably in want of money; a servant or slave, who has so much wit to strike in with him, and help to dupe his father; a braggadocio captain, a parasite, and a lady of pleasure.

"As for the poor honest maid, on whom the story is built, and who ought to be one of the principal actors in the play, she is commonly a mute in it: she has the breeding of the old Elizabeth way, for maids to be seen and not to be heard; and it is enough you know she is willing to be married, when the fifth act requires it.

"These are plots built after the Italian mode of houses,—you see through them all at once: the characters are indeed the imitation of Nature, but so narrow, as if they had imitated only an eye or an hand, and did not dare to venture on the lines of a face, or the proportion of a body.

"But in how strait a compass soever they have bounded their plots and characters, we will pass it by, if they have regularly pursued them, and perfectly observed those three Unities of Time, Place, and Action; the knowledge of which you say is derived to us from them. But in the first place give me leave to tell you, that the Unity of Place, however it might be practised by them, was never any of their rules: we neither find it in Aristotle, Horace, or any who have written of it, till in our age the French poets first made it a precept of the stage. The Unity of Time, even Terence himself, who was the best and most regular of them, has neglected: his *Heautontimorumenos,* or *Self-Punisher,* takes up visibly two days, therefore, says Scaliger; the two first acts concluding the first day, were acted overnight; the three last on the ensuing day; and Euripides, in tying himself to one day, has committed an absurdity never to be forgiven him; for in one of his tragedies he has made Theseus go from Athens to Thebes, which

11 ["The placing together of the actions."]

12 [Literally, "Boiled capon" ("tasty dish, luxury").]

13 ["Juno, goddess of childbirth, bring help."]

was about forty English miles, under the walls of it to give battle, and appear victorious in the next act; and yet, from the time of his departure to the return of the Nuntius, who gives the relation of his victory, Æthra and the Chorus have but thirty-six verses; that is not for every mile a verse.

"The like error is as evident in Terence his *Eunuch,* when Laches, the old man, enters in a mistake the house of Thais; where, betwixt his exit and the entrance of Pythias, who comes to give ample relation of the disorders he has raised within, Parmeno, who was left upon the stage, has not above five lines to speak. *C'est bien employer un temps si court,*[14] says the French poet, who furnished me with one of the observations: and almost all their tragedies will afford us examples of the like nature.

"'T is true, they have kept the continuity, or, as you called it, *liaison des scenes,* somewhat better: two do not perpetually come in together, talk, and go out together; and other two succeed them, and do the same throughout the act, which the English call by the name of single scenes; but the reason is, because they have seldom above two or three scenes, properly so called, in every act; for it is to be accounted a new scene, not every time the stage is empty; but every person who enters, though to others, makes it so; because he introduces a new business. Now the plots of their plays being narrow, and the persons few, one of their acts was written in a less compass than one of our well-wrought scenes; and yet they are often deficient even in this. To go no further than Terence; you find in the *Eunuch,* Antipho entering single in the midst of the third act, after Chremes and Pythias were gone off; in the same play you have likewise Dorias beginning the fourth act alone; and after she had made a relation of what was done at the Soldier's entertainment (which by the way was very inartificial, because she was presumed to speak directly to the audience, and to acquaint them with what was necessary to be known, but yet should have been so contrived by the poet as to have been told by persons of the drama to one another, and so by them to have come to the knowledge of the people), she quits the stage, and Phædria enters next, alone likewise: he also gives you an account of himself, and of his returning from the country, in monologue; to which unnatural way of narration Terence is subject in all his plays. In his *Adelphi,* or Brothers, Syrus and Demea enter after the scene was broken by the departure of Sostrata, Geta, and Canthara; and indeed you can scarce look into any of his comedies, where you will not presently discover the same interruption.

"But as they have failed both in laying of their plots, and managing of them, swerving from the rules of their own art by misrepresenting Nature to us, in which they have ill satisfied one intention of a play, which was delight; so in the instructive part they have erred worse: instead of punishing vice and rewarding virtue, they have often shown a prosperous wickedness, and an unhappy piety: they have set before us a bloody image of revenge in Medea, and given her dragons to convey her safe from punishment; a Priam and Astyanex murdered, and Cassandra ravished, and the lust and murder ending in the victory of him who acted them: in short, there is no indecorum in any of our modern plays, which if I would excuse, I could not shadow with some authority from the Ancients.

"And one farther note of them let me leave you: tragedies and comedies were not writ then as they are now, promiscuously, by the same person; but he who found his genius bending to the one, never attempted the other way. This is so plain, that I need not instance to you, that Aristophanes, Plautus, Terence, never any of them writ a tragedy; Æschylus, Euripides, Sophocles, and Seneca, never meddled with comedy: the sock and buskin were not worn by the same poet. Having then so much care to excel in one kind, very little is to be pardoned them, if they miscarried in it; and this would lead me to the consideration of their wit, had not Crites given me sufficient warning not to be too bold in my judgment of it; because, the languages being dead, and many of the customs and little accidents on which it depended lost to us, we are not competent judges of it. But though I grant that here and there we may miss the application of a proverb or a custom, yet a thing well said will be wit in all languages; and though it may lose something in the translation.

14 ["It is well to employ so short a time."]

yet to him who reads it in the original, 'tis still the same: he has an idea of its excellency, though it cannot pass from his mind into any other expression or words than those in which he finds it. When Phædria, in the *Eunuch,* had a command from his mistress to be absent two days, and, encouraging himself to go through with it, said, *Tandem ego non illa caream, si sit opus, vel totum triduum?* [15] Parmeno, to mock the softness of his master, lifting up his hands and eyes, cries out, as it were in admiration, *Hui! universum triduum!* [16] the elegancy of which *universum,* though it cannot be rendered in our language, yet leaves an impression on our souls: but this happens seldom in him; in Plautus oftener, who is infinitely too bold in his metaphors and coining words, out of which many times his wit is nothing; which questionless was one reason why Horace falls upon him so severely in those verses:

Sed proavi nostri Plautinos et numeros et
Laudavere sales, nimium patienter utrumque,
Ne dicam stolidè.[17]

For Horace himself was cautious to obtrude a new word on his readers, and makes custom and common use the best measure of receiving it into our writings:

Multa renascentur quæ nunc cecidere, cadentque
Quæ nunc sunt in honore vocabula, si volet usus,
Quem penes arbitrium est, et jus, et norma loquendi.[18]

"The not observing this rule is that which the world has blamed in our satirist, Cleveland: to express a thing hard and unnaturally, is his new way of elocution. 'Tis true, no poet but may sometimes use a catachresis: Virgil does it—

Mistaque ridenti colocasia fundet acantho—[19]

in his eclogue of *Pollio;* and in his 7th *Æneid:*

mirantur et undæ,
Miratur nemus insuetum fulgentia longe
Scuta virum fluvio pictasque innare carinas.[20]

And Ovid once so modestly, that he asks leave to do it:

quem, si verbo audacia detur,
Haud metuam summi dixisse Palatia cœli.[21]

calling the court of Jupiter by the name of Augustus his palace; though in another place he is more bold, where he says,—*et longas visent Capitolia pompas.*[22] But to do this always, and never be able to write a line without it, though it may be admired by some few pedants, will not pass upon those who know that wit is best conveyed to us in the most easy language; and is most to be admired when a great thought comes dressed in words so commonly received, that it is understood by the meanest apprehensions, as the best meat is the most easily digested: but we cannot read a verse of Cleveland's without making a face at it, as if every word were a pill to swallow: he gives us many times a hard nut to break our teeth, without a kernel for our pains. So that there is this difference betwixt his *Satires* and doctor Donne's; that the one gives us deep thoughts in common language, though rough cadence; the other gives us common thoughts in abstruse words: 'tis true, in some places his wit is independent of his words, as in that of the rebel Scot:

Had *Cain* been *Scot,* God would have chang'd his doom;
Not forc'd him wander, but confin'd him home.

"*Si sic omnia dixisset!* [23] This is wit in all languages: it is like Mercury, never to be lost or killed:—and so that other—

For beauty, like white powder, makes no noise,
And yet the silent hypocrite destroys.

You see, the last line is highly metaphorical, but it is so soft and gentle, that it does not shock us as we read it.

15 ["Shall I not do without her if it is necessary, even for a whole three days?"]
16 ["Alas, all of three days!"]
17 ["Our forefathers praised both the verses and witticisms of Plautus all too tolerantly, if I may not say stupidly."]
18 ["Many words will be revived which now have fallen into disuse and many will fall into disuse which are now accepted if practice demands, in whose power lie the choice, the right and the standard of language."]
19 ["And the colocasia will spread forth, mingled with the laughing acanthus."]
20 ["The woods and waters wonder at the gleam
Of shields, and painted ships, that stem the stream." (Dryden)]
21 ["If I may use so bold a figure of speech I should not hesitate to call the palace of the sky."]
22 ["And the capitol will see long processions."]
23 ["If only he had said everything in this way."]

"But, to return from whence I have digressed, to the consideration of the Ancients' writing, and their wit; of which by this time you will grant us in some measure to be fit judges. Though I see many excellent thoughts in Seneca, yet he of them who had a genius most proper for the stage, was Ovid; he had a way of writing so fit to stir up a pleasing admiration and concernment, which are the objects of a tragedy, and to show the various movements of a soul combating betwixt two different passions, that, had he lived in our age, or in his own could have writ with our advantages, no man but must have yielded to him; and therefore I am confident the *Medea* is none of his: for, though I esteem it for the gravity and sententiousness of it, which he himself concludes to be suitable to a tragedy, —*Omne genus scripti gravitate tragœdia vincit,*[24] —yet it moves not my soul enough to judge that he, who in the epic way wrote things so near the drama as the story of Myrrha, of Caunus and Biblis, and the rest, should stir up no more concernment where he most endeavoured it. The masterpiece of Seneca I hold to be that scene in the *Troades,* where Ulysses is seeking for Astyanax to kill him; there you see the tenderness of a mother so represented in Andromache, that it raises compassion to a high degree in the reader, and bears the nearest resemblance of anything in their tragedies to the excellent scenes of passion in Shakspeare, or in Fletcher: for love-scenes, you will find few among them; their tragic poets dealt not with that soft passion, but with lust, cruelty, revenge, ambition, and those bloody actions they produced; which were more capable of raising horror than compassion in an audience: leaving love untouched, whose gentleness would have tempered them, which is the most frequent of all the passions, and which, being the private concernment of every person, is soothed by viewing its own image in a public entertainment.

"Among their comedies, we find a scene or two of tenderness, and that where you would least expect it, in Plautus; but to speak generally, their lovers say little, when they see each other, but *anima mea vita mea;* Ζωὴ καὶ ψυχη,[25] as the women in Juvenal's time used to cry out in the fury of their kindness: then indeed to speak sense were an offence. Any sudden gust of passion (as an ecstasy of love in an unexpected meeting) cannot better be expressed than in a word and a sigh, breaking one another. Nature is dumb on such occasions; and to make her speak, would be to represent her unlike herself. But there are a thousand other concernments of lovers, as jealousies, complaints, contrivances, and the like, where not to open their minds at large to each other, were to be wanting to their own love, and to the expectation of the audience; who watch the movements of their minds, as much as the changes of their fortunes. For the imaging of the first is properly the work of a poet; the latter he borrows of the historian."

Eugenius was proceeding in that part of his discourse, when Crites interrupted him. "I see," said he, "Eugenius and I are never like to have this question decided betwixt us; for he maintains, the Moderns have acquired a new perfection in writing; I can only grant they have altered the mode of it. Homer described his heroes men of great appetites, lovers of beef broiled upon the coals, and good fellows; contrary to the practice of the French Romances, whose heroes neither eat, nor drink, nor sleep, for love. Virgil makes Æneas a bold avower of his own virtues:

Sum pius Æneas, fama super æthera notus;[26]

which in the civility of our poets is the character of a fanfaron or Hector: for with us the knight takes occasion to walk out, or sleep, to avoid the vanity of telling his own story, which the trusty 'squire is ever to perform for him. So in their love-scenes, of which Eugenius spoke last, the ancients were more hearty, we more talkative: they writ love as it was then the mode to make it; and I will grant thus much to Eugenius, that perhaps one of their poets had he lived in our age, *si foret hoc nostrum fato delapsus in œvum*[27] (as Horace says of Lucilius), he had altered many things; not that they were not natural before, but that he might accommodate himself to the age he lived in. Yet in the meantime, we are not to conclude any-

24 ["Tragedy exceeds every kind of writing in gravity."]

25 ["My soul, my life."]

26 ["I am dutiful Aeneas, whose fame is known above the heavens."]

27 ["If he had been dropped into our age by fate."]

thing rashly against those great men, but preserve to them the dignity of masters, and give that honour to their memories, *quos Libitina sacravit*,[28] part of which we expect may be paid to us in future times."

This moderation of Crites, as it was pleasing to all the company, so it put an end to that dispute; which Eugenius, who seemed to have the better of the argument, would urge no farther: but Lisideius, after he had acknowledged himself of Eugenius his opinion concerning the Ancient, yet told him, he had forborne, till his discourse were ended, to ask him why he preferred the English plays above those of other nations? and whether we ought not to submit our stage to the exactness of our next neighbours?

"Though," said Eugenius, "I am at all times ready to defend the honour of my country against the French, and to maintain, we are as well able to vanquish them with our pens, as our ancestors have been with their swords; yet, if you please," added he, looking upon Neander, "I will commit this cause to my friend's management; his opinion of our plays is the same with mine: and besides, there is no reason, that Crites and I, who have now left the stage, should reenter so suddenly upon it; which is against the laws of comedy."

"If the question had been stated," replied Lisideius, "who had writ best, the French or English, forty years ago, I should have been of your opinion, and adjudged the honour to our own nation; but since that time" (said he, turning towards Neander), "we have been so long together bad Englishmen that we had not leisure to be good poets. Beaumont, Fletcher, and Jonson (who were only capable of bringing us to that degree of perfection which we have), were just then leaving the world; as if (in an age of so much horror) wit, and those milder studies of humanity, had no farther business among us. But the Muses, who ever follow peace, went to plant in another country: it was then that the great Cardinal Richelieu began to take them into his protection; and that, by his encouragement, Corneille, and some other Frenchmen, reformed their theatre, which before was as much below ours, as it now surpasses it and the rest of Europe. But because Crites in his discourse for the Ancients has prevented me, by touching upon many rules of the stage which the Moderns have borrowed from them, I shall only, in short, demand of you, whether you are not convinced that of all nations the French have best observed them? In the Unity of Time you find them so scrupulous, that it yet remains a dispute among their poets, whether the artificial day of twelve hours, more or less, be not meant by Aristotle, rather than the natural one of twenty-four; and consequently, whether all plays ought not to be reduced into that compass. This I can testify, that in all their dramas writ within these last twenty years and upwards, I have not observed any that have extended the time to thirty hours: in the Unity of Place they are full as scrupulous; for many of their critics limit it to that very spot of ground where the play is supposed to begin; none of them, exceed the compass of the same town or city. The Unity of Action in all plays is yet more conspicuous; for they do not burden them with under-plots, as the English do: which is the reason why many scenes of our tragi-comedies carry on a design that is nothing of kin to the main plot; and that we see two distinct webs in a play, like those in ill-wrought stuffs; and two actions, that is, two plays, carried on together, to the confounding of the audience; who, before they are warm in their concernments for one part, are diverted to another; and by that means espouse the interest of neither. From hence likewise it arises that the one half of our actors are not known to the other. They keep their distances, as if they were Montagues and Capulets, and seldom begin an acquaintance till the last scene of the fifth act, when they are all to meet upon the stage. There is no theatre in the world has anything so absurd as the English tragi-comedy; 'tis a drama of our own invention, and the fashion of it is enough to proclaim it so; here a course of mirth, there another of sadness and passion, and a third of honour, and fourth a duel: thus, in two hours and a half, we run through all the fits of Bedlam. The French affords you as much variety on the same day, but they do it not so unseasonably, or *mal à propos*, as we: our poets present you the play and the farce together; and our stages still re-

[28] ["Which Libitina has consecrated."]

tain somewhat of the original civility of the *Red Bull:*

Atque ursum et pugiles media inter carmina poscunt.[29]

The end of tragedies or serious plays, says Aristotle, is to beget admiration, compassion, or concernment; but are not mirth and compassion things incompatible? and is it not evident that the poet must of necessity destroy the former by intermingling of the latter? that is, he must ruin the sole end and object of his tragedy, to introduce somewhat that is forced in, and is not of the body of it. Would you not think that physician mad, who, having prescribed a purge, should immediately order you to take restringents upon it?

"But to leave our plays, and return to theirs. I have noted one great advantage they have had in the plotting of their tragedies; that is, they are always grounded upon some known history: according to that of Horace, *Ex noto fictum carmen sequar,*[30] and in that they have so imitated the Ancients that they have surpassed them. For the Ancients, as was observed before, took for the foundation of their plays some poetical fiction, such as under that consideration could move but little concernment in the audience, because they already knew the event of it. But the French goes farther:

Atque ita mentitur, sic veris falsa remiscet
Primo ne medium, medio ne discrepet imum.[31]

He so interweaves truth with probable fiction that he puts a pleasing fallacy upon us; mends the intrigues of fate, and dispenses with the severity of history, to reward that virtue which has been rendered to us there unfortunate. Sometimes the story has left the success so doubtful that the writer is free, by the privilege of a poet, to take that which of two or more relations will best suit with his design: as for example, the death of Cyrus, whom Justin and some others report to have perished in the Scythian war, but Xenophon affirms to have died in his bed of extreme old age. Nay more, when the event is past dispute, even then we are willing to be deceived, and the poet, if he contrives it with appearance of truth, has all the audience of his party; at least during the time his play is acting: so naturally we are kind to virtue, when our own interest is not in question, that we take it up as the general concernment of mankind. On the other side, if you consider the historical plays of Shakspeare, they are rather so many chronicles of kings, or the business many times of thirty or forty years, cramped into a representation of two hours and a half; which is not to imitate or paint Nature, but rather to draw her in miniature, to take her in little; to look upon her through the wrong end of a perspective, and receive her images not only much less, but infinitely more imperfect than the life: this, instead of making a play delightful, renders it ridiculous:—

Quodcunque ostendis mihi sic, incredulus odi.[32]

For the spirit of man cannot be satisfied but with truth, or at least verisimility; and a poem is to contain, if not τὰ ἔτυμα, yet ἐτύμοισιν ὁμοῖα,[33] as one of the Greek poets has expressed it.

"Another thing in which the French differ from us and from the Spaniards, is that they do not embarrass, or cumber themselves with too much plot; they only represent so much of a story as will constitute one whole and great action sufficient for a play; we, who undertake more, do but multiply adventures; which, not being produced from one another, as effects from causes, but barely following, constitute many actions in the drama, and consequently make it many plays.

"But by pursuing close one argument, which is not cloyed with many turns, the French have gained more liberty for verse, in which they write; they have leisure to dwell on a subject which deserves it; and to represent the passions (which we have acknowledged to be the poet's work), without being hurried from one thing to another, as we are in the plays of Calderon, which we have seen lately upon our theatres under the name of Spanish plots. I have taken

29 ["And in the middle of plays they ask for a bear and boxers."]

30 ["Out of a well-known story, I should bring a poem."]

31 ["And he so lies and so mixes the false with the true that the middle part will not be inconsistent with the first part nor the last part with the middle."]

32 ["Whatever you show me in this way I find incredible and I hate."]

33 ["True things"—"things like the truth."]

notice but of one tragedy of ours, whose plot has that uniformity and unity of design in it, which I have commended in the French; and that is *Rollo,* or rather, under the name of Rollo, the Story of Bassianus and Geta in Herodian: there indeed the plot is neither large nor intricate, but just enough to fill the minds of the audience, not to cloy them. Besides, you see it founded upon the truth of history,—only the time of the action is not reduceable to the strictness of the rules; and you see in some places a little farce mingled, which is below the dignity of the other parts; and in this all our poets are extremely peccant: even Ben Jonson himself, in *Sejanus* and *Catiline,* has given us this oleo of a play, this unnatural mixture of comedy and tragedy; which to me sounds just as ridiculously as the history of David with the merry humours of Golias. In *Sejanus* you may take notice of the scene betwixt Livia and the physician, which is a pleasant satire upon the artificial helps of beauty: in *Catiline* you may see the parliament of women; the little envies of them to one another; and all that passes betwixt Curio and Fulvia: scenes admirable in their kind, but of an ill mingle with the rest.

"But I return again to the French writers, who, as I have said, do not burden themselves too much with plot, which has been reproached to them by an *ingenious person* of our nation as a fault; for, he says, they commonly make but one person considerable in a play; they dwell on him, and his concernments, while the rest of the persons are only subservient to set him off. If he intends this by it, that there is one person in the play who is of greater dignity than the rest, he must tax, not only theirs, but those of the Ancients, and which he would be loth to do, the best of ours; for it is impossible but that one person must be more conspicuous in it than any other, and consequently the greatest share in the action must devolve on him. We see it so in the management of all affairs; even in the most equal aristocracy, the balance cannot be so justly poised but some one will be superior to the rest, either in parts, fortune, interest, or the consideration of some glorious exploit; which will reduce the greatest part of business into his hands.

"But, if he would have us to imagine, that in exalting one character the rest of them are neglected, and that all of them have not some share or other in the action of the play, I desire him to produce any of Corneille's tragedies, wherein every person, like so many servants in a well-governed family, has not some employment, and who is not necessary to the carrying on of the plot, or at least to your understanding it.

"There are indeed some protatic persons in the Ancients, whom they make use of in their plays, either to hear or give the relation: but the French avoid this with great address, making their narrations only to, or by such, who are some way interested in the main design. And now I am speaking of relations, I cannot take a fitter opportunity to add this in favour of the French, that they often use them with better judgment and more *à propos* than the English do. Not that I commend narrations in general, —but there are two sorts of them. One, of those things which are antecedent to the play, and are related to make the conduct of it more clear to us. But 'tis a fault to choose such subjects for the stage as will force us on that rock because we see they are seldom listened to by the audience and that is many times the ruin of the play; for, being once let pass without attention, the audience can never recover themselves to understand the plot: and indeed it is somewhat unreasonable that they should be put to so much trouble, as that, to comprehend what passes in their sight, they must have recourse to what was done, perhaps, ten or twenty years ago.

"But there is another sort of relations, that is, of things happening in the action of the play, and supposed to be done behind the scenes; and this is many times both convenient and beautiful; for by it the French avoid the tumult to which we are subject in England, by representing duels, battles, and the like; which renders our stage too like the theatres where they fight prizes. For what is more ridiculous than to represent an army with a drum and five men behind it; all which the hero of the other side is to drive in before him; or to see a duel fought, and one slain with two or three thrusts of the foils, which we know are so blunted, that we might give a man an hour to kill another in good earnest with them.

"I have observed that in all our tragedies, the audience cannot forbear laughing when the actors are to die; it is the most comic part of the whole play. All *passions* may be lively represented on the stage, if to the well-writing of them the actor supplies a good commanded voice, and limbs that move easily, and without stiffness; but there are many *actions* which can never be imitated to a just height: dying especially is a thing which none but a Roman gladiator could naturally perform on the stage, when he did not imitate or represent, but naturally do it; and therefore it is better to omit the representation of it.

"The words of a good writer, which describe it lively, will make a deeper impression of belief in us than all the actor can persuade us to, when he seems to fall dead before us; as a poet in the description of a beautiful garden, or a meadow, will please our imagination more than the place itself can please our sight. When we see death represented, we are convinced it is but fiction; but when we hear it related, our eyes, the strongest witnesses, are wanting, which might have undeceived us; and we are all willing to favour the sleight, when the poet does not too grossly impose on us. They therefore who imagine these relations would make no concernment in the audience, are deceived, by confounding them with the other, which are of things antecedent to the play: those are made often in cold blood, as I may say, to the audience; but these are warmed with our concernments, which were before awakened in the play. What the philosophers say of motion, that, when it is once begun, it continues of itself, and will do so to eternity, without some stop put to it, is clearly true on this occasion: the soul being already moved with the characters and fortunes of those imaginary persons, continues going of its own accord; and we are no more weary to hear what becomes of them when they are not on the stage, than we are to listen to the news of an absent mistress. But it is objected, that if one part of the play may be related, then why not all? I answer, some parts of the action are more fit to be represented, some to be related. Corneille says judiciously, that the poet is not obliged to expose to view all particular actions which conduce to the principal: he ought to select such of them to be seen, which will appear with the greatest beauty, either by the magnificence of the show, or the vehemence of passions, which they produce, or some other charm which they have in them; and let the rest arrive to the audience by narration. 'Tis a great mistake in us to believe the French present no part of the action on the stage; every alteration or crossing of a design, every new-sprung passion, and turn of it, is a part of the action, and much the noblest, except we conceive nothing to be action till they come to blows; as if the painting of the hero's mind were not more properly the poet's work than the strength of his body. Nor does this anything contradict the opinion of Horace, where he tells us,

Segnius irritant animos demissa per aurem,
Quam quæ sunt oculis subjecta fidelibus.[34]

For he says immediately after,

Non tamen intus
Digna geri promes in scenam; multaq; tolles
Ex oculis, quæ mox narret facundia præsens.[35]

Among which many he recounts some:

Nec pueros coram populo Medea trucidet,
Aut in avem Progne mutetur, Cadmus in anguem,
etc.[36]

That is, those actions which by reason of their cruelty, will cause aversion in us, or by reason of their impossibility, unbelief, ought either wholly to be avoided by a poet, or only delivered by narration. To which we may have leave to add such as to avoid tumult (as was before hinted), or to reduce the plot into a more reasonable compass of time, or for defect of beauty in them, are rather to be related than presented to the eye. Examples of all these kinds are frequent, not only among all the Ancients, but in the best received of our English poets. We find Ben Jonson using them in his *Magnetic Lady*, where one comes out from dinner, and relates the quarrels and disorders of it, to save the undecent appearance of them on the stage, and to abbreviate the story; and this in express imitation of Terence, who had done the same before him in his *Eunuch*, where Pythias makes the

34 ["The things which are transmitted through the ear stir the mind less forcefully than the things which are set before the faithful eyes."]

35 ["You shall not bring on the stage things which should be done offstage; and you shall remove from my sight things which a ready eloquence will soon narrate."]

36 ["And Medea should not cut up her children in front of the audience, nor Procne be changed into a bird, Cadmus into a snake, etc."]

like relation of what had happened within at the Soldier's entertainment. The relations likewise of Sejanus's death, and the prodigies before it, are remarkable; the one of which was hid from sight, to avoid the horror and tumult of the representation; the other, to shun the introducing of things impossible to be believed. In that excellent play, *The King and no King*, Fletcher goes yet farther; for the whole unravelling of the plot is done by narration in the fifth act, after the manner of the Ancients; and it moves great concernment in the audience, though it be only a relation of what was done many years before the play. I could multiply other instances, but these are sufficient to prove that there is no error in choosing a subject which requires this sort of narrations; in the ill managing of them, there may.

"But I find I have been too long in this discourse, since the French have many other excellencies not common to us; as that you never see any of their plays end with a conversion, or simple change of will, which is the ordinary way which our poets use to end theirs. It shows little art in the conclusion of a dramatic poem, when they who have hindered the felicity during the four acts, desist from it in the fifth, without some powerful cause to take them off; and though I deny not but such reasons may be found, yet it is a path that is cautiously to be trod, and the poet is to be sure he convinces the audience that the motive is strong enough. As for example, the conversion of the Usurer in *The Scornful Lady* seems to me a little forced; for, being an Usurer, which implies a lover of money to the highest degree of covetousness (and such the poet has represented him), the account he gives for the sudden change is, that he has been duped by the wild young fellow; which in reason might render him more wary another time, and make him punish himself with harder fare and coarser clothes, to get it up again: but that he should look on it as a judgment, and so repent, we may expect to hear of in a sermon, but I should never endure it in a play.

"I pass by this; neither will I insist on the care they take that no person after his first entrance shall ever appear, but the business which brings him upon the stage shall be evident; which, if observed, must needs render all the events in the play more natural; for there you see the probability of every accident, in the cause that produced it; and that which appears chance in the play, will seem so reasonable to you, that you will there find it almost necessary: so that in the exits of the actors you have a clear account of their purpose and design in the next entrance (though, if the scene be well wrought, the event will commonly deceive you) for there is nothing so absurd, says Corneille, as for an actor to leave the stage only because he has no more to say.

"I should now speak of the beauty of their rhyme, and the just reason I have to prefer that way of writing in tragedies before ours in blank-verse; but because it is partly received by us, and therefore not altogether peculiar to them, I will say no more of it in relation to their plays. For our own, I doubt not but it will exceedingly beautify them; and I can see but one reason why it should not generally obtain, that is, because our poets write so ill in it. This indeed may prove a more prevailing argument than all others which are used to destroy it, and therefore I am only troubled when great and judicious poets, and those who are acknowledged such, have writ or spoke against it: as for others, they are to be answered by that one sentence of an ancient author:—*Sed ut primo ad consequendos eos quos priores ducimus, accendimur, ita ubi aut proeteriri, aut æquari eos posse desperavimus, studium cum spe senescit: quod, scilicet, assequi non potest, sequi desinit; . . . praeteritoque eo in quo eminere non possumus, aliquid in quo nitamur, conquirimus.*" [37]

Lisideius concluded in this manner; and Neander, after a little pause, thus answered him:

"I shall grant Lisideius, without much dispute, a great part of what he has urged against us; for I acknowledge that the French contrive their plots more regularly, and observe the laws of comedy, and decorum of the stage (to speak generally), with more exactness than the English. Farther, I deny not but he has taxed us

[37] ["But just as we are inflamed to follow those whom we consider foremost, so, when we despair that they can be either surpassed or equalled, our zeal wanes with our hope: for, to be sure, what it cannot attain it stops to follow . . . and when that in which we cannot excel is passed, we look for something in which to strive."]

justly in some irregularities of ours, which he has mentioned; yet, after all, I am of opinion that neither our faults nor their virtues are considerable enough to place them above us.

"For the lively imitation of Nature being in the definition of a play, those which best fulfil that law ought to be esteemed superior to the others. 'Tis true, those beauties of the French poesy are such as will raise perfection higher where it is, but are not sufficient to give it where it is not: they are indeed the beauties of a statue, but not of a man, because not animated with the soul of Poesy, which is imitation of humour and passions: and this Lisideius himself, or any other, however biassed to their party, cannot but acknowledge, if he will either compare the humours of our comedies, or the characters of our serious plays, with theirs. He that will look upon theirs which have been written till these last ten years, or thereabouts, will find it an hard matter to pick out two or three passable humours amongst them. Corneille himself, their arch-poet, what has he produced except *The Liar,* and you know how it was cried up in France; but when it came upon the English stage, though well translated, and that part of Dorant acted to so much advantage by Mr. Hart as I am confident it never received in its own country, the most favourable to it would not put it in competition with many of Fletcher's or Ben Jonson's. In the rest of Corneille's comedies you have little humour; he tells you himself, his way is, first to show two lovers in good intelligence with each other; in the working up of the play to embroil them by some mistake, and in the latter end to clear it, and reconcile them.

"But of late years Molière, the younger Corneille, Quinault, and some others, have been imitating afar off the quick turns and graces of the English stage. They have mixed their serious plays with mirth, like our tragi-comedies, since the death of Cardinal Richelieu; which Lisideius and many others not observing, have commended that in them for a virtue which they themselves no longer practise. Most of their new plays are, like some of ours, derived from the Spanish novels. There is scarce one of them without a veil, and a trusty Diego, who drolls much after the rate of *The Adventures.* But their humours, if I may grace them with that name, are so thin-sown, that never above one of them comes up in any play. I dare take upon me to find more variety of them in some one play of Ben Jonson's than in all theirs together; as he who has seen *The Alchemyst, The Silent Woman,* or *Bartholomew Fair,* cannot but acknowledge with me.

"I grant the French have performed what was possible on the ground-work of the Spanish plays; what was pleasant before, they have made regular: but there is not above one good play to be writ on all those plots; they are too much alike to please often; which we need not the experience of our own stage to justify. As for their new way of mingling mirth with serious plot, I do not, with Lisideius, condemn the thing, though I cannot approve their manner of doing it. He tells us, we cannot so speedily recollect ourselves after a scene of great passion and concernment, as to pass to another of mirth and humour, and to enjoy it with any relish: but why should he imagine the soul of man more heavy than his senses? Does not the eye pass from an unpleasant object to a pleasant in a much shorter time than is required to this? and does not the unpleasantness of the first commend the beauty of the latter? The old rule of logic might have convinced him, that contraries, when placed near, set off each other. A continued gravity keeps the spirit too much bent; we must refresh it sometimes, as we bait in a journey that we may go on with greater ease. A scene of mirth, mixed with tragedy, has the same effect upon us which our music has betwixt the acts; and that we find a relief to us from the best plots and language of the stage, if the discourses have been long. I must therefore have stronger arguments, ere I am convinced that compassion and mirth in the same subject destroy each other; and in the meantime cannot but conclude, to the honour of our nation, that we have invented, increased, and perfected a more pleasant way of writing for the stage, than was ever known to the Ancients or moderns of any nation, which is tragi-comedy.

"And this leads me to wonder why Lisideius and many others should cry up the barrenness of the French plots above the variety and copiousness of the English. Their plots are single; they carry on one design, which is pushed forward by all the actors. every scene in the play contributing and moving towards it. Our plays, besides the main design, have under-plots or by-concernments, of less considerable persons and intrigues, which are carried on with the motion of the main plot: just as they say the orb of the fixed stars, and those of the planets, though they have motions of their own, are whirled about by the motion of the *primum mobile,* in which they are contained. That similitude expresses much of the English stage; for if contrary motions may be found in nature to agree; if a planet can go east and west at the same time;—one way by virtue of his own motion, the other by the force of the First Mover, it will not be difficult to imagine how the under-plot, which is only different, not contrary to the great design, may naturally be conducted along with it.

"Eugenius has already shown us, from the confession of the French poets, that the Unity of Action is sufficiently preserved, if all the imperfect actions of the play are conducing to the main design; but when those petty intrigues of a play are so ill ordered, that they have no coherence with the other, I must grant that Lisideius has reason to tax that want of due connection; for co-ordination in a play is as dangerous and unnatural as in a state. In the meantime he must acknowledge, our variety, if well ordered, will afford a greater pleasure to the audience.

"As for his other argument, that by pursuing one single theme they gain an advantage to express and work up the passions, I wish any example he could bring from them would make it good; for I confess their verses are to me the coldest I have ever read. Neither, indeed, is it possible for them, in the way they take, so to express passion, as that the effects of it should appear in the concernment of an audience, their speeches being so many declamations, which tire us with the length; so that instead of persuading us to grieve for their imaginary heroes, we are concerned for our own trouble, as we are in tedious visits of bad company; we are in pain till they are gone. When the French stage came to be reformed by Cardinal Richelieu, those long harangues were introduced to comply with the gravity of a churchman. Look upon the *Cinna* and the *Pompey;* they are not so properly to be called plays, as long discourses of reason of state; and *Polieucte* in matters of religion is as solemn as the long stops upon our organs. Since that time it is grown into a custom, and their actors speak by the hour-glass, as our parsons do; nay, they account it the grace of their parts, and think themselves disparaged by the poet, if they may not twice or thrice in a play entertain the audience with a speech of an hundred or two hundred lines. I deny not but this may suit well enough with the French; for as we, who are a more sullen people, come to be diverted at our plays, so they, who are of an airy and gay temper, come thither to make themselves more serious: and this I conceive to be one reason why comedy is more pleasing to us, and tragedies to them. But to speak generally: it cannot be denied that short speeches and replies are more apt to move the passions and beget concernment in us, than the other; for it is unnatural for any one in a gust of passion to speak long together, or for another in the same condition to suffer him, without interruption. Grief and passion are like floods raised in little brooks by a sudden rain; they are quickly up; and if the concernment be poured unexpectedly in upon us, it overflows us: but a long sober shower gives them leisure to run out as they came in, without troubling the ordinary current. As for Comedy, repartee is one of its chiefest graces; the greatest pleasure of the audience is a chase of wit, kept up on both sides, and swiftly managed. And this our forefathers, if not we, have had in Fletcher's plays, to a much higher degree of perfection than the French poets can arrive at.

"There is another part of Lisideius his discourse, in which he has rather excused our neighbours, than commended them; that is, for aiming only to make one person considerable in their plays. 'Tis very true what he has urged, that one character in all plays, even without the poet's care, will have advantage of all the others; and that the design of the whole drama will chiefly depend on it. But this hinders not that there may be more shining characters in the play: many persons of a second magnitude, nay, some so very near, so almost equal to the first, that greatness may be opposed to greatness, and all the persons be made considerable, not only by their quality, but their action. 'Tis evident that the more the persons are, the greater will be the variety of the plot. If then the parts are managed so regularly, that the beauty of the whole be kept entire, and that the variety become not a perplexed and confused mass of accidents, you will find it infinitely pleasing to be led in a labyrinth of design, where you see some of your way before you, yet discern not the end till you arrive at it. And that all this is practicable, I can produce for examples many of our English plays: as *The Maid's Tragedy, The Alchemyst, The Silent Woman:* I was going to have named *The Fox,* but that the unity of design seems not exactly observed in it; for there appear two actions in the play; the first naturally ending with the fourth act; the second forced from it in the fifth; which yet is the less to be condemned in him, because the disguise of Volpone, though it suited not with his character as a crafty or covetous person, agreed well enough with that of a voluptuary; and by it the poet gained the end he aimed at, the punishment of vice, and the reward of virtue, which that disguise produced. So that to judge equally of it, it was an excellent fifth act, but not so naturally proceeding from the former.

"But to leave this, and pass to the latter part of Lisideius his discourse, which concerns relations: I must acknowledge with him, that the French have reason when they hide that part of the action which would occasion too much tumult on the stage, and choose rather to have it made known by narration to the audience. Farther, I think it very convenient, for the reasons he has given, that all incredible actions were removed; but, whether custom has so insinuated itself into our countrymen, or nature has so formed them to fierceness, I know not; but they will scarcely suffer combats and other objects of horror to be taken from them. And indeed, the indecency of tumults is all which can be objected against fighting: for why may not our imagination as well suffer itself to be deluded with the probability of it, as with any other thing in the play? For my part, I can with as great ease persuade myself that the blows which are struck, are given in good earnest, as I can, that they who strike them are kings or princes, or those persons which they represent. For objects of incredibility, I would be satisfied from Lisideius, whether we have any so removed from all appearance of truth, as are those of Corneille's *Andromede;* a play which has been frequented the most of any he has writ. If the Perseus, or the son of an heathen god, the Pegasus, and the Monster, were not capable to choke a strong belief, let him blame any representation of ours hereafter. Those indeed were objects of delight; yet the reason is the same as to the probability: for he makes it not a Ballette or masque, but a play, which is to resemble truth. But for death, that it ought not to be represented, I have, besides the arguments alleged by Lisideius, the authority of Ben Jonson, who has forborne it in his tragedies; for both the death of Sejanus and Catiline are related: though in the latter I cannot but observe one irregularity of that great poet; he has removed the scene in the same act from Rome to Catiline's army, and from thence again to Rome; and besides, has allowed a very inconsiderable time, after Catiline's speech, for the striking of the battle, and the return of Petreius, who is to relate the event of it to the senate: which I should not animadvert on him, who was otherwise a painful observer of τὸ πρέπον, or the *decorum* of the stage, if he had not used extreme severity in his judgment on the incomparable Shakspeare for the same fault.—To conclude on this subject of relations; if we are to be blamed for showing too much of the action, the French are as faulty for discovering too little of it: a mean betwixt both should be observed by every judicious writer, so as the audience may neither be left unsatisfied by not seeing what is beautiful, or shocked by beholding what is either incredible or undecent.

"I hope I have already proved in this discourse, that though we are not altogether so puncutal as the French, in observing the laws of Comedy, yet our errors are so few, and little, and those things wherein we excel them so considerable, that we ought of right to be preferred before them. But what will Lisideius say, if they themselves acknowledge they are too strictly tied up by those laws, for breaking which he has blamed the English? I will allege Corneille's words, as I find them in the end of his Discourse of the Three Unities:—*Il est facile aux spéculatifs d'estre sévères, etc.* ' 'Tis easy for speculative persons to judge severely; but if they would produce to public view ten or twelve pieces of this nature, they would perhaps give more latitude to the rules than I have done, when by experience they had known how much we are bound up and constrained by them, and how many beauties of the stage they banished from it.' To illustrate a little what he has said: By their servile observations of the Unities of Time and Place, and integrity of scenes, they have brought on themselves that dearth of plot, and narrowness of imagination, which may be observed in all their plays. How many beautiful accidents might naturally happen in two or three days, which cannot arrive with any probability in the compass of twenty-four hours? There is time to be allowed also for maturity of design, which, amongst great and prudent persons, such as are often represented in Tragedy, cannot, with any likelihood of truth, be brought to pass at so short a warning. Farther; by tying themselves strictly to the Unity of Place, and unbroken scenes, they are forced many times to omit some beauties which cannot be shown where the act began; but might, if the scene were interrupted, and the stage cleared for the persons to enter in another place; and therefore the French poets are often forced upon absurdities; for if the act begins in a chamber, all the persons in the play must have some business or other to come thither, or else they are not to be shown that act; and sometimes their characters are very unfitting to appear there. As, suppose it were the king's bed-chamber; yet the meanest man in the tragedy must come and dispatch his business there, rather than in the lobby or courtyard (which is fitter for him), for fear the stage should be cleared, and the scenes broken. Many times they fall by it in a greater inconvenience; for they keep their scenes unbroken, and yet change the place; as in one of their newest plays, where the act begins in the street. There a gentleman is to meet his friend; he sees him with his man, coming out from his father's house; they talk together, and the first goes out: the second, who is a lover, has made an appointment with his mistress; she appears at the window, and then we are to imagine the scene lies under it. This gentleman is called away, and leaves his servant with his mistress; presently her father is heard from within; the young lady is afraid the serving-man should be discovered, and thrusts him in through a door, which is supposed to be her closet. After this, the father enters to the daughter, and now the scene is in a house; for he is seeking from one room to another for this poor Philipin, or French Diego, who is heard from within, drolling and breaking many a miserable conceit upon his sad condition. In this ridiculous manner the play goes on, the stage being never empty all the while: so that the street, the window, the houses, and the closet, are made to walk about, and the persons to stand still. Now what, I beseech you, is more easy than to write a regular French play, or more difficult than to write an irregular English one, like those of Fletcher, or of Shakspeare?

"If they content themselves, as Corneille did, with some flat design, which, like an ill riddle, is found out ere it be half proposed, such plots we can make every way regular, as easily as they; but whene'er they endeavour to rise to any quick turns and counterturns of plot, as some of them have attempted, since Corneille's plays have been less in vogue, you see they write as irregularly as we, though they cover it more speciously. Hence the reason is perspicuous, why no French plays, when translated, have, or ever can succeed on the English stage. For, if you consider the plots, our own are fuller of variety; if the writing, ours are more quick and fuller of spirit; and therefore 'tis a strange mistake in those who decry the way of writing plays in verse, as if the English therein imitated the French. We have borrowed nothing from them; our plots are weaved in English looms: we endeavour therein to follow the variety and greatness of characters which are derived to us from Shakspeare and Fletcher; the copiousness and well-knitting of the intrigues we have from Jonson; and for the verse itself we have English precedents of elder date than any of Corneille's plays. Not to name our old comedies before Shakspeare, which were all writ in verse of six feet, or Alexandrines, such as the French now use, I can show in Shakspeare, many scenes of rhyme together, and the like in Ben Jonson's tragedies: in *Catiline* and *Sejanus* sometimes thirty or forty lines, I mean besides the Chorus, or the monologues; which, by the way, showed Ben no enemy to this way of writing, especially if you look upon his *Sad Shepherd*, which goes sometimes on rhyme, sometimes on blank verse, like an horse who eases himself on trot and amble. You find him likewise commending Fletcher's pastoral of *The Faithful Shepherdess,* which is for the most part rhyme, though not refined to that purity to which it hath since been brought. And these examples are enough to clear us from a servile imitation of the French.

"But to return whence I have digressed: I dare boldly affirm these two things of the English drama;—First, that we have many plays of ours as regular as any of theirs, and which, besides, have more variety of plot and characters; and secondly, that in most of the irregular plays of Shakspeare or Fletcher (for Ben Jonson's are for the most part regular), there is a more masculine fancy and greater spirit in the writing than there is in any of the French. I could produce, even in Shakspeare's and Fletcher's works, some plays which are almost exactly formed; as *The Merry Wives of Windsor,* and *The Scornful Lady:* but because (generally speaking) Shakspeare, who writ first, did not perfectly observe the laws of Comedy, and Fletcher, who came nearer to perfection, yet through carelessness made many faults; I will take the pattern of a perfect play from Ben Jonson, who was a careful and learned observer of the dramatic laws, and from all his comedies I shall select *The Silent Woman;* of which I will make a short examen, according to those rules which the French observe."

As Neander was beginning to examine *The Silent Woman,* Eugenius, looking earnestly upon him; "I beseech you, Neander," said he, "gratify the company, and me in particular, so far, as before you speak of the play, to give us a character of the author; and tell us frankly your opinion, whether you do not think all writers, both French and English, ought to give place to him."

"I fear," replied Neander, "that in obeying your commands I shall draw a little envy on myself. Besides, in performing them, it will be first necessary to speak somewhat of Shakspeare and Fletcher, his rivals in poesy; and one of them, in my opinion, at least his equal, perhaps his superior.

"To begin, then, with Shakspeare. He was the man who of all modern, and perhaps ancient poets, had the largest and most comprehensive soul. All the images of Nature were still present to him, and he drew them, not laboriously, but luckily; when he describes any thing, you more than see it, you feel it too. Those who accuse him to have wanted learning, give him the greater commendation: he was naturally learned; he needed not the spectacles of books to read Nature; he looked inwards, and found her there. I cannot say he is everywhere alike; were he so, I should do him injury to compare him with the greatest of mankind. He is many times flat, insipid; his comic wit degenerating into clenches, his serious swelling into bombast. But he is always great, when some great occasion is presented to him; no man can say he ever had a fit subject for his wit, and did not then raise himself as high above the rest of poets,

Quantum lenta solent inter viburna cupressi.[38]

The consideration of this made Mr. Hales of Eaton say, that there was no subject of which any poet ever writ, but he would produce it much better treated of in Shakspeare; and however others are now generally preferred before him, yet the age wherein he lived, which had contemporaries with him Fletcher and Jonson, never equalled them to him in their esteem: and in the last King's court, when Ben's reputation was at highest, Sir John Suckling, and with him the greater part of the courtiers, set our Shakspeare far above him.

"Beaumont and Fletcher, of whom I am next to speak, had, with the advantage of Shakspeare's wit, which was their precedent, great natural gifts, improved by study: Beaumont especially being so accurate a judge of plays, that Ben Jonson, while he lived, submitted all his writings to his censure, and, 'tis thought, used his judgment in correcting, if not contriving, all his plots. What value he had for him, appears by the verses he writ to him; and therefore I need speak no farther of it. The first play that brought Fletcher and him in esteem was their *Philaster:* for before that, they had written two or three very unsuccessfully, as the like is reported of Ben Jonson, before he writ *Every Man in his Humour*. Their plots were generally more regular than Shakspeare's, especially those which were made before Beaumont's

[38] ["As cypresses commonly do among pliant shrubs."]

death; and they understood and imitated the conversation of gentlemen much better; whose wild debaucheries, and quickness of wit in repartees, no poet can ever paint as they have done. Humour, which Ben Jonson derived from particular persons, they made it not their business to describe: they represented all the passions very likely, but above all, love. I am apt to believe the English language in them arrived to its highest perfection: what words have since been taken in, are rather superfluous than ornamental. Their plays are now the most pleasant and frequent entertainments of the stage; two of theirs being acted through the year for one of Shakspeare's or Jonson's: the reason is, because there is a certain gaiety in their comedies, and pathos in their more serious plays, which suit generally with all men's humours. Shakspeare's language is likewise a little obsolete, and Ben Jonson's wit comes short of theirs.

"As for Jonson, to whose character I am now arrived, if we look upon him while he was himself (for his last plays were but his dotages), I think him the most learned and judicious writer which any theatre ever had. He was a most severe judge of himself, as well as others. One cannot say he wanted wit, but rather that he was frugal of it. In his works you find little to retrench or alter. Wit, and language, and humour also in some measure, we had before him; but something of art was wanting to the Drama till he came. He managed his strength to more advantage than any who preceded him. You seldom find him making love in any of his scenes, or endeavouring to move the passions; his genius was too sullen and saturnine to do it gracefully, especially when he knew he came after those who had performed both to such an height. Humour was his proper sphere; and in that he delighted most to represent mechanic people. He was deeply conversant in the Ancients, both Greek and Latin, and he borrowed boldly from them: there is scarce a poet or historian among the Roman authors of those times whom he has not translated in *Sejanus* and *Catiline*. But he has done his robberies so openly, that one may see he fears not to be taxed by any law. He invades authors like a monarch; and what would be theft in other poets is only victory in him. With the spoils of these writers he so represents old Rome to us, in its rites, ceremonies, and customs, that if one of their poets had written either of his tragedies, we had seen less of it than in him. If there was any fault in his language, 'twas that he weaved it too closely and laboriously, in his serious plays: perhaps, too, he did a little too much Romanise our tongue, leaving the words which he translated almost as much Latin as he found them: wherein, though he learnedly followed the idiom of their language, he did not enough comply with the idiom of ours. If I would compare him with Shakspeare, I must acknowledge him the more correct poet, but Shakspeare the greater wit. Shakspeare was the Homer, or father of our dramatic poets; Jonson was the Virgil, the pattern of elaborate writing; I admire him, but I love Shakspeare. To conclude of him; as he has given us the most correct plays, so in the precepts which he has laid down in his *Discoveries*, we have as many and profitable rules for perfecting the stage, as any wherewith the French can furnish us.

"Having thus spoken of the author, I proceed to the examination of his comedy, *The Silent Woman*.

"EXAMEN OF *The Silent Woman*

"To begin first with the length of the action; it is so far from exceeding the compass of a natural day, that it takes not up an artificial one. 'Tis all included in the limits of three hours and a half, which is no more than is required for the presentment on the stage. A beauty perhaps not much observed; if it had, we should not have looked on the Spanish translation of *Five Hours* with so much wonder. The scene of it is laid in London; the latitude of place is almost as little as you can imagine; for it lies all within the compass of two houses, and after the first act, in one. The continuity of scenes is observed more than in any of our plays, except his own *Fox* and *Alchemyst*. They are not broken above twice or thrice at most in the whole comedy; and in the two best of Corneille's plays, the *Cid* and *Cinna*, they are interrupted once apiece. The action of the play is entirely one; the end or aim of which is the settling Morose's estate on Dauphine. The intrigue of it is the greatest and most noble of any pure unmixed comedy in any language;

you see in it many persons of various characters and humours, and all delightful: as first, Morose, or an old man, to whom all noise but his own talking is offensive. Some who would be thought critics, say this humour of his is forced: but to remove that objection, we may consider him first to be naturally of a delicate hearing, as many are, to whom all sharp sounds are unpleasant; and secondly, we may attribute much of it to the peevishness of his age, or the wayward authority of an old man in his own house, where he may make himself obeyed; and this the poet seems to allude to in his name Morose. Besides this, I am assured from divers persons, that Ben Jonson was actually acquainted with such a man, one altogether as ridiculous as he is here represented. Others say, it is not enough to find one man of such an humour; it must be common to more, and the more common the more natural. To prove this, they instance in the best of comical characters, Falstaff. There are many men resembling him; old, fat, merry, cowardly, drunken, amorous, vain, and lying. But to convince these people, I need but tell them, that humour is the ridiculous extravagance of conversation, wherein one man differs from all others. If then it be common, or communicated to many, how differs it from other men's? or what indeed causes it to be ridiculous so much as the singularity of it? As for Falstaff, he is not properly one humour, but a miscellany of humours or images, drawn from so many several men: that wherein he is singular is his wit, or those things he says *præter expectatum,* unexpected by the audience; his quick evasions, when you imagine him surprised, which, as they are extremely diverting of themselves, so receive a great addition from his person; for the very sight of such an unwieldy old debauched fellow is a comedy alone. And here, having a place so proper for it, I cannot but enlarge somewhat upon this subject of humour into which I am fallen. The ancients had little of it in their comedies; for the τὸ γελοῖον [39] of the Old Comedy, of which Aristophanes was chief, was not so much to imitate a man, as to make the people laugh at some odd conceit, which had commonly somewhat of unnatural or obscene in it. Thus, when you see Socrates brought upon the stage, you are not to imagine him made ridiculous by the imitation of his actions, but rather by making him perform something very unlike himself; something so childish and absurd, as by comparing it with the gravity of the true Socrates, makes a ridiculous object for the spectators. In their New Comedy which succeeded, the poets sought indeed to express the ἦθος,[40] as in their tragedies the πάθος [41] of mankind. But this ἦθος contained only the general characters of men and manners; as old men, lovers, serving-men, courtezans, parasites, and such other persons as we see in their comedies; all which they made alike: that is, one old man or father, one lover, one courtezan, so like another, as if the first of them had begot the rest of every sort: *Ex homine hunc natum dicas.*[42] The same custom they observed likewise in their tragedies. As for the French, though they have the word *humeur* among them, yet they have small use of it in their comedies or farces; they being but ill imitations of the *ridiculum,* or that which stirred up laughter in the Old Comedy. But among the English 'tis otherwise: where by humour is meant some extravagant habit, passion, or affection, particular (as I said before) to some one person, by the oddness of which, he is immediately distinguished from the rest of men; which being lively and naturally represented, most frequently begets that malicious pleasure in the audience which is testified by laughter; as all things which are deviations from customs are ever the aptest to produce it: though by the way this laughter is only accidental, as the person represented is fantastic or bizarre; but pleasure is essential to it, as the imitation of what is natural. The description of these humours, drawn from the knowledge and observation of particular persons, was the peculiar genius and talent of Ben Jonson; to whose play I now return.

"Besides Morose, there are at least nine or ten different characters and humours in *The Silent Woman;* all which persons have several concernments of their own, yet are all used by the poet to the conducting of the main design to perfection. I shall not waste time in com-

39 ["The laughable."]

40 ["Character."]

41 ["Emotion."]

42 ["You would say that one was born from the other."]

mending the writing of this play; but I will give you my opinion, that there is more wit and acuteness of fancy in it than in any of Ben Jonson's. Besides that he has here described the conversation of gentlemen in the persons of True-Wit, and his friends, with more gaiety, air, and freedom, than in the rest of his comedies. For the contrivance of the plot, 'tis extreme elaborate, and yet withal easy; for the λυσις, or untying of it, 'tis so admirable, that when it is done, no one of the audience would think the poet could have missed it; and yet it was concealed so much before the last scene, that any other way would sooner have entered into your thoughts. But I dare not take upon me to commend the fabric of it, because it is altogether so full of art, that I must unravel every scene in it to commend it as I ought. And this excellent contrivance is still the more to be admired, because 'tis comedy, where the persons are only of common rank, and their business private, not elevated by passions or high concernments, as in serious plays. Here every one is a proper judge of all he sees, nothing is represented but that with which he daily converses: so that by consequence all faults lie open to discovery, and few are pardonable. 'Tis this which Horace has judiciously observed:

Creditur, ex medio quia res arcessit, habere
Sudoris minimum; sed habet Comedia tanto
Plus oneris, quanto veniæ minus.[43]

"But our poet who was not ignorant of these difficulties, had prevailed himself of all advantages; as he who designs a large leap takes his rise from the highest ground. One of these advantages is that which Corneille has laid down as the greatest which can arrive to any poem, and which he himself could never compass above thrice in all his plays; viz. the making choice of some signal and long-expected day, whereon the action of the play is to depend. This day was that designed by Dauphine for the settling of his uncle's estate upon him; which to compass, he contrives to marry him. That the marriage had been plotted by him long beforehand, is made evident by what he tells True-Wit in the second act, that in one moment he had destroyed what he had been raising many months.

"There is another artifice of the poet, which I cannot here omit, because by the frequent practice of it in his comedies he has left it to us almost as a rule; that is, when he has any character or humour wherein he would show a *coup de Maistre,* or his highest skill, he recommends it to your observation by a pleasant description of it before the person first appears. Thus, in *Bartholomew Fair* he gives you the pictures of Numps and Cokes, and in this those of Daw, Lafoole, Morose, and the Collegiate Ladies; all which you hear described before you see them. So that before they come upon the stage, you have a longing expectation of them, which prepares you to receive them favourably; and when they are there, even from their first appearance you are so far acquainted with them, that nothing of their humour is lost to you.

"I will observe yet one thing further of this admirable plot; the business of it rises in every act. The second is greater than the first; the third than the second; and so forward to the fifth. There too you see, till the very last scene, new difficulties arising to obstruct the action of the play; and when the audience is brought into despair that the business can naturally be effected, then, and not before, the discovery is made. But that the poet might entertain you with more variety all this while, he reserves some new characters to show you, which he opens not till the second and third act. In the second Morose, Daw, the Barber, and Otter; in the third the Collegiate Ladies: all which he moves afterwards in by-walks, or under-plots, as diversions to the main design, lest it should grow tedious, though they are still naturally joined with it, and somewhere or other subservient to it. Thus, like a skilful chess-player, by little and little he draws out his men, and makes his pawns of use to his greater persons.

"If this comedy and some others of his were translated into French prose (which would now be no wonder to them, since Molière has lately given them plays out of verse, which have not displeased them), I believe the controversy would soon be decided betwixt the two nations, even making them the judges. But we need not call our heroes to our aid. Be it spoken to the

[43] ["Comedy is thought to require the least work because it draws its subjects from every-day life; but the less indulgence it has the more work it requires."]

honour of the English, our nation can never want in any age such who are able to dispute the empire of wit with any people in the universe. And though the fury of a civil war, and power for twenty years together abandoned to a barbarous race of men, enemies of all good learning, had buried the Muses under the ruins of monarchy; yet, with the restoration of our happiness, we see revived Poesy lifting up its head, and already shaking off the rubbish which lay so heavy on it. We have seen since his Majesty's return, many dramatic poems which yield not to those of any foreign nation, and which deserve all laurels but the English. I will set aside flattery and envy: it cannot be denied but we have had some little blemish either in the plot or writing of all those plays which have been made within these seven years (and perhaps there is no nation in the world so quick to discern them, or so difficult to pardon them, as ours:) yet if we can persuade ourselves to use the candour of that poet, who, though the most severe of critics, has left us this caution by which to moderate our censures—

> *ubi plura nitent in carmine, non ego paucis*
> *Offendar maculis;*—[44]

if, in consideration of their many and great beauties, we can wink at some slight and little imperfections, if we, I say, can be thus equal to ourselves, I ask no favour from the French. And if I do not venture upon any particular judgment of our late plays, 'tis out of the consideration which an ancient writer gives me: *vivorum, ut magna admiratio, ita censura difficilis:* [45] betwixt the extremes of admiration and malice, 'tis hard to judge uprightly of the living. Only I think it may be permitted me to say, that as it is no lessening to us to yield to some plays, and those not many, of our own nation in the last age, so can it be no addition to pronounce of our present poets, that they have far surpassed all the Ancients, and the modern writers of other countries."

This, my Lord, was the substance of what was then spoken on that occasion; and Lisideius, I think, was going to reply, when he was prevented thus by Crites: "I am confident," said he, "that the most material things that can be said have been already urged on either side; if they have not, I must beg of Lisideius that he will defer his answer till another time: for I confess I have a joint quarrel to you both, because you have concluded, without any reason given for it, that rhyme is proper for the stage. I will not dispute how ancient it hath been among us to write this way; perhaps our ancestors knew no better till Shakspeare's time. I will grant it was not altogether left by him, and that Fletcher and Ben Jonson used it frequently in their Pastorals, and sometimes in other plays. Farther, I will not argue whether we received it originally from our own countrymen, or from the French; for that is an inquiry of as little benefit, as theirs who, in the midst of the great Plague, were not so solicitous to provide against it, as to know whether we had it from the malignity of our own air, or by transportation from Holland. I have therefore only to affirm, that it is not allowable in serious plays; for comedies, I find you already concluding with me. To prove this, I might satisfy myself to tell you, how much in vain it is for you to strive against the stream of the people's inclination; the greatest part of which are prepossessed so much with those excellent plays of Shakspeare, Fletcher, and Ben Jonson, which have been written out of rhyme, that except you could bring them such as were written better in it, and those too by persons of equal reputation with them, it will be impossible for you to gain your cause with them, who will still be judges. This it is to which, in fine, all your reasons must submit. The unanimous consent of an audience is so powerful, that even Julius Cæsar (as Macrobius reports of him), when he was perpetual dictator, was not able to balance it on the other side; but when Laberius, a Roman Knight, at his request contended in the Mime with another poet, he was forced to cry out, *Etiam favente me victus es, Laberi.*[46] But I will not on this occasion take the advantage of the greater number, but only urge such reasons against rhyme, as I find in the writings of those who have argued for the other way. First then, I am of opinion, that rhyme is unnatural in a play, because dia-

[44] ["Where many beauties shine in a poem, I shall not be offended by little faults."]

[45] ["Just as admiration for the living is great so is criticism of them difficult."]

[46] ["Even with me on your side you were defeated. Laberius."]

logue there is presented as the effect of sudden thought: for a play is the imitation of Nature; and since no man without premeditation speaks in rhyme, neither ought he to do it on the stage. This hinders not but the fancy may be there elevated to an higher pitch of thought than it is in ordinary discourse; for there is a probability that men of excellent and quick parts may speak noble things *extempore:* but those thoughts are never fettered with the numbers or sound of verse without study, and therefore it cannot be but unnatural to present the most free way of speaking in that which is the most constrained. For this reason, says Aristotle, 'tis best to write tragedy in that kind of verse which is the least such, or which is nearest prose: and this amongst the Ancients was the iambic, and with us is blank verse, or the measure of verse kept exactly without rhyme. These numbers therefore are fittest for a play; the others for a paper of verses, or a poem; blank verse being as much below them as rhyme is improper for the Drama. And if it be objected that neither are blank verses made *extempore,* yet, as nearest nature, they are still to be preferred.—But there are two particular exceptions, which many besides myself have had to verse; by which it will appear yet more plainly how improper it is in plays. And the first of them is grounded on that very reason for which some have commended rhyme; they say, the quickness of repartees in argumentative scenes receives an ornament from verse. Now what is more unreasonable than to imagine that a man should not only light upon the wit, but the rhyme too, upon the sudden? This nicking of him who spoke before both in sound and measure, is so great an happiness, that you must at least suppose the persons of your play to be born poets: *Arcades omnes, et cantare pares, et respondere parati:* [47] they must have arrived to the degree of *quicquid conabar dicere;* [48]—to make verses almost whether they will or no. If they are any thing below this, it will look rather like the design of two, than the answer of one: it will appear that your actors hold intelligence together; that they perform their tricks like fortune-tellers, by confederacy. The hand of art will be too visible in it, against that maxim of all professions, *Ars est celare artem,*[49] that it is the greatest perfection of art to keep itself undiscovered. Nor will it serve you to object, that however you manage it, 'tis still known to be a play; and, consequently, the dialogue of two persons understood to be the labour of one poet. For a play is still an imitation of Nature; we know we are to be deceived, and we desire to be so; but no man ever was deceived but with a probability of truth; for who will suffer a gross lie to be fastened on him? Thus we sufficiently understand, that the scenes which represent cities and countries to us are not really such, but only painted on boards and canvas; but shall that excuse the ill painture or designment of them? Nay, rather ought they not be laboured with so much the more diligence and exactness, to help the imagination? since the mind of man does naturally tend to, and seek after truth; and therefore the nearer any thing comes to the imitation of it, the more it pleases.

"Thus, you see, your rhyme is incapable of expressing the greatest thoughts naturally, and the lowest it cannot with any grace: for what is more unbefitting the majesty of verse, than to call a servant, or bid a door be shut in rhyme? And yet this miserable necessity you are forced upon. But verse, you say, circumscribes a quick and luxuriant fancy, which would extend itself too far on every subject, did not the labour which is required to well-turned and polished rhyme, set bounds to it. Yet this argument, if granted, would only prove that we may write better in verse, but not more naturally. Neither is it able to evince that; for he who wants judgment to confine his fancy in blank verse, may want it as much in rhyme: and he who has it will avoid errors in both kinds. Latin verse was as great a confinement to the imagination of those poets, as rhyme to ours; and yet you find Ovid saying too much on every subject. *Nescivit* (says Seneca) *quod bene cessit relinquere*: [50] of which he gives you one famous instance in his description of the deluge:

Omnia pontus erat, deerant quoque litora ponto.
Now all was sea, nor had that sea a shore.

[47] ["Both young Arcadians, both alike inspired
To sing, and answer as the song requir'd."
(Dryden)]

[48] ["(of) singing what they attempted."]

[49] ["It is an art to conceal art."]

[50] ["He did not know how to leave off where he should have."]

Thus Ovid's fancy was not limited by verse, and Virgil needed not verse to have bounded his.

"In our own language we see Ben Jonson confining himself to what ought to be said, even in the liberty of blank verse; and yet Corneille, the most judicious of the French poets, is still varying the same sense an hundred ways, and dwelling eternally on the same subject, though confined by rhyme. Some other exceptions I have to verse; but being these I have named are for the most part already public, I conceive it reasonable they should first be answered."

"It concerns me less than any," said Neander (seeing he had ended), "to reply to this discourse; because when I should have proved that verse may be natural in plays, yet I should always be ready to confess, that those which I have written in this kind come short of that perfection which is required. Yet since you are pleased I should undertake this province, I will do it, though with all imaginable respect and deference, both to that person from whom you have borrowed your strongest arguments, and to whose judgment, when I have said all, I finally submit. But before I proceed to answer your objections, I must first remember you, that I exclude all Comedy from my defence; and next that I deny not but blank verse may be also used; and content myself only to assert, that in serious plays where the subject and characters are great, and the plot unmixed with mirth, which might allay or divert these concernments which are produced, rhyme is there as natural and more effectual than blank verse.

"And now having laid down this as a foundation,—to begin with Crites, I must crave leave to tell him, that some of his arguments against rhyme reach no farther than, from the faults or defects of ill rhyme, to conclude against the use of it in general. May not I conclude against blank verse by the same reason? If the words of some poets who write in it, are either ill chosen, or ill placed, which makes not only rhyme, but all kind of verse in any language unnatural, shall I, for their vicious affectation, condemn those excellent lines of Fletcher, which are written in that kind? Is there any thing in rhyme more constrained than this line in blank verse, *I heaven invoke, and strong resistance make?* where you see both the clauses are placed unnaturally, that is, contrary to the common way of speaking, and that without the excuse of a rhyme to cause it: yet you would think me very ridiculous, if I should accuse the stubbornness of blank verse for this, and not rather the stiffness of the poet. Therefore, Crites, you must either prove that words, though well chosen, and duly placed, yet render not rhyme natural in itself; or that, however natural and easy the rhyme may be, yet it is not proper for a play. If you insist on the former part, I would ask you, what other conditions are required to make rhyme natural in itself, besides an election of apt words, and a right dispositing of them? For the due choice of your words expresses your sense naturally, and the due placing them adapts the rhyme to it. If you object that one verse may be made for the sake of another, though both the words and rhyme be apt, I answer, it cannot possibly so fall out; for either there is a dependance of sense betwixt the first line and the second, or there is none: if there be that connection, then in the natural position of the words the latter line must of necessity flow from the former; if there be no dependance, yet still the due ordering of words makes the last line as natural in itself as the other: so that the necessity of a rhyme never forces any but bad or lazy writers to say what they would not otherwise. 'Tis true, there is both care and art required to write in verse. A good poet never concludes upon the first line, till he has sought out such a rhyme as may fit the sense, already prepared to heighten the second: many times the close of the sense falls into the middle of the next verse, or farther off, and he may often prevail himself of the same advantages in English which Virgil had in Latin; he may break off in the hemistich, and begin another line. Indeed, the not observing these two last things, makes plays which are writ in verse so tedious: for though, most commonly, the sense is to be confined to the couplet, yet nothing that does *perpetuo tenore fluere,* run in the same channel, can please always. 'Tis like the murmuring of a stream, which not varying in the fall, causes at first attention, at last drowsiness. Variety of cadences is the best rule; the greatest help to the actors, and refreshment to the audience.

"If then verse may be made natural in itself, how becomes it improper to a play? You say the stage is the representation of Nature, and no man in ordinary conversation speaks in rhyme. But you foresaw when you said this, that it might be answered—neither does any man speak in blank verse, or in measure without rhyme. Therefore you concluded, that which is nearest Nature is still to be preferred. But you took no notice that rhyme might be made as natural as blank verse, by the well placing of the words, etc. All the difference between them, when they are both correct, is, the sound in one, which the other wants; and if so, the sweetness of it, and all the advantage resulting from it, which are handled in the Preface to *The Rival Ladies,* will yet stand good. As for that place of Aristotle, where he says, plays should be writ in that kind of verse which is nearest prose, it makes little for you; blank verse being properly but measured prose. Now measure alone, in any modern language, does not constitute verse; those of the Ancients in Greek and Latin consisted in quantity of words, and a determinate number of feet. But when, by the inundation of the Goths and Vandals into Italy, new languages were brought in, and barbarously mingled with the Latin, of which the Italian, Spanish, French, and ours (made out of them and the Teutonic) are dialects, a new way of poesy was practised; new, I say, in those countries, for in all probability it was that of the conquerors in their own nations. This new way consisted in measure or number of feet, and rhyme; the sweetness of rhyme, and observation of accent, supplying the place of quantity in words, which could neither exactly be observed by those Barbarians, who knew not the rules of it, neither was it suitable to their tongues, as it has been to the Greek and Latin. No man is tied in modern poesy to observe any farther rule in the feet of his verse, but that they be dissyllables; whether spondee, trochee, or iambic, it matters not; only he is obliged to rhyme. Neither do the Spanish, French, Italian, or Germans, acknowledge at all, or very rarely, any such kind of poesy as blank verse amongst them. Therefore, at most 'tis but a poetic prose, a *sermo pedestris;* and as such, most fit for comedies, where I acknowledge rhyme to be improper. Farther; as to that quotation of Aristotle, our couplet verses may be rendered as near prose as blank verse itself, by using those advantages I lately named, as breaks in an hemistich, or running the sense into another line, thereby making art and order appear as loose and free as nature: or not tying ourselves to couplets strictly, we may use the benefit of the Pindaric way practised in *The Siege of Rhodes;* where the numbers vary, and the rhyme is disposed carelessly, and far from often chiming. Neither is that other advantage of the Ancients to be despised, of changing the kind of verse when they please, with the change of the scene, or some new entrance; for they confine not themselves always to iambics, but extend their liberty to all lyric numbers, and sometimes even to hexameter. But I need not go so far to prove that rhyme, as it succeeds to all other offices of Greek and Latin verse, so especially to this of plays, since the custom of all nations at this day confirms it, all the French, Italian, and Spanish tragedies are generally writ in it; and sure the universal consent of the most civilised parts of the world ought in this, as it doth in other customs, to include the rest.

"But perhaps you may tell me, I have proposed such a way to make rhyme natural, and consequently proper to plays, as is unpracticable; and that I shall scarce find six or eight lines together in any play, where the words are so placed and chosen as is required to make it natural. I answer, no poet need constrain himself at all times to it. It is enough he makes it his general rule; for I deny not but sometimes there may be a greatness in placing the words otherwise; and sometimes they may sound better, sometimes also the variety itself is excuse enough. But if, for the most part, the words be placed as they are in the negligence of prose, it is sufficient to denominate the way practicable; for we esteem that to be such, which in the trial oftener succeeds than misses. And thus far you may find the practice made good in many plays: where you do not, remember still, that if you cannot find six natural rhymes together, it will be as hard for you to produce as many lines in blank verse, even among the greatest of our poets, against which I cannot make some reasonable exception.

"And this, Sir, calls to my remembrance the beginning of your discourse, where you told us we should never find the audience favourable to this kind of writing, till we could produce as good plays in rhyme as Ben Jonson, Fletcher, and Shakespeare, had writ out of it. But it is to raise envy to the living, to compare them with the dead. They are honoured, and almost adored by us, as they deserve; neither do I know any so presumptuous of themselves as to contend with them. Yet give me leave to say thus much, without injury to their ashes; that not only we shall never equal them, but they could never equal themselves, were they to rise and write again. We acknowledge them our fathers in wit; but they have ruined their estates themselves, before they came to their children's hands. There is scarce an humour, a character, or any kind of plot, which they have not blown upon. All comes sullied or wasted to us: and were they to entertain this age, they could not make so plenteous treatments out of such decayed fortunes. This therefore will be a good argument to us, either not to write at all, or to attempt some other way. There is no bays to be expected in their walks: *tentanda via est, quà me quoque possum tollere humo.*[51]

"This way of writing in verse they have only left free to us; our age is arrived to a perfection in it, which they never knew; and which (if we may guess by what of theirs we have seen in verse, as *The Faithful Shepherdess,* and *Sad Shepherd*) 'tis probable they never could have reached. For the genius of every age is different; and though ours excel in this, I deny not but to imitate Nature in that perfection which they did in prose, is a greater commendation than to write in verse exactly. As for what you have added, that the people are not generally inclined to like this way; if it were true, it would be no wonder, that betwixt the shaking off an old habit, and the introducing of a new, there should be difficulty. Do we not see them stick to Hopkins' and Sternhold's psalms, and forsake those of David, I mean Sandys his translation of them? If by the people you understand the multitude, the οἱ πολλοί, 'tis no matter what they think; they are sometimes in the right, sometimes in the wrong: their judgment is a mere lottery. *Est ubi plebs rectè putat, est ubi peccat.*[52] Horace says it of the vulgar, judging poesy. But if you mean the mixed audience of the populace and the noblesse, I dare confidently affirm that a great part of the latter sort are already favourable to verse; and that no serious plays written since the King's return have been more kindly received by them than *The Siege of Rhodes,* the *Mustapha, The Indian Queen,* and *Indian Emperor.*

"But I come now to the inference of your first argument. You said the dialogue of plays is presented as the effect of sudden thought, but no man speaks suddenly, or *ex tempore,* in rhyme; and you inferred from thence, that rhyme, which you acknowledge to be proper to epic poesy, cannot equally be proper to dramatic, unless we could suppose all men born so much more than poets, that verses should be made in them, not by them.

"It has been formerly urged by you, and confessed by me, that since no man spoke any kind of verse *ex tempore,* that which was nearest Nature was to be preferred. I answer you, therefore, by distinguishing betwixt what is nearest to the nature of Comedy, which is the imitation of common persons and ordinary speaking, and what is nearest the nature of a serious play: this last is indeed the representation of Nature, but 'tis Nature wrought up to a higher pitch. The plot, the characters, the wit, the passions, the descriptions, are all exalted above the level of common converse, as high as the imagination of the poet can carry them, with proportion to verisimility. Tragedy, we know, is wont to image to us the minds and fortunes of noble persons, and to portray these exactly; heroic rhyme is nearest Nature, as being the noblest kind of modern verse.

Indignatur enim privatis et prope socco
Dignis carminibus narrari cœna Thyestœ[53]

says Horace: and in another place,

Effutire leves indigna tragœdia versus.[54]

Blank verse is acknowledged to be too low for a poem, nay more, for a paper of verses; but if too low for an ordinary sonnet, how much more for Tragedy, which is by Aristotle, in the dispute betwixt the epic poesy and the dramatic,

51 ["New ways I must attempt, my grov'ling name
To raise aloft." (Dryden)]

52 ["There is a time when the people think rightly, there is a time when they err."]

53 ["It is offensive for the banquet of Thyestes to be narrated in familiar verses that belong almost to comedy."]

54 ["It is not fitting for tragedy to babble forth light verse."]

for many reasons he there alleges, ranked above it?

"But setting this defence aside, your argument is almost as strong against the use of rhyme in poems as in plays; for the epic way is every where interlaced with dialogue, or discoursive scenes; and therefore you must either grant rhyme to be improper there, which is contrary to your assertion, or admit it into plays by the same title which you have given it to poems. For though Tragedy be justly preferred above the other, yet there is a great affinity between them, as may easily be discovered in that definition of a play which Lisideius gave us. The *genus* of them is the same, a just and lively image of human nature, in its actions, passions, and traverses of fortune: so is the end, namely, for the delight and benefit of mankind. The characters and persons are still the same, viz. the greatest of both sorts; only the manner of acquainting us with those actions, passions, and fortunes, is different. Tragedy performs it *viva voce*, or by action, in dialogue; wherein it excels the Epic Poem, which does it chiefly by narration, and therefore is not so lively an image of human nature. However, the agreement betwixt them is such, that if rhyme be proper for one, it must be for the other. Verse, 'tis true, is not the effect of sudden thought; but this hinders not that sudden thought may be represented in verse, since those thoughts are such as must be higher than Nature can raise them without premeditation, especially to a continuance of them, even out of verse; and consequently you cannot imagine them to have been sudden either in the poet or in the actors. A play, as I have said, to be like Nature, is to be set above it; as statues which are placed on high are made greater than the life, that they may descend to the sight in their just proportion.

"Perhaps I have insisted too long on this objection; but the clearing of it will make my stay shorter on the rest. You tell us, Crites, that rhyme appears most unnatural in repartees, or short replies: when he who answers, it being presumed he knew not what the other would say, yet makes up that part of the verse which was left incomplete, and supplies both the sound and measure of it. This, you say, looks rather like the confederacy of two, than the answer of one.

"This, I confess, is an objection which is in every one's mouth, who loves not rhyme: but suppose, I beseech you, the repartee were made only in blank verse, might not part of the same argument be turned against you? for the measure is as often supplied there as it is in rhyme; the latter half of the hemistich as commonly made up, or a second line subjoined as a reply to the former; which any one leaf in Jonson's plays will sufficiently clear to you. You will often find in the Greek tragedians, and in Seneca, that when a scene grows up into the warmth of repartees, which is the close fighting of it, the latter part of the trimeter is supplied by him who answers; and yet it was never observed as a fault in them by any of the ancient or modern critics. The case is the same in our verse, as it was in theirs; rhyme to us being in lieu of quantity to them. But if no latitude is to be allowed a poet, you take from him not only his licence of *quidlibet audendi*,[55] but you tie him up in a straiter compass than you would a philosopher. This is indeed *Musas colere severiores*.[56] You would have him follow Nature, but he must follow her on foot: you have dismounted him from his Pegasus. But you tell us, this supplying the last half of a verse, or adjoining a whole second to the former, looks more like the design of two, than the answer of one. Suppose we acknowledge it: how comes this confederacy to be more displeasing to you, than in a dance which is well contrived? You see there the united design of many persons to make up one figure: after they have separated themselves in many petty divisions, they rejoin one by one into a gross: the confederacy is plain amongst them, for chance could never produce anything so beautiful; and yet there is nothing in it, that shocks your sight. I acknowledge the hand of art appears in repartee, as of necessity it must in all kind of verse. But there is also the quick and poynant brevity of it (which is an high imitation of Nature in those sudden gusts of passion) to mingle with it; and this, joined with the cadency and sweetness of the rhyme, leaves nothing in the soul of the hearer to desire. 'Tis an art which appears; but it appears only like the shadowings of painture, which be-

55 ["Of taking any liberty."]

56 ["To worship the more serious Muses.']

ing to cause the rounding of it, cannot be absent; but while that is considered, they are lost: so while we attend to the other beauties of the matter, the care and labour of the rhyme is carried from us, or at least drowned in its own sweetness, as bees are sometimes buried in their honey. When a poet has found the repartee, the last perfection he can add to it, is to put it into verse. However good the thought may be, however apt the words in which 'tis couched, yet he finds himself at a little unrest, while rhyme is wanting: he cannot leave it till that comes naturally, and then is at ease, and sits down contented.

"From replies, which are the most elevated thoughts of verse, you pass to the most mean ones, those which are common with the lowest of household conversation. In these, you say, the majesty of verse suffers. You instance in the calling of a servant, or commanding a door to be shut, in rhyme. This, Crites, is a good observation of yours, but no argument: for it proves no more but that such thoughts should be waived, as often as may be, by the address of the poet. But suppose they are necessary in the places where he uses them, yet there is no need to put them into rhyme. He may place them in the beginning of a verse, and break it off, as unfit, when so debased, for any other use: or granting the worst,—that they require more room than the hemistich will allow, yet still there is a choice to be made of the best words, and least vulgar (provided they be apt) to express such thoughts. Many have blamed rhyme in general, for this fault, when the poet with a little care might have redressed it. But they do it with no more justice, than if English Poesy should be made ridiculous for the sake of the Water Poet's rhymes. Our language is noble, full, and significant; and I know not why he who is master of it may not clothe ordinary things in it as decently as the Latin, if he use the same diligence in his choice of words: *delectus verborum origo est eloquentiæ.*[57] It was the saying of Julius Cæsar, one so curious in his, that none of them can be changed but for a worse. One would think, *unlock the door,* was a thing as vulgar as could be spoken; and yet Seneca could make it sound high and lofty in his Latin:

> *Reserate clusos regii postes laris.*
> Set wide the palace gates.

"But I turn from this conception, both because it happens not above twice or thrice in any play that those vulgar thoughts are used; and then too, were there no other apology to be made, yet the necessity of them, which is alike in all kind of writing, may excuse them. Besides that the great eagerness and precipitation with which they are spoken makes us rather mind the substance than the dress; that for which they are spoken, rather than what is spoken. For they are always the effect of some hasty concernment, and something of consequence depends on them.

"Thus, Crites, I have endeavoured to answer your objections; it remains only that I should vindicate an argument for verse, which you have gone about to overthrow. It had formerly been said that the easiness of blank verse renders the poet too luxuriant, but that the labour of rhyme bounds and circumscribes an over-fruitful fancy; the sense there being commonly confined to the couplet, and the words so ordered that the rhyme naturally follows them, not they the rhyme. To this you answered, that it was no argument to the question in hand; for the dispute was not which way a man may write best, but which is most proper for the subject on which he writes.

"First, give me leave, Sir, to remember you, that the argument against which you raised this objection was only secondary: it was built on this hypothesis, that to write in verse was proper for serious plays. Which supposition being granted (as it was briefly made out in that discourse, by showing how verse might be made natural), it asserted, that this way of writing was an help to the poet's judgment, by putting bounds to a wild overflowing fancy. I think, therefore, it will not be hard for me to make good what it was to prove. But you add, that were this let pass, yet he who wants judgment in the liberty of his fancy, may as well show the defect of it when he is confined to verse; for he who has judgment will avoid errors, and he who has it not, will commit them in all kinds of writing.

"This argument, as you have taken it from a most acute person, so I confess it carries much

[57] ["Proper choice of words is the origin of eloquence."]

weight in it: but by using the word judgment here indefinitely, you seem to have put a fallacy upon us. I grant, he who has judgment, that is, so profound, so strong, so infallible a judgment, that he needs no helps to keep it always poised and upright, will commit no faults either in rhyme or out of it. And on the other extreme, he who has a judgment so weak and crazed that no helps can correct or amend it, shall write scurvily out of rhyme, and worse in it. But the first of these judgments is no where to be found, and the latter is not fit to write at all. To speak therefore of judgment as it is in the best poets; they who have the greatest proportion of it, want other helps than from it, within. As for example, you would be loth to say, that he who was endued with a sound judgment had no need of History, Geography, or Moral Philosophy, to write correctly. Judgment is indeed the master-workman in a play; but he requires many subordinate hands, many tools to his assistance. And verse I affirm to be one of these; 'tis a rule and line by which he keeps his building compact and even, which otherwise lawless imagination would raise either irregularly or loosely; at least, if the poet commits errors with this help, he would make greater and more without it: 'tis, in short, a slow and painful, but the surest kind of working. Ovid, whom you accuse for luxuriancy in verse, had perhaps been farther guilty of it, had he writ in prose. And for your instance of Ben Jonson, who, you say, writ exactly without the help of rhyme; you are to remember, 'tis only an aid to a luxuriant fancy, which his was not: as he did not want imagination, so none ever said he had much to spare. Neither was verse then refined so much to be an help to that age, as it is to ours. Thus then the second thoughts being usually the best, as receiving the maturist digestion from judgment, and the last and most mature product of those thoughts being artful and laboured verse, it may well be inferred, that verse is a great help to a luxuriant fancy; and this is what that argument which you opposed was to evince."

Neander was pursuing this discourse so eagerly, that Eugenius had called to him twice or thrice, ere he took notice that the barge stood still, and that they were at the foot of Somerset stairs, where they had appointed it to land. The company were all sorry to separate so soon, though a great part of the evening was already spent; and stood a-while looking back on the water, which the moonbeams played upon, and made it appear like floating quick-silver: at last they went up through a crowd of French people, who were merrily dancing in the open air, and nothing concerned for the noise of guns which had alarmed the town that afternoon. Walking thence together to the Piazze, they parted there; Eugenius and Lisideius to some pleasant appointment they had made, and Crites and Neander to their several lodgings.

SAMUEL TAYLOR COLERIDGE:

Occasion of the "Lyrical Ballads"*

During the first year that Mr. Wordsworth and I were neighbours, our conversations turned frequently on the two cardinal points of poetry, the power of exciting the sympathy of the reader by a faithful adherence to the truth of nature, and the power of giving the interest of novelty by the modifying colours of imagination. The sudden charm, which accidents of light and shade, which moon-light or sunset diffused over a known and familiar landscape, appeared to represent the practicability of combining both. These are the poetry of nature. The thought suggested itself—(to which of us I do not recollect)—that a series of poems might be composed of two sorts. In the one, the inci-

* Chapter XIV of *Biographia Literaria* (1817).

dents and agents were to be, in part at least, supernatural; and the excellence aimed at was to consist in the interesting of the affections by the dramatic truth of such emotions, as would naturally accompany such situations, supposing them real. And real in this sense they have been to every human being who, from whatever source of delusion, has at any time believed himself under supernatural agency. For the second class, subjects were to be chosen from ordinary life; the characters and incidents were to be such as will be found in every village and its vicinity, where there is a meditative and feeling mind to seek after them, or to notice them, when they present themselves.

In this idea originated the plan of the LYRICAL BALLADS; in which it was agreed, that my endeavours should be directed to persons and characters supernatural, or at least romantic; yet so as to transfer from our inward nature a human interest and a semblance of truth sufficient to procure for these shadows of imagination that willing suspension of disbelief for the moment, which constitutes poetic faith. Mr. Wordsworth, on the other hand, was to propose to himself as his object, to give the charm of novelty to things of every day, and to excite a feeling analogous to the supernatural, by awakening the mind's attention to the lethargy of custom, and directing it to the loveliness and the wonders of the world before us; an inexhaustible treasure, but for which, in consequence of the film of familiarity and selfish solicitude, we have eyes, yet see not, ears that hear not, and hearts that neither feel nor understand.

With this view I wrote THE ANCIENT MARINER, and was preparing among other poems, THE DARK LADIE, and the CHRISTABEL, in which I should have more nearly realized my ideal, than I had done in my first attempt. But Mr. Wordsworth's industry had proved so much more successful, and the number of his poems so much greater, that my compositions, instead of forming a balance, appeared rather an interpolation of heterogeneous matter. Mr. Wordsworth added two or three poems written in his own character, in the impassioned, lofty, and sustained diction, which is characteristic of his genius. In this form the LYRICAL BALLADS were published; and were presented by him, as an experiment, whether subjects, which from their nature rejected the usual ornaments and extra-colloquial style of poems in general, might not be so managed in the language of ordinary life as to produce the pleasurable interest, which it is the peculiar business of poetry to impart. To the second edition he added a preface of considerable length; in which, notwithstanding some passages of apparently a contrary import, he was understood to contend for the extension of this style to poetry of all kinds, and to reject as vicious and indefensible all phrases and forms of speech that were not included in what he (unfortunately, I think, adopting an equivocal expression) called the language of real life. From this preface, prefixed to poems in which it was impossible to deny the presence of original genius, however mistaken its direction might be deemed, arose the whole long-continued controversy. For from the conjunction of perceived power with supposed heresy I explain the inveteracy and in some instances, I grieve to say, the acrimonious passions, with which the controversy has been conducted by the assailants.

Had Mr. Wordsworth's poems been the silly, the childish things, which they were for a long time described as being: had they been really distinguished from the compositions of other poets merely by meanness of language and inanity of thought; had they indeed contained nothing more than what is found in the parodies and pretended imitations of them; they must have sunk at once, a dead weight, into the slough of oblivion, and have dragged the preface along with them. But year after year increased the number of Mr. Wordsworth's admirers. They were found too not in the lower classes of the reading public, but chiefly among young men of strong sensibility and meditative minds; and their admiration (inflamed perhaps in some degree by opposition) was distinguished by its intensity, I might almost say, by its religious fervour. These facts, and the intellectual energy of the author, which was more or less consciously felt, where it was outwardly and even boisterously denied, meeting with sentiments of aversion to his opinions, and of alarm at their consequences, produced an eddy of criticism, which would of itself have borne up the poems by the violence with which it whirled them round and round. With many parts of this preface in the sense attributed to them and which the words undoubtedly seem to authorize, I never concurred; but on the contrary objected to them as erroneous in principle, and as contradictory (in appearance at least) both to other parts of the same preface, and to the author's own practice in the greater part of the poems themselves. Mr. Wordsworth in his recent collection has, I find, degraded this prefatory disquisition to the end of his second volume, to be read or not at the reader's choice. But he has not, as far as I can discover, announced any change in his poetic creed. At all events, considering it as the source of a controversy, in which I have been honoured more than I deserve by the frequent conjunction of my name with his, I think it expedient to declare once for all, in what points I coincide with the opinions supported in that preface, and in what points I altogether differ. But in order to render myself intelligible I must previously, in as few words as possible, explain my views, first, of a Poem; and secondly, of Poetry itself, in kind, and in essence.

The office of philosophical disquisition consists in just distinction; while it is the privilege of the philosopher to preserve himself constantly aware, that distinction is not division. In order to obtain adequate notions of any truth, we must intellectually separate its distinguishable parts; and this is the technical process of philosophy. But having so done, we must then restore them in our conceptions to the unity, in which they actually co-exist; and this is the result of philosophy. A poem contains the same elements as a prose composition; the difference therefore must consist in a different combination of them, in consequence of a different object being proposed. According to the difference of the object will be the difference of the combination. It is possible, that the object may be merely to facilitate the recollection of any given facts or observations by artificial arrangement; and the composition will be a poem, merely because it is distinguished from prose by metre, or by rhyme, or by both conjointly. In this, the lowest sense, a man might attribute the name of a poem to the well-known enumeration of the days in the several months;

> Thirty days hath September,
> April, June, and November, &c.

and others of the same class and purpose. And as a particular pleasure is found in anticipating the recurrence of sounds and quantities, all compositions that have this charm super-added, whatever be their contents, *may* be entitled poems.

So much for the superficial form. A difference of object and contents supplies an additional ground of distinction. The immediate purpose may be the communication of truths; either of truth absolute and demonstrable, as in works of science; or of facts experienced and recorded, as in history. Pleasure, and that of the highest and most permanent kind, may result from the attainment of the end; but it is not itself the immediate end. In other works the communication of pleasure may be the immediate purpose; and though truth, either moral or intellectual, ought to be the ultimate end, yet this will distinguish the character of the author, not the class to which the work belongs. Blest indeed is that state of society, in which the immediate purpose would be baffled by the perversion of the proper ultimate end; in which no charm of diction or imagery could exempt the BATHYLLUS even of an Anacreon, or the ALEXIS of Virgil, from disgust and aversion!

But the communication of pleasure may be the immediate object of a work not metrically composed; and that object may have been in a high degree attained, as in novels and romances. Would then the mere superaddition of metre, with or without rhyme, entitle these to the name of poems? The answer is, that nothing can permanently please, which does not contain in itself the reason why it is so, and not otherwise. If metre be superadded, all other parts must be made consonant with it. They must be such, as to justify the perpetual and distinct attention to each part, which an exact correspondent recurrence of accent and sound are calculated to excite. The final definition then, so deduced, may be thus worded. A poem is that species of composition, which is opposed to works of science, by proposing for its *immediate* object pleasure, not truth; and from all other species—(having *this* object in common with it)—it is discriminated by proposing to itself such delight from the *whole*, as is compatible with a distinct gratification from each component *part*.

Controversy is not seldom excited in consequence of the disputants attaching each a different meaning to the same word; and in few instances has this been more striking, than in disputes concerning the present subject. If a man chooses to call every composition a poem, which is rhyme, or measure, or both, I must leave his opinion uncontroverted. The distinction is at least competent to characterize the writer's intention. If it were subjoined, that the whole is likewise entertaining or affecting, as a tale, or as a series of interesting reflections, I of course admit this as another fit ingredient of a poem, and an additional merit. But if the definition sought for be that of a *legitimate* poem, I answer it must be one, the parts of which mutually support and explain each other; all in their proportion harmonizing with, and supporting the purpose and known influences of metrical arrangement. The philosophic critics of all ages coincide with the ultimate judgment of all countries, in equally denying the praises of a just poem, on the one hand, to a series of striking lines or distiches, each of which, absorbing the whole attention of the reader to itself, becomes disjoined from its context, and forms a separate whole, instead of a harmonizing part; and on the other hand, to an unsustained composition, from which the reader collects rapidly the general result unattracted by the component parts. The reader should be carried forward, not merely or chiefly by the mechanical impulse of curiosity, or by a restless desire to arrive at the final solution; but by the pleasurable activity of mind excited by the attractions of the journey itself. Like the motion of a serpent, which the Egyptians made the emblem of intellectual power; or like the path of sound through the air;—at every step he pauses and half recedes, and from the retrogressive movement collects the force which again carries him onward. *Præcipitandus est liber spiritus,*[1] says Petronius most happily. The epithet, *liber,* here balances the preceding verb; and it is not easy to conceive more meaning condensed in fewer words.

But if this should be admitted as a satisfactory character of a poem, we have still to seek for a definition of poetry. The writings of Plato, and Jeremy Taylor, and Burnet's Theory of the Earth, furnish undeniable proofs that poetry of the highest kind may exist without metre, and even without the contradistinguishing objects of a poem. The first chapter of Isaiah—(indeed a very large portion of the whole book)—is poetry in the most emphatic sense; yet it would be not less irrational than strange to assert, that pleasure, and not truth was the immediate object of the prophet. In short, whatever specific import we attach to the word, Poetry, there will be found involved in it, as a necessary consequence, that a poem of any length neither can be, nor ought to be, all poetry. Yet if an harmonious whole is to be produced, the remaining parts must be preserved in keeping with the poetry; and this can be no otherwise effected than by such a studied selection and artificial arrangement, as will partake of one, though not a peculiar property of poetry. And this again can be no other than the property of exciting a more continuous and equal attention than the language of prose aims at, whether colloquial or written.

My own conclusions on the nature of poetry, in the strictest use of the word, have been in part anticipated in some of the remarks on the Fancy and Imagination in the early part of this work. What is poetry?—is so nearly the same question with, what is a poet?—that the answer to the one is involved in the solution of the other. For it is a distinction resulting from the poetic genius itself, which sustains and modifies the images, thoughts, and emotions of the poet's own mind.

The poet, described in ideal perfection, brings the whole soul of man into activity, with the subordination of its faculties to each other according to their relative worth and dignity. He diffuses a tone and spirit of unity, that blends, and (as it were) *fuses,* each into each, by that synthetic and magical power, to which I would exclusively appropriate the name of Imagination. This power, first put in action by the will and understanding, and retained under their irremissive, though gentle and unnoticed, control, *laxis effertur habenis,*[2] reveals itself in the balance or reconcilement of opposite or discordant qualities: of sameness, with difference; of the general with the concrete; the idea with

1 ["The free spirit must be swept onward."]

2 ["Carried along with loose reins."]

the image; the individual with the representative; the sense of novelty and freshness with old and familiar objects; a more than usual state of emotion with more than usual order; judgment ever awake and steady self-possession with enthusiasm and feeling profound or vehement; and while it blends and harmonizes the natural and the artificial, still subordinates art to nature; the manner to the matter; and our admiration of the poet to our sympathy with the poetry. Doubtless, as Sir John Davies observes of the soul—(and his words may with slight alteration be applied, and even more appropriately, to the poetic Imagination)—

Doubtless this could not be, but that she turns
  Bodies to *spirit* by sublimation strange,
As fire converts to fire the things it burns,
  As we our food into our nature change.

From their gross matter she abstracts *their* forms,
  And draws a kind of quintessence from things;
Which to her proper nature she transforms
  To bear them light on her celestial wings.

Thus does she, when from *individual states*
  She doth abstract the universal kinds;
Which then re-clothed in divers names and fates
  Steal access through the senses to our minds.

Finally, Good Sense is the Body of poetic genius, Fancy its Drapery, Motion its Life, and Imagination the Soul that is everywhere, and in each; and forms all into one graceful and intelligent whole.*

* "The imagination then I consider either as primary, or secondary. The primary Imagination I hold to be the living power and prime agent of all human perception, and as a repetition in the finite mind of the eternal act of creation in the infinite I AM. The secondary Imagination I consider as an echo of the former, co-existing with the conscious will, yet still as identical with the primary in the *kind* of its agency, and differing only in *degree*, and in the *mode* of its operation. It dissolves, diffuses, dissipates, in order to recreate: or where this process is rendered impossible, yet still at all events it struggles to idealize and to unify. It is essentially *vital*, even as all objects (as objects) are essentially fixed and dead.

"FANCY, on the contrary, has no other counters to play with, but fixities and definites. The fancy is indeed no other than a mode of memory emancipated from the order of time and space; while it is blended with, and modified by that empirical phenomenon of the will, which we express by the word Choice. But equally with the ordinary memory the Fancy must receive all its materials ready made from the law of association." [*Biog. Lit.*, Chapter XIII.]

SAMUEL TAYLOR COLERIDGE:

The Specific Symptoms of Poetic Power*

IN THE application of these principles to purposes of practical criticism, as employed in the appraisement of works more or less imperfect, I have endeavoured to discover what the qualities in a poem are, which may be deemed promises and specific symptoms of poetic power, as distinguished from general talent determined to poetic composition by accidental motives, by an act of the will, rather than by the inspiration of a genial and productive nature. In this investigation, I could not, I thought, do better, than keep before me the earliest work of the greatest genius, that perhaps human nature has yet produced, our *myriad-minded*[1] Shakespeare. I mean the VENUS AND ADONIS, and the LUCRECE; works which give at once strong promises of the strength, and yet obvious proofs of the immaturity, of his genius. From these I abstracted the following marks, as characteristics of original poetic genius in general.

1. In the VENUS AND ADONIS, the first and most obvious excellence is the perfect sweetness of the versification; its adaptation to the sub-

* Chapter XV of *Biographia Literaria* (1817).

[1] 'Ανὴρ μυριόνους, a phrase which I have borrowed from a Greek monk, who applies it to a Patriarch of Constantinople. I might have said, that I have reclaimed, rather than borrowed, it: for it seems to belong to Shakespeare, *de jure singulari, et ex privilegio naturæ.*

ject; and the power displayed in varying the march of the words without passing into a loftier and more majestic rhythm than was demanded by the thoughts, or permitted by the propriety of preserving a sense of melody predominant. The delight in richness and sweetness of sound, even to a faulty excess, if it be evidently original, and not the result of an easily imitable mechanism, I regard as a highly favourable promise in the compositions of a young man. The man that hath not music in his soul can indeed never be a genuine poet. Imagery,—(even taken from nature, much more when transplanted from books, as travels, voyages, and works of natural history),—affecting incidents, just thoughts, interesting personal or domestic feelings, and with these the art of their combination or inter-texture in the form of a poem, —may all by incessant effort be acquired as a trade, by a man of talent and much reading, who, as I once before observed, has mistaken an intense desire of poetic reputation for a natural poetic genius; the love of the arbitrary end for a possession of the peculiar means. But the sense of musical delight, with the power of producing it, is a gift of imagination; and this together with the power of reducing multitude into unity of effect, and modifying a series of thoughts by some one predominant thought or feeling, may be cultivated and improved, but can never be learned. It is in these that "*poeta nascitur non fit.*" [2]

2. A second promise of genius is the choice of subjects very remote from the private interests and circumstances of the writer himself. At least I have found, that where the subject is taken immediately from the author's personal sensations and experiences, the excellence of a particular poem is but an equivocal mark, and often a fallacious pledge, of genuine poetic power. We may perhaps remember the tale of the statuary, who had acquired considerable reputation for the legs of his goddesses, though the rest of the statue accorded but indifferently with ideal beauty; till his wife, elated by her husband's praises, modestly acknowledged that she had been his constant model. In the VENUS AND ADONIS this proof of poetic power exists even to excess. It is throughout as if a superior spirit more intuitive, more intimately conscious, even than the characters themselves, not only of every outward look and act, but of the flux and reflux of the mind in all its subtlest thoughts and feelings, were placing the whole before our view; himself meanwhile unparticipating in the passions, and actuated only by that pleasurable excitement, which had resulted from the energetic fervour of his own spirit in so vividly exhibiting what it had so accurately and profoundly contemplated. I think, I should have conjectured from these poems, that even then the great instinct, which impelled the poet to the drama, was secretly working in him, prompting him—by a series and never broken chain of imagery, always vivid and, because unbroken, often minute; by the highest effort of the picturesque in words, of which words are capable, higher perhaps than was ever realized by any other poet, even Dante not excepted; to provide a substitute for that visual language, that constant intervention and running comment by tone, look and gesture, which in his dramatic works he was entitled to expect from the players. His Venus and Adonis seem at once the characters themselves, and the whole representation of those characters by the most consummate actors. You seem to be told nothing, but to see and hear everything. Hence it is, from the perpetual activity of attention required on the part of the reader; from the rapid flow, the quick change, and the playful nature of the thoughts and images; and above all from the alienation, and, if I may hazard such an expression, the utter *aloofness* of the poet's own feelings, from those of which he is at once the painter and the analyst;—that though the very subject cannot but detract from the pleasure of a delicate mind, yet never was poem less dangerous on a moral account. Instead of doing as Ariosto, and as, still more offensively, Wieland has done, instead of degrading and deforming passion into appetite, the trials of love into the struggles of concupiscence;—Shakespeare has here represented the animal impulse itself, so as to preclude all sympathy with it, by dissipating the reader's notice among the thousand outward images, and now beautiful, now fanciful circumstances, which form its dresses and its scenery; or by diverting our attention from the main subject by those frequent witty or profound re-

[2] ["A poet is born, not made."]

flections, which the poet's ever active mind has deduced from, or connected with, the imagery and the incidents. The reader is forced into too much action to sympathize with the merely passive of our nature. As little can a mind thus roused and awakened be brooded on by mean and indistinct emotion, as the low, lazy mist can creep upon the surface of a lake, while a strong gale is driving it onward in waves and billows.

3. It has been before observed that images, however beautiful, though faithfully copied from nature, and as accurately represented in words, do not of themselves characterize the poet. They become proofs of original genius only as far as they are modified by a predominant passion; or by associated thoughts or images awakened by that passion; or when they have the effect of reducing multitude to unity, or succession to an instant; or lastly, when a human and intellectual life is transferred to them from the poet's own spirit,

Which shoots its being through earth, sea, and air.

In the two following lines for instance, there is nothing objectionable, nothing which would preclude them from forming, in their proper place, part of a descriptive poem:

Behold yon row of pines, that shorn and bow'd
Bend from the sea-blast, seen at twilight eve.

But with a small alteration of rhythm, the same words would be equally in their place in a book of topography, or in a descriptive tour. The same image will rise into semblance of poetry if thus conveyed:

Yon row of bleak and visionary pines,
By twilight glimpse discerned, mark! how they flee
From the fierce sea-blast, all their tresses wild
Streaming before them.

I have given this as an illustration, by no means as an instance, of that particular excellence which I had in view, and in which Shakespeare even in his earliest, as in his latest, works surpasses all other poets. It is by this, that he still gives a dignity and a passion to the objects which he presents. Unaided by any previous excitement, they burst upon us at once in life and in power,—

Full many a glorious morning have I seen
Flatter the mountain tops with sovereign eye.

Not mine own fears, nor the prophetic soul
Of the wide world dreaming on things to come— . . .
The mortal moon hath her eclipse endured,
And the sad augurs mock their own presage;
Incertainties now crown themselves assur'd,
And Peace proclaims olives of endless age.
Now with the drops of this most balmy time
My love looks fresh, and Death to me subscribes,
Since spite of him, I'll live in this poor rhyme,
While he insults o'er dull and speechless tribes.
And thou in this shalt find thy monument,
When tyrants' crests, and tombs of brass are spent.

As of higher worth, so doubtless still more characteristic of poetic genius does the imagery become, when it moulds and colours itself to the circumstances, passion, or character, present and foremost in the mind. For unrivalled instances of this excellence, the reader's own memory will refer him to the LEAR, OTHELLO, in short to which not of the *"great, ever living, dead man's"* dramatic works? *Inopem me copia fecit.*[3] How true it is to nature, he has himself finely expressed in the instance of love in his 98th Sonnet.

From you have I been absent in the spring,
When proud-pied April drest in all its trim,
Hath put a spirit of youth in every thing;
That heavy Saturn laugh'd and leap'd with him.
Yet nor the lays of birds, nor the sweet smell
Of different flowers in odour and in hue,
Could make me any summer's story tell,
Or from their proud lap pluck them, where they grew:
Nor did I wonder at the lilies white,
Nor praise the deep vermilion in the rose;
They were, tho' sweet, but figures of delight,
Drawn after you, you pattern of all those.
Yet seem'd it winter still, and, you away,
As with your shadow, I with these did play!

Scarcely less sure, or if a less valuable, not less indispensable mark

Γόνιμου μὲν ποιητοῦ———
———ὅστις ῥῆμα γενναῖον λάκοι,[4]

will the imagery supply, when, with more than the power of the painter, the poet gives us the

[3] ["The abundance leaves me helpless."]

[4] ["Of genuine poets—who's to utter the fitting word,"]

liveliest image of succession with the feeling of simultaneousness:—

With this, he breaketh from the sweet embrace
Of those fair arms, which bound him to her breast,
And homeward through the dark laund runs apace;— . . .
Look! how a bright star shooteth from the sky,
So glides he in the night from Venus' eye.

4. The last character I shall mention, which would prove indeed but little, except as taken conjointly with the former;—yet without which the former could scarce exist in a high degree, and (even if this were possible) would give promises only of transitory flashes and a meteoric power;—is depth, and energy of thought. No man was ever yet a great poet, without being at the same time a profound philosopher. For poetry is the blossom and the fragrancy of all human knowledge, human thoughts, human passions, emotions, language. In Shakespeare's poems the creative power and the intellectual energy wrestle as in a war embrace. Each in its excess of strength seems to threaten the extinction of the other. At length in the drama they were reconciled, and fought each with its shield before the breast of the other. Or like two rapid streams, that, at their first meeting within narrow and rocky banks, mutually strive to repel each other and intermix reluctantly and in tumult; but soon finding a wider channel and more yielding shores blend, and dilate, and flow on in one current and with one voice. The VENUS AND ADONIS did not perhaps allow the display of the deeper passions. But the story of Lucretia seems to favour and even demand their intensest workings. And yet we find in *Shakespeare's* management of the tale neither pathos, nor any other *dramatic* quality. There is the same minute and faithful imagery as in the former poem, in the same vivid colours, inspirited by the same impetuous vigour of thought, and diverging and contracting with the same activity of the assimilative and of the modifying faculties; and with a yet larger display, a yet wider range of knowledge and reflection; and lastly, with the same perfect dominion, often domination, over the whole world of language. What then shall we say? even this; that Shakespeare, no mere child of nature; no *automaton* of genius; no passive vehicle of inspiration, possessed by the spirit, not possessing it; first studied patiently, meditated deeply, understood minutely, till knowledge, become habitual and intuitive, wedded itself to his habitual feelings, and at length gave birth to that stupendous power, by which he stands alone, with no equal or second in his own class; to that power which seated him on one of the two glory-smitten summits of the poetic mountain, with Milton as his compeer, not rival. While the former darts himself forth, and passes into all the forms of human character and passion, the one Proteus of the fire and the flood; the other attracts all forms and things to himself, into the unity of his own ideal. All things and modes of action shape themselves anew in the being of Milton; while Shakespeare becomes all things, yet for ever remaining himself.* O what great men hast thou not produced, England, my country!—Truly indeed—

We must be free or die, who speak the tongue,
Which Shakespeare spake; the faith and morals hold,
Which Milton held. In every thing we are sprung
Of earth's first blood, have titles manifold.

* [A useful supplement to Coleridge's remarks about Shakespeare may be found in the following observations on organic form.

"The form is mechanic when on any given material we impress a pre-determined form, not necessarily arising out of the properties of the material, as when to a mass of wet clay we give whatever shape we wish it to retain when hardened. The organic form, on the other hand, is innate; it shapes as it develops itself from within, and the fullness of its development is one and the same with the perfection of its outward form. Such is the life, such the form. Nature, the prime genial artist, inexhaustible in diverse powers, is equally inexhaustible in forms. Each exterior is the physiognomy of the being within, its true image reflected and thrown out from the concave mirror. And even such is the appropriate excellence of her chosen poet, of our own Shakespeare, himself a nature humanized, a genial understanding directing self-consciously a power and an implicit wisdom deeper than consciousness."

"We call, for we see and feel, the swan and the dove both transcendently beautiful. As absurd as it would be to institute a comparison between their separate claims to beauty from any abstract rule common to both, without reference to the life and being of the animals themselves—say rather if, having first seen the dove, we abstracted its outlines, gave them a false generalization, called them principle or ideal of bird-beauty and then proceeded to criticize the swan or the eagle —not less absurd is it to pass judgment on the works of a poet on the mere ground that they have been called by the same class-name with the works of other poets of other times and circumstances, or any ground indeed save that of their inappropriateness to their own end and being, their want of significance, as symbol and physiognomy."

"In respect of style and versification, this play [*The Queen of Corinth*] and the following of *Bonduca* may be taken as the best, and yet as characteristic, specimens of Beaumont and Fletcher's dramas. I particularly instance the first scene of the *Bonduca*. Take Shakespeare's *Richard II*, and having selected some one scene of about the same number of lines, and consisting mostly of long speeches, compare it with the first scene in *Bonduca*,—not for the idle purpose of finding out which is the better, but in order to see and understand the difference. The latter, that of B. and F., you will find a well-arranged bed of flowers, each having its separate root, and its position determined aforehand by the will of the gardener,—each fresh plant a fresh volition. In the former you see an Indian fig-tree, as described by Milton;—all is growth, evolution, γένεσις;—each line, each work, almost, begets the following, and the will of the writer is an interfusion, a continuous agency, and not a series of separate acts. Shakespeare is the height, breadth, and depth of Genius: Beaumont and Fletcher the excellent mechanism, in juxtaposition and succession, of talent."

"What had a grammatical and logical consistency for the ear—what could be put together and represented to the eye—these poets [Beaumont and Fletcher] took from the ear and eye, unchecked by any intuition of an inward impossibility;—just as a man might put together a quarter of an orange, a quarter of an apple, and the like of a lemon and a pomgranate, and make it look like one round diverse-colored fruit. But nature, which works from within by evolution and assimilation according to a law, can not do so, nor could Shakespeare; for he too worked in the spirit of nature, by evolving the germ from within by the imaginative power according to an idea. For as the power of seeing is to light, so is an idea in mind to a law in nature. They are correlatives, which suppose each other."

(The first two of the above quotations are reprinted here by permission of the Harvard University Press from Thomas Middleton Raysor's edition of *Coleridge's Shakespearean Criticism*, 1930. The third and fourth are from Coleridge's *Notes and Lectures upon Shakespeare, and Some of the Old Poets and Dramatists, with Other Literary Remains, Complete Works*, ed. *Shedd*, 1871.)]

T. E. HULME: Romanticism and Classicism*

I WANT to maintain that after a hundred years of romanticism, we are in for a classical revival, and that the particular weapon of this new classical spirit, when it works in verse, will be fancy. And in this I imply the superiority of fancy—not superior generally or absolutely, for that would be obvious nonsense, but superior in the sense that we use the word good in empirical ethics—good for something, superior for something. I shall have to prove then two things, first that a classical revival is coming, and, secondly, for its particular purposes, fancy will be superior to imagination.

So banal have the terms Imagination and Fancy become that we imagine they must have always been in the language. Their history as two differing terms in the vocabulary of criticism is comparatively short. Originally, of course, they both mean the same thing; they first began to be differentiated by the German writers on aesthetics in the eighteenth century.

I know that in using the words "classic" and "romantic" I am doing a dangerous thing. They represent five or six different kinds of antitheses, and while I may be using them in one sense you may be interpreting them in another. In this present connection I am using them in a perfectly precise and limited sense. I ought really to have coined a couple of new words, but I prefer to use the ones I have used, as I then conform to the practice of the group of polemical writers who make most use of them at the present day, and have almost succeeded in making them political catchwords. I mean Maurras, Lasserre and all the group connected with *L'Action Française*.

At the present time this is the particular group with which the distinction is most vital. Because it has become a party symbol. If you asked a man of a certain set whether he preferred the

* "Romanticism and Classicism" is one of the pieces collected by Herbert Read in *Speculations: Essays on Humanism and the Philosophy of Art* (1924), the posthumous volume of the writings of T. E. Hulme (1883-1917). Mr. Read kindly corroborates the suggestion of the present editors that the probable date of composition is 1913-1914. The essay is here reprinted by permission of Harcourt, Brace and Company, Inc.

classics or the romantics, you could deduce from that what his politics were.

The best way of gliding into a proper definition of my terms would be to start with a set of people who are prepared to fight about it—for in them you will have no vagueness. (Other people take the infamous attitude of the person with catholic tastes who says he likes both.)

About a year ago, a man whose name I think was Fauchois gave a lecture at the Odéon on Racine, in the course of which he made some disparaging remarks about his dullness, lack of invention and the rest of it. This caused an immediate riot: fights took place all over the house; several people were arrested and imprisoned, and the rest of the series of lectures took place with hundreds of gendarmes and detectives scattered all over the place. These people interrupted because the classical ideal is a living thing to them and Racine is the great classic. That is what I call a real vital interest in literature. They regard romanticism as an awful disease from which France had just recovered.

The thing is complicated in their case by the fact that it was romanticism that made the revolution. They hate the revolution, so they hate romanticism.

I make no apology for dragging in politics here; romanticism both in England and France is associated with certain political views, and it is in taking a concrete example of the working out of a principle in action that you can get its best definition.

What was the positive principle behind all the other principles of '89? I am talking here of the revolution in as far as it was an idea; I leave out material causes—they only produce the forces. The barriers which could easily have resisted or guided these forces had been previously rotted away by ideas. This always seems to be the case in successful changes; the privileged class is beaten only when it has lost faith in itself, when it has itself been penetrated with the ideas which are working against it.

It was not the rights of man—that was a good solid practical war-cry. The thing which created enthusiasm, which made the revolution practically a new religion, was something more positive than that. People of all classes, people who stood to lose by it, were in a positive ferment about the idea of liberty. There must have been some idea which enabled them to think that something positive could come out of so essentially negative a thing. There was, and here I get my definition of romanticism. They had been taught by Rousseau that man was by nature good, that it was only bad laws and customs that had suppressed him. Remove all these and the infinite possibilities of man would have a chance. This is what made them think that something positive could come out of disorder, this is what created the religious enthusiasm. Here is the root of all romanticism: that man, the individual, is an infinite reservoir of possibilities; and if you can so rearrange society by the destruction of oppressive order then these possibilities will have a chance and you will get Progress.

One can define the classical quite clearly as the exact opposite to this. Man is an extraordinarily fixed and limited animal whose nature is absolutely constant. It is only by tradition and organisation that anything decent can be got out of him.

This view was a little shaken at the time of Darwin. You remember his particular hypothesis, that new species came into existence by the cumulative effect of small variations—this seems to admit the possibility of future progress. But at the present day the contrary hypothesis makes headway in the shape of De Vries's mutation theory, that each new species comes into existence, not gradually by the accumulation of small steps, but suddenly in a jump, a kind of sport, and that once in existence it remains absolutely fixed. This enables me to keep the classical view with an appearance of scientific backing.

Put shortly, these are the two views, then. One, that man is intrinsically good, spoilt by circumstance; and the other that he is intrinsically limited, but disciplined by order and tradition to something fairly decent. To the one party man's nature is like a well, to the other like a bucket. The view which regards man as a well, a reservoir full of possibilities, I call romantic; the one which regards him as a very finite and fixed creature, I call the classical.

One may note here that the Church has always taken the classical view since the defeat of the Pelagian heresy and the adoption of the sane classical dogma of original sin.

It would be a mistake to identify the classical

view with that of materialism. On the contrary it is absolutely identical with the normal religious attitude. I should put it in this way: That part of the fixed nature of man is the belief in the Deity. This should be as fixed and true for every man as belief in the existence of matter and in the objective world. It is parallel to appetite, the instinct of sex, and all the other fixed qualities. Now at certain times, by the use of either force or rhetoric, these instincts have been suppressed—in Florence under Savonarola, in Geneva under Calvin, and here under the Roundheads. The inevitable result of such a process is that the repressed instinct bursts out in some abnormal direction. So with religion. By the perverted rhetoric of Rationalism, your natural instincts are suppressed and you are converted into an agnostic. Just as in the case of the other instincts, Nature has her revenge. The instincts that find no right and proper outlet in religion must come out in some other way. You don't believe in a God, so you begin to believe that man is a god. You don't believe in Heaven, so you begin to believe in a heaven on earth. In other words, you get romanticism. The concepts that are right and proper in their own sphere are spread over, and so mess up, falsify and blur the clear outlines of human experience. It is like pouring a pot of treacle over the dinner table. Romanticism then, and this is the best definition I can give of it, is spilt religion.

I must now shirk the difficulty of saying exactly what I mean by romantic and classical in verse. I can only say that it means the result of these two attitudes towards the cosmos, towards man, in so far as it gets reflected in verse. The romantic, because he thinks man infinite, must always be talking about the infinite; and as there is always the bitter contrast between what you think you ought to be able to do and what man actually can, it always tends, in its later stages at any rate, to be gloomy. I really can't go any further than to say it is the reflection of these two temperaments, and point out examples of the different spirits. On the one hand I would take such diverse people as Horace, most of the Elizabethans and the writers of the Augustan age, and on the other side Lamartine, Hugo, parts of Keats, Coleridge, Byron, Shelley and Swinburne.

I know quite well that when people think of classical and romantic in verse, the contrast at once comes into their mind between, say, Racine and Shakespeare. I don't mean this; the dividing line that I intend is here misplaced a little from the true middle. That Racine is on the extreme classical side I agree, but if you call Shakespeare romantic, you are using a different definition to the one I give. You are thinking of the difference between classic and romantic as being merely one between restraint and exuberance. I should say with Nietzsche that there are two kinds of classicism, the static and the dynamic. Shakespeare is the classic of motion.

What I mean by classical in verse, then, is this. That even in the most imaginative flights there is always a holding back, a reservation. The classical poet never forgets this finiteness, this limit of man. He remembers always that he is mixed up with earth. He may jump, but he always returns back; he never flies away into the circumambient gas.

You might say if you wished that the whole of the romantic attitude seems to crystallise in verse round metaphors of flight. Hugo is always flying, flying over abysses, flying up into the eternal gases. The word infinite in every other line.

In the classical attitude you never seem to swing right along to the infinite nothing. If you say an extravagant thing which does exceed the limits inside which you know man to be fastened, yet there is always conveyed in some way at the end an impression of yourself standing outside it, and not quite believing it, or consciously putting it forward as a flourish. You never go blindly into an atmosphere more than the truth, an atmosphere too rarefied for man to breathe for long. You are always faithful to the conception of a limit. It is a question of pitch; in romantic verse you move at a certain pitch of rhetoric which you know, man being what he is, to be a little high-falutin. The kind of thing you get in Hugo or Swinburne. In the coming classical reaction that will feel just wrong. For an example of the opposite thing, a verse written in the proper classical spirit, I can take the song from Cymbeline beginning with "Fear no more the heat of the sun." I am just using this as a parable. I don't quite mean what I say here. Take the last two lines:

> Golden lads and lasses must,
> Like chimney sweepers come to dust.

Now, no romantic would have ever written that. Indeed, so ingrained is romanticism, so objectionable is this to it, that people have asserted that these were not part of the original song.

Apart from the pun, the thing that I think quite classical is the word lad. Your modern romantic could never write that. He would have to write golden youth, and take up the thing at least a couple of notes in pitch.

I want now to give the reasons which make me think that we are nearing the end of the romantic movement.

The first lies in the nature of any convention or tradition in art. A particular convention or attitude in art has a strict analogy to the phenomena of organic life. It grows old and decays. It has a definite period of life and must die. All the possible tunes get played on it and then it is exhausted; moreover its best period is its youngest. Take the case of the extraordinary efflorescence of verse in the Elizabethan period. All kinds of reasons have been given for this—the discovery of the new world and all the rest of it. There is a much simpler one. A new medium had been given them to play with—namely, blank verse. It was new and so it was easy to play new tunes on it.

The same law holds in other arts. All the masters of painting are born into the world at a time when the particular tradition from which they start is imperfect. The Florentine tradition was just short of full ripeness when Raphael came to Florence, the Bellinesque was still young when Titian was born in Venice. Landscape was still a toy or an appanage of figure-painting when Turner and Constable arose to reveal its independent power. When Turner and Constable had done with landscape they left little or nothing for their successors to do on the same lines. Each field of artistic activity is exhausted by the first great artist who gathers a full harvest from it.

This period of exhaustion seems to me to have been reached in romanticism. We shall not get any new efflorescence of verse until we get a new technique, a new convention, to turn ourselves loose in.

Objection might be taken to this. It might be said that a century as an organic unity doesn't exist, that I am being deluded by a wrong metaphor, that I am treating a collection of literary people as if they were an organism or state department. Whatever we may be in other things, an objector might urge, in literature in as far as we are anything at all—in as far as we are worth considering—we are individuals, we are persons, and as distinct persons we cannot be subordinated to any general treatment. At any period at any time, an individual poet may be a classic or a romantic just as he feels like it. You at any particular moment may think that you can stand outside a movement. You may think that as an individual you observe both the classic and the romantic spirit and decide from a purely detached point of view that one is superior to the other.

The answer to this is that no one, in a matter of judgment of beauty, can take a detached standpoint in this way. Just as physically you are not born that abstract entity, man, but the child of particular parents, so you are in matters of literary judgment. Your opinion is almost entirely of the literary history that came just before you, and you are governed by that whatever you may think. Take Spinoza's example of a stone falling to the ground. If it had a conscious mind it would, he said, think it was going to the ground because it wanted to. So you with your pretended free judgment about what is and what is not beautiful. The amount of freedom in man is much exaggerated. That we are free on certain rare occasions, both my religion and the views I get from metaphysics convince me. But many acts which we habitually label free are in reality automatic. It is quite possible for a man to write a book almost automatically. I have read several such products. Some observations were recorded more than twenty years ago by Robertson on reflex speech, and he found that in certain cases of dementia, where the people were quite unconscious so far as the exercise of reasoning went, that very intelligent answers were given to a succession of questions on politics and such matters. The meaning of these questions could not possibly have been understood. Language here acted after the manner of a reflex. So that certain extremely complex mechanisms, subtle enough to imitate beauty, can work by themselves—I certainly think that this is the case with judgments about beauty.

I can put the same thing in slightly different form. Here is a question of a conflict of two attitudes, as it might be of two techniques. The critic, while he has to admit that changes from one to the other occur, persists in regarding them as mere variations to a certain fixed normal, just as a pendulum swing. I admit the analogy of the pendulum as far as movement, but I deny the further consequence of the analogy, the existence of the point of rest, the normal point.

When I say that I dislike the romantics, I dissociate two things: the part of them in which they resemble all the great poets, and the part in which they differ and which gives them their character as romantics. It is this minor element which constitutes the particular note of a century, and which, while it excites contemporaries, annoys the next generation. It was precisely that quality in Pope which pleased his friends, which we detest. Now, anyone just before the romantics who felt that, could have predicted that a change was coming. It seems to me that we stand just in the same position now. I think that there is an increasing proportion of people who simply can't stand Swinburne.

When I say that there will be another classical revival I don't necessarily anticipate a return to Pope. I say merely that now is the time for such a revival. Given people of the necessary capacity, it may be a vital thing; without them we may get a formalism something like Pope. When it does come we may not even recognise it as classical. Although it will be classical it will be different because it has passed through a romantic period. To take a parallel example: I remember being very surprised, after seeing the Post Impressionists, to find in Maurice Denis's account of the matter that they consider themselves classical in the sense that they were trying to impose the same order on the mere flux of new material provided by the impressionist movement, that existed in the more limited materials of the painting before.

There is something now to be cleared away before I get on with my argument, which is that while romanticism is dead in reality, yet the critical attitude appropriate to it still continues to exist. To make this a little clearer: For every kind of verse, there is a corresponding receptive attitude. In a romantic period we demand from verse certain qualities. In a classical period we demand others. At the present time I should say that this receptive attitude has outlasted the thing from which it was formed. But while the romantic tradition has run dry, yet the critical attitude of mind, which demands romantic qualities from verse, still survives. So that if good classical verse were to be written tomorrow very few people would be able to stand it.

I object even to the best of the romantics. I object still more to the receptive attitude. I object to the sloppiness which doesn't consider that a poem is a poem unless it is moaning or whining about something or other. I always think in this connection of the last line of a poem of John Webster's which ends with a request I cordially endorse:

> End your moan and come away.

The thing has got so bad now that a poem which is all dry and hard, a properly classical poem, would not be considered poetry at all. How many people now can lay their hands on their hearts and say they like either Horace or Pope? They feel a kind of chill when they read them.

The dry hardness which you get in the classics is absolutely repugnant to them. Poetry that isn't damp isn't poetry at all. They cannot see that accurate description is a legitimate object of verse. Verse to them always means a bringing in of some of the emotions that are grouped round the word infinite.

The essence of poetry to most people is that it must lead them to a beyond of some kind. Verse strictly confined to the earthly and the definite (Keats is full of it) might seem to them to be excellent writing, excellent craftsmanship, but not poetry. So much has romanticism debauched us, that, without some form of vagueness, we deny the highest.

In the classic it is always the light of ordinary day, never the light that never was on land or sea. It is always perfectly human and never exaggerated: man is always man and never a god.

But the awful result of romanticism is that, accustomed to this strange light, you can never live without it. Its effect on you is that of a drug.

There is a general tendency to think that verse means little else than the expression of unsatisfied emotion. People say: "But how can you have verse without sentiment?" You see what it is: the prospect alarms them. A classical revival to them would mean the prospect of an arid desert and the death of poetry as they understand it, and could only come to fill the gap caused by that death. Exactly why this dry classical spirit should have a positive and legitimate necessity to express itself in poetry is utterly inconceivable to them. What this positive need is, I shall show later. It follows from the fact that there is another quality, not the emotion produced, which is at the root of excellence in verse. Before I get to this I am concerned with a negative thing, a theoretical point, a prejudice that stands in the way and is really at the bottom of this reluctance to understand classical verse.

It is an objection which ultimately I believe comes from a bad metaphysic of art. You are unable to admit the existence of beauty without the infinite being in some way or another dragged in.

I may quote for purposes of argument, as a typical example of this kind of attitude made vocal, the famous chapters in Ruskin's *Modern Painters,* Vol. II, on the imagination. I must say here, parenthetically, that I use this word without prejudice to the other discussion with which I shall end the paper. I only use the word here because it is Ruskin's word. All that I am concerned with just now is the attitude behind it, which I take to be the romantic.

> Imagination cannot but be serious; she sees too far, too darkly, too solemnly, too earnestly, ever to smile. There is something in the heart of everything, if we can reach it, that we shall not be inclined to laugh at. . . . Those who have so pierced and seen the melancholy deeps of things, are filled with intense passion and gentleness of sympathy. (Part III, Chap. III, §9.)
>
> There is in every word set down by the imaginative mind an awful undercurrent of meaning, and evidence and shadow upon it of the deep places out of which it has come. It is often obscure, often half-told; for he who wrote it, in his clear seeing of the things beneath, may have been impatient of detailed interpretation; for if we choose to dwell upon it and trace it, it will lead us always securely back to that metropolis of the soul's dominion from which we may follow out all the ways and tracks to its farthest coasts. (Part III, Chap. III, §5.)

Really in all these matters the act of judgment is an instinct, an absolutely unstateable thing akin to the art of the tea taster. But you must talk, and the only language you can use in this matter is that of analogy. I have no material clay to mould to the given shape; the only thing which one has for the purpose, and which acts as a substitute for it, a kind of mental clay, are certain metaphors modified into theories of aesthetic and rhetoric. A combination of these, while it cannot state the essentially unstateable intuition, can yet give you a sufficient analogy to enable you to see what it was and to recognise it on condition that you yourself have been in a similar state. Now these phrases of Ruskin's convey quite clearly to me his taste in the matter.

I see quite clearly that he thinks the best verse must be serious. That is a natural attitude for a man in the romantic period. But he is not content with saying that he prefers this kind of verse. He wants to deduce his opinion like his master, Coleridge, from some fixed principle which can be found by metaphysic.

Here is the last refuge of this romantic attitude. It proves itself to be not an attitude but a deduction from a fixed principle of the cosmos.

One of the main reasons for the existence of philosophy is not that it enables you to find truth (it can never do that) but that it does provide you a refuge for definitions. The usual idea of the thing is that it provides you with a fixed basis from which you can deduce the things you want in aesthetics. The process is the exact contrary. You start in the confusion of the fighting line, you retire from that just a little to the rear to recover, to get your weapons right. Quite plainly, without metaphor this—it provides you with an elaborate and precise language in which you really can explain definitely what you mean, but what you want to say is decided by other things. The ultimate reality is the hurly-burly, the struggle; the metaphysic is an adjunct to clear-headedness in it.

To get back to Ruskin and his objection to all that is not serious. It seems to me that involved in this is a bad metaphysical aesthetic. You have the metaphysic which in defining beauty or the nature of art always drags in the infinite. Particularly in Germany, the land where theories of aesthetics were first created, the romantic aesthetes collated all beauty to an impression of the infinite involved in the identification of our being in absolute spirit. In the least element of beauty we have a total intuition of the whole world. Every artist is a kind of pantheist.

Now it is quite obvious to anyone who holds this kind of theory that any poetry which confines itself to the finite can never be of the highest kind. It seems a contradiction in terms to them. And as in metaphysics you get the last refuge of a prejudice, so it is now necessary for me to refute this.

Here follows a tedious piece of dialectic, but it is necessary for my purpose. I must avoid two pitfalls in discussing the idea of beauty. On the one hand there is the old classical view which is supposed to define it as lying in conformity to certain standard fixed forms; and on the other hand there is the romantic view which drags in the infinite. I have got to find a metaphysic between these two which will enable me to hold consistently that a neo-classic verse of the type I have indicated involves no contradiction in terms. It is essential to prove that beauty may be in small, dry things.

The great aim is accurate, precise and definite description. The first thing is to recognise how extraordinarily difficult this is. It is no mere matter of carefulness; you have to use language, and language is by its very nature a communal thing; that is, it expresses never the exact thing but a compromise—that which is common to you, me and everybody. But each man sees a little differently, and to get out clearly and exactly what he does see, he must have a terrific struggle with language, whether it be with words or the technique of other arts. Language has its own special nature, its own conventions and communal ideas. It is only by a concentrated effort of the mind that you can hold it fixed to your own purpose. I always think that the fundamental process at the back of all the arts might be represented by the following metaphor. You know what I call architect's curves—flat pieces of wood with all different kinds of curvature. By a suitable selection from these you can draw approximately any curve you like. The artist I take to be the man who simply can't bear the idea of that "approximately." He will get the exact curve of what he sees whether it be an object or an idea in the mind. I shall here have to change my metaphor a little to get the process in his mind. Suppose that instead of your curved pieces of wood you have a springy piece of steel of the same types of curvature as the wood. Now the state of tension or concentration of mind, if he is doing anything really good in this struggle against the ingrained habit of the technique, may be represented by a man employing all his fingers to bend the steel out of its own curve and into the exact curve which you want. Something different to what it would assume naturally.

There are then two things to distinguish, first the particular faculty of mind to see things as they really are, and apart from the conventional ways in which you have been trained to see them. This is itself rare enough in all consciousness. Second, the concentrated state of mind, the grip over oneself which is necessary in the actual expression of what one sees. To prevent one falling into the conventional curves of ingrained technique, to hold on through infinite detail and trouble to the exact curve you want. Wherever you get this sincerity, you get the fundamental quality of good art without dragging in infinite or serious.

I can now get at that positive fundamental quality of verse which constitutes excellence, which has nothing to do with infinity, with mystery or with emotions.

This is the point I aim at, then, in my argument. I prophesy that a period of dry, hard, classical verse is coming. I have met the preliminary objection founded on the bad romantic aesthetic that in such verse, from which the infinite is excluded, you cannot have the essence of poetry at all.

After attempting to sketch out what this positive quality is, I can get on to the end of my paper in this way: That where you get this quality exhibited in the realm of the emotions you get imagination, and that where you get this quality exhibited in the contemplation of finite things you get fancy.

In prose as in algebra concrete things are embodied in signs or counters which are moved about according to rules, without being visual ised at all in the process. There are in prose certain type situations and arrangements of words, which move as automatically into certain other arrangements as do functions in algebra. One only changes the X's and the Y's back into physical things at the end of the process. Poetry, in one aspect at any rate, may be considered as an effort to avoid this characteristic of prose. It is not a counter language, but a visual concrete one. It is a compromise for a language of intuition which would hand over sensations bodily. It always endeavours to arrest you, and to make you continuously see a physical thing, to prevent you gliding through an abstract process. It chooses fresh epithets and fresh metaphors, not so much because they are new, and we are tired of the old, but because the old cease to convey a physical thing and become abstract counters. A poet says a ship "coursed the seas" to get a physical image, instead of the counter word "sailed." Visual meanings can only be transferred by the new bowl of metaphor; prose is an old pot that lets them leak out. Images in verse are not mere decoration, but the very essence of an intuitive language. Verse is a pedestrian taking you over the ground, prose—a train which delivers you at a destination.

I can now get on to a discussion of two words often used in this connection, "fresh" and "unexpected." You praise a thing for being "fresh." I understand what you mean, but the word besides conveying the truth conveys a secondary something which is certainly false. When you say a poem or drawing is fresh, and so good, the impression is somehow conveyed that the essential element of goodness is freshness, that it is good because it is fresh. Now this is certainly wrong, there is nothing particularly desirable about freshness *per se*. Works of art aren't eggs. Rather the contrary. It is simply an unfortunate necessity due to the nature of language and technique that the only way the element which does constitute goodness, the only way in which its presence can be detected externally, is by freshness. Freshness convinces you, you feel at once that the artist was in an actual physical state. You feel that for a minute. Real communication is so very rare, for plain speech is unconvincing. It is in this rare fact of communication that you get the root of aesthetic pleasure.

I shall maintain that wherever you get an extraordinary interest in a thing, a great zest in its contemplation which carries on the contemplator to accurate description in the sense of the word accurate I have just analysed, there you have sufficient justification for poetry. It must be an intense zest which heightens a thing out of the level of prose. I am using contemplation here just in the same way that Plato used it, only applied to a different subject; it is a detached interest. "The object of aesthetic contemplation is something framed apart by itself and regarded without memory or expectation, simply as being itself, as end not means, as individual not universal."

To take a concrete example. I am taking an extreme case. If you are walking behind a woman in the street, you notice the curious way in which the skirt rebounds from her heels. If that peculiar kind of motion becomes of such interest to you that you will search about until you can get the exact epithet which hits it off, there you have a properly aesthetic emotion. But it is the zest with which you look at the thing which decides you to make the effort. In this sense the feeling that was in Herrick's mind when he wrote "the tempestuous petticoat" was exactly the same as that which in bigger and vaguer matters makes the best romantic verse. It doesn't matter an atom that the emotion produced is not of dignified vagueness, but on the contrary amusing; the point is that exactly the same activity is at work as in the highest verse. That is the avoidance of conventional language in order to get the exact curve of the thing.

I have still to show that in the verse which is to come, fancy will be the necessary weapon of the classical school. The positive quality I have talked about can be manifested in ballad verse by extreme directness and simplicity, such as you get in "On Fair Kirkconnel Lea." But the particular verse we are going to get will be cheerful, dry and sophisticated, and here the necessary weapon of the positive quality must be fancy.

Subject doesn't matter; the quality in it is the same as you get in the more romantic people.

It isn't the scale or kind of emotion produced

that decides, but this one fact: Is there any real zest in it? Did the poet have an actually realised visual object before him in which he delighted? It doesn't matter if it were a lady's shoe or the starry heavens.

Fancy is not mere decoration added on to plain speech. Plain speech is essentially inaccurate. It is only by new metaphors, that is, by fancy, that it can be made precise.

When the analogy has not enough connection with the thing described to be quite parallel with it, where it overlays the thing it described and there is a certain excess, there you have the play of fancy—that I grant is inferior to imagination.

But where the analogy is every bit of it necessary for accurate description in the sense of the word accurate I have previously described, and your only objection to this kind of fancy is that it is not serious in the effect it produces, then I think the objection to be entirely invalid. If it is sincere in the accurate sense, when the whole of the analogy is necessary to get out the exact curve of the feeling or thing you want to express—there you seem to me to have the highest verse, even though the subject be trivial and the emotions of the infinite far away.

It is very difficult to use any terminology at all for this kind of thing. For whatever word you use is at once sentimentalised. Take Coleridge's word "vital." It is used loosely by all kinds of people who talk about art, to mean something vaguely and mysteriously significant. In fact, vital and mechanical is to them exactly the same antithesis as between good and bad.

Nothing of the kind; Coleridge uses it in a perfectly definite and what I call dry sense. It is just this: A mechanical complexity is the sum of its parts. Put them side by side and you get the whole. Now vital or organic is merely a convenient metaphor for a complexity of a different kind, that in which the parts cannot be said to be elements as each one is modified by the other's presence, and each one to a certain extent is the whole. The leg of a chair by itself is still a leg. My leg by itself wouldn't be.

Now the characteristic of the intellect is that it can only represent complexities of the mechanical kind. It can only make diagrams, and diagrams are essentially things whose parts are separate one from another. The intellect always analyses—when there is a synthesis it is baffled. That is why the artist's work seems mysterious. The intellect can't represent it. This is a necessary consequence of the particular nature of the intellect and the purposes for which it is formed. It doesn't mean that your synthesis is ineffable, simply that it can't be definitely stated.

Now this is all worked out in Bergson, the central feature of his whole philosophy. It is all based on the clear conception of these vital complexities which he calls "intensive" as opposed to the other kind which he calls "extensive," and the recognition of the fact that the intellect can only deal with the extensive multiplicity. To deal with the intensive you must use intuition.

Now, as I said before, Ruskin was perfectly aware of all this, but he had no such metaphysical background which would enable him to state definitely what he meant. The result is that he has to flounder about in a series of metaphors. A powerfully imaginative mind seizes and combines at the same instant all the important ideas of its poem or picture, and while it works with one of them, it is at the same instant working with and modifying all in their relation to it and never losing sight of their bearings on each other—as the motion of a snake's body goes through all parts at once and its volition acts at the same instant in coils which go contrary ways.

A romantic movement must have an end of the very nature of the thing. It may be deplored, but it can't be helped—wonder must cease to be wonder.

I guard myself here from all the consequences of the analogy, but it expresses at any rate the inevitableness of the process. A literature of wonder must have an end as inevitably as a strange land loses its strangeness when one lives in it. Think of the lost ecstasy of the Elizabethans. "Oh my America, my new found land," think of what it meant to them and of what it means to us. Wonder can only be the attitude of a man passing from one stage to another, it can never be a permanently fixed thing.

T. S. ELIOT: Hamlet and His Problems*

Few critics have ever admitted that *Hamlet* the play is the primary problem, and Hamlet the character only secondary. And Hamlet the character has had an especial temptation for that most dangerous type of critic: the critic with a mind which is naturally of the creative order, but which through some weakness in creative power exercises itself in criticism instead. These minds often find in Hamlet a vicarious existence for their own artistic realization. Such a mind had Goethe, who made of Hamlet a Werther; and such had Coleridge, who made of Hamlet a Coleridge; and probably neither of these men in writing about Hamlet remembered that his first business was to study a work of art. The kind of criticism that Goethe and Coleridge produced, in writing of Hamlet, is the most misleading kind possible. For they both possessed unquestionable critical insight, and both make their critical aberrations the more plausible by the substitution—of their own Hamlet for Shakespeare's—which their creative gift effects. We should be thankful that Walter Pater did not fix his attention on this play.

Two writers of our time, Mr. J. M. Robertson and Professor Stoll of the University of Minnesota, have issued small books which can be praised for moving in the other direction. Mr. Stoll performs a service in recalling to our attention the labours of the critics of the seventeenth and eighteenth centuries,[1] observing that they knew less about psychology than more recent Hamlet critics, but they were nearer in spirit to Shakespeare's art; and as they insisted on the importance of the effect of the whole rather than on the importance of the leading character, they were nearer, in their old-fashioned way, to the secret of dramatic art in general.

Qua work of art, the work of art cannot be interpreted; there is nothing to interpret; we can only criticize it according to standards, in comparison to other works of art; and for "interpretation" the chief task is the presentation of relevant historical facts which the reader is not assumed to know. Mr. Robertson points out, very pertinently, how critics have failed in their "interpretation" of *Hamlet* by ignoring what ought to be very obvious: that *Hamlet* is a stratification, that it represents the efforts of a series of men, each making what he could out of the work of his predecessors. The *Hamlet* of Shakespeare will appear to us very differently if, instead of treating the whole action of the play as due to Shakespeare's design, we perceive his *Hamlet* to be superposed upon much cruder material which persists even in the final form.

We know that there was an older play by Thomas Kyd, that extraordinary dramatic (if not poetic) genius who was in all probability the author of two plays so dissimilar as the *Spanish Tragedy* and *Arden of Feversham;* and what this play was like we can guess from three clues: from the *Spanish Tragedy* itself, from the tale of Belleforest upon which Kyd's *Hamlet* must have been based, and from a version acted in Germany in Shakespeare's lifetime which bears strong evidence of having been adapted from the earlier, not from the later, play. From these three sources it is clear that in the earlier play the motive was a revenge motive simply; that the action or delay is caused, as in the *Spanish Tragedy,* solely by the difficulty of as-

* "Hamlet and His Problems" first appeared in *The Athenaeum,* 16 September 1919, and is reprinted here from *Selected Essays: 1917-1932* by T. S. Eliot, Copyright, 1932, by Harcourt, Brace and Company, Inc. Mr. Eliot (*b.* 1888) is the author of *The Sacred Wood* (1920), *For Lancelot Andrewes* (1928), *John Dryden: the Poet, the Dramatist, the Critic* (1932), *The Use of Poetry and the Use of Criticism* (1933), *After Strange Gods* (1933), *Elizabethan Essays* (1934), and *Essays, Ancient and Modern* (1936).

[1] I have never, by the way, seen a cogent refutation of Thomas Rymer's objections to *Othello.*

sassinating a monarch surrounded by guards; and that the "madness" of Hamlet was feigned in order to escape suspicion, and successfully. In the final play of Shakespeare, on the other hand, there is a motive which is more important than that of revenge, and which explicitly "blunts" the latter; the delay in revenge is unexplained on grounds of necessity or expediency; and the effect of the "madness" is not to lull but to arouse the king's suspicion. The alteration is not complete enough, however, to be convincing. Furthermore, there are verbal parallels so close to the *Spanish Tragedy* as to leave no doubt that in places Shakespeare was merely *revising* the text of Kyd. And finally there are unexplained scenes—the Polonious-Laertes and the Polonius-Reynaldo scenes—for which there is little excuse; these scenes are not in the verse style of Kyd, and not beyond doubt in the style of Shakespeare. These Mr. Robertson believes to be scenes in the original play of Kyd reworked by a third hand, perhaps Chapman, before Shakespeare touched the play. And he concludes, with very strong show of reason, that the original play of Kyd was, like certain other revenge plays, in two parts of five acts each. The upshot of Mr. Robertson's examination is, we believe, irrefragable: that Shakespeare's *Hamlet*, so far as it is Shakespeare's, is a play dealing with the effect of a mother's guilt upon her son, and that Shakespeare was unable to impose this motive successfully upon the "intractable" material of the old play.

Of the intractability there can be no doubt. So far from being Shakespeare's masterpiece, the play is most certainly an artistic failure. In several ways the play is puzzling, and disquieting as is none of the others. Of all the plays it is the longest and is possibly the one on which Shakespeare spent most pains; and yet he has left in it superfluous and inconsistent scenes which even hasty revision should have noticed. The versification is variable. Lines like

Look, the morn, in russet mantle clad,
Walks o'er the dew of yon high eastern hill,

are of the Shakespeare of *Romeo and Juliet.* The lines in Act V. Sc. ii,

Sir, in my heart there was a kind of fighting
That would not let me sleep . . .
Up from my cabin,
My sea-gown scarf'd about me, in the dark
Grop'd I to find out them: had my desire;
Finger'd their packet;

are of his quite mature. Both workmanship and thought are in an unstable position. We are surely justified in attributing the play, with that other profoundly interesting play of "intractable" material and astonishing versification, *Measure for Measure,* to a period of crisis, after which follow the tragic successes which culminate in Coriolanus. *Coriolanus* may be not as "interesting" as *Hamlet,* but it is, with *Antony and Cleopatra,* Shakespeare's most assured artistic success. And probably more people have thought *Hamlet* a work of art because they found it interesting, than have found it interesting because it is a work of art. It is the "Mona Lisa" of literature.

The grounds of *Hamlet's* failure are not immediately obvious. Mr. Robertson is undoubtedly correct in concluding that the essential emotion of the play is the feeling of a son towards a guilty mother:

> [Hamlet's] tone is that of one who has suffered tortures on the score of his mother's degradation. . . . The guilt of a mother is an almost intolerable motive for drama, but it had to be maintained and emphasized to supply a psychological solution, or rather a hint of one.

This, however, is by no means the whole story. It is not merely the "guilt of a mother" that cannot be handled as Shakespeare handled the suspicion of Othello, the infatuation of Antony, or the pride of Coriolanus. The subject might conceivably have expanded into a tragedy like these, intelligible, self-complete, in the sunlight. *Hamlet,* like the sonnets, is full of some stuff that the writer could not drag to light, contemplate, or manipulate into art. And when we search for this feeling, we find it, as in the sonnets, very difficult to localize. You cannot point to it in the speeches; indeed, if you examine the two famous soliloquies you see the versification of Shakespeare, but a content which might be claimed by another, perhaps by the author of the *Revenge of Bussy d'Ambois,* Act V. Sc. i. We find Shakespeare's *Hamlet* not in the action, not in any quotations that we might select, so much as in an unmistakable tone which is unmistakably not in the earlier play.

The only way of expressing emotion in the form of art is by finding an "objective correlative"; in other words, a set of objects, a situation, a chain of events which shall be the formula of that *particular* emotion; such that when the external facts, which must terminate in sensory experience, are given, the emotion is immediately evoked. If you examine any of Shakespeare's more successful tragedies, you will find this exact equivalence; you will find that the state of mind of Lady Macbeth walking in her sleep has been communicated to you by a skilful accumulation of imagined sensory impressions; the words of Macbeth on hearing of his wife's death strike us as if, given the sequence of events, these words were automatically released by the last event in the series. The artistic "inevitability" lies in this complete adequacy of the external to the emotion; and this is precisely what is deficient in *Hamlet.* Hamlet (the man) is dominated by an emotion which is inexpressible, because it is in *excess* of the facts as they appear. And the supposed identity of Hamlet with his author is genuine to this point: that Hamlet's bafflement at the absence of objective equivalent to his feelings is a prolongation of the bafflement of his creator in the face of his artistic problem. Hamlet is up against the difficulty that his disgust is occasioned by his mother, but that his mother is not an adequate equivalent for it; his disgust envelops and exceeds her. It is thus a feeling which he cannot understand; he cannot objectify it, and it therefore remains to poison life and obstruct action. None of the possible actions can satisfy it; and nothing that Shakespeare can do with the plot can express Hamlet for him. And it must be noticed that the very nature of the *données* of the problem precludes objective equivalence. To have heightened the criminality of Gertrude would have been to provide the formula for a totally different emotion in Hamlet; it is just *because* her character is so negative and insignificant that she arouses in Hamlet the feeling which she is incapable of representing.

The "madness" of Hamlet lay to Shakespeare's hand; in the earlier play a simple ruse, and to the end, we may presume, understood as a ruse by the audience. For Shakespeare it is less than madness and more than feigned. The levity of Hamlet, his repetition of phrase, his puns, are not part of a deliberate plan of dissimulation, but a form of emotional relief. In the character Hamlet it is the buffoonery of an emotion which can find no outlet in action; in the dramatist it is the buffoonery of an emotion which he cannot express in art. The intense feeling, ecstatic or terrible, without an object or exceeding its object, is something which every person of sensibility has known; it is doubtless a subject of study for pathologists. It often occurs in adolescence: the ordinary person puts these feelings to sleep, or trims down his feelings to fit the business world; the artist keeps them alive by his ability to intensify the world to his emotions. The Hamlet of Laforgue is an adolescent; the Hamlet of Shakespeare is not, he has not that explanation and excuse. We must simply admit that here Shakespeare tackled a problem which proved too much for him. Why he attempted it at all is an insoluble puzzle; under compulsion of what experience he attempted to express the inexpressibly horrible, we cannot ever know. We need a great many facts in his biography; and we should like to know whether, and when, and after or at the same time as what personal experience, he read Montaigne, II. xii, *Apologie de Raimond Sebond.* We should have, finally, to know something which is by hypothesis unknowable, for we assume it to be an experience which, in the manner indicated, exceeded the facts. We should have to understand things which Shakespeare did not understand himself.

T. S. ELIOT: "Ulysses," Order, and Myth *

Mr. Joyce's book [1] has been out long enough for no more general expression of praise, or expostulation with its detractors, to be necessary; and it has not been out long enough for any attempt at a complete measurement of its place and significance to be possible. All that one can usefully do at this time, and it is a great deal to do, for such a book, is to elucidate any aspect of the book—and the number of aspects is indefinite—which has not yet been fixed. I hold this book to be the most important expression which the present age has found; it is a book to which we are all indebted, and from which none of us can escape. These are postulates for anything that I have to say about it, and I have no wish to waste the reader's time by elaborating my eulogies; it has given me all the surprise, delight, and terror that I can require, and I will leave it at that.

Amongst all the criticisms I have seen of the book, I have seen nothing—unless we except, in its way, M. Valery Larbaud's valuable paper which is rather an Introduction than a criticism—which seemed to me to appreciate the significance of the method employed—the parallel to the Odyssey, and the use of appropriate styles and symbols to each division. Yet one might expect this to be the first peculiarity to attract attention; but it has been treated as an amusing dodge, or scaffolding erected by the author for the purpose of disposing his realistic tale, of no interest in the completed structure. The criticism which Mr. Aldington directed upon *Ulysses* several years ago seems to me to fail by this oversight—but, as Mr. Aldington wrote before the complete work had appeared, fails more honourably than the attempts of those who had the whole book before them. Mr. Aldington treated Mr. Joyce as a prophet of chaos; and wailed at the flood of Dadaism which his prescient eye saw bursting forth at the tap of the magician's rod. Of course, the influence which Mr. Joyce's book may have is from my point of view an irrelevance. A very great book may have a very bad influence indeed; and a mediocre book may be in the event most salutary. The next generation is responsible for its own soul; a man of genius is responsible to his peers, not to a studio-full of uneducated and undisciplined coxcombs. Still, Mr. Aldington's pathetic solicitude for the half-witted seems to me to carry certain implications about the nature of the book itself to which I cannot assent; and this is the important issue. He finds the book, if I understand him, to be an invitation to chaos, and an expression of feelings which are perverse, partial, and a distortion of reality. But unless I quote Mr. Aldington's words I am likely to falsify. "I say, moreover," he says,[2] "that when Mr. Joyce, with his marvellous gifts, uses them to disgust us with mankind, he is doing something which is false and a libel on humanity." It is somewhat similar to the opinion of the urbane Thackeray upon Swift. "As for the moral, I think it horrible, shameful, unmanly, blasphemous; and giant and great as this Dean is, I say we should hoot him." (This, of the conclusion of the Voyage to the Houyhnhnms—which seems to me one of the greatest triumphs that the human soul has ever achieved.)—It is true that Thackeray later pays Swift one of the finest tributes that a man has ever given or received: "So great a man he seems to me that thinking of him is like thinking of an empire falling." And Mr. Aldington, in his time, is almost equally generous.)

Whether it is possible to libel humanity (in

* "'Ulysses,' Order, and Myth" first appeared in *The Dial*, November 1923, and it is reprinted here for the first time by permission of Mr. Eliot.

[1] *Ulysses*. By James Joyce. 8vo. 752 pages. Shakespeare and Company, Paris. Limited edition.

[2] *English Review*, April 1921.

distinction to libel in the usual sense, which is libelling an individual or a group in contrast with the rest of humanity) is a question for philosophical societies to discuss; but of course if *Ulysses* were a "libel" it would simply be a forged document, a powerless fraud, which would never have extracted from Mr. Aldington a moment's attention. I do not wish to linger over this point: the interesting question is that begged by Mr. Aldington when he refers to Mr. Joyce's "great *undisciplined* talent."

I think that Mr. Aldington and I are more or less agreed as to what we want in principle, and agreed to call it classicism. It is because of this agreement that I have chosen Mr. Aldington to attack on the present issue. We are agreed as to what we want, but not as to how to get it, or as to what contemporary writing exhibits a tendency in that direction. We agree, I hope, that "classicism" is not an alternative to "romanticism," as of political parties, Conservative and Liberal, Republican and Democrat, on a "turn-the-rascals-out" platform. It is a goal toward which all good literature strives, so far as it is good, according to the possibilities of its place and time. One can be "classical," in a sense, by turning away from nine-tenths of the material which lies at hand, and selecting only mummified stuff from a museum—like some contemporary writers, about whom one could say some nasty things in this connexion, if it were worth while (Mr. Aldington is not one of them). Or one can be classical in tendency by doing the best one can with the material at hand. The confusion springs from the fact that the term is applied to literature and to the whole complex of interests and modes of behaviour and society of which literature is a part; and it has not the same bearing in both applications. It is much easier to be a classicist in literary criticism than in creative art—because in criticism you are responsible only for what you want, and in creation you are responsible for what you can do with material which you must simply accept. And in this material I include the emotions and feelings of the writer himself, which, for that writer, are simply material which he must accept—not virtues to be enlarged or vices to be diminished. The question, then, about Mr. Joyce, is: how much living material does he deal with, and how does he deal with it: deal with, not as a legislator or exhorter, but as an artist?

It is here that Mr. Joyce's parallel use of the Odyssey has a great importance. It has the importance of a scientific discovery. No one else has built a novel upon such a foundation before: it has never before been necessary. I am not begging the question in calling *Ulysses* a "novel"; and if you call it an epic it will not matter. If it is not a novel, that is simply because the novel is a form which will no longer serve; it is because the novel, instead of being a form, was simply the expression of an age which had not sufficiently lost all form to feel the need of something stricter. Mr. Joyce has written one novel—*The Portrait;* Mr. Wyndham Lewis has written one novel—*Tarr.* I do not suppose that either of them will ever write another "novel." The novel ended with Flaubert and with James. It is, I think, because Mr. Joyce and Mr. Lewis, being "in advance" of their time, felt a conscious or probably unconscious dissatisfaction with the form, that their novels are more formless than those of a dozen clever writers who are unaware of its obsolescence.

In using the myth, in manipulating a continuous parallel between contemporaneity and antiquity, Mr. Joyce is pursuing a method which others must pursue after him. They will not be imitators, any more than the scientist who uses the discoveries of an Einstein in pursuing his own, independent, further investigations. It is simply a way of controlling, of ordering, of giving a shape and a significance to the immense panorama of futility and anarchy which is contemporary history. It is a method already adumbrated by Mr. Yeats, and of the need for which I believe Mr. Yeats to have been the first contemporary to be conscious. It is a method for which the horoscope is auspicious. Psychology (such as it is, and whether our reaction to it be comic or serious), ethnology, and *The Golden Bough* have concurred to make possible what was impossible even a few years ago. Instead of narrative method, we may now use the mythical method. It is, I seriously believe, a step toward making the modern world possible for art, toward that order and form which Mr. Aldington so earnestly desires. And only those who have won their own discipline in secret and without aid, in a world which offers very little assistance to that end, can be of any use in furthering this advance.

T. S. ELIOT: A Dialogue on Dramatic Poetry *

E: You were saying, *B,* that it was all very well for the older dramatic critics—you instanced Aristotle and Corneille and Dryden at random—to discuss the laws of drama as they did; that the problem is altogether different and infinitely more complicated for us. That fits in with a notion of my own, which I will expound in a moment; but first I should like to know what differences you find.

B: I need not go into the matter very deeply to persuade you of my contention. Take Aristotle first. He had only one type of drama to consider; he could work entirely within the "categories" of that drama; he did not have to consider or criticize the religious, ethical or artistic prejudices of his race. He did not have to like so many things as we have to like, merely because he did not know so many things. And the less you know and like, the easier to frame aesthetic laws. He did not have to consider either what is universal or what is necessary for the time. Hence he had a better chance of hitting on some of the universals and of knowing what was right for the time. And as for Dryden. I take Dryden because there is an obvious, a too obvious, hiatus between the Tudor-Jacobean drama and that of the Restoration. We know about the closing of the theatres, and so on; and we are apt to magnify the differences and difficulties. But the differences between Dryden and Jonson are nothing to the differences between ourselves, who are sitting here to discuss poetic drama and Mr. Shaw and Mr. Galsworthy and Sir Arthur Pinero and Mr. Jones and Mr. Arlen and Mr. Coward: all of whom are almost contemporary with us. For the world of Dryden on the one hand and the world of Shakespeare and Jonson on the other were much the same world, with similar religious, ethical and artistic presuppositions. But what have we in common with the distinguished playwrights whom I have just mentioned?

And, to return to Aristotle for a moment, consider how much more we know (unfortunately) about Greek drama than he did. Aristotle did not have to worry about the relation of drama to religion, about the traditional morality of the Hellenes, about the relation of art to politics; he did not have to struggle with German or Italian aesthetics; he did not have to read the (extremely interesting) works of Miss Harrison or Mr. Cornford, or the translations of Professor Murray, or wrinkle his brow over the antics of the Todas and the Veddahs. Nor did he have to reckon with the theatre as a paying proposition.

Similarly, neither Dryden, nor Corneille from whom he learned so much, was bothered by excessive knowledge about Greek civilization. They had the Greek and Latin classics to read, and were not aware of *all* the differences between Greek and Roman civilization and their own. As for us, we know too much, and are convinced of too little. Our literature is a substitute for religion, and so is our religion. We should do better if, instead of worrying about the place of drama in society, we simply decided what amused us. What is the purpose of the theatre except to amuse?

E: It is all very well to reduce the drama to "amusement." But it seems to me that that is

* "A Dialogue on Dramatic Poetry" first appeared as "A Dialogue on Poetic Drama" in conjunction with a new printing of Dryden's "Essay of Dramatic Poesie" in 1928. It is reprinted here from *Selected Essays: 1917-1932* by T. S. Eliot, Copyright, 1932, by Harcourt, Brace and Company, Inc.

just what has happened. I believe that the drama has something else to do except to divert us. What else does it do at the moment?

B: I have just given a list of dramatists. I admit that their intentions vary. Pinero, for instance, was concerned with setting, or, as is said in the barbarous jargon of our day, "posing" the problems of his generation. He was much more concerned with "posing" than with answering. Shaw, on the other hand, was much more concerned with answering than with "posing." Both of these accomplished writers had a strong ethical motive. This ethical motive is not apparent in Mr. Arlen or Mr. Coward. Their drama is pure "amusement." The two excesses go together. The whole question is, whom does the drama amuse? and what is the quality of the amusement?

C: I should not for my part admit that any of these people are concerned to amuse. There is no such thing as mere amusement. They are concerned with flattering the prejudices of the mob. And their own. I do not suppose for a moment that either Shaw, or Pinero, or Mr. Coward has ever spent one hour in the study of ethics. Their cleverness lies in finding out how their audiences would like to behave, and encouraging them to do it by exhibiting personages behaving in that way.

D: But why should a dramatist be expected to spend even five minutes in the study of ethics?

B: I consent. But they need to assume some moral attitude in common with their audience. Æschylus and Sophocles, the Elizabethans, and the Restoration dramatists had this. But this must be already given; it is not the job of the dramatist to impose it.

E: What is the moral attitude of Dryden's *Mr. Limberham?*

B: Impeccable. The morality of our Restoration drama cannot be impugned. It assumes orthodox Christian morality, and laughs (in its comedy) at human nature for not living up to it. It retains its respect for the divine by showing the failure of the human. The attitude of the Blasphemer towards Religion. It is only the irreligious who are shocked by blasphemy. Blasphemy is a sign of Faith. Imagine Mr. Shaw blaspheming! He could not. Our Restoration drama is all virtue. It depends upon virtue for its existence. The author of *The Queen was in the Parlour* does not depend upon virtue.

E: You are talking as if the drama was merely a matter of established morals. Let me for a moment transfer the discussion to the question of form. I speak as one who is satisfied neither by Elizabethan drama nor by Pinero or Barrie. A few years ago I—and you *B* and you *C* and *A*—was delighted by the Russian ballet. Here seemed to be everything that we wanted in drama, except the poetry. It did not teach any "lesson," but it had form. It seemed to revive the more formal element in drama for which we craved. I concede that the more recent ballets have not given me the same pleasure. But for that I blame Mr. Diaghilev, not the ballet in principle. If there is a future for drama, and particularly for poetic drama, will it not be in the direction indicated by the ballet? Is it not a question of form rather than ethics? And is not the question of verse drama versus prose drama a question of degree of form?

A: There I am inclined to support you. People have tended to think of verse as a restriction upon drama. They think that the emotional range, and the realistic truth, of drama is limited and circumscribed by verse. People were once content with verse in drama, they say, because they were content with a restricted and artificial range of emotion. Only prose can give the full gamut of modern feeling, can correspond to actuality. But is not every dramatic representation artificial? And are we not merely deceiving ourselves when we aim at greater and greater realism? Are we not contenting ourselves with appearances, instead of insisting upon fundamentals? Has human feeling altered much from Æschylus to ourselves? I maintain the contrary. I say that prose drama is merely a slight by-product of verse drama. The human soul, in intense emotion, strives to express itself in verse. It is not for me, but for the neurologists, to discover why this is so, and why and how feeling and rhythm are related. The tendency, at any rate, of prose drama is to emphasise the ephemeral and superficial; if we want to get at the permanent and universal we tend to express ourselves in verse.

D: But—to return to the point—can you hang all this on the ballet? How is the ballet concerned with the permanent and universal?

B: The ballet is valuable because it has, unconsciously, concerned itself with a permanent form; it is futile because it has concerned itself with the ephemeral in content. Apart from Stravinski, who is a real musician, and from Cocteau, who is a real playwright, what is the strength of the ballet? It is in a tradition, a training, an askesis, which, to be fair, is not of Russian but of Italian origin, and which ascends for several centuries. Sufficient to say that any efficient dancer has undergone a training which is like a moral training. Has any successful actor of our time undergone anything similar?

E: This seems to give me the opening for which I have been waiting. You all approve of the ballet because it is a system of physical training, of traditional, symbolical and highly skilled movements. It is a liturgy of very wide adaptability, and you seem to laud the liturgy rather than the variations. Very well. *B* has spoken of our knowledge of Greek antecedents to Greek drama, and has implied that we know more about that than Dryden, or Aristotle, or the Greek dramatists themselves. I say that the consummation of the drama, the perfect and ideal drama, is to be found in the ceremony of the Mass. I say, with the support of the scholars whom *B* mentions (and others), that drama springs from religious liturgy, and that it cannot afford to depart far from religious liturgy. I agree with *B* that the problem of drama was simpler for Aristotle and for Dryden and for Corneille than for us. They had only to take things as they found them. But when drama has ranged as far as it has in our own day, is not the only solution to return to religious liturgy? And the only dramatic satisfaction that I find now is in a High Mass well performed. Have you not there everything necessary? And indeed, if you consider the ritual of the Church during the cycle of the year, you have the complete drama represented. The Mass is a small drama, having all the unities; but in the Church year you have represented the full drama of creation.

B: The question is not, whether the Mass is dramatic, but what is the relation of the drama to the Mass? We must take things as we find them. Are we to say that our cravings for drama are fulfilled by the Mass? I believe that a cursory examination is enough for us to reply, No. For I once knew a man who held the same views that you appear to hold, *E*. He went to High Mass every Sunday, and was particular to find a church where he considered the Mass efficiently performed. And as I sometimes accompanied him, I can testify that the Mass gave him extreme, I may even say immoderate satisfaction. It was almost orgiastic. But when I came to consider his conduct, I realized that he was guilty of a *confusion des genres.* His attention was not on the meaning of the Mass, for he was not a believer but a Bergsonian; it was on the Art of the Mass. His dramatic desires were satisfied by the Mass, precisely because he was not interested in the Mass, but in the drama of it. Now what I maintain is, that you have no business to care about the Mass unless you are a believer. And even if you are a believer you will have dramatic desires which crave fulfilment otherwise. For man lives in various degrees. We need (as I believe, but you need not believe this for the purpose of my argument) religious faith. And we also need amusement (the quality of the amusement will, of course, not be unrelated to the quality of our religious belief). Literature can be no substitute for religion, not merely because we need religion, but because we need literature as well as religion. And religion is no more a substitute for drama than drama is a substitute for religion. If we can do without religion, then let us have the theatre without pretending that it *is* religion; and if we can do without drama, then let us not pretend that religion is drama.

For there is a difference in attention. If we are religious, then we shall only be aware of the Mass as art, in so far as it is badly done and interferes with our devotion consequently. A devout person, in assisting at Mass, is not in the frame of mind of a person attending a drama, for he is *participating*—and that makes all the difference. In participating we are supremely conscious of certain realities, and unconscious of others. But we are human beings, and crave representations in which we are conscious, and critical, of these other realities. We cannot be aware solely of divine realities. We must be aware also of human realities. And we crave some liturgy less divine, something in respect of which we shall be more spectators and less participants. Hence we want the human drama, related to the divine drama, but not the same, as well as the Mass.

E: You have admitted all that I expected, and more. That is the essential relation of drama to religious liturgy.

D: I have a suggestion to put forward. It is this: can we not take it that the form of the drama must vary from age to age in accordance with religious assumptions of the age? That is, that drama represents a relation of the human needs and satisfactions to the religious needs and satisfactions which the age provides. When the age has a set religious practice and belief, then the drama can and should tend towards realism, I say *towards,* I do not say arrive at. The more definite the religious and ethical principles, the more freely the drama can move towards what is now called photography. The more fluid, the more chaotic the religious and ethical beliefs, the more the drama must tend in the direction of liturgy. Thus there would be some constant relation between drama and the religion of the time. The movement, in the time of Dryden and indeed of Corneille, and indeed of Aristotle, was towards freedom. Perhaps our movement should be towards what we called, in touching upon the ballet, form?

E: An interesting theory, with no historical backing whatever, but concluding in exactly what I said myself. But if you want form, you must go deeper than dramatic technique.

C: I should like to make an interruption. If I do not make it now I shall probably forget to make it at all. You are all talking of form and content, of freedom and restriction, as if everything was indefinitely variable. You are not, like myself, students of the popular drama of the *faubourgs.* And what I there remark is the fixity of morality. The suburban drama has today fundamentally the same morality as it had in the days of *Arden of Feversham* and *The Yorkshire Tragedy.* I agree with *B* about Restoration comedy. It is a great tribute to Christian morality. Take the humour of our great English comedian, Ernie Lotinga. It is (if you like) bawdy. But such bawdiness is a tribute to, an acknowledgment of conventional British morality. I am a member of the Labour Party. I believe in the King and the Islington Empire. I do not believe in the plutocratic St. Moritzers for whom our popular dramatists cater. But what I was saying is that our suburban drama is morally sound, and out of such soundness poetry may come. Human nature does not change. Another port, please.

B: I suggest that I agree with the late William Archer about Elizabethan drama.

A, E, C, and *D:* What!

B: Yes. William Archer was a very honest man. As a dramatic critic he had one fault: he knew nothing about poetry. Furthermore, he made the egregious error of supposing that the dramatic merit of a dramatic work could be estimated without reference to its poetic merit. Henrik Ibsen certainly had more dramatic ability than Cyril Tourneur. But as Archer did not realize that dramatic and poetic ability are less different than chalk and cheese, he made the mistake of supposing that Ibsen was a greater dramatist than Tourneur. Greater if you like, but he will not last as long. For the greatest drama is poetic drama, and dramatic defects *can* be compensated by poetic excellence. Let us ignore Tourneur. We can cite Shakespeare.

C: Do you mean that Shakespeare is a greater dramatist than Ibsen, not by being a greater dramatist, but by being a greater poet?

B: That is precisely what I mean. For, on the other hand, what great poetry is not dramatic? Even the minor writers of the Greek Anthology, even Martial, are dramatic. Who is more dramatic than Homer or Dante? We are human beings, and in what are we more interested than in human action and human attitudes? Even when he assaults, and with supreme mastery, the divine mystery, does not Dante engage us in the question of the human attitude towards this mystery—which is dramatic? Shakespeare was a great dramatist and a great poet. But if you isolate poetry from drama completely, have you the right to say that Shakespeare was a greater dramatist than Ibsen, or than Shaw? Shaw is right about Shakespeare, for Shaw is no poet. I am not quite right there neither, for Shaw *was* a poet—until he was born, and the poet in Shaw was stillborn. Shaw has a great deal of poetry, but all stillborn; Shaw is dramatically precocious, and poetically less than immature. The best you can say for Shaw is that he seems not to have read all the popular handbooks on science that Mr. Wells and Bishop Barnes have read.

E: Yes, Shakespeare fails us, and Mr. Archer is right. William Archer is only wrong in having attacked the minor figures of Elizabethan drama and not having understood that he was obliged to attack Shakespeare as well. He was wrong, as you said, in thinking that drama and poetry are two different things. If he had seen that they are the same thing he would have had to admit that Cyril Tourneur is a great dramatist, that Jonson is a great dramatist, that Marlowe is a very great dramatist, that Webster is a great dramatist, and that Shakespeare is so great a dramatist, so great a poet, that even Mr. Archer should have removed his shoes, instead of evading the question, rather than ask Shakespeare to abide it. Shakespeare would have abidden it if Mr. William Archer had chosen to ask it. But he did not chose.

D: I think both *B* and *E* are rather muddled about the relation of poetry and drama, but especially *B*. Just as Archer made a mechanical separation, so *B* makes a mechanical reunion. Let us make it clearer by putting it about the other way, and taking up a point that *B* let slip. If drama tends to poetic drama, not by adding an embellishment and still less by limiting its scale, we should expect a dramatic poet like Shakespeare to write his finest poetry in his most dramatic scenes. And this is just what we do find: what makes it most dramatic is what makes it most poetic. No one ever points to certain plays of Shakespeare as being the most poetic, and to *other* plays as being the most dramatic. The same plays are the most poetic and the most dramatic, and this not by a concurrence of two activities, but by the full expansion of one and the same activity. I agree that the dramatist who is not a poet is so much the less a dramatist.

C: The odd thing about William Archer's book is that he did, to some extent, recognize poetry when he saw it; but at any rate when he was dealing with an Elizabethan like Chapman, whenever he comes across a passage of poetry, he refuses to believe that it is dramatic. If this is poetry, he seems to say, that proves that it is not drama. I remember that when I read the book I noticed that Archer could certainly have picked out un-dramatic or defectively dramatic passages from Chapman's plays: instead he selects that splendidly dramatic speech of Clermont on seeing the ghosts—as an example of "mild surprise"!

B: Perhaps the ghosts put him off.

E: Yet nothing is more dramatic than a ghost.

C: To sum up: there is no "relation" between poetry and drama. All poetry tends towards drama, and all drama towards poetry.

F: A neat and dangerous generalization. For you would admit that you enjoy a great deal of poetry in which hardly even your own practised eye could detect the "tendency" towards drama; and consequently you ought surely to be able to enjoy a great deal of drama which is unquestionably written in prose.

B: Of course he does. And some of the Elizabethan plays of which Mr. Archer disapproved are, in fact, bad plays. And a great many were also, as Mr. Shaw has observed, bad verse. Shaw points out that it is easier to write bad verse than good prose—which nobody ever denied; but it is easy for Shaw to write good prose and quite impossible for him to write good verse.

E: Running off on this wild-goose chase after William Archer, whom you might just as well have left alone, you have forgotten to tell us why Shakespeare fails us.

B: I mean that Archer's objections to Elizabethan drama were partly based upon a right instinct. He used some deplorable terms, such as "humanitarianism," in expressing his dislike. But had he observed that his fundamental objection applied as much to Shakespeare as to anybody, as much to the best as to the worst, he might have admitted an obligation to find another and profounder explanation for it.

A: Are we to infer that you criticize Shakespeare on the ground that his plays are not morally edifying?

B: In a sense, yes.

A: But a little while ago you were defending Restoration comedy against the charge of immorality and indecency.

B: Not against indecency, that was unnecessary. We all like its indecency when it is really witty, as it sometimes is. But the question of Wycherley and the question of Shakespeare are not on the same plane. Restoration comedy is a comedy of social manners. It presupposes the existence of a society, therefore of social and moral laws. (It owes much to Jonson, but little to Shakespeare—anyway, Shakespeare was too great to have much influence.) It laughs at the members of society who transgress its laws. The tragedy of Shakespeare goes much deeper and yet it tells us only that weakness of character leads to disaster. There is no background of social order such as you perceive behind Corneille and Sophocles.

C: Why should there be? You can't deduce from that that Shakespeare is inferior to Sophocles and Corneille.

B: No, I can't. All I know is that something is lacking, I am left dissatisfied and disturbed. I think there are other people who feel the same thing. So far as I can isolate Shakespeare, I prefer him to all other dramatists of every time. But I can not do that altogether; and I find the age of Shakespeare moved in a steady current, with back-eddies certainly, towards anarchy and chaos.

C: But that has nothing to do with the question.

B: Possibly not.

E: Surely the dramatic poet, being when and where he is, has no business with his own background. He can't help that, and his business is with the audience. The Elizabethan drama, or at any rate Shakespeare, was good enough to justify artistically its own background. But it does seem to me that it is as much the lack of moral and social conventions as the lack of artistic conventions that stands in the way of poetic drama today. Shaw is our greatest stage moralist, and his conventions are only negative: they consist in all the things he doesn't believe. But there again, Shaw cannot help that.

A: This sort of moralising censorship would leave us nothing. Are you prepared to say that you are the worse for having read Shakespeare and seen him played?

B: No.

A: Are you prepared to maintain that you are none the better, none the wiser, and none the happier for it?

B: No.

A: Very well. I have also heard you railing at Wagner as "pernicious." But you would not willingly resign your experience of Wagner either. Which seems to show that a world in which there was no art that was not morally edifying would be a very poor world indeed.

B: So it would. I would not suppress anything that is good measured by artistic standards. For there is always something to be learned from it. I would not have Shakespeare any different from what he is. But it is like life in general. There are heaps of things in the world which I should like to see changed; but in a world without Evil life would not be worth living.

E: Well, you have taken a long time to leave us just where we were before.

B: Not quite. You can never draw the line between aesthetic criticism and moral and social criticism; you cannot draw a line between criticism and metaphysics; you start with literary criticism, and however rigorous an aesthete you may be, you are over the frontier into something else sooner or later. The best you do is to accept these conditions and know what you are doing when you do it. And, on the other hand, you must know how and when to retrace your steps. You must be very nimble. I may begin by moral criticism of Shakespeare and pass over into aesthetic criticism, or vice versa.

E: And all you do is to lead the discussion astray.

C: I cannot agree with that wild generalisation about the anarchy of Elizabethan drama. In fact it would only make the present-day situation more puzzling. We seem to agree that the modern world is chaotic, and we are inclined to agree that its lack of social and moral conventions makes the task of the dramatic poet more difficult, if not impossible. But if the Elizabethan and Jacobean period was also a period of chaos, and yet produced great poetic drama, why cannot we?

B: I don't know.

C: You will have to qualify your statement about Elizabethan drama. You would have had to do that in any case, for there are a great many more things to take account of than this simple idea of decay. To begin with, there is no precedent for a nation having *two* great periods of drama. And its great period is always short, and is great because of a very small number of great dramatists. And a very great period of any kind of poetry is never repeated. Perhaps each great race has just strength enough for one period of literary supremacy.

D: If *C* is not side-tracked he will lead us presently into politics.

A: All this is true and perfectly commonplace. But it does not help. When it comes to the present age, we are not going to be deterred by a fatalistic philosophy of history from wanting a poetic drama, and from believing that there must be some way of getting it. Besides, the craving for poetic drama is permanent in human nature. At this point I suspect that *F* is waiting to let off on us what he calls the economic factors; and the state of the public, and the producers, and the cost of theatres; and the competition of cheap cinemas, et caetera. I believe that if you want a thing you can get it, and hang the economic factors.

F: And your way of getting it is to talk about it.

A: I like talking about things; it helps me to think.

C: I agree with *A,* whether he has thought about it or not. All this talk about periods of art is interesting and sometimes useful when we are occupied with the past, but is quite futile when we come to consider the present in relation to the future. Let us begin by observing the several kinds of way in which contemporary drama fails. There are the plays written by poets who have no knowledge of the stage: this kind has been sufficiently abused. There are the plays written by men who know the stage and are not poets. Of these two extremes I will only remark that experience proves that neither is of any pertinence to our present subject.

A: But what is our present subject?

C: The possibility of poetic drama.

G: You seem to have covered nearly the whole field of discussion of contemporary drama, except for the topics of Gordon Craig, Reinhardt, Meierhold, Sir Barry Jackson, the Old Vic, Eugene O'Neill, Pirandello and Toller. And we are not here concerned with methods of production—which rules out the first four of these names—but with the production of something to produce. I have only one suggestion to offer, but it will be the only practical suggestion that has been made. We should hire a barn or studio, and produce plays of our own, or even disjected scenes of plays and produce them by ourselves and only for ourselves, no friends to be admitted. We might learn at least by practice first whether we have anything in common, and second what forms of versification are possible. We must find a new form of verse which shall be as satisfactory a vehicle for us as blank verse was for the Elizabethans.

F: And I know what will happen. We shall start selling tickets in order to pay the costs, we shall then have to import plays in order to supply the demand, and we shall end with a perfectly conventional cosmopolitan little-theatre or Sunday-society performance.

C: One thing has struck me in this conversation. We started by speaking of Dryden, then passed to poetic drama in general; and we have not taken up one of the subjects that Dryden thought it worth while to discuss, and all of the subjects raised have been subjects that Dryden would never have thought of.

B: It is one thing to discuss the rules of an art when that art is alive, and quite another when it is dead. When there is a contemporary practice, the critic must start from that point, and all his criticism must return to it. Observe how confident Dryden is! Even the difference between the drama of his age and that of the Elizabethans, when the tumults and disorders of the Great Rebellion had hardly been subdued, seemed to him less important than they seemed to us. He admits that his age is inferior, essentially in the respects in which we find it inferior, to the preceding; yet he thought of his generation—and at bottom he must have been thinking, with justifiable pride, of himself—as improving and polishing the earlier drama in many ways. He is quite right: the relation of his drama to that of the Elizabethans should be conceived as he conceived it; the chasm is not so vast as it is usually taken to be; and the French influence was far less than it is supposed to be. But the questions which he discussed are not out of date.

E: The Unities of Place and Time, for instance. Dryden gives what is the soundest and most commonsense view possible for his time and place. But the Unities have for me, at least, a perpetual fascination. I believe they will be found highly desirable for the drama of the future. For one thing, we want more concentration. All plays are now much too long. I never go to the theatre, because I hate to hurry over my dinner, and I dislike to dine early. A continuous hour and a half of *intense* interest is what we need. No intervals, no chocolate-sellers or ignoble trays. The Unities do make for intensity, as does verse rhythm.

A: You think that we need stronger stimulants, in a shorter space of time, to get the same exaltation out of the theatre that a sensitive contemporary may be supposed to have got out of a tragedy by Shakespeare or even out of one by Dryden.

E: And meanwhile let us drink another glass of port to the memory of John Dryden.

E. M. FORSTER: The Plot*

"CHARACTER," says Aristotle, "gives us qualities, but it is in actions—what we do—that we are happy or the reverse." We have already decided that Aristotle is wrong and now we must face the consequences of disagreeing with him. "All human happiness and misery," says Aristotle, "take the form of action." We know better. We believe that happiness and misery exist in the secret life, which each of us leads privately and to which (in his characters) the novelist has access. And by the secret life we mean the life for which there is no external evidence, not, as is vulgarly supposed, that which is revealed by a chance word or a sigh. A chance word or sigh are just as much evidence as a speech or a murder: the life they reveal ceases to be secret and enters the realm of action.

There is, however, no occasion to be hard on Aristotle. He had read few novels and no modern ones—the *Odyssey* but not *Ulysses*—he was by temperament apathetic to secrecy, and indeed regarded the human mind as a sort of tub from which everything can finally be extracted; and when he wrote the words quoted above he had in view the drama, where, no doubt they hold true. In the drama all human happiness and misery does and must take the form of action. Otherwise its existence remains unknown, and this is the great difference between the drama and the novel.

* "The Plot" is the fifth chapter from *Aspects of the Novel*, by E. M. Forster, Copyright, 1927, by Harcourt, Brace and Company, Inc. Mr. Forster (*b.* 1879) is also the author of *Abinger Harvest* (1936) and *Virginia Woolf* (1942).

The speciality of the novel is that the writer can talk about his characters as well as through them or can arrange for us to listen when they talk to themselves. He has access to self-communings, and from that level he can descend even deeper and peer into the subconscious. A man does not talk to himself quite truly—not even to himself; the happiness or misery that he secretly feels proceed from causes that he cannot quite explain, because as soon as he raises them to the level of the explicable they lose their native quality. The novelist has a real pull here. He can show the subconscious short-circuiting straight into action (the dramatist can do this too); he can also show it in its relation to soliloquy. He commands all the secret life, and he must not be robbed of this privilege. "How did the writer know that?" it is sometimes said. "What's his standpoint? He is not being consistent, he's shifting his point of view from the limited to the omniscient, and now he's edging back again." Questions like these have too much the atmosphere of the law courts about them. All that matters to the reader is whether the shifting of attitude and the secret life are convincing, whether it is πιθανόν[1] in fact, and with his favourite word ringing in his ears Aristotle may retire.

However, he leaves us in some confusion, for what, with this enlargement of human nature, is going to become of the plot? In most literary works there are two elements: human individuals, whom we have recently discussed, and the element vaguely called art. Art we have also

1 ["Plausible."]

dallied with, but with a very low form of it: the story: the chopped-off length of the tapeworm of time. Now we arrive at a much higher aspect: the plot, and the plot, instead of finding human beings more or less cut to its requirements, as they are in the drama, finds them enormous, shadowy and intractable, and three-quarters hidden like an iceberg. In vain it points out to these unwieldy creatures the advantages of the triple process of complication, crisis, and solution so persuasively expounded by Aristotle. A few of them rise and comply, and a novel which ought to have been a play is the result. But there is no general response. They want to sit apart and brood or something, and the plot (whom I here visualize as a sort of higher government official) is concerned at their lack of public spirit: "This will not do," it seems to say. "Individualism is a most valuable quality; indeed my own position depends upon individuals; I have always admitted as much freely. Nevertheless there are certain limits, and those limits are being overstepped. Characters must not brood too long, they must not waste time running up and down ladders in their own insides, they must contribute, or higher interests will be jeopardised." How well one knows that phrase, "a contribution to the plot"! It is accorded, and of necessity, by the people in a drama: how necessary is it in a novel?

Let us define a plot. We have defined a story as a narrative of events arranged in their time-sequence. A plot is also a narrative of events, the emphasis falling on causality. "The king died and then the queen died," is a story. "The king died, and then the queen died of grief" is a plot. The time-sequence is preserved, but the sense of causality overshadows it. Or again: "The queen died, no one knew why, until it was discovered that it was through grief at the death of the king." This is a plot with a mystery in it, a form capable of high development. It suspends the time-sequence, it moves as far away from the story as its limitations will allow. Consider the death of the queen. If it is in a story we say "and then?" If it is in a plot we ask "why?" That is the fundamental difference between these two aspects of the novel. A plot cannot be told to a gaping audience of cave men or to a tyrannical sultan or to their modern descendant the movie-public. They can only be kept awake by "and then—and then—" They can only supply curiosity. But a plot demands intelligence and memory also.

Curiosity is one of the lowest of the human faculties. You will have noticed in daily life that when people are inquisitive they nearly always have bad memories and are usually stupid at bottom. The man who begins by asking you how many brothers and sisters you have, is never a sympathetic character, and if you meet him in a year's time he will probably ask you how many brothers and sisters you have, his mouth again sagging open, his eyes still bulging from his head. It is difficult to be friends with such a man, and for two inquisitive people to be friends must be impossible. Curiosity by itself takes us a very little way, nor does it take us far into the novel—only as far as the story. If we would grasp the plot we must add intelligence and memory.

Intelligence first. The intelligent novel-reader, unlike the inquisitive one who just runs his eye over a new fact, mentally picks it up. He sees it from two points of view: isolated, and related to the other facts that he has read on previous pages. Probably he does not understand it, but he does not expect to do so yet awhile. The facts in a highly organized novel (like *The Egoist*) are often of the nature of cross-correspondences and the ideal spectator cannot expect to view them properly until he is sitting up on a hill at the end. This element of surprise or mystery—the detective element as it is sometimes rather emptily called—is of great importance in a plot. It occurs through a suspension of the time-sequence; a mystery is a pocket in time, and it occurs crudely, as in "Why did the queen die?" and more subtly in half-explained gestures and words, the true meaning of which only dawns pages ahead. Mystery is essential to a plot, and cannot be appreciated without intelligence. To the curious it is just another "and then—" To appreciate a mystery, part of the mind must be left behind, brooding, while the other part goes marching on.

That brings us to our second qualification: memory.

Memory and intelligence are closely connected, for unless we remember we cannot understand. If by the time the queen dies we have forgotten the existence of the king we shall never make out what killed her. The plot-maker expects us to remember, we expect him to leave no loose ends. Every action or word ought to count; it ought to be economical and spare; even when complicated it should be organic and free from dead matter. It may be difficult or easy, it may and should contain mysteries, but it ought not to mislead. And over it, as it unfolds, will hover the memory of the reader (that dull glow of the mind of which intelligence is the bright advancing edge) and will constantly rearrange and reconsider, seeing new clues, new chains of cause and effect, and the final sense (if the plot has been a fine one) will not be of clues or chains, but of something aesthetically compact, something which might have been shown by the novelist straight away, only if he had shown it straight away it would never have become beautiful. We come up against beauty here—for the first time in our enquiry: beauty at which a novelist should never aim, though he fails if he does not achieve it. I will conduct beauty to her proper place later on. Meanwhile please accept her as part of a completed plot. She looks a little surprised at being there, but beauty ought to look a little surprised: it is the emotion that best suits her face, as Botticelli knew when he painted her risen from the waves, between the winds and the flowers. The beauty who does not look surprised, who accepts her position as her due—she reminds us too much of a prima donna.

But let us get back to the plot, and we will do so via George Meredith.

Meredith is not the great name he was twenty or thirty years ago, when much of the universe and all Cambridge trembled. I remember how depressed I used to be by a line in one of his poems: "We live but to be sword or block." I did not want to be either and I knew that I was not a sword. It seems though that there was no real cause for depression, for Meredith is himself now rather in the trough of a wave, and though fashion will turn and raise him a bit, he will never be the spiritual power he was about the year 1900. His philosophy has not worn well. His heavy attacks on sentimentality—they bore the present generation, which pursues the same quarry but with neater instruments, and is apt to suspect any one carrying a blunderbuss of being a sentimentalist himself. And his visions of Nature—they do not endure like Hardy's, there is too much Surrey about them, they are fluffy and lush. He could no more write the opening chapter of *The Return of the Native* than Box Hill could visit Salisbury Plain. What is really tragic and enduring in the scenery of England was hidden from him, and so is what is really tragic in life. When he gets serious and noble-minded there is a strident overtone, a bullying that becomes distressing. I feel indeed that he was like Tennyson in one respect: through not taking himself quietly enough he strained his inside. And his novels: most of the social values are faked. The tailors are not tailors, the cricket matches are not cricket, the railway trains do not even seem to be trains, the county families give the air of having been only just that moment unpacked, scarcely in position before the action starts, the straw still clinging to their beards. It is surely very odd, the social scene in which his characters are set: it is partly due to his fantasy, which is legitimate, but partly a chilly fake, and wrong. What with the faking, what with the preaching, which was never agreeable and is now said to be hollow, and what with the home counties posing as the universe, it is no wonder Meredith now lies in the trough. And yet he is in one way a great novelist. He is the finest contriver that English fiction has ever produced, and any lecture on plot must do homage to him.

Meredith's plots are not closely knit. We cannot describe the action of *Harry Richmond* in a phrase, as we can that of *Great Expectations,* though both books turn on the mistake made by a young man as to the sources of his fortune. A Meredithian plot is not a temple to the tragic or even to the comic Muse, but rather resembles a series of kiosks most artfully placed among wooded slopes, which his people reach by their own impetus, and from which they emerge with altered aspect. Incident springs out of character, and having occurred it alters that character. People and events are closely connected, and he does it by means of these contrivances. They are often delightful, sometimes touching, always unexpected. This shock, followed by the feeling, "Oh, that's all right," is a sign that all is well with the plot: characters, to be real, ought to run smoothly, but a plot ought to cause surprise. The horse-whipping of

Dr. Shrapnel in *Beauchamp's Career* is a surprise. We know that Everard Romfrey must dislike Shrapnel, must hate and misunderstand his radicalism, and be jealous of his influence over Beauchamp: we watch too the growth of the misunderstanding over Rosamund, we watch the intrigues of Cecil Baskelett. As far as characters go, Meredith plays with his cards on the table, but when the incident comes what a shock it gives us and the characters too! The tragicomic business of one old man whipping another from the highest motives—it reacts upon all their world, and transforms all the personages of the book. It is not the centre of *Beauchamp's Career,* which indeed has no centre. It is essentially a contrivance, a door through which the book is made to pass, emerging in an altered form. Towards the close, when Beauchamp is drowned and Shrapnel and Romfrey are reconciled over his body, there is an attempt to elevate the plot to Aristotelian symmetry, to turn the novel into a temple wherein dwells interpretation and peace. Meredith fails here: *Beauchamp's Career* remains a series of contrivances (the visit to France is another of them), but contrivances that spring from the characters and react upon them.

And now briefly to illustrate the mystery element in the plot: the formula of "The queen died, it was afterwards discovered through grief." I will take an example, not from Dickens (through *Great Expectations* provides a fine one), nor from Conan Doyle (whom my priggishness prevents me from enjoying), but again from Meredith: an example of a concealed emotion from the admirable plot of *The Egoist:* it occurs in the character of Laetitia Dale.

We are told, at first, all that passes in Laetitia's mind. Sir Willoughby has twice jilted her, she is sad, resigned. Then, for dramatic reasons, her mind is hidden from us, it develops naturally enough, but does not re-emerge until the great midnight scene where he asks her to marry him because he is not sure about Clara, and this time, a changed woman, Laetitia says "No." Meredith has concealed the change. It would have spoiled his high comedy if we had been kept in touch with it throughout. Sir Willoughby has to have a series of crashes, to catch at this and that, and find everything rickety. We should not enjoy the fun, in fact it would be boorish, if we saw the author preparing the booby traps beforehand, so Laetitia's apathy has been hidden from us. This is one of the countless examples in which either plot or character has to suffer, and Meredith with his unerring good sense here lets the plot triumph.

As an example of mistaken triumph, I think of a slip—it is no more than a slip—which Charlotte Brontë makes in *Villette.* She allows Lucy Snowe to conceal from the reader her discovery that Dr. John is the same as her old playmate Graham. When it comes out, we do get a good plot thrill, but too much at the expense of Lucy's character. She has seemed, up to then, the spirit of integrity, and has, as it were, laid herself under a moral obligation to narrate all that she knows. That she stoops to suppress is a little distressing, though the incident is too trivial to do her any permanent harm.

Sometimes a plot triumphs too completely. The characters have to suspend their natures at every turn, or else are so swept away by the course of Fate that our sense of their reality is weakened. We shall find instances of this in a writer who is far greater than Meredith, and yet less successful as a novelist—Thomas Hardy. Hardy seems to me essentially a poet, who conceives of his novels from an enormous height. They are to be tragedies or tragicomedies, they are to give out the sound of hammer-strokes as they proceed; in other words Hardy arranges events with emphasis on causality, the ground plan is a plot, and the characters are ordered to acquiesce in its requirements. Except in the person of Tess (who conveys the feeling that she is greater than destiny) this aspect of his work is unsatisfactory. His characters are involved in various snares, they are finally bound hand and foot, there is ceaseless emphasis on fate, and yet, for all the sacrifices made to it, we never see the action as a living thing as we see it in *Antigone* or *Berenice* or *The Cherry Orchard.* The fate above us, not the fate working through us—that is what is eminent and memorable in the Wessex novels. Egdon Heath before Eustacia Vye has set foot upon it. The woods without the Woodlanders. The downs above Budmouth Regis with the royal princesses, still asleep, driving across them through the dawn. Hardy's success in *The Dynasts* (where he uses another medium) is complete, there the hammer-strokes are heard, cause and effect enchain the characters despite their struggles, complete contact between the actors and the plot is established. But in the novels, though the same superb and terrible machine works, it never catches humanity in its teeth; there is some vital problem that has not been answered, or even posed, in the misfortunes of Jude the Obscure. In other words the characters have been required to contribute too much to the plot; except in their rustic humours, their vitality has been impoverished, they have gone dry and thin. This, as far as I can make out, is the flaw running through Hardy's novels: he has emphasized causality more strongly than his medium permits. As a poet and prophet and visualizer George Meredith is nothing by his side—just a suburban roarer—but Meredith did know what the novel could stand, where the plot could dun the characters for a contribution, where it must let them function as they liked. And the moral—well, I see no moral, because the work of Hardy is my home and that of Meredith cannot be: still the moral from the point of these lectures is again unfavourable to Aristotle. In the novel, all human happiness and misery does not take the form of action, it seeks means of expression other than through the plot, it must not be rigidly canalized.

In the losing battle that the plot fights with the characters, it often takes a cowardly revenge. Nearly all novels are feeble at the end. This is because the plot requires to be wound up. Why is this necessary? Why is there not a convention which allows a novelist to stop as soon as he feels muddled or bored? Alas, he has to round things off, and usually the characters go dead while he is at work, and our final impression of them is through deadness. *The Vicar of Wakefield* is in this way a typical novel, so clever and fresh in the first half, up to the painting of the family group with Mrs. Primrose as Venus, and then so wooden and imbecile. Incidents and people that occurred at first for their own sake now have to contribute to the dénouement. In the end even the author feels he is being a little foolish. "Nor can I go on," he says, "without a reflection on those accidental meetings which though they happen every day, seldom excite our surprise but upon some extraordinary occasion." Goldsmith is of course a light-weight, but most novels do fail here—there is this disastrous standstill while logic takes over the command from flesh and blood. If it was not for death and marriage I do not know how the average novelist would conclude. Death and marriage are almost his only connection between his characters and his plot, and the reader is more ready to meet him here, and take a bookish view of them, provided they occur later on in the book: the writer, poor fellow, must be allowed to finish up somehow, he has his living to get like any one else, so no wonder that nothing is heard but hammering and screwing.

This—as far as one can generalize—is the inherent defect of novels: they go off at the end: and there are two explanations of it: firstly, failure of pep, which threatens the novelist like all workers: and secondly, the difficulty which we have been discussing. The characters have been getting out of hand, laying foundations and declining to build on them afterwards, and now the novelist has to labour personally, in order that the job may be done to time. He pretends that the characters are acting for him. He keeps mentioning their names and using inverted commas. But the characters are gone or dead.

The plot, then, is the novel in its logical intellectual aspect: it requires mystery, but the mysteries are solved later on: the reader may be moving about in worlds unrealized, but the novelist has no misgivings. He is competent, poised above his work, throwing a beam of light here, popping on a cap of invisibility there, and (qua plot-maker) continually negotiating with himself qua character-monger as to the best effect to be produced. He plans his book beforehand: or anyhow he stands above it, his interest in cause and effect give him an air of predetermination.

And now we must ask ourselves whether the framework thus produced is the best possible for a novel. After all, why has a novel to be planned? Cannot it grow? Why need it close, as a play closes? Cannot it open out? Instead of standing above his work and controlling it, cannot the novelist throw himself into it and be carried along to some goal that he does not foresee? The plot is exciting and may be beautiful, yet is it not a fetich, borrowed from the drama, from the spatial limitations of the stage? Cannot fiction devise a framework that is not so logical yet more suitable to its genius?

Modern writers say that it can, and we will now examine a recent example—a violent onslaught on the plot as we have defined it: a constructive attempt to put something in the place of the plot.

I have already mentioned the novel in question: *Les Faux Monnayeurs* by André Gide. It contains within its covers both the methods. Gide has also published the diary he kept while he was writing the novel, and there is no reason why he should not publish in the future the impressions he had when rereading both the diary and the novel, and in the future-perfect a still more final synthesis in which the diary, the novel, and his impressions of both will interact. He is indeed a little more solemn than an author should be about the whole caboodle, but regarded as a caboodle it is excessively interesting, and repays careful study by critics.

We have, in the first place, a plot in *Les Faux Monnayeurs* of the logical objective type that we have been considering—a plot, or rather fragments of plots. The main fragment concerns a young man called Olivier—a charming, touching and lovable character, who misses happiness, and then recovers it after an excellently contrived dénouement; confers it also; this fragment has a wonderful radiance and "lives," if I may use so coarse a word, it is a successful creation on familiar lines. But it is by no means the centre of the book. No more are the other logical fragments—that which concerns Georges, Olivier's schoolboy brother, who passes false coin, and is instrumental in driving a fellow-pupil to suicide. (Gide gives us his sources for all this in his diary, he got the idea of Georges from a boy whom he caught trying to steal a book off a stall, the gang of coiners were caught at Roen, and the suicide of children took place at Clermont-Ferrand, etc.) Neither Olivier, nor Georges, nor Vincent a third brother, nor Bernard their friend is the centre of the book. We come nearer to it in Edouard. Edouard is a novelist. He bears the same relation to Gide as Clissold does to Wells. I dare not be more precise. Like Gide, he keeps a diary, like Gide he is writing a book called *Les Faux Monnayeurs,* and like Clissold he is disavowed. Edouard's diary is printed in full. It begins before the plot-fragments, continues during them, and forms the bulk of Gide's book. Edouard is not just a chronicler. He is an actor too; indeed it is he who rescues Olivier and is rescued by him; we leave those two in happiness.

But that is still not the centre. The nearest to the centre lies in a discussion about the art of the novel. Edouard is holding forth to Bernard his secretary and some friends. He has said (what we all accept as commonplace) that truth in life and truth in a novel are not identical, and then he goes on to say that he wants to write a book which shall include both sorts of truth.

"And what is its subject?" asked Sophroniska.

"There is none," said Edouard sharply. "My novel has no subject. No doubt that sounds foolish. Let us say, if you prefer, that it will not have 'a' subject. . . . 'A slice of life,' the naturalistic school used to say. The mistake that school made was always to cut its slice in the same direction, always lengthwise, in the direction of time. Why not cut it up and down? Or across? As for me, I don't want to cut it at all. You see what I mean. I want to put everything into my novel and not snip off my material either here or there. I have been working for a year, and there is nothing I haven't put in: all I see, all I know, all I can learn from other people's lives and my own."

"My poor man, you will bore your readers to death," cried Laura, unable to restrain her mirth.

"Not at all. To get my effect, I am inventing, as my central character, a novelist, and the subject of my book will be the struggle between what reality offers him and what he tries to make of the offer."

"Have you planned out this book?" asked Sophroniska, trying to keep grave.

"Of course not."

"Why 'of course'?"

"For a book of this type any plan would be unsuitable. The whole of it would go wrong if I decided any detail ahead. I am waiting for reality to dictate to me."

"But I thought you wanted to get away from reality."

"My novelist wants to get away, but I keep pulling him back. To tell the truth, this is my subject: the struggle between facts as proposed by reality, and the ideal reality."

"Very well. Tell it them, Bernard."

"*Les Faux Monnayeurs,*" said Bernard. "And now will you please tell us who these faux monnayeurs are."

"I haven't the least idea."

Bernard and Laura looked at each other and then at Sophroniska. There was the sound of a deep sigh.

The fact was that ideas about money, depreciation, inflation, forgery, etc., had gradually invaded Edouard's book—just as theories of clothing invade *Sartor Resartus* and even assume the functions of characters. "Has any of you ever had hold of a false coin?" he asked after a pause. "Image a ten-franc piece, gold, false. It is actually worth a couple of sous, but it will remain worth ten francs until it is found out. Suppose I begin with the idea that—"

"But why begin with an idea?" burst out Bernard, who was by now in a state of exasperation. "Why not begin with a fact? If you introduce the fact properly, the idea will follow of itself. If I was writing your *Faux Monnayeurs* I should begin with a piece of false money, with the ten-franc piece you were speaking of, and here it is!"

So saying, Bernard pulled a ten-franc piece out of his pocket and flung it on the table.

"There," he remarked. "It rings all right. I got it this morning from the grocer. It's worth more than a couple of sous, as it's coated in gold, but it's actually made of glass. It will become quite transparent in time. No—don't rub it—you're going to spoil my false coin."

Edouard had taken it and was examining it with the utmost attention.

"How did the grocer get it?"

"He doesn't know. He passed it on me for a joke, and then enlightened me, being a decent fellow. He let me have it for five francs. I thought that, since you were writing *Les Faux Monnayeurs,* you ought to see what false money is like, so I got it to show you. Now that you have looked at it, give it me back. I am sorry to see that reality has no interest for you."

"Yes," said Edouard: "it interests me, but it puts me out."

"That's a pity," remarked Bernard.[2]

This passage is the centre of the book. It contains the old thesis of truth in life versus truth in art, and illustrates it very neatly by the arrival of an actual false coin. What is new in it is the attempt to combine the two truths, the proposal that writers should mix themselves up in their material and be rolled over and over by it; they should not try to subdue any longer, they should hope to be subdued, to be carried away. As for a plot—to pot with the plot, break it up, boil it down. Let there be those "formidable erosions of contour" of which Nietzsche speaks. All that is prearranged is false.

Another distinguished critic has agreed with Gide—that old lady in the anecdote who was accused by her nieces of being illogical. For some time she could not be brought to understand what logic was, and when she grasped its true nature she was not so much angry as contemptuous. "Logic! Good gracious! What rubbish!" she exclaimed. "How can I tell what I think till I see what I say?" Her nieces, educated young women, thought that she was passée; she was really more up to date than they were.

Those who are in touch with contemporary France, say that the present generation follows the advice of Gide and the old lady and resolutely hurls itself into confusion, and indeed admires English novelists on the ground that they so seldom succeed in what they attempt. Compliments are always delightful, but this particular one is a bit of a backhander. It is like trying to lay an egg and being told you have produced a paraboloid—more curious than gratifying. And what results when you try to lay a paraboloid, I cannot conceive—perhaps the death of the hen. That seems the danger in Gide's position—he sets out to lay a paraboloid; he is not well advised, if he wants to write subconscious novels, to reason so lucidly and patiently about the subconscious; he is introducing mysticism at the wrong stage of the process. However that is his affair. As a critic he is most stimulating, and the various bundles of words he has called *Les Faux Monnayeurs* will be enjoyed by all who cannot tell what they think till they see what they say, or who weary of the tyranny by the plot and of its alternative, tyranny by characters.

There is clearly something else in view, some other aspect or aspects which we have yet to examine. We may suspect the claim to be consciously subconscious, nevertheless there is a vague and vast residue into which the subconscious enters. Poetry, religion, passion—we have

[2] Paraphrased from *Les Faux Monnayeurs,* pp. 238-246. My version, needless to say, conveys neither the subtlety nor the balance of the original.

not placed them yet, and since we are critics—only critics—we must try to place them, to catalogue the rainbow. We have already peeped and botanized upon our mothers' graves.

The numbering of the warp and woof of the rainbow must accordingly be attempted and we must now bring our minds to bear on the subject of fantasy.

E. M. W. TILLYARD: The Two Village Greens *

JOHNSON in attacking Lycidas provided a classic example of criticism that errs through a false assumption. *Lycidas* is an elegy; an elegy professes to lament the death of a revered or beloved person; and Johnson assumes that an elegy should be judged by the standards it professes. He found that *Lycidas* did not fulfil its professions:

> It is not to be considered as the effusion of real passion; for passion runs not after remote allusions and obscure opinions. . . . Where there is leisure for fiction, there is little grief.

Johnson assumed that *Lycidas* is what I shall call "direct" poetry or the poetry of "statement," and by such a standard he found it wanting. Actually the poem is far other than what it professes to be. Its main concern embraces vastly more than grief at the death of Edward King. It expresses a personal mental experience and a general moral truth. And it does so not by direct statement but obliquely by implication. This distinction between "direct" and "oblique" poetry will be elaborated in the next section. It suffices here to say that Johnson's attack is invalidated from the start because he has put the poem in the wrong category.

Critics today are not likely to make Johnson's specific error, but they are not always clear in their minds what degree of directness or obliquity they assume the poems they are judging to possess. They run the risk of going astray initially, just as Johnson did. And the danger of being deceived today by a specious obliquity may not be less than the converse one of being deceived by a specious directness. The distinction between "direct" and "oblique" poetry is not new, and must be familiar enough in some form or another, but as an important initial criterion I doubt if it has been clearly formulated or consciously applied to critical practice. This book suggests a scale ranging from the greatest possible directness to the greatest possible obliquity in poetry. Between the two extremes the gradations are of course innumerable; and the scale is only of the roughest. But still it should help to eliminate the mistake of judging poems by standards to which they have no reference.

But when you have fixed your poem in the scale, you have not begun seriously to criticise it. All you have done is to put it in a position where you can see it without a certain preliminary distortion. Now if you conclude that a poem is oblique, you are not likely to get very far with it until you discover what it is that has been given oblique expression. In writing a book on Milton I was confronted with this problem when I came to *Lycidas,* and flattered myself that I had got a little way behind that poem's façade. At any rate I was attempting a kind of criticism of which there is too little and whose possibilities are large. One object of this book is to exploit this kind of criticism through a series of practical demonstrations.

The relations of direct and oblique poetry

* "The Two Village Greens" is the Introductory section of *Poetry: Direct and Oblique,* first published in 1934 and published in a revised version in 1945. The later text is here reprinted by permission of the author and the publisher, Chatto & Windus. Mr. Tillyard (*b.* 1889) is also the author of *Milton* (1930), *The Miltonic Setting, Past and Present* (1938), *Shakespeare's Last Plays* (1938), *The Elizabethan World Picture* (1944), *Shakespeare's History Plays* (1944), and, with C. S. Lewis, *The Personal Heresy, a Controversy* (1939).

have their bearing on the general poetic health of a given epoch; including that of our own day; and I have inserted some historical comment, and drawn contemporary morals.

The terms "direct" and "oblique" poetry are a false contrast. All poetry is more or less oblique: there is no direct poetry. But the terms "less oblique" and "more oblique" would sound ridiculous; and the only way to be emphatic or even generally intelligible is by exaggeration to force a hypothetical but convenient contrast.

I use the words *direct, oblique, statement,* etc., in ways that are convenient rather than quite consistent. I make *direct statement,* or merely *statement,* or *directness,* stand for the same notion; as I make *oblique statement,* or *obliquity,* stand for the opposed notion.

2

A familiar contrast, directed usually to illustrating some differences between Augustan and Romantic styles of poetry, is that between Goldsmith's picture of Auburn in *The Deserted Village* and Blake's *Echoing Green* in *Songs of Innocence.* And these two pieces will serve neatly enough as text for the quite different contrast I have to explain. Here is Goldsmith's village-green with the pleasures that enlivened it:

How often have I loitered o'er the green,
Where humble happiness endeared each scene!
How often have I paused on every charm,
The sheltered cot, the cultivated farm,
The never-failing brook, the busy mill,
The decent church that topt the neighbouring hill,
The hawthorn bush, with seats beneath the shade,
For talking age and whispering lovers made!
How often have I blest the coming day,
When toil remitting lent its turn to play,
And all the village train from labour free
Led up their sports beneath the spreading tree,
While many a pastime circled in the shade,
The young contending as the old surveyed;
And many a gambol frolicked o'er the ground,
And slights of art and feats of strength went round;
And still as each repeated pleasure tired,
Succeeding sports the mirthful band inspired.

This is a fair example of the poetry of direct statement: it is to some degree concerned with what the words state as well as with what they imply. Had Goldsmith been describing one actual village, were it certain that he were describing an actual remembered scene at Lissoy, the element of statement would be solider than it is; and in that he is imagining his village on the analogy of a number of villages he has known, he is the less direct. But at least he wants the reader to think primarily of villages when he talks of Auburn; not of the Social Contract or of heavenly beatitude. We believe this because the formal parts of the poetry reinforce the statement rather than suggest thoughts alien to it. The couplets evolve in a simple explicatory sequence; they unfold the scene with no hint of ulterior meaning; their freshness and unobstructedness are those of the clear sunny day they describe. The vocabulary is as close to simple statement as Goldsmith's epoch allowed to anyone but a rebel; and when he is not simple, it is for convention's sake and not with any view to obliquity. Thus by "humble happiness" he probably means "humble, happy people," and by "talking age" he certainly means "garrulous old folk": but these phrases are no more than the poetic idiom of his day.

True, some obliquity cannot be denied. Goldsmith wants to say that he likes villagers to be hard-working and sober and to enjoy simple pleasures, and in that he says so, not by a general statement but through describing an imagined single occasion when the villagers enjoy these pleasures, he is being slightly oblique. And there is another, much more important example of obliquity. Goldsmith idealises his Auburn not only because this is how he would like villages to be, but because, feeling homesick for some place other than the one he is in, he must imagine his perfect refuge. Thus, when he says,

> And still as each repeated pleasure tired,
> Succeeding sports the mirthful band inspired,

he reveals himself day-dreaming of perpetually unexhausted pleasure, forgetful of the cruel actual law of diminishing returns.

For all this, Goldsmith's lines mainly concern their professed subject, village-life, and therefore exemplify the poetry of statement.

Here is Blake's village-green:

> The Sun does arise,
> And make happy the skies;

The merry bells ring
To welcome the Spring;
The skylark and thrush,
The birds of the bush,
Sing louder around
To the bells' chearful sound,
While our sports shall be seen
On the Echoing Green.

Old John, with white hair,
Does laugh away care,
Sitting under the oak,
Among the old folk.
They laugh at our play,
And soon they all say:
"Such, such were the joys
When we all, girls and boys,
In our youth time were seen
On the Echoing Green."

Till the little ones, weary,
No more can be merry;
The sun does descend,
And our sports have an end.
Round the laps of their mothers
Many sisters and brothers,
Like birds in their nest,
Are ready for rest,
And sport no more seen
On the darkening Green.

It is very easy to allow to Blake's lines just about the same amount of directness and obliquity as to Goldsmith's. Blake's is the greater mind, and of course he uses a different language; but he has every appearance of describing as real a village as Goldsmith's and of knowing quite as much about village games. The sunshine has got into Blake's verse no less than into Goldsmith's. Blake, too, is using his village to express approval of a way of life. He finds in the traditional village sports and pieties a type of his world of innocence, a wider notion perhaps than Goldsmith's more didactic approval. All this is true as far as it goes, and did it respond to our feelings about *The Echoing Green* we might be content with criticising the poem by standards of no profounder obliquity than satisfied *The Deserted Village.*

Now the statements that confront us in *The Echoing Green* have so solid an appearance, present so winningly confident a front, that it seems initially ridiculous not to take them as the poem's major concern. It is the structure that should first put us on our guard. Blake's three verses contrast emphatically with the leisurely roll-out of Goldsmith's couplets. Dawn in the first stanza. Why in the second does Old John sit under the oak? To keep off the noonday sun. Evening in the third. The form is a stylised day-cycle; and if we heed this form, some element of abstraction is set up against the concrete activities of the villagers. There is a careful balance of idea between opening and close: the echoing green becomes the darkening green to balance (though not for this reason only) the rising sun of the first line; the awakening birds in the first stanza are balanced by the simile "like birds in their nest" in the last. Congruently with the full noonday heat and light the old unfreeze and join their mirth to make up a full chorus with the children. Why all this ingenuity? Does it merely add a pleasing regularity to the statement, or is it a symptom of something else? The truth is that Blake is expressing an idea, an idea that has nothing in itself to do with birds, old and young folk, or village-greens, and one of those most common in Blake's poetical works. It is the idea that there is a virtue in desire satisfied. Though desire is not mentioned, yet the keynote of the poem is fruition. Nature fulfils itself in the cycle of a perfect day. Old John gets a perfect vicarious satisfaction, the little ones are utterly played out and ready for rest. And at the end the "echoing green" is the "darkening green" because its function is fulfilled. The very completeness of formal balance points the same way. The poem gives the sense of the perfectly grown apple that comes off at a touch of the hand. It expresses the profound peace of utterly gratified desire.

Thus explained, *The Echoing Green* is as nearly perfect an example of poetical obliquity as can be found. The main sense is stated in no particular whatever, but is diffused through every part of the poem and can be apprehended as a whole only through the synthesis of all those parts. The abstract idea, far from being stated, has been translated into completely concrete form; it has disappeared into apparently alien facts. Through its major obliquity *The Echoing Green* is in a different category from Goldsmith's lines and must be judged by different standards.

Even if this interpretation of *The Echoing Green* were wrong (and such bold guesses at obliquity are likely to please oneself better than others), the *principle* illustrated is not thereby invalidated. Those who reject this instance may find a better and agree that directness and obliquity must vary widely from poem to poem and that to judge an oblique poem as if it were direct, and the other way round, can only lead to disaster.

YVOR WINTERS:

The Experimental School in American Poetry *

AN ANALYTICAL SURVEY OF ITS STRUCTURAL METHODS, EXCLUSIVE OF METER

During the second and third decades of the twentieth century, the chief poetic talent of the United States took certain new directions, directions that appear to me in the main regrettable. The writers between Robinson and Frost, on the one hand, and Allen Tate and Howard Baker on the other, who remained relatively traditional in manner were with few exceptions minor or negligible; the more interesting writers, as I shall endeavor to show in these pages, were misguided, and in discussing them I shall have little to say of their talents, their ineliminable virtues, but shall rather take these for granted.

In order that I may evaluate the new structural methods, I shall have first to describe at least briefly the old. Inasmuch as a wider range of construction is possible in the short poem than in any of the longer literary forms, I shall deal with principles that are fundamental to all literary composition, and shall here and there have recourse to illustrations drawn from the novel or perhaps from the drama. The virtues of the traditional modes of construction will be indicated chiefly in connection with my discussion of the defects of the recent experimental modes.

* Yvor Winters (*b.* 1900) is the author of *Primitivism and Decadence: A Study of American Experimental Poetry* (1937), *Maule's Curse: Seven Studies in the History of American Obscurantism* (1938), and *The Anatomy of Nonsense* (1943), all republished in *In Defense of Reason* (1947). "The Experimental School in American Poetry," elements of which were printed in various book reviews in the late nineteen-twenties and early thirties, is reprinted from *Primitivism and Decadence* in *In Defense of Reason* by Yvor Winters, copyright, 1937, 1947, by Yvor Winters, and copyright, 1938, 1943, by *New Directions*, by permission of The Swallow Press and William Morrow and Company, Inc.

TYPE I: THE METHOD OF REPETITION

Kenneth Burke has named and described this method without evaluating it.[1] It is the simplest and most primitive method possible, and is still in common use; if limited to a short lyrical form, it may still be highly effective. It consists in a restatement in successive stanzas of a single theme, the terms, or images, being altered in each restatement. Two of the finest poems in the form are Nashe's poem on the plague (*Adieu! Farewell earth's bliss*) and Raleigh's poem entitled *The Lie.* In such a poem there is no rational necessity for any order of sequence, the order being determined wholly by the author's feeling about the graduation of importance or intensity. Nevertheless, such a poem rests on a formulable logic, however simple; that is, the theme can be paraphrased in general terms. Such a paraphrase, of course, is not the equivalent of a poem: a poem is more than its paraphrasable content. But, as we shall eventually see, many poems cannot be paraphrased and are therefore defective.

The method of repetition is essentially the same today as it has always been, if we confine our attention to the short poem. Of recent

[1] In *Counterstatement.* Harcourt, Brace and Co., 1932.

years, however, there has been a tendency to extend it into longer forms, with unfortunate results. Such extension is the chief method of Whitman, and results in a form both lax and diffuse. Such extension occurs even in many modern attempts at narrative, both in prose and in verse. To illustrate what I say, I shall venture to summarize the structural defects of the narrative poetry of Robinson Jeffers:

Mr. Jeffers is theologically some kind of monist. He envisages, as did Wordsworth, nature as Deity; but his Nature is the Nature of the text-book in physics and not that of the rambling botanist—Mr. Jeffers seems to have taken the terminology of modern physics more literally than it is meant by its creators. Nature, or God, is thus a kind of self-sufficient mechanism, of which man is a product, but from which man is cut off by his humanity (just what gave rise to this humanity, which is absolutely severed from all communication with God, is left for others to decide): as there is no mode of communication with God or from God, God is praised adequately only by the screaming demons that make up the atom. Man, if he accepts this dilemma as necessary, can choose between two modes of action: he may renounce God and rely upon his humanity, or he may renounce his humanity and rely upon God.

In the narratives preceding *Cawdor*[2] and in most of the lyrics, Mr. Jeffers preaches the second choice. In *Cawdor* and in *Thurso's Landing*,[3] he has attempted a compromise: that is, while the tragic characters recognize that the second choice would be the more reasonable, they make the first in a kind of half-hearted stubbornness. They insist on living, but without knowing why, and without any good to which to look forward save the final extinction in God, when it comes in God's time. Their stubbornness is meaningless.

Life as such is incest, an insidious and destructive evil. So much, says Mr. Jeffers by implication, for Greek and Christian ethics. Now the mysticism of such a man as San Juan de la Cruz offers at least the semblance of a spiritual, a human, discipline as a preliminary to union with Divinity; but for Mr. Jeffers a simple and mechanical device lies always ready; namely, suicide, a device to which he has, I believe, never resorted.

In refusing to take this step, however, Mr. Jeffers illustrates one of a very interesting series of romantic compromises. The romantic of the ecstatically pantheistic type denies life yet goes on living;[4] nearly all romantics decry the intellect and philosophy, yet they offer justifications, necessarily incoherent but none the less rational in intention, of their attitude; they are prone to belittle literary technique, yet they write, and too often with small efficiency; they preach, in the main, the doctrine of moral equivalence, yet their every action, whether private or literary, since it rests on a choice, is a denial of the doctrine. Not all romantics are guilty of all these forms of confusion, but the romantic who is guilty of all is more consistent than is he who is guilty only of some, for all inhere in each from a rational standpoint. And Mr. Jeffers, having decried human life, and having denied the worth of the rules of the game, endeavors to write narrative and dramatic poems, poems, in other words, dealing with people who are playing the game. Jesus, the hero of *Dear Judas*,[5] speaking apparently for Mr. Jeffers, says that the secret reason for the doctrine of forgiveness is that all men are driven to act as they do, by the mechanism-God, that they are entirely helpless; yet he adds in the next breath that this secret must be guarded, for if it were given out, men would run amuck—they would begin acting differently.[6]

The Women at Point Sur[7] is a perfect laboratory of Mr. Jeffers' philosophy and a perfect example of his narrative method. Barclay, an insane divine, preaches Mr. Jeffers' religion, and his disciples, acting upon it, become emotional mechanisms, lewd and twitching conglomerations of plexuses, their humanity annulled.

[2] *Cawdor and Other Poems*, by Robinson Jeffers. Horace Liveright, New York, 1928.

[3] *Thurso's Landing*, same. Liveright Inc., New York, 1932.

[4] Hart Crane, unlike Mr. Jeffers, demonstrated the seriousness of his conviction, but the demonstration did nothing to clarify his concepts.

[5] *Dear Judas*. Horace Liveright, 1929.

[6] This dilemma is not new in American literature. In the eighteenth century, Jonathan Edwards accomplished a revival in the Puritan Church, that is, induced large numbers of sinners to repent and enter the church, by preaching the doctrine of election and the inability to repent.

[7] *The Women at Point Sur*. Boni and Liveright, 1927.

Human experience in these circumstances, having necessarily and according to the doctrine, no meaning, there can be no necessary sequence of events: every act is equivalent to every other; every act is devoid of consequence and occurs in a perfect vacuum; most of the incidents could be shuffled about into different sequences without violating anything save Mr. Jeffers' sense of their relative intensity.

Since the poem is his, of course, this sense may appear a legitimate criterion; the point is, that this is not a narrative nor a dramatic but is a lyrical criterion. A successful lyrical poem of one hundred and seventy-five pages is unlikely, for the essence of lyrical expression is concentration; but it is at least hypothetically possible. The difficulty here is that the lyric achieves its effect by the generalization of experience (that is, the motivation of the lyric is stated or implied in a summary form, and is ordinarily not given in detailed narrative) and by the concentration of expression; lyrical poetry tends to be expository. Narrative can survive fairly well without distinction of style, provided the narrative logic is complete and compelling, as in the works of Balzac, though this occurs most often in prose. Now Mr. Jeffers, as I have pointed out, has abandoned narrative logic with the theory of ethics, and he has never, in addition, achieved a distinguished style: his writing, line by line, is pretentious trash. There are a few good phrases, but they are very few, and none is first-rate.

Mr. Jeffers has no method of sustaining his lyric, then, other than the employment of an accidental (that is, a non-narrative and repetitious) series of anecdotes (that is, of details that are lyrically impure, details clogged with too much information to be able to function properly as lyrical details); his philosophical doctrine and his artistic dilemma alike decree that these shall be at an hysterical pitch of feeling. By this method, Mr. Jeffers continually *lays claim* to extreme feeling, which has no support whether of structure or of detail and which is therefore simply unmastered and self-inflicted hysteria.

Cawdor contains a plot which in its rough outlines might be sound, and *Cawdor* likewise contains his best poetry: the lines describing the seals at dawn, especially, are very good. But the plot is blurred for lack of style and for lack of moral intelligence on the part of the author. As in *Thurso's Landing,* of which the writing is much worse, the protagonists desire to live as the result of a perfectly unreasoning and meaningless stubbornness, and their actions are correspondingly obscure. Mr. Jeffers will not even admit the comprehensible motive of cowardice. In *The Tower beyond Tragedy,*[8] Mr. Jeffers takes one of the very best of ready-made plots, the Orestes-Clytemnestra situation, the peculiar strength of which lies in the fact that Orestes is forced to choose between two crimes, the murder of his mother and the failure to avenge his father. But at the very last moment, in Mr. Jeffers' version, Orestes is converted to Mr. Jeffers' religion and goes off explaining to Electra (who has just tried to seduce him) that though men may think he is fleeing from the furies, he is really doing no more than drift up to the mountains to meditate on the stars. And the preceding action is, of course, rendered meaningless.

Dear Judas is a kind of dilution of *The Women at Point Sur,* with Jesus as Barclay, and with a less detailed background. *The Loving Shepherdess*[9] deals with a girl who knows herself doomed to die at a certain time in childbirth, and who wanders over the countryside caring for a small and diminishing flock of sheep in an anguish of devotion. The events here also are anecdotal and reversible, and the feeling is lyrical or nothing. The heroine is turned cruelly from door to door, and the sheep fall one by one before the reader's eyes, the sheep and the doors constituting the matter of the narrative; until finally the girl dies in a ditch in an impossible effort to give birth to her child.

TYPE II: THE LOGICAL METHOD

By the logical method of composition, I mean simply explicitly rational progression from one detail to another: the poem has a clearly evident expository structure. Marvell's poem *To His Coy Mistress,* as Mr. T. S. Eliot has said, has something of the structure of a syllogism, if the relationships only of the three paragraphs

[8] In the volume called *The Women at Point Sur,* previously mentioned.

[9] In the volume entitled *Dear Judas.*

to each other be considered:[10] within each paragraph the structure is repetitive. The logical method is a late and sophisticated procedure that in Europe is most widespread in the sixteenth and seventeenth centuries, though it appears earlier and continues later. It was exploited, mastered, and frequently debauched by the English Metaphysical School, for example, though it was not invariably employed by them.

Sometimes in the Metaphysical poets, frequently in the dramatists contemporary with them, and far too often in the poetry of the twentieth century, the logical structure becomes a shell empty of logic but exploiting certain elusive types of feeling. The forms of pseudo-logic I shall reserve for treatment under another heading.

By stretching our category a trifle we may include under this heading poems *implicitly* rational, provided the implications of rationality are at all points clear. William Carlos Williams' poem, *On the Road to the Contagious Hospital*, may serve as an example.[11] On the other hand, Rimbaud's *Larme*, a poem which, like that of Dr. Williams, describes a landscape, is unformulable: it is an example of what Kenneth Burke has called qualitative progression, a type of procedure that I shall consider later. The poem by Williams, though its subject is simple, is a poem of directed meditation; the poem by Rimbaud is one of non-rational and hallucinatory terror.

TYPE III: NARRATIVE

Narrative achieves coherence largely through a feeling that the events of a sequence are necessary parts of a causative chain, or plausible interferences with a natural causative chain. In this it is similar to logic. The hero, being what he is and in a given situation, seems to act naturally or unnaturally; if his action seems natural, and is in addition reasonably interesting and, from an ethical point of view, important, the narrative is in the main successful. To this extent, Mr. Kenneth Burke is wrong, I believe, in censuring nineteenth century fiction for its concern with what he calls the psychology of the hero as opposed to the concern with the psychology of the audience:[12] by the former, he means the plausibility of the portrait; by the latter the concern with those rhetorical devices which please and surprise the reader, devices, for example, of the type of which Fielding was a consummate master. Mr. Burke overlooks the facts that rhetoric cannot exist without a subject matter, and that the subject matter of fiction is narration, that, in short, the author's most important instrument for controlling the attitude of the audience is precisely the psychology of the hero. Mr. Burke is right, however, in that there are other, less important but necessary means of controlling the attitude of the audience, and that most of the standard fiction of the nineteenth century, sometimes for neglecting them, sometimes for utilizing them badly, suffers considerably.

Mr. Burke, in his own compositions, with a precocious security that is discouraging, reverses the Victorian formula: in his novel, *Towards a Better Life*,[13] he concentrates on the sentence, or occasionally on the paragraph, that is, on the incidental. He has attained what appears to be his chief end: he has made himself quotable. His book contains some good aphorisms and many bad; it contains some excellent interludes, such as the fable of the scholar with the face like a vegetable, or the paragraph on Voltaire. Any of these felicities may be removed from their context with perfect impunity, for there really is no context: *Towards a Better Life*, as a whole, is duller than Thackeray. On the other hand, such writers as Jane Austen and Edith Wharton are likely to be wittier than Mr. Burke; but their wit, like that of Molière, is not often separable from their context, since it is primarily a context that they are creating.

Short sketches in prose often deal with the revelation of a situation instead of with the development of one. The result is static, but if the prose is skillful and does not run to excessive length, it may be successful: Cunninghame Graham's *At Dalmary*[14] is a fine example. Other

[10] *Selected Essays*, by T. S. Eliot. Harcourt, Brace and Co., New York, 1932.

[11] *Spring and All*, by William Carlos Williams, Contact Editions, Paris.

[12] In the volume called *Counterstatement*, already mentioned.

[13] *Towards a Better Life*, by Kenneth Burke. Harcourt, Brace and Co., New York, 1932.

[14] *Hope*, by Cunninghame Graham. Duckworth, London.

things being equal, however (which, of course, they never are), action should lend power. In a short narrative poem it matters little whether the situation be revealed or developed: the force of the poetic language can raise the statement to great impressiveness either way; in fact the process of revelation itself may take on in a short poem a quality profoundly dramatic.[15] The famous English Ballad, *Edward,* Mr. E. A. Robinson's *Luke Havergal,*[16] *Her Going* [17] by Agnes Lee, are all examples of revelation at a high level of excellence. Mr. Robinson's *Eros Turannos* [16] is a fine example of development within a short form.

The coherence of character may be demonstrated, as in the novels of Henry James, in a closed, or dramatic plot, in which personage acts upon personage, and in which accident and mechanical change play little part; or the personage may prove himself coherent in a struggle with pure accident, as in Defoe, who pits Moll Flanders against the wilderness of London, or as in Melville, who pits Ahab against the complex wilderness of the sea, of brute nature, and of moral evil; or there may be, as in Mrs. Wharton, a merging of the two extremes: in Mrs. Wharton, the impersonal adversary is usually represented by a human being such as Undine Spragg or the elder Raycie, who is morally or intellectually undeveloped, so that the protagonist is unable to cope with him in human terms. The novel is not the drama, and to demand of it dramatic plot appears to me unreasonable. The form permits the treatment of a great deal of material impossible in the drama, and the material, since it is important in human life, ought to be treated. It is certain, however, that narrative requires coherence of character, and coherence necessitates change. Fielding is dull in bulk because his characters do not develop and because his incidents are without meaning except as anecdotal excuses for the exercise of style. Defoe's rhetoric is less agile, but his conception is more solid.

[15] It is curious that this procedure if employed in a long form, such as the novel or the play, tends to degenerate into bald melodrama; it is the essential, for example, of detective fiction. On the other hand, it is in a large part the form of *The Ambassadors,* the revelation in this, however, motivating further development.

[16] *Collected Poems,* by E. A. Robinson. Macmillan.

[17] *Faces and Open Doors,* by Agnes Lee. R. F. Seymour, Chicago, 1932.

In addition to having greater range, the novel of accident may have advantages over the dramatic novel which are perhaps too seldom considered. The author is less likely to be restricted to the exact contents of the minds of his characters, and so he may have greater opportunity to exhibit, directly or indirectly, his own attitudes, which, in most cases, may be more complex than the attitudes of his characters. Fielding, for example, would have been seriously embarrassed to treat Tom Jones from the point of view of Tom Jones. Melville accomplishes even more with his personal freedom than does Fielding. The superstition that the author should write wholly from within the minds of his characters appears to have grown up largely as a reaction to the degeneration of Fieldingese among the Victorians, notably Thackeray and Dickens, and perhaps Meredith, and perhaps in part as a result of the achievements in the newer mode by Flaubert and by Henry James. Flaubert is misleading, however, in that the perfection and subtlety of his style introduces an important element from without the consciousness of the character in a manner that may be overlooked; and James is misleading not only in this respect but because his characters are usually almost as highly developed as the author himself, so that the two are frequently all but indistinguishable. The superstition is reduced to absurdity in some of Mr. Hemingway's short stories about prize-fighters and bull-fighters, whose views of their own experience are about as valuable as the views of the Sunbonnet Babies or of Little Black Sambo.

Theoretically, that fictional convention should be most desirable which should allow the author to deal with a character from a position formally outside the mind of the character, and which should allow him to analyze, summarize, and arrange material as author, and without regard to the way in which the character might be supposed to have perceived the material originally. This procedure should permit the greatest possibility of rhetorical range; should permit the direct play of the intelligence of the author, over and above the intelligence and limitations of the character; it should permit the greatest possible attention to what Mr. Kenneth Burke has called the psychology of the audience in so far as it is separable from what he calls the psychology of the hero: Mr. Burke, in fact, in his own novel, *Towards a Better Life*, employs a modified stream-of-consciousness convention, thus limiting the rhetorical range very narrowly, and confining himself to a very narrow aspect of the psychology of the hero, so far as the construction of his work as a whole is concerned, and in a large measure as regards all relationships beyond those within the individual sentence. The convention which I should recommend is that of the first-rate biography or history (Johnson's *Lives*, for example, or Hume, or Macaulay) instead of the various post-Joycean conventions now prevalent. Exposition may be made an art; so may historical summary; in fact, the greatest prose in existence is that of the greatest expository writers. The novel should not forego these sources of strength. If it be argued that the first aim of the novelist is to reach a public from whom the great expositors are isolated by their virtues, then the novelist is in exactly that measure unworthy of serious discussion. My recommendation is not made wholly in the absence of examples, however: allowances made for individual limitations of scope and defects of procedure, Jane Austen, Melville, Hawthorne, Henry James, Fielding, and Defoe may be called to serve; Edith Wharton at her best, in such performances as *Brunner Sisters* and *False Dawn*, as *The Valley of Decision* and *The Age of Innocence*, is nearly the perfect example.

TYPE IV: PSEUDO-REFERENCE

Every line or passage of good poetry, every good poetic phrase, communicates a certain quality of feeling as well as a certain paraphrasable content. It would be possible to write a poem unimpeachable as to rational sequence, yet wholly inconsecutive in feeling or even devoid of feeling. Meredith and Browning often display both defects. Chapman's *Hero and Leander* is a rational continuation of Marlowe's beginning, but the break in feeling is notorious.

Suppose that we imagine the reversal of this formula, retaining in our language coherence of feeling, but as far as possible reducing rational coherence. The reduction may be accomplished in either of two ways: (1) we may retain the syntactic forms and much of the vocabulary of rational coherence, thus aiming to exploit the feeling of rational coherence in its absence or at least in excess of its presence; or (2) we may abandon all pretence of rational coherence. The first of these methods I have called *pseudo-reference* and shall treat in this section. The second I shall reserve for the next section.

Pseudo-reference takes a good many forms. I shall list as many forms as I have observed. My list will probably not be complete, but it will be nearly enough complete to illustrate the principle and to provide a basis of further observation.

1. *Grammatical coherence in excess of, or in the absence of, rational coherence.* This may mean no more than a slight excess of grammatical machinery, a minor redundancy. Thus Miss Moore, in *Black Earth:*

> *I do these*
> *things* which I do, *which please*
> *no one but myself.*[18]

The words which I have set in Roman are redundant. Again, in *Reinforcements,*[19] Miss Moore writes:

> *the future of time is determined by*
> *the power of volition*

when she means:

> *volition determines the future.*

Miss Moore is usually ironic when writing thus, but not always; and I confess that it appears to me a somewhat facile and diffuse kind of irony, for the instrument of irony (the poetry) is weakened in the interests of irony. It is an example of what I shall have repeated occasion to refer to as the fallacy of expressive, or imitative, form; the procedure in which the form succumbs to the raw material of the poem. It is as if Dryden had descended to imitating Shadwell's style in his efforts to turn it to ridicule.

Closely related to this procedure, but much more audacious, is the maintenance of grammatical coherence when there is no coherence of thought or very little. Hart Crane, for ex-

[18] *Observations*, by Marianne Moore. The Dial Press, New York, 1924.

[19] *Observations*, by Marianne Moore. The Dial Press, New York, 1942.

ample, has placed at the beginning of his poem, *For the Marriage of Faustus and Helen,*[20] the following quotation from Ben Jonson's play, *The Alchemist:*

And so we may arrive by Talmud skill
And profane Greek to raise the building up
Of Helen's house against the Ismaelite,
King of Thogarma, and his habergeons
Brimstony, blue and fiery; and the force
Of King Abaddon, and the beast of Cittim;
Which Rabbi David Kimchi, Onkelos,
And Aben Ezra do interpret Rome.[21]

This is one of the numerous passages in the play, in which the characters speak nonsense purporting to contain deep alchemical secrets or to express a feignedly distraught state of mind: this particular passage serves both functions at once. The nonsense is necessary to Jonson's plot; the reader recognizes the necessity and can make no objection, so that he is forced to accept with unalloyed pleasure whatever elusive but apparently real poetic implications there may be in such a passage, since he receives these implications absolutely gratis. The technique of expressive form, to which I have alluded, is here forced upon Jonson in a measure by the dramatic medium, for the characters must be represented in their own persons; this may or may not indicate a defect in the medium itself, as compared to other methods of satire, but at any rate there is no misuse of the medium. Jonson appears, then, to have been wholly aware of this procedure, which is usually regarded as a Mallarmean or Rimbaldian innovation, and Crane appears to have found at least one of his chief models for this kind of writing in Jonson. Jonson differs from Crane in that he does not employ the method when writing in his own name, but merely employs it to characterize his cozeners.

The two sections in blank verse of *Faustus and Helen* resemble Jonson's nonsense very closely. For example:

The mind is brushed by sparrow wings;
Numbers, rebuffed by asphalt, crowd
The margins of the day, accent the curbs,
Conveying divers dawns on every corner
To druggist, barber, and tobacconist,
Until the graduate opacities of evening
Take them away as suddenly to somewhere
Virginal, perhaps, less fragmentary, cool.[22]

This is perfectly grammatical, and if not examined too carefully may appear more or less comprehensible. But the activities of the numbers, if the entire sentence is surveyed, appear wholly obscure. If one suppose *numbers* to be a synonym for *numbers of persons,* for *crowds,* one or two points are cleared up, but no more. If one suppose the numbers to be the mathematical abstractions of modern life, structural, temporal, financial, and others similar, there is greater clarity; but the first five lines are so precious and indirect as to be somewhat obscure, and the last three lines are perfectly obscure.

There is a pleasanter example of the same kind of writing in a shorter poem by Crane, and from the same volume, the poem called *Sunday Morning Apples:*

A boy runs with a dog before the sun, straddling
Spontaneities that form their independent orbits,
Their own perennials of light
In the valley where you live
(called Brandywine.)

The second line, taken in conjunction with the first, conveys the action of the boy, but it does

[20] *White Buildings,* by Hart Crane. Boni and Liveright, New York, 1926.

[21] Act IV: 3.

[22] [The correction which follows appears in "A Foreword" to *Maule's Curse,* and is here reprinted by request of the author. "In discussing a passage quoted from the opening of Hart Crane's poem, *For the Marriage of Faustus and Helen,* I complained of the obscurity of the lines beginning, 'Numbers rebuffed by asphalt,' and said that the numbers might refer to numbers of people or to the mathematical abstractions of modern life, but that either interpretation left the passage imperfectly comprehensible. Now I was wrong, and in justice to Crane, I ought to correct the error. The numbers in question refer to the sparrows' wings in the preceding line, and by extension, to the sparrows, and with this understanding the passage is perfectly clear. Crane is in a good measure to blame for the difficulty, for the grammatical reference here and throughout the poem is of the loosest, and . . . there are elements in the passage that actively support the second interpretation and that would no doubt be a sufficient justification of the second interpretation if that interpretation clarified the passage within itself. My error does not, I believe, invalidate my general criticism of Crane, for the type of obscurity which I mistakenly found in this passage is certainly to be found elsewhere in Crane, though commonly in shorter fragments, and I see no reason to believe that I was mistaken in regard to other passages which I found obscure."]

so indirectly and by suggestion. What it says, if we consider rational content alone, is really indecipherable. One can, of course, make a rational paraphrase, but one can do it, not by seeking the rational content of the lines, but by seeking suggestions as to the boy's behavior, and by then making a rational statement regarding it. The line has a certain loveliness and conveys what it sets out to convey: the objection which I should make to it is that it goes through certain motions that are only half effective. A greater poet would have made the rational formula count rationally, at the same time that he was utilizing suggestion; he would thus have achieved a more concentrated poetry.

2. *Transference of Values from one field of experience to another and unrelated field.* I shall illustrate this procedure with passages from Crane's poem, *The Dance.*[23] The poem opens with the description of a journey first by canoe up the Hudson, then on foot into the mountains. As the protagonist, or narrator, proceeds on his way, he appears to proceed likewise into the past, until he arrives at the scene of an Indian dance, at which a chieftain, Maquokeeta, is being burned at the stake. The poem from this point on deals with the death and apotheosis of Maquokeeta, the apotheosis taking the form of a union with Pocahontas, who has been introduced in this poem and in the poem preceding, *The River,* as a kind of mythic deity representing the American soil. The following passage is the climax and the most striking moment in the poem:

O, like the lizard in the furious noon,
That drops his legs and colors in the sun,
—And laughs, pure serpent, Time itself, and moon
Of his own fate, I saw thy change begun!

And saw thee dive to kiss that destiny
Like one white meteor, sacrosanct and blent
At last with all that's consummate and free
There where the first and last gods keep thy tent.

The remainder of the poem develops the same theme and the same mood. The following phrases are typical:

Thy freedom is her largesse, Prince . . .
And are her perfect brows to thine? . . .

[23] From *The Bridge,* by Hart Crane. Horace Liveright, New York, 1930.

The difficulty resides in the meaning of the union. It may be regarded in either of two ways: as the simple annihilation and dissolution in the soil of Maquokeeta, or as the entrance into another and superior mode of life. There is no possible compromise.

If we select the former alternative, the language of mystical and physical union has no relationship to the event: it is language carried over, with all or a good deal of its connotation, from two entirely different realms of experience. The passage is thus parasitic for its effect upon feelings unrelated to its theme. The words *consummate and free,* for example, carry the connotations common to them, but their rational meaning in this context is *terminated and dissipated. Sacrosanct,* similarly, while carrying certain feelings from its religious past, would mean *devoid of human meaning,* or, more concisely, *devoid of meaning.* Similarly, *perfect,* in the last line quoted, carries feelings from love poetry, but it would actually signify *meaningless.* In other words, extinction is beatitude. But this is nonsense: extinction is extinction. If there is a state of beatitude, it is a state; that is, it is not extinction.

If we accept the second alternative and assume that some really mystical experience is implied, there is nothing in the poem or elsewhere in Crane's work to give us a clue to the nature of the experience. The only possible conclusion is that he was confused as to his own feelings and did not bother to find out what he was really talking about. That odd bits of this obscurity can be glossed I am fully aware; but it cannot be cleaned up to an extent even moderately satisfactory. There is a wide margin of obscurity and of meaningless excitement, despite a certain splendor of language which may at times move one to forget, or to try to forget, what the poem lacks.

Further, there seems actually little doubt that Crane did confuse in some way the ideas of extinction and of beatitude, and that he was an enthusiastic pantheistical mystic. The mere fact that beatitude is represented in this poem by the union with Pocahontas, who stands for the soil of America, is evidence in itself; and further evidence may be found in *The River* and in some of the shorter poems. But one does not create a religion and a conception of immortality by simply naming the soil Pocahontas and by then writing love poetry to the Indian girl who bore that name. Crane repeatedly refers to an idea which he cannot define and which probably never had even potential existence.

A similar difficulty occurs in *Atlantis,* the final section of *The Bridge,* the sequence of which *The Dance* and *The River* are central parts. The Brooklyn Bridge is seen in a kind of vision or hallucination as the new Atlantis, the future America. The language is ecstatic; at certain moments and in certain ways it comes near to being the most brilliant language in Crane's work:

Like hails, farewells—up planet-sequined heights
Some trillion whispering hammers glimmer Tyre:
Serenely, sharply up the long anvil cry
Of inchling aeons silence rivets Troy. . . .

But the only poetic embodiment of the future, the only source of the ecstasy, is a quantitative vision of bigger cities with higher buildings. One can read a certain amount of allegory into this, but in so far as one makes the allegory definite or comprehensible, one will depart from the text; the enthusiasm again is obscure.

3. *Reference to a non-existent plot.* This is most easily illustrated by selections from T. S. Eliot. I quote from *Gerontion:* [24]

To be eaten, to be divided, to be drunk
Among whispers; by Mr. Silvero
With caressing hands, at Limoges
Who walked all night in the next room;
By Hakagawa, bowing among the Titians;
By Madame de Tornquist, in the dark room
Shifting the candles; Fräulein von Kulp
Who turned in the hall, one hand on the door.

Each one of these persons is denoted in the performance of an act, and each act, save possibly that of Hakagawa, implies an anterior situation, is a link in a chain of action; even that of Hakagawa implies an anterior and unexplained personality. Yet we have no hint of the nature of the history implied. A feeling is claimed by the poet, the motivation, or meaning, of which is with-held, and of which in all likelihood he has no clearer notion than his readers can have. I do not wish to seem to insist that Mr. Eliot should have recounted the past histories in order to perfect this particular poem. Given the convention, the modus operandi, the obscurity is inevitable, and compared to the obscurity which we have just seen in Crane, it is relatively innocent. But obscurity it is: discreetly modulated diffuseness. A more direct and economical convention seems to me preferable.

Mr. Eliot does much the same thing, but less skillfully, elsewhere. The following passage is from *Burbank with a Baedeker; Bleistein with a Cigar:* [25]

Burbank crossed a little bridge,
  Descending at a small hotel;
Princess Volupine arrived,
  They were together, and he fell.

What is the significance of the facts in the first two lines? They have no real value as perception: the notation is too perfunctory. They must have some value as information, as such details might have value, for example, in a detective story, if they are to have any value at all. Yet they have no bearing on what follows; in fact, most of what follows is obscure in exactly the same way. They are not even necessary to what occurs in the next two lines, for Princess Volupine might just as well have encountered him anywhere else and after any other transit.

4. *Explicit Reference to a non-existent symbolic value.* The following lines are taken from a poem entitled *Museum,*[26] by Mr. Alan Porter:

The day was empty. Very pale with dust,
A chalk road set its finger at the moors.
The drab, damp air so blanketed the town
Never an oak swung leather leaf. The chimneys
Pushed up their pillars at the loose-hung sky;
And through the haze, along the ragstone houses,
Red lichens dulled to a rotten-apple brown. . . .

Suddenly turning a byeway corner, a cripple,
Bloodless with age, lumbered along the road.
The motes of dust whirled at his iron-shod crutches
And quickly settled. A dog whined. The old
Cripple looked round, and, seeing no man, gave
A quick, small piping chuckle, swung a pace,
And stopped to look about and laugh again.
"That," said a girl in a flat voice, "is God."
Her mother made no answer; she remembered,
"I knew an old lame beggar who went mad."

[24] *Poems 1909-1925,* by T. S. Eliot.

[25] *Poems 1909-1925,* by T. S. Eliot.

[26] *Signature of Pain,* by Alan Porter. The John Day Company, New York, 1931.

He lumbered along the road and turned a corner.
His tapping faded and the day was death.

This poem is ably written and has an unusually fine texture; in fact, it is the texture of the entire work which provides the effective setting for the factitious comment on the beggar, and the comment is introduced with great skill. The landscape is intense and mysterious, as if with meaning withheld. In such a setting, the likening of the beggar to God appears, for an instant, portentous, but only for an instant, for there is no discernible basis for the likening. The beggar is treated as if he were symbolic of something, whereas he is really symbolic of nothing that one can discover. The introduction of the beggar appears to be a very skillful piece of sleight-of-hand; yet it is not an incidental detail of the description, but is rather the climax of the description, the theme of the poem. We have, in other words, a rather fine poem about nothing.

5. *Implicit Reference to a non-existent symbolic value.* It may be difficult at times to distinguish this type of pseudo-reference from the last or from the type which I have designated under the heading of transferred value. I shall merely endeavor to select examples as obvious as possible.

There is, in the first place, such a thing as implicit reference to a genuine symbolic value. The second sonnet in Heredia's *Trophées,* the sonnet entitled *Némée,* describes the slaying of the Nemean lion by Hercules. Hercules is the typical hero; the slaying of the lion is the heroic task; the fleeing peasant is the common mortal for whom the task is performed. It is nakedly and obviously allegorical, yet there is no statement within the poem of the allegorical intention: it is our familiarity with the myth and with other similar myths which makes us recognize the poem as allegory. Similarly, there is no statement of allegorical intention within Blake's poem, *The Tiger:* the recognition of the intention is due to Blake's having been fairly explicit in other works.

Further, it is possible to describe an item with no past history in such a way that it will have a significance fairly general. This is the procedure of a handful of the best poems of the Imagist movement; for example, of Dr. Williams' poem, *On the Road to the Contagious Hospital.* Thus Miss Moore describes a parakeet, in the poem entitled *My Apish Cousins:*

the parakeet,
trivial and humdrum on examination,
destroying
bark and portions of the food it could not eat.

There is also the legitimate field of purely descriptive poetry, with no general significance and no claim to any. For examples, one could cite many passages from *The Seasons,* or from Crabbe. There is no attempt in such poetry to communicate any feeling save the author's interest in visible beauties. Such poetry can scarcely rise to the greatest heights, but within its field it is sound, and it can, as in some of Crabbe's descriptions, especially of the sea, achieve surprising power. There is a good deal of this sort of thing scattered through English literature.

Growing out of these two types of poetry (that which refers to a genuine symbolic value, but implicitly, and the purely descriptive), there is a sentimental and more or less spurious variety, a good deal of which was recently fostered by the Imagist movement, but which actually antedates the Imagist movement by more than a century.

This poetry describes landscape or other material, sometimes very ably, but assumes a quality or intensity of feeling of which the source is largely obscure. Thus in Collins' *Ode to Evening* we find a melancholy which at moments, as in the description of the bat, verges on disorder, and which at all times is far too profound to arise from an evening landscape alone. Collins' bat differs from Miss Moore's parakeet in this: that the parakeet is a genuine example of the way in which the exotic may become humdrum with familiarity—there is, in other words, a real perception of the bird involved, which does not exceed the order of experience which the bird may reasonably represent; whereas Collins' bat is not mad nor a sufficient motive for madness, but is used to express a state of mind irrelevant to him. It is as if a man should murder his mother, and then, to express his feelings, write *Ode to Thunder.* Or rather, it is as if a man should murder his mother with no consciousness of the act, but with all of the consequent suffering, and should then so express himself. A symbol is used to embody a feeling neither relevant to the symbol nor relevant to anything else of which the poet is conscious: the poet expresses his feeling as best he is able without understanding it. Collins in this poem, and in his odes to the disembodied passions, is perhaps the first purely romantic poet and one of the best. He does not, like Gray, retain amid his melancholy any of the classical gift for generalization, and he has provided the language with no familiar quotations. Shelley's *Ode to the West Wind,* and in a measure Keats' *Ode to the Nightingale,* are examples of the same procedure; namely, of expressing a feeling, not as among the traditional poets in terms of its motive, but in terms of something irrelevant or largely so, commonly landscape. No landscape, in itself, is an adequate motive for the feelings expressed in such poems as these; an appropriate landscape merely brings to mind certain feelings and is used as a symbol for their communication. The procedure can be defended on the grounds that the feeling may be universal and that the individual reader is at liberty to supply his own motive; but the procedure nevertheless does not make for so concentrated a poetry as the earlier method, and as an act of moral contemplation the poem is incomplete and may even be misleading and dangerous.

H. D. employs a formula nearly identical with that of Collins in most of her poems. In describing a Greek landscape, she frequently writes as if it had some intrinsic virtue automatically evoked by a perception of its qualities as landscape but more important than these qualities in themselves. It is not Greek history or civilization with which she is concerned, or most often it is not: the material is simple and more or less ideally bucolic. Frequently the ecstasy (the quality of feeling assumed is nearly identical in most of her poems) is evoked merely by rocks, sea, and islands. But it would not be evoked by any rock, sea, or islands: they must be Greek. But why must they be Greek? Because of Athenian civilization? If so, why the to-do about material irrelevant to Athenian civilization? There is some wholly obscure attachment on the poet's part to anything Greek, regardless of its value: the mention of anything Greek is sufficient to release her very intense feeling. But since the relationship between the feeling and the Greek landscape has no comprehensible source and is very strong, one must call it sentimental.

This is not to say that all her poetry is spoiled by it: much of it is spoiled and nearly all is tainted, but the taint is sometimes very slight; and the description, in addition, is sometimes very fine. Exotic landscapes of one kind or another have been employed in exactly this fashion for about a century, and, in America, the American landscape has been so employed by such writers as Whitman, Sandburg, Crane, and Williams.

6. *Explicit Reference to a non-existent or obscure principle of motivation.* This may at times be hard to distinguish from almost any of the types of obscurity which I have described, but there are to be found occasionally passages of pseudo-reference which will fit into scarcely any other category. Bearing in mind the fundamental obscurity of *The Dance,* by Hart Crane, an obscurity which I have already discussed at some length, let us consider these two lines from it:

> Mythical brows we saw retiring—loth,
> Disturbed, and destined, into denser green.

This passage depends for its effect wholly upon the feeling of motivation.

The mythical has rational content for the believer in myths or for him who can find an idea embodied in the myth. The major Greek divinities exist for us chiefly as allegorical embodiments of more or less Platonic ideas. What myths have we in mind here? None. Or none unless it be the myth of Pocahontas, which, as we have seen, is irreducible to any idea. There is merely a feeling of mythicalness.

Loth, disturbed, destined are words of motivation; that is, each one implies a motive. But the nature of the motive is not given in the poem, nor is it deducible from the poem nor from the body of Crane's work. In fact, it is much easier to read some sort of general meaning into these lines in isolation than in their context, which has already been discussed.

Such terms give, then, a feeling of reasonable motivation unreasonably obscured. The poet speaks as if he had knowledge incommunicable to us, but of which he is able to communicate the resultant feelings. There is a feeling of mystery back of an emotion which the poet endeavors to render with precision. It is a skillful indulgence in irresponsibility. The skill is admirable, but not the irresponsibility. The poetry has a ghostly quality, as if it were only half there.

7. *Reference to a purely private symbolic value.* A poet, sometimes because of the limitations of his education, and sometimes for other reasons, may center his feelings in symbols shared with no one, or perhaps only with a small group. The private symbol may or may not refer to a clear concept or understanding. If it does so refer and the poetry is otherwise good, readers are likely eventually to familiarize themselves with the symbols; in fact brilliant writing alone will suffice to this end, as witness the efforts that have been made to clarify the essentially obscure concepts of Blake and of Yeats. A certain amount of this kind of thing, in fact, is probably inevitable in any poet, and sometimes, as in the references to private experience in the sonnets of Shakespeare, the obscurity, as a result of the accidents of history, can never be penetrated.

I have illustrated one extreme type of pseudo-reference with a passage from Ben Jonson; I might have utilized also the "mad songs" of the sixteenth and seventeenth centuries, such as were written by Shakespeare, Fletcher, and Herrick. Samuel Johnson wrote thus in his *Life of Dryden:* "Dryden delighted to tread upon the brink of meaning, where light and darkness mingle. . . . This inclination sometimes produced nonsense, which he knew; and sometimes it issued in absurdity, of which perhaps he was not conscious." The method appears, then, to have been for a long time one of the recognized potentialities of poetic writing, but to have been more or less checked by the widespread command of rational subject matter.

It should naturally have been released, as it appears to have been, by a period of amateur mysticism, of inspiration for its own sake, by a tendency such as that which we have for some years past observed, to an increasingly great preoccupation with the fringe of consciousness, to an increasing emphasis on the concept of continuous experience, a tendency to identify, under the influence, perhaps, of scientific or of romantic monism, subconscious stimuli and reactions with occult inspiration, to confuse the divine and the visceral, and to employ in writing from such attitudes as this confusion might provide, a language previously reserved to the religious mystics. Such a change would involve along its way such indefinable philosophies as Bergsonism [27] and Transcendentalism,[28] such half-metaphorical sciences as psychoanalysis, and especially the popular myths and superstitions which they and the more reputable sciences have engendered. In such an intellectual milieu, semi-automatic writing begins to appear a legitimate and even a superior method.

Emerson, in *Merlin,* for example, gives this account of the bard's activity:

> He shall not his brain encumber
> With the coil of rhythm and number;
> But, leaving rule and pale forethought,
> He shall aye climb
> For his rhyme.
> "Pass in, pass in," the angels say,
> "In to the upper doors,
> Nor count compartments of the floors,
> But mount to paradise
> By the stairway of surprise."

Just how much Emerson meant by this passage it would be hard to say; it is always hard to say just how much Emerson meant, and perhaps would have been hardest for Emerson. Mr. Tate reduces Emerson's Transcendentalism [29] to this formula: ". . . In Emerson, man is greater than any idea, and being the Over-Soul is potentially perfect; there is no struggle because—I state the Emersonian doctrine, which is very slippery, in its extreme terms—because there is no possibility of error. There is no drama in human character, because there is no tragic fault."

To continue with extreme terms—which will give us, if not what Emerson desired, the results which his doctrine and others similar have encouraged—we arrive at these conclusions: If there is no possibility of error, the revision of

[27] *Le Bergsonisme,* by Julien Benda. Mercure de France, 1926. Also "Flux and Blur in Contemporary Art," by John Crowe Ransom in *The Sewanee Review,* July, 1929.

[28] H. B. Parkes on Emerson, in the *Hound and Horn,* Summer, 1932.

[29] "New England Culture and Emily Dickinson," by Allen Tate. *The Symposium,* April, 1932.

judgment is meaningless; immediate inspiration is correct; but immediate inspiration amounts to the same thing as unrevised reactions to stimuli; unrevised reactions are mechanical; man in a state of perfection is an automaton; an automatic man is insane. Hence, Emerson's perfect man is a madman.

The important thing about all this is not Emerson's originality, but his complete lack of any: exactly the same conclusions are deducible from the *Essay on Man,* and the convictions which lead to them one meets everywhere in the eighteenth, nineteenth, and twentieth centuries.

Dr. W. C. Williams, for example, who, like Emerson, does not practice unreservedly what he preaches, but who more perhaps than any writer living encourages in his juniors a profound conviction of their natural rightness, a sentimental debauchery of self-indulgence, is able to write as follows: "It is the same thing you'll see in a brigand, a criminal of the grade of Gerald Chapman, some of the major industrial leaders, old-fashioned kings, the Norsemen, drunkards and the best poets. . . . Poetry is imposed on an age by men intent on something else, whose primary cleanliness of mind makes them automatically first-rate." [30]

A few months later Dr. Williams writes of and to his young admirers somewhat querulously: [31] "Instead of that—Lord how serious it sounds—let's play tiddly-winks with the syllables. . . . Experiment we must have, but it seems to me that a number of the younger writers has forgotten that writing doesn't mean just inventing new ways to say 'So's your Old Man.' I swear I myself can't make out for the life of me what many of them are talking about, and I have a will to understand them that they will not find in many another." He demands substance, not realizing that his own teachings have done their very respectable bit toward cutting the young men off from any.

The Emersonian and allied doctrines differ in their moral implications very little from any form of Quietism or even from the more respectable and Catholic forms of mysticism. If we add to the doctrine the belief in pantheism—that is, the belief that the Over-Soul is the Universe, that body and soul are one—we have the basis for the more or less Freudian mysticism of the surrealists and such of their disciples as Eugene Jolas; we have also—probably—a rough notion of Hart Crane's mysticism. There is the danger for the Quietist that the promptings of the Devil or of the viscera may be mistaken for the promptings of God. The pantheistic mystic identifies God, Devil, and viscera as a point of doctrine: he is more interested in the promptings of the "subconscious" mind than of the conscious, in the half-grasped intention, in the fleeting relationship, than in that which is wholly understood. He is interested in getting just as far off in the direction of the uncontrolled, the meaningless, as he can possibly get and still have the pleasure of talking about it. He is frequently more interested in the psychology of sleeping than in the psychology of waking; [32] he would if he could devote himself to exploring that realm of experience which he shares with sea-anemones, cabbages, and onions, in preference to exploring the realm of experience shared specifically with men.

So far as my own perceptions are able to guide me, it appears that the writers employing such methods are writing a little too much as Jonson's alchemist spoke, with a philosophical background insusceptible of definition, despite their apparently careful references to it, but as their own dupes, not to dupe others. They have revised Baudelaire's dictum that the poet should be the hypnotist and somnambulist combined; he should now be the cozener and the cozened. Crane, despite his genius, and the same is true of Mr. James Joyce, appears to answer Ben Jonson's scoundrels across the centuries, and in their own language, but like a somnambulist under their control.

This kind of writing is not a "new kind of poetry," as it has been called perennially since Verlaine discovered it in Rimbaud. It is the old kind of poetry with half the meaning removed. Its strangeness comes from its thinness.

[30] *Blues* (published by C. H. Ford, at Columbus, Miss.) for May, 1929.

[31] *Blues* for Autumn of 1930. The reference to the game of tiddly-winks will be clear only to those persons familiar with the imitators of Mr. James Joyce's fourth prose work, exclusive of *Exiles,* entitled *Finnegans Wake.*

[32] Cf. Mr. James Joyce's *Finnegans Wake,* and the voluminous works by Mr. Joyce's apologists and imitators.

Indubitable genius has been expended upon poetry of this type, and much of the poetry so written will more than likely have a long life, and quite justly, but the nature of the poetry should be recognized: it can do us no good to be the dupes of men who do not understand themselves.

TYPE V: QUALITATIVE PROGRESSION

The term *qualitative progression* I am borrowing from Mr. Kenneth Burke's volume of criticism, *Counterstatement,* to which I have already had several occasions to refer. This method arises from the same attitudes as the last, and it resembles the last except that it makes no attempt whatever at a rational progression. Mr. Pound's *Cantos* [33] are the perfect example of the form; they make no unfulfilled claims to matter not in the poetry, or at any rate relatively few and slight claims. Mr. Pound proceeds from image to image wholly through the coherence of feeling: his sole principle of unity is mood, carefully established and varied. That is, each statement he makes is reasonable in itself, but the progression from statement to statement is not reasonable: it is the progression either of random conversation or of revery. This kind of progression might be based upon an implicit rationality; in such a case the rationality of the progression becomes clearly evident before the poem has gone very far and is never thereafter lost sight of; in a poem of any length such implicit rationality would have to be supported by explicit exposition. But in Mr. Pound's poem I can find few implicit themes of any great clarity, and fewer still that are explicit.[34]

The principle of selection being less definite, the selection of details is presumably less rigid, though many of the details display a fine quality. The symbolic range is therefore reduced, since the form reduces the importance of selectiveness, or self-directed action. The movement is proportionately slow and wavering—indeed is frequently shuffling and undistinguished—and the range of material handled is limited: I do not mean that the poetry cannot refer to a great many types of actions and persons, but that it can find in them little variety of value—it refers to them all in the same way, that is, casually. Mr. Pound resembles a village loafer who sees much and understands little.

The following passage, however, the opening of the fourth *Canto,* illustrates this kind of poetry at its best:

Palace in smoky light,
Troy but a heap of smouldering boundary stones,
ANAXIFORMINGES! Aurunculeia!
Hear me. Cadmus of Golden Prows!
The silver mirrors catch the bright stones and flare,
Dawn, to our waking, drifts in the cool green light;
Dew-haze blurs, in the grass, pale ankles moving.
Beat, beat, whirr, thud, in the soft turf under the apple-trees,
Choros nympharum, goat-foot, with the pale foot alternate;
Crescent of blue-shot waters, green-gold in the shallows,
A black cock crows in the sea-foam;
And by the curved, carved foot of the couch, claw-foot and lion-head, an old man seated
Speaking in the low drone . . . :
Ityn
Et ter flebiliter, Ityn, Ityn!
And she went towards the window and cast her down

[33] *A Draft of XXX Cantos,* by Ezra Pound. Hours Press, 15 rue Guenegaud, Paris, 1930.

[34] Mr. Pound, writing in the *New English Weekly,* Vol. III, No. 4, of remarks similar to the above which I published in the *Hound and Horn* for the Spring of 1933, states: "I am convinced that one should not as a general rule reply to critics or defend works in process of being written. On the other hand, if one prints fragments of a work one perhaps owes the benevolent reader enough explanation to prevent his wasting time in unnecessary misunderstanding.

"The nadir of solemn and elaborate imbecility is reached by Mr. Winters in an American publication where he deplores my 'abandonment of logic in the Cantos,' presumably because he has never read my prose criticism and has never heard of the ideographic method, and thinks logic is limited to a few 'forms of logic' which better minds were already finding inadequate to the mental needs of the XIIIth century."

As to the particular defects of scholarship which Mr. Pound attributes to me, he is, alas, mistaken. For the rest, one may only say that civilization rests on the recognition that language possesses both connotative and denotative powers; that the abandonment of one in a poem impoverishes the poem to that extent; and that the abandonment of the denotative, or rational, in particular, and in a pure state, results in one's losing the only means available for checking up on the qualitative or "ideographic" sequences to see if they really are coherent in more than vague feeling. Mr. Pound, in other words, has no way of knowing whether he can think or not.

"And the while, the while swallows crying:
Ityn!
"It is Cabestan's heart in the dish."
"It is Cabestan's heart in the dish?
"No other taste shall change this."

The loveliness of such poetry appears to me indubitable, but it is merely a blur of revery: its tenuity becomes apparent if one compares it, for example, to the poetry of Paul Valéry, which achieves effects of imagery, particularly of atmospheric imagery, quite as extraordinary, along with precision, depth of meaning, and the power that comes of close and inalterable organization, and, though Mr. Pound's admirers have given him a great name as a metrist, with incomparably finer effects of sound.

Mr. Kenneth Burke defines the qualitative progression [35] by means of a very fine analysis of the preparation for the ghost in *Hamlet* and by reference to the porter scene in *Macbeth,* and then proceeds to the public house scene in *The Waste Land* [36] as if it were equally valid. Actually, the qualitative progression in Shakespeare is peripheral, the central movement of each play being dependent upon what Mr. Burke calls the psychology of the hero, or narrative logic, and so firmly dependent that occasional excursions into the rationally irrelevant can be managed with no loss of force, whereas in *The Waste Land* the qualitative progression is central: it is as if we should have a dislocated series of scenes from *Hamlet* without the prince himself, or with too slight an account of his history for his presence to be helpful. The difference between Mr. Eliot and Mr. Pound is this: that in *The Waste Land,* the prince is briefly introduced in the footnotes, whereas it is to be doubted that Mr. Pound could manage such an introduction were he so inclined. And the allegorical interpretation, or the germ of one, which Mr. Eliot has provided helps very little in the organization of the poem itself. To guess that the rain has a certain allegorical meaning when the rain is so indifferently described, or to guess at the allegorical relationships as a scholar might guess at the connections between a dozen odd pages recovered from a lost folio, is of very small aid to ourselves or to the poet.

[35] *Counterstatement,* page 38 and thereafter.
[36] *Poems 1909-25,* by T. S. Eliot.

If Mr. Eliot and Mr. Pound have employed conventions that can be likened to revery or to random conversation, Rimbaud and Mr. Joyce have gone farther. I quote Rimbaud's *Larme:*

Loin des oiseaux, des troupeaux, des villageoises,
Je buvais accroupi dans quelque bruyère
Entourée de tendres bois de noisetiers,
Par un brouillard d'après-midi tiède et vert.

Que pouvais-je boire dans cette jeune Oise,
Ormeaux sans voix, gazon sans fleurs, ciel couvert:
Que tirais-je à la gourde de colocase?
Quelque liqueur d'or, fade et qui fait suer.

Tel, j'eusse été mauvaise enseigne d'auberge.
Puis l'orage changea le ciel, jusqu'au soir.
Ce furent des pays noirs, des lacs, des perches,
Des colonnades sous la nuit bleue, des gares.

L'eau des bois se perdait sur les sables vierges,
Le vent, du ciel, jetait des glaçons aux mares . . .
Or! tel qu'un pêcheur d'or ou de coquillages,
Dire que je n'ai pas eu souci de boire!

The feelings of this poem are perhaps those attendant upon dream, delirium, or insanity. The coming of night and the storm is an intensification of the mood; the protagonist is suddenly sucked deeper in the direction of complete unconsciousness, and the terror becomes more profound.

In *Finnegans Wake,* by James Joyce, the dream convention is unmistakable. It penetrates the entire texture of the work, not only the syntax but the words themselves, which are broken down and recombined in surprising ways.

This unbalance of the reasonable and the non-reasonable, whether the non-reason be of the type which I am now discussing or of the pseudo-referent type, is a vice wherever it occurs, and in the experimental writers who have worked very far in this direction, it is, along with Laforguian irony, which I shall discuss separately, one of the two most significant vices of style now flourishing. The reasons have already been mentioned here and there, but I shall summarize them.

Since only one aspect of language, the connotative, is being utilized, less can be said in a given number of words than if the denotative aspect were being fully utilized at the same time. The convention thus tends to diffuseness. Further, when the denotative power of language is impaired, the connotative becomes proportionately parasitic upon denotations in previous contexts, for words cannot have associations without meanings; and if the denotative power of language could be wholly eliminated, the connotative would be eliminated at the same stroke, for it is the nature of associations that they are associated with something. This means that non-rational writing, far from requiring greater literary independence than the traditional modes, encourages a quality of writing that is relatively derivative and insecure.

Since one of the means to coherence, or form, is impaired, form itself is enfeebled. In so far as form is enfeebled, precision of detail is enfeebled, for details receive precision from the structure in which they function just as they may be employed to give that structure precision; to say that detail is enfeebled is to say that the power of discrimination is enfeebled. Mr. Joyce's new prose has sensitivity, for Mr. Joyce is a man of genius, but it is the sensitivity of a plasmodium, in which every cell squirms independently though much like every other. This statement is a very slight exaggeration if certain chapters are considered, notably the chapter entitled *Anna Livia Plurabelle,* but for the greater part it is no exaggeration.

The procedure leads to indiscriminateness at every turn. Mr. Joyce endeavors to express disintegration by breaking down his form, by experiencing disintegration before our very eyes, but this destroys much of his power of expression. Of course he controls the extent to which he impairs his form, but this merely means that he is willing to sacrifice just so much power of expression—in an effort to express something—and no more. He is like Whitman trying to express a loose America by writing loose poetry. This fallacy, the fallacy of expressive, or imitative, form, recurs constantly in modern literature.

Anna Livia Plurabelle is in a sense a modern equivalent of Gray's *Elegy,* one in which the form is expressive of the theme to an unfortunate extent; it blurs the values of all experience in the fact of change, and is unable, because of its inability to deal with rational experience, to distinguish between village Cromwells and the real article, between Othello on the one hand and on the other hand Shem and Shaun. It leads to the unlimited subdivision of feelings into sensory details till perception is lost, instead of to the summary and ordering of perception; it leads to disorganization and unintelligence. In Mr. Joyce we may observe the decay of genius. To the form of decay his genius lends a beguiling iridescence, and to his genius the decay lends a quality of novelty, which endanger the literature of our time by rendering decay attractive.

Mr. T. S. Eliot, in his introduction to the *Anabase* of St. Jean Perse,[37] has written: "There is a logic of the imagination as well as a logic of concepts. People who do not appreciate poetry always find it difficult to distinguish between order and chaos in the arrangement of images." Later in the same essay he says: "I believe that this is a piece of writing of the same importance as the later work of Mr. James Joyce, as valuable as *Anna Livia Plurabelle.* And this is a high estimate indeed."

The logic in the arrangement of images of which Mr. Eliot speaks either is formulable, is not formulable, or is formulated. If it is neither formulated nor formulable (and he admits that it is not formulated), the word *logic* is used figuratively, to indicate qualitative progression, and the figure is one which it is hard to pardon a professed classicist for using at the present time. If the logic is formulable, there is no need for an apology and there is no excuse for the reference to *Anna Livia Plurabelle;* and there is reason to wonder why no formulation is given or suggested by the critic. Mr. Eliot has reference obviously, merely to the type of graduated progression of feeling that we have been discussing, and the poem shares the weakness of other works already discussed.

Mr. Eliot's remarks are typical of the evasive dallying practiced by the greater number of even the most lucid and reactionary critics of our time when dealing with a practical problem of criticism. It is well enough to defend Christian morality and to speak of tradition, but forms must be defined and recognized or the darkness remains. A classicist may admire the sensibilities of Joyce and Perse with perfect consistency (though beyond a certain point not with per-

[37] *Anabasis,* a poem by St. Jean Perse, with translation and Preface by T. S. Eliot. Faber and Faber, London, 1930.

fect taste), but he cannot with consistency justify the forms which those sensibilities have taken.

If the reader is curious to compare with the *Anabase* a prose work of comparable length and subject in the traditional manner, he will find a specimen of the highest merit in *The Destruction of Tenochtitlan*[38] by William Carlos Williams, which, like the *Anabase*, deals with the military conquest of an exotic nation, but which utilizes not only qualitative progression but every other mode proper to narrative and in a masterly way. The form is exact; the rhetoric is varied and powerful; the details, unlike those of the *Anabase*, are exact both as description and, where symbolic force is intended, as symbols. Displaying fullness and precision of meaning, it is in no wise "strange" and has been ignored. But its heroic prose is superior to the prose of *Anabase* and of *Anna Livia Plurabelle*, is superior in all likelihood to nearly any other prose of our time and to most of the verse.

The so-called stream-of-consciousness convention of the contemporary novel is a form of qualitative progression. It may or may not be used to reveal a plot, but at best the revelation can be fragmentary since the convention excludes certain important functions of prose—summary, whether narrative or expository, being the chief. It approximates the manner of the chain of thought as it might be imagined in the mind of the protagonist: that is, it tends away from the reconsidered, the revised, and tends toward the fallacy of imitative form, which I have remarked in the work of Joyce and of Whitman.[39] It emphasizes, wittingly or not, abject imitation at the expense of art; it is technically naturalism; it emphasizes to the last degree the psychology of the hero, but the least interesting aspect of it, the accidental. Mr. Kenneth Burke, in his novel, *Toward a Better Life*[40] thus falls into the very pit which he has labored most diligently to avoid: he expands his entire rhetorical energy on his sentences, but lets his story run loosely through the mind of his hero. The quality of the detail is expository and aphoristic; the structure is not expository but is qualitative. One feels a discrepancy between the detail and the form; the detail appears labored, the form careless and confused.

The convention of reminiscence, a form of the stream-of-consciousness technique, which is employed by Mr. Burke and by others, has a defect peculiar to itself alone. It commonly involves the assumption, at the beginning of a story, of the state of feeling proper to the conclusion; then by means of revelation, detail by detail, the feeling is justified. In other words, the initial situations are befogged by unexplained feeling, and the feeling does not develop in a clean relationship to the events. The result is usually a kind of diffuse lyricism.

TYPE VI: THE ALTERNATION OF METHOD

Two or more methods may be used in formal arrangements. In a play or novel, where there is plenty of room for change, a great many modes of procedure may be employed. In a lyrical poem there will seldom be more than two. In Marvell's *To His Coy Mistress*, for example, the progression from stanza to stanza is logical, but within each stanza the progression is repetitive.

Mallarmé's *L'Après-Midi d'un Faune* illustrates a method toward which various writers have tended; namely to shift out of the logical into the pseudo-referent or qualitative, back into the logical, and so on, but at irregular intervals. The appearance of shifting may be due, of course, to my own inability to follow the argument, but it appears to be a real shifting. The faun recounts his adventure, trying to philosophize concerning it: hence narrative alternates with what should be exposition, but actually both narrative and exposition move in a more or less dreamy fashion at times, so that the

[38] *In the American Grain*, by W. C. Williams. A. and C. Boni, New York, 1925.

[39] This law of literary aesthetics has never that I know been stated explicitly. It might be thus formulated: Form is expressive invariably of the state of mind of the author; a state of formlessness is legitimate subject matter for literature, and in fact all subject matter, as such, is relatively formless; but the author must endeavor to give form, or meaning, to the formless—in so far as he endeavors that his own state of mind may imitate or approximate the condition of the matter, he is surrendering to the matter instead of mastering it. Form, in so far as it endeavors to imitate the formless, destroys itself.

[40] Op. cit.

cleavage in method does not coincide with the cleavage in subject matter.

TYPE VII: THE DOUBLE MOOD

A short poem or passage may be composed of alternating passages of two distinct and more or less opposed types of feeling, or of two types of feeling combined and without discernible alternation. A long poem may involve many types of feeling, but where two types alone are involved, one of them is usually ironic: it is with this situation in particular that I am here concerned. Byron, for example, commonly builds up a somewhat grandiloquent effect only to demolish it by ridicule or by ludicrous anticlimax. His effects are crude in the main, the poems being ill-written, but he was the first poet to embody on a pretentious scale, and to popularize, this common modern attitude.

The particular form which his method has taken in modern poetry is closely related to the poetry of Jules Laforgue, though Laforgue is not in every case an influence. I quote Laforgue's *Complainte du Printemps:*

> Permettez, ô sirène,
> Voici que votre haleine
> Embaume la verveine;
> C'est le printemps qui s'amène!
>
> —Ce système, en effet, ramène le printemps,
> Avec son impudent cortège d'excitants.
>
> Otez donc ces mitaines;
> Et n'ayes, inhumaine,
> Que mes soupirs pour traîne:
> Ous'qu'il y a de la gêne . . .
>
> —Ah! yeux bleus méditant sur l'ennui de leur art!
> Et vous, jeunes divins, aux soirs crus de hasard!
>
> Du géant à la naine,
> Vois, tout bon sire entraine
> Quelque contemporaine,
> Prendre l'air, par hygiène . . .
>
> —Mais vous saignez ainsi pour l'amour de l'exil!
> Pour l'amour de l'Amour! D'ailleurs, ainsi soit-il . . .
>
> T'ai-je fait de la peine?
> Oh! viens vers les fontaines
> Où tournent les phalènes
> Des nuits Elyséennes!
>
> —Pimbèche aux yeux vaincus, bellâtre aux beaux jarrets,
> Donnez votre fumier à la fleur du Regret.
>
> Voilà que son haleine
> N'embaum' plus la verveine!
> Drôle de phénomène . . .
> Hein, à l'année prochaine?
>
> Vierges d'hier, ce soir traîneuses de foetus,
> A genoux! voici l'heure où se plaint l'Angélus.
>
> Nous n'irons plus au bois,
> Les pins sont éternels,
> Les cors ont des appels! . . .
> Neiges des pâles mois,
> Vous serez mon missel!
> —Jusqu'au jour du dégel.

The opposition and cancellation of the two moods is so obvious as to need no particular comment: there is romantic nostalgia (romantic because it has no discernible object, is a form of unmotivated feeling) canceled by an immature irony (immature because it depends upon the obviously but insignificantly ridiculous, as in the third quatrain, or upon a kind of physical detail which is likely to cause pain to the adolescent but which is not likely to interest the mature, as in couplets four and five). The application of the irony, in turn, deepens the nostalgia, as in the fourth quatrain and the conclusion. It is the formula for adolescent disillusionment: the unhappily "cynical" reaction to the loss of a feeling not worth having.

A few years earlier than Laforgue, Tristan Corbière had employed the same procedure in a few poems, most vigorously in *Un Jeune Qui S'en Va,* but from his greatest work (*La Rapsode Foraine* and *Cris d'Aveugle,* two poems which are probably superior to any French verse of the nineteenth century save the best of Baudelaire), it is either absent or has lost itself amid an extremely complex cluster of feelings.

Previously to Corbière, Gautier had written in much the same fashion, but usually of very different subjects. His *Nostalgies des Obélisques* are examples. They consist of two poems, monologues spoken by two Egyptian obelisks, one of which has been transported to Paris and compares the Parisian and Egyptian scenes, lamenting the loss of the latter, the other of which remains behind, only to make the same comparison but to long for Paris. The alternations are almost mathematically balanced, though occasionally both moods will rest on a single image, as when an Egyptian animal performs a grotesquely ludicrous action in magnificent language. There is not, in Gautier, the adolescent mood of Laforgue, for Gautier was a vastly abler rhetorician and was too astute to give way to such a mood, but there is no meaning to his experience, as it appears in such poems, outside of the contrast, and the contrast is painfully precise. Gautier resembles a child fascinated by the task of separating and arranging exactly, blocks of exactly two colors. The moral sense of such a poet is too simple to hold the interest for many readings. Mr. Eliot in his quatrains employed the same formula; in fact several of his most striking lines are translated or imitated from *Emaux et Camées*.[41]

Similar to Laforgue's use of this kind of irony is Mr. Pound's use of it in *Hugh Selwyn Mauberly*.[42] The two attitudes at variance in this sequence are a nostalgic longing of which the visible object is the society of the Pre-Raphaelites and of the related poets of the nineties, and a compensatory irony which admits the mediocrity of that society or which at least ridicules its mediocre aspects. Even in the midst of the most biting comment, the yearning is unabated:

> The Burne-Jones cartons
> Have preserved her eyes;
> Still, at the Tate, they teach
> Cophetua to rhapsodize;
>
> Thin, like brook-water,
> With a vacant gaze.
> The English Rubaiyat was still-born
> In those days.[43]

And again, to quote an entire poem:

> Among the pickled foetuses and bottled bones
> Engaged in perfecting the catalogue,
> I found the last scion of the
> Senatorial families of Strassbourg, Monsieur Verog.
>
> For two hours he talked of Gallifet;
> Of Dowson; of the Rhymers' Club;
> Told me how Johnson (Lionel) died
> By falling from a high stool in a pub . . .
>
> But showed no trace of alcohol
> At the autopsy, privately performed—
> Tissues preserved—the pure mind
> Arose toward Newman as the whiskey warmed.
>
> Dowson found harlots cheaper than hotels;
> Headlam for uplift; image impartially imbued
> With raptures for Bacchus, Terpsichore, and the
> Church
> So spoke the author of "The Dorian Mood,"
>
> M. Verog, out of step with the decade,
> Detached from his contemporaries,
> Neglected by the young,
> Because of these reveries.[44]

As so often happens when this kind of irony occurs, the poem is guilty of a certain amount both of doggerel and of verbosity. It is not without virtues, however; and it is not the best poem in the sequence. It is worth noting that the two moods are not precisely separable here, as in so much of Eliot and of Gautier, but are usually coincident. This likewise is true of the irony of Wallace Stevens.

Mr. Stevens' commonest method of ironic comment is to parody his own style, with respect to its slight affectation of elegance; or perhaps it were more accurate to say that this affectation itself is a parody, however slight, of the purity of his style in its best moments. The parody frequently involves an excess of alliteration, as in the opening lines of the poem entitled *Of the Manner of Addressing Clouds:*[45]

> Gloomy grammarians in golden gowns,
> Meekly you keep the mortal rendezvous. . . .

The same device is more obviously employed in *The Comedian as the Letter C*, in which appears an explicit statement of the source of the irony, his inability to justify the practice of his art, his own lack of respect for what he is doing, and in which the irony frequently descends to the tawdry. In some poems he is entirely free of the quality, as, for examples, in *Sunday Morning, Death of a Soldier, Of Heaven Considered as a Tomb*. In such work, and in those poems

[41] *Poems 1909-25*, by T. S. Eliot: the series of poems in octosyllabic quatrains, of which the most successful is "Sweeney among the Nightingales."

[42] "Hugh Selwyn Mauberly," by Ezra Pound. Included in *Personae*, by Ezra Pound. Boni and Liveright, New York, 1926.

[43] "Yeux Glauges," from *Mauberly*.

[44] "*Siena Mi Fe': Disfecemi Maremma.*" The same.

[45] This poem and others by the same author may be found in *Harmonium*, by Wallace Stevens. Alfred A. Knopf, New York, 1931.

such as that last quoted and, to choose a more ambitious example, *Le Monocle de Mon Oncle,* in which the admixture is very slight, he is probably the greatest poet of his generation.

The double mood is not strictly post-romantic, either in English or in French, nor is ironic poetry, but both are perhaps more frequently so, and in pre-romantic poetry neither is employed for the purpose which I have been describing. For instance, in Dryden's *MacFlecknoe,* the combination of the heroic style and the satirical intention constitutes a kind of double mood, but there is no mutual cancellation; the same is true of Pope's *Dunciad,* of *La Pucelle* by Voltaire, and of a good many other poems. Churchill's *Dedication to Warburton,* in its semblance of eulogy actually covering a very bitter attack, employs both irony (as distinct from satire) and something that might be called a double mood. But in all of these examples, the poet is perfectly secure in his own feelings; he is attacking something or someone else from a point of view which he regards as tenable. The essence of romantic irony, on the other hand, is this: that the poet ridicules himself for a kind or degree of feeling which he can neither approve nor control; so that the irony is simply the act of confessing a state of moral insecurity which the poet sees no way to improve.[46]

A twentieth century ironist who resembles the earlier ironists instead of her contemporaries is Miss Marianne Moore. If one can trust the evidence of her earlier and shorter poems, she stems from the early Elizabethan epigrammatists. Turberville, a few years before Spenser and Sidney, writes *To One of Little Wit:*

I thee advise
If thou be wise
To keep thy wit
Though it be small.
'Tis hard to get
And far to fet—
'Twas ever yet
Dear'st ware of all.

[46] The relationship and partial indebtedness of this technical analysis of romantic irony to Irving Babbitt's more general treatment of the same subject in *Rousseau and Romanticism* will be evident to anyone familiar with the latter.

Miss Moore writes *To an Intramural Rat:*[47]

You make me think of many men
Once met, to be forgot again,
  Or merely resurrected
In a parenthesis of wit
That found them hastening through it
  Too brisk to be inspected.

In Miss Moore's later work, the same quality is developed through a very elaborate structure, in which the magnificent and the curious are combined with the ironical and the ludicrous: I have in mind in particular such poems as *My Apish Cousins* (later entitled *The Monkeys*), *New York, A Grave,* and *Black Earth.* These poems illustrate perfectly Miss Moore's virtues: unshakeable certainty of intention, a diction at once magnificent and ironic (her cat, for example, in *My Apish Cousins,* raises Gautier's formula for fantastic zoology into the realm of high art), and the fairly consistent control of an elaborate rhetoric. They suggest her weaknesses, which are more evident in other poems: a tendency to a rhetoric more complex than her matter, a tendency to be led astray by opportunities for description, and a tendency to base her security on a view of manners instead of morals.

The romantic antithesis of moods is the central theme of Joyce's *Ulysses,* which, at the same time, is rendered diffuse by a stream-of-consciousness technique and by the fallacy of imitative form.[48] The book has great virtues, which its admirers have long since fully enumerated, but it lacks final precision both of form and of feeling. It is adolescent as Laforgue is adolescent; it is ironic about feelings which are not worth the irony.

Mr. Kenneth Burke's novel, *Towards a Better Life,* displays the same kind of irony, which adds to the confusion coming from other sources which I have already mentioned. Mr. Burke, instead of giving us the progression of a narrative, endeavors, as I have said, to give us a progression of pure feeling. Frequently there is not even progression; we have merely a repetitious series of Laforguian antitheses.

[47] *Observations,* by Marianne Moore. The Dial Press, New York, 1924.

[48] *Ulysses,* by James Joyce. Shakespeare and Co., Paris.

Mr. Burke, in his volume of criticism, *Counter-statement*, offers the best defense with which I am familiar, of the attitudes to which I am now objecting.[49] He writes: "The ironist is essentially *impure*, even in the chemical sense of purity, since he is divided. He must deprecate his own enthusiasms, and distrust his own resentments. He will unite waveringly, as the components of his attitude, 'dignity, repugnance, the problematical, and art.' To the slogan-minded, the ralliers about a flag, the marchers who convert a simple idea into a simple action, he is an 'outsider.' Yet he must observe them with nostalgia, he must feel a kind of awe for their fertile assurance, even while remaining on the alert to stifle it with irony each time he discovers it growing in unsuspected quarters within himself."

In admitting no distinction save that between the ironist and the slogan-minded, Mr. Burke himself verges upon a dangerous enthusiasm, perhaps even upon a slogan. The whole issue comes down to the question of how carefully one is willing to scrutinize his feelings and correct them. Miss Rowena Lockett once remarked to me that Laforgue resembles a person who speaks with undue harshness and then apologizes; whereas he should have made the necessary subtractions before speaking. The objection implies an attitude more sceptical and cautious than that of Mr. Burke; instead of irony as the remedy for the unsatisfactory feeling, it recommends the waste-basket and a new beginning. And this recommendation has its basis not only in morality but in aesthetics: the romantic ironists whom I have cited write imperfectly in proportion to their irony; their attitude, which is a corruption of feeling, entails a corruption of style—that is, the irony is an admission of careless feeling, which is to say careless writing, and the stylist is weak in proportion to the grounds for his irony. To see this, one has only to compare the best work of these writers to the best of Churchill, Pope, Gay, Marot, or Voltaire.

Mr. Burke states elsewhere:[50] "The 'sum total of art' relieves the artist of the need of seeing life steadily and seeing it whole. He will presumably desire to be as comprehensive as he can, but what he lacks in adjustability can be supplied by another artist affirming some other pattern with equal conviction."

Except for the likelihood that two opposite excesses may not be equivalent to something intelligent, Mr. Burke's statement may up to a certain point be well enough for Society (whatever the word may mean in this connection), but from the standpoint of the individual seeking to train himself, it is not very helpful.

Mr. Burke does give the artist a morality, however: he bases it upon what he believes Society needs: "Alignment of forces. On the side of the practical: efficiency, prosperity, material acquisitions, increased consumption, 'new needs,' expansion, higher standards of living, progressive rather than regressive evolutions, in short ubiquitous optimism. . . . On the side of the aesthetic (the Bohemian): inefficiency, indolence, dissipation, vacillation, mockery, distrust, 'hypochondria,' non-conformity, bad sportsmanship, in short, negativism." We have here a summary of the basic notion of all of Mr. Burke's writings, the doctrine of balanced excess. Perhaps they will balance each other, and perhaps not, but suppose a man should desire to be intelligent with regard to himself alone; suppose, in other words, a particular artist should lack entirely the high altruism which Mr. Burke demands of him—of what value will he find Mr. Burke's morality? Mr. Burke's doctrine, in the realms of art and of morality, is really the least sceptical, the most self-confident possible: no point of view is tenable and hence no feeling is adequately motivated; all feeling is thus seen to be excessive, and neither more nor less excessive than any other, for there is no standard of measurement; any excess can be cancelled by an opposite excess, which is automatically equal, and careful evaluation, as it is impossible, is likewise unnecessary.

I have stated the matter very baldly, but quite fairly. Any artist holding Mr. Burke's views, in so far as he is an artist, will be restrained more or less by his natural feeling for rightness of expression; but as the theory does not, if pushed to its conclusions, admit the existence of rightness, the theory encourages shoddy writing and shoddy living. The hero of Mr. Burke's novel

49 In the essay on *Thomas Mann and André Gide*, pages 116 and following.

50 *Counterstatement*, the chapter called *Lexicon Rhetoricae*, page 231.

goes mad, for the reason that, the need of judgment having been removed by his (and Mr. Burke's) theories, the power of judgment atrophies; yet Mr. Burke continues to preach the doctrine which brought him to this end.

The perfect embodiment of Mr. Burke's doctrines, whether as an individual man, or as an allegorical representation of Society, is that Shan O'Neale who flourished in Ireland in the sixteenth century, and whose character David Hume has described as follows in his *History of England:* "He was a man equally noted for his pride, his violence, his debaucheries, and his hatred of the English nation. He is said to have put some of his followers to death because they endeavored to introduce the use of bread after the English fashion. Though so violent an enemy to luxury, he was extremely addicted to riot; and was accustomed, after his intemperance had thrown him into a fever, to plunge his body into the mire, that he might allay the flame which he had raised by former excesses."

R. P. BLACKMUR: A Critic's Job of Work *

CRITICISM, I take it, is the formal discourse of an amateur. When there is enough love and enough knowledge represented in the discourse it is a self-sufficient but by no means an isolated art. It witnesses constantly in its own life its interdependence with the other arts. It lays out the terms and parallels of appreciation from the outside in order to convict itself of internal intimacy; it names and arranges what it knows and loves, and searches endlessly with every fresh impulse or impression for better names and more orderly arrangements. It is only in this sense that poetry (or some other art) is a criticism of life; poetry names and arranges, and thus arrests and transfixes its subject in a form which has a life of its own forever separate but springing from the life which confronts it. Poetry is life at the remove of form and meaning; not life lived but life framed and identified. So the criticism of poetry is bound to be occupied at once with the terms and modes by which the remove was made and with the relation between—in the ambiguous stock phrase—content and form; which is to say with the establishment and appreciation of human or moral value. It will be the underlying effort of this essay to indicate approaches to criticism wherein these two problems—of form and value—will appear inextricable but not confused—like the stones in an arch or the timbers in a building.

These approaches—these we wish to eulogise—are not the only ones, nor the only good ones, nor are they complete. No approach opens on anything except from its own point of view and in terms of its own prepossessions. Let us set against each other for a time the facts of various approaches to see whether there is a residue, not of fact but of principle.

The approaches to—or the escapes from—the central work of criticism are as various as the heresies of the Christian church, and like them testify to occasional needs, fanatic emphasis, special interest, or intellectual pride, all flowing from and even the worst of them enlightening the same body of insight. Every critic like every theologian and every philosopher is a casuist in spite of himself. To escape or surmount the discontinuity of knowledge, each resorts to a particular heresy and makes it predominant and even omnivorous.[1]

For most minds, once doctrine is sighted and

* "A Critic's Job of Work" first appeared in *The Double Agent: Essays in Craft and Elucidation* (1935), and is reprinted here by permission of Mr. Blackmur. Mr. Blackmur (*b.* 1904) is also the author of *The Expense of Greatness* (1940), and editor of Henry James's critical prefaces, *The Art of the Novel* (1934).

[1] The rashest heresy of our day and climate is that exemplified by T. S. Eliot when he postulates an orthodoxy which exists whether anyone knows it or not.

is held to be the completion of insight, the doctrinal mode of thinking seems the only one possible. When doctrine totters it seems it can fall only into the gulf of bewilderment; few minds risk the fall; most seize the remnants and swear the edifice remains, when doctrine becomes intolerable dogma.[2] All fall notwithstanding; for as knowledge itself is a fall from the paradise of undifferentiated sensation, so equally every formula of knowledge must fall the moment too much weight is laid upon it—the moment it becomes omnivorous and pretends to be omnipotent—the moment, in short, it is taken literally. Literal knowledge is dead knowledge; and the worst bewilderment—which is always only comparative—is better than death. Yet no form, no formula, of knowledge ought to be surrendered merely because it runs the risk in bad or desperate hands of being used literally; and similarly, in our own thinking, whether it is carried to the point of formal discourse or not, we cannot only afford, we ought scrupulously to risk the use of any concept that seems propitious or helpful in getting over gaps. Only the use should be consciously provisional, speculative, and dramatic. The end-virtue of humility comes only after a long train of humiliations; and the chief labour of humbling is the constant, resourceful restoration of ignorance.

The classic contemporary example of use and misuse is attached to the name of Freud. Freud himself has constantly emphasised the provisional, dramatic character of his speculations: they are employed as imaginative illumination, to be relied on no more and no less than the sailor relies upon his buoys and beacons.[3] But the impetus of Freud was so great that a school of literalists arose with all the mad consequence of schism and heresy and fundamentalism which have no more honorable place in the scientific than the artistic imagination. Elsewhere, from one point of view, Caesarism in Rome and Berlin is only the literalist conception of the need for a positive state. So, too, the economic insights of Marxism, merely by being taken literally in their own field, are held to affect the subject and value of the arts, where actually they offer only a limited field of interest and enliven an irrelevant purpose. It is an amusing exercise—as it refreshes the terms of bewilderment and provides a common clue to the secrets of all the modes of thinking—to restore the insights of Freud and Fascism and Marxism to the terms of the Church; when the sexual drama in Freud becomes the drama of original sin, and the politics of Hitler and Lenin becomes the politics of the City of God in the sense that theology provides both the sanctions of economics and the values of culture. Controversy is in terms absolutely held, when the problems argued are falsely conceived because necessarily abstracted from "real" experience. The vital or fatal nexus is in interest and emotion and is established when the terms can be represented dramatically, almost, as it were for their own sakes alone and with only a pious or ritualistic regard for the doctrines in which they are clothed. The simple, and fatal, example is in the glory men attach to war; the vital, but precarious example, is in the intermittent conception of free institutions and the persistent reformulation of the myth of reason. Then the doctrines do not matter, since they are taken only for what they are worth (whatever rhetorical pretensions to the contrary) as guides and props, as aids to navigation. What does matter is the experience, the life represented and the value discovered, and both dramatised or enacted under the banner of doctrine. All banners are wrong-headed, but they make rallying points, free the impulse to cry out, and give meaning to the cry itself simply by making it seem appropriate.

It is on some analogue or parallel to these remarks alone that we understand and use the thought and art of those whose doctrines differ from our own. We either discount, absorb, or dominate the doctrine for the sake of the life that goes with it, for the sake of what is *formed* in the progressive act of thinking. When we do more—when we refine or elaborate the abstracted notion of form—we play a different game, which has merit of its own like chess, but which applied to the world we live in produces false dilemmas like solipsism and infant damnation.

[2] Baudelaire's sonnet *Le Gouffre* dramatises this sentiment at once as he saw it surmounted in Pascal and as it occurred insurmountably in himself.

[3] Santayana's essay "A Long Way Round to Nirvana" (in *Some Turns of Thought in Modern Philosophy*) illustrates the poetic-philosophic character of Freud's insight into death by setting up its analogue in Indian philosophy; and by his comparison only adds to the stimulus of Freud.

There is, taking solipsism for example, a fundamental distinction. Because of the logical doctrine prepared to support it, technical philosophers employ years [4] to get around the impasse in which it leaves them; whereas men of poetic imagination merely use it for the dramatic insight it contains—as Eliot uses it in the last section of the *Wasteland;* or as, say, everyone uses the residual mythology of the Greek religion—which its priests nevertheless used as literal sanctions for blood and power.

Fortunately, there exist archetypes of unindoctrinated thinking. Let us incline our minds like reflectors to catch the light of the early Plato and the whole Montaigne. Is not the inexhaustible stimulus and fertility of the Dialogues and the Essays due as much as anything to the absence of positive doctrine? Is it not that the early Plato always holds conflicting ideas in shifting balance, presenting them in contest and evolution, with victory only the last shift? Is it not that Montaigne is always making room for another idea, and implying always a third for provisional, adjudicating irony? Are not the forms of both men themselves ironic, betraying in its most intimate recesses the duplicity of every thought, pointing it out, so to speak, in the act of self-incrimination, and showing it not paled on a pin but in the buff life? . . . Such an approach, such an attempt at vivid questing, borrowed and no doubt adulterated by our own needs, is the only rational approach to the multiplication of doctrine and arrogant technologies which fills out the body of critical thinking. Anything else is a succumbing, not an approach; and it is surely the commonest of ironies to observe a man altogether out of his depth do his cause fatal harm merely because, having once succumbed to an idea, he thinks it necessary to stick to it. Thought is a beacon not a life-raft, and to confuse the functions is tragic. The tragic character of thought—as any perspective will show—is that it takes a rigid mould too soon; chooses destiny like a Calvinist, in infancy, instead of waiting slowly for old age, and hence for the most part works against the world, good sense, and its own object: as anyone may see by taking a perspective of any given idea of democracy, of justice, or the nature of the creative act.

Imaginative scepticism and dramatic irony—the modes of Montaigne and Plato—keep the mind athletic and the spirit on the stretch. Hence the juvenescence of the *Tempest,* and hence, too, perhaps, the air almost of precocity in *Back to Methuselah.* Hence, at any rate, the sustaining power of such varied works as *The Brothers Karamazoff, Cousine Bette,* and *The Magic Mountain.* Dante, whom the faithful might take to the contrary, is yet "the chief imagination of Christendom"; he took his doctrine once and for all from the Church and from St. Thomas and used it as a foil (in the painter's sense) to give recessiveness, background, and contrast. Virgil and Aristotle, Beatrice and Bertrans de Born, have in their way as much importance as St. Thomas and the Church. It was this security of reference that made Dante so much more a free spirit than were, say, Swift and Laurence Sterne. Dante had a habit (not a theory) of imagination which enabled him to dramatise with equal ardour and effect what his doctrine blessed, what it assailed, and what, at heart, it was indifferent to. Doctrine was the seed and structure of vision, and for his poems (at least to us) never more. The Divine Comedy no less than the Dialogues and the Essays is a true Speculum Mentis.

With lesser thinkers and lesser artists—and in the defective works of the greater—we have in reading, in criticising, to supply the scepticism and the irony, or, as may be, the imagination and the drama, to the degree, which cannot be complete since then we should have had no prompts, that they are lacking. We have to rub the looking-glass clear. With Hamlet, for example, we have to struggle and guess to bring the motive out of obscurity: a struggle which, aiming at the wrong end, the psychoanalysts have darkened with counsel. With Shelley we have to flesh out the Platonic Ideas, as with Blake we have to cut away, since it cannot be dramatised, all the excrescence of doctrine. With Baudelaire we have sometimes to struggle with and sometimes to suppress the problem of belief, working out the irony implicit in either attitude. Similarly, with a writer like Pascal, in order to get the most out of him, in order to compose

[4] Santayana found it necessary to resort to his only sustained labour of dialectic, *Scepticism and Animal Faith,* which, though a beautiful monument of intellectual play, is ultimately valuable for its *incidental* moral wisdom.

an artistic judgment, we must consider such an idea as that of the necessity of the wager, not solemnly as Pascal took it, but as a dramatised possibility, a savage, but provisional irony; and we need to show that the scepticisms of Montaigne and Pascal are not at all the same thing—that where one produced serenity the other produced excruciation.

Again, speaking of André Gide, we should remind ourselves not that he has been the apologist of homosexuality, not that he has become a communist, but that he is par excellence the French puritan chastened by the wisdom of the body, and that he has thus an acutely scrupulous ethical sensibility. It is by acknowledging the sensibility that we feel the impact of the apologetics and the political conversion. Another necessity in the apprehension of Gide might be put as the recognition of similarity in difference of the precocious small boys in Dostoieffsky and Gide, e.g. Kolya in *Karamazoff* and young George in *The Counterfeiters:* they are small, cruel engines, all naked sensibility and no scruple, demoniacally possessed, and used to keep things going. And these in turn may remind us of another writer who had a predilection for presenting the *terrible* quality of the young intelligence: of Henry James, of the children in *The Turn of the Screw,* of Maisie, and all the rest, all beautifully efficient agents of dramatic judgment and action, in that they take all things seriously for themselves, with the least prejudice of preparation, candidly, with an intelligence life has not yet violated.

Such feats of agility and attention as these remarks illustrate seem facile and even commonplace, and from facile points of view there is no need to take them otherwise. Taken superficially they provide escape from the whole labour of specific understanding; or, worse, they provide an easy vault from casual interpretation to an omnivorous world-view. We might take solemnly and as of universal application the two notions of demonic possession and inviolate intelligence in the children of Gide, Dostoieffsky, and James, and on that frail nexus build an unassailable theory of the sources of art, wisdom, and value; unassailable because affording only a stereotyped vision, like that of conservative capitalism, without reference in the real world. The maturity of Shakespeare and of Gertrude Stein would then be found on the same childish level.

But we need not go so far in order to draw back. The modes of Montaigne and Plato contain their own safety. Any single insight is good only at and up to a certain point of development and not beyond, which is to say that it is a provisional and tentative and highly selective approach to its field. Furthermore, no observation, no collection of observations, ever tells the whole story; there is always room for more, and at the hypothetical limit of attention and interest there will always remain, quite untouched, the thing itself. Thus the complex character—I say nothing of the value—of the remarks above reveals itself. They flow from a dramatic combination of all the skills and conventions of the thinking mind. They are commonplace only as criticism—as an end-product of function. Like walking, criticism is a pretty nearly universal art; both require a constant intricate shifting and catching of balance; neither can be questioned much in process; and few perform either really well. For either a new terrain is fatiguing and awkward, and in our day most men prefer paved walks or some form of rapid transit—some easy theory or outmastering dogma. A good critic keeps his criticism from becoming either instinctive or vicarious, and the labour of his understanding is always specific, like the art which he examines; and he knows that the sum of his best work comes only to the pedagogy of elucidation and appreciation. He observes facts and he delights in discriminations. The object remains, and should remain, itself, only made more available and seen in a clearer light. The imagination of Dante is for us only equal to what we can know of it at a given time.

Which brings us to what, as T. S. Eliot would say,[5] I have been leading up to all the time, and what has indeed been said several times by the way. Any rational approach is valid to literature and may be properly called critical which

[5] . . . that when "morals cease to be a matter of tradition and orthodoxy—that is, of the habits of the community formulated, corrected, and elevated by the continuous thought and direction of the Church—and when each man is to elaborate his own, then *personality* becomes a thing of alarming importance." (*After Strange Gods.*) Thus Mr. Eliot becomes one of those viewers-with-alarm whose next step forward is the very hysteria of disorder they wish to escape. The hysteria of institutions is more dreadful than that of individuals.

fastens at any point upon the work itself. The utility of a given approach depends partly upon the strength of the mind making it and partly upon the recognition of the limits appropriate to it. Limits may be of scope, degree, or relevance, and may be either plainly laid out by the critic himself, or may be determined by his readers; and it is, by our argument, the latter case that commonly falls, since an active mind tends to overestimate the scope of its tools and to take as necessary those doctrinal considerations which habit has made seem instinctive. No critic is required to limit himself to a single approach, nor is he likely to be able to do so; facts cannot be exhibited without comment, and comment involves the generality of the mind. Furthermore, a consciously complex approach like that of Kenneth Burke or T. S. Eliot, by setting up parallels of reference, affords a more flexible, more available, more stimulating standard of judgment—though of course at a greater risk of prejudice—than a single approach. What produces the evil of stultification and the malice of controversy is the confused approach, when the limits are not seen because they tend to cancel each other out, and the driving power becomes emotional.

The worse evil of fanatic falsification—of arrogant irrationality and barbarism in all its forms—arises when a body of criticism is governed by an *idée fixe,* a really exaggerated heresy, when a notion of genuine but small scope is taken literally as of universal application. This is the body of tendentious criticism where, since something is assumed proved before the evidence is in, distortion, vitiation, and absolute assertion become supreme virtues. I cannot help feeling that such writers as Maritain and Massis —no less than Nordau before them—are tendentious in this sense. But even here, in this worst order of criticism, there is a taint of legitimacy. Once we reduce, in a man like Irving Babbitt, the magnitude of application of such notions as the inner check and the higher will, which were for Babbitt paramount—that is, when we determine the limits within which he really worked —then the massive erudition and acute observation with which his work is packed become permanently available.

And there is no good to be got in objecting to and disallowing those orders of criticism which have an ulterior purpose. Ulterior is not in itself a pejorative, but only so when applied to an enemy. Since criticism is not autonomous—not a light but a process of elucidation—it cannot avoid discovering constantly within itself a purpose or purposes ulterior in the good sense. The danger is in not knowing what is ulterior and what is not, which is much the same as the cognate danger in the arts themselves. The arts serve purposes beyond themselves; the purposes of what they dramatise or represent at that remove from the flux which gives them order and meaning and value; and to deny those purposes is like asserting that the function of a handsaw is to hang above a bench and that to cut wood is to belittle it. But the purposes are varied and so bound in his subject that the artist cannot always design for them. The critic, if that is his bent, may concern himself with those purposes or with some one among them which obsess him; but he must be certain to distinguish between what is genuinely ulterior to the works he examines and what is merely irrelevant; and he must further not assume except within the realm of his special argument that other purposes either do not exist or are negligible or that the works may not be profitably discussed apart from ulterior purposes and as examples of dramatic possibility alone.

2

Three examples of contemporary criticism primarily concerned with the ulterior purposes of literature should, set side by side, exhibit both the defects and the unchastened virtues of that approach; though they must do so only tentatively and somewhat invidiously—with an exaggeration for effect. Each work is assumed to be a representative ornament of its kind, carrying within it the seeds of its own death and multiplication. Let us take then, with an eye sharpened by the dangers involved, Santayana's essay on Lucretius (in *Three Philosophical poets*), Van Wyck Brooks' *Pilgrimage of Henry James,* and Granville Hicks' *The Great Tradition.* Though that of the third is more obvious in our predicament, the urgency in the approach is equal in all three.

Santayana's essay represents a conversion or transvaluation of an actually poetic ordering of nature to the terms of a moral philosophy which, whatever its own responsibilities, is free of the special responsibility of poetry. So ably and so persuasively is it composed, his picture seems complete and to contain so much of what was important in Lucretius that *De Rerum Natura* itself can be left behind. The philosophical nature of the insight, its moral scope and defect, the influence upon it of the Democritan atom, once grasped intellectually as Santayana shows us how to grasp them, seem a good substitute for the poem and far more available. But, what Santayana remembers but does not here emphasise since it was beyond his immediate interest, there is no vicar for poetry on earth. Poetry is idiom, a special and fresh saying, and cannot for its life be said otherwise; and there is, finally, as much difference between words used about a poem and the poem as there is between words used about a painting and the painting. The gap is absolute. Yet I do not mean to suggest that Santayana's essay—that any philosophical criticism—is beside the point. It is true that the essay may be taken as a venture in philosophy for its own sake, but it is also true that it reveals a body of facts about an ulterior purpose in Lucretius' poem—doubtless the very purpose Lucretius himself would have chosen to see enhanced. If we return to the poem it will be warmer as the facts come alive in verse. The re-conversion comes naturally in this instance in that, through idioms differently construed but equally imaginative, philosophy and poetry both buttress and express moral value. The one enacts or represents in the flesh what the other reduces to principle or raises to the ideal. The only precaution the critic of poetry need take is negative: that neither poetry nor philosophy can ever fully satisfy the other's purposes, though each may seem to do so if taken in an ulterior fashion. The relationship is mutual but not equivalent.

When we turn deliberately from Santayana on Lucretius to Van Wyck Brooks on Henry James, we turn from the consideration of the rational ulterior purpose of art to the consideration of the irrational underlying predicament of the artist himself, not only as it predicts his art and is reflected in it, but also, and in effect predominantly, as it represents the conditioning of nineteenth century American culture. The consideration is sociological, the method of approach that of literary psychology, and the burden obsessive. The conversion is from literary to biographical values. Art is taken not as the objectification or mirroring of social experience but as a personal expression and escape-fantasy of the artist's personal life in dramatic extension. The point for emphasis is that the cultural situation of Henry James' America stultified the expression and made every escape ineffectual —even that of Europe. This theme—the private tragedy of the unsuccessful artist—was one of Henry James' own; but James saw it as typical or universal—as a characteristic tragedy of the human spirit—illustrated, as it happened for him, against the Anglo-American background. Brooks, taking the same theme, raises it to an obsession, an omnivorous concept, under which all other themes can be subsumed. Applied to American cultural history, such obsessive thinking is suggestive in the very exaggeration of its terms, and applied to the predicament of Henry James the man it dramatically emphasises—uses for all and more than it is worth—an obvious conflict that tormented him. As history or as biography the book is a persuasive imaginative picture, although clearly not the only one to be seen. Used as a nexus between James the man and the novels themselves, the book has only possible relevance and cannot be held as material. *Hamlet,* by a similar argument, could be shown to be an unsuccessful expression of Shakespeare's personality. To remain useful in the field of literary criticism, Brooks' notions ought to be kept parallel to James' novels but never allowed to merge with them. The corrective, the proof of the gap, is perhaps in the great air of freedom and sway of mastery that pervades the Prefaces James wrote to his collected edition. For James art was enough because it moulded and mirrored and valued all the life he knew. What Brooks' parallel strictures can do is to help us decide from another point of view whether to choose the values James dramatised. They cannot affect or elucidate but rather—if the gap is closed by will—obfuscate the values themselves.

In short, the order of criticism of which Brooks is a masterly exponent, and which we may call the psycho-sociological order, is primarily and in the end concerned less with the purposes, ulterior or not, of the arts than with some of the ulterior *uses* to which the arts can be appropriately put. Only what is said in the meantime, by the way—and does not depend upon the essence of argument but only accompanies it—can be applied to the arts themselves. There is nothing, it should be added, in Brooks' writings to show that he believes otherwise or would claim more; he is content with that scope and degree of value to which his method and the strength of his mind limit him; and his value is the greater and more urgent for that.

Such tacit humility, such implicit admission of contingency, are not immediate characteristics of Granville Hicks' *The Great Tradition,* though they may, so serious is his purpose, be merely virtues of which he deliberately, for the time being and in order to gain his point, deprives himself of the benefit. If that is so, however expedient his tactics may seem on the short view they will defeat him on the long. But let us examine the book on the ground of our present concern alone. Like Brooks, Hicks presents an interpretation of American literature since the Civil War, dealing with the whole body rather than single figures. Like Brooks he has a touchstone in an obsessive idea, but where we may say that Brooks *uses* his idea—as we think for more than it is worth—we must say that Hicks is victimised by his idea to the point where the travail of judgment is suspended and becomes the mere reiteration of a formula. He judges literature as it expressed or failed to express the economic conflict of classes sharpened by the industrial revolution, and he judges individual writers as they used or did not use an ideology resembling the Marxist analysis as prime clue to the clear representation of social drama. Thus Howells comes off better than Henry James, and Frank Norris better than Mark Twain, and, in our own day, Dos Passos is stuck on a thin eminence that must alarm him.

Controversy is not here a profitable exercise, but it may be said for the sake of the record that although every period of history presents a class struggle, some far more acute than our own, the themes of great art have seldom lent themselves to propaganda for an economic insight, finding, as it happened, religious, moral, or psychological—that is to say, interpretative—insights more appropriate impulses. If *Piers Plowman* dealt with the class struggle, *The Canterbury Tales* did not, and Hicks would be hard put, if he looked sharp, to make out a better case of social implication in Dostoieffsky than in Henry James.

What vitiates *The Great Tradition* is its tendentiousness. Nothing could be more exciting, nothing more vital, than a book by Hicks which discovered and examined the facts of a literature whose major theme hung on an honest, dramatic view of the class struggle—and there is indeed such a literature now emerging from the depression. And on the other hand it would be worth while to have Hicks sharpen his teeth on all the fraudulent or pseudo art which actually slanders the terms of the class and every other struggle.

The book with which he presents us performs a very different operation. There is an initial hortatory assumption that American literature ought to represent the class struggle from a Marxist view point, and that it ought thus to be the spur and guide to political action. Proceeding, the point is either proved or the literature dismissed and its authors slandered. Hicks is not disengaging for emphasis and contemporary need an ulterior purpose; he is not writing criticism at all; he is writing a fanatic's history and a casuist's polemic, with the probable result—which is what was meant by suggesting above that he had misconceived his tactics—that he will convert no one who retains the least love of literature or the least knowledge of the themes which engage the most of life. It should be emphasised that there is no more quarrel with Hicks' economic insight as such than there was with the insights of Santayana and Van Wyck Brooks. The quarrel is deeper. While it is true and good that the arts may be used to illustrate social propaganda—though it is not a great use—you can no more use an economic insight as your chief critical tool than you can make much out of the Mass by submitting the doctrine of transubstantiation to chemical analysis.

These three writers have one great formal fact in common, which they illustrate as differently as may be. They are concerned with the separable content of literature, with what may be said without consideration of its specific setting and apparition in a form; which is why, perhaps, all three leave literature so soon behind. The quantity of what can be said directly about the content alone of a given work of art is seldom great, but the least saying may be the innervation of an infinite intellectual structure, which however valuable in itself, has for the most part only an asserted relation with the works from which it springs. The sense of continuous relationship, of sustained contact, with the works nominally in hand is rare and when found uncommonly exhilarating; it is the fine object of criticism: as it seems to put us in direct possession of the principles whereby the works move without injuring or disintegrating the body of the works themselves. This sense of intimacy by inner contact cannot arise from methods of approach which hinge on seized separable content. We have constantly—if our interest is really in literature—to prod ourselves back, to remind ourselves that there was a poem, a play, or a novel of some initial and we hope terminal concern, or we have to falsify facts and set up fictions [6] to the effect that no matter what we are saying we are really talking about art after all. The question must often be whether the prodding and reminding is worth the labour, whether we might not better assign the works that require it to a different category than that of criticism.

3

Similar strictures and identical precautions are necessary in thinking of other, quite different approaches to criticism, where if there are no ulterior purposes to allow for there are other no less limiting features—there are certainly such, for example, for me in thinking of my own. The ulterior motive, or the limiting feature, which ever it is, is a variable constant. One does not always know what it is, nor what nor how much work it does; but one always knows it is there—for strength or weakness. It may be only the strength of emphasis—which is necessarily distortion; or it may be the worse strength of a simplifying formula, which skeletonises and transforms what we want to recognise in the flesh. It may be only the weakness of what is unfinished, undeveloped, or unseen—the weakness that follows on emphasis; or it may be the weakness that shows when pertinent things are deliberately dismissed or ignored, which is the corresponding weakness of the mind strong in formula. No mind can avoid distortion and formula altogether, nor would wish to; but most minds rush to the defence of qualities they think cannot be avoided, and that, in itself, is an ulterior motive, a limiting feature of the mind that rushes. I say nothing of one's personal prepossessions, of the damage of one's private experience, of the malice and false tolerance they inculcate into judgment. I know that my own essays suffer variously, but I cannot bring myself to specify the indulgences I would ask; mostly, I hope, that general indulgence which consists in the task of bringing my distortions and emphases and opinions into balance with other distortions, other emphases, and better opinions.

But rather than myself, let us examine briefly, because of their differences from each other and from the three critics already handled, the modes of approach to the act of criticism and habits of critical work of I. A. Richards, Kenneth Burke, and S. Foster Damon. It is to characterise them and to judge the *character* of their work—its typical scope and value—that we want to examine them. With the objective validity of their varying theories we are not much here concerned. Objective standards of criticism, as we hope them to exist at all, must have an existence anterior and superior to the practice of particular critics. The personal element in a given critic—what he happens to know and happens to be able to understand—is strong or obstinate enough to reach into his aesthetic theories; and as most critics do not have the coherence of philosophers it seems doubtful if any outsider could ever reach the same conclusions as the critic did by adopting his aesthetics. Aesthetics sometimes seems only as implicit in the practice of criticism as the

[6] Such a fiction, if not consciously so contrived, is the fiction of the organic continuity of all literature as expounded by T. S. Eliot in his essay, "Tradition and the Individual Talent." The locus is famous and represents that each new work of art slightly alters the relationships among the whole order of existing works. The notion has truth, but it is a mathematical truth and has little relevance to the arts. Used as Eliot uses it, it is an experimental conceit and pushes the mind forward. Taken seriously it is bad constitutional law, in the sense that it would provoke numberless artificial and insoluble problems.

atomic physics is present in sunlight when you feel it.

But some critics deliberately expand the theoretic phase of every practical problem. There is a tendency to urge the scientific principle and the statistical method, and in doing so to bring in the whole assorted world of thought. That Mr. Richards, who is an admirable critic and whose love and knowledge of poetry are incontestable, is a victim of the expansiveness of his mind in these directions, is what characterises, and reduces, the scope of his work as literary criticism. It is possible that he ought not to be called a literary critic at all. If we list the titles of his books we are in a quandary: *The Foundations of Aesthetics, The Meaning of Meaning* (these with C. K. Ogden), *The Principles of Literary Criticism, Science and Poetry, Practical Criticism, Mencius on the Mind,* and *Coleridge on Imagination.* The apparatus is so vast, so labyrinthine, so inclusive—and the amount of actual literary criticism is so small that it seems almost a by-product instead of the central target. The slightest volume, physically, *Science and Poetry,* contains proportionally the most literary criticism, and contains, curiously, his one obvious failure in appreciation—since amply redressed,—his misjudgment of the nature of Yeats' poetry. His work is for the most part *about* a department of the mind which includes the pedagogy of sensibility and the practice of literary criticism. The matters he investigates are the problems of belief, of meaning, of communication, of the nature of controversy, and of poetic language as the supreme mode of imagination. The discussion of these problems is made to focus for the most part on poetry because poetry provides the only great monuments of imagination available to verbal imagination. His bottom contention might I think be put as this: that words have a synergical power, in the realms of feeling, emotion, and value, to create a reality, or the sense of it, not contained in the words separately; and that the power and the reality as experienced in great poetry make the chief source of meaning and value for the life we live. This contention I share; except that I should wish to put on the same level, as sources of meaning and value, modes of imagination that have no medium in words—though words may call on them—and are not susceptible of verbal reformulation: the modes of great acting, architecture, music, and painting. Thus I can assent to Mr. Richards' positive statement of the task of criticism, because I can add to it positive tasks in analogous fields: "To recall that poetry is the supreme use of language, man's chief co-ordinating instrument, in the service of the most integral purposes of life; and to explore, with thoroughness, the intricacies of the modes of language as working modes of the mind." But I want this criticism, engaged in this task, constantly to be confronted with examples of poetry, and I want it so for the very practical purpose of assisting in pretty immediate appreciation of the use, meaning, and value of the language in that particular poetry. I want it to assist in doing for me what it actually assists Mr. Richards in doing, whatever that is, when he is reading poetry for its own sake.

Mr. Richards wants it to do that, too, but he wants it to do a great deal else first. Before it gets to actual poetry (from which it is said to spring) he wants literary criticism to become something else and much more: he wants it to become, indeed, the master department of the mind. As we become aware of the scope of poetry, we see, according to Mr. Richards, that "the study of the modes of language becomes, as it attempts to be thorough, the most fundamental and extensive of all inquiries. It is no preliminary or preparation for other profounder studies. . . . The very formation of the objects which these studies propose to examine takes place through the processes (of which imagination and fancy are modes) by which the words they use acquire their meanings. Criticism is the science of these meanings. . . . Critics in the future must have a theoretical equipment which has not been felt to be necessary in the past. . . . But the critical equipment will not be *primarily* philosophical. It will be rather a command *of the methods of general linguistic analysis.*" [7] I think we may take it that *Mencius on the Mind* is an example of the kind of excursion on which Mr. Richards would lead us. It is an excursion into multiple definition, and it is a good one if that is where you want to go and are in no hurry to come back: you learn the enormous variety and complexity of the opera-

[7] All quoted material is from the last four pages of *Coleridge on Imagination.*

tions possible in the process of verbally describing and defining brief passages of imaginative language and the equal variety and complexity of the result; you learn the practical impossibility of verbally ascertaining what an author means—and you hear nothing of the other ways of apprehending meaning at all. The instance is in the translation of Mencius, because Mr. Richards happens to be interested in Mencius, and because it is easy to see the difficulties of translating Chinese; but the principles and method of application would work as well on passages from Milton or Rudyard Kipling. The real point of Mr. Richards' book is the impossibility of understanding, short of a lifetime's analysis and compensation, the mechanism of meaning in even a small body of work. There is no question of the exemplary value and stimulus of Mr. Richards' work; but there is no question either that few would care to emulate him for any purpose of literary criticism. In the first place it would take too long, and in the second he does not answer the questions literary criticism would put. The literal adoption of Mr. Richards' approach to literary criticism would stultify the very power it was aimed to enhance—the power of imaginative apprehension, of imaginative coordination of varied and separate elements. Mr. Richards' work is something to be aware of, but deep awareness is the limit of use. It is notable that in his admirable incidental criticism of such poets as Eliot, Lawrence, Yeats, and Hopkins, Mr. Richards does not himself find it necessary to be more than aware of his own doctrines of linguistic analysis. As philosophy from Descartes to Bradley transformed itself into a study of the modes of knowing, Mr. Richards would transform literary criticism into the science of linguistics. Epistemology is a great subject, and so is linguistics; but they come neither in first nor final places; the one is only a fragment of wisdom and the other only a fraction of the means of understanding. Literary criticism is not a science—though it may be the object of one; and to try to make it one is to turn it upside down. Right side up, Mr. Richards' contribution shrinks in weight and dominion but remains intact and preserves its importance. We may conclude that it was the newness of his view that led him to exaggerate it, and we ought to add the probability that had he not exaggerated it we should never have seen either that it was new or valuable at all.

From another point of view than that of literary criticism, and as a contribution to a psychological theory of knowledge, Mr. Richards' work is not heretical, but is integral and integrating, and especially when it incorporates poetry into its procedure; but from our point of view the heresy is profound—and is far more distorting than the heresies of Santayana, Brooks, and Hicks, which carry with them obviously the impetus for their correction. Because it is possible to apply scientific methods to the language of poetry, and because scientific methods engross their subject matter, Mr. Richards places the whole burden of criticism in the application of a scientific approach, and asserts it to be an implement for the judgment of poetry. Actually, it can handle only the language and its words and cannot touch—except by assertion—the imaginative product of the words which is poetry: which is the object revealed or elucidated by criticism. Criticism must be concerned, first and last—whatever comes between—with the poem as it is read and as what it represents is felt. As no amount of physics and physiology can explain the *feeling* of things seen as green or even certify their existence, so no amount of linguistic analysis can explain the *feeling* or existence of a poem. Yet the physics in the one case and the linguistics in the other may be useful both to the poet and the reader. It may be useful, for example, in extracting the facts of meaning from a poem, to show that, whether the poet was aware of it or not, the semantic history of a word was so and so; but only if the semantics can be resolved into the ambiguities and precisions created by the poem. Similarly with any branch of linguistics; and similarly with the applications of psychology—Mr. Richards' other emphasis. No statistical description can either explain or demean a poem unless the description is translated back to the imaginative apprehension or feeling which must have taken place without it. The light of science is parallel or in the background where feeling or meaning is concerned. The Oedipus complex does not explain *Oedipus Rex;* not that Mr. Richards would think it did. Otherwise he could not believe that "poetry is the supreme use of language" and more, could not convey in his comments on T. S. Eliot's *Ash Wednesday* the actuality of his belief that poetry is the supreme use.

It is the interest and fascination of Mr. Richards' work in reference to different levels of sensibility, including the poetic, that has given him both a wide and a penetrating influence. No literary critic can escape his influence; an influence that stimulates the mind as much as anything by showing the sheer excitement as well as the profundity of the problems of language—many of which he has himself made genuine problems, at least for readers of poetry: an influence, obviously, worth deliberately incorporating by reducing it to one's own size and needs. In T. S. Eliot the influence is conspicuous if slight. Mr. Kenneth Burke is considerably indebted, partly directly to Mr. Richards, partly to the influences which acted upon Mr. Richards (as Bentham's theory of Fictions) and partly to the frame of mind which helped mould them both. But Mr. Burke is clearly a different person—and different from anyone writing today; and the virtues, the defects, and the élan of his criticism are his own.

Some years ago, when Mr. Burke was an animating influence on the staff of *The Dial*, Miss Marianne Moore published a poem in that magazine called "Picking and Choosing" which contained the following lines.

and Burke is a
psychologist—of acute and raccoon-
like curiosity. *Summa diligentia;*
to the humbug, whose name is so very amusing—very young
and ve-
ry rushed, Caesar crossed the Alps on the 'top of a
diligence.' We are not daft about the meaning but this
familiarity
with wrong meanings puzzles one.

In the index of Miss Moore's *Observations*, we find under Burke that the reference is to Edmund, but it is really to Kenneth just the same. There is no acuter curiosity than Mr. Burke's engaged in associating the meanings, right and wrong, of the business of literature with the business of life and vice versa. No one has a greater awareness—not even Mr. Richards—of the important part wrong meanings play in establishing the consistency of right ones. The writer of whom he reminds us, for the buoyancy and sheer remarkableness of his speculations, is Charles Santiago Saunders Peirce; one is enlivened by them without any *necessary* reference to their truth; hence they have truth for their own purposes, that is, for their own uses. Into what these purposes or uses are it is our present business to inquire.

As Mr. Richards in fact uses literature as a springboard or source for a scientific method of a philosophy of value, Mr. Burke uses literature, not only as a springboard but also as a resort or home, for a philosophy or psychology of moral possibility. Literature is the hold-all and the persuasive form for the patterns of possibility. In literature we see unique possibilities enacted, actualised, and in the moral and psychological philosophies we see the types of possibility generalised, see their abstracted, convertible forms. In some literature, and in some aspects of most literature of either great magnitude or great possibility, we see, so to speak, the enactment or dramatic representation of the type or patterns. Thus Mr. Burke can make a thrilling intellectual pursuit of the subintelligent writing of Erskine Caldwell: where he shows that Caldwell gains a great effect of humanity by putting in *none himself*, appealing to the reader's common stock: i.e., what is called for so desperately by the pattern of the story must needs be generously supplied. Exactly as thrilling is his demonstration of the great emotional role of the outsider as played in the supremely intelligent works of Thomas Mann and André Gide. His common illustrations of the pervasive spread of symbolic pattern are drawn from Shakespeare and from the type of the popular or pulp press. I think that on the whole his method could be applied with equal fruitfulness either to Shakespeare, Dashiell Hammet, or Marie Corelli; as indeed he does apply it with equal force both to the field of anarchic private morals and to the outline of a secular conversion to Communism—as in, respectively, *Toward a Better Life* and *Permanence and Change*.

The real harvest that we barn from Mr. Burke's writings is his presentation of the types of ways the mind works in the written word. He is more interested in the psychological means of the meaning, and how it might mean (and often really does) something else, than in the meaning itself. Like Mr. Richards, but for another purpose, he is engaged largely in the meaning of meaning, and is therefore much bound up with considerations of language, but on the plane of emotional and intellectual patterns rather than on the emotional plane; which is why his essays deal with literature (or other writings) as it dramatises or unfolds character (a character is a pattern of emotions and notions) rather than with lyric or meditative poetry which is Mr. Richards' field. So we find language containing felt character as well as felt coordination. The representation of character, and of aspiration and symbol, must always be rhetorical; and therefore we find that for Mr. Burke the rightly rhetorical is the profoundly hortatory. Thus literature may be seen as an inexhaustible reservoir of moral or character philosophies in action.

It is the technique of such philosophies that Mr. Burke explores, as he pursues it through curiosities of development and conversion and duplicity; it is the technique of the notions that may be put into or taken out of literature, but it is only a part of the technique of literature itself. The final reference is to the psychological and moral possibilities of the mind, and these certainly do not exhaust the technique or the reality of literature. The reality in literature is an object of contemplation and of feeling, like the reality of a picture or a cathedral, not a route of speculation. If we remember this and make the appropriate reductions here as elsewhere, Mr. Burke's essays become as pertinent to literary criticism as they are to the general ethical play of the mind. Otherwise they become too much a methodology for its own sake on the one hand, and too much a philosophy at one remove on the other. A man writes as he can; but those who use his writings have the further responsibility of redefining their scope, an operation (of which Mr. Burke is a master) which alone uses them to the full.

It is in relation to these examples which I have so unjustly held up of the philosophical, the sociological or historical, the tendentious, the semasiological, and the psychological approaches to criticism that I wish to examine an example of what composes, after all, the great bulk of serious writings about literature: a work of literary scholarship. Upon scholarship all other forms of literary criticism depend, so long as they are criticism, in much the same way that architecture depends on engineering. The great editors of the last century—men such as Dyce and Skeat and Gifford and Furness—performed work as valuable to the use of literature, and with far less complement of harm, as men like Hazlitt and Arnold and Pater. Scholarship, being bent on the collection, arrangement, and scrutiny of facts, has the positive advantage over other forms of criticism that it is a co-operative labour, and may be completed and corrected by subsequent scholars; and it has the negative advantage that it is not bound to investigate the mysteries of meaning or to connect literature with other departments of life—it has only to furnish the factual materials for such investigations and connections. It is not surprising to find that the great scholars are sometimes good critics, though usually in restricted fields; and it is a fact, on the other hand, that the great critics are themselves either good scholars or know how to take great advantage of scholarship. Perhaps we may put it that for the most part dead critics remain alive in us to the extent that they form part of our scholarship. It is Dr. Johnson's statements of fact that we preserve of him as a critic; his opinions have long since become a part of that imaginative structure, his personality. A last fact about scholarship is this, that so far as its conclusions are sound they are subject to use and digestion not debate by those outside the fold. And of bad scholarship as of bad criticism we have only to find means to minimise what we cannot destroy.

It is difficult to find an example of scholarship pure and simple, of high character, which can be made to seem relevant to the discussion in hand. What I want is to bring into the discussion the omnipresence of scholarship as a background and its immediate and necessary availability to every other mode of approach. What I want is almost anonymous. Failing that, I choose S. Foster Damon's *William Blake* (as I might have taken J. L. Lowe's *Road to Xanadu*) which, because of its special subject matter, brings its scholarship a little nearer the terms of discussion than a Shakespeare commentary would have done. The scholar's major problem with Blake happened to be one which many scholars could not handle, some refused to see, and some fumbled. A great part of Blake's meaning is not open to ordinarily well-instructed readers, but must be brought out by the detailed solution of something very like an enormous and enormously complicated acrostic puzzle. Not only earnest scrutiny of the poems as printed, but also a study of Blake's reading, a reconstruction of habits of thought, and an industrious piecing together into a consistent key of thousands of clues throughout the work, were necessary before many even of the simplest appearing poems could be explained. It is one thing to explain a mystical poet, like Crashaw, who was attached to a recognised church, and difficult enough; but it is a far more difficult thing to explain a mystical poet like Blake, who was so much an eclectic in his sources that his mystery as well as his apprehension of it was practically his own. All Mr. Damon had to go on besides the texts, and the small body of previous scholarship that was pertinent, were the general outlines of insight to which all mystics apparently adhere. The only explanation would be in the facts of what Blake meant to mean when he habitually said one thing in order to hide and enhance another; and in order to be convincing—poetry being what it is—the facts adduced had to be self-evident. It is not a question here whether the mystery enlightened was worth it. The result for emphasis is that Mr. Damon made Blake exactly what he seemed least to be, perhaps the most intellectually consistent of the greater poets in English. Since the chief weapons used are the extended facts of scholarship, the picture Mr. Damon produced cannot be destroyed even though later and other scholarship modifies, re-arranges, or adds to it with different or other facts. The only suspicion that might attach is that the picture is too consistent and that the facts are made to tell too much, and direct, but instructed, apprehension not enough.

My point about Mr. Damon's work is typical and double. First, that the same sort of work, the adduction of ultimately self-evident facts, can be done and must be done in other kinds of poetry than Blake's. Blake is merely an extreme and obvious example of an unusually difficult poet who hid his facts on purpose. The work must be done to the appropriate degree of digging out the facts in all orders of poetry—and especially perhaps in contemporary poetry, where we tend to let the work go either because it seems too easy or because it seems supererogatory. Self-evident facts are paradoxically the hardest to come by; they are not evident till they are seen; yet the meaning of a poem—the part of it which is intellectually formulable—must invariably depend on this order of facts, the facts about the meanings of the elements aside from their final meaning in combination. The rest of the poem, what it is, what it shows, its final value as a created emotion, its meanings, if you like, *as* a poem, cannot in the more serious orders of poetry develop itself to the full without this factual or intellectual meaning to show the way. The other point is already made, and has been made before in this essay, but it may still be emphasised. Although the scholarly account is indispensable it does not tell the whole story. It is only the basis and perhaps ultimately the residue of all the other stories. But it must be seen to first.

My own approach, such as it is, and if it can be named, does not tell the whole story either; the reader is conscientiously left with the poem with the real work yet to do; and I wish to advance it—as indeed I have been advancing it *seriatim*—only in connection with the reduced and compensated approaches I have laid out; and I expect, too, that if my approach is used at all it will require its own reduction as well as its compensations. Which is why this essay has taken its present form, preferring for once, in the realm of theory and apologetics, the implicit to the explicit statement. It is, I suppose, an approach to literary criticism—to the discourse of an amateur—primarily through the technique, in the widest sense of that word, of the examples handled; technique on the plane of words and even of linguistics in Mr. Richards' sense, but also technique on the plane of intellectual and emotional patterns in Mr. Burke's sense, and technique, too, in that there is a technique of securing and arranging and representing a fundamental view of life. The advantage of the technical approach is I think double. It readily admits other approaches and is anxious to be complemented by them. Furthermore, in a sense, it is able to incorporate the technical aspect, which always exists, of what is secured by other approaches—as I have argued elsewhere that so unpromising a matter as T. S.

Eliot's religious convictions may be profitably considered as a dominant element in his technique of revealing the actual. The second advantage of the technical approach is a consequence of the first; it treats of nothing in literature except in its capacity of reduction to literary fact, which is where it resembles scholarship, only passing beyond it in that its facts are usually further into the heart of the literature than the facts of most scholarship. Aristotle, curiously, is here the type and master; as the *Poetics* is nothing but a collection and explanation of the facts of Greek poetry, it is the factual aspect that is invariably produced. The rest of the labour is in the effort to find understandable terms to fit the composition of the facts. After all, it is only the facts about a poem, a play, a novel, that can be reduced to tractable form, talked about, and examined; the rest is the product of the facts, from the technical point of view, and not a product but the thing itself from its own point of view. The rest, whatever it is, can only be known, not talked about.

But facts are not simple or easy to come at; not all the facts will appear to one mind, and the same facts appear differently in the light of different minds. No attention is undivided, no single approach sufficient, no predilection guaranteed, when facts or what their arrangements create are in question. In short, for the arts, *mere* technical scrutiny of any order, is not enough without the direct apprehension—which may come first or last—to which all scrutinies that show facts contribute.

It may be that there are principles that cover both the direct apprehension and the labour of providing modes for the understanding of the expressive arts. If so, they are Socratic and found within, and subject to the fundamental scepticism as in Montaigne. There must be seeds, let us say—seeds, germs, beginning forms upon which I can rely and to which I resort. When I use a word, an image, a notion, there must be in its small nodular apparent form, as in the peas I am testing on my desk, at least prophetically, the whole future growth, the whole harvested life; and not rhetorically nor in a formula, but stubbornly, pervasively, heart-hidden, materially, in both the anterior and the eventual prospect as well as in the small handled form of the nub. What is it, what are they, these seeds of understanding? And if I know, are they logical? Do they take the processional form of the words I use? Or do they take a form like that of the silver backing a glass, a dark that enholds all brightness? Is every metaphor—and the assertion of understanding is our great metaphor—mixed by the necessity of its intention? What is the mixture of a word, an image, a notion?

The mixture, if I may start a hare so late, the mixture, even in the fresh use of an old word, is made in the pre-conscious, and is by hypothesis unascertainable. But let us not use hypotheses, let us not desire to ascertain. By intuition we adventure in the pre-conscious; and there, where the adventure is, there is no need or suspicion of certainty or meaning; there is the living, expanding, *prescient* substance without the tags and handles of conscious form. Art is the looking-glass of the pre-conscious, and when it is deepest seems to participate in it sensibly. Or, better, for purposes of criticism, our sensibility resumes the division of the senses and faculties at the same time that it preens itself into conscious form. Criticism may have as an object the establishment and evaluation (comparison and analysis) of the modes of making the pre-conscious *consciously* available.

But this emphasis upon the pre-conscious need not be insisted on; once recognised it may be tacitly assumed, and the effort of the mind will be, as it were, restored to its own plane—only a little sensitive to the tap-roots below. On its own plane—that is the plane where almost everything is taken for granted in order to assume adequate implementation in handling what is taken for granted by others; where because you can list the items of your bewilderment and can move from one to another you assert that the achievement of motion is the experience of order;—where, therefore, you must adopt always an attitude of provisional scepticism; where, imperatively, you must scrutinise until you have revealed, if it is there, the inscrutable divination, or, if it is not, the void of personal ambition; where, finally, you must stop short only when you have, with all the facts you can muster, indicated, surrounded, detached, somehow found the way demonstrably to get at, in pretty conscious terms which others may use, the substance of your chosen case.

L. C. KNIGHTS:

Restoration Comedy: The Reality and the Myth *

HENRY JAMES—whose "social comedy" may be allowed to provide a standard of maturity—once remarked that he found Congreve "insufferable," [1] and perhaps the first thing to say of Restoration drama—tragedy as well as comedy—is that the bulk of it is insufferably dull. There are long stretches of boredom to be found in the lower ranges of Elizabethan drama, but there is nothing comparable to the unmitigated fatigue that awaits the reader of *Love in a Tub, Sir Martin Mar-all, Mr. Limberham, The Relapse,* or *The Mourning Bride.* And who returns to Dryden's heroic plays with renewed zest? The superiority of the common run of plays in the first period to that of the second is, at all events, a commonplace. It should be equally commonplace that the strength of the Elizabethan drama lies partly in the kind and scope—the quality and variety—of the interests that the playwrights were able to enlist, partly in the idiom that they had at their command: the drama drew on a vigorous non-dramatic literature, and literature in general was in close relation with non-literary interests and a rich common language. That is not the whole story, but it is an important part of it, and it seems profitable, in a discussion of Restoration comedy, to keep these facts in mind for comparison. Ever since Collier published *A Short View of the Profaneness and Immorality of the English Stage* opponents of Restoration comedy have conducted their case almost entirely in moral terms, and it has been easy for recent critics, rightly discarding Lamb's obvious subterfuge, to turn the moral argument upside down, to find freedom of manners where Macaulay found licentiousness. "Morals" are, in the long run, decidedly relevant—but only in the long run: literary criticism has prior claims. If, to start with, we try to see the comedy of manners in relation to its contemporary non-dramatic literature—to take its bearings in the general culture of the time—we may at least make possible a free and critical approach.

During the forty years that followed the Restoration, English literature, English culture, was "upper-class" to an extent that it had never been before, and was not, after Addison, to be again. "Now if they ask me," said Dryden, "whence it is that our conversation is so much refined? I must freely and without flattery, ascribe it to the court," and his insistence, as a writer, on "the benefit of converse" with his courtly patrons was not merely dedicatory fulsomeness; the influence of the current conception of "the gentleman" is shown plainly enough by the urbane ease of his critical prefaces; and Dryden's non-dramatic prose is fairly representative of the new age.[2]

It is this that explains why, if one comes to Restoration literature after some familiarity with the Elizabethans, the first impression made by the language is likely to be a sense of what has been lost; the disintegration of the old cultural unity has plainly resulted in impoverishment. The speech of the educated is now remote from the speech of the people (Bunyan's huge sales were, until the eighteenth century, outside "the circumference of wit"), and idiomatic vig-

* "Restoration Comedy: The Reality and the Myth" first appeared in *Scrutiny,* and was later included in *Explorations: Essays in Criticism Mainly on the Literature of the Seventeenth Century* (1946), from which it is here reprinted by permission of George W. Stewart, Publisher, Inc. Mr. Knights (*b.* 1906) is also the author of *Drama and Society in the Age of Jonson* (1937).

1 *Letters,* Vol. I, p. 140.

2 On "the last and greatest advantage of our writing, which proceeds from *conversation,*" see in particular the *Defence of the Epilogue.* And the dialogue form in which Dryden cast the *Essay of Dramatic Poesy* was not unrecognizably far from actuality.

our and evocative power seem to have gone out of the literarv medium. But there was gain as well as loss. The common mode of Restoration prose—for there is now a common mode, a norm—was not evolved merely in the interests of good form and polite intercourse; it had behind it a more serious pressure. When, in 1667, Sprat attacked "this vicious abundance of phrase . . . this volubility of tongue, which makes so great a noise in the world," he had in mind the needs of scientific inquiry and rational discussion. "They have therefore," he said of the Royal Society, "been most rigorous in putting in execution the only remedy that can be found for this *extravagance,* and that has been a constant resolution to reject all amplifications, digressions, and swellings of style; to return back to the primitive purity and shortness, when men delivered so many *things* almost in an equal number of *words.* They have exacted from all their members a close, naked, natural way of speaking, positive expressions, clear senses, a native easiness, bringing all things as near the mathematical plainness as they can." [3] For the first time the English language was made—and to some extent made consciously—an instrument for rational dissection.

When once the aversion to bear uneasiness taketh place in a man's mind, it doth so check all the passions, that they are dampt into a kind of indifference; they grow faint and languishing, and come to be subordinate to that fundamental maxim, of not purchasing any thing at the price of a difficulty. This made that he had as little eagerness to oblige, as he had to hurt men; the motive of his giving bounties was rather to make men less uneasy to him, than more easy to themselves; and yet no ill-nature all this while. He would slide from an asking face, and could guess very well. It was throwing a man off from his shoulders, that leaned upon them with his whole weight; so that the party was not gladder to receive, than he was to give.

This is from Halifax's *Character of Charles II,* and the even tone, the sinuous ease of movement and the clarity of the analysis mark the passage as unmistakably post-Restoration. Halifax, of course, is in some ways an unusually handsome representative of his age; he is racy (the apt adjective is supplied by his editor, H. C. Foxcroft) as well as polite. But the achievement represented by his style was far from being a merely individual achievement. The shrewd and subtle portrait of Charles II is unlike anything that had appeared in English before his time, and it could only have appeared when it did.

[3] *The History of the Royal Society of London:* Spingarn, *Critical Essays of the Seventeenth Century,* Vol. II, pp. 112 ff.

Now an upper-class culture that produced *Absalom and Achitophel, The Character of a Trimmer,* Dryden's critical prefaces and Locke's *Second Treatise of Government,* may have been limited, but it was not altogether decadent. If the drama is inferior it is not because it represents—by Elizabethan standards—a limited culture, but because it represents contemporary culture so inadequately; it has no significant relation with the best thought of the time. Heroic tragedy is decadent because it is factitious; it substitutes violent emotionalism for emotion, the purple patch for poetry, and its rhetoric, unlike Elizabethan dramatic rhetoric, has no connexion with the congenial non-dramatic modes of the age; it is artificial in a completely damaging sense, *and by contemporary standards.* If we look for an early illustration of the bad mid-eighteenth-century conception of poetry as something applied from the outside [4] we find it in Dryden's verse plays, where he adopts canons of style that he would not have dreamed of applying—apart from his Odes—in his non-dramatic verse. Tragedy, he said, "is naturally pompous and magnificent." Nothing in English literature is more surprising—if we stop to consider—than the complete discrepancy between the sinewy ease of Dryden's satires and the stiff opaqueness of his dramatic verse; and "the lofty style," since it cannot modulate, is always coming down with a bump.

I'm pleased and pained, since first her eyes I saw,
As I were stung with some tarantula.
Arms, and the dusty field, I less admire,
And soften strangely in some new desire;
Honour burns in me not so fiercely bright,
But pales as fires when mastered by the light:
Even while I speak and look, I change yet more,
And now am nothing that I was before.

[4] ". . . enriching every subject (otherwise dry and barren) with a pomp of diction and luxuriant harmony of numbers."—Gray's note to *The Progress of Poesy,* 1754.

I'm numbed, and fixed, and scarce my eyeballs move;
I fear it is the lethargy of love! [5]

It is only in the easy strength of occasional lines ("A good, luxurious, palatable faith") that we hear his natural voice. In the plays as a whole—each made up of a succession of "great" moments and heroic postures—the "nature" that is "wrought up to a higher pitch" [6] bears little resemblance to the Nature that was to figure so largely in the Augustan code.

This, or a similar account, would probably be accepted by all critics of the Restoration heroic play. What is not commonly recognized (it is, at all events, not said) is that the comedy of manners exhibits a parallel attenuation and enfeeblement of what the age, taken as a whole, had to offer. I am not, for the moment, referring to the moral or social code expressed. The observation to start from is that the prose in which Restoration comedy is written—select which dramatist you like—is poor and inexpressive in comparison with the staple non-dramatic prose.

Congreve is usually accepted as the most brilliant stylist of the five or six comic dramatists who count. But place beside the extract quoted from Halifax a passage or two from *Love for Love* or *The Way of the World* (it makes no difference whether the speaker is Scandal or Mirabell), and Congreve's style shows as nerveless in the comparison:

A mender of reputations! ay, just as he is a keeper of secrets, another virtue that he sets up for in the same manner. For the rogue will speak aloud in the posture of a whisper; and deny a woman's name, while he gives you the marks of her person: he will forswear receiving a letter from her, and at the same time show you her hand in the superscription; and yet perhaps he has counterfeited the hand too, and sworn to a truth; but he hopes not to be believed; and refuses the reputation of a lady's favour, as a doctor says *No* to a bishopric, only that it may be granted him. In short, he is a public professor of secrecy, and makes proclamation that he holds private intelligence.

A. To give t' other his due, he has something of good nature, and does not always want wit.

B. Not always: but as often as his memory fails him, and his common-place of comparisons. He is a fool with a good memory, and some few scraps of other folks' wit. He is one whose conversation can never be approved, yet it is now and then to be endured. He has indeed one good quality, he is not exceptious; for he so passionately affects the reputation of understanding raillery, that he will construe an affront into a jest; and call downright rudeness and ill language, satire and fire.

This reminds me of Arnold's definition of Macaulayese, "the external characteristic being a hard metallic movement with nothing of the soft play of life, and the internal characteristic being a perpetual semblance of hitting the right nail on the head without the reality." Both construction and movement are so far from being expressive *of* anything in particular that the main function of some words is, it seems, to complete an antithesis or to display a riddling wit.[7] The verbal pattern appears at times to be completely unrelated to a mode of perceiving. The passages quoted have an air of preening themselves on their acute discriminations, but the antitheses are mechanical, and the pattern is monotonously repeated: "She has beauty enough to make any man think she has wit; and complaisance enough not to contradict him who should tell her so"—the common form soon loses the sting of surprise. Burnet can write in an antithetical style which also penetrates:

And tho' he desired to become absolute, and to overturn both our religion and our laws, yet he would neither run the risk, nor give himself the trouble, which so great a design required. He had an appearance of gentleness in his outward deportment: but he seemed to have no bowels nor tenderness in his nature: and in the end of his life he became cruel.[8]

[5] *The Conquest of Granada*, Part I, III, i.

[6] ". . . the nature of a serious play; this last is indeed the representation of nature, but 'tis nature wrought up to a higher pitch."—*Of Dramatic Poesy*. The final paragraph of the Preface to *Religio Laici* has some interesting remarks in this connexion; e.g. "The florid, elevated, and figurative way is for the passions."

[7] *The Old Bachelor* shows the riddles in the process of manufacture. *Bellmour:* He is the drum to his own praise—the only implement of a soldier he resembles; like that, being full of blustering noise and emptiness. *Sharper:* And like that, of no use but to be beaten, etc.

[8] I quote from Professor Nichol Smith's excellent anthology, *Characters from the Histories and Memoirs of the Seventeenth Century* (Clarendon Press), p. 222.

The nearest approach to subtlety that Congreve's style allows is represented by such things as this:

Fainall. You are a gallant man, Mirabell; and though you may have cruelty enough not to satisfy a lady's longing, you have too much generosity not to be tender of her honour. Yet you speak with an indifference which seems to be affected, and confesses you are conscious of a negligence.

Mirabell. You pursue the argument with a distrust that seems to be unaffected, and confess you are conscious of a concern for which the lady is more indebted to you than is your wife.

It isn't, really, very subtle. As for the "wit," when it isn't merely verbal and obvious ("Fruitful, the head fruitful;—that bodes horns; the fruit of the head is horns," etc.) it is hopelessly dependent on convention.

She that marries a fool, Sir Sampson, forfeits the reputation of her honesty or understanding: and she that marries a very witty man is a slave to the severity and insolent conduct of her husband. I should like a man of wit for a lover, because I would have such a man in my power; but I would no more be his wife than his enemy. For his malice is not a more terrible consequence of his aversion than his jealousy is of his love.

An intelligent husband, you see, must be jealous; take away that entertaining assumption and the point is blunted. Halifax is a witty writer, but his wit springs naturally from the situation he is concerned with and illuminates it:—"A partner in government is so unnatural a thing that it is a squint-eyed allegiance which must be paid to such a double-bottomed monarchy." [9] Congreve's wit is entirely self-regarding.

If there were space to discuss the manner of Wycherley, Etherege and Vanbrugh, it is a similar account that would have to be given. I am not suggesting that they write in a completely indistinguishable common mode (though they all have passages that might come from any play); but in essentials—in the way in which they use their similes and antitheses, in the conception of "style" and "wit" that they exhibit—they all stand together. Not one of them has achieved a genuinely sensitive and individual mode of expression; and in each the pattern of the prose inhibits any but the narrowest—and the most devastatingly *expected*—response. That, I should claim, is the judgment to which an analysis of their prose inevitably leads. The trouble is not that the Restoration comic writers deal with a limited number of themes, but that they bring to bear a miserably limited set of attitudes. And these, in turn, are factitious to exactly the same degree as the prose is artificial and non-representative of the current non-dramatic medium.

2

Apart from the presentation of incidental and unrelated "wit" (which soon becomes as tiring as the epigrams of the "good talker"), Restoration comedy has two main interests—the behaviour of the polite and of pretenders to politeness, and some aspects of sexual relationships. Critics have made out a case for finding in one or other of these themes a unifying principle and a serious base for the comedy of manners. According to Miss Lynch, the "thoroughly conventionalized social mode" of the courtly circle "was discovered to have manifestly comic aspects, both when awkwardly misinterpreted, and when completely fulfilled through personalities to which, however, it could not give complete expression," [10] and both these discrepancies were exploited by Etherege and his successors. Bonamy Dobrée, attributing to the comic dramatists "a deep curiosity, and a desire to try new ways of living," finds that "the distinguishing characteristic of Restoration comedy down to Congreve is that it is concerned with the attempt to rationalize sexual relationships. It is this that makes it different from any other comedy that has ever been written. . . . It said in effect, 'Here is life lived upon certain assumptions; see what it becomes.' It also dealt, as no other comedy has ever done, with a subject that arose directly out of this, namely sex-antagonism, a consequence of the experimental freedom allowed to women, which gave matter for some of its most brilliant scenes." [11]

These accounts, as developed, certainly look impressive, and if Restoration comedy really

[9] Also from *The Character of a Trimmer:*—". . . the indecent courtship of some silken divines, who, one would think, did practise to bow at the altar, only to learn to make the better legs at Court."

[10] K. M. Lynch, *The Social Mode of Restoration Comedy*, p. 216.

[11] Bonamy Dobrée, *Restoration Comedy*, pp. 22-23

answered to them—if it had something fresh and penetrating to say on sex and social relations—there would be no need to complain, even if one found the "solutions" distasteful. But Miss Lynch's case, at all events, depends on a vigorous reading into the plays of values which are not there, values which could not possibly be expressed, in fact, in the prose of any of the dramatists. (The candid reader can turn up the passages selected by Miss Lynch in support of her argument, and see if they are not all in the factitious, superficial mode that I have described.)

We may consider, by way of illustration, Etherege's *The Man of Mode.* When the play opens, Dorimant ("the finest of all fine gentlemen in Restoration comedy") is trying to rid himself of an old mistress, Mrs. Loveit, before taking up with a new, Bellinda, whilst Young Bellair, in love with Emilia, is trying to find some way out of marrying Harriet, an heiress whom his father has brought to town for him. The entertainment is made up of these two sets of complications, together with an exhibition of the would-be modishness of Sir Fopling Flutter. Events move fast. After a night spent in various sociabilities Dorimant keeps an appointment with Bellinda at 5 A.M. Letting her out of his lodgings an hour or so later, and swearing to be discreet "By all the Joys I have had, and those you keep in store," he is surprised by his companions, and in the resulting confusion Bellinda finds herself paying an unwilling visit to Mrs. Loveit. Dorimant appears and is rated by the women before he "flings off." Meanwhile Young Bellair and Emilia have secretly married. Dorimant, his equanimity recovered, turns up for the exposure, followed by his mistresses. The lovers are forgiven, the mistresses are huddled off the stage, and it is decided that Dorimant, who, the previous day, had ingratiated himself with Harriet's mother, and whose "soul has quite given up her liberty," shall be allowed to pay court to the heiress.

It seems to me that what the play provides—apart from the briskly handled intrigue—is a demonstration of the physical stamina of Dorimant. But Miss Lynch sees further. For her, Dorimant is "the fine flowering of Restoration culture." Illustrating her theory of the double standard, she remarks: "We laugh at Sir Fopling Flutter because he so clumsily parodies social fashions which Dorimant interprets with unfailing grace and distinction. We laugh at Dorimant because his assumed affectation admits of so poor and incomplete an expression of an attractive and vigorous personality." [12] The "unfailing grace and distinction" are perhaps not much in evidence in Dorimant's spiteful treatment of Mrs. Loveit; [13] but even if we ignore those brutish scenes we are forced to ask, How do we know that there *is* this "attractive and vigorous personality" beneath the conventional forms? Dorimant's intrigues are of no more human significance than those of a barn-yard cock, and as for what Miss Lynch calls "his really serious affair with Harriet" (I feel this deserves a *sic*), it is purely theatrical, and the "pangs of love" are expressed in nothing but the conventional formulae: "She's gone, but she has left a pleasing Image of herself behind that wanders in my Soul." The answer to the question posed is that Miss Lynch's account is a mere assumption. Nothing that Dorimant actually *says* will warrant it—and nothing in the whole of Restoration comedy—in the words actually spoken—allows us a glimpse of those other "personalities" to which the conventional social modes "could not give complete expression." The "real values" [14] simply are not there.

A minor point can be made in passing. It is just possible to claim that Restoration comedy contains "social criticism" in its handling of "the vulgar." "Come, Mr. Sharper," says Congreve's Bellinda, "you and I will take a turn, and laugh at the vulgar; both the great vulgar and the small," and Etherege's Lady Townley expresses the common attitude of the polite to-

[12] *The Social Mode of Restoration Comedy,* p. 181.

[13] See II, ii and V, i, where Dorimant, trying to force a quarrel with Mrs. Loveit, attributes to her a fondness for Sir Fopling. The first of these scenes was too much for Etherege, and he makes Bellinda say:

> He's given me the proof which I desired of his love,
> But 'tis a proof of his ill nature too.
> I wish I had not seen him use her so.

But this is soon forgotten, and we are not, of course, called on to register an unfavourable judgment of Dorimant.

[14] "The love affairs of Courtal and Ariana, Freeman and Gatty [in *She Wou'd if She Cou'd*] are similarly embarrassed by social convention. . . . The conduct of these polite lovers acquires comic vitality through the continually suggested opposition of artificial and real values."—*Op. cit.,* p. 152.

wards the social nuisances: "We should love wit, but for variety be able to divert ourselves with the extravagancies of those who want it." The butts, unfortunately, are only shown as fools by the discrepancy between their ambitions and their achievements, not because their ambitions are puerile. The subject is hardly worth discussing, since it is obviously nothing but an easily satisfied sense of superiority that is diverted by the "variety" of a constant succession of Dapperwits, Froths and Fopling Flutters. "When a humour takes in London," Tom Brown remarked, "they ride it to death ere they leave it. The primitive Christians were not persecuted with half that variety as the poor unthinking beaus are tormented with upon the theatre. . . . A huge great muff, and a gaudy ribbon hanging at a bully's backside, is an excellent jest, and new-invented curses, as, Stap my vitals, damn my diaphragm, slit my wind pipe, sink me ten thousand fathom deep, rig up a new beau, though in the main 'tis but the same everlasting coxcomb." [15]

3

In the matter of sexual relations Restoration comedy is entirely dominated by a narrow set of conventions. The objection that it is only certain characters, not the dramatists themselves, who accept them can be more freely encountered when the assumptions that are expressed most frequently have been briefly illustrated.

The first convention is, of course, that constancy in love, especially in marriage, is a bore. Vanbrugh, who was the most uneasy if not the most honest of the comic dramatists (I think that in *The Provok'd Wife* he shows as unusually honest), unambiguously attributes this attitude to Sir John Brute:

> What cloying meat is love—when matrimony's the sauce to it! Two years marriage has debauch'd my five senses. . . . No boy was ever so weary of his tutor, no girl of her bib, no nun of doing penance, or old maid of being chaste, as I am of being married. Sure there's a secret curse entail'd upon the very name of wife!
>
> The woman's well enough; she has no vice that I know of, but she's a wife, and—damn a wife! [16]

What Vanbrugh saw as a fit sentiment for Sir John had by that time (1697) served the Restoration stage—without change—for thirty years. In *She Wou'd if She Cou'd* Etherege had exhibited Sir Oliver Cockwood in an identical vein: "A pox of this tying man and woman together, for better, for worse." "To have a mistress love thee entirely" is "a damn'd trouble." "There are sots that would think themselves happy in such a Lady; but to a true bred Gentleman all lawful solace is abomination." [17] If Sir Oliver is a fool it is only because he is a trifle gross in his expression. "If you did but know, Madam," says the polite Freeman, "what an odious thing it is to be thought to love a Wife in good Company." [18] And the convention is constantly turning up in Congreve. "There is no creature perfectly civil but a husband," explains Mrs. Frail, "for in a little time he grows only rude to his wife, and that is the highest good breeding, for it begets his civility to other people." [19] "Marry her! Marry her!" Fainall advises Mirabell. "Be half as well acquainted with her charms, as you are with her defects, and my life on't, you are your own man again." [20] And Witwoud: "A wit should no more be sincere than a woman constant; one argues a decay of parts, as t'other of beauty." [21] Appetite, it seems (and this is the second assumption), needs perpetually fresh stimulus. This is the faith of Rhodophil in *Marriage à la Mode* and of Constant in *The Provok'd Wife,* as well as of Wycherley's old procuress, Mrs. Joyner. "If our wives would suffer us but now and then to make excursions," Rhodophil explains to Palamede, "the benefit of our variety would be theirs; instead of one continued, lazy, tired love, they would, in their turns, have twenty vigorous, fresh, and active lovers." [22] "Would anything but a madman complain of uncertainty?" asks Congreve's Angelica, for "security is an insipid thing, and the overtaking and possessing of a

[15] Tom Brown, *Works,* Vol. III, *Amusements Comical and Serious,* "At the Playhouse," p. 39.

[16] *The Provok'd Wife,* I, i; II, i.

[17] *She Wou'd if She Cou'd,* I, i; III, iii.

[18] *Ibid.,* III, iii.

[19] *Love for Love,* I, ii.

[20] *The Way of the World,* I, ii.

[21] *Ibid.*

[22] *Marriage à la Mode,* II, i. Cf. *The Provok'd Wife,* III, i: *Constant,* "There's a poor sordid slavery in marriage, that turns the flowing tide of honour, and sinks us to the lowest ebb of infamy. 'Tis a corrupted soil: Ill-nature, sloth, cowardice, and dirt, are all its prod uct."

wish, discovers the folly of the chase." [23] And Fainall, in *The Way of the World*, speaks for a large class when he hints at a liking for sauce —a little gentleman's relish—to his seductions: "I'd no more play with a man that slighted his ill fortune than I'd make love to a woman who under-valued the loss of her reputation." [24] Fainall, of course, is what he is, but the attitude that makes sexual pleasure "the bliss," that makes woman "delicious"—something to be savoured—as well as "damned" and "destructive," demands, for its support, "the pleasure of a chase." [25]

> Would you long preserve your lover?
>   Would you still his goddess reign?
> Never let him all discover,
>   Never let him much obtain.[26]

Restoration comedy used to be considered outrageously outspoken, but such stuff as this, far from being "outspoken," hovers on the outskirts of sexual relations, and sees nothing but the titillation of appetite (" 'Tis not the success," Collier observed, "but the manner of gaining it which is all in all").[27] Sex is a hook baited with tempting morsels; [28] it is a thirst quencher; [29] it is a cordial; [30] it is a dish to feed on; [31] it is a bunch of grapes; [32] it is anything but sex.

(This, of course, explains why some people can combine a delighted approval of Restoration comedy with an unbalanced repugnance for such modern literature as deals sincerely and realistically with sexual relationships.)

Now the objection referred to above was that sentiments such as these are not offered for straightforward acceptance. Many of them are attributed to characters plainly marked as Wicked (Maskwell, for example, is the black-a-vised villain of melodrama), or, more frequently, as trivial, and the dramatist can therefore dissociate himself. He may even be engaged in showing his audience the explicit, logical consequences of the half-unconscious premises on which they base their own lives, saying, as Mr. Dobrée has it, "Here is life lived upon certain assumptions; see what it becomes." To this there are several answers. The first is that reflexions of the kind that I have quoted are indistinguishable in tone and style from the general epigrammatic stock-in-trade (the audience was not altogether to be blamed if, as Congreve complained, they could not at first "distinguish betwixt the character of a Witwoud and a Lovewit"); and they are largely "exhibited," just as all the self-conscious witticisms are exhibited, for the sake of their immediate "comic" effect. One has only to note the laughter of a contemporary audience at a revival, and the places where the splutters occur, to realize how much of the fun provides a rather gross example of tendency wit.[33] The same attitudes, moreover, are manipulated again and again, turning up with the stale monotony of jokes on postcards, and the play that is made with them demands only the easiest, the most superficial, response. But it is, after all, useless to argue about the degree of detachment, the angle at

[23] *Love for Love*, IV, iii.

[24] *The Way of the World*, I, i.

[25] *The Old Bachelor*, I, i; III, ii ("O thou delicious, damned, dear, destructive woman!"); IV, ii.

[26] *Ibid.*, II, ii.

[27] *A Short View of the Profaneness and Immorality of the English Stage*, Fifth Edition, 1738, p. 116.

[28] " 'Tis true you are so eager in pursuit of the temptation, that you save the devil the trouble of leading you into it: nor is it out of discretion that you don't swallow the very hook yourselves have baited, but . . . what you meant for a whet turns the edge of your puny stomachs."—*The Old Bachelor*, I, i. "Strike Heartwell home, before the bait's worn off the hook. Age will come. He nibbled fairly yesterday, and no doubt will be eager enough today to swallow the temptation."—*Ibid.*, III, i.

[29] "What was my pleasure is become my duty: and I have as little stomach to her now as if I were her husband. . . . Pox on't! that a man can't drink without quenching his thirst."—*The Double-Dealer*, III, i.

[30] "You must get you a mistress, Rhodophil. That, indeed, is living upon cordials; but, as fast as one fails, you must supply it with another."—*Marriage à la Mode*, I, i.

[31] "Because our husbands cannot feed on one dish, therefore we must be starved."—*Ibid.*, III, i.

[32] "The only way to keep us new to one another, is never to enjoy, as they keep grapes, by hanging them upon a line; they must touch nothing, if you would preserve them fresh."—*Ibid*, V, i.

[33] The Freudian "censor" is at times projected in the form of the stage puritan. The plays written soon after the Commonwealth period appealed to Royalist prejudice by satirizing the "seemingly precise"; and even later, when "the bonfires of devotion," "the bellows of zeal," were forgotten, a good deal of the self-conscious swagger of indecency seems to have been directed against "our protestant husbands," city merchants, aldermen and the like; the "daring" effect was intensified by postulating a shockable audience somewhere—not necessarily in the theatre. Not that the really obscene jokes were merely bravado: Collier quite rightly remarked that "the modern poets seem to use smut as the old ones did Machines, to relieve a fainting situation."—*A Short View*, Fifth Edition, p. 4.

which these attitudes and assumptions are presented. As soon as one selects a particular comedy for that exercise one realizes that all is equally grist to the mill and that the dramatist (there is no need, here, to make distinctions) has no coherent attitude of his own. A consistent artistic purpose would not be content to express itself in a style that allows so limited, so local an effect.

But it is the triviality that one comes back to. In Dryden's *Marriage à la Mode* the characters accept the usual conventions: constancy is dull, and love only thrives on variety.

Palamede. O, now I have found it! you dislike her for no other reason but because she's your wife.

Rhodophil. And is not that enough? All that I know of her perfections now, is only by memory . . . At last we arrived at that point, that there was nothing left in us to make us new to one another . . .

Palamede. The truth is, your disease is very desperate; but, though you cannot be cured, you may be patched up a little: you must get you a mistress, Rhodophil. That, indeed, is living upon cordials; but, as fast as one fails, you must supply it with another.

The mistress that Rhodophil selects is Melantha, whom Palamede is to marry; Palamede falls in love with Doralice, Rhodophil's wife, and the ensuing complications provide sufficient entertainment (the grotto scene, III, ii, is really funny). Mr. Dobrée, however, regards the play as a witty exposure of the impossibility of rationalizing sex relations, as Palamede and Rhodophil attempt to rationalize them. Dryden "laughs morality back into its rightful place, as the scheme which ultimately makes life most comfortable." [34] But what Dryden actually does is to *use* the conventions for the amusement they afford, not to examine them. The level at which the play works is fairly indicated by the opening song:

Why should a foolish marriage vow,
  Which long ago was made,
Oblige us to each other now,
  When passion is decayed?
We loved, and we loved, as long as we could,
  'Til our love was loved out in us both;
But our marriage is dead, when the pleasure is fled:
  'Twas pleasure first made it an oath.

If I have pleasures for a friend,
  And further love in store,
What wrong has he, whose joys did end,
  And who could give no more?
'Tis a madness that he should be jealous of me,
  Or that I should bar him of another:
For all we can gain, is to give ourselves pain,
  When neither can hinder the other.

The lovers make no attempt to "rationalize sex" for the simple reason that genuine sexual feelings no more enter into the play as a whole than feelings of any kind enter into the song. (The obviously faked emotions of the heroic plot are, after all, relevant—and betraying.) And according to Mr. Dobrée, "In one sense the whole idea of Restoration comedy is summed up in the opening song of *Marriage à la Mode*.[35]

In a sense, too, Mr. Dobrée is right. Restoration comedy nowhere provides us with much more of the essential stuff of human experience than we have there. Even Congreve, by common account the best of the comic writers, is no exception. I have said that his verbal pattern often seems to be quite unrelated to an individual mode of perceiving. At best it registers a very limited mode. Restoration prose is all "social" in its tone, implications and general tenor, but Congreve's observation is *merely* of the public surface. And Congreve, too, relies on the conventional assumptions. In *The Way of the World*, it is true, they are mainly given to the bad and the foolish to express: it is Fainall who discourses on the pleasures of disliking one's wife, and Witwoud who maintains that only old age and ugliness ensure constancy. And Mirabell, who is explicitly opposed to some aspects of contemporary manners, goes through the common forms in a tone of rather weary aloofness: "I wonder, Fainall, that you who are married, and of consequence should be discreet, will suffer your wife to be of such a party." But Congreve himself is not above raising a cheap snigger; [36] and, above all, the characters with some life in them have nothing to fall back on—nothing, that is, except the conventional, and

[34] *Restoration Comedy*, p. 133.

[35] *Ibid.*, p. 106.

[36] Ay there's my grief; that's the sad change of life,
  To lose my title, and yet keep my wife.
The Way of the World, II, ii

conventionally limited, pleasures of sex. Millamant, who says she loathes the country and hates the town, expects to draw vitality from the excitement of incessant solicitation:

> I'll be solicited to the very last, nay, and afterwards . . . I should think I was poor and had nothing to bestow, if I were reduced to an inglorious ease, and freed from the agreeable fatigues of solicitation. . . . Oh, I hate a lover that can dare to think he draws a moment's air, independent of the bounty of his mistress. There is not so impudent a thing in nature, as the saucy look of an assured man, confident of success. The pedantic arrogance of a very husband has not so pragmatical an air.

Everyone seems to have found Millamant intelligent and attractive, but her attitude is not far removed from that expressed in

> Would you long preserve your lover?
> Would you still his goddess reign?

and she shares with characters who are decidedly not attractive a disproportionate belief in "the pleasure of a chase." Which is not surprising in view of her other occupations and resources; visiting, writing and receiving letters, tea-parties and small talk make up a round that is never for a moment enlivened by the play of genuine intelligence.[37] And although Congreve recognizes, at times, the triviality of his characters,[38] it is to the world whose confines were the Court, the drawing-room, the play-house and the park —a world completely lacking the real sophistication and self-knowledge that might, in some measure, have redeemed it—that he limits his appeal.

It is, indeed, hard to resist the conclusion that "society"—the smart town society that sought entertainment at the theatres—was fundamentally bored.[39] In *The Man of Mode* Emilia remarks of Medley, "I love to hear him talk o' the intrigues, let 'em be never so dull in themselves, he'll make 'em pleasant i' the relation," and the idiotic conversation that follows (II, i), affording us a glimpse of what Miss Lynch calls "the most brilliant society which Restoration comedy has to offer,"[40] suggests in more than one way how badly society *needed* to be entertained. It is the boredom—the constant need for titillation—that helps to explain not only the heroic "heightening" of emotion, but the various scenic effects, the devices of staging and costume that became popular at this period. (Charles II "almost died of laughing" at Nell Gwynn's enormous hat.) The conventions—of sexual pursuit, and so on—were an attempt to make life interesting—an impossible job for those who were aware of so limited a range of human potentialities.

The dominating mood of Restoration comedy is, by common account, a cynical one. But one cannot even say that there is here, in contrast to naïve Romantic fervours, the tough strength of disillusion. If—recognizing that there is a place in the educational process for, say, La Rochefoucauld—one finds the "cynicism" of the plays distasteful, it is because it is easy and superficial; the attitudes that we are presented with are based on so meagre an amount of observation and experience. Thus, "Elle retrouvait dans l'adultère toutes les platitudes du mariage" has, superficially, much the same meaning as, "I find now, by sad experience, that a mistress is much more chargeable than a wife, and after a little time too, grows full as dull and insignificant." But whereas the first sentence has behind it the whole of *Madame Bovary*, the second comes from *Sir Martin Mar-all*, which (although Dryden shares the honours with the Duke of Newcastle) is perhaps the stupidest play I have ever read, and the context is imbecility.

But the superficiality is betrayed at every turn —by the obvious rhythms of the interspersed songs, as well as by the artificial elegance of the prose. And the cynicism is closely allied with—merges into—sentimentality. One thinks of the

[37] As Lady Brute remarks, "After all, a woman's life would be a dull business, if it were not for the men . . . We shou'd never blame Fate for the shortness of our days; our time would hang wretchedly upon our hands." —*The Provok'd Wife*, III, iii.

[38] *Mirabell:* You had the leisure to entertain a herd of fools; things who visit you from their excessive idleness; bestowing on your easiness that time which is the encumbrance of their lives. How can you find delight in such society?—*The Way of the World*, II, i.

[39] The constitution, habits and demands of the theatre audience are admirably illustrated by Alexandre Beljame in that neglected classic of scholarship, *Le Public et les Hommes de Lettres en Angleterre au Dix-Huitième Siècle*, 1660-1740. See also C. V. Deane, *Dramatic Theory and the Rhymed Heroic Play*, Chapter I, Section 6.

[40] *The Social Mode of Restoration Comedy*, p. 177.

sentimentally conceived Fidelia in the resolutely "tough" *Plain Dealer;* and there is no doubt that the audience was meant to respond sympathetically when, at the end of *Love for Love,* Angelica declared her love for Valentine: "Had I the world to give you, it could not make me worthy of so generous a passion; here's my hand, my heart was always yours, and struggled very hard to make this utmost trial of your virtue." There is, of course, a good deal of loose emotion in the heroic plays, written—it is useful to remember—for the same audience:

I'm numbed, and fixed, and scarce my eyeballs
  move;
I fear it is the lethargy of love!
'Tis he; I feel him now in every part:
Like a new lord he vaunts about my heart;
Surveys, in state, each corner of my breast,
While poor fierce I, that was, am dispossessed.[41]

A secret pleasure trickles through my veins:
It works about the inlets of my soul,
To feel thy touch, and pity tempts the pass:
But the tough metal of my heart resists;
'Tis warmed with the soft fire, not melted down.[42]

"Feeling," in Dryden's serious plays, is fairly represented by such passages as these, and Dryden, we know, was not alone in admiring the Fletcherian "pathos." But it is the lyric verse of the period that provides the strongest confirmatory evidence of the kind of bad taste that is in question. It is not merely that in Etherege, Sedley and Dorset the feeling comes from much nearer the surface than in the Metaphysicals and the Caroline poets, intellectual "wit" no longer strengthens and controls the feeling. Conventional attitudes are rigged out in a conventional vocabulary and conventional images. (The stock outfit—the "fair eyes" that "wound," the "pleasing pains," the "sighs and tears," the "bleeding hearts" and "flaming darts"—can be studied in any anthology.[43]) There is, in consequence, a pervasive strain of sentimental vulgarity.

Farewell, ungrateful traitor!
  Farewell, my perjured swain!
Let never injured creature
  Believe a man again.
The pleasure of possessing
Surpasses all expressing,
But 'tis too short a blessing,
  And love too long a pain.

. . . . . .

The passion you pretended,
  Was only to obtain;
But when the charm is ended,
  The charmer you disdain.
Your love by ours we measure
Till we have lost our treasure,
But dying is a pleasure
  When living is a pain.

This piece of music-hall sentiment comes from Dryden's *The Spanish Friar,* and it does not stand alone. The mode that was to produce, among other things of equal merit, "When lovely woman stoops to folly," had its origin in the lyrics of the Restoration period. Most of these were written by the group connected with the theatres, and they serve to underline the essential criticism of the plays. The criticism that defenders of Restoration comedy need to answer is not that the comedies are "immoral," but that they are trivial, gross and dull.

[41] *The Conquest of Granada,* Part I, III, i.

[42] *Don Sebastian,* III, i.

[43] See, for example, Aphra Behn's "Love in fantastic triumph sate," Buckingham's *To his Mistress* ("Phyllis, though your all powerful charms"), Dryden's "Ask not the cause why sullen spring," and "Ah, how sweet it is to love," and Sedley's *To Chloris*—all in *The Oxford Book of English Verse,* or Ault's *Seventeenth Century Lyrics.*

JOHN CROWE RANSOM: A Poem Nearly Anonymous *

IT WAS published in 1638, in the darkness preceding our incomparable modernity. Its origins were about as unlikely as they could be, for it was only one of the exhibits in a memorial garland, a common academic sort of volume. It appeared there without a title and signed only by a pair of initials, though now we know it both by a name and by an author. Often we choose to think of it as the work of a famous poet, which it was not; done by an apprentice of nearly thirty, who was still purifying his taste upon an astonishingly arduous diet of literary exercises; the fame which was to shine backwards upon this poem, and to be not very different from the fame which he steadily intended, being as distant as it was great. Unfortunately it is one of the poems which we think we know best. Upon it is imposed the weight of many perfect glosses, respecting its occasion, literary sources, classical and contemporary allusions, exhausting us certainly and exhausting, for a good many persons, the poem. But I am bound to consider that any triteness which comes to mind with mention of the poem is a property of our own registration, and does not affect its freshness, which is perennial. The poem is young, brilliant, insubordinate. In it is an artist who wrestles with an almost insuperable problem, and is kinsman to some tortured modern artists. It has something in common with, for example, *The Waste Land*. In short, the poem is *Lycidas*.

A symbol is a great convenience in discussion, and therefore I will find one in the half-way anonymity of the poem; symbolic of the poet's admirable understanding of his art, and symbolic of the tradition that governed the art on the whole in one of its flourishing periods. Anonymity, of some real if not literal sort, is a condition of poetry. A good poem, even if it is signed with a full and well-known name, intends as a work of art to lose the identity of the author; that is, it means to represent him not actualized, like an eye-witness testifying in court and held strictly by zealous counsel to the point at issue, but freed from his juridical or prose self and taking an ideal or fictitious personality; otherwise his evidence amounts the less to poetry. Poets may go to universities and, if they take to education, increase greatly the stock of ideal selves into which they may pass for the purpose of being poetical. If on the other hand they insist too narrowly on their own identity and their own story, inspired by a simple but mistaken theory of art, they find their little poetic fountains drying up within them. Milton set out to write a poem mourning a friend and poet who had died; in order to do it he became a Greek shepherd, mourning another one. It was not that authority attached particularly to the discourse of a Greek shepherd; the Greek shepherd in his own person would have been hopeless; but Milton as a Greek shepherd was delivered from being Milton the scrivener's son, the Master of Arts from Cambridge, the handsome and finicky young man, and that was the point. In proceeding to his Master's degree he had made studies which gave him dramatic insight into many parts foreign to his own personal experience; which was precisely the technical resource he had required the moment he determined to be a poet. Such a training was almost the regular and unremarked procedure with the poets of his time. Today young men and women, as noble as Milton, those in university circles as much as those out of them, try to become poets on another plan, and with rather less success. They write their autobiographies, following perhaps the

* "A Poem Nearly Anonymous" is reprinted from *The World's Body* by John Crowe Ransom; copyright 1938 by Charles Scribner's Sons; used by permission of the publishers, Charles Scribner's Sons. Mr. Ransom (*b.* 1888) is also the author of *God Without Thunder: an Unorthodox Defense of Orthodoxy* (1930) and *The New Criticism* (1941).

example of Wordsworth, which on the whole may have been unfortunate for the prosperity of the art; or they write some of their intenser experiences, their loves, pities, griefs, and religious ecstasies; but too literally, faithfully, piously, ingenuously. They seem to want to do without wit and playfulness, dramatic sense, detachment, and it cuts them off from the practice of an art.

Briefly, it was Milton's intention to be always anonymous as a poet, rarely as a writer of prose. The poet must suppress the man, or the man would suppress the poet. What he wanted to say for himself, or for his principles, became eligible for poetry only when it became what the poet, the *dramatis persona* so to speak, might want to say for himself. The poet could not be directed to express faithfully and pointedly the man; nor was it for the sake of "expression" that the man abdicated in favor of the poet.

Strictly speaking, this may be a half-truth. But if we regard with a reformer's eye the decay, in our time, of poetry, it becomes almost the whole truth we are called to utter. I do not mind putting it flatly; nor drawing the conclusion that poetry appeared to the apprentice Milton, before it could appear anything else, and before it could come into proper existence at all, as a sort of exercise, very difficult, and at first sight rather beside the point. It was of course an exercise in pure linguistic technique, or metrics; it was also an exercise in the technique of what our critics of fiction refer to as "point of view." And probably we shall never find a better locus than *Lycidas* for exhibiting at once the poet and the man, the technique and the personal interest, bound up tightly and contending all but equally; the strain of contraries, the not quite resolvable dualism, that is art.

For we must begin with a remark quite unsuitable for those moderns to whom "expression" seems the essential quality of poetry. *Lycidas* is a literary exercise; and so is almost any other poem earlier than the eighteenth century; the craftsmanship, the formal quality which is written on it, is meant to have high visibility. Take elegy, for example. According to the gentle and extremely masculine tradition which once governed these matters, performance is not rated by the rending of garments, heartbreak, verisimilitude of desolation. After all, an artist is standing before the public, and bears the character of a qualified spokesman, and a male. Let him somewhat loudly sweep the strings, even the tender human ones, but not without being almost military and superficial in his restraint; like the pomp at the funeral of the king, whom everybody mourns publicly and nobody privately. Milton made a great point of observing the proprieties of verse. He had told Diodati, as plainly as Latin elegiacs allowed, that "expression" was not one of the satisfactions which they permitted to the poet: "You want to know in verse how much I love and cherish you; believe me that you will scarcely discover this in verse, for love like ours is not contained within cold measures, it does not come to hobbled feet." As for memorial verse, he had already written, in English or Latin, for the University beadle, the University carrier, the Vice-Chancellor, his niece the Fair Infant Dying of a Cough, the Marchioness of Winchester, the Bishop of Winchester, the Bishop of Ely; he was yet to write for his Diodati, and for Mrs. Katharine Thomason. All these poems are exercises, and some are very playful indeed. There is no great raw grief apparent ever, and sometimes, very likely, no great grief. For Lycidas he mourns with a very technical piety.

Let us go directly to the poem's metre—though this feature may seem a bristling technicality, and the sort of thing the tender reader may think he ought to be spared. I do not wish to be brutal, but I am afraid that metre is fundamental in the problem posed to the artist as poet. During the long apprenticeship Milton was the experimentalist, trying nearly everything. He does not ordinarily, in the Minor Poems, repeat himself metrically; another poem means another metre, and the new metre will scarcely satisfy him any better than the last one did. Evidently Milton never found the metre in which as a highly individual poet he could feel easy, and to which he was prepared to entrust his serious work, until he had taken the ragged blank verse of contemporary drama and had done something to it; tightening it up into a medium which was hard enough to exhibit form, and plastic enough to give him freedom. In other words, it defined the poet as somebody with a clipped, sonorous, figurative manner of speaking; but it also gave a possible if indirect utterance to the natural man. Here let us ask the question always in order against a Milton poem: What was the historic metrical pattern already before him, and what are the liberties he takes with it? For he does not cut patterns out of the whole cloth, but always takes an existing pattern; stretches it dangerously close to the limits that the pattern will permit without ceasing to be a pattern; and never brings himself to the point of defying that restraint which patterns inflict upon him, and composing something altogether unpatterned. That is to say, he tends habitually towards the formlessness which is modern, without quite caring to arrive at that destination. It is the principle we are interested in, not the literal answer to the question, which I will try to get over briefly.

The answer given by the Milton scholars, those who know their Italian, might well be that in this poem he made a very free adaptation of the canzone. This was a stanza of indeterminate length, running it might be to twenty lines or so, marked by some intricate rhyming scheme, and by a small number of six-syllable lines inserted among the ten-syllable lines which constituted the staple. The poet was free to make up his own stanza but, once that was given, had to keep it uniform throughout the poem. Milton employs it with almost destructive freedom, as we shall see. Yet, on the other hand, the correct stanza materials are there, and we can at least say that any one of the stanzas or paragraphs might make a passable canzone. And lest his irregularities be imputed to incompetence, we must observe the loving exactitude of his line-structure, that fundamental unit of any prosody, within the stanzas. He counts his syllables, he takes no liberties there: consisting with our rather fixed impression that he scarcely knew how in all his poetry to admit an imperfect line.

The Milton scholars know their Italian, and have me at a disadvantage. Milton knew his Italian. But he also knew his Spenser, and knowing that, it seems unnecessary to inquire whether he knew his Italian too; for he had only to adapt a famous Spenserian stanza, and his acquaintance with the canzone becomes really immaterial. I imagine this point has a slight importance. It would have something to do with the problem of the English poet who wants to employ an English technique in addressing himself to an English public which can be expected to know its English formal tradition. Spenser anticipated Milton by employing the canzone effectively in at least two considerable poems; they were not elegies, but at least they were marriage hymns. In 1596 he published his *Prothalamion,* upon the occasion of a noble alliance; the stanzas are exactly uniform, and they compose an admirable exercise in Italian canzoni. But he had published in 1595 his *Epithalamion,* upon the occasion of his own wedding, which is much more to Milton's purpose, and ours. Here are ten eighteen-line stanzas, but here are also twelve nineteen-line stanzas, and one of seventeen lines; and one of the eighteen-line stanzas does not agree in pattern with the others. If these details escape the modern reader, it is not at all certain that they were missed by Spenser's public. I should like to think that the poetical consciousness of the aristocratic literati of that age was a state of mind having metrical form in its foreground, and Spenser intended frankly to make use of the situation. Perhaps he calculated that if they would go to the trouble to analyze a poem composed of intricate but regular canzoni, they might go to still greater pains to analyze a poem whose canzoni were subtly irregular. I suppose this was something of a miscalculation, like other of his plans. But if it were a just calculation: then the advantage to be reaped by their going to such pains—it was their advantage as much as his—was the sort of addition to total effect which a labor of love can furnish. A public like Spenser's, if we are to construe it at its best, participates in the poem as does the author, and it is unfortunate if there lives today some modern Spenser who does not hope for such a reward to his efforts. But probably the sad truth is that a subtle art is unlikely in the first place, whose artist does not reckon upon the background of a severe technical tradition, and the prospect of a substantial public body of appreciation.

The enterprising Spenser prepared the way for the daring Milton, who remarks the liberties which his celebrated exemplar has taken and carries his own liberties further, to a point just this side of anarchy. The eleven stanzas of *Lycidas* occupy 193 lines, but are grossly unequal and unlike. Such stanzas are not in strictness stanzas at all; Milton has all but scrapped the stanza in its proper sense as a formal and binding element. But there is perhaps an even more startling lapse. Within the poem are ten lines which do not rhyme at all, and which technically do not belong therefore in any stanza, nor in the poem.

Now we may well imagine that the unrhymed lines did not escape Milton's notice, and also that he did not mean nor hope that they should escape ours. The opening line of the poem is unrhymed, which is fair warning. The ten unrhymed lines should be conspicuous among the 183 rhymed ones, like so many bachelors at a picnic of fast-mated families. Let us ask what readers of *Lycidas* have detected them, and we shall see what readers are equipped with the right sensibility for an effect in form. And if the effect in this case is an effect of prose formlessness, and if nevertheless it is deliberate, we had better ask ourselves what Milton wanted with it.

It is tempting to the imperious individualism of the modern reader, especially if he has heard somewhere about the enormous egoism of John Milton, to say that the "expression" in these lines must have seemed to their author "inevitable," and superior to any obligation to the law of the form. Just as we find them, they had leapt out of the tense creative fury of the poet, notable, possibly prophetic; and what higher considerations were there anywhere requiring him in cold blood to alter them? But that does not make sense as an account of the poetic processes of a Milton. The ten lines, as it happens, look at them hard as we like, do not seem more important than ten others, and are not the lines by which he could have set special store. As a matter of fact, he might have altered them easily, tinkering with them as long as necessary in order to bring them within the metre, and they would scarcely have been, by whatever standard, any the worse. So great is the suggestibility of the poet's mind, the associability of ideas, the margin in the meaning of words. It is the inexperienced artist who attributes sanctity to some detail of his inspiration. You may ask him to write a poem which will make sense and make metre at the same time, but in the performance he will sacrifice one or the other; the consequence will be good sense and lame metre, or good metre and nonsense; if he is a man of interests and convictions, the former. But the competent artist is as sure of his second thoughts as of his first ones. In fact, surer, if anything; second thoughts tend to be the richer, for in order to get them he has to break up the obvious trains of association and explore more widely. Milton was not enamored of the ten lines, and they stand out from their context by no peculiar quality of their own but only because they do not belong to it metrically. Therefore I would say that they constitute the gesture of his rebellion against the formalism of his art, but not the rebellion itself. They are defiances, showing the man unwilling to give way to the poet; they are not based upon a special issue but upon surliness, and general principles. It is a fateful moment. At this critical stage in the poet's career, when he has come to the end of the period of Minor Poems, and is turning over in his head the grand subjects out of which he will produce great poems, he is uneasy, sceptical, about the whole foundation of poetry as an art. He has a lordly contempt for its tedious formalities, and is determined to show what he can do with only half trying to attend to them. Or he thinks they are definitely bad, and proposes to see if it is not better to shove them aside.

In this uncertainty he is a modern poet. In the irregular stanzas and the rhymeless lines is registered the ravage of his modernity; it has bit into him as it never did into Spenser. And we imagine him thinking to himself, precisely like some modern poets we know, that he could no longer endure the look of perfect regimentation which sat upon the poor ideas objectified before him upon the page of poetry, as if that carried with it a reflection upon their sincerity. I will go further. It is not merely easy for a technician to write in smooth metres; it is perhaps easier than to write in rough ones, after he has once started; but when he has written smoothly, and contemplates his work, he is capable actually, if he is a modern poet, of going over it laboriously and roughening it. I venture to think that just such a practice, speaking very broadly, obtained in the composition of *Lycidas;* that it was written smooth and rewritten rough; which was treason.

I will make a summary statement which is true to the best of my knowledge. There did not at the time anywhere exist in English, among the poems done by competent technical poets, another poem so wilful and illegal in form as this one.

An art never possesses the "sincerity" that consists in speaking one's mind, that is, in expressing one's first impression before it has time to grow cold. This sincerity is spontaneity, the most characteristic quality in modern poetry. Art is long, and time is fleeting, and we have grown too impatient to relish more than the first motions towards poetic effect. The English and American Imagists exploited and consolidated this temper, which was no longer hospitable to a finished art. In their defence it may be said with justice that the writing of formal poetry, which they interrupted, was becoming a tedious parlor performance in which the poet made much ado about saying nothing of importance, while the man behind him quite escaped acquaintance through sheer lack of force. The verslibrists were determined to be bright, and fresh, and innocent of deep and ulterior designs; but their prose art was an anomaly. It wore out, and strict artistic economy has had a certain recovery; nothing like a complete one, for they left their mark upon our poetry, and I shall certainly not be so dogmatic as to say it has been entirely unfortunate.

It depends ultimately on taste whether we prefer prose to poetry, or prefer even a mixture of prose and poetry. Let us suppose two gentlemen talking a little wildly over their cups, until Mr. A insults Mr. B. Now if B is a modern man, he immediately strikes A down, with his knife if it happens to be in his hand, or his stick, or his fist. He has acted spontaneously, with a right and quick instinct, and he is admired for it. (I do not mean to raise any moral issues with my analogy.) But if the time is about a century or two earlier, B steps back and says drily: "My seconds will wait upon you, Sir." The next dawn A and B repair to the grove, attended by their respective partisans, draw their rapiers, and with great ceremony set in to kill each other. Or apparently they do; but if they are not really prepared to be hurt, nor to hurt each other, but are only passing the time until they are informed that their honors are satisfied, it is a bogus and ineffective action and the serious spectators feel cheated; that represents the sort of art against which the free versifiers revolted. If they fight till A puts his steel through the vitals of B, or *vice versa,* the spectators are well rewarded, and the ceremonial has justified itself, though it took time; that stands for the true art. But if they lose their tempers on the field and begin to curse, and kick, and throw stones and clods at each other, they are behaving too spontaneously for a formal occasion. Why were they not spontaneous yesterday if that was their intention? They will have to be recalled to the occasion and come to a conclusion under the terms nominated; and here we have the mixed affair of poetry and prose, a problem in taste; here, I am afraid, we have *Lycidas.*

At any rate Milton thought something of the kind. For he never repeated his bold experiment; and he felt at the time that it was not an altogether successful experiment. The last stanzas become much more patterned, and in the postscript Milton refers to the whole monody as the song of an "uncouth Swain," who has been "with eager thought warbling his *Dorick* lay." That is descriptive and deprecatory.

There is another possibility. Milton had much of the modern poet's awareness of his public; in this case the awareness of a public not quite capable of his own sustained artistic detachment. What sort of poem would it like? Too perfect an art might look cold and dead; and though an elegy had to be about the dead, it did not want itself to look dead, but to display incessant energy. So he read the formal poem he had written, and deformed it; or he had read other formal poems, like the *Epithalamion,* and remarked that the public, an increasingly mixed lot, thought them a little dull, and he now, as he composed his own poem, remembered to write into it plenty of formlessness. "The formalism," he was thinking, "if unrelieved, will dull the perceptions of my reader, and unprepare him for my surprises, and my tireless fertility. Therefore let him sense an exciting combat between the artist and the man, and let the man interrupt with his prose (comparative prose) the pretty passages of the artist." In that case the artist was only pretending to give way to the man, calculating with the cunning of a psychologist, perhaps of a dramatist, and violating the law of his art entirely for its public effect; a Jesuit of an artist. But the Jesuit, according to the Protestant tradition which reaches me, and which I will trust to the extent of this argument, has an excessive respect for the depravity of the humanity he ministers to, and he needs beyond other priests to be firmly grounded in his principles, lest from fighting the devil with fire he change his own element insensibly, become himself a fallen angel, and bear the reputation of one. The best thing to say for Milton is that his principles were strong, and he did not again so flagrantly betray them.

But if the poem is a literary exercise, it does not consist only in a game of metrical hide-and-seek, played between the long lines and short lines, the rhymed and unrhymed. It is also a poem in a certain literary "type," with conventions of subject-matter and style. Milton set out to make it a pastoral elegy, and felt honor-bound to use the conventions which had developed in the pastoral elegies of the Greeks, of Virgil, of the Italians, of Spenser; possibly of the French. The course of the poem in outline therefore is not highly "creative," but rather commonplace and in order, when the dead shepherd is remembered and his virtues published; when nature is made to lament him, and the streams to dry up in sympathy; when the guardian nymphs are asked why they have not saved him; when the untimeliness of his doom is moralized; when the corrupt church is reproached; when the flowers are gathered for the hearse; and finally when it appears to the mourners that they must cease, since he is not dead, but translated into a higher region, where he lives in bliss of a not definitive sort. In the pastoral elegy at large one of my friends distinguishes eleven different topics of discourse, and points out that Milton, for doubtless the first time in this literature, manages to "drag them all into one poem"; a distinction for him, though perhaps a doubtful one. But in doing so he simply fills up the poem; there are no other topics in it. And where is Milton the individualist, whose metrical departures would seem to have advertised a performance which in some to-be-unfolded manner will be revolutionary?

When we attempt to define the poetic "quality" of this poet's performances, we are forced to confess that it consists largely in pure eclecticism; here is a poet who can simply lay more of his predecessors under tribute than another. This is not to deny that he does a good job of it. He assimilates what he receives, and adapts it infallibly to the business in hand, where scraps fuse into integer, and the awkward articulations cannot be detected. His second-hand effects are not as good as new but better; the features of pastoral elegy are not as pretty in *Lycidas* as they were in Moschus, or Virgil, or Spenser, but prettier; though generically, and even in considerable detail, the same features. We remember after all that Milton intended his effects; and among others, this one of indebtedness to models. He expected that the reader should observe his eclecticism, he was scarcely alarmed lest it be mistaken for plagiarism. It is because of something mean in our modernism, or at least in that of our critics, that we, if we had composed the poem, would have found such an expectancy tainted with such an alarm. Like all the artists of the Renaissance, Milton hankered honestly after "Fame"; but he was not infected with our gross modern concept of "originality." The æsthetic of this point is perfectly rational. If a whole series of artists in turn develop the same subject, it is to the last one's advantage that he may absorb the others, in addition to being in whatever pointed or subtle manner his own specific self. His work becomes the climax of a tradition, and is better than the work of an earlier artist in the series. Unfortunately, there will come perhaps the day when there is no artist prepared to carry on the tradition; or, more simply, when the tradition has gone far enough and is not worth carrying further; that is, when it is worn out as a "heuristic" principle, and confines more than it frees the spirit. (Very few pastoral elegies can have been written since *Lycidas* in our language; very few critics can have deplored this.) On that day the art will need its revolutionist, to start another tradition. It is a bold step for the artist to take, and Milton did not think it needful to take it here. The revolutionist who does not succeed must descend to the rating, for history, of rebel; the fool of a wrong political intuition.

But revolutions, for all that, little and private ones if not big and general ones, come frequently into a healthy literary history, in which variety is a matter of course. The poet may do better with a make-believe of his own than with a time-honored one. There is no theoretical limit upon the variety of literary types, and each good type permits of many explorers, but tends at last to be exhausted. The point of view of Greek shepherds, as romantic innocents and rustics, is excellent, and offers a wide range of poetic discourse concerning friendship, love, nature, and even, a startling innovation of the Italian pastoralists, the "ruin of the clergy." The point of view of the amorous cavalier presenting his compliments and reproaches to his lady is also a good one; it ran through many hundreds of lyrics in the sixteenth and seventeenth centuries, and is still better than no point of view at all, which we find in some very young poet speaking in his own person to his own love. The studied "conceit" of the seventeenth century offered another field of discourse in which poetic exercises took place; logical and academic, but having rich possibilities, and eligible even for religious experiences. The sonnet is primarily a metrical form, but behind it there is an ideal and rather formidable speaker, far from actual, who must get what he has to say into a very small space and, according to the rules, into a very concise style of utterance. The ballad offers a point of view quite alien to the ordinary cultivated poet, because speaking in that form he must divest himself of the impedimenta of learning and go primitive. All these forms lend themselves to individual variations and innovations; call for them, in fact, in the course of time, when the poet can find no fresh experience within the usual thing. It is entirely according to the æsthetic of this art if a poet wants to enter the book of literature with a series of Choctaw incantations, provided he is steeped in Choctaw experience and able to make a substantial exhibit; or with a set of poems from the character of a mere Shropshire lad; or from that of a dry New England countryman. It is important mostly that the poet know his part and speak it fluently.

Of Milton's "style," in the sense of beauty of sound, imagery, syntax and dystax, idiom, I am quite unprepared to be very analytic. It is a grand style; which is to say, I suppose, that it is *the* grand style, or as much a grand style as English poets have known: the style produced out of the poet's remembrance of his classical models, chiefly Virgil. Milton has not been the only English poet to learn from Virgil, but he is doubtless the one who learned the most. Until the nineteenth century Virgil was perhaps the greatest external influence upon English literature. Dryden venerated but could not translate him:

> . . . must confess to my shame, that I have not been able to Translate any part of him so well, as to make him appear wholly like himself. For where the Original is close, no Version can reach it in the same compass. Hannibal Caro's, in the Italian, is the nearest, the most Poetical, and the most Sonorous of any Translation of the Æneid's; yet, though he takes the advantage of blank Verse, he commonly allows two lines for one of Virgil, and does not always hit his sence. . . . Virgil, therefore, being so very sparing of his words, and leaving so much to be imagined by the Reader, can never be translated as he ought, in any modern Tongue. To make him Copious, is to alter his Character; and to translate him Line for Line is impossible; because the Latin is naturally a more succinct Language than either the Italian, Spanish, French, or even than the English (which, by reason of its Monosyllables, is far the most compendious of them). Virgil is much the closest of any Roman Poet, and the Latin Hexameter has more Feet than the English Heroick.

But in spite of the unfitness of an uninflected language like English, poets have occasionally managed a Virgilian style in it. We think at once of Marlowe. Naturally, it was not entirely beyond Shakespeare's powers; but Shakespeare at his highest pitch likes to rely on fury and hyperbole rather than the "smoothness" and "majesty" which Dryden commends in Virgil. Shakespeare writes:

> Rumble thy bellyful! Spit, fire! Spout, rain!

and

> You sulphurous and thought-executing fires,
> Vaunt-couriers of oak-cleaving thunderbolts,
> Singe my white head!

which is in a sublime style but not, if we care to be precise, the grand style. But Milton very nearly commanded this style. And with reason; for he had written Minor Poems in Latin as well as Minor Poems in English, and they were perhaps the more important item in his apprenticeship. This is one of the consequences:

> But now my Oate proceeds,
> And listens to the Herald of the Sea,
> That came in *Neptune's* plea,

He ask'd the Waves, and ask'd the Fellon winds,
What hard mishap hath doom'd this gentle swain?
And question'd every gust of rugged wings
That blows from off each beaked Promontory,
They knew not of his story,
And sage *Hippotades* their answer brings,
That not a blast was from his dungeon stray'd,
The Ayr was calm, and on the level brine,
Sleek *Panope* with all her sisters play'd.
It was that fatall and perfidious Bark
Built in th'eclipse, and rigg'd with curses dark,
That sunk so low that sacred head of thine.

It is probable that no other English poet has this mastery of the Virgilian effect; it is much more Virgilian, too, than the later effect which Milton has in the lines of the *Paradise Lost,* where the great departure from the epical substance of the Virgil makes it needful to depart from the poetic tone. But Milton proves here that he had fairly mastered it. He had simply learned to know it in the Latin—learning by the long way of performance as well as by the short one of observation—and then transferred it to his native English; where it becomes a heightened effect, because this language is not accustomed at once to ease and condensation like this, and there is little competition. The great repute of the Miltonic style—or styles, variants of a style —in our literature is a consequence of the scarcity of Miltons; that is, of poets who have mastered the technique of Latin poetry before they have turned to their own.

But the author of *Lycidas,* attended into his project by so much of the baggage of tradition, cannot, by a universal way of thinking, have felt, exactly, free. I shall risk saying that he was not free. Little chance there for him to express the interests, the causes, which he personally and powerfully was developing; the poem too occasional and too formal for that. Of course the occasion was a fundamental one, it was no less than Death; and there is nobody so aggressive and self-assured but he must come to terms with that occasion. But a philosophy of death seems mostly to nullify, with its irony, the philosophy of life. Milton was yet very much alive, and in fact he regarded himself as having scarcely begun to live. The poem is almost wasted if we are seeking to determine to what extent it permitted Milton to unburden his heart.

But not quite. The passage on mortality is tense; Professor Tillyard finds the man in it. It goes into a passage on the immortality of the just man's Fame, which gives Milton's Platonic version of the ends of Puritanism. More important perhaps is the kind of expressiveness which appears in the speech of Peter. The freedom with which Milton abuses the false shepherds surpasses anything which his predecessors in this vein had indulged. He drops his Latinity for plain speech, where he can express a Milton who is angry, violent, and perhaps a little bit vulgar. It is the first time in his career that we have seen in him a taste for writing at this level. With modern readers it may be greatly to his credit as a natural man that he can feel strongly and hit hard. Later, in the period of his controversial prose, we get more of it, until we have had quite enough of this natural man. In the *Paradise Lost* we will get some "strong" passages again, but they are not Milton's response to his own immediate situation, they are dramatically appropriate, and the persons and scenes of the drama are probably remote enough to bring the passages under the precise head of artistic effect. This may be thought to hold for *Lycidas,* since it is Peter speaking in a pastoral part, and Peter still represents his villains as shepherds; but I feel that Peter sounds like another Puritan zealot, and less than apostolic.

Before I offer some generalizations about the poet and his art, I wish to refer, finally, to a feature of *Lycidas* which critics have rarely mentioned, and which most readers of my acquaintance, I believe, have never noticed, but which is technically astonishing all the same, and ought to initiate an important speculation upon the intentions of this poet. Pastoral elegies are dramatic monologues, giving the words of a single shepherd upon a single occasion; or they are dialogues giving, like so much printed drama, the speeches of several shepherds in a single scene. They may have prologues, perhaps so denominated in the text, and printed in italics, or in a body separate from the elegy proper; and likewise epilogues; the prologues and epilogues being the author's envelope of narrative within which is inserted the elegy. The composition is straightforward and explicitly logical.

Milton's elegy is otherwise. It begins without preamble as a monologue, and continues so through the former and bitterer half of the passage on Fame:

> But the fair Guerdon when we hope to find,
> And think to burst out into sudden blaze,
> Comes the blind *Fury* with th'abhorred shears,
> And slits the thin spun life. . . .

At this point comes an incredible interpolation:

> . . . But not the praise,
> *Phœbus* repli'd, and touch'd my trembling ears . . .

And Phœbus concludes the stanza; after which the shepherd apologizes to his pastoral Muses for the interruption and proceeds with his monologue. But dramatic monologue has turned for a moment into narrative. The narrative breaks the monologue several times more, presenting action sometimes in the present tense, sometimes in the past. And the final stanza gives a pure narrative conclusion in the past, without the typographical separateness of an epilogue; it is the one which contains Milton's apology for the "Dorick" quality of his performance, and promises that the author will yet appear in a serious and mature light as he has scarcely done on this occasion.

Such a breach in the logic of composition would denote, in another work, an amateurism below the level of publication. I do not know whether our failure to notice it is because we have been intoxicated by the wine of the poetry, or dulled by the drum-fire of the scholars' glosses, or intimidated by the sense that the poem is Milton's. Certainly it is Milton's; therefore it was intended; and what could have been in his mind? I have a suggestion. A feature that obeys the canon of logic is only the mere instance of a universal convention, while the one that violates the canon is an indestructibly private thing. The poor "instance" would like so much to attain to the dignity of a particular. If Milton had respected the rule of composition, he must have appeared as any other author of pastoral elegy, whereas in his disrespect of it he can be the person, the John Milton who is different, and dangerous, and very likely to become famous. (It is ironical that the lapse in question celebrates Fame.) The logical difficulties in the work of an artist capable of perfect logic may be the insignia of an individuality which would otherwise have to be left to the goodness of the imagination; and that is a calculation which lies, I think, under much modern art. There are living poets, and writers of fiction, and critics at the service of both, who have a perfect understanding of the principle. The incoherence or "difficulty" in the work is not necessarily to be attributed to the unresourcefulness of the artist, as if he could not have straightened everything out if he had desired, but sometimes to his choice. Under this head comes that licentious typography in which we may find one of the really magnificent manifestations of our modernity. The author is like some gentleman in the world of fashion who is thoroughly initiated, yet takes great pains to break the rule somewhere in order that nobody will make the mistake of not remarking his personality. If there is any force in this way of reasoning, we may believe that Milton's bold play with the forms of discourse constitutes simply one more item in his general insubordinacy. He does not propose to be buried beneath his own elegy. Now he had done a thing somewhat on the order of the present breach in his *L'Allegro* and *Il Penseroso.* There is a comparative simplicity to these pieces amounting almost to obviousness, but they are saved in several ways. For one thing, they are twin poems, and the parallelism or contrast is very intricate. More to our point, there is a certain lack of definition in the substantive detail; long sentences with difficult grammatical references, and uncertainty as to whether the invocation has passed into the action, and as to just where we are in the action. That trick was like the present one, indicating that the man is getting ahead of the poet, who is not being allowed to assimilate the matter into his formal style.

More accurately, of course, *they would like to indicate it;* the poet being really a party to the illusion. Therefore he lays himself open to the charge of being too cunning, and of overreaching himself; the effect is not heroic but mock-heroic. The excited Milton, breathless, and breaking through the logic of composition, is charming at first; but as soon as we are forced to reflect that he counterfeited the excitement, we are pained and let down. The whole poem is properly an illusion, but a deliberate and honest one, to which we consent, and through which we follow the poet because it enables him to do things not possible if he were presenting actuality. At some moments we may grow excited and tempted to forget that it is illusion, as the untrained spectator may forget and hiss the villain at the theatre. But we are quickly reminded of our proper attitude. If the author tends to forget, all the more if he pretends to forget, we would recall him to the situation too. Such license we do not accord to poets and dramatists, but only to novelists, whose art is young. And even these, or the best of these, seem now determined, for the sake of their artistic integrity, to surrender it.

So *Lycidas,* for the most part a work of great art, is sometimes artful and tricky. We are disturbingly conscious of a man behind the artist. But the critic will always find too many and too perfect beauties in it ever to deal with it very harshly.

WILLIAM EMPSON: Marvell's Garden*

THE IDEAL SIMPLICITY APPROACHED BY RESOLVING CONTRADICTIONS

The chief point of the poem is to contrast and reconcile conscious and unconscious states, intuitive and intellectual modes of apprehension; and yet that distinction is never made, perhaps could not have been made; his thought is implied by his metaphors. There is something very Far-Eastern about this; I was set to work on the poem by Dr. Richards' recent discussion of a philosophical argument in Mencius. The Oxford edition notes bring out a crucial double meaning (so that this at least is not my own fancy) in the most analytical statement of the poem, about the Mind—

> Annihilating all that's made
> To a green thought in a green shade.

"Either 'reducing the whole material world to nothing material, i.e. to a green thought,' or 'considering the material world as of no value compared to a green thought' "; either contemplating everything or shutting everything out. This combines the idea of the conscious mind, including everything because understanding it, and that of the unconscious animal nature, including everything because in harmony with it. Evidently the object of such a fundamental contradiction (seen in the etymology: turning all *ad nihil, to* nothing, and *to* a thought) is to deny its reality; the point is not that these two are essentially different but that they must cease to be different so far as either is to be known. So far as he has achieved his state of ecstasy he combines them, he is "neither conscious nor not conscious," like the seventh Buddhist state of enlightenment. This gives its point, I think, to the other ambiguity, clear from the context, as to whether the *all* considered was *made* in the mind of the author or the Creator; to so peculiarly "creative" a knower there is little difference between the two. Here as usual with "profound" remarks the strength of the thing is to combine unusually intellectual with unusually primitive ideas; thought about the conditions of knowledge with a magical idea that the adept controls the external world by thought.

The vehemence of the couplet, and this hint of physical power in thought itself (in the same way as the next line gives it colour), may hint at an idea that one would like to feel was present, as otherwise it is the only main idea about Nature that the poem leaves out; that of the

* "Marvell's Garden" first appeared in a much shorter version in *Scrutiny*, and later in the volume compiled by F. R. Leavis under the title *Determinations* (1934). The present, considerably extended version is the fourth essay in *English Pastoral Poetry*, and is reprinted here by permission of the publishers, W. W. Norton & Company, Inc., New York; copyright, 1938, by the publishers. Mr. Empson (*b.* 1906) is also the author of *Seven Types of Ambiguity* (1930).

Hymn to David and *The Ancient Mariner*, the Orpheus idea, that by delight in Nature when terrible man gains strength to control it. This grand theme too has a root in magic; it is an important version of the idea of the man powerful because he has included everything in himself, is still strong, one would think, among the mountain climbers and often the scientists, and deserves a few examples here. I call it the idea of the *Hymn to David,* though being hidden behind the religious one it is nowhere overtly stated, except perhaps in the line

Praise above all, for praise prevails.

David is a case of Orpheus-like behaviour because his music restrained the madness of Saul.

His furious foes no more maligned
When he such melody divined,
And sense and soul detained;

By *divining*—intuiting—the harmony behind the universe he "makes it divine," rather as to discover a law of nature is to "give nature laws," and this restrains the madman who embodies the unruled forces of nature from killing him. The main argument of the verses describing nature (or nature as described by David) is that the violence of Nature is an expression of her adoration of God, and therefore that the man of prayer who also adores God delights in it and can control it.

Strong the gier eagle on his sail
Strong against tide, th' enormous whale
Emerges, as he goes.

But stronger still, in earth or air
Or in the sea, the man of prayer,
And far beneath the tide.

The feeling is chiefly carried by the sound; long Latin words are packed into the short lines against a short one-syllable rhyming word full of consonants; it is like dancing in heavy skirts; he juggles with the whole cumbrous complexity of the world. The *Mariner* makes a more conscious and direct use of the theme, but in some degree runs away from it at the end. The reason it was a magical crime for a sailor to kill the albatross is that it both occurs among terrible scenes of Nature and symbolises man's power to extract life from them, so ought doubly to be delighted in. So long as the Mariner is horrified by the creatures of the calm he is their slave; he is set free to act, in the supreme verses of the poem, as soon as he delights in them. The final moral is

He prayeth best, that loveth best
All things both great and small.

But that copybook maxim is fine only if you can hold it firmly together with such verses as this, which Coleridge later omitted:

The very deeps did rot; oh Christ
That such a thing could be;
Yea, slimy things did crawl with legs
Upon the slimy sea.

And it was these creatures, as he insisted in the margin by giving the same name to both, that the Mariner blessed unaware when he discovered their beauty. This is what Coleridge meant by alternately saying that the poem has too much of the moral and too little; knowing what the conventional phrases of modern Christianity ought to mean he thought he could shift to a conventional moral that needs to be based upon the real one. Byron's nature-poetry gives more obvious examples of the theme; he likes to compare a storm on the Jura or what not to a woman whom, we are to feel, only Byron could dominate. Poe was startled and liberated by it into a symbol of his own achievement; the sailor in *The Maelstrom* is so horrified as to be frozen, through a trick of neurosis, into idle curiosity, and this becomes a scientific interest in the portent which shows him the way to escape from it.

Nature when terrible is no theme of Marvell's, and he gets this note of triumph rather from using nature when peaceful to control the world of man.

How safe, methinks, and strong, behind
These Trees have I encamp'd my Mind;
Where Beauty, aiming at the Heart,
Bends in some Tree its useless Dart;
And where the World no certain Shot
Can make, or me it toucheth not.
But I on it securely play,
And gaul its Horsemen all the Day.

The masculine energy of the last couplet is balanced immediately by an acceptance of Nature more masochist than passive, in which he becomes Christ with both the nails and the thorns. (*Appleton House*, lxxvi.)

> Bind me ye *Woodbines* in your 'twines,
> Curle me about ye gadding *Vines,*
> And Oh so close your Circles lace,
> That I may never leave this Place:
> But, lest your Fetters prove too weak,
> Ere I your Silken Bondage break,
> Do you, *O Brambles,* chain me too,
> And courteous *Briars* nail me through.

He does not deify himself more actively, and in any case the theme of the *Garden* is a repose.

> How vainly men themselves amaze
> To win the Palm, or Oke, or Bayes;
> And their uncessant Labours see
> Crown'd from some single Herb or Tree.
> Whose short and narrow verged Shade
> Does prudently their Toyles upbraid;
> While all Flow'rs and all Trees do close
> To weave the Garlands of repose.

This first verse comes nearest to stating what seems the essential distinction, with that between powers inherent and power worked out in practice, being a general and feeling one could be; in this ideal case, so the wit of the thing claims, the power to have been a general is already satisfied in the garden. "Unemployment" is too painful and normal even in the fullest life for such a theme to be trivial. But self-knowledge is possible in such a state so far as the unruly impulses are digested, ordered, made transparent, not by their being known, at the time, as unruly. Consciousness no longer makes an important distinction; the impulses, since they must be balanced already, neither need it to put them right nor are put wrong by the way it forces across their boundaries. They let themselves be known because they are not altered by being known, because their principle of indeterminacy no longer acts. This idea is important for all the versions of pastoral, for the pastoral figure is always ready to be the critic; he not only includes everything but may in some unexpected way know it.

Another range of his knowledge might be mentioned here. I am not sure what arrangement of flower-beds is described in the last verse, but it seems clear that the sun goes through the "zodiac" of flowers in one day, and that the bees too, in going from one bed to another, reminding us of the labours of the first verse, pass all summer in a day. They compute their time as well as we in that though their lives are shorter they too contract all experience into it, and this makes the poet watch over large periods of time as well as space. So far he becomes Nature, he becomes permanent. It is a graceful finale to the all-in-one theme, but not, I think, very important; the crisis of the poem is in the middle.

Once you accept the Oxford edition's note you may as well apply it to the whole verse.

> Meanwhile the Mind, from pleasure less,
> Withdraws into its happiness;
> The Mind, that Ocean where each kind
> Does streight its own resemblance find;
> Yet it creates, transcending these,
> Far other worlds, and other Seas,
> Annihilating . . .

From pleasure less. Either "from the lessening of pleasure"—"we are quiet in the country, but our dullness gives a sober and self-knowing happiness, more intellectual than that of the over-stimulated pleasures of the town" or "made less by this pleasure"—"The pleasures of the country give a repose and intellectual release which make me less intellectual, make my mind less worrying and introspective." This is the same puzzle as to the consciousness of the thought; the ambiguity gives two meanings to pleasure, corresponding to his Puritan ambivalence about it, and to the opposition between pleasure and happiness. *Happiness,* again, names a conscious state, and yet involves the idea of things falling right, happening so, not being ordered by an anxiety of the conscious reason. (So that as a rule it is a weak word; it is by seeming to look at it hard and bring out its implications that the verse here makes it act as a strong one.)

The same doubt gives all their grandeur to the next lines. The sea if calm reflects everything near it; the mind as knower is a conscious mirror. Somewhere in the sea are sea-lions and -horses and everything else, though they are different from land ones; the unconsciousness is unplumbed and pathless, and there is no instinct so strange among the beasts that it lacks its fantastic echo in the mind. In the first version thoughts are shadows, in the second (like the *green thought*) they are as solid as what they image; and yet they still correspond to some thing in the outer world, so that the poet's intuition is comparable to pure knowledge. This metaphor may reflect back so that *withdraws* means the tide going down; the *mind* is *less* now, but will return, and it is now that one can see the rock-pools. On the Freudian view of an Ocean, *withdraws* would make this repose in Nature a return to the womb; anyway it may mean either "withdraws into self-contemplation" or "withdraws altogether, into its mysterious processes of digestion." *Streight* may mean "packed together," in the microcosm, or "at once"; the beasts see their reflection (perhaps the root idea of the metaphor) as soon as they look for it; the calm of Nature gives the poet an immediate self-knowledge. But we have already had two entrancingly witty verses about the sublimation of sexual desire into a taste for Nature (I should not say that this theme was the main emotional drive behind the poem, but it takes up a large part of its overt thought), and the *kinds* look for their *resemblance,* in practice, out of a desire for *creation;* in the mind, at this fertile time for the poet, they can *find* it "at once," being "packed together." The transition from the beast and its reflection to the two pairing beasts implies a transition from the correspondences of thought with fact to those of thought with thought, to find which is to be creative; there is necessarily here a suggestion of rising from one "level" of thought to another; and in the next couplet not only does the mind transcend the world it mirrors, but a sea, to which it is parallel, transcends both land and sea too, which implies self-consciousness and all the antinomies of philosophy. Whether or not you give *transcendent* the technical sense "predicable of all categories" makes no great difference; in including everything in itself the mind includes as a detail itself and all its inclusions. And it is true that the sea reflects the *other worlds* of the stars; Donne's metaphor of the globe is in the background. Yet even here the double meaning is not lost; all land-beasts have their sea-beasts, but the sea also has the kraken; in the depths as well as the transcendence of the mind are things stranger than all the kinds of the world.

Miss M. C. Bradbrook has pointed out to me that the next verse, while less triumphant, gives the process a more firmly religious interpretation.

> Here at the Fountains sliding foot,
> Or by some Fruit-trees mossy root,
> Casting the Bodies Vest aside,
> My Soul into the boughs does glide;
> There like a Bird it sits, and sings,
> Then whets, and combs its silver Wings;
> And, till prepar'd for longer flight,
> Waves in its Plumes the various Light.

The bird is the dove of the Holy Spirit and carries a suggestion of the rainbow of the covenant. By becoming inherent in everything he becomes a soul not pantheist but clearly above and apart from the world even while still living in it. Yet the paradoxes are still firmly maintained here, and the soul is as solid as the green thought. The next verse returns naturally and still with exultation to the jokes in favour of solitude against women.

Green takes on great weight here, as Miss Sackville West pointed out, because it has been a pet word of Marvell's before. To list the uses before the satires may seem an affectation of pedantry, but shows how often the word was used; and they are pleasant things to look up. In the Oxford text: pages 12, I.23; 17, I.18; 25, I.ii; 27, I.4; 38, I.3; 45, I.3; 46, I.25; 48, I.18; 49, I.48; 70, I.376; 71, I.390; 74, I.510; 122, I.2. Less rich uses: 15, I.18; 21, I.44; 30, I.55; 42, I.14; 69, I.339; 74, II.484, 496; 78, I.628; 85, I.82; 89, I.94; 108, I.196. It is connected here with grass, buds, children, an as yet virginal prospect of sexuality, and the peasant stock from which the great families emerge. The "unfathomable" grass makes the soil fertile and shows it to be so; it is the humble, permanent, undeveloped nature which sustains everything, and to which everything must return. No doubt D. H. Lawrence was right when he spoke up for Leaves of Grass against Whitman and said they felt themselves to be very aristocratic, but that too is eminently a pastoral fancy. Children are connected with this both as buds, and because of their contact with Nature (as in Wordsworth), and unique fitness for Heaven (as in the Gospels).

> The tawny mowers enter next,
> Who seem like Israelites to be,
> Walking on foot through a green sea,

connects greenness with oceans and gives it a magical security;

> And in the greenness of the grass
> Did see my hopes as in a glass

connects greenness with mirrors and the partial knowledge of the mind. The complex of ideas he concentrates into this passage, in fact, had been worked out already, and in a context that shows how firmly these ideas about Nature were connected with direct pastoral. The poem indeed comes immediately after a pastoral series about the mower of grass.

> I am the Mower Damon, known
> Through all the Meadows I have mown;
> On me the Morn her dew distills
> Before her darling Daffodils.

In these meadows he feels he has left his mark on a great territory, if not on everything, and as a typical figure he has mown all the meadows of the world; in either case Nature gives him regal and magical honours, and I suppose he is not only the ruler but the executioner of the daffodils—the Clown as Death.

> Only for him no Cure is found,
> Whom Juliana's Eyes do wound.
> 'Tis death alone that this must do:
> For Death thou art a Mower too.

He provides indeed more conscious and comic mixtures of heroic and pastoral:

> every Mower's wholesome heat
> Smelled like an Alexander's sweat.

It is his grand attack on gardens which introduces both the connection through wit between the love of woman and of nature, which is handled so firmly in the *Garden:*

> No white nor red was ever seen
> So am'rous as this lovely green:

—and the belief that the fruitful attitude to Nature is the passive one:

> His [the gardener's] green *Seraglio* has its
> Eunuchs too;
> Lest any Tyrant him outdoe.
> And in the Cherry he does Nature vex,
> To procreate without a Sex.
> 'Tis all enforced; the Fountain and the Grot;
> While the sweet Fields do lye forgot;
> Where willing Nature does to all dispence
> A wild and fragrant Innocence:
> And *Fauns* and *Faryes* do the Meadows till,
> More by their presence than their skill.

It is Marvell himself who tills the Garden by these magical and contemplative powers.

Grass indeed comes to be taken for granted as the symbol of pastoral humility:

> Unhappy Birds! what does it boot
> To build below the Grasses' Root;
> When Lowness is unsafe as Hight,
> And Chance o'ertakes what scapeth Spight?

It is a humility of Nature from which she is still higher than man, so that the grasshoppers preach to him from their pinnacles:

> And now to the Abyss I pass
> Of that unfathomable Grass,
> Where men like Grashoppers appear,
> But Grashoppers are Gyants there;
> They, in their squeking Laugh, contemn
> Us as we walk more low than them:
> And, from the Precipices tall
> Of the green spire's, to us do call.

It seems also to be an obscure merit of grass that it produces "hay," which was the name of a country dance, so that the humility is gaiety.

> With this the golden fleece I shear
> Of all these Closes ev'ry Year,
> And though in Wool more poor than they,
> Yet I am richer far in Hay.

To nineteenth-century taste the only really poetical verse of the poem is the central fifth of the nine; I have been discussing the sixth, whose dramatic position is an illustration of its very penetrating theory. The first four are a crescendo of wit, on the themes "success or failure is not important, only the repose that follows the exercise of one's powers" and "women, I am pleased to say, are no longer interesting to me, because nature is more beautiful." One effect of the wit is to admit, and so make charming, the impertinence of the second of these, which indeed the first puts in its place; it is only for a time, and after effort among human beings, that he can enjoy solitude. The value of these moments made it fitting to pretend they were eternal; and yet the lightness of his expression of their sense of power is more intelligent, and so more convincing, than Wordsworth's solemnity on the same theme, because it does not forget the opposing forces.

> When we have run our Passions heat,
> Love hither makes his best retreat.
> The *Gods*, that mortal beauty chase,
> Still in a Tree did end their race.
> *Apollo* hunted *Daphne* so,
> Only that she might Laurel grow,
> And *Pan* did after *Syrinx* speed,
> Not as a Nymph, but for a Reed.

The energy and delight of the conceit has been sharpened or keyed up here till it seems to burst and transform itself; it dissolves in the next verse into the style of Keats. So his observation of the garden might mount to an ecstasy which disregarded it; he seems in this next verse to imitate the process he has described, to enjoy in a receptive state the exhilaration which an exercise of wit has achieved. But striking as the change of style is, it is unfair to empty the verse of thought and treat it as random description; what happens is that he steps back from overt classical conceits to a rich and intuitive use of Christian imagery. When people treat it as the one good "bit" of the poem one does not know whether they have recognised that the Alpha and Omega of the verse are the Apple and the Fall.

> What wond'rous Life in this I lead!
> Ripe Apples drop about my head;
> The Luscious Clusters of the Vine
> Upon my Mouth do crush their Wine;
> The Nectaren, and curious Peach,
> Into my hands themselves do reach;
> Stumbling on Melons, as I pass,
> Insnar'd with Flow'rs, I fall on Grass.

Melon, again, is the Greek for apple; "all flesh is *grass*" and its own *flowers* here are the snakes in it that stopped Eurydice. Mere grapes are at once the primitive and the innocent wine; the *nectar* of Eden, and yet the blood of sacrifice. *Curious* could mean "rich and strange" (Nature), "improved by care" (art) or "inquisitive" (feeling towards me, since nature is a mirror, as I do towards her). All the eatable beauties give themselves so as to lose themselves, like a lover, with a forceful generosity; like a lover they *ensnare* him. It is the triumph of the attempt to impose a sexual interest upon nature; there need be no more Puritanism in this use of sacrificial ideas than is already inherent in the praise of solitude; and it is because his repose in the orchard hints at such a variety of emotions that he is contemplating *all that's made.* Sensibility here repeats what wit said in the verse before; he tosses into the fantastic treasure-chest of the poem's thought all the pathos and dignity that Milton was to feel in his more celebrated Garden; and it is while this is going on, we are told in the next verse, that the mind performs its ambiguous and memorable *withdrawal.* For each of the three central verses he gives a twist to the screw of the microscope and is living in another world.

I must go back to the *annihilating* lines, whose method is less uncommon. Similar ideas and tricks of language are used in Donne's *Exstasie,* where various puns impose on us the idea that an adequate success in love is a kind of knowledge which transcends the barriers of the ordinary kind. There is again some doubt how far the author knew what he was doing.

> As our blood labours to beget
> Spirits, as like souls as it can, . . .
> So must pure louers' soules descend. . . .

To the modern reader this is a pun on the senses "subtle material essence" (e.g. "spirits of salt") and "non-material unit of life"; it seems used with as much "wit" as the other puns, to trick us into feeling that soul and body may be interfused. The Oxford edition notes make clear that to Donne this was neither a pun nor a sophistry; "The spirits . . . are the thin and active part of the blood, and are of a kind of middle nature, between soul and body" (Sermons); one view of them was that there was a hierarchy of more and more spiritual ones. It is curious how the change in the word leaves the poetry unaffected; by Swift's time the two senses were an absurd accident from which one could get ironies against materialism. No doubt in some important senses Donne was right, but however supported by Cambridge Platonism it is a genuine primitive use of the word. Whereas he would certainly have known there was a pun on "sense" even if he took it for granted. "Our bodies why do we forbeare?"

> We owe them thankes, because they thus,
> Did us, to us, at first convey,

> Yielded their forces, sense, to us,
> Nor are dross to us, but allay.

The antithesis for *allay* makes it mean "alloy," a less valuable substance put into their gold to strengthen it for practical use; *allay* could mean "keeping the spiritual pleasure from being too great, more than our strength could bear," which goes with "alloy," then, behind that, "relief to the pain of desire," which makes the flesh less unimportant. This is reinforced by the special meaning of sense ("the wanton stings and motions of the 's' "). That rich word confuses the pleasure and the knowledge given the senses (Donne wants to imply they are mutually dependent) and suggests that soul and body are in a healthy intuitive relation—"plenty of sense." The use of *sense* for sensibleness became stronger later in the century, but it is already clearly an element in the word—for example in saying "there is no sense" in a statement when it has meaning but is not sensible. "We could not know each other at all without sensations, therefore cannot know each other fully without sensuality, nor would it be sensible to try to do so."

The poem uses the word again later, and there the sexual meaning is clear.

> So must pure louers soules descend
> To affections, and to faculties,
> Which sense may reach and apprehend,
> Else a great Prince in prison lies.
> To our bodies turn we then. . . .

Affections are "loves," "weaknesses," and in the philosophical sense "physical effects." *Apprehend* means "know" and by derivation "clutch," and *reach* would go with either, which gives sense a sort of bridge between its meanings.

It is possible that Donne means to throw in a pun on "know," as in "Adam knew his wife."

> Wee then, who are this new soule, know,
> Of what we are compos'd, and made,
> For, the Atomies of which we grow,
> Are soules, which no change can invade.

Know is isolated by the comma ("know each other"), and *of* may then take a step towards "by means of." Then, with Donne's usual leap in pretending to give a reason, he makes each soul entirely immaterial; "the intellectual knowledge has, for us, all the advantages of the physical one, even granted that they are distinguishable." If he did this it would have to be done consciously and wilfully.

One should not of course take such poetry as only a clever game. This truth-seeking idea seems fundamental to the European convention of love-poetry; love is always idealised as a source of knowledge not only of the other party but of oneself and of the world:

> This Exstasie doth unperplex

because it makes the disparate impulses of the human creature not merely open to the prying of the mind but prepared for its intrusion. It is along these lines, I think, that D. H. Lawrence's hatred of the whole conception might be answered, or rather that he answered it himself. On the other hand, I think Donne felt quite casual about these particular tricks; the juggle with *sense* has the same graceful impudence as his frankly absurd arguments. M. Legouis may be right in saying that he set out merely to dramatise the process of seduction; it is only clear that he found the argument fascinating and believed that it had some truth in some cases. He did not think it so false as to depend on his puns, even where he recognised them; he may well have understood what the puns themselves depend upon. They insist on relics of primitive thought in civilised language, and thereby force the language to break down its later distinctions and return to ideas natural to the human mind. Dr. Richards' account of romantic nature poetry in *Coleridge on Imagination* is a very good example; the personalised Nature is treated both as external to man and as created by an instinct of the mind, and by tricks of language these are made to seem the same. But if they were simply called the same we would not so easily be satisfied by the tricks. What we feel is that though they are essentially unlike they are practically unlike in different degrees at different times; a supreme condition can therefore be imagined, though not attained, in which they are essentially like. (To put it like this is no doubt to evade a philosophic issue.) A hint of the supreme condition is thus found in the actual one (this makes the actual one include everything in itself), but this apparently exalted claim is essentially joined to humility; it is effective only through the admission that it is only a hint.

Something of the tone of pastoral is therefore inherent in the claim; the fault of the Wordsworthian method seems to be that it does not show this.

I shall add here a pun from *As You Like It*, which shows how the same issue may be raised by a casual joke. The pun in its context makes a contradiction, and this is felt to show an intuitive grasp of some of the puzzles of the context. Fortunately there is no doubt that a pun is meant because the text insists upon it; the *N.E.D.* shows that the modern spelling, though used loosely, already made the distinction. Apart from facsimiles no edition that I have seen has yet printed the text. The point of the two spellings is to show that the two senses are at work; it is none the less fair to take the senses the other way round. (This is from the Folio; there is no Quarto.)

CLOWN. . . . truly, I would the Gods hadde made thee poeticall.

AUDREY. I do not know what Poetical is: is it honest in word and deed: is it a true thing?

CLOWN. No trulie: for the truest poetrie is the most faining, and Louers are given to Poetrie: and what they sweare in Poetrie, may be said as Louers, they do feigne.

AUDREY. Do you wish then that the Gods had made me Poetical?

CLOWN. I do truly: for thou swear'st to me thou art honest: Now if thou wert a Poet, I might haue some hope thou didst feigne.

"A material fool" is the pleased judgment of the listening Jaques; he feels that there is a complete copy of the human world among fools, as of beasts among sea-beasts. This indeed is one of the assumptions of pastoral, that you can say everything about complex people by a complete consideration of simple people. The jokes are mainly carried on by puns on "honest"—chastity in women, truth in speech, simplicity in clowns, and the hearty sense "generous because free from hypocrisy"; my point is the pun on "fain" (*desiring*) and "feign" (*pretend*; in lovers *pretend honest desire*). The doubt of the poet's honesty is referred to the broader doubt of his self-knowledge, just as *honest* itself shifts from "truth-telling" to "sincere in his own mind." The pun itself is common, though I think it is only here, where it enriches the thought so much, that Shakespeare spelt it out for the reader.

EGEUS. Thou hast by moonelight at her window sang
With faining voice, verses of faining love,
And stolne the impression of her fantasie.

He feigns true love because he would fain possess her; the word *love* itself may be used of a desire not permanent or generous; Egeus would call that a feigning love even if Nature deceives both of them, and the man thinks himself sincere. The easy but capacious mind of Spenser takes this for granted (F.Q., V.xii. 36; Hymn to Love, 216); nobody pretends without purpose, so it is a useful trick of language. Touchstone's use of it about poetry is more searching.

The root of the joke is that a physical desire drives the human creature to a spiritual one. The best poetry is the most genuinely passionate (fain) but there may be two pretences (feign), that the desire felt for this woman is spiritual and that any woman is the object of so spiritual a desire. "To write poetry is not the quickest way to satisfy desire; there must be some other impulse behind the convention of love-poetry; something feigned in the choice of topic; some other thing of which they are fain." As for the distinction between their rôles as poets and lovers, both senses may apply to them in both, also to *swearing*, since "go to hell" is spontaneous, not meant, not meant to deceive, and a sort of feigning in which you are fain of what you feign. For that matter they are wooing the reader even if they are not trying to seduce a mistress; the process at its simplest involves desire and detachment, nature and sophistication; levels mysteriously inter-related which a sane man separates only for a joke. Touchstone's pretence of acidity allows of a real plea for his own case because it implies that the most refined desires are inherent in the plainest, and would be false if they weren't; he shows a staircase by giving the two lowest steps, lust and cheating. In the Marvell and Donne examples it is the top of the staircase that is in question, but the same method is used to define it. Two ideas are united which in normal use are contradictory, and our machinery of interpretation so acts that we feel there is a series of senses in which they could be more and more truly combined. This is clearest in what Mr. James Smith defined as metaphysical conceits, those that genuinely sum up a metaphysical problem. The top and next steps in the Aristotelian staircase about form and matter, for example, would be pure form and the material, already form, which it informs. Donne is using this when he calls each lover's soul the body of the other's; the fact that we do not believe that the lovers are in this condition does not keep us from a feeling of belief in the conceit, because we believe in the staircase which it defines; the lovers appear as conscious of the staircase and higher up on it than most. Nor for that matter do we believe that the clown is at the bottom of his staircase; his understanding of it acts as a proof that he isn't. A good case of a poem with some doubt about the staircase it requires is provided by Shakespeare's *Phoenix and Turtle;* it depends on the same ideas as Donne's *First Anniversary*, but gets very different feelings out of them. The entire flatness of the use of the convention makes it seem first an engagingly simpleminded piece of "idealism" and then, since the union of the birds is likely after all to be of a simple kind, an expression of cultivated and good-humoured sensuality; this does not by any means destroy the pathetic dignity of the close. There is a suggestion that the author finds the convention fascinating but absurd, which he shows mainly by his sound-effects. This seems to me intentional, very delightful, and not a thing that Chapman (who has been suggested as the author) could possibly have done. It is clear here that once you cease to impose a staircase the thing shifts from heroic to mock-pastoral. Some such idea needs to be added to Mr. James Smith's account (perhaps he would call it obvious) because otherwise there seems no way of putting in a judgment of value; on his account a metaphysical conceit is essentially a vivid statement of a puzzle, and in practice it is more.

I should say that this process is at work in much poetry that does not seem ambiguous at all, and shall pursue the question into Homer as the fountainhead of simplicity. This may also throw some light on the obscure connection between heroic and pastoral; the fact seems to be that both rely on a "complex in simple" formula.

One idea essential to a primitive epic style is that the good is not separable (anyway at first level judgments) from a life of straightforward worldly success in which you keep certain rules; the plain satisfactions are good in themselves and make great the men who enjoy them. From this comes the "sense of glory" and of controlling nature by delight in it. It is absurd to call this a "premoralistic" view, since the rules may demand great sacrifices and it is shameful not to keep them; there is merely a naive view of the nature of good. (Both a limitation of the things that are good and a partial failure to separate the idea of good from the idea of those things.) The naive view is so often more true than the sophisticated ones that this comes in later ages to take on an air of massive grandeur; it gives a feeling of freedom from humbug which is undoubtedly noble, and the Homeric heroes support this by the far from savage trait of questioning the beliefs they still die for. Stock epithets about "the good wine" or "the well-built gates" imply "so one always rightly feels"; such a thing essentially has virtue in it, *is* a piece of virtue; a later reader feels this to be symbolic, a process of packing all the sorts of good into a simple one. Material things are taken as part of a moral admiration, and to a later reader (with less pride, for example, in the fact that his culture uses iron) this seems an inspiriting moral paradox like those of pastoral—"to one who knows how to live the ideal is easily reached." It is assumed that Ajax is still enormously grand when he cooks his dinner; the later reader feels he must really be very grand not to lose his dignity, whereas at the time it was a thing of some splendour to have so much dinner to cook or such implements to do it with. This comes to have the same effect as a pretence of pastoral humility in the author. Also the heroic individual has an enormous effect on everything in sight, gods and men, and yet finds everything of manageable dimensions; the later reader feels that this belongs to a village society rather than a large-town one. Certainly the heroes are not grand merely because they are brave; they can run away like other people, and say so more frankly. Indeed a great part of their dignity comes from the naive freshness with which they can jump from one level of argument to another, and this leaves room for the effects I am considering.

Thus the puzzles become more obvious later, but this is not to say they were not used at the start. The heroes are given a directly moral grandeur by the perpetual clashes between free-will and necessity, symbolised by their relations with the gods, out of which they construct their speeches; they fight on when certain of failure and kill each other with the apology that they too are fated, and such fore-knowledge as they have makes them half divine. It is very curious that what is supposed to be another branch of the same race, when it arrived in India, had none of this interest in the problems of freewill; the dignity of the heroes in the Mahabarata is based on puzzles about the One and the Many. Nor did it develop later; the Buddha was once actually faced with the problem of freewill raised so starkly by his system, and brushed it aside on grounds of morality; I understand that all Buddhist theologians have ignored the issue. Whereas all new ideas in Europe, Christianity and the sciences in turn, have been taken as new problems about necessity and free-will. Thus the reason why the Homeric *but* where one expects "and" has so much poetic force is that it implies some argument, such as all the characters are happy with, and the argument would lead you to other levels of thought. (This acts as a feeling that the two things put together are vividly different in themselves.) "He spoke, and held still his hand upon the silvery hilt, and thrust back the great sword into the scabbard, nor did he disobey the order of Minerva; but she had gone to Olympus, to the mansions of aegis-bearing Jove, amongst the other deities." *But* makes her already indifferent; the puzzle about how far men are free and how far the gods are only forces in their minds is thrust upon your attention. Also there is a strong feeling in the epic that the heroes are too great to kill each other for detested Helen and the unnecessary recovery of corpses ("Nor do I fear so much about the dead body of Patroclus, which will quickly satiate the dogs and birds of the Trojans, as much as I fear for my own head, lest it suffer anything, and for thine") and yet that only this would display their greatness; a rich contradiction on which to build a hierarchy of value. I began by saying that such writing was based on a naive idea of the nature of good, but in fact other ideas of good are implicit in it; Shakespeare's *Troilus and Cressida* is often taken as a sort of parody of the *Iliad,* but there is little in it that Homer did not imply. What becomes strange to a more sophisticated society is the order in which the ideas can be built up; in such a society everybody has been told some refined ideas about good (or what not) and wants them put in at once; to take a simple thing and imply a hierarchy in it can then only be done in a strange world like that of Milton's Adam or a convention like that of pastoral. To say this is to echo what many of Homer's critics, including Milton himself, have said about the peculiar advantage he got from his date, and I am only trying to show that it fits in with my theory.

I have not been able to say what machinery erects a staircase on a contradiction, but then the only essential for the poet is to give the reader a chance to build an interesting one; there are continual opportunities in the most normal uses of language. Any statement of identity between terms already defined ("God is love") is a contradiction because you already know they are not identical; you have to ignore senses that would be unimportant ("the first cause was a creative impulse") and there are likely to be degrees in which the two may be called identical which lead to different important senses. That the process is not simple is obvious when you turn them round; "love is God" would be quite different. "Might is Right" and "Right is Might" were felt to be clear and opposite statements of ethical theory, and it is not clear how this was possible. It is no good to read them as "if a man has might, then he has right," etc.; a supporter of this opinion would say that if a man has no might he has no right, and the two sentences are still identical. The same applies to the similar interpretations "Might is a member of the class Right," etc.; it would be the only member of its class. I think these are at work; the analogy of the second word to an adjective in this version shows how the first is felt to be the more solid and unchangeable. But the second word is in fact belittled rather than made inclusive. Yet you cannot read them simply as substitutions; "always say might instead of right; there is no reason for not making a full use of power" and "never calculate chances; to be in the right is the only thing to be considered." These are present and seem to control the senses from the back, but the subdued word is still there and is not negated. *Right* in the first is some sort of justification and *might* in the second some sort of hope or claim. "A great and crowded nation has the right to expand"; "because we have right on our side we are certain to win." A vague sense that "is" has other uses than the expression of identity makes us ready to find meanings in such sentences; this may well have been the historical reason why it was too convenient to be simplified. But the principle of language that makes the two different is simply a traffic rule; the two words are felt to cover some of the same ground and in some cases of conflict the first has the right of way.

It might I think also be argued that any contradiction implies a regress, though not one definite one. To say that it is always an example of the supreme process of seeing the Many as One is to ignore the differences in the feelings aroused by different examples; but there may always be a less ambitious process at work that uses similar machinery. The pretence that two words are identical acts as a hint that they have been fitted into some system, in which each key word is dependent on the others, like the parts of an organism; admittedly, the words are not the same but they have been "unified." One characteristic of an organism is that you can only change it (as a whole and without killing it) by a process like edging up a chimney in rock-climbing; one element must be changed to the small extent that the elasticity of the system allows and then the others must be changed to fit it. So to find your way into the interpretation seems essentially a process of shifting the words again and again. This at least describes the sense of richness (readiness for argument not pursued) in such language and the fact that one ambiguity, even though obtained in several parallel words, is not enough for it.

That this talk about a hierarchy of "levels" is vague I can cheerfully admit; the idea is generally vague in the authors who use it, and none the less powerful for being left in a suggestive form. But the three central verses of the Marvell poem are at least a definite example; in the course of suggesting various interlocking hierarchies (knowing that you know that you know, reconciling the remaining unconscious with the increasing consciousness, uniting in various degrees perception and creation, the one and the many), it does in fact rise through a hierarchy of three sharply contrasted styles and with them give a more and more inclusive account of the mind's relation to Nature. Only a metaphysical poet with so perfect a sense of form and so complete a control over the tricks of the style, at the end of its development, could actually dramatise these hints as he gave them.

DAVID DAICHES: Character*

SHOULD the personalities of characters in fiction emerge from a chronological account of a group of events and the characters' reactions to those events, or is it the duty of the novelist to take time off, as it were, in order to give a rounded description of the characters at the point when they are introduced into the story? Novelists have employed either of these two methods, and some have employed both at once. Sometimes the character as we see him first is a shadowy and indeterminate creature, but after his reactions to a chronological series

* "Character" is the second chapter of *The Novel and the Modern World* (1939), reprinted here by permission of the author and the director of the University of Chicago Press. Mr. Daiches (*b.* 1912) is also the author of *The Place of Meaning in Poetry* (1935), *New Literary Values* (1936), *Literature and Society* (1938), *Poetry and the Modern World* (1941), *Virginia Woolf* (1942), and *Robert Louis Stevenson* (1948).

of events have been presented we feel that he is now a living personality. In other novels we are given a descriptive portrait of the character first, so that we know what to expect, and the resulting actions and reactions of the character provide a filling-in and elaboration whose justness we can appreciate by comparison with the original portrait.

In Thomas Hardy's *Mayor of Casterbridge* there is no set description of Michael Henchard's character at the beginning of the book or, indeed, anywhere else. In the first chapter he is simply a young man, and Hardy continues to call him "the man" until the first episode is concluded. True, we have an account of Michael's physical appearance ("The man was of fine figure, swarthy, and stern in aspect," etc.) but that is all. There is no hint of his real nature—his personality. That emerges as the story proceeds—emerges from the story itself, from the account of what Michael does, and the way in which he reacts to the doings of others. It might be argued that his character is not fully presented until the story is concluded, and the only way Hardy has by then managed to give us a full view of his character has been by taking him through a long and varied sequence of events. Any criterion of consistency we may apply can concern only the relation of one action or reaction of Michael to another; there can be no referring back to an original prose portrait, because the author has not given us one.

That is one way of presenting character. The other, and perhaps the commoner, way is illustrated as well as anywhere in the third chapter of Trollope's *Barchester Towers*. The chapter is entitled "Dr. and Mrs. Proudie" and is a complete formal account of the characters of Dr. Proudie and his wife. First a general sketch of Dr. Proudie's personality and habits of mind, then an account of his career, then further expansion of his present nature and attitude. Then Mrs. Proudie is taken up and similarly treated. By the end of the chapter we know exactly who and what these two characters are: we know no more about their characters at the end of the book—we have only seen the application to particular events of the general principles already enunciated. The interest of the book lies in these events and in our noting and approving how the characters run true to form throughout.

Most effective of all from the point of view of those whose chief interest in fiction lies in its psychological aspects is the technique which combines the foregoing two methods. Any one of Jane Austen's novels would provide a good example of this. *Emma,* for example, begins as follows:

> Emma Woodhouse, handsome, clever, and rich, with a comfortable home and happy disposition, seemed to unite some of the best blessings of existence; and had lived nearly twenty-one years in the world with very little to distress or vex her. . . .
>
> The real evils . . . of Emma's situation were the power of having rather too much her own way, and a disposition to think a little too well of herself; these were the disadvantages which threatened alloy to her many enjoyments. The danger, however, was at present so unperceived, that they did not by any means rank as misfortunes with her. . . .

And so on. In the first chapter we are given a fairly adequate sketch of Emma's character and circumstances. Yet we do not know Emma completely. A full understanding of her nature comes only after we have watched her reactions to the events which constitute the story and have studied her own part in the shaping of those events. Jane Austen has availed herself of both of our two methods: she starts with the inset character sketch, yet it is not complete, even as a character sketch, until we have seen Emma in her relations with Harriet Smith, Jane Fairfax, Mr. Elton, Mr. Knightley, and others. Whether or not there comes a point in the course of the novel, before the actual conclusion, where we feel that we know the real Emma, is a matter that individual readers may wrangle over; what concerns us here is to notice Jane Austen's method of showing us the kind of person that Emma is. Trollope shows us a known constant in varied circumstances, and our pleasure lies in recognizing the truth of the resulting description of behavior. Jane Austen shows us a partially known variant (variant for the reader just because partially known) in varied circumstances, and our pleasure lies in the progressively enhanced knowledge of that variant which the resulting description of behavior brings us —until there comes a point at which the variant becomes a constant, as we know the limiting bounds within which it moves. Hardy shows us an unknown defining itself by its reactions to the circumstances with which it is brought into contact. In all three cases a consistent character portrait emerges, but in each case the method of portraying—and the point at which the portrait is complete—is different. It might be noted that in Jane Austen's case minor characters are often portrayed by the first method: Mr. Woodhouse, for example, is presented complete at his first appearance and is made to act consistently throughout.

These two methods, separately or in combination, have been the stock methods of presenting character in fiction from the beginnings of the novel until modern times. Their prototypes are, respectively, the "Character" as practiced originally by Theophrastus and widely imitated in France and England in the seventeenth century, and the simple adventure story. You put a character into a story, or you arrange a story so that a character emerges—to make a very blunt distinction. In recent times, partly as a result of increased speculation into the nature of states of consciousness, writers have become dissatisfied with these traditional methods. They have realized that a psychologically accurate account of what a man is at any given moment can be given neither in terms of a static description of his character nor in terms of a group of chronologically arranged reactions to a series of circumstances. They have become interested in those aspects of consciousness which cannot be viewed as a progression of individual and self-existing moments, but which are essentially dynamic rather than static in nature and are independent of the given moment. The present moment is specious; it denotes the ever fluid passing of the "already" into the "not yet," and therefore retrospect and anticipation constitute the very essence of consciousness at any specified time. In other words, the relation of consciousness to time is not the simple one of events to time, but is independent of chronological sequence in a way that events are not. Further, the quality of my experience of any new phenomenon (and hence my reaction to any new circumstance) is conditioned by a group of similar experiences scattered up and down through past time, the association of which with the present experience is what makes the present experience what it is. A novelist might try to indicate this by such digression as, "That reminded him of . . . ," or "There flashed through his brain a memory of . . . ," or similar formulas, but modern writers have come to feel that this is too clumsy and artificial a way of expressing the mind's independence of chronological sequence. Some more fluid technique must be devised which will enable the author to utilize constantly those ever present contacts with the past which constitute the very stuff of consciousness. The static character sketch is, in the view of these writers, an arbitrary formalization of the real facts, while, on the other hand, to make the presentation of states of mind dependent on the step-by-step relation of a sequence of events in time is to impose on the mental activity of men a servile dependence on chronology which is not in accordance with psychological fact. It was as a way out of this difficulty (arising from a new realization of the complex and fluid nature of consciousness and the desire to utilize this realization in the portrayal of character) that the "stream of consciousness" technique was introduced into fiction.

Looked at from one point of view, the "stream of consciousness" technique is a means of escape from the tyranny of the time dimension. It is not only in distinct memories that the past impinges on the present, but also in much vaguer and more subtle ways, our mind floating off down some channel superficially irrelevant but really having a definite starting-off place from the initial situation; so that in presenting the characters' reactions to events, the author will show us states of mind being modified by associations and recollections deriving from the present situation (in a sense *creating* the present situation) but referring to a constantly shifting series of events in the past. Now, if this presentation of a state of mind is done with care and skill, the author will be able to kill two birds with one stone: he will be able to indicate the precise nature of the present experience of his character and at the same time he will be giving, incidentally, facts about the character's life previous to this moment—previous, in all probability, to the moment at which the book opens; and thus though the chronological scheme of the novel may comprise only a very limited time, one day, for example, the characters will emerge complete, both historically and psychologically.

This technique is, as has been mentioned, an extension of the more traditional memory digression. But a story which claims to unite in mutual progress the event and the character's reaction to the event, so that the mental picture is always dependent on the physical situation, can exploit the points in consciousness where the past impinges on, and indeed conditions, the present only as a digression, as an exception to the rule, which will become wearisome and disintegrating to the story if indulged in to any extent. What the "stream of consciousness" technique enables the writer to do is to claim a validity for these references and impingements, a validity in their own right as it were, because it is through their means that the story is presented completely and welded into a unity. The new method of describing states of mind becomes a new technique of story-telling.

Consider the actual story in Virginia's Woolf's *Mrs. Dalloway*. If we were to judge it by the chronological time scheme, we should say that it was the story of one day in the life of a middle-aged woman. But it is not that: the story embraces much of Mrs. Dalloway's past life and her relations with other characters in the past as well as in the present, so that, even judging the story on the simple narrative level, we can see that it is more than the story of one day's activity. This inclusion of so much of Mrs. Dalloway's past life is made possible by the way in which her ever-changing state of mind is described. True, the time sequence is marked off almost rigidly by such an obvious device as the striking of clocks (we shall discuss this point in more detail in a later chapter); but the very reason why the chronological framework has to be kept so constantly before the reader's attention is just because it is a framework, and nothing more. It is not the substance of the story, as it would be in any traditional novel; it is the mere skeleton which supports the living flesh and blood of the novel. Fixing her character physically at a given point in time and space, Mrs. Woolf is free to follow the character's "stream of consciousness" up and down in these two dimensions. It is as though we are led away up a winding tributary, but, having previously marked with some easily distinguished object the point where the tributary joins the main stream, we are able to find our way back at any moment. The significance of a novel like *Mrs. Dalloway* lies—to continue the metaphor—in the tributaries explored rather than in the main stream. The main stream is important only because it is from it that we take our bearings and with reference to it that we chart our position at any given moment. The line along which we move in the traditional chronological novel becomes, in a novel of this kind, one of the axes of a graph on which the curve of our journey is plotted, and we refer to the axis only when we want to check up on our position.

Thus the "stream of consciousness" technique is not simply a method of describing states of mind, because the method has implications for the whole technique of narrative and character drawing. If we ask ourselves why Joyce in *Ulysses* is able, while confining his chronological framework to the events of a single day, to relate so much more than merely the events of that single day and to make his hero perhaps the most complete and rounded character in all fiction, the answer lies in the potentialities—potentialities for narrative as well as for psychological analysis—of this new method of describing mental attitudes.

But the advantages for psychological analysis need not be minimized. The realization, which this technique implies, of the fact that personality is in a constant state of unstable equilibrium, that a mood is never anything static but a fluid pattern "mixing memory with desire," marks an important new development in the tradition of psychological fiction that has come down to us from Richardson. Richardson tried to present immediately the mood and thought of his characters by weaving his novels out of their letters. The defect here, from the modern standpoint, is that letters written to a given correspondent are bound to be subject to rigid formal limitations which prohibit the direct and adequate expression of states of mind. Only formalized aspects of an attitude can be expressed to any given audience (as every audience, even if the letter is a letter to the press, is a strictly defined and limited audience) however indefatigable a correspondent the character may be. The inhibiting effect of the audience would make the epistolary technique unacceptable to the modern psychological novelist. The diary would seem a more helpful device here than the letter; but the author will always be at a loss to render convincing the desire of the character to express completely and effectively his states of mind with reference to the given circumstances. No, if the characters are not to be either incredibly frank and self-conscious letter-writers or continuously introverted egoists, the responsibility for putting the "stream of consciousness" onto paper must not be laid on the characters but assumed in full by the author. The technique of Dorothy Richardson or Virginia Woolf or James Joyce is in this respect no more "real" than any other: it is a convention like other conventions, and it depends on our acceptance of the author's omniscience with no limitation whatsoever; but, once the convention is accepted, it makes possible the presentation of aspects of personality and of states of mind which were not possible in fiction utilizing other techniques and other conventions.

That we are what we are in virtue of what we have been is an obvious platitude; but the full utilization of the psychological aspects of this fact to build up a new technique in fiction is a comparatively recent development in the history of literature. The wheel has come full circle since the days when seventeenth-century wits wrote "characters" of types or eccentrics. Novelists who employ the "stream of consciousness" technique would deny that character *portrayal* is possible for the fiction writer at all: character is a process not a state, and the truth about men's reactions to their environment—and what is a man's character but his reactions to environment, actual and potential?—can be presented only through some attempt to show this process at work. An understanding of this view can help us to understand one of the main directive forces at work in contemporary fiction.

If we may return for a moment to the two traditional methods of presenting character discussed at the beginning of this chapter—the complete initial portrait followed by events which confirm the portrait and the emergence of the complete character from the action—we may note that a third method is frequently distinguished by students of fiction. This is the method which shows the character changing or developing, so that while the initial portrait is valid with reference to the situation presented at the beginning of the novel, it ceases to be valid by the time the novel is concluded. As a result of the circumstances in which the character finds himself throughout the course of the story, his nature is modified and we are finally confronted with a different person from the one we met at the beginning. Now, to distinguish this method as essentially a different technique seems to be the result of a certain confusion. It is of course possible to make a character really change in the course of the action: we know how in many popular novels the villain reforms at the end and becomes a good man. But such sudden and radical change as this—we recall Mr. Alfred Jingle's distressing conversion at the end of the *Pickwick Papers*—is never convincing in terms of psychological probability. Development, however, as distinct from such crude change, is more regular in good fiction. This is in essence but one aspect of our second method, when the character, incompletely presented at the beginning, does not emerge completely until the action has taken place. The final character is different, in the sense that events have made actual elements in his nature which before were only potential. The completeness of a character is judged by the degree to which its potentialities are realized. Thus, one reason why there is no complete portrayal at the beginning, why the portrayal is not complete until after we have seen the character in action, may be because the character was not meant to be a complete character until after these events had brought to light what was hitherto dormant. There is such a thing as an incomplete character in life. It may be such a character that the author introduces to us at the beginning of his story, while eventually we see the character made complete by experience. It will be seen that this is a modification of what we have called the second method rather than a quite separate method.

This point may be made clearer if we take an example from drama, where this development is more regular. Take the stock example of *King Lear*. King Lear is a different man at the end of the play from the man he was in Act I. Experience has altered his attitude, and we can actually see that process of modification at work throughout the play. Yet the circumstances presented in the play do not so much *change* Lear's character as bring out aspects of it which hitherto events had not conspired to release. This is a very different thing from the formal conversion of a villain to a reformed character. A character is not fully revealed until brought into the necessary testing circumstances, and an author can introduce us to a character either before or after he has met with such circumstances. There is a difference between change as the fulfilment of latent potentialities and change as the entire alteration of what previously existed. Consider Jane Austen's *Emma* again. True, Emma's character develops: she is more sensible in her attitude to specific things when we leave her than she was when we found her. But this is simply because her inherent common sense, a characteristic of hers all along, has had an opportunity of confronting experiences with which she was hitherto unfamiliar. Her rationality has applied itself to new premises and made the necessary deductions; and in the future she will always be in possession of those deductions. The change in Emma is of course very trivial when compared with that in Lear; but the difference is one of degree and not of kind. (Changes which are a result of physical or biological development are naturally in quite a different category. An adult is a different character from the child he once was. It might even be argued that for the purposes of plot in fiction they represent two separate characters. Novels whose central figure is shown progressing from infancy to manhood are liable to be episodic; no single presentation of character emerges from the work as a whole.)

What has the "stream of consciousness" technique to offer in presenting development in character? The situation here is very different from that present with either of the traditional methods; because by the adequate exploitation of states of mind and by following up all the paths suggested by the impinging of the past, in its multifarious variety, on the present, the nature of potentiality in character can be indicated even without our being shown the occurrence of events that would make those potentialities actual. The most interesting case in point here is the character of Stephen Dedalus in *Ulysses*. We see Stephen still a young man, immature, foolish, in many respects undeveloped. We are not shown him at all in his maturity—nothing in the book anticipates that day in June, 1904. Yet the fulness of implication provided by Joyce's method of presenting the consciousness of his characters is such that by the time the book closes we know the whole of Stephen, even though the whole of him is not yet, as it were, made actual. We can see the germ of the future in the present and without looking beyond the present. In Mrs. Dalloway, too, though the method is applied to her very much less intensely (and she is already a woman near the end of her life), we have a feeling by the end of the book that we know not only what she is and has been but what she might have been—we know all the unfulfilled possibilities in her character. In a character whose life is almost complete, unfulfilled possibilities are mere "might have beens"; in a character who has not yet reached complete maturity, such potentialities reveal also what may be.

If Joyce's method had been applied to the character of Lear it would have been possible, within a chronological framework comprising one day in Lear's life before the tragedy occurred, to make the reader aware of those potentialities in his character that in the play we do not see until they are made actual by events. The "stream of consciousness" method, at its most subtle and most intense, is able to achieve by depth what the traditional method achieves by extension. It provides a method of presenting character outside time and place, in the double sense that, first, it separates the presentation of consciousness from the chronological sequence of events, and, second, it enables the quality of a given state of mind to be investigated so completely, by means of pursuing to their end the remote mental associations and suggestions, that we do not need to wait for time to make the potential actual before we can see the whole.

CLEANTH BROOKS: The Language of Paradox *

Few of us are prepared to accept the statement that the language of poetry is the language of paradox. Paradox is the language of sophistry, hard, bright, witty; it is hardly the language of the soul. We are willing to allow that paradox is a permissible weapon which a Chesterton may on occasion exploit. We may permit it in epigram, a special subvariety of poetry; and in satire, which though useful, we are hardly willing to allow to be poetry at all. Our prejudices force us to regard paradox as intellectual rather than emotional, clever rather than profound, rational rather than divinely irrational.

Yet there is a sense in which paradox is the language appropriate and inevitable to poetry. It is the scientist whose truth requires a language purged of every trace of paradox; apparently the truth which the poet utters can be approached only in terms of paradox. I overstate the case, to be sure; it is possible that the title of this paper is itself to be treated as merely a paradox. Certainly, the paper itself will appear to many people as merely a piece of special case-making, specious rather than convincing. But there are reasons for thinking that the overstatement which I propose may light up some elements in the nature of poetry which tend to be overlooked.

The case of William Wordsworth, for instance, is instructive on this point. His poetry would not appear to promise many examples of the language of paradox. He usually prefers the direct attack. He insists on simplicity; he distrusts whatever seems sophistical. And yet the typical Wordsworth poem is based upon a paradoxical situation. Consider his celebrated

> It is a beauteous evening, calm and free,
> The holy time is quiet as a Nun
> Breathless with adoration. . . .

The poet is filled with worship, but the girl who walks beside him is not worshipping. The implication is that she should respond to the holy time, and become like the evening itself, nunlike; but she seems less worshipful than inanimate nature itself. Yet

> If thou appear untouched by solemn thought,
> Thy nature is not therefore less divine:
> Thou liest in Abraham's bosom all the year,
> And worship'st at the temple's inner shrine,
> God being with thee when we know it not.

The underlying paradox (of which the enthusiastic reader may well be unconscious) is nevertheless thoroughly necessary, even for the reader. Why does the innocent girl worship more deeply than the self-conscious poet who walks beside her? Because she is filled with an unconscious sympathy for *all* of nature, not merely the grandiose and solemn. One remembers the lines from Wordsworth's friend, Coleridge:

> He prayeth best, who loveth best
> All things both great and small.

Her unconscious sympathy is the unconscious worship. She is in communion with nature "all the year," and her devotion is continual whereas that of the poet is sporadic and momentary. But we have not done with the paradox yet. It not only underlies the poem, but something of the paradox informs the poem, though, since this is Wordsworth, rather timidly. The comparison of the evening to the nun actually has more than one dimension. The calm of the evening obviously means "worship," even to the dull-

* "The Language of Paradox" first appeared in *The Language of Poetry* (1942), a symposium, and is here reprinted by permission of The Princeton University Press. It has since been reprinted, with slight changes, as the first chapter of Mr. Brooks' volume, *The Well Wrought Urn* (1947). Mr. Brooks (*b.* 1906) is also the author of *Modern Poetry and the Tradition* (1939) and co-editor of *Understanding Poetry* (1938), *Understanding Fiction* (1943), and *Understanding Drama* (1945).

witted and insensitive. It corresponds to the trappings of the nun, visible to everyone. Thus, it suggests not merely holiness, but, in the total poem, even a hint of pharisaical holiness, with which the girl's careless innocence, itself a symbol of her continual secret worship, stands in contrast.

Or consider Wordsworth's sonnet, "Composed upon Westminster Bridge." I believe that most of us will agree that it is one of Wordsworth's most successful poems; yet most students have the greatest difficulty in accounting for its goodness. The attempt to account for it on the grounds of nobility of sentiment soon breaks down. On this level, the poem merely says: that the city in the morning light presents a picture which is majestic and touching to all but the most dull of soul; but the poem says very little more about the sight: the city is beautiful in the morning light and it is awfully still. The attempt to make a case for the poem in terms of the brilliance of its images also quickly breaks down: the student searches for graphic details in vain; there are next to no realistic touches. In fact, the poet simply huddles the details together:

> . . . silent, bare
> Ships, towers, domes, theatres, and temples lie
> Open unto the fields. . . .

We get a blurred impression—points of roofs and pinnacles along the skyline, all twinkling in the morning light. More than that, the sonnet as a whole contains some very flat writing and some well-worn comparisons.

The reader may ask: where, then, does the poem get its power? It gets it, it seems to me, from the paradoxical situation out of which the poem arises. Wordsworth is honestly surprised, and he manages to get some sense of awed surprise into the poem. It is odd to the poet that the city should be able to "wear the beauty of the morning" at all. Mount Snowden, Skiddaw, Mont Blanc—these wear it by natural right, but surely not grimy, feverish London. This is the point of the almost shocked exclamation

> Never did sun more beautifully steep
> In his first splendour, *valley, rock,* or *hill.* . . .

The "smokeless air" reveals a city which the poet did not know existed: man-made London is a part of nature too, is lighted by the sun of nature, and lighted to as beautiful effect.

> The river glideth at his own sweet will. . . .

A river is the most "natural" thing that one can imagine; it has the elasticity, the curved line of nature itself. The poet had never been able to regard this one as a real river—now, uncluttered by barges, the river reveals itself as a natural thing, not at all disciplined into a rigid and mechanical pattern: it is like the daffodils, or the mountain brooks, artless, and whimsical, and "natural" as they. The poem closes, you will remember, as follows:

> Dear God! the very houses seem asleep;
> And all that mighty heart is lying still!

The city, in the poet's insight of the morning, has earned its right to be considered organic, not merely mechanical. That is why the stale metaphor of the sleeping houses is strangely renewed. The most exciting thing that the poet can say about the houses is that they are *asleep.* He has been in the habit of counting them dead—as just mechanical and inanimate; to say they are "asleep" is to say that they are alive, that they participate in the life of nature. In the same way, the tired old metaphor which sees a great city as a pulsating heart of empire becomes revivified. It is only when the poet sees the city under the semblance of death that he can see it as actually alive—quick with the only life which he can accept, the organic life of "nature."

It is not my intention to exaggerate Wordsworth's own consciousness of the paradox involved. In this poem, he prefers, as is usual with him, the frontal attack. But the situation is paradoxical here as in so many of his poems. In his preface to the second edition of the *Lyrical Ballads* Wordsworth stated that his general purpose was "to choose incidents and situations from common life" but so to treat them that "ordinary things should be presented to the mind in an unusual aspect." Coleridge was to state the purpose for him later, in terms which make even more evident Wordsworth's exploitation of the paradoxical: "Mr. Wordsworth . . . was to propose to himself as his object, to give the charm of novelty to things of every day, and to excite a feeling analogous to the supernatural, by awakening the mind's attention to the lethargy of custom, and directing it to the loveliness and the wonders of the world before us. . . ." Wordsworth in short was consciously attempting to show his audience that the common was really uncommon, the prosaic was really poetic.

Coleridge's terms, "the charm of novelty to things of every day," "awakening the mind," suggest the Romantic preoccupation with wonder—the surprise, the revelation which puts the tarnished familiar world in a new light. This may well be the *raison d'etre* of most Romantic paradoxes; and yet the neoclassic poets use paradox for much the same reason. Consider Pope's lines from "The Essay on Man":

> In doubt his Mind or Body to prefer;
> Born but to die, and reas'ning but to err;
> Alike in ignorance, his Reason such,
> Whether he thinks too little, or too much. . . .
>
> Created half to rise, and half to fall;
> Great Lord of all things, yet a Prey to all;
> Sole Judge of Truth, in endless Error hurl'd;
> The Glory, Jest, and Riddle of the world!

Here, it is true, the paradoxes insist on the irony, rather than on the wonder. But Pope too might have claimed that he was treating the things of every day, man himself, and awakening his mind so that he would view himself in a new and blinding light. Thus, there is a certain awed wonder in Pope just as there is a certain trace of irony implicit in the Wordsworth sonnets. There is, of course, no reason why they should not occur together; and they do. Wonder and irony merge in many of the lyrics of Blake; they merge in Coleridge's *Ancient Mariner*. The variations in emphasis are numerous. Gray's "Elegy" uses a typical Wordsworth "situation" with the rural scene and with peasants contemplated in the light of their "betters." But in the "Elegy" the balance is heavily tilted in the direction of irony, the revelation an ironic rather than a startling one:

> Can storied urn or animated bust
> Back to its mansion call the fleeting breath?
> Can Honour's voice provoke the silent dust,
> Or Flatt'ry sooth the dull cold ear of Death?

But I am not here interested in the possible variations; I am interested rather in our seeing that the paradoxes spring from the very nature of the poet's language: it is a language in which the connotations play as great a part as the denotations. And I do not mean that the connotations are important as supplying some sort of frill or trimming, something external to the real matter in hand. I mean that the poet does not use a notation at all—as the scientist may properly be said to do so. The poet, within limits, has to make up his language as he goes.

T. S. Eliot somewhere refers to "That perpetual slight alteration of language, words perpetually juxtaposed in new and sudden combinations," which occurs in poetry. It *is* perpetual; it cannot be kept out of the poem; it can only be directed and controlled. The tendency of science is necessarily to stabilize terms, to freeze them into strict denotations; the poet's tendency is by contrast disruptive. His terms are continually modifying each other, and thus violating their dictionary meanings. To take a very simple example, consider the adjectives in the first lines of Wordsworth's evening sonnet: *beauteous, calm, free, holy, quiet, breathless*. The juxtapositions are hardly startling; and yet notice this: the evening is like a nun breathless with adoration. The adjective "breathless" suggests tremendous excitement; and yet the evening is not only quiet but *calm*. There is no final contradiction, to be sure: it is *that* kind of calm and *that* kind of excitement, and the two states may well occur together. But the poet has no one term. Even if he had a polysyllabic technical term, the term would not provide the solution for his problem. He must work by contradiction and qualification.

We may approach the problem in this way: the poet has to work by analogies. All of the subtler states of emotion, as I. A. Richards has pointed out, necessarily demand metaphor for their expression. The poet must work by analogies, but the metaphors do not lie in the same plane or fit neatly edge to edge. There is a continual tilting of the planes; necessary overlappings, discrepancies, contradictions. Even the most direct and simple poet is forced into paradoxes far more often than we think, if we are sufficiently alive to what he is doing.[1]

But in dilating on the difficulties of the poet's task, I do not want to leave the impression that it is a task which necessarily defeats him, or even that with his method he may not win to a fine precision. To use Shakespeare's figure, he can

with assays of bias
By indirections find direction out.

Shakespeare had in mind the game of lawn-bowls in which the bowl is distorted, a circumstance which allows the skilful player to bowl a curve. To elaborate the figure, science makes use of the perfect sphere and its attack can be direct. The method of art can, I believe, never be direct—is always indirect. The serious difficulties will occur only when he confuses his game with that of science and mistakes the nature of his appropriate instrument. Mr. Stuart Chase a few years ago, with a touching naiveté, urged us to take the distortion out of the bowl—to treat language like notation.

I have said that even the apparently simple and straightforward poet is forced into paradoxes by the nature of his instrument. Seeing this, we should not be surprised to find poets who consciously employ it to gain a compression and precision otherwise unobtainable. Such a method, like any other, carries with it its own perils. But the dangers are not overpowering; the poem is not predetermined to a shallow and glittering sophistry. The method is an extension of the normal language of poetry, not a perversion of it.

[1] All metaphor, of course, involves some element of paradox, for metaphor by its very nature cannot give a strictly point-to-point analogy with no element of discrepancy and contradiction between the items compared. Indeed, even Dr. Johnson drew the line in practice far short of general agreement between the items compared: he refused to allow that Addison's famous angel simile was a real simile. Marlborough directing the battle and the angel directing the storm were too closely parallel. The items compared—the tenor and the vehicle—had to "contradict" each other sharply, and in this contradiction lies the element of paradox which this paper attempts to emphasize. For the strategy of this paper, I have felt justified in making such an emphasis. But it is only fair to say that I should prefer as a matter of general practice to approach many of the problems raised in this paper as problems of metaphor; that is, I have no desire to force the application of the term "paradox" on every case of discrepancy.

I should like to refer you to a concrete case. Donne's "Canonization" ought to provide a sufficiently extreme instance.

For Godsake hold your tongue, and let me love,
Or chide my palsie, or my gout,
My five gray haires, or ruin'd fortune flout,
With wealth your state, your minde with Arts improve,
Take you a course, get you a place,
Observe his honour, or his grace,
Or the Kings reall, or his stamped face
Contemplate, what you will, approve,
So you will let me love.

Alas, alas, who's injur'd by my love?
What merchants ships have my sighs drown'd?
Who saies my teares have overflow'd his ground?
When did my colds a forward spring remove?
When did the heats which my veines fill
Adde one more to the plaguie Bill?
Soldiers finde warres, and Lawyers finde out still
Litigious men, which quarrels move,
Though she and I do love.

Call us what you will, wee are made such by love;
Call her one, mee another flye,
We'are Tapers too, and at our owne cost die,
And wee in us finde the'Eagle and the Dove.
The Phoenix ridle hath more wit
By us, we two being one, are it.
So to one neutrall thing both sexes fit,
We dye and rise the same, and prove
Mysterious by this love.

Wee can dye by it, if not live by love,
And if unfit for tombes and hearse
Our legend bee, it will be fit for verse;
And if no peece of Chronicle wee prove,
We'll build in sonnets pretty roomes;
As well a well wrought urne becomes
The greatest ashes, as halfe-acre tombes,
And by these hymnes, all shall approve
Us Canoniz'd for Love:

And thus invoke us; You whom reverend love
Made one anothers hermitage;
You, to whom love was peace, that now is rage;
Who did the whole worlds soule contract, and drove
Into the glasses of your eyes
(So made such mirrors, and such spies,
That they did all to you epitomize,)
Countries, Townes, Courts: Beg from above
A patterne of your love!

The basic metaphor which underlies the poem (and which is reflected in the title) involves a sort of paradox. For the poet daringly treats profane love as if it were divine love. The canonization is not that of a pair of holy anchorites who have renounced the world and the flesh. The hermitage of each is the other's body; but they do renounce the world, and so their title to sainthood is cunningly argued. The poem then is a parody of Christian sainthood; but it is an intensely serious parody of a sort that modern man, habituated as he is to an easy yes or no, can hardly understand. He refuses to accept the paradox as a serious rhetorical device; and since he is able to accept it only as a cheap trick, he is forced into this dilemma. Either: Donne does not take love seriously; here he is merely sharpening his wit as a sort of mechanical exercise. Or: Donne does not take sainthood seriously; here he is merely indulging in a cynical and bawdy parody.

Neither account is true; a reading of the poem will show that Donne takes both love and religion seriously; it will show, further, that the paradox is here his inevitable instrument. But to see this plainly will require a closer reading than most of us give to poetry.

The poem opens dramatically on a note of exasperation. The "you" whom the speaker addresses is not a friend, who is objecting to the speaker's love affair. At any rate, the person represents the practical world which regards love as a silly affectation. To use the metaphor on which the poem is built, the friend represents the secular world which the lovers have renounced.

Donne begins to suggest this metaphor in the first stanza by the contemptuous alternatives which he suggests to the friend

> . . . chide my palsy, or my gout,
> My five gray haires, or ruin'd fortune flout . . .

The implications are: (1) All right, consider my love as an infirmity, as a disease, if you will, but confine yourself to my other infirmities, my palsy, my approaching old age, my ruined fortune. You stand a better chance of curing those; in chiding me for this one, you are simply wasting your time as well as mine. (2) Why don't you pay attention to your own welfare—go on and get wealth and honor for yourself. What should you care if I do give these up in pursuing my love?

The two main categories of secular success are neatly, and contemptuously epitomized in the line

> Or the Kings reall, or his stamped face.

Cultivate the court and gaze at the king's face there, or, if you prefer, get into business and look at his face stamped on coins. But let me alone.

This conflict between the "real" world and the lover absorbed in the world of love runs through the poem; it dominates the second stanza in which the torments of love, so vivid to the lover, affect the real world not at all—

> What merchants ships have my sighs drown'd?

It is touched on in the fourth stanza in the contrast between the word "Chronicle" which suggests secular history with its pomp and magnificence, the history of kings and princes, and the word "sonnets" with its suggestions of trivial and precious intricacy. The conflict appears again in the last stanza, only to be resolved when the unworldly lovers, love's saints who have given up the world, paradoxically achieve a more intense world. But here the paradox is still contained in, and supported by, the dominant metaphor: so does the holy anchorite win a better world by giving up this one.

But before going on to discuss this development of the theme, it is important to see what else the second stanza does. For it is in this second stanza and the third, that the poet shifts the tone of the poem, modulating from the note of irritation with which the poem opens into the quite different tone with which it closes.

Donne accomplishes the modulation of tone by what may be called an analysis of love-metaphor. Here, as in many of his poems, he shows that he is thoroughly self-conscious about what he is doing. This second stanza he fills with the conventionalized figures of the Petrarchan tradition: the wind of lovers' sighs, the floods of lovers' tears, etc.—extravagant figures with which the contemptuous secular friend might be expected to tease the lover. The implication is that the poet himself recognizes the absurdity of the Petrarchan love metaphors. But what of it? The very absurdity of the jargon which lovers are expected to talk makes for his argument: their love, however absurd it may appear to the world, does no harm to the world. The practical friend need have no fears: there will still be wars to fight and lawsuits to argue.

The opening of the third stanza suggests that this vein of irony is to be maintained. The poet points out to his friend the infinite fund of such absurdities which can be applied to lovers:

Call her one, mee another flye,
We'are Tapers too, and at our owne cost die. . . .

For that matter, the lovers can conjure up for themselves plenty of such fantastic comparisons: *they* know what the world thinks of them. But these figures of the third stanza are no longer the threadbare Petrarchan conventionalities; they have sharpness and bite. The last one, the likening of the lovers to the phoenix, is fully serious, and with it, the tone has shifted from ironic banter into a defiant but controlled tenderness.

The effect of this implied awareness of the lovers' apparent madness is to cleanse and revivify metaphor; to indicate the sense in which the poet accepts it, and thus to prepare us for accepting seriously the fine and seriously intended metaphors which dominate the last two stanzas of the poem.

The opening line of the fourth stanza,

Wee can dye by it, if not live by love,

achieves an effect of tenderness and deliberate resolution. The lovers are ready to die to the world; they are committed; they are not callow but confident. (The basic metaphor of the saint, one notices, is being carried on; the lovers in their renunciation of the world, have something of the confident resolution of the saint. By the bye, the word "legend"—

. . . if unfit for tombes and hearse
Our legend bee—

in Donne's time meant "the life of a saint.") The lovers are willing to forego the ponderous and stately chronicle and to accept the trifling and insubstantial "sonnet" instead; but then if the urn be well-wrought it provides a finer memorial for one's ashes than does the pompous and grotesque monument. With the finely contemptuous, yet quiet phrase, "half-acre tombes," the world which the lovers reject expands into something gross and vulgar. But the figure works further; the pretty sonnets will not merely hold their ashes as a decent earthly memorial. Their legend, their story, will gain them canonization; and approved as love's saints, other lovers will invoke them.

In this last stanza, the theme receives a final complication. The lovers in rejecting life actually win to the most intense life. This paradox has been hinted at earlier in the phoenix metaphor. Here it receives a powerful dramatization. The lovers in becoming hermits, find that they have not lost the world, but have gained the world in each other, now a more intense, more meaningful world. Donne is not content to treat the lovers' discovery as something which comes to them passively, but rather as something which they actively achieve. They are like the saint, God's athlete:

Who did the whole worlds soule *contract*, and *drove*
Into the glasses of your eyes. . . .

The image is that of a violent squeezing as of a powerful hand. And what do the lovers "drive" into each other's eyes? The "Countries, Townes," and "Courts," which they renounced in the first stanza of the poem. The unworldly lovers thus become the most "worldly" of all.

The tone with which the poem closes is one of triumphant achievement, but the tone is a development contributed to by various earlier elements. One of the more important elements which works toward our acceptance of the final paradox is the figure of the phoenix, which will bear a little further analysis.

The comparison of the lovers to the phoenix is very skilfully related to the two earlier comparisons, that in which the lovers are like burning tapers, and that in which they are like the eagle and the dove. The phoenix comparison gathers up both: the phoenix is a bird, and like the tapers, it burns. We have a selected series of items: the phoenix figure seems to come in a natural stream of association. "Call us what you will," the lover says, and rattles off in his desperation the first comparisons that occur to him. The comparison to the phoenix seems thus merely another outlandish one, the most outrageous of all. But it is this most fantastic one, stumbled over apparently in his haste, that the poet goes on to develop. It really describes the lovers best and justifies their renunciation. For the phoenix is not two but one, "we two being one, are it"; and it burns, not like the taper at its own cost, but to live again. Its death is life: "Wee dye and rise the same. . . ." The poet literally justifies the fantastic assertion. In the sixteenth and seventeenth centuries to "die" means to experience the consummation of the act of love. The lovers after the act are the same. Their love is not exhausted in mere lust. This is their title to canonization. Their love is like the phoenix.

I hope that I do not seem to juggle the meaning of *die*. The meaning that I have cited can be abundantly justified in the literature of the period; Shakespeare uses "die" in this sense; so does Dryden. Moreover, I do not think that I give it undue emphasis. The word is in a crucial position. On it is pivoted the transition to the next stanza,

> Wee can dye by it, if not live by love,
> And if unfit for tombes. . . .

Most important of all, the sexual submeaning of "die" does not contradict the other meanings: the poet is saying: "Our death is really a more intense life"; "We can afford to trade life (the world) for death (love), for that death is the consummation of life"; "After all, one does not expect to live *by* love, one expects, and wants, to die *by* it." But in the total passage he is also saying "Because our love is not mundane, we can give up the world"; "because our love is not merely lust, we can give up the other lusts, the lust for wealth and power"; "because," and this is said with a little vein of irony as by one who knows the world too well, "because our love can outlast its consummation, we are a minor miracle; we are love's saints." This passage with its ironical tenderness and its realism feeds and supports the brilliant paradox with which the poem closes.

There is one more factor in developing and sustaining the final effect. The poem is an instance of the doctrine which it asserts; it is both the assertion and the realization of the assertion. The poet has actually before our eyes built within the song the "pretty room" with which he says the lovers can be content. The poem itself is the well-wrought urn which can hold the lovers' ashes and which will not suffer in comparison with the prince's "half-acre tomb."

And how necessary are the paradoxes? Donne might have said directly, "Love in a cottage is enough." "The Canonization" contains this admirable thesis, but it contains a great deal more. He might have been as forthright as a later lyricist who wrote, "We'll build a sweet little nest, / Somewhere out in the West, / And let the rest of the world go by." He might even have imitated that more metaphysical lyric, which maintains, "You're the cream in my coffee." "The Canonization" touches on all these observations, but it goes beyond them, not merely in dignity, but in precision.

I submit that the only way by which the poet could say what "The Canonization" says is by paradox. More direct methods may be tempting, but all of them enfeeble and distort what is to be said. This statement may seem the less surprising when we reflect on how many of the important things which the poet has to say have to be said by means of paradox:—most of the language of lovers is such; "The Canonization" is a good example; most of the language of religion: "He who would save his life must lose it"; "The last shall be first." Indeed, almost any insight important enough to warrant a great poem apparently has to be stated in such terms. Deprived of the character of paradox with its twin concomitants of irony and wonder, the matter of Donne's poem unravels into "facts," biological, sociological, and economic. What happens to Donne's lovers if we consider them "scientifically," without benefit of the supernaturalism which the poet confers upon them? [2]

[2] In this paper I have not attempted to distinguish between kinds of paradoxes. Obviously, they do not stand on the same level: for example, there are doctrinal paradoxes such as the Christian mystery of the Trinity; there are philosophical paradoxes such as are found in Kant's antinomies; there are rhetorical paradoxes, themselves of innumerable kinds. An elaborate classification of types would be out of place in a paper of this sort; nor have I cared to take up here the problem of the relation of poetry to philosophy and religion. But the statement that the poet confers upon facts a "supernaturalism" does call for further comment. Perhaps something like "super-positivism" should be substituted for "supernaturalism." The point that I have in mind is related to the discussion of positivism in Mr. Allen Tate's recent *Reason in Madness:* "There are 'two doctrines,' [I. A. Richards] says, which have tended to flourish independently—" and yet, neither is intelligible apart from Imagination.

"The two doctrines can be stated as follows:

"1. The mind of the poet at moments . . . gains an insight into reality, reads Nature as a symbol of some-

Well, what happens to Shakespeare's lovers, for Shakespeare uses the basic metaphor of "The Canonization" in his *Romeo and Juliet?* In their first conversation, you remember, the lovers play with the analogy between the lover and the pilgrim to the Holy Land. Juliet says:

For saints have hands that pilgrims' hands do touch
And palm to palm is holy palmers' kiss.

Considered scientifically, the lovers become Mr. Aldous Huxley's animals, "quietly sweating, palm to palm."

For us today, Donne's imagination seems obsessed with the problem of unity: the sense in which the lovers become one—the sense in which the soul is united with God. Frequently, as we have seen, one type of union becomes a metaphor for the other. It may not be too far-fetched to see both as instances of, and metaphors for, the union which the creative imagination itself effects. For that fusion is not logical; it apparently violates science and commonsense; it welds together the discordant and the contradictory. Coleridge has of course given us the classic description of its nature and power. It "reveals itself in the balance or reconcilement of opposite or discordant qualities: of sameness, with difference; of the general, with the concrete; the idea, with the image; the individual, with the representative; the sense of novelty and freshness, with old and familiar objects; a more than usual state of emotion, with more than usual order. . . ." It is a great and illuminating statement, but it is a series of paradoxes. Apparently Coleridge could describe the effect of the imagination in no other way.

thing behind or within Nature not ordinarily perceived.

"2. The mind of the poet creates a Nature into which his own feelings, his aspirations and apprehensions, are projected."

"Now," continues Mr. Tate, "the positivist sciences have denied all validity to the first doctrine." The poet is left, consequently, to "project" his fancies. They have no objective validity. Yet the world in which we live (not to be confused with the abstractions from it made by the various sciences) requires both the first *and* second doctrine. It is a concrete world in which man requires the "complete knowledge" which Mr. Tate holds that poetry gives. And yet the two doctrines constitute a pair of antinomies which can be reconciled only in the doctrine of the Imagination to which Richards refers. The whole passage in *Reason and Madness* and the chapter of Richards' *Coleridge on Imagination* there discussed should be read in this connection.

Shakespeare, in one of his poems, has given a description that oddly parallels that of Coleridge.

Reason in itself confounded,
Saw Division grow together,
To themselves yet either neither,
Simple were so well compounded.

I do not know what his "The Phoenix and the Turtle" celebrates. Perhaps it *was* written to honor the marriage of Sir John Salisbury and Ursula Stanley; or perhaps the phoenix is Lucy, Countess of Bedford; or perhaps the poem is merely an essay on Platonic love. But the scholars themselves are so uncertain, that I think we will do little violence to established habits of thinking, if we boldly preempt the poem for our own purposes. Certainly the poem is an instance of that magic power which Coleridge sought to describe. I propose that we take it for a moment as a poem about that power:

So they loved as love in twaine,
Had the essence but in one,
Two distincts, Division none,
Number there in love was slaine.

Hearts remote, yet not asunder;
Distance and no space was seene,
Twixts the *Turtle* and his Queene;
But in them it were a wonder. . . .

Propertie was thus appalled,
That the selfe was not the same;
Single Natures double name,
Neither two nor one was called.

Precisely! The nature is single, one, unified. But the name is double, and today with our multiplication of sciences, it is multiple. If the poet is to be true to his poetry, he must call it neither two nor one: the paradox is his only solution. The difficulty has intensified since Shakespeare's day: the timid poet, when confronted with the problem of "Single Natures double name," has too often funked it. A history of poetry from Dryden's time to our own might bear as its subtitle "The Half-Hearted Phoenix."

In Shakespeare's poem, you will remember that at the union of the phoenix and the turtle, Reason is "in itselfe confounded"; but it recovers to admit its own bankruptcy,

Love hath Reason, Reason none,
If what parts, can so remaine . . .

and it is Reason which goes on to utter the beautiful threnos with which the poem concludes:

Beautie, Truth, and Raritie,
Grace in all simplicitie,
Here enclosede, in cinders lie. . . .

Truth may seem, but cannot be;
Beauty brag, but 'tis not she;
Truth and beauty buried be.

To this urne let those repaire,
That are either true or faire,
For these dead Birds, sigh a prayer.

Having preempted the poem for our own purposes, it may not be too outrageous to go on to deduce one further observation. The urn to which we are summoned, the urn which holds the ashes of the phoenix, is like the well-wrought urn of Donne's "Canonization" which holds the phoenix-lovers' ashes; it is the poem itself. One is reminded of still another urn, Keats's Grecian urn, which contained for Keats, Truth and Beauty as Shakespeare's urn encloses "Beautie, Truth, and Raritie." But there is a sense in which all such well-wrought urns contain the ashes of a phoenix. The urns are not meant for memorial purposes only, though that often seems to be their chief significance to the professors of literature. The phoenix rises from its ashes; or ought to rise; but it will not arise merely for our sifting and measuring the ashes, or testing them for their chemical content. We must be prepared to accept the paradox of the imagination itself; else "Beautie, Truth, and Raritie" remain enclosed in their cinders and we shall end with essential cinders, for all our pains.

ROBERT PENN WARREN: Pure and Impure Poetry*

CRITICS are rarely faithful to their labels and their special strategies. Usually the critic will confess that no one strategy—the psychological, the moralistic, the formalistic, the historical—or combination of strategies, will quite work the defeat of the poem. For the poem is like the monstrous Orillo in Boiardo's *Orlando Inamorato*. When the sword lops off any member of the monster, that member is immediately rejoined to the body, and the monster is as formidable as ever. But the poem is even more formidable than the monster, for Orillo's adversary finally gained a victory by an astonishing feat of dexterity: he slashed off both the monster's arms and quick as a wink seized them and flung them into the river. The critic who vaingloriously trusts his method to account for the poem, to exhaust the poem, is trying to emulate this dexterity: he thinks that he, too, can win by throwing the lopped-off arms into the river. But he is doomed to failure. Neither fire nor water will suffice to prevent the rejoining of the mutilated members to the monstrous torso. There is only one way to conquer the monster: you must eat it, bones, blood, skin, pelt, and gristle. And even then the monster is not dead, for it lives in you, is assimilated into you, and you are different, and somewhat monstrous yourself, for having eaten it.

So the monster will always win, and the critic knows this. He does not want to win. He knows that he must always play stooge to the monster. All he wants to do is to give the monster a chance to exhibit again its miraculous power.

With this fable, I shall begin by observing that poetry wants to be pure. And it always suc-

* "Pure and Impure Poetry" was first published in *The Kenyon Review*, Spring 1943, and is reprinted here by permission of the editor and the author. Mr. Warren (*b.* 1905) is co-editor of *Understanding Poetry* (1938) and *Understanding Fiction* (1943). His many critical essays will presently be published in a collected form.

ceeds in this ambition. In so far as we have poetry at all, it is always pure poetry; that is, it is not non-poetry. The poetry of Shakespeare, the poetry of Pope, the poetry of Herrick, is pure, in so far as it is poetry at all. We call the poetry "higher" or "lower," we say "more powerful" or "less powerful" about it, and we are, no doubt, quite right in doing so. The souls that form the great rose of Paradise are seated in banks and tiers of ascending blessedness, but they are all saved, they are all perfectly happy; they are all "pure," for they have all been purged of mortal taint. This is not to say, however, that if we get poetry from one source, such a single source, say Shakespeare, should suffice us in as much as we can always appeal to it, or that, since all poetry is equally pure, we engage in a superfluous labor in trying to explore or create new sources of poetry. No, for we can remember that every soul in the great rose is precious in the eyes of God. No soul is the substitute for another.

Poetry wants to be pure, but poems do not. At least, most of them do not want to be too pure. The poems want to give us poetry, which is pure, and the elements of a poem, in so far as it is a good poem, will work together toward that end, but many of the elements, taken in themselves, may actually seem to contradict that end, or be neutral toward the achieving of that end. Are we then to conclude that, because neutral or recalcitrant elements appear in poems, even in poems called great, these elements are simply an index to human frailty, that in a perfect world there would be no dross in poems which would, then, be perfectly pure? No, it does not seem to be merely the fault of our world, for the poems include, deliberately, more of the so-called dross than would appear necessary. They are not even as pure as they might be in this imperfect world. They mar themselves with cacophonies, jagged rhythms, ugly words and ugly thoughts, colloquialisms, clichés, sterile technical terms, head work and argument, self-contradictions, clevernesses, irony, realism—all things which call us back to the world of prose and imperfection.

Sometimes a poet will reflect on this state of affairs, and grieve. He will decide that he, at least, will try to make one poem as pure as possible. So he writes:

> Now sleeps the crimson petal, now the white;
> Nor waves the cypress in the palace walk;
> Nor winks the gold fin in the porphyry font:
> The firefly wakens: waken thou with me.

We know the famous garden. We know how all nature conspires here to express the purity of the moment: how the milk-white peacock glimmers like a ghost, and how like a ghost the unnamed "she" glimmers on to her tryst; how earth lies "all Danaë to the stars," as the beloved's heart lies open to the lover; and how, in the end, the lily folds up her sweetness, "and slips into the bosom of the lake," as the lovers are lost in the sweet dissolution of love.

And we know another poet and another garden. Or perhaps it is the same garden, after all:

> I arise from dreams of thee
> In the first sweet sleep of night,
> When the winds are breathing low
> And the stars are shining bright.
> I arise from dreams of thee,
> And a spirit in my feet
> Hath led me—who knows how?
> To thy chamber window, Sweet!

We remember how, again, all nature conspires, how the wandering airs "faint," how the Champak's odors "pine," how the nightingale's complaint "dies upon her heart," as the lover will die upon the beloved's heart. Nature here strains out of nature, it wants to be called by another name, it wants to spiritualize itself by calling itself another name. How does the lover get to the chamber window? He refuses to say how, in his semi-somnambulistic daze, he got there. He blames, he says, "a spirit in my feet," and hastens to disavow any knowledge of how that spirit operates. In any case, he arrives at the chamber window. Subsequent events and the lover's reaction toward them are somewhat hazy. We only know that the lover, who faints and fails at the opening of the last stanza, and who asks to be lifted from the grass by a more enterprising beloved, is in a condition of delectable passivity, in which distinctions blur out in the "purity" of the moment.

Let us turn to another garden: the place, Verona; the time, a summer night, with full moon. The lover speaks:

> But soft! what light through yonder window breaks?
> It is the east. . . .

But we know the rest, and know that this garden, in which nature for the moment conspires again with the lover, is the most famous of them all, for the scene is justly admired for its purity of effect, for giving us the very essence of young, untarnished love. Nature conspires beneficently here, but we may chance to remember that beyond the garden wall strolls Mercutio, who can celebrate Queen Mab, but who is always aware that nature has other names as well as the names the pure poets and pure lovers put upon her. And we remember that Mercutio outside the wall, has just said:

> . . . 'twould anger him
> To raise a spirit in his mistress's circle
> Of some strange nature, letting it there stand
> Till she had laid it and conjured it down.

Mercutio has made a joke, a bawdy joke. That is bad enough, but worse, he has made his joke witty and, worst of all, intellectually complicated in its form. Realism, wit, intellectual complication—these are the enemies of the garden purity.

But the poet has not only let us see Mercutio outside the garden wall. Within the garden itself, when the lover invokes nature, when he spiritualizes and innocently trusts her, and says,

> Lady, by yonder blessed moon I swear,

the lady herself replies,

> O, swear not by the moon, the inconstant moon,
> That monthly changes in her circled orb.

The lady distrusts "pure" poems, nature spiritualized into forgetfulness. She has, as it were, a rigorous taste in metaphor, too; she brings a logical criticism to bear on the metaphor which is too easy; the metaphor must prove itself to her, must be willing to subject itself to scrutiny beyond the moment's enthusiasm. She injects the impurity of an intellectual style into the lover's pure poem.

And we must not forget the voice of the nurse, who calls from within, a voice which, we discover, is the voice of expediency, of half-measures, of the view that circumstances alter cases—the voice of prose and imperfection.

It is time to ask ourselves if the celebrated poetry of this scene, which as poetry is pure, exists despite the impurities of the total composition, if the effect would be more purely poetic were the nurse and Mercutio absent and the lady a more sympathetic critic of pure poems. I do not think so. The effect might even be more vulnerable poetically if the impurities were purged away. Mercutio, the lady, and the nurse are critics of the lover, who believes in pure poems, but perhaps they are necessary. Perhaps the lover can only be accepted in their context. The poet seems to say: "I know the worst that can be said on this subject, and I am giving fair warning. Read at your own risk." So the poetry arises from a recalcitrant and contradictory context; and finally involves that context.

Let us return to one of the other gardens, in which there is no Mercutio or nurse, and in which the lady is more sympathetic. Let us mar its purity by installing Mercutio in the shrubbery, from which the poet was so careful to banish him. You can hear his comment when the lover says:

> And a spirit in my feet
> Hath led me—who knows how?
> To thy chamber window, Sweet!

And we can guess what the wicked tongue would have to say in response to the last stanza.

It may be that the poet should have made his peace early with Mercutio, and have appealed to his better nature. For Mercutio seems to be glad to cooperate with a poet. But he must be invited; otherwise, he is apt to show a streak of merry vindictiveness about the finished product. Poems are vulnerable enough at best. Bright reason mocks them like sun from a wintry sky. They are easily left naked to laughter when leaves fall in the garden and the cold winds come. Therefore, they need all the friends they can get, and Mercutio, who is an ally of reason and who himself is given to mocking laughter, is a good friend for a poem to have.

On what terms does a poet make his peace with Mercutio? There are about as many sets of terms as there are good poets. I know that I have loaded the answer with the word *good* here, that I have implied a scale of excellence based, in part at least, on degree of complication. I shall return to this question. For the moment, however, let us examine a poem whose apparent innocence and simple lyric cry should earn it a place in any anthology of "pure poetry."

Western wind, when wilt thou blow
  That the small rain down can rain?
Christ, that my love were in my arms
  And I in my bed again!

The lover, grieving for the absent beloved, cries out for relief. Several kinds of relief are involved in the appeal to the wind. First there is the relief that would be had from the sympathetic manifestation of nature. The lover, in his perturbation of spirit, invokes the perturbations of nature. He exclaims,

Western wind, when wilt thou blow

and Lear exclaims,

Blow, winds, and crack your cheeks! rage! blow!

Second, there is the relief that would be had by the fulfillment of grief—the frost of grief, the drouth of grief broken, the full anguish expressed, then the violence allayed in the peace of tears. Third, there is the relief that would be had in the excitement and fulfillment of love itself. There seems to be a contrast between the first two types of relief and the third type; speaking loosely, we may say that the first two types are romantic and general, the third type realistic and specific. So much for the first two lines.

In the last two lines, the lover cries out for the specific solace of his case: reunion with his beloved. But there is a difference between the two lines. The first is general, and romantic. The phrase "in my arms" does not seem to mean exactly what it says. True, it has a literal meaning, if we can look close at the words, but it is hard to look close because of the romantic aura—the spiritualized mist about them.[1] But with the last line the perfectly literal meaning suddenly comes into sharp focus. The mist is rifted and we can look straight at the words, which, we discover with a slight shock of surprise, do mean exactly what they say. The last line is realistic and specific. It is not even content to say,

And I in bed again!

It is, rather, more scrupulously specific, and says,

And I in *my* bed again! [2]

All of this does not go to say that the realistic elements here are to be taken as cancelling, or negating, the romantic elements. There is no ironical leer. The poem is not a celebration of carnality. It is a faithful lover who speaks. He is faithful to the absent beloved, and he is also faithful to the full experience of love. That is, he does not abstract one aspect of the experience and call it the whole experience. He does not strain nature out of nature; he does not over-spiritualize nature. This nameless poet would never have said, in the happier days of his love, that he had been led to his Sweet's chamber window by "a spirit in my feet"; and he certainly would not have added the coy disavowal, "who knows how?" But because the nameless poet refused to over-spiritualize nature, we can accept the spirituality of the poem.

Another poem gives us another problem.

Ah, what avails the sceptered race,
  Ah, what the form divine!
What every virtue, every grace!
  Rose Aylmer, all were thine.

Rose Aylmer, whom those wakeful eyes
  May weep, but never see,
A night of memories and of sighs
  I consecrate to thee.

This is another poem about lost love: a "soft" subject. Now to one kind of poet the soft subject presents a sore temptation. Because it is soft in its natural state, he is inclined to feel that to get at its poetic essence he must make

[1] It may be objected here that I am reading the phrase "in my arms" as a 20th Century reader. I confess the fact. Certainly, several centuries have passed since the composition of the little poem, and those centuries have thickened the romantic mist about the words, but it is scarcely to be believed that the 16th Century was the clear, literal Eden dawn of poetry when words walked without the fig leaf.

[2] In connection with the word *my* in this line, we may also feel it helps to set over the comfort and satisfaction there specified against the bad weather of the first two lines. We may also glance at the word *small* in the second line. It is the scrupulous word, the word that, realistically, makes us believe in the rain. But, too, it is broader in its function. The storm which the lover invokes will not rend the firmament, it will not end the world; it will simply bring down the "small" rain, a credible rain.

it softer still, that he must insist on its softness, that he must render it as "pure" as possible. At first glance, it may seem that Landor is trying to do just that. What he says seems to be emphatic, unqualified, and open. Not every power, grace, and virtue could avail to preserve his love. That statement insists on the pathetic contrast. And in the next stanza, wakefulness and tearfulness are mentioned quite unashamedly, along with memories and sighs. It is all blurted out, as pure as possible.

But only in the paraphrase is it "blurted." The actual quality of the first stanza is hard, not soft. It is a chiseled stanza, in which formality is insisted upon. We may observe the balance of the first and second lines; the balance of the first half with the second half of the third line, which recapitulates the structure of the first two lines; the balance of the two parts of the last line, though here the balance is merely a rhythmical and not a sense balance as in the preceding instances; the binders of discreet alliteration, repetition, and assonance. The stanza is built up, as it were, of units which are firmly defined and sharply separated, phrase by phrase, line by line. We have the formal control of the soft subject, ritual and not surrender.

But in the second stanza the rigor of this formality is somewhat abated, as the more general, speculative emphasis (why cannot pomp, virtue, and grace avail?) gives way to the personal emphasis, as though the repetition of the beloved's name had, momentarily, released the flood of feeling. The first line of the second stanza spills over into the second; the "wakeful eyes" as subject find their verb in the next line, "weep," and the *wake-weep* alliteration, along with the rest after *weep,* points up the disintegration of the line, just as it emphasizes the situation. Then with the phrase "but never see" falling away from the long thrust of the rhetorical structure to the pause after *weep,* the poem seems to go completely soft, the frame is broken. But, even as the poet insists on "memories and sighs" in the last two lines he restores the balance. Notice the understatement of "A night." It says: "I know that life is a fairly complicated affair, and that I am committed to it and to its complications. I intend to stand by my commitment, as a man of integrity, that is, to live despite the grief. Since life is complicated, I cannot, if I am to live, spare too much time for indulging grief. I can give *a* night, but not all nights." The lover, like the hero of Frost's poem "Stopping by Woods on a Winter Evening," tears himself from the temptation of staring into the treacherous, delicious blackness, for he, too, has "promises to keep." Or he resembles the Homeric heroes who, after the perilous passage is made, after their energy has saved their lives, and after they have beached their craft and eaten their meal, can then set aside an hour before sleep to mourn the comrades lost by the way—the heroes who, as Aldous Huxley says, understand realistically a whole truth as contrasted with a half-truth.

Is this a denial of the depth and sincerity of the grief? The soft reader, who wants the poem pure, may be inclined to say so. But let us look at the last line to see what it gives us in answer to this question. The answer seems to lie in the word *consecrate.* The meter thrusts this word at us; we observe that two of the three metrical accents in the line fall on syllables of this word forcing it beyond its prose emphasis. The word is important and the importance is justified, for the word tells us that the single night is not merely a lapse into weakness, a trivial event to be forgotten when the weakness is overcome. It is, rather, an event of the most extreme and focal importance, an event formally dedicated, "set apart for sacred uses," an event by which other events are to be measured. So the word *consecrate* formalizes, philosophizes, ritualizes the grief; it specifies what style in the first stanza has implied.

But here is another poem of grief, grief at the death of a child:

There was such speed in her little body,
And such lightness in her footfall,
It is no wonder that her brown study
Astonishes us all.

Her wars were bruited in our high window.
We looked among orchard trees and beyond
Where she took arms against her shadow,
Or harried unto the pond

The lazy geese, like a snow cloud
Dripping their snow on the green grass,
Tricking and stopping, sleepy and proud,
Who cried in goose, Alas,

For the tireless heart within the little
Lady with rod that made them rise
From their noon apple dreams, and scuttle
Goose-fashion under the skies!

But now go the bells, and we are ready;
In one house we are sternly stopped
To say we are vexed at her brown study,
Lying so primly propped.

Another soft subject, softer, if anything, than the subject of "Rose Aylmer," and it presents the same problem. But the problem is solved in a different way.

The first stanza is based on two time-honored clichés: first, "Heaven, won't that child ever be still, she is driving me distracted"; and second, "She was such an active, healthy-looking child, would you've ever thought she would just up and die?" In fact, the whole poem develops these clichés, and exploits, in a backhand fashion, the ironies implicit in their inter-relation. And in this connection, we may note that the fact of the clichés, rather than more original or profound observations, at the root of the poem is important; there is in the poem the contrast between the staleness of the clichés and the shock of the reality. Further, we may note that the second cliché is an answer, savagely ironical in itself, to the first: the child you wished would be still *is* still, despite all that activity which your adult occupations deplored.

But such a savage irony is not the game here. It is too desperate, too naked, in a word, too pure. And ultimately, it is, in a sense, a meaningless irony if left in its pure state, because it depends on a mechanical, accidental contrast in nature, void of moral content. The poem is concerned with modifications and modulations of this brute, basic irony, modulations and modifications contingent upon an attitude taken toward it by a responsible human being, the speaker of the poem. The savagery is masked, or ameliorated.

In this connection, we may observe, first, the phrase "brown study." It is not the "frosted flower," the "marmoreal immobility," or any one of a thousand such phrases which would aim for the pure effect. It is merely the brown study which astonishes—a phrase which denies, as it were, the finality of the situation, underplays the pathos, and merely reminds one of those moments of childish pensiveness into which the grown-up cannot penetrate. And the phrase itself is a cliché—the common now echoed in the uncommon.

Next, we may observe that stanzas two, three, and four simply document, with a busy yet wavering rhythm (one sentence runs through the three stanzas) the tireless naughtiness which was once the cause of rebuke, the naughtiness which disturbed the mature goings-on in the room with the "high window." But the naughtiness has been transmuted, by events just transpired, into a kind of fanciful story-book dream-world, in which geese are whiter than nature, and the grass greener, in which geese speak in goose language, saying "Alas," and have apple dreams. It is a drowsy, delicious world, in which the geese are bigger than life, and more important. It is an unreal (now unreal because lost), stylized world. Notice how the phrase "the little lady with rod" works: the detached, grown-up primness of "little lady"; the formal, stiff effect gained by the omission of the article before *rod;* the slightly unnatural use of the word *rod* itself, which sets some distance between us and the scene (perhaps with the hint of the fairy story, a magic wand, or a magic rod—not a common, every-day stick). But the stanzas tie back into the premises of the poem in other ways. The little girl, in her naughtiness, warred against her shadow. Is it crowding matters too hard to surmise that the shadow here achieves a sort of covert symbolic significance? The little girl lost her war against her "shadow," which was always with her. Certainly the phrase "tireless heart" has some rich connotations. And the geese which say "Alas!" conspire with the family to deplore the excessive activity of the child. (They do not conspire to express the present grief, only the past vexation—an inversion of the method of the pastoral elegy, or of the method of the first two garden poems.)

The business of the three stanzas, then, may be said to be twofold. First, they make us believe more fully in the child and therefore in the fact of the grief itself. They "prove" the grief, and they show the deliciousness of the lost world which will never look the same from the high window. Second, and contrariwise, they "transcend" the grief, or at least give a hint of a means for transcending the immediate anguish: the lost world is, in one sense, redeemed out of time, it enters the pages of the picture book where geese speak, where the untrue is true, where the fleeting is fixed. What was had cannot, after all, be lost. (By way of comparison—a comparison which, because extreme, may be helpful—I cite the transcendence in *La Récherche du Temps Perdu.*) The three stanzas, then, to state it in another way, have validated the first stanza and have prepared for the last.

The three stanzas have made it possible for us to say, when the bell tolls, "we are ready." Some kind of terms, perhaps not the best terms possible but some kind, have been made with the savage underlying irony. But the terms arrived at do not prevent the occasion from being a "stern" one. The transcendence is not absolute, and in the end is possible only because of an exercise of will and self-control. Because we control ourselves, we can say "vexed" and not some big word. And the word itself picks up the first of the domestic clichés on which the poem is based—the outburst of impatience at the naughty child who, by dying, has performed her most serious piece of naughtiness. But now the word comes to us charged with the burden of the poem, and further, as re-echoed here by the phrase "brown study," charged by the sentence in which it occurs: we are gathered formally, ritualistically, sternly together to say the word *vexed.*[3] *Vexed* becomes the ritualistic, the summarizing word.

I have used the words *pure* and *impure* often in the foregoing pages, and I confess that I have used them rather loosely. But perhaps it has been evident that I have meant something like this: the pure poem tries to be pure by excluding, more or less rigidly, certain elements which might qualify or contradict its original impulse. In other words, the pure poems want to be, and desperately, all of a piece. It has also been evident, no doubt, that the kinds of impurity which are admitted or excluded by the various little anthology pieces which have been analyzed, are different in the different poems. This is only to be expected, for there is not one doctrine of "pure poetry"—not one definition of what constitutes impurity in poems—but many. And not all of the doctrines are recent. When, for example, one cites Poe as the father of *the* doctrine of pure poetry, one is in error; Poe simply fathered *a* particular doctrine of pure poetry. One can find other doctrines of purity long antedating Poe. When Sir Philip Sidney, for example, legislated against tragi-comedy, he was repeating a current doctrine of purity. When Ben Jonson told William Drummond that Donne, for not keeping of accent, deserved hanging, he was defending another kind of purity, and when Dryden spoke to save the ear of the fair sex from metaphysical perplexities in amorous poems, he was defending another kind of purity, just as he was defending another when he defined the nature of the heroic drama. The 18th Century had a doctrine of pure poetry, which may be summed up under the word *sublimity*, but which involved two corollary doctrines, one concerning diction and the other concerning imagery. But at the same time that this century, by means of these corollary doctrines, was tidying up and purifying, as Mr. Monk and Mr. Henn have indicated, the doctrine derived from Longinus, it was admitting into the drama certain impurities which the theorists of the heroic drama would not have admitted.[4]

But when we think of the modern doctrine of pure poetry, we usually think of Poe, as critic and poet, perhaps of Shelley, of the Symbolists, of the Abbé Brémond, perhaps of Pater, and certainly of George Moore and the Imagists. We know Poe's position: the long poem is "a flat contradiction in terms," because intense excite-

[3] It might be profitable, in contrast with this poem, to analyze "After the Burial," by James Russell Lowell, a poem which is identical in situation. But in Lowell's poem the savagery of the irony is unqualified. In fact, the whole poem insists, quite literally, that qualification is impossible: the scheme of the poem is to set up the brute fact of death against possible consolations. It insists on "tears," the "thin-worn locket," the "anguish of deathless hair," "the smallness of the child's grave," the "little shoe in the corner." It is a poem which, we might say, does not progress, but ends where it begins, resting in the savage irony from which it stems; or we might say that it is a poem without any "insides" for the hero of the poem is not attempting to do anything about the problem which confronts him—it is a poem without issue, without conflict, a poem of unconditional surrender. In other words, it tries to be a pure poem, pure grief, absolutely inconsolable. It is a strident poem, and strident in its rhythms. The fact that we know this poem to be an expression of a bereavement historically real makes it an embarrassing poem, as well. It is a naked poem.

[4] Samuel Holt Monk: *The Sublime: a Study of Critical Theories in XVIII-Century England,* and T. R. Henn: *Longinus and English Criticism.*

ment, which is essential in poetry, cannot be long maintained; the moral sense and the intellect function more satisfactorily in prose than in poetry, and, in fact, "Truth" and the "Passions," which are for Poe associated with intellect and the moral sense, may actually be inimical to poetry; vagueness, suggestiveness, are central virtues, for poetry has for "its object an *indefinite* instead of a *definite* pleasure"; poetry is not supposed to undergo close inspection, only a cursory glance, for it, "above all things, is a beautiful painting whose tints, to minute inspection, are confusion worse confounded, but start out boldly to the cursory glance of the connoisseur"; poetry aspires toward music, since it is concerned with "indefinite sensations, to which music is an *essential,* since the comprehension of sweet sound is our most indefinite conception"; melancholy is the most poetical effect and enters into all the higher manifestations of beauty. We know, too, the Abbé Brémond's mystical interpretation, and the preface to George Moore's anthology, and the Imagist manifesto.

But these views are not identical. Shelley, for instance, delights in the imprecision praised and practiced by Poe, but he has an enormous appetite for "Truth" and the "Passions," which are, except for purposes of contrast, excluded by Poe. The Imagist manifesto, while excluding ideas, endorses precision rather than vagueness in rendering the image, and admits diction and objects which would have seemed impure to Poe and to many poets of the 19th Century, and does not take much stock in the importance of verbal music. George Moore emphasizes the objective aspect of his pure poetry, which he describes as "something which the poet creates outside his own personality," and this is opposed to the subjective emphasis in Poe and Shelley; but he shares with both an emphasis on verbal music, and with the former a distaste for ideas.

But more recently, the notion of poetic purity has emerged in other contexts, contexts which sometimes obscure the connection of the new theories with the older theories. For instance Max Eastman has a theory. "Pure poetry," he says in *The Literary Mind,* "is the pure effort to heighten consciousness." Mr. Eastman, we discover elsewhere in his book, would ban idea from poetry, but his motive is different from, say, the motive of Poe, and the difference is important: Poe would kick out the ideas because the ideas hurt the poetry, and Mr. Eastman would kick out the ideas because the poetry hurts the ideas. Only the scientist, he tells us, is entitled to have ideas on any subject, and the rest of the citizenry must wait to be told what attitude to take toward the ideas which they are not permitted to have except at secondhand. Literary truth, he says, is truth which is "uncertain or comparatively unimportant." But he assigns the poet a function—to heighten consciousness. But in the light of this context we would have to rewrite his original definition: pure poetry is the pure effort to heighten consciousness, but the consciousness which is heightened must not have any connection with ideas, must involve no attitude toward any ideas.

Furthermore, to assist the poet in fulfilling the assigned function, Mr. Eastman gives him a somewhat sketchy doctrine of "pure" poetic diction. For instance, the word *bloated* is not admissable into a poem because it is, as he testifies, "sacred to the memory of dead fish," and the word *tangy* is, though he knows not exactly how, "intrinsically poetic." The notion of a vocabulary which is intrinsically poetic seems, with Mr. Eastman, to mean a vocabulary which indicates agreeable or beautiful objects. So we might rewrite the original definition to read: pure poetry is the pure effort to heighten consciousness, but the consciousness which is heightened must be a consciousness exclusively of agreeable or beautiful objects—certainly not a consciousness of any ideas.

In a recent book, *The Idiom of Poetry,* Frederick Pottle has discussed the question of pure poetry. He distinguishes another type of pure poetry in addition to the types already mentioned. He calls it the "Elliptical," and would include in it symbolist and metaphysical poetry (old and new) and some work by poets such as Collins, Blake, and Browning. He observes—without any pejorative implication, for he is a critical relativist and scarcely permits himself the luxury of evaluative judgments—that the contemporary product differs from older examples of the elliptical type in that "the modern poet goes much farther in employing private experiences or ideas than would formerly have been thought legitimate." To the common reader, he says, "the prime characteristic of this kind of poetry is not the nature of its imagery but its obscurity: its urgent suggestion that you add something to the poem without telling you what that something is." This omitted "something" he interprets as the prose "frame," to use his word, the statement of the occasion, the logical or narrative transitions, the generalized application derived from the poem, etc. In other words, this type of pure poetry contends that "the effect would be more powerful if we could somehow manage to feel the images fully and accurately without having the effect diluted by any words put in to give us a 'meaning'—that is, if we could expel all the talk *about* the imaginative realization and have the pure realization itself." [5]

For the moment I shall pass the question of the accuracy of Mr. Pottle's description of the impulse of Elliptical Poetry and present the question which ultimately concerns him. How pure does poetry need to be in practice? That is the question which Mr. Pottle asks. He answers by saying that a great degree of impurity *may* be admitted, and cites our famous didactic poems, *The Faerie Queene, The Essay on Man, The Vanity of Human Wishes, The Excursion.* That is the only answer which the relativist, and nominalist, can give. Then he turns to what he calls the hardest question in the theory of poetry: what kind of prosaism is acceptable and what is not? His answer, which he advances very modestly, is this:

> . . . the element of prose is innocent and even salutary when it appears as—take your choice of three metaphors—a background on which the images are projected, or a frame in which they are shown, or a thread on which they are strung In short, when it serves a *structural* purpose. Prose in a poem seems offensive to me when . . . the prosaisms are sharp, obvious, individual, and ranked coordinately with the images.

At first glance this looks plausible, and the critic has used the sanctified word *structural.* But at second glance we may begin to wonder what the sanctified word means to the critic. It means something rather mechanical—background, frame, thread. The structure is a showcase, say a jeweler's showcase, in which the little jewels of poetry are exhibited, the images. The showcase shouldn't be ornamental itself ("sharp, obvious, individual," Mr. Pottle says), for it would then distract us from the jewels; it should be chastely designed, and the jewels should repose on black velvet and not on flowered chintz. But Mr. Pottle doesn't ask what the relation among the bright jewels should be. Apparently, not only does the showcase bear no relation to the jewels, but the jewels bear no relation to each other. Each one is a shining little focus of heightened consciousness, or pure realization, existing for itself alone. Or perhaps he should desire that they be arranged in some mechanical pattern, such a pattern, perhaps, as would make it easier for the eye to travel from one little jewel to the next when the time comes to move on. Structure becomes here simply a device of salesmanship, a well-arranged showcase.

It is all mechanical. And this means that Mr. Pottle, after all, is himself an exponent of pure poetry. He locates the poetry simply in the images, the nodes of "pure realization." This means that what he calls the "element of prose" includes definition of situation, movement of narrative, logical transition, factual description, generalization, ideas. Such things, for him, do not participate in the poetic effect of the poem; in fact, they work against the poetic effect, and so, though necessary as a frame, should be kept from being "sharp, obvious, individual." [6]

[5] F. W. Bateson, in *English Poetry and the English Language,* discusses the impulse in contemporary poetry. Tennyson, he points out in connection with "The Sailor Boy," dilutes his poetry by telling a story as well as writing a poem, and "a shorter poem would have spoilt his story." The claims of prose conquer the claims of poetry. Of the Victorians in general: "The dramatic and narrative framework of their poems, by circumventing the disconcerting plunges into *medias res* which are the essence of poetry, brings it down to a level of prose. The reader knows where he is; it serves the purpose of introduction and note." Such introduction and notes in the body of the poem itself are exactly what Mr. Pottle says is missing in Elliptical Poetry. Mr. Bateson agrees with Poe in accepting intensity as the criterion of the poetic effect, and in accepting the corollary that a poem should be short. But he, contradicting Poe, seems to admire precise and complicated incidental effects.

[6] Several other difficulties concerning Mr. Pottle's statement may suggest themselves. First, since he seems to infer that the poetic essence resides in the image, what view would he take of meter and rhythm? His statement, strictly construed, would mean that these factors do not participate in the poetic effect, but are simply part of the frame. Second, what view of dramatic poetry is implied? It seems again that a strict interpretation would mean that the story and the images

I have referred to *The Idiom of Poetry*, first, because it is such an admirable and provocative book, sane, lucid, generous-spirited, and second, because, to my mind, it illustrates the insidiousness with which a doctrine of pure poetry can penetrate into the theory of a critic who is suspicious of such a doctrine. Furthermore, I have felt that Mr. Pottle's analysis might help me to define the common denominator of the various doctrines of pure poetry.

That common denominator seems to be the belief that poetry is an essence that is to be located at some particular place in a poem, or in some particular element. The exponent of pure poetry persuades himself that he has determined the particular something in which the poetry inheres, and then proceeds to decree that poems shall be composed, as nearly as possible, of that element and of nothing else. If we add up the things excluded by various critics and practitioners, we get a list about like this:

1. ideas, truths, generalizations, "meaning"
2. precise, complicated, "intellectual" images
3. unbeautiful, disagreeable, or neutral materials
4. situation, narrative, logical transition
5. realistic details, exact descriptions, realism in general
6. shifts in tone or mood
7. irony
8. metrical variation, dramatic adaptations of rhythm, cacophony, etc.
9. meter itself
10. subjective and personal elements

No one theory of pure poetry excludes all of these items, and, as a matter of fact, the items listed are not on the same level of importance. Nor do the items always bear the same interpretation. For example, if one item seems to be central to discussions of pure poetry, it is the first: "ideas," it is said, "are not involved in the poetic effect, and may even be inimical to it." But this view can be interpreted in a variety of ways. If it is interpreted as simply meaning that the paraphrase of a poem is not equivalent to the poem, that the poetic gist is not to be defined as the statement embodied in the poem with the sugar-coating as bait, then the view can be held by opponents as well as exponents of any theory of pure poetry. We might scale down from this interpretation to the other extreme interpretation that the poem should merely give the sharp image in isolation. But there are many complicated and confused variations possible between the two extremes. There is, for example, the interpretation that "ideas," though they are not involved in the poetic effect, must appear in poems to provide, as Mr. Pottle's prosaisms do, a kind of frame, or thread, for the poetry—a spine to support the poetic flesh or a Christmas tree on which the baubles of poetry are hung.[7] T. S. Eliot has said something of this sort:

> The chief use of the "meaning" of a poem, in the ordinary sense, may be (for here again I am speaking of some kinds of poetry and not all) to satisfy one habit of the reader, to keep his mind diverted and quiet, while the poem does its work upon him: much as the imaginary burglar is always provided with a bit of nice meat for the house-dog.

Here, it would seem, Mr. Eliot has simply inverted the old sugar-coated pill theory: the idea becomes the sugar-coating and the "poetry" becomes the medicine. This seems to say that the idea in a poem does not participate in the poetic effect, and seems to commit Mr. Eliot to a theory of pure poetry. But to do justice to the quotation, we should first observe that the parenthesis indicates that the writer is referring to some sort of provisional and superficial distinction and not to a fundamental one, and second observe that the passage is out of its context. In the context, Mr. Eliot goes on to say that some poets "become impatient of this 'meaning' [explicit statement of ideas in logical order] which seems superfluous, and perceive possibilities of intensity through its elimination." This

bear no essential relation to each other, that the story is simply part of the frame. That is the story, characters, rhythms, and ideas, are on one level and the images, in which the poetry inheres, are on another. But Miss Spurgeon, Mr. Knight, and other critics have given us some reason for holding that the images do bear some relation to the business of the other items. In fact, all of the items, as M. Maritain has said, "feelings, ideas, representations, are for the artist merely materials and means, still symbols." That is, they are all elements in a single expressive structure.

[7] Such an interpretation seems to find a parallel in E. M. Forster's treatment of plot in fiction. Plot in his theory becomes a mere spine and does not really participate, except in a narrow, formal sense, in the fictional effect. By his inversion of the Aristotelian principle, the plot becomes merely a necessary evil.

may mean either of two things. It may mean that ideas do not participate in the poetic effect, or it may mean, though they do participate in the poetic effect, they need not appear in the poem in an explicit and argued form. And this second reading would scarcely be a doctrine of pure poetry at all, for it would involve poetic casuistry and not poetic principle.

We might, however, illustrate the second interpretation by glancing at Marvell's "Horatian Ode" on Cromwell. Marvell does not give us narrative; he does not give us an account of the issues behind the Civil War; he does not state the two competing ideas which are dramatized in the poem, the idea of "sanction" and the idea of "efficiency." But the effect of the poem does involve these two factors; the special reserved, scarcely resolved, irony, which is realized in the historical situation, is an irony derived from unstated materials and ideas. It is, to use Mr. Pottle's term again, a pure poem in so far as it is elliptical in method, but it is anything but a pure poem if by purity we mean the exclusion of idea from participation in the poetic effect. And Mr. Eliot's own practice implies that he believes that ideas do participate in the poetic effect. Otherwise, why did he put the clues to his ideas in the notes at the end of the *Waste Land* after so carefully excluding any explicit statement of them from the body of the poem? If he is regarding those ideas as mere bait—the "bit of nice meat for the house-dog"—he has put the ideas in a peculiar place, in the back of the book—like giving the dog the meat on the way out of the house with the swag or giving the mouse the cheese after he is in the trap. All this would lead one to the speculation that Marvell and Mr. Eliot have purged away statement of ideas from their poems, not because they wanted the ideas to participate less in the poetry, but because they wanted them to participate more fully, intensely, and immediately. This impulse, then, would account for the characteristic type of image, types in which precision, complication, and complicated intellectual relation to the theme are exploited; in other words, they are trying—whatever may be their final success—to carry the movement of mind to the center of the process. On these grounds they are the exact opposite of poets who, presumably on grounds of purity, exclude the movement of mind from the center of the poetic process—from the internal structure of the poem—but pay their respect to it as a kind of footnote, or gloss, or application coming at the end. Marvell and Eliot, by their cutting away of frame, are trying to emphasize the participation of ideas in the poetic process. Then Elliptical Poetry is not, as Mr. Pottle says it is, a pure poetry at all if we regard intention; the elliptical poet is elliptical for purposes of inclusion, not exclusion.

But waiving the question of Elliptical Poetry, no one of the other theories does—or could—exclude all the items on the list above. And that fact may instruct us. If all of these items were excluded, we might not have any poem at all. For instance, we know how some critics have pointed out that even in the strictest imagist poetry idea creeps in—when the image leaves its natural habitat and enters a poem it begins to "mean" something. The attempt to read ideas out of the poetic party violates the unity of our being and the unity of our experience. "For this reason," as Santayana puts it, "philosophy, when a poet is not mindless, enters inevitably into his poetry, since it has entered into his life; or rather, the detail of things and the detail of ideas pass equally into his verse, when both alike lie in the path that has led him to his ideal. To object to theory in poetry would be like objecting to words there; for words, too, are symbols without the sensuous character of the things they stand for; and yet it is only by the net of new connections which words throw over things, in recalling them, that poetry arises at all. Poetry is an attenuation, a rehandling, an echo of crude experience; it is itself a theoretic vision of things at arm's length." Does this not lead us to the conclusion that poetry does not inhere in any particular element but depends upon the set of relationships, the structure, which we call the poem?

Then the question arises: what elements cannot be used in such a structure? I should answer that nothing that is available in human experience is to be legislated out of poetry. This does not mean that anything can be used in *any* poem, or that some materials or elements may not prove more recalcitrant than others, or that it might not be easy to have too much of some things. But it does mean that, granted certain contexts, any sort of material, a chemical formula for instance, might appear functionally in a poem. It also may mean that, other things being equal, the greatness of a poet depends upon the extent of the area of experience which he can master poetically.

Can we make any generalizations about the nature of the poetic structure? First, it involves resistances, at various levels. There is the tension between the rhythm of the poem and the rhythm of speech (a tension which is very low at the extreme of free verse and at the extreme of verse such as that of "Ulalume," which verges toward a walloping doggerel); between the formality of the rhythm and the informality of the language; between the particular and the general, the concrete and the abstract; between the elements of even the simplest metaphor; between the beautiful and the ugly; between ideas (as in Marvell's poem); between the elements involved in irony (as in "Bells for John Whiteside's Daughter" or "Rose Aylmer"); between prosisms and poeticisms (as in "Western Wind"). This list is not intended to be exhaustive; it is intended to be merely suggestive. But it may be taken to imply that the poet is like the jiujitsu expert; he wins by utilizing the resistance of his opponent—the materials of the poem. In other words, a poem, to be good, must earn itself. It is a motion toward a point of rest, but if it is not a resisted motion, it is motion of no consequence. For example, a poem which depends upon stock materials and stock responses is simply a toboggan slide, or a fall through space. And the good poem must, in some way, involve the resistances; it must carry something of the context of its own creation; it must come to terms with Mercutio. This is another way of saying that a good poem involves the participation of the reader; it must, as Coleridge puts it, make the reader into "an active creative being." Perhaps we can see this most readily in the case of tragedy: the definition of good or evil is not a "given" in tragedy, it is something to be earned in the process, and even the tragic villain must be "loved." We must kill him, as Brutus killed Caesar, not as butchers but as sacrificers. And all of this adds up to the fact that the structure is a dramatic structure, a movement through action toward rest, through complication toward simplicity of effect.

In the foregoing discussion, I have deliberately omitted reference to another type of pure poetry, a type which, in the context of the present war, may well become dominant. Perhaps the most sensible description of this type can be found in an essay by Herbert Muller:

> If it is not the primary business of the poet to be eloquent about these matters [faith and ideals], it still does not follow that he has more dignity or wisdom than those who are, or that he should have more sophistication. At any rate the fact is that almost all poets of the past did freely make large, simple statements, and not in their prosy or lax moments.

Mr. Muller then goes on to illustrate by quoting three famous, large, simple statements:

> In la sua voluntade e nostra pace

and

> We are such stuff
> As dreams are made on; and our little lives
> Are rounded with a sleep.

and

> The mind is its own place, and in itself
> Can make a heaven of hell, a hell of heaven.

Mr. Muller is here attacking the critical emphasis on ironic tension in poetry. His attack really involves two lines of argument. First, the poet is not wiser than the statesman, philosopher, or saint, people who are eloquent about faith and ideals and who say what they mean, without benefit of irony. This Platonic (or pseudo-Platonic) line of argument is, I think, off the point in the present context. Second, the poets of the past who have made large, simple affirmations have said what they meant. This line of argument is very much on the point.

Poets *have* tried very hard, for thousands of years, to say what they mean. But they have not only tried to say what they mean, they have tried to prove what they mean. The saint proves his vision by stepping cheerfully into the fires. The poet, somewhat less spectacularly, proves his vision by submitting it to the fires of irony—to the drama of his structure—in the hope that the fires will refine it. In other words, the poet wishes to indicate that his vision has been earned, that it can survive reference to the complexities and contradictions of experience. And irony is one such device of reference.

In this connection let us look at the first of Mr. Muller's exhibits. The famous line occurs in Canto III of the *Paradiso.* It is spoken by Piccarda Donati, in answer to Dante's question as to why she does not desire to rise higher than her present sphere, the sphere of the moon. But it expresses, in unequivocal terms, a central theme of the *Commedia,* as of Christian experience. On the one hand, it may be a pious truism, fit for sampler work, and on the other hand, it may be a burning conviction, tested and earned. Dante, in his poem, sets out to show how it has been earned and tested. One set of ironic tensions, for instance, which centers about this theme concerns the opposition between the notion of human justice and the notion of divine justice. The story of Paolo and Francesca is so warm, appealing, and pathetic in its human terms and their punishment so savage and unrelenting, so incommensurable, it seems, with the fault, that Dante, torn by the conflict, falls down as a dead body falls. Or Farinata, the enemy of Dante's house, is presented by the poet in terms of his human grandeur, which now, in Hell, is transmuted into a superhuman grandeur,

> com' avesse l'inferno in gran dispitto.[8]

Ulysses remains a hero, a hero who should draw special applause from Dante, who defined the temporal end of man as the conquest of knowledge. But Ulysses is damned, as the great Brutus is damned, who hangs from the jaws of the fiend in the lowest pit of traitors. So divine justice is set over against human pathos, human dignity, human grandeur, human intellect, human justice. And we recall how Virgil, more than once, reminds Dante that he must not apply human standards to the sights he sees. It is this long conflict, which appears in many forms, this ironic tension, which finally gives body to the simple eloquence of the line in question; the statement is meaningful, not for what it says, but for what has gone before. It is earned. It has been earned by the entire poem.

I do not want to misrepresent Mr. Muller. He does follow his quotations by the sentence: "If they are properly qualified in the work as a whole, they may still be taken straight, they *are* [he italicizes the word] taken so in recollection as in their immediate impact." But can this line be taken so in recollection, and was it taken so in its "immediate impact"? And if one does take it so, is he not violating, very definitely, the poet's meaning, for the poet means the *poem,* he doesn't mean the line.

It would be interesting to try to develop the contexts of the other passages which Mr. Muller quotes. But in any case, he was simply trying, in his essay, to guard against what he considered to be, rightly or wrongly, a too narrow description of poetry; he was not trying to legislate all poetry into the type of simple eloquence, the unqualified statement of "faith and ideas." But we have already witnessed certain, probably preliminary, attempts to legislate literature into becoming a simple, unqualified, "pure" statement of faith and ideal. We have seen the writers of the 1920's called the "irresponsibles." We have seen writers such as Proust, Eliot, Dreiser, and Faulkner, called writers of the "death drive." Why are these writers condemned? Because they have tried, within the limits of their gifts, to remain faithful to the complexities of the problems with which they were dealing, because they refused to take the easy statement as solution, because they tried to define the context in which, and the terms by which, faith and ideals could be earned. But this method will scarcely satisfy the mind which is hot for certainties; to that mind it will seem merely an index to lukewarmness, indecision, disunity, treason. The new theory of purity would purge out all complexities and all ironies and all self-criticism. And this theory will forget that the hand-me-down faith, the hand-me-down ideals, no matter what the professed content, is in the end not only meaningless but vicious. It is vicious because, as parody, it is the enemy of all faith.

[8] ["As if he held Hell in great contempt."]

JOSEPH FRANK: Spatial Form in Modern Literature*

LESSING'S *Laokoon*, André Gide once remarked, is one of those books it is good to reiterate or contradict every thirty years. Despite this excellent advice, neither of these attitudes toward *Laokoon* has been adopted by modern writers.[1] Lessing's attempt to define the limits of literature and the plastic arts has become a dead issue—one to which respectful reference is occasionally made, but which no longer has any fecundating influence on esthetic thinking. One can understand how this came about in the nineteenth century, with its passion for historicism, but it is not so easy to understand at present when so many writers on esthetic problems are occupied with questions of form. To a historian of literature or the plastic arts, Lessing's effort to define the unalterable laws of these mediums may well have seemed quixotic; but modern critics, no longer overawed by the bugbear of historical method, have begun to take up again the problems he tried to solve.

Lessing's own solution to these problems seems, at first glance, to have little relation to modern esthetic thinking. The arguments of *Laokoon* were directed against the pictorial poetry of his time, which has long since ceased to interest the modern sensibility; and many of its conclusions about the plastic arts grew out of a now-antiquated archeology, which, to make matters worse, Lessing knew mainly at second-hand. But it was precisely his quixotic attempt to rise above history, to define the unalterable laws of esthetic perception rather than to attack or defend any particular school, which gives his work the perennial freshness to which André Gide alluded. Since the validity of his central thesis does not depend on its relationship to the literary movements of his time, or on the extent of his first-hand acquaintanceship with the art works of antiquity, it may be taken up apart from these circumstances and used in the analysis of later developments.

In *Laokoon* Lessing fuses two currents of thought that were of great importance in the cultural history of his time. The archeological researches of Winckelmann, his contemporary, had stimulated a passionate interest in Greek culture among the Germans. Lessing went back to Homer, Aristotle and the Greek tragedians, using his first-hand knowledge to attack the distorted critical theories, supposedly based on classical authority, which had filtered into France through Italian commentators and then taken hold in Germany. At the same time, as Wilhelm Dilthey points out in his famous essay on Lessing, Locke and the empirical school of English philosophy had given a new impulse to esthetic speculation. Locke tried to solve the problem of knowledge by breaking down complex ideas into simple elements of sensation, and then examining the operations of the mind to see how these sensations were combined to form ideas. This method was soon taken over by the estheticians, who, instead of laying down rules for beauty, began to analyze esthetic perception. Writers like Shaftesbury, Hogarth, Hutcheson and Burke, to mention only a few, concerned themselves with the precise character and combination of impressions that gave esthetic pleas-

* "Spatial Form in Modern Literature" appeared in *The Sewanee Review*, Spring, Summer, and Autumn 1945. Mr. Frank (*b.* 1918) has kindly revised and condensed his essay for its present publication, and it is printed in its new form here by his permission and by permission of the editor of *The Sewanee Review*.

[1] Irving Babbitt, in 1910, wrote *The New Laokoon* with the intention of doing for modern art what Lessing had done for the art of his own day. Briefly, Babbitt's thesis was that, just as the confusion of *genres* in Lessing's time could be traced to a false theory of imitation, so the artistic aberrations of our own time could be traced to a false theory of spontaneity. Babbitt's argument, however, has nothing to do with Lessing's theories. The discussion of Lessing in the first half of the book merely reinforces the analogy between Lessing's purpose and Babbitt's own.

ure to the sensibility. Lessing's friend and critical ally, Mendelssohn, popularized this method of dealing with esthetic problems in Germany; Lessing himself was a close student of these works and many others in the same general spirit. *Laokoon,* as a result, stands at the confluence of these intellectual currents: Lessing analyzes the laws of esthetic perception, shows how they prescribe necessary limitations to literature and the plastic arts, and then demonstrates how Greek writers and painters, especially Homer, created masterpieces by obeying these laws.

His argument starts from the simple observation that literature and the plastic arts, working through different sensuous mediums, must therefore differ in the fundamental laws governing their creation. "If it is true," Lessing wrote, "that painting and poetry in their imitations make use of entirely different means or symbols—the first, namely, of form and color in space, the second of articulated sounds in time—if these symbols indisputably require a suitable relation to the thing symbolized, then it is clear that symbols arranged in juxtaposition can only express subjects of which the wholes or parts exist in juxtaposition; while consecutive symbols can only express subjects of which the wholes or parts are themselves consecutive." Lessing, of course, did not originate this distinction, which has been traced as far back as classical antiquity. His contribution was to raise it from an isolated insight into a universal critical principle, in this way carrying to their logical conclusion the efforts of French classical critics to define the immutable laws of art as laid down by "la raison."

Form in the plastic arts, according to Lessing, is necessarily spatial, because the visible aspect of objects can best be presented juxtaposed in an instant of time. Literature, on the other hand, makes use of language, composed of a succession of words proceeding through time; and it follows that literary form, to harmonize with the essential quality of its medium, must be based primarily on some form of narrative sequence. Lessing used this argument to attack two artistic genres highly popular in his day: pictorial poetry and allegorical painting. The pictorial poet tried to paint with words, the allegorical painter to tell a story in visible images; both were doomed to fail because their aims contradicted the fundamental properties of their mediums. No matter how accurate and vivid a verbal description might be, Lessing argued, it could not give the unified impression of a visible object; no matter how skillfully figures might be chosen and arranged, a painting or piece of sculpture could not successfully set forth the various stages of an action.

Lessing develops his argument by attempting to prove that the Greeks, with an unfailing sense of esthetic propriety, respected the limits imposed on different art mediums by the conditions of human perception. The importance of Lessing's distinction, however, does not depend on these ramifications of his argument, nor even on his specific judgments of individual writers or artists. Various critics have quarrelled with one or another of these judgments, thinking that in doing so they were in some way undermining Lessing's position; but such a belief is based on a misunderstanding of *Laokoon's* importance in the history of esthetic theory. Lessing's insights may be used solely as instruments of analysis, without proceeding to judge the value of individual works by how closely they adhere to the norms he laid down; and unless this is done, as a matter of fact, the real meaning of *Laokoon* cannot be understood. For what Lessing offered was not a new set of opinions but a new conception of esthetic form.

The conception of esthetic form inherited by the eighteenth century from the Renaissance was a purely external one. Classical literature—or what was known of it—was presumed to have reached perfection, and later writers could do little better than imitate its example. A horde of commentators and critics had deduced certain rules from the classical masterpieces—rules like the Aristotelian unities, of which Aristotle had never heard—and modern writers were warned to obey these rules if they wished to appeal to a cultivated public. Gradually, these rules hardened to an external mold into which the material of a literary work had to be poured: the form of a work was nothing but the technical arrangement dictated by the rules. Such a mechanical notion of esthetic form, however, led to serious perversions of taste—Shakespeare was considered a barbarian even by so sophisticated a writer as Voltaire, and Pope found it necessary in translating Homer to do a good deal of editing. Lessing's point of view, breaking sharply with this external conception of form, marks out the road for esthetic speculation to follow in the future.

For Lessing, as we have seen, esthetic form is not an external arrangement provided by a set of traditional rules: it is the relation between the sensuous nature of the art medium and the conditions of human perception. Just as the natural man of the eighteenth century was not to be bound by traditional political forms, but was to create them in accordance with his own nature, so art was to create its own forms out of itself rather than accepting them ready-made from the practice of the past. Criticism was not to prescribe rules for art, but was to explore the necessary laws by which art governs itself. No longer was esthetic form confused with the mere externals of technique—it was not a strait-jacket into which the artist, willy-nilly, had to force his creative ideas, but issued spontaneously from the organization of the art work as it presented itself to perception. Time and space were the two extremes defining the limits of literature and the plastic arts in their relation to sensuous perception; and it is possible, following Lessing's example, to trace the evolution of art forms by their oscillations between these two poles.[2]

The purpose of the present essay is to apply Lessing's method to modern literature—to trace the evolution of form in modern poetry and, more particularly, in the novel. The first two sections will try to show that modern literature, exemplified by such writers as T. S. Eliot, Ezra Pound, Marcel Proust and James Joyce, is moving in the direction of spatial form. This means that the reader is intended to apprehend their work spatially, in a moment of time, rather than as a sequence. So far as the novel is concerned, this tendency reaches its culmination in Djuna Barnes's remarkable book *Nightwood*, which has never received the critical attention it deserves.[3] Finally, since changes in esthetic form always involve major changes in the sensibility of a particular cultural period, an effort will be made to outline the spiritual attitudes that have led to the predominance of spatial form.

1

Modern Anglo-American poetry received its initial impetus from the Imagist movement of the years directly preceding and following the first World War. Imagism was important not for any actual poetry written by Imagist poets—no one knew quite what an Imagist poet was—but rather because it opened the way for later developments by its clean break with sentimental Victorian verbiage. The critical writings of Ezra Pound, the leading theoretician of Imagism, are an astonishing farrago of keen esthetic perceptions thrown in among a series of boyishly naughty remarks, whose chief purpose, it would seem, is to *épater le bourgeois*—to startle the stuffed shirts. But Pound's definition of the image, perhaps the keenest of his perceptions, is of fundamental importance for any discussion of modern literary form. "An image," Pound wrote, "is that which presents an intellectual and emotional complex in an instant of time." The implications of this definition should be noted—an image is defined, not as a pictorial reproduction, but as the unification of disparate ideas and emotions into a complex presented spatially in an instant of time. Such a complex is not to proceed discursively, according to the laws of language, but is rather to strike the

[2] German art criticism in the last few decades has experienced a veritable renaissance along the lines marked out by Lessing. Following the lead of Alois Riegl, the immediate predecessor of those writers who later occupied themselves with tracing the history of form in the plastic arts, German scholars traced the changing apprehensions of space which they saw at the root of changes in esthetic form. The next step was to connect the change in the apprehension of space with broader changes in the history of culture. Finally, the inquiry was broadened out to take in not only the plastic arts but also literature and music—thus bringing in the category of time—and even the varying conceptions of space and time in philosophical thought as parallel developments to changes in art forms. The most extensive attempt at such a synthesis has been made by Dagobert Frey in his brilliant and suggestive book *Gotik und Renaissance*, published in 1929. An excellent brief account of this movement may be found in *Die Philosophie der Kunstgeschichte in der Gegenwart*, by Walter Passarge.

Mention should also be made at this point of Edwin Muir's *Structure of the Novel*, the only work in English, so far as is known to the present writer, that attempts to discuss form in literature in terms of space and time.

[3] As originally published, this essay contained a detailed analysis of *Nightwood* which has been eliminated from the present version. Interested readers are referred to *The Sewanee Review*, Summer, 1945.

reader's sensibility with an instantaneous impact. Pound stresses this aspect by adding, in a later passage, that only the instantaneous presentation of such complexes gives "that sense of sudden liberation; that sense of freedom from time limits and space limits; that sense of sudden growth, which we experience in the presence of the greatest works of art."

At the very outset, therefore, modern poetry championed a poetic method in direct contradiction to the way in which, according to Lessing, language had to be perceived. By comparing Pound's definition of the image with Eliot's well-known description of the psychology of the poetic process, we can see clearly how profoundly this conception has influenced our modern idea of the nature of poetry. For Eliot, the distinctive quality of a poetic sensibility is its capacity to form new wholes, to fuse seemingly disparate experiences into an organic unity. The ordinary man, Eliot writes, "falls in love, or reads Spinoza, and these two experiences have nothing to do with each other, or with the noise of the typewriter or the smell of cooking; in the mind of the poet these experiences are always forming new wholes." Pound, to be sure, had attempted to define the image in terms of its esthetic attributes, while Eliot, in this passage, is describing its psychological origins; but the result in a poem was likely to be the same.

This view of the nature of poetry immediately gave rise to numerous problems. How was more than one image to be included in a poem? If the chief value of an image was its capacity to present an intellectual and emotional complex simultaneously, to link up images would clearly destroy most of their efficacy. Or was the poem itself one vast image, whose individual components were to be apprehended as a unity? But then it would be necessary to overcome the inherent consecutiveness of language, frustrating the reader's normal expectation of a sequence and forcing him to perceive the elements of the poem as juxtaposed in space rather than unrolling in time.

This is precisely what Eliot and Pound attempted in their major works. Both poets, in their earlier work, still retained some elements of conventional structure. Their poems were looked upon as daring and revolutionary chiefly because of technical matters, like the loosening of metrical pattern and the handling of subjects ordinarily considered non-poetic. Perhaps this is less true of Eliot than of Pound, especially the Eliot of the more complex early works like "Prufrock," "Gerontion" and "Portrait of a Lady"; but even here, although the sections of the poem are not governed by syntactical logic, the skeleton of an implied narrative structure is always present. The reader of "Prufrock" is swept up in a narrative movement from the very first lines:

> Let us go then, you and I,
> When the evening . . .

And the reader, accompanying Prufrock, finally arrives at their mutual destination:

> In the room the women come and go
> Talking of Michelangelo.

At this point the poem becomes a series of more or less isolated fragments, each stating some aspect of Prufrock's emotional dilemma; but the fragments are now localized and focused on a specific set of circumstances: the reader can organize them by referring to the implied situation. The same method is employed in "Portrait of a Lady," while in "Gerontion" the reader is specifically told that he has been reading the "thoughts of a dry brain in a dry season"—the stream-of-consciousness of "an old man in a dry month, being read to by a boy, waiting for rain." In both cases there is a perceptible framework around which the seemingly disconnected passages of the poem can be organized. This was one reason why Pound's "Mauberly" and Eliot's early work were first regarded, not as forerunners of a new poetic form, but as latter-day *vers de société*—witty, disillusioned, with a somewhat brittle charm, but lacking that quality of "high seriousness" that Matthew Arnold had selected as the touchstone of poetic excellence. These poems were considered unusual mainly because *vers de société* had long fallen out of fashion; there was little difficulty in accepting them as an entertaining departure from the grand style of the nineteenth century. In the "Cantos" and "The Waste Land," however, it should have been clear that a radical transformation was taking place in esthetic structure; but this transformation has been touched on only peripherally by modern critics. R. P. Blackmur comes closest to the central problem while analyzing what he calls Pound's "anecdotal" method. The special form of the "Cantos," Blackmur explains, "is that of the anecdote begun in one place, taken up in one or more other places, and finished, if at all, in still another. This deliberate disconnectedness, this art of a thing continually alluding to itself, continually breaking off short, is the method by which the 'Cantos' tie themselves together. So soon as the reader's mind is concerted with the material of the poem, Mr. Pound deliberately disconcerts it, either by introducing fresh and disjunct material or by reverting to old and, apparently, equally disjunct material." Blackmur's remarks apply equally well to "The Waste Land," where syntactical sequence is given up for a structure depending on the perception of relationships between disconnected word-groups. To be properly understood, these word-groups must be juxtaposed with one another and perceived simultaneously; only when this is done can they be adequately understood; for while they follow one another in time, their meaning does not depend on this temporal relationship. The one difficulty of these poems which no amount of textual exegesis can wholly overcome is the internal conflict between the time-logic of language and the space-logic implicit in the modern conception of the nature of poetry.

Esthetic form in modern poetry, then, is based on a space-logic which demands a complete reorientation in the reader's attitude towards language. Since the primary reference of any word-group is to something inside the poem itself, language in modern poetry is really reflexive: the meaning-relationship is completed only by the simultaneous perception in space of word-groups which, when read consecutively in time, have no comprehensible relation to each other. Instead of the instinctive and immediate reference of words and word-groups to the objects or events they symbolize, and the construction of meaning from the sequence of these references, modern poetry asks its readers to suspend the process of individual reference temporarily until the entire pattern of internal references can be apprehended as a unity. This explanation, of course, is the extreme statement of an ideal condition rather than of an actually existing state of affairs; but the conception of poetic form that runs through Mallarmé to Pound and Eliot, and which has left its traces on a whole generation of modern poets, can be formulated only in terms of the principle of reflexive reference. And this principle is the link connecting the esthetic development of modern poetry with similar experiments in the modern novel.

2

For a study of esthetic form in the modern novel, Flaubert's famous county fair scene in *Madame Bovary* is a convenient point of departure. This scene has justly been praised for its mordant caricature of bourgeois pomposity, its portrayal—unusually sympathetic for Flaubert—of the bewildered old servant, and its burlesque of the pseudo-romantic rhetoric by which Rodolphe woos the sentimental Emma. At present, it is enough to notice the method by which Flaubert handles the scene—a method we might as well call cinematographic, since this analogy comes immediately to mind. As Flaubert sets the scene, there is action going on simultaneously at three levels, and the physical position of each level is a fair index to its spiritual significance. On the lowest plane, there is the surging, jostling mob in the street, mingling with the livestock brought to the exhibition; raised slightly above the street by a platform are the speech-making officials, bombastically reeling off platitudes to the attentive multitudes; and on the highest level of all, from a window overlooking the spectacle, Rodolphe and Emma are watching the proceedings and carrying on their amorous conversation in phrases as stilted as those regaling the crowds. Albert Thibaudet has compared this scene to the medieval mystery play in which various related actions occur simultaneously on different stage levels; but this acute comparison refers to Flaubert's intention rather than to his method. "Everything should sound simultaneously," Flaubert later wrote, in commenting on this scene; "one should hear the bellowing of the cattle, the whisperings of the lovers and the rhetoric of the officials all at the same time."

But since language proceeds in time, it is impossible to approach this simultaneity of perception except by breaking up temporal sequence. And this is exactly what Flaubert does: he dissolves sequence by cutting back and forth between the various levels of action in a slowly-rising crescendo until—at the climax of the scene—Rodolphe's Chateaubriandesque phrases are read at almost the same moment as the names of prize winners for raising the best pigs. Flaubert takes care to underline this satiric similarity by description, as well as by juxtaposition, as if afraid the reflexive relations of the two actions would not be grasped: "From magnetism, by slow degrees, Rodolphe had arrived at affinities, and while M. le Président was citing Cincinnatus at his plow, Diocletian planting his cabbages and the emperors of China ushering in the new year with sowing-festivals, the young man was explaining to the young woman that these irresistible attractions sprang from some anterior existence."

This scene illustrates, on a small scale, what we mean by the spatialization of form in a novel. For the duration of the scene, at least, the time-flow of the narrative is halted; attention is fixed on the interplay of relationships within the limited time-area. These relationships are juxtaposed independently of narrative progress; the full significance of the scene is given only by the reflexive relations among the units of meaning. In Flaubert's scene, however, the unit of meaning is not, as in modern poetry, a word-group or a fragment of an anecdote; it is the totality of each level of action taken as an integer: the unit is so large that the scene can be read with an illusion of complete understanding, yet with a total unawareness of the "dialectic of platitude" (Thibaudet) interweaving all levels and finally linking them together with devastating irony. In other words, the struggle towards spatial form in Pound and Eliot resulted in the disappearance of coherent sequence after a few lines; but the novel, with its larger unit of meaning, can preserve coherent sequence within the unit of meaning and break up only the time-flow of narrative. (Because of this difference, readers of modern poetry are practically forced to read reflexively to get any literal sense, while readers of a novel like *Nightwood*, for example, are led to expect narrative sequence by the deceptive normality of language sequence within the unit of meaning.) But this does not affect the parallel between esthetic form in modern poetry and the form of Flaubert's scene: both can be properly understood only when their units of meaning are apprehended reflexively, in an instant of time.

Flaubert's scene, although interesting in itself, is of minor importance to his novel as a whole, and is skillfully blended back into the main narrative structure after fulfilling its satiric function. Flaubert's method, however, was taken over by James Joyce and applied on a gigantic scale in the composition of *Ulysses.* Joyce composed his novel of an infinite number of references and cross-references which relate to one another independently of the time-sequence of the narrative; these references must be connected by the reader and viewed as a whole before the book fits together into any meaningful pattern. Ultimately, if we are to believe Stuart Gilbert, these systems of reference form a complete picture of practically everything under the sun—from the stages of man's life and the organs of the human body to the colors of the spectrum; but these structures are far more important for Joyce, as Harry Levin has remarked, than they could ever possibly be for the reader. Students of Joyce, fascinated by his erudition, have usually applied themselves to exegesis, unfortunately neglecting the problem of form with which we are concerned.

Joyce's most obvious intention in *Ulysses* is to give the reader a picture of Dublin seen as a whole—to re-create the sights and sounds, the people and places of a typical Dublin day, much as Flaubert had re-created his provincial county fair. Like Flaubert, Joyce wanted his depiction to have the same unified impact, the same sense of simultaneous activity occurring in different places. Joyce, as a matter of fact, frequently makes use of the same method as Flaubert—cutting back and forth between different actions occurring at the same time—and usually does so to obtain the same ironic effect. But Joyce had the problem of creating this impression of simultaneity for the life of a whole teeming city, and of maintaining it—or rather of strengthening it—through hundreds of pages that must be read as a sequence. To meet this problem, Joyce was forced to go far beyond what Flaubert had done: while Flaubert had maintained a clear-cut narrative line except in the county-fair scene, Joyce breaks up his narrative and transforms the very structure of his novel into an instrument of his esthetic intention.

Joyce, we know, conceived *Ulysses* as a modern epic. In the epic, as Stephen Dedalus tells us in *The Portrait of the Artist as a Young Man,* "the personality of the artist, at first sight a cry or a cadence and then a fluid and lambent narrative, finally refines itself out of existence, impersonalizes itself, so to speak . . . the artist, like the God of creation, remains within or beyond or above his handiwork, invisible, refined out of existence, indifferent, paring his fingernails." The epic, for Joyce, is thus synonymous with the complete self-effacement of the author; and with his usual uncompromising rigor, Joyce carries this implication further than anyone had dared before. He assumes, for one thing, that his readers are Dubliners, intimately acquainted with Dublin life and the personal history of his characters. This allows him to refrain from giving any direct information about his characters, for such information would immediately have betrayed the presence of an omniscient author. What Joyce does, instead, is to present the elements of his narrative—the relations between Stephen and his family, between Bloom and his wife, between Stephen and Bloom and the Dedalus family—in fragments, as they are thrown out unexplained in the course of casual conversation, or as they lie embedded in the various strata of symbolic reference; and the same is true of all the allusions to Dublin life, history, and the external events of the twenty-four hours during which the novel takes place. In other words, all the factual background—so conveniently summarized for the reader in an ordinary novel—must be reconstructed from fragments, sometimes hundreds of pages apart, scattered through the book. As a result, the reader is forced to read *Ulysses* in exactly the same manner as he reads modern poetry—continually fitting fragments together and keeping allusions in mind until, by reflexive reference, he can link them to their complements.

Joyce intended, in this way, to build up in the reader's mind a sense of Dublin as a totality, including all the relations of the characters to one another and all the events which enter their consciousness. As the reader progresses through the novel, connecting allusions and references spatially, gradually becoming aware of the pattern of relationships, this sense was to be imperceptibly acquired; and at the conclusion of the novel, it might almost be said, Joyce literally wanted the reader to become a Dubliner. For this is what Joyce demands: that the reader have at hand the same instinctive knowledge of Dublin life, the same sense of Dublin as a huge, surrounding organism, which the Dubliner possesses as a birthright. Such knowledge, at any one moment of time, gives him a knowledge of Dublin's past and present as a whole; and it is only by such knowledge that the reader, like the characters, can place all the references in their proper context. This, it should be realized, is practically the equivalent of saying that Joyce cannot be read—he can only be re-read. A knowledge of the whole is essential to an understanding of any part; but unless one is a Dubliner, such knowledge can be obtained only after the book has been read and all the references fitted into their proper place and grasped as a unity. Although the burdens placed on the reader by this method of composition may seem insuperable, the fact remains that Joyce, in his unbelievably laborious fragmentation of narrative structure, proceeded on the assumption that a unified spatial apprehension of his work would ultimately be possible.

In a far more subtle manner than with Flaubert and Joyce, the same principle of composition is at work in Marcel Proust. Since Proust himself tells us that, before all else, his novel will have imprinted on it "a form which usually remains invisible, the form of Time," it may seem strange to speak of Proust in connection with spatial form. Almost without exception, he has been considered the novelist of time *par excellence,* the literary interpreter of that Bergsonian "real time" which, when intuited by the sensibility, places us in contact with ultimate reality. To stop at this point, however, is to miss what Proust himself considered the deepest significance of his work. Obsessed with the ineluctability of time, Proust was suddenly visited by certain mystical experiences that he describes in detail in "Le temps retrouvé," the last volume of his multi-volumed work. These experiences, by providing him with a technique for transcending time, seemed to free him from time's domination; and in writing a novel, in which he would translate the extra-temporal qualities of these experiences to the level of esthetic form, he hoped to reveal their nature to the world. For like a true artist, he did not only wish to explain them conceptually—he wanted the world to feel the exact emotional impact he had felt himself.

To define how this is done, one must first understand clearly the precise nature of the Proustian revelation. Each such experience, Proust tells us, is marked by a feeling that "the permanent essence of things, usually concealed, is set free and our true self, which had long seemed dead but was not dead in other ways, awakes, takes on fresh life as it receives the celestial nourishment brought to it." This celestial nourishment consists of some sound, or odor, or other sensory stimulus, "sensed anew, simultaneously in the present and the past." But why should these moments seem so overwhelmingly valuable that Proust calls them celestial? Because, Proust observes, the imagination can only operate on the past; the material presented to the imagination, therefore, lacks any sensuous immediacy. But at certain moments, the physical sensations of the past came flooding back to fuse with the present; and in these moments, Proust believed, he grasped a reality "real without being of the present moment, ideal but not abstract." Only in these moments did he attain his most cherished ambition—"to seize, isolate, immobilize for the duration of a lightning flash" what otherwise he could not apprehend, "namely: a fragment of time in its pure state." For a person experiencing this moment, Proust adds, the word "death" no longer has meaning. "Situated outside the scope of time, what could he fear from the future?"

The significance of this experience, though obscurely hinted at throughout the book, is made explicit only in the concluding pages describing the final appearance of the narrator at the reception of the Princesse de Guermantes. The narrator decides to dedicate the remainder of his life to re-creating these experiences in a work of art; and this work will differ essentially from all others because, at its foundation, will be a vision of reality refracted through an extra-temporal perspective. Many critics, viewing Proust as the last and most debilitated of a long line of neurasthenic esthetes, have found in this decision to create a work of art merely the final step in his flight from the burdens of reality. Edmund Wilson links up this view with Proust's ambition to conquer time, assuming that Proust hoped to oppose time by establishing something—a work of art—impervious to its flux; but this scarcely does justice to Proust's own conviction, expressed with special intensity in the last volume of his work, that he was fulfilling a prophetic mission. It was not the work of art *qua* work of art that Proust cared about (his contempt for the horde of faddish scribblers was unbounded) but a work of art that should stand as a monument to his personal conquest of time. His own work could do this, however, not simply because it was a work of art, and like all works of art presumably timeless, but because it was a work that communicated the Proustian vision by a method compelling the reader to experience its full emotional significance.

The prototype of this method, like the analysis of the revelatory moment, occurs during the reception at the Princesse de Guermantes. After spending years in a sanatorium, losing touch almost completely with the fashionable world of the earlier volumes, the narrator comes out of seclusion to attend the reception. His first reaction is one of bewilderment at the striking changes in social position and the even more striking changes in character and personality among his former friends. In the opinion of some socially-minded critics, Proust's intention in this scene was to portray the invasion of French aristocratic society by the upper bourgeoisie, and the gradual breakdown of all social and moral standards caused by the first World War. No doubt this process is incidentally described at some length; but as the narrator takes great pains to tell us, it is far from being the most important meaning of the scene for him. What strikes the narrator, almost with the force of a blow, is this: In trying to recognize old friends under the masks which, as he feels, the years have welded to them, he is jolted for the first time into a consciousness of the passage of time. When a young man addresses the narrator respectfully, instead of familiarly, as if he were an elderly gentleman, the narrator realizes suddenly that he has become an elderly gentleman; but for him the passage of time had gone unperceived up until that moment. To become conscious of time, the narrator begins to understand, it had first been necessary to remove himself from his accustomed environment—or, what amounts to the same thing, from the stream of time acting on that environment—and then to plunge back into the stream after a lapse of years. In so doing, the narrator found himself presented with two images—the world as he had formerly known it, and the world, transformed by time, that he now saw before him; when these two images are juxtaposed, the narrator discovers, the passage of time is suddenly experienced through its visible effects. Habit, that universal soporific, ordinarily conceals the passage of time from those who have gone their accustomed ways, for at any one moment of time the changes are so minute as to be imperceptible. "Other people," Proust writes, "never cease to change places in relation to ourselves. In the imperceptible, but eternal march of the world, we regard them as motionless in a moment of vision, too short for us to perceive the motion that is sweeping them on. But we have only to select in our memory two pictures taken of them at different moments, close enough together however for them not to have altered in themselves—perceptibly, that is to say—and the difference between the two pictures is a measure of the displacement that they have undergone in relation to us." By comparing these two images in a moment of time, the passage of time can be experienced concretely through the impact of its visible effects on the sensibility; it is no longer merely a gap counted off in numbers. This discovery provides the narrator with a method which, in T. S. Eliot's phrase, is an "objective correlative" enabling him to evoke through the medium of a work of art the visionary apprehension of the fragment of "pure time" intuited in the revelatory moment.

When the narrator discovers this method of communicating his experience of the revelatory moment, he decides, as we have already said, to incorporate it in a novel. But the novel the narrator decides to write has just been finished by the reader; and its form is controlled by the method that the narrator has outlined in its concluding pages. The reader, in other words, was substituted for the narrator, and was placed by the author throughout the book in the same position as the narrator occupies before his own experience at the reception of the Princesse de Guermantes. This is done by the discontinuous presentation of character—a simple device which, nevertheless, is the clue to the form of Proust's vast structure. Every reader soon notices that Proust does not follow any of his characters through the whole course of his novel: they appear and re-appear in various stages of their lives, but hundreds of pages sometimes go by between the time they are last seen and the time they re-appear; and when they do turn up again, the passage of time has invariably changed them in some decisive way. Instead of submerging the reader in the stream of time, that is, presenting him with characters that develop progressively, in a continuous line of development, Proust confronts the reader with various snapshots of the characters "motionless in a moment of vision" at different stages in their lives; and the reader, in juxtaposing these images, experiences the effects of the passage of time exactly as the narrator had done. As he had promised, therefore, Proust does stamp his novel indelibly with the form of time; but we are now in a position to understand exactly what he meant by the promise.

To experience the passage of time, Proust learned, it was necessary to rise above it, and to grasp both past and present simultaneously in a moment of what he called "pure time." But "pure time," obviously, is not time at all—it is perception in a moment of time, that is, space. By the discontinuous presentation of character, Proust forces the reader to juxtapose disparate images of his characters spatially, in a moment of time, so that the experience of time's passage will be fully communicated to their sensibility. There is a striking analogy here between Proust's method and that of his beloved Impressionist painters which goes far deeper than the usual comments about the "impressionism" of Proust's style. The Impressionist painters juxtaposed pure tones on the canvas, instead of mixing them on the palette, in order to leave the blending of colors to the eye of the spectator. Similarly, Proust gives us what might be called pure views of his characters—views of them "motionless in a moment of vision" in various phases of their lives—and allows the sensibility of the reader to fuse these views into a unity. Proust's purpose is only achieved, therefore, when these units of meaning are referred to each other reflexively in a moment of time. This is no doubt what Ramon Fernandez had in mind when, in a striking footnote to an essay on Proust, he threw out the following observation: "In general, [Proust's] manner of making contact with his 'durée' is quite Bergsonian (see the episode of the madeleine), but the reactions of his intelligence on his sensibility, which determine the curve of his work, would orient him rather towards a *spatialisation* of time and memory." (Italics in text.) Consequently, as with Joyce and the modern poets, we see that spatial form is also the structural scaffolding of Proust's labyrinthine masterpiece.

3

Granted that the works already considered are similar in their structure, that they all have in common the quality of spatial form, the question immediately arises: How can we account for this surprising unanimity? To answer this question satisfactorily, we must first widen the bounds of our analysis and consider the more general question of the relation of art forms to the cultural climates in which they are created. This latter question has attracted students of the fine arts at least since the time of Herder and Winckelmann; but it was not until the turn of the last century that a systematic study of the problem was begun. Stimulated by Hegel's masterly analysis of art styles as the sensuous objectification of various attitudes towards the universe, a group of German art-scholars and critics concentrated on the problem of form in the plastic arts, working out different categories of form, tracing in detail the shift from one type of form to another, and attempting to account for these changes in general cultural terms. T. E. Hulme, one of the few writers in English to have concerned himself seriously with these problems, turned for guidance to this group of German scholars and critics; and we can do no better than follow his example.

There is one writer in particular who exercised a strong influence on Hulme and, through Hulme by way of Eliot, possibly on the whole of modern English critical writing. This writer is Wilhelm Worringer, the author of a book entitled *Abstraktion und Einfühlung*—literally translated, *Abstraction and Empathy*—which is subtitled *A Contribution to the Psychology of Style;* and it is in Worringer's book that we shall find the clue to our own problem of spatial form.[4] Originally published in 1908, as its author's doctoral dissertation, the book went through numerous editions—a fact which, as Worringer claims in the preface to the third edition, proves that his subject was not merely academic but touched on problems vital to the modern sensibility. Another proof of this point, Worringer further remarks, is that, while he and other scholars were examining and re-evaluating neglected styles, creative artists were turning to these styles for inspiration, finding in them an esthetic form better adaped to the needs of their sensibility than the conventional naturalism of the nineteenth century. Although Worringer's work is impeccably scholastic, confining itself strictly to the past and excluding all but the briefest references to contemporary work, his claim is quite justified: a reader cannot help being struck by the relevance of Worringer's theories to the most fundamental problems of modern art. It is this relevance, along with a powerful and incisive style, which gives the book its notable atmosphere of intellectual excitement and discovery—an air which makes the reading of it, even today, an exhilarating experience.

In his book, Worringer proposes to explain why, throughout the history of the plastic arts, there has been a continual alternation between naturalistic and non-naturalistic styles. During periods of naturalism—the classical age of Greek sculpture and architecture, the Italian Renaissance, the art of Western Europe to the end of the nineteenth century—the artist strives to represent the objective, three-dimensional world of ordinary experience, and to reproduce with loving accuracy the processes of organic nature, among which man is included. On the other hand, during periods of non-naturalism—

[4] Although two of Worringer's books have been translated into English, *Abstraktion und Einfühlung* can, unfortunately, be read only in German. However, the second section of Hulme's essay on "Modern Art," pp. 82-91 of *Speculations*, is, as Hulme says, "practically an abstract of Worringer's views." These are the views presented in *Abstraktion und Einfühlung.*

the art of primitive peoples, Egyptian monumental sculpture, Oriental art, Byzantine art, Gothic sculpture, the art of the twentieth century—the artist abandons the three-dimensional world and returns to the plane, reduces organic nature, including man, to linear-geometrical forms, and frequently abandons the organic world altogether for one of pure lines, forms and colors. While there are, of course, vast differences between the art-products of various periods lumped together under both these categories, the basic similarities between the works in one category, and their basic opposition, taken as a group, to all the works in the other category, are no less striking and instructive. We have here, according to Worringer, a fundamental polarity between two distinct methods of creation in the plastic arts; and neither can be set up as the norm to which the other must adhere.

From the Renaissance to the close of the nineteenth century, however, it was customary to accept naturalism, understood in this broad sense, as the standard for the plastic arts. Non-naturalism was looked upon as a barbarous aberration caused by technical incapacity: it was inconceivable that artists should have violated the canons of naturalism if they had not been forced to do so by a low level of cultural development. Franz Wickhoff, a famous Austrian art-historian of the old school, called non-naturalistic art the "delightful stammering of children"; and this opinion, although it has lost all cogency with artists themselves, would probably find some acceptance among the educated public even at this late date. To combat this invidious elevation of naturalism as an eternal esthetic standard, Worringer makes use of the concept of *Kunstwollen,* or will-to-art, originally employed by another famous Austrian scholar, Alois Riegl. The impulse to creation in the plastic arts, Riegl believed, was not primarily an urge towards the imitation of natural objects; for if this were true, esthetic value would be identical with skill in naturalistic reproduction, and the best works of art would be those which most skillfully duplicated the appearances of the natural world. Instead, Riegl postulated what he called an absolute will-to-art, or, better still, will-to-form; this absolute will-to-form is the element common to all activity in the plastic arts, but it cannot be identified with any particular style. All styles are, as a matter of fact, modifications of this absolute will-to-form as it finds expression in diverse fashions throughout the course of history. The importance of this concept, Worringer points out, is that it shifted the center of gravity in the study of styles from a purely mechanical causation—the state of technical artistic knowledge at the time the style flourished—to a cause based on the purposeful employment of the will-to-form. "The peculiarities of style in past eras," Worringer writes, "can be traced back, not to any deficiency in knowledge, but to a differently directed will-to-art." From this point of view, it is impossible to regard non-naturalism as a grotesquely unsuccessful attempt to reproduce natural appearances: it has no interest in such reproduction, and cannot be judged as if attempting to compete with naturalism on its own terms. Both types of art, created to satisfy different spiritual needs, can only be understood if we examine the climates of feeling which have led to the predominance of the one or the other form at different times.

Once this conclusion is accepted, it is only a short step to the heart of Worringer's book—his discussion of the spiritual conditions which have impelled the will-to-art to move either in the direction of naturalism or non-naturalism. When naturalism is the reigning art style, according to Worringer, we find that it is created by cultures which have achieved an equilibrium with the natural environment of which they are part. Like the Greeks of the classical period, they feel themselves part of organic nature, or, like modern man from the Renaissance to the close of the nineteenth century, they are convinced of their ability to dominate the natural world. In either case, the organic world of nature holds no terrors for them: they have what Worringer calls a *Vertraulichkeitsverhältnis*—a relationship of confidence and intimacy—with the universe; and the result, in art, is a naturalism which delights in reproducing the forms and appearances of the objective, three-dimensional organic world. Following Riegl, however, Worringer warns us not to confuse this delight in the organic exhibited by naturalism with a mere impulse towards imitation. Although the imitation of natural forms and objects is a by-product of naturalism, what we enjoy is not the imitation *per se*, but our heightened sense of active participation in the organic; and it is this sense which, by demanding satisfaction, turns the will-to-art in the direction of naturalism when man and the universe are in harmonious relation.

On the other hand, when the relationship between man and the universe is one of disharmony and disequilibrium, we find that non-naturalistic, abstract styles are always produced. To primitive peoples the external world is an incomprehensible chaos, an utterly meaningless confusion of occurrences and sensations. Clearly, peoples at this level of cultural development would take no pleasure in an objective presentation of the organic: the world of their ordinary experience is a world of fear, and the representation of this world in art would merely intensify their terror. Their will-to-art, instead of turning towards naturalism, goes in the opposite direction: it reduces the appearances of the natural world to linear-geometrical forms—forms which have the stability, the harmony and the sense of order which primitive man cannot find in the flux of phenomena as, to quote Hart Crane, they "plunge in silence by." Non-naturalistic styles are also produced, at a higher level of cultural development, in periods which, like the Byzantine and the Gothic, are dominated by a religion that completely rejects the natural world as a realm of evil and imperfection. Instead of depicting natural appearances in all their overwhelming vitality, the will-to-art turns toward their spiritualization, towards the elimination of mass and corporeality, towards an approximation of the eternal, ethereal tranquillity of other-worldly existence. In both cases—the primitive and the transcendental—the will-to-art, in conformity with the prevalent climate of feeling, diverges from naturalism to create esthetic forms that will satisfy the spiritual needs of their creators; and in both cases these forms are characterized by an emphasis on linear-geometrical patterns, on an elimination of objective, three-dimensional shapes and objective, three-dimensional space, on the dominance of the plane in all types of plastic art.[5]

It is a simple matter to apply Worringer's observations to modern developments in the plastic arts. At a time like the present, a time when, as the psychologist Erich Fromm has told us, man is trying to escape from freedom because he no longer feels able to cope with the bewildering complexities of megalopolitan existence, it should be no surprise that artists—always the most sensitive barometers of cultural change—have turned for inspiration to the styles of periods ruled by similar climates of feeling; and the results of this process on the plastic arts are too obvious to need any detailed comment. But, as T. E. Hulme was one of the first to realize, esthetic form in modern literature could be expected to undergo a similar change in response to the same climate of feeling. Hulme's most interesting essay, "Romanticism and Classicism," is an attempt to define this change as it affected literary form. Unfortunately, Hulme lacked any adequate concept of esthetic form in literature, and he mistakenly tried to compensate for this deficiency by adopting ideas used by the French critics Pierre Lasserre and Charles Maurras in their attack on Romanticism. For political as well as literary reasons, these writers had bitterly criticized the French Romantics on every conceivable ground, much as Irving Babbitt was to do with Romanticism in general some years later; but what most impressed Hulme in the writing of the French critics was their denunciation of romantic subjectivity, of the unrestrained emotionalism which the Romantics sometimes fobbed off as literature. Non-naturalistic art, Hulme had noticed, in its suppression of the organic also suppressed the subjective and the personal as modern man understood them; the corresponding style in literature would also be impersonal and objective, or at least would not be "like pouring a pot of treacle over the dinner table"; it would have a "dry hardness," the hardness of Pope and Horace, as against "the sloppiness which doesn't consider that a poem is a poem

[5] To forestall objections, it might be pointed out that neither Worringer nor the present writer regard these distinctions as absolute in any but a theoretical sense. These different styles are ideal constructions, to which the art of various periods has approximated in greater or lesser degree. Elements of both styles may be found in all periods; cultures are spoken of as creating one or the other on the basis of predominance, not of absolute exclusion. The entire second portion of Worringer's book, which is outside the scope of our discussion, traces the actual degree of dominance and interpenetration of both styles in the plastic arts of selected cultures.

unless it is moaning or whining about something or other." And, Hulme concludes, "I prophesy that a period of dry, hard, classical verse is coming." Although this prophecy may seem to have struck remarkably close to home, from Hulme's own poems we know he was thinking of something resembling Imagism rather than the later influence of Donne and the Metaphysicals; but regardless of the accuracy of his prediction, his adoption of the classic-romantic antithesis could only confuse the issue. Instead of following Worringer's lead, and attempting to work out some precise notion of the literary form that would parallel the changes taking place in modern art, Hulme gives us a vague description of this literary form as being "dry and hard" in quality, tacking this description on to a totally different set of problems by calling the form "classical" as well. Hulme's great merit lies in having been among the first to realize that literary form would undergo a change similar to changes in the plastic arts; but he failed to define this literary form with any exactitude. To do so, we must go back to Worringer and take up where Hulme's happy but fragmentary intuitions left off.

Because literature is a time-art, Hulme might have taken his point of departure, as we shall do, from Worringer's discussion of the disappearance of depth in non-naturalistic art. The general reasons for this development have already been explained; but Worringer analyzes this point with great particularity, and in doing so throws out a remark of first importance for the understanding of spatial form in modern literature. "Space filled with atmospheric light," Worringer writes, "which binds objects together and cancels out their individual self-containedness, imparts a temporal value (*Zeitlichkeitswert*) to things, drawing them into the cosmic merry-go-round of appearances." Presenting objects in depth gives them a time-value, or perhaps we should say accentuates their time-value, because it connects them with the real world in which events occur; and since time is the very condition of that flux and change which, as we have seen, man wants to escape from when he is in a condition of disequilibrium with nature, non-naturalistic styles shun the dimension of depth and prefer the plane. For when depth disappears and objects are presented in one plane, their simultaneous apprehension as part of a timeless unity is obviously made easier. Although, to come back to Lessing, the plastic arts are absolutely spatial when compared to literature, we now see that they have been more or less spatial in the course of their inner evolution, depending on the extent to which the representation of three-dimensionality was favored or avoided. This means, paradoxically, that the plastic arts have been most spatial when they did not represent the depth dimension and least spatial when they did, since a greater degree of time-value always accompanies the presentation of three-dimensionality.[6]

In a non-naturalistic style, then, the inherent spatiality of the plastic arts is accentuated by the effort to remove all traces of time-value; and since modern art is non-naturalistic, we can say that it is moving in the direction of increased spatiality. The significance of spatial form in modern literature now becomes clear: it is the exact complement in literature, on the plane of esthetic form, to the developments that have taken place in the plastic arts. Spatial form is the literary development that Hulme was looking for but did not know how to find. In both artistic mediums, one naturally spatial and the other naturally temporal, the evolution of esthetic form in the twentieth century has been absolutely identical: both have moved to overcome, so far as possible, the time-elements involved in their perception; and the reason for this identity is that both are rooted in the same spiritual and emotional climate—a climate

[6] Dagobert Frey, whose book *Gotik und Renaissance* we have already mentioned, takes over Lessing's categories of space and time and demonstrates in detail that, from a perceptual point of view, the plastic arts can be more or less spatial, and literature—not to mention music—more or less temporal. Frey, however, calls the planimetric, non-naturalistic art of the Middle Ages temporal because, to understand the *meaning* of the symbols compressed in the picture-plane, the eye must go from one to the other in time and read the symbols as if they were the letters of a word or the parts of a sentence.

While this is unquestionably true, the fact remains that, aside from the question of content, the planimetric art of the Middle Ages created geometric forms on the plane from which all trace of time-value had been removed. Events in the life of Christ, for example, though they may have occurred at different times, are juxtaposed on the same picture-plane and apprehended simultaneously as part of a stylized visual pattern. For this reason, we cannot accept Frey's terminology as adequate to describe the most important perceptual quality of medieval art.

which, as it affects the sensibility of all artists, must also affect the forms they create in every medium. On a purely formal plane, therefore, by demonstrating the complete congruity of esthetic form in modern art with the form of modern literature, we have laid bare what Worringer would call the "psychological" roots of spatial form in modern literature. But for a true psychology of style, as Worringer reminds us in the remarks quoted at the head of this section, the "formal value" must be shown "to be an accurate expression of the inner value, in such a way that duality of form and content cease to exist." What elements can be discovered in the content of the works we have discussed that will resolve this duality?

In the case of Proust, we have already answered this question by showing that his use of spatial form arose from an attempt to communicate the extra-temporal quality of his revelatory moments. Ernst Robert Curtius, at the conclusion of his penetrating study of Proust, calls him a Platonist; and this term is quite accurate if we take Curtius to mean that, like Plato, Proust found his ultimate value in an existence that had wrenched itself free from all submission to the flux of the temporal. Proust, it is not generally realized, was an ardent student of philosophy as well as a neurasthenic esthete; he was fully aware of the philosophic implications of his own literary productions. By conceptualizing these implications for us in his analysis of the revelatory moment, Proust himself explained to the reader the unity between form and content in his masterwork.

With our other writers, however, the problem is a good deal more complex. Where Proust had been concerned with an individual revelation, restricted, in his work, to the sphere of the narrator's personal experience, the other writers all move out beyond the personal into the wider reaches of history: all deal, in one way or another, with the clash of historical perspectives induced by the identification of contemporary figures and events with various historical prototypes. This is evident in the "Cantos," in "The Waste Land" and in *Ulysses,* for the chief source of meaning in all three is the sense of ironic dissimilarity and yet of profound human continuity between the modern protagonists and their long-dead exemplars. A similar palimpsest effect is found in *Nightwood,* where Dr. O'Connor is continually drawing on his "prehistoric memory" for images and metaphors, weaving the past in with the present and identifying the two. Allen Tate, speaking of the "Cantos," writes that Ezra Pound's "powerful juxtapositions of the ancient, the Renaissance, and the modern worlds reduce all three elements to an unhistorical miscellany, timeless and without origin"; and this is called "the peculiarly modern quality of Mr. Pound." But it is, as well, the peculiarly modern quality of all the works we have before us—they all maintain a continual juxtaposition between aspects of the past and present, in such a way that both are fused in one comprehensive view; and both Tiresias and Dr. O'Connor—the central figures of the works in which they appear—are the focus of consciousness in these works precisely because they transcend historical limits and encompass all times. (Leopold Bloom, of course, does the same thing; but Joyce, maintaining the traditions of naturalism, makes Bloom the unconscious bearer of his own immortality.) By this juxtaposition of past and present, as Allen Tate realized, history becomes unhistorical: it is no longer seen as an objective, causal progression in time, with distinctly marked-out differences between each period, but is sensed as a continuum in which distinctions between past and present are obliterated. Just as the dimension of depth has vanished from the plastic arts, so the dimension of depth has vanished from history as it forms the content of these works: past and present are seen spatially, locked in a timeless unity which, while it may accentuate surface differences, eliminates any feeling of historical sequence by the very act of juxtaposition. The objective historical imagination, on which modern man has prided himself, and which he has cultivated so carefully since the Renaissance, is transformed in these writers into the mythical imagination for which historical time does not exist—the imagination that sees the actions and events of a particular time merely as the bodying forth of eternal prototypes. These prototypes are created by transmuting the time-world of history into the timeless world of myth. And it is this timeless world of myth, forming the common content of modern literature, which finds its appropriate esthetic expression in spatial form.

W. K. WIMSATT, JR.:

The Structure of the "Concrete Universal" in Literature *

THE CENTRAL argument of this essay, concerning what I shall, taking a term from Hegel, call the "concrete universal," proceeds from the observation that literary theorists have from early times to the present persisted in making statements which in their contexts seem to mean that a work of literary art is in some peculiar sense a very individual thing or a very universal thing or both. What that paradox can mean, or what important fact behind the paradox has been discerned by such various critics as Aristotle, Plotinus, Hegel, Whitehead, and Ransom, it will be the purpose of the essay to inquire, and by the inquiry to discuss not only a significant feature of metaphysical poetics from Aristotle to the present day but the relation between metaphysical poetics and more practical and specific rhetorical analysis. In the brief historical survey which forms one part of this essay it will not be my purpose to suggest that any of these writers meant exactly what I shall mean in later parts where I describe the structure of poetry. Yet throughout the essay I shall proceed on the theory not only that men have at different times used the same terms and have meant differently, but that they have sometimes used different terms and have meant the same or somewhat the same. In other words, I assume that there is continuity in the problems of criticism, and that a person who studies poetry today has a legitimate interest in what Plato said about poetry.

The view of common terms and their relations to classes of things from which I shall start is roughly that which one may read in the logic of J. S. Mill, a view which is not much different from the semantic view of today and for most purposes not much different from the Aristotelian and scholastic view. Mill speaks of the word and its denotation and connotation (the term, referent and reference of Ogden and Richards) (the sign, denotatum and designatum of Charles W. Morris). The denotation is the *it*, the individual thing or the aggregate of things to which the term may refer; the connotation is the *what*, the quality or classification inferred for the it, or implicitly predicated by the application of the term or the giving of the name.[1] The main difference between all modern positivistic, nominalistic and semantic systems and the scholastic and classical systems is that the older ones stress the similarity of the individuals denoted by the common term and hence the real universality of meaning, while the modern systems stress the differences in the individuals, the constant flux even of each individual in time and space and its kinetic structure, and hence infer only an approximate or nominal universality of meaning and a convenience rather than a truth in the use of general terms. A further difference lies in the view of how the individual is related to the various connotations of terms which may be applied to it. That is, to the question: What is it? the older writers seem to hold there is but one (essentially right) answer, while the moderns accept as many answers as there are classes to which the individual may be assigned (an indefinite number). The older writers speak of a proper essence or whatness of the individual, a quality which in some cases at least is that designated by the class name most commonly

* "The Structure of the 'Concrete Universal' in Literature" first appeared in *Publications of the Modern Language Association*, March 1947, and is reprinted here with some minor revisions by permission of the editors and the author. W. K. Wimsatt, Jr. (*b.* 1907), is the author of *The Prose Style of Samuel Johnson* (1941).

[1] The terms "denotation" and "connotation" are commonly and loosely used by literary critics to distinguish the dictionary meaning of a term (denotation) from the vaguer aura of suggestion (connotation). But both these are parts of the connotation in the logical sense.

applied to the individual: a bench is a bench, essentially a bench, accidentally a heavy wooden object or a thing made by a carpenter.[2] "When we say *what* it is," observes Aristotle, "we do not say 'white' or 'hot' or 'three cubits long,' but 'a man' or 'a god.' " And this view is also a habit scarcely avoidable in daily thinking, especially when we think of living things or of artifacts, things made by us or our fellows for a purpose. What is it? Bench, we think, is an adequate answer. An assemblage of sticks painted green, we consider freakish. Why this should be so is a question which—even though one avoid the metaphysical problem of "essence" —one must consider in discussing the structure of the "concrete universal."

2

Whether or not one believes in universals, one may see the persistence in literary criticism of a theory that poetry presents the concrete and the universal, or the individual and the universal, or an object which in a mysterious and special way is both highly general and highly particular. The doctrine is implicit in Aristotle's two statements that poetry imitates action and that poetry tends to express the universal. It is implicit again at the end of the classic period in the doctrine of Plotinus, who in his later writing on beauty, reverses the Platonic objection that art does not know the ultimate reality of the forms. Plotinus arrives at the view that the artist by a kind of by-pass of the inferior natural productions of the world soul reaches straight to the forms that lie behind in the divine intelligence.[3] Another version of the classic theory, with affinities for Plotinus, lies in the scholastic phrase *resplendentia formae.*

Cicero's account of how Zeuxis painted an ideal Helen from the five most beautiful virgins of Crotona is a typical development of the less mystic Aristotelian theory, in effect the familiar neo-classic theory found in Du Fresnoy's *Art of Painting,* in the writings of Johnson, especially in the tulip passage in *Rasselas,* and in the *Discourses* and *Idlers* of Reynolds. The business of the poet is not to number the streaks of the tulip; it is to give us not the individual, but the species. The same thing is stated in a more complicated way by Kant in telling how the imagination constructs the "aesthetical normal Idea":

> It is the image for the whole race, which floats among all the variously different intuitions of individuals, which nature takes as archetype in her productions of the same species, but which seems not to be fully reached in any individual case.

And Hegel's account is as follows:

> The work of art is not only for the *sensuous* apprehension as sensuous object, but its position is of such a kind that as sensuous it is at the same time essentially addressed to the *mind.*
>
> In comparison with the show or semblance of immediate sensuous existence or of historical narrative, the artistic semblance has the advantage that in itself it points beyond self, and refers us away from itself to something spiritual which it is meant to bring before the mind's eye. . . . The hard rind of nature and the common world give the mind more trouble in breaking through to the idea than do the products of art.

The excellence of Shakespeare, says Coleridge, consists in a "union and interpenetration of the universal and particular." In one terminology or another this idea of a concrete universal is found in most metaphysical aesthetic of the eighteenth and nineteenth centuries.

Even more noteworthy perhaps is the persistence of the doctrine in certain quarters today. A subtle semanticist such as Professor Morris writes: "In the apprehension of the iconic sign there is both a mediated and an immediate taking account of certain properties." And "The semantical rule for the use of icons is that they denote those objects which have the characteristics which they themselves have—or more

[2] Cf. Mortimer J. Adler, *Problems for Thomists, The Problem of Species* (New York, 1940), pp. 24-25; Jacques Maritain, *An Introduction to Logic* (New York, 1937), pp. 12-13. But see a neo-scholastic statement of the opposite view, John J. Toohey, "What are the Predicables," *The New Scholasticism,* x (July, 1936), 260-261; and cf. Joseph Fröbes, *Tractatus Logicae Formalis* (Rome, 1940), pp. 24-25.

[3] "The arts are not to be slighted on the ground that they create by imitation of natural objects; for, to begin with, these natural objects are themselves imitations; then, we must recognize that they give no bare reproduction of the thing seen but go back to the ideas from which Nature itself derives" (*Enneads,* v, viii, 1, *Plotinus—The Fifth Ennead,* trans. Stephen MacKenna [London, 1926], p. 74).

usually a certain specified set of their characteristics." And in a similar vein Professor Whitehead writes:

Thus "art" in the general sense which I require is any selection by which the concrete facts are so arranged as to elicit attention to particular values which are realisable by them.

We want the concrete fact with a high light thrown on what is relevant to its preciousness.

The concrete facts in a special way embody and draw attention to an aspect of themselves (a value), the universal. A more elaborate form of the doctrine and a determined attempt to clarify the paradox involved in it, is to be found in the writings of a literary critic, Mr. John Crowe Ransom, who speaks of the argument of a poem (the universal) and a local texture or tissue of concrete irrelevance. Another literary critic, Mr. Allen Tate, manipulating the logical terms "extension" and "intension," has arrived at the concept of "tension" in poetry. "Extension," as logicians use the word, is the range of individuals denoted by a term (denotation); "intension" is the total of qualities connoted (connotation). In the ordinary or logical use of the terms, extension and intension are of inverse relationship—the wider the one, the shallower the other. A poem, says Mr. Tate, as I interpret him, is a verbal structure which in some peculiar way has both a very wide extension and a very deep intension.

Not all these theories of the concrete universal lay equal stress on the two sides of the paradox, and it seems indicative of the vitality of the theory and of the truth implicit in it, that the two sides have been capable of exaggeration into antithetic schools and theories of poetry. For Du Fresnoy, Johnson and Reynolds poetry and painting give the universal; the less said about the particulars the better. This is the neo-classic theory, the illustrations of which we seek in Pope's *Essay on Man* or in Johnson's *Ramblers*, where the ideas are moral and general and concerned with "nature," "one clear, unchanged, and universal light." [4] The opposite theory is the romantic, which had notable expression in England, a few years before Johnson wrote *Rasselas*, in Joseph Warton's *Essay on Pope:*

A minute and particular enumeration of circumstances judiciously selected, is what chiefly discriminates poetry from history, and renders the former, for that reason, a more close and faithful representation of nature than the latter.

And Blake's marginal criticism of Reynolds was: "THIS Man was Hired to Depress art." "To Generalize is to be an Idiot. To Particularize is the Alone Distinction of Merit. General Knowledges are those Knowledges that Idiots possess." "Sacrifice the Parts; What becomes of the whole?" The line from Warton's *Essay* to Croce's *Aesthetic* seems a straight and obvious one, from Thomson's specific descriptions of flowers to the individual act of intuition-expression which is art—its opposite and enemy being the concept or generality.[5] The two views of art (two that can be held by different theorists about the same works of art) may be startlingly contrasted in the following passages about fictitious character—one a well-known statement by Johnson, the other by the philosopher of the *élan vital.*

[Shakespeare's] characters are not modified by the customs of particular places, unpractised by the rest of the world; by the peculiarities of studies or professions, which can operate but upon small numbers; or by the accidents of transient fashions or temporary opinions: they are the genuine progeny of common humanity, such as the world will always supply, and observation will always find. His persons act and speak by the influence of those general passions and principles by which all minds are agitated, and the whole system of life is continued in motion. In the writings of other poets a

[4] At least the ideas are general as far as such a thing is possible. I have contended elsewhere (*The Prose Style of Samuel Johnson* [New Haven, 1941], p. 96) that Johnson was the only neo-classicist who managed even to approximate the kind of writing described in the theory, and the *Ramblers* suffer as art for that very reason. A neo-classicist like Pope, in *The Rape of the Lock*, will be as particular as any romantic poet, only about different things, as Hazlitt so well describes his poetry, not about tempests but about tea-cups. All great poetry would seem to be alike in respect to the concrete and the universal; it is a balance.

[5] It is true that Croce has protested: "Ce qu'on démontre comme inconciliable avec le principe de la pure intuition, ce n'est pas l'universalité, mais la valeur intellectualiste et transcendante donnée dans l'art à l'universalité, sous la forme de l'allegorie ou du symbole. . . ." ("Le Caractère de Totalité de l'Expression Artistique," in *Bréviaire d'Esthétique*, trad. Georges Bourgin [Paris, 1923], p. 170.) But the main drift of his better-known *Aesthetic* is against the concept and the generality.

character is too often an individual; in those of Shakespeare it is commonly a species.

Hence it follows that art always aims at what is *individual.* What the artist fixes on his canvas is something he has seen at a certain spot, on a certain day, at a certain hour, with a colouring that will never be seen again. What the poet sings of is a certain mood which was his, and his alone, and which will never return. . . . Nothing could be more unique than the character of Hamlet. Though he may resemble other men in some respects, it is clearly not on that account that he interests us most.[6]

Other critics, notably the most ancient and the most modern (Aristotle, Morris, Whitehead, Ransom) have tried to hold the extremes together. Neither of the extremes gives a good account of art and each leads out of art. The theory of particularity leads to individuality and originality (Edward Young was another eighteenth-century Crocean), then to the idiosyncratic and the unintelligible and to the psychology of the author, which is not in the work of art and is not a standard for judgment. The theory of universality as it appears in Johnson and Reynolds leads to platitude and to a standard of material objectivity, the average tulip, the average human form, some sort of average.[7]

3

"Just representations of general nature," said Johnson, and it ought to be noted, though it perhaps rarely is, that two kinds of generality are involved, as indeed they are in the whole neoclassic theory of generality. There is the generality of logic or classification, of the more general as opposed to the more specific, "essential" generality, one might say. And there is the generality of literal truth to nature, "existential" generality. The assumption in neo-classic theory seems to be that these two must coincide. As a matter of fact they may and often do, but need not. Thus: "purple cow" is a more general (less specific) term and concept than "tan cow with a broken horn," yet the latter is more general or true to nature. We have, in short, realism or fantasy, and in either there may be various degrees of the specific or general. We have *A Journal of the Plague Year* and *The Rambler, Gulliver's Travels* and *Rasselas.* The fact that there are a greater number of "vicissitudes" and "miscarriages" (favorite *Rambler* events) in human experience than plagues at London, that there are more tan cows than tan cows with broken horns, makes it true in a sense that a greater degree of essential generality involves a greater degree of existential. But in this sense the most real concept is simply that of "being."

The question is how a work of literature can be either more individual (unique) or more universal than other kinds of writing, or how it can combine the individual and the universal more than other kinds. Every description in words, so far as it is a direct description (The barn is red and square) is a generalization. That is the nature of words. There are no individuals conveyed in words but only more or less specific generalizations, so that Johnson is right, though we have to ask him what degree of verbal generality makes art, and whether "tulip" is a better or more important generality than "tulip with ten streaks," or whether "beauty" is not in fact a much more impressive generality than "tulip." On the other hand, one cannot deny that in some sense there are more tulips in poetry than pure abstracted beauty. So that Bergson is right too; only we shall have to ask him what degree of specificity in verbal description makes art. And he can never claim complete specificity or individuality, even for Hamlet.

If he could, if a work of literary art could be looked on as an artifact or concrete physical work, the paradox for the student of universals would return from the opposite direction even more forcibly—as it does in fact for theorists of graphic art. If Reynolds' picture "The Age of Innocence" presents a species or universal, what species does it present? Not an Aristotelian essence—"man," or "humanity"—nor even a more specific kind of being such as "woman-

[6] Henri Bergson, *Laughter, An Essay on the Meaning of the Comic* (New York, 1928), pp. 161-162.

[7] Roger Fry in his Introduction to Reynolds' *Third Discourse* argues that the species presented in painting are not those of the natural, but those of the social world, as king, knight, beggar (*Discourses,* ed. Roger Fry, London, 1905, p. 46). And a modern critic of sculpture, R. H. Wilenski, offers what is perhaps the last retreat of the doctrine of universals in visual art: not man, flower or animal but the forms of life analogous in (i.e. common to) man, flower and animal are abstracted and presented pure in sculptural art (R. H. Wilenski, *The Meaning of Modern Sculpture* [London, 1939], pp. 159-160).

hood." For then the picture would present the same universal as Reynolds' portrait of Mrs. Siddons as "The Tragic Muse," and all differences between "The Age of Innocence" and "The Tragic Muse" would be aesthetically irrelevant. Does the picture then present girlhood, or barefoot girlhood, or barefoot girlhood in a white dress against a gloomy background? All three are equally valid universals (despite the fact that makeshift phrases are required to express two of them), and all three are presented by the picture. Or is it the title which tells us what universal is presented, "The Age of Innocence," and without the title should we not know the universal? The question will be: What in the individual work of art demands that we attribute to it one universal rather than another?

We may answer that for poetry it is the generalizing power of words already mentioned, and go on to decide that what distinguishes poetry from scientific or logical discourse is a degree of irrelevant concreteness in descriptive details. This is in effect what Mr. Ransom says in his doctrine of argument and local irrelevance, but the doctrine bears a suspicious resemblance to an ancient and now rather thoroughly discredited theory, that of ornamental metaphor. The argument, says Mr. Ransom, is the prose or scientific meaning, what the poem has in common with other kinds of writing. The irrelevance is a texture of concreteness which does not contribute anything to the argument but is somehow enjoyable or valuable for its own sake, the vehicle of a metaphor which one boards heedless of where it runs, whether crosstown or downtown—just for the ride. So Mr. Ransom nurses and refines the argument, and on one page he makes the remark that the poet searches for "suitability" in his particular phrases, and by suitability Mr. Ransom means "the propriety which consists in their denoting the particularity which really belongs to the logical object." [8] But the difference between "propriety" and relevance in such a context is not easy to see. And relevance is logic. The fact is that all concrete illustration has about it something of the irrelevant. An apple falling from a tree illustrates gravity, but apple and tree are irrelevant to the pure theory of gravity. It may be that what happens in a poem is that the apple and the tree are somehow made more than usually relevant.

Such a theory, not that of Johnson and Reynolds, not that of Warton and Bergson, not quite that of Mr. Ransom, is what I would suggest—yet less as a novelty than as something already widely implicit in recent poetical analyses and exegeses, in those of Mr. Empson, for instance, Mr. Tate, Mr. Blackmur, Mr. Brooks, and Mr. R. P. Warren. If a work of literature is not in a simple sense either more individual or more universal than other kinds of writing, it may yet be such an individual or such a complex of meaning that it has a special relation to the world of universals. Some acute remarks on this subject were made by Ruskin in a chapter of *Modern Painters* neglected today perhaps because of its distasteful ingredient of "noble emotion." Poetry, says Ruskin in criticizing Reynolds' *Idlers,* is not distinguished from history by the omission of details, nor for that matter by the mere addition of details. "It is not the multiplication of details which constitutes history—there must be something either in the nature of the details themselves, or the method of using them, which invests them with poetical power." Their nature, one may add, as assumed through their relation to one another, a relation which may also be called the method of using them. The poetic character of details consists not in what they say directly and explicitly (as if roses and moonlight were poetic) but in what by their arrangement they *show* implicitly.

4

The question of the concrete and universal in art is closely related to that of unity, and unity in works of art is in turn only to be understood in terms of unity in the world of nature, a concept too often taken for granted. At the risk of being tedious, I shall offer a few epistemological and ontological generalizations: The world before our eyes and other senses if not a con-

[8] *The New Criticism* (Norfolk, 1941), p. 315. Mr. Maritain, coming from a different direction, arrives at somewhat the same poser. "If it pleases a futurist to paint a lady with only one eye, or a quarter of an eye, nobody denies him such a right: all one is entitled to require—and here is the whole problem—is that the quarter eye is all the lady needs *in the given case*" (*Art and Scholasticism* [New York, 1937], p. 28). Here indeed is the whole problem. Long ago Aristotle said, "Not to know that a hind has no horns is a less serious matter than to paint it inartistically" (*Poetics*, xxv, 5).

tinuum in the Platonic sense of a complete chain of being (with purple cows) is a continuum in the sense that the parts we call objects (unities) are jammed close together. There are no spaces separating the objects. We separate and perceive unities with our minds, and while homogeneity and detachability are partly our standards (the diamond from the clay, the head from the body, and the parts of an atom from one another), yet in the endless conflux and overlapping of objects, it is another standard, that of organized heterogeneity (in the human artifact, in the chemical structure, and in the living organism) which is a more profound standard of unity. If a man could come *ex vacuo* into our known and familiar landscape and if he began to classify objects (compressing into a few moments the experience of a child's first years), he might first make a rude division into the moving and the stationary, and in the first class he would put animals, birds, streams, leaves blown by the wind, butterflies and mowing machines; and in the second he would put trees, rocks, fences, hills and houses. On closer inspection, however, he would find great ontological gaps between rocks and trees and between butterflies and blown leaves and at the same time cross-affinities between the members of his first two superficial classes. He would see that rocks and streams, trees and butterflies, houses and mowing machines have deeper and more complex qualities in common than motion and rest. He would reclassify.

Not so much the looseness or removability of the typewriter on the desk as its organization makes us consider it an *it;* its organization and its place beside the telephone and lamp make us say it is a typewriter.[9] It is a complex artifact, so special and different, that its very structure and use by human beings points to the class in which we must put it. It is a "concrete universal." In fact, if it is so constructed that its values may be directly inspected, if its use shines through it, there may be question whether it is not a work of art. The artist, we are told, puts a frame around his picture or a pedestal under his statue, to remind us that it is isolated from us or is to be taken as a sign of itself and of other denotata like it. With a piece of black velvet under it, the typewriter may well take its place in an exhibition on 53rd Street to illustrate the relation between art and industrial design.

[9] If we perceive and classify objects according to their heterogeneous unities, we perceive and classify them also according to their spacing against the background of potentiality (that is, the frequency of their occurrence in reality) and according to their importance in a given human context. Reflections of this fact may be seen in what seem to us the strangely concrete vocabularies of primitive peoples and in such word-group survivals in our own language as *horse, mare, stallion, foal, colt.* Cf. Otto Jespersen, *Language* (London, 1922), pp. 430-431. Cf. Locke, *Human Understanding,* II, xxii, 5.

5

"One," observes Ben Jonson, thinking of literature, "One is considerable two waies: either, as it is only separate, and by it self: or as being compos'd of many parts, it beginnes to be one as those parts grow or are wrought together."[10] A literary work of art is a complex of detail (an artifact, if we may be allowed that metaphor for what is only a verbal object), a composition so complicated of human values that its interpretation is dictated by the understanding of it, and so complicated as to seem in the highest degree individual—a concrete universal. We are accustomed to being told, for example, that what makes a character in fiction or drama vital is a certain fullness or rotundity: that the character has many sides. Thus E. M. Forster:

> We may divide characters into flat and round. Flat characters were called "humours" in the seventeenth century, and are sometimes called types, and sometimes caricatures. In their purest form, they are constructed round a single idea or quality: when there is more than one factor in them, we get the beginning of the curve towards the round. The really flat character can be expressed in one sentence such as "I never will desert Mr. Micawber."

It remains to be said, however, that the many traits of the round character (if indeed it is one character and not a hodge-podge) are harmonized or unified, and that if this is so, then all the traits are chosen by a principle, just as are the traits of the flat character. Yet it cannot be that the difference between the round and flat character is simply numerical; the difference cannot be merely that the presiding principle is illustrated by more examples in the

[10] *Discoveries,* ed. Maurice Castelain (Paris, 1906), p. 139. Jonson translates from Heinsius.

round character. Something further must be supposed—a special interrelation in the traits of the round character. Bobadil is an example of the *miles gloriosus*,[11] a flat humour. He swears by "The foot of Pharaoh," takes tobacco, borrows money from his landlady, is found lying on a bench fully dressed with a hangover, brags about his feats at the siege of Strigonium, beats Cob a poor water carrier, and so on. It is possible that he has numerically as many traits as Falstaff, one of the most vital of all characters. But one of the differences between Falstaff and Bobadil is that the things Falstaff says are funny; the things Bobadil says are not. Compared to Falstaff, Bobadil is unconscious, an opaque butt. There is the vitality of consciousness in Falstaff. And further there is the crowning complexity of self-consciousness. The fact that Morgann could devote a book to arguing that Falstaff is not a coward, that lately Professor Wilson has argued that at Gadshill Falstaff may exhibit " 'all the common symptoms of the malady' of cowardice" and at the same time persuade the audience that he has " 'never once lost his self-possession,' " the fact that one can conceive that Falstaff in the Gadshill running-away scene really knows that his assailants are the Prince and Poins—all this shows that in Falstaff there is a kind of interrelation among his attributes, his cowardice, his wit, his debauchery, his presumption, that makes them in a special way an organic harmony. He is a rounded character not only in the sense that he is gross (a fact which may have tempted critics to speak of a rounded character) or in the sense that he is a bigger bundle of attributes, stuffed more full, than Bobadil or Ralph Roister Doister; but in the sense that his attributes make a circuit and connection. A kind of awareness of self (a very high and human characteristic), with a pleasure in the fact, is perhaps the central principle which instead of simplifying the attributes gives each one a special function in the whole, a double or reflex value. Falstaff or such a character of self-conscious "infinite variety"[12] as Cleopatra are concrete universals because they have no class names, only their own proper ones, yet are structures of such precise variety and centrality that each demands a special interpretation—which none can name—in the realm of human values. They are individuals with a highlight.

Character is one type of concrete universal; there are perhaps other types, as many perhaps as the central terms of criticism; but most can be learned I believe by examination of metaphor—the structure most characteristic of concentrated poetry. The language of poets, said Shelley, "is vitally metaphorical: that is, it marks the before unapprehended relations of things and perpetuates their apprehension." Wordsworth spoke of the abstracting and modifying powers of the imagination. And long ago Aristotle said that the greatest thing was the use of metaphor, because it meant an eye for resemblances. Even the simplest form of metaphor or simile ("My love is like a red, red rose") presents us with a special and creative, in fact a concrete, kind of abstraction different from that of science. For behind a metaphor lies a resemblance between two classes, and hence a more general third class (perhaps bridging a gap wide in the pattern of actual things), but nevertheless a literal real class. This class is unnamed and most likely remains unnamed and is apprehended only through the metaphor. It is a new conception for which there is no other expression. Keats discovering Homer is like a traveler in the realms of gold, like an astronomer who discovers a planet, like Cortez gazing at the Pacific. The title of the sonnet, "On First Looking into Chapman's Homer," seems to furnish not so much the subject of the poem as a fourth member of a central metaphor, the real subject of the poem being an abstraction, a certain kind of thrill in discovering, for which there is no name and no other description, only the four members of the metaphor pointing, as to the center of their pattern. The point of the poem seems to lie somewhere outside both vehicle and tenor.

To take a more complicated instance, Wordsworth's "Solitary Reaper" has the same basic metaphorical structure, the girl alone reaping and singing, and the two bird images, the nightingale in Arabian sands and the cuckoo among the Hebrides, the three figures serving the parallel or metaphorical function of bringing out the

[11] ["boastful soldier."]

[12] I do not mean that self-consciousness is the only principle of complexity in character, yet a degree of it I suspect will be found in all the richest characters.

abstraction of loneliness, remoteness, mysterious charm in the singing. But there is also a kind of third-dimensional significance, in the fact that one bird is far out in the northern sea, the other far off in southern sands, a fact which is not part of the comparison between the birds and the girl. By an implication cutting across the plane of logic of the metaphor, the girl and the two birds suggest extension in space, universality and world communion—an effect supported by other details of the poem such as the overflowing of the vale profound, the mystery of the Erse song, the bearing of the song away in the witness' heart, the past and future themes which the girl may be singing. Thus a central abstraction is created, of communion, telepathy in solitude, the prophetic soul of the wide world dreaming on things to come—an abstraction which is the effect not wholly of the metaphor elaborated logically (in a metaphysical way) but of a working on two axes, by association rather than by logic, by a three-dimensional complexity of structure.

To take yet a third instance, metaphoric structure may appear where we are less likely to realize it explicitly—in poetic narratives, for example, elliptically concealed in the more obvious narrative outlines. "I can bring you," writes Mr. Max Eastman, "examples of diction that is metrical but not metaphoric—a great part of the popular ballads, for example—and you can hardly deny that they too are poetic." But the best story poems may be analyzed, I believe, as metaphors without expressed tenors, as symbols which speak for themselves. "La Belle Dame Sans Merci," for example (if a literary ballad may be taken), is about a knight, by profession a man of action, but sensitive, like the lily and the rose, and about a faery lady with wild, wild eyes. At a more abstract level, it is about the loss of self in the mysterious lure of beauty—whether woman, poetry, or poppy. It sings the irretrievable departure from practical normality (the squirrel's granary is full), the wan isolation after ecstasy. Each reader will experience the poem at his own level of experience or at several. A good story poem is like a stone thrown into a pond, into our minds, where ever widening concentric circles of meaning go out—and this because of the structure of the story.

"A poem should not mean but be." It is an epigram worth quoting in every essay on poetry. And the poet "nothing affirmeth, and therefore never lieth." "Sit quidvis," said Horace, "simplex dumtaxat et unum." [13] It seems almost the reverse of the truth. "Complex dumtaxat et unum" [14] would be better. Every good poem is a complex poem and may be demonstrated so by rhetorical analysis. And further it is only in virtue of its complexity that it has artistic unity. Without complexity it could have the unity of a cobblestone but not that of a typewriter. A newspaper poem by Edgar Guest [15] does not have such heterogeneous unity, and hence does not have unity in the artistic sense. It is this truth which is expressed by Aristotle when he says that ontological beauty is based on unity in variety, and by Coleridge when he says that "The Beautiful, contemplated in its essentials, that is, in *kind* and not in *degree*, is that in which the *many*, still seen as many becomes one," and that a work of art is "rich in proportion to the variety of parts which it holds in unity."

The difference between art and other intuition, says Croce, is quantitative, in the degree of complexity of the intuition. To which one must answer that the difference is quantitative only if we think of art *qua* intuition. The degree of complexity does not make art more an intuition (if it is an intuition) than other intuitions, but it does make it art. Unified concrete complexity is precisely the structural specific difference between art and other forms of knowledge. The objection of the Crocean critic to the view that art involves concepts is that the artist

[13] ["Let each thing be only simple and a unit."]

[14] ["Only complex and a unit."]

[15] A reader whose judgment I esteem tells me that such a name appears in a serious discussion of poetics anomalously and in bad taste. I have allowed it to remain (in preference to some more dignified name of mediocrity) precisely because I wish to insist on the existence of badness in poetry and so to establish an antithetic point of reference for the discussion of goodness. Relativistic argument often creates an illusion in its own favor by moving steadily in a realm of great and nearly great art. See, for example, George Boas, *A Primer for Critics* (Baltimore, 1937), where a cartoon by Daumier appears toward the end as a startling approach to the vulgar. The purpose of my essay is not judicial but theoretical, that is, not to exhibit original discoveries in taste, but to show the relationship between examples acknowledged to lie in the realms of the good and the bad.

has nothing to do with the concept; it is invented and imposed by the critic. Thus Mrs. E. R. Dodds argues against Coleridge:

Where the poet is unconscious of the concept it is because he does not possess it as a concept. It is something built upon his work, formulated from it afterwards, by the philosopher. Wordsworth did not impersonate "anile dotage abandoned by judgment." He expressed an experience; and Coleridge defined the experience by a concept. . . . Shakespeare did not "study mankind in the Idea of a human race"; but the idea may be formed by a philosopher from Shakespeare's "studies," as also from his individuals the idea of certain types may be formed.

And A. C. Bradley writes about Shelley's theory.

The specific way of imagination is not to clothe in imagery consciously held ideas; it is to produce *half-consciously* a matter from which, when produced, the reader may, if he chooses, extract ideas. Poetry (I must exaggerate to be clear), psychologically considered, is not the *expression* of ideas or of a view of life; it is their discovery or creation, or rather both discovery and creation in one.

Half-consciously. These italics are mine. Both Mrs. Dodds and Professor Bradley are concerned to know whether the poet was conscious of his concept, a question no one will ever be able to answer except about one's own poems, and which, being a private question, one can scarcely offer as a norm for criticizing the poem. "If he chooses," then, says Professor Bradley, the reader may "extract ideas." But Professor Bradley does not make it clear whether the reader who understands the poem is free to choose or not to choose to extract an idea, or free to choose which idea he shall extract. Certainly he is not. If he chooses to extract an idea, the reason must be that there is something in the poem which warrants the idea. What that thing is, what idea or concept it warrants and how, is the objective matter of criticism. Whether we have ready (as we certainly shall not have) other words, one-word synonyms, for the concept, is a matter of the limitation of language. Whether the poet formulated concepts or wrote altogether unconscious of concepts or intuitions, whether he wrote in a trance at the dictation of spirits, is a matter of author psychology, of genetics and inspiration, not of the structure, value, and definition of poems.

6

The discussion so far has been a rhetorical one, that is, one about the relations of parts and whole, and most objective analysis of poetry is in fact rhetorical. It is easier to show how poetry works than to show why anyone should want it to work in a given way; it is easier to show its structure than its value. Rhetorical theory of poetry has always tended to separate from axiological, technique from worth. But the very structure of poems as concrete and universal, it seems to me, is the principle by which the two may be kept together. If it be granted that the "subject matter" of poetry is in a broad sense the moral realm, human actions as good or bad, with all their associated feelings, all the cognition and imagination that goes with happiness and suffering (if poetry submits "the shews of things to the desires of the Mind"), then the rhetorical structure of the concrete universal, the complexity and unity of the poem, is also its maturity or sophistication or richness or depth, and hence its value. Complexity of form is sophistication of content. The newspaper poetry of Edgar Guest lacks heterogeneous unity, or at least the high degree of heterogeneous unity which makes poetry. Almost any critic, I trust, will admit that it lacks maturity. One must further insist on the interdependence, in a sense the identity, of these two lacks. It is precisely in lacking maturity that such poetry lacks unity, in lacking unity that it lacks maturity. The unity and maturity of good poems are two sides of the same thing. The kind of unity which we look for and find in poetry (that of the typewriter rather than that of the cobblestone) is attained only through a degree of complexity in design which itself involves maturity and richness. For a visual diagram of the metaphysics of poetry one might write vertically the word complexity, a column, and give it a head with Janus faces, one looking in the rhetorical direction, unity, and the other in the axiological, maturity.

And this may show how poetry can be concerned with moral values, yet not be moral, how it can be flowers of evil. Mr. Eliot (in explaining his distaste for Shelley) has distinguished between beliefs which are "tenable" and those which are "acceptable." Mr. Norman Foerster has offered somewhat the same distinction in saying that "Tintern Abbey" may not be philosophically "sound" but that it is philosophically "vital." Schiller said that the crime of theft is offensive to both taste and morals, but that of murder, though worse morally, is not so bad aesthetically. The truth perhaps is that there are some sins which are sophisticated, some which are naive, some mature and some childishly simple. And so of virtues—some are complex enough to be interesting, some not so. And this distinction may be applied, I believe, whether one adopt a Christian ethic (of will) or a strictly Socratic ethic (of knowledge). When the young man in *Locksley Hall* muses:

As the husband is, the wife is: thou art mated with a clown,
And the grossness of his nature will have weight to drag thee down.
He will hold thee, when his passion shall have spent its novel force,
Something better than his dog, a little dearer than his horse,

he is not only a very bad young man but a very callow one. There is a shallow simplicity about this poem that is expressed even in its rhythm. No irony or other element of complexity or tension advises us that we are not to share the young man's experience to the full and approve it. This young man is quite a different sort of sinner from, let us say, the Antony of Shakespeare's play. By any ethical standard at all what Antony does to Fulvia, to Octavia especially, to his political allegiance, to himself, to Cleopatra even, must be bad. Yet the death of Antony and of Cleopatra is in the high Roman fashion, what's brave, what's noble. "For it is great To do that thing that ends all other deeds, Which shackles accidents, and bolts up change." We are called upon to admire Antony and Cleopatra. In short, the play is immoral.[16] The play, however, is great poetry because of the complexity of its immorality—if one may venture the phrase, its mature immorality. The death of Antony and Cleopatra is the climax of a subtle blend of human richness—of imperial extravagance and the opulence of burnished thrones, of drink and surfeits that rot themselves with motion, of the versatility, perverseness and charm of a woman, the infatuation, gallantry and bravery of a grizzled warrior.

[16] There is of course another view, that the play is moral sheerly through its tragic outcome. Thus Croce: "The tragedy of *Anthony and Cleopatra* is composed of the violent sense of pleasure, and its power to bind and to dominate, coupled with a shudder at its abject effects of dissolution and of death" (*Ariosto, Shakespeare and Corneille* [London, 1920], p. 242).

7

A criticism of structure and of value is an objective criticism. It rests on facts of human psychology (as that a man may love a woman so well as to give up empires), facts, which though psychological, yet are so well acknowledged as to lie in the realm of what may be called public psychology—a realm which one should distinguish from the private realm of the author's psychology and from the equally private realm of the individual reader's psychology (the vivid pictures which poetry or stories are supposed to create in the imagination, or the venerable action of catharsis—all that poetry is said to *do* rather than to *be*). Such a criticism, again, is objective and absolute, as distinguished from the relative criticism of idiom and period. I mean that this criticism will notice that Pope is different from Shakespeare, but will notice even more attentively that Shakespeare is different from Taylor the Water Poet and Pope different from Sir Richard Blackmore. Such a criticism will be interested to analyze the latter two differences and see what these differences have in common and what Shakespeare and Pope have in common, and it will not despair of describing that similarity (that formula or character of great poetry) even though the terms be abstract and difficult—for the proof will always be found in specific analysis of a good poem. Or, if we are told that there is no universal agreement about what is good—that Pope has not been steadily held in esteem, that Shakespeare has been considered a barbarian, the objective analyst of structures can at least say (and it seems much to say) that he is describing a class of poems, those which through a peculiar complexity possess unity and maturity and in a special way can be called both individual and universal. Among all recorded "poems," this class is of a relative rarity, and further the members of this class will be found in an impressive way to coincide with the members of the class "poems which have by some body of critics, some age of educated readers, been called great." It is not possible to analyze the poems of Sir Richard Blackmore and of Edgar Guest so as to show that they belong to the class of the individual and universal.

The function of the objective critic is by approximate descriptions of poems, or multiple restatements of their meaning, to aid other readers to come to an intuitive and full realization of poems themselves and hence to know good poems and distinguish them from bad ones. It is of course impossible to tell all about a poem in other words. Croce tells us, as we should expect him to, of the "impossibility of ever rendering in logical terms the full effect of any poetry or of other artistic work." "Criticism, nevertheless," he tells us, ". . . performs its own office, which is to discern and to point out exactly where lies the poetical motive and to formulate the divisions which aid in distinguishing what is proper to every work." The situation is something like this: In each poem there is something (an individual intuition—or a concept) which can never be expressed in other terms. It is like the square root of two or like π, which cannot be expressed by rational numbers, but only as their *limit.* Criticism of poetry is like 1.414 . . . or 3.1416 . . . , not all it would be, yet all that can be had and very useful.

3. END

SIR PHILIP SIDNEY: An Apologie for Poetrie*

When the right vertuous Edward Wotton, and I, were at the Emperors Court together, wee gave our selves to learne horsemanship of John Pietro Pugliano: one that with great commendation had the place of an Esquire in his stable. And hee, according to the fertilnes of the Italian wit, did not onely afoord us the demonstration of his practise, but sought to enrich our mindes with the contemplations therein, which hee thought most precious. But with none I remember mine eares were at any time more loden, then when (either angred with slowe paiment, or mooved with our learner-like admiration,) he exercised his speech in the prayse of his facultie. Hee sayd, Souldiours were the noblest estate of mankinde, and horsemen, the noblest of Souldiours. Hee sayde, they were the Maisters of warre, and ornaments of peace: speedy goers, and strong abiders, triumphers both in Camps and Courts. Nay, to so unbeleeved a poynt hee proceeded, as that no earthly thing bred such wonder to a Prince, as to be a good horseman. Skill of government, was but a Pedanteria in comparison: then would hee adde certaine prayses, by telling what a peerlesse beast a horse was. The onely serviceable Courtier without flattery, the beast of most beutie, faithfulnes, courage, and such more, that if I had not beene a peece of a Logician before I came to him, I think he would have perswaded mee to have wished my selfe a horse. But thus much at least with his no fewe words hee drave into me, that selfe-love is better than any building to make that seeme gorgious, wherein our selves are parties. Wherein, if Pugliano his strong affection and weake arguments will not satisfie you, I wil give you a neerer example of my selfe, who (I knowe not by what mischance) in these my not old yeres and idelest times, having slipt into the title of a Poet, am provoked to say somthing unto you in the defence of that my unelected vocation, which if I handle with more good will then good reasons, beare with me, sith the scholler is to be pardoned that foloweth the steppes of his Maister. And yet I must say, that as I have just cause to make a pittiful defence of poore Poetry, which from almost the highest estimation of learning, is fallen to be the laughingstocke of children. So have I need to bring some more availeable proofes: sith the former is by no man barred of his deserved credite, the silly latter hath had even the names of Philosophers used to the defacing of it, with great danger of civill war among the Muses. And first, truly to al them that professing learning inveigh against Poetry, may justly be objected, that they goe very neer to ungratfulnes, to seek to deface that, which in the noblest nations and languages that are knowne, hath been the first light-giver to ignorance, and first Nurse, whose milk by little and little enabled them to feed afterwards of tougher knowledges: and will they now play the Hedghog, that being received into the den, drave out his host? or rather the Vipers, that with theyr birth kill their Parents? Let learned Greece in any of her manifold Sciences, be able to shew me one booke, before Musæus, Homer, and Hesiodus, all three nothing els but Poets. Nay, let any historie be brought, that can say any Writers were there before them, if they were not men of the same skil, as Orpheus, Linus, and some other are named: who having beene the first of that Country, that made pens deliverers of their knowledge to their posterity, may justly challenge to bee called their Fathers in learning: for not only in time they had this priority (although in it self antiquity be vener-

* Written in the early 1580's, Sidney's essay was not published until 1595, when different publishers, Ponsonby and Olney, issued different versions, with different titles—*The Defence of Poesie* and *An Apologie for Poetrie.* Ours is the Olney text.

able) but went before them, as causes to drawe with their charming sweetnes, the wild untamed wits to an admiration of knowledge. So as Amphion was sayde to move stones with his Poetrie, to build Thebes. And Orpheus to be listened to by beastes, indeed, stony and beastly people. So among the Romans were Livius, Andronicus, and Ennius. So in the Italian language, the first that made it aspire to be a Treasure-house of Science, where the Poets Dante, Boccace, and Petrarch. So in our English were Gower and Chawcer.

After whom, encouraged and delighted with theyr excellent foregoing, others have followed, to beautifie our mother tongue, as wel in the same kinde as in other Arts. This did so notably shewe it selfe, that the Phylosophers of Greece, durst not a long time appeare to the worlde but under the masks of Poets. So Thales, Empedocles, and Parmenides, sange their naturall Phylosophie in verses: so did Pythagoras and Phocilides their morral counsells: so did Tirteus in war matters, and Solon in matters of policie: or rather, they beeing Poets, dyd exercise their delightful vaine in those points of highest knowledge, which before them lay hid to the world. For that wise Solon was directly a Poet, it is manifest, having written in verse, the notable fable of the Atlantick Iland, which was continued by Plato.

And truely, even Plato, whosoever well considereth, shall find, that in the body of his work, though the inside and strength were Philosophy, the skinne as it were and beautie, depended most of Poetrie: for all standeth upon Dialogues, wherein he faineth many honest Burgesses of Athens to speake of such matters, that if they had been sette on the racke, they would never have confessed them. Besides, his poetical describing the circumstances of their meetings, as the well ordering of a banquet, the delicacie of a walke, with enterlacing meere tales, as Giges Ring, and others, which who knoweth not to be flowers of Poetrie, did never walke into Appolos Garden.

And even Historiographers (although theyr lippes sounde of things doone, and veritie be written in theyr fore-heads,) have been glad to borrow both fashion, and perchance weight of Poets. So Herodotus entituled his Historie, by the name of the nine Muses: and both he and all the rest that followed him, either stole or usurped of Poetrie, their passionate describing of passions, the many particularities of battailes, which no man could affirme: or if that be denied me, long Orations put in the mouthes of great Kings and Captaines, which it is certaine they never pronounced. So that truely, neyther Phylosopher nor Historiographer, coulde at the first have entred into the gates of populer judgements, if they had not taken a great pasport of Poetry, which in all Nations at this day wher learning florisheth not, is plaine to be seene: in all which they have some feeling of Poetry. In Turky, besides their lawe-giving Divines, they have no other Writers but Poets. In our neighbour Countrey Ireland, where truelie learning goeth very bare, yet are theyr Poets held in a devoute reverence. Even among the most barbarous and simple Indians where no writing is, yet have they their Poets, who make and sing songs which they call Areytos, both of theyr Auncestors deedes, and praises of theyr Gods. A sufficient probabilitie, that if ever learning come among them, it must be by having theyr hard dull wits softened and sharpened with the sweete delights of Poetrie. For untill they find a pleasure in the exercises of the minde, great promises of much knowledge, will little perswade them, that knowe not the fruites of knowledge. In Wales, the true remnant of the auncient Brittons, as there are good authorities to shewe the long time they had Poets, which they called Bardes: so thorough all the conquests of Romaines, Saxons, Danes, and Normans, some of whom did seeke to ruine all memory of learning from among them, yet doo their Poets even to this day, last; so as it is not more notable in soone beginning then in long continuing. But since the Authors of most of our Sciences were the Romans, and before them the Greekes, let us a little stand uppon their authorities, but even so farre as to see, what names they have given unto this now scorned skill.

Among the Romans a Poet was called Vates, which is as much as a Diviner, Fore-seer, or Prophet, as by his conjoyned wordes Vaticinium and Vaticinari, is manifest: so heavenly a title did that excellent people bestow upon his hartravishing knowledge. And so farre were they carried into the admiration thereof, that they thought in the chaunceable hitting uppon any such verses great fore-tokens of their following fortunes were placed. Whereupon grew the worde of Sortes Virgilianæ, when by suddaine opening Virgils booke, they lighted upon any verse of hys making, whereof the histories of the Emperors lives are full, as of Albinus the Governour of our Iland, who in his childehoode mette with this verse

Arma amens capio nec sat rationis in armis.[1]

And in his age performed it, which although it were a very vaine, and godles superstition, as also it was to think that spirits were commaunded by such verses, whereupon this word charmes, derived of Carmina commeth, so yet serveth it to shew the great reverence those wits were helde in. And altogether not without ground, since both the Oracles of *Delphos* and Sibillas prophecies, were wholy delivered in verses. For that same exquisite observing of number and measure in words, and that high flying liberty of conceit proper to the Poet, did seeme to have some dyvine force in it.

And may not I presume a little further, to shew the reasonablenes of this worde Vates? And say that the holy Davids Psalmes are a divine Poem? If I doo, I shall not do it without the testimonie of great learned men, both auncient and moderne: but even the name Psalmes will speake for mee, which being interpreted, is nothing but songes; then that it is fully written in meeter, as all learned Hebricians agree, although the rules be not yet fully found. Lastly and principally, his handeling his prophecy, which is meerely poetical. For what els is the awaking his musicall instruments? The often and free changing of persons? His notable Prosopopeias, when he maketh you as it were, see God comming in his Majestie. His telling of the Beastes joyfulnes and hills leaping, but a heavenlie poesie: wherein almost hee sheweth himself a passionate lover, of that unspeakable and everlasting beautie to be seen by the eyes of the minde, onely cleered by fayth. But truely nowe having named him, I feare mee I seeme to prophane that holy name, applying it to Poetrie, which is among us throwne downe to so ridiculous an estimation: but they that with quiet judgements will looke a little deeper into it, shall finde the end and working of it such, as beeing rightly applyed, deserveth not to bee scourged out of the Church of God.

But now, let us see how the Greekes named it, and howe they deemed of it. The Greekes called him a Poet, which name, hath as the most excellent, gone thorough other Languages. It commeth of this word *Poiein,* which is, to make: wherein I know not whether by lucke or wisedome, wee Englishmen have mette with the Greekes, in calling him a maker: which name, how high and incomparable a title it is, I had rather were knowne by marking the scope of other Sciences, then by my partiall allegation.

There is no Arte delivered to mankinde, that hath not the wordes of Nature for his principall object, without which they could not consist, and on which they so depend, as they become Actors and Players as it were, of what Nature will have set foorth. So doth the Astronomer looke upon the starres, and by that he seeth, setteth downe what order Nature hath taken therein. So doe the Geometrician, and Arithmetician, in their diverse sorts of quantities. So doth the Musitian in times, tel you which by nature agree, which not. The naturall Philosopher thereon hath his name, and the Morrall Philosopher standeth upon the naturall vertues, vices, and passions of man; and followe Nature (saith hee) therein, and thou shalt not erre. The Lawyer sayth what men have determined. The Historian what men have done. The Grammarian speaketh onely of the rules of speech, and the Rethorician, and Logitian, considering what in Nature will soonest prove and perswade, thereon give artificial rules, which still are compassed within the circle of a question, according to the proposed matter. The Phisition waigheth the nature of a mans bodie, and the nature of things helpeful, or hurtefull into it. And the Metaphisick, though it be in the seconde and abstract notions, and therefore be counted supernaturall: yet doth hee indeede builde upon the depth of Nature: onely the Poet, disdayning to be tied to any such subjection, lifted up with the vigor of his owne invention, dooth growe in effect, another nature, in making things either better than Nature bringeth forth, or quite a newe formes such as never were in Nature, as the Heroes, Demigods, Cyclops, Chimeras, Furies, and such like: so as hee goeth hand in hand with Nature, not in-

[1] ["In my frenzy I take up arms, but I am not in control of my senses."]

closed within the narrow warrant of her guifts, but freely ranging onely within the Zodiack of his owne wit.

Nature never set forth the earth in so rich tapistry, as divers Poets have done, neither with plesant rivers, fruitful trees, sweet smelling flowers: nor whatsoever els may make the too much loved earth more lovely. Her world is brasen, the Poets only deliver a golden: but let those things alone and goe to man, for whom as the other things are, so it seemeth in him her uttermost cunning is imployed, and knowe whether shee have brought foorth so true a lover as Theagines, so constant a friende as Pilades, so valiant a man as Orlando, so right a Prince as Xenophons Cyrus: so excellent a man every way, as Virgils Aeneas: neither let this be jestingly conceived, because the works of the one be essentiall: the other, in imitation or fiction, for any understanding knoweth the skil of the Artificer: standeth in that Idea or fore-conceite of the work, and not in the work it selfe. And that the Poet hath that Idea, is manifest, by delivering them forth in such excellencie as hee hath imagined them. Which delivering forth also, is not wholie imaginative, as we are wont to say by them that build Castles in the ayre: but so farre substantially it worketh, not onely to make a Cyrus, which had been but a particuler excellencie, as Nature might have done, but to bestow a Cyrus upon the worlde, to make many Cyrus's, if they wil learne aright, why, and how that Maker made him.

Neyther let it be deemed too sawcie a comparison to ballance the highest poynt of mans wit with the efficacie of Nature: but rather give right honor to the heavenly Maker of that maker: who having made man to his owne likenes, set him beyond and over all the workes of that second nature, which in nothing hee sheweth so much as in Poetrie: when with the force of a divine breath, he bringeth things forth far surpassing her dooings, with no small argument to the incredulous of that first accursed fall of Adam: sith our erected wit, maketh us know what perfection is, and yet our infected will, keepeth us from reaching unto it. But these arguments wil by fewe be understood, and by fewer granted. Thus much (I hope) will be given me, that the Greekes with some probabilitie of reason, gave him the name above all names of learning. Now let us goe to a more ordinary opening of him, that the trueth may be more palpable: and so I hope, though we get not so unmatched a praise as the Etimologie of his names wil grant, yet his very description, which no man will denie, shall not justly be barred from a principall commendation.

Poesie therefore is an arte of imitation, for so Aristotle termeth it in his word *Mimesis* that is to say, a representing, counterfetting, or figuring foorth: to speake metaphorically, a speaking picture: with this end, to teach and delight; of this have beene three severall kindes. The chiefe both in antiquitie and excellencie, were they that did imitate the inconceivable excellencies of GOD. Such were, David in his Psalmes, Salomon in his song of Songs, in his Ecclesiastes, and Proverbs: Moses and Bebora in theyr Hymnes, and the writer of Job; which beside other, the learned Emanuell Tremilius and Franciscus Junius, doe entitle the poeticall part of the Scripture. Against these none will speake that hath the holie Ghost in due holy reverence.

In this kinde, though in a full wrong divinitie, were Orpheus, Amphion, Homer in his hymes, and many other, both Greekes and Romaines: and this Poesie must be used, by whosoever will follow S. James his counsell, in singing Psalmes when they are merry: and I knowe is used with the fruite of comfort by some, when in sorrowfull pangs of their death-bringing sinnes, they find the consolation of the never-leaving goodnesse.

The second kinde, is of them that deale with matters Philosophicall; eyther morrall, as Tirteus, Phocilides and Cato, or naturall, as Lucretius and Virgils Georgicks: or Astronomicall, as Manilius, and Pontanus: or historical, as Lucan: which who mislike, the faulte is in their judgements quite out of taste, and not in the sweet foode of sweetly uttered knowledge. But because thys second sorte is wrapped within the folde of the proposed subject, and takes not the course of his owne invention, whether they properly be Poets or no, let Gramarians dispute: and goe to the thyrd, indeed right Poets, of whom chiefly this question ariseth; betwixt whom, and these second is such a kinde of difference, as betwixt the meaner sort of Painters, (who counterfet onely such faces as are sette before them) and the more excellent: who having no law but wit, bestow that in cullours upon you which is fittest for the eye to see: as the constant, though lamenting looke of Lucrecia, when she punished in her selfe an others fault.

Wherein he painteth not Lucrecia whom he never sawe, but painteth the outwarde beauty of such a vertue: for these third be they which most properly do imitate to teach and delight, and to imitate, borrow nothing of what is, hath been, or shall be: but range onely rayned with learned discretion, into the divine consideration of what may be, and should be. These bee they, that as the first and most noble sorte, may justly bee termed *Vates,* so these are waited on in the excellen[te]st languages and best understandings, with the fore described name of Poets: for these indeede doo meerely make to imitate: and imitate both to delight and teach: and delight to move men to take that goodnes in hande, which without delight they would flye as from a stranger. And teach, to make them know that goodnes whereunto they are mooved, which being the noblest scope to which ever any learning was directed, yet want there not idle tongues to barke at them. These be subdivided into sundry more speciall denominations. The most notable bee the Heroick, Lirick, Tragick, Comick, Satirick, Iambick, Elegiack, Pastorall, and certaine others. Some of these being termed according to the matter they deale with, some by the sorts of verses they liked best to write in, for indeede the greatest part of Poets have apparelled their poeticall inventions in that numbrous kinde of writing which is called verse: indeed but apparelled, verse being but an ornament and no cause to Poetry: sith there have beene many most excellent Poets, that never versified, and now swarme many versifiers that neede never aunswere to the name of Poets. For Xenophon, who did imitate so excellently, as to give us *effigiem justi imperij,* the portraiture of a just Empire under the name of Cyrus, (as Cicero sayth of him) made therein an absolute heroicall Poem.

So did Heliodorus in his sugred invention of that picture of love in Theagines and Cariclea, and yet both these writ in Prose: which I speak to shew, that it is not riming and versing that maketh a Poet, no more then a long gowne maketh an Advocate: who though he pleaded in armor should be an Advocate and no Souldier. But it is that fayning notable images of vertues, vices, or what els, with that delightfull teaching which must be the right describing note to know a Poet by: although indeed the Senate of Poets hath chosen verse as their fittest rayment, meaning, as in matter they passed all in all, so in maner to goe beyond them: not speaking (table talke fashion or like men in a dreame,) words as they chanceably fall from the mouth, but peyzing each sillable of each worde by just proportion according to the dignitie of the subject.

Nowe therefore it shall not bee amisse first to waigh this latter sort of Poetrie by his works, and then by his partes; and if in neyther of these Anatomies hee be condemnable, I hope wee shall obtaine a more favourable sentence. This purifing of wit, this enritching of memory, enabling of judgment, and enlarging of conceyt, which commonly we call learning, under what name soever it com forth, or to what immediat end soever it be directed, the final end is, to lead and draw us to as high a perfection, as our degenerate soules made worse by theyr clayey lodgings, can be capable of. This according to the inclination of the man, bred many formed impressions, for some that thought this felicity principally to be gotten by knowledge, and no knowledge to be so high and heavenly, as acquaintance with the starres, gave themselves to Astronomie; others, perswading themselves to be Demigods if they knewe the causes of things, became naturall and supernaturall Philosophers, some an admirable delight drew to Musicke: and some, the certainty of demonstration, to the Mathematickes. But all, one, and other, having this scope to knowe, and by knowledge to lift up the mind from the dungeon of the body, to the enjoying his owne divine essence. But when by the ballance of experience it was found, that the Astronomer looking to the starres might fall into a ditch, that the enquiring Philosopher might be blinde in himselfe, and the Mathematician might draw foorth a straight line with a crooked hart: then loe, did proofe the over ruler of opinions, make manifest, that all these are but serving Sciences, which as they have each a private end in themselves, so yet are they all directed to the highest end of the mistres Knowledge, by the Greekes called *Arkitecktonike*, which stands, (as I thinke) in the knowledge of a mans selfe, in the Ethicke and politick consideration, with the end of well dooing and not of well knowing onely; even as the Sadlers next end is to make a good saddle: but his farther end, to serve a nobler facultie, which is horsemanship, so the horsemans to souldiery, and the Souldier not onely to have the skill, but to performe the practise of a Souldier: so that the ending end of all earthly learning, being vertuous action, those skilles that most serve to bring forth that, have a most just title to bee Princes over all the rest: wherein if wee can shewe the Poets noblenes, by setting him before his other Competitors, among whom as principall challengers step forth the morrall Philosophers, whom me thinketh, I see comming towards me with a sullen gravity, as though they could not abide vice by day light, rudely clothed for to witnes outwardly their contempt of outward things, with bookes in their hands agaynst glory, whereto they sette theyr names, sophistically speaking against subtility, and angry with any man in whom they see the foule fault of anger: these men casting larges as they goe, of Definitions, Divisions, and Distinctions, with a scornefull interogative, doe soberly aske, whether it bee possible to finde any path, so ready to leade a man to vertue, as that which teacheth what vertue is? and teacheth it not onely by delivering forth his very being, his causes, and effects: but also, by making known his enemie vice, which must be destroyed, and his combersome servant Passion, which must be maistered, by shewing the generalities that contayneth it, and the specialities that are derived from it. Lastly, by playne setting downe, how it extendeth it selfe out of the limits of a mans own little world, to the government of families, and maintayning of publique societies.

The Historian, scarcely giveth leysure to the Moralist, to say so much, but that he loden with old Mouse-eaten records, authorising himselfe (for the most part) upon other histories, whose greatest authorities, are built upon the notable foundation of Heare-say, having much a-doe to accord differing Writers, and to pick trueth out of partiality, better acquainted with a thousande yeeres a goe, then with the present age: and yet better knowing how this world goeth, then how his owne wit runneth: curious for antiquities, and inquisitive of novelties, a wonder to young folkes, and a tyrant in table talke, denieth in a great chafe, that any man for teaching of vertue, and vertuous actions, is comparable to him. I am *Lux vitæ, Temporum Magistra, Vita memoriæ, Nuncia vetustatis, &c.*[2]

The Phylosopher (sayth hee) teacheth a disputative vertue, but I doe an active: his vertue is excellent in the dangerlesse Academie of Plato, but mine sheweth foorth her honorable face, in the battailes of Marathon, Pharsalia, Poitiers, and Agincourt. Hee teacheth vertue by certaine abstract considerations, but I onely bid you follow the footing of them that have gone before you. Olde-aged experience, goeth beyond the fine-witted Phylosopher, but I give the experience of many ages. Lastly, if he make the Song-booke, I put the learners hande to the Lute: and if hee be the guide, I am the light.

Then woulde hee alledge you innumerable examples, conferring storie by storie, how much the wisest Senatours and Princes, have beene directed by the credite of history, as Brutus, Alphonsus of Aragon, and who not, if need bee? At length, the long lyne of theyr disputation maketh a poynt in thys, that the one giveth the precept, and the other the example.

Nowe, whom shall wee finde (sith the question standeth for the highest forme in the Schoole of learning) to bee Moderator? Trulie, as me seemeth, the Poet; and if not a Moderator, even the man that ought to carrie the title from them both, and much more from all other serving Sciences. Therefore compare we the Poet with the Historian, and with the Morrall Phylosopher, and, if hee goe beyond them both, no other humaine skill can match him. For as for the Divine, with all reverence it is ever to be excepted, not only for having his scope as far beyonde any of these, as eternitie exceedeth a moment, but even for passing each of these in themselves.

And for the Lawyer, though Jus bee the Daughter of Justice, and Justice the chiefe of Vertues, yet because hee seeketh to make men good, rather *Formidine pœnæ*, then *Virtutis amore*,[3] or to say righter, dooth not indevour to make men good, but that their evill hurt not

[2] ["The light of life, the instructress of the ages, the life of memory, the messenger of antiquity."]

[3] ["Through fear of punishment" (rather than) "through love of virtue."]

others: having no care so hee be a good Cittizen; how bad a man he be. Therefore, as our wickedness maketh him necessarie, and necessitie maketh him honorable, so is hee not in the deepest trueth to stande in rancke with these; who all indevour to take naughtines away, and plant goodnesse even in the secretest cabinet of our soules. And these foure are all, that any way deale in that consideration of mens manners, which being the supreme knowledge, they that best breed it, deserve the best commendation.

The Philosopher therfore and the Historian, are they which would win the gole: the one by precept, the other by example. But both not having both, doe both halte. For the Philosopher, setting downe with thorny argument the bare rule, is so hard of utterance, and so mistie to bee conceived, that one that hath no other guide but him, shall wade in him till hee be olde, before he shall finde sufficient cause to bee honest: for his knowledge standeth so upon the abstract and generall, that happie is that man who may understande him, and more happie, that can applye what hee dooth understand.

On the other side, the Historian wanting the precept, is so tyed, not to what shoulde bee, but to what is, to the particular truth of things, and not to the general reason of things, that hys example draweth no necessary consequence and therefore a lesse fruitfull doctrine.

Nowe dooth the peerelesse Poet performe both: for whatsoever the Philosopher sayth should be doone, hee giveth a perfect picture of it in some one, by whom hee presupposeth it was done. So as hee coupleth the generall notion with the particuler example. A perfect picture I say, for hee yeeldeth to the powers of the minde, an image of that whereof the Philosopher bestoweth but a woordish description: which dooth neyther strike, pierce, nor possesse the sight of the soule, so much as that other dooth.

For as in outward things, to a man that had never seene an Elephant or a Rinoceros, who should tell him most exquisitely all theyr shapes, cullour, bignesse, and perticular markes: or of a gorgeous Pallace, the Architecture, with declaring the full beauties, might well make the hearer able to repeate as it were by rote, all hee had heard, yet should never satisfie his inward conceits, with being witnes to it self of a true lively knowledge: but the same man, as soone as hee might see those beasts well painted, or the house wel in moddel, should straightwaies grow without need of any description, to a judicial comprehending of them, so no doubt the Philosopher with his learned definition, bee it of vertue, vices, matters of publick policie, or privat government, replenisheth the memory with many infallible grounds of wisdom: which notwithstanding, lye darke before the imaginative and judging powre, if they bee not illuminated or figured foorth by the speaking picture of Poesie.

Tullie taketh much paynes and many times not without poeticall helpes, to make us knowe the force love of our Countrey hath in us. Let us but heare old Anchises speaking in the middest of Troyes flames, or see Ulisses in the fulnes of all Calipso's delights, bewayle his absence from barraine and beggerly Ithaca. Anger the Stoicks say, was a short maddnes, let but Sophocles bring you Ajax on a stage, killing and whipping Sheepe and Oxen, thinking them the Army of Greeks, with theyr Chiefetaines Agamemnon and Menelaus, and tell mee if you have not a more familiar insight into anger, then finding in the Schoolemen his Genus and difference. See whether wisdome and temperance in Ulisses and Diomedes, valure in Achilles, friendship in Nisus and Eurialus, even to an ignoraunt man, carry not an apparent shyning: and contrarily, the remorse of conscience in Oedipus, the soone repenting pride of Agamemnon, the selfe-devouring crueltie in his Father Atreus, the violence of ambition in the two Theban brothers, the sowre-sweetnes of revenge in Medæa, and to fall lower, the Terentian Gnato, and our Chaucers Pandar, so exprest, that we nowe use their names to signifie their trades. And finally, all vertues, vices, and passions, so in their own naturall seates layd to the viewe, that wee seeme not to heare of them, but cleerely to see through them. But even in the most excellent determination of goodnes, what Philosophers counsell can so redily direct a Prince, as the fayned Cyrus in Xenophon? or a vertuous man in all fortunes, as Aeneas in Virgill? or a whole Common-wealth, as the way of Sir Thomas Moores *Eutopia?* I say the way, because where Sir Thomas Moore erred, it was the fault of the man and not of the Poet, for that way of patterning a Common-wealth was most absolute, though hee perchaunce hath not so absolutely perfourmed it: for the question is, whether the fayned image of Poesie, or the regular instruction of Philosophy, hath the more force in teaching: wherein if the Philosophers have more rightly shewed themselves Philosophers, then the Poets have obtained to the high top of their profession as in truth,

> ——*Mediocribus esse poetis,*
> *Non Diji, non homines, non concessere Columnæ:* [4]

It is I say againe, not the fault of the Art, but that by fewe men that Arte can bee accomplished.

Certainly, even our Saviour Christ could as well have given, the morrall common places of uncharitablenes and humblenes, as the divine narration of Dives and Lazarus: or of disobedience and mercy, as that heavenly discourse of the lost Child and the gratious Father; but that hys through-searching wisdom, knewe the estate of Dives burning in hell, and of Lazarus being in Abrahams bosome, would more constantly (as it were) inhabit both the memory and judgment. Truly, for my selfe, mee seemes I see before my eyes the lost Childes disdainefull prodigality, turned to envie a Swines dinner: which by the learned Divines, are thought not historicall acts, but instructing Parables. For conclusion, I say the Philosopher teacheth, but he teacheth obscurely, so as the learned onely can understande him: that is to say, he teacheth them that are already taught, but the Poet is the foode for the tenderest stomacks, the Poet is indeed the right Popular Philosopher, whereof Esops tales give good proofe: whose pretty Allegories, stealing under the formall tales of Beastes, make many, more beastly then Beasts, begin to heare the sound of vertue from these dumbe speakers.

But now may it be alledged, that if this imagining of matters be so fitte for the imagination, then must the Historian needs surpasse, who bringeth you images of true matters, such as indeede were doone, and not such as fantastically or falsely may be suggested to have been doone. Truely Aristotle himselfe in his discourse of Poesie, plainely determineth this question, saying, that Poetry is *Philosophoteron* and *Spoudaioteron,* that is to say, it is more Philosophicall, and more studiously serious, then history. His reason is, because Poesie dealeth with *Katholon,* that is to say, with the universall consideration; and the history with *Kathekaston,* the perticuler; nowe sayth he, the universall wayes what is fit to bee sayd or done, eyther in likelihood or necessity, (which the Poesie considereth in his imposed names), and the perticuler, onely mark's whether Alcibiades did, or suffered, this or that. Thus farre Aristotle: which reason of his, (as all his) is most full of reason. For indeed, if the question were whether it were better to have a perticuler acte truly or falsly set down: there is no doubt which is to be chosen, no more then whether you had rather have Vespasians picture right as hee was, or at the Painters pleasure nothing resembling. But if the question be for your owne use and learning, whether it be better to have it set downe as it should be, or as it was: then certainely is more doctrinable the fained Cirus of Xenophon then the true Cyrus in Justine: and the fayned Aeneas in Virgil, then the right Aeneas in Dares Phrigius.

As to a Lady that desired to fashion her countenance to the best grace, a Painter should more benefite her to portrait a most sweet face, wryting Canidia upon it, then to paynt Canidia as she was, who Horace sweareth, was foule and ill favoured.

If the Poet doe his part a-right, he will shew you in Tantalus, Atreus, and such like, nothing that is not to be shunned. In Cyrus, Aeneas, Ulisses, each thing to be followed; where the Historian, bound to tell things as things were, cannot be liberall (without hee will be poeticall) of a perfect patterne; but as in Alexander or Scipio himselfe, shew dooings, some to be liked, some to be misliked. And then how will you discerne, what to followe but by your owne discretion, which you had without reading Quintus Curtius? And whereas a man may say, though in universall consideration of doctrine the Poet prevaileth; yet that the historie, in his saying such a thing was doone, doth warrant a man more in that hee shall follow.

The aunswere is manifest, that if hee stande upon that was; as if hee should argue, because

[4] ["Neither gods, nor men, nor booksellers have granted poets the right to be mediocre."]

it rayned yesterday, therefore it shoulde rayne to-day, then indeede it hath some advantage to a grose conceite: but if he know an example onlie, informes a conjectured likelihood, and so goe by reason, the Poet dooth so farre exceede him, as hee is to frame his example to that which is most reasonable: be it in warlike, politick, or private matters; where the Historian in his bare *Was,* hath many times that which wee call fortune, to over-rule the best wisdome. Manie times, he must tell events, whereof he can yeelde no cause: or if hee doe, it must be poeticall; for that a fayned example, hath as much force to teach, as a true example: (for as for to moove, it is cleere, sith the fayned may bee tuned to the highest key of passion) let us take one example, wherein a Poet and a Historian doe concur.

Herodotus and Justine do both testifie, that Zopirus, King Darius faithful servaunt, seeing his Maister long resisted by the rebellious Babilonians, fayned himselfe in extreame disgrace of his King: for verifying of which, he caused his owne nose and eares to be cut off: and so flying to the Babylonians, was received: and for his knowne valour, so far credited, that hee did finde meanes to deliver them over to Darius. Much like matter doth Livie record of Tarquinius and his sonne. Xenophon excellently faineth such another stratageme, performed by Abradates in Cyrus behalfe. Now would I fayne know, if occasion bee presented unto you, to serve your Prince by such an honest dissimulation, why you doe not as well learne it of Xenophons fiction, as of the others verity: and truely so much the better, as you shall save your nose by the bargaine: for Abradates did not counterfet so far. So then the best of the Historian, is subject to the Poet; for whatsoever action, or faction, whatsoever counsell, pollicy, or warre stratagem, the Historian is bound to recite, that may the Poet (if he list) with his imitation make his own; beautifying it both for further teaching, and more delighting, as it pleaseth him: having all, from Dante his heaven, to hys hell, under the authoritie of his penne. Which if I be asked what Poets have done so, as I might well name some, yet say I, and say againe, I speak of the Arte, and not of the Artificer.

Nowe, to that which commonly is attributed to the prayse of histories, in respect of the notable learning is gotten by marking the successe, as though therein a man should see vertue exalted, and vice punished. Truely that commendation is peculiar to Poetrie, and farre off from History. For indeede Poetrie ever setteth vertue so out in her best cullours, making Fortune her wel-wayting hand-mayd, that one must needs be enamored of her. Well may you see Ulisses in a storme, and in other hard plights; but they are but exercises of patience and magnanimitie, to make them shine the more in the neere-following prosperitie. And of the contrarie part, if evill men come to the stage, they ever goe out (as the Tragedie Writer answered, to one that misliked the shew of such persons) so manacled, as they little animate folkes to followe them. But the Historian, beeing captived to the trueth of a foolish world, is many times a terror from well dooing, and an incouragement to unbrideled wickedness.

For, see wee not valiant Milciades rot in his fetters? The just Phocion, and the accomplished Socrates, put to death like Traytors? The cruell Severus live prosperously? The excellent Severus miserably murthered? Sylla and Marius dying in theyr beddes? Pompey and Cicero slaine then, when they would have thought exile a happinesse?

See wee not vertuous Cato driven to kyll himselfe? and rebell Cæsar so advaunced, that his name yet after 1600 years, lasteth in the highest honor? And marke but even Cæsars own words of the fore-named Sylla, (who in that onely did honestly, to put downe his dishonest tyrannie,) *Literas nescivit,*[5] as if want of learning caused him to doe well. Hee meant it not by Poetrie, which not content with earthly plagues, deviseth new punishments in hel for Tyrants; nor yet by Philosophie, which teacheth *Occidendos esse,*[6] but no doubt by skill in Historie: for that indeede can affoord your Cipselus, Periander, Phalaris, Dionisius, and I know not how many more of the same kennell, that speede well enough in theyr abhominable unjustice or usurpation. I conclude therefore, that hee excelleth Historie, not onely in furnishing the minde with knowledge, but in setting it forward, to that which deserveth to be called and accounted good: which setting forward, and mooving to

[5] ["He was ignorant of letters."]

[6] ["(that) they are to be killed."]

well dooing, indeed setteth the Lawrell crowne upon the Poet as victorious, not onely of the Historian, but over the Phylosopher: howsoever in teaching it may bee questionable.

For suppose it be granted, (that which I suppose with great reason may be denied,) that the Philosopher in respect of his methodical proceeding, doth teach more perfectly then the Poet: yet do I thinke, that no man is so much *Philophilosophos,* as to compare the Philosopher in mooving, with the Poet.

And that mooving is of a higher degree then teaching, it may by this appeare: that is wel nigh the cause and the effect of teaching. For who will be taught, if hee bee not mooved with desire to be taught? and what so much good doth that teaching bring forth, (I speak still of morall doctrine) as that it mooveth one to doe that which it dooth teach? for as Aristotle sayth, it is not *Gnosis,* but *Praxis* must be the fruit. And howe *Praxis* cannot be, without being mooved to practise, it is no hard matter to consider.

The Philosopher sheweth you the way, hee informeth you of the particularities, as well of the tediousnes of the way, as of the pleasant lodging you shall have when your journey is ended, as of the many byturnings that may divert you from your way. But this is to no man but to him that will read him, and read him with attentive studious painfulnes. Which constant desire, whosoever hath in him, hath already past halfe the hardnes of the way, and therefore is beholding to the Philosopher but for the other halfe. Nay truely, learned men have learnedly thought, that where once reason hath so much overmastred passion, as that the minde hath a free desire to doe well, the inward light each minde hath in it selfe, is as good as a Philosophers booke; seeing in nature we know it is wel, to doe well, and what is well, and what is evill, although not in the words of Arte, which Philosophers bestowe upon us. For out of naturall conceit, the Philosophers drew it, but to be moved to doe that which we know, or to be mooved with desire to knowe, *Hoc opus: Hic labor est.*[7]

Nowe therein of all Sciences, (I speak still of humane, and according to the humane conceits) is our Poet the Monarch. For he dooth not only show the way, but giveth so sweete a prospect into the way, as will intice any man to enter into it. Nay, he dooth as if your journey should lye through a fayre Vineyard, at the first give you a cluster of Grapes: that full of that taste, you may long to passe further. He beginneth not with obscure definitions, which must blur the margent with interpretations, and load the memory with doubtfulnesse: but hee commeth to you with words sent in delightfull proportion, either accompanied with, or prepared for the well inchaunting skill of Musicke; and with a tale forsooth he commeth unto you: with a tale which holdeth children from play, and old men from the chimney corner. And pretending no more, doth intende the winning of the mind from wickednesse to vertue: even as the childe is often brought to take most wholsom things, by hiding them in such other as have a pleasant tast: which if one should beginne to tell them, the nature of Aloes, or Rubarb they shoulde receive, woulde sooner take their Phisicke at their eares, then at their mouth. So is it in men (most of which are childish in the best things, till they bee cradled in their graves,) glad they will be to heare the tales of Hercules, Achilles, Cyrus, and Aeneas: and hearing them, must needs heare the right description of wisdom, valure, and justice; which, if they had been barely, that is to say, Philosophically set out, they would sweare they bee brought to schoole againe.

That imitation whereof Poetry is, hath the most conveniency to Nature of all other, in somuch, that as Aristotle sayth, those things which in themselves are horrible, as cruell battailes, unnaturall Monsters, are made in poeticall imitation delightfull. Truely I have knowen men, that even with reading *Amadis de Gaule,* (which God knoweth wanteth much of a perfect Poesie) have found their harts mooved to the exercise of courtesie, liberalitie, and especially courage.

Who readeth Aeneas carrying olde Anchises on his back, that wisheth not it were his fortune to perfourme so excellent an acte? Whom doe not the words of Turnus moove? (the tale of Turnus, having planted his image in the imagination,)

> ——————*Fugientem hæc terra videbit,*
> *Usque adeone mori miserum est?*———[8]

[7] ["In this the task and mighty labor lies."]

[8] ["Will this land see him fleeing? Is it then such a wretched thing to die?"]

Where the Philosophers, as they scorne to delight, so must they bee content little to moove: saving wrangling, whether Vertue bee the chiefe, or the onely good: whether the contemplative, or the active life doe excell: which Plato and Boethius well knew, and therefore made Mistres Philosophy, very often borrow the masking rayment of Poesie. For even those harde harted evill men, who thinke vertue a schoole name, and knowe no other good, but *indulgere genio,*[9] and therefore despise the austere admonitions of the Philosopher, and feele not the inward reason they stand upon; yet will be content to be delighted: which is all the good felow Poet seemeth to promise: and so steale to see the forme of goodnes (which seene they cannot but love) ere themselves be aware, as if they tooke a medicine of Cherries. Infinite proofes of the strange effects of this poeticall invention might be alledged, onely two shall serve, which are so often remembred, as I thinke all men knowe them.

The one of Menenius Agrippa, who when the whole people of Rome had resolutely devided themselves from the Senate, with apparent shew of utter ruine: though hee were (for that time) an excellent Oratour, came not among them, upon trust of figurative speeches, or cunning insinuations: and much lesse, with farre set Maximes of Phylosophie, which (especially if they were Platonick,) they must have learned Geometrie before they could well have conceived: but forsooth he behaves himselfe, like a homely, and familiar Poet. Hee telleth them a tale, that there was a time, when all the parts of the body made a mutinous conspiracie against the belly, which they thought devoured the fruits of each others labour: they concluded they would let so unprofitable a spender starve. In the end, to be short, (for the tale is notorious, and as notorious that it was a tale,) with punishing the belly, they plagued themselves. This applied by him, wrought such effect in the people, as I never read, that ever words brought forth but then, so suddaine and so good an alteration: for upon reasonable conditions, a perfect reconcilement ensued. The other is of Nathan the Prophet, who when the holie David had so far forsaken God, as to confirme adulterie with murther: when hee was to doe the tenderest office of a friende, in laying his owne shame before his eyes, sent by God to call againe so chosen a servant: how doth he it? but by telling of a man, whose beloved Lambe was ungratefullie taken from his bosome: the applycation most divinely true, but the discourse itselfe, fayned: which made David, (I speake of the second and instrumentall cause) as in a glasse, to see his own filthines, as that heavenly Psalme of mercie wel testifieth.

By these therefore examples and reasons, I think it may be manifest, that the Poet with that same hand of delight, both draw the mind more effectually, then any other Arte dooth, and so a conclusion not unfitlie ensueth: that as vertue is the most excellent resting place for all worldlie learning to make his end of: so Poetrie, beeing the most familiar to teach it, and most princelie to move towards it, in the most excellent work, is the most excellent workman. But I am content, not onely to decipher him by his workes, (although works in commendation or disprayse, must ever holde an high authority,) but more narrowly will examine his parts: so that (as in a man) though altogether may carry a presence ful of majestie and beautie, perchance in some one defectious peece, we may find a blemish: now in his parts, kinds, or *Species,* (as you list to terme them) it is to be noted that some Poesies have coupled together two or three kindes, as Tragicall and Comicall, wher-upon is risen, the Tragi-comicall. Some in the like manner have mingled Prose and Verse, as Sanazzar and Boetius. Some have mingled matters Heroicall and Pastorall. But that commeth all to one in this question, for if severed they be good, the conjunction cannot be hurtfull. Therefore perchaunce forgetting some, and leaving some as needlesse to be remembred, it shall not be amisse in a worde to cite the speciall kindes, to see what faults may be found in the right use of them.

Is it then the Pastorall Poem which is misliked? (for perchance, where the hedge is lowest, they will soonest leape over.) Is the poore pype disdained, which sometime out of Melibeus mouth, can shewe the miserie of people, under hard Lords, or ravening Souldiours? And again, by Titirus, what blessedness is derived to them that lye lowest from the goodnesse of them that sit highest? Sometimes, under the prettie tales of Wolves and Sheepe, can include the whole

[9] ["to indulge their inclination(s)."]

considerations of wrong dooing and patience. Sometimes shew, that contention for trifles, can get but a trifling victorie. Where perchaunce a man may see, that even Alexander and Darius, when they strave who should be Cocke of this worlds dunghill, the benefit they got, was, that the after-livers may say,

Hæc memini et victum frustra contendere Thirsin:
Ex illo Coridon, Coridon est tempore nobis.[10]

Or is it the lamenting Elegiack, which in a kinde hart would moove rather pitty then blame, who bewailes with the great Philosopher Heraclitus, the weakenes of man-kind, and the wretchednes of the world: who surely is to be praysed, either for compassionate accompanying just causes of lamentation, or for rightly paynting out how weake be the passions of wofulnesse. Is it the bitter, but wholsome Iambick, which rubs the galled minde, in making shame the trumpet of villanie, with bolde and open crying out against naughtines; Or the Satirick, who

Omne vafer vitium, ridenti tangit amico? [11]

who sportingly never leaveth, until hee make a man laugh at folly, and at length ashamed, to laugh at himselfe: which he cannot avoyd, without avoyding the follie. Who while

Circum præcordia ludit,[12]

giveth us to feele, how many head-aches a passionate life bringeth us to. How when all is done,

Est ulubris animus si nos non deficit æquus? [13]

No perchance it is the Comick, whom naughtie Play-makers and Stage-keepers, have justly made odious. To the argument of abuse, I will answer after. Onely thus much now is to be said, that the Comedy is an imitation of the common errors of our life, which he representeth, in the most ridiculous and scornefull sort that may be. So as it is impossible, that any beholder can be content to be such a one.

Now, as in Geometry, the oblique must be knowne as wel as the right: and in Arithmetick, the odde as well as the even, so in the actions of our life, who seeth not the filthines of evil, wanteth a great foile to perceive the beauty of vertue. This doth the Comedy handle so in our private and domestical matters, as with hearing it, we get as it were an experience, what is to be looked for of a nigardly Demea: of a crafty Danus: of a flattering Gnato: of a vaine glorious Thraso: and not onely to know what effects are to be expected, but to know who be such, by the signifying badge given them by the Comedian. And little reason hath any man to say, that men learne evill by seeing it so set out: sith as I sayd before, there is no man living, but by the force trueth hath in nature, no sooner seeth these men play their parts, but wisheth them in *Pistrinum:* although perchance the sack of his owne faults, lye so behinde his back, that he seeth not himselfe daunce the same measure: whereto, yet nothing can more open his eyes, then to finde his own actions contemptibly set forth. So that the right use of Comedy will (I thinke) by no body be blamed, and much lesse of the high and excellent Tragedy, that openeth the greatest wounds, and sheweth forth the Vlcers, that are covered with Tissue: that maketh Kinges feare to be Tyrants, and Tyrants manifest their tirannicall humors: that with sturring the affects of admiration and commiseration, teacheth, the uncertainety of this world, and upon how weake foundations guilden roofes are builded. That maketh us knowe,

Qui sceptra sævus, duro imperio regit,
Timet timentes, metus in authorem redit.[14]

But how much it can moove, Plutarch yeeldeth a notable testimonie, of the abhominable Tyrant, Alexander Pheræus; from whose eyes, a Tragedy wel made, and represented, drewe aboundance of teares: who without all pitty, had murthered infinite nombers, and some of his owne blood. So as he, that was not ashamed to make matters for Tragedies, yet coulde not resist the sweet violence of a Tragedie.

And if it wrought no further good in him, it was, that he in despight of himselfe, withdrewe himselfe from harkening to that, which might

[10] ["I remember these things, and that Thirsis competed in vain and was defeated: From that time Coridon has to us been Coridon."]

[11] ["In his cleverness he touches upon every fault of his laughing friend."]

[12] ["He plays about the heart."]

[13] ["(What we are looking for) is at Ulubrae if we do not lack a tranquil mind."]

[14] ["He who wields a scepter harshly and severely fears those who fear, and dread turns back upon its author."]

mollifie his hardened heart. But it is not the Tragedy they doe mislike: For it were too absurd to cast out so excellent a representation of whatsoever is most worthy to be learned. Is it the Liricke that most displeaseth, who with his tuned Lyre, and wel accorded voyce, giveth praise, the reward of vertue, to vertuous acts? who gives morall precepts, and naturall Problemes, who sometimes rayseth up his voice to the height of the heavens, in singing the laudes of the immortall God. Certainly I must confesse my own barbarousnes, I never heard the olde song of Percy and Duglas, that I found not my heart mooved more then with a Trumpet: and yet is it sung but by some blinde Crouder, with no rougher voyce, then rude stile: which being so evill apparrelled in the dust and cobwebbes of that uncivill age, what would it worke trymmed in the gorgeous eloquence of Pindar? In Hungary I have seene it the manner at all Feasts, and other such meetings, to have songes of their Auncestours valour; which that right Souldierlike Nation thinck the chiefest kindlers of brave courage. The incomparable Lacedemonians, did not only carry that kinde of Musicke ever with them to the field, but even at home, as such songs were made, so were they all content to bee the singers of them, when the lusty men were to tell what they dyd, the olde men, what they had done, and the young men what they wold doe. And where a man may say, that Pindar many times prayseth highly victories of small moment, matters rather of sport then vertue: as it may be aunswered, it was the fault of the Poet, and not of the Poetry; so indeede, the chiefe fault was in the tyme and custome of the Greekes, who set those toyes at so high a price, that Phillip of Macedon reckoned a horserace wonne at Olimpus, among hys three fearefull felicities. But as the unimitable Pindar often did, so is that kinde most capable and most fit, to awake the thoughts from the sleep of idlenes, to imbrace honorable enterprises.

There rests the Heroicall, whose very name (I thinke) should daunt all back-biters; for by what conceit can a tongue be directed to speak evill of that, which draweth with it, no lesse Champions then Achilles, Cyrus, Aeneas, Turnus, Tideus, and Rinaldo? who doth not onely teach and move to a truth, but teacheth and mooveth to the most high and excellent truth. Who maketh magnanimity and justice shine, throughout all misty fearefulnes and foggy desires. Who, if the saying of Plato and Tullie bee true, that who could see Vertue, would be wonderfully ravished with the love of her beauty: this man sets her out to make her more lovely in her holyday apparell, to the eye of any that will daine, not to disdaine, untill they understand. But if anything be already sayd in the defence of sweete Poetry, all concurreth to the maintaining the Heroicall, which is not onely a kinde, but the best, and most accomplished kinde of Poetry. For as the image of each action styrreth and instructeth the mind, so the loftie image of such Worthies, most inflameth the mind with desire to be worthy, and informes with counsel how to be worthy. Only let Aeneas be worne in the tablet of your memory, how he governeth himselfe in the ruine of his Country, in the preserving his old Father, and carrying away his religious ceremonies: in obeying the Gods commandement to leave Dido, though not onely all passionate kindenes, but even the humane consideration of vertuous gratefulnes, would have craved other of him. How in storms, howe in sports, howe in warre, howe in peace, how a fugitive, how victorious, how besiedged, how besiedging, howe to strangers, howe to allyes, how to enemies, howe to his owne: lastly, how in his inward selfe, and how in his outward government. And I thinke, in a minde not prejudiced with a prejudicating humor, hee will be found in excellencie fruitefull: yea, even as Horace sayth

Melius Chrisippo et Crantore.[15]

But truely I imagine, it falleth out with these Poet-whyppers, as with some good women, who often are sicke, but in fayth they cannot tel where. So the name of Poetrie is odious to them, but neither his cause, nor effects, neither the sum that containes him, nor the particularities descending from him, give any fast handle to their carping disprayse.

Sith then Poetrie is of all humane learning the most auncient, and of most fatherly antiquitie, as from whence other learnings have taken theyr beginnings: sith it is so universall, that no learned Nation dooth despise it, nor no barbarous Nation is without it: sith both Roman

15 ["Better than Chrisippo and Crantor."]

and Greek gave divine names unto it: the one of prophecying, the other of making. And that indeede, that name of making is fit for him; considering, that where as other Arts retaine themselves within their subject, and receive as it were, their beeing from it: the Poet onely, bringeth his owne stuffe, and dooth not learne a conceite out of a matter, but maketh matter for a conceite: Sith neither his description, nor his ende, contayneth any evill, the thing described cannot be evill: Sith his effects be so good as to teach goodnes and to delight the learners: Sith therein, (namely in morrall doctrine, the chiefe of all knowledges,) hee dooth not onely farre passe the Historian, but for instructing, is well nigh comparable to the Philosopher: and for moving, leaves him behind him: Sith the holy scripture (wherein there is no uncleannes) hath whole parts in it poeticall. And that even our Saviour Christ, vouchsafed to use the flowers of it: Sith all his kindes are not onlie in their united formes, but in their severed dissections fully commendable, I think, (and think I thinke rightly) the Lawrell crowne appointed for tryumphing Captaines, doth worthilie (of al other learnings) honor the Poets tryumph. But because wee have eares aswell as tongues, and that the lightest reasons that may be, will seeme to weigh greatly, if nothing be put in the counter-balance: let us heare, and aswell as wee can ponder, what objections may bee made against this Arte, which may be worthy, eyther of yeelding, or answering.

First truely I note, not onely in these *Mysomousoi* Poet-haters, but in all that kinde of people, who seek a prayse by dispraysing others, that they doe prodigally spend a great many wandering wordes, in quips, and scoffes; carping and taunting at each thing, which by styrring the Spleene, may stay the braine from a thorough beholding the worthines of the subject.

Those kinde of objections, as they are full of very idle easines, sith there is nothing of so sacred a majestie, but that an itching tongue may rubbe it selfe upon it: so deserve they no other answer, but in steed of laughing at the jest, to laugh at the jester. Wee know a playing wit, can prayse the discretion of an Asse; the comfortablenes of being in debt, and the jolly commoditie of beeing sick of the plague. So of the contrary side, if we will turne Ovids verse,

Ut lateat virtus, proximitate mali,

that good lye hid in neerenesse of the evill: Agrippa will be as merry in showing the vanitie of Science, as Erasmus was in commending of follie. Neyther shall any man or matter escape some touch of these smyling raylers. But for Erasmus and Agrippa, they had another foundation then the superficiall part would promise. Mary, these other pleasant Fault-finders, who wil correct the Verbe, before they understande the Noune, and confute others knowledge before they confirme theyr owne: I would have them onely remember, that scoffing commeth not of wisedom. So as the best title in true English they gette with their merriments, is to be called good fooles: for so have our grave Forefathers ever termed that humorous kinde of jesters: but that which gyveth greatest scope to their scorning humors, is ryming and versing. It is already sayde (and as I think, trulie sayde) it is not ryming and versing, that maketh Poesie. One may bee a Poet without versing, and a versifier without Poetry. But yet, presuppose it were inseparable (as indeede it seemeth Scaliger judgeth) truelie it were an inseparable commendation. For if *Oratio,* next to *Ratio,* Speech next to Reason, bee the greatest gyft bestowed upon mortalitie: that can not be praiselesse, which dooth most pollish that blessing of speech, which considers each word, not only (as a man may say) by his forcible qualitie, but by his best measured quantitie, carrying even in themselves, a Harmonie: (without (perchaunce) Number, Measure, Order, Proportion, be in our time growne odious.) But lay a side the just prayse it hath, by beeing the onely fit speech for Musick, (Musick I say, the most divine striker of the sences:) thus much is undoubtedly true, that if reading bee foolish, without remembring, memorie being the onely treasurer of knowled[g]e, those words which are fittest for memory, are likewise most convenient for knowledge.

Now, that Verse farre exceedeth Prose in the knitting up of the memory, the reason is manifest. The words, (besides theyr delight which hath a great affinitie to memory,) beeing so set, as one word cannot be lost, but the whole worke failes: which accuseth it selfe, calleth the remembrance backe to it selfe, and so most strongly confirmeth it; besides, one word so as it were begetting another, as be it in ryme or measured verse, by the former a man shall have a neere gesse to the follower: lastly, even they that have taught the Art of memory, have shewed nothing so apt for it, as a certaine roome devided into many places well and throughly knowne. Now, that hath the verse in effect perfectly; every word having his naturall seate, which seate, must needes make the words remembred. But what needeth more in a thing so knowne to all men? who is it that ever was a scholler, that doth not carry away some verses of Virgill, Horace, or Cato, which in his youth he learned, and even to his old age serve him for howrely lessons? but the fitnes it hath for memory, is notably proved by all delivery of Arts: wherein for the most part, from Grammar, to Logick, Mathematick, Phisick, and the rest, the rules chiefely necessary to bee borne away, are compiled in verses. So that, verse being in it selfe sweete and orderly, and beeing best for memory, the onely handle of knowledge, it must be in jest that any man can speake against it. Nowe then goe wee to the most important imputations laid to the poore Poets, for ought I can yet learne, they are these, first, that there beeing many other more fruitefull knowledges, a man might better spend his tyme in them, then in this. Secondly, that it is the mother of lyes. Thirdly, that it is the Nurse of abuse, infecting us with many pestilent desires: with a Syrens sweetnes, drawing the mind to the Serpents tayle of sinfull fancy. And heerein especially, Comedies give the largest field to erre, as Chaucer sayth: howe both in other Nations and in ours, before Poets did soften us, we were full of courage, given to martiall exercises; the pillers of manlyke liberty, and not lulled a sleepe in shady idlenes with Poets pastimes. And lastly, and chiefely, they cry out with an open mouth, as if they out shot Robin Hood, that Plato banished them out of hys Common-wealth. Truely, this is much, if there be much truth in it. First to the first: that a man might better spend his time, is a reason indeede: but it doth (as they say) but *Petere principium:* [16] for if it be as I affirme, that no learning is so good, as that which teacheth and mooveth to vertue; and that none can both teach and move thereto so much as Poetry: then is the conclusion manifest, that Incke and Paper cannot be to a more profitable purpose employed. And certainly, though a man should graunt their first assumption, it should followe (me thinkes) very unwillingly, that good is not good, because better is better. But I still and utterly denye, that there is sprong out of earth a more fruitefull knowledge. To the second therefore, that they should be the principall lyars; I aunswere paradoxically, but truely, I thinke truely; that of all Writers under the sunne, the Poet is the least lier; and though he would, as a Poet can scarcely be a lyer, the Astronomer, with his cosen the Geometrician, can hardly escape, when they take upon them to measure the height of the starres.

How often, thinke you, doe the Phisitians lye, when they aver things, good for sicknesses, which afterwards send Charon a great nomber of soules drown[e]d in a potion before they come to his Ferry. And no lesse of the rest, which take upon them to affirme. Now, for the Poet, he nothing affirmes, and therefore never lyeth. For, as I take it, to lye, is to affirme that to be true which is false. So as the other Artists, and especially the Historian, affirming many things, can in the cloudy knowledge of mankinde, hardly escape from many lyes. But the Poet (as I sayd before) never affirmeth. The Poet never maketh any circles about your imagination, to conjure you to beleeve for true what he writes. Hee citeth not authorities of other Histories, but even for hys entry, calleth the sweete Muses to inspire into him a good invention: in troth, not labouring to tell you what is, or is not, but what should or should not be: and therefore, though he recount things not true, yet because hee telleth them not for true, he lyeth not, without we will say, that Nathan, lyed in his speech, before alledged to David. Which as a wicked man durst scarce say, so think I none so simple would say, that Esope lyed in the tales of his beasts: for who thinks that Esope writ it for actually true, were well worthy to have his name c[h]ronicled among the beastes hee writeth of.

What childe is there, that comming to a Play, and seeing Thebes written in great Letters upon an olde doore, doth beleeve that it is Thebes? If then, a man can arive, at that childs age, to

[16] ["Revert to the beginning."]

know that the poets persons and dooings, are but pictures what should be, and not stories what have beene, they will never give the lye, to things not affirmatively, but allegorically, and figurativelie written. And therefore, as in Historie, looking for trueth, they goe away full fraught with falsehood: so in Poesie, looking for fiction, they shal use the narration, but as an imaginative groundplot of a profitable invention.

But heereto is replyed, that the Poets gyve names to men they write of, which argueth a conceite of an actuall truth, and so, not being true, prooves a falsehood. And doth the Lawyer lye then, when under the names of *John a stile* and *John a noakes,* hee puts his case? But that is easily answered. Theyr naming of men, is but to make theyr picture the more lively, and not to builde any historie: paynting men, they cannot leave men namelesse. We see we cannot play at Chesse, but that wee must give names to our Chesse-men; and yet mee thinks, hee were a very partiall Champion of truth, that would say we lyed, for giving a peece of wood, the reverend title of a Bishop. The Poet nameth Cyrus or Aeneas, no other way, then to shewe, what men of theyr fames, fortunes, and estates, should doe.

Their third is, how much it abuseth mens wit, trayning it to wanton sinfulness, and lustfull love: for indeed that is the principall, if not the onely abuse I can heare alledged. They say, the Comedies rather teach, then reprehend, amorous conceits. They say, the Lirick, is larded with passionate Sonnets. The Elegiack, weepes the want of his mistresse. And that even to the Heroical, Cupid hath ambitiously climed. Alas Love, I would, thou couldest as well defende thy selfe, as thou canst offende others. I would those, on whom thou doost attend, could eyther put thee away, or yeelde good reason, why they keepe thee. But grant love of beautie, to be a beastlie fault, (although it be very hard, sith onely man, and no beast, hath that gyft, to discerne beauty.) Grant, that lovely name of Love, to deserve all hatefull reproches: (although even some of my Maisters the Phylosophers, spent a good deale of theyr Lamp-oyle, in setting foorth the excellencie of it.) Grant, I say, whatsoever they wil have granted; that not onely love, but lust, but vanitie, but, (if they list) scurrilitie, possesseth many leaves of the Poets bookes: yet thinke I, when this is granted, they will finde, theyr sentence may with good manners, put the last words foremost: and not say, that Poetrie abuseth mans wit, but that, mans wit abuseth Poetrie.

For I will not denie, but that mans wit may make Poesie, (which should be *Eikastike,* which some learned have defined, figuring foorth good things,) to be *Phantastike:* which doth contrariwise, infect the fancie with unworthy objects. As the Painter, that shoulde give to the eye, eyther some excellent perspective, or some fine picture, fit for building or fortification: or contayning in it some notable example, as Abraham, sacrificing his Sonne Isaack, Judith killing Holofernes, David fighting with Goliath, may leave those, and please an ill-pleased eye, with wanton shewes of better hidden matters. But what, shall the abuse of a thing, make the right use odious? Nay truely, though I yeeld, that Poesie may not onely be abused, but that beeing abused, by the reason of his sweete charming force, it can doe more hurt than any other Armie of words: yet shall it be so far from concluding, that the abuse, should give reproch to the abused, that contrariwise it is a good reason, that whatsoever being abused, dooth most harme, beeing rightly used: (and upon the right use each thing conceiveth his title) doth most good.

Doe wee not see the skill of Phisick, (the best rampire to our often-assaulted bodies) beeing abused, teach poyson the most violent destroyer? Dooth not knowledge of Law, whose end is, to even and right all things being abused, grow the crooked fosterer of horrible injuries? Doth not (to goe to the highest) Gods word abused, breed heresie? and his Name abused, become blasphemie? Truely, a needle cannot doe much hurt, and as truely, (with leave of Ladies be it spoken) it cannot doe much good. With a sword, thou maist kill thy Father, and with a sword thou maist defende thy Prince and Country. So that, as in their calling Poets the Fathers of lyes, they say nothing: so in this theyr argument of abuse, they proove the commendation.

They alledge heere-with, that before Poets beganne to be in price, our Nation, hath set their harts delight upon action, and not upon imagination: rather doing things worthy to bee written, then writing things fitte to be done. What that before tyme was, I thinke scarcely

Sphinx can tell: Sith no memory is so auncient, that hath the precedence of Poetrie. And certaine it is, that in our plainest homelines, yet never was the Albion Nation without Poetrie. Mary, thys argument, though it bee leaveld against Poetrie, yet is it indeed, a chaine-shot against all learning, or bookishnes, as they commonly tearme it. Of such minde were certaine Goethes, of whom it is written, that having in the spoile of a famous Citie, taken a fayre librarie: one hangman (bee like fitte to execute the fruites of their wits) who had murthered a great number of bodies, would have set fire on it: no sayde another, very gravely, take heede what you doe, for whyle they are busie about these toyes, wee shall with more leysure conquer their Countries.

This indeede is the ordinary doctrine of ignorance, and many wordes sometymes I have heard spent in it: but because this reason is generally against all learning, aswell as Poetrie; or rather, all learning but Poetry: because it were too large a digression, to handle, or at least, too superfluous: (sith it is manifest, that all government of action, is to be gotten by knowledg, and knowledge best, by gathering many knowledges, which is, reading,) I onely with Horace, to him that is of that opinion,

Iubeo stultum esse libenter; [17]

for as for Poetrie it selfe, it is the freest from thys objection. For Poetrie is the companion of the Campes.

I dare undertake, *Orlando Furioso,* or honest King Arthur, will never displease a Souldier: but the quiddity of *Ens,* and *Prima materia,* will hardely agree with a Corslet: and therefore, as I said in the beginning, even Turks and Tartares are delighted with Poets. Homer, a Greek, florished, before Greece flourished. And if to a slight conjecture, a conjecture may be opposed: truly it may seeme, that as by him, their learned men, tooke almost their first light of knowledge, so their active men, received their first notions of courage. Onlie Alexanders example may serve, who by Plutarch is accounted of such vertue, that Fortune was not his guide, but his footestoole: whose acts speake for him, though Plutarch did not: indeede, the Phœnix of warlike Princes. This Alexander, left his Schoole-maister, living Aristotle, behinde him, but tooke deade Homer with him: he put the Philosopher Calisthenes to death, for his seeming philosophicall, indeed mutinous stubburnnes. But the chiefe thing he ever was heard to wish for, was, that Homer had been alive. He well found he received more graverie of minde, bye the patterne of Achilles, then by hearing the definition of Fortitude: and therefore, if Cato misliked Fulvius, for carying Ennius with him to the fielde, it may be aunswered, that if Cato misliked it, the noble Fulvius liked it, or els he had not doone it: for it was not the excellent Cato Uticensis, (whose authority I would much more have reverenced,) but it was the former: in truth, a bitter punisher of faults, but else, a man that had never wel sacrificed to the Graces. Hee misliked and cryed out upon all Greeke learning, and yet being 80. yeeres olde, began to learne it. Be-like, fearing that Pluto understood not Latine. Indeede, the Romaine lawes allowed, no person to be carried to the warres, but hee that was in the Souldiers role: and therefore, though Cato misliked his unmustered person, hee misliked not his worke. And if hee had, Scipio Nasica judged by common consent, the best Romaine, loved him. Both the other Scipio Brothers, who had by their vertues no lesse surnames, then of Asia, and Affrick, so loved him, that they caused his body to be buried in their Sepulcher. So as Cato, his authoritie being but against his person, and that aunswered, with so farre greater then himselfe, is heerein of no validitie. But now indeede my burthen is great; now Plato his name is layde upon mee, whom I must confesse, of all Philosophers, I have ever esteemed most worthy of reverence, and with great reason: Sith of all Philosophers, he is the most poeticall. Yet if he will defile the Fountaine, out of which his flowing streames have proceeded, let us boldly examine with what reasons hee did it. First truly, a man might maliciously object, that Plato being a Philosopher was a naturall enemie of Poets: for indeede, after the Philosophers, had picked out of the sweete misteries of Poetrie, the right discerning true points of knowledge, they forthwith putting it in method, and making a Schoole-arte of that which the Poets did onely teach, by a divine delightfulnes, beginning to spurne at their guides, like ungratefull Prentises, were not con-

[17] ["I order him to be stupid, and gladly so."]

tent to set up shops for themselves, but sought by all meanes to discredit their Maisters. Which by the force of delight being barred them, the lesse they could overthrow them, the more they hated them. For indeede, they found for Homer, seaven Cities strove, who should have him for their Citizen: where many Citties banished Philosophers, as not fitte members to live among them. For onely repeating certaine of Euripides verses, many Athenians had their lyves saved of the Siracusians: when the Athenians themselves, thought many Philosophers, unwoorthie to live.

Certaine Poets, as Simonides, and Pindarus had so prevailed with Hiero the first, that of a Tirant they made him a just King, where Plato could do so little with Dionisius, that he himselfe, of a Philosopher, was made a slave. But who should doe thus, I confesse, should requite the objections made against Poets, with like cavillation against Philosophers, as likewise one should doe, that should bid one read Phædrus, or Symposium in Plato, or the discourse of love in Plutarch, and see whether any Poet doe authorize abhominable filthines, as they doe. Againe, a man might aske out of what Commonwealth Plato did banish them? insooth, thence where he himselfe alloweth communitie of women: So as belike, this banishment grewe not for effeminate wantonnes, sith little should poeticall Sonnets be hurtfull, when a man might have what woman he listed. But I honor philosophicall instructions, and blesse the wits which bred them: so as they be not abused, which is likewise stretched to Poetrie.

S. Paule himselfe, (who yet for the credite of Poets) alledgeth twise two Poets, and one of them by the name of a Prophet, setteth a watchword upon Philosophy, indeede upon the abuse. So dooth Plato, upon the abuse, not upon Poetrie. Plato found fault, that the Poets of his time, filled the worlde, with wrong opinions of the Gods, making light tales of that unspotted essence; and therefore, would not have the youth depraved with such opinions. Heerin may much be said, let this suffice: the Poets did not induce such opinions, but dyd imitate those opinions already induced. For all the Greek stories can well testifie, that the very religion of that time, stoode upon many, and many-fashioned Gods, not taught so by the Poets, but followed, according to their nature of imitation. Who list, may reade in Plutarch, the discourses of Isis and Osiris, of the cause why Oracles ceased, of the divine providence; and see, whether the Theologie of that nation, stood not upon such dreames, which the Poets indeed supersticiously observed, and truly, (sith they had not the light of Christ,) did much better in it than the Philosophers, who shaking off superstition, brought in Atheisme. Plato therefore, (whose authoritie I had much rather justly conster, then unjustly resist,) meant not in general of Poets, in those words of which Julius Scaliger saith *Qua authoritate, barbari quidam, atque hispidi, abuti velint, ad Poetas é republica exigendos;* [18] but only meant, to drive out those wrong opinions of the Deitie (whereof now, without further law, Christianity hath taken away all the hurtful beliefe,) perchance (as he thought) norished by the then esteemed Poets. And a man need goe no further then to Plato himselfe, to know his meaning: who in his Dialogue called Ion, giveth high, and rightly divine commendation to Poetrie. So as Plato, banishing the abuse, not the thing, not banishing it, but giving due honor unto it, shall be our Patron, and not our adversarie. For indeed I had much rather, (sith truly I may doe it) shew theyr mistaking of Plato, (under whose Lyons skin they would make an Asselike braying against Poesie,) then goe about to overthrow his authority, whom the wiser a man is, the more just cause he shall find to have in admiration: especially, sith he attributeth unto Poesie, more then my selfe doe; namely, to be a very inspiring of a divine force, farre above mans wit; as in the aforenamed Dialogue is apparent.

Of the other side, who wold shew the honors, have been by the best sort of judgements granted them, a whole Sea of examples woulde present themselves. Alexanders, Cæsars, Scipios, al favorers of Poets. Lelius, called the Romane Socrates, himselfe a Poet: so as part of *Heautontimorumenon* in Terence, was supposed to be made by him. And even the Greek Socrates, whom Apollo confirmed to be the onely wise man, is sayde to have spent part of his old tyme, in putting Esops fables into verses. And therefore, full evill should it become his scholler Plato, to put such words in his Maisters mouth,

[18] ["Which authority certain crude barbarians wished to abuse in order to drive poets out of the state."]

against Poets. But what need more? Aristotle writes the Arte of Poesie: and why if it should not be written? Plutarch teacheth the use to be gathered of them, and how if they should not be read? And who reades Plutarchs eyther historie or philosophy, shall finde, hee trymmeth both theyr garments, with gards of Poesie. But I list not to defend Poesie, with the helpe of her underling, Historiography. Let it suffise, that it is a fit soyle for prayse to dwell upon: and what dispraise may set upon it, is eyther easily overcome, or transformed into just commendation. So that, sith the excellencies of it, may be so easily, and so justly confirmed, and the low-creeping objections, so soone troden downe; it not being an Art of lyes, but of true doctrine: not of effeminatenes, but of notable stirring of courage: not of abusing mans witte, but of strengthning mans wit: not banished, but honored by Plato: let us rather plant more Laurels, for to engarland our Poets heads, (which honor of beeing laureat, as besides them, onely tryumphant Captaines weare, is a sufficient authority, to shewe the price they ought to be had in,) then suffer the ill-favouring breath of such wrong-speakers, once to blowe upon the cleere springs of Poesie.

But sith I have runne so long a careere in this matter, me thinks, before I give my penne a fulle stop, it shal be but a little more lost time, to inquire, why England, (the Mother of excellent mindes,) shoulde bee growne so hard a step-mother to Poets, who certainly in wit ought to passe all other: sith all onely proceedeth from their wit, being indeede makers of themselves, not takers of others. How can I but exclaime,

Musa mihi causas memora, quo numine læso.[19]

Sweete Poesie, that hath aunciently had Kings, Emperors, Senators, great Captaines, such, as besides a thousand others, David, Adrian, Sophocles, Germanicus, not onely to favour Poets, but to be Poets. And of our neerer times, can present for her Patrons, a Robert, king of Sicil, the great king Francis of France, King James of Scotland. Such Cardinals as Bembus, and Bibiena. Such famous Preachers and Teachers, as Beza and Melancthon. So learned Philosophers, as Fracastorius and Scaliger. So great Orators, as Pontanus and Muretus. So piercing wits, as George Buchanan. So grave Counsellors, as besides many, but before all, that Hospitall of Fraunce: then whom, (I thinke) that Realme never brought forth a more accomplished judgement: more firmely builded upon vertue. I say these, with numbers of others, not onely to read others Poesies, but to poetise for others reading, that Poesie thus embraced in all other places, should onely finde in our time, a hard welcome in England, I thinke the very earth lamenteth it, and therefore decketh our Soyle with fewer Laurels then it was accustomed. For heertofore, Poets have in England also florished. And which is to be noted, even in those times, when the trumpet of Mars did sounde loudest. And now, that an overfaint quietnes should seeme to strew the house for Poets, they are almost in as good reputation, as the Mountibancks at Venice. Truly even that, as of the one side, it giveth great praise to Poesie, which like Venus, (but to better purpose) hath rather be troubled in the net with Mars, then enjoy the homelie quiet of Vulcan: so serves it for a peece of reason, why they are lesse gratefull to idle England, which nowe can scarce endure the payne of a pen. Upon this, necessarily followeth, that base men, with servile wits undertake it: who think it inough, if they can be rewarded of the Printer. And so as Epaminondas is sayd, with the honor of his vertue, to have made an office, by his exercising it, which before was contemptible, to become highly respected: so these, no more but setting their names to it, by their owne disgracefulnes, disgrace the most gracefull Poesie. For now, as if all the Muses were gotte with childe, to bring foorth bastard Poets, without any commission, they doe poste over the banckes of Helicon, tyll they make the readers more weary than Post-horses: while in the mean tyme, they

Queis meliore luto finxit præcordia Titan,[20]

are better content, to suppresse the out-flowing of their wit, then by publishing them, to bee accounted Knight of the same order. But I, that before ever I durst aspire unto the dignitie, am admitted into the company of the Paper-blurers, doe finde the very true cause of our wanting estimation, is want of desert: taking upon us

[19] ["Oh Muse, recount to me what divinity was offended."]

[20] ["Whose soul the Titan has shaped of finer clay."]

to be Poets, in despight of Pallas. Nowe, wherein we want desert, were a thanke-worthy labour to expresse: but if I knew, I should have mended my selfe. But I, as I never desired the title, so have I neglected the meanes to come by it. Onely over-mastred by some thoughts, I yeelded an inckie tribute unto them. Mary, they that delight in Poesie it selfe, should seeke to knowe what they doe, and how they doe; and especially, looke themselves in an unflattering Glasse of reason, if they bee inclinable unto it. For Poesie, must not be drawne by the eares, it must bee gently led, or rather, it must lead. Which was partly the cause, that made the auncient-learned affirme, it was a divine gift, and no humaine skill: sith all other knowledges, lie ready for any that hath strength of witte: A Poet, no industrie can make, if his owne Genius bee not carried unto it: and therefore is it an old proverbe, *Orator fit; Poeta nascitur.* Yet confesse I alwayes, that as the firtilest ground must bee manured, so must the highest flying wit, have a Dedalus to guide him. That Dedalus, they say, both in this, and in other, hath three wings, to beare it selfe up into the ayre of due commendation: that is, Arte, Imitation, and Exercise. But these, neyther artificiall rules, nor imitative patternes, we much cumber our selves withall. Exercise indeede wee doe, but that, very forebackwardly: for where we should exercise to know, wee exercise as having knowne: and so is oure braine delivered of much matter, which never was begotten by knowledge. For, there being two principal parts, matter to be expressed by wordes, and words to expresse the matter, in neyther, wee use Arte, or Imitation, rightly. Our matter is *Quodlibit* indeed, though wrongly perfourming Ovids verse,

> *Quicquid conabar dicere versus erit:* [21]

never marshalling it into an assured rancke, that almost the readers cannot tell where to finde themselves.

Chaucer undoubtedly did excellently in hys *Troylus and Cresseid;* of whom, truly I know not, whether to mervaile more, either that he in that mistie time, could see so clearely, or that wee in this cleare age, walke so stumblingly after him. Yet had he great wants, fitte to be forgiven, in so reverent antiquity. I account the *Mirrour of Magistrates,* meetely furnished of beautiful parts; and in the Earle of Surries *Liricks,* many things tasting of a noble birth, and worthy of a noble minde. The *Sheapheards Kalender,* hath much Poetrie in his Eglogues: indeede worthy the reading if I be not deceived. That same framing of his stile, to an old rustick language, I dare not alowe, sith neyther Theocritus in Greeke, Virgill in Latine, nor Sanazar in Italian, did affect it. Besides these, doe I not remember to have seene but fewe, (to speake boldely) printed, that have poeticall sinnewes in them: for proofe whereof, let but most of the verses bee put in Prose, and then aske the meaning: and it will be found, that one verse did but beget another, without ordering at the first, what should be at the last: which becomes a confused masse of words, with a tingling sound of ryme, barely accompanied with reason.

Our Tragedies, and Comedies, (not without cause cried out against,) observing rules, neyther of honest civilitie, nor of skilfull Poetrie, excepting *Gorboduck,* (againe, I say, of those that I have seen,) which notwithstanding, as it is full of stately speeches, and well sounding Phrases, clyming to the height of Seneca his stile, and as full of notable moralitie, which it doth most delightfully teach; and so obtayne the very end of Poesie: yet in troth it is very defectious in the circumstaunces; which greeveth mee, because it might not remaine as an exact model of all Tragedies. For it is faulty both in place, and time, the two necessary companions of all corporall actions. For where the stage should alwaies represent but one place, and the uttermost time presupposed in it, should be, both by Aristotles precept, and common reason, but one day: there is both many dayes, and many places, inartificially imagined. But if it be so in *Gorboduck,* how much more in al the rest? where you shal have Asia of the one side, and Affrick of the other, and so many other under-kingdoms, that the Player, when he commeth in, must ever begin with telling where he is: or els, the tale wil not be conceived. Now ye shal have three Ladies, walke to gather flowers, and then we must beleeve the stage to be a Garden. By and by, we heare newes of shipwracke in the same place, and then wee are to blame, if we accept it not for a Rock.

[21] ["Whatever I attempted to say was verse."]

Upon the backe of that, comes out a hideous Monster, with fire and smoke, and then the miserable beholders, are bounde to take it for a Cave. While in the meantime, two Armies flye in, represented with foure swords and bucklers, and then what harde heart will not receive it for a pitched fielde? Now, of time they are much more liberall, for ordinary it is that two young Princes fall in love. After many traverces, she is got with childe, delivered of a faire boy, he is lost, groweth a man, falls in love, and is ready to get another child, and all this in two hours space: which how absurd it is in sence, even sence may imagine, and Arte hath taught, and all auncient examples justified: and at this day, the ordinary Players in Italie, wil not erre in. Yet wil some bring in an example of *Eunuchus* in Terence, that containeth matter of two dayes, yet far short of twenty yeeres. True it is, and so was it to be playd in two daies, and so fitted to the time it set forth. And though Plautus hath in one place done amisse, let us hit with him, and not misse with him. But they wil say, how then shal we set forth a story, which containeth both many places, and many times? And doe they not knowe, that a Tragedie is tied to the lawes of Poesie, and not of Historie? not bound to follow the storie, but having liberty, either to faine a quite newe matter, or to frame the history, to the most tragicall conveniencie. Againe, many things may be told, which cannot be shewed, if they knowe the difference betwixt reporting and representing. As for example, I may speake, (though I am heere) of Peru, and in speech, digresse from that, to the description of Calicut: but in action, I cannot represent it without Pacolets horse: and so was the manner the Auncients tooke, by some *Nuncius,* to recount thinges done in former time, or other place. Lastly, if they wil represent an history, they must not (as Horace saith) beginne *Ab ovo,*[22] but they must come to the principall poynt of that one action, which they wil represent. By example this wil be best expressed. I have a story of young Polidorus, delivered for safeties sake, with great riches, by his Father Priamus to Polimnestor king of Thrace, in the Troyan war time: Hee after some yeeres, hearing the over-throwe of Priamus, for to make the treasure his owne, murthereth the child: the body of the child is taken up [by] Hecuba; shee the same day, findeth a slight to bee revenged most cruelly of the Tyrant: where nowe would one of our Tragedy writers begin, but with the delivery of the childe? Then should he sayle over into Thrace, and so spend I know not how many yeeres, and travaile numbers of places. But where dooth Euripides? Even with the finding of the body, leaving the rest to be tolde by the spirit of Polidorus. This need no further to be inlarged, the dullest wit may conceive it. But besides these grosse absurdities, how all theyr Playes be neither right Tragedies, nor right Comedies: mingling Kings and Clownes, not because the matter so carrieth it: but thrust in Clownes by head and shoulders, to play a part in majesticall matters, with neither decencie, nor discretion. So as neither the admiration and commiseration, nor the right sportfulnes, is by their mungrell Tragy-comedie obtained. I know Apuleius did some-what so, but that is a thing recounted with space of time, not represented in one moment: and I knowe, the Auncients have one or two examples of Tragy-comedies, as Plautus hath *Amphitrio:* But if we marke them well, we shall find, that they never, or very daintily, match Horn-pypes and Funeralls. So falleth it out, that having indeed no right Comedy, in that comicall part of our Tragedy, we have nothing but scurrility, unwoorthy of any chast eares: or some extreame shew of doltishnes, indeed fit to lift up a loude laughter, and nothing els: where the whole tract of a Comedy, shoulde be full of delight, as the Tragedy shoulde be still maintained, in a well raised admiration. But our Comedians, thinke there is no delight without laughter, which is very wrong, for though laughter may come with delight, yet commeth it not of delight: as though delight should be the cause of laughter, but well may one thing breed both together: nay, rather in themselves, they have as it were, a kind of contrarietie; for delight we scarcely doe, but in things that have a conveniencie to our selves, or to the general nature: laughter, almost ever commeth, of things most disproportioned to our selves, and nature. Delight hath a joy in it, either permanent, or present. Laughter, hath onely a scornful tickling.

For example, we are ravished with delight to see a faire woman, and yet are far from being

22 ["From the egg."]

moved to laughter. We laugh at deformed creatures, wherein certainely we cannot delight. We delight in good chaunces, we laugh at mischaunces; we delight to heare the happines of our friends, or Country; at which he were worthy to be laughed at, that would laugh; wee shall contrarily laugh sometimes, to finde a matter quite mistaken, and goe downe the hill agaynst the byas, in the mouth of some such men, as for the respect of them, one shal be hartely sorry, yet he cannot chuse but laugh; and so is rather pained, then delighted with laughter. Yet deny I not, but that they may goe well together, for as in Alexanders picture well set out, wee delight without laughter, and in twenty mad Anticks we laugh without delight: so in Hercules, painted with his great beard, and furious countenance, in womans attire, spinning at Omphales commaundement, it breedeth both delight and laughter. For the representing of so strange a power in love, procureth delight: and the scornefulnes of the action, stirreth laughter. But I speake to this purpose, that all the end of the comicall part, bee not upon such scornefull matters, as stirreth laughter onely: but mixt with it, that delightful teaching which is the end of Poesie. And the great fault even in that point of laughter, and forbidden plainely by Aristotle, is, that they styrre laughter in sinfull things; which are rather execrable then ridiculous: or in miserable, which are rather to be pittied than scorned. For what is it to make folkes gape at a wretched Begger, or a beggerly Clowne? or against lawe of hospitality, to jest at straungers, because they speake not English so well as wee doe? what do we learne, sith it is certaine

> (*Nil habet infœlix paupertas durius in se,*)
> *Quam quod ridiculos homines facit.*——[23]

But rather a busy loving Courtier, a hartles threatening Thraso. A selfe-wise-seeming schoolemaster. A awry-transformed Traveller. These, if we sawe walke in stage names, which wee play naturally, therein were delightfull laughter, and teaching delightfulnes: as in the other, the Tragedies of Buchanan, doe justly bring forth a divine admiration. But I have lavished out too many wordes of this play matter. I doe it because as they are excelling parts of Poesie, so is there none so much used in England, and none can be more pittifully abused. Which like an unmannerly Daughter, shewing a bad education, causeth her mother Poesies honesty, to bee called in question. Other sorts of Poetry almost have we none, but that Lyricall kind of Songs and Sonnets: which, Lord, if he gave us so good mindes, how well it might be imployed, and with howe heavenly fruite, both private and publique, in singing the prayses of the immortall beauty: the immortall goodnes of that God, who gyveth us hands to write, and wits to conceive, of which we might well want words, but never matter, of which, we could turne our eies to nothing, but we should ever have new budding occasions. But truely many of such writings, as come under the banner of unresistable love, if I were a Mistres, would never perswade mee they were in love: so coldely they apply fiery speeches, as men that had rather red Lovers writings; and so caught up certaine swelling phrases, which hang together, like a man which once tolde mee, the winde was at North, West, and by South, because he would be sure to name windes enowe: then that in truth they feele those passions, which easily (as I think) may be bewrayed, by that same forciblenes, or Energia, (as the Greekes cal it) of the writer. But let this bee a sufficient, though short note, that wee misse the right use of the materiall point of Poesie.

Now, for the out-side of it, which is words, or (as I may tearme it) Diction, it is even well worse. So is that honny-flowing Matron Eloquence, apparelled, or rather disguised, in a Curtizan-like painted affectation: one time with so farre fette words, they may seeme Monsters: but must seeme straungers to any poore English man. Another tyme, with coursing of a Letter, as if they were bound to followe the method of a Dictionary: an other tyme, with figures and flowers, extreamelie winter-starved. But I would this fault were only peculier to Versifiers, and had not as large possession among Prose-printers; and, (which is to be mervailed) among many Schollers, and, (which is to be pittied) among some Preachers. Truly I could wish, if at least I might be so bold, to wish in a thing beyond the reach of my capacity, the diligent imitators of Tullie, and Demosthenes, (most worthy to be imitated) did not so much keep,

[23] ["Unhappy poverty has nothing harder in it than that it makes men ridiculous."]

Nizolian Paper-bookes of their figures and phrases, as by attentive translation (as it were) devoure them whole, and make them wholly theirs: For nowe they cast Sugar and Spice, upon every dish that is served to the table; Like those Indians, not content to weare eare-rings at the fit and naturall place of the eares, but they will thrust Jewels through their nose, and lippes because they will be sure to be fine.

Tullie, when he was to drive out Cateline, as it were with a Thunderbolt of eloquence, often used that figure of repitition, *Vivit vivit? imo Senatum venit &c.*[24] Indeed, inflamed with a well-grounded rage, hee would have his words (as it were) double out of his mouth: and so doe that artificially, which we see men doe in choller naturally. And wee, having noted the grace of those words, hale them in sometime to a familier Epistle, when it were to too much choller to be chollerick. Now for similitudes, in certaine printed discourses, I thinke all Herbarists, all stories of Beasts, Foules, and Fishes, are rifled up, that they come in multitudes, to waite upon any of our conceits; which certainly is as absurd a surfet to the eares, as is possible: for the force of a similitude, not being to proove anything to a contrary Disputer, but onely to explane to a willing hearer, when that is done, the rest is a most tedious pratling: rather over-swaying the memory from the purpose whereto they were applyed, then any whit informing the judgement, already eyther satisfied, or by similitudes not to be satis-fied. For my part, I doe not doubt, when Antonius and Crassus, the great forefathers of Cicero in eloquence, the one (as Cicero testifieth of them) pretended not to know Arte, the other, not to set by it: because with a playne sensiblenes, they might win credit of popular eares; which credit, is the neerest step to perswasion: which perswasion, is the chiefe marke of Oratory; I doe not doubt (I say) but that they used these tracks very sparingly, which who doth generally use, any man may see doth daunce to his owne musick: and so be noted by the audience, more careful to speake curiously, then to speake truly.

Undoubtedly, (at least to my opinion undoubtedly,) I have found in divers smally learned Courtiers, a more sounde stile, then in some professors of learning: of which I can gesse no other cause, but that the Courtier following that which by practise hee findeth fittest to nature, therein, (though he know it not,) doth according to Art, though not by Art: where the other, using Art to shew Art, and not to hide Art, (as in these cases he should doe) flyeth from nature, and indeede abuseth Art.

But what? me thinkes I deserve to be pounded, for straying from Poetrie to Oratorie: but both have such an affinity in this wordish consideration, that I thinke this digression, will make my meaning receive the fuller understanding: which is not to take upon me to teach Poets howe they should doe, but onely finding my selfe sick among the rest, to shewe some one or two spots of the common infection, growne among the most part of Writers: that acknowledging our selves somewhat awry, we may bend to the right use both of matter and manner; whereto our language gyveth us great occasion, beeing indeed capable of any excellent exercising of it. I know, some will say it is a mingled language. And why not so much the better, taking the best of both the other? Another will say it wanteth Grammer. Nay truly, it hath that prayse, that it wanteth not Grammer: for Grammer it might have, but it needes it not; beeing so easie of it selfe, and so voyd of those cumbersome differences of Cases, Genders, Moodes, and Tenses, which I thinke was a peece of the Tower of Babilons curse, that a man should be put to schoole to learne his mother-tongue. But for the uttering sweetly, and properly the conceits of the minde, which is the end of speech, that hath it equally with any other tongue in the world: and is particulerly happy, in compositions of two or three words together, neere the Greeke, far beyond the Latine: which is one of the greatest beauties can be in a language.

Now, of versifying there are two sorts, the one Auncient, the other Moderne: the Auncient marked the quantitie of each silable, and according to that, framed his verse: the Moderne, observing onely number, (with some regarde of the accent,) the chiefe life of it, standeth in that lyke sounding of the words, which we call Ryme. Whether of these be the most excellent, would beare many speeches. The Auncient, (no doubt) more fit for Musick, both words and tune ob-

[24] ["He lives, he lives? Why, he actually comes into the senate."]

serving quantity, and more fit lively to expresse divers passions, by the low and lofty sounde of the well-weyed silable. The latter likewise, with hys Ryme, striketh a certaine musick to the eare: and in fine, sith it dooth delight, though by another way, it obtaines the same purpose: there beeing in eyther sweetnes, and wanting in neither majestie. Truely the English, before any other vulgar language I know, is fit for both sorts: for, for the Ancient, the Italian is so full of Vowels, that it must ever be cumbred with Elisions. The Dutch, so of the other side with Consonants, that they cannot yeeld the sweet slyding, fit for a Verse. The French, in his whole language, hath not one word, that hath his accent in the last silable saving two, called Antepenultima, and little more hath the Spanish: and therefore, very gracelesly may they use Dactiles. The English is subject to none of these defects.

Nowe, for the ryme, though wee doe not observe quantity, yet wee observe the accent very precisely: which other languages, eyther cannot doe, or will not doe so absolutely. That Cæsura, or breathing place in the middest of the verse, neither Italian nor Spanish have, the French, and we, never almost fayle of. Lastly, even the very ryme it selfe, the Italian cannot put in the last silable, by the French named the Masculine ryme, but still in the next to the last, which the French call the Female; or the next before that, which the Italians terme *Sdrucciola.* The example of the former, is *Buono, Suono,* of the *Sdrucciola, Femina, Semina.* The French, of the other side, hath both the Male, as *Bon, Son,* and the Female, as *Plaise, Taise.* But the *Sdrucciola,* hee hath not: where the English hath all three, as *Due, True, Father, Rather, Motion, Potion;* with much more which might be sayd, but that I finde already, the triflingnes of this discourse, is much too much enlarged. So that sith the ever-praise-worthy Poesie, is full of vertue-breeding delightfulnes, and voyde of no gyfte, that ought to be in the noble name of learning: sith the blames laid against it, are either false, or feeble: sith the cause why it is not esteemed in Englande, is the fault of Poet-apes, not Poets: sith lastly, our tongue is most fit to honor Poesie, and to bee honored by Poesie, I conjure you all, that have had the evill lucke to reade this incke-wasting toy of mine, even in the name of the nyne Muses, no more to scorne the sacred misteries of Poesie: no more to laugh at the name of Poets, as though they were next inheritours to Fooles: no more to jest at the reverent title of a Rymer: but to beleeve with Aristotle, that they were the auncient Treasurers, of the Græcians Divinity. To beleeve with Bembus, that that they were first bringers in of all civilitie. To beleeve with Scaliger, that no Philosophers precepts can sooner make you an honest man, then the reading of Virgill. To beleeve with Clauserus, the Translator of Cornutus, that it pleased the heavenly Deitie, by Hesiod and Homer, under the vayle of fables, to give us all knowledge, Logick, Rethorick, Philosophy, naturall, and morall; and *Quid non?* To believe with me, that there are many misteries contained in Poetrie, which of purpose were written darkely, least by prophane wits, it should bee abused. To believe with Landin, that they are so beloved of the Gods, that whatsoever they write, proceeds of a divine fury. Lastly, to beleeve themselves, when they tell you they will make you immortall, by their verses.

Thus doing, your name shal florish in the Printers shoppes; thus doing, you shall bee of kinne to many a poetical Preface; thus doing, you shall be most fayre, most ritch, most wise, most all, you shall dwell upon Superlatives. Thus dooing, though you be *Libertino patre natus,*[25] you shall suddenly grow *Hercules proles:*[26]

Si quid mea carmina possunt.[27]

Thus doing, your soule shal be placed with Dantes Beatrix, or Virgils Anchises. But if, (fie of such a but) you be borne so neere the dull making Cataphract of Nilus, that you cannot heare the Plannet-like Musick of Poetrie, if you have so earth-creeping a mind, that it cannot lift it selfe up, to looke to the sky of Poetry: or rather, by a certaine rusticall disdaine, will become such a Mome, as to be a Momus of Poetry: then, though I will not wish unto you, the Asses eares of Midas, nor to bee driven by

25 ["Born of a freedman."]
26 ["Hercules' offspring."]
27 ["If my poetry wields any power."]

a Poets verses, (as Bubonax was) to hang himselfe, nor to be rimed to death, as is sayd to be doone in Ireland: yet thus much curse I must send you in the behalfe of all Poets, that while you live, you live in love, and never get favour, for lacking skill of a Sonnet: and when you die, your memory die from the earth, for want of an Epitaph.

ALEXANDER POPE: An Essay on Criticism*

PART I

'Tis hard to say, if greater want of skill
Appear in writing or in judging ill;
But, of the two, less dang'rous is th' offence
To tire our patience, than mislead our sense:
Some few in that, but numbers err in this,
Ten censure wrong for one who writes amiss;
A fool might once himself alone expose;
Now one in verse makes many more in prose.
'Tis with our judgments as our watches, none
Go just alike, yet each believes his own.
In poets as true genius is but rare,
True taste as seldom is the critic's share;
Both must alike from heav'n derive their light,
These born to judge, as well as those to write.
Let such teach others who themselves excel,
And censure freely, who have written well.
Authors are partial to their wit, 'tis true,
But are not critics to their judgment too?
Yet, if we look more closely, we shall find
Most have the seeds of judgment in their mind.
Nature affords at least a glimm'ring light;
The lines, tho' touch'd but faintly are drawn right:
But as the slightest sketch, if justly trac'd,
Is by ill colouring but the more disgrac'd,
So by false learning is good sense defac'd:
Some are bewilder'd in the maze of schools,
And some made coxcombs Nature meant but fools:
In search of wit, these lose their common sense,
And then turn critics in their own defence:
Each burns alike, who can, or cannot write,
Or with a rival's, or an eunuch's spite.
All fools have still an itching to deride,
And fain would be upon the laughing side.
If Maevius scribble in Apollo's spite,
There are who judge still worse than he can write.
Some have at first for wits, then poets past,
Turn'd critics next, and prov'd plain fools at last.
Some neither can for wits nor critics pass,
As heavy mules are neither horse nor ass.
Those half-learn's witlings, num'rous in our isle,
As half-form'd insects on the banks of Nile;
Unfinish'd things, one knows not what to call,
Their generation's so equivocal;
To tell them would a hundred tongues require,
Or one vain wit's, that might a hundred tire.
But you who seek to give and merit fame,
And justly bear a Critic's noble name,
Be sure yourself and your own reach to know,
How far your genius, taste, and learning go;
Launch not beyond your depth, but be discreet,
And mark that point where sense and dulness meet.
Nature to all things fix'd the limits fit,
And wisely curb'd proud man's pretending wit.
As on the land while here the ocean gains,
In other parts it leaves wide sandy plains;
Thus in the soul while memory prevails,
The solid pow'r of understanding fails;
Where beams of warm imagination play,
The memory's soft figures melt away.
One science only will one genius fit;
So vast is art, so narrow human wit:
Not only bounded to peculiar arts,
But oft' in those confin'd to single parts.
Like kings we lose the conquests gain'd before,
By vain ambition still to make them more:

* "An Essay on Criticism" was first published in 1711, but it may have been composed as early as 1707.

Each might his sev'ral province well command,
Would all but stoop to what they understand.
First follow Nature, and your judgment frame
By her just standard, which is still the same:
Unerring Nature! still divinely bright,
One clear, unchang'd, and universal light,
Life, force, and beauty, must to all impart,
At once the source, and end, and test of art.
Art from that fund each just supply provides;
Works without show, and without pomp presides:
In some fair body thus th' informing soul
With spirits feeds, with vigour fills the whole;
Each motion guides, and ev'ry nerve sustains,
Itself unseen, but in th' effects remains.
Some, to whom Heav'n in wit has been profuse,
Want as much more, to turn it to its use;
For wit and judgment often are at strife,
Tho' meant each other's aid, like man and wife.
'Tis more to guide, than spur the Muse's steed;
Restrain his fury, than provoke his speed:
The winged courser, like a gen'rous horse,
Shows most true mettle when you check his course.
Those Rules of old discover'd, not devis'd,
Are Nature still, but Nature methodiz'd:
Nature, like liberty, is but restrain'd
By the same laws which first herself ordain'd.
Hear how learn'd Greece her useful rules indites,
When to repress, and when indulge our flights:
High on Parnassus' top her sons she show'd,
And pointed out those arduous paths they trod;
Held from afar, aloft, th' immortal prize,
And urg'd the rest by equal steps to rise.
Just precepts thus from great examples giv'n,
She drew from them what they deriv'd from Heav'n;
The gen'rous critic fann'd the poet's fire,
And taught the world with reason to admire.
Then Criticism the Muse's handmaid prov'd,
To dress her charms, and make her more belov'd:
But following wits from that intention stray'd;
Who could not win the mistress, woo'd the maid;
Against the poets their own arms they turn'd,
Sure to hate most the men from whom they learn'd.
So modern 'pothecaries, taught the art
By doctors' bills to play the doctor's part,
Bold in the practice of mistaken rules,
Prescribe, apply, and call their masters fools.
Some on the leaves of ancient authors prey;
Nor time nor moths e'er spoil'd so much as they:
Some dryly plain, without invention's aid,
Write dull receipts how poems may be made;
These leave the sense, their learning to display,
And those explain the meaning quite away.
You then whose judgment the right course would steer,
Know well each ancient's proper character;
His fable, subject, scope in ev'ry page;
Religion, country, genius of his age:
Without all these at once before your eyes,
Cavil you may, but never criticise.
Be Homer's works your study and delight,
Read them by day, and meditate by night;
Thence form your judgment, thence your maxims bring,
And trace the Muses upward to their spring.
Still with itself compar'd, his text peruse;
And let your comment be the Mantuan Muse.
When first young Maro in his boundless mind
A work t' outlast immortal Rome design'd,
Perhaps he seem'd above the critic's law,
And but from Nature's fountain scorn'd to draw:
But when t' examine every part he came,
Nature and Homer were, he found, the same.
Convinc'd, amaz'd, he checks the bold design,
And rules as strict his labour'd work confine
As if the Stagyrite o'erlook'd each line.
Learn hence for ancient rules a just esteem;
To copy Nature is to copy them.
Some beauties yet no precepts can declare,
For there's a happiness as well as care.
Music resembles poetry; in each
Are nameless graces which no methods teach,
And which a master-hand alone can reach.
If, where the rules not far enough extend,
(Since rules were made but to promote their end)
Some lucky licence answer to the full
Th' intent propos'd, that licence is a rule.
Thus Pegasus, a nearer way to take,
May boldly deviate from the common track.
Great wits sometimes may gloriously offend,
And rise to faults true critics dare not mend;
From vulgar bounds with brave disorder part,
And snatch a grace beyond the reach of art,
Which, without passing thro' the judgment, gains
The heart, and all its end at once attains.
In prospects thus some objects please our eyes,
Which out of Nature's common order rise,

The shapeless rock, or hanging precipice.
But tho' the Ancients thus their rules invade,
(As kings dispense with laws themselves have made)
Moderns, beware! or if you must offend
Against the precept, ne'er transgress its end;
Let it be seldom, and compell'd by need;
And have, at least, their precedent to plead;
The critic else proceeds without remorse,
Seizes your fame, and puts his laws in force.
I know there are, to whose presumptuous thoughts
Those freer beauties, ev'n in them, seem faults.
Some figures monstrous and mis-shap'd appear,
Consider'd singly, or beheld too near,
Which, but proportion'd to their light, or place,
Due distance reconciles to form and grace.
A prudent chief not always must display
His pow'rs in equal ranks, and fair array,
But with th' occasion and the place comply,
Conceal his force, nay, seem sometimes to fly.
Those oft' are stratagems which errors seem,
Nor is it Homer nods but we that dream.
Still green with bays each ancient altar stands,
Above the reach of sacrilegious hands;
Secure from flames, from envy's fiercer rage,
Destructive war, and all-involving age.
See, from each clime, the learn'd their incense bring;
Hear, in all tongues consenting Pæans ring!
In praise so just let ev'ry voice be join'd,
And fill the gen'ral chorus of mankind.
Hail, Bards triumphant! born in happier days;
Immortal heirs of universal praise!
Whose honours with increase of ages grow,
As streams roll down, enlarging as they flow;
Nations unborn your mighty names shall sound,
And worlds applaud, that must not yet be found!
O may some spark of your celestial fire,
The last, the meanest of your sons inspire,
(That on weak wings, from far, pursues your flights;
Glows while he reads, but trembles as he writes,)
To teach vain wits a science little known,
T' admire superior sense, and doubt their own!

PART II

Of all the causes which conspire to blind
Man's erring judgment, and misguide the mind,
What the weak head with strongest bias rules,
Is pride, the never-failing vice of fools.
Whatever Nature has in worth deni'd,
She gives in large recruits of needful pride;
For as in bodies, thus in souls, we find
What wants in blood and spirits, swell'd with wind:
Pride, where wit fails, steps in to our defence,
And fills up all the mighty void of sense:
If once right reason drives that cloud away,
Truth breaks upon us with resistless day.
Trust not yourself; but, your defects to know,
Make use of ev'ry friend—and ev'ry foe.
A little learning is a dang'rous thing;
Drink deep, or taste not the Pierian spring:
There shallow draughts intoxicate the brain,
And drinking largely sobers us again.
Fir'd at first sight with what the Muse imparts,
In fearless youth we tempt the heights of arts,
While from the bounded level of our mind,
Short views we take, nor see the lengths behind;
But more advanc'd, behold with strange surprise,
New distant scenes of endless science rise!
So pleas'd at first the tow'ring Alps we try,
Mount o'er the vales, and seem to tread the sky,
Th' eternal snows appear already past,
And the first clouds and mountains seem the last:
But those attain'd, we tremble to survey
The growing labours of the lengthen'd way;
Th' increasing prospect tires our wand'ring eyes,
Hills peep o'er hills, and Alps on Alps arise!
A perfect judge will read each work of wit
With the same spirit that its author writ;
Survey the whole, nor seek slight faults to find
Where Nature moves, and rapture warms the mind;
Nor lose for that malignant dull delight,
The gen'rous pleasure to be charm'd with wit.
But in such lays as neither ebb nor flow,
Correctly cold, and regularly low,
That, shunning faults, one quiet tenour keep,
We cannot blame indeed—but we may sleep.
In wit, as Nature, what affects our hearts
Is not th' exactness of peculiar parts;
'Tis not a lip, or eye, we beauty call,
But the joint force and full result of all.
Thus when we view some well-proportion'd dome,
(The world's just wonder, and ev'n thine, O Rome!)

No single parts unequally surprise,
All comes united to th' admiring eyes;
No monstrous height, or breadth, or length, appear;
The whole at once is bold, and regular.
Whoever thinks a faultless piece to see,
Thinks what ne'er was, nor is, nor e'er shall be.
In ev'ry work regard the writer's end,
Since none can compass more than they intend;
And if the means be just, the conduct true,
Applause, in spite of trivial faults, is due.
As men of breeding, sometimes men of wit,
T' avoid great errors, must the less commit;
Neglect the rules each verbal critic lays,
For not to know some trifles is a praise.
Most critics, fond of some subservient art,
Still make the whole depend upon a part:
They talk of principles, but notions prize,
And all to one lov'd folly sacrifice.
Once on a time, La Mancha's Knight, they say,
A certain bard encount'ring on the way,
Discours'd in terms as just, with looks as sage,
As e'er could Dennis, of the Grecian stage;
Concluding all were desp'rate sots and fools,
Who durst depart from Aristotle's rules.
Our author, happy in a judge so nice,
Produc'd his play, and begg'd the Knight's advice;
Made him observe the subject, and the plot,
The manners, passions, unities; what not?
All which, exact to rule, were brought about,
Were but a combat in the lists left out.
"What! leave the combat out?" exclaims the Knight.
"Yes, or we must renounce the Stagyrite."
"Not so, by Heav'n!" (he answers in a rage)
"Knights, squires, and steeds, must enter on the stage."
"So vast a throng, the stage can ne'er contain."
"Then build a new, or act it in a plain."
Thus critics of less judgment than caprice,
Curious, not knowing, not exact but nice,
Form short ideas, and offend in arts
(As most in manners) by a love to parts.
Some to Conceit alone their taste confine,
And glitt'ring thoughts struck out at ev'ry line;
Pleas'd with a work where nothing's just or fit;
One glaring chaos and wild heap of wit.
Poets, like painters, thus unskill'd to trace
The naked nature, and the living grace,
With golds and jewels cover ev'ry part,
And hide with ornaments their want of art.
True wit is Nature to advantage dress'd;
What oft' was thought, but ne'er so well express'd;
Something, whose truth convinc'd at sight we find,
That gives us back the image of our mind.
As shades more sweetly recommend the light,
So modest plainness sets off sprightly wit:
For works may have more wit than does them good,
As bodies perish thro' excess of blood.
Others for Language all their care express,
And value books, as women men, for dress:
Their praise is still,—the style is excellent;
The sense, they humbly take upon content.
Words are like leaves, and where they most abound,
Much fruit of sense beneath is rarely found.
False eloquence, like the prismatic glass,
Its gaudy colours spreads on ev'ry place;
The face of Nature we no more survey,
All glares alike, without distinction gay;
But true expression, like th' unchanging sun,
Clears and improves whate'er it shines upon,
It gilds all objects, but it alters none.
Expression is the dress of thought, and still
Appears more decent, as more suitable:
A vile conceit in pompous words express'd
Is like a clown in regal purple dress'd:
For diff'rent styles with diff'rent subjects sort,
As several garbs with country, town, and court.
Some by old words to fame have made pretence,
Ancients in praise, mere Moderns in their sense;
Such labour'd nothings, in so strange a style,
Amaze th' unlearn'd, and make the learned smile.
Unlucky, as Fungoso in the play,
These sparks with aukward vanity display
What the fine gentleman wore yesterday;
And but so mimic ancient wits at best,
As apes our grandsires, in their doublets drest.
In words, as fashions, the same rule will hold;
Alike fantastic, if too new, or old:
Be not the first by whom the new are try'd,
Nor yet the last to lay the old aside.
But most by Numbers judge a poet's song,
And smooth or rough, with them, is right or wrong:

In the bright Muse, tho' thousand charms conspire,
Her voice is all these tuneful fools admire;
Who haunt Parnassus but to please their ear,
Not mend their minds; as some to church repair
Not for the doctrine, but the music there.
These equal syllables alone require,
Tho' oft' the ear the open vowels tire;
While expletives their feeble aid do join,
And ten low words oft' creep in one dull line:
While they ring round the same unvary'd chimes,
With sure returns of still expected rhymes;
Where'er you find "the cooling western breeze,"
In the next line, it "whispers thro' the trees:"
If crystal streams "with pleasing murmurs creep,"
The reader's threaten'd (not in vain) with "sleep:"
Then, at the last and only couplet, fraught
With some unmeaning thing they call a thought,
A needless Alexandrine ends the song,
That, like a wounded snake, drags its slow length along.
Leave such to tune their own dull rhymes, and know
What's roundly smooth, or languishingly slow;
And praise the easy vigour of a line
Where Denham's strength, and Waller's sweetness join.
True ease in writing comes from art, not chance,
As those move easiest who have learn'd to dance.
'Tis not enough no harshness gives offence;
The sound must seem an echo to the sense.
Soft is the strain when zephyr gently blows,
And the smooth stream in smoother numbers flows;
But when loud surges lash the sounding shore,
The hoarse, rough verse should like the torrent roar:
When Ajax strives some rock's vast weight to throw,
The line too labours, and the words move slow:
Not so when swift Camilla scours the plain,
Flies o'er th' unbending corn, and skims along the main.
Hear how Timotheus' vary'd lays surprise,
And bid alternate passions fall and rise,
While at each change, the son of Libyan Jove
Now burns with glory, and then melts with love;
Now his fierce eyes with sparkling fury glow,
Now sighs steal out, and tears begin to flow:
Persians and Greeks like turns of Nature found,
And the world's victor stood subdu'd by sound!
The pow'r of music all our hearts allow,
And what Timotheus was, is Dryden now.
  Avoid extremes, and shun the fault of such
Who still are pleas'd too little or too much.
At ev'ry trifle scorn to take offence,
That always shews great pride, or little sense:
Those heads, as stomachs, are not sure the best,
Which nauseate all, and nothing can digest.
Yet let not each gay turn thy rapture move;
For fools admire, but men of sense approve:
As things seem large which we thro' mists descry,
Dulness is ever apt to magnify.
  Some foreign writers, some our own despise;
The Ancients only, or the moderns prize.
Thus wit, like faith, by each man is apply'd
To one small sect, and all are damn'd beside.
Meanly they seek the blessing to confine,
And force that sun but on a part to shine,
Which not alone the southern wit sublimes,
But ripens spirits in cold northern climes;
Which, from the first has shone on ages past,
Enlights the present, and shall warm the last;
Tho' each may feel increases and decays,
And see now clearer and now darker days;
Regard not then if wit be old or new,
But blame the false, and value still the true.
  Some ne'er advance a judgment of their own,
But catch the spreading notion of the town;
They reason and conclude by precedent,
And own stale nonsense which they ne'er invent.
Some judge of authors' names, not works, and then
Nor praise nor blame the writings, but the men.
Of all this servile herd, the worst is he
That in proud dulness joins with quality;
A constant critic at the great man's board,
To fetch and carry nonsense for my Lord.
What woful stuff this madrigal would be,
In some starv'd hackney sonnetteer, or me!
But let a lord once own the happy lines,
How the wit brightens! how the style refines!
Before his sacred name flies ev'ry fault,
And each exalted stanza teems with thought!
  The vulgar thus thro' imitation err,
As oft the learn'd by being singular;
So much they scorn the crowd, that if the throng
By chance go right, they purposely go wrong:

So schismatics the plain believers quit,
And are but damn'd for having too much wit.
Some praise at morning what they blame at night,
But always think the last opinion right.
A muse by these is like a mistress us'd,
This hour she's idoliz'd, the next abus'd;
While their weak heads, like towns unfortify'd,
'Twixt sense and nonsense daily change their side.
Ask them the cause; they're wiser still they say;
And still tomorrow's wiser than today.
We think our fathers fools, so wise we grow;
Our wiser sons, no doubt, will think us so.
Once school-divines this zealous isle o'erspread;
Who knew most Sentences, was deepest read:
Faith, gospel, all, seem'd made to be disputed,
And none had sense enough to be confuted.
Scotists and Thomists, now in peace remain,
Amidst their kindred cobwebs in Duck Lane.
If faith itself has diff'rent dresses worn,
What wonder modes in wit should take their turn?
Oft' leaving what is natural and fit,
The current folly proves the ready wit;
And authors think their reputation safe,
Which lives as long as fools are pleas'd to laugh.

Some, valuing those of their own side or mind,
Still make themselves the measure of mankind:
Fondly we think we honour merit then,
When we but praise ourselves in other men.
Parties in wit attend on those of state,
And public faction doubles private hate.
Pride, malice, folly, against Dryden rose,
In various shapes of parsons, critics, beaus;
But sense surviv'd when merry jests were past;
For rising merit will buoy up at last.
Might he return, and bless once more our eyes,
New Blackmores and new Milbourns must arise:
Nay, should great Homer lift his awful head,
Zoilus again would start up from the dead.
Envy will merit, as its shade, pursue;
But like a shadow, proves the substance true:
For envy'd wit, like Sol eclips'd, makes known
Th' opposing body's grossness, not its own.
When first that sun too pow'rful beams displays,
It draws up vapours which obscure its rays;
But ev'n those clouds at last adorn its way,
Reflect new glories, and augment the day.

Be thou the first true merit to befriend;
His praise is lost, who stays till all commend.
Short is the date, alas! of modern rhymes,
And 'tis but just to let them live betimes.
No longer now that golden age appears,
When patriarch wits surviv'd a thousand years;
Now length of fame (our second life) is lost,
And bare threescore is all ev'n that can boast;
Our sons their fathers' failing language see,
And such as Chaucer is, shall Dryden be.
So when the faithful pencil has design'd
Some bright idea of the master's mind,
Where a new world leaps out at his command,
And ready Nature waits upon his hand;
When the ripe colours soften and unite,
And sweetly melt into just shade and light;
When mellowing years their full perfection give,
And each bold figure just begins to live,
The treach'rous colours the fair art betray,
And all the bright creation fades away!

Unhappy wit, like most mistaken things,
Atones not for that envy which it brings;
In youth alone its empty praise we boast,
But soon the short-liv'd vanity is lost;
Like some fair flow'r the early spring supplies,
That gaily blooms, but ev'n in blooming dies.
What is this wit, which must our cares employ?
The owner's wife, that other men enjoy;
Then most our trouble still when most admir'd,
And still the more we give, the more requir'd;
Whose fame with pains we guard, but lose with ease,
Sure some to vex, but never all to please;
'Tis what the vicious fear, the virtuous shun,
By fools 'tis hated, and by knaves undone!

If wit so much from ign'rance undergo,
Ah, let not learning too commence its foe!
Of old, those met rewards who could excel,
And such were prais'd who but endeavour'd well:
Tho' triumphs were to gen'rals only due,
Crowns were reserv'd to grace the soldiers too.
Now, they who reach Parnassus' lofty crown,
Employ their pains to spurn some others down;
And while self-love each jealous writer rules,
Contending wits become the sport of fools;
But still the worst with most regret commend,
For each ill author is as bad a friend.
To what base ends, and by what abject ways,
Are mortals urg'd thro' sacred lust of praise!

Ah, ne'er so dire a thirst of glory boast,
Nor in the critic let the man be lost.
Good nature and good sense must ever join;
To err is human, to forgive, divine.
But if in noble minds some dregs remain
Not yet purg'd off, of spleen and sour disdain,
Discharge that rage on more provoking crimes,
Nor fear a dearth in these flagitious times.
No pardon vile obscenity should find,
Tho' wit and art conspire to move your mind;
But dulness with obscenity must prove
As shameful sure as impotence in love.
In the fat age of pleasure, wealth, and ease,
Sprung the rank weed, and thriv'd with large increase:
When love was all an easy monarch's care;
Seldom at council, never in a war,
Jilts rul'd the state, and statesmen farces writ;
Nay, wits had pensions, and young lords had wit;
The fair sat panting at a courtier's play,
And not a mask went unimprov'd away;
The modest fan was lifted up no more,
And virgins smil'd at what they blush'd before.
The foll'wing licence of a foreign reign
Did all the dregs of bold Socinus drain;
Then unbelieving priests reform'd the nation,
And taught more pleasant methods of salvation;
Where Heaven's free subjects might their rights dispute,
Lest God himself should seem too absolute:
Pulpits their sacred satire learn'd to spare,
And Vice admir'd to find a flatt'rer there!
Encourag'd thus, Wit's Titans braved the skies,
And the press groan'd with licens'd blasphemies.
These monsters, Critics! with your darts engage,
Here point your thunder, and exhaust your rage!
Yet shun their fault, who, scandalously nice,
Will needs mistake an author into vice:
All seems infected that th' infected spy,
As all looks yellow to the jaundic'd eye.

PART III

Learn then what morals critics ought to show,
For 'tis but half a judge's task, to know.
'Tis not enough, taste, judgment, learning, join;
In all you speak, let truth and candour shine,
That not alone what to your sense is due
All may allow, but seek your friendship too.
Be silent always when you doubt your sense,
And speak, tho' sure, with seeming diffidence:
Some positive, persisting fops we know,
Who, if once wrong, will needs be always so;
But you with pleasure own your errors past,
And make each day a critique on the last.
'Tis not enough your counsel still be true;
Blunt truths more mischief than nice falsehoods do;
Men must be taught as if you taught them not,
And things unknown propos'd as things forgot.
Without good-breeding truth is disapprov'd;
That only makes superior sense belov'd.
Be niggards of advice on no pretence,
For the worst avarice is that of sense.
With mean complaisance ne'er betray your trust,
Nor be so civil as to prove unjust.
Fear not the anger of the wise to raise;
Those best can bear reproof, who merit praise.
'Twere well might critics still this freedom take,
But Appius reddens at each word you speak,
And stares, tremendous, with a threat'ning eye,
Like some fierce tyrant in old tapestry.
Fear most to tax an Honourable fool,
Whose right it is, uncensur'd, to be dull:
Such, without wit, are poets when they please,
As without learning they can take degrees.
Leave dang'rous truths to unsuccessful satires,
And flattery to fulsome dedicators,
Whom, when they praise, the world believes no more,
Than when they promise to give scribbling o'er.
'Tis best sometimes your censure to restrain,
And charitably let the dull be vain;
Your silence there is better than your spite,
For who can rail so long as they can write?
Still humming on, their drowsy course they keep,
And lash'd so long, like tops, are lash'd asleep.
False steps but help them to renew the race,
As, after stumbling, jades will mend their pace.
What crowds of these, impenitently bold,
In sounds and jingling syllables grown old,
Still run on poets in a raging vein,
Ev'n to the dregs and squeezing of the brain,
Strain out the last dull droppings of their sense,
And rhyme with all the rage of impotence.
Such shameless bards we have; and yet, 'tis true,
There are as mad, abandon'd critics too.

The bookful blockhead, ignorantly read,
With loads of learned lumber in his head,
With his own tongue still edifies his ears,
And always list'ning to himself appears:
All books he reads, and all he reads assails,
From Dryden's Fables down to Durfey's Tales.
With him most authors steal their works, or buy;
Garth did not write his own Dispensary.
Name a new play, and he's the poet's friend,
Nay, show'd his faults—but when would poets mend?
No place so sacred from such fops is barr'd,
Nor is Paul's church more safe than Paul's churchyard:
Nay, fly to altars, there they'll talk you dead;
For fools rush in where angels fear to tread.
Distrustful sense with modest caution speaks,
It still looks home, and short excursions makes;
But rattling nonsense in full volleys breaks,
And never shock'd, and never turn'd aside,
Bursts out, resistless, with a thund'ring tide.

But where's the man, who counsel can bestow,
Still pleas'd to teach, and yet not proud to know?
Unbiass'd, or by favour, or by spite,
Not dully prepossess'd, nor blindly right;
Tho' learn'd, well-bred; and tho' well-bred, sincere;
Modestly bold, and humanly severe;
Who to a friend his faults can freely show,
And gladly praise the merit of a foe?
Bles'd with a taste exact, yet unconfin'd;
A knowledge both of books and human-kind;
Gen'rous converse; a soul exempt from pride;
And love to praise, with reason on his side?

Such once were Critics; such the happy few
Athens and Rome in better ages knew.
The mighty Stagyrite first left the shore,
Spread all his sails, and durst the deeps explore;
He steer'd securely, and discover'd far,
Led by the light of the Maeonian star.
Poets, a race long unconfin'd and free,
Still fond and proud of savage liberty,
Receiv'd his laws, and stood convinc'd 'twas fit,
Who conquer'd Nature, should preside o'er wit.

Horace still charms with graceful negligence,
And without method talks us into sense;
Will, like a friend, familiarly convey
The truest notions in the easiest way.
He, who supreme in judgment, as in wit,
Might boldly censure, as he boldly writ,
Yet judg'd with coolness, tho' he sung with fire;
His precepts teach but what his works inspire.
Our critics take a contrary extreme,
They judge with fury, but they write with phlegm:
Nor suffers Horace more in wrong translations
By wits, than critics in as wrong quotations.

See Dionysius Homer's thoughts refine,
And call new beauties forth from ev'ry line!

Fancy and art in gay Petronius please,
The scholar's learning, with the courtier's ease.

In grave Quintilian's copious work, we find
The justest rules, and clearest method join'd.
Thus useful arms in magazines we place,
All rang'd in order, and dispos'd with grace;
But less to please the eye, than arm the hand,
Still fit for use, and ready at command.

Thee, bold Longinus! all the Nine inspire,
And bless their critic with a poet's fire:
An ardent judge, who, zealous in his trust,
With warmth gives sentence, yet is always just;
Whose own example strengthens all his laws;
And is himself that great Sublime he draws.

Thus long succeeding critics justly reign'd,
Licence repress'd, and useful laws ordain'd.
Learning and Rome alike in empire grew,
And arts still follow'd where her Eagles flew;
From the same foes, at last, both felt their doom,
And the same age saw Learning fall, and Rome.
With Tyranny, then Superstition join'd,
As that the body, this enslav'd the mind;
Much was believ'd, but little understood,
And to be dull was constru'd to be good;
A second deluge Learning thus o'er-run,
And the Monks finish'd what the Goths begun.

At length Erasmus, that great injur'd name,
(The glory of the priesthood, and the shame!)
Stemm'd the wild torrent of a barb'rous age,
And drove those holy Vandals off the stage.

But see! each Muse, in Leo's golden days,
Starts from her trance, and trims her wither'd bays;
Rome's ancient Genius, o'er its ruins spread,
Shakes off the dust, and rears his rev'rend head.
Then Sculpture and her sister arts revive;
Stones leap'd to form, and rocks began to live;
With sweeter notes each rising temple rung;
A Raphael painted, and a Vida sung.

Immortal Vida: on whose honour'd brow
The poet's bays and critic's ivy grow:
Cremona now shall ever boast thy name,
As next in place to Mantua, next in fame!
But soon by impious arms from Latium chas'd,
Their ancient bounds the banish'd Muses pass'd:
Thence arts o'er all the northern world advance,
But critic learning flourish'd most in France;
The rules a nation, born to serve, obeys;
And Boileau still in right of Horace sways.
But we, brave Britons, foreign laws despis'd,
And kept unconquer'd, and unciviliz'd;
Fierce for the liberties of wit, and bold,
We still defy'd the Romans, as of old.
Yet some there were, among the sounder few
Of those who less presum'd, and better knew,
Who durst assert the juster ancient cause,
And here restor'd Wit's fundamental laws.
Such was the Muse, whose rules and practice tell
"Nature's chief master-piece is writing well."
Such was Roscommon, not more learn'd than good,
With manners gen'rous as his noble blood;
To him the wit of Greece and Rome was known,
And ev'ry author's merit, but his own.
Such late was Walsh—the Muse's judge and friend,
Who justly knew to blame or to commend;
To failings mild, but zealous for desert;
The clearest head, and the sincerest heart.
Thus humble praise, lamented Shade! receive;
This praise at least a grateful Muse may give:
The Muse, whose early voice you taught to sing,
Prescrib'd her heights, and prun'd her tender wing,
(Her guide now lost) no more attempts to rise,
But in low numbers short excursions tries;
Content, if hence th' unlearn'd their wants may view,
The learn'd reflect on what before they knew:
Careless of censure, nor too fond of fame;
Still pleas'd to praise, yet not afraid to blame;
Averse alike to flatter, or offend;
Not free from faults, nor yet too vain to mend.

DAVID HUME: Of the Standard of Taste*

THE GREAT variety of Taste, as well as of opinion, which prevails in the world, is too obvious not to have fallen under every one's observation. Men of the most confined knowledge are able to remark a difference of taste in the narrow circle of their acquaintance, even where the persons have been educated under the same government, and have early imbibed the same prejudices. But those, who can enlarge their view to contemplate distant nations and remote ages, are still more surprized at the great inconsistence and contrariety. We are apt to call *barbarous* whatever departs widely from our own taste and apprehension: But soon find the epithet of reproach retorted on us. And the highest arrogance and self-conceit is at last startled, on observing an equal assurance on all sides, and scruples, amidst such a contest of sentiment, to pronounce positively in its own favour.

As this variety of taste is obvious to the most careless enquirer; so will it be found, on examination, to be still greater in reality than in appearance. The sentiments of men often differ with regard to beauty and deformity of all kinds, even while their general discourse is the same. There are certain terms in every language, which import blame, and others praise; and all men, who use the same tongue, must agree in their application of them. Every voice is united in applauding elegance, propriety, simplicity, spirit in writing; and in blaming fustian, affec-

* "Of the Standard of Taste" first appeared in Hume's *Four Dissertations* (1757) and later appeared as Essay XXIII in Volume III of the Green and Grose edition of Hume's *Essays Moral, Political, and Literary* (1875) from which it is here reprinted.

tation, coldness, and a false brilliancy: But when critics come to particulars, this seeming unanimity vanishes; and it is found, that they had affixed a very different meaning to their expressions. In all matters of opinion and science, the case is opposite: The difference among men is there oftener found to lie in generals than in particulars; and to be less in reality than in appearance. An explanation of the terms commonly ends the controversy; and the disputants are surprized to find, that they had been quarrelling, while at bottom they agreed in their judgment.

Those who found morality on sentiment, more than on reason, are inclined to comprehend ethics under the former observation, and to maintain, that, in all questions, which regard conduct and manners, the difference among men is really greater than at first sight it appears. It is indeed obvious, that writers of all nations and all ages concur in applauding justice, humanity, magnanimity, prudence, veracity; and in blaming the opposite qualities. Even poets and other authors, whose compositions are chiefly calculated to please the imagination, are yet found, from Homer down to Fenelon, to inculcate the same moral precepts, and to bestow their applause and blame on the same virtues and vices. This great unanimity is usually ascribed to the influence of plain reason; which, in all these cases, maintains similar sentiments in all men, and prevents those controversies, to which the abstract sciences are so much exposed. So far as the unanimity is real, this account may be admitted as satisfactory: But we must also allow that some part of the seeming harmony in morals may be accounted for from the very nature of language. The word *virtue*, with its equivalent in every tongue, implies praise; as that of *vice* does blame: And no one, without the most obvious and grossest impropriety, could affix reproach to a term, which in general acceptation is understood in a good sense; or bestow applause, where the idiom requires disapprobation. Homer's general precepts, where he delivers any such, will never be controverted; but it is obvious, that, when he draws particular pictures of manners, and represents heroism in Achilles and prudence in Ulysses, he intermixes a much greater degree of ferocity in the former, and of cunning and fraud in the latter, than Fenelon would admit of. The sage Ulysses in the Greek poet seems to delight in lies and fictions, and often employs them without any necessity or even advantage: But his more scrupulous son, in the French epic writer, exposes himself to the most imminent perils, rather than depart from the most exact line of truth and veracity.

The admirers and followers of the *Alcoran* insist on the excellent moral precepts interspersed throughout that wild and absurd performance. But it is to be supposed, that the Arabic words, which correspond to the English, equity, justice, temperance, meekness, charity, were such as, from the constant use of that tongue, must always be taken in a good sense; and it would have argued the greatest ignorance, not of morals, but of language, to have mentioned them with any epithets, besides those of applause and approbation. But would we know, whether the pretended prophet had really attained a just sentiment of morals? Let us attend to his narration; and we shall soon find, that he bestows praise on such instances of treachery, inhumanity, cruelty, revenge, bigotry, as are utterly incompatible with civilized society. No steady rule of right seems there to be attained to; and every action is blamed or praised, so far only as it is beneficial or hurtful to the true believers.

The merit of delivering true general precepts in ethics is indeed very small. Whoever recommends any moral virtues, really does no more than is implied in the terms themselves. That people, who invented the word *charity*, and used it in a good sense, inculcated more clearly and much more efficaciously, the precept, *be charitable*, than any pretended legislator or prophet, who should insert such a *maxim* in his writings. Of all expressions, those, which, together with their other meaning, imply a degree either of blame or approbation, are the least liable to be perverted or mistaken.

It is natural for us to seek a *Standard of Taste;* a rule, by which the various sentiments of men may be reconciled; at least, a decision afforded, confirming one sentiment, and condemning another.

There is a species of philosophy, which cuts off all hopes of success in such an attempt, and represents the impossibility of ever attaining any standard of taste. The difference, it is said, is very wide between judgment and sentiment. All sentiment is right; because sentiment has a reference to nothing beyond itself, and is always real, wherever a man is conscious of it. But all determinations of the understanding are not right; because they have a reference to something beyond themselves, to wit, real matter of fact; and are not always conformable to that standard. Among a thousand different opinions which different men may entertain of the same subject, there is one, and but one, that is just and true; and the only difficulty is to fix and ascertain it. On the contrary, a thousand different sentiments, excited by the same object, are all right: Because no sentiment represents what is really in the object. It only marks a certain conformity or relation between the object and the organs or faculties of the mind; and if that conformity did not really exist, the sentiment could never possibly have being. Beauty is no quality in things themselves: It exists merely in the mind which contemplates them; and each mind perceives a different beauty. One person may even perceive deformity, where another is sensible of beauty; and every individual ought to acquiesce in his own sentiment, without pretending to regulate those of others. To seek the real beauty, or real deformity, is as fruitless an enquiry, as to pretend to ascertain the real sweet or real bitter. According to the disposition of the organs, the same object may be both sweet and bitter; and the proverb has justly determined it to be fruitless to dispute concerning tastes. It is very natural, and even quite necessary, to extend this axiom to mental, as well as bodily taste; and thus common sense, which is so often at variance with philosophy, especially with the sceptical kind, is found, in one instance at least, to agree in pronouncing the same decision.

But though this axiom, by passing into a proverb, seems to have attained the sanction of common sense; there is certainly a species of common sense which opposes it, at least serves to modify and restrain it. Whoever would assert an equality of genius and elegance between Ogilby and Milton, or Bunyan and Addison, would be thought to defend no less an extravagance, than if he had maintained a mole-hill to be as high as Teneriffe, or a pond as extensive as the ocean. Though there may be found persons, who give the preference to the former authors, no one pays attention to such a taste; and we pronounce without scruple the sentiment of these pretended critics to be absurd and ridiculous. The principle of the natural equality of tastes is then totally forgot, and while we admit it on some occasions, where the objects seem near an equality, it appears an extravagant paradox, or rather a palpable absurdity, where objects so disproportioned are compared together.

It is evident that none of the rules of composition are fixed by reasoning *a priori,* or can be esteemed abstract conclusions of the understanding, from comparing those habitudes and relations of ideas, which are eternal and immutable. Their foundation is the same with that of all the practical sciences, experience; nor are they any thing but general observations, concerning what has been universally found to please in all countries and in all ages. Many of the beauties of poetry and even of eloquence are founded on falsehood and fiction, on hyperboles, metaphors, and an abuse or perversion of terms from their natural meaning. To check the sallies of the imagination, and to reduce every expression to geometrical truth and exactness, would be the most contrary to the laws of criticism; because it would produce a work, which, by universal experience, has been found the most insipid and disagreeable. But though poetry can never submit to exact truth, it must be confined by rules of art, discovered to the author either by genius or observation. If some negligent or irregular writers have pleased, they have not pleased by their transgressions of rule or order, but in spite of these transgressions: They have possessed other beauties, which were conformable to just criticism; and the force of these beauties has been able to overpower censure, and give the mind a satisfaction superior to the disgust arising from the blemishes. Ariosto pleases; but not by his monstrous and improbable fictions, by his bizarre mixture of the serious and comic styles, by the want of coherence in his stories, or by the continual interruptions of his narration. He charms by the force and clearness of his expression, by the readiness and variety of his inventions, and by his natural pictures of the passions, especially those of the gay and amorous kind: And however his faults may diminish our satisfaction, they are not able entirely to destroy it. Did our pleasure really arise from those parts of his poem, which we denominate faults, this would be no objection to criticism in general: It would only be an objection to those particular rules of criticism, which would establish such circumstances to be faults, and would represent them as universally blameable. If they are found to please, they cannot be faults; let the pleasure, which they produce, be ever so unexpected and unaccountable.

But though all the general rules of art are founded only on experience and on the observation of the common sentiments of human nature, we must not imagine, that, on every occasion, the feelings of men will be conformable to these rules. Those finer emotions of the mind are of a very tender and delicate nature, and require the concurrence of many favourable circumstances to make them play with facility and exactness, according to their general and established principles. The least exterior hindrance to such small springs, or the least internal disorder, disturbs their motion, and confounds the operation of the whole machine. When we would make an experiment of this nature, and would try the force of any beauty or deformity, we must choose with care a proper time and place, and bring the fancy to a suitable situation and disposition. A perfect serenity of mind, a recollection of thought, a due attention to the object; if any of these circumstances be wanting, our experiment will be fallacious, and we shall be unable to judge of the catholic and universal beauty. The relation, which nature has placed between the form and the sentiment, will at least be more obscure; and it will require greater accuracy to trace and discern it. We shall be able to ascertain its influence not so much from the operation of each particular beauty, as from the durable admiration, which attends those works, that have survived all the caprices of mode and fashion, all the mistakes of ignorance and envy.

The same Homer, who pleased at Athens and Rome two thousand years ago, is still admired at Paris and at London. All the changes of climate, government, religion, and language, have not been able to obscure his glory. Authority or prejudice may give a temporary vogue to a bad poet or orator; but his reputation will never be durable or general. When his compositions are examined by posterity or by foreigners, the enchantment is dissipated, and his faults appear in their true colours. On the contrary, a real genius, the longer his works endure, and the more wide they are spread, the more sincere is the admiration which he meets with. Envy and jealousy have too much place in a narrow circle; and even familiar acquaintance with his person may diminish the applause due to his performances: But when these obstructions are removed, the beauties, which are naturally fitted to excite agreeable sentiments, immediately display their energy; and while the world endures, they maintain their authority over the minds of men.

It appears then, that, amidst all the variety and caprice of taste, there are certain general principles of approbation or blame, whose influence a careful eye may trace in all operations of the mind. Some particular forms or qualities, from the original structure of the internal fabric, are calculated to please, and others displease; and if they fail of their effect in any particular instance, it is from some apparent defect or imperfection in the organ. A man in a fever would not insist on his palate as able to decide concerning flavours; nor would one, affected with the jaundice, pretend to give a verdict with regard to colours. In each creature, there is a sound and defective state; and the former alone can be supposed to afford us a true standard of taste and sentiment. If, in the sound state of the organ, there be an entire or a considerable uniformity of sentiment among men, we may thence derive an idea of the perfect beauty; in like manner as the appearance of objects in day-light, to the eye of a man in health, is denominated their true and real colour, even while colour is allowed to be merely a phantasm of the senses.

Many and frequent are the defects in the internal organs which prevent or weaken the influence of those general principles, on which depends our sentiment of beauty or deformity. Though some objects, by the structure of the mind, be naturally calculated to give pleasure, it is not to be expected, that in every individual the pleasure will be equally felt. Particular incidents and situations occur, which either throw a false light on the objects, or hinder the true from conveying to the imagination the proper sentiment and perception.

One obvious cause, why many feel not the proper sentiment of beauty, is the want of that *delicacy* of imagination, which is requisite to convey a sensibility of those finer emotions. This delicacy every one pretends to: Every one talks of it; and would reduce every kind of taste or sentiment to its standard. But as our intention in this essay is to mingle some light of the understanding with the feeling of sentiment, it will be proper to give a more accurate definition of delicacy, than has hitherto been attempted. And not to draw our philosophy from too profound a source, we shall have recourse to a noted story in *Don Quixote*.

It is with good reason, says Sancho to the squire with the great nose, that I pretend to have a judgment in wine: This is a quality hereditary in our family. Two of my kinsmen were once called to give their opinion of a hogshead, which was supposed to be excellent, being old and of a good vintage. One of them tastes it; considers it; and after mature reflection pronounces the wine to be good, were it not for a small taste of leather, which he perceived in it. The other, after using the same precautions, gives also his verdict in favour of the wine; but with the reserve of a taste of iron, which he could easily distinguish. You cannot imagine how much they were both ridiculed for their judgment. But who laughed in the end? On emptying the hogshead, there was found at the bottom, an old key with a leathern thong tied to it.

The great resemblance between mental and bodily taste will easily teach us to apply this story. Though it be certain that beauty and deformity, more than sweet and bitter, are not qualities in objects, but belong entirely to the sentiment, internal or external; it must be allowed, that there are certain qualities in objects, which are fitted by nature to produce those particular feelings. Now as these qualities may be found in a small degree, or may be mixed and confounded with each other, it often happens, that the taste is not affected with such minute qualities, or is not able to distinguish all the particular flavours, amidst the disorder, in which they are presented. Where the organs are so fine, as to allow nothing to escape them; and at the same time so exact as to perceive every ingredient in the composition: This we call delicacy of taste, where we employ these terms in the literal or metaphorical sense. Here then the general rules of beauty are of use; being drawn from established models, and from the observation of what pleases or displeases, when presented singly and in a high degree: And if the same qualities, in a continued composition and in a smaller degree, affect not the organs with a sensible delight or uneasiness, we exclude the person from all pretensions to this delicacy. To produce these general rules or avowed patterns of composition is like finding the key with the leathern thong; which justified the verdict of Sancho's kinsmen, and confounded those pretended judges who had condemned them. Though the hogshead had never been emptied, the taste of the one was still equally delicate, and that of the other equally dull and languid: But it would have been more difficult to have proved the superiority of the former, to the conviction of every by-stander. In like manner, though the beauties of writing had never been methodized, or reduced to general principles; though no excellent models had ever been acknowledged; the different degrees of taste would still have subsisted, and the judgment of one man been preferable to that of another; but it would not have been so easy to silence the bad critic, who might always insist upon his particular sentiment, and refuse to submit to his antagonist. But when we show him an avowed principle of art; when we illustrate this principle by examples, whose operation, from his own particular taste, he acknowledges to be conformable to the principle; when we prove, that the same principle may be applied to the present case, where he did not perceive or feel its influence: He must conclude, upon the whole, that the fault lies in himself, and that he wants the delicacy, which is requisite to make him sensible of every beauty and every blemish, in any composition or discourse.

It is acknowledged to be the perfection of every sense or faculty, to perceive with exactness its most minute objects, and allow nothing to escape its notice and observation. The smaller the objects are, which become sensible to the eye, the finer is that organ, and the more elaborate its make and composition. A good palate is not tried by strong flavours; but by a mixture of small ingredients, where we are still sensible of each part, notwithstanding its minuteness and its confusion with the rest. In like manner, a quick and acute perception of beauty and deformity must be the perfection of our mental taste; nor can a man be satisfied with himself while he suspects, that any excellence or blemish in a discourse has passed him unobserved. In this case, the perfection of the man, and the perfection of the sense or feeling, are found to be united. A very delicate palate, on many occasions, may be a great inconvenience both to a man himself and to his friends: But a delicate taste of wit or beauty must always be a desirable quality; because it is the source of all the finest and most innocent enjoyments, of which human nature is susceptible. In this decision the sentiments of all mankind are agreed. Wherever you can ascertain a delicacy of taste, it is sure to meet with approbation; and the best way of ascertaining it is to appeal to those models and principles, which have been established by the uniform consent and experience of nations and ages.

But though there be naturally a wide difference in point of delicacy between one person and another, nothing tends further to encrease and improve this talent, than *practice* in a particular art, and the frequent survey or contemplation of a particular species of beauty. When objects of any kind are first presented to the eye or imagination, the sentiment, which attends them, is obscure and confused; and the mind is, in a great measure, incapable of pronouncing concerning their merits or defects. The taste cannot perceive the several excellences of the performance; much less distinguish the particular character of each excellency, and ascertain its quality and degree. If it pronounce the whole in general to be beautiful or deformed, it is the utmost that can be expected; and even this judgment, a person, so unpractised, will be apt to deliver with great hesitation and reserve. But allow him to acquire experience in those objects, his feeling becomes more exact and nice: He not only perceives the beauties and defects of each part, but marks the distinguishing species of each quality, and assigns it suitable praise or blame. A clear and distinct sentiment attends him through the whole survey of the objects; and he discerns that very degree and kind of approbation or displeasure, which each part is naturally fitted to produce. The mist dissipates, which seemed formerly to hang over the object: The organ acquires greater perfection in its operations; and can pronounce, without danger of mistake, concerning the merits of every performance. In a word, the same address and dexterity, which practice gives to the execution of any work, is also acquired by the same means, in the judging of it.

So advantageous is practice to the discernment of beauty, that, before we can give judgment on any work of importance, it will even be requisite, that that very individual performance be more than once perused by us, and be surveyed in different lights with attention and deliberation. There is a flutter or hurry of thought which attends the first perusal of any piece, and which confounds the genuine sentiment of beauty. The relation of the parts is not discerned: The true characters of style are little distinguished: The several perfections and defects seem wrapped up in a species of confusion, and present themselves indistinctly to the imagination. Not to mention, that there is a species of beauty, which, as it is florid and superficial, pleases at first; but being found incompatible with a just expression either of reason or passion, soon palls upon the taste, and is then rejected with disdain, at least rated at a much lower value.

It is impossible to continue in the practice of contemplating any order of beauty, without being frequently obliged to form *comparisons* between the several species and degrees of excellence, and estimating their proportion to each other. A man, who has had no opportunity of comparing the different kinds of beauty, is indeed totally unqualified to pronounce an opinion with regard to any object presented to him. By comparison alone we fix the epithets of praise or blame, and learn how to assign the due degree of each. The coarsest daubing contains a certain lustre of colours and exactness of imitation, which are so far beauties, and would affect the mind of a peasant or Indian with the highest admiration. The most vulgar ballads are not entirely destitute of harmony or nature; and none but a person, familiarized to superior beauties, would pronounce their numbers harsh, or narration uninteresting. A great inferiority of beauty gives pain to a person conversant in the highest excellence of the kind, and is for that reason pronounced a deformity: As the most finished object, with which we are acquainted, is naturally supposed to have reached the pinnacle of perfection, and to be entitled to the highest applause. One acustomed to see, and examine, and weigh the several performances, admired in different ages and nations, can only rate the merits of a work exhibited to his view, and assign its proper rank among the productions of genius.

But to enable a critic the more fully to execute this undertaking, he must preserve his mind free from all *prejudice,* and allow nothing to enter into his consideration, but the very object which is submitted to his examination. We may observe, that every work of art, in order to produce its due effect on the mind, must be surveyed in a certain point of view, and cannot be fully relished by persons, whose situation, real or imaginary, is not conformable to that which is required by the performance. An orator addresses himself to a particular audience, and must have a regard to their particular genius, interests, opinions, passions, and prejudices; otherwise he hopes in vain to govern their resolutions, and inflame their affections. Should they even have entertained some prepossessions against him, however unreasonable, he must not overlook this disadvantage; but, before he enters upon the subject, must endeavour to conciliate their affection, and acquire their good graces. A critic of a different age or nation, who should peruse this discourse, must have all these circumstances in his eye, and must place himself in the same situation as the audience, in order to form a true judgment of the oration. In like manner, when any work is addressed to the public, though I should have a friendship or enmity with the author, I must depart from this situation; and considering myself as a man in general, forget, if possible, my individual being and my peculiar circumstances. A person influenced by prejudice, complies not with this condition; but obstinately maintains his natural position, without placing himself in that point of view, which the performance supposes. If the work be addressed to persons of a different age or nation, he makes no allowance for their peculiar views and prejudices; but, full of the manners of his own age and country, rashly condemns what seemed admirable in the eyes of those for whom alone the discourse was calculated. If the work be executed for the public, he never sufficiently enlarges his comprehension, or forgets his interest as a friend or enemy, as a rival or commentator. By this means, his sentiments are perverted; nor have the same beauties and blemishes the same influence upon him, as if he had imposed a proper violence on his imagination, and had forgotten himself for a moment. So far his taste evidently departs from the true standard; and of consequence loses all credit and authority.

It is well known, that in all questions, submitted to the understanding, prejudice is destructive of sound judgment, and perverts all operations of the intellectual faculties: It is no less contrary to good taste; nor has it less influence to corrupt our sentiment of beauty. It belongs to *good sense* to check its influence in both cases; and in this respect, as well as in many others, reason, if not an essential part of taste, is at least requisite to the operations of this latter faculty. In all the nobler productions of genius, there is a mutual relation and correspondence of parts; nor can either the beauties or blemishes be perceived by him, whose thought is not capacious enough to comprehend all those parts, and compare them with each other, in order to perceive the consistence and uniformity of the whole. Every work of art has also a certain end or purpose, for which it is calculated; and is to be deemed more or less perfect, as it is more or less fitted to attain this end. The object of eloquence is to persuade, of history to instruct, of poetry to please by means of the passions and the imagination. These ends we must carry constantly in our view, when we peruse any performance; and we must be able to judge how far the means employed are adapted to their respective purposes. Besides every kind of composition, even the most poetical, is nothing but a chain of propositions and reasonings; not always, indeed, the justest and most exact, but still plausible and specious, however disguised by the colouring of the imagination. The persons introduced in tragedy and epic poetry, must be represented as reasoning, and thinking, and concluding, and acting, suitably to their character and circumstances; and without judgment, as well as taste and invention, a poet can never hope to succeed in so delicate an undertaking. Not to mention, that the same excellence of faculties which contributes to the improvement of reason, the same clearness of conception, the same exactness of distinction, the same vivacity of apprehension, are essential to the operations of true taste, and are its infallible concomitants. It seldom, or never happens, that a man of sense, who has experience in any art, cannot judge of its beauty; and it is no less rare to meet with a man who has a just taste without a sound understanding.

Thus, though the principles of taste be universal, and, nearly, if not entirely the same in all men; yet few are qualified to give judgment on any work of art, or establish their own sentiment as the standard of beauty. The organs of internal sensation are seldom so perfect as to allow the general principles their full play, and produce a feeling correspondent to those principles. They either labour under some defect, or are vitiated by some disorder; and by that means, excite a sentiment, which may be pronounced erroneous. When the critic has no delicacy, he judges without any distinction, and is only affected by the grosser and more palpable qualities of the object: The finer touches pass unnoticed and disregarded. Where he is not aided by practice, his verdict is attended with confusion and hesitation. Where no comparison has been employed, the most frivolous beauties, such as rather merit the name of defects, are the objects of his admiration. Where he lies under the influence of prejudice, all his natural sentiments are perverted. Where good sense is wanting, he is not qualified to discern the beauties of design and reasoning, which are the highest and most excellent. Under some or other of these imperfections, the generality of men labour; and hence a true judge in the finer arts is observed, even during the most polished ages, to be so rare a character: Strong sense, united to delicate sentiment, improved by practice, perfected by comparison, and cleared of all prejudice, can alone entitle critics to this valuable character; and the joint verdict of such, wherever they are to be found, is the true standard of taste and beauty.

But where are such critics to be found? By what marks are they to be known? How distinguish them from pretenders? These questions are embarrassing; and seem to throw us back into the same uncertainty, from which, during the course of this essay, we have endeavoured to extricate ourselves.

But if we consider the matter aright, these are questions of fact, not of sentiment. Whether any particular person be endowed with good sense and a delicate imagination, free from prejudice, may often be the subject of dispute, and be liable to great discussion and enquiry: But that such a character is valuable and estimable will be agreed in by all mankind. Where these doubts occur, men can do no more than in other disputable questions, which are submitted to the understanding: They must produce the best arguments, that their invention suggests to them; they must acknowledge a true and decisive standard to exist somewhere, to wit, real existence and matter of fact; and they must have indulgence to such as differ from them in their appeals to this standard. It is sufficient for our present purpose, if we have proved, that the taste of all individuals is not upon an equal footing, and that some men in general, however difficult to be particularly pitched upon, will be acknowledged by universal sentiment to have a preference above others.

But in reality the difficulty of finding, even in particulars, the standard of taste, is not so great as it is represented. Though in speculation, we may readily avow a certain criterion in science and deny it in sentiment, the matter is found in practice to be much more hard to ascertain in the former case than in the latter. Theories of abstract philosophy, systems of profound theology, have prevailed during one age: In a successive period, these have been universally exploded: Their absurdity has been detected: Other theories and systems have supplied their place, which again gave place to their successors: And nothing has been experienced more liable to the revolutions of chance and fashion than these pretended decisions of science. The case is not the same with beauties of eloquence and poetry. Just expressions of passion and nature are sure, after a little time, to gain public applause, which they maintain for ever. Aristotle, and Plato, and Epicurus, and Descartes, may successively yield to each other: But Terence and Virgil maintain an universal, undisputed empire over the minds of men. The abstract philosophy of Cicero has lost its credit: The vehemence of his oratory is still the object of our admiration.

Though men of delicate taste be rare, they are easily to be distinguished in society, by the soundness of their understanding and the superiority of their faculties above the rest of mankind. The ascendant, which they acquire, gives a prevalence to that lively approbation, with which they receive any productions of genius, and renders it generally predominant. Many men, when left to themselves, have but a faint and dubious perception of beauty, who yet are capable of relishing any fine stroke, which is pointed out to them. Every convert to the admiration of the real poet or orator is the cause of some new conversion. And though prejudices may prevail for a time, they never unite in celebrating any rival to the true genius, but yield at last to the force of nature and just sentiment. Thus, though a civilized nation may easily be mistaken in the choice of their admired philosopher, they never have been found long to err, in their affection for a favorite epic or tragic author.

But notwithstanding all our endeavours to fix a standard of taste, and reconcile the discordant apprehensions of men, there still remain two sources of variation, which are not sufficient indeed to confound all the boundaries of beauty and deformity, but will often serve to produce a difference in the degrees of our approbation or blame. The one is the different humours of particular men; the other, the particular manners and opinions of our age and country. The general principles of taste are uniform in human nature: Where men vary in their judgments, some defect or perversion in the faculties may commonly be remarked; proceeding either from prejudice, from want of practice, or want of delicacy; and there is just reason for approving one taste, and condemning another. But where there is such a diversity in the internal frame or external situation as is entirely blameless on both sides, and leaves no room to give one the preference above the other; in that case a certain degree of diversity in judgment is unavoidable, and we seek in vain for a standard, by which we can reconcile the contrary sentiments.

A young man, whose passions are warm, will be more sensibly touched with amorous and tender images, than a man more advanced in years, who takes pleasure in wise, philosophical reflections concerning the conduct of life and moderation of the passions. At twenty, Ovid may be the favourite author; Horace at forty; and perhaps Tacitus at fifty. Vainly would we, in such cases, endeavour to enter into the sentiments of others, and divest ourselves of those propensities, which are natural to us. We choose our favourite author as we do our friend, from a conformity of humour and disposition. Mirth or passion, sentiment or reflection; whichever of these most predominates in our temper, it gives us a peculiar sympathy with the writer who resembles us.

One person is more pleased with the sublime; another with the tender; a third with raillery. One has a strong sensibility to blemishes, and is extremely studious of correctness: Another has a more lively feeling of beauties, and pardons twenty absurdities and defects for one elevated or pathetic stroke. The ear of this man is entirely turned towards conciseness and energy; that man is delighted with a copious, rich, and harmonious expression. Simplicity is affected by one; ornament by another. Comedy, tragedy, satire, odes, have each its partizans, who prefer that particular species of writing to all others. It is plainly an error in a critic, to confine his approbation to one species or style of writing, and condemn all the rest. But it is almost impossible not to feel a predilection for that which suits our particular turn and disposition. Such preferences are innocent and unavoidable, and can never reasonably be the object of dispute, because there is no standard, by which they can be decided.

For a like reason, we are more pleased, in the course of our reading, with pictures and characters, that resemble objects which are found in our own age or country, than with those which describe a different set of customs. It is not without some effort, that we reconcile ourselves to the simplicity of ancient manners, and behold princesses carrying water from the spring, and kings and heroes dressing their own victuals. We may allow in general, that the representation of such manners is no fault in the author, nor deformity in the piece; but we are not so sensibly touched with them. For this reason, comedy is not easily transferred from one age or nation to another. A Frenchman or Englishman is not pleased with the *Andria* of Terence, or *Clitia* of Machiavel; where the fine lady, upon whom all the play turns, never once appears to the spectators, but is always kept behind the scenes, suitably to the reserved humour of the ancient Greeks and modern Italians. A man of learning and reflection can make allowance for these peculiarities of manners; but a common audience can never divest themselves so far of their usual ideas and sentiments, as to relish pictures which in no wise resemble them.

But here there occurs a reflection, which may, perhaps, be useful in examining the celebrated controversy concerning ancient and modern learning; where we often find the one side excusing any seeming absurdity in the ancients from the manners of the age, and the other refusing to admit this excuse, or at least, admitting it only as an apology for the author, not for the performance. In my opinion, the proper boundaries in this subject have seldom been fixed between the contending parties. Where any innocent peculiarities of manners are represented, such as those above mentioned, they ought certainly to be admitted; and a man, who is shocked with them, gives an evident proof of false delicacy and refinement. The poet's *monument more durable than brass,* must fall to the ground like common brick or clay, were men to make no allowance for the continual revolutions of manners and customs, and would admit of nothing but what was suitable to the prevailing fashion. Must we throw aside the pictures of our ancestors, because of their ruffs and fardingales? But where the ideas of morality and decency alter from one age to another, and where vicious manners are described, without being marked with the proper characters of blame and disapprobation; this must be allowed to disfigure the poem, and to be a real deformity. I cannot, nor is it proper I should, enter into such sentiments; and however I may excuse the poet, on account of the manners of his age, I never can relish the composition. The want of humanity and of decency, so conspicuous in the characters drawn by several of the ancient poets, even sometimes by Homer and the Greek tragedians, diminishes considerably the merit of their noble performances, and gives modern authors an advantage over them. We are not interested in the fortunes and sentiments of such rough heroes: We are displeased to find the limits of vice and virtue so much confounded: And whatever indulgence we may give to the writer on account of his prejudices, we cannot prevail on ourselves to enter into his sentiments, or bear an affection to characters, which we plainly discover to be blameable.

The case is not the same with moral principles, as with speculative opinions of any kind. These are in continual flux and revolution. The son embraces a different system from the father. Nay, there scarcely is any man, who can boast of great constance and uniformity in this particular. Whatever speculative errors may be found in the polite writings of any age or country, they detract but little from the value of those compositions. There needs but a certain turn of thought or imagination to make us enter into all the opinions, which then prevailed, and relish the sentiments or conclusions derived from them. But a very violent effort is requisite to change our judgment of manners, and excite sentiments of approbation or blame, love or hatred, different from those to which the mind from long custom has been familiarized. And where a man is confident of the rectitude of that moral standard, by which he judges, he is justly jealous of it, and will not pervert the sentiments of his heart for a moment, in complaisance to any writer whatsoever.

Of all speculative errors, those, which regard religion, are the most excusable in compositions of genius; nor is it ever permitted to judge of the civility or wisdom of any people, or even of single persons, by the grossness or refinement of their theological principles. The same good sense, that directs men in the ordinary occurrences of life, is not hearkened to in religious matters, which are supposed to be placed altogether above the cognizance of human reason. On this account, all the absurdities of the pagan system of theology must be overlooked by every critic, who would pretend to form a just notion of ancient poetry; and our posterity, in their turn, must have the same indulgence to their forefathers. No religious principles can ever be imputed as a fault to any poet, while they remain merely principles, and take no such strong possession of his heart, as to lay him under the imputation of *bigotry* or *superstition*. Where that happens, they confound the sentiments of morality, and alter the natural boundaries of vice and virtue. They are therefore eternal blemishes, according to the principle above mentioned; nor are the prejudices and false opinions of the age sufficient to justify them.

It is essential to the Roman Catholic religion to inspire a violent hatred of every other worship, and to represent all pagans, mahometans, and heretics as the objects of divine wrath and vengeance. Such sentiments, though they are in reality very blameable, are considered as virtues by the zealots of that communion, and are represented in their tragedies and epic poems as a kind of divine heroism. This bigotry has disfigured two very fine tragedies of the French theatre, *Polieucte* and *Athalia;* where an intemperate zeal for particular modes of worship is set off with all the pomp imaginable, and forms the predominant character of the heroes. "What is this," says the sublime Joad to Josabet, finding her in discourse with Mathan, the priest of Baal, "does the daughter of David speak to this traitor? Are you not afraid, lest the earth should open and pour forth flames to devour you both? Or lest these holy walls should fall and crush you together? What is his purpose? Why comes that enemy of God hither to poison the air, which we breathe, with his horrid presence?" Such sentiments are received with great applause on the theatre of Paris; but at London the spectators would be full as much pleased to hear Achilles tell Agamemnon, that he was a dog in his forehead, and a deer in his heart, or Jupiter threaten Juno with a sound drubbing, if she will not be quiet.

Religious principles are also a blemish in any polite composition, when they rise up to superstition, and intrude themselves into every sentiment, however remote from any connection with religion. It is no excuse for the poet, that the customs of his country had burthened life with so many religious ceremonies and observances, that no part of it was exempt from that yoke. It must for ever be ridiculous in Petrarch to compare his mistress Laura, to Jesus Christ. Nor is it less ridiculous in that agreeable libertine, Boccace, very seriously to give thanks to God Almighty and the ladies, for their assistance in defending him against his enemies.

SAMUEL JOHNSON: Gray*

THOMAS GRAY, the son of Mr. Philip Gray, a scrivener of London, was born in Cornhill, November 26, 1716. His grammatical education he received at Eton under the care of Mr. Antrobus, his mother's brother, then assistant to Dr. George; and when he left school, in 1734, entered a pensioner at Peterhouse in Cambridge.

The transition from the school to the college is, to most young scholars, the time from which they date their years of manhood, liberty, and happiness; but Gray seems to have been very little delighted with academical gratifications; he liked at Cambridge neither the mode of life nor the fashion of study, and lived sullenly on to the time when his attendance on lectures was no longer required. As he intended to profess the Common Law, he took no degree.

When he had been at Cambridge about five years, Mr. Horace Walpole, whose friendship he had gained at Eton, invited him to travel with

* "Gray" was one of the last of Johnson's Prefaces to *The English Poets* (1779-1781) to be written, and appeared in the tenth and final volume of the series, which was then revised as *Lives of the Poets* (1783).

him as his companion. They wandered through France into Italy; and Gray's Letters contain a very pleasing account of many parts of their journey. But unequal friendships are easily dissolved: at Florence they quarrelled, and parted; and Mr. Walpole is now content to have it told that it was by his fault. If we look however with prejudice on the world, we shall find that men, whose consciousness of their own merit sets them above the compliances of servility, are apt enough in their association with superiors to watch their own dignity with troublesome and punctilious jealousy, and in the fervour of independence to exact that attention which they refuse to pay. Part they did, whatever was the quarrel, and the rest of their travels was doubtless more unpleasant to them both. Gray continued his journey in a manner suitable to his own little fortune, with only an occasional servant.

He returned to England in September 1741, and in about two months afterwards buried his father; who had, by an injudicious waste of money upon a new house, so much lessened his fortune, that Gray thought himself too poor to study the law. He therefore retired to Cambridge, where he soon after became Bachelor of Civil Law; and where, without liking the place or its inhabitants, or professing to like them, he passed, except a short residence in London, the rest of his life.

About this time he was deprived of Mr. West, the son of a chancellor of Ireland, a friend on whom he appears to have set a high value, and who deserved his esteem by the powers which he shews in his Letters, and in the *Ode to May*, which Mr. Mason has preserved, as well as by the sincerity with which, when Gray sent him part of *Agrippina*, a tragedy that he had just begun, he gave an opinion which probably intercepted the progress of the work, and which the judgement of every reader will confirm. It was certainly no loss to the English stage that *Agrippina* was never finished.

In this year (1742) Gray seems first to have applied himself seriously to poetry; for in this year were produced the *Ode to Spring*, his *Prospect of Eton*, and his *Ode to Adversity*. He began likewise a Latin poem, *De Principiis Cogitandi.*

It may be collected from the narrative of Mr. Mason, that his first ambition was to have excelled in Latin poetry: perhaps it were reasonable to wish that he had prosecuted his design; for though there is at present some embarrassment in his phrase, and some harshness in his Lyrick numbers, his copiousness of language is such as very few possess; and his lines, even when imperfect, discover a writer whom practice would quickly have made skilful.

He now lived on at Peterhouse, very little solicitous what others did or thought, and cultivated his mind and enlarged his views without any other purpose than of improving and amusing himself; when Mr. Mason, being elected fellow of Pembroke-hall, brought him a companion who was afterwards to be his editor, and whose fondness and fidelity has kindled in him a zeal of admiration, which cannot be reasonably expected from the neutrality of a stranger and the coldness of a critick.

In this retirement he wrote (1747) an ode on *The Death of Mr. Walpole's Cat;* and the year afterwards attempted a poem of more importance, on *Government and Education,* of which the fragments which remain have many excellent lines.

His next production (1750) was his farfamed *Elegy in the Church-yard*, which, finding its way into a Magazine, first, I believe, made him known to the publick.

An invitation from Lady Cobham about this time gave occasion to an odd composition called *A Long Story,* which adds little to Gray's character.

Several of his pieces were published (1753), with designs, by Mr. Bentley; and, that they might in some form or other make a book, only one side of each leaf was printed. I believe the poems and the plates recommended each other so well, that the whole impression was soon bought. This year he lost his mother.

Some time afterwards (1756) some young men of the college, whose chambers were near his, diverted themselves with disturbing him by frequent and troublesome noises, and, as is said, by pranks yet more offensive and contemptuous. This insolence, having endured it a while, he represented to the governors of the society, among whom perhaps he had no friends; and, finding his complaint little regarded, removed himself to Pembroke-hall.

In 1757 he published *The Progress of Poetry* and *The Bard,* two compositions at which the readers of poetry were at first content to gaze in mute amazement. Some that tried them confessed their inability to understand them, though Warburton said that they were understood as well as the works of Milton and Shakespeare, which it is the fashion to admire. Garrick wrote a few lines in their praise. Some hardy champions undertook to rescue them from neglect, and in a short time many were content to be shewn beauties which they could not see.

Gray's reputation was now so high, that after the death of Cibber, he had the honour of refusing the laurel, which was then bestowed on Mr. Whitehead.

His curiosity, not long after, drew him away from Cambridge to a lodging near the Museum, where he resided near three years, reading and transcribing; and, so far as can be discovered, very little affected by two odes on *Oblivion* and *Obscurity,* in which his Lyrick performances were ridiculed with much contempt and much ingenuity.

When the Professor of Modern History at Cambridge died, he was, as he says, *cockered and spirited up,* till he asked it of lord Bute, who sent him a civil refusal; and the place was given to Mr. Brocket, the tutor of Sir James Lowther.

His constitution was weak, and believing that his health was promoted by exercise and change of place, he undertook (1765) a journey into Scotland, of which his account, so far as it extends, is very curious and elegant; for as his comprehension was ample, his curiosity extended to all the works of art, all the appearances of nature, and all the monuments of past events. He naturally contracted a friendship with Dr. Beattie, whom he found a poet, a philosopher, and a good man. The Mareschal College at Aberdeen offered him the degree of Doctor of Laws, which, having omitted to take it at Cambridge, he thought it decent to refuse.

What he had formerly solicited in vain, was at last given him without solicitation. The Professorship of History became again vacant, and he received (1768) an offer of it from the duke of Grafton. He accepted, and retained it to his death; always designing lectures, but never reading them; uneasy at his neglect of duty, and appeasing his uneasiness with designs of reformation, and with a resolution which he believed himself to have made of resigning the office, if he found himself unable to discharge it.

Ill health made another journey necessary, and he visited (1769) Westmoreland and Cumberland. He that reads his epistolary narration wishes, that to travel, and to tell his travels, had been more of his employment; but it is by studying at home that we must obtain the ability of travelling with intelligence and improvement.

His travels and his studies were now near their end. The gout, of which he had sustained many weak attacks, fell upon his stomach, and, yielding to no medicines, produced strong convulsions, which (July 30, 1771) terminated in death.

His character I am willing to adopt, as Mr. Mason has done, from a Letter written to my friend Mr. Boswell, by the Rev. Mr. Temple, rector of St. Gluvias in Cornwall; and am as willing as his warmest well-wisher to believe it true.

"Perhaps he was the most learned man in Europe. He was equally acquainted with the elegant and profound parts of science, and that not superficially but thoroughly. He knew every branch of history, both natural and civil; had read all the original historians of England, France, and Italy; and was a great antiquarian. Criticism, metaphysicks, morals, politicks, made a principal part of his study; voyages and travels of all sorts were his favourite amusements; and he had a fine taste in painting, prints, architecture, and gardening. With such a fund of knowledge, his conversation must have been equally instructing and entertaining; but he was also a good man, a man of virtue and humanity. There is no character without some speck, some imperfection; and I think the greatest defect in his was an affectation in delicacy, or rather effeminacy, and a visible fastidiousness, or contempt and disdain of his inferiors in science. He also had, in some degree, that weakness which disgusted Voltaire so much in Mr. Congreve: though he seemed to value others chiefly according to the progress they had made in knowledge, yet he could not bear to be considered himself merely as a man of letters; and though without birth, or fortune, or station, his desire was to be looked upon as a private independent gentleman, who read for his amusement. Perhaps it may be said, What signifies so much knowledge, when it produced so little? Is it worth taking so much pains to leave no memorial but a few poems? But let it be considered that Mr. Gray was, to others, at least innocently employed; to himself, certainly beneficially. His time passed agreeably; he was every day making some new acquisition in science; his mind was enlarged, his heart softened, his virtue strengthened; the world and mankind were shewn to him without a mask; and he was taught to consider every thing as trifling, and unworthy of the attention of a wise man, except the pursuit of knowledge and practice of virtue, in that state wherein God hath placed us."

To this character Mr. Mason has added a more particular account of Gray's skill in zoology. He has remarked, that Gray's effeminacy was affected most *before those whom he did not wish to please;* and that he is unjustly charged with making knowledge his sole reason of preference, as he paid his esteem to none whom he did not likewise believe to be good.

What has occurred to me, from the slight inspection of his Letters in which my undertaking has engaged me, is, that his mind had a large grasp; that his curiosity was unlimited, and his judgement cultivated; that he was a man likely to love much where he loved at all, but that he was fastidious and hard to please. His contempt however is often employed, where I hope it will be approved, upon scepticism and infidelity. His short account of Shaftesbury I will insert.

"You say you cannot conceive how lord Shaftesbury came to be a philosopher in vogue; I will tell you: first, he was a lord; secondly, he was as vain as any of his readers; thirdly, men are very prone to believe what they do not understand; fourthly, they will believe any thing at all, provided they are under no obligation to believe it; fifthly, they love to take a new road, even when that road leads no where; sixthly, he was reckoned a fine writer, and seems always to mean more than he said. Would you have any more reasons? An interval of above forty years has pretty well destroyed the charm. A dead lord ranks with commoners: vanity is no longer interested in the matter; for a new road is become an old one."

Mr. Mason has added, from his own knowledge, that though Gray was poor, he was not eager of money; and that, out of the little that he had, he was very willing to help the necessitous.

As a writer he had this peculiarity, that he did not write his pieces first rudely, and then correct them, but laboured every line as it arose in the train of composition; and he had a notion not very peculiar, that he could not write but at certain times, or at happy moments; a fantastick foppery, to which my kindness for a man of learning and of virtue wishes him to have been superior.

Gray's Poetry is now to be considered; and I hope not to be looked on as an enemy to his name, if I confess that I contemplate it with less pleasure than his life.

His *Ode on Spring* has something poetical, both in the language and the thought; but the language is too luxuriant, and the thoughts have nothing new. There has of late arisen a practice of giving to adjectives, derived from substantives, the termination of participles; such as the *cultured* plain, the *daisied* bank; but I was sorry to see, in the lines of a scholar like Gray, the *honied* Spring. The morality is natural, but too stale; the conclusion is pretty.

The poem on the *Cat* was doubtless by its author considered as a trifle, but it is not a happy trifle. In the first stanza *the azure flowers* that *blow,* shew resolutely a rhyme is sometimes made when it cannot easily be found. *Selima,* the *Cat,* is called a nymph, with some violence both to language and sense; but there is good use made of it when it is done; for of the two lines,

> What female heart can gold despise?
> What cat's averse to fish?

the first relates merely to the nymph, and the second only to the cat. The sixth stanza contains a melancholy truth, that *a favourite has no friend;* but the last ends in a pointed sentence of no relation to the purpose; if *what glistered* had been *gold,* the cat would not have gone into the water; and, if she had, would not less have been drowned.

The *Prospect of Eton College* suggests nothing to Gray, which every beholder does not equally think and feel. His supplication to father *Thames*, to tell him who drives the hoop or tosses the ball, is useless and puerile. Father *Thames* has no better means of knowing than himself. His epithet *buxom health* is not elegant; he seems not to understand the word. Gray thought his language more poetical as it was more remote from common use: finding in Dryden *honey redolent of Spring*, an expression that reaches the utmost limits of our language, Gray drove it a little more beyond apprehension, by making *gales* to be *redolent of joy and youth.*

Of the *Ode on Adversity*, the hint was at first taken from *O Diva, gratum quae regis Antium;* [1] but Gray has excelled his original by the variety of his sentiments, and by their moral application. Of this piece, at once poetical and rational, I will not by slight objections violate the dignity.

My process has now brought me to the *Wonderful Wonder of Wonders*, the two Sister Odes; by which, though either vulgar ignorance or common sense at first universally rejected them, many have been since persuaded to think themselves delighted. I am one of those that are willing to be pleased, and therefore would gladly find the meaning of the first stanza of *The Progress of Poetry.*

Gray seems in his rapture to confound the images of *spreading sound and running water.* A *stream of music* may be allowed; but where does *Musick*, however *smooth and strong*, after having visited the *verdant vales, rowl down the steep amain*, so as that *rocks and nodding groves rebellow to the roar?* If this be said of *Musick*, it is nonsense; if it be said of *Water*, it is nothing to the purpose.

The second stanza, exhibiting Mars's car and Jove's eagle, is unworthy of further notice. Criticism disdains to chase a schoolboy to his common-places.

To the third it may likewise be objected, that it is drawn from Mythology, though such as may be more easily assimilated to real life. Idalia's *velvet-green* has something of cant. An epithet or metaphor drawn from Nature ennobles Art; an epithet or metaphor drawn from Art degrades Nature. Gray is too fond of words arbitrarily compounded. *Many-twinkling* was formerly censured as not analogical; we may say *many-spotted*, but scarcely *many-spotting.* This stanza, however, has something pleasing.

Of the second ternary of stanzas, the first endeavours to tell something, and would have told it, had it not been crossed by Hyperion: the second describes well enough the universal prevalence of Poetry; but I am afraid that the conclusion will not rise from the premises. The caverns of the North and the plains of Chili are not the residences of *Glory and generous Shame.* But that Poetry and Virtue go always together is an opinion so pleasing, that I can forgive him who resolves to think it true.

The third stanza sounds big with *Delphi*, and *Egean*, and *Ilissus*, and *Meander*, and *hallowed fountain* and *solemn sound;* but in all Gray's odes there is a kind of cumbrous splendour which we wish away. His position is at last false: in the time of Dante and Petrarch, from whom he derives our first school of Poetry, Italy was overrun by *tyrant power* and *coward vice;* nor was our state much better when we first borrowed the Italian arts.

Of the third ternary, the first gives a mythological birth of Shakespeare. What is said of that mighty genius is true; but is not said happily: the real effects of this poetical power are put out of sight by the pomp of machinery. Where truth is sufficient to fill the mind, fiction is worse than useless; the counterfeit debases the genuine.

His account of Milton's blindness, if we suppose it caused by study in the formation of his poem, a supposition surely allowable, is poetically true, and happily imagined. But the *car* of Dryden, with his *two coursers*, has nothing in it peculiar; it is a car in which any other rider may be placed.

The Bard appears, at the first view, to be, as Algarotti and others have remarked, an imitation of the prophecy of Nereus. Algarotti thinks it superior to its original; and, if preference depends only on the imagery and animation of the two poems, his judgement is right. There is in *The Bard* more force, more thought, and more variety. But to copy is less than to invent, and the copy has been unhappily produced at a wrong time. The fiction of Horace was to the Romans credible; but its revival disgusts us

[1] ["O Goddess who ruleth over pleasing Antium."]

with apparent and unconquerable falsehood. *Incredulus odi.*[2]

To select a singular event, and swell it to a giant's bulk by fabulous appendages of spectres and predictions, has little difficulty, for he that forsakes the probable may always find the marvellous. And it has little use; we are affected only as we believe; we are improved only as we find something to be imitated or declined. I do not see that *The Bard* promotes any truth, moral or political.

His stanzas are too long, especially his epodes; the ode is finished before the ear has learned its measures, and consequently before it can receive pleasure from their consonance and recurrence.

Of the first stanza the abrupt beginning has been celebrated; but technical beauties can give praise only to the inventor. It is in the power of any man to rush abruptly upon his subject, that has read the ballad of *Johnny Armstrong,*

Is there ever a man in all Scotland—

The initial resemblances, or alliterations, *ruin, ruthless, helm or hauberk,* are below the grandeur of a poem that endeavours at sublimity.

In the second stanza *The Bard* is well described; but in the third we have the puerilities of obsolete mythology. When we are told that *Cadwallo hush'd the stormy main,* and that *Modred* made *huge Plinlimmon bow his cloud-top'd head,* attention recoils from the repetition of a tale that, even when it was first heard, was heard with scorn.

The *weaving* of the *winding sheet* he borrowed, as he owns, from the northern Bards; but their texture, however, was very properly the work of female powers, as the art of spinning the thread of life in another mythology. Theft is always dangerous; Gray has made weavers of slaughtered bards, by a fiction outrageous and incongruous. They are then called upon to *Weave the warp, and weave the woof,* perhaps with no great propriety; for it is by crossing the *woof* with the *warp* that men *weave* the *web* or piece; and the first line was dearly bought by the admission of its wretched correspondent, *Give ample room and verge enough.* He has, however, no other line as bad.

The third stanza of the second ternary is commended, I think, beyond its merit. The personification is indistinct. *Thirst* and *Hunger* are not alike; and their features, to make the imagery perfect, should have been discriminated. We are told, in the same stanza, how *towers* are *fed.* But I will no longer look for particular faults; yet let it be observed that the ode might have been concluded with an action of better example; but suicide is always to be had, without expense of thought.

These odes are marked by glittering accumulations of ungraceful ornaments; they strike, rather than please; the images are magnified by affectation; the language is laboured into harshness. The mind of the writer seems to work with unnatural violence. *Double, double, toil and trouble.* He has a kind of strutting dignity, and is tall by walking on tiptoe. His art and his struggle are too visible, and there is too little appearance of ease and nature.

To say that he has no beauties, would be unjust: a man like him, of great learning and great industry, could not but produce something valuable. When he pleases least, it can only be said that a good design was ill directed.

His translations of Northern and Welsh poetry deserve praise; the imagery is preserved, perhaps often improved; but the language is unlike the language of other poets.

In the character of his *Elegy* I rejoice to concur with the common reader; for by the common sense of readers uncorrupted with literary prejudices, after all the refinements of subtilty and the dogmatism of learning, must be finally decided all claim to poetical honours. The *Church-yard* abounds with images which find a mirrour in every mind, and with sentiments to which every bosom returns an echo. The four stanzas beginning *Yet even these bones,* are to me original: I have never seen the notions in any other place; yet he that reads them here, persuades himself that he has always felt them. Had Gray written often thus, it had been vain to blame, and useless to praise him.

[2] ["I hate because I cannot believe."]

PERCY BYSSHE SHELLEY: A Defence of Poetry*

According to one mode of regarding those two classes of mental action, which are called reason and imagination, the former may be considered as mind contemplating the relations borne by one thought to another, however produced, and the latter, as mind acting upon those thoughts so as to colour them with its own light, and composing from them, as from elements, other thoughts, each containing within itself the principle of its own integrity. The one is the τὸ ποιειν,[1] or the principle of synthesis, and has for its objects those forms which are common to universal nature and existence itself; the other is the τὸ λογιζειν,[2] or principle of analysis, and its action regards the relations of things simply as relations; considering thoughts, not in their integral unity, but as the algebraical representations which conduct to certain general results. Reason is the enumeration of quantities already known; imagination is the perception of the value of those quantities, both separately and as a whole. Reason respects the differences, and imagination the similitudes of things. Reason is to imagination as the instrument to the agent, as the body to the spirit, as the shadow to the substance.

Poetry, in a general sense, may be defined to be "the expression of the imagination"; and poetry is connate with the origin of man. Man is an instrument over which a series of external and internal impressions are driven, like the alternations of an ever-changing wind over an Æolian lyre, which move it by their motion to ever-changing melody. But there is a principle within the human being, and perhaps within all sentient beings, which acts otherwise than in the lyre, and produces not melody alone, but harmony, by an internal adjustment of the sounds or motions thus excited to the impressions which excite them. It is as if the lyre could accommodate its chords to the motions of that which strikes them, in a determined proportion of sound; even as the musician can accommodate his voice to the sound of the lyre. A child at play by itself will express its delight by its voice and motions; and every inflexion of tone and every gesture will bear exact relation to a corresponding antitype in the pleasurable impressions which awakened it; it will be the reflected image of that impression; and as the lyre trembles and sounds after the wind has died away, so the child seeks, by prolonging in its voice and motions the duration of the effect, to prolong also a consciousness of the cause. In relation to the objects which delight a child, these expressions are, what poetry is to higher objects. The savage (for the savage is to ages what the child is to years) expresses the emotions produced in him by surrounding objects in a similar manner; and language and gesture, together with plastic or pictorial imitation, become the image of the combined effect of those objects, and of his apprehension of them. Man in society, with all his passions and his pleasures, next becomes the object of the passions and pleasures of man; an additional class of emotions produces an augmented treasure of expressions; and language, gesture, and the imitative arts, become at once the representation and the medium, the pencil and the picture, the chisel and the statue, the chord and the harmony. The social sympathies, or those laws from which, as from its elements, society results, begin to develop themselves from the moment that two human beings co-exist; the future is contained within the present, as the plant within the seed; and equality, diversity, unity, contrast, mutual dependence, become the principles alone capable of affording the motives according to which the

* "A Defence of Poetry" was written in 1821, but it was not published until 1840, and then, presumably, in a rather different form.

[1] ["to make."] [2] ["to reason."]

will of a social being is determined to action, inasmuch as he is social; and constitute pleasure in sensation, virtue in sentiment, beauty in art, truth in reasoning, and love in the intercourse of kind. Hence men, even in the infancy of society, observe a certain order in their words and actions, distinct from that of the objects and the impressions represented by them, all expression being subject to the laws of that from which it proceeds. But let us dismiss those more general considerations which might involve an inquiry into the principles of society itself, and restrict our view to the manner in which the imagination is expressed upon its forms.

In the youth of the world, men dance and sing and imitate natural objects, observing in these actions, as in all others, a certain rhythm or order. And, although all men observe a similar, they observe not the same order, in the motions of the dance, in the melody of the song, in the combinations of language, in the series of their imitations of natural objects. For there is a certain order or rhythm belonging to each of these classes of mimetic representation, from which the hearer and the spectator receive an intenser and purer pleasure than from any other: the sense of an approximation to this order has been called taste by modern writers. Every man in the infancy of art, observes an order which approximates more or less closely to that from which this highest delight results: but the diversity is not sufficiently marked, as that its gradations should be sensible, except in those instances where the predominance of this faculty of approximation to the beautiful (for so we may be permitted to name the relation between this highest pleasure and its cause) is very great. Those in whom it exists in excess are poets, in the most universal sense of the word; and the pleasure resulting from the manner in which they express the influence of society or nature upon their own minds, communicates itself to others, and gathers a sort of reduplication from that community. Their language is vitally metaphorical; that is, it marks the before unapprehended relations of things and perpetuates their apprehension, until the words which represent them, become, through time, signs for portions or classes of thoughts instead of pictures of integral thoughts; and then if no new poets should arise to create afresh the associations which have been thus disorganized, language will be dead to all the nobler purposes of human intercourse. These similitudes or relations are finely said by Lord Bacon to be "the same footsteps of nature impressed upon the various subjects of the world"—and he considers the faculty which perceives them as the storehouse of axioms common to all knowledge. In the infancy of society every author is necessarily a poet, because language itself is poetry; and to be a poet is to apprehend the true and the beautiful, in a word, the good which exists in the relation, subsisting, first between existence and perception, and secondly between perception and expression. Every original language near to its source is in itself the chaos of a cyclic poem: the copiousness of lexicography and the distinctions of grammar are the works of a later age, and are merely the catalogue and the form of the creations of poetry.

But poets, or those who imagine and express this indestructible order, are not only the authors of language and of music, of the dance, and architecture, and statuary, and painting: they are the institutors of laws, and the founders of civil society, and the inventors of the arts of life, and the teachers, who draw into a certain propinquity with the beautiful and the true, that partial apprehension of the agencies of the invisible world which is called religion. Hence all original religions are allegorical, or susceptible of allegory, and, like Janus, have a double face of false and true. Poets, according to the circumstances of the age and nation in which they appeared, were called, in the earlier epochs of the world, legislators, or prophets: a poet essentially comprises and unites both these characters. For he not only beholds intensely the present as it is, and discovers those laws according to which present things ought to be ordered, but he beholds the future in the present, and his thoughts are the germs of the flower and the fruit of latest time. Not that I assert poets to be prophets in the gross sense of the word, or that they can foretell the form as surely as they foreknow the spirit of events: such is the pretence of superstition, which would make poetry an attribute of prophecy, rather than prophecy an attribute to poetry. A poet participates in the eternal, the infinite, and the one; as far as relates to his conceptions, time and place and number are not. The grammatical forms which express the moods of time, and the difference of persons, and the distinction of place, are convertible with respect to the highest poetry without injuring it as poetry; and the choruses of Æschylus, and the Book of Job, and Dante's Paradise, would afford, more than any other writings, examples of this fact, if the limits of this essay did not forbid citation. The creations of sculpture, painting, and music are illustrations still more decisive.

Language, colour, form, and religious and civil habits of action, are all the instruments and materials of poetry; they may be called poetry by that figure of speech which considers the effect as a synonym of the cause. But poetry in a more restricted sense expresses those arrangements of language, and especially metrical language, which are created by that imperial faculty, whose throne is curtained within the invisible nature of man. And this springs from the nature itself of language, which is a more direct representation of the actions and passions of our internal being, and is susceptible of more various and delicate combinations, than colour, form, or motion, and is more plastic and obedient to the control of that faculty of which it is the creation. For language is arbitrarily produced by the imagination, and has relation to thoughts alone; but all other materials, instruments, and conditions of art have relations among each other, which limit and interpose between conception and expression. The former is as a mirror which reflects, the latter as a cloud which enfeebles, the light of which both are mediums of communication. Hence the fame of sculptors, painters, and musicians, although the intrinsic powers of the great masters of these arts may yield in no degree to that of those who have employed language as the hieroglyphic of their thoughts, has never equalled that of poets in the restricted sense of the term; as two performers of equal skill will produce unequal effects from a guitar and a harp. The fame of legislators and founders of religions, so long as their institutions last, alone seems to exceed that of poets in the restricted sense; but it can scarcely be a question, whether, if we deduct the celebrity which their flattery of the gross opinions of the vulgar usually conciliates, together with that which belonged to them in their higher character of poets, any excess will remain.

We have thus circumscribed the word poetry within the limits of that art which is the most familiar and the most perfect expression of the faculty itself. It is necessary, however, to make the circle still narrower, and to determine the distinction between measured and unmeasured language; for the popular division into prose and verse is inadmissible in accurate philosophy.

Sounds as well as thoughts have relation both between each other and towards that which they represent, and a perception of the order of those relations has always been found connected with a perception of the order of the relations of thoughts. Hence the language of poets has ever affected a certain uniform and harmonious recurrence of sound, without which it were not poetry, and which is scarcely less indispensable to the communication of its influence, than the words themselves, without reference to that peculiar order. Hence the vanity of translation; it were as wise to cast a violet into a crucible that you might discover the formal principle of its colour and odour, as seek to transfuse from one language into another the creations of a poet. The plant must spring again from its seed, or it will bear no flower—and this is the burthen of the curse of Babel.

An observation of the regular mode of the recurrence of harmony in the language of poetical minds, together with its relation to music, produced metre, or a certain system of traditional forms of harmony and language. Yet it is by no means essential that a poet should accommodate his language to this traditional form, so that the harmony, which is its spirit, be observed. The practice is indeed convenient and popular, and to be preferred, especially in such composition as includes much action: but every great poet must inevitably innovate upon the example of his predecessors in the exact structure of his peculiar versification. The distinction between poets and prose writers is a vulgar error. The distinction between philosophers and poets has been anticipated. Plato was essentially a poet—the truth and splendour of his imagery, and the melody of his language, are the most intense that it is possible to conceive. He rejected the measure of the epic, dramatic, and lyrical forms, because he sought to kindle a harmony in thoughts divested of shape and action, and he forebore to invent any regular plan of rhythm which would include, under determinate forms, the varied pauses of his style. Cicero sought to imitate the cadence of his periods, but with little success. Lord Bacon was a poet. His language has a sweet and majestic rhythm, which satisfies the sense, no less than the almost superhuman wisdom of his philosophy satisfies the intellect; it is a strain which distends, and then bursts the circumference of the reader's mind, and pours itself forth together with it into the universal element with which it has perpetual sympathy. All the authors of revolutions in opinion are not only necessarily poets as they are inventors, nor even as their words unveil the permanent analogy of things by images which participate in the life of truth; but as their periods are harmonious and rhythmical, and contain in themselves the elements of verse; being the echo of the eternal music. Nor are those supreme poets, who have employed traditional forms of rhythm on account of the form and action of their subjects, less capable of perceiving and teaching the truth of things, than those who have omitted that form. Shakespeare, Dante, and Milton (to confine ourselves to modern writers) are philosophers of the very loftiest power.

A poem is the very image of life expressed in its eternal truth. There is this difference between a story and a poem, that a story is a catalogue of detached facts, which have no other connection than time, place, circumstance, cause and effect; the other is the creation of actions according to the unchangeable forms of human nature, as existing in the mind of the Creator, which is itself the image of all other minds. The one is partial, and applies only to a definite period of time, and a certain combination of events which can never again recur; the other is universal, and contains within itself the germ of a relation to whatever motives or actions have place in the possible varieties of human nature. Time, which destroys the beauty and the use of the story of particular facts, stripped of the poetry which should invest them, augments that of poetry, and for ever develops new and wonderful applications of the eternal truth which it contains. Hence epitomes have been called the moths of just history; they eat out the poetry of it. A story of particular facts is as a mirror which obscures and distorts that which should be beautiful: poetry is a mirror which makes beautiful that which is distorted.

The parts of a composition may be poetical, without the composition as a whole being a poem. A single sentence may be considered as a whole, though it may be found in the midst of a series of unassimilated portions; a single word even may be a spark of inextinguishable thought. And thus all the great historians, Herodotus, Plutarch, Livy, were poets; and although the plan of these writers, especially that of Livy, restrained them from developing this faculty in its highest degree, they made copious and ample amends for their subjection, by filling all the interstices of their subjects with living images.

Having determined what is poetry, and who are poets, let us proceed to estimate its effects upon society.

Poetry is ever accompanied with pleasure: all spirits on which it falls open themselves to receive the wisdom which is mingled with its delight. In the infancy of the world, neither poets themselves nor their auditors are fully aware of the excellence of poetry: for it acts in a divine and unapprehended manner, beyond and above consciousness; and it is reserved for future generations to contemplate and measure the mighty cause and effect in all the strength and splendour of their union. Even in modern times, no living poet ever arrived at the fullness of his fame; the jury which sits in judgment upon a poet, belonging as he does to all time, must be composed of his peers: it must be impanelled by Time from the selectest of the wise of many generations. A poet is a nightingale, who sits in darkness and sings to cheer its own solitude with sweet sounds; his auditors are as men entranced by the melody of an unseen musician, who feel that they are moved and softened, yet know not whence or why. The poems of Homer and his contemporaries were the delight of infant Greece; they were the elements of that social system which is the column upon which all succeding civilization has reposed. Homer embodied the ideal perfection of his age in human character; nor can we doubt that those who read his verses were awakened to an ambition of becoming like Achilles, Hector, and Ulysses: the truth and beauty of friendship, patriotism, and persevering devotion to an object, were unveiled to the depths in these immortal creations: the sentiments of the auditors must have been refined and enlarged by a sympathy with such great and lovely impersonations, until from admiring they imitated, and from imitation they identified themselves with the objects of their admiration. Nor let it be objected, that these characters are remote from moral perfection, and that they can by no means be considered as edifying patterns for general imitation. Every epoch, under names more or less specious, has deified its peculiar errors; Revenge is the naked idol of the worship of a semi-barbarous age; and Self-deceit is the veiled image of unknown evil, before which luxury and satiety lie prostrate. But a poet considers the vices of his contemporaries the temporary dress in which his creations must be arrayed, and which cover without concealing the eternal proportions of their beauty. An epic or dramatic personage is understood to wear them around his soul, as he may the ancient armour or the modern uniform around his body; whilst it is easy to conceive a dress more graceful than either. The beauty of the internal nature cannot be so far concealed by its accidental vesture, but that the spirit of its form shall communicate itself to the very disguise, and indicate the shape it hides from the manner in which it is worn. A majestic form and graceful motions will express themselves through the most barbarous and tasteless costume. Few poets of the highest class have chosen to exhibit the beauty of their conceptions in its naked truth and splendour; and it is doubtful whether the alloy of costume, habit, etc., be not necessary to temper this planetary music for mortal ears.

The whole objection, however, of the immorality of poetry rests upon a misconception of the manner in which poetry acts to produce the moral improvement of man. Ethical science arranges the elements which poetry has created, and propounds schemes and proposes examples of civil and domestic life: nor is it for want of admirable doctrines that men hate, and despise, and censure, and deceive, and subjugate one another. But poetry acts in another and diviner manner. It awakens and enlarges the mind itself by rendering it the receptacle of a thousand unapprehended combinations of thought. Poetry lifts the veil from the hidden beauty of the world, and makes familiar objects be as if they were not familiar; it reproduces all that it represents, and the impersonations clothed in its Elysian light stand thenceforward in the minds of those who have once contemplated them, as memorials of that gentle and exalted content which extends itself over all thoughts and actions with which it co-exists. The great secret of morals is love; or a going out of our nature, and an identification of ourselevs with the beautiful which exists in thought, action, or person, not our own. A man, to be greatly good, must imagine intensely and comprehensively; he must put himself in the place of another and of many others; the pains and pleasures of his species must become his own. The great instrument of moral good is the imagination; and poetry administers to the effect by acting upon the cause. Poetry enlarges the circumference of the imagination by replenishing it with thoughts of ever new delight, which have the power of attracting and assimilating to their own nature all other thoughts, and which form new intervals and interstices whose void for ever craves fresh food. Poetry strengthens the faculty which is the organ of the moral nature of man, in the same manner as exercise strengthens a limb. A poet therefore would do ill to embody his own conceptions of right and wrong, which are usually those of his place and time, in his poetical creations, which participate in neither. By this assumption of the inferior office of interpreting the effect, in which perhaps after all he might acquit himself but imperfectly, he would resign a glory in a participation in the cause. There was little danger that Homer, or any of the eternal poets, should have so far misunderstood themselves as to have abdicated this throne of their widest dominion. Those in whom the poetical faculty, though great, is less intense, as Euripides, Lucan, Tasso, Spenser, have frequently affected a moral aim, and the effect of their poetry is diminished in exact proportion to the degree in which they compel us to advert to this purpose.

Homer and the cyclic poets were followed at a certain interval by the dramatic and lyrical poets of Athens, who flourished contemporaneously with all that is most perfect in the kindred expressions of the poetical faculty; architecture, painting, music, the dance, sculpture, philosophy, and we may add, the forms of civil life. For although the scheme of Athenian society was deformed by many imperfections which the poetry existing in chivalry and Christianity has erased from the habits and institutions of modern Europe, yet never at any other period has so much energy, beauty, and virtue been developed; never was blind strength and stubborn form so disciplined and rendered subject to the will of man, or that will less repugnant to the dictates of the beautiful and the true, as during the century which preceded the death of Socrates. Of no other epoch in the history of our species have we records and fragments stamped so visibly with the image of the divinity in man. But it is poetry alone, in form, in action, or in language, which has rendered this epoch memorable above all others, and the storehouse of examples to everlasting time. For written poetry existed at that epoch simultaneously with the other arts, and it is an idle inquiry to demand which gave and which received the light, which all, as from a common focus, have scattered over the darkest periods of succeeding time. We know no more of cause and effect than a constant conjunction of events: poetry is ever found to coexist with whatever other arts contribute to the happiness and perfection of man. I appeal to what has already been established to distinguish between the cause and the effect.

It was at the period here adverted to, that the drama had its birth; and however a succeeding writer may have equalled or surpassed those few great specimens of the Athenian drama which have been preserved to us, it is indisputable that the art itself never was understood or practised according to the true philosophy of it, as at Athens. For the Athenians employed language, action, music, painting, the dance, and religious institutions, to produce a common effect in the representation of the highest idealisms of passion and of power; each division in the art was made perfect in its kind by artists of the most consummate skill, and was disciplined into a beautiful proportion and unity one towards the other. On the modern stage a few only of the elements capable of expressing the image of the poet's conception are employed at once. We have tragedy without music and dancing; and music and dancing without the highest impersonations of which they are the fit accompaniment, and both without religion and solemnity. Religious institution has indeed been usually banished from the stage. Our system of divesting the actor's face of a mask, on which the many expressions appropriated to his dramatic character might be moulded into one permanent and unchanging expression, is favourable only to a partial and inharmonious effect; it is fit for nothing but a monologue, where all the attention may be directed to some great master of ideal mimicry. The modern practice of blending comedy with tragedy, though liable to great abuse in point of practice, is undoubtedly an extension of the dramatic circle; but the comedy should be as in *King Lear*, universal, ideal, and sublime. It is perhaps the intervention of this principle which determines the balance in favour of *King Lear* against the *Œdipus Tyrannus* or the *Agamemnon*, or, if you will, the trilogies with which they are connected; unless the intense power of the choral poetry, especially that of the latter, should be considered as restoring the equilibrium. *King Lear*, if it can sustain this comparison, may be judged to be the most perfect specimen of the dramatic art existing in the world; in spite of the narrow conditions to which the poet was subjected by the ignorance of the philosophy of the drama which has prevailed in modern Europe. Calderon, in his religious *Autos*, has attempted to fulfil some of the high conditions of dramatic representation neglected by Shakespeare; such as the establishing a relation between the drama and religion, and the accommodating them to music and dancing; but he omits the observation of conditions still more important, and more is lost than gained by the substitution of the rigidly-defined and ever-repeated idealisms of a distorted superstition for the living impersonations of the truth of human passion.

But I digress.—The connection of scenic exhibitions with the improvement or corruption of the manners of men, has been universally recognized; in other words, the presence or absence of poetry in its most perfect and universal form has been found to be connected with good and evil in conduct or habit. The corruption which has been imputed to the drama as an effect, begins, when the poetry employed in its constitution ends: I appeal to the history of manners whether the periods of the growth of the one and the decline of the other have not corresponded with an exactness equal to any example of moral cause and effect.

The drama at Athens, or wheresoever else it may have approached to its perfection, ever co-existed with the moral and intellectual greatness of the age. The tragedies of the Athenian poets are as mirrors in which the spectator beholds himself, under a thin disguise of circumstance, stript of all but that ideal perfection and energy which every one feels to be the internal type of all that he loves, admires, and would become. The imagination is enlarged by a sympathy with pains and passions so mighty, that they distend in their conception the capacity of that by which they are conceived; the good affections are strengthened by pity, indignation, terror and sorrow; and an exalted calm is prolonged from the satiety of this high exercise of them into the tumult of familiar life: even crime is disarmed of half its horror and all its contagion by being represented as the fatal consequence of the unfathomable agencies of nature; error is thus divested of its wilfulness; men can no longer cherish it as the creation of their choice. In a drama of the highest order there is little food for censure or hatred; it teaches rather self-knowledge and self-respect. Neither the eye nor the mind can see itself, unless reflected upon that which it resembles. The drama, so long as it continues to express poetry, is as a prismatic and many-sided mirror, which collects the brightest rays of human nature and divides and reproduces them from the simplicity of these elementary forms, and touches them with majesty and beauty, and multiplies all that it reflects, and endows it with the power of propagating its like wherever it may fall.

But in periods of the decay of social life, the drama sympathizes with that decay. Tragedy becomes a cold imitation of the form of the great masterpieces of antiquity, divested of all harmonious accompaniment of the kindred arts, and often the very form misunderstood, or a weak attempt to teach certain doctrines, which the writer considers as moral truth; and which are usually no more than specious flatteries of some gross vice or weakness, with which the author, in common with his auditors, are infected. Hence what has been called the classical and domestic drama. Addison's *Cato* is a specimen of the one; and would it were not superfluous to cite examples of the other! To such purposes poetry cannot be made subservient. Poetry is a sword of lightning, ever unsheathed, which consumes the scabbard that would contain it. And thus we observe that all dramatic writings of this nature are unimaginative in a singular degree; they affect sentiment and passion, which, divested of imagination, are other names for caprice and appetite. The period in our own history of the grossest degradation of the drama is the reign of Charles II, when all forms in which poetry had been accustomed to be expressed became hymns to the triumph of kingly power over liberty and virtue. Milton stood alone illuminating an age unworthy of him. At such periods the calculating principle pervades all the forms of dramatic exhibition, and poetry ceases to be expressed upon them. Comedy loses its ideal universality: wit succeeds to humour; we laugh from self-complacency and triumph, instead of pleasure; malignity, sarcasm, and contempt succeed to sympathetic merriment; we hardly laugh, but we smile. Obscenity, which is ever blasphemy against the divine beauty in life, becomes, from the very veil which it assumes, more active if less disgusting: it is a monster for which the corruption of society for ever brings forth new food, which it devours in secret.

The drama being that form under which a greater number of modes of expression of poetry are susceptible of being combined than any other, the connexion of poetry and social good is more observable in the drama than in whatever other form. And it is indisputable that the highest perfection of human society has ever corresponded with the highest dramatic excellence; and that the corruption or extinction of the drama in a nation where it has once flourished, is a mark of a corruption of manners, and an extinction of the energies which sustain the soul of social life. But, as Machiavelli says of political institutions, that life may be preserved and renewed, if men should arise capable of bringing back the drama to its principles. And this is true with respect to poetry in its most extended sense: all language, institution and form, require not only to be produced but to be sustained: the office and character of a poet participates in the divine nature as regards providence, no less than as regards creation.

Civil war, the spoils of Asia, and the fatal predominance first of the Macedonian, and then of the Roman arms, were so many symbols of the extinction or suspension of the creative faculty in Greece. The bucolic writers, who found patronage under the lettered tyrants of Sicily and Egypt, were the latest representatives of its most glorious reign. Their poetry is intensely melodious; like the odour of the tuberose, it overcomes and sickens the spirit with excess of sweetness; while the poetry of the preceding age was as a meadow-gale of June, which mingles the fragrance of all the flowers of the field, and adds a quickening and harmonizing spirit of its own which endows the sense with a power of sustaining its extreme delight. The bucolic and erotic delicacy in written poetry is correlative with that softness in statuary, music, and the kindred arts, and even in manners and institutions, which distinguished the epoch to which I now refer. Nor is it the poetic faculty itself, or any mis-application of it, to which this want of harmony is to be imputed. An equal sensibility to the inflence of the senses and the affections is to be found in the writings of Homer and Sophocles: the former, especially, has clothed sensual and pathetic images with irresistible attractions. Their superiority over these succeeding writers consists in the presence of those thoughts which belong to the inner faculties of our nature, not in the absence of those which are connected with the external: their incomparable perfection consists in a harmony of the union of all. It is not what the erotic poets have, but what they have not, in which their imperfection consists. It is not inasmuch as they were poets, but inasmuch as they were not poets, that they can be considered with any plausibility as connected with the corruption of their age. Had that corruption availed so as to extinguish in them the sensibility to pleasure, passion, and natural scenery, which is imputed to them as an imperfection, the last triumph of evil would have been achieved. For the end of social corruption is to destroy all sensibility to pleasure; and, therefore, it is corruption. It begins at the imagination and the intellect as at the core, and distributes itself thence as a paralysing venom, through the affections into the very appetites, until all become a torpid mass in which hardly sense survives. At the approach of such a period, poetry ever addresses itself to those faculties which are the last to be destroyed, and its voice is heard, like the footsteps of Astræa departing from the world. Poetry ever communicates all the pleasure which men are capable of receiving: it is ever still the light of life; the source of whatever of beautiful or generous or true can have place in an evil time. It will readily be confessed that those among the luxurious citizens of Syracuse and Alexandria, who were delighted with the poems of Theocritus, were less cold, cruel, and sensual than the remnant of their tribe. But corruption must utterly have destroyed the fabric of human society before poetry can ever cease. The sacred links of that chain have never been entirely disjoined, which descending through the minds of many men is attached to those great minds, whence as from a magnet the invisible effluence is sent forth, which at once connects, animates, and sustains the life of all. It is the faculty which contains within itself the seeds at once of its own and of social renovation. And let us not circumscribe the effects of the bucolic and erotic poetry within the limits of the sensibility of those to whom it was addressed. They may have perceived the beauty of those immortal compositions, simply as fragments and isolated portions: those who are more finely organized, or, born in a happier age, may recognize them as episodes to that great poem, which all poets, like the co-operating thoughts of one great mind, have built up since the beginning of the world.

The same revolutions within a narrower sphere had place in ancient Rome; but the actions and forms of its social life never seem to have been perfectly saturated with the poetical element. The Romans appear to have considered the Greeks as the selectest treasuries of the selectest forms of manners and of nature, and to have abstained from creating in measured language, sculpture, music, or architecture, anything which might bear a particular relation to their own condition, whilst it should bear a general one to the universal constitution of the world. But we judge from partial evidence, and we judge perhaps partially. Ennius, Varro, Pacuvius, and Accius, all great poets, have been lost. Lucretius is in the highest, and Virgil in a very high sense, a creator. The chosen delicacy of expressions of the latter, are as a mist of light which conceal from us the intense and exceeding truth of his conceptions of nature. Livy is instinct with poetry. Yet Horace, Catullus, Ovid, and generally the other great writers of the Virgilian age, saw man and nature in the mirror of Greece. The institutions also, and the religion of Rome, were less poetical than those of Greece, as the shadow is less vivid than the substance. Hence poetry in Rome seemed to follow, rather than accompany, the perfection of political and domestic society. The true poetry of Rome lived in its institutions; for whatever of beautiful, true, and majestic, they contained, could have sprung only from the faculty which creates the order in which they consist. The life of Camillus, the death of Regulus; the expectation of the senators, in their godlike state, of the victorious Gauls; the refusal of the republic to make peace with Hannibal, after the battle of Cannæ, were not the consequences of a refined calculation of the probable personal advantage to result from such a rhythm and order in the shows of life, to those who were at once the poets and the actors of these immortal dramas. The imagination beholding the beauty of this order, created it out of itself according to its own idea; the consequence was empire, and the reward ever-living fame. These things are not the less poetry, *quia carent vate sacro*.[3] They are the episodes of that cyclic poem written by Time upon the memories of men. The Past, like an inspired rhapsodist, fills the theatre of everlasting generations with their harmony.

At length the ancient system of religion and manners had fulfilled the circle of its revolutions. And the world would have fallen into utter anarchy and darkness, but that there were found poets among the authors of the Christian and chivalric systems of manners and religion, who created forms of opinion and action never before conceived; which, copied into the imaginations of men, became as generals to the bewildered armies of their thoughts. It is foreign to the present purpose to touch upon the evil produced by these systems: except that we protest, on the ground of the principles already established, that no portion of it can be attributed to the poetry they contain.

It is probable that the poetry of Moses, Job, David, Solomon, and Isaiah had produced a great effect upon the mind of Jesus and his disciples. The scattered fragments preserved to us by the biographers of this extraordinary person, are all instinct with the most vivid poetry. But his doctrines seem to have been quickly distorted. At a certain period after the prevalence of a system of opinions founded upon those promulgated by him, the three forms into which Plato had distributed the faculties of mind underwent a sort of apotheosis, and became the object of the worship of the civilized world. Here it is to be confessed that "Light seems to thicken," and

> The crow makes wing to the rooky wood,
> Good things of day begin to droop and drowse,
> And night's black agents to their preys do rouse.

But mark how beautiful an order has sprung from the dust and blood of this fierce chaos! how the world, as from a resurrection, balancing itself on the golden wings of knowledge and of hope, has reassumed its yet unwearied flight into the heaven of time. Listen to the music, unheard by outward ears, which is as a ceaseless and invisible wind, nourishing its everlasting course with strength and swiftness.

The poetry in the doctrines of Jesus Christ, and the mythology and institutions of the Celtic conquerors of the Roman empire, outlived the darkness and the convulsions connected with their growth and victory, and blended themselves in a new fabric of manners and opinion. It is an error to impute the ignorance of the dark ages to the Christian doctrines or the predominance of the Celtic nations. Whatever of evil their agencies may have contained sprang from the extinction of the poetical principle, connected with the progress of despotism and superstition. Men, from causes too intricate to be here discussed, had become insensible and selfish: their own will had become feeble, and yet they were its slaves, and thence the slaves of the will of others: lust, fear, avarice, cruelty, and fraud, characterized a race amongst whom no one was to be found capable of *creating* in form, language, or institution. The moral anomalies of such a state of society are not justly to

3 ["Because they lack the divine poet."]

be charged upon any class of events immediately connected with them, and those events are most entitled to our approbation which could dissolve it most expeditiously. It is unfortunate for those who cannot distinguish words from thoughts, that many of these anomalies have been incorporated into our popular religion.

It was not until the eleventh century that the effects of the poetry of the Christian and chivalric systems began to manifest themselves. The principle of equality had been discovered and applied by Plato in his *Republic*, as the theoretical rule of the mode in which the materials of pleasure and of power produced by the common skill and labour of human beings ought to be distributed among them. The limitations of this rule were asserted by him to be determined only by the sensibility of each, or the utility to result to all. Plato, following the doctrines of Timæus and Pythagoras, taught also a moral and intellectual system of doctrine, comprehending at once the past, the present, and the future condition of man. Jesus Christ divulged the sacred and eternal truths contained in these views to mankind, and Christianity, in its abstract purity, became the exoteric expression of the esoteric doctrines of the poetry and wisdom of antiquity. The incorporation of the Celtic nations with the exhausted population of the south, impressed upon it the figure of the poetry existing in their mythology and institutions. The result was a sum of the action and reaction of all the causes included in it; for it may be assumed as a maxim that no nation or religion can supersede any other without incorporating into itself a portion of that which it supersedes. The abolition of personal and domestic slavery, and the emancipation of women from a great part of the degrading restraints of antiquity, were among the consequences of these events.

The abolition of personal slavery is the basis of the highest political hope that it can enter into the mind of man to conceive. The freedom of women produced the poetry of sexual love. Love became a religion, the idols of whose worship were ever present. It was as if the statues of Apollo and the Muses had been endowed with life and motion, and had walked forth among their worshippers; so that earth became peopled by the inhabitants of a diviner world. The familiar appearance and proceedings of life became wonderful and heavenly, and a paradise was created as out of the wrecks of Eden. And as this creation itself is poetry, so its creators were poets; and language was the instrument of their art: "Galeotto fù il libro, e chi lo scrisse." [4] The Provençal Trouveurs, or inventors, preceded Petrarch, whose verses are as spells, which unseal the inmost enchanted fountains of the delight which is in the grief of love. It is impossible to feel them without becoming a portion of that beauty which we contemplate: it were superfluous to explain how the gentleness and the elevation of mind connected with these sacred emotions can render men more amiable, more generous and wise, and lift them out of the dull vapours of the little world of self. Dante understood the secret things of love even more than Petrarch. His *Vita Nuova* is an inexhaustible fountain of purity of sentiment and language: it is the idealized history of that period, and those intervals of his life which were dedicated to love. His apotheosis of Beatrice in Paradise, and the gradations of his own love and her loveliness, by which as by steps he feigns himself to have ascended to the throne of the Supreme Cause, is the most glorious imagination of modern poetry. The acutest critics have justly reversed the judgment of the vulgar, and the order of the great acts of the *Divine Drama*, in the measure of the admiration which they accord to the Hell, Purgatory, and Paradise. The latter is a perpetual hymn of everlasting love. Love, which found a worthy poet in Plato alone of all the ancients, has been celebrated by a chorus of the greatest writers of the renovated world; and the music has penetrated the caverns of society, and its echoes still drown the dissonance of arms and superstition. At successive intervals, Ariosto, Tasso, Shakespeare, Spenser, Calderon, Rousseau, and the great writers of our own age, have celebrated the dominion of love, planting as it were trophies in the human mind of that sublimest victory over sensuality and force. The true relation borne to each other by the sexes into which human kind is distributed has become less misunderstood; and if the error which confounded diversity with inequality of the powers of the two sexes has been partially recognized in the opinions and institutions of modern Europe, we owe this great benefit to the worship

[4] ["Galeotto was the book and the one who wrote it."]

of which chivalry was the law, and poets the prophets.

The poetry of Dante may be considered as the bridge thrown over the stream of time, which unites the modern and ancient world. The distorted notions of invisible things which Dante and his rival Milton have idealized, are merely the mask and the mantle in which these great poets walk through eternity enveloped and disguised. It is a difficult question to determine how far they were conscious of the distinction which must have subsisted in their minds between their own creeds and that of the people. Dante at least appears to wish to mark the full extent of it by placing Riphæus, whom Virgil calls *justissimus unus,*[5] in Paradise, and observing a most heretical caprice in his distribution of rewards and punishments. And Milton's poem contains within itself a philosophical refutation of that system, of which, by a strange and natural antithesis, it has been a chief popular support. Nothing can exceed the energy and magnificence of the character of Satan as expressed in *Paradise Lost.* It is a mistake to suppose that he could ever have been intended for the popular personification of evil. Implacable hate, patient cunning, and a sleepless refinement of device to inflict the extremest anguish on an enemy, these things are evil; and, although venial in a slave, are not to be forgiven in a tyrant; although redeemed by much that ennobles his defeat in one subdued, are marked by all that dishonours his conquest in the victor. Milton's Devil as a moral being is as far superior to his God, as one who perseveres in some purpose which he has conceived to be excellent in spite of adversity and torture, is to one who in the cold security of undoubted triumph inflicts the most horrible revenge upon his enemy, not from any mistaken notion of inducing him to repent of a perseverance in enmity, but with the alleged design of exasperating him to deserve new torments. Milton has so far violated the popular creed (if this shall be judged to be a violation) as to have alleged no superiority of moral virtue to his God over his Devil. And this bold neglect of a direct moral purpose is the most decisive proof of the supremacy of Milton's genius. He mingled as it were the elements of human nature as colours upon a single pallet, and arranged them in the composition of his great picture according to the laws of epic truth; that is, according to the laws of that principle by which a series of actions of the external universe and of intelligent and ethical beings is calculated to excite the sympathy of succeeding generations of mankind. The *Divina Commedia* and *Paradise Lost* have conferred upon modern mythology a systematic form; and when change and time shall have added one more superstition to the mass of those which have arisen and decayed upon the earth, commentators will be learnedly employed in elucidating the religion of ancestral Europe, only not utterly forgotten because it will have been stamped with the eternity of genius.

[5] ["The one most just."]

Homer was the first and Dante the second epic poet: that is, the second poet, the series of whose creations bore a defined and intelligible relation to the knowledge and sentiment and religion of the age in which he lived, and of the ages which followed it, developing itself in correspondence with their development. For Lucretius had limed the wings of his swift spirit in the dregs of the sensible world; and Virgil, with a modesty that ill became his genius, had affected the fame of an imitator, even whilst he created anew all that he copied; and none among the flock of mock-birds, though their notes were sweet, Apollonius Rhodius, Quintus Calaber, Nonnus, Lucan, Statius, or Claudian, have sought even to fulfil a single condition of epic truth. Milton was the third epic poet. For if the title of epic in its highest sense be refused to the *Æneid,* still less can it be conceded to the *Orlando Furioso,* the *Gerusalemme Liberata,* the *Lusiad,* or the *Fairy Queen.*

Dante and Milton were both deeply penetrated with the ancient religion of the civilized world; and its spirit exists in their poetry probably in the same proportion as its forms survived in the unreformed worship of modern Europe. The one preceded and the other followed the Reformation at almost equal intervals. Dante was the first religious reformer, and Luther surpassed him rather in the rudeness and acrimony, than in the boldness of his censures of papal usurpation. Dante was the first awakener of entranced Europe; he created a language, in itself music and persuasion, out of a chaos of inharmonious barbarisms. He was the congregator of those great spirits who presided over the resurrection of learning; the Lucifer of that starry flock which in the thirteenth century shone forth from republican Italy, as from a heaven, into the darkness of the benighted world. His very words are instinct with spirit; each is as a spark, a burning atom of inextinguishable thought; and many yet lie covered in the ashes of their birth, and pregnant with the lightning which has yet found no conductor. All high poetry is infinite; it is as the first acorn, which contained all oaks potentially. Veil after veil may be undrawn, and the inmost naked beauty of the meaning never exposed. A great poem is a fountain for ever overflowing with the waters of wisdom and delight; and after one person and one age has exhausted all its divine effluence which their peculiar relations enable them to share, another and yet another succeeds, and new relations are ever developed, the source of an unforeseen and an unconceived delight.

The age immediately succeeding to that of Dante, Petrarch, and Boccaccio, was characterized by a revival of painting, sculpture, and architecture. Chaucer caught the sacred inspiration, and the superstructure of English literature is based upon the materials of Italian invention.

But let us not be betrayed from a defence into a critical history of poetry and its influence on society. Be it enough to have pointed out the effects of poets, in the large and true sense of the word, upon their own and all succeeding times.

But poets have been challenged to resign the civic crown to reasoners and mechanists on another plea. It is admitted that the exercise of the imagination is most delightful, but it is alleged that that of reason is more useful. Let us examine as the grounds of this distinction what is here meant by utility. Pleasure or good, in a general sense, is that which the consciousness of a sensitive and intelligent being seeks, and in which, when found, it acquiesces. There are two kinds of pleasure, one durable, universal, and permanent; the other transitory and particular. Utility may either express the means of producing the former or the latter. In the former sense, whatever strengthens and purifies the affections, enlarges the imagination, and adds spirit to sense, is useful. But a narrower meaning may be assigned to the word utility, confining it to express that which banishes the importunity of the wants of our animal nature, the surrounding men with security of life, the dispersing the grosser delusions of superstition, and the conciliating such a degree of mutual forbearance among men as may consist with the motives of personal advantage.

Undoubtedly the promoters of utility, in this limited sense, have their appointed office in society. They follow the footsteps of poets, and copy the sketches of their creations into the book of common life. They make space, and give time. Their exertions are of the highest value, so long as they confine their administration of the concerns of the inferior powers of our nature within the limits due to the superior ones. But whilst the sceptic destroys gross superstitions, let him spare to deface, as some of the French writers have defaced, the eternal truths charactered upon the imaginations of men. Whilst the mechanist abridges, and the political economist combines labour, let them beware that their speculations, for want of correspondence with those first principles which belong to the imagination, do not tend, as they have in modern England, to exasperate at once the extremes of luxury and want. They have exemplified the saying, "To him that hath, more shall be given; and from him that hath not, the little that he hath shall be taken away." The rich have become richer, and the poor have become poorer; and the vessel of the state is driven between the Scylla and Charybdis of anarchy and despotism. Such are the effects which must ever flow from an unmitigated exercise of the calculating faculty.

It is difficult to define pleasure in its highest sense; the definition involving a number of apparent paradoxes. For, from an inexplicable defect of harmony in the constitution of human nature, the pain of the inferior is frequently connected with the pleasures of the superior portions of our being. Sorrow, terror, anguish, despair itself, are often the chosen expressions of an approximation to the highest good. Our sympathy in tragic fiction depends on this principle; tragedy delights by affording a shadow of the pleasure which exists in pain. This is the source also of the melancholy which is inseparable from the sweetest melody. The pleasure that is in sorrow is sweeter than the pleasure of pleasure itself. And hence the saying, "It is better to go to the house of mourning, than to the house of mirth." Not that this highest species of pleasure is necessarily linked with pain. The delight of love and friendship, the ecstasy of the admiration of nature, the joy of the perception and still more of the creation of poetry, is often wholly unalloyed.

The production and assurance of pleasure in this highest sense is true utility. Those who produce and preserve this pleasure are poets or poetical philosophers.

The exertions of Locke, Hume, Gibbon, Voltaire, Rousseau,[6] and their disciples, in favour of oppressed and deluded humanity, are entitled to the gratitude of mankind. Yet it is easy to calculate the degree of moral and intellectual improvement which the world would have exhibited, had they never lived. A little more nonsense would have been talked for a century or two; and perhaps a few more men, women, and children burnt as heretics. We might not at this moment have been congratulating each other on the abolition of the Inquisition in Spain. But it exceeds all imagination to conceive what would have been the moral condition of the world if neither Dante, Petrarch, Boccaccio, Chaucer, Shakespeare, Calderon, Lord Bacon, nor Milton, had ever existed; if Raphael and Michael Angelo had never been born; if the Hebrew poetry had never been translated; if a revival of the study of Greek literature had never taken place; if no monuments of ancient sculpture had been handed down to us; and if the poetry of the religion of the ancient world had been extinguished together with its belief. The human mind could never, except by the intervention of these excitements, have been awakened to the invention of the grosser sciences, and that application of analytical reasoning to the aberrations of society, which it is now attempted to exalt over the direct expression of the inventive and creative faclty itself.

We have more moral, political, and historical wisdom than we know how to reduce into practice; we have more scientific and economical knowledge than can be accommodated to the just distribution of the produce which it multiplies. The poetry in these systems of thought is concealed by the accumulation of facts and calculating processes. There is no want of knowledge respecting what is wisest and best in morals, government, and political economy, or at least, what is wiser and better than what men now practise and endure. But we let "*I dare not* wait upon *I would*, like the poor cat in the adage." We want the creative faculty to imagine that which we know; we want the generous impulse to act that which we imagine; we want the poetry of life: our calculations have outrun conception; we have eaten more than we can digest. The cultivation of those sciences which have enlarged the limits of the empire of men over the external world, has, for want of the poetical faculty, proportionally circumscribed those of the internal world; and man, having enslaved the elements, remains himself a slave. To what but a cultivation of the mechanical arts in a degree disproportioned to the presence of the creative faculty, which is the basis of all knowledge, is to be attributed the abuse of all invention for abridging and combining labour, to the exasperation of the inequality of mankind? From what other cause has it arisen that the discoveries which should have lightened, have added a weight to the curse imposed on Adam? Poetry, and the principle of Self, of which money is the visible incarnation, are the God and Mammon of the world.

The functions of the Poetical faculty are twofold; by one it creates new materials of knowledge, and power, and pleasure; by the other it engenders in the mind a desire to reproduce and arrange them according to a certain rhythm and order which may be called the beautiful and the good. The cultivation of poetry is never more to be desired than at periods when, from an excess of the selfish and calculating principle, the accumulation of the materials of external life exceed the quantity of the power of assimilating them to the internal laws of human nature. The body has then become too unwieldy for that which animates it.

Poetry is indeed something divine. It is at once the centre and circumference of knowledge; it is that which comprehends all science, and that to which all science must be referred. It is at the same time the root and blossom of all other systems of thought; it is that from which all spring, and that which adorns all; and that

[6] Although Rousseau has been thus classed, he was essentially a poet. The others, even Voltaire, were mere reasoners. (Shelley.)

which, if blighted, denies the fruit and the seed, and withholds from the barren world the nourishment and the succession of the scions of the tree of life. It is the perfect and consummate surface and bloom of all things; it is as the odour and the colour of the rose to the texture of the elements which compose it, as the form and splendour of unfaded beauty to the secrets of anatomy and corruption. What were virtue, love, patriotism, friendship—what were the scenery of this beautiful universe which we inhabit; what were our consolations on this side of the grave—and what were our aspirations beyond it, if poetry did not ascend to bring light and fire from those eternal regions where the owl-winged faculty of calculation dare not ever soar? Poetry is not like reasoning, a power to be exerted according to the determination of the will. A man cannot say, "I will compose poetry." The greatest poet even cannot say it; for the mind in creation is as a fading coal, which some invisible influence, like an inconstant wind, awakens to transitory brightness; this power arises from within, like the colour of a flower which fades and changes as it is developed, and the conscious portions of our natures are unprophetic either of its approach or its departure. Could this influence be durable in its original purity and force, it is impossible to predict the greatness of the results; but when composition begins, inspiration is already on the decline, and the most glorious poetry that has ever been communicated to the world is probably a feeble shadow of the original conceptions of the poet. I appeal to the greatest poets of the present day, whether it is not an error to assert that the finest passages of poetry are produced by labour and study. The toil and the delay recommended by critics can be justly interpreted to mean no more than a careful observation of the inspired moments, and an artificial connexion of the spaces between their suggestions by the intertexture of conventional expressions; a necessity only imposed by the limitedness of the poetical faculty itself: for Milton conceived the *Paradise Lost* as a whole before he executed it in portions. We have his own authority also for the muse having "dictated" to him the "unpremeditated song." And let this be an answer to those who would allege the fifty-six various readings of the first line of the *Orlando Furioso*. Compositions so produced are to poetry what mosaic is to painting. This instinct and intuition of the poetical faculty is still more observable in the plastic and pictorial arts: a great statue or picture grows under the power of the artist as a child in the mother's womb; and the very mind which directs the hands in formation is incapable of accounting to itself for the origin, the gradations, or the media of the process.

Poetry is the record of the best and happiest moments of the happiest and best minds. We are aware of evanescent visitations of thought and feeling sometimes associated with place or person, sometimes regarding our own mind alone, and always arising unforeseen and departing unbidden, but elevating and delightful beyond all expression: so that even in the desire and the regret they leave, there cannot but be pleasure, participating as it does in the nature of its object. It is as it were the interpenetration of a diviner nature through our own; but its footsteps are like those of a wind over the sea, which the coming calm erases, and whose traces remain only as on the wrinkled sands which pave it. These and corresponding conditions of being are experienced principally by those of the most delicate sensibility and the most enlarged imagination; and the state of mind produced by them is at war with every base desire. The enthusiasm of virtue, love, patriotism, and friendship is essentially linked with such emotions; and whilst they last, self appears as what it is, an atom to a universe. Poets are not only subject to these experiences as spirits of the most refined organization, but they can colour all that they combine with the evanescent hues of this ethereal world; a word, a trait in the representation of a scene or a passion will touch the enchanted chord, and reanimate, in those who have ever experienced these emotions, the sleeping, the cold, the buried image of the past. Poetry thus makes immortal all that is best and most beautiful in the world; it arrests the vanishing apparitions which haunt the interluminations of life, and veiling them, or in language or in form, sends them forth among mankind, bearing sweet news of kindred joy to those with whom their sisters abide—abide, because there is no portal of expression from the caverns of the spirit which they inhabit into the universe of things. Poetry redeems from decay the visitations of the divinity in man.

Poetry turns all things to loveliness; it exalts the beauty of that which is most beautiful, and it adds beauty to that which is most deformed; it marries exultation and horror, grief and pleasure, eternity and change; it subdues to union under its light yoke all irreconcilable things. It transmutes all that it touches, and every form moving within the radiance of its presence is changed by wondrous sympathy to an incarnation of the spirit which it breathes: its secret alchemy turns to potable gold the poisonous waters which flow from death through life; it strips the veil of familiarity from the world, and lays bare the naked and sleeping beauty, which is the spirit of its forms.

All things exist as they are perceived: at least in relation to the percipient. "The mind is its own place, and of itself can make a heaven of hell, a hell of heaven." But poetry defeats the curse which binds us to be subjected to the accident of surrounding impressions. And whether it spreads its own figured curtain, or withdraws life's dark veil from before the scene of things, it equally creates for us a being within our being. It makes us the inhabitants of a world to which the familiar world is a chaos. It reproduces the common universe of which we are portions and percipients, and it purges from our inward sight the film of familiarity which obscures from us the wonder of our being. It compels us to feel that which we perceive, and to imagine that which we know. It creates anew the universe, after it has been annihilated in our minds by the recurrence of impressions blunted by reiteration. It justifies the bold and true words of Tasso—*Non merita nome di creatore, se non Iddio ed il Poeta.*[7]

A poet, as he is the author to others of the highest wisdom, pleasure, virtue, and glory, so he ought personally to be the happiest, the best, the wisest, and the most illustrious of men. As to his glory, let time be challenged to declare whether the frame of any other institutor of human life be comparable to that of a poet. That he is the wisest, the happiest, and the best, inasmuch as he is a poet, is equally incontrovertible: the greatest poets have been men of the most spotless virtue, of the most consummate prudence, and, if we would look into the interior of their lives, the most fortunate of men: and the exceptions, as they regard those who possessed the poetic faculty in a high yet inferior degree, will be found on consideration to confine rather than destroy the rule. Let us for a moment stoop to the arbitration of popular breath, and usurping and uniting in our own persons the incompatible characters of accuser, witness, judge, and executioner, let us decide without trial, testimony, or form, that certain motives of those who are "there sitting where we dare not soar," are reprehensible. Let us assume that Homer was a drunkard, that Virgil was a flatterer, that Horace was a coward, that Tasso was a madman, that Lord Bacon was a peculator, that Raphael was a libertine, that Spenser was a poet laureate. It is inconsistent with this division of our subject to cite living poets, but posterity has done ample justice to the great names now referred to. Their errors have been weighed and found to have been dust in the balance; if their sins "were as scarlet, they are now white as snow"; they have been washed in the blood of the mediator and redeemer, Time. Observe in what a ludicrous chaos the imputations of real or fictitious crime have been confused in the contemporary calumnies against poetry and poets; consider how little is, as it appears—or appears, as it is; look to your own motives, and judge not, lest ye be judged.

Poetry, as has been said, differs in this respect from logic, that it is not subject to the control of the active powers of the mind, and that its birth and recurrence have no necessary connexion with the consciousness or will. It is presumptuous to determine that these are the necessary conditions of all mental causation, when mental effects are experienced unsusceptible of being referred to them. The frequent recurrence of the poetical power, it is obvious to suppose, may produce in the mind a habit of order and harmony correlative with its own nature and with its effects upon other minds. But in the intervals of inspiration, and they may be frequent without being durable, a poet becomes a man, and is abandoned to the sudden reflux of the influences under which others habitually live. But as he is more delicately organized

[7] ["None but God and the Poet deserves the name of creator."]

than other men, and sensible to pain and pleasure, both his own and that of others, in a degree unknown to them, he will avoid the one and pursue the other with an ardour proportioned to this difference. And he renders himself obnoxious to calumny, when he neglects to observe the circumstances under which these objects of universal pursuit and flight have disguised themselves in one another's garments.

But there is nothing necessarily evil in this error, and thus cruelty, envy, revenge, avarice, and the passions purely evil, have never formed any portion of the popular imputations on the lives of poets.

I have thought it most favourable to the cause of truth to set down these remarks according to the order in which they were suggested to my mind, by a consideration of the subject itself, instead of observing the formality of a polemical reply; but if the view which they contain be just, they will be found to involve a refutation of the arguers against poetry, so far at least as regards the first division of the subject. I can readily conjecture what should have moved the gall of some learned and intelligent writers who quarrel with certain versifiers; I confess myself, like them, unwilling to be stunned by the Theseids of the hoarse Codri of the day. Bavius and Mævius undoubtedly are, as they ever were, insufferable persons. But it belongs to a philosophical critic to distinguish rather than confound.

The first part of these remarks has related to poetry in its elements and principles; and it has been shown, as well as the narrow limits assigned them would permit, that what is called poetry, in a restricted sense, has a common source with all other forms of order and of beauty, according to which the materials of human life are susceptible of being arranged, and which is poetry in an universal sense.

The second part will have for its object an application of these principles to the present state of the cultivation of poetry, and a defence of the attempt to idealize the modern forms of manners and opinions, and compel them into a subordination to the imaginative and creative faculty. For the literature of England, an energetic development of which has ever preceded or accompanied a great and free development of the national will, has arisen as it were from a new birth. In spite of the low-thoughted envy which would undervalue contemporary merit, our own will be a memorable age in intellectual achievements, and we live among such philosophers and poets as surpass beyond comparison any who have appeared since the last national struggle for civil and religious liberty. The most unfailing herald, companion, and follower of the awakening of a great people to work a beneficial change in opinion or institution, is poetry. At such periods there is an accumulation of the power of communicating and receiving intense and impassioned conceptions respecting man and nature. The persons in whom this power resides, may often, as far as regards many portions of their nature, have little apparent correspondence with that spirit of good of which they are the ministers. But even whilst they deny and abjure, they are yet compelled to serve, the power which is seated on the throne of their own soul. It is impossible to read the compositions of the most celebrated writers of the present day without being startled with the electric life which burns within their words. They measure the circumference and sound the depths of human nature with a comprehensive and all-penetrating spirit, and they are themselves perhaps the most sincerely astonished at its manifestations; for it is less their spirit than the spirit of the age. Poets are the hierophants of an unapprehended inspiration; the mirrors of the gigantic shadows which futurity casts upon the present; the words which express what they understand not; the trumpets which sing to battle, and feel not what they inspire; the influence which is moved not, but moves. Poets are the unacknowledged legislators of the world.

THOMAS DE QUINCEY:

On the Knocking at the Gate in "Macbeth"*

FROM my boyish days I had always felt a great perplexity on one point in *Macbeth*. It was this:—the knocking at the gate which succeeds to the murder of Duncan produced to my feelings an effect for which I never could account. The effect was that it reflected back upon the murderer a peculiar awfulness and a depth of solemnity; yet, however obstinately I endeavored with my understanding to comprehend this, for many years I never could see *why* it should produce such an effect.

Here I pause for one moment to exhort the reader never to pay any attention to his understanding when it stands in opposition to any other faculty of his mind. The mere understanding, however useful and indispensable, is the meanest faculty in the human mind and the most to be distrusted; and yet the great majority of people trust to nothing else,—which may do for ordinary life, but not for philosophical purposes. Of this, out of ten thousand instances that I might produce, I will cite one. Ask of any person whatsoever who is not previously prepared for the demand by a knowledge of perspective, to draw in the rudest way the commonest appearance which depends upon the laws of that science—as, for instance, to represent the effect of two walls standing at right angles to each other, or the appearance of the houses on each side of a street, as seen by a person looking down the street from one extremity. Now, in all cases, unless the person has happened to observe in pictures how it is that artists produce these effects, he will be utterly unable to make the smallest approximation to it. Yet why? For he has actually seen the effect every day of his life. The reason is that he allows his understanding to overrule his eyes. His understanding, which includes no intuitive knowledge of the laws of vision, can furnish him with no reason why a line which is known and can be proved to be a horizontal line should not *appear* a horizontal line; a line that made any angle with the perpendicular less than a right angle would seem to him to indicate that his houses were all tumbling down together. Accordingly he makes the line of his houses a horizontal line, and fails of course to produce the effect demanded. Here then is one instance out of many, in which not only the understanding is allowed to overrule the eyes, but where the understanding is positively allowed to obliterate the eyes, as it were; for not only does the man believe the evidence of his understanding in opposition to that of his eyes, but (what is monstrous) the idiot is not aware that his eyes ever gave such evidence. He does not know that he has seen (and therefore *quoad* his consciousness has *not* seen) that which he *has* seen every day of his life.

But to return from this digression. My understanding could furnish no reason why the knocking at the gate in *Macbeth* should produce any effect, direct or reflected. In fact, my understanding said positively that it could *not* produce any effect. But I knew better; I felt that it did; and I waited and clung to the problem until further knowledge should enable me to solve it. At length, in 1812, Mr. Williams made his *début* on the stage of Ratcliffe Highway, and executed those unparalleled murders which have procured for him such a brilliant and undying reputation. On which murders, by the way, I must observe, that in one respect they have had an ill effect, by making the connoisseur in murder very fastidious in his taste, and dissatisfied with anything that has been since done in that line. All other murders look pale by the deep crimson of his; and, as an amateur once said

* This essay was first published in *The London Magazine*, October 1823.

to me in a querulous tone, "There has been absolutely nothing *doing* since his time, or nothing that's worth speaking of." But this is wrong, for it is unreasonable to expect all men to be great artists, and born with the genius of Mr. Williams. Now it will be remembered that in the first of these murders (that of the Marrs) the same incident (of a knocking at the door soon after the work of extermination was complete) did actually occur which the genius of Shakespeare has invented; and all good judges, and the most eminent dilettanti, acknowledged the felicity of Shakespeare's suggestion as soon as it was actually realized. Here, then, was a fresh proof that I had the right in relying on my own feeling in opposition to my understanding; and again I set myself to study the problem. At length I solved it to my own satisfaction; and my solution is this:—Murder, in ordinary cases, where the sympathy is wholly directed to the case of the murdered person, is an incident of coarse and vulgar horror; and for this reason,—that it flings the interest exclusively upon the natural but ignoble instinct by which we cleave to life; an instinct which, as being indispensable to the primal law of self-preservation, is the same in kind (though different in degree) amongst all living creatures. This instinct, therefore, because it annihilates all distinctions, and degrades the greatest of men to the level of "the poor beetle that we tread on," exhibits human nature in its most abject and humiliating attitude. Such an attitude would little suit the purposes of the poet. What then must he do? He must throw the interest on the murderer. Our sympathy must be with *him* (of course I mean a sympathy of comprehension, a sympathy by which we enter into his feelings, and are made to understand them—not a sympathy of pity or approbation).[1] In the murdered person all strife of thought, all flux and reflux of passion and of purpose, are crushed by one overwhelming panic; the fear of instant death smites him "with its petrific mace." But in the murderer, such a murderer as a poet will condescend to, there must be raging some great storm of passion—jealousy, ambition, vengeance, hatred—which will create a hell within him; and into this hell we are to look.

In *Macbeth*, for the sake of gratifying his now enormous and teeming faculty of creation, Shakespeare has introduced two murderers; and, as usual in his hands, they are remarkably discriminated; but—though in Macbeth the strife of mind is greater than in his wife, the tiger spirit not so awake, and his feelings caught chiefly by contagion from her—yet, as both were finally involved in the guilt of murder, the murderous mind of necessity is finally to be presumed in both. This was to be expressed; and on its own account, as well as to make it a more proportionable antagonist to the unoffending nature of their victim, "the gracious Duncan," and adequately to expound "the deep damnation of his taking off," this was to be expressed with peculiar energy. We were to be made to feel that the human nature—i.e., the divine nature of love and mercy, spread through the hearts of all creatures, and seldom utterly withdrawn from man—was gone, vanished, extinct, and that the fiendish nature had taken its place. And, as this effect is marvellously accomplished in the *dialogues* and *soliloquies* themselves, so it is finally consummated by the expedient under consideration; and it is to this that I now solicit the reader's attention. If the reader has ever witnessed a wife, daughter, or sister, in a fainting fit, he may chance to have observed that the most affecting moment in such a spectacle is that in which a sigh and a stirring announce the recommencement of suspended life. Or, if the reader has ever been present in a vast metropolis on the day when some great national idol was carried in funeral pomp to his grave, and, chancing to walk near the course through which it passed, has felt powerfully, in the silence and desertion of the streets and in the stagnation of ordinary business, the deep interest which at that moment was possessing the heart of man,—if all at once he should hear the death-like stillness broken up by the sound of wheels rattling away from the scene, and making known that the transitory vision was dissolved, he will be aware

[1] It seems almost ludicrous to guard and explain my use of a word in a situation where it would naturally explain itself. But it has become necessary to do so, in consequence of the unscholarlike use of the word sympathy, at present so general, by which, instead of taking it in its proper sense, as the act of reproducing in our minds the feelings of another, whether for hatred, indignation, love, pity, or approbation, it is made a mere synonym of the word *pity;* and hence, instead of saying, "sympathy *with* another," many writers adopt the monstrous barbarism of "sympathy *for* another."

that at no moment was his sense of the complete suspension and pause in ordinary human concerns so full and affecting as at that moment when the suspension ceases, and the goings-on of human life are suddenly resumed. All action in any direction is best expounded, measured, and made apprehensible, by reaction. Now apply this to the case in *Macbeth.* Here, as I have said, the retiring of the human heart and the entrance of the fiendish heart was to be expressed and made sensible. Another world has stepped in; and the murderers are taken out of the region of human things, human purposes, human desires. They are transfigured: Lady Macbeth is "unsexed"; Macbeth has forgot that he was born of woman; both are conformed to the image of devils; and the world of devils is suddenly revealed. But how shall this be conveyed and made palpable? In order that a new world may step in, this world must for a time disappear. The murderers, and the murder, must be insulated—cut off by an immeasurable gulf from the ordinary tide and succession of human affairs—locked up and sequestered in some deep recess; we must be made sensible that the world of ordinary life is suddenly arrested—laid asleep—tranced—racked into a dread armistice; time must be annihilated, relation to things without abolished; and all must pass self-withdrawn into a deep syncope and suspension of earthly passion. Hence it is that, when the deed is done, when the work of darkness is perfect, then the world of darkness passes away like a pageantry in the clouds: the knocking at the gate is heard, and it makes known audibly that the reaction has commenced; the human has made its reflux upon the fiendish; the pulses of life are beginning to beat again; and the re-establishment of the goings-on of the world in which we live first makes us profoundly sensible of the awful parenthesis that had suspended them.

O mighty poet! Thy works are not as those of other men, simply and merely great works of art, but are also like the phenomena of nature, like the sun and the sea, the stars and the flowers, like frost and snow, rain and dew, hailstorm and thunder, which are to be studied with entire submission of our own faculties, and in the perfect faith that in them there can be no too much or too little, nothing useless or inert, but that, the farther we press in our discoveries, the more we shall see proofs of design and self-supporting arrangement where the careless eye had seen nothing but accident!

THOMAS DE QUINCEY: The Literature of Knowledge and the Literature of Power*

WHAT is it that we mean by *literature?* Popularly, and amongst the thoughtless, it is held to include everything that is printed in a book. Little logic is required to disturb *that* definition; the most thoughtless person is easily made aware, that in the idea of *literature,* one essential element is,—some relation to a general and common interest of man, so that, what applies only to a local, or professional, or merely personal interest, even though presenting itself in the shape of a book, will not belong to literature. So far the definition is easily narrowed; and it is as easily expanded. For not only is much that takes a station in books not literature; but inversely, much that really *is* literature never reaches a station in books. The weekly sermons of Christendom, that vast pulpit literature which acts so extensively upon the popular mind—to warn, to uphold, to renew, to comfort, to alarm, does not attain the sanctuary of libraries in the ten-thousandth part of its extent. The drama again, as for in-

* This is a section of De Quincey's review of "The Works of Alexander Pope, Esquire. By W. Roscoe, Esq." which first appeared in *The North British Review,* August 1848.

stance, the finest of Shakespeare's plays in England, and all leading Athenian plays in the noontide of the Attic stage, operated as a literature on the public mind, and were (according to the strictest letter of that term) *published* through the audiences that witnessed [1] their representation some time before they were published as things to be read; and they were published in this scenical mode of publication with much more effect than they could have had as books, during ages of costly copying, or of costly printing.

Books, therefore, do not suggest an idea coextensive and interchangeable with the idea of literature; since much literature, scenic, forensic, or didactic (as from lecturers and public orators), may never come into books; and much that *does* come into books, may connect itself with no literary interest.[2] But a far more important correction, applicable to the common vague idea of literature, is to be sought—not so much in a better definition of literature, as in a sharper distinction of the two functions which it fulfils. In that great social organ, which, collectively, we call literature, there may be distinguished two separate offices that may blend and often *do* so, but capable, severally, of a severe insulation, and naturally fitted for reciprocal repulsion. There is, first, the literature of *knowledge;* and, secondly, the literature of *power.* The function of the first is—to *teach;* the function of the second is—to *move:* the first is a rudder; the second, an oar or a sail. The first speaks to the *mere* discursive understanding; the second speaks ultimately, it may happen, to the higher understanding or reason, but always *through* affections of pleasure and sympathy. Remotely, it may travel towards an object seated in what Lord Bacon calls *dry* light; but, proximately, it does and must operate, else it ceases to be a literature of *power,* on and through that *humid* light which clothes itself in the mists and glittering *iris* of human passions, desires, and genial emotions. Men have so little reflected on the higher functions of literature, as to find it a paradox if one should describe it as a mean or subordinate purpose of books to give information. But this is a paradox only in the sense which makes it honorable to be paradoxical. Whenever we talk in ordinary language of seeking information or gaining knowledge, we understand the words as connected with something of absolute novelty. But it is the grandeur of all truth, which *can* occupy a very high place in human interests, that it is never absolutely novel to the meanest of minds: it exists eternally by way of germ or latent principle in the lowest as in the highest, needing to be developed, but never to be planted. To be capable of transplantation is the immediate criterion of a truth that ranges on a lower scale. Besides which, there is a rarer thing than truth, namely, *power,* or deep sympathy with truth. What is the effect, for instance, upon society, of children? By the pity, by the tenderness, and by the peculiar modes of admiration, which connect themselves with the helplessness, with the innocence, and with the simplicity of children, not only are the primal affections strengthened and continually renewed, but the qualities which are dearest in the sight of heaven—the frailty, for instance, which appeals to forbearance; the innocence which symbolizes the heavenly, and the simplicity which is most alien from the worldly, are kept up in perpetual remembrance, and their ideals are continually refreshed. A purpose of the same nature is answered by the higher literature, viz., the literature of power. What do you learn from *Paradise Lost?* Nothing at all. What do you learn from a cookery-book? Something new—something that you did not know before, in every paragraph. But would you therefore put the wretched cookery-book on a higher level of estimation than the divine poem? What you own to Milton is not any knowledge, of which a million separate items are still but a million of advancing steps on the same earthly level; what you owe, is *power,* that is, exercise and expan-

[1] Charles I, for example, when Prince of Wales, and many others in his father's court, gained their known familiarity with Shakespeare—not through the original quartos, so slenderly diffused, nor through the first folio of 1623, but through the court representations of his chief dramas at Whitehall.

[2] What are called the *Blue Books,* by which title are understood the folio Reports issued every session of Parliament by committees of the two Houses, and stitched into blue covers,—though often sneered at by the ignorant as so much waste paper, will be acknowledged gratefully by those who have used them diligently, as the main well-heads of all accurate information as to the Great Britain of this day. As an immense depository of faithful (*and not superannuated*) statistics, they are indispensable to the honest student. But no man would therefore class the *Blue Books* as literature.

sion to your own latent capacity of sympathy with the infinite, where every pulse and each separate influx is a step upwards—a step ascending as upon a Jacob's ladder from earth to mysterious altitudes above the earth. *All* the steps of knowledge, from first to last, carry you further on the same plane, but could never raise you one foot above your ancient level of earth: whereas, the very *first* step in power is a flight —is an ascending movement into another element where earth is forgotten.

Were it not that human sensibilities are ventilated and continually called out into exercise by the great phenomena of infancy, or of real life as it moves through chance and change, or of literature as it recombines these elements in the mimicries of poetry, romance, &c., it is certain that, like any animal power or muscular energy falling into disuse, all such sensibilities would gradually droop and dwindle. It is in relation to these great *moral* capacities of man that the literature of power, as contradistinguished from that of knowledge, lives and has its field of action. It is concerned with what is highest in man; for the Scriptures themselves never condescended to deal by suggestion or cooperation, with the mere discursive understanding: when speaking of man in his intellectual capacity, the Scriptures speak not of the understanding, but of "*the understanding heart,*"—making the heart, i.e., the great *intuitive* (or non-discursive) organ, to be the interchangeable formula for man in his highest state of capacity for the infinite. Tragedy, romance, fairy tale, or epopee, all alike restore to man's mind the ideals of justice, of hope, of truth, of mercy, of retribution, which else (left to the support of daily life in its realities) would languish for want of sufficient illustration. What is meant, for instance, by *poetic justice?*—It does not mean a justice that differs by its object from the ordinary justice of human jurisprudence; for then it must be confessedly a very bad kind of justice; but it means a justice that differs from common forensic justice by the degree in which it *attains* its object, a justice that is more omnipotent over its own ends, as dealing—not with the refractory elements of earthly life—but with the elements of its own creation, and with materials flexible to its own purest preconceptions. It is certain that, were it not for the literature of power, these ideals would often remain amongst us as mere arid notional forms; whereas, by the creative forces of man put forth in literature, they gain a vernal life of restoration, and germinate into vital activities.

The commonest novel, by moving in alliance with human fears and hopes, with human instincts of wrong and right, sustains and quickens those affections. Calling them into action, it rescues them from torpor. And hence the preeminency over all authors that merely *teach,* of the meanest that *moves;* or that teaches, if at all, indirectly *by* moving. The very highest work that has ever existed in the literature of knowledge, is but a *provisional* work: a book upon trial and sufferance, and *quamdiu bene se gesserit.* Let its teaching be even partially revised, let it be but expanded, nay, even let its teaching be but placed in a better order, and instantly it is superseded. Whereas the feeblest works in the literature of power, surviving at all, survive as finished and unalterable amongst men. For instance, the *Principia* of Sir Isaac Newton was a book *militant* on earth from the first. In all stages of its progress it would have to fight for its existence: first, as regards absolute truth; secondly, when that combat was over, as regards its form or mode of presenting the truth. And as soon as a La Place, or anybody else, builds higher upon the foundations laid by this book, effectually he throws it out of the sunshine into decay and darkness; by weapons won from this book he superannuates and destroys this book, so that soon the name of Newton remains, as a mere *nominis umbra,* but his book, as a living power, has transmigrated into other forms. Now, on the contrary, the *Iliad,* the *Prometheus* of Æschylus,—the *Othello* or *King Lear,*—the *Hamlet* or *Macbeth,*—and the *Paradise Lost,* are not militant but triumphant for ever as long as the languages exist in which they speak or can be taught to speak. They never *can* transmigrate into new incarnations. To reproduce *these* in new forms, or variations, even if in some things they should be improved, would be to plagiarize. A good steam-engine is properly superseded by a better. But one lovely pastoral valley is not superseded by another, nor a statue of Praxiteles by a statue of Michael Angelo. These things are separated not by imparity, but by disparity. They are not thought of as unequal under the same standard, but as different in *kind*, and if otherwise equal, as equal under a different standard. Human works of immortal beauty and works of nature in one respect stand on the same footing; they never absolutely repeat each other; never approach so near as not to differ; and they differ not as better and worse, or simply by more and less: they differ by undecipherable and incommunicable differences, that cannot be caught by mimicries, that cannot be reflected in the mirror or copies, that cannot become ponderable in the scales of vulgar comparison.

Applying these principles to Pope, as a representative of fine literature in general, we would wish to remark the claim which he has, or which an equal writer has, to the attention and jealous winnowing of those critics, in particular, who watch over public morals. Clergymen, and all the organs of public criticism put in motion by clergymen, are more especially concerned in the just appreciation of such writers, if the two canons are remembered, which we have endeavored to illustrate, viz., that all works in this class, as opposed to those in the literature of knowledge, first, work by far deeper agencies; and, secondly, are more permanent; in the strictest sense they are κτήματα ἐς ἀεί [3]: and what evil they do, or what good they do, is commensurate with the national language, sometimes long after the nation has departed. At this hour, five hundred years since their creation, the tales of Chaucer, never equalled on this earth for their tenderness, and for life of picturesqueness, are read familiarly by many in the charming language of their natal day, and by others in the modernizations of Dryden, of Pope, and Wordsworth. At this hour, one thousand eight hundred years since their creation, the Pagan tales of Ovid, never equalled on this earth for the gaiety of their movement and the capricious graces of their narrative, are read by all Christendom. This man's people and their monuments are dust; but *he* is alive: he has survived them, as he told us that he had it in his commission to do, by a thousand years; "and *shall* a thousand more."

[3] ["Possessions forever."]

All the literature of knowledge builds only ground-nests, that are swept away by floods, or confounded by the plough; but the literature of power builds nests in aërial altitudes of temples sacred from violation, or of forests inaccessible to fraud. *This* is a great prerogative of the *power* literature; and it is a greater which lies in the mode of its influence. The *knowledge* literature, like the fashion of this world, passeth away. An Encyclopædia is its abstract; and, in this respect, it may be taken for its speaking symbol—that, before one generation has passed, an Encyclopædia is superannuated; for it speaks through the dead memory and unimpassioned understanding, which have not the repose of higher faculties, but are continually enlarging and varying their phylacteries. But all literature, properly so called—literature κατ' ἐξοχήν,[4] for the very reason that it is so much more durable than the literature of knowledge, is (and by the very same proportion it is) more intense and electrically searching in its impressions. The directions in which the tragedy of this planet has trained our human feelings to play, and the combinations into which the poetry of this planet has thrown our human passions of love and hatred, of admiration and contempt, exercise a power bad or good over human life, that cannot be contemplated, when stretching through many generations, without a sentiment allied to awe.[5] And of this let every one be assured—that he owes to the impassioned books which he has read, many a thousand more of emotions than he can consciously trace back to them. Dim by their origination, these emotions yet arise in him, and mould him through life like forgotten incidents of his childhood.

[4] i.e., great literature.

[5] The reason why the broad distinctions between the two literatures of power and knowledge so little fix the attention, lies in the fact, that a vast proportion of books—history, biography, travels, miscellaneous essays, &c., lying in a middle zone, confound these distinctions by interblending them. All that we call "amusement" or "entertainment," is a diluted form of the power belonging to passion, and also a mixed form; and where threads of direct *instruction* intermingle in the texture with these threads of *power*, this absorption of the duality into one representative *nuance* neutralizes the separate perception of either. Fused into a *tertium quid*, or neutral state, they disappear to the popular eye as the repelling forces, which, in fact, they are.

EDGAR ALLAN POE: The Poetic Principle*

IN SPEAKING of the Poetic Principle, I have no design to be either thorough or profound. While discussing, very much at random, the essentiality of what we call Poetry, my principal purpose will be to cite for consideration some few of those minor English or American poems which best suit my own taste, or which, upon my own fancy, have left the most definite impression. By "minor poems" I mean, of course, poems of little length. And here, in the beginning, permit me to say a few words in regard to a somewhat peculiar principle, which, whether rightfully or wrongfully, has always had its influence in my own critical estimate of the poem. I hold that a long poem does not exist. I maintain that the phrase, "a long poem," is simply a flat contradiction in terms.

I need scarcely observe that a poem deserves its title only inasmuch as it excites, by elevating the soul. The value of the poem is in the ratio of this elevating excitement. But all excitements are, through a psychal necessity, transient. That degree of excitement which would entitle a poem to be so called at all cannot be sustained throughout a composition of any great length. After the lapse of half an hour, at the very utmost, it flags—fails—a revulsion ensues—and then the poem is, in effect, and in fact, no longer such.

There are, no doubt, many who have found difficulty in reconciling the critical dictum that the *Paradise Lost* is to be devoutly admired throughout, with the absolute impossibility of maintaining for it, during perusal, the amount of enthusiasm which that critical dictum would demand. This great work, in fact, is to be regarded as poetical, only when, losing sight of that vital requisite in all works of Art, Unity, we view it merely as a series of minor poems. If, to preserve its Unity—its totality of effect or impression—we read it (as would be necessary) at a single sitting, the result is but a constant alternation of excitement and depression. After a passage of what we feel to be true poetry, there follows, inevitably, a passage of platitude which no critical pre-judgment can force us to admire; but if, upon completing the work, we read it again omitting the first book—that is to say, commencing with the second—we shall be surprised at now finding that admirable which we before condemned—that damnable which we had previously so much admired. It follows from all this that the ultimate, aggregate, or absolute effect of even the best epic under the sun, is a nullity:—and this is precisely the fact.

In regard to the *Iliad*, we have, if not positive proof, at least very good reason, for believing it intended as a series of lyrics; but, granting the epic intention, I can say only that the work is based in an imperfect sense of Art. The modern epic is, of the supposititious ancient model, but an inconsiderate and blindfold imitation. But the day of these artistic anomalies is over. If, at any time, any very long poem *were* popular in reality, which I doubt, it is at least clear that no very long poem will ever be popular again.

That the extent of a poetical work is, *ceteris paribus*,[1] the measure of its merit, seems undoubtedly, when we thus state it, a proposition sufficiently absurd—yet we are indebted for it to the Quarterly Reviews. Surely there can be nothing in mere *size*, abstractly considered—there can be nothing in mere *bulk*, so far as a volume is concerned, which has so continuously elicited admiration from these saturnine pam-

* "The Poetic Principle" was first published in *Sartain's Union Magazine*, October 1850. It is reprinted here from the E. C. Stedman and G. E. Woodberry edition of Poe's *Works* (1894-95).

1 ["Other things being equal."]

phlets! A mountain, to be sure, by the mere sentiment of physical magnitude which it conveys, *does* impress us with a sense of the sublime —but no man is impressed after *this* fashion by the material grandeur of even *The Columbiad*. Even the Quarterlies have not instructed us to be so impressed by it. *As yet,* they have not *insisted* on our estimating Lamartine by the cubic foot, or Pollok by the pound—but what else are we to *infer* from their continued prating about "sustained effort"? If, by "sustained effort," any little gentleman has accomplished an epic, let us frankly commend him for the effort —if this indeed be a thing commendable—but let us forbear praising the epic on the effort's account. It is to be hoped that common sense, in the time to come, will prefer deciding upon a work of art, rather by the impression it makes, by the effect it produces, than by the time it took to impress the effect or by the amount of "sustained effort" which had been found necessary in effecting the impression. The fact is, that perseverance is one thing, and genius quite another—nor can all the Quarterlies in Christendom confound them. By-and-by, this proposition, with many which I have been just urging, will be received as self-evident. In the mean time, by being generally condemned as falsities, they will not be essentially damaged as truths.

On the other hand, it is clear that a poem may be improperly brief. Undue brevity degenerates into mere epigrammatism. A *very* short poem, while now and then producing a brilliant or vivid, never produces a profound or enduring effect. There must be the steady pressing down of the stamp upon the wax. Béranger has wrought innumerable things, pungent and spirit-stirring; but, in general, they have been too imponderous to stamp themselves deeply into the public attention; and thus, as so many feathers of fancy, have been blown aloft only to be whistled down the wind.

A remarkable instance of the effect of undue brevity in depressing a poem—in keeping it out of the popular view—is afforded by the following exquisite little serenade:

I arise from dreams of thee
  In the first sweet sleep of night,
When the winds are breathing low,
  And the stars are shining bright;
I arise from dreams of thee,
  And a spirit in my feet
Hath led me—who knows how?—
  To thy chamber-window, sweet!

The wandering airs, they faint
  On the dark, the silent stream;
The champak odors fail
  Like sweet thoughts in a dream;
The nightingale's complaint,
  It dies upon her heart,
As I must die on thine,
  Oh, beloved as thou art!

Oh, lift me from the grass!
  I die! I faint! I fail!
Let thy love in kisses rain
  On my lips and eyelids pale.
My cheek is cold and white, alas!
  My heart beats loud and fast:
Oh! press it close to thine again,
  Where it will break at last!

Very few, perhaps, are familiar with these lines—yet no less a poet than Shelley is their author. Their warm, yet delicate and ethereal imagination will be appreciated by all—but by none so thoroughly as by him who has himself arisen from sweet dreams of one beloved to bathe in the aromatic air of a southern midsummer night.

One of the finest poems by Willis—the very best in my opinion, which he has ever written— has, no doubt, through this same defect of undue brevity, been kept back from its proper position, not less in the critical than in the popular view.

The shadows lay along Broadway,
  'Twas near the twilight tide,
And slowly there a lady fair
  Was walking in her pride.
Alone walked she; but, viewlessly,
  Walked spirits at her side.

Peace charmed the street beneath her feet
  And Honor charmed the air;
And all astir looked kind on her,
  And called her good as fair,
For all God ever gave to her
  She kept with chary care.

She kept with care her beauties rare
  From lovers warm and true,
For her heart was cold to all but gold,
  And the rich came not to woo—
But honored well are charms to sell
  If priests the selling do.

Now walking there was one more fair—
  A slight girl, lily pale;
And she had unseen company
  To make the spirit quail:
'Twixt Want and Scorn she walked forlorn,
  And nothing could avail.

No mercy now can clear her brow
  For this world's peace to pray;
For, as love's wild prayer dissolved in air,
  Her woman's heart gave way!—
But the sin forgiven by Christ in heaven
  By man is cursed alway!

In this composition we find it difficult to recognize the Willis who has written so many mere "verses of society." The lines are not only richly ideal, but full of energy; while they breathe an earnestness—an evident sincerity of sentiment—for which we look in vain throughout all the other works of this author.

While the epic mania—while the idea that, to merit in poetry, prolixity is indispensable—has, for some years past, been gradually dying out of the public mind, by mere dint of its own absurdity—we find it succeeded by a heresy too palpably false to be long tolerated, but one which, in the brief period it has already endured, may be said to have accomplished more in the corruption of our Poetical Literature than all its other enemies combined. I allude to the heresy of *The Didactic.* It has been assumed, tacitly and avowedly, directly and indirectly, that the ultimate object of all Poetry is Truth. Every poem, it is said, should inculcate a moral; and by this moral is the poetical merit of the work to be adjudged. We Americans, especially, have patronized this happy idea; and we Bostonians, very especially, have developed it in full. We have taken it into our heads that to write a poem simply for the poem's sake, and to acknowledge such to have been our design, would be to confess ourselves radically wanting in the true Poetic dignity and force:—but the simple fact is, that, would we but permit ourselves to look into our own souls, we should immediately there discover that under the sun there neither exists nor *can* exist any work more thoroughly dignified—more supremely noble than this very poem—this poem *per se*—this poem which is a poem and nothing more—this poem written solely for the poem's sake.

With as deep a reverence for the True as ever inspired the bosom of man, I would, nevertheless, limit, in some measure, its modes of inculcation. I would limit to enforce them. I would not enfeeble them by dissipation. The demands of Truth are severe. She has no sympathy with the myrtles. All *that* which is so indispensable in Song, is precisely all *that* with which *she* has nothing whatever to do. It is but making her a flaunting paradox, to wreathe her in gems and flowers. In enforcing a truth, we need severity rather than efflorescence of language. We must be simple, precise, terse. We must be cool, calm, unimpassioned. In a word, we must be in that mood which, as nearly as possible, is the exact converse of the poetical. He must be blind, indeed, who does not perceive the radical and chasmal differences between the truthful and the poetical modes of inculcation. He must be theory-mad beyond redemption who, in spite of these differences, shall still persist in attempting to reconcile the obstinate oils and waters of Poetry and Truth.

Dividing the world of mind into its three most obvious distinctions, we have the Pure Intellect, Taste, and the Moral Sense. I place Taste in the middle, because it is just this position which in the mind it occupies. It holds intimate relations with either extreme; but from the Moral Sense is separated by so faint a difference that Aristotle has not hesitated to place some of its operations among the virtues themselves. Nevertheless, we find the *offices* of the trio marked with a sufficient distinction. Just as the Intellect concerns itself with Truth, so Taste informs us of the Beautiful, while the Moral Sense is regardful of Duty. Of this latter, while Conscience teaches the obligation, and Reason the expediency, Taste contents herself with displaying the charms:—waging war upon Vice solely on the ground of her deformity—her disproportion, her animosity to the fitting, to the appropriate, to the harmonious—in a word, to Beauty.

An immortal instinct, deep within the spirit of man, is thus, plainly, a sense of the Beautiful. This it is which administers to his delight in the manifold forms, and sounds, and odors, and sentiments amid which he exists. And just as the lily is repeated in the lake, or the eyes of Amaryllis in the mirror, so is the mere oral or written repetition of these forms, and sounds, and colors, and odors, and sentiments, a duplicate source of delight. But this mere repetition is not poetry. He who shall simply sing, with however glowing enthusiasm, or with however vivid a truth of description, of the sights, and sounds, and odors, and colors, and sentiments, which greet *him* in common with all mankind—he, I say, has yet failed to prove his divine title. There is still a something in the distance which he has been unable to attain. We have still a thirst unquenchable, to allay which he has not shown us the crystal springs. This thirst belongs to the immortality of Man. It is at once a consequence and an indication of his perennial existence. It is the desire of the moth for the star. It is no mere appreciation of the Beauty before us—but a wild effort to reach the Beauty above. Inspired by an ecstatic prescience of the glories beyond the grave, we struggle, by multiform combinations among the things and thoughts of Time, to attain a portion of that Loveliness whose very elements, perhaps, appertain to eternity alone. And thus when by Poetry—or when by Music, the most entrancing of the Poetic moods—we find ourselves melted into tears—not as the Abbaté Gravina supposes—through excess of pleasure, but through a certain, petulant, impatient sorrow at our inability to grasp *now*, wholly, here on earth, at once and forever, those divine and rapturous joys, of which *through* the poem, or *through* the music, we attain to but brief and indeterminate glimpses.

The struggle to apprehend the supernal Loveliness—this struggle, on the part of souls fittingly constituted—has given to the world all *that* which it (the world) has ever been enabled at once to understand and *to feel* as poetic.

The Poetic Sentiment, of course, may develop itself in various modes—in Painting, in Sculpture, in Architecture, in the Dance—very especially in Music—and very peculiarly, and with a wide field, in the composition of the Landscape Garden. Our present theme, however, has regard only to its manifestation in words. And here let me speak briefly on the topic of rhythm. Contenting myself with the certainty that Music, in its various modes of metre, rhythm, and rhyme, is of so vast a moment in Poetry as never to be wisely rejected—is so vitally important an adjunct, that he is simply silly who declines its assistance—I will not now pause to maintain its absolute essentiality. It is in Music, perhaps, that the soul most nearly attains the great end for which, when inspired by the Poetic Sentiment, it struggles—the creation of supernal Beauty. It *may* be, indeed, that here this sublime end is, now and then, attained *in fact.* We are often made to feel, with a shivering delight, that from an earthly harp are stricken notes which *cannot* have been unfamiliar to the angels. And thus there can be little doubt that in the union of Poetry with Music in its popular sense, we shall find the widest field for the Poetic development. The old Bards and Minnesingers had advantages which we do not possess—and Thomas Moore, singing his own songs, was, in the most legitimate manner, perfecting them as poems.

To recapitulate, then:—I would define, in brief, the Poetry of words as *The Rhythmical Creation of Beauty*. Its sole arbiter is Taste. With the Intellect or with the Conscience, it has only collateral relations. Unless incidentally, it has no concern whatever either with Duty or with Truth.

A few words, however, in explanation. *That* pleasure which is at once the most pure, the most elevating, and the most intense, is derived, I maintain, from the contemplation of the Beautiful. In the contemplation of Beauty we alone find it possible to attain that pleasurable elevation, or excitement, *of the soul,* which we recognize as the Poetic Sentiment, and which is so easily distinguished from Truth, which is the satisfaction of the Reason, or from Passion, which is the excitement of the heart. I make Beauty, therefore—using the word as inclusive of the sublime—I make Beauty the province of the poem, simply because it is an obvious rule of Art that effects should be made to spring as directly as possible from their causes:—no one as yet having been weak enough to deny that the peculiar elevation in question is at least *most readily* attainable in the poem. It by no means follows, however, that the incitements of Passion, or the precepts of Duty, or even the lessons of Truth, may not be introduced into a poem, and with advantage; for they may subserve, incidentally, in various ways, the general purposes of the work:—but the true artist will always contrive to tone them down in proper subjection to that *Beauty* which is the atmosphere and the real essence of the poem.

I cannot better introduce the few poems, which I shall present for your consideration, than by the citation of the "Proem" to Mr. Longfellow's "Waif":

The day is done, and the darkness
  Falls from the wings of Night,
As a feather is wafted downward
  From an eagle in his flight.

I see the lights of the village
  Gleam through the rain and the mist,
And a feeling of sadness comes o'er me,
  That my soul cannot resist:

A feeling of sadness and longing,
  That is not akin to pain,
And resembles sorrow only
  As the mist resembles the rain.

Come, read to me some poem,
  Some simple and heartfelt lay,
That shall soothe this restless feeling,
  And banish the thoughts of day.

Not from the grand old masters,
  Not from the bards sublime,
Whose distant footsteps echo
  Through the corridors of Time.

For, like strains of martial music,
  Their mighty thoughts suggest
Life's endless toil and endeavor;
  And tonight I long for rest.

Read from some humbler poet,
  Whose songs gushed from his heart,
As showers from the clouds of summer,
  Or tears from the eyelids start;

Who, through long days of labor,
  And nights devoid of ease,
Still heard in his soul the music
  Of wonderful melodies.

Such songs have power to quiet
  The restless pulse of care,
And come like the benediction
  That follows after prayer.

Then read from the treasured volume
  The poem of thy choice,
And lend to the rhyme of the poet
  The beauty of thy voice.

And the night shall be filled with music,
  And the cares that infest the day,
Shall fold their tents, like the Arabs,
  And as silently steal away.

With no great range of imagination, these lines have been justly admired for their delicacy of expression. Some of the images are very effective. Nothing can be better than—

the bards sublime
Whose distant footsteps echo
  Through the corridors of Time.

The idea of the last quatrain is also very effective. The poem, on the whole, however, is chiefly to be admired for the graceful *insouciance* of its metre, so well in accordance with the character of the sentiments, and especially for the *ease* of the general manner. This "ease," or naturalness, in a literary style, it has long been the fashion to regard as ease in appearance alone—as a point of really difficult attainment. But not so:—a natural manner is difficult only to him who should never meddle with it—to the unnatural. It is but the result of writing with the understanding, or with the instinct, that *the tone*, in composition, should always be that which the mass of mankind would adopt—and must perpetually vary, of course, with the occasion. The author who, after the fashion of the "North American Review," should be, upon *all* occasions, merely "quiet," must necessarily, upon *many* occasions, be simply silly, or stupid; and has no more right to be considered "easy," or "natural," than a Cockney exquisite, or than the sleeping Beauty in the wax-works.

Among the minor poems of Bryant, none has so much impressed me as the one which he entitles "June." I quote only a portion of it:—

There, through the long, long summer hours,
    The golden light should lie,
And thick young herbs and groups of flowers
    Stand in their beauty by.
The oriole should build and tell
His love-tale, close beside my cell;
    The idle butterfly
Should rest him there, and there be heard
The housewife-bee and humming-bird.

And what if cheerful shouts at noon
    Come, from the village sent,
Or songs of maids, beneath the moon,
    With fairy laughter blent?

And what if, in the evening light,
Betrothèd lovers walk in sight
Of my low monument?
I would the lovely scene around
Might know no sadder sight nor sound.

I know that I no more should see
The season's glorious show,
Nor would its brightness shine for me,
Nor its wild music flow;
But if, around my place of sleep,
The friends I love should come to weep,
They might not haste to go.
Soft airs, and song, and light, and bloom
Should keep them lingering by my tomb.

These to their softened hearts should bear
The thought of what has been,
And speak of one who cannot share
The gladness of the scene;
Whose part, in all the pomp that fills
The circuit of the summer hills,
Is—that his grave is green;
And deeply would their hearts rejoice
To hear again his living voice.

The rhythmical flow, here, is even voluptuous—nothing could be more melodious. The poem has always affected me in a remarkable manner. The intense melancholy which seems to well up, perforce, to the surface of all the poet's cheerful sayings about his grave, we find thrilling us to the soul—while there is the truest poetic elevation in the thrill. The impression left is one of a pleasurable sadness. And if, in the remaining compositions which I shall introduce to you, there be more or less of a similar tone always apparent, let me remind you that (how or why we know not) this certain taint of sadness is inseparably connected with all the higher manifestations of true Beauty. It is, nevertheless,

A feeling of sadness and longing
That is not akin to pain,
And resembles sorrow only
As the mist resembles the rain.

The taint of which I speak is clearly perceptible even in a poem so full of brilliancy and spirit as the "Health" of Edward Coate Pinkney:

I fill this cup to one made up
Of loveliness alone,
A woman, of her gentle sex
The seeming paragon;
To whom the better elements
And kindly stars have given
A form so fair, that, like the air,
'Tis less of earth than heaven.

Her every tone is music's own,
Like those of morning birds,
And something more than melody
Dwells ever in her words;
The coinage of her heart are they,
And from her lips each flows
As one may see the burdened bee
Forth issue from the rose.

Affections are as thoughts to her,
The measures of her hours;
Her feelings have the fragrancy,
The freshness of young flowers;
And lovely passions, changing oft,
So fill her, she appears
The image of themselves by turns,—
The idol of past years!

Of her bright face one glance will trace
A picture on the brain,
And of her voice in echoing hearts
A sound must long remain;
But memory, such as mine of her,
So very much endears,
When death is nigh my latest sigh
Will not be life's, but hers.

I fill this cup to one made up
Of loveliness alone,
A woman, of her gentle sex
The seeming paragon—
Her health! and would on earth there stood
Some more of such a frame,
That life might be all poetry,
And weariness a name.

It was the misfortune of Mr. Pinkney to have been born too far south. Had he been a New Englander, it is probable that he would have been ranked as the first of American lyrists, by that magnanimous cabal which has so long controlled the destinies of American Letters, in conducting the thing called the "North American Review." The poem just cited is especially beautiful; but the poetic elevation which it induces, we must refer chiefly to our sympathy in the poet's enthusiasm. We pardon his hyperboles for the evident earnestness with which they are uttered.

It was by no means my design, however, to expatiate upon the *merits* of what I should read you. These will necessarily speak for themselves. Boccalini, in his "Advertisements from Parnassus," tells us that Zoilus once presented Apollo a very caustic criticism upon a very admirable book:—whereupon the god asked him for the beauties of the work. He replied that he only busied himself about the errors. On hearing this, Apollo, handing him a sack of unwinnowed wheat, bade him pick out *all the chaff* for his reward.

Now this fable answers very well as a hit at the critics—but I am by no means sure that the god was in the right. I am by no means certain that the true limits of the critical duty are not grossly misunderstood. Excellence, in a poem especially, may be considered in the light of an axiom, which need only be properly *put*, to become self-evident. It is *not* excellence if it require to be demonstrated as such:—and thus, to point out too particularly the merits of a work of Art is to admit that they are *not* merits altogether.

Among the "Melodies" of Thomas Moore, is one whose distinguished character as a poem proper seems to have been singularly left out of view. I allude to his lines beginning—"Come, rest in this bosom." The intense energy of their expression is not surpassed by anything in Byron. There are two of the lines in which a sentiment is conveyed that embodies the *all in all* of the divine passion of love—a sentiment which, perhaps, has found its echo in more, and in more passionate, human hearts than any other single sentiment ever embodied in words:

Come, rest in this bosom, my own stricken deer,
Though the herd have fled from thee, thy home is still here;
Here still is the smile, that no cloud can o'ercast,
And a heart and a hand all thy own to the last.

Oh! what was love made for, if 'tis not the same
Through joy and through torment, through glory and shame?
I know not, I ask not, if guilt's in that heart,
I but know that I love thee, whatever thou art.

Thou hast called me thy Angel in moments of bliss,
And thy Angel I'll be, 'mid the horrors of this,—
Through the furnace, unshrinking, thy steps to pursue,
And shield thee, and save thee,—or perish there too!

It has been the fashion, of late days, to deny Moore imagination, while granting him fancy —a distinction originating with Coleridge—than whom no man more fully comprehended the great powers of Moore. The fact is, that the fancy of this poet so far predominates over all his other faculties, and over the fancy of all other men, as to have induced, very naturally, the idea that he is fanciful *only*. But never was there a greater mistake. Never was a grosser wrong done the fame of a true poet. In the compass of the English language I can call to mind no poem more profoundly—more weirdly *imaginative,* in the best sense, than the lines commencing—"I would I were by that dim lake"—which are the composition of Thomas Moore. I regret that I am unable to remember them.

One of the noblest—and, speaking of fancy, one of the most singularly fanciful of modern poets, was Thomas Hood. His "Fair Ines" had always, for me, an inexpressible charm:

O saw ye not fair Ines?
She's gone into the West,
To dazzle when the sun is down,
And rob the world of rest:
She took our daylight with her,
The smiles that we love best,
With morning blushes on her cheek,
And pearls upon her breast.

O turn again, fair Ines,
Before the fall of night,
For fear the Moon should shine alone,
And stars unrivalled bright;
And blessèd will the lover be
That walks beneath their light,
And breathes the love against thy cheek
I dare not even write!

Would I had been, fair Ines,
That gallant cavalier,
Who rode so gaily by thy side,
And whispered thee so near!
Were there no bonny dames at home,
Or no true lovers here,
That he should cross the seas to win
The dearest of the dear?

I saw thee, lovely Ines,
Descend along the shore,
With bands of noble gentlemen,
And banners waved before;

And gentle youth and maidens gay,
  And snowy plumes they wore;
It would have been a beauteous dream,
  If it had been no more!

Alas, alas, fair Ines,
  She went away with song,
With Music waiting on her steps,
  And shoutings of the throng;
But some were sad, and felt no mirth,
  But only Music's wrong,
In sounds that sang Farewell, Farewell,
  To her you've loved so long.

Farewell, farewell, fair Ines,
  That vessel never bore
So fair a lady on its deck,
  Nor danced so light before,—
Alas for pleasure on the sea,
  And sorrow on the shore!
The smile that blest one lover's heart
  Has broken many more!

"The Haunted House," by the same author, is one of the truest poems ever written—one of the *truest*—one of the most unexceptionable—one of the most thoroughly artistic, both in its theme and in its execution. It is, moreover, powerfully ideal—imaginative. I regret that its length renders it unsuitable for the purposes of this Lecture. In place of it, permit me to offer the universally appreciated "Bridge of Sighs."

One more Unfortunate,
Weary of breath,
Rashly importunate,
Gone to her death!

Take her up tenderly,
Lift her with care;—
Fashioned so slenderly,
Young, and so fair!

Look at her garments
Clinging like cerements;
Whilst the wave constantly
Drips from her clothing;
Take her up instantly,
Loving, not loathing.

Touch her not scornfully;
Think of her mournfully,
Gently and humanly;
Not of the stains of her,
All that remains of her
Now is pure womanly.

Make no deep scrutiny
Into her mutiny
Rash and undutiful;
Past all dishonor,
Death has left on her
Only the beautiful.

Still, for all slips of hers,
One of Eve's family—
Wipe those poor lips of hers
Oozing so clammily.
Loop up her tresses
Escaped from the comb,
Her fair auburn tresses;
Whilst wonderment guesses
Where was her home?

Who was her father?
Who was her mother?
Had she a sister?
Had she a brother?
Or was there a dearer one
Still, and a nearer one
Yet, than all other?

Alas! for the rarity
Of Christian charity
Under the sun!
Oh! it was pitiful!
Near a whole city full,
Home she had none.

Sisterly, brotherly,
Fatherly, motherly
Feelings had changed:
Love, by harsh evidence,
Thrown from its eminence;
Even God's providence
Seeming estranged.

Where the lamps quiver
So far in the river,
With many a light
From window and casement,
From garret to basement,
She stood, with amazement,
Houseless by night.

The bleak wind of March
Made her tremble and shiver;
But not the dark arch,
Or the black flowing river:
Mad from life's history,
Glad to death's mystery,
Swift to be hurled—
Anywhere, anywhere
Out of the world!

In she plunged boldly,
No matter how coldly
The rough river ran,—
Over the brink of it,
Picture it,—think of it,
Dissolute Man!
Lave in it, drink of it
Then, if you can!

Take her up tenderly
Lift her with care
Fashion'd so slenderly,
Young, and so fair!

Ere her limbs frigidly
Stiffen too rigidly,
Decently,—kindly,—
Smoothe, and compose them;
And her eyes, close them,
Staring so blindly!

Dreadfully staring
Through muddy impurity,
As when with the daring
Last look of despairing
Fixed on futurity.

Perishing gloomily,
Spurred by contumely,
Cold inhumanity,
Burning insanity,
Into her rest.—
Cross her hands humbly,
As if praying dumbly,
Over her breast!

Owning her weakness,
Her evil behavior,
And leaving, with meekness,
Her sins to her Savior!

The vigor of this poem is no less remarkable than its pathos. The versification, although carrying the fanciful to the very verge of the fantastic, is nevertheless admirably adapted to the wild insanity which is the thesis of the poem.

Among the minor poems of Lord Byron, is one which has never received from the critics the praise which it undoubtedly deserves:

Though the day of my destiny's over,
And the star of my fate hath declined,
Thy soft heart refused to discover
The faults which so many could find;
Though thy soul with my grief was acquainted,
It shrunk not to share it with me,
And the love which my spirit hath painted
It never hath found but in *thee.*

Then when nature around me is smiling,
The last smile which answers to mine,
I do not believe it beguiling,
Because it reminds me of thine;
And when winds are at war with the ocean,
As the breasts I believed in with me,
If their billows excite an emotion,
It is that they bear me from *thee.*

Though the rock of my last hope is shivered,
And its fragments are sunk in the wave,
Though I feel that my soul is delivered
To pain—it shall not be its slave.
There is many a pang to pursue me:
They may crush, but they shall not contemn—
They may torture, but shall not subdue me—
'Tis of *thee* that I think—not of them.

Though human, thou didst not deceive me,
Though woman, thou didst not forsake,
Though loved, thou forborest to grieve me,
Though slandered, thou never couldst shake,—
Though trusted, thou didst not disclaim me,
Though parted, it was not to fly,
Though watchful, 'twas not to defame me,
Nor mute, that the world might belie.

Yet I blame not the world, nor despise it,
Nor the war of the many with one—
If my soul was not fitted to prize it,
'Twas folly not sooner to shun:
And if dearly that error hath cost me,
And more than I once could foresee,
I have found that whatever it lost me,
It could not deprive me of *thee.*

From the wreck of the past, which hath perished,
Thus much I at least may recall,
It hath taught me that which I most cherished,
Deserved to be dearest of all:
In the desert a fountain is springing,
In the wide waste there still is a tree,
And a bird in the solitude singing,
Which speaks to my spirit of *thee.*

Although the rhythm here is one of the most difficult, the versification could scarcely be improved. No nobler *theme* ever engaged the pen of poet. It is the soul-elevating idea, that no man can consider himself entitled to complain of Fate while, in his adversity, he still retains the unwavering love of woman.

From Alfred Tennyson—although in perfect sincerity I regard him as the noblest poet that ever lived—I have left myself time to cite only a very brief specimen. I call him, and *think* him, the noblest of poets—*not* because the impressions he produces are, at *all* times, the most profound—*not* because the poetical excitement which he induces is, at *all* times, the most intense—but because it *is*, at all times, the most ethereal—in other words, the most elevating and the most pure. No poet is so little of the earth, earthy. What I am about to read is from his last long poem, "The Princess":

Tears, idle tears, I know not what they mean,
Tears from the depth of some divine despair
Rise in the heart, and gather to the eyes,
In looking on the happy autumn fields,
And thinking of the days that are no more.

Fresh as the first beam glittering on a sail
That brings our friends up from the underworld,
Sad as the last which reddens over one
That sinks with all we love below the verge;
So sad, so fresh, the days that are no more.

Ah, sad and strange as in dark summer dawns
The earliest pipe of half-awaken'd birds
To dying ears, when unto dying eyes
The casement slowly grows a glimmering square;
So sad, so strange, the days that are no more.

Dear as remembered kisses after death,
And sweet as those by hopeless fancy feigned
On lips that are for others; deep as love,
Deep as first love, and wild with all regret;
O Death in Life, the days that are no more.

Thus, although in a very cursory and imperfect manner, I have endeavored to convey to you my conception of the Poetic Principle. It has been my purpose to suggest that, while this Principle itself is, strictly and simply, the Human Aspiration for Supernal Beauty, the manifestation of the Principle is always found in *an elevating excitement of the Soul*—quite independent of that passion which is the intoxication of the Heart—or of that truth which is the satisfaction of the Reason. For, in regard to Passion, alas! its tendency is to degrade, rather than to elevate the Soul. Love, on the contrary—Love—the true, the divine Eros—the Uranian, as distinguished from the Dionæan Venus—is unquestionably the purest and truest of all poetical themes. And in regard to Truth—if, to be sure, through the attainment of a truth, we are led to perceive a harmony where none was apparent before, we experience, at once, the true poetical effect—but this effect is referable to the harmony alone, and not in the least degree to the truth which merely served to render the harmony manifest.

We shall reach, however, more immediately a distinct conception of what the true Poetry is, by mere reference to a few of the simple elements which induce in the Poet himself the true poetical effect. He recognizes the ambrosia which nourishes his soul, in the bright orbs that shine in Heaven—in the volutes of the flower—in the clustering of low shrubberies—in the waving of the grain-fields—in the slanting of tall, Eastern trees—in the blue distance of mountains—in the grouping of clouds—in the twinkling of half-hidden brooks—in the gleaming of silver rivers—in the repose of sequestered lakes—in the star-mirroring depths of lonely wells. He perceives it in the songs of birds—in the harp of Æolus—in the sighing of the night-wind—in the repining voice of the forest—in the surf that complains to the shore—in the fresh breath of the woods—in the scent of the violet—in the voluptuous perfume of the hyacinth—in the suggestive odor that comes to him, at eventide, from far-distant, undiscovered islands, over dim oceans, illimitable and unexplored. He owns it in all noble thoughts—in all unworldly motives—in all holy impulses—in all chivalrous, generous, and self-sacrificing deeds. He feels it in the beauty of woman—in the grace of her step—in the lustre of her eye—in the melody of her voice—in her soft laughter—in her sigh—in the harmony of the rustling of her robes. He deeply feels it in her winning endearments—in her burning enthusiasms—in her gentle charities—in her meek and devotional endurances—but above all—ah, far above all—he kneels to it—he worships it in the faith, in the purity, in the strength, in the altogether divine majesty—of her *love*.

Let me conclude—by the recitation of yet another brief poem—one very different in character from any that I have before quoted. It is by Motherwell, and is called "The Song of the Cavalier." With our modern and altogether rational ideas of the absurdity and impiety of warfare, we are not precisely in that frame of mind best adapted to sympathize with the sentiments, and thus to appreciate the real excellence of the poem. To do this fully, we must identify ourselves, in fancy, with the soul of the old cavalier.

Then mounte! then mounte, brave gallants, all,
  And don your helmes amaine:
Death's couriers, Fame and Honor, call
  Us to the field againe.

No shrewish teares shall fill our eye
  When the sword-hilt's in our hand,—
Heart-whole we'll part, and no whit sighe
  For the fayrest of the land;
Let piping swaine, and craven wight,
  Thus weepe and puling crye,
Our business is like men to fight,
  And hero-like to die!

WALTER PATER: Conclusion*

Λέγει που Ἡράκλειτος ὅτι πάντα χωρεῖ καὶ οὐδὲν μένει [1]

TO REGARD all things and principles of things as inconstant modes or fashions has more and more become the tendency of modern thought. Let us begin with that which is without—our physical life. Fix upon it in one of its more exquisite intervals, the moment, for instance, of delicious recoil from the flood of water in summer heat. What is the whole physical life in that moment but a combination of natural elements to which science gives their names? But these elements, phosphorus and lime and delicate fibres, are present not in the human body alone: we detect them in places most remote from it. Our physical life is a perpetual motion of them—the passage of the blood, the wasting and repairing of the lenses of the eye, the modification of the tissues of the brain by every ray of light and sound—processes which science reduces to simpler and more elementary forces. Like the elements of which we are composed, the action of these forces extends beyond us; it rusts iron and ripens corn. Far out on every side of us those elements are broadcast, driven by many forces; and birth and gesture and death and the springing of violets from the grave are but a few out of ten thousand resultant combinations. That clear, perpetual outline of face and limb is but an image of ours, under which we group them—a design in a web, the actual threads of which pass out beyond it. This at least of flamelike our life has, that it is but the concurrence, renewed from moment to moment, of forces parting sooner or later on their ways.

Or if we begin with the inward world of thought and feeling, the whirlpool is still more rapid, the flame more eager and devouring. There it is no longer the gradual darkening of the eye and fading of colour from the wall,—the movement of the shore-side, where the water flows down indeed, though in apparent rest,—but the race of the mid-stream, a drift of momentary acts of sight and passion and thought. At first sight experience seems to bury us under a flood of external objects, pressing upon us with a sharp and importunate reality, calling us out of ourselves in a thousand forms of action. But when reflexion begins to act upon those objects they are dissipated under its influence; the cohesive force seems suspended like a trick of magic; each object is loosed into a group of impressions—colour, odour, texture—in the mind of the observer. And if we continue to

* *Studies in the History of the Renaissance*, of which this is the Conclusion, first appeared in 1873. To the third edition, of 1888, Pater appended the following note: "This brief 'Conclusion' was omitted in the second edition of this book, as I conceived it might possibly mislead some of those young men into whose hands it might fall. On the whole, I have thought it best to reprint it here, with some slight changes which bring it closer to my original meaning. I have dealt more fully in *Marius the Epicurean* with the thoughts suggested by it." We reprint the version included in the third edition.

[1] ["Heraclitus somewhere says that all things move and nothing stays."]

dwell in thought on this world, not of objects in the solidity with which language invests them, but of impressions unstable, flickering, inconsistent, which burn and are extinguished with our consciousness of them, it contracts still further; the whole scope of observation is dwarfed to the narrow chamber of the individual mind. Experience, already reduced to a swarm of impressions, is ringed round for each one of us by that thick wall of personality through which no real voice has ever pierced on its way to us, or from us to that which we can only conjecture to be without. Every one of those impressions is the impression of the individual in his isolation, each mind keeping as a solitary prisoner its own dream of a world. Analysis goes a step farther still, and assures us that those impressions of the individual mind to which, for each one of us, experience dwindles down, are in perpetual flight; that each of them is limited by time, and that as time is infinitely divisible, each of them is infinitely divisible also; all that is actual in it being a single moment, gone while we try to apprehend it, of which it may ever be more truly said that it has ceased to be than that it is. To such a tremulous wisp constantly reforming itself on the stream, to a single sharp impression, with a sense in it, a relic more or less fleeting, of such moments gone by, what is real in our life fines itself down. It is with this movement, with the passage and dissolution of impressions, images, sensations, that analysis leaves off—that continual vanishing away, that strange, perpetual, weaving and unweaving of ourselves.

Philosophiren, says Novalis, *ist dephlegmatisiren, vivificiren.* The service of philosophy, of speculative culture, towards the human spirit is to rouse, to startle it into sharp and eager observation. Every moment some form grows perfect in hand or face; some tone on the hills or the sea is choicer than the rest; some mood of passion or insight or intellectual excitement is irresistibly real and attractive for us,—for that moment only. Not the fruit of experience, but experience itself, is the end. A counted number of pulses only is given to us of a variegated, dramatic life. How may we see in them all that is to be seen in them by the finest senses? How shall we pass most swiftly from point to point, and be present always at the focus where the greatest number of vital forces unite in their purest energy?

To burn always with this hard, gemlike flame, to maintain this ecstasy, is success in life. In a sense it might even be said that our failure is to form habits: for, after all, habit is relative to a stereotyped world, and meantime it is only the roughness of the eye that makes any two persons, things, situations, seem alike. While all melts under our feet, we may well catch at any exquisite passion, or any contribution to knowledge that seems by a lifted horizon to set the spirit free for a moment, or any stirring of the senses, strange dyes, strange colours, and curious odours, or work of the artist's hands, or the face of one's friend. Not to discriminate every moment some passionate attitude in those about us, and in the brilliancy of their gifts some tragic dividing of forces on their ways, is, on this short day of frost and sun, to sleep before evening. With this sense of the splendour of our experience and of its awful brevity, gathering all we are into one desperate effort to see and touch, we shall hardly have time to make theories about the things we see and touch. What we have to do is to be for ever curiously testing new opinions and courting new impressions, never acquiescing in a facile orthodoxy of Comte, or of Hegel, or of our own. Philosophical theories or ideas, as points of view, instruments of criticism, may help us to gather up what might otherwise pass unregarded by us. "Philosophy is the microscope of thought." The theory or idea or system which requires of us the sacrifice of any part of this experience, in consideration of some interest into which we cannot enter, or some abstract theory we have not identified with ourselves, or what is only conventional, has no real claim upon us.

One of the most beautiful passages in the writings of Rousseau is that in the sixth book of the *Confessions,* where he describes the awakening in him of the literary sense. An undefinable taint of death had always clung about him, and now in early manhood he believed himself smitten by mortal disease. He asked himself how he might make as much as possible of the interval that remained; and he was not biassed by anything in his previous life when he decided that it must be by intellectual excitement, which he found just then in the clear, fresh writings of Voltaire. Well! we are all *condamnés,* as Victor Hugo says: we are all under sentence of death but with a sort of indefinite reprieve—*les hommes sont tous condamnés à mort avec des sursis indéfinis:* we have an interval, and then our place knows us no more. Some spend this interval in listlessness, some in high passions, the wisest, at least among "the children of this world," in art and song. For our one chance lies in expanding that interval, in getting as many pulsations as possible into the given time. Great passions may give us this quickened sense of life, ecstasy and sorrow of love, the various forms of enthusiastic activity, disinterested or otherwise, which come naturally to many of us. Only be sure it is passion—that it does yield you this fruit of a quickened, multiplied consciousness. Of this wisdom, the poetic passion, the desire of beauty, the love of art for art's sake, has most; for art comes to you professing frankly to give nothing but the highest quality to your moments as they pass, and simply for those moments' sake.

MATTHEW ARNOLD: The Study of Poetry*

"The future of poetry is immense, because in poetry, where it is worthy of its high destinies, our race, as time goes on, will find an ever surer and surer stay. There is not a creed which is not shaken, not an accredited dogma which is not shown to be questionable, not a received tradition which does not threaten to dissolve. Our religion has materialised itself in the fact, in the supposed fact; it has attached its emotion to the fact, and now the fact is failing it. But for poetry the idea is everything; the rest is a world of illusion, of divine illusion. Poetry attaches its emotion to the idea; the idea *is* the fact. The strongest part of our religion today is its unconscious poetry."

Let me be permitted to quote these words of my own, as uttering the thought which should, in my opinion, go with us and govern us in all our study of poetry. In the present work it is the course of one great contributory stream to the world-river of poetry that we are invited to follow. We are here invited to trace the stream of English poetry. But whether we set ourselves, as here, to follow only one of the several streams that make the mighty river of poetry, or whether we seek to know them all, our governing thought should be the same. We should conceive of poetry worthily, and more highly than it has been the custom to conceive of it. We should conceive of it as capable of higher uses, and called to higher destinies, than those which in general men have assigned to it hitherto. More and more mankind will discover that we have to turn to poetry to interpret life for us, to console us, to sustain us. Without poetry, our science will appear incomplete; and most of what now passes with us for religion and philosophy will be replaced by poetry. Science, I say, will appear incomplete without it. For finely and truly does Wordsworth call poetry "the impassioned expression which is in the countenance of all science"; and what is a countenance without its expression? Again, Wordsworth finely and truly calls poetry "the breath and finer spirit of all knowledge"; our religion, parading evidences such as those on which the popular mind relies now; our philosophy, pluming itself on its reasonings about causation and finite and infinite being; what are they but the shadows and dreams and false shows of knowledge? The day will come when we shall wonder at ourselves for having trusted to them, for having taken them seriously; and the more we perceive their hollowness, the more we shall prize "the breath

* "The Study of Poetry" was first published in 1880 as the general introduction to Ward's anthology of *The English Poets.* It is reprinted here by courtesy of The Macmillan Company of New York.

and finer spirit of knowledge" offered to us by poetry.

But if we conceive thus highly of the destinies of poetry, we must also set our standard for poetry high, since poetry, to be capable of fulfilling such high destinies, must be poetry of a high order of excellence. We must accustom ourselves to a high standard and to a strict judgment. Sainte-Beuve relates that Napoleon one day said, when somebody was spoken of in his presence as a charlatan: "Charlatan as much as you please; but where is there *not* charlatanism?"—"Yes," answers Sainte-Beuve, "in politics, in the art of governing mankind, that is perhaps true. But in the order of thought, in art, the glory, the eternal honour is that charlatanism shall find no entrance; herein lies the inviolableness of that noble portion of man's being." It is admirably said, and let us hold fast to it. In poetry, which is thought and art in one, it is the glory, the eternal honour, that charlatanism shall find no entrance; that this noble sphere be kept inviolate and inviolable. Charlatanism is for confusing or obliterating the distinctions between excellent and inferior, sound and unsound or only half-sound, true and untrue or only half-true. It is charlatanism, conscious or unconscious, whenever we confuse or obliterate these. And in poetry, more than anywhere else, it is unpermissible to confuse or obliterate them. For in poetry the distinction between excellent and inferior, sound and unsound or only half-sound, true and untrue or only half-true, is of paramount importance. It is of paramount importance because of the high destinies of poetry. In poetry, as in criticism of life under the conditions fixed for such a criticism by the laws of poetic truth and poetic beauty, the spirit of our race will find, we have said, as time goes on and as other helps fail, its consolation and stay. But the consolation and stay will be of power in proportion to the power of the criticism of life. And the criticism of life will be of power in proportion as the poetry conveying it is excellent rather than inferior, sound rather than unsound or half-sound, true rather than untrue or half-true.

The best poetry is what we want; the best poetry will be found to have a power of forming, sustaining, and delighting us, as nothing else can. A clearer, deeper sense of the best in poetry, and of the strength and joy to be drawn from it, is the most precious benefit which we can gather from a poetical collection such as the present. And yet in the very nature and conduct of such a collection there is inevitably something which tends to obscure in us the consciousness of what our benefit should be, and to distract us from the pursuit of it. We should therefore steadily set it before our minds at the outset, and should compel ourselves to revert constantly to the thought of it as we proceed.

Yes; constantly in reading poetry, a sense for the best, the really excellent, and of the strength and joy to be drawn from it, should be present in our minds and should govern our estimate of what we read. But this real estimate, the only true one, is liable to be superseded, if we are not watchful, by two other kinds of estimate, the historic estimate and the personal estimate, both of which are fallacious. A poet or a poem may count to us historically, they may count to us on grounds personal to ourselves, and they may count to us really. They may count to us historically. The course of development of a nation's language, thought, and poetry, is profoundly interesting; and by regarding a poet's work as a stage in this course of development we may easily bring ourselves to make it of more importance as poetry than in itself it really is, we may come to use a language of quite exaggerated praise in criticising it; in short, to over-rate it. So arises in our poetic judgments the fallacy caused by the estimate which we may call historic. Then, again, a poet or poem may count to us on grounds personal to ourselves. Our personal affinities, likings and circumstances, have great power to sway our estimate of this or that poet's work, and to make us attach more importance to it as poetry than in itself it really possesses, because to us it is, or has been, of high importance. Here also we over-rate the object of our interest, and apply to it a language of praise which is quite exaggerated. And thus we get the source of a second fallacy in our poetic judgments—the fallacy caused by an estimate which we may call personal.

Both fallacies are natural. It is evident how naturally the study of the history and development of poetry may incline a man to pause over reputations and works once conspicuous but now obscure, and to quarrel with a careless public for skipping, in obedience to mere tradition and habit, from one famous name or work in its national poetry to another, ignorant of what it misses, and of the reason for keeping what it keeps, and of the whole process of growth in its poetry. The French have become diligent students of their own early poetry, which they long neglected; the study makes many of them dissatisfied with their so-called classical poetry, the court-tragedy of the seventeenth century, a poetry which Pellisson long ago reproached with its want of the true poetic stamp, with its *politesse stérile et rampante,* but which nevertheless has reigned in France as absolutely as if it had been the perfection of classical poetry indeed. The dissatisfaction is natural; yet a lively and accomplished critic, M. Charles d'Héricault, the editor of Clément Marot, goes too far when he says that "the cloud of glory playing round a classic is a mist as dangerous to the future of a literature as it is intolerable for the purposes of history." "It hinders," he goes on, "it hinders us from seeing more than one single point, the culminating and exceptional point; the summary, fictitious and arbitrary, of a thought and of a work. It substitutes a halo for a physiognomy, it puts a statue where there was once a man, and hiding from us all trace of the labour, the attempts, the weaknesses, the failures, it claims not study but veneration; it does not show us how the thing is done, it imposes upon us a model. Above all, for the historian this creation of classic personages is inadmissible; for it withdraws the poet from his time, from his proper life, it breaks historical relationships, it blinds criticism by conventional admiration, and renders the investigation of literary origins unacceptable. It gives us a human personage no longer but a God seated immovable amidst His perfect work, like Jupiter on Olympus; and hardly will it be possible for the young student to whom such work is exhibited at such a distance from him, to believe that it did not issue ready made from that divine head."

All this is brilliantly and tellingly said, but we must plead for a distinction. Everything depends on the reality of a poet's classic character. If he is a dubious classic, let us sift him; if he is a false classic, let us explode him. But if he is a real classic, if his work belongs to the class of the very best (for this is the true and right meaning of the word *classic, classical*), then the great thing for us is to feel and enjoy his work as deeply as ever we can, and to appreciate the wide difference between it and all work which has not the same high character. This is what is salutary, this is what is formative; this is the great benefit to be got from the study of poetry. Everything which interferes with it, which hinders it, is injurious. True, we must read our classic with open eyes, and not with eyes blinded with superstition; we must perceive when his work comes short, when it drops out of the class of the very best, and we must rate it, in such cases, at its proper value. But the use of this negative criticism is not in itself, it is entirely in its enabling us to have a clearer sense and a deeper enjoyment of what is truly excellent. To trace the labour, the attempts, the weaknesses, the failures of a genuine classic, to acquaint oneself with his time and his life and his historical relationships, is mere literary dilettantism unless it has that clear sense and deeper enjoyment for its end. It may be said that the more we know about a classic the better we shall enjoy him; and, if we lived as long as Methuselah and had all of us heads of perfect clearness and wills of perfect steadfastness, this might be true in fact as it is plausible in theory. But the case here is much the same as the case with the Greek and Latin studies of our schoolboys. The elaborate philological groundwork which we require them to lay is in theory an admirable preparation for appreciating the Greek and Latin authors worthily. The more thoroughly we lay the groundwork, the better we shall be able, it may be said, to enjoy the authors. True, if time were not so short, and schoolboys' wits not so soon tired and their power of attention exhausted; only, as it is, the elaborate philological preparation goes on, but the authors are little known and less enjoyed. So with the investigator of "historic origins" in poetry. He ought to enjoy the true classic all the better for his investigations; he often is distracted from the enjoyment of the best, and with the less good he overbusies himself, and is prone to over-rate it in proportion to the trouble which it has cost him.

The idea of tracing historic origins and his

torical relationships cannot be absent from a compilation like the present. And naturally the poets to be exhibited in it will be assigned to those persons for exhibition who are known to prize them highly, rather than to those who have no special inclination towards them. Moreover, the very occupation with an author, and the business of exhibiting him, disposes us to affirm and amplify his importance. In the present work, therefore, we are sure of frequent temptation to adopt the historic estimate, or the personal estimate, and to forget the real estimate; which latter, nevertheless, we must employ if we are to make poetry yield us its full benefit. So high is that benefit, the benefit of clearly feeling and of deeply enjoying the really excellent, the truly classic in poetry, that we do well, I say, to set it fixedly before our minds as our object in studying poets and poetry, and to make the desire of attaining it the one principle to which, as the *Imitation* says, whatever we may read or come to know, we always return. *Cum multa legeris et cognoveris, ad unum semper oportet redire principium.*

The historic estimate is likely in especial to affect our judgment and our language when we are dealing with ancient poets; the personal estimate when we are dealing with poets our contemporaries, or at any rate modern. The exaggerations due to the historic estimate are not in themselves, perhaps, of very much gravity. Their report hardly enters the general ear; probably they do not always impose even on the literary men who adopt them. But they lead to a dangerous abuse of language. So we hear Cædmon, amongst our own poets, compared to Milton. I have already noticed the enthusiasm of one accomplished French critic for "historic origins." Another eminent French critic, M. Vitet, comments upon that famous document of the early poetry of his nation, the *Chanson de Roland.* It is indeed a most interesting document. The *joculator* or *jongleur Taillefer,* who was with William the Conqueror's army at Hastings, marched before the Norman troops, so said the tradition, singing "of Charlemagne and of Roland and of Oliver, and of the vassals who died at Roncevaux"; and it is suggested that in the *Chanson de Roland* by one Turoldus or Théroulde, a poem preserved in a manuscript of the twelfth century in the Bodleian Library at Oxford, we have certainly the matter, perhaps even some of the words, of the chant which Taillefer sang. The poem has vigour and freshness; it is not without pathos. But M. Vitet is not satisfied with seeing in it a document of some poetic value, and of very high historic and linguistic value; he sees in it a grand and beautiful work, a monument of epic genius. In its general design he finds the grandiose conception, in its details he finds the constant union of simplicity with greatness, which are the marks, he truly says, of the genuine epic, and distinguish it from the artificial epic of literary ages. One thinks of Homer; this is the sort of praise which is given to Homer, and justly given. Higher praise there cannot well be, and it is the praise due to epic poetry of the highest order only, and to no other. Let us try, then, the *Chanson de Roland* at its best. Roland, mortally wounded, lay himself down under a pine-tree, with his face turned towards Spain and the enemy—

De plusurs choses à remembrer li prist,
De tantes teres cume li bers cunquist,
De dulce France, des humes de sun lign,
De Carlemagne sun seignor ki l'nurrit.[1]

That is primitive work, I repeat, with an undeniable poetic quality of its own. It deserves such praise, and such praise is sufficient for it. But now turn to Homer—

Ὡς φάτο· τοὺς δ ἤδη κατέχεν φυσίζοος αἶα
ἐν Λακεδαίμονι αὖθι, φίλῃ ἐν πατρίδι γαίῃ.[2]

We are here in another world, another order of poetry altogether; here is rightly due such supreme praise as that which M. Vitet gives to the *Chanson de Roland.* If our words are to have any meaning, if our judgments are to have any solidity, we must not heap that supreme praise upon poetry of an order immeasurably inferior.

Indeed there can be no more useful help for discovering what poetry belongs to the class of the truly excellent, and can therefore do us most good, than to have always in one's mind lines and expressions of the great masters, and to

1 ["And he began to recall many things, The many countries the knight had conquered, Sweet France, the men of his lineage, Charlemagne, his lord who brought him up."]

2 ["So she said; but the life-giving earth already held them fast in Lacedaemon, their dear native land."]

apply them as a touchstone to other poetry. Of course we are not to require this other poetry to resemble them; it may be very dissimilar. But if we have any tact we shall find them, when we have lodged them well in our minds, an infallible touchstone for detecting the presence or absence of high poetic quality, and also the degree of this quality, in all other poetry which we may place beside them. Short passages, even single lines, will serve our turn quite sufficiently. Take the two lines which I have just quoted from Homer, the poet's comment on Helen's mention of her brothers;—or take his

Α δειλώ, τί σφῶϊ δόμεν Πηλῆϊ ἄνακτι
Θνητῷ; ὑμεῖς δ' ἐστὸν ἀγήρω τ' ἀθανάτω τε.
ἦ ἵνα δυστήνοισι μετ' ἀνδράσιν ἄλγε' ἔχητον; [3]

the address of Zeus to the horses of Peleus;—or take finally his

Καὶ σέ, γέρον, τὸ πρὶν μὲν ἀκούομεν ὄλβιον εἶναι· [4]

the words of Achilles to Priam, a suppliant before him. Take that incomparable line and a half of Dante, Ugolino's tremendous words—

Io no piangeva; sì dentro impietrai.
Piangevan elli . . . [5]

take the lovely words of Beatrice to Virgil—

Io son fatta da Dio, sua mercè, tale,
Che la vostra miseria non mi tange,
Nè fiamma d'esto incendio non m'assale . . . [6]

take the simple, but perfect, single line—

In la sua volontade è nostra pace. [7]

Take of Shakespeare a line or two of Henry the Fourth's expostulation with sleep—

Wilt thou upon the high and giddy mast
Seal up the ship-boy's eyes, and rock his brains
In cradle of the rude imperious surge . . .

and take, as well, Hamlet's dying request to Horatio—

If thou didst ever hold me in thy heart,
Absent thee from felicity awhile,
And in this harsh world draw thy breath in pain
To tell my story . . .

Take of Milton that Miltonic passage:

Darken'd so, yet shone
Above them all the archangel; but his face
Deep scars of thunder had intrench'd, and care
Sat on his faded cheek . . .

add two such lines as

And courage never to submit or yield
And what is else not to be overcome . . .

and finish with the exquisite close to the loss of Proserpine, the loss

. . . which cost Ceres all that pain
To seek her through the world.

These few lines, if we have tact and can use them, are enough even of themselves to keep clear and sound our judgments about poetry, to save us from fallacious estimates of it, to conduct us to a real estimate.

The specimens I have quoted differ widely from one another, but they have in common this: the possession of the very highest poetical quality. If we are thoroughly penetrated by their power, we shall find that we have acquired a sense enabling us, whatever poetry may be laid before us, to feel the degree in which a high poetical quality is present or wanting there. Critics give themselves great labour to draw out what in the abstract constitutes the characters of a high quality of poetry. It is much better simply to have recourse to concrete examples;—to take specimens of poetry of the high, the very highest quality, and to say: The characters of a high quality of poetry are what is expressed *there.* They are far better recognized by being felt in the verse of the master, than by being perused in the prose of the critic. Nevertheless if we are urgently pressed to give some critical account of them, we may safely, perhaps, venture on laying down, not indeed how and why the characters arise, but where and in what they arise. They are in the matter and substance of the poetry, and they are in its manner and style. Both of these, the substance and matter on the

[3] ["Ah, wretched pair, why did we give you to King Peleus, a mortal, while you are immortal and forever young? Was it that among ill-fated men you should suffer?"]

[4] ["And you, old man, as we have heard, were happy in former times."]

[5] ["I did not weep, so grew to stone within. They wept. . . ."]

[6] ["God, in his mercy, has so made me that your misery does not touch me, nor the flame of this fire assail me."]

[7] ["In His will is our peace."]

one hand, the style and manner on the other, have a mark, an accent, of high beauty, worth, and power. But if we are asked to define this mark and accent in the abstract, our answer must be: No, for we should thereby be darkening the question, not clearing it. The mark and accent are as given by the substance and matter of that poetry, by the style and manner of that poetry, and of all other poetry which is akin to it in quality.

Only one thing we may add as to the substance and matter of poetry, guiding ourselves by Aristotle's profound observation that the superiority of poetry over history consists in its possessing a higher truth and a higher seriousness (ψιλοσοψώτερον χαὶ σπουδαιότερον). Let us add, therefore, to what we have said, this: that the substance and matter of the best poetry acquire their special character from possessing, in an eminent degree, truth and seriousness. We may add yet further, what is in itself evident, that to the style and manner of the best poetry their special character, their accent, is given by their diction, and, even yet more, by their movement. And though we distinguish between the two characters, the two accents, of superiority, yet they are nevertheless vitally connected one with the other. The superior character of truth and seriousness, in the matter and substance of the best poetry, is inseparable from the superiority of diction and movement marking its style and manner. The two superiorities are closely related, and are in steadfast proportion one to the other. So far as high poetic truth and seriousness are wanting to a poet's matter and substance, so far also, we may be sure, will a high poetic stamp of diction and movement be wanting to his style and manner. In proportion as this high stamp of diction and movement, again, is absent from a poet's style and manner, we shall find, also, that high poetic truth and seriousness are absent from his substance and matter.

So stated, these are but dry generalities; their whole force lies in their application. And I could wish every student of poetry to make the application of them for himself. Made by himself, the application would impress itself upon his mind far more deeply than made by me. Neither will my limits allow me to make any full application of the generalities above propounded; but in the hope of bringing out, at any rate, some significance in them, and of establishing an important principle more firmly by their means, I will, in the space which remains to me, follow rapidly from the commencement the course of our English poetry with them in my view.

Once more I return to the early poetry of France, with which our own poetry, in its origins, is indissolubly connected. In the twelfth and thirteenth centuries, that seed-time of all modern language and literature, the poetry of France had a clear predominance in Europe. Of the two divisions of that poetry, its productions in the *langue d'oil* and its productions in the *langue d'oc*, the poetry of the *langue d'oc*, of southern France, of the troubadours, is of importance because of its effect on Italian literature;—the first literature of modern Europe to strike the true and grand note, and to bring forth, as in Dante and Petrarch it brought forth, classics. But the predominance of French poetry in Europe, during the twelfth and thirteenth centuries, is due to its poetry of the *langue d'oil*, the poetry of northern France and of the tongue which is now the French language. In the twelfth century the bloom of this romance-poetry was earlier and stronger in England, at the court of our Anglo-Norman kings, than in France itself. But it was a bloom of French poetry; and as our native poetry formed itself, it formed itself out of this. The romance-poems which took possession of the heart and imagination of Europe in the twelfth and thirteenth centuries are French; "they are," as Southey justly says, "the pride of French literature, nor have we anything which can be placed in competition with them." Themes were supplied from all quarters; but the romance-setting which was common to them all, and which gained the ear of Europe, was French. This constituted for the French poetry, literature, and language, at the height of the Middle Age, an unchallenged predominance. The Italian Brunetto Latini, the master of Dante, wrote his *Treasure* in French because, he says, "la parleure en est plus délitable et plus commune à toutes gens." In the same century, the thirteenth, the French romance-writer, Christian of Troyes, formulates the claims, in chivalry and letters, of France, his native country, as follows:—

Or vous ert par ce livre apris,
Que Gresse ot de chevalerie
Le premier los et de clergie;
Puis vint chevalerie à Rome,
Et de la clergie la some,
Qui ore est en France venue.
Diex doinst qu'ele i soit retenue,
Et que li lius li abelisse
Tant que de France n'isse
L'onor qui s'i est arestée!

"Now by this book you will learn that first Greece had the renown for chivalry and letters: then chivalry and the primacy in letters passed to Rome, and now it is come to France. God grant it may be kept there; and that the place may please it so well, that the honour which has come to make stay in France may never depart thence!"

Yet it is now all gone, this French romance-poetry of which the weight of substance and the power of style are not unfairly represented by this extract from Christian of Troyes. Only by means of the historic estimate can we persuade ourselves not to think that any of it is of poetical importance.

But in the fourteenth century there comes an Englishman nourished on this poetry, taught his trade by this poetry, getting words, rhyme, metre from this poetry; for even of that stanza which the Italians used, and which Chaucer derived immediately from the Italians, the basis and suggestion was probably given in France. Chaucer (I have already named him) fascinated his contemporaries, but so too did Christian of Troyes and Wolfram of Eschenbach. Chaucer's power of fascination, however, is enduring; his poetical importance does not need the assistance of the historic estimate; it is real. He is a genuine source of joy and strength, which is flowing still for us and will flow always. He will be read, as time goes on, far more generally than he is read now. His language is a cause of difficulty for us; but so also, and I think in quite as great a degree, is the language of Burns. In Chaucer's case, as in that of Burns, it is a difficulty to be unhesitatingly accepted and overcome.

If we ask ourselves wherein consists the immense superiority of Chaucer's poetry over the romance-poetry—why it is that in passing from this to Chaucer we suddenly feel ourselves to be in another world, we shall find that his superiority is both in the substance of his poetry and in the style of his poetry. His superiority in substance is given by his large, free, simple, clear yet kindly view of human life,—so unlike the total want, in the romance-poets, of all intelligent command of it. Chaucer has not their helplessness; he has gained the power to survey the world from a central, a truly human point of view. We have only to call to mind the Prologue to *The Canterbury Tales.* The right comment upon it is Dryden's: "It is sufficient to say, according to the proverb, that *here is God's plenty.*" And again: "He is a perpetual fountain of good sense." It is by a large, free, sound representation of things, that poetry, this high criticism of life, has truth of substance; and Chaucer's poetry has truth of substance.

Of his style and manner, if we think first of the romance-poetry and then of Chaucer's divine liquidness of diction, his divine fluidity of movement, it is difficult to speak temperately. They are irresistible, and justify all the rapture with which his successors speak of his "gold dew-drops of speech." Johnson misses the point entirely when he finds fault with Dryden for ascribing to Chaucer the first refinement of our numbers, and says that Gower also can show smooth numbers and easy rhymes. The refinement of our numbers means something far more than this. A nation may have versifiers with smooth numbers and easy rhymes, and yet may have no real poetry at all. Chaucer is the father of our splendid English poetry; he is our "well of English undefiled," because by the lovely charm of his diction, the lovely charm of his movement, he makes an epoch and founds a tradition. In Spenser, Shakespeare, Milton, Keats, we can follow the tradition of the liquid diction, the fluid movement of Chaucer; at one time it is his liquid diction of which in these poets we feel the virtue, and at another time it is his fluid movement. And the virtue is irresistible.

Bounded as is my space, I must yet find room for an example of Chaucer's virtue, as I have given examples to show the virtue of the great classics. I feel disposed to say that a single line is enough to show the charm of Chaucer's verse; that merely one line like this—

> O martyr souded in virginitee!

has a virtue of manner and movement such as we shall not find in all the verse of romance-poetry;—but this is saying nothing. The virtue is such as we shall not find, perhaps, in all English poetry, outside the poets whom I have named as the special inheritors of Chaucer's tradition. A single line, however, is too little if we have not the strain of Chaucer's verse well in our memory; let us take a stanza. It is from *The Prioress's Tale,* the story of the Christian child murdered in a Jewry—

> My throte is cut unto my nekke-bone
> Saidè this child, and as by way of kinde
> I should have deyd, yea, longè time agone;
> But Jesu Christ, as ye in bookès finde,
> Will that his glory last and be in minde,
> And for the worship of his mother dere
> Yet may I sing *O Alma* loud and clere.

Wordsworth has modernised this Tale, and to feel how delicate and evanescent is the charm of verse, we have only to read Wordsworth's first three lines of this stanza after Chaucer's—

> My throat is cut unto the bone, I trow,
> Said this young child, and by the law of kind
> I should have died, yea, many hours ago.

The charm is departed. It is often said that the power of liquidness and fluidity in Chaucer's verse was dependent upon a free, a licentious dealing with language, such as is now impossible; upon a liberty, such as Burns too enjoyed, of making words like *neck, bird,* into a dissyllable by adding to them, and words like *cause, rhyme,* into a dissyllable by sounding the *e* mute. It is true that Chaucer's fluidity is conjoined with this liberty, and is admirably served by it; but we ought not to say that it was dependent upon it. It was dependent upon his talent. Other poets with a like liberty do not attain to the fluidity of Chaucer; Burns himself does not attain to it. Poets, again, who have a talent akin to Chaucer's, such as Shakespeare or Keats, have known how to attain his fluidity without the like liberty.

And yet Chaucer is not one of the great classics. His poetry transcends and effaces, easily and without effort, all the romance-poetry of Catholic Christendom; it transcends and effaces all the English poetry contemporary with it, it transcends and effaces all the English poetry subsequent to it down to the age of Elizabeth. Of such avail is poetic truth of substance, in its natural and necessary union with poetic truth of style. And yet, I say, Chaucer is not one of the great classics. He has not their accent. What is wanting to him is suggested by the mere mention of the name of the first great classic of Christendom, the immortal poet who died eighty years before Chaucer,—Dante. The accent of such verse as

> *In la sua volontage è nostra pace . . .*

is altogether beyond Chaucer's reach; we praise him, but we feel that this accent is out of the question for him. It may be said that it was necessarily out of the reach of any poet in the England of that stage of growth. Possibly; but we are to adopt a real, not a historic, estimate of poetry. However we may account for its absence, something is wanting, then, to the poetry of Chaucer, which poetry must have before it can be placed in the glorious class of the best. And there is no doubt what that something is. It is the σπουδαιότης the high and excellent seriousness, which Aristotle assigns as one of the grand virtues of poetry. The substance of Chaucer's poetry, his view of things and his criticism of life, has largeness, freedom, shrewdness, benignity; but it has not this high seriousness. Homer's criticism of life has it, Dante's has it, Shakespeare's has it. It is this chiefly which gives to our spirits what they can rest upon; and with the increasing demands of our modern ages upon poetry, this virtue of giving us what we can rest upon will be more and more highly esteemed. A voice from the slums of Paris, fifty or sixty years after Chaucer, the voice of poor Villon out of his life of riot and crime, has at its happy moments (as, for instance, in the last stanza of *La Belle Heaulmière*) more of this important poetic virtue of seriousness than all the productions of Chaucer. But its apparition in Villon, and in men like Villon, is fitful; the greatness of the great poets, the power of their criticism of life, is that their virtue is sustained.

To our praise, therefore, of Chaucer as a poet there must be this limitation; he lacks the high seriousness of the great classics, and therewith an important part of their virtue. Still, the main fact for us to bear in mind about Chaucer is his sterling value according to that real estimate which we firmly adopt for all poets. He has poetic truth of substance, though he has not high poetic seriousness, and corresponding to his truth of substance he has an exquisite virtue of style and manner. With him is born our real poetry.

For my present purpose I need not dwell on our Elizabethan poetry, or on the continuation and close of this poetry in Milton. We all of us profess to be agreed in the estimate of this poetry; we all of us recognise it as great poetry, our greatest, and Shakespeare and Milton as our poetical classics. The real estimate, here, has universal currency. With the next age of our poetry divergency and difficulty begin. An historic estimate of that poetry has established itself; and the question is, whether it will be found to coincide with the real estimate.

The age of Dryden, together with our whole eighteenth century which followed it, sincerely believed itself to have produced poetical classics of its own, and even to have made advance, in poetry, beyond all its predecessors. Dryden regards as not seriously disputable the opinion "that the sweetness of English verse was never understood or practised by our fathers." Cowley could see nothing at all in Chaucer's poetry. Dryden heartily admired it, and, as we have seen, praised its matter admirably; but of its exquisite manner and movement all he can find to say is that "there is the rude sweetness of a Scotch tune in it, which is natural and pleasing, though not perfect." Addison, wishing to praise Chaucer's numbers, compares them with Dryden's own. And all through the eighteenth century, and down even into our own times, the stereotyped phrase of approbation for good verse found in our early poetry has been, that it even approached the verse of Dryden, Addison, Pope, and Johnson.

Are Dryden and Pope poetical classics? Is the historic estimate, which represents them as such, and which has been so long established that it cannot easily give way, the real estimate? Wordsworth and Coleridge, as is well known, denied it; but the authority of Wordsworth and Coleridge does not weigh much with the young generation, and there are many signs to show that the eighteenth century and its judgments are coming into favour again. Are the favourite poets of the eighteenth century classics?

It is impossible within my present limits to discuss the question fully. And what man of letters would not shrink from seeming to dispose dictatorially of the claims of two men who are, at any rate, such masters in letters as Dryden and Pope; two men of such admirable talent, both of them, and one of them, Dryden, a man, on all sides, of such energetic and genial power? And yet, if we are to gain the full benefit from poetry, we must have the real estimate of it. I cast about for some mode of arriving, in the present case, at such an estimate without offence. And perhaps the best way is to begin, as it is easy to begin, with cordial praise.

When we find Chapman, the Elizabethan translator of Homer, expressing himself in his preface thus: "Though truth in her very nakedness sits in so deep a pit, that from Gades to Aurora and Ganges few eyes can sound her, I hope yet those few here will so discover and confirm that, the date being out of her darkness in this morning of our poet, he shall now gird his temples with the sun,"—we pronounce that such a prose is intolerable. When we find Milton writing: "And long it was not after, when I was confirmed in this opinion, that he, who would not be frustrate of his hope to write well hereafter in laudable things, ought himself to be a true poem,"—we pronounce that such a prose has its own grandeur, but that it is obsolete and inconvenient. But when we find Dryden telling us: "What Virgil wrote in the vigour of his age, in plenty and at ease, I have undertaken to translate in my declining years; struggling with wants, oppressed with sickness, curbed in my genius, liable to be misconstrued in all I write,"—then we exclaim that here at last we have the true English prose, a prose such as we would all gladly use if we only knew how. Yet Dryden was Milton's contemporary.

But after the Restoration the time had come when our nation felt the imperious need of a fit prose. So, too, the time had likewise come when our nation felt the imperious need of freeing itself from the absorbing preoccupation which religion in the Puritan age had exercised. It was impossible that this freedom should be brought about without some negative excess, without some neglect and impairment of the religious life of the soul; and the spiritual history of the eighteenth century shows us that the freedom was not achieved without them. Still, the freedom was achieved; the preoccupation, an undoubtedly baneful and retarding one if it had continued, was got rid of. And as with religion amongst us at that period, so it was also with letters. A fit prose was a necessity; but it was impossible that a fit prose should establish itself amongst us without some touch of frost to the imaginative life of the soul. The needful qualities for a fit prose are regularity, uniformity, precision, balance. The men of letters, whose destiny it may be to bring their nation to the attainment of a fit prose, must of necessity, whether they work in prose or in verse, give a predominating, an almost exclusive attention to the qualities of regularity, uniformity, precision, balance. But an almost exclusive attention to these qualities involves some repression and silencing of poetry.

We are to regard Dryden as the puissant and glorious founder, Pope as the splendid high priest, of our age of prose and reason, of our excellent and indispensable eighteenth century. For the purposes of their mission and destiny their poetry, like their prose, is admirable. Do you ask me whether Dryden's verse, take it almost where you will, is not good?

> A milk-white Hind, immortal and unchanged,
> Fed on the lawns and in the forest ranged.

I answer: Admirable for the purposes of the inaugurator of an age of prose and reason. Do you ask me whether Pope's verse, take it almost where you will, is not good?

> To Hounslow Heath I point, and Banstead Down
> Thence comes your mutton, and these chicks my own.

I answer: Admirable for the purposes of the high priest of an age of prose and reason. But do you ask me whether such verse proceeds from men with an adequate poetic criticism of life, from men whose criticism of life has a high seriousness, or even, without that high seriousness, has poetic largeness, freedom, insight, benignity? Do you ask me whether the application of ideas to life in the verse of these men, often a powerful application, no doubt, is a powerful *poetic* application? Do you ask me whether the poetry of these men has either the matter or the inseparable manner of such an adequate poetic criticism; whether it has the accent of

> Absent thee from felicity awhile . . .

or of

> And what is else not to be overcome . . .

or of

> O Martyr souded in virginitee!

I answer: It has not and cannot have them; it is the poetry of the builders of an age of prose and reason. Though they may write in verse, though they may in a certain sense be masters of the art of versification, Dryden and Pope are not classics of our poetry, they are classics of our prose.

Gray is our poetical classic of that literature and age; the position of Gray is singular, and demands a word of notice here. He has not the volume or the power of poets who, coming in times more favourable, have attained to an independent criticism of life. But he lived with the great poets, he lived, above all, with the Greeks, through perpetually studying and enjoying them; and he caught their poetic point of view for regarding life, caught their poetic manner. The point of view and the manner are not self-sprung in him, he caught them of others; and he had not the free and abundant use of them. But, whereas Addison and Pope never had the use of them, Gray had the use of them at times. He is the scantiest and frailest of classics in our poetry, but he is a classic.

And now, after Gray, we are met, as we draw towards the end of the eighteenth century, we are met by the great name of Burns. We enter now on times where the personal estimate of poets begins to be rife, and where the real estimate of them is not reached without difficulty. But in spite of the disturbing pressures of personal partiality, of national partiality, let us try to reach a real estimate of the poetry of Burns.

By his English poetry Burns in general belongs to the eighteenth century, and has little importance for us.

Mark ruffian Violence, distain'd with crimes,
Rousing elate in these degenerate times;
View unsuspecting Innocence a prey,
As guileful Fraud points out the erring way;
While subtle Litigation's pliant tongue
The life-blood equal sucks of Right and Wrong!

Evidently this is not the real Burns, or his name and fame would have disappeared long ago. Nor is Clarinda's love-poet, Sylvander, the real Burns either. But he tells us himself: "These English songs gravel me to death. I have not the command of the language that I have of my native tongue. In fact, I think that my ideas are more barren in English than in Scotch. I have been at *Duncan Gray* to dress it in English, but all I can do is desperately stupid." We English turn naturally, in Burns, to the poems in our own language, because we can read them easily; but in those poems we have not the real Burns.

The real Burns is of course in his Scotch poems. Let us boldly say that of much of this poetry, a poetry dealing perpetually with Scotch drink, Scotch religion, and Scotch manners, a Scotchman's estimate is apt to be personal. A Scotchman is used to this world of Scotch drink, Scotch religion, and Scotch manners; he has a tenderness for it; he meets its poet half way. In this tender mood he reads pieces like the *Holy Fair* or *Halloween.* But this world of Scotch drink, Scotch religion, and Scotch manners is against a poet, not for him, when it is not a partial countryman who reads him; for in itself it is not a beautiful world, and no one can deny that it is of advantage to a poet to deal with a beautiful world. Burns's world of Scotch drink, Scotch religion, and Scotch manners is often a harsh, a sordid, a repulsive world: even the world of his *Cotter's Saturday Night* is not a beautiful world. No doubt a poet's criticism of life may have such truth and power that it triumphs over its world and delights us. Burns may triumph over his world, often he does triumph over his world, but let us observe how and where. Burns is the first case we have had where the bias of the personal estimate tends to mislead; let us look at him closely, he can bear it.

Many of his admirers will tell us that we have Burns, convivial, genuine, delightful, here—

Leeze me on drink! it gies us mair
  Than either school or college;
It kindles wit, it waukens lair,
  It pangs us fou o' knowledge.
Be't whisky gill or penny wheep
  Or ony stronger potion,
It never fails, on drinking deep,
  To kittle up our notion
    By night or day.

There is a great deal of that sort of thing in Burns, and it is unsatisfactory, not because it is bacchanalian poetry, but because it has not that accent of sincerity which bacchanalian poetry, to do it justice, very often has. There is something in it of bravado, something which makes us feel that we have not the man speaking to us with his real voice; something, therefore, poetically unsound.

With still more confidence will his admirers tell us that we have the genuine Burns, the great poet, when his strain asserts the independence, equality, dignity, of men, as in the famous song *For a' that, and a' that*—

A prince can mak' a belted knight,
  A marquis, duke, and a' that;
But an honest man's aboon his might,
  Guid faith he mauna fa' that!
    For a' that, and a' that,
      Their dignities, and a' that,
    The pith o' sense, and pride o' worth,
      Are higher rank than a' that.

Here they find his grand, genuine touches; and still more, when this puissant genius, who so often set morality at defiance, falls moralising—

The sacred lowe o' weel-placed love
  Luxuriantly indulge it;
But never tempt th' illicit rove,
  Tho' naething should divulge it.
I waive the quantum o' the sin,
  The hazard o' concealing,
But och! it hardens a' within,
  And petrifies the feeling.

Or in a higher strain—

Who made the heart, 'tis He alone
  Decidedly can try us;
He knows each chord, its various tone;
  Each spring, its various bias.

Then at the balance let's be mute,
We never can adjust it;
What's *done* we partly may compute,
But know not what's resisted.

Or in a better strain yet, a strain, his admirers will say, unsurpassable—

To make a happy fire-side clime
To weans and wife,
That's the true pathos and sublime
Of human life.

There is criticism of life for you, the admirers of Burns will say to us; there is the application of ideas to life! There is, undoubtedly. The doctrine of the last-quoted lines coincides almost exactly with what was the aim and end, Xenophon tells us, of all the teaching of Socrates. And the application is a powerful one; made by a man of vigorous understanding, and (need I say?) a master of language.

But for supreme poetical success more is required than the powerful application of ideas to life; it must be an application under the conditions fixed by the laws of poetic truth and poetic beauty. Those laws fix as an essential condition, in the poet's treatment of such matters as are here in question, high seriousness;—the high seriousness which comes from absolute sincerity. The accent of high seriousness, born of absolute sincerity, is what gives to such verse as

In la sua volontade è nostra pace . . .

to such criticism of life as Dante's, its power. Is this accent felt in the passages which I have been quoting from Burns? Surely not; surely, if our sense is quick, we must perceive that we have not in those passages a voice from the very inmost soul of the genuine Burns; he is not speaking to us from these depths, he is more or less preaching. And the compensation for admiring such passages less, from missing the perfect poetic accent in them, will be that we shall admire more the poetry where that accent is found.

No; Burns, like Chaucer, comes short of the high seriousness of the great classics, and the virtue of matter and manner which goes with that high seriousness is wanting to his work. At moments he touches it in a profound and passionate melancholy, as in those four immortal lines taken by Byron as a motto for *The Bride of Abydos,* but which have in them a depth of poetic quality such as resides in no verse of Byron's own—

Had we never loved sae kindly,
Had we never loved sae blindly,
Never met, or never parted,
We had ne'er been broken-hearted.

But a whole poem of that quality Burns cannot make; the rest, in the *Farewell to Nancy,* is verbiage.

We arrive best at the real estimate of Burns, I think, by conceiving his work as having truth of matter and truth of manner, but not the accent or the poetic virtue of the highest masters. His genuine criticism of life, when the sheer poet in him speaks, is ironic; it is not—

Thou Power Supreme, whose mighty scheme
These woes of mine fulfil,
Here firm I rest, they must be best
Because they are Thy will!

It is far rather: *Whistle owre the lave o't!* Yet we may say of him as of Chaucer, that of life and the world, as they come before him, his view is large, free, shrewd, benignant,—truly poetic therefore; and his manner of rendering what he sees is to match. But we must note, at the same time, his great difference from Chaucer. The freedom of Chaucer is heightened, in Burns, by a fiery, reckless energy; the benignity of Chaucer deepens, in Burns, into an overwhelming sense of the pathos of things;—of the pathos of human nature, the pathos, also, of non-human nature. Instead of the fluidity of Chaucer's manner, the manner of Burns has spring, boundless swiftness. Burns is by far the greater force, though he has perhaps less charm. The world of Chaucer is fairer, richer, more significant than that of Burns; but when the largeness and freedom of Burns get full sweep, as in *Tam o' Shanter*, or still more in that puissant and splendid production, *The Jolly Beggars,* his world may be what it will, his poetic genius triumphs over it. In the world of *The Jolly Beggars* there is more than hideousness and squalor, there is bestiality; yet the piece is a superb poetic success. It has a breadth, truth, and power which make the famous scene in Auerbach's Cellar, of Goethe's *Faust,* seem artificial and tame beside it, and which are only matched by Shakespeare and Aristophanes.

Here, where his largeness and freedom serve him so admirably, and also in those poems and songs where to shrewdness he adds infinite archness and wit, and to benignity infinite pathos, where his manner is flawless, and a perfect poetic whole is the result,—in things like the address to the mouse whose home he had ruined, in things like *Duncan Gray, Tam Glen, Whistle and I'll come to you my Lad, Auld Lang Syne* (this list might be made much longer),—here we have the genuine Burns, of whom the real estimate must be high indeed. Not a classic, nor with the excellent σπουδαιότης of the great classics, nor with a verse rising to a criticism of life and a virtue like theirs; but a poet with thorough truth of substance and an answering truth of style, giving us a poetry sound to the core. We all of us have a leaning towards the pathetic, and may be inclined perhaps to prize Burns most for his touches of piercing, sometimes almost intolerable, pathos; for verse like—

> We twa hae paidl'd i' the burn
> From mornin' sun till dine;
> But seas between us braid hae roar'd
> Sin auld lang syne . . .

where he is as lovely as he is sound. But perhaps it is by the perfection of soundness of his lighter and archer masterpieces that he is poetically most wholesome for us. For the votary misled by a personal estimate of Shelley, as so many of us have been, are, and will be,—of that beautiful spirit building his many-coloured haze of words and images

> pinnacled dim in the intense inane—

no contact can be wholesomer than the contact with Burns at his archest and soundest. Side by side with the

> On the brink of the night and the morning
> My coursers are wont to respire,
> But the Earth has just whispered a warning
> That their flight must be swifter than fire . . .

of *Prometheus Unbound,* how salutary, how very salutary, to place this from *Tam Glen*—

> My minnie does constantly deave me
> And bids me beware o' young men;
> They flatter, she says, to deceive me;
> But wha can think sae o' Tam Glen?

But we enter on burning ground as we approach the poetry of times so near to us—poetry like that of Byron, Shelley, and Wordsworth—of which the estimates are so often not only personal, but personal with passion. For my purpose, it is enough to have taken the single case of Burns, the first poet we come to of whose work the estimate formed is evidently apt to be personal, and to have suggested how we may proceed, using the poetry of the great classics as a sort of touchstone, to correct this estimate, as we had previously corrected by the same means the historic estimate where we met with it. A collection like the present, with its succession of celebrated names and celebrated poems, offers a good opportunity to us for resolutely endeavouring to make our estimates of poetry real. I have sought to point out a method which will help us in making them so, and to exhibit it in use so far as to put any one who likes in a way of applying it for himself.

At any rate the end to which the method and the estimate are designed to lead, and from leading to which, if they do lead to it, they get their whole value,—the benefit of being able clearly to feel and deeply to enjoy the best, the truly classic, in poetry,—is an end, let me say it once more at parting, of supreme importance. We are often told that an era is opening in which we are to see multitudes of a common sort of readers, and masses of a common sort of literature; that such readers do not want and could not relish anything better than such literature, and that to provide it is becoming a vast and profitable industry. Even if good literature entirely lost currency with the world, it would still be abundantly worth while to continue to enjoy it by oneself. But it never will lose currency with the world, in spite of momentary appearances; it never will lose supremacy. Currency and supremacy are insured to it, not indeed by the world's deliberate and conscious choice, but by something far deeper,—by the instinct of self-preservation in humanity.

WILLIAM BUTLER YEATS: The Tragic Theatre*

I DID not find a word in the printed criticism of Synge's *Deirdre of the Sorrows* about the qualities that made certain moments seem to me the noblest tragedy, and the play was judged by what seemed to me but wheels and pulleys necessary to the effect, but in themselves nothing.

Upon the other hand, those who spoke to me of the play never spoke of these wheels and pulleys, but if they cared at all for the play, cared for the things I cared for. One's own world of painters, of poets, of good talkers, of ladies who delight in Ricard's portraits or Debussy's music, all those whose senses feel instantly every change in our mother the moon, saw the stage one way; and those others who look at plays every night, who tell the general playgoer whether this play or that play is to his taste, saw it in a way so different that there is certainly some body of dogma—whether in the instincts or in the memory—pushing the ways apart. A printed criticism, for instance, found but one dramatic moment, that when Deirdre in the second act overhears her lover say that he may grow weary of her; and not one—if I remember rightly—chose for praise or explanation the third act which alone had satisfied the author, or contained in any abundance those sentences that were quoted at the fall of the curtain and for days after.

Deirdre and her lover, as Synge tells the tale, returned to Ireland, though it was nearly certain they would die there, because death was better than broken love, and at the side of the open grave that had been dug for one and would serve for both, quarrelled, losing all they had given their life to keep. "Is it not a hard thing that we should miss the safety of the grave and we trampling its edge?" That in Deirdre's cry at the outset of a reverie of passion that mounts and mounts till grief itself has carried her beyond grief into pure contemplation. Up to this the play had been a Master's unfinished work, monotonous and melancholy, ill-arranged, little more than a sketch of what it would have grown to, but now I listened breathless to sentences that may never pass away, and as they filled or dwindled in their civility of sorrow, the player, whose art had seemed clumsy and incomplete, like the writing itself, ascended into that tragic ecstasy which is the best that art—perhaps that life—can give. And at last when Deirdre, in the paroxysm before she took her life, touched with compassionate fingers him that had killed her lover, we knew that the player had become, if but for a moment, the creature of that noble mind which had gathered its art in waste islands, and we too were carried beyond time and persons to where passion, living through its thousand purgatorial years, as in the wink of an eye, becomes wisdom; and it was as though we too had touched and felt and seen a disembodied thing.

One dogma of the printed criticism is that if a play does not contain definite character, its constitution is not strong enough for the stage, and that the dramatic moment is always the contest of character with character.

In poetical drama there is, it is held, an antithesis between character and lyric poetry, for lyric poetry—however much it move you when read out of a book—can, as these critics think, but encumber the action. Yet when we go back a few centuries and enter the great periods of drama, character grows less and sometimes disappears, and there is much lyric feeling, and at times a lyric measure will be wrought into the

* Yeats gives 1910 as the date of composition of "The Tragic Theatre." It first appeared in *The Cutting of an Agate* (1912), and is reprinted here from Yeats's *Essays* (1924), by permission of The Macmillan Company of New York, publishers. Yeats was also the author of *Discoveries* (1907), *Essays: 1931-1936* (1937), *Letters to the New Island* (1934), *On the Boiler* (1939), and *Letters on Poetry . . . to Dorothy Wellesley* (1940), but much of his best criticism is contained in his *Autobiographies* (1938).

dialogue, a flowing measure that had well-befitted music, or that more lumbering one of the sonnet. Suddenly it strikes us that character is continuously present in comedy alone, and that there is much tragedy, that of Corneille, that of Racine, that of Greece and Rome, where its place is taken by passions and motives, one person being jealous, another full of love or remorse or pride or anger. In writers of tragicomedy (and Shakespeare is always a writer of tragi-comedy) there is indeed character, but we notice that it is in the moments of comedy that character is defined, in Hamlet's gaiety let us say; while amid the great moments, when Timon orders his tomb, when Hamlet cries to Horatio "absent thee from felicity awhile," when Antony names "Of many thousand kisses the poor last," all is lyricism, unmixed passion, "the integrity of fire." Nor does character ever attain to complete definition in these lamps ready for the taper, no matter how circumstantial and gradual the opening of events, as it does in Falstaff who has no passionate purpose to fulfil, or as it does in Henry the Fifth whose poetry, never touched by lyric heat, is oratorical; nor when the tragic reverie is at its height do we say, "How well that man is realised, I should know him were I to meet him in the street," for it is always ourselves that we see upon the stage, and should it be a tragedy of love we renew, it may be, some loyalty of our youth, and go from the theatre with our eyes dim for an old love's sake.

I think it was while rehearsing a translation of *Les Fourberies de Scapin* in Dublin, and noticing how passionless it all was, that I saw what should have been plain from the first line I had written, that tragedy must always be a drowning and breaking of the dykes that separate man from man, and that it is upon these dykes comedy keeps house. But I was not certain of the site of that house (one always hesitates when there is no testimony but one's own); till somebody told me of a certain letter of Congreve's. He describes the external and superficial expressions of "humour" on which farce is founded and then defines "humour" itself—the foundation of comedy—as a "singular and unavoidable way of doing anything peculiar to one man only, by which his speech and actions are distinguished from all other men," and adds to it that "passions are too powerful in the sex to let humour have its course," or as I would rather put it, that you can find but little of what we call character in unspoiled youth, whatever be the sex, for as he indeed shows in another sentence, it grows with time like the ash of a burning stick, and strengthens towards middle life till there is little else at seventy years.

Since then I have discovered an antagonism between all the old art and our new art of comedy and understand why I hated at nineteen years Thackeray's novels and the new French painting. A big picture of cocottes sitting at little tables outside a cafe, by some follower of Manet's, was exhibited at the Royal Hibernian Academy while I was a student at a life class there, and I was miserable for days. I found no desirable place, no man I could have wished to be, no woman I could have loved, no Golden Age, no lure for secret hope, no adventure with myself for theme out of that endless tale I told myself all day long. Years after I saw the *Olympia* of Manet at the Luxembourg and watched it without hostility indeed, but as I might some incomparable talker whose precision of gesture gave me pleasure, though I did not understand his language. I returned to it again and again at intervals of years, saying to myself, "some day I will understand"; and yet, it was not until Sir Hugh Lane brought the *Eva Gonzales* to Dublin, and I had said to myself, "How perfectly that woman is realised as distinct from all other women that have lived or shall live" that I understood I was carrying on in my own mind that quarrel between a tragedian and a comedian which the Devil on Two Sticks in Le Sage showed to the young man who had climbed through the window.

There is an art of the flood, the art of Titian when his "Ariosto," and his Bacchus and Ariadne, gives new images to the dreams of youth, and of Shakespeare when he shows us Hamlet broken away from life by the passionate hesitations of his reverie. And we call this art poetical, because we must bring more to it than our daily mood if we would take our pleasure; and because it takes delight in the moment of exaltation, of excitement, of dreaming (or in the capacity for it, as in that still face of "Ariosto's" that is like some vessel soon to be full of wine). And there is an art that we call real, because character can only express itself perfectly in a real world, being that world's creature, and because we understand it best through a delicate discrimination of the senses which is but entire wakefulness, the daily mood grown cold and crystalline.

We may not find either mood in its purity, but in mainly tragic art one distinguishes devices to exclude or lessen character, to diminish the power of that daily mood, to cheat or blind its too clear perception. If the real world is not altogether rejected, it is but touched here and there, and into the places we have left empty we summon rhythm, balance, pattern, images that remind us of vast passions, the vagueness of past times, all the chimeras that haunt the edge of trance; and if we are painters, we shall express personal emotion through ideal form, a symbolism handled by the generations, a mask from whose eyes the disembodied looks, a style that remembers many masters that it may escape contemporary suggestion; or we shall leave out some element of reality as in Byzantine painting, where there is no mass, nothing in relief; and so it is that in the supreme moment of tragic art there comes upon one that strange sensation as though the hair of one's head stood up. And when we love, if it be in the excitement of youth, do we not also, that the flood may find no stone to convulse, no wall to narrow it, exclude character or the signs of it by choosing that beauty which seems unearthly because the individual woman is lost amid the labyrinth of its lines as though life were trembling into stillness and silence, or at last folding itself away? Some little irrelevance of line, some promise of character to come, may indeed put us at our ease, "give more interest" as the humour of the old man with the basket does to Cleopatra's dying; but should it come as we had dreamed in love's frenzy to our dying for that woman's sake, we would find that the discord had its value from the tune. Nor have we chosen illusion in choosing the outward sign of that moral genius that lives among the subtlety of the passions, and can for her moment make her of the one mind with great artists and poets. In the studio we may indeed say to one another "character is the only beauty," but when we chose a wife, as when we go to the gymnasium to be shaped for woman's eyes, we remember academic form, even though we enlarge a little the point of interest and chose "a painter's beauty," finding it the more easy to believe in the fire because it has made ashes.

When we look at the faces of the old tragic paintings, whether it is in Titian or in some painter of mediaeval China, we find there sadness and gravity, a certain emptiness even, as of a mind that waited the supreme crisis (and indeed it seems at times as if the graphic art, unlike poetry which sings the crisis itself, were the celebration of waiting). Whereas in modern art, whether in Japan or Europe, "vitality" (is not that the great word of the studios?), the energy, that is to say, which is under the command of our common moments, sings, laughs, chatters or looks its busy thoughts.

Certainly we have here the Tree of Life and that of The Knowledge of Good and Evil which is rooted in our interests, and if we have forgotten their differing virtues it is surely because we have taken delight in a confusion of crossing branches. Tragic art, passionate art, the drowner of dykes, the confounder of understanding, moves us by setting us to reverie, by alluring us almost to the intensity of trance. The persons upon the stage, let us say, greaten till they are humanity itself. We feel our minds expand convulsively or spread out slowly like some moon-brightened image-crowded sea. That which is before our eyes perpetually vanishes and returns again in the midst of the excitement it creates, and the more enthralling it is, the more do we forget it.

I. A. RICHARDS: Science and Poetry*

The future of poetry is immense, because in poetry, where it is worthy of its high destinies, our race, as time goes on, will find an ever surer and surer stay. There is not a creed which is not shaken, not an accredited dogma which is not shown to be questionable, not a received tradition which does not threaten to dissolve. Our religion has materialised itself in the fact, in the supposed fact; it has attached its emotion to the fact, and now the fact is failing it. But for poetry the idea is everything.—MATTHEW ARNOLD

1

THE GENERAL SITUATION

MAN'S prospects are not at present so rosy that he can neglect any means of improving them. He has recently made a number of changes in his customs and ways of life, partly with intention, partly by accident. These changes are involving such widespread further changes that the fairly near future is likely to see an almost complete reorganization of our lives, in their intimate aspects as much as in their public. Man himself is changing, together with his circumstances; he has changed in the past, it is true, but never perhaps so swiftly. His circumstances are not known ever to have changed so much or so suddenly before, with psychological as well as with economic, social and political dangers. This suddenness threatens us. Some parts of human nature resist change more than others. We risk disaster if some of our customs change while others which should change with them stay as they are.

Habits that have endured for many thousands of years are not easy to throw off—least of all when they are habits of thought and when they do not come into open conflict with changing circumstances, or do not clearly involve us in loss or inconvenience. Yet the loss may be great without our knowing anything about it. Before 1590 no one knew how inconvenient were our natural habits of thought about the ways in which a stone may fall; yet the modern world began when Galileo discovered what really happens. Before 1800 only persons thought to be crazy knew that ordinary traditional ideas as to cleanliness are dangerously inadequate. The infant's average "expectation of life" has increased by about 30 years since Lister upset them. Nobody before Sir Ronald Ross knew what were the consequences of thinking about malaria in terms of influences and miasmas instead of in terms of mosquitoes. The Roman Empire might perhaps have still been flourishing if some one had found this out before A.D. 100.

With such examples all about us we can no longer, in any department of life, so easily accept what was good enough for our fathers as good enough for ourselves or for our children. We are forced to wonder whether our ideas, even upon subjects apparently of little practical importance, such as poetry, may not be dangerously inadequate. It becomes indeed somewhat alarming to recognize, as we must, that our habits of thought remain, as regards most of our affairs, much as they were 5,000 years ago. The Sciences are, of course, simply the exceptions to this rule. Outside the Sciences—and the greater part of our thinking still goes on outside the Sciences—we think very much as our ancestors thought a hundred or two hundred

* "Science and Poetry" first appeared in 1926, and is reprinted here by permission of the publishers, W. W. Norton & Company, Inc., New York; copyright, 1926, by the publishers. I. A. Richards (*b.* 1893) is a co-author of *The Foundations of Aesthetics* (1922) and *The Meaning of Meaning: A Study of the Influence of Language upon Thought and of the Science of Symbolism* (1923), and the author of *Principles of Literary Criticism: A Study of Literary Judgment* (1929), *Mencius on the Mind: Experiments in Multiple Definition* (1932), *Basic Rules of Reason* (1933), *Coleridge on the Imagination* (1934), *How to Read a Page* (1942), and of various experiments in Basic English.

generations ago. Certainly this is so as regards official views about poetry. Is it not possible that these are wrong, as wrong as most ideas of an equally hoary antiquity? Is it not possible that to the men of the future our life today will seem a continual, ceaseless disaster due only to our own stupidity, to the nervelessness with which we accept and transmit ideas which do not apply and never have applied to anything?

The average educated man is growing more conscious, an extraordinarily significant change. It is probably due to the fact that his life is becoming more complex, more intricate, his desires and needs more varied and more apt to conflict. And as he becomes more conscious he can no longer be content to drift in unreflecting obedience to custom. He is forced to reflect. And if reflection often takes the form of inconclusive worrying, that is no more than might be expected in view of the unparalleled difficulty of the task. To live reasonably is much more difficult today than it was in Dr. Johnson's time, and even then, as Boswell shows, it was difficult enough.

To live reasonably is not to live by reason alone—the mistake is easy, and, if carried far, disastrous—but to live in a way of which reason, a clear full sense of the whole situation, would approve. And the most important part of the whole situation, as always, is ourselves, our own psychological make-up. The more we learn about the physical world, about our bodies, for example, the more points we find at which our ordinary behaviour is out of accord with the facts, inapplicable, wasteful, disadvantageous, dangerous or absurd. Witness our habit of boiling our vegetables. We have still to learn how to feed ourselves satisfactorily. Similarly, the little that is yet known about the mind already shows that our ways of thinking and feeling about very many of the things with which we concern ourselves are out of accord with the facts. This is pre-eminently true of our ways of thinking and feeling about poetry. We think and talk in terms of states of affairs which have never existed. We attribute to ourselves and to things, powers which neither we nor they possess. And equally we overlook or misuse powers which are all-important to us.

Day by day, in recent years, man is getting more out of place in Nature. Where he is going to he does not yet know, he has not yet decided. As a consequence he finds life more and more bewildering, more and more difficult to live coherently. Thus he turns to consider himself, his own nature. For the first step towards a reasonable way of life is a better understanding of human nature.

It has long been recognized that if only something could be done in psychology remotely comparable to what has been achieved in physics, practical consequences might be expected even more remarkable than any that the engineer can contrive. The first positive steps in the science of the mind have been slow in coming, but already they are beginning to change man's whole outlook.

2

THE POETIC EXPERIENCE

Extraordinary claims have often been made for poetry—Matthew Arnold's words quoted at the head of this essay are an example—claims which very many people are inclined to view with astonishment or with the smile which tolerance gives to the enthusiast. Indeed a more representative modern view would be that the future of poetry is *nil.* Peacock's conclusion in his *The Four Ages of Poetry* finds a more general acceptance. "A poet in our times is a semi-barbarian in a civilized community. He lives in the days that are past. . . . In whatever degree poetry is cultivated, it must necessarily be to the neglect of some branch of useful study: and it is a lamentable thing to see minds, capable of better things, running to seed in the specious indolence of these empty aimless mockeries of intellectual exertion. Poetry was the mental rattle that awakened the attention of intellect in the infancy of civil society: but for the maturity of mind to make a serious business of the playthings of its childhood, is as absurd as for a grown man to rub his gums with coral, and cry to be charmed asleep by the jingle of silver bells." And with more regret many others—Keats was among them—have thought that the inevitable effect of the advance of science would be to destroy the possibility of poetry.

What is the truth in this matter? How is our estimate of poetry going to be affected by science? And how will poetry itself be influenced?

The extreme importance which has in the past been assigned to poetry is a fact which must be accounted for whether we conclude that it was rightly assigned or not, and whether we consider that poetry will continue to be held in such esteem or not. It indicates that the case for poetry, whether right or wrong, is one which turns on momentous issues. We shall not have dealt adequately with it unless we have raised questions of great significance.

Very much toil has gone to the endeavour to explain the high place of poetry in human affairs, with, on the whole, few satisfactory or convincing results. This is not surprising. For in order to show how poetry is important it is first necessary to discover to some extent what it is. Until recently this preliminary task could only be very incompletely carried out; the psychology of instinct and emotion was too little advanced; and, moreover, the wild speculations natural in pre-scientific enquiry definitely stood in the way. Neither the professional psychologist, whose interest in poetry is frequently not intense, nor the man of letters, who as a rule has no adequate ideas of the mind as a whole, has been equipped for the investigation. Both a passionate knowledge of poetry and a capacity for dispassionate psychological analysis are required if it is to be satisfactorily prosecuted.

It will be best to begin by asking "What *kind of a thing*, in the widest sense, is poetry?" When we have answered this we shall be ready to ask "How can we use and misuse it?" and "What reasons are there for thinking it valuable?"

Let us take an experience, ten minutes of a person's life, and describe it in broad outline. It is now possible to indicate its general structure, to point out what is important in it, what trivial and accessory, which features depend upon which, how it has arisen, and how it is probably going to influence his future experience. There are, of course, wide gaps in this description, none the less it *is* at last possible to understand in general how the mind works in an experience, and what sort of stream of events the experience is.

A poem, let us say Wordsworth's *Westminster Bridge* sonnet, is such an experience, it is the experience the right kind of reader has when he peruses the verses. And the first step to an understanding of the place and future of poetry in human affairs is to see what the general structure of such an experience is. Let us begin by reading it very slowly, preferably aloud, giving every syllable time to make its full effect upon us. And let us read it experimentally, repeating it, varying our tone of voice until we are satisfied that we have caught its rhythm as well as we are able, and—whether our reading is such as to please other people or not—we ourselves at least are certain how it should "go."

Earth has not anything to show more fair:
Dull would he be of soul who could pass by
A sight so touching in its majesty:
This City now doth like a garment wear
The beauty of the morning: silent, bare,
Ships, towers, domes, theatres and temples lie
Open to the fields, and to the sky;
All bright and glittering in the smokeless air.
Never did sun more beautifully steep
In his first splendour valley, rock or hill;
Ne'er saw I, never felt, a calm so deep!
The river glideth at its own sweet will:
Dear God! the very houses seem asleep
And all that mighty heart is lying still!

We may best make our analysis of the experience that arises through reading these lines from the surface inwards, to speak metaphorically. The surface is the impression of the printed words on the retina. This sets up an agitation which we must follow as it goes deeper and deeper.

The first things to occur (if they do not, the rest of the experience will be gravely inadequate) are the sound of the words "in the mind's ear" and the feel of the words imaginarily spoken.[1] These together give the *full body*, as it were, to the words, and it is with the full bodies of words that the poet works, not with their printed signs. But many people lose nearly everything in poetry through these indispensable parts escaping them.

Next arise various pictures "in the mind's eye"; not of words but of things for which the words stand; perhaps of ships, perhaps of hills; and together with them, it may be, other images of various sorts. Images of what it feels like to stand leaning on the parapet of Westminster

[1] The view of the mind-body problem assumed here is defended and maintained with references to the contemporary authorities who hold it, in *The Meaning of Psychology* by C. K. Ogden, Chapter II. (London, Kegan Paul; New York, Harpers; 1926.)

Bridge. Perhaps that odd thing an image of "silence." But, unlike the image-bodies of the words themselves, those other images of things are not vitally important. Those who have them may very well think them indispensable, and *for them* they may be necessary; but other people may not require them at all. This is a point at which differences between individual minds are very marked.

Thence onwards the agitation which is the experience divides into a major and a minor branch, though the two streams have innumerable interconnections and influence one another intimately. Indeed it is only as an expositor's artifice that we may speak of them as two streams.

The minor branch we may call the intellectual stream; the other, which we may call the active, or emotional, stream, is made up of the play of our interests.

The intellectual stream is fairly easy to follow; it follows itself, so to speak; but it is the less important of the two. In poetry it matters only *as a means;* it directs and excites the active stream. It is made up of thoughts, which are not static little entities that bob up into consciousness and down again out of it, but fluent happenings, events, which reflect or point to the things the thoughts are of. Exactly how they do this is a matter which is still much disputed.

This pointing to or reflecting things is all that thoughts do. They appear to do much more; which is our chief illusion. The realm of thought is never a sovereign state. Our thoughts are the servants of our interests, and even when they seem to rebel it is usually our interests that are in disorder. Our thoughts are pointers and it is the other, the active, stream which deals with the things which thoughts reflect or point to.

Some people who read verse (they do not often read much of it) are so constituted that very little more happens than this intellectual stream of thoughts. It is perhaps superfluous to point out that they miss the real poem. To exaggerate this part of the experience, and give it too much importance on its own account, is a notable current tendency, and for many people explains why they do not read poetry.

The active branch is what really matters; for from it all the energy of the whole agitation comes. The thinking which goes on is somewhat like the play of an ingenious and invaluable "governor" run by, but controlling, the main machine. Every experience is essentially some interest or group of interests swinging back to rest.

To understand what an interest is we should picture the mind as a system of very delicately poised balances, a system which so long as we are in health is constantly growing. Every situation we come into disturbs some of these balances to some degree. The ways in which they swing back to a new equipoise are the impulses with which we respond to the situation. And the chief balances in the system are our chief interests.

Suppose that we carry a magnetic compass about in the neighbourhood of powerful magnets. The needle waggles as we move and comes to rest pointing in a new direction whenever we stand still in a new position. Suppose that instead of a single compass we carry an arrangement of many magnetic needles, large and small, swung so that they influence one another, some able only to swing horizontally, others vertically, others hung freely. As we move, the perturbations in this system will be very complicated. But for every position in which we place it there will be a final position of rest for all the needles into which they will in the end settle down, a general poise for the whole system. But even a slight displacement may set the whole assemblage of needles busily readjusting themselves.

One further complication. Suppose that while all the needles influence one another, some of them respond only to some of the outer magnets among which the system is moving. The reader can easily draw a diagram if his imagination needs a visual support.

The mind is not unlike such a system if we imagine it to be incredibly complex. The needles are our interests, varying in their importance, that is in the degree to which any movement they make involves movement in the other needles. Each new disequilibrium, which a shift of position, a fresh situation, entails, corresponds to a need: and the wagglings which ensue as the system rearranges itself are our responses, the impulses through which we seek to meet the need. Often the new poise is not found until long after the original disturbance. Thus states of strain can arise which last for years.

The child comes into the world as a comparatively simple arrangement. Few things affect him comparatively speaking, and his responses also are few and simple, but he very quickly becomes more complicated. His recurrent needs for food and for various attentions are constantly setting all his needles swinging. Little by little separate needs become departmentalized as it were, sub-systems are formed; hunger causes one set of responses, the sight of his toys another, loud noises yet another, and so on. But the sub-systems never become quite independent. So he grows up, becoming susceptible to ever more numerous and more delicate influences.

He grows more discriminating in some respects, he is thrown out of equilibrium by slighter differences in his situation. In other respects he becomes more stable. From time to time, through growth, fresh interests develop; sex is the outstanding example. His needs increase, he becomes capable of being upset by quite new causes, he becomes responsive to quite new aspects of the situation.

This development takes a very indirect course. It would be still more erratic if society did not mould and remould him at every stage, reorganising him incompletely two or three times over before he grows up. He reaches maturity in the form of a vast assemblage of major and minor interests, partly a chaos, partly a system, with some tracts of his personality fully developed and free to respond, others tangled and jammed in all kinds of accidental ways. It is this incredibly complex assemblage of interests to which the printed poem has to appeal. Sometimes the poem is itself the influence which disturbs us, sometimes it is merely the means by which an already existing disturbance can right itself. More usually perhaps it is both at once.

We must picture then the stream of the poetic experience as the swinging back into equilibrium of these disturbed interests. We are reading the poem in the first place only because we are in some way interested in doing so, only because some interest is attempting to regain its poise thereby. And whatever happens as we read happens only for a similar reason. We understand the words (the intellectual branch of the stream goes on its way successfully) only because an interest is reacting through that means, and all the rest of the experience is equally but more evidently our adaptation working itself out.

The rest of the experience is made up of emotions and attitudes. Emotions are what the reaction, with its reverberations in bodily changes, feels like. Attitudes are the impulses towards one kind of behaviour or another which are set ready by the response. They are, as it were, its outward going part.[2] Sometimes, as here in *Westminster Bridge,* they are very easily overlooked. But consider a simpler case—a fit of laughter which it is absolutely essential to conceal, in Church or during a solemn interview, for example. You contrive not to laugh; but there is no doubt about the activity of the impulses in their restricted form. The much more subtle and elaborate impulses which a poem excites are not different in principle. They do not show themselves as a rule, they do not come out into the open, largely because they are so complex. When they have adjusted themselves to one another and become organized into a coherent whole, the needs concerned may be satisfied. *In a fully developed man a state of readiness for action will take the place of action when the full appropriate situation for action is not present.* The essential peculiarity of poetry as of all the arts is that the full appropriate situation is *not* present. It is an *actor* we are seeing upon the stage, not Hamlet. So readiness for action takes the place of actual behaviour.

This is the main plan then of the experience. Signs on the retina, taken up by sets of needs (remember how many other impressions all day long remain entirely *unnoticed* because no interest responds to them); thence an elaborate agitation of impulses, one branch of which is *thoughts* of what the words mean, the other an emotional response leading to the development of *attitudes,* preparations, that is, for action which may or may not take place; the two branches being in intimate connection.

We must look now a little more closely at these connections. It may seem odd that we do not more definitely make the thoughts the rulers and causes of the rest of the response. To do

[2] For a further discussion of attitudes see the author's *Principles of Literary Criticism,* Chapter XV (International Library of Psychology).

just this has been in fact the grand error of traditional psychology. Man prefers to stress the features which distinguish him from monkey, and chief among these are his intellectual capacities. Important though they are, he has given them a rank to which they are not entitled. Intellect is an adjunct to the interests, a means by which they adjust themselves more successfully. Man is not in any sense primarily an intelligence; he is a system of interests. Intelligence helps man but does not run him.

Partly through this natural mistake, and partly because intellectual operations are so much easier to study, the whole traditional analysis of the working of the mind has been turned upside down. It is largely as a remedy from the difficulties which this mistake involves that poetry may have so much importance in the future. But let us look again more closely at the poetic experience.

In the first place, why is it essential in reading poetry to give the words their full imagined sound and body? What is meant by saying that the poet works with this sound and body? The answer is that even before the words have been intellectually understood and the thoughts they occasion formed and followed, the movement and sound of the words is playing deeply and intimately upon the interests. How this happens is a matter which has yet to be successfully investigated, but that it happens no sensitive reader of poetry doubts. A good deal of poetry and even some great poetry exists (e.g., some of Shakespeare's Songs and, in a different way, much of the best of Swinburne) in which the sense of the words can be *almost* entirely missed or neglected without loss. Never perhaps entirely without effort, however; though sometimes with advantage. But the plain fact that the relative importance of grasping the sense of the words may vary (compare Browning's *Before* with his *After*) is enough for our purpose here.

In nearly all poetry the sound and feel of the words, what is often called the *form* of the poem in opposition to its *content*, get to work first, and the sense in which the words are taken is subtly influenced by this fact. Most words are ambiguous as regards their plain sense, especially in poetry. We can take them as we please in a variety of senses. The sense we are pleased to choose is the one which most suits the impulses already stirred through the form of the verse. The same thing can be noticed in conversation. Not the strict logical sense of what is said, but the tone of voice and the occasion are the primary factors by which we interpret. Science, it is worth noting, endeavours with increasing success to bar out these factors. We believe a scientist because he can substantiate his remarks, not because he is eloquent or forcible in his enunciation. In fact, we distrust him when he seems to be influencing us by his manner.

In its use of words poetry is just the reverse of science. Very definite thoughts do occur, but not because the words are so chosen as logically to bar out all possibilities but one. No. But because the manner, the tone of voice, the cadence and the rhythm play upon our interests and make *them* pick out from among an indefinite number of possibilities the precise particular thought which they need. This is why poetical descriptions often seem so much more accurate than prose descriptions. Language logically and scientifically used cannot describe a landscape or a face. To do so it would need a prodigious apparatus of names for shades and nuances, for precise particular qualities. These names do not exist, so other means have to be used. The poet, even when, like Ruskin or De Quincey, he writes in prose, makes the reader pick out the precise particular sense required from an indefinite number of possible senses which a word, phrase or sentence may carry. The means by which he does this are many and varied. Some of them have been mentioned above, but the way in which he uses them is the poet's own secret, something which cannot be taught. He knows how to do it, but he does not himself know how it is done.

Misunderstanding and under-estimation of poetry is mainly due to over-estimation of the thought in it. We can see still more clearly that thought is not the prime factor if we consider for a moment not the experience of the reader but that of the poet. Why does the poet use these words and no others? Not because they stand for a series of thoughts which in themselves are what he is concerned to communicate. It is never what a poem *says* which matters, but what it *is*. The poet is not writing as a scientist. He uses these words because the interests which the situation calls into play combine to bring them, just in this form, into his consciousness *as a means of ordering, controlling and consolidating* the whole experience. The experience itself, the tide of impulses sweeping through the mind, is the source and the sanction of the words. They represent this experience itself, not any set of perceptions or reflections, though often to a reader who approaches the poem wrongly they will seem to be only a series of remarks about other things. But to a suitable reader the words—if they actually spring from experience and are not due to verbal habits, to the desire to be effective, to factitious excogitation, to imitation, to irrelevant contrivances, or to any other of the failings which prevent most people from writing poetry—the words will reproduce in his mind a similar play of interests putting him for the while into a similar situation and leading to the same response.

Why this should happen is still somewhat of a mystery. An extraordinarily intricate concourse of impulses brings the words together. Then in another mind the affair in part reverses itself, the words bring into being a similar concourse of impulses. The words which seem to be the effect of the experience in the first instance, seem to become the cause of a similar experience in the second. A very odd thing to happen, not exactly paralleled outside communication. But this description is not quite accurate. The words, as we have seen, are not simply the effect in one case, nor the cause in the other. In both cases they are the part of the experience which binds it together, which gives it a definite structure and keeps it from being a mere welter of disconnected impulses. They are *the key,* to borrow a useful metaphor from McDougall, for this particular combination of impulses. So regarded, it is less strange that what the poet wrote should reproduce his experience in the mind of the reader.

3

WHAT IS VALUABLE?

Enough perhaps as to the kind of thing a poem is, as to the general structure of these experiences. Let us now turn to the further questions "Of what use is it?" "Why and how is it valuable?"

The first point to be made is that poetic experiences are valuable (when they are) in the same ways as any other experiences. They are to be judged by the same standards. What are these?

Extraordinarily diverse views have been held upon this point. Very naturally, since such very different ideas have been entertained as to what kind of thing an experience is. For our opinions as to the differences between good and bad experiences depend inevitably upon what we take an experience to be. As fashions have changed in psychology men's ethical theories have followed suit. When a created, simple and eternal soul was the pivotal point, Good was conformity with the will of the creator, Evil was rebellion. When the associationist psychologists substituted a swarm of sensations and images for the soul, Good became pleasure and Evil became pain, and so on. A long chapter of the history of opinions has still to be written tracing these changes. Now that the mind is seen to be a hierarchy of interests, what will for this account be the difference between Good and Evil?

It is the difference between free and wasteful organization, between fullness and narrowness of life. For if the mind is a system of interests, and if an experience is their play, the worth of any experience is a matter of the degree to which the mind, through this experience attains a complete equilibrium.

This is a first approximation. It needs qualifying and expanding if it is to become a satisfactory theory. Let us see how some of these amendments would run.

Consider an hour of any person's life. It holds out innumerable possibilities. Which of these are realized depends upon two main groups of factors:—the external situation in which he is living, his surroundings, including the other people with whom he is in contact; and, secondly, his psychological make-up. The first of these, the external situation, is sometimes given too much importance. We have only to notice what very different experiences different people undergo when in closely similar situations to recognize this fact. A situation which is dulness itself for one may be full of excitement for another.

What an individual responds to is not the whole situation but a selection from it, and as a rule few people make the same selection. What is selected is decided by the organization of the individual's interests.

Now let us simplify the case by supposing that nothing which happens during this hour is going to have any further consequences either in our hypothetical person's life or in anyone else's. He is going to cease to exist when the clock strikes—but for our purposes he must be imagined not to know this—and no one is to be a whit better or worse whatever he thinks, feels or does during the hour. What shall we say it would be best for him, if he could, to do?

We need not bother to imagine the detail of the external situation or the character of the man. We can answer our question in general terms without doing so. The man has a certain definite instinctive make-up—the result of his past history, including his heredity. There will be many things which he cannot do which another man could, and many things which he cannot do in this situation, whatever it is, which he could do in other situations. But given this particular man in this particular situation, our question is, which of the possibilities open to him would be better than which others? How would we as friendly observers like to see him living?

Setting pain aside, we may perhaps agree that torpor would be the worst choice. Complete inertness, lifelessness, would be the sorriest spectacle—anticipating too nearly and unnecessarily what is to happen when the hour strikes. We can then perhaps agree, though here more resistance from preconceived ideas may be encountered, that the best choice would be the opposite of torpor, that is to say the fullest, keenest, most active and complete kind of life.

Such a life is one which brings into play as many as possible of the *positive* interests. We can leave out the negative interests. It would be a pity for our friend to be frightened or disgusted even for a minute of his precious hour.

But this is not all. It is not enough that many interests should be stirred. There is a more important point to be noted.

The Gods approve
The depth and not the tumult of the soul.

The interests must come into play and remain in play with as little conflict among themselves as possible. In other words, the experience must be organized so as to give all the impulses of which it is composed the greatest possible degree of freedom.[3]

It is in this respect that people differ most from one another. It is this which separates the good life from the bad. Far more life is wasted through muddled mental organization than through lack of opportunity. Conflicts between different impulses are the greatest evils which afflict mankind.

The best life then which we can wish for our friend will be one in which as much as possible of himself is engaged (as many of his impulses as possible). And this with as little conflict, as little mutual interference between different sub-systems of his activities as there can be. The more he lives and the less he thwarts himself, the better. That briefly is our answer as psychologists, as outside observers abstractly describing the state of affairs. And if it is asked, what does such life feel like, how is it to live through? the answer is that it feels like and is the experience of poetry.

There are two ways in which conflict can be avoided or overcome. By conquest and by conciliation. One or other of the contesting impulses can be suppressed, or they can come to a mutual arrangement, they can adjust themselves to one another. We owe to psycho-analysis—at present still a rather undisciplined branch of psychology—a great deal of striking evidence as to the extreme difficulty of suppressing any vigorous impulse. When it seems to be suppressed it is often found to be really as active as ever, but in some other form, generally a troublesome one. Persistent mental imbalances are the source of nearly all our troubles. For this reason, as well as for the simpler reason that suppression is wasteful of life, conciliation is always to be preferred to conquest. People who are always winning victories over themselves might equally well be described as always enslaving themselves. Their lives become unnecessarily narrow. The minds of many saints

[3] See *The Foundations of Aesthetics,* by C. K. Ogden, James Wood and the author, pp. 74 ff. for a description of such experience.

have been like wells; they should have been like lakes or like the sea.

Unfortunately, most of us, left to ourselves, have no option but to go in for extensive attempts at self-conquest. It is our only means of escape from chaos. Our impulses must have some order, some organisation, or we do not live ten minutes without disaster. In the past, Tradition, a kind of Treaty of Versailles assigning frontiers and spheres of influence to the different interests, and based chiefly upon conquest, ordered our lives in a moderately satisfactory manner. But Tradition is weakening. Moral authorities are not as well backed by beliefs as they were; their sanctions are declining in force. We are in need of something to take the place of the old order. Not in need of a new balance of power, a new arrangement of conquests, but of a League of Nations for the moral ordering of the impulses; a new order based on conciliation, not on attempted suppression.

Only the rarest individuals hitherto have achieved this new order, and never yet perhaps completely. But many have achieved it for a brief while, for a particular phase of experience, and many have recorded it for these phases.

Of these records poetry consists.

But before going on to this new point let us return for a moment to our hypothetical friend who is enjoying his last hour, and suppose this limitation removed. Instead of such an hour let us consider any hour, one which has consequences for his future and for other people. Let us consider any piece of any life. How far is our argument affected? Will our standards of good and evil be altered?

Clearly the case now is, in certain respects, different; it is much more complicated. We have to take these consequences into account. We have to regard his experience not in itself alone, but as a piece of his life and as a probable factor in other people's situations. If we are to approve of the experience, it must not only be full of life and free from conflict, but it must be likely to lead to other experiences, both his own and those of other people, also full of life and free from conflict. And often, in actual fact, it has to be less full of life and more restricted than it might be in order to ensure these results. A momentary individual good has often to be sacrificed for the sake of a later or a general good. Conflicts are often necessary in order that they should not occur later. The mutual adjustment of conflicting impulses may take time, and an acute struggle may be the only way in which they learn to co-operate peacefully in the future.

But all these complications and qualifications do not disturb the conclusion we arrived at through considering the simpler case. A good experience is still one full of life, in the sense which we have explained, or derivatively one conducive to experiences full of life. An evil experience is one which is self-thwarting or conducive to stultifying conflicts. So far then, all is sound and shipshape in the argument, and we can go on to consider the poet.

4

THE COMMAND OF LIFE

The chief characteristic of poets is their amazing *command* of words. This is not a mere matter of vocabulary, though it is significant that Shakespeare's vocabulary is the richest and most varied that any Englishman has ever used. It is not the quantity of words a writer has at his disposal, but the way in which he disposes them that gives him his rank as a poet. His sense of how they modify one another, how their separate effects in the mind combine, how they fit into the whole response, is what matters. As a rule the poet is not conscious of the reason why just these words and no others best serve. They fall into their place without his conscious control, and a feeling of rightness, of inevitability is commonly his sole conscious ground for his certainty that he has ordered them aright. It would as a rule be idle to ask him why he used a particular rhythm or a particular epithet. He might give reasons, but they would probably be mere rationalizations having nothing to do with the matter. For the choice of the rhythm or the epithet was not an intellectual matter (though it may be capable of an intellectual justification), but was due to an instinctive impulse seeking to confirm itself, or to order itself with its fellows.

It is very important to realize how deep are the motives which govern the poet's use of words. No study of other poets which is not an impassioned study will help him. He can learn much from other poets, but only by letting them influence him deeply, not by any superficial examination of their style. For the motives which shape a poem spring from the root of the mind. The poet's style is the direct outcome of the way in which his interests are organized. That amazing capacity of his for ordering speech is only a part of a more amazing capacity for ordering his experience.

This is the explanation of the fact that poetry cannot be written by cunning and study, by craft and contrivance. To a superficial glance the productions of the mere scholar, steeped in the poetry of the past, and animated by intense emulation and a passionate desire to place himself among the poets, will often look extraordinarily like poetry. His words may seem as subtly and delicately ordered as words can be, his epithets as happy, his transitions as daring, his simplicity as perfect. By every intellectual test he may succeed. But unless the ordering of the words sprang, not from knowledge of the technique of poetry added to a desire to write some, but from an actual supreme ordering of *experience*, a closer approach to his work will betray it. Characteristically its rhythm will give it away. For rhythm is no matter of tricks with syllables, but directly reflects personality. It is not separable from the words to which it belongs. Moving rhythm in poetry arises only from genuinely stirred impulses, and is a more subtle index than any other to the order of the interests.

Poetry, in other words, cannot be imitated; it cannot be faked so as to baffle the only test that ought ever to be applied. It is unfortunately true that this test is often very difficult to apply. And it is sometimes hard to know whether the test has or has not been applied. For the test is this—that only genuine poetry will give to the reader who approaches it in the proper manner a response which is as passionate, noble and serene as the experience of the poet, the master of speech because he is the master of experience itself. But it is easy to read carelessly and shallowly, and easy to mistake for the response something which does not properly belong to it at all. By careless reading we miss what is in the poem. And in some states of mind, for example, when intoxicated, the silliest doggerel may seem sublime. What happened was not due to the doggerel but to the drink.

With these general considerations in mind we may turn now from the question—What can the dawning science of psychology tell us about poetry?—to the allied questions—How is science in general, and the new outlook upon the world which it induces, already affecting poetry, and to what extent may science make obsolete the poetry of the past? To answer these questions we need to sketch some of the changes which have recently come about in our world-picture, and to consider anew what it is that we demand from poetry.

5

THE NEUTRALISATION OF NATURE

The poets are failing us, or we them, if after reading them we do not find ourselves changed; not with a temporary change, such as luncheon or slumber will produce, from which we inevitably work back to the *status quo ante,* but with a permanent alteration of our possibilities as responsive individuals in good or bad adjustment to an all but overwhelming concourse of stimulations. How many living poets have the power to make such deep changes? Let us set aside youthful enthusiasm; there is a time in most lives when, rightly enough, Mr. Masefield, Mr. Kipling, Mr. Drinkwater, or even Mr. Noyes or Mr. Studdert Kennedy may profoundly affect the awakening mind; it is being introduced to poetry. Later on, looking back, we can see that any one of a hundred other poets would have served as well or better. Let us consider only the experienced, the fairly hardened reader, who is familiar with a great deal of the poetry of the past.

Contemporary poetry which will, accidents apart, modify the attitudes of this reader must be such as could not have been written in another age than our own. It must have sprung in part from the contemporary situation. It must correspond to needs, impulses, attitudes, which did not arise in the same fashion for poets in the past, and criticism also must take notice of the contemporary situation. Our attitudes to man, to nature, and to the universe change with every generation, and have changed with unusual violence in recent years. We cannot leave these changes out of account in judging modern poetry. When attitudes are changing neither criticism nor poetry can remain stationary. To those who realise what the poet is this will be obvious; but all literary history bears it out.

It would be of little use to give a list of the chief recent intellectual revolutions and to attempt to deduce therefrom what must be happening to poetry. The effects upon our attitudes of changes of opinion are too complex to be calculated so. What we have to consider is not men's current opinions but their attitudes—how they feel about this or that as part of the world; what relative importance its different aspects have for them; what they are prepared to sacrifice for what; what they trust, what they are frightened by, what they desire. To discover these things we must go to the poets. Unless they are failing us, they will show us just these things.

They will *show* them, but, of course, they will not state them. Their poetry will not be *about* their attitudes in the sense in which a treatise on anatomy is about the structure of the body. Their poetry will arise out of their attitudes and will evoke them in an adequate reader, but, as a rule, it will not mention any attitudes. We must, of course, expect occasional essays in verse upon psychological topics, but these should not mislead us. Most of the attitudes with which poetry is concerned are indescribable—because psychology is still in a primitive stage—and can only be named or spoken about as the attitude of this poem or that. The poem, the actual experience as it forms itself in the mind of the fit reader, controlling his responses to the world and ordering his impulses, is our best evidence as to how other men feel about things; and we read it, if we are serious, partly to discover how life seems to another, partly to try how his attitudes suit us, engaged as we also are in the same enterprise.

Although we cannot—for lack of a sufficient psychology—describe attitudes in terms which do not apply also to others which we are not considering, and although we cannot deduce a poet's attitudes from the general intellectual background, none the less, after reading his poetry, when his experience has become our own, we can sometimes profitably look round us to see why these attitudes should be so very different, in some ways, from those we find in the poetry of 100 or 1,000 years ago. In so doing we gain a means of indicating what these attitudes are, useful both for those who are constitutionally unable to read poetry (an increasing number), and for those victims of education who neglect modern poetry because they "don't know what to make of it."

What, then, has been happening to the intellectual background, to the world-picture, and in what ways may changes here have caused a reorganization of our attitudes?

The central dominant change may be described as the *Neutralisation of Nature,* the transference from the Magical View of the world to the scientific, a change so great that it is perhaps only paralleled historically by the change, from whatever adumbration of a world-picture preceded the Magical View, to the Magical View itself. By the Magical View I mean, roughly, the belief in a world of Spirits and Powers which control events, and which can be evoked and, to some extent, controlled themselves by human practices. The belief in Inspiration and the beliefs underlying Ritual are representative parts of this view. It has been decaying slowly for some 300 years, but its definite overthrow has taken place only in the last 60. Vestiges and survivals of it prompt and direct a great part of our daily affairs, but it is no longer the world-picture which an informed mind most easily accepts. There is some evidence that Poetry, together with the other Arts, arose with this Magical View. It is a possibility to be seriously considered that Poetry may pass away with it.

The reasons for the downfall of the Magical View are familiar. It seems to have arisen as a consequence of an increase in man's knowledge of and command over nature (the discovery of agriculture). It fell through the extension of that knowledge of and command over nature. Throughout its (10,000 years?) reign its stability has been due to its capacity for satisfying men's emotional needs through its adequacy as an object for their attitudes. We must remember that human attitudes have developed always *inside* the social group; they are what a man feels, the mainsprings of his behaviour towards his fellow-men, and they have only a limited field of applicability. Thus the Magical View, being an interpretation of nature in terms of man's own most intimate and most important affairs, very soon came to suit man's emotional make-up better than any other view possibly could. The attraction of the Magical View lay very little in the actual command over nature which it gave. That Galton was the first person to test the efficacy of prayer experimentally is an indication of this. What did give the Magical View its standing was the ease and adequacy with which the universe therein presented could be emotionally handled, the scope offered for man's love and hatred, for his terror as well as for his hope and his despair. It gave life a shape, a sharpness, and a coherence that no other means could so easily secure.

In its place we have the universe of the mathematician, a field for the tracing out of ever wider and more general uniformities. A field in which intellectual certainty is, almost for the first time, available, and on an unlimited scale. Also the despondencies, the emotional excitements accompanying research and discovery, again on an unprecedented scale. Thus a number of men who might in other times have been poets are today in bio-chemical laboratories—a fact of which we might avail ourselves, did we feel the need, in defence of an alleged present poverty in poetry. But apart from these thrills, what has the world-picture of science to do with human emotions? A god voluntarily or involuntarily subjected to the General Theory of Relativity does not make an emotional appeal. So this form of compromise fails. Various emergent deities have been suggested—by Mr. Wells, by Professors Alexander and Lloyd Morgan—but, alas! the reasons for suggesting them have become too clear and conscious. They are there to meet a demand, not to make one; they do not do the work for which they were invented.

The revolution brought about by science is, in short, too drastic to be met by any such half-measures. It touches the central principle by which the Mind has been deliberately organized in the past, and no alteration in beliefs, however great, will restore equilibrium while that principle is retained. I come now to the main purport of these remarks.

Ever since man first grew self-conscious and reflective he has supposed that his feelings, his attitudes, and his conduct spring from his knowledge. That as far as he could it would be wise for him to organise himself in this way, with knowledge [4] as the foundation on which should rest feeling, attitude, and behaviour. In point of fact, he never has been so organised, knowledge having been until recently too scarce; but he has constantly been persuaded that he was built on this plan, and has endeavoured to carry the structure further on these lines. He has sought for knowledge, supposing that it would itself *directly* excite a right orientation to existence, supposing that, if he only knew what the world was like, this knowledge in itself would show him how to feel towards it, what attitudes to adopt, and with what aims to live. He has constantly called what he found in this quest, "knowledge," unaware that it was hardly ever pure, unaware that his feelings, attitudes, and behaviour were *already* orientated by his physiological and social needs, and were themselves, for the most part, the sources of whatever it was that he supposed himself to be knowing.

Suddenly, not long ago, he began to get genuine knowledge on a large scale. The process went faster and faster; it snow-balled. Now he has to face the fact that the edifices of supposed knowledge, with which he has for so long buttressed and supported his attitudes, will no longer stand up, and, at the same time, he has to recognise that pure knowledge is irrelevant to his aims, that it has no *direct* bearing upon what he should feel, or what he should attempt to do.

For science, which is simply our most elaborate way of *pointing* to things systematically, tells us and can tell us nothing about the nature of things in any *ultimate* sense. It can never answer any question of the form: *What* is so and so? It can only tell us *how* so and so behaves. And it does not attempt to do more than this. Nor, indeed, can more than this be done. Those ancient, deeply troubling, formulations that begin with "What" and "Why" prove, when we examine them, to be not questions at all; but requests—for emotional satisfaction. They indicate our desire not for knowledge but for assurance,[5] a point which appears clearly when

[4] I.e. thoughts which are both true and evidenced, in the narrower, stricter senses. For a discussion of some relevant senses of "truth" and "knowledge" see *Principles of Literary Criticism*, Chapters XXXIII and XXXIV.

[5] On this point the study of the child's questions included in *The Language and Thought of the Child* by J. Piaget (Kegan Paul, 1926), is illuminating.

we look into the "How" of questions and requests, of knowledge and desire. Science can tell us about man's place in the universe and his chances; that the place is precarious, and the chances problematical. It can enormously increase our chances if we can make wise use of it. But it cannot tell us what we are or what this world is; not because these are in any sense insoluble questions, but because they are not questions at all.[6] And if science cannot answer these pseudo-questions no more can philosophy or religion. So that all the varied answers which have for ages been regarded as the keys of wisdom are dissolving together.

The result is a biological crisis which is not likely to be decided without trouble. It is one which we can, perhaps, decide for ourselves, partly by thinking, partly by reorganising our minds in other ways; if we do not it may be decided for us, not in the way we should choose. While it lasts it puts a strain on each individual and upon society, which is part of the explanation of many modern difficulties, the difficulties of the poet in particular, to come back to our present subject. I have not really been far away.

6

POETRY AND BELIEFS

The business of the poet, as we have seen, is to give order and coherence, and so freedom, to a body of experience. To do so through words which act as its skeleton, as a structure by which the impulses which make up the experience are adjusted to one another and act together. The means by which words do this are many and varied. To work them out is a problem for psychology. A beginning has been indicated above, but only a beginning. What little can be done shows already that most critical dogmas of the past are either false or nonsense. A little knowledge is not here a danger, but clears the air in a remarkable way.

Roughly and inadequately, even in the light of our present knowledge, we can say that words work in the poem in two main fashions. As sensory stimuli and as (in the *widest* sense) symbols. We must refrain from considering the sensory side of the poem, remarking only that it is *not* in the least independent of the other side, and that it has for definite reasons prior importance in most poetry. We must confine ourselves to the other function of words in the poem, or rather, omitting much that is of secondary relevance, to one form of that function, let me call it *pseudo-statement.*

It will be admitted—by those who distinguish between scientific statement, where truth is ultimately a matter of verification as this is understood in the laboratory, and emotive utterance, where "truth" is primarily acceptability *by* some attitude, and more remotely is the acceptability *of* this attitude itself—that it is *not* the poet's business to make true statements. Yet poetry has constantly the air of making statements, and important ones; which is one reason why some mathematicians cannot read it. They find the alleged statements to be *false.* It will be agreed that their approach to poetry and their expectations from it are mistaken. But what exactly is the other, the right, the poetic, approach and how does it differ from the mathematical?

The poetic approach evidently limits the framework of possible consequences into which the pseudo-statement is taken. For the scientific approach this framework is unlimited. Any and every consequence is relevant. If any of the consequences of a statement conflicts with acknowledged fact then so much the worse for the statement. Not so with the pseudo-statement when poetically approached. The problem is—just how does the limitation work? The usual account is in terms of a supposed universe of discourse, a world of make-believe, of imagination, of recognised fictions common to the poet and his readers. A pseudo-statement which fits into this system of assumptions would be regarded as "poetically true"; one which does not, as "poetically false." This attempt to treat "poetic truth" on the model of general "coherence theories" is very natural for certain schools of logicians; but is inadequate, on the wrong lines from the outset. To mention two objections out of many; there is no means of discovering what the "universe of discourse" is on any occasion, and the kind of coherence which must hold within it, supposing it to be discoverable, is not

[6] The remarks of Wittgenstein (*Tractatus Logico-Philosophicus,* 6.5, 6.52), which superficially resemble this, should be consulted, if only to show how important the *context* of a statement may be; for what is said above should lead not towards but away from all forms of mysticism.

an affair of logical relations. Attempt to define the system of propositions into which

O Rose, thou art sick!

must fit, and the logical relations which must hold between them if it is to be "poetically true"; the absurdity of the theory becomes evident.

We must look further. In the poetic approach the relevant consequences are not logical or to be arrived at by a partial relaxation of logic. Except occasionally and by accident logic does not enter at all. They are the consequences which arise through our emotional organisation. The acceptance which a pseudo-statement receives is entirely governed by its effects upon our feelings and attitudes. Logic only comes in, if at all, in subordination, as a servant to our emotional response. It is an unruly servant, however, as poets and readers are constantly discovering. A pseudo-statement is "true" if it suits and serves some attitude or links together attitudes which on other grounds are desirable. This kind of truth is so opposed to scientific truth that it is a pity to use so similar a word, but at present it is difficult to avoid the malpractice.[7]

This brief analysis may be sufficient to indicate the fundamental disparity and opposition between pseudo-statements as they occur in poetry and statements as they occur in science. A pseudo-statement is a form of words which is justified entirely by its effect in releasing or organising our impulses and attitudes (due regard being had for the better or worse organisations of these *inter se*); a statement, on the other hand, is justified by its truth, i.e. its correspondence, in a highly technical sense, with the fact to which it points.

Statements true and false alike do of course constantly touch off attitudes and action. Our daily practical existence is largely guided by them. On the whole true statements are of more service to us than false ones. None the less we do not and, at present, cannot order our emotions and attitudes by true statements alone. Nor is there any probability that we ever shall contrive to do so. This is one of the great new dangers to which civilisation is exposed. Countless pseudo-statements—about God, about the universe, about human nature, the relations of mind to mind, about the soul, its rank and destiny—pseudo-statements which are pivotal points in the organisation of the mind, vital to its well-being, have suddenly become, for sincere, honest and informal minds, impossible to believe. For centuries they have been believed; now they are gone, irrecoverably; and the knowledge which has killed them is not of a kind upon which an equally fine organisation of the mind can be based.

This is the contemporary situation. The remedy, since there is no prospect of our gaining adequate knowledge, and since indeed it is fairly clear that genuine knowledge cannot serve us here and can only increase our practical control of Nature, is to cut our pseudo-statements free from belief, and yet retain them, in this released state, as the main instruments by which we order our attitudes to one another and to the world. Not so desperate a remedy as may appear, for poetry conclusively shows that even the most important among our attitudes can be aroused and maintained without any belief entering in at all. Those of Tragedy, for example. We need no beliefs, and indeed we must have none, if we are to read *King Lear*. Pseudo-statements to which we attach no belief and statements proper such as science provides cannot conflict. It is only when we introduce illicit beliefs into poetry that danger arises. To do so is from this point of view a profanation of poetry.

Yet an important branch of criticism which has attracted the best talents from prehistoric times until today consists of the endeavour to persuade men that the functions of science and poetry are identical, or that the one is a "higher form" of the other, or that they conflict and we must choose between them.

The root of this persistent endeavour has still to be mentioned; it is the same as that from which the Magical View of the world arose. If we give to a pseudo-statement the kind of unqualified acceptance which belongs by right only to certified scientific statements, if we can contrive to do this, the impulses and attitudes with which we respond to it gain a notable stability and vigour. Briefly, if we can contrive to believe poetry, then the world *seems*, while we do so, to be transfigured. It used to be compara-

[7] For an account of the various senses of truth and of the ways in which they may be distinguished in discussion cf. *The Meaning of Meaning*, by C. K. Ogden and the author, Chapters VII and X.

tively easy to do this, and the habit has become well established. With the extension of science and the neutralisation of nature it has become difficult as well as dangerous. Yet it is still alluring; it has many analogies with drug-taking. Hence the endeavours of the critics referred to. Various subterfuges have been devised along the lines of regarding Poetic Truth as figurative, symbolic; or as more immediate, as a truth of Intuition, not of reason; or as a higher form of the same truth as reason yields. Such attempts to use poetry as a denial or as a corrective of science are very common. One point can be made against them all: they are never worked out in detail. There is no equivalent to Mill's *Logic* expounding any such view. The language in which they are framed is usually a blend of obsolete psychology and emotive exclamations.

The long-established and much-encouraged habit of giving to emotive utterances—whether pseudo-statements simple, or looser and larger wholes taken as saying something figuratively—the kind of assent which we give to established facts, has for most people debilitated a wide range of their responses. A few scientists, caught young and brought up in the laboratory, are free from it; but then, as a rule, they pay no *serious* attention to poetry. For most men the recognition of the neutrality of nature brings about—through this habit—a divorce from poetry. They are so used to having their responses propped up by beliefs, however vague, that when these shadowy supports are removed they are no longer able to respond. Their attitudes to so many things have been forced in the past, over-encouraged. And when the world-picture ceases to assist there is a collapse. Over whole tracts of natural emotional response we are today like a bed of dahlias whose sticks have been removed. And this effect of the neutralisation of nature is only in its beginnings. Consider the probable effects upon love-poetry in the near future of the kind of enquiry into basic human constitution exemplified by psychoanalysis.

A sense of desolation, of uncertainty, of futility, of the groundlessness of aspirations, of the vanity of endeavour, and a thirst for a life-giving water which seems suddenly to have failed, are the signs in consciousness of this necessary reorganisation of our lives.[8] Our attitudes and impulses are being compelled to become self-supporting; they are being driven back upon their biological justification, made once again sufficient to themselves. And the only impulses which seem strong enough to continue unflagging are commonly so crude that, to more finely developed individuals, they hardly seem worth having. Such people cannot live by warmth, food, fighting, drink and sex alone. Those who are least affected by the change are those who are emotionally least removed from the animals. As we shall see at the close of this essay, even a considerable poet may attempt to find relief by a reversion to primitive mentality.

It is important to diagnose the disease correctly and to put the blame in the right quarter. Usually it is some alleged "materialism" of science which is denounced. This mistake is due partly to clumsy thinking, but chiefly to relics of the Magical View. For even if the Universe were "spiritual" all through (whatever that assertion might mean; all such assertions are probably nonsense), that would not make it any more accordant to human attitudes. It is not what the universe is made of but how it works, the law it follows, which makes knowledge of it incapable of spurring on our emotional responses, and further the nature of knowledge itself makes it inadequate. The contact with things which we therein establish is too sketchy and indirect to help us. We are beginning to know too much about the bond which unites the mind to its object in knowledge for that old dream of a perfect knowledge which would guarantee perfect life to retain its sanction. What was thought to be pure knowledge, we see now to have been shot through with hope and desire, with fear and wonder, and these intrusive elements indeed gave it all its power to support our lives. In knowledge, in the "How?" of

[8] To those familiar with Mr. Eliot's *The Waste Land*, my indebtedness to it at this point will be evident. He seems to me by this poem, to have performed two considerable services for this generation. He has given a perfect emotive description of a state of mind which is probably inevitable for a while to all meditative people. Secondly, by effecting a complete severance between his poetry and *all* beliefs, and this without any weakening of the poetry, he has realised what might otherwise have remained largely a speculative possibility, and has shown the way to the only solution of these difficulties. "In the destructive element immerse. That is the way."

events, we can find hints by which to take advantage of circumstances in our favour and avoid mischances. But we cannot get from it a *raison d'être* or a justification of more than a relatively lowly kind of life.

The justification, or the reverse, of any attitude lies, not in the object, but in itself, in its serviceableness to the whole personality. Upon its place in the whole system of attitudes, which is the personality, all its worth depends. This is true equally for the subtle, finely compounded attitudes of the civilised individual as for the simpler attitudes of the child.

In brief, experience is its own justification; and this fact must be faced, although sometimes —by a lover, for example—it may be very difficult to accept. Once it is faced, it is apparent that all the attitudes to other human beings and to the world in all its aspects, which have been serviceable to humanity, remain as they were, as valuable as ever. Hesitation felt in admitting this is a measure of the strength of the evil habit we have described. But many of these attitudes, valuable as ever, are, now that they are being set free, more difficult to maintain, because we still hunger after a basis in belief.

7

SOME CONTEMPORARY POETS

It is time to turn to those living poets through study of whose work these reflections have arisen. Mr. Hardy is for every reason the poet with whom it is most natural to begin. Not only does his work span the whole period in which what I have called the neutralisation of nature was finally effected, but it has throughout definitely reflected that change. Short essays in verse are fairly frequent among his *Collected Poems,* essays almost always dealing with this very topic; but these, however suggestive, are not the ground for singling him out as the poet who has most fully and courageously accepted the contemporary background; nor are the poems which are most definitely *about* the neutrality of nature the ground for the assertion. There is an opportunity for a misunderstanding at this point. The ground is the tone, the handling and the rhythm of poems which treat other subjects, for example *The Self Unseeing, The Voice, A Broken Appointment,* and preeminently *After a Journey.* A poem does not necessarily accept the situation because it gives it explicit recognition, but only through the precise mutation of the attitudes of which it is composed. Mr. Middleton Murry, against whose recent positions parts of this essay may be suspected by the reader to be aimed, has best pointed out, in his *Aspects of Literature,* how peculiarly "adequate to what we know and have suffered" Mr. Hardy's poetry is. "His reaction to an episode has behind it and within it a reaction to the universe." This is not as I should put it were I making a statement; but read as a pseudo-statement, emotively, it is excellent; it makes us remember how we felt. Actually it describes just what Hardy, at his best, does not do. He makes no reaction to the universe, recognising it as something to which no reaction is more relevant than another. Mr. Murry is again well inspired, this time both emotively and scientifically, when he says: "Mr. Hardy stands high above all other modern poets by the deliberate purity of his responsiveness. The contagion of the world's slow stain has not touched him; from the first he held aloof from the general conspiracy to forget in which not only those who are professional optimists take a part." These extracts (from a writer more agonisingly aware than others that some strange change has befallen man in this generation, though his diagnosis is, I believe, mistaken) indicate very well Mr. Hardy's place and rank in English poetry. He is the poet who has most steadily refused to be comforted. The comfort of forgetfulness, the comfort of beliefs, he has put both these away. Hence his singular preoccupation with death; because it is in the contemplation of death that the necessity for human attitudes, in the face of an indifferent universe, to become self-supporting is felt most poignantly. Only the greatest tragic poets have achieved an equally self-reliant and immitigable acceptance.

From Mr. Hardy to Mr. De la Mare may seem a large transition, though readers of Mr. De la Mare's later work will agree that there are interesting resemblances—in *Who's That* and in other poems in *The Veil* where Mr. De la Mare is notably less himself than when writing at his best. In his best poetry, in *The Pigs and the Charcoal Burner,* in *John Mouldy,* no intimation of the contemporary situation sounds. He is writing of, and from, a world which knows nothing of these difficulties, a world of pure phantasy for which the distinction between knowledge and feeling has not yet dawned. When in other poems, more reflective, in *The Tryst,* for example, Mr. De la Mare does seem to be directly facing the indifference of the universe towards "poor mortal longingness" a curious thing happens. His utterance, in spite of his words, becomes not at all a recognition of this indifference, but voices instead an impulse to turn away, to forget it, to seek shelter in the warmth of his own familiar thickets of dreams, not to stay out in the wind. His rhythm, that indescribable personal note which clings to all his best poetry, is a lulling rhythm, an anodyne, an opiate, it gives sleep and visions, phantasmagoria; but it does not give *vision,* it does not awaken. Even when he most appears to be contemplating the fate of the modern, "whom the words of the wise have made sad," the drift of his verse is still "seeking after that sweet golden clime" where the mental traveller's journey *begins.*

There is one exception to this charge (for in a sense it is an adverse criticism, though not one to be pressed except against a great poet), there is one poem in which there is no such reluctance to bear the blast—*The Mad Prince's Song* in *Peacock Pie.* But here the spirit of the poem, the impulse which gives it life, comes from a poet who more than most refused to take shelter; *The Mad Prince's Song* derives from *Hamlet.*

Mr. Yeats and Mr. Lawrence present two further ways of dodging those difficulties which come from being born into this generation rather than into some earlier age. Mr. De la Mare takes shelter in the dream-world of the child, Mr. Yeats retires into black velvet curtains and the visions of the Hermetist, and Mr. Lawrence makes a magnificent attempt to reconstruct in himself the mentality of the Bushman. There are other modes of escape open to the poet. Mr. Blundell, to name one other poet only, goes into the country, but few people follow him there in his spirit, whereas Mr. Yeats and Mr. Lawrence, whether they are widely read or not, do represent tendencies among the defeated which are only too easily observable.

Mr. Yeats' work from the beginning was a repudiation of the most active contemporary interests. But at first the poet of *The Wanderings of Usheen, The Stolen Child* and *Innisfree* turned away from contemporary civilisation in favour of a world which he knew perfectly, the world of folk-lore as it is accepted, neither with belief nor disbelief, by the peasant. Folk-lore and the Irish landscape, its winds, woods, waters, islets, and seagulls, and for a while an unusually simple and direct kind of love poetry in which he became something more than a minor poet, these were his refuge. Later, after a drawn battle with the drama, he made a more violent repudiation, not merely of current civilisation but of life itself, in favour of a supernatural world. But the world of the "eternal moods," of supernal essences and immortal beings is not, like the Irish peasant stories and the Irish landscape, part of his natural and familiar experience. Now he turns to a world of symbolic phantasmagoria about which he is desperately uncertain. He is uncertain because he has adopted as a technique of inspiration the use of trance, of dissociated phases of consciousness, and the revelations given in these dissociated states are insufficiently connected with normal experience. This, in part, explains the weakness of Mr. Yeats' transcendental poetry. A deliberate reversal of the natural relations of thought and feeling is the rest of the explanation. Mr. Yeats takes certain feelings—feelings of conviction attaching to certain visions—as evidence for the thoughts which he supposes his visions to symbolize. To Mr. Yeats the value of *The Phases of the Moon* lies not in any attitudes which it arouses or embodies but in the doctrine which for an initiate it promulgates.

The resort to trance, and the effort to discover a new world-picture to replace that given by science are the two most significant points for our purpose in Mr. Yeats' work. A third might be the singularly bitter contempt for the generality of mankind which occasionally appears.

The doctrinal problem arises again, but in a clearer form with Mr. Lawrence. But here (Mr. Yeats' promised treatise on the states of the soul has not yet appeared) we have the advantage of an elaborate prose exposition, *Phantasia of the Unconscious,* of the positions which so many of the poems advocate. It is not unfair to put the matter in this way, since there is little doubt possible that the bulk of Mr. Lawrence's published verse is prose, scientific prose too, jottings, in fact, from a psychologist's notebook, with a commentary interspersed. Due allowance being made for the extreme psychological interest of these observations, there remains the task of explaining how the poet who wrote the *Ballad of Another Ophelia* and *Aware,* and, above all, *The White Peacock,* should have wandered, through his own zeal misdirected, so far from the paths which once appeared to be his alone to open.

Mr. Lawrence's revolt against civilisation seems to have been originally spontaneous, an emotional revulsion free from *ad hoc* beliefs. It sprang directly from experience. He came to abhor all the attitudes men adopt, not through the direct prompting of their instincts, but because of the supposed nature of the objects to which they are directed. The conventions, the idealizations, which come between man and man and between man and woman, which often queer the pitch for the natural responses, seemed to him the source of all evil. Part of his revolt was certainly justified. These idealisations—representative examples are the dogma of the equality of man and the doctrine that Love is primarily sympathy—are beliefs illicitly interpolated in order to support and strengthen attitudes in the manner discussed at length above. And Mr. Lawrence's original rejection of a morality not self-supporting but based upon beliefs, makes his work an admirable illustration of my main thesis. But two simple and avoidable mistakes deprived his revolt of the greater part of its value. He overlooked the fact that such beliefs commonly arise because the attitudes they support are already existent. He assumed that a bad basis for an attitude meant a bad attitude. In general, it does mean a forced attitude, but that is another matter. Secondly, he tried to cure the disease by introducing other beliefs of his own manufacture in place of the conventional beliefs and in support of very different attitudes.

The genesis of these beliefs is extremely interesting as an illustration of primitive mentality. Since the attitudes on which he fell back are those of a very early stage of human development, it is not surprising that the means by which he has supported them should be of the same era, or that the world-picture which he has worked out should be similar to that described in *The Golden Bough.* The mental process at work is schematically as follows: First, undergo an intense emotion, located with unusual definiteness in the body, which can be described as "a feeling *as though* the solar plexus were connected by a current of dark passional energy with another person." Those whose emotions tend to be localised will be familiar with such feelings. The second step is to say "I must trust my feelings." The third is to call the feeling an intuition. The last is to say "*I know* that my solar plexus is, etc." By this means we arrive at indubitable knowledge that the sun's energy is recruited from the life on the earth and that the astronomers are wrong in what they say about the moon, and so on.

The illicit steps in the argument are not quite so evident as they appear to be in this analysis. To distinguish an intuition *of* an emotion from an intuition *by* it is not always easy, nor is a description of an emotion always in practice distinguishable from an emotion. Certainly we must trust our feelings—in the sense of acting upon them. We have nothing else to trust. And to confuse this trusting with believing an emotive description of them is a mistake which all traditional codes of morality encourage us to commit.

The significance of such similar disasters in the work of poets so unlike and yet so greatly gifted as Mr. Yeats and Mr. Lawrence is noteworthy. For each the traditional scaffolding of conventional beliefs have proved unsatisfying, unworkable as a basis for their attitudes. Each has sought, in very different directions it is true, a new set of beliefs as a remedy. For neither has the world-picture of science seemed a possible substitute. And neither seems to have envisaged the possibility of a poetry which is independent of all beliefs, probably because, however much they differ, both are very serious poets. A great deal of poetry can, of course, be written for which total independence of all beliefs is an easy matter. But it is never poetry of the more important kind, because the temptation to introduce beliefs is a sign and measure of the importance of the attitudes involved. At present it is not primarily religious beliefs, in the stricter sense of the word, which are most likely to be concerned. Emphases alter surprisingly. University societies founded fifteen years ago, for example, to discuss religion, are usually found to be discussing sex today. And serious love poetry, which is independent of beliefs of one kind or another, traditional or eccentric, is extremely rare.

Yet the necessity for independence is increasing. This is not to say that traditional poetry, into which beliefs readily enter, is becoming obsolete; it is merely becoming more and more difficult to approach without confusion; it demands a greater imaginative effort, a greater purity in the reader.

We must distinguish here, however. There are many feelings and attitudes which, though in the past supported by beliefs now untenable, can survive their removal because they have other, more natural, supports and spring directly from the necessities of existence. To the extent to which they have been undistorted by the beliefs which have gathered round them they will remain as before. But there are other attitudes which are very largely the product of belief and have no other support. These will lapse if the changes here forecast continue. With their disappearance some forms of poetry—much minor devotional verse, for example—will become obsolete. And with the unravelling of the intellect *versus* emotion entanglement, there will be cases where even literature to which immense value has been assigned—the speculative portions of the work of Dostoevsky may be instanced—will lose much of its interest, except for the history of the mind. It was because he belonged to our age that Dostoevsky had to wrestle so terribly in these toils. A poet today, whose integrity is equal to that of the greater poets of the past, is inevitably plagued by the problem of thought and feeling as poets have never been plagued before.

A pioneer in modern research upon the origins of culture was asked recently whether his work had any bearing upon religion. He replied that it had, but that at present he was engaged merely in "getting the guns into position." The same answer might be given with regard to the probable consequences of recent progress in psychology, not only for religion but for the whole fabric of our traditional beliefs about ourselves. In many quarters there is a tendency to suppose that the series of attacks upon received ideas which began, shall we say, with Galileo and rose to a climax with Darwinism, has overreached itself with Einstein and Eddington, and that the battle is now due to die down. This view seems to be too optimistic. The most dangerous of the sciences is only now beginning to come into action. I am thinking less of Psycho-analysis or of Behaviourism than of the whole subject which includes them. It is very probable that the Hindenburg Line to which the defence of our traditions retired as a result of the onslaughts of the last century will be blown up in the near future. If this should happen a mental chaos such as man has never experienced may be expected. We shall then be thrown back, as Mathew Arnold foresaw, upon poetry. It is capable of saving us; it is a perfectly possible means of overcoming chaos. But whether man is capable of the reorientation required, whether he can loosen in time the entanglement with belief which now takes from poetry half its power and would then take all, is another question, and too large for the scope of this essay.

I. A. RICHARDS: Sense and Feeling*

My belief is that there every one is under the sway of preferences deeply rooted within, into the hands of which he unwittingly plays as he pursues his speculation. When there are such good grounds for distrust, only a tepid feeling of indulgence is possible towards the results of one's own mental labours. But I hasten to add that such self-criticism does not render obligatory any special tolerance of divergent opinions. One may inexorably reject theories that are contradicted by the very first steps in the analysis of observation, and yet at the same time be aware that those one holds oneself have only a tentative validity.

—FREUD, *Beyond the Pleasure Principle*

SO FAR we have been concerned with some of the snares that waylay the apprehension and judgment of the *sense* of poetry,[1] treated more or less in isolation from its other kinds of meaning. But the *interferences* with one another of these various meanings give rise to more formidable difficulties. A mistake as to the general intention of a passage can obviously twist its sense for us, and its tone and feeling, almost out of recognition. If we supposed, for example, that *Poem I* should be read, not as a passage from an Epic, but as a piece of dramatic verse put in the mouth either of a prosing bore, or of a juvenile enthusiast, our apprehension of its tone and feeling would obviously be changed, and our judgment of it, though still perhaps adverse, would be based upon different considerations. The different intentions attributed to *Poem II* by readers who take it to express on the one hand "a deep passion for real life" (2.61) and on the other "an atmosphere of quietness and uninterrupted peace" (2.71) reflect themselves in the different descriptions they give of its tone ("breathless tumultuous music,"

* "Sense and Feeling" is the third chapter of Part III of *Practical Criticism* (1929) and, together with the extended footnote from the Introduction, it is reprinted here by permission of Harcourt, Brace and Company, Inc.

[1] [In the "Introductory" section of *Practical Criticism*, Mr. Richards writes as follows:

"The following seem to be the chief difficulties of criticism or, at least, those which we shall have most occasion to consider here:—

"A. First must come the difficulty of *making out the plain sense* of poetry. The most disturbing and impressive fact brought out by this experiment is that a large proportion of average-to-good (and in some cases, certainly, devoted) readers of poetry frequently and repeatedly *fail to understand it,* both as a statement and as an expression. They fail to make out its prose sense, its plain, overt meaning, as a set of ordinary, intelligible, English sentences, taken quite apart from any further poetic significance. And equally, they misapprehend its feeling, its tone, and its intention. They would travesty it in a paraphrase. They fail to construe it just as a schoolboy fails to construe a piece of Caesar. How serious in its effects in different instances this failure may be, we shall have to consider with care. It is not confined to one class of readers; not only those whom we would suspect fall victims. Nor is it only the most abstruse poetry which so betrays us. In fact, to set down, for once, the brutal truth, no immunity is possessed on any occasion, not by the most reputable scholar, from this or any other of these critical dangers.

"B. Parallel to, and not unconnected with, these difficulties of interpreting the meaning are the difficulties of *sensuous* apprehension. Words in sequence have a form to the mind's ear and the mind's tongue and larynx, even when silently read. They have a movement and may have a rhythm. The gulf is wide between a reader who naturally and immediately perceives this form and movement (by a conjunction of sensory, intellectual and emotional sagacity) and another reader, who either ignores it or has to build it up laboriously with finger-counting, table-tapping and the rest; and this difference has most far-reaching effects.

"C. Next may come those difficulties that are connected with the place of *imagery,* principally visual imagery, in poetic reading. They arise in part from the incurable fact that we differ immensely in our capacity to visualise, and to produce imagery of the other senses. Also the importance of our imagery as a whole, as well as of some pet particular type of image, in our mental lives varies surprisingly. Some minds can do nothing and get nowhere without images; others seem to be able to do everything and get anywhere, reach any and every state of thought and feeling without making use of them. Poets on the whole (though by no means all poets always) may be suspected of exceptional imaging capacity, and some readers are constitutionally prone to stress the place of imagery in reading, to pay great attention to it, and even to judge the value of "delicate movement with clear, fine tone,[2] gravity and steadiness"). More plainly the rather one-sided debates about the intentions of *Poems VIII* and *XIII* reveal how much this major aspect, as it were, influences the minor aspects, through which the major aspect, one would suppose, must be apprehended. The rapidity with which many readers leap to a conviction as to a poem's general intention, and the ease with which this assumption can distort their whole reading, is one of the most interesting features in the protocols. And its moral is perhaps as important as any that can be drawn. With most good poetry more than one look is needed before we can be sure of the intention, and sometimes everything else in the poem must become clear to us before this.

Tone, as a distinct character in a poem, is less easy to discuss than the others, and its importance may easily be overlooked. Yet poetry, which has no other very remarkable qualities, may sometimes take very high rank simply because the poet's attitude to his listeners—in view of what he has to say—is so perfect. Gray and Dryden are notable examples. Gray's *Elegy*, indeed, might stand as a supreme instance to show how powerful an exquisitely adjusted tone may be. It would be difficult to maintain that the thought in this poem is either striking or original,[3] or that its feeling is exceptional. It em-

the poetry by the images it excites in them. But images are erratic things; lively images aroused in one mind need have no similarity to the equally lively images stirred by the same line of poetry in another, and neither set need have anything to do with any images which may have existed in the poet's mind. Here is a troublesome source of critical deviations.

"D. Thirdly, more obviously, we have to note the powerful very pervasive influence of *mnemonic irrelevances.* These are misleading effects of the reader's being reminded of some personal scene or adventure, erratic associations, the interference of emotional reverberations from a past which may have nothing to do with the poem. Relevance is not an easy notion to define or to apply, though some instances of irrelevant intrusions are among the simplest of all accidents to diagnose.

"E. More puzzling and more interesting are the critical traps that surround what may be called *Stock Responses.* These have their opportunity whenever a poem seems to, or does, involve views and emotions already fully prepared in the reader's mind, so that what happens appears to be more of the reader's doing than the poet's. The button is pressed, and then the author's work is done, for immediately the record starts playing in quasi- (or total) independence of the poem which is supposed to be its origin or instrument.

Whenever this lamentable redistribution of the poet's and reader's share in the labour of poetry occurs, or is in danger of occurring, we require to be especially on our guard. Every kind of injustice may be committed as well by those who just escape as by those who are caught.

"F. *Sentimentality* is a peril that needs less comment here. It is a question of the due measure of response. This over-facility in certain emotional directions is the Scylla whose Charybdis is—

"G. *Inhibition.* This, as much as Sentimentality, is a positive phenomenon, though less studied until recent years and somewhat masked under the title of Hardness of Heart. But neither can well be considered in isolation.

"H. *Doctrinal Adhesions* present another troublesome problem. Very much poetry—religious poetry may be instanced—seems to contain or imply views and beliefs, true or false, about the world. If this be so, what bearing has the truth-value of the views upon the worth of the poetry? Even if it be not so, if the beliefs are not really contained or implied, but only seem so to a non-poetical reading, what should be the bearing of the reader's conviction, if any, upon his estimate of the poetry? Has poetry anything to say; if not, why not, and if so, how? Difficulties at this point are a fertile source of confusion and erratic judgment.

"I. Passing now to a different order of difficulties, the effects of *technical presuppositions* have to be noted. When something has once been well done in a certain fashion we tend to expect similar things to be done in the future in the same fashion, and are disappointed or do not recognise them if they are done differently. Conversely, a technique which has shown its ineptitude for one purpose tends to become discredited for all. Both are cases of mistaking means for ends. Whenever we attempt to judge poetry from outside by technical details we are putting means before ends, and—such is our ignorance of cause and effect in poetry—we shall be lucky if we do not make even worse blunders. We have to try to avoid judging pianists by their hair.

"J. Finally, *general critical preconceptions* (prior demands made upon poetry as a result of theories—conscious or unconscious—about its nature and value), intervene endlessly, as the history of criticism shows only too well, between the reader and the poem. Like an unlucky dietetic formula they may cut him off from what he is starving for, even when it is at his very lips.

"These difficulties, as will have been observed, are not unconnected with one another and indeed overlap. They might have been collected under more heads or fewer. Yet, if we set aside certain extreme twists or trends of the personality (for example, blinding narcissism or grovelling self-abasement—aberrations, temporary or permanent, of the self-regarding sentiment) together with undue accumulations or depletions of energy, I believe that most of the principal obstacles and causes of failure may without much straining be brought under these ten heads. But they are too roughly sketched here for this to be judged. . . ."]

[2] "Tone" in a quite different sense here, of course; but these descriptions of the qualities of the verse sounds do enable us to infer differences in the way the reader feels that he is being addressed.

[3] The originality of the thoughts and that of the expression are to be distinguished here. "The four

bodies a sequence of reflections and attitudes that under similar conditions arise readily in any contemplative mind. Their character as commonplaces, needless to say, does not make them any less important, and the *Elegy* may usefully remind us that boldness and originality are not necessities for great poetry. But these thoughts and feelings, in part because of their significance and their nearness to us, are peculiarly difficult to express without faults of tone. If we are forced to express them we can hardly escape pitching them in a key which "overdoes" them, or we take refuge in an elliptic mode of utterance—hinting them rather than rendering them to avoid offence either to others or to ourselves. Gray, however, without overstressing any point, composes a long address, perfectly accommodating his familiar feelings towards the subject and his awareness of the inevitable triteness of the only possible reflections, to the discriminating attention of his audience. And this is the source of his triumph, which we may misunderstand if we treat it simply as a question of "style." Indeed, many of the secrets of "style" could, I believe, be shown to be matters of tone, of the perfect recognition of the writer's relation to the reader in view of what is being said and their joint feelings about it.

Much popular verse, of the type with which the name of Wilcox is nowadays somewhat unfairly associated, fails more in this respect than in any other. It "overdoes" what it attempts, and so insults the reader. And such overstressing is often a very delicate indication of the rank of the author. When a commonplace, either of thought or feeling, is delivered with an air appropriate to a fresh discovery or a revelation, we can properly grow suspicious. For by the tone in which a great writer handles these familiar things we can tell whether they have their due place in the whole fabric of his thought and feeling and whether, therefore, he has the right to our attention. Good manners, fundamentally, are a reflection of our sense of proportion, and faults of tone are much more than mere superficial blemishes. They may indicate a very deep disorder.

The importance of tone appears clearly if we reflect how comparatively easy it is to acquire acceptable doctrines and how difficult to avoid mistakes in tone.

We must distinguish, however, between what may be called fundamental manners and the code that rules in any given period. Good manners for the eighteenth century may be atrocious by twentieth-century standards, or *vice versa*, and not only in literary matters. There are more than a few verses in *The Rape of the Lock*, for example, which would be thought in very poor taste if they were written today. But the codes that rule wit are peculiarly variable. Of all literary products jokes are the most apt to become "flat" and tasteless with the passage of time.

Eighteenth-century verse writers, on the whole, rarely forget the reader. They paid him, indeed, rather too much deference, a result of the social character of the period. In comparison, Swinburne and Shelley often show atrocious manners as poets; [4] they please themselves and continually neglect the reader. Not that good tone requires that the reader be remembered always, much less that he be constantly flattered. But the occasions on which he is ignored must be exciting enough to excuse the poet's rapt oblivion. Faults of tone, especially over-insistence and condescension, can ruin poetry which might otherwise have had value, though usually, as I have suggested, they betoken fatal disabilities in the poet. They may, however, be due to clumsiness only. The poet has to find some equivalent for the gestures and intonations which in ordinary speech so often look after this whole matter, and this translation may at times ask for special discernment and tolerance in the reader. It will have been noticed that the reception of *Poems V* and *VII* was very largely determined by the readers' estimation of their tone (5.5, 5.8, 5.81, 7.4, 7.43, 7.6). But in judging such ques-

stanzas beginning, *Yet e'en these bones*, are to me, original: I have never seen the notions in any other place; yet he that reads them here persuades himself that he has always felt them." Dr. Johnson may be right in this, but I find it hard not to believe that the notions in these four stanzas have not been familiar to many who neither knew the *Elegy* nor received them from those who did.

[4] Unless we suppose that we are not so much being addressed as invited to stand by the poet's side and harangue the multitude with him. Tone in Swinburne frequently lapses altogether; he has neither good nor bad manners, but simply none. This, perhaps, aristocratic trait in part excuses his long-windedness, for example.

tions we must remember, though it is not at all easy to do so, that tone is not independent of the other kinds of meaning. We can allow a poet to address us as though we were somewhat his inferiors if what he has to say convinces us of his right to do so. But when what he offers us is within our own compass, we may be excused if we grow resentful. The subtleties possible here can easily be imagined, and some effects that may seem very mysterious until we look into them from this point of view can then be explained. Questions of tone arise, of course, whether the reader is ostensibly addressed in the second person or not. The reader can be as grossly insulted in a third-person narrative or in an Elegy, by underrating his sensitiveness or intelligence for example, as by any direct rudeness.

But the most curious and puzzling cases of mutual dependence between different kinds of meaning occur with sense and feeling. They are, as a rule, interlinked and combined very closely, and the exact dissection of the one from the other is sometimes an impossible and always an extremely delicate and perilous operation. But the effort to separate these forms of meaning is instructive, and can help us both to see why misunderstandings of all kinds are so frequent, and to devise educational methods that will make them less common.

Let us set one complication aside at once. The *sound* of a word has plainly much to do with the feeling it evokes, above all when it occurs in the organised context of a passage of verse. Let us postpone—so far as we can—all consideration of this whole *sensuous* aspect of words (including their character as products of the speech-organs and their associated dance-movement) until the following Chapter, where the difficulties of the apprehension of poetic form must be tackled. In practice, of course, the sound is very important, as one of the causes (together with the word's history, its semantics, its usual applications and contexts and its special context in the poem) of the feeling it carries. But here let us confine our attention to the relations between sense and feeling and to the ways in which the feeling may be, in various degrees, dependent on the sense. And let us be careful to remember that we are concerned, firstly, with the feeling actually aroused by the word in the poem, not with the feelings the word might have in other contexts, or the feeling it generally has, or the feeling it "ought to have," though these may with advantage be remembered, for a word's feeling is often determined in part by its sense in other contexts.[5]

Even the evident complexities of this subject are prodigious, and it must be left for some treatise of the future on the Emotive Functions of Language to display in full their tedium, their beauty, and their supreme significance.[6] Here three main situations can alone be discussed, three types of the interrelation of sense and feeling.

Type I.—This is the most obvious case where the feeling is generated by and governed by the sense. The feeling evoked is the result of apprehending the sense. As examples, "miraculous" and "sorcery" may serve (*Poem X*). Given the apprehension of their sense, the feeling follows, and as a rule the two, sense and feeling, seem to form an indissoluble whole.

Type II.—Here there is an equally close tie, but fixed the other way round. For the word first expresses a feeling, and such sense as it conveys is derived from the feeling. "Gorgeous" (*Poem X*) is an excellent example; its sense is "being of a kind to excite such and such feelings." The description of the feelings would have to be long and include mention of a tendency to contempt, grudging admiration, and a certain richness and fullness and, perhaps, satiation. "Gorgeous," it will be noticed, is a representative "aesthetic" or "projectile" adjective.[7] It registers a "projection" of feeling, and may be considered along with "beautiful," "pleasant" and "good" in some of their uses.

Type III.—Here sense and feeling are less closely knit: their alliance comes about through their context. "Sprawling" may be taken as an example. Its sense (in *Poem X*) may be indi-

[5] On the semantic aspects of this, Owen Barfield, *History in English Words*, may be profitably consulted. His *Poetic Diction* is less satisfactory, owing to an unfortunate attempt to construct a philosophical account of meaning—an account which blurs the distinction between thought and feeling and reduces the many-sided subject of Meaning to a matter of one aspect only, namely, semantics.

[6] If we reflect, for example, upon the emotive formulae in the liturgies of various religions, we shall not underrate the importance of this topic.

[7] Like most projectile adjectives it is applied to very different things by different people.

cated as an absence of symmetry, regularity, poise, and coherence, and a stretched and loose disposition of parts. I have been careful here to use only neutral (or nearly neutral) words, in order not to import the feeling in my paraphrase of the sense. The feeling of "sprawling" here is a mixture of good-humoured mockery and affected commiseration. And this feeling arises from the sense of the word only through the influence of the rest of the poem. It does not derive at all inevitably from the sense of the word considered by itself. One test by which we can distinguish Type III from Type I is by noticing that very special circumstances would be needed to make "miraculous" evoke quite another set of feelings, whereas no great change need be imagined for "sprawling" to excite feelings either of contempt or of easeful relaxation. As 10.55 puts it, "A drunken man sprawls and totters," and 10.57 has some other association, though what it is, is open to conjecture.

The looser relation described in Type III is of course the usual condition in poetry. Its separation from Type I [8] is a matter only of degree, for no word carries a fixed feeling quite irrespective of its context. But the distinction between words whose feeling tends to dominate their context and words of a more malleable nature is useful, for upon it most mistakes in apprehending feeling turn. The last two lines of Donne's Sonnet (3.12, 3.31, 3.41), the last verse but one of *Poem VII* (7.4, 7.43, 7.53), "boom," "poised," and "tinkling" in *Poem VIII* (8.1, 8.11, 8.13), "immortal" in *Poem XI* (11.2, 11.4, 11.421), and "rude" in *Poem XIII* (13.7, 13.73), provide some examples upon which to test the distinction. Is the pull exerted by the context (and in these cases the whole of the rest of the poem is the context) sufficient to overcome what may be described as the normal separate feeling of the questionable word? Can this pull bring it in, as an item either in accordance or in due contrast to the rest? Or does the word resist, stay outside, or wrench the rest of the poem into crudity or confusion? To triumph over the resistances of words may sometimes be considered the measure of a poet's power (Shakespeare being the obvious example), but more often it is the measure of his discretion, and a reader who is aware of the complexity and delicacy of the reconciliations of diverse feelings that poetry effects will walk as carefully.

The influence of the rest of the poem upon the single word or phrase is exerted in two ways—directly between feelings and indirectly through sense. The feelings already occupying the mind limit the possibilities of the new word; they may tinge it, they may bring out one of its possible feelings with an added tang of contrast. Words, as we all recognise, are as ambiguous in their feeling as in their sense; but, though we can track down their equivocations of sense to some extent, we are comparatively helpless with their ambiguities of feeling. We only know that words are chameleon-like in their feeling, governed in an irregular fashion by their surroundings. In this "psychical relativity" words may be compared with colours, but of the laws governing the effects of collocation and admixture hardly anything is known.

It is more interesting, therefore, to consider the other way in which the feeling of a phrase or word is controlled by the context—through the transactions between parts of the sense in the whole passage. On this much more can be said, for here the whole apparatus of our verbal and logical intelligence can be brought to bear. When a phrase strikes us as particularly happy, or particularly unfortunate, we can usually contrive, by examining the fabric of the sense into which it fits, to find rational grounds for our approval or dislike. And we often seem to see clearly why the emotional effect should be just what it is. But there is an odd fact to be noted which may make us hesitate. The phrase commonly is accepted or rejected, and its feeling merged, for good or ill, into the poem long before the discursive intelligence has performed its task of working out the cross-implications, affiliations and discrepancies of senses which later on may seem the explanation of its success or failure.

Three conjectures may be offered to account for an instantaneity which has led many critics to under-value the work of intellectual analysis in the reading of poetry. It may be that the ap-

[8] These types of situation are not mutually exclusive. The same word may give rise simultaneously to situations of Types I and II. We are often unable to say which of the two, sense or feeling, is the dominant partner, both views being possible. The dilemma may be a tribute to our insight rather than a sign of its deficiency, for both views may be true.

prehension of a network of logical relations between ideas is one thing and that the analysis and clear formulation of them is quite another, and that the first may often be easy and instantaneous when the second is difficult and laborious. This seems likely, and many parallel cases can be found. A cricketer, for example, can judge a ball without in the least being able to describe its flight, or say how or why he meets it as he does. Secondly, if, as seems possible, some degree of "dissociation" occurs in the reading of poetry, we may actually, while under the influence of the poem, apprehend more than we are able to recall when we come to reflect upon it out of the "trance" afterwards. This conjecture, however, seems extravagant. Thirdly, the compression of poetic language tends to obstruct the discursive intelligence that works by spreading ideas out and separating their parts. But this very concentration may assist immediate, instantaneous, apprehension. Nowhere but in poetry, unless in mathematics, do we meet with ideas so closely packed together, so tightly woven.

An instance may assist us to keep in touch with the observable facts while considering this obscure but important matter. The point is worth some trouble, for it is cardinal to any account of how poetry is read and why misunderstandings both of sense and feeling are so common and so difficult to avoid. The second line of the last verse of *Poem X* will serve our purpose:—

O frail steel tissues of the sun—

It will be agreed that the sense here is intricate, and that when it is analysed out it shows a rational correspondence with the feeling which those readers who accept the line as one of the felicities of the poem may be supposed to have experienced. Let me give a fairly detailed analysis, first asking any reader who approves of the line to consider how much logical structure the sense seems to him to have *as he reads* (not when he reflects). How far does this logical structure which appears to him while reading seem the source of the feeling of the words? Does it not rather remain in a vague background, more a possibility than an actuality?

"Tissue," to begin with the noun, has a double sense; firstly, "cloth of steel" in extension from "cloth of gold" or "cloth of silver," the cold, metallic, inorganic quality of the fabric being perhaps important; secondly, "thin, soft, semi-transparent" as with tissue-paper. "Steel" is also present as a sense-metaphor of Aristotle's second kind, when the transference is from *species* to *genus*, steel a particular kind of strong material being used to stand for any material strong enough to hold together, as it appears, the immensity of the cloud-structure. The colour suggestion of "steel" is also relevant. "Frail" echoes the semi-transparency of "tissue," the diaphanousness, and the impending dissolution too. "Of the sun" it may be added runs parallel to "of the silk worm," *i.e.*, produced by the sun. I give such an elaborate explanation partly because of the many readers (10.42) who had difficulty in making out this line.

It is safe, perhaps, to affirm that few readers will become clearly aware of more than a small part of these fibrillar articulations and correspondences of the sense until they deliberately question the line and think it over. Yet it can be accepted (and, I must add, rejected) with certainty and conviction on the strength of what seems the merest glimpse of its sense. Moreover, a definite and relevant feeling can be aroused at once. In fact, a feeling that is quite pertinent seems often to precede any clear grasping of the sense. And most readers will admit that, *as a rule*, the full sense, analysed and clearly articulated, never comes to their consciousness; yet they may get the feeling perfectly. The reception of *Poems I* and *V* was largely determined by whether the readers responded first to sense or to feeling. (Compare 1.17 and 1.3; and 5.81, 5.38 and 5.53. Also 7.43.) Still more does all this apply to *tone*.

I am far from wishing to quarrel with this summary kind of reading when it is practised by highly competent readers. A mere glimpse, to the right kind of eye, may be amply sufficient, but the dangers to those who are less quick and sensitive are obvious. Dangers both of a false understanding of the sense and of a distorted development of feeling. The corrective, in ideal perfection, is equally obvious—exercise in analysis and cultivation of the habit of regarding poetry as capable of explanation. But in practice the corrective has its own dangers. It has not been enough recognised in schools that making a paraphrase or gloss for any poem worth reading is a delicate exercise. Recalling some of the atrocities which teachers sometimes permit themselves, one is tempted to believe that the remedy might be worse than the disease. The risk of supposing that the feelings which the logical expansion of a poetic phrase excites must be those which the phrase was created to convey is very great. We easily substitute a bad piece of prose for the poem—a peculiarly damaging form of attack upon poetry. Furthermore, we must recognise that a single paraphrase will rarely indicate more than a single partial aspect of a poem. We often need one form of paraphrase to elucidate its sense and quite another to suggest its feeling. Since the only cure that can be suggested for the general unintelligibility of poetry that the protocols exhibit is some more enlightened use of interpretation exercised in our schools, it is worth while to consider what means are available for developing this power of apprehending both sense and feeling in teachers and pupils alike. It may be remarked that this is not a matter which concerns poetry only, though incapacity, obtuseness and failure in discrimination most appear through poetry, the most concentrated and delicate form of human utterance.

If we compare our powers of analysing sense and feeling we shall recognise at once that feeling, in contrast with sense, is a will-o'-the-wisp. We have a marvellous apparatus of inter-engaging and overlapping symbols for handling and elucidating sense, a logical machine of great sensitiveness and power, equipped with automatic safety devices and danger signals in the form of contradictions. Logical language has even reached such a high state of development that it can now be used to improve and extend itself, and may in time be made self-running and even fool-proof. For handling feeling we have nothing at all comparable. We have to rely upon introspection, a few clumsy descriptive names for emotions, some scores of aesthetic adjectives and the indirect resources of poetry, resources at the disposal of a few men only, and for them only in exceptional hours. Introspection has become a by-word, even where intellectual and sensory products and processes are concerned, but it is even more untrustworthy when applied to feelings. For a feeling even more than an idea or an image tends to vanish as we turn our introspective attention upon it. We have to catch it by the tip of its tail as it decamps. Furthermore, even when we are partially successful in catching it, we do not yet know how to analyse it. Analysis is a matter of separating out its attributes and no one knows yet what attributes a feeling may have, what their system of interconnections is, or which are important, which trivial.

This, it may be hoped, matters less than might be supposed. For if we had to wait until psychology had conquered *this* territory we might reasonably despair. But we shall find encouragement if we look more closely into the methods by which we do actually—in spite of the backwardness of psychology—contrive to discriminate between feelings, and it is not impossible that by so doing we may be able to give psychology a leg up.

We do somehow manage to discuss our feelings, sometimes with remarkable facility and success. We say things about them sometimes that seem to be subtle and recondite, and yet true. We do this in spite of our feebleness in introspection and our ignorance of the general nature of feelings. How do we come to be so knowledgeable and clever? Psychologists have never, I think, resolutely faced this question of how we know so much about ourselves that does not find any way at present into their text-books. Put shortly, the answer seems to be that this knowledge is lying dormant in the dictionary. Language has become its repository, a record, a reflection, as it were, of human nature.

No one who uses a dictionary—for other than orthographic purposes—can have escaped the shock of discovering how very far ahead of us our words often are. How subtly they already record distinctions towards which we are still groping. And many young philologists and grammarians must have indulged dreams of bringing some of this wisdom into the ordered system of science. If we could read this reflection of our minds aright, we might learn nearly as much about ourselves as we shall ever wish to know; we should certainly increase enormously our power of handling our knowledge. Many of the distinctions words convey have been arrived at and recorded by methods no single mind could apply, complex methods that are, as yet, not well understood. But our understanding of them is improving—psychology has notably helped here—and our power of interpreting the psychological records embodied in words is increasing and capable of immense increase in the future. Among the means to this end a combination or co-operation of psychology and literary analysis, or criticism, seems the most hopeful. Neither alone can do much, both together may go far. There is a possibility that something parallel to the recent advances in physics might be achieved if we could combine them. As geology, in the early stages of inquiry into radioactivity, came in to supply evidence that experiments could not elicit, so the records, hidden not in rocks but in words, and accessible only to literary penetration, may combine [9] with groping psychological analysis to produce results as yet unprofitable to conjecture.

From these high speculations let us come back nearer to the problem of sense and feeling. How actually do we enquire into the feeling a word (or phrase) carries? How we enquire into its sense is not so difficult to make out. We utter the word or phrase and note the thoughts it arouses, being careful to keep them in the context of the other thoughts aroused by the whole passage. We then attempt, by a well-recognised and elaborate technique, to construct a definition, choosing from among several methods to suit our purpose and the situation. If we still have any difficulty in distinguishing the precise sense, we can put definite questions, we can substitute other words—which the dictionary will supply—that in part arouse the same thoughts. We note the samenesses and differences and plot the position of the thought we wish to define with regard to these other thoughts.

In these and other ways we exploit the syntactical suppleness of language and its overlapping vocabulary to disentangle sense, but if we consider how far the same resources are available for disentangling feeling we find a difference. There is, it is true, a department of language, a certain selection of the dictionary, which can be applied in the same fashion. There are the names of the emotions and of the emotional attitudes—*anger, fear, joy, sorrow . . .*; *hope, surprise, discouragement, dread. . . .* And the derivative [10] adjectives, verbs and adverbs, *enthusiastic, passionate, tender . . .*; *startle, delight, distress . . .*; *mournfully, eagerly, gaily. . . .* Moreover, we have the special apparatus of the aesthetic or "projectile" adjectives. We express our feeling by describing the object which excites it as *splendid, glorious, ugly, horrid, lovely, pretty . . .* words which really indicate not so much the nature of the object as the character of our feeling towards it. Thus we obtain an indirect notion for our feelings by projecting them rather than describing them. But we use this notation in a very unsystematic fashion, though a very curious and interesting order may be sometimes glimpsed behind it. Some of these words, for example, may be used together, while others bar one another out. A thing may be both grand and sublime, it can be glorious and beautiful, or gorgeous and ugly; but it can hardly be both pretty and beautiful, it can certainly not be pretty and sublime. These accordances and incompatibilities reflect the organisation of our feelings, the relations that hold between them. But our power to take advantage of this linguistic reflection of our emotional constitution is at present very limited—perhaps because so little work has been done upon this subject. And it is when we attempt to describe the difference between the feelings which *pretty* and *beautiful* express, for example, that we discover how unsatisfactory are the verbal resources expressly allocated to this purpose.

There is, of course, a certain apparatus of qualifying words and phrases that we use rather speculatively and uncertainly to describe feelings. We can say of a feeling that it is *elevated* or *gross*, or *tenuous*, or *calm*, or *grave*, or *expansive*. Most of these are clearly metaphorical expressions, words whose sense has not normally anything to do with feeling, transferred and applied to feeling on account of some glimpsed or supposed character in the feeling analogous to a character in the object the word usually describes. Sometimes the analogy is close—*fleeting, massive, intense, constricting*—and our slight knowledge of the physiology of emotions may also help us here. But often the resemblance

[9] This inquiry will not be so much a matter of semantics (though semantics obviously provide invaluable information) as of a comparative study of the resources (direct and indirect) available in different languages and periods for psychological purposes.

[10] Logically, not grammatically, derivative, of course.

or analogy is remote and will not bear pressing. It is hard to be certain what is being said when a feeling is described as *profound,* or *vital.* Perhaps very little indeed, may be being said. And often, if we look closely, the metaphor turns out to be not a prose or *sense* metaphor at all but an *emotive* metaphor. The difference between these is worth some reflection.[11]

A metaphor is a shift, a carrying over of a word from its normal use to a new use. In a sense metaphor the shift of the word is occasioned and justified by a similarity or analogy *between the object* it is usually applied to and the new object. In an emotive metaphor the shift occurs through some similarity *between the feelings* the new situation and the normal situation arouse. The same word may, in different contexts, be either a sense or an emotive metaphor. If you call a man a swine, for example, it may be because his features resemble those of a pig, but it may be because you have towards him something of the feeling you conventionally have towards pigs, or because you propose, if possible, to excite those feelings. Both metaphorical shifts may be combined simultaneously, and they often are. But in studying our methods of describing feelings they have to be distinguished. Consider, for example, *profound,* one of the commonest terms by which we attempt to describe emotions. When we use it we may be doing either of two things, or both together. We may be simply inviting from our reader the awed respectful feelings he usually has towards other things that are said to be profound—deep lakes, vast chasms in the earth, night, human error, the wisdom of sages, and so forth. Often we can obtain this respect for our feeling without requiring the reader to consider the feeling itself in any fashion, and in fact while discouraging investigation. This is the simplest type of emotive metaphor. Or we may be asking him to recognise that our feeling has in some (undefined) way something of the character of other profound things—that it is not easily explored, for example, that it may contain all kinds of things, or that it is easy to get lost in it. This is the sense metaphor. Usually the two are combined, without analysis of either. It is not a very encouraging sign of our general intelligence, or of our emotional discrimination, that this word has been found invaluable by many popular critics and preachers. I must take some credit for charity in not citing a collection of examples that lies upon my table.

Most descriptions of feelings, and nearly all subtle descriptions, are metaphorical and of the combined type. The power to analyse explicitly the ground of the transference is not widely possessed in any high degree, and it is less exercised both in school-training and in general discussion than might be wished. A better understanding of metaphor is one of the aims which an improved curriculum of literary studies might well set before itself. But a writer may use a metaphor and a reader take both its sense and feeling correctly without either writer or reader being capable of explaining how it works. Such explanations are a special branch of the critic's business. Conversely, however acute and penetrating a reader may be, it does not follow that he will be able to create good metaphorical language himself. It is one thing to be able to analyse resemblances and analogies when they have first been seized and recorded by someone else; it is quite another thing to effect the discovery and integration oneself.

This brings us obviously back to the poet, one of whose gifts, ordinarily, is just this command of original metaphor. From the technical point of view indeed the poet's task is constantly (though not only) that of finding ways and means of controlling feeling through metaphor. He has to be expert, if not in describing feeling, in presenting it, and presenting and describing are here rather near together. Even in the case of *profound,* dissected above, there was a third possibility. The word may instigate in the reader an echo, a shadow-semblance of the emotion it describes. He may find a sympathetic pulse awaken in his bosom, and feel serious, self-conscious and responsible, at grips with Destiny. If so, the word may in part have presented the feeling as well as described it. Any lively, close, realistic thought of an emotion is so apt to revive it that most descriptions that are at all concrete or intimate, that do succeed in "putting it before one," also reinstate it.

Of the two kinds of paraphrasing which, we

[11] Some further explanations of this distinction will be found in *Principles,* p. 240, and in *The Meaning of Meaning,* Ch. VI.

suggested, might be made more use of in our schools—the one to exhibit the sense of a poem, the other to portray its feeling—the first requires only an intelligent use of the dictionary, logical acumen, a command of syntax, and pertinacity. The second demands qualities of sensitiveness and imagination, the power to use remote experience and to create metaphors, gifts which may seem to belong by birthright to the poet alone. It may seem strange to suggest that these gifts could be developed by school training, but remembering the original endowment of average children and comparing it with the obtuseness of the sample adult, the proposal (if we can guard against some of the dangers hinted at above), may not in the end prove to be so unduly optimistic. It was partly to show the need and to suggest the possibility of improved methods in education that my documentation in Part II was extended to such length.

KENNETH BURKE: Antony in Behalf of the Play*

At times when the standards of criticism are set by a *receptive* class, as in the decadent stages of feudalism, the emphasis of the critic tends to be placed upon *consumption.* Matters of "appreciation" and "enjoyment" are the touchstones. Conversely, in the Art for Art's Sake movement of recent decades, we find the emphasis placed almost wholly upon *production.* Our practical inventors and business promoters of this period tended to emphasize the productive factor, assuming that in the large the matter of consumption would take care of itself—and there was a corresponding trend in aesthetics, with the essence of art being seen in the "self-expression" of the artist.

Today, in nonliterary fields, we are stressing neither production nor consumption, but the *integration* of the two. And in the aesthetic field, this emphasis might be paralleled by a tendency to consider literature, not as a creator's device for self-expression, nor as an audience's device for amusement or instruction, but as a communicative relationship between writer and audience, with both parties actively participating. In such an approach, the poet's "self-expression" or the audience's "appreciation" will necessarily figure, but the main emphasis will be elsewhere.

This reader-writer relationship is emphasized in the following article, which is an imaginary speech by Antony. Instead of addressing the mob, as he is pictured in the third act of *Julius Caesar,* he turns to the audience. And instead of being a dramatic character *within* the play, he is here made to speak as a critical commentator *upon* the play, explaining its mechanism and its virtues. Thus we have a tale from Shakespeare, retold, not as a plot but from the standpoint of the rhetorician, who is concerned with a work's processes of appeal.

Act III, Scene ii. *Antony has entered with the body of Caesar. Brutus has made his defense before the people, has won their sympathies to the cause of the conspirators, and has departed.*

Antony: Friends, Romans, Countrymen . . . one—two—three syllables: hence in this progression, a magic formula. "Romans" to fit the conditions of the play; "countrymen" the better to identify the play-mob with the mob in the pit—for we are in the Renaissance, at that point when Europe's vast national integers are taking shape, and all the wisdom that comes of the body is to be obscured by our putting in place of the body the political corpus, while we try

* "Antony in Behalf of the Play" first appeared in *The Southern Review,* Autumn 1935, and was later included in *The Philosophy of Literary Form: Studies of Symbolic Action* (1941). It is reprinted here by permission of the author and the editors of the Louisiana State University Press. Mr. Burke (*b.* 1897) is also the author of *Counter-Statement* (1931), *Permanence and Change: An Anatomy of Purpose* (1935), *Attitudes Toward History* (1937), and *A Grammar of Motives* (1945).

to run this bigger hulk with the instincts for the little one—the Hobbesian metaphor—and the gloomy error has exalted us, so that no word handles as much, and as quickly, and as inexpressibly, as this word "countrymen," which must really mean, if pragmatic results are the test, that there is glory solely in being outdone by those within our own borders. Anyway, consider how much better my one-two-three arrangement is than was the opining salutation in Brutus' speech: "Romans, countrymen, lovers." He is an orator—but because you of England have thought the untrustworthy Latins eloquent, and because you don't think you are nearly so clever as you'd like to be, I shall seem closer to you if I apologize for bluntness. Yet how much more competent my opening syllables are: how much *truer*, since true to the process of a spell, stressing a charm's *threeness.*

My Elizabethan audience, under the guise of facing a Roman mob I confront you at a most complicated moment. As a matter of fact, up to this point in our play you have been treated most outrageously. It can honestly be said that, in no major particular, have you been granted those clear and simple responses to which, as customers, you might feel yourselves entitled. Instead, your author has kept you in as vacillating a condition as this very Roman mob you have been watching with so little respect. I doubt if he distinguishes between the two of you. All that I as Antony do to this play-mob, as a character-recipe I do to you. He would play upon you; he would seem to know your stops; he would sound you from your lowest note to the top of your compass. He thinks you as easy to be played upon as a pipe.

Oh, there have been signs you recognize quickly, that you might feel familiar with the road upon which you have been stumbling. The conspirators have met during storms and in the "vile contagion of the night." They have pulled caps over their eyes. One plucked at another's sleeve. Such labels are easily read by anyone. The streets of Rome have bristled with bad omens. Caesar's wife has cried in sleep that they are murdering Caesar. Outlandish astronomical and biologic marvels have occurred—to point the direction of our plot and give it weight by implicating the very heavens. And finally, Caesar was struck with daggers. Yet these standard things have lured you into a region where you are not competent at all.

Consider the burden you now carry, as I step before the play-mob with the fresh-murdered body of Caesar. We have established a Caesar-principle and a Brutus-principle, though I blush to consider some of the devices whereby the two principles have been set into your minds. Realize for what slight reasons you have been willing to let Caesar die. (The conspirators would not so much as touch him until you also had been brought into their band. And when Casca shouted, "Speak, hands, for me!" stabbing great Caesar, those homicidal hands spoke for you also.) First, we had the portents, beginning with the soothsayer's admonition that Caesar beware the Ides of March. In showing how things were going, these signs prepared you somewhat to go in the same direction.

But in addition, *your sympathies have been poisoned.* Caesar a conqueror, a monarch by reason of his attainments? Yet he was deaf in one ear. He had the falling-sickness, and "swounded" from the intense strain of refusing a crown he coveted. "He had a fever when he was in Spain," cried out "like a sick girl," his feebleness amazing Cassius. Cassius was a better swimmer than Caesar—and when the two of them had leaped into the Tiber on a dare, Cassius had to pull out Caesar, to whom he must "bend his body if Caesar carelessly but nod on him." His wife is barren. For all his determination to be bold, there is a timid and superstitious trait in him. And worst, for an emperor, on a night of storm and portents he appeared on the stage in his nightgown—so let him die. For such reasons as these you are willing to put a knife through the ribs of Caesar.

Still, you are sorry for Caesar. We cannot profitably build a play around the horror of a murder if you do not care whether the murdered man lives or dies. So we had to do something for Caesar—and you would be ashamed if you stopped to consider what we did. I believe we made Caesar appealing by proxy. That is: I, Antony, am a loyal follower of Caesar; you love me for a good fellow, since I am expansive, hearty, much as you would be after not too heavy a meal; and as one given to pleasure, I am not likely to lie awake at night plotting you injury. If such a man loves Caesar, his love lifts up Caesar in your eyes.

I serve a double purpose. Not only do I let Caesar shine a bit warmly by his reflection of my glow, but when the actual *persona* of Caesar-principle is dispatched by daggers, the principle lives on in me, who continue the function of Caesar in the play. In the next act, the fourth, the *persona* itself will reappear momentarily as a ghost in Brutus' tent—but on the whole, after Caesar's death, I am the plot-substitute for Caesar. No wonder Brutus, in his address to the play-mob but a short time ago, told them that only Caesar's vices had been slain, while his virtues lived on, still active. So they do, in me, whom you like because I am marked by so serviceable a trait as loyalty. And when this play is over, Antony alone of the major characters will live; for you like to have about you such a man as might keep guard at the door while you sleep. Given certain conceptions of danger, I become the sign of safety. A little sunshine-thought, to take home with you after these many slaughterings. Only as much of the Caesar-principle as will let you relax, is left to bid you good-night—and the Brutus-principle will have died to purchase you this handsome privilege.

I grant that on this last score I am not the perfect recipe. My author has provided purer comfort-recipes for you elsewhere. I show a little too much aptitude at deception, but you should not hold that against me. This trait was merely a by-product of my place in the story: it arose from the fact that upon me fell the burden of keeping things going, and the plottiness of our drama makes naturally for plotting. Besides, recall that I was wholly the reveler as long as Caesar lived. Once he is dead, it is no longer so necessary that I be likable in Caesar's behalf and warm him by my warmth. Henceforth I am no mere Caesar-adjunct, but the very vessel of the Caesar-principle. So, in expanding to my expanded rôle, I must break the former mold somewhat. Let *savants* explain the change by saying that carefree Antony was made a sober man, and a bitter one, by the death of Caesar. But it is an obvious fact that if an important cog in the plot vanishes in the very middle of our drama, something has to take its place. In deputizing for Caesar, I found it impossible to remain completely Antony. Let *savants* explain my altered psychology as they will—*I* know it was a playwright's necessity.

You have been made conspirators in a murder. For this transgression, there must be some expiative beast brought up for sacrifice. Such requirements guided us in the mixing of the Brutus-recipe, for it is Brutus that must die to absolve you of your stabbing an emperor who was deaf in one ear and whose wife was sterile. But let us be fair. There is also the fact that you wrested certain political prerogatives from King John, and have been taught to cherish them. Here also was a source of conviction to be tapped as an ingredient in our formula. We discredited Caesar from the very opening of the play, even before he had appeared (significant timing), by letting you see the tribunes angry with certain commoners who were too cordial in their preparations for the return of Caesar after victory. Caesar, it seems, would try to retract your *Magna Carta* from the Romans. Conversely, it is the Brutus-recipe that would prevent this threatened undoing of English political emancipation. So we make Brutus honorable in your eyes by starting his conduct primarily from this fear, which is always your fear as regards conditions in the contemporary state. He is virtuous because he does for Romans what you want your popular leaders to do for you. He takes on the nobility that comes of being good for private enterprise.

On the other hand, he is a conspirator; hence from the general censure takes corruption. For tough Casca is a Brutus-adjunct; and lean, envious Cassius; and Decius the flatterer. Here are qualities which, if lodged in any but yourselves, are not comforting to contemplate—hence are "vices." Brutus' acts, though done in a good cause, have shadiness. One cannot be stealthy as a thief without partially earning the kind of judgments that are laid against thieves. Nobleness, yes, but dirty business. And if his wife, Portia, speaks for him by her deep affection (as I obediently did for Caesar), note that she is allowed to show this affection only at those moments when he is sinisterly engaged, and answers her evasively. That is: her *love* is conveyed by her *misgivings,* as she worries because her once regular husband roams about at night, in "rheumy and unpurged air" sucking up "the humours of the dank morning," so that even the quality of swamps is drawn upon to discredit Brutus a little, right when Portia is loving him. All told: a fit expiative offering for our offense of murder: worthy, since he was noble and aroused affection, yet yieldable on good legalistic grounds, since he was a conspirator, like a bog. In weeping for his death, you will be sweetly absolved.

At this particular point in the play, however, as I rise to address you, accompanied by Caesar's corse, Brutus has just confronted the play-mob, stated before them the case of the conspirators, and been exonerated. They have clamored their approval. They are convinced that Caesar would have been a tyrant. And they have shouted to the Brutus-principle, who must die for you, "Live, Brutus! live! live!" It is my task, as I stand before the play-mob, to contrive a *peripety* for my audience, reversing the arrows of your expectations. When my speech is finished, we must have set you to making the preparations for Brutus' death.

Well, a dramatist is a *professional* gambler. He prefers playing with loaded dice. And don't think that we should try to bring about this reversal without first making sure that we had furtively dealt ourselves some trumps. We have stacked the cards a little—not so shamelessly as some of our rival Shake-scenes might have done, but enough. Here, I believe, we have drawn from the well of magic. As follows:

Recall how, in the early rites of communion, whereby one man's interests were made identical with another's, the risks of competitive harms were eliminated by a partnership, a partnership established by three distinct symbolic acts: the sharing of one's wife, the exchanging of blood, the sitting down together at table. Of these, the sharing of the wife is dead, buried beneath notions of virtue that go with later concepts of ownership. Yet we give you something similar, in Caesar's dying words, "*Et tu, Brute?* Then fall, Caesar!" which suggests that in Caesar's pain there is more than the pain of knives, there is the pain of wrenched intimacy, eliciting a rebuke almost Christlike in its replacing of vengefulness with sorrow, as the victim saw that "Caesar's angel" was among his slayers. At this moment Caesar becomes great—for he must die well, at the expense of Brutus. They had shared affection; hence a promise contracted within the deep-lying terms of magic had been violated.

As for the rites at table: When the conspirators had come, to make sure that Caesar would be on hand at the Senate to be murdered, Caesar welcomed them heartily: "Good friends, go in, and taste some wine with me." And lastly, as for the blood-communion, how grimly it is vivified and mocked (in pious profanation) when the conspirators, at Brutus' word, bathe in the blood of Caesar's wounds. Three magic formulae, outraged—thus Shakespeare speaks to you in accents you had heard while not listening.

I now stand before you, assigned to the definite task of contriving our peripety, turning the arrows of your future while apparently engaged only in turning those of this unruly play-mob. I shall, by what immediately follows, proclaim myself in all thoroughness the Caesar-principle perpetuated. Here I fulfill the pledge I gave when first I came upon the stage after Caesar's murder. I came ostensibly to reassure the conspirators that I was ready to make peace with them, now that the offense was definitely beyond reparation. I shook hands with them, one after the other—but in the very act of doing so, I forgot them, and fell to musing aloud upon the destroyed magnificence of Caesar. In this way I signaled you to the effect that I was not turning against Caesar, even while "shaking the bloody fingers of his foes." (You wanted me to remain with Caesar, since that has been established as my part in this play. I have been given my label—and like children, you insist that a thing's *true* name is the name you first heard it called by. In your insistence that I remain allied with Caesar, repeating my number, you are grateful for the little cue I give you by my absent-minded musings over Caesar's body. In your satisfaction at receiving from me this sign, to restate my identity even as I make peace with the conspirators, you do not stop to ask why the conspirators should not interpret this sign precisely as you do. Your concern with your own aesthetic problem leads you to overlook this straining of verisimilitude, as we thought you would. We judged that, in your eagerness to receive the clue, you would not be overexacting as regard our manner of conveying it.)

Brutus, you will remember, had asked the

mob to weigh what he said, and to judge his statements as critics. But, as a matter of fact, he gave them no opportunity to follow his advice. He told them to choose, then stated the issue in such a way that there was no choice. Those that love Rome, he said, must agree that Caesar should have been killed. Those that do not love Rome, should object. If there are any that do not love Rome, let them step forward in protest. No move—hence, the killing is endorsed.

And now, my countrymen, hear me ask the play-mob to lend me their ears, as I proceed to lay before you a plot in miniature. It will not be a very difficult pattern that I ask you to appreciate: a rudimentary piece of translation, by which I awaken in you the satisfactions of authorship, as you hear me say one thing and know that I mean another. "I come to bury Caesar, not to praise him"—whereat I praise him so roundly that all the vigor of the Caesar-principle is brought to life again.

. . . if I were dispos'd to stir
Your heart and minds to mutiny and rage,
I should do Brutus wrong, and Cassius wrong . . .

Whereat I stir hearts and minds to mutiny and rage. And as the pattern grows clear, I can subtilize it, making Brutus and his band dishonorable by calling them all, all honorable men. And by the time I mentioned Caesar's will, saying that I would not read it because it would inflame the people, in accordance with the pattern you wait to hear me read the will. You hear them entreat me, you hear me refuse. Then you observe me stepping down, to be among them, that I may better "realize" Caesar's death from them, and make them tearful coroners while I appraise the wounds:

If you have tears, prepare to shed them now.
You all do know this mantle: I remember
The first time ever Caesar put it on;
'Twas on a summer's evening in his tent,
That day he overcame the Nervii.
Look! in this place ran Cassius' dagger through:
See what a rent the envious Casca made:
Through this the well-beloved Brutus stabb'd;
And, as he pluck'd his cursed steel away,
Mark how the blood of Caesar follow'd it,
As rushing out of doors, to be resolv'd
If Brutus so unkindly knock'd or no;
For Brutus, as you know, was Caesar's angel:
Judge, O you gods! how dearly Caesar lov'd him.
This was the most unkindest cut of all;
For when the noble Caesar saw him stab,
Ingratitude, more strong than traitors' arms,
Quite vanquish'd him: then burst his mighty heart;
And, in his mantle muffling up his face,
Even at the base of Pompey's statue,
Which all the while ran blood, great Caesar fell.
O! what a fall was there, my countrymen;
Then I, and you, and all of us fell down,
Whilst bloody treason flourish'd over us.
O! now you weep, and I perceive you feel
The dint of pity; these are gracious drops.
Kind souls, what! weep you when you but behold
Our Caesar's vesture wounded? Look you here,
Here is himself, marr'd, as you see, with traitors.

You see my "transference," as I turn from the mantle to the dead man that had worn the mantle. You see the play-mob grow *inflamed* under my talk of *pity* (remember our pattern). There is loud talk of mutiny; the people are about to rush away in anger—but we would "consolidate" our position. And now, rounding out the pattern, I return to the matter of the will, which I had refused to read:

Why, friends, you go to do you know not what.
Wherein hath Caesar thus deserv'd your loves?
Alas! you know not: I must tell you then.
You have forgot the will I told you of.

Whereupon I read them the will of a rich philanthropist—and their vindictiveness against the conspirators is complete. You have been engrossed—faugh! you demons, how you do love plottings, for all your censure of plotters. Or is it machinery that delights you—and are you pleased with joining me to make a smoothly running engine of fatality?

Cassius was right in proposing that they slay me, along with Caesar. But Brutus held it was enough to slay the *persona* of the Caesar-principle, on the ground that the *adjunct* would subside through want of its source:

Our course will seem too bloody, Caius Cassius,
To cut the head off and then hack the limbs, . . .
For Antony is but a limb of Caesar. . . .
And, for Mark Antony, think not of him;
For he can do no more than Caesar's arm
When Caesar's head is off.

So the Brutus-principle slays half the Caesar-principle, and spares the other half that will in turn destroy it.

Recall these steps: How first, after the murder, I had sent word by a servant offering to join the cause of the conspirators, if they would guarantee me safety. How I fell to musing over the body of Caesar. How, after *exeunt all but Antony*, I had let loose my full-throated venom:

O! pardon me, thou bleeding piece of earth,
That I am meek and gentle with these butchers;
Thou art the ruins of the noblest man
That ever lived in the tide of times.
Woe to the hand that shed this costly blood!
Over thy wounds now do I prophesy,
Which like dumb mouths do ope their ruby lips,
To beg the voice and utterance of my tongue,
A curse shall light upon the limbs of men;
Domestic fury and fierce civil strife
Shall cumber all the parts of Italy;
Blood and destruction shall be so in use,
And dreadful objects so familiar,
That mothers shall but smile when they behold
Their infants quarter'd with the hands of war;
All pity chok'd with custom of fell deeds:
And Caesar's spirit, ranging for revenge,
With Ate by his side come hot from hell,
Shall in these confines with a monarch's voice
Cry "Havoc!" and let slip the dogs of war;
That this foul deed shall smell above the earth
With carrion men, groaning for burial.

Then, in my speech before the Romans, I fulfilled my promises, starting those processes by which the Brutus-principle, which killed the Caesar-*persona,* is driven to his death by the Caesar-adjunct.

Thank us for this growing thing by growing with it—and in the following scene we shall allow you to squeeze the last available sum of emotion from the mounting sequence, causing it to drip, not by still hotter pressure, but by a sudden cooling. Prominent among the conspirators, there was a certain Cinna. Now another Cinna comes upon the stage, Cinna the poet, ludicrous, the cartoon of a poet, the aesthete, such as you have long before now been taught to laugh at (our author is treading on safe ground here). He is an earnest but ineffectual wretch, who probably knows a good line when he sees it, and would doubtless have been entranced to write just such verses as Shakespeare wrote; and perhaps he might even have written them had he known, like Shakespeare, how to draw finesses from toughnesses. Yet our dramatist betrays him for the delectation of you, my stinking audience, makes him your laughing stock, ridicules one of his own Guild for your benefit, though you have no desire whatever to write like Shakespeare, would much rather eat beef than hear a play, but cannot go on eating beef forever, and so come here occasionally, demanding firm, beefy diction. The mob stumbles upon this Cinna, overwhelming him. First Citizen, Second Citizen, Third Citizen, and Fourth Citizen each ask him a different question, all at the same time, insisting imperiously that he answer without delay. It is all quite hilarious, as Cinna is in a daze, comically. And when they ask him his name, and he says with assurance, "Cinna," they start pawing at him in earnest—and when he begs them for a little accuracy, insisting that he is not Cinna the conspirator but Cinna the poet, they unanswerably answer that they abominate the name, and so will pummel him for his verses, and the act ends with the brawling group moving from the stage. You somehow know that the poetic Cinna will suffer no fundamental harm. He will merely be slain-notslain, like a clown hit by cannon balls —yet by this let-down we have reaffirmed in another way the grim intentions of the mob. We have clinched the arrows of your expectancy, incidentally easing our obligations as regard the opening of Act IV.

You will be still more wisely handled by what follows, as our Great Demagogue continues to manipulate your minds. I think particularly of the second scene of the next act, weighted by the steadily organized pressure of events. You will witness a startling quarrel between Brutus and Cassius. After this violence and the sad reconciliation (these men are disintegrating), there will be a contrasted descent to soft tearfulness, as Brutus' drowsy servant plays him a disconsolate little tune in the dead of night (Portia is dead)—and the servant is drowsy, that he may fall asleep as Varro and Claudius have done; then with three men sleeping (and you drooping in sympathy) and Brutus alone awake, there will be, all about, a sleepiness, and a Brutus-loneliness—whereat the Caesar-*persona,* now as a ghost, may return to indicate, by a vague prophecy, that all will be ended for Brutus at Philippi.

PAUL ELMER MORE: How to Read "Lycidas"*

AFTER passing, as I might say, through the valley of the shadow of death, after months of physical prostration when reading of any sort was beyond the strength of a depleted brain, the poet to whom I turned instinctively with the first renewal of health was Milton. And so I have been reading Milton again and books about him, with the old zest I had as a boy, and with an added joy of almost tremulous excitement such as a miser might feel at the rediscovery of a treasure of gold stolen from him and long buried out of sight. But with this delight have been mingled certain scruples which vexed me a little more than they did in the old days. Again, as many times before, on laying down one of the poems the familiar words of Tennyson would come unbidden to my mind:

O mighty-mouth'd inventor of harmonies,
O skill'd to sing of Time or Eternity,
God-gifted organ-voice of England,
Milton, a name to resound for ages.

Of the mighty harmonies there would be no doubt; God-gifted voice certainly, organ-voice certainly, for those who have ears to hear. If any one in English, Milton had the divine craft of words, the mastery of sonorous speech. His is not Shakespeare's incalculable gift; it lacks the element of magic that captures us in Shakespeare; it is, or soon after his earliest experiments it was, an art that came by reflection, and as we read him we imagine that we might by equal deliberation attain the same perfection—only we never do attain it. And something of this distinction Milton himself seems to have felt when he wrote of Shakespeare:

For whil'st to th' shame of slow-endeavoring Art
Thy easie numbers flow.

The same distinction, I think, was present to Irving Babbitt when he spoke, as I have heard him do more than once, of his experience in quoting. It was Babbitt's custom in the first draught of his essays to cite from memory, and then, before printing, to verify the quotation by reference to the text. He would find occasionally that even his retentive memory had slipped and that he had substituted a word of his own for the poet's. And sometimes, he would say, he could not see that the substitution was inferior to the original—except in the case of Shakespeare. He never made a change in Shakespeare's language but some force or charm was lost. That was not so even with Milton.—Such a difference exists between the seemingly careless spontaneity and the elaborated art of our two supreme masters of poetical diction; and he would be a rash judge who should say that the advantage was all on one side or the other.

But to return to the question that vexed my mood of acquiescent joy. God-gifted organ-voice Milton possessed in full measure—but "voice of England"? Does he speak for the whole of England, or, that being scarcely possible, does he speak from the heart of England giving articulate expression to that central quality which has made England what we know and love? And by his influence did he maintain that balance and moderation, that sense of law enveloping the individual, which made of Falkland a true type of the Englishman that was to be? Here the question begins with style, but extends beyond mere style to psychology and to principles of government and life.

*"How to Read 'Lycidas'" first appeared in *The American Review*, May 1936, and was later included in the final volume of criticism by Paul Elmer More (1864-1937), *On Being Human* (1936). It is reprinted here by permission of the Princeton University Press. More's criticism is contained in the eleven volumes of the *Shelburne Essays* (1904-1921) and the three volumes of *New Shelburne Essays* (1928-1936).

Now, if there be any hesitation with me to accept Milton's style as the norm of good English, it is certainly not on the ground of that "dissociation of sensibility" which draws a school of modern critics and poets to repudiate what may be called the Miltonic line of development and to seek their parentage in Shakespeare and Donne and the "Metaphysicals." If I understand what the leader of that Choir means by this rather obscure phrase, it is that Milton by conscious choice and judgement dissociated his mind from one whole range of perceptions, refusing to respond to them emotionally as foreign to his fixed theory of values, and by the same deliberate act of selection created a more or less artificial language; whereas the poets proceeding from Donne held their sensibility open to any and every perception and employed words to convey the sharp immediate impression of each fact of sense and experience without discrimination. The distinction is valid, and it is interesting; for the "modernist" in poetry it is of vital significance. But I am not sure that the "dissociation of sensibility," so taken, has been the source of dead monotony and of verbal unreality in our literature; and I am sure that if Milton failed in national leadership it was not for this reason. Rather I should say that his influence in this respect has made for sanity and form and for limitations which are characteristically English. Rather I should maintain that Milton's failure, so far as he failed, was owing to something essentially un-English, or only partially English, to something belonging to his individual temperament, which passed into his philosophy of life and diverted a noble love of liberty into a morbid and isolating passion. Here too Milton was clear-headed in his application of the law to others, but curiously perverse when his own interests were affected. In the second of the sonnets on the book called *Tetrachordon,* he berates his fellow countrymen as "Owels and Cuckoos, Asses, Apes and Doggs" for the very reason that they have lost the true meaning of liberty, while they

bawle for freedom in this senceless mood,
And still revolt when truth would set them free.
Licence they mean when they cry libertie;
For who loves that, must first be wise and good;
But from that mark, how far they roave we see
For all this waste of wealth, and loss of blood.

That is sound doctrine, but—alas to say it!—Milton did not see how apt would be the retort, *de te fabula;* how easy the reply: License he meant when he cried liberty.

This book called *Tetrachordon,* written by Milton himself, was the second of his treatises on divorce, and is a bitter invective against those who, by opposing the facile freedom of marital separation, enslave the soul under man-made laws, forgetting that which "makes us holiest and likest to God's immortal image," and who, for the law of liberty, set up "that which makes us most conformable and captive to civil and subordinate precepts: . . . although indeed no ordinance, human or from heaven, can bind against the good of man." By "the good of man," as Mr. Tillyard observes in his comment on the passage, Milton means what elsewhere he calls "nature"—damnable word, I add, into which have been distilled all the fallacies of human wit through thousands of years. If you track the word down through its many ambiguities, you will discover that in the end it signifies that which a man temperamentally and personally desires as distinguished from that which is prescribed for him by human rule or divine precept. So it was that Milton, fretted and humiliated because his wife, finding existence with him intolerable, left him and ran away home,—so it was that incontinently he rebelled against the human and divine laws of marriage, and wrote his pleas for freedom of divorce as complying with natural law and the good of man. If ever there was a case of liberty becoming license, it was here. However they may have differed in other respects, in this quality Milton resembled Shelley: they both identified what they desired at any moment with the natural good of man; they both made self-righteousness the law of right.

That was the beginning of Milton's public career and of his prose writings, and it was typical of what ensued. If the bishops in any way interfered with his personal idea of worship, then down with episcopacy and away with the Church; if the monarchical form of government hampered his political independence, then down with monarchy and away with the Constitution. There is no more painful reading in English literature than these apologies for free divorce and regicide which occupied the greatest genius of the age between *Lycidas* and *Paradise Lost,* and the style in which they are written is as heavy and un-English as their spirit is perverse. There are purple patches scattered through these treatises, which are all that most readers know of Milton's prose and which would give the impression that he is as magnificent here as in his verse; but if these passages are examined it will be found that, taken apart from their context, they are expressions of personal ambition, legitimate in itself and magnificent in its devotion to the aim of a poet, while all about them floats and rages a sea of rebellious discontent. I will not endorse Hilaire Belloc's sweeping condemnation of the prose works, but in the mass they do certainly form a repellent body of reading. Following the ideas of the tractates through the surging verbiage, one is reminded of the monsters in the account of creation, "wallowing unweildie" in

> the vast immeasurable Abyss
> Outrageous as a Sea, dark, wasteful, wilde,
> Up from the bottom turn'd by furious windes.

There is something disconcerting in the spectacle of a supreme artist, as Milton was in his verse, so losing his craftsmanship in another medium; what I would insist on is that the very style of his prose has a close relation to the fact that when he passes from imagination to theory his voice is not that of his people but of an exasperated individual. The seventeenth century, with all its greatness, is an age of frustration, filled with fine promises that, except in the field of science, came to no fruition, replete with noble utterance that somehow failed to convince. In the Church, in the State, in society, the one thing needed and not found was a commanding genius that should have been indeed the voice of England. It is the tragedy of the time that he who had the genius so to speak should have wasted his energies in querulous complaints against what was, and in the future was to show itself, the true spirit of the land. In a word that spirit may be described precisely as liberty not license, as centrality, not dissent.

But I am not concerned to pass judgement on Milton's character and its effect upon his work as a whole; that is a longer theme than I care now to discuss. What I started out to do was to consider one small piece of his output, the *Lycidas,* and to ask myself how it should be read. To this question, at least in its acuter form, I was moved by chancing to take up at the same time Mr. Tillyard's estimation of the poem and Dr. Johnson's. As a whole I should regard Mr. Tillyard's *Milton* as about the best book we have on the man and the poet, a study admirable for its scholarship and discrimination, and particularly notable for its treatment of the philosophical problems raised by *Paradise Lost,* such as Milton's conception of the nature of evil and the cause of man's fall. Now to Mr. Tillyard "*Lycidas* is the last and greatest English poem of Milton's youth; though shorter, it is greater than *Comus,* written with newly won but complete mastery and expressing a mental experience both valuable and profound." That is a sentiment with which my own judgement is in perfect accord; indeed, I should go further and hold it to be the greatest short poem of any author in English, the very criterion and touchstone of poetical taste. Yet with that opinion I have felt bound to remember the sweeping condemnation of Johnson, to whom "the diction" of the poem "is harsh, the rhymes uncertain, and the numbers unpleasing." It is without passion and without art. In part no doubt Johnson's lack of appreciation can be set down to his known deficiency in the higher faculty of imagination. His comment on the diction and rhythm does nothing more than indicate a certain insensitiveness to the finer and more delicate effects of poetry in general. But one cannot read the whole essay without perceiving that his hostile criticism of the art of *Lycidas* sprang not so much from his miscomprehension and aesthetic obtuseness as from hostility to the poet and to all that Milton as a man stood for. Touching Milton's plea for looser laws of divorce, the neglect of which by the ruling Presbyterians turned him against that sect, Johnson observes, and justly: "He that changes his party by his humor is not more virtuous than he that changes it by his interest; he loves himself rather than truth." As for the political tirades, Johnson in his attack ran true to form: "Milton's republicanism was . . . founded in an envious hatred of greatness, and a sullen desire of independence. . . . He hated monarchs in the State, and prelates in the Church; for he hated all whom he was required to obey. . . . He felt not so much the love of liberty as repugnance to authority." Now for myself I do not like Belloc's summary and contemptuous dismissal of Milton as "a man rotten with the two worst vices: falsehood and pride"; for somehow one shrinks from using such language of a very great poet. To Johnson's charge, on the contrary, I can subscribe without reservation (indeed I have already said much the same thing in weaker language), and I do not see how the charge, in substance, can be countered by any impartial student of Milton's life. But to Johnson the faults of the man were ruinous to the earlier work of the poet, and he denounced *Lycidas* because he read into it the author's ecclesiastical and political heresies; whereas I must reject the maker whilst admiring what he has made. And there the difficulty lies—or has lain for me: how can one make so complete a separation between Milton the destroyer of Church and State, and Milton the artist? how is one to read *Lycidas?*

That particular difficulty, it will be observed, opens up into one of the major problems of criticism in general: the relation between the content of a poem and the art of a poem independent of its content. In the beginning, when that distinction first presented itself to the Greek mind, it took a very simple form and indeed was scarcely a question at all: the *Iliad* and the *Odyssey* were valued primarily, not for their charm and interest, but because in them the statesman, the soldier, the athlete, the man who desired to live honourably, could find the wisest precepts and the best models. For later times, and for us of the West, the principle involved was formulated by Horace in his famous saying that the most successful poet was he who knew how to mix the *utile* and the *dulce*. What Horace meant by the *dulce* is clear enough; it is just that in a poem which gives pleasure to the reader. And what he meant by the *utile* is equally clear; it is that in a poem from which we draw instruction. So in one of the *Epistles* he tells a friend, held in Rome by the practice of declaiming, no doubt about the schools of philosophy, that he is in the country reading Homer, who is a better teacher than all the philosophers:

Qui, quid sit pulchrum, quid turpe, quid utile, quid non,
Plenius ac melius Chrysippo et Crantore dicit.[1]

In exactly that form the question reached the renaissance critics, with the emphasis still heavily on the *utile*. So Puttenham, to name a single example, thinks it necessary to preface his treatise on *The Arte of English Poesie* with a long apology, wherein is shown how "poets were the first priests, the first prophets, the first legislators and politicians in the world," as seen in Homer, Orpheus, Amphion, and the rest. You are back a thousand years and more, and might be reading one of the ancient Greek commentators. But a change came with the advent of the romantic movement. The *utile* and the *dulce* took on new significance, and the old division was sharpened to something like an absolute contrast between two irreconcilable criteria of excellence. The *utile* was broadened so as to embrace the whole substance of a poem whether instructive or not, its sense or meaning. The *dulce* on the other side was refined to a conception of pure poetry, the quintessence of art, as a sort of abstract entity which could be felt and judged somehow apart from any articulate thought or story conveyed; indeed the ideal poem would be a succession of beautiful words with no meaning at all. Such a thesis, badly stated, is manifestly bare nonsense; but practically the early romantics applied it to criticism by taking *Kubla Khan* as the ideal poem, because, while the content was no more than the shimmering matter of a dream, it reeked of that mysterious entity called pure poetry. And it was not so long ago that the theory flared up again in France under the impulse of the Abbé Bremond's monograph on *La Poésie pure*. The discussion that ensued was confused by the Abbé's association of aesthetic rapture with a mystical view of the function of prayer. More illuminating, to me at least, is T. S. Eliot's pursuit and final rejection of the same ideal of absolute poetry. In his earlier essays, particularly those on Seneca, Shakespeare, and Dante, you will see him eagerly pursuing this *ignis fatuus* as the ultimate standard of value. In the first of those studies he ranks Shakespeare and Dante

[1] ["He expresses more fully and accurately than Chrysippo and Crantor what is noble, what is base, what is useful and what is not."]

together as the supreme poets of the world, and the two are equally great though the Italian has taken up into the *Commedia* the profoundest wisdom of human experience as expounded in the Thomistic theology, whereas the Englishman has no interpretation of life's riddle beyond the stale platitudes of Seneca. "Perhaps it was Shakespeare's special rôle in history to have effected this peculiar union—perhaps it is a part of his special eminence to have expressed an inferior philosophy in the greatest poetry." It is true that Mr. Eliot has his reservations in supporting this romantic dream of pure poetry which came to him from certain early and, as I think, unfortunate associations. It is more important to note that in his latest enunciation he has worked himself quite clear of the disturbing inheritance. There lies before me now his recently published volume of *Essays Ancient and Modern,* and in the opening paragraph of one of the "modern" (that is, hitherto unprinted) essays I am held by this sentence: "The 'greatness' of literature cannot be determined solely by literary standards; though we must remember that whether it is literature or not can be determined only by literary standards." That I take to be a complete truth perfectly expressed; and the whole essay on "Religion and Literature" is a masterly application of this sentence to modern currents in verse and fiction. It is the critic come to full maturity after years of probation.

And so, to apply this canon of taste to *Lycidas,* it may be possible for a young man, enamoured of the sheer beauty of words and untroubled as yet by the graver issues of life, to enjoy the marvellous art of the poem with no thought of what the poem means if connected with the poet's place in the word of ideas and action. But such a rupture between the form and the substance of literature cannot long be maintained with the ripening of experience. Sooner or later we are bound to make up our account with the law of taste so ably formulated: "The 'greatness' of literature cannot be determined solely by literary standards; though one must remember that whether it is literature or not can be determined only by literary standards." That *Lycidas* is literature, poetry and not mere verse, depends on the language, the images, the form, on that mysterious working of the imagination which we can feel but cannot ultimately analyse or adequately describe; that it is great literature must depend on the junction of such qualities with nobility of content. And such nobility is there, in full measure.

The poem is an elegy prompted by the drowning of a college friend of the author. It has been the complaint of more than one critic that the expression of grief has little of that warmth which might be expected from such a subject. Dr. Johnson can find no "effusion of real passion, for passion runs not after remote allusions and obscure opinions." Against this charge of frigidity Mr. Tillyard contends with great acumen that the true theme of the poem is not the death of Edward King at all, but the possible death of the poet himself. Milton was writing just before he set out on his voyage to Italy, when such an adventure was more or less perilous and the chance of shipwreck and drowning might very well have occupied his mind. So taken, the charge of coldness towards a friend might be changed to one of cowardice or egotism. But Milton was no coward and, however he may have shown himself elsewhere, the note of egotism is relieved by the artful, though doubtless unconscious transference of anxiety for himself to sorrow for another. And it was not the mere termination of life that made him anxious, but the fear that his one all-absorbing passion might so be left unfulfilled. To understand his state of mind and the emotion that was impelling him to write, the elegy should be read in the light of those passages of self-dedication scattered through his prose works. These purple patches laid upon the coarse cloth of controversy are too well known to need repeating here. The keynote is given by the words inserted in the gross *Apology for Smectymnuus:*

> He who would not be frustrate of his hope to write well hereafter in laudable things, ought himself to be a true poem; that is, a composition and pattern of the best and honourablest things; not presuming to sing high praises of heroic men, or famous cities, unless he have in himself the experience and the practice of all that which is praiseworthy.

And joined with this personal ambition was the conviction that no loftier or purer service could be rendered to one's country and to the world than such a work as he was preparing himself to produce. Under the spell of a great heroic poem the mind of the people would respond in efforts towards great and heroic living. That was Milton's faith. It was the spirit of the reformer engrafted upon the temperament of the artist. In such a profession, wherein personal glory is identified with public welfare, pride with humility, there lurks, let us admit, a subtle danger; to fall short of brilliant success must leave the professor a monument of ridicule, like the mountains in labour that brought forth only a mouse. But, on the other hand, such a purpose, if carried through valiantly to a successful issue, makes the ordinary ambition of the artist and poet to appear in comparison no more than a cheap display of vanity. And Milton had the courage of conviction and the genius to succeed. In the history of English letters there is nothing like this determination carried through from youth to age, except the solemn dedication of Wordsworth to a similar purpose. All this must be read into *Lycidas.* Under the pretext of grief for the loss of a comrade in hope the poem is in reality as it were the quintessence of those prose passages through which there speaks a self-confidence as sublime as it was justified.

It is in the light of this life-long ambition that we should read the savage attack on the abuses in Church and State which raises the note of elegy to the "higher mood" of righteous indignation:

Last came and last did go,
The Pilot of the *Galilean* lake. . . .
He shook his Miter'd locks, and stern bespake,
How well could I have spar'd for thee, young swain,
Anow of such as for their bellies sake,
Creep and intrude, and climb into the fold? . . .
But that two-handed engine at the door,
Stands ready to smite once, and smite no more.

And apart from any theory of episcopacy and royalty the abuses were there and cried out for remedy. Laud knew them as well as did Baxter, Charles as well as Cromwell; but none but Milton possessed the "dread voice" which—alas, but for defects of temper!—might have done so much to set them right.

In this light also we should interpret the allegorical symbolism of the poem:

The hungry Sheep look up, and are not fed.

To Dr. Johnson all this masquerade of sheep and shepherds is "easy, vulgar, and therefore disgusting," a cheap device of images without passion and without art. Johnson had good reason to be suspicious of a *genre* that has invited so many weak poets to indulge in flim-flam. But he should not have forgotten how all through the Old Testament, from the call that came to Amos, "who was among the herdmen of Tekoa," and all through the New Testament, from the angelic vision that broke upon the shepherds who were "abiding in the field" about Bethlehem to the parable that Jesus spake to his disciples, "I am the good shepherd and know my sheep," —how all through the Bible this pastoral allegory of the Church runs like the very music of religion.

These were the thoughts that haunted the memory of the poet when he linked himself with his friend as shepherds:

Together both, ere the high Lawns appear'd
Under the opening eye-lids of the morn,
We drove a field.

Together they were practising their "rural ditties" in preparation for the louder chant that was to stir the nation from its ignoble lethargy, when one of the twain was washed away by the sounding sea, and his voice forever silenced. And what if a like fate awaited the other, who also was about to start on a voyage? "What boots it with incessant care . . . to meditate the thankless Muse," of what avail to "live laborious dayes," when just as we

think to burst out into sudden blaze,
Comes the blind *Fury* with th' abhorred shears,
And slits the thin spun life?

"But not the praise," he exclaims; the reward and the outcome are not confined to this world nor are they measured by success "on mortal soil," but in heaven before the "witness of all judging *Jove.*" I do not know how others are affected, but I can never peruse the climax of the poem without a thrill such as scarcely any other verses of the language excite.

Weep no more, woful Shepherds, weep no more,
For *Lycidas* your sorrow is not dead,
Sunk though he be beneath the watry floar,
So sinks the day-star in the Ocean bed,

And yet anon repairs his drooping head,
And tricks his beams, and with new spangled Ore,
Flames in the forehead of the morning sky:
So *Lycidas* sunk low, but mounted high,
Through the dear might of him that walk'd the waves
Where other groves, and other streams along,
With *Nectar* pure his oozy Lock's he laves,
And hears the unexpressive nuptiall Song,
In the blest Kingdoms meek of joy and love.
There entertain him all the Saints above,
In solemn troops, and sweet Societies
That sing, and singing in their glory move,
And wipe the tears for ever from his eyes.

Milton always rang true when he wrote of the world to come, but never before nor after did he attain quite this elevation, or achieve so realistic an expression of the invisible mysteries wrapt in the future. A few of his contemporaries possessed this power of giving substance to the hopes of eternity—notably Vaughan—but none of them approaches the master. And in later times the art was simply lost. Choose the best of the modern, Newman for instance in *The Dream of Gerontius,* and they will appear cold and unconvincing beside Milton. Nor did any of the great poets of the earlier ages of faith quite equal him in this field. I would not compare the few lines of an elegy with the mighty structure of Dante's *Paradiso,* but for myself at least there is no single incident in Dante's voyage through the celestial spheres that touches me with the shock of actuality like that which I feel when I read *Lycidas.* I am not competent to explain by what devices, by what choice of words, Milton obtains his sublime effect. It would be easy of course, if it seemed worth while, to point to the rich manipulation of vowel sounds in this or that verse, to note the startling obviousness of the allusion to the might of him that walked the waves, but the final alchemy of art escapes such an analysis; indeed I question whether any skill of criticism can penetrate to the heart of that mystery of the word which we call inspiration, and leave at that. But one phase of Milton's method impresses me: the fact that his images are borrowed from the simplest commonplaces of faith,—the return of dawn after the sinking of the sun in the ocean stream, the tears wiped away, the heavenly choiring of the blest. A comparison of Newman's attempt to translate the subtler speculations of theology into a poetic account of the soul's awakening after death shows how inevitably right was Milton's choice. There are regions of spiritual experience where the untutored imagination of the people goes deeper into reality than all the groping wisdom of philosophy.

One thing in the end is certain, the "greatness" of *Lycidas* is determined by an intimate marriage of form and matter, expression and substance. He who would read the poem worthily must see this, and must be equally sensitive to the delicacy of its art and to the sublimity of its ideas. This does not mean that he will forget or slur over the disagreeable traits of the poet's character or the repulsiveness of his ecclesiastical and political theories. But for our good fortune what repels us in the man and roused Johnson to a fury of protest is reserved for his prose and is excluded from his poetry—not completely indeed, for, not to mention the more outrageous sonnets, occasionally, the bitterness of his disappointed soul breaks out in his later works, yet to such an extent that it is not impossible to keep the poet and the controversialist apart as two almost separate powers. That divorce has its unhappy aspect; for one thing it debars Milton, in his total effect, from being accepted as the voice of England. But it leaves to him the high credit of having raised in *Paradise Lost,* to the honour of his native land, the one monumentally successful product of that humanistic culture of the Renaissance in which originality of genius and faithfulness to the classical tradition are combined in perfect union. And for *Lycidas* there is this further apology, that the elegy was composed before Milton's splendid spirit of liberty was exacerbated by opposition into petulant license, when his personal pride flamed with a yet undiverted zeal to make of his own life a true poem and so to train himself for creating such a work of art as would lift his people from the ugly slough of faction and greed, where they were grovelling, into the finer atmosphere where pure religion and the love of beauty might flourish together.

HARRY LEVIN: Literature as an Institution*

1

THE CONTRIBUTION OF TAINE

"LITERATURE is the expression of society, as speech is the expression of man." In this aphorism the Vicomte de Bonald summed up one of the bitter lessons that the French Revolution had taught the world. With the opening year of the nineteenth century, and the return of the Emigration, coincided a two-volume study by Madame de Staël: *De la Littérature considérée dans ses rapports avec les institutions sociales*. This was not the first time, of course, that some relationship had been glimpsed. Renaissance humanism, fighting out the invidious quarrel between ancient and modern literatures, had concluded that each was the unique creation of its period, and had adumbrated a historical point of view. Romantic nationalism, seeking to undermine the prestige of the neo-classic school and to revive the native traditions of various countries, was now elaborating a series of geographical comparisons. It was left for Hippolyte Taine—in the vanguard of a third intellectual movement, scientific positivism—to formulate a sociological approach. To the historical and geographical factors, the occasional efforts of earlier critics to discuss literature in terms of "moment" and "race," he added a third conception, which completed and finally eclipsed them. "Milieu," as he conceived it, is the link between literary criticism and the social sciences. Thus Taine raised a host of new problems by settling an old one.

When Taine's history of English literature appeared, it smelled—to a contemporary reader, Amiel—like the exhalations from a laboratory. To that sensitive Swiss idealist, it conveyed a whiff of "the literature of the future in the American style," of "the death of poetry flayed and anatomized by science." This "intrusion of technology into literature," as Amiel was shrewd enough to observe, is a responsibility which Taine shares with Balzac and Stendhal. As Taine self-consciously remarked, "From the novel to criticism and from criticism to the novel, the distance at present is not very great." Taine's critical theory is grounded upon the practice of the realists, while their novels are nothing if not critical. His recognition of the social forces behind literature coincides with their resolution to embody those forces in their works. The first to acknowledge Stendhal as a master, he welcomed Flaubert as a colleague and lived to find Zola among his disciples. "When M. Taine studies Balzac," Zola acknowledged, "he does exactly what Balzac himself does when he studies Père Grandet." There is no better way to bridge the distance between criticism and the novel, or to scrutinize the presuppositions of modern literature, than by a brief reconsideration of Taine's critical method.

A tougher-minded reader than Amiel, Flaubert, noted in 1864 that—whatever the *Histoire de la littérature anglaise* left unsettled—it got rid of the uncritical notion that books dropped like meteorites from the sky. The social basis of art might thereafter be overlooked, but it could hardly be disputed. Any lingering belief in poetic inspiration could hardly withstand the higher criticism that had disposed of spontaneous generation and was disposing of divine revelation. When Renan, proclaiming his disbelief in

* "Literature as an Institution" first appeared in *Accent*, Spring 1946, and is an abridged version of the Introduction to Mr. Levin's study of the novel, *The Gates of Horn*, to be published by the Oxford University Press. It is reprinted here by permission of Mr. Levin, Mr. Kerker Quinn, and the editors of the Oxford University Press. Mr. Levin (*b.* 1912) is the author of *The Broken Column: A Study of Romantic Hellenism* (1931) and *James Joyce: A Critical Introduction* (1941), and editor of *The Selected Works of Ben Jonson* (1938) and *The Portable James Joyce* (1947).

mysteries, depicted Jesus as the son of man and analyzed the origins of Christianity, then Taine could depict genius as the outgrowth of environment and analyze the origins of literature. On the whole, though critics have deplored the crudity of his analyses and scholars have challenged the accuracy of his facts, his working hypothesis has won acceptance. He has become the stock example of a rigorous determinist—especially for those who think determinism is a modern version of fatalism. Taine's determinism, however, is simply an intensive application of the intellectual curiosity of his age. It is no philosopher's attempt to encroach upon the freedom of the artist's will; it is simply a historian's consciousness of what the past has already determined.

As for Taine's rigor, a more thoroughgoing historical materialist, George Plekhanov, has gone so far as to accuse him of arrant idealism. A recent artist-philosopher, Jean-Paul Sartre, describes Taine's empiricism as an unsuccessful effort to set up a realistic system of metaphysics. Actually his position is that of most realists, so outrageous to their early readers and so tame to later critics. His method explained too much to satisfy his contemporaries; it has not explained enough to satisfy ours. Confronted with the provocative statement, "Vice and virtue are products like vitriol and sugar," we are not shocked by the audacity that reduces moral issues to chemical formulæ; we are amused at the naiveté that undertakes to solve them both by a single equation. Taine's introduction to his history of English literature, which abounds in dogmas of this sort, is rather a manifesto than a methodology. If, reading on, we expect the history to practise what the introduction preaches, we are amiably disappointed. Each successive author is more freely individualized. How does Taine's all-determining scheme meet its severest test? With Shakespeare, he explains, after canvassing the material factors, "all comes from within—I mean from his soul and his genius; circumstances and externals have contributed but little to his development."

The loophole that enables Taine to avoid the strict consequences of his three determinants is a fourth—a loose system of psychology. Psychology takes over where sociology has given up, and the sociologist has shown surprisingly little interest in classes or institutions. He has viewed history as a parade of influential individuals, themselves the creatures of historical influences. To understand their achievements is "a problem in psychological mechanics." The psychologist must disclose their ruling passions; he must hit upon that magnificent obsession, that "master faculty" which conditions have created within the soul of every great man. Let us not be put off by the circular logic, the mechanical apparatus, and the scientific jargon: Taine, conscientious child of his temperament and time, was an ardent individualist. His theory of character owes quite as much to Balzac as his theory of environment owes to Stendhal. Had it been the other way around, had he combined Stendhal's psychological insight with Balzac's sociological outlook, he might have been a better critic. His portrait of Balzac, for better or worse, is as monomaniacal as Balzac's portrait of Grandet.

Psychology is a knife, Dostoevsky warns us, which cuts two ways. We may look for a man in his books, or we may look to the man for the explanation of his books. Taine's is the more dangerous way: to deduce the qualities of a work from a presupposition about the author. The whole *Comédie humaine* follows from the consideration that Balzac was a business man, and Livy's history is what you might expect from a writer who was really an orator. This mode of critical characterization must perforce be limited to a few broad strokes, much too exaggerated and impressionistic to be compared with the detailed nuances of Sainte-Beuve's portraiture. Most of Taine's figures bear a strong family likeness. He is most adroit at bringing out the generic traits of English literature: the response to nature, the puritan strain, the fact—in short—that it was written by Englishmen. He himself, true to his theories, remains an intransigent Frenchman, and his history—to the point where he abandons Tennyson for Musset and recrosses the channel—remains a traveller's survey of a foreign culture. Why, in spite of all temptations to interpret other cultures, should Taine have been attracted to England?

Taine's critical faculties were conditioned not by science but by romanticism, and who was

Taine to repudiate his own conditioning? Madame de Staël had been drawn to Germany, and Melchior de Vogué would soon be seeking the Russian soul, but English was for most Frenchmen the typically romantic literature. France had been the Bastille of classicism, while Britain had never been enslaved to the rules; untamed nature, in Saxon garb, resisted the shackles of Norman constraint. It took very little perception of the technique of English poetry for Taine to prefer blank verse to alexandrines. Form, as he construed it, was a body of artificial restrictions which inhibited free expression, and which English men of letters had somehow succeeded in doing without. One might almost say that they had developed a literature of pure content. "Not in Greece, nor in Italy, nor in Spain, nor in France," said Taine, "has an art been seen which tried so boldly to express the soul and the most intimate depths of the soul, the reality and the whole reality." What seemed to him so unprecedented is, on closer scrutiny, a complex tradition. Elizabethan drama is so much more baroque than the succinct tragedies of Racine that Taine missed its pattern altogether, and believed he was facing a chaos of first-hand and unconstrained realities. His impressions were those of Fielding's barber Partridge at the play, wholly taken in by theatrical make-believe, naively mistaking the actors for the characters they represent, quixotically confusing literature with life.

2

SOCIOLOGICAL CRITICISM AND SOCIAL CRITICS

Remembering Lamb's essay on the artificiality of Restoration comedy, we cannot share Taine's facile assumption that the English stage received and retained "the exact imprint of the century and the nation." We cannot accept this free translation of Hamlet's impulse to give "the very age and body of the time his form and pressure." We can admit that Taine was less of a critic than a historian, but we cannot forgive him for being such an uncritical historian. His professed willingness to trade quantities of charters for the letters of Saint Paul or the memoirs of Cellini does not indicate a literary taste; it merely states a preference for human documents as against constitutional documents. In exploiting literature for purposes of historical documentation, Taine uncovered a new mine of priceless source material. But he never learned the difference between ore and craftsmanship. In his *Philosophie de l'art,* to be sure, he could no longer sidestep esthetic and technical discussion. He was forced to concede that art could be idealistic as well as realistic, and to place Greek sculpture at a farther remove from reality than Flemish painting. This concession allowed him to turn his back on the sculpture, and to reconstruct, with a freer hand than ever, the moment, the race, and the milieu of ancient Greece.

The serious objection to environmentalism is that it failed to distinguish, not between one personality and another, but between personality and art. It encouraged scholars to write literary histories which, as Ferdinand Brunetière pointed out, were nothing but chronological dictionaries of literary biography. It discouraged the realization, which Brunetière called the evolution of *genres,* that literary technique had a history of its own. It advanced a brilliant generalization, and established—as first-rate ideas will do in second-rate minds—a rule of thumb. The incidental and qualified extent to which books epitomize their epoch may vary from one example to the next. Taine's successors made no allowances for the permutations of form; rather they industrialized his process for extracting the contents of the books. The prevailing aim of literary historiography, under the sponsorship of Gustave Lanson in France and other professors elsewhere, has been a kind of illustrated supplement to history. Academic research has concentrated so heavily on the backgrounds of literature that the foreground has been almost obliterated.

Meanwhile Taine's influence has been felt in the wider areas of criticism, and here it has been subordinated to political ends. Taine himself was bitterly anti-political. He did not realize the importance of ideas until he had lost faith in his own: originally he had been a proponent of the doctrines of the *philosophes,* which he blamed in his later studies, *Les Origines de la France contemporaine,* for instigating the revolution of 1789. It was a Danish critic, closely associated with Ibsen, Nietzsche, and the controversies of the eighties, who broadened the range and narrowed the tendency of literary history. For politics, and for literature too, Georg Brandes had more feeling than Taine. A cosmopolitan liberal, deeply suspicious of the ascendancy of Prussia, he found a touchstone for the romanticists in their struggles or compromises with clerical reaction and the authority of the state. Byron and Heine were his urbane prophets, the Schlegels were renegades, and the revolution of 1848 was the anticlimax toward which his *Main Currents of Nineteenth Century Literature* moved. Where a book had been an end-product to Taine, to Brandes it was continuing force, and the critic's added function was to chart its repercussions.

Both aspects have been duly stressed in the critical interpretation of American writers—their reactions to their environment and their contributions to the liberal tradition. Our foremost literary historian, V. L. Parrington, extended and modified Taine's formula to fit our problems, dramatizing New England puritanism from the standpoint of western populism, and pitting a heroic Jefferson against a sinister Hamilton. His title, *Main Currents in American Thought,* conveyed a fraternal salute to Brandes, and denoted an additional qualification. Parrington got around Taine's difficulty—the difficulty of using imaginative writers as historical sources—by drawing upon the moralists and the publicists. His chapters on Roger Williams and John Marshall are ample and rewarding; his accounts of Poe and Henry James are so trivial that they might better have been omitted. The latest period is inevitably the hardest, and his last volume is posthumous and fragmentary, but it seems to mark an increasing conflict between artistic and political standards. Granville Hicks, going over the same ground, was able to resolve that conflict by the simple device of discarding artistic standards.

Mr. Hicks, if he still adheres to his somewhat elusive conception of *The Great Tradition,* is a Marxist critic in the sense that Parrington was a Jeffersonian critic. The choice between them is largely a matter of political standards. Jeffersonianism, naturally the most favorable climate in which to discuss American literature, has been taken in vain so often that it has begun to resist definition. Marxism, by redefining milieu in economic terms, has presented a more rigorous theory of historical causation than Taine's and a more ruthless canon of political allegiance than Brandes'. It has introduced criticism to a sociological system which is highly illuminating and a social doctrine which is highly controversial. It has tightened the relations between literature and life by oversimplifying them beyond recognition. In this respect Karl Marx, as he occasionally confessed, was no Marxist: he repeatedly cautioned his followers against expecting the arts to show a neat conformity with his views. Perhaps if he had written his projected study of Balzac, he would have bequeathed them a critical method. For lack of one, they took what was available. Marxist criticism superimposed its socialistic doctrine on the deterministic method, and judged according to Marx what it had interpreted according to Taine.

Extension and modification have added their corollary to Taine's method: the relations between literature and society are reciprocal. Literature is not only the effect of social causes; it is also the cause of social effects. The critic may investigate its causes, as Taine tried to do; or he may, like Brandes and others, be more interested in its effects. So long as he is correlating works of art with trends of history, his function is relatively clear. It becomes less clear as he encounters his contemporaries, and as the issues become more immediate. He is then concerned, no longer with a secure past, but with a problematic future. An insecure present may commit him to some special partisanship, Marxist or otherwise, and incline him to judge each new work by its possible effect—whether it will advance or hinder his party's program. Since art can be a weapon, among other things, it will be judged in the heat of the battle by its polemical possibilities. We need not deny the relevance or significance of such judgments; we need only recognize that they carry us beyond the limits of esthetic questions into the field of moral values. There are times when criticism cannot conveniently stop at the border. Whenever there are boundary disputes, questions involving propaganda or regulation, we may be called upon to go afield. We shall be safe while we are aware that virtue and beauty are as intimately related as beauty and truth, and as eternally distinct.

3

THE ROLE OF CONVENTION

It was as if Taine had discovered that the earth was round, without realizing that another continent lay between Europe and Asia. The distance was longer, the route more devious, than sociological criticism had anticipated. Not that the intervening territory was unexplored; but those who had explored it most thoroughly were isolationists. Those who were most familiar with the techniques and traditions of literature were least conscious of its social responsibilities. Most of them were writers themselves, lacking in critical method perhaps, yet possessing the very skills and insights that the methodologists lacked. A few were philosophers, striving—on the high plane of idealism—toward a historical synthesis of the arts. Their concept of expressive form, inherited by the esthetic of Croce from the literary history of Francesco de Sanctis, resembles the "organic principle" that Anglo-American criticism inherits from the theory of Coleridge, the preaching of Emerson, and the practice of Thoreau. By whichever name, it is too sensitive an instrument to be used effectively, except by acute critics on acknowledged masterpieces. With cruder material, in unskilled hands, its insistence on the uniqueness of each work of art and its acceptance of the artist at his own evaluation dissolve into esthetic impressionism and romantic hero-worship.

While this school is responsible for many admirable critiques, it has never produced that "new criticism" which the late J. E. Spingarn tried vainly to define. Conceiving art as the fullest expression of individuality, it has disregarded the more analytic approaches. Taine's school, though less discriminating, has been more influential, because it conceives art as a collective expression of society. The fallacy in this conception—we have already seen—is to equate art with society, to assume a one-to-one correspondence between a book and its subject-matter, to accept the literature of an age as a complete and exact replica of the age itself. One way or another, literature is bound to tell the truth; but it has told the whole truth very seldom, and nothing but the truth hardly ever; some things are bound to be left out, and others to be exaggerated in the telling. Sins of omission can usually be traced to some restriction in the artist's freedom of speech, his range of experience, or his control of his medium. Sins of commission are inherent in the nature of his materials. The literary historian must reckon with these changing degrees of restriction and exaggeration. Literary history, if it is to be accurate, must be always correcting its aim.

To mention one conspicuous case, the relations between the sexes have received a vast—possibly a disproportionate—amount of attention from writers. From their miscellaneous and contradictory testimony it would be rash to infer very much, without allowing for the artistic taboos of one period or the exhibitionism of another. An enterprising sociologist, by measuring the exposed portions of the human figure in various paintings, has arrived at a quantitative historical index of comparative sensuality. What inference could not be drawn, by some future sciolist, from the preponderance of detective stories on the shelves of our circulating libraries? Those volumes testify, for us, to the colorless comfort of their readers' lives. We are aware, because we are not dependent on literary evidence, that ours is no unparalleled epoch of domestic crime—of utterly ineffectual police, of criminals who bear all the earmarks of innocence, and of detectives whose nonchalance is only equalled by their erudition. These, we are smugly aware, have not much more significance than the counters of a complicated game. Nevertheless, it is disturbing to imagine what literal-minded critics may deduce when the rules of the game have been forgotten. It suggests that we ourselves may be misreading other books through our ignorance of the lost conventions on which they hinge.

Convention may be described as a necessary difference between art and life. Some differences, strictly speaking, may be quite unnecessary: deliberate sallies of the imagination, unconscious effects of miscalculation or misunderstanding. But art must also differ from life for technical reasons: limitations of form, difficulties of expression. The artist, powerless to overcome these obstacles by himself, must have the assistance of his audience. They must agree to take certain formalities and assumptions for granted, to take the word for the deed or the shading for the shadow. The result of their unspoken agreement is a compromise between the possibilities of life and the exigencies of art. Goethe might have been speaking of convention when he said, "*In der Beschränkung zeigt sich erst der Meister.*" [1] Limitation has often been a source of new forms, and difficulty—as the defenders of rhyme have argued, from Samuel Daniel to Paul Valéry—has prompted poets to their most felicitous expressions. Without some sort of conventionalization art could hardly exist. It exists by making virtues of necessities; after the necessities disappear, we forget the conventions. After perspective is invented, we misjudge the primitives; after scenery is set up, we challenge the unities. And Taine, forgetting that feminine roles were played by boys, is appalled at finding masculine traits in Elizabethan heroines.

His former classmate, Francisque Sarcey, who became—through forty years of playgoing—the most practical of critics, might have supplied the needed correction for Taine's theories. "It is inadequate to repeat that the theater is a representation of human life," Sarcey had learned. "It would be a more precise definition to say that dramatic art is the sum of conventions, universal or local, eternal or temporary, which help —when human life is represented on the stage —to give a public the illusion of truth." This illusion may be sustained in the novel more easily than on the stage; but it is still an illusion, as Maupassant frankly admitted. Although drama may be the most conventional of literary forms, and fiction the least, even fiction is not entirely free. Even Proust, the most unconventional of novelists, must resort to the convention of eavesdropping in order to sustain the needs of first-person narrative. We need not condone such melodramatic stratagems; we can observe that the modern novel has endeavored to get along without them; upon fuller consideration we may even conclude that the whole modern movement of realism, technically considered, is an endeavor to emancipate literature from the sway of conventions.

1 ["Mastery becomes evident only under limitations."]

4

TOWARD AN INSTITUTIONAL METHOD

This provisional conclusion would explain why literary historians, under the influence of realism, have slighted literary form. In their impatience to lay bare the so-called content of a work, they have missed a more revealing characteristic: the way the artist handles the appropriate conventions. Whether it is possible, or even desirable, to eliminate artifice from art—that is one of the largest questions that criticism must face. But realistic novelists who declare their intentions of transcribing life have an obvious advantage over realistic critics who expect every book to be a literal transcript. Stendhal, when he declares that "a novel is a mirror riding along a highway," is in a position to fulfil his picaresque intention. When Taine echoes this precept, defining the novel as "a kind of portable mirror which can be conveyed everywhere, and which is most convenient for reflecting all aspects of nature and life," he puts the mirror before the horse. He is then embarrassed to discover so few reflections of the *ancien régime* in French novels of the eighteenth century. His revulsion from neo-classical generalities and his preference for descriptive details carry him back across the channel, from Marmontel and Crébillon *fils* to Fielding and Smollett. Some mirrors, Taine finally discovered, are less reliable than others.

The metaphor of the mirror held up to nature, the idea that literature reflects life, was mentioned by Plato only to be rejected. By the time of Cicero it was already a commonplace of criticism. It was applied by the ancients to comedy, the original vehicle of realism; later it became a byword for artistic didacticism, for the medieval zeal to see vice exposed and virtue emulated. When Shakespeare invoked it, he had a definite purpose which those who quote him commonly ignore. Hamlet is not merely describing a play, he is exhorting the players. His advice is a critique of bad acting as well as an apology for the theater, a protest against unnatural conventions as well as a plea for realism. Like modern critics who derive their metaphors from photography, he implies a further comparison with more conventionalized modes of art—particularly with painting. To hold up a photograph or a mirror, as it were, is to compare the "abstract and brief chronicles of the time" with the distorted journeywork that "imitated humanity so abominably." Art should be a reflection of life, we are advised, not a distortion—as it has all too frequently been. Criticism, in assuming that art invariably reflects and forgetting that it frequently distorts, wafts us through the looking-glass into a sphere of its own, where everything is clear and cool, logical and literal, and more surrealistic than real.

In questioning the attempts of scholars to utilize Shakespeare as the mirror of his time, Professor Stoll has reminded them that their business is to separate historical fact from literary illusion, to distinguish the object from its reflected image. Literature, instead of reflecting life, refracts it. Our task, in any given case, is to determine the angle of refraction. Since the angle depends upon the density of the medium, it is always shifting, and the task is never easy. We are aided today, however, by a more flexible and accurate kind of critical apparatus than Taine was able to employ. An acquaintance with artistic conventions, which can best be acquired through comparative studies in technique, should complement an awareness of social backgrounds. "Literature is complementary to life." This formula of Lanson's is broad enough to include the important proviso that there is room in the world of art for ideals and projects, fantasies and anxieties, which do not ordinarily find a habitation in the world of reality. But, in recognizing that literature adds something to life or that it subtracts something from life, we must not overlook the most important consideration of all—that literature is at all times an intrinsic part of life. It is, if we can work out the implications of Leslie Stephen's phrase, "a particular function of the whole social organism."

The organic character of this relationship has been most explicitly formulated by a statesman and historian, Prosper de Barante. Writing of the ideas behind the French revolution while they were still fresh in men's minds, his comprehension of their political interplay was broader than Taine's. "In the absence of regular institutions," wrote Barante, "literature became one." The truth, though it has long been obscured by a welter of personalities and technicalities, is that literature has always been an institution. Like other institutions, the church or the law, it cherishes a unique phase of human experience and controls a special body of precedents and devices; it tends to incorporate a self-perpetuating discipline, while responding to the main currents of each succeeding period; it is continually accessible to all the impulses of life at large, but it must translate them into its own terms and adapt them to its peculiar forms. Once we have grasped this fact, we begin to perceive how art may belong to society and yet be autonomous within its own limits, and are no longer puzzled by the apparent polarity of social and formal criticism. These, in the last analysis, are complementary frames of reference whereby we may discriminate the complexities of a work of art. In multiplying these discriminations between external impulses and internal peculiarities—in other words, between the effects of environment and convention—our ultimate justification is to understand the vital process to which they are both indispensable.

To consider the novel as an institution, then, imposes no dogma, exacts no sacrifice, and excludes none of the critical methods that have proved illuminating in the past. If it tends to subordinate the writer's personality to his achievement, it requires no further apology, for criticism has long been unduly subordinated to biography. The tendency of the romanticists to live their writings and write their lives, and the consequent success of their critics as biographers, did much to justify this subordination; but even Sainte-Beuve's "natural history of souls," though it unified and clarified an author's works by fitting them into the pattern of his career, was too ready to dismiss their purely artistic qualities as "rhetoric." More recently the doctrines of Freud, while imposing a topheavy vocabulary upon the discussion of art, have been used to corroborate and systematize the sporadic intuitions of artists; but the psychologists, like the sociologists, have been more interested in utilizing books for documentary purposes than in exploring their intrinsic nature. Meanwhile, on the popular level, the confusion between a novelist and his novels has been consciously exploited. A series of novelized biographies, calling itself *Le Roman des grandes existences,* invites the common reader to proceed from "the prodigious life of Balzac" through "the mournful life of Baudelaire" to "the wise and merry life of Montaigne."

If fiction has seldom been discussed on a plane commensurate with its achievements, it is because we are too often sidetracked by personalities. If, with Henry James, we recognize the novelist's intention as a figure in a carpet, we must recognize that he is guided by his material, his training, his commission, by the size and shape of his loom, and by his imagination to the extent that it accepts and masters those elements. Psychology—illuminating as it has been—has treated literature too often as a record of personal idiosyncrasies, too seldom as the basis of a collective consciousness. Yet it is on that basis that the greatest writers have functioned. Their originality has been an ability to "seize on the public mind," in Bagehot's opinion; conventions have changed and styles have developed as lesser writers caught "the traditional rhythm of an age." The irreducible element of individual talent would seem to play the same role in the evolution of *genres* that natural selection plays in the origin of species. Amid the mutations of modern individualism, we may very conceivably have overstressed the private aspects of writing. One convenience of the institutional method is that it gives due credit to the never-ending collaboration between writer and public. It sees no reason to ignore what is relevant in the psychological prepossessions of the craftsman, and it knows that he is ultimately to be judged by the technical resources of his craftsmanship; but it attains its clearest and most comprehensive scope by centering on his craft—on his social status and his historical function as participant in a skilled group and a living tradition.

When Edgar Quinet announced a course at the Collège de France in *La Littérature et les institutions comparées de l'Europe méridionelle,* he was requested by Guizot's ministry to omit the word "institutions" and to limit himself to purely literary discussion. When he replied that this would be impossible, his course was suspended, and his further efforts went directly into those reform agitations which culminated in the democratic revolution of the following year, 1848. Thereby proceeding from sociological to social criticism, he demonstrated anew what French critics and novelists have understood particularly well—the dynamic interaction between ideas and events. In a time which has seen that demonstration repeated on so vast a scale, the institutional forces that impinge upon literature are self-evident. The responsibilities that literature owes to itself, and the special allegiance it exacts from us, should also become apparent when we conceive it as an institution in its own right. The misleading dichotomy between substance and form, which permits literary historians, like Parrington, to dismiss "belletristic philandering," and esthetic impressionists, like Mr. R. P. Blackmur, to dispose of "separable content," should disappear as soon as abstract categories are dropped and concrete relations are taken up. And the jurisdictional conflict between truth and beauty should dissolve when esthetics discovers the truth about beauty; when criticism becomes—as Bacon intended, and Renan and Sainte-Beuve remembered, and all too many other critics have forgotten—the science of art.

WESTMAR COLLEGE LIBRARY